HISTORIC DOCUMENTS OF 1980

Cumulative Index 1976-80

Congressional Quarterly Inc.

Printed in the United States of America

Congressional Quarterly Inc.
1414 22nd St. N.W., Washington, D.C. 20037

The Library of Congress cataloged the first issue of this title as follows:

Historic documents.   1972—
    Washington. Congressional Quarterly Inc.

    1. United States—Politics and government—1945— —Yearbooks.
2. World politics—1945— —Yearbooks. I.Congressional Quarterly Inc.

E839.5.H57   917.3′03′9205   72-97888
ISBN 0-87187-169-6

FOREWORD

Publication of *Historic Documents of 1980* carries through a ninth year the project launched by Congressional Quarterly with *Historic Documents 1972*. The purpose of this continuing series of volumes is to give students, scholars, librarians, journalists and citizens convenient access to documents of basic importance in the broad range of public affairs.

To place the documents in perspective, each entry is preceded by a brief introduction containing background materials, in some cases a short summary of the document itself and, where necessary, relevant subsequent developments. We believe these introductions will prove increasingly useful in future years when the events and questions now covered are less fresh in one's memory and the documents may be difficult to find or unobtainable.

When Americans look back on 1980, two events are likely to stand out: the continuing effort to free 52 hostages held in Iran and the election of a new president. As if to underscore how closely the hostage crisis and the election were intertwined, the hostages finally were freed the following year, minutes after President Reagan took office. But the groundwork for their release had been prepared during 1980, first with an unsuccessful rescue attempt and then with an on-again, off-again series of secret negotiations that ultimately brought success.

Although President Carter may have been hurt by his inability to win an earlier release for the hostages, most observers felt that other factors — notably voter dissatisfaction with Carter's handling of the economy — probably accounted for his defeat. Whatever the cause, Reagan's landslide victory over an incumbent president capped the remarkable career of a movie actor turned politician.

The natural world also made history in 1980, partly through mankind's efforts to learn more about it. The dazzling flight of Voyager I through the rings of Saturn provided an uplift to American morale. On the other hand, the spectacular and destructive eruption of Mount St. Helens was a somber reminder of the limits to technological achievement.

These and other developments added substantially to the usual outpouring of presidential statements, court decisions, committee reports, special studies and speeches of national or international importance. We have selected for inclusion in this book as many as possible of the documents that in our judgment will be of more than transitory interest. Where space limitations prevented reproduction of the full texts, the excerpts used were chosen to set forth the essential and, at the same time, to preserve the flavor of the materials.

John L. Moore
Editor

Washington, D.C.
February 1981

Historic Documents of 1980

Editor: John L. Moore
Assistant Editor: Sari Horwitz
Contributors: Michael J. Glennon, James R. Ingram,
   W. Allan Wilbur
Editorial Coordinator: Carolyn Goldinger
Cumulative Index: Diane Huffman
Production Manager: I. D. Fuller
Assistant Production Manager: Maceo Mayo

Book Department

How to Use This Book

The documents are arranged in chronological order. If you know the approximate date of the report, speech, statement, court decision or other document you are looking for, glance through the titles for that month in the Table of Contents below.

If the Table of Contents does not lead you directly to the document you want, make a double check by turning to the subject Index at the end of the book. There you may find references not only to the particular document you seek but also to other entries on the same or a related subject. The Index in this volume is a **five-year cumulative index** of Historic Documents covering the years 1976-1980. The introduction to each document is printed in italic type. The document itself, printed in roman type, follows the spelling, capitalization and punctuation of the original or official copy. Where the full text is not given, omissions of material are indicated by the customary ellipsis points.

TABLE OF CONTENTS

January

February

March

April

May

June

July

August

September

October

November

December

HISTORIC
DOCUMENTS
OF
1980

January

ISLAMIC PARLEYS
ON AFGHAN CRISIS
January 12, 27-29; May 16-22, 1980

Delegates to the Islamic foreign ministers conference, at an emergency session in January and again at the 11th Islamic Conference in May, approved resolutions condemning military intervention in Afghanistan by the Soviet Union.

Foreign ministers at the emergency meeting Jan. 27-29 called the invasion "a flagrant violation of international law." Again condemning the Soviet action, the ministers at the regular parley May 16-22 also proposed a mediation plan. Both meetings were held in Islamabad, Pakistan.

Ignoring both the resolutions of condemnation and the offer of mediation, the Soviet Union continued to deny that aggression had taken place. The Soviet invasion of Afghanistan began with an airlift of Russian troops into the country Dec. 26, 1979. By mid-1980, the Soviets were attempting to consolidate their occupation in the face of sporadic resistance by Afghan rebel groups.

Emergency Session

The January emergency session of the Islamic foreign ministers' conference was called by Bangladesh, reportedly at the request of Pakistan and Saudi Arabia, after the Soviet Union had vetoed a United Nations Security Council resolution calling for withdrawal of Soviet troops from Afghanistan. (The U.N. General Assembly later adopted a resolution deploring the Soviet intervention.)

3

Pakistani President Zia ul-Haq and the foreign ministers of Gambia, Malaysia and Morocco, in speeches at the opening session of the session, urged outright condemnation of the Soviet intervention in Afghanistan. But in an effort to obtain broader unity among both conservative and leftist Islamic countries, the conference delegates broadened the language of the resolution, calling upon Islamic nations to unite against the "hegemonistic ambitions of global powers."

President Zia ul-Haq also called for an Islamic collective defense arrangement to deter future invasions of Moslem nations, but he provided no specific details of his plan.

Other Resolutions

The emergency meeting also suspended Afghanistan from membership in the Islamic conference group and called upon other Islamic nations "to withhold recognition from the illegal regime in Afghanistan . . . until the complete withdrawal of Soviet troops."

In other resolutions, the delegates to the conference:

● *Urged member states to boycott the 1980 summer Olympic games in Moscow, unless Soviet troops withdrew from Afghanistan.*

● *Adopted a resolution expressing the hope that the United States and Iran "would resolve the outstanding differences between themselves by peaceful means."* (Historic Documents of 1979, p. 867)

● *Condemned the Israeli-Egyptian peace treaty and demanded Israeli withdrawal from East Jerusalem. The Middle East resolutions also were seen by observers as attempts to broaden consensus at the emergency session.* (Peace treaty, Historic Documents of 1979, p. 223)

May Conference

Resolutions adopted at the May meeting not only condemned the Soviet invasion but also proposed a mediation plan. The delegates recommended that a committee composed of the foreign ministers of Iran and Pakistan and the secretary general of the Islamic conference be authorized to open negotiations with all parties involved in the dispute.

The decision to try to open talks with the Soviet Union and the Soviet-installed government in Kabul was seen by some observers as a significant retreat from actions taken by the foreign ministers at their emergency session in January. But Agha Shahi, Pakistan's chief foreign policy adviser and conference chairman, called the mediation plan "a major step forward in the search for a political solution of the problem."

Delegates from 39 Islamic countries attended the 11th Islamic Conference in May. In addition to actions concerning the Soviet invasion of Afghanistan, the delegates:

● Called for the restoration of the national rights of the Palestinians, including the right to statehood and self-determination.

● Unanimously condemned the attempt of the United States to rescue American hostages held in Iran.

● Opposed any action that threatened the territorial integrity or independence of Iran and warned against imposition of economic sanctions against that country.

Brezhnev Interview

Leonid I. Brezhnev, the Soviet leader, in an interview Jan. 12 released by Tass, the Russian news agency, asserted that Soviet troops had been invited into Afghanistan "on the request of its government to defend the national independence, freedom and honor of its country from armed aggressive actions from outside."

Background

The Organization of Islamic Conference, formed in 1966 to oppose Israel, had 42 member countries until Egypt was expelled in 1978 for its initiative in achieving peace with Israel. The conference included politically diverse nations, from conservative oil-rich states such as Saudi Arabia to leftist Arab states such as Syria and Iraq. Consequently, unity on political issues was difficult for the conference to achieve.

> *Following are the texts of the resolutions of the Islamic foreign ministers conference adopted Jan. 29 and May 22, 1980, condemning Soviet intervention in Afghanistan and offering to mediate the crisis; and an interview with Leonid I. Brezhnev released Jan. 12, 1980, by Tass, the Russian news agency, setting forth the Soviet view of the military action in Afghanistan.* (Boldface headings in brackets have been added by Congressional Quarterly to highlight the organization of the texts.):

JANUARY 29 RESOLUTION

The first extraordinary session of the Islamic Conference of Foreign Ministers meeting in Islamabad from 7 to 9 Rabi al Awwal, corresponding to 27 to 29 January 1980,

IN PURSUANCE of the principles and objectives of the Organization of the Islamic Conference, and the provisions of resolutions adopted by Islamic summit conference, emphasizing the common objectives and destiny of the peoples of the Islamic nation,

RECALLING IN PARTICULAR the basic principles of the nonaligned movement of which Afghanistan is a founding member,

EXPRESSING ITS DEEP CONCERN at the dangerous escalation of tension, intensification of rivalry and increased recourse to military intervention and interference in the internal affairs of states, particularly the Islamic states,

EXPRESSING THE DETERMINATION of the governments and peoples of member states to reject all forms and types of foreign occupation and expansion and the race for spheres of influence, thereby strengthening the sovereignty of peoples and the independence of states,

SERIOUSLY CONCERNED over the Soviet armed intervention in Afghanistan and the effect of this interference on the will of the Moslem people of Afghanistan to exercise their right to determine their political future,

CONSIDERING that the continuing presence of Soviet troops in Afghanistan, its attempt at imposing the fait accompli and the military operations of these troops against the Afghan people flout international covenants and norms and blatantly violate human rights,

REAFFIRMING THE DETERMINATION of Islamic states to pursue a nonaligned policy in respect of superpower conflict and to protect Moslem people from the adverse effects of the cold war between these states,

FULLY AWARE of the immense financial burden borne by neighboring countries of Afghanistan, in particular the Islamic Republic of Pakistan, as a result of the asylum it provides to hundreds of thousands of Afghan people, old men, women and children, driven away by the Soviet military occupation,

AFFIRMING that the Soviet occupation of Afghanistan constitutes a violation of its independence, and aggression against the liberty of its people and a flagrant violation of all international covenants and norms, as well as a serious threat to peace and security in the region and throughout the world,

1. CONDEMNS the Soviet military aggression against the Afghan people, denounces and deplores it as a flagrant violation of international laws, covenants, and norms, primarily the Charter of the United Nations, which condemned this aggression in its Resolution No. ES-6/2 of 14 January 1980 and the charter of the Organization of the Islamic Conference, and calls upon all peoples and governments throughout the world to persist in condemning this aggression and denouncing it as an aggression against human rights and a violation of the freedoms of people, which cannot be ignored;

2. DEMANDS the immediate and unconditional withdrawal of all Soviet troops stationed on Afghan territories, and reiterates that Soviet

troops should refrain from acts of oppression and tyranny against the Afghan people and their struggling sons until the departure of the last Soviet soldier from Afghan territory, and urges all countries and peoples to secure the Soviet withdrawal through all possible means;

3. SUSPENDS the membership of Afghanistan in the Organization of the Islamic conference;

4. INVITES the member states to withhold recognition to the illegal regime in Afghanistan and sever diplomatic relations with that country until the complete withdrawal of Soviet troops from Afghanistan;

5. CALLS UPON all member states to stop all aid and all forms of assistance given to the present regime of Afghanistan by member states;

6. URGES all states and people throughout the world to support the Afghan people and provide assistance and succor to the refugees whom aggression has driven away from their homes;

7. RECOMMENDS to all member states to affirm their solidarity with the Afghan people in their just struggle to safeguard their faith, national independence and territorial integrity and to recover their right to determine their destiny;

8. SOLEMNLY DECLARES its complete solidarity with the Islamic countries neighboring Afghanistan against any threat to their security and well-being and calls upon states of the Islamic Conference to resolutely support and extend all possible cooperation to these countries in their efforts to fully safeguard their sovereignty, national independence and territorial integrity;

9. AUTHORIZES the secretary to receive contributions from member states, organizations and individuals and to disperse the amounts to the authorities concerned on the recommendations of a committee of three member states to be established by him in consultation with the states concerned;

10. CALLS UPON member states to envisage through appropriate bodies the nonparticipation in Olympic Games being held in Moscow in July 1980 until the Soviet Union in compliance with the call of the U.N. General Assembly and the Islamic Conference withdraws all its troops forthwith from Afghanistan;

11. MANDATES the secretary general of the Organization of the Islamic Conference to follow up the implementation of these resolutions and report thereon to the eleventh session of the Islamic Conference of Foreign Ministers.

MAY 22 RESOLUTION

EXPRESSING its deep conviction that termination of Soviet military intervention in Afghanistan and respect for the political independence, sovereignty and nonaligned status of Afghanistan and for the inalienable

national right of the Afghan people to choose their own political and
socio-economic system and form of government without outside interference or coercion are imperative for bringing about conditions of peace
and stability in the region and for defusing current international tensions;

SERIOUSLY CONCERNED at the sufferings of the Afghan people
and at the continuing influx of Afghan refugees into Pakistan and
Iran;

DEEPLY CONSCIOUS of the objective enshrined in the charter of
the Islamic conference requiring the member states to strengthen the
struggle of all Moslem peoples with a view to safeguarding their dignity,
independence and national rights;

CALLING UPON all states to respect the sovereignty, territorial integrity, political independence, nonaligned status and Islamic identity
of Afghanistan;

REAFFIRMING the determination of the Islamic states to pursue
a policy of nonalignment and to oppose superpower interference in the
affairs of Islamic countries;

EXPRESSING its hope that the nonaligned movement will play an
active role in the search for a comprehensive solution to the Afghan
crisis consistent with this resolution in order to strengthen peace and
stability in the region and in the world and the purposes and objectives
of the movement;

1. REAFFIRMS the resolution on the Soviet military intervention
in Afghanistan and on its ensuing effects, adopted at the extraordinary
session of the Islamic conference;

2. EXPRESSES its deep concern at the continued Soviet military
presence in Afghanistan;

3. REITERATES its demand for the immediate, total and unconditional withdrawal of all Soviet troops stationed on the territory of
Afghanistan;

4. REAFFIRMS respect for the inalienable national right of the people
of Afghanistan to determine their own form of government and choose
their economic, political and social system free from outside interference
or coercion;

5. STRONGLY URGES the creation of the right conditions that would
permit the early return of the Afghan refugees to their homeland in
security and honor;

6. REITERATES its appeal to all states and peoples to provide assistance in order to alleviate the sufferings of the Afghan refugees;

7. DECIDES, in order to give effect to the provisions of this resolution,
to establish a committee comprising the foreign ministers of the Islamic
Republic of Iran and the Islamic Republic of Pakistan and the Secretary
General of the Organization of the Islamic Conference to seek ways
and means, including appropriate consultations as well as the convening
of an international conference under the auspices of the United Nations
or otherwise, for a comprehensive solution of the grave crisis with respect
to Afghanistan, provided that it is not inconsistent with this resolution.

BREZHNEV INTERVIEW

Q: Leonid Ilyich, how do you evaluate the present international situation, especially in the light of the American administration's latest steps?

A: The consistent and creative pursuance by our party of the course of peace, detente and disarmament, of implementing the Peace Program set forth by 24th and 25th Congresses of the Communist Party of the Soviet Union, has made it possible to achieve much. Broadly speaking, the main accomplishment is that we have succeeded in breaking the tragic cycle: world war, brief spell of peace, world war again. We, the Soviet people, our friends — the peoples of fraternal socialist countries — and all those who have struggled and continue to struggle for peace, for detente, for the peaceful coexistence of states with different social systems have a right to be proud of this historic result.

The situation, unfortunately, has noticeably deteriorated at the junction of the seventies and the eighties, and the peoples must know the truth about who is responsible for this. I will answer without any reservations: The imperialist forces, first of all definite circles in the United States, are to blame for this. The blame is on all those who see in the relaxation of tension an obstacle to their aggressive plans, to the whipping up of militaristic psychosis and to interference in the internal affairs of other peoples. The blame is on those who have a deeply ingrained habit of behaving in a cavalier manner with other states and of acting in the international arena in a way as though everything is permitted them.

It has been clear for some time that the leading circles of the United States and of some other NATO countries have embarked on a course hostile to the cause of detente, a course of spiralling the arms race and leading to a growth of the war danger. The beginning of this was laid already in 1978, at the May session of the NATO Council in Washington, where the automatic growth of the military budgets of NATO member-countries until the end of the 20th century was approved. Lately, militaristic tendencies in the policy of the United States find their expression also in the acceleration of new long-term arms programs, in the creation of new military bases far beyond the United States, including the Middle East and the Indian Ocean area, in the forming of the so-called "quick reaction corps," this instrument of the policy of military interference.

[SALT II Treaty]

Now, take such an important document as the SALT-II Treaty. Its implementation would have opened the way to big steps in the field of disarmament. As is known, this treaty received support throughout

9

the whole world, including the NATO allies of the United States and broad circles of the international public. And what did the Carter Administration do with it? Hardly was the treaty signed when people in the United States began discrediting it. As for the process of ratification, the opponents of the treaty — not without the connivance of government circles in the United States — actually began using it to complicate the treaty's ratification to the utmost. By his recent decision to freeze indefinitely the debate on the SALT-II Treaty in the Senate, President Carter added one more touch to this unseemly process.

It was the United States that, in December 1979, forced on its NATO allies the decision to deploy in a number of West European countries new, medium-range nuclear missile arms, this leading to a new spiral of the arms race. Washington virtually muzzled those of its allies who inclined to positively respond to the Soviet Union's constructive proposals to hold talks on this matter.

[Afghanistan]

Today the opponents of peace and detente are trying to speculate on the events in Afghanistan. Mountains of lies are being built up around these events, and a shameless anti-Soviet campaign is being mounted. What has really happened in Afghanistan?

A revolution took place there in April 1978. The Afghan people took their destiny into their hands and embarked on the road of independence and freedom. As it has always been in history, the forces of the past ganged up against the revolution. The people of Afghanistan, of course, could have coped with them themselves. But from the very first days of the revolution it encountered an external aggression and rude interference from outside into their internal affairs.

Thousands and tens of thousands of insurgents, armed and trained abroad, and whole armed units were sent into the territory of Afghanistan. In effect, imperialism, together with its accomplices, launched an undeclared war against revolutionary Afghanistan.

Afghanistan persistently demanded an end to the aggression and that it be allowed to build its new life in peace. Resisting the external aggression, the Afghan leadership, during the lifetime of President [Nur Mohammad] Taraki and then later, repeatedly asked the Soviet Union for assistance. On our part, we warned those concerned that if the aggression did not stop, we would not abandon the Afghan people at a time of trial. As is known, we stand by what we say.

The actions of the aggressors against Afghanistan were assisted by [Hafizullah] Amin, who, upon seizing power, launched cruel repressions against broad segments of Afghan society, against party and military cadres, against representatives of the intelligentsia and the Moslem clergy, that is, exactly against those segments on which the April Revolution relied. And the people under the leadership of the People's

Democratic Party headed by Babrak Karmal rose against this Amin tyranny and put an end to it. Now in Washington and some other capitals they are mourning over Amin. This exposes their hypocricy with particular clarity. Where were these mourners when Amin was conducting his mass repressions, when he forcibly removed and unlawfully murdered Taraki, the founder of the new Afghan State?

The unceasing armed intervention, the well advanced plot by external forces of reaction created a real threat that Afghanistan would lose its independence and be turned into an imperialist military bridgehead on our country's southern border. In other words, the time came when we could no longer fail to respond to the request of the government of friendly Afghanistan. To have acted otherwise would have meant leaving Afghanistan prey to imperialism and allowing the aggressive forces to repeat in that country what they had succeeded in doing, for instance, in Chile where the people's freedom was drowned in blood. To act otherwise would have meant to watch passively the origination on our southern border of a seat of serious danger to the security of the Soviet state.

[Soviet-Afghan Treaty]

When making the request to us, Afghanistan proceeded from clear-cut provisions of the Treaty of Friendship, Good-Neighbourliness and Cooperation, concluded by Afghanistan with the USSR on December 1978, on the right of each state, in accordance with the United Nations Charter, to individual or collective self-defense, a right that other states have exercised more than once.

It was no simple decision for us to send Soviet military contingents to Afghanistan. But the party's Central Committee and the Soviet Government acted in full awareness of their responsibility and took into account the entire sum total of circumstances. The only task given to the Soviet contingents is to assist the Afghans in repulsing the aggression from outside. They will be fully withdrawn from Afghanistan once the causes that made the Afghan leadership request their introduction disappear.

It is deliberately and unscrupulously that the imperialist and also the Peking propaganda distort the Soviet Union's role in Afghan affairs.

It goes without saying that there has been no Soviet "intervention" or "aggression" at all. Oh, there is another thing: We are helping the new Afghanistan, on the request of its government, to defend the national independence, freedom and honor of its country from armed aggressive actions from outside.

The national interests or security of the United States of America and other states are not affected in any way by the events in Afghanistan. All attempts to portray matters otherwise are sheer nonsense. These attempts are being made with ill intent, with the aim of making the fulfillment of their own imperialist plans easier.

[False Allegations]

Also absolutely false are the allegations that the Soviet Union has some expansionist plans in respect to Pakistan, Iran or other countries of that area. The policy and psychology of colonialists is alien to us. We are not coveting the lands or wealth of others. It is the colonialists who are attracted by the smell of oil.

Outright hypocritical are the attempts to talk at length about the "Soviet threat of peace" and to pose as observers of international morals by those whose record includes the "dirty war" against Vietnam, who did not move a finger when the Chinese aggressors made their armed intrusion into Socialist Vietnam, who for decades have kept a military base on Cuban soil contrary to the will of its people and government, who are engaged in saber-rattling, who are threatening to impose a blockade and are exerting open military pressure on the revolutionary Iranian people by sending to the shores of Iran a naval armada armed with atomic weapons and including a considerable part of the U.S. carrier force.

And one last point must be made in this connection. Interference in the internal affairs of Afghanistan is really taking place, and even such an august and respected institution as the United Nations organization is being used for this. Indeed, can the discussion of the so-called "Afghan question" at the United Nations, contrary to objections by the government of Afghanistan, be described in any other way than a rude flouting of the sovereign rights of the Afghan state?

For the Afghan government and its responsible representative in the United Nations organization are stating for all to hear: Leave us alone; the Soviet military contingents were brought in at our request and in accordance with the Soviet-Afghan Treaty and Article 51 of the United Nations Charter.

Meantime, under the cover of the clamor, assistance is being increased to those elements that are intruding into Afghanistan and perpetrating aggressive actions against the legitimate government. The White House recently openly announced its decision to expand the supply to these elements of military equipment and everything necessary for hostile activities. The Western press reports that during his talks in Peking the U.S. Defense Secretary colluded with the Chinese leadership on the coordination of such actions.

Concluding the Afghan theme, it must be said that there is nothing surprising in the hostile reaction of imperialist forces to the events in Afghanistan. The crux of the matter is that the card on which the imperialists and their accomplices had counted was trumped there.

In short, the events in Afghanistan are not the true cause of the present complication of the international situation. If there were no Afghanistan, certain circles in the United States and in NATO would have surely found another pretext to aggravate the situation in the world.

[Cold War Language]

Finally, the entire sum total of the American Administration's steps in connection with the events in Afghanistan — the freezing of the SALT-II Treaty, refusal to deliver to the USSR a number of commodities, including grain, in accordance with some already concluded contracts, the termination of talks with the Soviet Union on a number of questions of bilateral relations and so on, shows that Washington again, like decades ago, is trying to speak with us in the language of the Cold War. In this the Carter Administration is displaying contempt for important interstate documents and is disrupting established ties in the field of science, culture and human contacts.

It is difficult even to enumerate the number of treaties, intergovernmental agreements, accords and understandings reached between our two countries on questions of mutual relations in various fields that have been arbitrarily and unilaterally violated lately by the government of President Carter. Of course, we will manage without these ties with the United States. In fact, we never sought these ties as some sort of a favor to us, believing that this is a mutually advantageous matter meeting the mutual interests of the peoples of our countries, first of all in the context of strengthening peace.

But the arrogation by Washington of some sort of a "right" to "reward" or "punish" independent sovereign states raises a question of a principled character. In effect, by such actions the U.S. Government deals a blow at the orderly international system of legal relations among states.

[Unreliable Partner]

As a result of the Carter Administration's action the impression is increasingly forming in the world of the United States as an absolutely unreliable partner in inter-state ties, as a state whose leadership, prompted by some whim, caprice or emotional outbursts, or by considerations of narrowly understood immediate advantage, is capable at any moment of violating its international obligations and canceling treaties and agreements signed by it. There is hardly any need to explain what a dangerous destabilizing impact this has on the entire international situation, the more so that this is the behavior of the leadership of a big influential power from which the peoples have the right to expect a well-considered and responsible policy.

But, of course, these actions of the U.S. Administration will not inflict on us the damage obviously hoped for by their initiators. The cynical estimates concerning the worsening of the food situation in the Soviet Union as a result of the U.S. refusal to sell us grain are based on nonsensical notions about our economic potential. The Soviet people have sufficient possibilities to live and work calmly, to fulfill our plans, to raise our living standards. In particular, I can assure you that the

13

plans to provide Soviet people with bread and bakery products will not be lessened by a single kilogram.

We can regard the actions of the American Administration only as a poorly weighed attempt to use the events in Afghanistan for blocking international efforts to lessen the military danger, to strengthen peace, to restrict the arms race, in short for blocking the attainment of aims in which humankind is vitally interested.

The unilateral measures taken by the United States are tantamount to serious miscalculations in politics. Like a boomerang, they will hit back at their initiators, if not today then tomorrow.

Now if all these sallies against our policy are intended to check our mettle, this means that the experience of history is totally ignored. When the world's first socialist state was born in 1917, our people did not ask anybody's permission. And now, too, they decide themselves what their way of life is to be. Imperialism tried to put us to test already at the dawn of Soviet government, and everybody remembers what came out of this. The fascist aggressors tried to break us in the bloodiest war ever experienced by humankind. But they suffered a defeat. We were subjected to trials in the years of the Cold War, when the world was being pushed to the brink of the precipice, when one international crisis was engineered after another. But then, too, nobody succeeded in making us waver. It is very useful to remember this today.

Q: What, in your opinion, are the prospects of the development of the situation in Europe?

A: The situation in Europe today is much better than it was, say, in the early 1970s. But, of course, Washington's latest irresponsible actions are making themselves felt here as well. The United States is not content with doing almost everything to poison Soviet-American relations. It would like to spoil also the relations of West European countries with the Soviet Union, relations in which, as is known, many useful things were achieved during the past decade. The United States is trying to undermine the spirit and essence of the Helsinki Final Act, which has become a recognized milestone in strengthening security and developing peaceful cooperation on the continent. Last but not least, by its steps directed at aggravating the international situation, Washington pursues the aim of putting under the European states, first of all its own allies.

But the cardinal interests of the European peoples are unbreakably connected with detente. The Europeans have already come to know its beneficial fruits from their own experience. They are inhabitants of a continent that has been marked more than once by devastating wars, and they are by no means prepared, and we are convinced of this, to embark on a road of ventures at the bidding of politicians from across the ocean. It is impossible to believe that there can be states in Europe that would wish to throw the fruit of detente under the feet of those who are ready to trample them. Western states, and the United States as well, need detente in Europe by no means to a lesser extent than the socialist countries or the Soviet Union.

[Future Peace]

Much of a constructive nature can be accomplished in Europe for the good of peace in the near future, in particular, in connection with the forthcoming meeting in Madrid and the proposal by Warsaw Treaty countries to hold a conference on military detente and disarmament. We resolutely are for consolidating and multiplying everything positive that has been created over the years in the European continent through the collective efforts of states, big and small. We will further pursue a policy of peace and friendship between peoples.

In stark contrast to Washington's present extremist position, our position is to continue the talks started in recent years along many directions, with the aim of stopping the arms race. This, naturally, also applies to problems of lessening military confrontation in Europe.

I repeat: We are for talks, but for honest and equal talks, for observance of the principle of equal security. It is exactly such talks that we recently proposed to start on the question of medium-range nuclear arms. Nobody can expect the Soviet Union to accept NATO's terms, designed for conducting talks from positions of strength. The present position of NATO countries makes talks on this problem impossible. We formally told the U.S. Government about all this a number of days ago.

We look into the future with optimism. It is a well-founded optimism. We understand that the deliberate aggravation of the international situation by American imperialism expresses its displeasure at the consolidation of the positions of socialism, the upsurge of the national liberation movement, the strengthening of forces coming out for detente and peace. We know that the will of the peoples has cleared, through all obstacles, a road for a positive direction in world affairs that is well expressed by the word "detente." This policy has deep roots. It is supported by mighty forces, and this policy has every chance to remain the leading tendency in relations between states.

Our people and our country are firmly advancing along the road of communist construction, fulfilling the assignments of the Tenth Five-Year Plan, the tasks set by the party. Soviet people and our friends abroad can rest assured that the Leninist foreign policy course is unflagging. It was defined by the decisions of CPSU congresses and is being embodied in all our foreign policy activities. This course combines consistent peaceableness with a firm rebuff to aggression. It has justified itself in past decades and we will adhere to it further. No one will push us off this course.

REPORT ON SMOKING BY WOMEN
January 14, 1980

In a report released Jan. 14, Dr. Julius B. Richmond, U.S. surgeon general, warned that lung cancer would overtake breast cancer as the leading cancer-related cause of death among women. "Within three years," the report stated, "the lung cancer death rate is expected to surpass that for breast cancer."

The 400-page report, entitled "The Health Consequences of Smoking for Women," said that women who smoked as men did incurred the same health risks. The surgeon general's report shattered the myth that women were not so susceptible as men to the health problems caused by smoking. It said that "is an illusion reflecting the fact that women lagged one-quarter century behind men in their widespread use of cigarettes."

The report also concluded that:
● Smoking is a threat to pregnant women and to the well-being of their newborn infants.

● Women's smoking habits — the reasons for starting, continuing, stopping or failing to quit — may not be precisely the same as for men. The report called for research to clarify the differences.

● The percentage of adolescent female smokers — ages 17-19 — has remained constant and is higher than that of males in the same age group.

● Low-tar and nicotine cigarettes do not reduce significantly the health hazards associated with smoking.

Annual Report

The document was the 12th annual report to Congress on smoking made by the Department of Health, Education and Welfare (now the Department of Health and Human Services) as required by the 1969 Public Health Cigarette Smoking Act (PL 91-222). Previous studies of smokers focused on men, the report said, because large numbers of women did not take up smoking until World War II. Women who smoked "are now only in their thirties, forties and fifties," the report stated, adding that "[a]s these women grow older, and continue to smoke, their burden of smoking-related disease will grow larger."

The report did not present completely new findings. It was, however, a comprehensive synthesis of scientific documents pertaining to women and smoking brought together for the first time in one study.

Patricia Roberts Harris, secretary of Health, Education and Welfare, noted in a cover letter accompanying the report that it was "one of the most alarming in the series." But Harris did not attend the ceremony at which the report was presented. The outspoken criticism of smoking by her predecessor as secretary, Joseph A. Califano Jr., had aroused the ire of the tobacco industry.

Pregnancy and Smoking

Pregnant women who smoke, the report asserted, run a greater risk of problems before, during and after childbirth. They have greater frequency of spontaneous abortions or of delivering babies with below average weight.

"Scientific studies encompassing various races and ethnic groups, cultures and countries, involving hundreds of thousands of pregnancies," the report continued, "have shown that cigarette smoking during pregnancy significantly affects the unborn fetus and the newborn baby. These damaging effects have been repeatedly shown to operate independently of all other factors which influence the outcome of pregnancy. The effects are increased by heavier smoking and are reduced if a women stops smoking during pregnancy."

The study also stated that the long-term growth and intellectual development of children born to smoking mothers may be adversely affected.

Adolescent Smokers

One of the significant findings was that while smoking had declined among both male and female smokers in the population at large over the preceding few years the percentage of adolescent female smokers,

17 to 19, had remained steady and exceeded that of male smokers of the same age.

Noting that health damage due to cigarette smoking increased when a person began smoking at an early age, the report acknowledged that the reasons were "far from clear" why a higher proportion of teen-age girls than teen-age boys smoked. But the report suggested that "smoking patterns among girls correlate with parental, peer and sibling smoking habits, educational level, type of school curriculum, academic performance, socioeconomic status, and other forms of substance abuse. . . ."

Low Tar Cigarettes

The study also cautioned that smokers who switched to low tar and nicotine cigarettes did not eliminate health hazards. Although filter tips reduced the amounts of tar and nicotine taken into the system, the report said, many filter cigarettes conveyed higher levels of other harmful substances into the system — particularly carbon monoxide.

Even the lowest yield filter cigarettes presented "very much higher" health hazards for men and women than smoking no cigarettes at all, the report said. "The single most effective way for both men and women smokers to reduce the hazards associated with cigarettes is to quit smoking."

Reaction

The Tobacco Institute — the Washington, D.C.-based association representing the tobacco industry — called the report simplistic.

Connie Drath, assistant to the president of the institute, said the increase in lung cancer among women could be the result of "better detection methods." She added that the increase could even be smaller than the surgeon general's report indicated, but she offered no data to support her statement.

Drath also said she doubted the report had established any relationship between smoking mothers and the mental and physical development of their children.

> *Following are excerpts from the texts of a cover letter by Patricia Roberts Harris, secretary of Health, Education and Welfare, and the 12th annual report on smoking of the U.S. surgeon general, "The Health Consequences of Smoking for Women," both released Jan. 14, 1980. (Boldface headings in brackets have been added by Congressional Quarterly to highlight the organization of the text.):*

LETTER OF TRANSMITTAL

The Honorable Thomas P. O'Neill, Jr.
Speaker of the House of Representatives
Washington, D.C. 20515

Dear Mr. Speaker:

I hereby submit the 12th annual report that the Department of Health, Education, and Welfare (DHEW) has prepared for Congress as required by the Public Health Cigarette Smoking Act of 1969, Public Law 91-222, and its predecessor, the Federal Cigarette Labeling and Advertising Act. This report is one of the most alarming in the series.

It clearly establishes that women smokers face the same risks as men smokers of lung cancer, heart disease, lung disease and other consequences. Perhaps more disheartening is the harm which mothers' smoking causes to their unborn babies and infants.

The report is not all bad news. It presents recent data showing that women are turning away from smoking in response to the warnings of government, voluntary agencies and physicians. The precipitate rise in women's deaths from lung cancer and chronic lung disease demand that this trend away from cigarettes be accelerated. Our scientists expect that by 1983, the lung cancer death rate will exceed that of any other type of cancer among women.

Citizens of our free society may decide for themselves whether to smoke cigarettes. The health consequences of this decision make it imperative for their government to assure that the decision is an informed one. This series of reports is one way in which DHEW is striving to meet this critical responsibility.

Sincerely yours,

Patricia Roberts Harris

WOMEN AND SMOKING

[Introduction]

This report is more than a factual review of the health consequences of smoking for women. It is a document which challenges our society and, in particular, our medical and public health communities.

This report points out that the first signs of an epidemic of smoking-related disease among women are now appearing. Because women's cigarette use did not become widespread until the onset of World War

II, those women with the greatest intensity of smoking are now only in their thirties, forties, and fifties. As these women grow older, and continue to smoke, their burden of smoking-related disease will grow larger. Cigarette smoking now contributes to one-fifth of the newly diagnosed cases of cancer and one-quarter of all cancer deaths among women — more cancer and more cancer deaths among women than can be atttributed to any other known agent. Within three years, the lung cancer death rate is expected to surpass that for breast cancer. A similar epidemic of chronic obstructive lung disease among women has also begun.

Four main themes emerge from this report to guide future public health efforts.

First, women are not immune to the damaging effects of smoking already documented for men. The apparently lower susceptibility to smoking related diseases among women smokers is an illusion reflecting the fact that women lagged one-quarter century behind men in their widespread use of cigarettes.

Second, cigarette smoking is a major threat to the outcome of pregnancy and well-being of the newborn baby.

Third, women may not start smoking, continue to smoke, quit smoking, or fail to quit smoking for precisely the same reasons as men. Unless future research clarifies these differences, we will find it difficult to prevent initiation or to promote cessation of cigarette smoking among women.

Fourth, the reduction of cigarette smoking is the keystone in our nation's long term strategy to promote a healthy lifestyle for women and men of all races and ethnic groups.

The Fallacy of Women's Immunity

All of the major prospective studies of smoking and mortality have reached consistent conclusions. Death rates from coronary heart disease, chronic lung disease, lung cancer, and overall mortality rates are significantly increased among both women and men smokers. These risks increase with the amount smoked, duration of smoking, depth of inhalation, and the "tar" and nicotine delivery of the cigarette smoked.

In these studies, conducted during the past three decades, relative mortality risks among female smokers appeared to be less than those of male smokers. It is now clear, however, that these studies were comparing the death rates of a generation of established, lifelong male smokers with a generation of women who had not yet taken up smoking with full intensity. Even those older women who reported smoking a large number of cigarettes per day had not smoked cigarettes in the same way as their male counterparts. Now that the cigarette smoking characteristics of women and men are becoming increasingly similar, their relative risks of smoking-related illness will become increasingly similar.

21

This fallacy of women's apparent immunity is clearly illustrated by differences in the timing of the growth in lung cancer among men and women in this century. Lung cancer deaths among males began to increase during the 1930s, as those men who had converted from other forms of tobacco to cigarette smoking before the turn of the century gradually accumulated decades of inhaled tobacco exposure. By the time of the first retrospective studies of smoking and lung cancer in 1950, two entire generations of men had already become lifelong cigarette smokers. Relatively few women from these generations smoked cigarettes, and even fewer had smoked cigarettes since their adolescence. Those young women who had taken up smoking intensively during World War II were only in their twenties and thirties. In 1950, women accounted for less than one in twelve deaths from lung cancer.

Thereafter, the age adjusted lung cancer death rate among women accelerated, and the male predominance in lung cancer declined. Lung cancer surpassed uterine cervical cancer as a cause of death in women. By 1968, as the findings of many large population prospective studies were being published, women accounted for one-sixth of all lung cancer deaths. These studies found that women cigarette smokers had 2.5 to 5 times greater death rates from lung cancer than women nonsmokers. By 1979, women accounted for fully one-fourth all lung cancer deaths. Over the next few years, women cigarette smokers' risk of lung cancer death will approach 8 to 12 times that of women nonsmokers, the same relative risk as that of men.

Lung cancer has four main histological types: epidermoid, small cell, adenocarcinoma, and large cell carcinoma. As several studies have shown, the incidence of each of these types of lung cancer displays a clear relationship to cigarette smoking among both men and women. Epidermoid and small cell lung cancer appear to be more prominent among men, while adenocarcinoma of the lung now appears to be more prominent among women.

The recent acceleration of lung cancer incidence among women has in fact been more rapid than the corresponding growth of lung cancer among men in the 1930s. Again, this difference in the initial rate of acceleration of lung cancer incidence does not refute the demonstrated causal relation between cigarette smoking and lung cancer among both sexes. Instead, differences in the rate of increase of lung cancer incidence may reflect changes in the carcinogenic properties of cigarette smoke, the style of cigarette smoking, or the interaction of cigarette smoking with other environmental hazards. It is noteworthy that those men who died of lung cancer in the 1930s came from a generation that had gradually converted to cigarettes from other, non-inhaled forms of tobacco. By contrast, the first regular tobacco users among women were almost exclusively cigarette smokers.

The 1979 Report on Smoking and Health documented numerous instances where cigarette smoking adds to the hazards of the workplace environment among men. Among women, this report reveals two such occupational exposures — asbestos and cotton dust — which have been clearly demonstrated to interact with cigarette smoking. The fact that evidence is limited among women does not imply that women are protected from the dangerous interactions of smoking and occupational exposures.

Pregnancy, Infant Health, and Reproduction

Scientific studies encompassing various races and ethnic groups, cultures and countries, involving hundreds of thousands of pregnancies, have shown that cigarette smoking during pregnancy significantly affects the unborn fetus and the newborn baby. These damaging effects have been repeatedly shown to operate independently of all other factors which influence the outcome of pregnancy. The effects are increased by heavier smoking and are reduced if a woman stops smoking during pregnancy.

Numerous toxic substances in cigarette smoke, such as nicotine and hydrogen cyanide, cross the placenta to affect the fetus directly. The carbon monoxide from cigarette smoke is transported into the fetal blood and deprives the growing baby of oxygen. Fetal growth is directly retarded. The resulting reduction in fetal weight and size has many unfortunate consequences. Women who smoke cigarettes during pregnancy have more spontaneous abortions, and a greater incidence of bleeding during pregnancy, premature and prolonged rupture of amniotic membranes, abruptio placentae and placenta previa. Women who smoke cigarettes during pregnancy have more fetal and neonatal deaths than nonsmoking pregnant women. A relation between maternal smoking and Sudden Infant Death Syndrome has now been established.

[DIRECT HARMFUL EFFECTS]

The direct harmful effects of smoking on the fetus have long term consequences. Children of mothers who smoked during pregnancy lag measurably in physical growth; there may also be effects on behavior and cognitive development. The extent of these deficiencies increases with the number of cigarettes smoked.

The damaging effects of maternal smoking on infants are not restricted to pregnancy. Nicotine, a known poison, is found in the breast milk of smoking mothers. Children whose parents smoke cigarettes have more respiratory infections and more hospitalizations in the first year of life.

Women who smoke cigarettes have more than three times the risk of dying of stroke due to subarachnoid hermorrhage, and as much as two times the risk of dying of heart attack in comparison to nonsmoking women. The use of oral contraceptives in addition to smoking, however, causes a markedly increased risk, including a 22-fold increase in the risk of subarachnoid hemorrhagic stroke and a 20-fold increase in heart attack in heavy smokers.

Why Do Women Smoke?

Cigarette consumption in this country is now declining. Annual per capita consumption has decreased from 4,258 in 1965 to an estimated 3,900 in 1979. From 1965 to 1979, the proportion of adult male cigarette smokers declined from 51 to 37 percent. Not only have millions of men quit smoking, but the rate of initiation of smoking among adolescent males has now slowed.

From 1965 to 1976, the proportion of adult women cigarette smokers remained virtually unchanged at 32 to 33 percent. Since 1976, however, the proportion of adult women cigarette smokers appears to have declined to 28 percent. Although adult women are now beginning to quit smoking at rates comparable to adult men, the rate of initiation of smoking among younger women has not declined.

This report documents numerous differences by sex in the perceived role of cigarette smoking, in attitudes toward health and lifestyle, and in methods of coping with stress, anger, and boredom. Yet the significance of these differences, and their relation to differences in smoking patterns, remains poorly understood.

Although it is frequently observed that women in organized smoking cessation programs have more severe withdrawal symptoms and lower rates of successful quitting than men, these observations have not been systematically confirmed for the general population. In the past, women may have attempted to quit or succeeded in quitting smoking less frequently than men. The recent decline in the proportion of women smokers, however, suggests that women's attempted and successful quitting rates have now increased.

Although weight gain is a frequently cited consequence of quitting smoking, the association of weight gain with cessation of smoking has not been the subject of sufficient scrutiny. Controlled studies with careful measurement on representative populations of women do not exist. The impact of the fear of weight gain after quitting has not been adequately examined. If weight gain does result from cessation of smoking, its exact mechanism must be determined.

Even more problematic are marked differences by sex in the distribution of smoking prevalence by occupation. Men with advanced education and professional occupations have taken the lead in quitting smoking, but women in administrative and managerial positions have relatively high smoking prevalence rates. Although 20 percent or fewer male physicians smoke, the proportions of cigarette smokers among women health professionals, especially nurses and psychologists, remain disturbingly high.

Recent changes in smoking prevalence among black women and men have paralleled those of the general population. From 1965 to 1979, the proportion of black women cigarette smokers declined from 34 to 29 percent, while the proportion of black men smokers declined from 61 to 42 percent. However, differences by race in the onset, maintenance, and cessation of smoking have not been adequately explored. Little is known about cigarette smoking among other ethnic and minority groups.

Adolescent Smoking

The health consequences of smoking evolve over a lifetime. Evidence continues to accumulate, for example, that cigarette smoking produces measurable lung changes even in childhood and young adulthood. Young cigarette smokers of both sexes show more evidence of small airway dysfunction, and a higher prevalence of cough, wheezing, phlegm production, and other respiratory symptoms. The health damage due to cigarette smoking increases when an individual begins regular smoking earlier in life. Yet, as this report documents, the average age of onset of regular smoking among women has continuously declined during the last 50 years, and continues to decline.

According to a recent survey by the National Institute of Education, cigarette smoking among adolescent girls now exceeds that among adolescent boys. In the 17-19 year age group, there are almost 5 female cigarette smokers for every 4 male cigarette smokers. The causes of this inversion are far from clear. We do not yet understand the signal events in the initiation of smoking among young women. It is possible that parents set examples concerning lifestyle, health attitude, and risk-taking much earlier in childhood. The beginning of junior high school or entrance into the work force may be equally critical events. We do not know enough about an adolescent's sense of competence and self-mastery, and how these roles differ among women and men. Although smoking patterns among girls correlate with parental, peer and sibling smoking habits, educational level, type of school curriculum, academic performance, socioeconomic status, and other forms of substance abuse, the practical significance of these empirical correlations is unclear.

Women and the Changing Cigarette

As this report documents, the proportion of men and women smokers using brands with lowered "tar" and nicotine continues to grow. Adolescents of both sexes have followed this trend, to the point where nonfilter cigarettes are relatively rare among young adults.

Although the preponderance of scientific evidence continues to suggest that cigarettes with lower "tar" and nicotine are less hazardous, four serious warnings are in order.

First, the reported "tar" and nicotine deliveries of cigarettes are standardized machine measurements. They do not necessarily represent the smoker's actual intake of these substances. Evidence is now mounting that individuals who switch to cigarettes with lowered "tar" and nicotine inhale more deeply, smoke a greater proportion of their cigarettes, and in some cases smoke more cigarettes.

Second, "tar" and nicotine are not the only dangerous chemical components of cigarette smoke. Many conventional filter cigarettes, in fact, may deliver more carbon monoxide than nonfilter cigarettes.

Third, it has not been established that lower "tar" and nicotine cigarettes have less harmful effects on the unborn fetus and baby; on women and men at high risk for developing coronary heart disease, such as those with elevated cholesterol or high blood pressure; or on workers with adverse occupational exposures. It has not been established that switching to a lower "tar" and nicotine cigarette has any salutory effect on individuals who already have smoking-related illnesses, such as coronary heart disease, chronic bronchitis, and emphysema.

Fourth, even the lowest yield cigarettes present health hazards for both women and men that are very much higher than smoking no cigarettes at all.

The single most effective way for both women and men smokers to reduce the hazards associated with cigarettes is to quit smoking.

As this report demonstrates, little is known about the effects of these product changes on the initiation, maintenance and cessation of smoking, particularly among women. It has not been determined whether the availability of cigarettes with lowered "tar" and nicotine has made it easier for young women to experiment with and become addicted to cigarettes. It is not known whether smokers of the lowest yield cigarettes are more or less likely to attempt to quit, or to succeed in quitting, than smokers of conventional filtertip or nonfilter cigarettes. The extent to which the act of switching to a lower "tar" cigarette may serve as a substitute for quitting may differ among women and men.

Public Health Responsibilities

This report ... has confirmed in every way the judgement of the World Health Organization, that there can no longer be any doubt among informed people that cigarette smoking is a major and removable cause of ill health and premature death.

Each individual woman must make her own decision about this significant health issue. Secretary Harris has noted that the role of the Government, and all responsible health professionals, is to assure that this decision is an informed one. In issuing this report, we hope to help the public health community accomplish this purpose.

Julius B. Richmond, M.D.
Assistant Secretary for
Health and Surgeon General

STATE OF THE UNION ADDRESS, ACCOMPANYING MESSAGE

January 21 and 23, 1980

Responding forcefully to the Soviet armed intervention in Afghanistan, President Carter in his State of the Union address Jan. 23 said that the United States was prepared to go to war if necessary to protect its security interests in the Persian Gulf region.

The most direct challenge to the nation, the president said, came from the Soviet Union because its "radical and aggressive" invasion of Afghanistan "could pose the most serious threat to the peace since the Second World War."

Carter's State of the Union address, delivered before a joint session of Congress and televised nationally, repeatedly was interrupted by thunderclaps of applause. The address focused on foreign policy. A 75-page written message Carter had sent Congress on Jan. 21 contained his administration's detailed proposals.

'Carter Doctrine'

In his speech, Carter said that "An attempt by any outside force to gain control of the Persian Gulf region will be regarded as an assault on the vital interests of the United States of America, and such an assault will be repelled by any means necessary, including military force." Reporters and analysts were quick to refer to the blunt warning as the "Carter doctrine."

As he delivered his address, observers said, the president seemed to be riding the crest of a wave of strong national sentiment. The mood, they believed, was evoked not only by the Soviet military action that began Dec. 26, 1979, but also by the seizure of more than 50 American hostages in Tehran, Iran, on Nov. 4, 1979. (Historic Documents of 1979, pp. 867, 965)

Written Message

In the detailed, written message, Carter told Congress he was limiting his major domestic proposals. Administration officials said the initiatives were fewer than usual because in an election year Congress would have only 80 working days.

The message did, however, contain five major legislative proposals:
●A new program to assist utilities in converting from oil and natural gas to coal. The program would provide utilities with $12 billion in grants and loans over a decade.
●New legislative authority for the general revenue-sharing program for state and local governments.
●A standby gasoline rationing plan that the president said he would send Congress under authority of 1979 legislation (PL 96-102).
●The reorganization of the Nuclear Regulatory Commission (NRC) to strengthen the role of the chairman and legislation to launch the first comprehensive nuclear waste management program.
●Expansion (by $2 billion over two years) of the youth employment program to provide basic skills and work experience to more than 1.5 million additional disadvantaged young people annually.

U.S.-Soviet Relations

Before the State of the Union address, the president had imposed a number of economic sanctions against the Soviet Union, including an embargo on new sales to Russia of grain and other agricultural goods and such high technology items as computers, and a ban on Soviet fishing within U.S. territorial waters.

In the address, Carter also called for a U.S. boycott of the 1980 Summer Olympics scheduled to be held in Moscow. He asserted that "neither the American people nor I will support sending an Olympic team to Moscow" while Soviet forces remained in Afghanistan.

He asked Congress to remove "unwarranted restrictions" on U.S. intelligence-gathering capabilities, to reinstate national registration for the military draft, and, "as the first order of business," to approve an economic and military aid package "designed to assist Pakistan to defend itself."

Many analysts believed that the shifts in U.S. foreign policy Carter enunciated had been evolving over a number of months. The changes coalesced, they believed, with the crises in the Middle East and Southwest Asia. At the very least, the period known as "détente" in U.S.-Soviet relations clearly had come to an end, and it appeared highly uncertain what would follow. Virtually lost in the shuffle was the SALT II treaty that until the Afghanistan invasion had ranked as one of Carter's highest priorities. The president made only a brief mention of the treaty. (SALT II, Historic Documents of 1979, p. 413)

Hostages in Iran

Although overshadowed in the State of the Union address by Soviet military moves in Afghanistan, the continued holding of 50 American hostages by Iranian militants at the U.S. Embassy in Tehran was noted by Carter.

The president repeated earlier warnings that "a severe price will be paid" if the hostages were harmed, and he again attempted to tell the Iranians that the real danger "lies in the north, in the Soviet Union and from the Soviet troops now in Afghanistan, and that the unwarranted Iranian quarrel with the United States hampers their response to this far greater danger to them."

National Defense

Carter asked Congress to approve a fiscal 1981 defense budget that would provide a 5 percent increase in new budget authority, after allowing for inflation. As a candidate for president, Carter had vowed to cut $5 billion to $7 billion each year from the defense budget.

He also listed steps he was taking to strengthen U.S. defense forces, including development of the cruise missile and the M-X mobile intercontinental missile, an increased U.S. presence in the Indian Ocean, a search for permanent air and naval facilities in the Middle East, and the assembling of "rapid deployment forces." The latter, Carter said, "could range in size from a few ships or air squadrons to formations as large as 100,000 men, together with their support." The new forces would be prepared, the president said, "for rapid deployment to any region of strategic significance."

Reaction

The immediate reaction to the president's hard-hitting speech was largely favorable. The Wall Street Journal *in an editorial said that "in the new tone of Mr. Carter's speech, and in his new willingness to face up to decisions . . . , we find a considerably hopeful sign." But the newspaper said the speech had "an element of bravado. It is not entirely believable, especially since it is far from clear that he would have the forces at his disposal to do anything effective."*

An early call for caution was sounded by George F. Kennan, a historian and former U.S. ambassador to Soviet Russia and Yugoslavia. In an article published in The New York Times *Feb. 1 and widely quoted,*

Kennan wrote that the official response to the Afghanistan invasion had "revealed a disquieting lack of balance." Questioning official assumptions of "the Soviet motivation," Kennan wrote, "If there was ever a time for realism, prudence and restraint in American statesmanship, it is this one."

Following are the text of President Carter's nationally televised State of the Union address to Congress Jan. 23, and excerpts from his more detailed written message sent to Congress Jan. 21. (Boldface headings in brackets have been added by Congressional Quarterly to highlight the organization of the texts.):

STATE OF THE UNION ADDRESS

Mr. President, Mr. Speaker, Members of the 96th Congress, fellow citizens:

This last few months has not been an easy time for any of us. As we meet tonight, it has never been more clear that the state of our Union depends on the state of the world. And tonight, as throughout our own generation, freedom and peace in the world depend on the state of our Union.

The 1980's have been born in turmoil, strife, and change. This is a time of challenge to our interests and our values and it's a time that tests our wisdom and our skills.

At this time in Iran, 50 Americans are still held captive, innocent victims of terrorism and anarchy. Also at this moment, massive Soviet troops are attempting to subjugate the fiercely independent and deeply religious people of Afghanistan. These two acts — one of international terrorism and one of military aggression — present a serious challenge to the United States of America and indeed to all the nations of the world. Together, we will meet these threats to peace.

I'm determined that the United States will remain the strongest of all nations, but our power will never be used to initiate a threat to the security of any nation or to the rights of any human being. We seek to be and to remain secure — a nation at peace in a stable world. But to be secure we must face the world as it is.

[Three Developments]

Three basic developments have helped to shape our challenges: the steady growth and increased projection of Soviet military power beyond its own borders; the overwhelming dependence of the Western democracies on oil supplies from the Middle East; and the press of social and religious and economic and political change in the many nations of the developing world, exemplified by the revolution in Iran.

Each of these factors is important in its own right. Each interacts with the others. All must be faced together, squarely and courageously. We will face these challenges, and we will meet them with the best that is in us. And we will not fail.

In response to the abhorrent act in Iran, our Nation has never been aroused and unified so greatly in peacetime. Our position is clear. The United States will not yield to blackmail.

We continue to pursue these specific goals: first, to protect the present and long-range interests of the United States; secondly, to preserve the lives of the American hostages and to secure, as quickly as possible, their safe release, if possible, to avoid bloodshed which might further endanger the lives of our fellow citizens; to enlist the help of other nations in condemning this act of violence, which is shocking and violates the moral and the legal standards of a civilized world; and also to convince and to persuade the Iranian leaders that the real danger to their nation lies in the north, in the Soviet Union and from the Soviet troops now in Afghanistan, and that the unwarranted Iranian quarrel with the United States hampers their response to this far greater danger to them.

If the American hostages are harmed, a severe price will be paid. We will never rest until every one of the American hostages are released.

[Soviet Challenge]

But now we face a broader and more fundamental challenge in this region because of the recent military action of the Soviet Union.

Now, as during the last 3-1/2 decades, the relationship between our country, the United States of America, and the Soviet Union is the most critical factor in determining whether the world will live at peace or be engulfed in global conflict.

Since the end of the Second World War, America has led other nations in meeting the challenge of mounting Soviet power. This has not been a simple or a static relationship. Between us there has been cooperation, there has been competition, and at times there has been confrontation.

In the 1940's we took the lead in creating the Atlantic Alliance in response to the Soviet Union's suppression and then consolidation of its East European empire and the resulting threat of the Warsaw Pact to Western Europe.

In the 1950's we helped to contain further Soviet challenges in Korea and in the Middle East, and we rearmed to assure the continuation of that containment.

In the 1960's we met the Soviet challenges in Berlin, and we faced the Cuban missile crisis. And we sought to engage the Soviet Union in the important task of moving beyond the cold war and away from confrontation.

And in the 1970's three American Presidents negotiated with the Soviet leaders in attempts to halt the growth of the nuclear arms race. We sought to establish rules of behavior that would reduce the risks of conflict, and we searched for areas of cooperation that could make our relations reciprocal and productive, not only for the sake of our two nations but for the security and peace of the entire world.

[Two Commitments]

In all these actions, we have maintained two commitments: to be ready to meet any challenge by Soviet military power, and to develop ways to resolve disputes and to keep the peace.

Preventing nuclear war is the foremost responsibility of the two superpowers. That's why we've negotiated the strategic arms limitation treaties — SALT I and SALT II. Especially now, in a time of great tension, observing the mutual constraints imposed by the terms of these treaties will be in the best interest of both countries and will help to preserve world peace. I will consult very closely with the Congress on this matter as we strive to control nuclear weapons. That effort to control nuclear weapons will not be abandoned.

We superpowers also have the responsibility to exercise restraint in the use of our great military force. The integrity and the independence of weaker nations must not be threatened. They must know that in our presence they are secure.

But now the Soviet Union has taken a radical and an aggressive new step. It's using its great military power against a relatively defenseless nation. The implications of the Soviet invasion of Afghanistan could pose the most serious threat to the peace since the Second World War.

The vast majority of nations on Earth have condemned this latest Soviet attempt to extend its colonial domination of others and have demanded the immediate withdrawal of Soviet troops. The Moslem world is especially and justifiably outraged by this aggression against an Islamic people. No action of a world power has ever been so quickly and so overwhelmingly condemned. But verbal condemnation is not enough. The Soviet Union must pay a concrete price for their aggression.

[Economic Penalties Imposed]

While this invasion continues, we and the other nations of the world cannot conduct business as usual with the Soviet Union. That's why the United States has imposed stiff economic penalties on the Soviet Union. I will not issue any permits for Soviet ships to fish in the coastal waters of the United States. I've cut Soviet access to high-technology equipment and to agricultural products. I've limited other commerce with the Soviet Union, and I've asked our allies and friends to join with us in restraining their own trade with the Soviets and not to replace our own embargoed items. And I have notified the Olympic Committee that with Soviet invading forces in Afghanistan, neither the American people nor I will support sending an Olympic team to Moscow.

The Soviet Union is going to have to answer some basic questions: Will it help promote a more stable international environment in which its own legitimate, peaceful concerns can be pursued? Or will it continue to expand its military power far beyond its genuine security needs, and use that power for colonial conquest? The Soviet Union must realize that its decision to use military force in Afghanistan will be costly to every political and economic relationship it values.

[Importance of Region]

The region which is now threatened by Soviet troops in Afghanistan is of great strategic importance: It contains more than two-thirds of the world's exportable oil. The Soviet effort to dominate Afghanistan has brought Soviet military forces to within 300 miles of the Indian Ocean and close to the Straits of Hormuz, a waterway through which most of the world's oil must flow. The Soviet Union is now attempting to consolidate a strategic position, therefore, that poses a grave threat to the free movement of Middle East oil.

This situation demands careful thought, steady nerves, and resolute action, not only for this year but for many years to come. It demands collective efforts to meet this new threat to security in the Persian Gulf and in Southwest Asia. It demands the participation of all those who rely on oil from the Middle East and who are concerned with global peace and stability. And it demands consultation and close cooperation with countries in the area which might be threatened.

Meeting this challenge will take national will, diplomatic and political wisdom, economic sacrifice, and, of course, military capability. We must call on the best that is in us to preserve the security of this crucial region.

[Warning]

Let our position be absolutely clear: An attempt by any outside force to gain control of the Persian Gulf region will be regarded as an assault on the vital interests of the United States of America, and such an assault will be repelled by any means necessary, including military force.

During the past 3 years, you have joined with me to improve our own security and the prospects for peace, not only in the vital oil-producing area of the Persian Gulf region but around the world. We've increased annually our real commitment for defense, and we will sustain this increase of effort throughout the Five Year Defense Program. It's imperative that Congress approve this strong defense budget for 1981, encompassing a 5-percent real growth in authorizations, without any reduction.

We are also improving our capability to deploy U.S. military forces rapidly to distant areas. We've helped to strengthen NATO and our other alliances, and recently we and other NATO members have decided to develop and to deploy modernized, intermediate-range nuclear forces to meet an unwarranted and increased threat from the nuclear weapons of the Soviet Union.

[Middle East]

We are working with our allies to prevent conflict in the Middle East. The peace treaty between Egypt and Israel is a notable achievement which represents a strategic asset for America and which also enhances prospects for regional and world peace. We are now engaged in further negotiations to provide full autonomy for the people of the West Bank and Gaza, to resolve the Palestinian issue in all its aspects, and to preserve the peace and security of Israel. Let no one doubt our commitment to the security of Israel. In a few days we will observe an historic event when Israel makes another major withdrawal from the Sinai and when ambassadors will be exchanged between Israel and Egypt.

We've also expanded our own sphere of friendship. Our deep commitment to human rights and to meeting human needs has improved our relationship with much of the Third World. Our decision to normalize relations with the People's Republic of China will help to preserve peace and stability in Asia and in the Western Pacific.

We've increased and strengthened our naval presence in the Indian Ocean, and we are now making arrangements for key naval and air facilities to be used by our forces in the region of northeast Africa and the Persian Gulf.

[Pakistan]

We've reconfirmed our 1959 agreement to help Pakistan preserve its independence and its integrity. The United States will take action consistent with our own laws to assist Pakistan in resisting any outside aggression. And I'm asking the Congress specifically to reaffirm this agreement. I'm also working, along with the leaders of other nations, to provide additional military and economic aid for Pakistan. That request will come to you in just a few days.

In the weeks ahead, we will further strengthen political and military ties with other nations in the region. We believe that there are no irreconcilable differences between us and any Islamic nation. We respect the faith of Islam, and we are ready to cooperate with all Moslem countries.

Finally, we are prepared to work with other countries in the region to share a cooperative security framework that respects differing values and political beliefs, yet which enhances the independence, security, and prosperity of all.

All these efforts combined emphasize our dedication to defend and preserve the vital interests of the region and of the nation which we represent and those of our allies — in Europe and the Pacific, and also in the parts of the world which have such great strategic importance to us, stretching especially through the Middle East and Southwest Asia. With your help, I will pursue these efforts with vigor and with determination. You and I will act as necessary to protect and to preserve our Nation's security.

[Selective Service and Intelligence]

The men and women of America's Armed Forces are on duty tonight in many parts of the world. I'm proud of the job they are doing, and I know you share that pride. I believe that our volunteer forces are adequate for current defense needs, and I hope that it will not become necessary to impose a draft. However, we must be prepared for that possibility. For this reason, I have determined that the Selective Service System must now be revitalized. I will send legislation and budget proposals to the Congress next month so that we can begin registration and then meet future mobilization needs rapidly if they arise.

We also need clear and quick passage of a new charter to define the legal authority and accountability of our intelligence agencies. We will guarantee that abuses do not recur, but we must tighten our controls on sensitive intelligence information, and we need to remove unwarranted restraints on America's ability to collect intelligence.

The decade ahead will be a time of rapid change, as nations everywhere seek to deal with new problems and age-old tensions. But America need have no fear. We can thrive in a world of change if we remain true to our values and actively engaged in promoting world peace. We will continue to work as we have for peace in the Middle East and southern Africa. We will continue to build our ties with developing nations, respecting and helping to strengthen their national independence which they have struggled so hard to achieve. And we will continue to support the growth of democracy and the protection of human rights.

[Human Rights]

In repressive regimes, popular frustrations often have no outlet except through violence. But when peoples and their governments can approach their problems together through open, democratic methods, the basis for stability and peace is far more solid and far more enduring. That is why our support for human rights in other countries is in our own national interest as well as part of our own national character.

Peace — a peace that preserves freedom — remains America's first goal. In the coming years, as a mighty nation we will continue to pursue peace. But to be strong abroad we must be strong at home. And in order to be strong, we must continue to face up to the difficult issues that confront us as a nation today.

The crises in Iran and Afghanistan have dramatized a very important lesson: Our excessive dependence on foreign oil is a clear and present danger to our nation's security. The need has never been more urgent. At long last, we must have a clear, comprehensive energy policy for the United States.

[Energy Conservation]

As you well know, I have been working with the Congress in a concentrated and persistent way over the past 3 years to meet this need. We have made progress together. But Congress must act promptly now to complete final action on this vital energy legislation. Our Nation will then have a major conservation effort, important initiatives to develop solar power, realistic pricing based on the true value of oil, strong incentives for the production of coal and other fossil fuels in the United States, and our Nation's most massive peacetime investment in the development of synthetic fuels.

The American people are making progress in energy conservation. Last year we reduced overall petroleum consumption by 8 percent and gasoline consumption by 5 percent below what it was the year before. Now we must do more.

After consultation with the Governors, we will set gasoline conservation goals for each of the 50 States, and I will make them mandatory if these goals are not met.

I've established an import ceiling for 1980 of 8.2 million barrels a day — well below the level of foreign oil purchases in 1977. I expect our imports to be much lower than this, but the ceiling will be enforced by an oil import fee if necessary. I'm prepared to lower these imports still further if the other oil-consuming countries will join us in a fair and mutual reduction. If we have a serious shortage, I will not hesitate to impose mandatory gasoline rationing immediately.

The single biggest factor in the inflation rate last year, the increase in the inflation rate last year, was from one cause: the skyrocketing prices of OPEC oil. We must take whatever actions are necessary to reduce our dependence on foreign oil — and at the same time reduce inflation.

As individuals and as families, few of us can produce energy by ourselves. But all of us can conserve energy — every one of us, every day of our lives. Tonight I call on you — in fact, all of the people of America — to help óur Nation. Conserve energy. Eliminate waste. Make 1980 indeed a year of energy conservation.

[Economy]

Of course, we must take other actions to strengthen our Nation's economy.

First, we will continue to reduce the deficit and then to balance the Federal budget.

Second, as we continue to work with business to hold down prices, we'll build also on the historic national accord with organized labor to restrain pay increases in a fair fight against inflation.

Third, we will continue our successful efforts to cut paperwork and to dismantle unnecessary Government regulation.

Fourth, we will continue our progress in providing jobs for America, concentrating on a major new program to provide training and work for our young people, especially minority youth. It has been said that "a mind is a terrible thing to waste." We will give our young people new hope for jobs and a better life in the 1980's.

And fifth, we must use the decade of the 1980's to attack the basic structural weaknesses and problems in our economy through measures to increase productivity, savings, and investment.

With these energy and economic policies, we will make America even stronger at home in this decade — just as our foreign and defense policies will make us stronger and safer throughout the world. We will never abandon our struggle for a just and a decent society here at home. That's the heart of America — and it's the source of our ability to inspire other people to defend their own rights abroad.

Our material resources, great as they are, are limited. Our problems are too complex for simple slogans or for quick solutions. We cannot solve them without effort and sacrifice. Walter Lippmann once reminded us, "You took the good things for granted. Now you must earn them again. For every right that you cherish, you have a duty which you must fulfill. For every good which you wish to preserve, you will have to sacrifice your comfort and your ease. There is nothing for nothing any longer."

[Formidable Challenges]

Our challenges are formidable. But there's a new spirit of unity and resolve in our country. We move into the 1980's with confidence and hope and a bright vision of the America we want: an America strong and free, an America at peace, an America with equal rights for all citizens — and for women, guaranteed in the United States Constitution — an America with jobs and good health and good education for every citizen, an America with a clean and bountiful life in our cities and

37

on our farms, an America that helps to feed the world, an America secure in filling its own energy needs, an America of justice, tolerance and compassion. For this vision to come true, we must sacrifice, but this national commitment will be an exciting enterprise that will unify our people.

Together as one people, let us work to build our strength at home, and together as one indivisible union, let us seek peace and security throughout the world.

Together let us make of this time of challenge and danger a decade of national resolve and of brave achievement.

Thank you very much.

ACCOMPANYING MESSAGE

To the Congress of the United States:

My State of the Union Address will be devoted to a discussion of the most important challenges facing our country as we enter the 1980's.

Over the coming year, those challenges will receive my highest priority and greatest efforts. However, there will also be many other significant areas which will receive my personal commitment, as well as that of my Administration, during the 2nd Session of the 96th Congress.

It is important that Congress, along with the public, be aware of these other vital areas of concern as they listen to my State of the Union Address. In that way, the context of the Address, and my Administration's full message for 1980, can best be understood.

For that reason, I am sending this State of the Union Message to the Congress today, several days before my State of the Union Address.

Congress

During the last three years, my Administration has developed a very cooperative and productive record with Congress. Landmark legislation has been enacted; major domestic and international problems have been addressed directly and resolved; and a spirit of mutual trust and respect has been restored to Executive-Legislative relations. Indeed, in no other three-year period in our recent past has there been a comparable record of progress and achievement for the American people.

But much more remains to be done. We cannot afford to rest on our record. We cannot fail to complete the agenda begun in the 1970's; we cannot ignore the new challenges of the 1980's.

By continuing to work together, my Administration and the Congress can meet these goals. Our cooperative efforts can help to ensure stable prices and economic growth; a return to energy security; an efficient, responsive government; a strong, unsurpassed defense capability; and world peace.

The program that I have placed before the Congress since 1977, combined with the few new initiatives I will be placing before the Congress this year, will enable us to reach these goals. Our task in this Session is to complete the work on that program. I have no doubt that we can do it. There is no time to waste.

Record of Progress

When I took office in 1977, our Nation faced a number of serious domestic and international problems:

* the economy had still not recovered from the most serious recession since World War II;

* unemployment was near 8%, and almost 8 million American workers were unemployed;

* no national energy policy existed, and our dependence on foreign oil was rapidly increasing;

* public trust in the integrity and openness of the government was extremely low;

* the Federal government was operating inefficiently in administering essential programs and policies;

* major social problems were being ignored or poorly addressed by the Federal government;

* our defense posture was declining as a result of a continuously shrinking defense budget;

* the strength of the NATO Alliance was at a post-World War II low;

* tensions between Israel and Egypt threatened another Middle East war; and

* America's resolve to oppose international aggression and human rights violations was under serious question.

Over the past 36 months, clear progress has been made in solving the challenges we found in January of 1977:

* the unemployment rate at the end of last year of 5.9%, representing a 25% decrease in three years; 9 million jobs have been created, and more Americans, 98 million, are at work than at any time in our history;

* major parts of a comprehensive energy program have been enacted; a Department of Energy has been established to administer the program; and Congress is on the verge of enacting the remaining major parts of the energy program;

* confidence in the government's integrity has been restored, and respect for the government's openness and fairness has been renewed;

* the government has been made more effective and efficient: the Civil Service system was completely reformed for the first time this

century; 13 reorganization initiatives have been proposed to the Congress, approved, and implemented, two new Cabinet departments have been created to consolidate and streamline the government's handling of energy and education problems; inspectors general have been placed in each Cabinet department to combat fraud, waste and other abuses; zero-based budgeting practices have been instituted throughout the Federal government; cash management reforms have saved hundreds of millions of dollars; the process of issuing regulations has been reformed to eliminate unneeded and incomprehensible regulations; procedures have been established to assure citizen participation in government; and the airline industry has been deregulated, at enormous savings to the consumer.

• critical social problems, many long ignored by the Federal government, have been addressed directly and boldly: an urban policy was developed and implemented, reversing the decline in our urban areas; the Food Stamp program has been expanded and the purchase requirement eliminated; the Social Security System was refinanced to put it on a sound financial basis; the Humphrey-Hawkins Full Employment Act was enacted; Federal assistance for education was expanded by 75%; the minimum wage was increased to levels needed to ease the effects of inflation; affirmative action has been pursued aggressively — more blacks, Hispanics and women have been appointed to senior government positions and to judgeships than at any other time in our history; the ERA ratification deadline was extended to aid the ratification effort; and minority business procurement by the Federal government has more than doubled;

• the decline in defense spending has been reversed; defense spending has increased at a real rate of over 3% in 1979, and I am proposing a real increase in the defense spending level of more than 20% over the next 5 years;

• the NATO Alliance has been revitalized and strengthened through substantially increased resources, new deterrent weapons, and improved coordination; increased emphasis has also been given to conventional force capabilities to meet crises in other areas of the world;

• Egypt and Israel have ended more than 30 years of war through a Peace Treaty that also established a framework for comprehensive peace in the Middle East;

• the commitment of our Nation to pursue human rights throughout the world, in nations which are friendly and those which are not, has been made clear to all;

• our resolve to oppose aggression, such as the illegal invasion of the Soviet Union into Afghanistan, has been supported by tough action.

Legislative Priorities

In the coming legislative session, the last in this Presidential term, I am deeply committed to finishing the agenda that I have placed before the Congress. That agenda has been comprehensive and demanding, but it has also been absolutely essential for our Nation's well-being.

I do not plan to add significantly to the agenda this year. Because of the importance of enacting the proposals already before the Congress, and the relatively short Congressional session facing us, I will be limiting my major *new* proposals to a critical few:

- Youth Employment;
- General Revenue Sharing;
- Utility Oil Use Reduction;
- Nuclear Waste Management and Nuclear Regulatory Commission Reorganization;
- Standby Gasoline Rationing Plan; and
- Initiatives implementing my response to the Soviet invasion of Afghanistan.

I am convinced that these new initiatives, along with the major proposals I previously made to the Congress, can be enacted this year, if we have a dedicated, all-out effort on the part of the Administration and the Congress. I pledge such an effort on my part, and that of my Administration. . . .

My highest legislative priorities in each of these areas this year will be:

Ensuring Economic Strength

- *The FY 1981 Budget* — This is a responsible, restrained budget, whose enactment will help control Federal spending, significantly reduce the Federal deficit, and aid in our fight against inflation.
- *Hospital Cost Containment* — This long overdue legislation is a major weapon in our fight against inflation; it will save consumers more billions of dollars and is the single most important anti-inflation bill before the Congress.
- *Youth Education, Training and Employment Program* — This new initiative, which is designed to educate and train youth to secure and hold meaningful jobs, will provide enhanced opportunities for disadvantaged youth as well as improve the productivity of our work force.

Creating Energy Security for Our Nation

- *Windfall Profits Tax* — The size of this important energy and tax measure has been agreed to by the conferees, but it is imperative that final agreement on a tax reflecting sound energy policy occur at the outset of this session and that Congress act promptly on that agreement.
- *Energy Mobilization Board* — It is also essential that this vital measure in the effort to eliminate unnecessary red tape in the construction

41

of needed energy facilities be agreed to promptly by the conferees and the Congress, without substantive waivers of law.

• *Energy Security Corporation* — The conferees and the Congress also need to act expeditiously on this legislation. This bill is critical to our Nation's beginning a serious, massive program to develop alternative energy fuels so that our dependence on foreign oil can be severely reduced. It is necessary to remove this critical national effort from the constraints which can bind government agencies.

This legislation contains, as well, vital energy conservation and gasohol provisions. They are needed if we are to move forward in our national efforts in these areas.

• *Utility Oil Use Reduction* — This new initiative will aid in the effort to reduce our reliance on oil by requiring our Nation's utilities to substantially convert from oil to coal-burning or other energy facilities by our Nation's utilities over a defined timetable. This bill is a key tool in our effort to increase the use of coal, our most abundant natural fuel source.

• *Standby Gasoline Rationing Plan* — Under the legislation enacted last year, I will propose to the Congress a Standby Gasoline Rationing Plan; its prompt approval will be required if we are to be prepared for a significant energy supply interruption.

Enhancing Basic Human and Social Needs

• *National Health Plan* — The time for improving the health care provided to our citizens is long overdue, and I am convinced that the health plan I proposed last year provides a realistic, affordable and beneficial way of providing our citizens with the health care they need and deserve. It will provide millions of low-income Americans with health coverage for the first time, improved Medicare coverage for the elderly, and protect every American against the disastrous costs of extended illness. . . .

• *Welfare Reform* — Our nation's welfare system remains a disgrace to both the recipient and the taxpayers. It encourages family instability and encourages waste. It is a crazy-quilt of differing provisions from state-to-state. The House has approved a sound welfare reform proposal. I call upon the Senate to act rapidly on this issue so that welfare reform can become a reality this Session.

• *General Revenue Sharing* — I will propose a reauthorization of this important program to our state and local governments, in order to continue providing them with the funds that they depend upon to meet essential social and operating needs. . . .

• *Countercyclical Revenue Sharing* — I will again work with the Congress to provide the aid needed to help our most financially pressed local areas. The Senate has already acted and I urge prompt House passage early in the Session.

- *Low-Income Energy Assistance* — I am committed to seeking authority to continue the low-income assistance program enacted at my request last year to give the poor protection against rising energy costs.

- *Economic Development* — This legislation will reauthorize and improve the government's ability to provide economic development assistance. It is a key ingredient in implementing both my urban and rural policy and I urge prompt action on it by the House-Senate Conference.

[More Efficient and Effective Government]

- *Regulatory Reform* — I will continue to pursue efforts to eliminate unnecessary regulatory burdens, and will concentrate on seeking approval this year of my regulatory process reform bill, my trucking and rail deregulation proposals, my banking reform measures, and passage of sunset legislation and communications reform measures. Progress has been made on each of these during the First Session. Final passage should come before this Session ends.

- *Nuclear Regulatory Commission Reorganization* — As I stated in responding to the Kemeny Commission Report, I will propose a reorganization of the Nuclear Regulatory Commission in order to improve its management and its emergency operating capabilities. This is an essential step to the improvement of safety in the nuclear industry.

[Protecting Our Rights and Liberties]

- *Equal Rights Amendment* — While the Congress has passed the Equal Rights Amendment, and the possibiility for ratification now lies with the State Legislatures, it is essential that the Members of Congress help with their State Legislatures. Toward that end, we will be working with Members from States which have not yet been [sic] ratified. We cannot stand tall as a Nation seeking to enhance human rights at home as long as we deny it to American women here at home.

- *Fair Housing* — I will continue to press for enactment of this important civil rights initiative; it will enable the government to enforce our fair housing laws effectively and promptly. It is the most critical civil rights legislation before the Congress in years. The promise of equal housing opportunity has been far too long an empty promise. This bill will help make that promise a reality.

- *Intelligence Charters* — I have already proposed a legislative charter for the FBI; I will soon be proposing a legislative charter for the intelligence community. These charters will protect our citizens' rights while enabling the agencies to meet their responsibilities.

[Natural Resources]

- *Alaska D-2 Lands* — My highest environmental priority in this Congress continues to be enactment of legislation that will preserve and protect Alaska lands. I urge the Senate to follow the House's lead in this area.
- *Oil and Hazardous Wastes Superfund* — This program is needed to mitigate the effects of oil hazardous substance spills and releases from uncontrolled hazardous waste dumps, which is a growing national problem.
- *Nuclear Waste Management* — I will propose a series of legislative and administrative initiatives to implement our Nation's first comprehensive nuclear waste program.

Building America's Military Strength

- *Defense Department Authorizations and Appropriations* — I will be proposing a defense budget containing a 3.3% real growth in outlays. It is essential that the Congress support an increase of that amount if we are to strengthen our defense capabilities.

Working to Resolve International Disputes

- *Refugee Legislation and Funding* — This legislation is necessary to improve our refugee program and to provide needed domestic assistance to refugees. Prompt House action would assure that we have a sound framework within which to accommodate the increasing flow of refugees.

[International Economic Problems]

- *Bilateral and Multilateral Foreign Assistance* — I will be proposing foreign assistance legislation which provides the authority needed to carry forward a cooperative relationship with a large number of developing nations. Prompt Congressional action is essential.
- *China Trade Agreement* — I will be seeking early approval by the Congress of the Trade Agreement reached with China; the Agreement represents a major step forward in the process toward improved economic relations with China.

[Democratic Institutions and Human Rights]

- *Special International Security Assistance for Pakistan* — I am sending to Congress a military and economic assistance program to enable Pakistan to strengthen its defenses. Prompt enactment will be one of my highest legislative priorities.
- *Human Rights Conventions* — I will continue to press the Senate to ratify five key human rights treaties — the American Convention

on Human Rights, the Convention on Racial Discrimination, the UN Covenants on Civil and Political Rights, and on Economic and Social and Cultural Rights, and the Genocide Convention.

[Preventing the Spread of Nuclear Weapons]

● *SALT II* — I firmly believe that SALT II is in our Nation's security interest and that it will add significantly to the control of nuclear weapons. But because of the Soviet invasion of Afghanistan, I do not believe it is advisable to have the Senate consider the Treaty now.

I. Ensuring Economic Strength

My economic program, since I took office, has been designed to achieve several goals:

—restore and continue economic growth;

—reduce unemployment; and

—restrain inflation. . . .

Inflation

Inflation continues to be our most serious economic problem. Restraining inflation remains my highest domestic priority.

Inflation at the current, unacceptably high levels is the direct result of economic problems that have been building, virtually without letup, for over a decade. There are no easy answers, or quick solutions to inflation. It cannot be eliminated overnight; its roots in our economy are too deep, its causes are too pervasive and complex. We know we cannot spend our way out of this problem.

But there is hope — for a gradual reduction in the inflation rate, for an easing of the economic pressures causing inflation.

The hope lies in a program of public and private restraint in the short-run and a program to attack the structural causes of inflation over the longer-run. This is the policy I have pursued and will continue to pursue.

Last year was an especially difficult time for anti-inflation policies. OPEC increased its prices by more than 80% and thus added more than three points to the inflation rate. If energy price increases are excluded, inflation last year would have been nearly three percentage points lower.

The biggest challenge to anti-inflation policy is to keep energy price increases from doing permanent damage, to prevent a dangerous acceleration of the wage-price spiral. My program has been successful in accomplishing this. Inflation will slow this year. In 1981 it should be even lower. This progress is the result of our persistence in the battle against inflation on many fronts:

45

Budget Restraint: The budget deficit for FY 1979 was lowered to $27.7 billion, more than 50% below the FY 1976 level.

Regulatory Reform: The flood of new, costly government regulations was slowed as our procedures to ensure that we achieve our regulatory goals in the most cost-effective manner took hold.

Wage-Price Guidelines: The guideline standards were followed by the vast majority of unions which negotiated contracts and by nearly every major corporation in the country.

Energy: The energy legislation put into place over the past two years began to reduce our dependence on foreign oil and our consumption of such important energy fuels as gasoline, thereby reducing the ability of oil producing nations to disrupt our economy.

Productivity: We began to introduce policies to increase industrial innovation and thereby productivity; the decline in productivity growth must be reversed if we are to improve our real living standards over the long term.

In 1980, with the Congress' cooperation, we will continue our aggressive fight against inflation on each of these major fronts:

Budget Restraint: The deficit for the FY 1981 budget will be less than half of the FY 1980 budget deficit and will represent a 75% reduction from the deficit I inherited.

Regulatory Reform: We will be pursuing deregulation legislation for the trucking, rail, banking and communications industries, as well as regulatory management reform legislation; these bills will enable us to further eliminate unnecessary regulatory burdens.

Labor Accord: The Pay Advisory and Price Advisory Committees, established as a result of last year's historic Accord with organized labor will enable us to better implement, and coordinate with both labor and business, the private restraint necessary as part of our anti-inflation efforts. . . .

Energy: We expect to enact major energy legislation — the Windfall Profits Tax, the Energy Mobilization Board, and the Energy Security Corporation — early in this Session; this legislation, when combined with the voluntary and mandatory energy conservation measures that will take an even stronger hold this year, should enable us to further reduce our dependence on foreign oil.

Productivity: We will be implementing our industrial innovation program and further expanding our commitment in the budget to research and development.

Council on Wage and Price Stability

The Council on Wage and Price Stability has played a vital role in our anti-inflation efforts. The Council and its staff have lead responsibility within the Executive branch for implementing the voluntary wage and price monitoring program. Without the Council's continuing role, the anti-inflation effort could not begin to assess whether the private sector is cooperating with our standards. . . .

The 1981 Budget

The budget I will send to the Congress for FY 1981 will meet this Nation's critical needs; and it will continue the sound budgetary policies that my Administration has pursued throughout my term in office.

No single year's budget can accurately portray the philosophy of an Administration. However, there is a clear pattern in the budgets I have proposed — restraint in spending, coupled with careful targeting of resources to areas of greatest need. My 1981 budget continues this pattern by lowering the deficit roughly $50 billion below what it was when I ran for office. At the same time, I will recommend increases for programs of critical national concern.

Last year, my budget was austere. I proposed eliminating some programs and reducing spending for others; and these tough decisions have proven correct and have provided the country with clear benefits. I am pleased that the Congress approved my budget in virtually the form I proposed. As a result of our actions, the rate of Federal spending growth has been slowed. Just as importantly, the widespread expectation that the Federal budget would continue its upward spiral unchecked has been proven false. We have moved on to the path necessary for achieving a balanced budget in the very near future. And we have helped the fight against inflation.

The 1981 Budget will continue my policy of restraint. Real growth in spending will be close to zero. The deficit will be cut by more than half from last year. The deficit as a percent of the budget and of GNP will be at the second lowest point in this decade. We will have the smallest deficit in seven years. And if the economy were to continue to grow at a rate which held the unemployment rate at the current level, *this* budget would be in surplus. . . .

Fiscal Policy

As President, I have been concerned about the tax burden on our citizens and have, as a result, worked with the Congress to enact two major tax cuts. In 1977, I proposed, and Congress passed, an $8 billion individual tax cut as part of the economic stimulus package. In 1978, I proposed, and Congress passed, a $21 billion individual and business tax cut. This year, those two cuts will reduce Americans' tax burden by $31 billion.

I recognize that there is interest in another tax cut this year, but my 1981 budget proposes no tax cuts. As long as double-digit inflation continues and there is no sign of a recession, our top budgetary priority must be reduction of the deficit.

Over the long run, continued tight control over budget expenditures will hold down the share of Federal spending in GNP. Inflation, on the other hand, is raising the percentage of national income collected in taxes. Over time, because of these two developments, tax reductions will be possible while still maintaining the fiscal restraint needed to control inflation. However, the timing and structure of any tax reductions is of critical importance and must be dictated by our economic circumstances: the urgency of the anti-inflation fight requires that we defer such tax reductions at this time.

Tax reductions put into effect prematurely, and under the wrong economic conditions, could make inflation worse by overstimulating the economy. Inflation is still running at unacceptably high levels.

Virtually all economic forecasters predict the onset of a mild recession and my Administration's estimates of budget receipts and expenditures in the FY 1981 budget assume a recession. However, none of the current economic statistics yet show any overall economic decline. In recent months the economy has displayed much more strength than earlier forecasts had predicted. Forecasts of impending recession may therefore prove to be as wrong as previous ones. Employment has held up well — in part due to unsatisfactory productivity performance. To enact tax cuts now would run a serious risk of adding inflationary demand pressures to an economy which continues to grow more strongly than predicted by the forecasts. With the present high inflation, we cannot afford that risk.

When tax reductions are timely, they should be designed insofar as possible in a way that achieves multiple objectives — not only reducing the tax burden and stimulating growth, but raising investment and productivity and reducing inflation as well. . . .

Employment

My Administration, working closely with Congress, has made significant progress in reducing the serious unemployment problems that existed three years ago.

● The December unemployment rate of 5.9% represents a 25% reduction from the December 1976 rate.

● Over 9.2 million more people have jobs than before the beginning of the Administration.

● Total employment has reached an all-time high of 98 million in December.

● Nonwhite employment has increased by 1.4 million persons or 15.5%.

● Adult female employment has increased by 5 million persons.

● Employment of black teenagers, which had actually decreased during the 1969-1975 period, has increased by more than 15% since I took office. Although unemployment rates for all youth, especially minority youth, are still too high, progress has been made.

We will continue to make progress in the 1980's as a result of the framework which has already been established and which will be strengthened this year.

• The Comprehensive Employment and Training Act (CETA) was reauthorized in 1978 for four years.

• The Humphrey-Hawkins Full Employment Act became law after many years of effort.

• The Private Sector Initiatives Program, a new partnership between the government and the private sector to assist the most disadvantaged unemployed, is being successfully implemented.

• A targeted jobs tax credit has been enacted to provide employers with the economic incentives needed to increase their hiring of unemployed low-income youth and others who historically have difficulty finding jobs.

• A massive effort to reduce the problems causing excessive youth unemployment rates is being strengthened and revitalized this year with a new $2 billion youth education, training, and employment program. . . .

Youth Employment

The fact that we have had persistently high unemployment among poor and minority youth for three decades demonstrates clearly the inadequacies of our system for teaching, training and helping young people to find and keep decent jobs.

The economic challenges of the 1980's will require the energy and commitment of the entire American work force. We cannot afford to waste anyone's talents.

If we are to become the society of our ideals, we must provide economic opportunity for all.

My Administration is committed to a renewed national effort to remove any unnecessary obstacles to a productive life for every American.

Over the past three years, we have developed a solid record. We have incresed resources for youth employment and training programs from $2.5 to over $4 billion. We have conducted the largest experimental youth program effort ever attempted. We have reduced overall youth unemployment rates by 15%. But this is not good enough. Youth unemployment, especially for the poor and minorities, is still unacceptably high.

Based on the experience we have gained over the past three years, and on the advice of the thousands of Americans who helped the Vice President's Task Force on Youth Employment over the past nine months, my Administration has devised a new approach, which I announced two weeks ago. Under my program, the most significant new domestic initiative I will be sending to Congress this year, the Federal government will be making its most comprehensive effort ever to eradicate the causes of excessive and harmful youth unemployment.

By 1982 this new program will have increased Federal resources committed to reducing youth unemployment by $2 billion, to a total of $6 billion. The program will have two key components: for in-school youth, we will have a major effort through the Department of Education to teach basic skills to low-achieving youth in junior and senior high schools located in low-income communities, while providing work experience and training after school hours. For disadvantaged out-of-school youth, we will provide, through the Department of Labor, redesigned and expanded work experience and training programs, as well as basic skills programs managed by the Department of Education.

The Department of Education's basic education and skill training program, when fully implemented, will provide basic education and employment skills to approximately 1 million low-achieving junior and senior high school students in about 3,000 of the poorest urban and rural school districts around the country. . . .

Trade

This past year was one of unmatched and historic achievement for a vital component of the U.S. economy — exports and trade. In 1979, nearly 3 million jobs in our manufacturing industries, or one out of every seven jobs in manufacturing, depended upon our export performance in overseas markets.

Our exports were a key contributor to the growth of the U.S. economy in 1979.

Exports of agricultural and industrial goods grew by an unparalleled $35 billion, reaching a level of $180 billion. This represented an increase of 25% over exports in 1978. This record increase in exports, coupled with a slower rate of growth of imports, resulted in substantial improvements of $5 billion in our balance of trade. Futhermore, a rapid growth of service exports in 1979 led to a $13 billion improvement in the current account, bringing that account from a deficit in 1978 to near balance in 1979.

I expect that in 1980 our exports will continue to strengthen and that, if we can continue to further conserve and limit imports of oil, we will further improve our trade balance position and that of the dollar. The future for American exports is bright, and will remain so, despite the necessity of suspending certain exports to the Soviet Union. . . .

Small Business

This year marks the high point of three years of accomplishment for small business under my Administration, and the beginning of a decade of continuing effort to strengthen this large and vital sector of our economy.

The White House Conference on Small Business, which I convened eighteen months ago and which has just concluded its deliberations, fulfills a pledge I made in 1976 that the voice of small business would be heard in my Administration. In anticipation of the Conference, I called on the head of every executive department and agency to propose at least one initiative of benefit to small business. Over 160 separate initiatives have been proposed and are under examination, and many of them have already been put in effect. . . .

We have also increased Small Business Administration lending activity, from $1.8 billion in 1976 to $3.1 billion in 1979, an increase of 72%. Since 1977 we have more than doubled Federal purchases of goods and services from minority firms from $1.1 billion to $2.5 billion in 1979. I am confident that such purchases will exceed $3.5 billion this year.

I have put into place a comprehensive policy to strengthen the role of women in business, and have directed Federal agencies to take affirmative action to include women in management assistance and other business-related programs. . . .

Finally, last week I sent to the Congress a Message on Small Business to emphasize the vital importance of small business and to report to you on the steps we have already taken and plan to take in 1980 to strengthen small business.

Minority Business

From the beginning of my term, I have worked with the Congress to increase opportunities for minority business. As a result of our efforts, enormous progress has been made in the last three years:

• Federal procurement from minority-owned firms has increased by nearly two and a half times;

• Federal deposits in minority-owned banks have nearly doubled;

• minority ownership of radio and television stations has increased by 65%;

• almost 15% of the funds spent under the Local Public Works Act of 1977 went to minority-owned firms;

• the Section 8(a) program operated by the Small Business Administration has been reformed and strengthened.

This year, my Administration is committed to expanding upon the progress made to date. This year, I am committed to more than tripling the 1977 level of federal procurement from minority-owned firms, and I have no doubt we can meet that goal.

My 1981 budget improves the targeting of Small Business Administration loans to minority-owned businesses. We will also expand management, technical, and training assistance for minority firms and provide substantial funding increases for minority capital development under the SBA's minority enterprise small business investment company (MESBIC) program. . . .

Women in Business

Last year I announced a new policy to strengthen and foster the growth of women-owned businesses. My new budget includes funds to make this policy a reality by increasing SBA direct loans to women by 50%, by assisting women in gaining access to sources of financing, and by expanding management and technical assistance to women. By insuring that women have fuller access to opportunitities to start and maintain their own enterprises, we will start a genuine momentum to take full advantage of the contribution which women can make to the growth and productivity of our economy.

II. Creating Energy Security

Since I took office, my highest legislative priorities have involved the development of our Nation's first comprehensive energy policy. The struggle to achieve that policy has been difficult for all of us, but the accomplishments of the past three years leave no doubt that our country is finally serious about the problems caused by our over-dependence on foreign oil. The accomplishments can be lost, however, and the progress stopped, if we fail to move forward even further this year. There is no single panacea that will solve our energy crisis. We must rely on and encourage multiple forms of production — coal, crude oil, natural gas, solar, nuclear, synthetics — and conservation.

It is therefore essential that Congress enact the major energy bills I proposed last year; and their enactment will be my most immediate and highest legislative priority this year.

Windfall Profits Tax

My highest, most immediate legislative priority during this Session is prompt passage of a sound windfall profits tax on crude oil.

Last April, I proposed a tough windfall profits tax to recoup a portion of the unearned income that would accrue to the oil companies as a result of the phased decontrol of domestic crude oil prices and OPEC price increases. It is essential that these revenues be invested on behalf of all Americans to help us become an energy secure nation. The revenues from the tax will be used to support key national energy goals: low-income energy assistance, improved and expanded mass transit and energy supply and conservation programs.

The windfall tax that I proposed was also carefully designed to provide incentives needed to increase domestic oil production. Under my proposal, we expect a [1 million] barrel per day increase in domestic production due to decontrol and higher world prices. Without any windfall profits tax production would be only marginally higher by 1985.

The American people clearly want and our national energy needs clearly require — a tough windfall tax. We cannot afford further delay. . . .

Energy Mobilization Board

Last July, together with a comprehensive energy program, I asked Congress to join with me to create an Energy Mobilization Board (EMB). The Board can cut through burdensome and unnecessary red tape and reach prompt decisions on designated priority energy projects. Decision-making can be streamlined without overriding of substantive law, which I strongly oppose. The Board is a key element of our strategy to attain energy security by cutting foreign oil imports in the coming years. Prompt passage of the EMB is one of my highest priorities this year, and I urge the Congress to complete its action on this proposal without delay.

Energy Security Corporation

Last year, I proposed the creation of an Energy Security Corporation to lead our national effort to develop and produce synthetic fuels, coal-based synthetics, oil shale and biomass. The Corporation would be an independent body, chartered by the government and authorized to use a variety of financing tools — principally price guarantees, Federal purchases, and loan guarantees — to stimulate private sector development of synthetic energy alternatives to imported oil.

I have recommended that the Corporation be given a goal to develop the capacity to produce 1.75 million barrels per day of synthetic fuels, oil shale, and biomass by 1990. With an ability to produce commercially synthetic alternatives to foreign crude oil, our Nation will have effectively capped the price which foreign oil producers can charge for crude oil.

We cannot do the job we must do for our Nation's security by operating this program from within the government. The Corporation can much more easily obtain the needed talent and operate without the constraints binding a government agency.

Enactment of the legislation containing the Energy Security Corporation is one of my highest legislative priorities for this Session. I urge the conferees to complete this work expeditiously so that the Corporation can open its doors as early as possible this year.

Reduction in Utility Oil Use

I will soon send to the Congress legislation which will assist utilities in the use of coal, and encourage them to retire existing oil burning plants for generating electricity. The Department of Energy and my staff have worked very closely with Congressional energy leadership over the last several months to develop a legislative proposal which can be acted upon quickly.

My proposed utility oil use reduction legislation will help us to achieve two of our basic energy goals — decreasing our dependence on foreign oil and increasing our production of more abundant and secure energy supplies, such as coal. For that reason, passage of this legislation will be one of my highest energy priorities this year.

Gasoline Rationing

I will soon be sending to Congress for its approval a standby gasoline rationing plan, under the authority of legislation I signed into law last year. In developing this plan, we have given priority attention to accommodating essential gasoline usage, bearing in mind the need to design a plan which is workable and which can be put into place quickly if a severe emergency arises.

I recognize the difficulty of developing a plan that meets the many competing State and local concerns. Last year's experience demonstrated that difficulty very well. I am determined, as I am certain Congress is, to avoid repeating it.

My Administration will work very closely with Congress on the standby plan. I hope the Congress will recognize the overriding national importance of emergency preparedness and will take action early to approve my proposed plan.

I do not intend, under our current supply conditions, to implement a rationing program. But we can no longer afford to be unprepared for the possibility of further severe interruptions in energy supplies.

Energy Conservation

In my very first energy address to the Nation in April 1977, I stressed the importance of conservation as the cornerstone of our national energy policy. It is the cheapest and fastest means of reducing our dependence on imported oil and it constitutes an alternative source of supply. To the extent that we conserve — in our homes, factories, cars, and public buildings — we make the task of providing secure sources of energy for the future that much more attainable.

In November 1978, I signed into law our country's first energy conservation tax credits. These provide up to $300 for home conservation investments, and an additional 10 % investment tax credit for industrial investments in energy efficient equipment. At the same time, we put in place a requirement that utilities provide energy audits for their customers and offer to arrange financing. We also established stiff taxes on new gas guzzling automobiles. As a result of my April 1977 initiatives, we are also providing a total of $900 million over three years to weatherize schools and hospitals across the Nation.

Last July, I proposed a program to provide $5.8 billion over the next decade to subsidize interest rates on homeowner loans for conservation investments. This program will be targeted to low- and moderate-income homeowners and apartment owners for whom the tax credits are less effective as an incentive. Under this program it is expected that consumers' total monthly bills will decline since the financial savings resulting from lower energy use will be greater than the monthly payments on the subsidized loans.

I consider this new program to be an essential piece of my overall conservation strategy and urge the House-Senate Conference Committee now working on the bill containing this provision to complete work promptly.

Energy conservation must also go forward at the State and local levels. To help that important effort, I am again urging Congress to pass my proposal, under the authority of the proposed Energy Management and Partnership Act, to provide grants to local governments to meet national energy conservation goals.

Solar Energy

Last June, I sent the Congress a Message on Solar Energy outlining my Administration's solar program and setting a national goal for the year 2000 of deriving 20% of this Nation's energy from solar and renewable resources. A firm and ambitious course — not only by the Federal government but also by State and local governments, private industry, academia and private citizens — is required to reach this goal.

As part of my solar program announced in June, I proposed a number of initiatives to the Congress to assist in solar energy development. Among those were the establishment of a Solar Energy Development Bank funded at $150 million per year to provide subsidized loans for the installation of solar equipment on homes and commercial structures, and additional tax credits for passive solar construction, wood stoves, industrial and agricultural solar applications, and gasohol. These initiatives have yet to be enacted by the Congress and I urge prompt action on these measures to help speed the penetration of solar technologies in the marketplace.

In addition, my FY 1980 program for solar energy exceeded $1 billion government-wide. This is more than three times greater than the program in place when I took office. In FY 1981 government-wide expenditures for solar and renewable energy will be nearly $1.4 billion and will include programs administered by the Departments of Energy, Agriculture, Interior, Defense, State, Housing and Urban Development, and the Tennessee Valley Authority. The Federal solar program has as its overall objectives, the emphasis on basic research and development of solar technologies not currently economic such as photovoltaics, where electricity is generated directly from the sun, and the provision of funding and technical information to accelerate the use of marketable solar technologies which are available now. Solar heat and hot water and wood energy are among these technologies.

We will continue to work with the Congress this session on passage of critical solar energy legislation. We are making progress on the transition away from our dependence on fossil fuels and towards the widespread use of renewable sources of energy. We must maintain an aggressive policy to achieve this transition.

Nuclear Safety

Immediately following the accident at Three Mile Island, I established a Presidential Commission, chaired by the President of Dartmouth College, to report to me on actions needed to prevent recurrence of this kind of accident. Safety is and will remain my Administration's primary priority in the regulation and management of nuclear power. I have taken steps to correct virtually all problems identified by the Kemeny Commission and have acted to implement most of its specific recommendations, including:

• A reorganization of the NRC to strengthen the role of the Chairman. I will soon send to Congress a reorganization plan to give the Chairman power to select key personnel and act on behalf of the Commission during an emergency.

• Appointment of a new Chairman of the NRC from outside the agency when the next vacancy occurs. In the meantime, I have designated Commissioner Ahearne as Chairman with a mandate to initiate changes needed to assure the safety of nuclear power plant operations.

• Direction to the Federal Emergency Management Agency to lead all off-site emergency activities and review all emergency plans in States with operating reactors by June.

• A request to the NRC to accelerate its program to place a resident Federal inspector at every reactor site, and to upgrade training and evaluation programs for reactor operators.

I endorsed the approach the NRC adopted to pause in licensing, but have urged the Commission to complete its work as quickly as possible, and in any event no later than June of this year.

Once we have instituted the necessary reforms to assure safety, we must resume the licensing process promptly so that the new plants which we need to reduce our dependence on foreign oil can be built and operated. Nuclear power is an option that we should keep open.

Gasohol

I have recently proposed a program to accelerate dramatically America's production and use of gasohol, as yet another important way on which we can wage — and win — our energy war.

My Administration is commited to a program which will provide between $8.5 billion and $12.8 billion of assistance to stimulate production of alcohol fuels over the coming decade. We will quadruple current gasohol production capacity by the end of this year. During 1981, we should be capable of producing ethanol at an annual rate of 500 million gallons — more than six times the current rate. If this entire amount of ethanol were turned into gasohol, it would replace almost 10% of our anticipated demand for unleaded gasoline in 1981. . . .

III. Enhancing Basic Human and Social Needs

For too many years immediately preceding my Administration, too many of our Nation's basic human and social needs were being ignored or dealt with insensitively by the Federal government. Over the past three years, we have significantly increased funding for many of the vital programs in these areas; developed new programs where needs were unaddressed; targeted Federal support to those individuals and areas most in need of our assistance; and removed barriers that have unnecessarily kept many disadvantaged citizens from obtaining aid for their most basic needs.

Our efforts over the past three years have produced clear progress in our effort to solve some of the country's fundamental human and social problems. The Administration and the Congress, working together, have demonstrated that government must and can meet our citizens' basic human and social needs in a responsible and compassionate way.

But there is an unfinished agenda still before the Congress. If we are to meet our obligations to help all Americans realize the dreams of sound health care, decent housing, effective social services, a good education, and a meaningful job, we still have important legislation to enact this year. The legislation is before the Congress, and I will be working with you toward its enactment.

HEALTH

National Health Plan

Last June, I proposed to Congress a National Health Plan which will enable the country to reach the goal of comprehensive, universal health care coverage. The legislation I submitted lays the foundation for this comprehensive plan and addresses the most serious problems of health financing and delivery. It is realistic, affordable, and enactable. It does not overpromise or overspend, and, as a result, can be the solution to the thirty years of Congressional battles on national health insurance. My Plan includes the following key features:

● nearly 15 million additional poor would receive fully-subsidized comprehensive coverage;

● pre-natal and delivery services are provided for all pregnant women and coverage is provided for all acute care for infants in their first year of life.

● the elderly and disabled would have a limit of $1,250 placed on annual out-of-pocket medical expenses and would no longer face limits on hospital coverage;

- all full-time employees and their families would receive insurance against at least major medical expenses under mandated employer coverage;
- Medicare and Medicaid would be combined and expanded into an umbrella Federal program, Healthcare, for increased program efficiency, accountability and uniformity; and
- strong cost controls and health system reforms would be implemented initiatives, including greater incentives for Health Maintenance Organizations.

If enacted this year, my Plan would begin providing benefits in 1983. . . .

Hospital Cost Containment

Hospital Cost Containment remains the single most important piece of legislation that the Congress can pass to demonstrate its commitment to fight inflation. This legislative initiative will save billions of dollars for our Nation's consumers by eliminating unnecessary and wasteful hospital services. . . .

Maternal and Child Health

Ensuring a healthy start in life for children remains not only a high priority of my Administration, but also one of the most cost effective forms of health care.

When I took office, immunization levels for preventable childhood diseases had fallen to 70%. As a result of a concerted nationwide effort during my Administration, I am pleased to report that now at least 90% of children under 15, and virtually all school-age children are immunized. In addition, reported cases of measles and mumps are at their lowest levels ever.

Under the National Health Plan I have proposed, there will be no cost-sharing for prenatal and delivery services for all pregnant women and for acute care provided to infants in their first year of life. These preventive services are recognized to have extremely high returns in terms of improved newborn and long-term child health.

Under the Child Health Assurance Program (CHAP) legislation which I have already submitted to this Congress, an additional two million low-income children under 18 will become eligible for Medicaid benefits, which will include special health assessments. CHAP will also improve the continuity of care for the nearly 14 million children now eligible for Medicaid. An additional 100,000 low-income pregnant women will become eligible for prenatal care under the proposal. We must work together this year to enact CHAP and thereby provide millions of needy children with essential health services. . . .

[Services to the Poor and Underserved]

My health proposals for FY 1981 will place high priority on expanding other improvements which have been made during my Administration in the access and continuity of care for medically underserved groups. I will propose substantially increased funding for the most successful programs in this area, including Community and Migrant Health Centers, and the National Health Service Corps program, which places health professionals in rural and urban medically underserved areas. In addition, I am proposing legislation to make coverage of clinics providing comprehensive primary care services a mandatory benefit under Medicaid.

Mental Health

Last year, I submitted a Mental Health Message to Congress and proposed the Mental Health Systems Act, which is based upon recommendations of my Commission on Mental Health. The Act is designed to inaugurate a new era of Federal and State partnership in the planning and provision of mental health services. In addition, the Act specifically provides for prevention and support services to the chronically mentally ill, to prevent unnecessary institutionalization, prevention services, and for the development of community-based mental health services. . . .

Worker Health and Safety

My Administration will continue to enforce fully laws protecting worker health and safety in a sensible and efficient manner. We will be making further efforts to eliminate frivolous and unneeded rules, while concentrating greater enforcement efforts on the most dangerous and particularly the most unhealthy occupational environments. More effective management of our worker safety programs will serve the interest that both labor and management have in better working conditions.

Drug Abuse Prevention

At the beginning of my Administration there were over a half million heroin addicts in the United States. Our continued emphasis on reducing the supply of heroin, as well as providing treatment and rehabilitation to its victims, has reduced the heroin addict population to 380,000, reduced the number of heroin overdose deaths by 80%, and reduced the number of heroin related injuries by 50%. However, drug abuse in many forms continues to detract from the quality of life and is of great concern to us and the people of all nations.

I am particularly concerned over the increasing quantities of heroin originating in Iran and Southwest Asia and we will continue to be especially alert to this threat in 1980. During 1980, we will also strive to reduce the supply of illegal drugs, both at their overseas sources and within the United States. While continuing a comprehensive treatment program, our priority will be to reduce drug abuse among adolescents. One of the important goals of my Administration at the beginning of this decade is to change the social acceptance of drug use.

Food and Nutrition

Building on the comprehensive reform of the Food Stamp Program that I proposed and Congress passed in 1977, my Administration and the Congress worked together last year to enact several other important changes in the Program. These changes will further simplify administration and reduce fraud and error, will make the program more responsive to the needs of the elderly and disabled, and will increase the cap on allowable program expenditures. In this session, I will continue to work with the Congress to achieve additional improvements in the Food Stamp Program and to eliminate permanently the expenditure cap. I will also propose this year that Congress pass the Administration's Child Nutrition Amendments to target assistance under our school meal programs to those most in need.

EDUCATION

The stern challenges of the 80's place new demands on every sector of our society. Education is the insurance we have to provide the talent and capability to meet every demand on our National agenda. The challenge of the 80's in education is to see that quantity education becomes quality education. That is a challenge we can meet. Last year, my Administration and the Congress successfully collaborated to create a new Department of Education. The Department will give education a stronger voice at the Federal level, while at the same time reserving the actual control and operation of education to states, localities, and private institutions. . . .

To ensure adequate financial resources for education, I have requested, since taking office, an overall increase in Federal aid to education of 75% above the previous Administration's last budget. Many programs, including those serving disadvantaged and handicapped students and those providing financial aid to students enrolled in postsecondary education, have benefited from ever larger percentage increases during my Administration.

My FY 1981 budget request in education will represent a generous increase over last year's budget. There will be particularly significant increases in a number of programs serving special populations, in addition to the major new program designed to give youth the basic skills needed to get and keep a job. I am also recommending a substantial increase in the programs which deal with international education, to improve our understanding of other nations.

In addition, proposals I submitted last July to reauthorize the Higher Education Act are still under consideration in the Congress. The center-piece of my proposals for the student financial aid programs is a major reform of the student loan programs. My proposal would, for the first time, provide a comprehensive program of loans from the Federal government for higher education students who need them. Our proposals would eliminate much of the paperwork and confusion that have plagued students, parents, and colleges by mandating a single application form for all Federal need-based assistance. . . .

INCOME SECURITY

Welfare Reform

Last year, I proposed a welfare reform package which offers solutions to some of the most urgent problems in our welfare system. This proposal is embodied in two bills — The Work and Training Opportunities Act and The Social Welfare Reform Amendments Act. Within the framework of our present welfare system, my reform proposals offer achievable means to increase self-sufficiency through work rather than welfare, more adequate assistance to people unable to work, the removal of inequities in coverage under current programs, and fiscal relief needed by States and localities.

Our current welfare system is long overdue for serious reform; the system is wasteful and not fully effective. The legislation I have proposed will help eliminate inequities by establishing a national minimum benefit, and by directly relating benefit levels to the poverty threshold. It will reduce program complexity, which leads to inefficiency and waste, by simplifying and coordinating administration among different programs.

Last year the House passed The Social Welfare Reform Amendments Act, which addresses the major problems in our cash assistance programs. This year, we must continue this momentum toward welfare reform. I am determined to do whatever I can to help enact the two bills needed for the most comprehensive reform of the welfare system in our history.

Child Welfare

My Administration has worked closely with the Congress on legislation which is designed to improve greatly the child welfare services and foster care programs and to create a Federal system of adoption assistance. The work of the Congress on this legislation is now almost completed. The well-being of children in need of homes and their permanent placement are primary concerns of my Administration, and I am determined to see improvement in the system which cares for these children. This legislation will help ensure that.

Low-Income Energy Assistance

Last year, I proposed a program to provide a total of $2.4 billion per year to low-income households which are hardest hit by rising energy bills. With Congress' cooperation, we were able to move quickly to provide $1.6 billion for assistance needed this winter. Of that amount $1.2 billion was provided for grants to eligible households and $400 million for an energy crisis assistance program. The first checks were received by eligible families and individuals in early January.

I have already proposed, and will continue to press for, legislation which provides $2.4 billion a year for low-income energy assistance. Funding from this program will come from the Windfall Profits Tax. Continuing this assistance is one of my high priorities in this session of Congress.

Social Security

I have been deeply committed to restoring the public's confidence and trust in the Social Security System. With the passage of the Social Security Amendments of 1977, the financial stability of the system was improved. Each month 35 million Americans receive pension and disability checks. They can rely on doing so without fear of interruption.

We must, however, address the continuing financial viability of the Social Security System in light of changing economic circumstances. We must also review the equity of the sex-related distinctions contained in the system's benefit provisions.

To help ensure the system's viability, I will propose legislation to permit borrowing among the separate trust funds. This measure will strengthen the Social Security System for current and future beneficiaries. I will also review closely the work of several major study groups, and will consult with experts in the Department of Health and Human Services and the Congress to assess their recommendations.

Disability Insurance Reforms

As a result of the legislation we enacted in 1977, which strengthened the financing of the Social Security System, the Social Security disability insurance program is now in stable financial condition. Last year, my Administration proposed modifications in the program to further improve its administration and to increase incentives for disabled beneficiaries to seek rehabilitation and to return to work. In 1980, we will work with the Congress to enact these reforms. I hope the Congress will stay as close as possible to my original proposal.

HOUSING

My Administration has brought improved stability to the Nation's housing market. Housing starts from 1977 through 1979 averaged more than 1.9 million units per year. We have been and remain committed to assuring the availability of an adequate level of mortgage credit during a period of record high interest rates. Toward that goal, we developed the six-month money market certificate and broadened the secondary market activity of the Government National Mortgage Association and the Federal Home Loan Mortgage Corporation. Most recently, the bank regulators introduced two and one-half year certificates which should become valuable sources of funds for savings institutions, enabling them to continue a high level of mortgage lending.

I am pleased that our anti-inflation policies have begun to slow the rate of growth in home prices. . . .

Neighborhood Development

Neighborhood development is an essential component of my policies designed to revitalize our Nation's urban areas. My Administration has taken a number of steps to assist non-governmental, neighborhood groups carry out community improvement plans.

In Fiscal Year 1981, I will propose increased funding for the Neighborhood Self-Help Development Program. This program aims to build the capacity of independent, neighborhood organizations to implement conservation and revitalization projects in low- and moderate-income neighborhoods.

In 1980, I will strongly support the renewal of the Home Mortgage Disclosure Act in order to encourage neighborhood reinvestment. My Administration will also continue to support fully the neighborhood reinvestment actions of independent regulatory agencies, such as the Federal Home Loan Bank Board's Community Investment Fund.

TRANSPORTATION

A major goal during the 1980's is to bring about a dramatic increase in the economic and energy efficiency of our transportation systems. While this Nation's transportation facilities are among the best in the world, they were planned, designed and constructed in an era of abundant and cheap energy. The country now faces a totally different situation of scarce and increasingly expensive energy. To help combat this problem, I have proposed to use $16.5 billion over the next decade from the windfall profits tax revenues to increase the energy efficiency of transportation. Of that, $13 billion would be allocated to increase transit capacity; $2.5 billion would be directed to promote the energy-efficient use of the automobile; and $1 billion for research on automotive fuel efficiency. I urge the Congress to enact this proposal without delay.

To further promote energy conservation, stimulate urban growth and create new employment opportunities in the inner cities, I urge the Congress to support mass transportation authorization legislation. This year I will seek reauthorization and extension of the public transportation grant program.

With the assistance of the Congress, we have taken a number of positive steps to reform outmoded transportation regulation. The Airline Deregulation Act of 1978 is working well, with reduced passenger fares per mile, and with the airlines better able to withstand the effects of recession and fuel price increases than would have otherwise been possible. To continue that type of progress, last year I submitted truck and rail regulatory reform bills and I am committed to seeking their enactment in 1980. These important bills will save consumers billions of dollars annually and reduce wasted fuel consumption.

To further improve America's railroads, I have introduced legislation to direct Federal railroad financial assistance toward restructuring of failing railroads and improved employment efficiency.

I will also ask Congress to increase funding for and extend the life of the Northeast Corridor Improvement Project to improve passenger rail services in the Northeast. . . .

SPECIAL NEEDS

Women

The efforts of my Administration over the last several years have been concentrated on providing American women with a full range of opportunities. Programmatic initiatives have been developed to overcome the widespread discrimination and disparities which women have faced in education, in health, and in employment. . . .

Refugees

In 1979 my Administration made significant progress in resolving a number of problems arising from the increase in refugees. Last March, I proposed comprehensive refugee legislation, and I regard its passage as a high priority this year. The legislation — which is the first comprehensive reform of our refugee immigration and domestic resettlement policies in twenty-eight years — will bring common sense and cohesion to an unnecessarily fragmented approach to international and domestic refugee needs. Under vigorous new leadership, the Office of the U.S. Coordinator for Refugee Affairs, which I created last year, will aggressively address the needs of refugees at home and abroad. We will also encourage greater cooperation with the private sector and other actions to ensure successful refugee resettlement.

Veterans

As our commitment to peace and our national security remains as strong as ever, so too is our Nation's obligation to those whose past service to our country helped to keep peace in the world. For that reason, my Administration's commitment to the needs of America's veterans will remain a high priority. . . .

GOVERNMENT ASSISTANCE

[State and Local Governments]

Since taking office, I have been strongly committed to strengthening the fiscal condition of our Nation's State and local governments. I have accomplished this goal by maintaining consistent and strong economic growth, and by encouraging economic development of local communities, and by supporting the General Revenue Sharing and Counter-Cyclical Fiscal Assistance programs.

General Revenue Sharing

This year I will propose the renewal of General Revenue Sharing. My Administration's proposal will forge a closer partnership among the Federal, State and local governments and will further emphasize the pivotal role of the States in our Federal system. My proposal for GRS renewal also will provide additional aid to the cities and counties that are most strained fiscally.

I will soon send legislation to Congress that will extend GRS for five years at the current funding level of $6.9 billion. One-third of the money will be provided to State governments on the basis of the current distribution formula. . . .

Two-thirds of GRS payments will be provided to local governments on the basis of population, tax effort and per capita income. While I will propose retention of the basic distribution formula for local governments, I also will propose a number of modest formula changes to provide greater aid to localities with large service responsibilities and with insufficient fiscal resources. . . .

[Counter-Cyclical and Targeted Fiscal Aid]

Last year, I submitted to Congress a two-part fiscal aid package designed to strengthen further the fiscal condition of our Nation's States and localities. The first part of this legislation provided standby counter-cyclical legislation to protect States and localities from unexpected changes in the national economy. The second part provided transitional highly targeted fiscal assistance in FY 1980 to only the most distressed local governments.

Substantial progress has been made on this legislation in the past year. The Senate passed legislation providing both targeted fiscal assistance and counter-cyclical aid in August, 1979, and similar legislation is now ready for House action. It is important that Congress complete its action on this legislation early this year.

URBAN POLICY

Two years ago, I proposed the Nation's first comprehensive urban policy. That policy involved more than one hundred improvements in existing Federal programs, four new Executive Orders and nineteen pieces of urban-oriented legislation. With Congress' cooperation, fifteen of these bills have now been signed into law. Additional action is expected to put into place more of these proposals this year.

Economic Development

One of the principal goals of my domestic policy has been to strengthen the private sector economic base of our Nation's economically troubled urban and rural areas. With Congress' cooperation, we have substantially expanded the Federal government's economic development programs and provided new tax incentives for private investment in urban and rural communities. These programs have helped many communities to attract new private sector jobs and investments and to retain the jobs and investments that already are in place.

When I took office, the Federal government was spending less than $300 million annually on economic development programs, and only $60 million of those funds in our Nation's urban areas. My FY 1980 budget requested more than $1.5 billion for economic development grants, loans and interest subsidies and more than $2.5 billion for loan guarantees. Approximately 60% of these funds will be spent in our Nation's urban areas. My FY 1981 budget continues these programs at these already high levels. In addition, we have extended the 10% investment credit to include rehabilitation of existing industrial facilities as well as new construction.

This year we need to continue our progess by extending and expanding the programs of the Economic Development Administration. With Congress' cooperation, this legislation already has passed both the House and the Senate. Both the House and the Senate bills include the key elements of my original National Development Bank proposal and provide a substantial expansion of the economic development grant, loan, loan guarantee and interest subsidy programs of the Federal government. This legislation is vitally important to the economic revitalization and redevelopment of our Nation's economically troubled urban and rural areas. I am hopeful that the conferees will complete their work shortly so that we can get these essential programs underway.

I continue to believe that the development of private sector investment and jobs is the key to revitalizing our Nation's economically depressed urban and rural areas. To ensure that the necessary economic development goes forward, the Congress must enact legislation reauthorizing the programs of the Economic Development Administration. That legislation is now in Conference, and I urge the conferees to complete their work soon, so that we can provide a foundation for the economic development of our Nation in the 1980's.

Community Development

The partnership among Federal, State and local governments to revitalize our Nation's communities has been a high priority of my Administration. When I took office, I proposed a substantial expansion of the Community Development Block Grant (CDBG) program and the enactment of a new $400 million Urban Development Action Grant (UDAG) program. Both of these programs have provided essential community and economic development assistance to our Nation's cities and counties.

This year, I will ask Congress to reauthorize both the CDBG and UDAG programs. I will propose the the CDBG program be reauthorized for three more years, and that a $150 million increase in funding be provided for FY 1981. I also will propose that the UDAG program be extended for three years, and that $675 million be provided for this program in the upcoming fiscal year. These actions should help our Nation's cities and counties to continue the progress they have made in the last three years.

Rural Policy

Since the beginning of my Administration, we have taken steps to address the pressing needs of a changing and rapidly growing rural America. For many rural areas, and for most rural residents, the last decade was a time of rapid growth and development. While this growth and development has produced higher income and increased jobs in rural communities, it has also created substantial housing, energy, transportation, health, and management problems.

Last December I announced our Small Community and Rural Development Policy, which is the culmination of several years' work and is designed to address these pressing problems now affecting rural areas. The major elements of the policy involve:

—Creation of the position of Under Secretary of Agriculture for Small Community and Rural Development to provide leadership in carrying out this policy.

—Establishment of an inter-agency working group to assist in the implementation of this policy.

—Appointment of a citizens Advisory Council to advise the President on the performance of the Federal government in the implementation of this policy and to recommend needed changes.

—An invitation to the Nation's government-formed rural development councils to work in partnership with Federal agencies in delivering State and Federal programs to rural areas.

—A directive to the working group to annually review existing and proposed policies, programs, and budget levels to determine their adequacy in meeting rural needs and fulfilling the policy objectives and principles. . . .

CONSUMERS

Consumer Representation

Last September I signed an Executive Order designed to strengthen and coordinate Federal consumer programs and to establish procedures to improve and facilitate consumer participation in government decisionmaking. Under the Order, each Federal agency must adopt and implement its own strong consumer program.

I also established an interagency Council to coordinate the Agencies' actions in responding to the Executive Order. This year, under the leadership of my Special Assistant for Consumer Affairs we will be working to make certain that the Order is faithfully implemented and that consumers receive better protection and assistance from Federal agencies.

My Administration will continue to support efforts to provide financial assistance in regulatory proceedings to citizen groups, small businesses and others whose participation is limited by their economic circumstances. These programs are needed to balance the regulatory process by assuring opportunities for broad public involvement in these proceedings.

Finally the Administration will continue to support reform of class-action procedures to ease the unnecessary burdens and costs of class actions, while at the same time preventing their use as an harassment technique.

National Consumer Cooperative Bank

My Administration worked closely with the Congress to create the National Consumer Cooperative Bank. The Bank is to provide loans, loan guarantees, and other financial services to non-profit consumer cooperatives, operating in such areas as food, housing, health, and auto repair.

To demonstrate my commitment to this innovative institution, I have signed legislation increasing appropriations for the Bank from $4 million in fiscal 1979 to $74 million in fiscal 1980. Legislation has also been signed adding two members to the Bank's board of directors — one to represent the interests of small business and one to represent the general public.

This year we will continue our efforts with Congress to make the Bank a strong and vital resource for consumers.

Consumer Services Information

Genuine competition is lacking in many service industries because consumers generally lack comparative cost and quality information. To help alleviate this problem, my Administration will assist non-profit groups and State and local government agencies to develop local consumer information systems to provide accurate cost and quality data on locally provided services. An essential part of this effort will be an evaluation of the impact of better consumer information on inflation and productivity in the service sector.

SCIENCE

Science and Technology

Since the beginning of my Administration, I have been committed to strengthening our Nation's research and development capability and to advancing those areas of science and technology which are vital to our economic and social well-being. That commitment has been reflected in: a 40% increase in basic research funding, resulting in the highest research and development funding in our Nation's history; a new Automotive Research initiative in which the industry, in partnership with the Federal government, will undertake basic research essential to help improve future automobiles; an acceleration of scientific and technological exchanges with the People's Republic of China; a major review of space activities and needs, resulting in a 60% increase in space funding and in the development of a space policy that will set the direction of our space efforts over the next decade; and a major new program to encourage industrial innovation.

Each of the undertakings will be pursued, in cooperation with the Congress, in this year.

Space

The diversity of our activities in space shows that space technology has become an integral part of our lives — in communications, in remote sensing for defense and civilian purposes, and in studies of the earth and the universe. Guided by a sound, aggressive, and fiscally responsible space policy, my Administration has undertaken a concerted effort to support and further our space activities.

During my Administration, the expenditures for Federal space programs have increased by 75%. Much of this increase is to meet the increasingly operational nature of our space activities. Nearly half of our expenditures are now for defense purposes; photo-reconnaissance satellites, for example, are enormously important in stabilizing world affairs and thereby make a significant contribution to the security of all nations. And my new initiative to establish an oceanic satellite system will provide invaluable ocean data for both the civil and defense sectors, thereby avoiding unnecessary duplication. . . .

ARTS & HUMANITIES

Arts

The arts provide fundamental enrichment for our Nation. The National Endowment for the Arts has played a major role in focusing public attention on the arts. In doing so, the Endowment has brought wider audiences from all parts of the country into contact with all of the arts.

Since the beginning of my term, I have increased the government's support for the Endowment's activities. I will continue that record of expanded support again this year. This will enable the Endowment to strengthen its efforts to open the arts to new audiences, new forums, and new parts of the country.

Humanities

The humanities play a vital role in deepening our understanding of culture and society. To enable the National Endowment for the Humanities to continue its important efforts, I will again be proposing increased funding for the Endowment.

While maintaining the on-going programs aiding scholarly research, education, and cultural interpretation, the Endowment will use these increased funds to augment its support for:

• research designed to increased our understanding of the traditions, cultures, and directions of countries in the Third World;

• studies exploring the complex public and ethical issues created by an increasingly technological society; and

• efforts to preserve the priceless documents and other materials that constitute the heritage of this Nation and of its regional and ethnic communities. . . .

DISTRICT OF COLUMBIA

No longer is our Nation's Capital a convenient target for misdirected political attacks. My Administration has developed a partnership for progress with the District of Columbia.

My Administration worked with the last Congress to pass a proposed Constitutional amendment granting full voting representation to the citizens of our Nation's Capital. The ratification process for this proposed amendment has begun and I urge the State legislatures which have not ratified the resolution to join those which have. We will continue our efforts this year in the ratification effort. . . .

COMMISSION ON THE HOLOCAUST

Last year, I received and approved the recommendations of the President's Commission on the Holocaust, which I established to assess how our government might officially recognize, for the first time, the tragedy of the Holocaust. I will shortly be appointing a Council of distinguished Americans to develop ways to implement the Commission's proposals. . . .

IV. Making Government Effective and Efficient

One of my major commitments as a candidate was to make the Federal government more effective and efficient. Over the past three years, with Congress' help, I believe that enormous progress has been made toward that goal. Reforms thought to be impossible — such as Civil Service Reform — have been enacted. Regulatory burdens — such as airline regulation and government paperwork — have been reduced or eliminated. This coming year, I intend to work with the Congress to improve further the government's ability to serve the nation effectively.

Government Reorganization

One of my highest priorities has been to improve the quality and efficiency of Federal programs through reorganization. Since I took office, we have submitted 13 reorganization initiatives to Congress, and Congress has approved all of them. These initiatives have strengthened the Federal government's capacity to deal effectively with such critical issues as energy, civil service, disaster relief, civil rights, international development assistance, education and trade.

In 1979, Congress approved legislation that I sought to consolidate education programs in a new Cabinet department. The Department of Education will provide full-time leadership, improved management and direct accountability for its performance to me, to the Congress and to those involved in education at every level.

This month I put into effect a major reorganization of the Federal government's trade functions approved by Congress last year. In conjunction with the Multilateral Trade Negotiations Agreements this reorganization will ensure that expanded trade opportunities for American business abroad are fully realized, and that my goal of trade expansion is given a higher priority by the Federal government.

Organizational initiatives are also an important part of my energy program. We have consolidated enforcement functions for the Alaska Natural Gas Transportation System under a single Federal Inspector to ensure timely completion of the natural gas pipeline. To reduce our dependence on foreign oil, I have proposed the creation of an Energy Mobilization Board which will expedite Federal, State, and local decisions on proposed energy facilities. I am also urging the Congress to approve creation of an Energy Security Corporation to spur development of a domestic fuels industry.

This year I will propose to Congress another significant reorganization: a plan which will strengthen the internal management and effectiveness of the Nuclear Regulatory Commission. Safety is our highest concern in regulating nuclear power development, and my reorganization plan will help improve the NRC's ability to ensure nuclear safety. . . .

Civil Service and Compensation Reform

In March 1978 I said that civil service reform would be the centerpiece of my government reorganization efforts. The Congress supported it, and I am pleased to report it is working very well. In the first real test of the reform act, over 98% of the eligible top-level managers joined the Senior Executive Service, choosing the challenge and accountability demanded by this new corps of top executives. The Office of Personnel Management, the Merit Systems Protection Board, and the Federal Labor Relations Authority authorized by the Act have operated effectively in their first year. And the agencies throughout the government continue to make substantial progress in implementing the other important civil service reforms. For the first time in the hundred year history of the civil service system Federal employees can get and hold jobs, and be paid, on the basis of actual on-the-job performance — not merely length of service.

Last year, I asked the Congress to take the next step in my Federal Employee Compensation Reform Message. I urged you to pass a pay reform bill which would modernize the Federal compensation system. This legislation is fair to Federal employees and to American taxpayers alike. Our white collar, blue collar and military compensation systems must be reformed in order to make certain that we neither overpay nor underpay Federal employees. It is a fair bill, and one which will help restore public confidence in the Federal service. I urge Congressional action on it.

Regulatory Reform

Over the past three years, we have put into place a comprehensive program to overhaul the Federal regulatory establishment, and eliminate unnecessary regulatory burdens. For 1980, I am determined to continue the progress of this effort; it is the most important part of my ongoing campaign to make our government more efficient and effective.

Airline deregulation. The Airline Deregulation Act of 1978 has revolutionized air transportation. In the first year of its operation, the new environment of free competition created by the law produced a record number of flights and passengers, a much wider variety of service packages, and a savings of approximately $2.5 billion in the fares paid by the travelling public. Under the Act, regulatory controls will continue to be relaxed, until in 1985, the CAB itself will be completely phased out of existence.

Trucking deregulation. The trucking industry is enmeshed in detailed regulations that control the routes truckers can drive and the goods they can carry. In addition, truckers are allowed to fix prices through industry rate bureaus. This regulatory system works to stifle competition, waste fuel, reduce service to small towns, and inflate prices.

My appointees to the Interstate Commerce Commission have started modernizing the system, but we need legislation to provide comprehensive reform. I have submitted a bill to open up entry, lift restrictions on the goods truckers may haul and the routes they may use, promote vigorous price competition, reduce regulatory delays, and improve safety on the road.

This bill is an important step in fighting inflation, and I look forward to passage of a sound bill by early summer. If appropriate legislation is not enacted, I would expect the ICC to proceed under its authority to implement reform initiatives.

In addition, we need legislation to increase competition in the household moving industry. The Senate recently passed a constructive bill, and I urge the House to strengthen and pass it.

Railroad deregulation. Railroads have traditionally been one of the most overregulated industries in America. As a result, management initiative, service, and competitive pricing have been stifled. Railroad plants and equipment have deteriorated, and the average railroad industry rate of return on investment is far too low. My Administration will continue to work to eliminate these wasteful conditions and the regulatory structure which helps cause them. Our principal weapon in that effort is the railroad deregulation bill that I proposed last year. Enactment of significant railroad deregulation legislation this year is essential to restoring our railroad system to its former strength.

Financial institutions regulation. Last year the combination of deposit rate ceilings and outmoded restrictions on the asset powers of thrift institutions produced severe inequities for the small saver, substantial savings outflows from many thrift institutions, and disruptions in the availability of mortgage credit. Contrary to its intended purpose, the Regulation Q system has contributed to the cyclical nature of the housing market and has destabilized the flow of mortgage funds. In a related area, changing competitive relationships, as well as innovations in the market, have increased inequities and produced a continuing decline in Federal Reserve membership. Now is the time to take the actions necessary to prepare for the financial environment of the 1980's.

The Congress passed legislation in 1979 which increased the ability of many Americans to obtain mortgage credit. In addition, the Congress made major progress toward enactment of the historic financial reform legislation I proposed last year.

This year we will work closely with Congress to achieve final approval of our financial reform objectives: the phaseout of Regulation Q deposit rate ceilings, the broadening of the asset and liability process of thrift institutions, the approval of legislation to stem the decline in Federal Reserve membership, and the elimination of other unwarranted regulatory restraints. Prompt action is necessary to avert a significant decline in Federal Reserve membership and to assure a fair rate of return to the saver, a steadier flow of housing credit, and a stable financial environment for all classes of depository institutions.

This spring I will submit to the Congress the Administration's findings on the McFadden Act and other geographic restraints on banking activity.

Telecommunications deregulation. Technological advances, such as satellites, computers, and microwave relays, have made it practical to move much of the telecommunications industry from a regulated monopoly to a deregulated, competitive market. This shift is already underway and is benefitting individual customers as well as companies.

Toward that end, I will continue to support strongly ongoing efforts in Congress to pass a bill that will encourage and protect competition, remove needless regulation, and maintain universal, reliable service. In addition, we need this legislation to smooth the transition to a competitive environment by protecting workers' rights, ensuring against any large increases for rural telephone rates and providing needed national security and emergency preparedness powers.

Regulation Reform Act. In March of 1979, I sent to Congress the Regulation Reform Act. When enacted, this bill will assure that new and existing regulations will be rigorously scrutinized before they can be issued or retained, that wasteful delays are eliminated from the regulatory process, that key regulatory officials be selected purely on grounds of integrity and competence, and that the public will be assured meaningful opportunities to participate in regulatory decision-making. The reform steps I have taken administratively have already avoided billions of dollars in unnecessary regulatory costs, erased thousands of useless regulations from the books of OSHA and other agencies, and opened up the regulatory process across the Executive Branch. Enactment of my regulatory reform bill legislation is needed in this Congress, to strengthen these reforms, and extend their benefits to the independent regulatory commissions.

Presidential oversight of regulation. Many regulatory programs are vital to the protection of the health, safety and welfare of our citizens.

These we must manage effectively, while cutting out wasteful red tape, rigidity, and costs imposed on industry and the public, and enhancing opportunities for public participation in decision-making. . . .

Legislative Veto. While supporting the Regulation Reform Act, I will strongly oppose proposals that would undermine the ability of the President to manage the regulatory process, or would cripple the effectiveness of needed programs. In particular, my Administration will oppose proposals to subject individual agency rules to veto by one or two houses of Congress, to transfer regulatory policy decision-making authority to the Federal courts, and to create rigid statutory procedures for Presidential supervision of Executive Branch regulatory agencies.

This last year has seen Congress besieged by assaults on various important regulatory statutes, especially the Federal Trade Commission Act, seeking groundless exemptions, crippling loopholes, and unprecedented Congressional interference with ongoing proceedings. I will resist strenuously all such efforts to confuse special interest pressure with regulatory reform.

Communications

My highest priority in the communications area is passage of regulatory reform legislation covering the telecommunications industry. In addition, in 1980 we will continue our program to make the media more diverse and to ensure that the public gets the full benefit of the advances in communications technologies. Administration efforts include:

● working to increase minority participation; already our program has helped produce a two-thirds increase in minority ownership of broadcast stations, and we will continue that progress;

● working with the Federal Communications Commission to continue to eliminate needless paperwork and regulations;

● pursuing plans to open up channels for as many as 1,000 new radio stations, to improve service to rural areas and provide more opportunities for minorities;

● developing proposals to improve the way frequencies are assigned, including incentives for users to conserve the increasingly crowded radio spectrum;

● encouraging the use of satellites, cable TV, and other technologies to deliver public services and to improve rural communications;

● working with Congress and the FCC to protect First Amendment rights and the free flow of information, through such measures as my bill on police searches of newsrooms; and

● continuing to support a strong, independent public broadcasting system and working to increase its coverage to reach all Americans.

In addition, I will submit to the Senate, later this year, the Treaty and Protocol that resulted from the World Administrative Radio Conference concluded in Geneva in December. This conference, and the follow-up conferences that will be held in the next few years, will determine the utilization of the radio spectrum for the rest of the century. We prepared for this conference for over two years; our delegation has secured for the United States all allocations necessary for its civilian and military services while also responding to the legitimate needs of the Third World nations.

Sunset

We will continue to work with Congress to pass sunset legislation. This legislation will overcome the inertia that lets Federal programs continue when they have outlived their purpose. It will ensure that Congress regularly reviews programs to decide whether they should be changed or eliminated. A comprehensive sunset bill, with a strong mechanism to force action when programs need change, is a vital building-block toward making the government more efficient. . . .

Lobby Reform

The American people have a right to know what significant influences affect their national legislature. The proliferation of well-financed, organizational lobbying activities during recent years has demonstrated the clear need for reform of the outdated and ineffective lobby disclosure law now in effect. This year my Administration will again work with Congress to pass a sound lobby law reform bill — one that respects the First Amendment rights of all Americans and minimizes paperwork burdens, yet allows meaningful disclosures.

Public Financing of Congressional Elections

The impact of special interest contributions on congressional campaigns has grown dramatically in recent years. It is time to adopt public financing for congressional elections before it is too late. Such public financing will avoid even the appearance of undue special interest influence, and will allow worthy candidates without adequate funds to run for Congress. I urge the Congress to act on this legislation.

Judicial Reform

In my Civil Justice Reform Message last year, I made proposals to increase the efficiency, cut the cost, and enhance the integrity of our Federal court system. Last year, I signed the Federal Magistrates Act of 1979. Both the Senate and the House have passed the Dispute Resolution Act, which would develop simple and informal means of resolving citizen disputes, and I look forward to early final action on this legislation. The Federal Courts Improvement Act has passed the

Senate, and I urge the House to act on it early in this session. I hope that the Congress will also pass the other bills recommended in my Message, such as the one which would curtail diversity jurisdiction.

LEAA

LEAA's potential to improve and strengthen State and local criminal justice programs has never been realized. Two years ago, I proposed far-reaching reforms in its structure and programs. Last month, Congress passed, and I signed, a bill which incorporated most of those reforms and which reauthorized LEAA for four more years. These reforms will preclude excessive expenditure of funds for equipment, enable better information and research about crime problems and permit funding only of innovative programs which have a high probability or record of proven success. . . .

Patent Reform

As part of the Industrial Innovation policy that I announced last year, we will be seeking to reform our patent laws in a way which will spur creativity and invention. The Administration will be working with Congress to develop a single policy to guide the Departments and Agencies dealing with patents resulting from federally-sponsored research. Such uniform treatment should encourage the commercial use of discoveries while protecting the taxpayers' investment.

V. Protecting Basic Rights and Liberties

Since taking office, I have worked to protect and enhance the basic rights and liberties guaranteed to Americans under the Constitution and our other laws. With your cooperation, we have made important progress in this area. This year, though, important work remains to be done if our goal of ensuring equality and basic freedoms for all Americans is to be realized. The dream of equal opportunity remains unfulfilled. I will do whatever I can to bring that dream closer to realization.

Equal Rights Amendment

I am committed as strongly as possible to the ratification of the Equal Rights Amendment. Its ratification this year will be one of my highest priorities.

As a result of our efforts in 1978, the Equal Rights Amendment's deadline for ratification was extended for three years. We have now two years and three States left. We cannot afford any delay in marshalling our resources and efforts to obtain the ratification of those three additional States. With your help, I believe we can succeed this year.

Although the Congress has no official role in the ratification process at this point, you do have the ability to affect public opinion and the support of State Legislators for the Amendment. I urge Members from States which have not yet ratified the Equal Rights Amendment to use that ability.

Civil Rights

The completion of the civil rights reorganization and significant operational improvements in the agencies that carry out equal employment opportunity functions have enabled the federal government to shift its focus for the first time to large-scale enforcement efforts. These have been buttressed by our vigorous and successful posture in several landmark affirmative action cases. At the same time, the reorganization mandate to eliminate unnecessary costs, paperwork and other burdens to businesses is being vigorously implemented by the Equal Employment Opportunity Commission. That will continue with increased resources this year.

To make certain that civil rights activities are given the highest priority in the Agencies, we have created a civil rights unit in the Office of Management and Budget. This new unit will monitor civil rights enforcement and advise the Director of OMB on the funding and management resources needed for effective enforcement.

Martin Luther King, Jr.

Dr. Martin Luther King, Jr. led this Nation's effort to provide all its citizens with civil rights and equal opportunities....As one of our Nation's most outstanding leaders, it is appropriate that his birthday be commemorated as a national holiday, and I will continue to work with the Congress to enact legislation that will achieve this goal.

Fair Housing

Enforcement of laws against housing discrimination has lagged in comparison with the employment area. Because there is no adequate enforcement mechanism, Title VIII of the Civil Rights Act, which prohibits discrimination in housing, has been largely ineffective. I have strongly supported legislation which seeks to provide the Department of Housing and Urban Development with the power to hold administrative hearings and to issue "cease and desist orders" in cases where Title VIII has been violated. We will continue to work with the Congress during 1980 to enact this long-overdue authority. Its enactment will continue to be my highest legislative priority in the civil rights area.

Intelligence Charters

A legislative charter for the intelligence agencies and a charter for the FBI are long overdue. The failure to define in law the duties and responsibilities of these agencies had made possible some of the abuses which have occurred in recent years.

Several months ago, I submitted to the Congress a legislative charter for the FBI which protects the rights of our citizens while preserving the Bureau's ability to meet its important responsibilities. In 1980, we will continue to work with the Congress toward enactment of this legislation.

Events of the past year indicate the need for a strengthened and clearly defined role for our intelligence community. On the basis of the sound consultative work done already with Congress, I plan to submit a proposed charter early this year.

Hatch Act Reform

Federal employees who work in non-sensitive positions should have the right to participate in off-the-job political activities. My Administration will continue to support legislation which would reform the Hatch Act to accomplish this goal, and would prevent any on-the-job political abuse.

Criminal Code

The Federal criminal laws are often archaic, frequently contradictory and imprecise, and clearly in need of revision and codification. My Administration will continue to work with the Congress to develop a Federal criminal code which simplifies and clarifies our criminal laws, while maintaining our basic civil liberties and protections.

Labor Law Reform

Our labor laws are vital to ensuring that a sound labor-management relationship exists in collective bargaining. Efforts to abuse those labor laws, especially by unduly slowing or blocking their implementation, have increased in recent years. As a result, a reform of our labor laws is badly needed to guarantee that their intended spirit is fully observed and enforced. . . .

Handicapped

During my Administration, we have made great strides toward ending discrimination against handicapped people through broadened employment opportunities, educational opportunities, and greater access to public facilities and services. Just after I came to office, the Department of Health, Education and Welfare issued the first regulations on Section 504 of the Rehabilitation Act. Since then, numerous other Federal agencies have issued final regulations, and we expect to have regulations from all the necessary agencies by the end of 1980.

Last year I supported legislation which would prohibit discrimination against the handicapped in private employment and housing. I will continue to support that initiative this year and to clarify legislative and administrative uncertainty about provisions of the Acts affecting the rights or programs affecting handicapped individuals. . . .

Privacy

Changes in our society are threatening the rights to personal privacy. Government and private institutions collect increasing amounts of information about individuals. Many decisions that once were made face-to-face are now based on recorded data, and modern technology allows this data to be transferred throughout the country instantaneously. Much of this information must be collected and used to enforce the laws, provide financial services, and for other important services. However, these needs must be balanced against the right to privacy and against the harm that unfair uses of information can cause.

Last year, I announced the government's first comprehensive privacy program, building on legislation already passed to prevent improper use of wiretaps and improper access to personal bank records. This new program has five separate bills — establishing privacy safeguards for medical, research, bank, insurance, and credit records and providing special protections, modeled on the wiretap laws, for electronic funds transfer systems. In addition, I have proposed legislation limiting police searches of newsrooms to deal with the problems created by the Supreme Court's *Stanford Daily* decision. . . .

VI. [Protecting our Natural Resources]

Two of our Nation's greatest natural resources are our environment and our fertile agricultural capacity. Since I have been in office, I have worked with the Congress to preserve, protect and where appropriate, develop our natural resources. In the environmental areas, I have been concerned about the importance of preserving a clean environment, and have taken a number of major actions designed to foster such an environment.

In the agricultural area, I have taken the steps needed to improve farm incomes and increase our agricultural production to record levels. With your help we can continue to make progress in both of these areas in 1980.

Environment

Balancing the need for resource development and conservation has been a major environmental theme of my Administration. I remain strongly convinced that this Nation can have economic and energy development and adequate environmental protection. As we open the decade of the 80's, all Americans can be proud of their natural and cultural heritage which continues to satisfy economic, recreational, and spiritual requirements.

1980 is the tenth anniversary of a decade of environmental awareness that began on Earth Day, 1970. During this past decade, monumental legislative achievements have occurred. These include: the National Environmental Policy Act, the Clean Air and Clean Water Acts, additions to our National Parks, Trails, and River Systems, and the Endangered Species Act. I was pleased to sign into law the reauthorization of the Endangered Species Act last year. During 1980 as we celebrate this tenth anniversary let us rededicate ourselves to the creation and maintenance of a safe and healthy environment, to the wise use and development of our natural resources, to the fair implementation of environmental statutes, to preserving unique wildlife resources, and to even greater achievements for improving the quality of life for all Americans.

During the next year, my Administration will vigorously pursue the protection of Alaskan lands; the implementation of an effective water resources policy; a careful implementation of domestic energy production programs, with proper regard for environmental values; a review of wilderness potential on the public lands; creation of a hazardous waste management program; fisheries development and coastal management policies.

Alaska Lands

Passage of legislation which adequately resolves the allocation of Federal lands in Alaska continues to be my highest environmental priority. At stake is the fate of tens of millions of acres of beautiful land, outstanding and unique wildlife populations, native cultures, and the opportunity to ensure that future generations of Americans will be able to experience and benefit from these nationally significant resources.

The proposals which I have supported in the 95th Congress, and again during the first session of this Congress, assure that Alaska's great national treasures can be preserved, while providing for increased domestic energy production and for the economic needs of all Alaskans.

In addition to recommendations for designating National Parks, Wildlife Refuges, Wilderness Areas, National Forests, and Wild and Scenic Rivers on the Federal lands in Alaska, I have or will be proposing aggressive but environmentally sensitive oil and gas development programs in Alaska's outer continental shelf and National Petroleum Reserve. My Administration is also stepping up the transfer of 103 million acres of Federal land to the State of Alaska and 44 million acres to Alaskan natives so that both the State of Alaska and the Native Corporations can build their economic base.

However, in order to maintain the proper balance between resource protection and development in Alaska, the Congress must now enact the comprehensive legislation which has been before that body for over two years. The 96th Congress will soon be asked to vote on what clearly amounts to the conservation decision of the century. . . .

Hazardous Waste/Toxic Substances

One of the most important environmental and public health issues facing our Nation is the threat caused by the improper disposal of hazardous substances. Accidents like those at Love Canal and Valley of the Drums have highlighted the inadequacy of the existing laws and inability of governments at all levels to respond quickly and efficiently to these dangerous incidents. In the coming years, there may be thousands of hazardous waste sites which will need attention, the cost of which could be enormous. Clearly an effective public policy is needed to deal with this situation.

Last June, I submitted to Congress a comprehensive $1.6 billion legislative proposal that establishes a system to deal with releases from uncontrollable hazardous waste sites as well as spills of oil and hazardous substances. This system includes provisions for emergency government response, effective enforcement, liability and in some cases, economic compensation. The system also calls for a partnership with the States in cleaning up and containing this problem. This legislation is absolutely essential if we are to meet our responsibilities to the public and I urge the Congress to act on it expeditiously.

Nuclear Waste Management

The problems related to the management, disposal and storage of nuclear wastes remains one of the most serious problems with nuclear power. My Administration has been deeply concerned with this problem for the past three years. An exhaustive study and review of this problem has been undertaken by the Administration over the past year.

Based on the findings and recommendations of that study, I will soon be proposing to Congress comprehensive legislation that deals directly with this problem. My proposals, if enacted, will represent the biggest step forward in the area of nuclear waste management since the dawn of the nuclear age. I urge the Congress to take action in this area this year.

RARE II

In 1979, I submitted to Congress my recommendations on wilderness for the National Forests under the RARE II procedure. These proposals include 15.4 million acres of new wilderness — the most desirable areas within the vast review. Over 10 million acres are undergoing further study. In addition, I directed the Forest Service to release for multiple use management the 36 million acres of land that was designated for non-wilderness. I urge the Congress to approve my recommendations this year.

Water Policy Legislation

Sound water management is vital to the economic and environmental health of our Nation.

Administrative implementation of the comprehensive water policy initiatives which I announced in June of 1978 is nearing completion. We will continue to work with the Congress to pass legislation needed to improve further Federal water resources programs and to support the States in their primary responsibilities for water allocation and management.

I am pleased that last fall the Senate authorized an expanded grant program to the States for water management and water conservation technical assistance, and I expect the House to soon pass this legislation. The cost sharing bill which I have proposed is critically needed to give the States a more effective voice in setting water project priorities in state and Federal water policy decisions.

I believe the establishment of an independent review unit in the Water Resources Council is essential, and I urge the Congress to act quickly on the pending authorization. The independent review unit will provide an objective, impartial, technical analysis to the Administration and to the Congress, of water projects proposed for authorization or new-start construction funding. This information will enable the Administration and the Congress to make better informed decisions on where to invest the taxpayers' water resource dollars.

It should be clear that my Administration supports sound water resources development, and has taken several steps to improve the quality of projects sent to Congress for authorization and funding. I am concerned that the water projects authorization bills now under consideration by Congress threaten to overturn the progress made in recent years. I urge the Congress to give this legislation the careful and thoughtful scrutiny required by our joint commitment to restraining Federal spending and ensuring a sound environment.

Fisheries Development

Last May, my Administration proposed a fisheries development policy that recognized both the importance of the U.S. commercial fishing industry to the Nation's economy and that fish is an important food source. This policy includes a recognition of the potential for fisheries expansion within the Nation's 200-mile fisheries conservation zone, and the importance of the Federal government's creating a positive climate for fisheries development. In conjunction with this policy, my Administration has sent a legislative proposal on fisheries development to the Congress.

It is time that the United States begin taking action to more fully utilize the fisheries resources of the 200-mile economic zone. I urge the Congress to join with me in this effort.

AGRICULTURE

Agricultural Progress

While much work remains to be done, America's agriculture is by far the best in the world. Efforts made by my Administration, in cooperation with Congress, to secure economic stability for the farmer, have produced results.

In 1979, we experienced another record year for farm production. Net farm income jumped to $32 billion in 1979, a $4 billion increase over 1978. Agricultural exports also reached new highs, rising 18% in 1979 to $32 billion. Despite the suspension of exports to the Soviet Union, we can expect a continued healthy export picture for our Nation's farmers.

Last year the Secretary of Agriculture travelled around the country and conducted an extraordinarily detailed and creative dialogue with the Nation's farmers. He obtained invaluable suggestions on economic and social issues concerning farm life; as we prepare our farm program for this year and beyond, the advice of our Nation's farmers will clearly be reflected in the policies we develop with the Congress.

Soviet Grain Suspension

In response to the Soviet armed invasion of Afghanistan on Christmas Eve, I took several actions to demonstrate our Nation's resolve to resist such hostile acts of aggression against a sovereign, independent nation. One of the most important of these actions was the suspension of grain sales to the Soviet Union beyond the 8 million tons provided under our 1975 grains agreement. The Soviet Union had intended to purchase an estimated 25 million tons of U.S. wheat and feed grains. Thus, the suspension of sales above the 8 million ton agreement level is expected to result in the freeing of about 17 million tons.

My decision to suspend these sales was a difficult one, but a necessary one. We could not continue to do business as usual with the Soviet Union while it is invading an independent, sovereign nation in an area of the world of strategic importance to the United States....

To protect American farmers from the price depressing effects of the grain suspension, I directed the Secretary of Agriculture to take several actions:

• The Commodity Credit Corporation will assume the contractual obligations for grain previously committed for shipment to the Soviet Union.

• The Department of Agriculture, acting through the Commodity Credit Corporation, will purchase wheat contracted for export to the Soviet Union for the purpose of forming an emergency international wheat reserve. In this connection, I will propose legislation authorizing release of this wheat for international aid purposes.

• To encourage farmers to place additional grain in the farmer-held grain reserve, the Secretary of Agriculture has made several modifications in that important program.

• The Commodity Credit Corporation will purchase corn at the local level to alleviate the congestion within the transportation system caused by the refusal of the International Longshoremen's Association to load grain up to the 8 million metric ton level.

In combination, these actions are expected to isolate from the market an amount of grain equivalent to that not shipped to the Soviet Union, thereby avoiding a decline in grain prices. I am pleased to report that these actions are having the desired results and that American farmers are being protected from the effects of the suspension.

If further actions are necessary to insure that American agriculture does not bear a disproportionately large share of the burden associated with this action, I will not hesitate to take them.

Crop Insurance

We now have an assortment of Federal loan, grant and insurance programs designed to protect farmers from the economic risks associated with natural disasters. We recognized early in my Administration that these programs were in serious need of reform. They are marked by many shortcomings: inconsistencies in eligibility, inequities in the level of benefits to producers of different crops, and inefficiencies in the use of taxpayer money. Recent evidence of abuse in the agricultural disaster loan programs provides further evidence of the need for this reform.

I have sent the Congress a proposal to consolidate these authorities in the form of an all-risk comprehensive insurance program. Congress has made clear progress in devising an improved crop insurance program, but work remains to be done. I urge the Congress to finish its work on this legislation as soon as possible.

International Emergency Wheat Reserve

The Congress has not yet acted on the proposal I made in the last Session to create an International Emergency Wheat Reserve. This reserve of up to 4 million tons of wheat would be used to assure recipient nations that we will meet our international food aid commitments. The suspension of further grain sales to the Soviet Union provides an appropriate opportunity to provide this authority, and thereby establish guidelines for the release of wheat now being acquired by the Commodity Credit Corporation.

Foreign Policy

From the time I assumed office three years ago this month, I have stressed the need for this country to assert a leading role in a world undergoing the most extensive and intensive change in human history.

My policies have been directed in particular at three areas of change:

—the steady growth and increased projection abroad of Soviet military power — power that has grown faster than our own over the past two decades.

—the overwhelming dependence of Western nations, which now increasingly includes the United States, on vital oil supplies from the Middle East.

—the pressures of change in many nations of the developing world, including the year old revolution in Iran and uncertainty about the future in many other countries.

As a result of those fundamental facts, we face some of the most serious challenges in the history of this Nation. The Soviet invasion of Afghanistan is a threat to global peace, to East-West relations, and to regional stability and to the flow of oil. As the unprecedented and overwhelming vote in the General Assembly demonstrated, countries across the world — and particularly the non-aligned — regard the Soviet invasion as a threat to their independence and security. Turmoil within the region adjacent to the Persian Gulf poses risks for the security and prosperity of every Western nation and thus for the entire global economy. The continuing holding of American hostages in Iran is both an affront to civilized people everywhere, and a serious impediment to meeting the self-evident threat to widely-shared common interests — including those of Iran. . . .

[National Security — Military Strength]

The maintenance of national security is my first concern, as it has been for every President before me.

As I stated one year ago in Atlanta: "This is still a world of danger, a world in which democracy and freedom are still challenged, a world in which peace must be re-won every day."

We must have both the military power and the political will to deter our adversaries and to support our friends and allies.

We must pay whatever price is required to remain the strongest nation in the world. That price has increased as the military power of our major adversary has grown and its readiness to use that power been made all too evident in Afghanistan.

The U.S.-Soviet Relationship

We are demonstrating to the Soviet Union across a broad front that it will pay a heavy price for its aggression in terms of our relationship. Throughout the last decades U.S.-Soviet relations have been a mixture of cooperation and competition. The Soviet attack on Afghanistan and the ruthless extermination of its government have highlighted in the starkest terms the darker side of their policies — going well beyond competition and the legitimate pursuit of national interest, and violating all norms of international law and practice.

This attempt to subjugate an independent, non-aligned Islamic people is a callous violation of international law and the United Nations Charter, two fundamentals of international order. Hence, it is also a dangerous threat to world peace. For the first time since World War II, the Soviets have sent combat forces into an area that was not previously under their control, into a non-aligned and sovereign state.

On January 4 I therefore announced a number of measures, including the reduction of grain sales and the curtailment of trade and technology transfer, designed to demonstrate our firm opposition to Soviet actions in Afghanistan and to underscore our belief that in the face of this blatant transgression of international law, it was impossible to conduct business as usual. I have also been in consultation with our allies and with countries in the region regarding additional multilateral measures that might be taken to register our disapproval and bolster security in Southwest Asia. I have been heartened by the support expressed for our position, and by the fact that such support has been tangible, as well as moral.

The destruction of the independence of Afghanistan government and the occupation by the Soviet Union has altered the strategic situation in that part of the world in a very ominous fashion. It has brought the Soviet Union within striking distance of the Indian Ocean and even the Persian Gulf.

It has eliminated a buffer between the Soviet Union and Pakistan and presented a new threat to Iran. These two countries are now far more vulnerable to Soviet political intimidation. If that intimidation were to prove effective, the Soviet Union might well control an area of vital strategic and economic significance to the survival of Western Europe, the Far East, and ultimately the United States.

It is clear that the entire subcontinent of Asia and specifically Pakistan is threatened. Therefore, I am asking Congress, as the first order of business, to pass an economic and military aid package designed to assist Pakistan defend itself.

Defense Budget

For many years the Soviets have steadily increased their real defense spending, expanded their strategic forces, strengthened their forces in

Europe and Asia, and enhanced their capability for projecting military force around the world directly or through the use of proxies. Afghanistan dramatizes the vastly increased military power of the Soviet Union.

The Soviet Union has built a war machine far beyond any reasonable requirements for their own defense and security. In contrast, our own defense spending declined in real terms every year from 1968 through 1976.

We have reversed this decline in our own effort. Every year since 1976 there has been a real increase in our defense spending — and our lead has encouraged increases by our allies. With the support of the Congress, we must and will make an even greater effort in the years ahead. . . .

Strategic Forces

We are strengthening each of the three legs of our strategic forces. The cruise missile production which will begin next year will modernize our strategic air deterrent. B-52 capabilities will also be improved. These steps will maintain and enhance the B-52 fleet by improving its ability to deliver weapons against increasingly heavily defended targets.

We are also modernizing our strategic submarine missile force. The first new Trident submarine has already been launched and will begin sea trials this year. The second Trident will be launched in the spring of 1980. The first of our new Trident missiles, with a range of more than 4,000 miles, have already begun operational patrols in Poseidon submarines.

The new MX missile will enhance the survivability of our land-based intercontinental ballistic missile force. This is why I decided last spring to produce this missile and selected the basing mode best suited to enhance its capability. Further the MX will strengthen our capability to attack a wide variety of Soviet targets.

Our new systems will enable U.S. strategic forces to maintain equivalence in the face of the mounting Soviet challenge. We would however need an even greater investment in strategic systems to meet the likely Soviet buildup without SALT.

Forces for NATO

We are greatly accelerating our ability to reinforce Western Europe with massive ground and air forces in a crisis. We are undertaking a major modernization program for the Army's weapons and equipment, adding armor, firepower, and tactical mobility.

We are prepositioning more heavy equipment in Europe to help us cope with attacks with little warning, and greatly strengthening our airlift and sealift capabilities.

We are also improving our tactical air forces — buying about 1,700 new fighter and attack aircraft over the next five years — and increasing the number of Air Force fighter wings by over 10%.

We are accelerating the rate at which we can move combat aircraft to Europe to cope with any surprise attack, and adding to the number of shelters at European airbases to prevent our aircraft from being destroyed on the ground.

Rapid Deployment Forces

We are systematically enhancing our ability to respond rapidly to non-NATO contingencies wherever required by our commitments or when our vital interests are threatened.

The rapid deployment forces we are assembling will be extraordinarily flexible: They could range in size from a few ships or air squadrons to formations as large as 100,000 men, together with their support. Our forces will be prepared for rapid deployment to any region of strategic significance.

Among the specific initiatives we are taking to help us respond to crises outside of Europe are:

—the development and production of a new fleet of large cargo aircraft with intercontinental range;

—the design and procurement of a force of Maritime Prepositioning Ships that will carry heavy equipment and supplies for the three Marine Corps brigades. . . .

Naval Forces

Seapower is indispensable to our global position — in peace and also in war. Our shipbuilding program will sustain a 550-ship Navy in the 1990's and we will continue to build the most capable ships afloat.

The program I have proposed will assure the ability of our Navy to operate in high threat areas, to maintain control of the seas and protect vital lines of communication — both military and economic — and to provide the strong maritime component of our rapid deployment forces. This is essential for operations in remote areas of the world, where we cannot predict far in advance the precise location of trouble, or preposition equipment on land.

Military Personnel

No matter how capable or advanced our weapons systems, our military security depends on the abilities, the training and the dedication of the people who serve in our armed forces. I am determined to recruit and to retain under any foreseeable circumstances an ample level of such skilled and experienced military personnel.

We have enhanced our readiness and combat endurance by improving the Reserve Components. All reservists are assigned to units structured to complement and provide needed depth to our active forces. Some reserve personnel have also now been equipped with new equipment.

Mobilization Planning

I have also launched a major effort to establish a coherent and practical basis for all government mobilization planning. Begun last May, this is the first such effort conducted at Presidential level since World War II. It involves virtually every Federal agency, with the aim of improved efficiency and readiness.

Our Intelligence Posture

Our national interests are critically dependent on a strong and effective intelligence capability. We will not shortchange the intelligence capabilities needed to assure our national security. Maintenance of and continued improvements in our multi-faceted intelligence effort are essential if we are to cope successfully with the turbulence and uncertainties of today's world.

The intelligence budget I have submitted to the Congress responds to our needs in a responsible way, providing for significant growth over the Fiscal Year 1980 budget. This growth will enable us to develop new technical means of intelligence collection while also assuring that the more traditional methods of intelligence work are also given proper stress. We must continue to integrate both modes of collection in our analyses.

It is imperative that we now move forward promptly within the context of effective Congressional oversight to provide America's intelligence community with Charters which can permit it to operate more effectively and within a national concern codified by law.

Regional Policies

Every President for over three decades has recognized that America's interests are global and that we must pursue a global foreign policy.

Two world wars have made clear our stake in Western Europe and the North Atlantic area. We are also inextricably linked with the Far East — politically, economically, and militarily. In both of these, the United States has a permanent presence and security commitments which would be automatically triggered. We have become increasingly conscious of our growing interests in a third area — the Middle East and the Persian Gulf area.

We have vital stakes in other major regions of the world as well. We have long recognized that in an era of interdependence, our own security and prosperity depend upon a larger common effort with friends and allies throughout the world.

The Atlantic Alliance

At the outset of this Administration I emphasized the primacy of our Atlantic relationship in this country's national security agenda. We have made important progress toward making the Atlantic Alliance still more effective in a changing security environment.

We are meeting the Soviet challenge in a number of important ways:

First, there is a recognition among our allies that mutual security is a responsibility to be shared by all. We are each committed to increase national defense expenditures by 3% per year. There remains much work to be done in strengthening NATO's conventional defense; the work proceeding under the Alliance's Long Term Defense Program will help achieve this objective.

Last month, we and our NATO allies took an historic step in Alliance security policies with the decision to improve substantially our theater nuclear capabilities. The theater nuclear force modernization (TNF) program, which includes deployment of improved Pershing ballistic missiles and of ground-launched cruise missiles in Europe, received the unanimous support of our allies. The accelerated deployment of Soviet SS-20 MIRVed missiles made this modernization step essential. TNF deployments will give the Alliance an important retaliatory option that will make clear to the Soviets that they cannot wage a nuclear war in Europe and expect that Soviet territory will remain unscathed.

While we move forward with our necessary defense efforts in Europe, we are also proceeding with our efforts to improve European security through arms control.

As an integral part of the NATO TNF decisions, the Alliance has made it clear that it is prepared to negotiate limitations on long-range theater nuclear missiles.

On our part, our TNF modernization efforts will make possible a streamlining of our nuclear weapons stockpile in Europe, allowing us to withdraw 1,000 nuclear warheads over the next year.

In the Mutual and Balanced Force Reduction talks, we and our allies have recently put forward new proposals that are designed to simplify the negotiations and improve the prospect for early progress in limiting conventional military forces in Europe.

In a very real sense the accomplishments of the past year answered a critical question concerning NATO's future: can the Western Alliance, which has provided the foundation for one of the longest periods of peace and prosperity that Europe has ever enjoyed, still summon the essential cohesion, relevance, and resolve to deal with fundamental security issues likely to affect its member nations well into the next century? NATO's consensus in favor of modernizing and negotiating about its nuclear arsenal while continuing to improve conventional forces, dramatized Allied capacity to respond effectively to both the military and political threats posed by the Soviet Union.

Relations with our allies and friends in Europe are taking on ever broader dimensions. Our security agenda remains central; we are addressing new concerns as well. . . .

Asia

The United States is a Pacific nation, as much as it is an Atlantic nation. Our interests in Asia are as important to us as our interests in Europe. Our trade with Asia is even greater than our trade with Europe. We have pursued and maintained these interests on the basis of a stable balance of power in the region. Our partnership and alliance with Japan is central to our Asian policy. We are strengthening our new relationship with China. We have expanded our ties with the Association of South East Asian Nations (ASEAN) and its member governments. . . .

Asian Security

The balance of power is fundamental to Asian security. We have maintained that balance through a strong United States military posture in the region, as well as close ties with our allies, Japan, Australia, New Zealand and Korea. Over the past year I have worked to stabilize the United States military presence in Asia by concluding an amended base agreement with the Philippines that will last until 1991. We have fostered the closest degree of security cooperation with Japan in the history of our two nations — exemplified by joint planning for the defense of Japan, increased Japanese contributions to United States base costs in Japan, and large-scale Japanese purchases of United States defense equipment. After examining in detail new intelligence estimates of North Korean military strength, I decided to maintain our troop strength in the Republic of Korea at its present level until at least 1981. The reaffirmation of our commitment to Korean security has been of great importance to the Koreans as they make necessary political adjustments in the wake of President Park's assassination.

Response by nations in East Asia to the Soviet aggression in Afghanistan has been gratifying. Australia in particular deserves recognition for the forthright stand it has taken. Japan and the ASEAN nations have also been strongly supportive.

China

Over the last year we have expanded our new relationship with the People's Republic of China to ensure that where our interests coincide, our separate actions will be mutually reinforcing. To this end we have enhanced our consultative relationship. We have also sought to develop an enduring institutional framework in the economic, cultural, scientific, and trade areas.

This process has been facilitated by the successful visits of Vice Premier Deng to the United States and Vice President Mondale to China; through the signing of over 15 commercial, scientific, and cultural agreements; through numerous Cabinet-level visits; and through a significant expansion of trade and the flow of people between our two countries.

During Secretary of Defense Brown's recent trip to the People's Republic of China, wide-ranging talks were held on global and regional issues, arms control, technology transfer, and ways to sustain bilateral contacts. Although we may differ with the Chinese on some issues, our views coincide on many important issues, particularly with respect to the implications for the region of the Soviet invasion of Afghanistan.

In 1980 I look forward to passage by Congress early in the year of the China Trade Agreement and of authorization of OPIC operations in China; we plan to conclude civil aviation, maritime, and textile agreements; and continue to expand our commercial, cultural, and scientific relations, particularly through ExImBank credits to the People's Republic of China.

Southeast Asia

The countries comprising ASEAN are central to United States interests in Southeast Asia.

Throughout the past year, our relations with ASEAN have continued to expand as our consultative arrangements were strengthened.

The stability and prosperity of Southeast Asia have been severely challenged by Soviet-supported Vietnamese aggression in Cambodia. During this year we will continue to encourage a political settlement in Cambodia which will permit that nation to be governed by leaders of its own choice. We have taken all prudent steps possible to deter Vietnamese attacks on Thai territory by increasing our support to the Thais, and by direct warnings to Vietnam and the U.S.S.R. The other members of ASEAN have stood firmly behind Thailand, and this in great measure has helped to contain the conflict. We have been gratified by Thailand's courageous and humane acceptance of the Cambodian refugees.

Middle East — Persian Gulf — South Asia

Events in Iran and Afghanistan have dramatized for us the critical importance for American security and prosperity of the area running from the Middle East through the Persian Gulf to South Asia. This region provides two-thirds of the world's oil exports, supplying most of the energy needs of our allies in Europe and Japan. It has been a scene of almost constant conflict between nations, and of serious internal instability within many countries. And now one of its nations has been invaded by the Soviet Union.

We are dealing with these multiple challenges in a number of ways.

Middle East

First, it has been a key goal of my Administration since 1977 to promote an enduring resolution of the Arab-Israeli conflict — which is so essential to bringing stability and peace to the entire region. Following the Camp David Summit of August 1978, in March 1979, I helped bring about the signing of a peace treaty between Egypt and Israel — the first time in 30 years of Middle East conflict that peace had shined with such a bright and promising flame. At the historic signing ceremony at the White House, Prime Minister Begin and President Sadat repeated their Camp David pledge to work for full autonomy for the West Bank and Gaza.

Since then Egypt and Israel have been working to complete this part of the Camp David framework and to provide an opportunity for the Palestinian people to participate in determining their future. I strongly support these efforts, and have pledged that we will be a full partner in the autonomy negotiations. We will continue to work vigorously for a comprehensive peace in the Middle East, building on the unprecedented achievements at Camp David.

At the same time, I have reinforced America's commitment to Israel's security, and to the right of all nations in the area to live at peace with their neighbors, within secure and recognized frontiers.

Persian Gulf

In recent years as our own fuel imports have soared, the Persian Gulf has become vital to the United States as it has been to many of our friends and allies. Over the longer term, the world's dependence on Persian Gulf oil is likely to increase. The denial of these oil supplies — to us or to others — would threaten our security and provoke an economic crisis greater than that of the Great Depression 50 years ago, with a fundamental change in the way we live.

Twin threats to the flow of oil — from regional instability and now potentially from the Soviet Union — require that we firmly defend our vital interests when threatened.

In the past year, we have begun to increase our capacity to project military power into the Persian Gulf region, and are engaged in explorations of increased use of military facilities in the area. We have increased our naval presence in the Indian Ocean. We have been working with countries in the region on shared security concerns. Our rapid deployment forces, as described earlier, could be used in support of friendly governments in the Gulf and Southwest Asian region, as well as in other areas.

South Asia

The overwhelming challenge in this region will be dealing with the new situation posed by Soviet aggression in Afghanistan. We must help the regional states develop a capability to withstand Soviet pressures in a strengthened framework for cooperation in the region. We want to cooperate with all the states of the region in this regard — with India and Pakistan, with Sri Lanka, Bangladesh and Nepal.

In this new situation, we are proposing to the Congress a military and economic assistance program to enable Pakistan to buttress its defenses. This is a matter of the most urgent concern, and I strongly urge the earliest possible approval by the House and Senate. We are also working closely with other friends of Pakistan to increase the resources available for Pakistan's development and security.

We are also pursuing the possibility of gaining access to military facilities in the region in time of trouble. We are prepared to work closely with our friends in the region, on a cooperative basis, to do whatever is required to ensure that aggressors would bear heavy costs so that further aggression is deterred.

A high priority for us in the region is to manage our nuclear concerns with India and Pakistan in ways that are compatible with our global and regional priorities. The changed security situation in South Asia arising from the Soviet invasion of Afghanistan calls for legislative action to allow renewed assistance to Pakistan. But this in no way diminishes our commitment to work to prevent nuclear weapons proliferation, in Pakistan or elsewhere.

Steady growth of our economic assistance is also essential if the countries of South Asia are to achieve growth and true stability.

Africa

A peaceful transition to majority rule in Southern Africa continues to be a major goal of the United States. We gave our fullest support to the successful British drive to reach an agreement among all parties in Rhodesia. The process of implementation will not be easy, but the path is now open to a peaceful outcome. With our European allies, Canada and the African states directly concerned we also are making progress toward independence and majority rule for Namibia. The momentum resulting from successful resolution of the Rhodesian conflict should aid in these initiatives.

Congressional support for the Executive Branch decision to maintain sanctions on Rhodesia until the parties reached agreement on a ceasefire and an impartial elections process had begun was instrumental in creating the conditions necessary for agreement. Now that the United States, European trading partners and the surrounding African states have lifted sanctions, the process of economic reconstruction in Rhodesia — soon to be Zimbabwe — can begin.

With the creation of an independent Zimbabwe after many years of fighting, we will be prepared to cooperate in a coherent multi-donor development plan for the poor nations in the Southern Africa region. . . .

North Africa

In 1979 the United States moved to help a long-standing friend by strengthening our arms supply relationship with Morocco. In assisting Morocco to deal with attacks inside its internationally recognized frontiers, we seek conditions of greater security and confidence in which a political settlement of the Western Sahara conflict can be effectively pursued. Though not itself a mediator, the United States in the months ahead will encourage the countries in the area to resolve their differences peacefully in order that the vast economic potential of North Africa can be exploited for the well-being of the people living there.

Latin America

Since my inauguration, I have worked hard to forge a new, collaborative relationship with the nations of Latin America and the Caribbean — one resting on a firm commitment to human rights, democratization, economic development and non-intervention. The events of 1979 — even the turbulence in Central America and the Caribbean — presented us with opportunities to move toward these goals.

There was encouraging progress in the area of human rights and democratization in the Western Hemisphere this past year. The inauguration of a new democracy in Ecuador, and the strong effort by the Andean countries to preserve democracy in Bolivia were positive steps.

During 1979, I met with the President of Mexico twice to discuss the opportunities and difficult issues before our two countries. We have taken worthwhile steps, including an agreement on natural gas and on trade.

On October 1, Vice President Mondale and many leaders from Latin America traveled to Panama to celebrate the coming into force of the Panama Canal Treaties. The transition to a new relationship and a new structure to manage the Canal was smooth and effective because of the contributions and the mutual respect between Panamanians and Americans. . . .

The International Economy

A growing defense effort and a vigorous foreign policy rest upon a strong economy here in the United States. And the strength of our own economy depends upon our ability to lead and compete in the international market place.

Energy

An essential lesson to be drawn from Iran is that there are compelling foreign policy, as well as domestic economic reasons for lessening our dependence on foreign oil.

In response to a series of United States proposals, the industrial countries adopted in 1979 a cooperative energy strategy for the 1980's. Its main elements are collective restraint on oil imports; intensified efforts to conserve oil and boost production of conventional substitutes for oil; and collaborative research, development and commercialization of new fuel technologies.

At the Tokyo Economic Summit in June, the heads of government of the seven major industrial democracies agreed that they must take responsibility for curbing oil demand. By the end of the year, 20 industrialized nations, members of the International Energy Association, had agreed not only to enforce equitably allocated ceilings on their oil imports, but to create a system for quickly adjusting the ceilings to changes in world oil supply. Completion of the detailed agreements to execute the global oil demand-allocation process is at the head of the international energy agenda for 1980.

At the 1980 Economic Summit in Venice, I intend to propose further joint action to smooth the transition from oil to more abundant fuels and to slow the growth in oil prices.

In support of the international oil strategy, the Administration and the United States coal industry are launching joint marketing efforts to make this country a major exporter of steam coal. With assurance of reliable United States coal supply at competitive prices, many of the electric power plants to be built in the 1980's and 1990's can be coal-fired rather than oil-burning. Coal exports will help us pay for our declining but costly oil imports.

A new source of natural gas supply for the United States — Mexico — was opened through the conclusion of government-to-government negotiations. Through close cooperation with our northern neighbor, Canada, the Administration cleared the way for expanding the flow of Canadian natural gas to the United States and for private development of the Alaskan gas pipeline across Canada to the lower 48 states.

We continue to believe that nuclear power will play an essential role in meeting the energy needs of many nations, but with effective safeguards against the proliferation of nuclear weapons.

International Monetary Policy

We are moving forcefully to establish the fundamental economic conditions for a strong dollar. In 1979 the balance of payments was in approximate balance for the first time in three years, despite substantially higher oil import costs. Our anti-inflationary economic policies and strong energy program should provide a basis for further improvement. Of course, the outcome depends in part also upon responsible pricing behavior by OPEC and other oil producers.

We support the efforts under way to strengthen the international monetary system. I urge the Congress to enact promptly legislation permitting the United States to increase its quota in the International

Monetary Fund (IMF) as part of the general expansion of Fund resources. We welcome the measures being taken by the IMF to improve its ability to promote sound economic and exchange rate policies in all member countries. We also welcome the study of the possible establishment of a "substitution account" to strengthen the international monetary system by promoting the role of the Special Drawing Right as the principal reserve asset in the system.

Trade

Under the direction of my Special Trade Representative, we brought to a successful conclusion the multilateral trade negotiations, the most ambitious set of negotiations to reduce barriers to international trade in a decade. The resulting "MTN" agreements, covering a broad spectrum of trade issues, were concluded and ratified by overwhelming majorities of the United States Congress. These binding commitments, signed by all the major trading nations, provide the framework for a new era in international trading relations with them and with the developing nations. This makes clear my resolve and that of the American people to resist the dangers of protectionism.

The reorganization of the Federal government trade agencies which I directed will assure more effective and prompt governmental action to exploit the export opportunities afforded by the MTN. The plan, approved by Congress this fall, establishes a strong, authoritative voice in the Executive Office of the President to provide coherence and leadership to United States trade policy, negotiations, and the implementation of the MTN trade codes. The reorganization establishes the Office of the U.S. Trade Representative and strengthens the Commerce Department.

Sugar

In 1979, Congress ratified the International Sugar Agreement, thus fulfilling a major commitment of this Administration. The agreement is an important element in our international commodity policy with far-reaching implications for our relations with developing countries, particularly sugar producers in Latin America. . . .

Tin

At year's end, Congress approved stockpile disposal legislation which will permit the General Services Administration to sell 30,000 metric tons of tin from our strategic stockpile and contribute up to 5,000 metric tons to the International Tin Organization's (ITO) buffer stock. This fulfills a United States pledge made during the Conference on International Economic Cooperation and represents a major step forward in our relations with producing countries in the developing world. . . .

Common Fund

The United States joined members of the United Nations Conference on Trade and Development, both developed and developing nations, in negotiating an agreement on the framework of a Common Fund to help international commodity agreements stabilize the prices of raw materials. Negotiations are now underway on the final articles of agreement of the Fund. . . .

Economic Cooperation With Developing Nations

Our relations with the developing nations are of central importance to the United States. The fabric of our relations with these countries has both political and economic dimensions, as we witnessed in recent weeks when nations of the Third World took the lead in condemning the Soviet invasion of Afghanistan. . . .

Food — The War on Hunger

One of the main economic problems facing developing countries is lagging food production. We must help these countries meet this problem — not only so that their peoples will be free from the threat of continuing hunger, but also so that their societies will be strong enough to resist external pressure. I have directed that United States bilateral and multilateral aid be geared increasingly to this goal, as recommended by our Hunger Commission, chaired by Sol Linowitz; we are urging other donor countries to join in more effective efforts to this end.

Good progress has been made since the Tokyo Economic Summit called for increased effort on this front. The World Bank is giving this problem top priority, as are some other donor countries. The resources of the consultative Group on International Agricultural Research will be doubled over a five-year period. The work of our own Institute of Scientific and Technological Cooperation will further strengthen the search for relevant new agricultural technologies.

The Human Dimension of Foreign Policy

Human Rights

The ultimate aim of our foreign policy must be to preserve freedom for ourselves and to expand freedom for others. This is a matter both of national principle and of national interest. For we believe that free and open societies are not only better able to meet the rising expectations of their people; they are also better able to accommodate often conflicting internal pressures before popular frustrations explode in violent and radical directions.

We do not seek to impose our system or institutions on others. Rather, we seek to support, in practical and concrete ways, the efforts of other nations to build their own institutions in ways that will meet the irrepressible human drive for freedom and justice.

Human rights policy commands the strong support of our citizens, and of the Congress. The world climate increasingly favors human rights progress.

Despite new turbulence and conflict, the past year featured some encouraging positive developments. We cannot and should not claim credit for them. But it is clear that we are part of a growing movement. During 1979, we saw:

—The further strengthening of democratic practices in Spain and Portugal, with free elections in both countries;

—The disappearance of several of the world's most repressive regimes;

—The freeing of political prisoners in Asia, Africa, and Latin America;

—A return to democratic rule in several Latin American countries and widespread progress in reducing human rights violations in the region;

—The growing strength of international human rights institutions. The Inter-American Court of Human Rights held its first meeting. Preparations began for another conference to review compliance with the Helsinki accords, to be held in Madrid this November. The OAU took long strides toward establishing a human rights commission for Africa. UN bodies became increasingly active in their human rights efforts. . . .

Humanitarian Aid

The mass exodus of refugees from Vietnam reached a crescendo in summer 1979 with over 65,000 people a month fleeing repression and economic privation. Most fled by boat, and many were lost at sea. In July, at a special UN meeting on refugees, Vice President Mondale presented a major United States program to rescue and help support and resettle the new refugee population. I doubled to 14,000 a month the number of Indochinese refugees the United States, in accord with our finest traditions, would absorb over the year ahead.

The Vietnamese invasion of Kampuchea in late 1978 gravely jeopardized the supply of food for the already decimated and brutalized Khmer people. In October, I announced that the United States would pay one-third of the costs of the international relief program mounted jointly by UNICEF and the International Committee of the Red Cross. Leaders of thirty-five church and voluntary agencies, with White House encouragement, are engaged in their own large fund-raising program for refugees. . . .

The Control of Nuclear Weapons

Together with our friends and allies, we are striving to build a world in which peoples with diverse interests can live freely and prosper. But all that humankind has achieved to date, all that we are seeking to accomplish, and human existence itself can be undone in an instant — in the catastrophe of a nuclear war.

Thus one of the central objectives of my Administration has been to control the proliferation of nuclear weapons to those nations which do not have them, and their further development by the existing nuclear powers — notably the Soviet Union and the United States.

Non-Proliferation

I entered office committed to assert American leadership in stemming the proliferation of nuclear weapons — which could create fundamental new instabilities in critical regions of the world, and threaten the security of the United States. This should not and cannot be done unilaterally. The cooperation of other suppliers of nuclear technology and materials is needed. This issue must not become a North-South confrontation. . . .

Limitations on Strategic Arms

The most prominent of our nuclear arms control efforts is, of course, SALT II.

The signing of the Treaty brought to an end painstaking negotiations carried out under three administrations of both parties.

—SALT II is in our mutual interest; it is neither an American favor to the Soviet Union nor a Soviet favor to the United States.

—Ratification of the SALT II Treaty would represent a major step forward in restraining the continued growth of Soviet strategic forces. . . .

Conclusion

As we enter the decade of the 1980's, we face challenges both at home and abroad which will test our qualities as a people — our toughness and willingness to sacrifice for larger goals, our courage and our vision.

For this Nation to remain secure, for this country to prosper, we must rise above narrow interests. The dangers of disunity are self-evident in a world of major power confrontation. The rewards of a new national consensus and sense of purpose are equally clear.

We have new support in the world for our purposes of national independence and individual human dignity. We have a new will at home to do what is required to keep us the strongest nation on earth.

We must move together into this decade with the strength which comes from realization of the dangers before us and from the confidence that together we can overcome them.

JIMMY CARTER

The White House
January 21, 1980

SAKHAROV BANISHMENT

January 22, 1980

The Soviet Union Jan. 22 stripped Andrei D. Sakharov, noted physicist and human rights advocate, of all of his state awards and honors and sent him from Moscow into internal exile at Gorky — a city 250 miles east of Moscow closed to western visitors.

A leading figure in Russia's development of the hydrogen bomb, Sakharov and his wife, Yelena Bonner, had been critics of the Soviet government's denial of human rights. It had been presumed that Sakharov's international reputation would protect him from arrest.

The eviction of the Sakharovs was seen as part of the Soviet reaction to a chill in U.S.-Soviet relations following the Russian invasion of Afghanistan in December 1979. (Historic Documents of 1979, p. 965) *President Carter — an outspoken supporter of human rights and of dissidents within the Soviet Union — had sent Sakharov a personal letter in 1977 expressing support for his human rights activities.*

Despite exile and other restrictions, Sakharov published a copyrighted open letter in The New York Times *June 8 urging greater world pressure on the Soviet Union to withdraw from Afghanistan. He supported a boycott of the 1980 Summer Olympic Games in Moscow, saying, "[e]very spectator or athlete who comes to the Olympics will be giving indirect support to Soviet military policies."*

Sakharov Statement

Although Sakharov was confined to Gorky, his wife was allowed to return to Moscow periodically. On one such trip she brought a Jan.

27 statement in which Sakharov said that "[t]he actions of the Soviet authorities are a gross violation of my basic right to receive and disseminate information...." He explained that he had been "arrested on the streets" and "[o]n the same day, with my wife ... I was taken by special flight to Gorky, where the city's deputy procurator explained the conditions the regime decreed for me — constant observation, prohibition against leaving the city limits, prohibition against meeting with foreigners and 'criminal elements,' prohibitions against correspondence and telephone conversations with foreigners, including scientific and purely personal correspondence and telephone calls."

He was instructed to report three times a month to the police with the threat of arrest for non-compliance, the Russian scientist reported, adding that "[e]ven in prison, there is more possibility of communication with the outside world." Referring to the plight of government critics within the Soviet Union, Sakharov said his eviction was "making possible further repressive measures against all dissident groups in the country."

Tass Statement

Tass, the Soviet news agency, in a statement released the day of Sakharov's arrest, charged that the physicist had "been conducting subversive activities against the Soviet state for a number of years. He was repeatedly warned ... about the impermissibility of such activities. Ignoring these warnings, Sakharov lately embarked on the road of open calls to reactionary circles of imperialist states to interfere in the U.S.S.R.'s internal affairs."

Other Arrests

The Soviet move against Sakharov signaled a crackdown on other dissidents in the country. A week before his banishment Sakharov reported the arrest Jan. 14 of a Lithuanian nationalist who had called for the independence of Lithuania from the Soviet Union.

Sakharov's June 8 open letter named 21 dissidents recently arrested in Russia.

Moreover, the resignation of Vladimir Kirillin from high government posts shortly after Sakharov's exile suggested to some experts a Communist Party crackdown. Deputy chairman of the Council of Ministers and chairman of the State Committee for Science and Technology, Kirillin had favored increased contacts with the West.

The Soviet Academy of Sciences, whose membership included the nation's leading academicians, concluded its meeting Feb. 8 without discussion or action on Sakharov's continued membership in that prestigious body. Political expulsion — except for the Stalin era — had been rare during its 256-year history.

U.S. Reaction

The Carter administration issued a statement Jan. 22 deploring Sakharov's arrest and exile. His fate, the statement said, "is cause for deepest concern for all free societies where his courageous struggle for basic rights and dignity is celebrated."

President Carter Jan. 23 said the action of the Soviet government "arouses worldwide indignation." Carter asserted that the treatment of Sakharov was "a scar on their system that ... Soviet leaders cannot erase by hurling abuse at him and seeking to mask the truth."

Other protests were made by Great Britain, the Netherlands and by the human rights organization, Amnesty International.

Following are the texts of President Jimmy Carter's remarks Jan. 23, 1980, deploring the arrest and exile of Andrei D. Sakharov; and Sakharov's statement of Jan. 27, 1980, as translated from the Russian by The New York Times, *describing his arrest and exile and criticizing Soviet policy in Afghanistan and the treatment of dissidents within the Soviet Union. (Boldface headings in brackets have been added by Congressional Quarterly to highlight the organization of the texts.):*

CARTER'S JAN. 23 REMARKS

The decision by Soviet authorities to deprive Nobel laureate Andrei Sakharov of his honors and to send him into exile arouses worldwide indignation. This denial of basic freedoms is a direct violation of the Helsinki Accords and a blow to the aspirations of all mankind to establish respect for human rights. The American people join with free men and women everywhere in condemning this act.

We must, at the same time, ask why the Soviet Union has chosen this moment to persecute this great man. What has he done in the past few months that is in any way different from what he was doing for the past 20 years? Why the need to silence him now? Is it because of the invasion and occupation of Afghanistan?

Just as we have welcomed [Alexander] Solzhenitsyn, [Joseph] Brodsky, [Mstislav] Rostropovich, and thousands of others who have fled Soviet oppression, so we would welcome Dr. Sakharov. It is part of our proud and sacred heritage.

The arrest of Dr. Sakharov is a scar on their system that the Soviet leaders cannot erase by hurling abuse at him and seeking to mask the truth. His voice may be silenced in exile, but the truths he has spoken serve as a monument to his courage and an inspiration to man's enduring quest for dignity and freedom.

SAKHAROV'S JAN. 27 STATEMENT

On Jan. 22, I was arrested on the street and taken to the office of the Procuracy of the U.S.S.R. A. Rekunkov, first deputy procurator general of the U.S.S.R., informed me that I was being deprived of my titles of Hero of Socialist Labor, of all decorations and prize awards, by decree of the Presidium of the Supreme Soviet of the U.S.S.R. I was asked to return the medals and orders and certificates, but I refused, believing that I was given them for good reason. Rekunkov also informed me of the decision to banish me to the city of Gorky, which is closed to foreigners.

On the same day, with my wife, Yelena Bonner, who was allowed to go with me, I was taken by special flight to Gorky, where the city's deputy procurator explained the conditions of the regime decreed for me — constant observation, prohibition against leaving the city limits, prohibition against meeting with foreigners and "criminal elements," prohibition against correspondence and telephone conversations with foreigners, including scientific and purely personal correspondence and telephone calls, even with my children and grandchildren, Matvei, 6, and Ana, 4. I was instructed to report three times a month to the police, with the threat of arrest in case of noncompliance.

[Imposed Isolation]

The authorities are thus imposing on us complete isolation from the outside world. The house is surrounded 24 hours a day by police and KGB details, which pose obstacles to visits to us by anyone, including our friends. Telephone connections with Moscow and Leningrad are completely blocked. We have not been able to call even my wife's mother, to tell her how we were. I was not able to call a physicist colleague, a highly respected Soviet scholar. These restrictions also apply to my wife, who is supposedly "free." She sent a telegram to our children in the United States, but there was no answer, so she is deprived of contact with the children.

Even in prison, there is more possibility of communication with the outside world.

No longer youngsters and not in the best of health, we are completely deprived of help from our friends, of medical help from our doctors.

These repressive actions against me were undertaken at a time of general worsening of the international situation and of intensification in the persecution of dissidents within the country.

The worsening of the international situation was caused by actions of the U.S.S.R., which is doing the following:

1. Launching in Europe a broad and demagogic campaign with the aim of strengthening its military superiority.

2. Trying to destroy the recently outlined peace opportunities in the Middle East and southern Africa.

3. Supporting terrorist regimes in Ethiopia and some other countries.

4. Maintaining military units in Cuba.

5. Supporting the actions of quasigovernmental terrorists in Iran who have violated the basic principles of diplomatic work.

6. The culmination of this dangerous policy was the invasion of Afghanistan, where Soviet soldiers are waging merciless war against insurgents, against the Afghan people.

Within the country, the authorities have taken new action against the core of the human rights movement. [Tatyana] Velikanova and [Viktor] Nekipelov have been arrested. [Malva] Landa has been threatened with arrest. The magazine Poiski [Searches] is being broken up. [Valery] Abramkin, [Viktor] Sokirko, [Yuri] Grimm have been arrested.

The movement for religious freedom is being persecuted and the clergymen [Dmitri] Dudko and [Glep] Yakunin have been arrested. [Lev] Regelson has been arrested. Trials and arrests are proceeding in the Ukraine and in the Baltic. Repression has increased against the Crimean Tatars; Reshat Dzhemilyov has been convicted.

[Government Repression]

The actions of the authorities against me in this situation are aimed at making the continuation of my public activities completely impossible. They are aimed at humiliating and discrediting me and at the same time making possible further repressive measures against all dissident groups in the country, with less possibility of the world's finding out about them, and further international adventures.

On Jan. 24 *Izvestia* published an article containing slander against me and a deliberate distortion of my position. My position remains unchanged. I am for a pluralistic, open society, both democratic and just; for convergence, disarmament and peace; for the defense of human rights in the whole world — in our country, in the countries of Eastern Europe, in Indonesia, China, Chile, everywhere; for a worldwide amnesty for prisoners of conscience; for doing away with the death penalty. I am for giving priority to the problems of peace, the problem of averting thermonuclear war.

From the article in *Izvestia* it is apparent that the main reason for the repression against me at this particularly anxious time was my position condemning the intervention in Afghanistan, which is a threat to the entire world, and demanding the withdrawal of Soviet troops from that country, perhaps with their replacement by United Nations units (see my interview with *The New York Times* and with American television), as well as my having joined in a document on the subject issued by the Moscow Helsinki group.

Being in a state of complete isolation and anxiety for members of my family and for my daughter-in-law, Liza Alekseyeva — to whom

I am no longer able to provide any protection — I demand that they be given an opportunity immediately to leave the U.S.S.R. and join their children and grandchildren. Although my wife is technically free, I will, of course, be afraid not only for her health, but for her life, if she is forced to travel to them [word illegible] (unfortunately, we know that the [state security] organs are capable of applying Mafia-like techniques).

The actions of the Soviet authorities are a gross violation of my basic right to receive and disseminate information (Article 19 of the Universal Declaration of Human Rights). Soviet representatives are trying to calm world public opinion by saying that I will be able to continue scientific work and that there is no threat of criminal prosecution against me. But I am prepared to stand public and open trial. I do not need a gilded cage. I need the right to fulfill my public duty as my conscience dictates.

I am grateful to all those who have come to my defense. My fate has been a happy one — I succeeded in being heard. But I ask everyone not to forget those who have selflessly served and are still serving in the defense of human rights, those whom I mentioned in this letter and all those whom I did not mention.

ANDREI SAKHAROV
Gorky, Jan. 27, 1980

CARTER'S BUDGET MESSAGES
January 28 and March 31, 1980

President Carter on Jan. 28 sent Congress his regular fiscal 1981 budget requests calling for outlays of $615.8 billion and anticipating a deficit of $15.8 billion. Just two months later, however, on March 31, the president submitted a revised budget envisioning outlays of $611.5 billion and revenues of $628 billion, thus projecting a surplus of $16.5 billion.

The budget reversal — from a deficit to a surplus — was the centerpiece of a package of anti-inflationary measures announced by Carter on March 14. It was the outcome of a round of White House economic policy making that began in February, less than three weeks after the president's original fiscal 1981 budget had been unveiled. (Anti-inflation package, p. 243)

The surplus projected in President Carter's revised budget was only the second in 12 years — fiscal 1969 had ended with a surplus of $3.2 billion. It reflected not only spending cuts, as the Carter administration stressed, but also new revenues. They included $12.6 billion from a gasoline conservation fee of 10 cents a gallon, which Carter had imposed, and $3.4 billion from a new withholding tax on interest and dividends, which he had asked Congress to approve.

January Budget

In his Jan. 28 message, Carter said his fiscal 1981 budget "continued the strategy of restraint" that he had proposed in his fiscal 1980 budget.

(Historic Documents of 1979, p. 9) *Anticipating revenues of $600 billion, Carter's January budget projected a $52 billion spending increase that would have represented a 9 percent rate of federal spending growth. "After allowing for inflation," the president said, "the budget is virtually level with 1980 spending." The $15.8 billion deficit projected in the January budget, Carter said, would be the lowest in seven years.*

The January budget called for $15 billion in increases in military, energy and intelligence activities. It held domestic spending, however, to about the same level as in fiscal 1980. While social programs would merely keep pace with inflation, military spending would rise by 3.3 percent.

The emphasis in the budget for the Defense Department was on the nation's nuclear deterrent, the combat readiness of forces in Europe and the military's ability to respond to crises elsewhere in the world. "I cannot ignore," the president said, "the implications of terrorism in Iran or Soviet aggression in Afghanistan."

Besides defense, the only area of the budget to propose substantial increases in spending was scientific research, especially basic research. Funding for the National Science Foundation would grow by 17 percent, exceeding $1 billion for the first time. In his Jan. 28 budget message, Carter said, "The payoff, particularly for basic research, is long-term, but immense."

Revised Budget

The revised budget, which the president sent Congress March 31, was prepared by the administration in close consultation with Democratic leaders in both chambers of Congress. It was believed that the sharp fiscal restraint demonstrated by the budget surplus, coupled with strong monetary actions by the Federal Reserve Board, would reverse the upward course of prices. The Consumer Price Index, the most widely watched measure of inflation, had reached an annualized rate of 18.2 percent in the first two months of 1980.

The revised budget contemplated new revenues in fiscal 1981 amounting to $28 billion. They included not only receipts from new taxes but also about $12 billion estimated to result from the effect of inflation on the income tax.

As the new budget was being made public March 31, James T. McIntyre Jr., director of the Office of Management and Budget, told reporters that the budget reductions were "fair." He added, "No single interest or set of recipients will bear a disproportionate share of the austerity."

Many of the spending cuts were achieved by the deferral or reduction of new programs proposed in the January budget. Some of the largest *reductions were $1.7 billion for state revenue sharing, $900 million for welfare reform, $850 million for the Young Adult Conservation Corps and for countercyclical CETA jobs, and $800 million achieved by delaying purchases of oil for the strategic petroleum reserve.*

Reaction

Many economists and key members of the nation's financial community reacted favorably to the president's updated budget. However, some analysts believed that since the deficit in Carter's January budget was relatively small to begin with, the impact of "balancing the budget" would be more cosmetic than real. A number of liberals, members of Congress from urban areas and special interest groups attacked the March 31 plan. "Nothing like this has taken place, ever," Sen. Daniel Patrick Moynihan, D-N.Y., told reporters, adding that New York City and state would lose 15 percent of their revenues. And Lane Kirkland, president of the AFL-CIO, charged that the new plan would put 500,000 Americans out of work. Kirkland called the drive for a balanced budget "Hooverist Republican" economics.

Some of the most conservative members of Congress also opposed the new plan, on the ground that the budget was balanced by raising taxes, not by cutting government spending.

Following are the texts of President Carter's Jan. 28, 1980, fiscal 1981 budget message to Congress and of his March 31, 1980, revised budget message:

JANUARY BUDGET MESSAGE

To the Congress of the United States:

This budget for 1981 is prudent and responsible. It continues the strategy of restraint that I proposed, and the Congress accepted, for the 1980 budget. At the same time it proposes selected, essential increases in areas of high priority and great national concern. In this way it seeks a balance between our needs for budgetary restraint and our needs for specific expenditures. I expect the Congress to support it.

Total outlays for 1981 proposed by this budget are $615.8 billion, an increase of 9%. After allowing for inflation, this budget is virtually level with 1980 spending. Total receipts for 1981 are estimated to be $600 billion. In view of current economic conditions, the only major revenue proposal included in the budget is my windfall profit tax now before the Congress.

Thus, I am proposing a deficit of $15.8 billion, the lowest deficit in 7 years. This reduces the deficit by 60% in comparison to 1980. More significantly, it is $50 billion less than when I first ran for the Presidency. As a percentage of the budget, and of the gross national product, the 1981 deficit is the second lowest of the last decade.

Economic projections deeply affect this budget. It appears today that the long economic recovery occurring throughout my first term may falter this year. I have therefore assumed that there will be some decline in GNP during the course of 1980, followed by renewed but moderate growth in 1981. As a result, budget receipts will be reduced and certain expenditures will increase automatically. This is why the 1981 budget is in deficit. If, contrary to our assumptions, the economy were to perform strongly enough to keep the unemployment rate at its current level, the 1981 budget would be in surplus.

[Tax Reductions]

We must monitor the economic outlook carefully. If the economy begins to deteriorate significantly, I will consider tax reductions and temporary spending programs for job creation targeted toward particular sectors of economic stress. But I believe current economic conditions argue for restraint.

I believe that this judgment and this budget recognize that equitable budget restraint is essential in our efforts to control inflation; that the unemployed should not bear the costs of our anti-inflation efforts; and most importantly, that we continue to pursue the goals of full employment, price stability, and balanced growth. The fiscal and program policies in this budget are essential, I believe, if we are to move rapidly toward these goals in the 1980's.

Indeed, the restraint proposed in this budget is essential to achieve these goals. The unacceptably high inflation now prevailing is clearly due to many, deeply imbedded, long-term forces. Countering this inflation involves sustained action across a wide spectrum.

● We must reduce our dependence upon foreign oil.

● We must enhance our economy's productivity.

● We must continue our efforts to foster competition and innovation through further deregulation.

● We must sustain compliance with the administration's wage and price guidelines.

But none of these efforts can succeed unless Federal spending is controlled. By continuing a clear and consistent policy of restraint, the 1981 budget insures that the Federal budget will not be an inflationary force in the economy.

Although I have kept spending in this budget from rising in real terms, I have found it necessary to increase funds in a few critical areas. The most important of these are defense, energy, basic research, and the training and employment of our Nation's young people.

Defense

The long decline in real spending for defense that began in 1969 has been reversed. The uncertain and sometimes hostile world we live in requires that we continue to rebuild our defense forces. The United States will continue to seek peaceful means to settle international disputes. But I cannot ignore the major increases in Soviet military spending that have taken place inexorably over the past 20 years. I cannot ignore our commitment to our NATO allies for mutual real increases in our investment in national defense. I cannot ignore the implications of terrorism in Iran, or Soviet aggression in Afghanistan.

Therefore, my budget proposes a defense program in 1981 of $158.2 billion in budget authority, an increase of over 5% in real terms. Outlays for defense will be $142.7 billion, a real increase of over 3%.

Moreover, I am committed as a matter of fundamental policy to continued real increases in defense; and I plan increases in my defense budgets through 1985. Over the period 1981-85, I am proposing that the defense program level of the United States increase by $90 billion.

Energy

This budget reflects the important progress made by my administration toward a broad and practical program dealing with the energy problems the Nation will face in the next decade. I am confident, and the 1981 budget assumes, that early in the 1980 session the Congress will pass the crucial measures I proposed last year: the windfall profit tax, the Energy Security Corporation, the conservation measures, and the Energy Mobilization Board.

With this budget we will have put into place an energy program composed of the following elements:

(1) *Realistic pricing and fair taxes.* — My decontrol decision of last April is now in effect. It is painful, and no one can pretend otherwise. But we cannot have an energy program that maintains illusions. Energy is not cheap, and we must accept that fact.

My windfall profit tax, to be passed early this year, retains a portion of the profits from energy price increases for the public. This will insure that increased energy prices will lead to new public investment in energy production. It will insure also that the burdens of higher energy costs are fairly shared.

(2) *Conservation.* — The 1981 budget allocates resources for tax incentives, low-interest subsidized loans, and other measures to stimulate more conservation. Conservation is the quickest and cheapest step we can take to confront our energy problem.

(3) *Production.* — This budget anticipates the creation of the Energy Security Corporation to facilitate the development of synthetic fuels and a major new gasohol program. It also supports continued new investments in those energy initiatives begun in the last two budgets. We are significantly increasing our expenditures on fossil fuels, on solar energy, and on nuclear fission. Nuclear fission research, on the other hand, declines, while greater emphasis is placed on solving the current problems of nuclear power.

(4) *Protection.* — As we adjust to the new energy realities, we must continue to protect those who are most vulnerable. The 1981 budget continues to provide funds for the poor to weatherize their homes; funds to enable the most disadvantaged Americans to cope with the rising cost of energy; and funds for energy crisis assistance.

My energy program is, of necessity, a long-term one. But if it is sustained through the new decade, we will reduce consumption, increase production from domestic sources, and promote alternate forms of energy. We will significantly reduce our dangerous reliance upon foreign oil. We will remove a major source of inflation. Our economy and our Nation will emerge from the 1980's stronger than they are now.

Basic Research

In the long run, economic growth depends critically on technological development. For many years, this country has led the world in producing new technology. We are in danger of losing this leadership. The 1981 budget continues my long-standing commitment to reverse the trends of the past two decades and provide for major and sustained increases — above the rate of inflation — for research and development programs. Obligations for research and development will increase by 13%, for basic research by 12%. Since 1978, obligations for basic research will have increased by 40%. I believe that these are among the most important expenditures we can make. The payoff, particularly for basic research, is long-term, but immense. We benefit today — in new industries, in millions of jobs, in lives saved, and in lives protected — from the investments in science made decades ago. We must continue such investments today to reap similar returns tomorrow.

The Budget Totals
[In billions of dollars]

	1979 actual	1980 estimate	1981 estimate	1982 estimate	1983 estimate
Budget receipts	466	524	600	691	799
Budget outlays	494	564	616	686	774
Surplus or deficit (−)	− 28	− 40	− 16	+ 5	+ 25
Budget authority	557	654	696	775	868

[Human Resources]

My budget, restrained as it is, provides needed support to those Americans who are most in need. Most of the increase in the 1981 budget over 1980 is due to the automatic cost-of-living increases in entitlement programs that provide income to the poor and the elderly. I have continued and improved these programs. In addition, I have proposed discretionary increases in a wide range of programs affecting those in our society who are the most disadvantaged.

The budget includes $687 million for proposals to expand health services to the poor and the underserved, including $403 million to provide medicaid eligibility for 2 million additional low-income children and approximately 100,000 pregnant women. The budget also includes a 24% increase in subsidized housing programs and a 24% increase in elementary and secondary education programs for the disadvantaged. Overall, I am proposing an increase of $7 billion in aid to the poor to protect them against the effects of inflation.

At the same time, I am proposing a major initiative that will enable our Nation's disadvantaged youth to receive a strong basic education, to find and keep a job. This is a critically important time for this initiative. In the 1980's, the number of youths entering the labor market will fall. If the young people of the 1980's are prepared, they will be able to find good jobs and build productive lives. My initiative will make this preparation possible. It will couple a strong emphasis on basic education with significant employment opportunity. For those young people who participate, the programs will be tough and challenging. But they will be extremely worthwhile. Those who complete them will have a major advantage where it counts — in the permanent job market. I consider this investment in human resources for the 1980's to be as important as the investments I am proposing for basic research. It is an investment in our most precious resource — the energies and talents of America's young people.

Agriculture

Because of the aggression by the Soviet Union against Afghanistan, I concluded that we could not now permit that country to benefit from our productive agriculture. On January 4, I announced the suspension of shipments of grain, soybeans, and their byproducts to the Soviet Union. This budget reflects the steps necessary to avoid the devastating effects such action could have had on our farmers and grain shippers. Specifically, the Secretary of Agriculture will:

• purchase contracts entered into with the Soviet Union at prices at or above those prevailing on January 4;

• if necessary, take title to the grain intended for export to the Soviet Union and isolate it from the market;

• purchase up to 4 million metric tons of wheat for an international food aid reserve;

• increase the loan level for feed grains and wheat by 10 and 15 cents per bushel, respectively; and

● modify the farmer-owned grain reserve to encourage farmers to place additional grain in the reserve.

On January 19, I announced, as additional steps to avoid the impact of suspension of shipments, that the Government would:

● increase the 1980 and 1981 Public Law 480 programs in order to increase grain shipments abroad; and

● purchase corn directly at local levels to stabilize cash markets and alleviate transportation backups.

I stand ready to take further steps if these actions prove insufficient.

Other Commitments

In other important areas, the 1981 budget reflects the reorganization accomplishments of the administration; continues the significant progress already experienced in urban and community development; expresses my commitments to welfare reform and a national health plan, programs that will begin in future budget years; and reaffirms my dedication to improved Federal budgeting and management.

The budget anticipates that my welfare reform proposals will take full effect in 1982, and my national health plan proposal in 1983. Taken together, these programs provide income support and assured health care to all Americans in need. My national health plan — which will be phased into operation prudently, consistent with the state of our economy — minimizes direct governmental control over health care, restrains the growth of Government, and provides maximum individual choice. I am continuing to seek enactment of my hospital cost containment proposal, which I believe is an essential part of any national health plan. When fully enacted, these two proposals — welfare reform and the national health plan — will significantly and permanently improve the lives and prospects of all Americans.

The 1981 budget includes a $15.5 billion allocation for the new Department of Education, which the Congress has approved. The establishment of this Department will require a great deal of effort in the short run, but it will give our system of education the consistent attention and high priority it deserves.

This budget also continues the improvement in the budget process I promised 4 years ago. In the 1979 budget we introduced zero-base budgeting, a system we have now used in three budgets to assure the allocation of scarce public resources to the most critical areas. Last year, in the 1980 budget, we moved to multiyear budgeting. My budget again this year shows not only decisions for 1981, but the effect of those decisions — in detail — for 1982 and 1983. To the extent feasible, the multiyear budget projects also the future costs of programs such as the national health plan, welfare reform, defense, energy, and research and development.

This year I have installed a central system to control the use of Federal credit. In the past, too much has escaped the normal discipline of the budget. This system, which is now in place, recommends specific credit limitations for most credit programs.

The new system of credit control will permit both the administration and the Congress to improve their understanding of the credit programs, to measure their important effects, and to determine appropriate levels of credit activity.

The Credit Budget Totals

[In billions of dollars]

	1979 actual	1980 estimate	1981 estimate
New direct loan obligations	51.4	59.7	60.7
New loan guarantee commitments	74.7	75.2	81.4
Total	126.1	134.9	142.1

This budget reflects continued efforts to improve financial management in Government and to stop illegal or improper use of taxpayers' money. We are achieving major savings from better cash management and stronger internal auditing in Federal agencies.

Conclusions

Proposing a responsible Federal budget is a fundamental task of public leadership. The budget must reconcile a broad range of legitimate claims for resources with the needs of the economy and the burdens on the taxpayer. Simultaneously, it must:

• respect past commitments in its allocations to social security, to veterans, and to the elderly;

• meet the needs of the present for defense, unemployment benefits, and health services; and

• invest in the future through research and development, energy programs, and education.

The budget must do all of these things specifically and in detail. A budget rests on specific proposals related to specific costs, not on rhetoric.

A budget also rests on policy. And this budget contains important policy decisions — major departures, new initiatives, larger and longer-term commitments. Each stands on its own merit. Yet taken together all of the proposals in this budget can also be characterized in a more general way. They reflect the maturing of the administration's basic, consistent underlying policy themes: restraint in budgeting the taxpayers' dollars; the strengthening of our defense; providing energy for the future;

improving opportunities for the Nation's youth; and making Government work better.

Ours is a great and complex nation. The existing arrangements in our society are the result of complex, not always consistent decisions of the past, emerging from a democratic people. Change is sometimes slow because it rests on consent. But intelligent, consistent leadership, persistently applied, can bring about change in policies and further the well-being of our society and of its people. I believe that this budget, and those I have submitted in the past, support the fundamental policies that will prepare America for the new decade.

JIMMY CARTER

January 28, 1980

REVISED BUDGET MESSAGE

To the Congress of the United States:

During the first two months of the year, inflation took another sharp upward leap, both in the United States and abroad. Actual prices and interest rates worsened, along with expectations about future inflation. Continued price increases of the size we have experienced would do grave harm to American society and the American economy.

OPEC's December oil price discussions in Caracas proved inconclusive, and world oil price increases were far beyond expectations. But inflation outside of the energy sector also rose. The American economy continued to be unexpectedly strong. Consumer demand and business investment remained at higher levels than predicted. Since the Federal Reserve continued, correctly, to restrict the growth of the money supply, the surge in inflation and credit demands produced a sharp upward spiral in interest rates.

To reverse these dangerous trends, I announced a five-point anti-inflation program. This program consists of spending cuts necessary to balance the budget for 1981, additional restraints on credit, wage and price actions, further energy conservation measures, and structural changes to enhance productivity, savings, and research and development.

These measures are interrelated and interdependent. Taken together they will be more than the sum of their parts. They will not reduce inflation immediately, but together they will produce a significant decline in inflation as the year progresses.

[Spending Cut]

At the center of this policy is my decision to cut Federal spending so as to balance the 1981 budget. In January, I submitted to the Congress a budget for 1981 that provided for substantial restraints on Federal spending and the lowest deficit in 7 years. After adjustment for inflation, the 1981 spending level was virtually level with that for

1980. It was a budget that followed in every respect the policies of restraint I have set during the past three years. However, in view of the continued high level of economic activity, and what has recently happened to inflation and interest rates, I have had to consider new policies. I must now ask the Congress and the American people to support a revised budget that is even more restrained and austere.

Let me first explain the extraordinary way in which my budget reduction proposals have been developed.

[Joint Product]

The budget, as it is finally enacted, is — as it should be under our Constitution — the joint product of the Congress and the executive branch. Because of the great importance we attach to reduced spending, the leadership of the Congress and I have done everything within our power to reach general understandings in advance on reduction proposals. I and senior members of my Administration met with Members of the Congress hour after hour, literally day and night, in order to reach consensus. The importance of cutting spending to achieve a balanced budget was never seriously in dispute. But agreements on the approach necessary to achieve this balance were not easy to reach. They could be worked out only through a lengthy and sometimes tedious process of consultation.

The revision of the 1981 budget that accompanies this message describes my proposals for increased budget discipline. The principal actions are:

—deferral, reduction, or cancellation of most of the new and expanded programs originally proposed in the 1981 budget;

—a cut in expenditures for personnel, operations, and maintenance throughout the government;

—an immediate limitation on Federal civilian employment, and rigid maintenance of employment ceilings to ensure that there will be at least 20,000 fewer Federal employees by the end of fiscal year 1980 than there are now;

—a reduction in ongoing spending programs throughout the Federal Government;

—re-emphasis of the savings and revenue measures submitted in the January budget, including hospital cost containment, Federal pay reform, and cash management reforms;

—defense efficiencies and savings that do not affect military readiness and are consistent with my continued commitment to real increases in defense spending;

—a 15% reduction in the use of consultants throughout the Federal establishment; and

—a freeze on basic salary increases for senior executive branch officials and members of the White House staff.

These budgetary decreases are being supplemented by a series of actions taken by the Federal Reserve to achieve greater restraint on the expansion of credit in the private sector. Some of these actions have been taken under the authority granted by the Credit Control Act of 1969. The measures taken by the Federal Reserve will help to reduce inflation by slowing the growth of business loans and some forms of consumer credit.

In addition to the actions of the Federal Reserve on private credit, the Administration will increase restraint of Federal credit programs:

—Federal loan guarantees will be cut by $4 billion in fiscal year 1981.

—My new system to control Federal credit activities will be strengthened by expanding significantly the amount of Federal insurance and guarantee activity subject to limits within the system.

I urge the Congress to include Federal credit limitations in the concurrent budget resolutions. These measures will enable the Federal Government to control more effectively total lending and loan guarantee activity.

[Oil Tax]

As part of this anti-inflation program, I have used my existing authorities to impose a gasoline conservation fee on imported oil. In the budget revisions, I am proposing to replace this fee with an ad valorem equivalent gasoline tax that, at current prices, will yield 10 cents per gallon. I am also proposing the withholding of taxes on interest and dividend payments at the source to ensure that Federal income taxes owed on those payments are in fact paid, and paid promptly. The resulting receipts will *not* be used to balance the 1981 budget. They will not be used as a substitute for necessary spending cuts. Rather, these receipts will give the budget, which will be balanced independently of these sources of income, a margin of safety. This will ensure that the budget will remain in balance if estimates change in a way that cannot be predicted now.

Success in reducing spending to achieve a balanced budget will require prompt action by the Congress. To achieve substantial outlay savings for 1981, the Congress must act before the fiscal year begins. I particularly urge prompt and constructive action on rescissions of 1980 budget authority, so as to produce outlay reductions at least equal to my proposals. I also urge prompt enactment of proposals to modify certain programs that now have two automatic inflation adjustments a year so that they conform to the normal practice of annual adjustments.

I will do everything in my power to ensure that my budget proposals are realized. I repeat that I intend to veto any legislation that threatens the spending reductions required for a balanced budget. I will use the powers available to me to defer spending or to rescind funds. If adequate steps are not being taken by the Congress to achieve the required fiscal restraint, I intend to seek from the Congress a temporary grant of extraordinary budget restraint powers.

Revised Budget Outlook

[In billions of dollars]

	1979	1980	1981	1982	1983
Budget receipts	465.9	532.4	628.0	724.8	837.8
Budget outlays	493.7	568.9	611.5	683.3	759.0
Surplus or deficit (−)	− 27.7	− 36.5	16.5	41.5	78.9
Budget authority	556.7	665.8	691.3	777.3	849.1

[Worldwide Inflation]

We are not alone in facing recent rapid inflation at annual rates nearing 20%. Wholesale prices have been increasing at annual rates in excess of 25% in Italy, Great Britain, and Japan. Even in Germany increases have been over 13%. Many other countries are responding as we are, by re-evaluating their budgets and seeking reductions.

There are no quick or easy answers to this worldwide inflation. It is deep-rooted, the result of many forces built up over the past decade and a half. No single measure — by itself — will stop inflation. My five-point program to strengthen the fight against inflation has as an essential element the spending reductions needed for a balanced 1981 budget. Those who say that we cannot stop inflation simply by balancing the 1981 budget miss the point. Balancing the budget is not a cure-all, but it *is* an essential element in the more comprehensive program. I believe that no overall anti-inflation program can work until the Federal Government has demonstrated to the American people that it will discipline its own spending and its own borrowing — not just for one year or two, but as a long-term policy.

JIMMY CARTER

March 31, 1980.

DEFENSE POSTURE REPORT

January 29, 1980

In his annual report on U.S. military posture released Jan. 29, Defense Secretary Harold Brown said the United States had to improve its military ability "to move with great power and speed on a worldwide basis."

Soviet military growth, the danger of conflicts abroad and the lag in U.S. readiness required that the nation improve its ability to move men and materiel rapidly with air and ground support, Brown said.

The 300-page posture statement presented by Brown before the House Armed Services Committee kicked off the Carter administration's battle to win defense spending increases averaging 4.6 percent over each of the ensuing five years.

Air Force Gen. David C. Jones, chairman of the Joint Chiefs of Staff, appeared with Secretary Brown before the House committee to explain a Carter budget request for $142.7 billion in 1981.

Despite some liberal opposition, the holding of American hostages in Iran and the Soviet invasion of Afghanistan in December 1979 overrode objections to higher defense spending, and the House and Senate supported the president's proposal with some modifications.

Rapid Deployment Force

Carter's major defense initiative was a proposed $10 billion plan to increase U.S. capability to send "rapid deployment forces" (RDFs) to *areas outside Europe. In fiscal 1981, $294.5 million would be spent on the program.*

Emphasis in the new military budget also was on arms purchases, research and development, building up North Atlantic Treaty Organization (NATO) forces, building new warships and increasing military pay.

Soviet Arms Buildup

A Soviet arms buildup, Brown said, went beyond any reasonable national security need. He told the House Armed Services Committee that Russia might be increasing its military forces to enable it to fight on three fronts at once. (U.S. strategy had been to maintain a capacity to meet one and one-half non-nuclear crises simultaneously.) Brown said: "Without reducing the large forces stationed in Eastern Europe, the Soviets have tripled the size of their forces in the Far East, and they are developing naval and other capabilities that will permit them to operate well beyond the periphery of the USSR. Their posture, overall, has grown more modern, and parts of it have reached a high state of combat readiness. We no longer can preclude their being able to operate simultaneously in several different parts of the world."

The report also cited the Soviet threat to the sea lanes and underscored U.S. dependence on them for oil supplies. It said the United States hoped to counter the threat with construction of more AEGIS anti-aircraft missile cruisers to blunt Soviet use of the Backfire bomber as an anti-ship weapon.

According to the report, the Soviet Union spent 11 to 14 percent of its gross national product (GNP) on defense. The United States, with a gross national product twice as large, spent 5 percent of its GNP on defense.

Nuclear Weapons

Within the previous 15 years, the posture report said, the Soviet Union had achieved parity with the United States in nuclear missiles. The secretary cautioned, however, that "[w]ithin a year or two," the Minuteman and Titan land-based missiles would be "put . . . at risk" because the Soviet Union's missiles had increased in number, reliability, accuracy and warhead yield. The U.S. program to build and deploy the mobile MX missile, Brown said, would restore the balance in nuclear weaponry and maintain the integrity of the U.S. "triad" concept — that is, a capacity to launch land-based missiles as well as submarine- and air-launched nuclear warheads.

Brown also said in the report that the United States did "not plan to match the Soviet program system by system or warhead by warhead" but he noted that "[m]odernization of the long-range theater nuclear forces will ... provide a firm foundation for the pursuit of serious arms control negotiations on this subject. ..."

Turning Point

The United States may well have reached a critical turning point in its history, Brown observed, emphasizing that the nation faced a decision with respect to its defense posture that no longer could be deferred.

He continued, "We must decide now whether we intend to remain the strongest nation in the world. The alternative is to let ourselves slip into inferiority, into a position of weakness in a harsh world where principles unsupported by power are victimized, and to become a nation with more of a past than a future. I reject that alternative. ..."

Following are excerpts from the Department of Defense Annual Report, released Jan. 29, 1980, urging higher defense spending to improve the U.S. military posture. (Boldface headings in brackets have been added by Congressional Quarterly to highlight the organization of the text.):

[Overview]

...[T]his year's Five-Year Defense Program [FYDP] projects a substantial increase in real defense resources over the next five years, as compared with last year's FYDP. This does not reflect a single sudden change in the world situation, or a sudden conversion on the part of the Administration. It is an example of executive leadership by President Carter in responding to the adverse trends in the military balance, and to increased dangers to U.S. interests in several parts of the world, reflected most recently in Iran and Afghanistan. These dangers did not develop suddenly during 1979; they have been apparent as trends for several years. It was to respond to them that the increased defense budgets of the last two years, the three percent NATO commitment, and the parallel tracks of military strength and arms control have been pursued by this Administration.

During the past year, we have reevaluated our needs and concluded we need more military capabilities of particular kinds, and need to ensure that we obtain them despite the uncertainties about inflation rates and despite the differences over program detail that we sometimes have with the Congress. During this same year, public perceptions of our needs have begun to catch up with the facts. A new consensus is forming around the President's leadership.

THE SOVIET UNION

In 1979, the Soviet military effort was about 50 percent larger than our own, measured by what it would cost to buy Soviet programs (including personnel) in the U.S. economy. We now estimate that the Soviets are using somewhere between 11 and 14 percent of their Gross National Product for defense purposes, compared with our five percent (of a U.S. GNP nearly twice as large).

The difference between Soviet and U.S. investments in military goods (R&D, procurement, and military construction) is even larger. In the past decade, Soviet investment has been cumulatively about 27 percent larger than ours. In 1979 alone, it was probably greater by 85 percent. The consequences of that investment are now becoming evident.

In strategic nuclear forces, the Soviets have come from a position of substantial numerical inferiority 15 years ago to one of parity today — and a potential for strategic advantage if we fail to respond with adequate programs of our own. Their forces have improved in quality as well as in numbers. They have deployed two new generations of ICBMs and SLBMs, and are working on a further generation — each generation being of increased sophistication and capability. Of greatest concern, they have deployed highly accurate, MIRVed ICBMs with the potential of threatening the survivability of our ICBM silos.

In addition to this buildup in their central strategic systems, the Soviets have modernized both their intermediate-range and their tactical nuclear forces. The MIRVed and mobile SS-20 ballistic missile and the BACKFIRE bomber are the most disturbing components of this ambitious program.

At the same time, Soviet ground and tactical air forces in Eastern Europe are excessively large and much too offensively oriented to serve primarily as a counterweight to NATO capabilities, let alone as occupation troops. Similarly, Soviet forces in the Far East are geographically positioned, exercised, and apparently designed for offensive operations. I should note, however, that many of the divisions in the Far East are less than fully combat-ready.

Some components of the increasingly modern Soviet navy are intended for the direct defense of the USSR. Other parts are designed for anti-submarine warfare and the interdiction of the major sea lanes. Still other parts are clearly intended for the long-range projection of Soviet military power. The Soviets have consistently sought to use air and naval facilities overseas, and they have expanded their capability for long-range sealift and airlift as well. There has been recent evidence that they intend to use their airborne divisions for power projection — in the Arab-Israeli October war of 1973 and in Afghanistan in 1979-80.

Although the Soviets have not shown much restraint in their defense decisions, they have been willing to negotiate arms control agreements that promote strategic stability. SALT II is just such an agreement.

It serves our national security interest — even more so when the Soviets are aggressive — but the timing of its ratification must defer to the urgent need that we assess and respond to Soviet actions in Afghanistan.

SALT II remains in our interest for five basic reasons:

—It will actually reduce the strategic forces of the Soviet Union and put a ceiling on the future strategic forces of both superpowers.

—It will impose important qualitative constraints on the strategic competition. In particular, it will constrain Soviet ICBM fractionation and the number of their MIRVed ICBM launchers, where their present momentum would otherwise give them much larger numbers during the period of the Treaty.

—It will bring greater predictability to the nuclear relationship between the two sides, and thereby facilitate our own defense planning.

—We will be better able to monitor Soviet strategic forces with the treaty than without it.

—We can continue the programs we need for our own strategic forces and for our allies under the treaty, but our efforts will cost billions less than would be likely without the treaty.

SALT II, in short, will increase our security and help to reduce one of our major defense problems.

INTERNATIONAL TURBULENCE

Largely for economic reasons, the United States has become heavily involved outside its traditional areas of concern in Europe, Latin America, and the Far East. Some of these other areas are now suffering increased turbulence from within as well as from the intervention of the Soviet Union.

Nowhere is this more the case than in the Middle East. The region has become a breeding ground for internal upheaval — as has already occurred in Iran — for war, terrorism, and subversion. Temporary disruptions or a more permanent decline in the supply of oil from the Persian Gulf could easily occur as a consequence. The Soviet invasion of Afghanistan, its footholds in South Yemen and the Horn of Africa, and the Soviet naval presence in the Red Sea and the Indian Ocean, only make a volatile situation potentially even more explosive.

Africa has become a major source of oil and other minerals for our economy. The main oil routes from the Persian Gulf to Europe and America run along its coasts. Yet internal strife wracks parts of the continent, and there is a continuing danger of more to come. Existing conflicts have already been exacerbated by a Cuban expeditionary force of perhaps 36,000 men in two principal areas, by Soviet military assistance to the more radical factions and regimes on the continent, and by the presence of Soviet and East European advisers. These conflicts may be settled short of critical damage to our economic and other ties, but we cannot count on it.

Cuba has already shown its willingness to exploit the forces of change in the Caribbean for its own ends. The grave dangers associated with further subversion should persuade Havana and Moscow that non-intervention is in order. But there is no certainty that they will see the virtues of restraint.

At the same time, we have to allow for the possibility that the tragic conflict between Communist states in Southeast Asia will spill over into Thailand. And we must still take precautions against the substantial expansion in the armed forces of North Korea that has been going on during the last decade.

As a result of these developments, our defense establishment could be faced with an almost unprecedented number of demands. And some of those demands could arise more or less simultaneously. To meet them, we must solve a number of immediate and longer-term problems.

THE STRATEGIC NUCLEAR PROBLEM

We have recognized for many years that our strategic nuclear capabilities could deter only a small number of contingencies. But there can be no doubt that these capabilities still provide the foundation on which our security rests. Without them, the Soviet Union could threaten the extinction of the United States and its allies. With them, our other forces become meaningful instruments of military and political power.

With the growth of Soviet strategic capabilities, we have concluded that credible deterrence depends on our ability:

—first, to maintain the second-strike forces necessary to attack a comprehensive set of targets, including targets of political and military as well as of economic value;

—second, to withhold retaliation against selected targets;

—third, to cover at all times a sizeable percentage of the Soviet economic base, so that these targets could be destroyed, if necessary; and fourth,

—to hold the elements of a reserve force for a substantial period after a strategic exchange.

Such a capability and such flexibility should enable us to prevent an enemy from achieving any meaningful advantage. To provide those features and to assure maintenance of our confidence in the deterrent, despite possible attempts to destroy its components or defend against them, we also maintain a TRIAD of strategic offensive forces with ICBMs, submarine-launched ballistic missiles, and bombers.

The Soviets are attempting to undermine that confidence by deploying a threat to our ICBMs. That threat is only now beginning to become a reality. But within another year or two, we can expect the Soviets to have the necessary combination of ICBM reliability, numbers, warhead yields, and accuracies to put most of our MINUTEMAN and TITAN silos at risk.

The hypothetical ability of the Soviets to destroy even 90 percent or more of our ICBM warheads is not the same thing as a disarming first strike nor even, by itself, a major Soviet military advantage — though, if we do not respond, it will create perceptual problems. The vulnerability of our ICBMs does not mean an increased probability of a Soviet surprise attack. But it does mean that a significant part of the TRIAD would be eroded, and that the Soviets would be encouraged to undermine the rest of it.

Accordingly, we will proceed with the development of the mobile MX so as to restore the survivability of the ICBM leg of the TRIAD. At the same time, we will continue to modernize the other two legs of the TRIAD. Providing that we do, the Soviets, even in the most desperate of circumstances, should not have any incentive to launch a nuclear attack on the United States or its strategic forces.

THE THEATER NUCLEAR PROBLEM

Even with these programs, we will not have overcome all our nuclear problems. The Soviets have already undertaken a major modernization of their theater nuclear forces. In particular, they have introduced the SS-20, a MIRVed and mobile intermediate-range ballistic missile (IRBM), and the BACKFIRE, a medium bomber.

With these new and more accurate weapons, the Soviets might make the mistaken judgment that they could threaten our allies without fear of retaliatory attacks on their territory, especially if they did not threaten to attack U.S. forces or territory. To avoid any such error of perception, we are proceeding with the development of two land-based, longer range, mobile missiles: the PERSHING II and the Ground-Launched Cruise Missile (GLCM). In accord with the NATO Ministerial decision of last December 12, we will deploy them in Great Britain and on the European continent.

We do not plan to match the Soviet program system by system or warhead by warhead, which might be construed as an attempt to create a European nuclear balance separate from the overall strategic relationship — and thus as risking "decoupling." Instead, we seek to strengthen the linkage of U.S. strategic forces to the defense of Europe. Modernization of the long-range theater nuclear forces will also provide a firm foundation for the pursuit of serious arms control negotiations on this subject with the Soviet Union. The United States is prepared to undertake such negotiations within the framework of SALT III.

THE NON-NUCLEAR PROBLEM

Our conventional force problems — and the requirements for the corresponding forces — are more complex because we must deal not only with the Soviet Union, but also with all the other manifestations of international turbulence. Ever since 1969, we have defined non-nuclear adequacy as the capability to deal simultaneously with one major and one minor contingency in conjunction with our allies. In order to achieve the necessary capability, we have depended primarily on our allies to man the forward defense lines in peacetime. This, in turn, has permitted us to organize a centrally located reinforcement capability of ground and tactical air forces, naval forces for sea control and power projection, and a backup capability of National Guard and Reserve forces. To move the forces, we have relied on airlift and sealift. By using materiel prepositioned overseas in theaters where the probability of conflict is significant, attacks with little warning a danger, and the consequences of conflict most severe, we save on lift and increase reinforcement rates enormously.

Although, during the past decade, we never acquired all the readiness and mobility required by this strategy, we were not penalized for it because our potential enemies were relatively sluggish, and we were not put to the test by contingencies outside of Southeast Asia. But now times are changing. Without reducing the large forces stationed in Eastern Europe, the Soviets have tripled the size of their forces in the Far East, and they are developing naval and other capabilities that will permit them to operate well beyond the periphery of the USSR. Their posture, overall, has grown more modern, and parts of it have reached a high state of combat readiness. We no longer can preclude their being able to operate simultaneously in several different parts of the world. Thanks largely to their assistance, lesser Communist powers such as North Korea, Vietnam, and Cuba — and some non-Communist ones such as Iraq — also have acquired relatively modern capabilities. These developments, combined with a number of internal and international disputes in areas of great interest to the United States, are beginning to put heavy pressure on our non-nuclear posture.

In Eastern Europe, the Soviets are improving their ability to launch heavy attacks against NATO with little advance preparation and warning. In Asia, the Vietnamese occupation of Cambodia poses a threat to Thailand's security and contains the seeds of great power confrontation. The long-term North Korean military buildup, and the political turmoil in South Korea inevitably raise doubts about the future stability of the Korean peninsula.

[U.S. RESPONSE IN EUROPE]

We have responded to the threat in Europe with the NATO-wide Long-Term Defense Program (LTDP) which includes a major U.S. effort to expand the size and pace of its ground and tactical air deployments to Europe. At the same time, the situation in Asia has caused us first to stabilize our deployments there, and then to increase them somewhat.

Our current force structure — and I emphasize force structure — is sufficient for both these purposes. But the deployments in Europe and the Western Pacific, combined with the strategic reserve we hold in the CONUS (Continental United States) for the reinforcement of our forward-based forces, absorb the bulk of our non-nuclear capabilities. Moreover, even if contingencies in Europe and North Asia were our only concern, the modernization of Soviet forces in Eastern Europe and the North Korean buildup would have required substantial increases in our defense budget. Indeed, they had already led us to pledge to our NATO allies, and program real increments of three percent a year in our defense outlays. Now, in addition, we have to allow for the dangers that could arise in the Middle East, the Caribbean, and elsewhere, as well as for the continued Soviet buildup.

At present, we cannot foresee clearcut and plausible contingencies in these regions on the basis of which we should plan and program major increases in our non-nuclear force structure. And there remains still a great deal we can do to get more combat capability out of the forces we already have in hand. But the necessary actions, while not spectacular, will be expensive. We need to increase the speed with which we can deploy our forces — through increased airlift and sealift capabilities, through the further prepositioning of materiel, and through the assurance of transit and basing rights in emergencies. We need to modernize the equipment of our ground and air forces. And we need to expand our naval construction program to assure the future offensive and defensive capabilities of our naval forces.

Assuming our allies in Europe and Asia continue to join with us in increasing their defense efforts, their forces — in conjunction with ours — should provide a solid foundation for deterrence in these two vital theaters. I myself would prefer to see the allies provide themselves with a greater margin of safety in Europe, and I remain concerned about the situation on the NATO flanks. As a consequence, we are considering plans to preposition additional equipment in the vicinity of the northern flank, and we will continue to commit elements of our ground and tactical air in the defense of both flanks, as necessary. Exercises to test these capabilities on the flanks have been augmented.

In Central Europe, NATO will be much more nearly in balance with the Warsaw Pact within the next few years, provided that the allies proceed with their modernization and our programs for the rapid deployment of reinforcements are brought to fruition. However, even with these improvements, NATO will not have as high a level of confidence as I would like of containing a large attack by the Pact launched with little preparation and warning. I should add that the Soviets could not have high confidence of a breakthrough either — on the assumption that U.S. reinforcements would arrive on time and could sustain themselves adequately in combat.

[ASIA AND OTHER CONTINGENCIES]

In Asia, the growth in North Korean capabilities remains a matter of deep concern. However, I do not see why the combination of strong South Korean forces, extensive fortifications, and deployed U.S. capabilities cannot frustrate a North Korean attack — provided that we are able to reinforce our deployed capabilities with considerable speed.

To deal with other contingencies, we have already designated specific units as components of our Rapid Deployment Forces (RDF). These forces exist, and need not be increased; they include units of all the Services. The composition of the forces deployed will vary depending on the nature and location of the crisis. But these units will not be able to respond adequately to the demands that may be placed on them unless we are able to improve their combat readiness and alert status, and particularly unless we can move them in force and with great rapidity to an area of crisis.

Conflict in one or more of these theaters would place heavy burdens on our Navy general purpose forces, since we would need to use the sea lanes extensively after only a few days or weeks for the reinforcement and support of our combat units overseas. Accordingly, sea control — followed or accompanied by power projection — could occupy the Navy on virtually a worldwide basis.

Our current general purpose naval forces should be able to hold Soviet surface combatants north of the Greenland-Iceland-United Kingdom (GIUK) line in the North Atlantic, subject Soviet submarines and older aircraft to significant attrition if they should attempt to come south of that line, and provide close-in protection to capital ships and, in conjunction with allies, to convoys. U.S. and other allied forces should also be able to establish the necessary control of the Mediterranean and close down the main exits from the Sea of Okhotsk and the Sea of Japan into the Pacific. The Navy would be able to concentrate forces for offensive battle group operations in higher threat areas as well.

Under these conditions, we would expect essential supplies to get through. However, with the appearance of the BACKFIRE bomber in increasing numbers, Soviet naval aviation could come to be a bigger threat to our sea lines of communication and naval forces than Soviet submarines. Although we have AEGIS ships under construction to counter this growing threat, we still lack sufficient defenses against massed missile and bomber attacks on convoys and battle groups.

THE PROGRAMS

It should be evident from this review of our problems that we need to make major improvements in our defense posture over and above those we have already programmed. The difficulties do not lie so much with our future strategic nuclear posture; provided the SALT II treaty is ratified we already have sufficient programs well underway to deal with our vulnerabilities — including MX, TRIDENT, and cruise missiles. In the absence of SALT, however, we will have to do more. And whatever the outcome of SALT II, we need to shore up our theater nuclear posture in Europe with GLCM and PERSHING II, which will not be cheap. Most important of all, we must increase the deployment, modernization, readiness, mobility, and sustainability of our non-nuclear forces. This must be done as part of our alliance strategies in Europe and Northeast Asia — and with our allies there carrying an increasing share of the burden. In other parts of the world, the military capabilities of those countries threatened by Soviet-supported external attack must be strengthened. At least as important, their own internal stability must be enhanced by economic and political means. And, to assure the U.S. capability to offset Soviet intervention, our own rapid deployment capability must be improved.

We have already expanded slightly the size of our naval Middle East Task Force which operates in the vicinity of the Persian Gulf, and the Navy has increased the number of ship-days it is spending in the Indian Ocean. We plan to increase that presence at sea, and to improve our ability to deploy and sustain land-based forces as well. A Rapid Deployment Joint Task Force (JTF) Headquarters comprising personnel from all four Services, has been established at Readiness Command in Florida, with a small element in Washington. Its first commander, appointed in December, 1979, is a Marine Corps lieutenant general. Its function is to do contingency planning for areas where there are few or no U.S. forces permanently stationed. If one of the contingencies should occur, the previously planned forces would be assigned to the JTF, and deployed — with the JTF commander assuming operational command. At the President's direction, we have also established a permanent, full-time Caribbean Joint Task Force Headquarters at Key West, Florida, begun the expansion of our military exercises in the Caribbean region, increased the surveillance of Cuba, and taken other measures to assure that, in the President's words, "no Soviet unit in Cuba can be used as a combat force to threaten the security of the United States or any other nation in this hemisphere."

At present, we appear to have enough divisions and tactical air wings to meet current international demands, even if those demands should include more or less simultaneous crises in Europe and the Persian Gulf, or in Europe and Korea. However, we need to improve the capability and deployability of our ground and air forces. To strengthen those units oriented to Europe, we are modernizing the Army's weapons and equipment by adding armor, firepower, and tactical mobility. We are also prepositioning more heavy equipment in Europe so that we can rapidly reinforce our ground units there. In a crisis, virtually all we would have to move to NATO's Central Region would be the men. Their equipment would be waiting for them.

We are also improving our tactical air forces by programming about 1,700 new aircraft over the next five years. At the same time, we are accelerating the rate at which we can move fighters quickly to Europe to cope with any surprise attack. And we are increasing the number of shelters at airbases there so as to prevent our aircraft from being destroyed on the ground by enemy attacks.

[IMMEDIATE DANGERS]

Many of the most immediate dangers to our interests lie outside of Europe. To help us cope with these other demands, we are launching two major initiatives. The first will lead to a force of Maritime Prepositioning Ships which will carry in dehumidified storage the heavy equipment and supplies for three Marine brigades. During peacetime, these ships will be stationed in waters near areas where U.S. forces might be needed. Though not designed for the Marines' traditional mission of amphibious assault landings against enemy opposition (a capability we will continue to maintain with other ships), they will be able to debark their equipment over the beach if no port is available. Marine Corps personnel (and equipment not well suited to storage) will, as necessary, be airlifted to the vicinity of the ships, where they will marry up with their gear and be ready for combat on short notice. Thus the Maritime Prepositioning Ships will enable us rapidly to deploy armored and mobile forces outside of Europe.

The other major initiative entails the development and production of a new fleet of large cargo aircraft able to carry Army equipment, including tanks, over intercontinental distances. This will greatly expand our outsize airlift capacity worldwide. As one example, these aircraft could be used initially to deliver the largest equipment of the advanced forces sent to secure airbases near the ports or beaches needed by the Maritime Prepositioning Ships to deliver their heavy gear. They would enable us to make simultaneous deployments to Europe and elsewhere, should the crises be concurrent (as is quite likely). After this initial phase, they would assist in additional force deployments, resupply, and intra-theater movements if needed.

As I noted in my review, our non-NATO needs center not so much on additional combat forces as on our ability to move suitably trained and equipped forces over great distances quickly enough so that they can be of real use at the point of crisis. In some cases, their arrival might turn the tide of battle; in other cases — we would hope in most cases — they would deter the outbreak of fighting in the first place.

We have, in addition, the special problems of the Navy. I believe we can meet the future demands for sea control and power projection — and hence for presence — with a force of about 550 active and reserve ships (if they are of the right kind), about the size of the fleet we will have by 1984. However, we must deal with the growing

BACKFIRE threat and the continued aging of our surface combatants and supply ships. To do so, we are programming the construction of 97 new ships over the next five years. Within that total we will be placing a relatively heavy emphasis on new guided missile AEGIS ships to defend against aerodynamic attacks. I should note, however, that such ships though necessary, are expensive. They challenge our ability to build and maintain as large a fleet as we need. To cope with that challenge, our program includes three new ship designs that will assure adequate fleet size and fighting power at reasonable cost. One will be a major fleet escort, another an anti-submarine frigate, and the third a nuclear-powered attack submarine.

We have made progress in raising the combat skills of our military personnel during the last three years, and I do not foresee any major problem in that area — unless rapidly rising fuel costs force us to reduce flying hours and steaming days below current levels. However, we continue to have problems with materiel readiness, in part because of the advanced equipment coming into the forces. Increasingly capable military forces need increasing levels of support. Such support is particularly important for units that we may want to deploy and operate on short notice. Accordingly, funds for operation and maintenance receive important emphasis from the Department of Defense — and deserve full support from the Congress.

How much combat sustaining capability we should keep on hand is one of the most difficult questions facing us in the present situation. Not only do we live with uncertainty about the nature of the wars we might be called upon to fight; there is even greater uncertainty about their duration. In the circumstances, our currently planned war reserve procurement program (which would provide a large stock of modern munitions by FY 1987, coupled with existing inventories of older and less effective items) entails what we judge to be an acceptable level of risk. In addition, we need to refurbish our options for rapid and complete or graduated mobilization of our resources.

[PERSONNEL NEEDS]

Finally, we are encountering problems in satisfying our personnel needs. Our active-duty personnel are only slightly below the strength authorized by the Congress, and the overall quality of the people entering the Services compares favorably with our intake from the draft prior to Vietnam. But in 1979, for the first time since the advent of the All-Volunteer Force (AVF), all the Services fell short of their recruiting goals; and we are now encountering increased difficulty retraining personnel in areas of skill where the private sector of the economy also has a strong interest. However, we have made progress in recruiting for the Reserve Component, and Individual Ready Reserve (IRR) strengths are increasing.

Peacetime conscription is by no means an obvious solution to our current personnel problems. These problems have more to do with the retention of skilled and experienced personnel who already have six to twelve years of service, than with recruits. We need, accordingly, to expand current efforts to improve our recruiting and retention performance. Our principal approach is to devote significant additional resources to first-term reenlistment bonuses. This is a relatively efficient way of improving enlisted retention; it significantly decreases requirements for both new accessions and career reenlistments. In addition, the budget reflects legislation that provides for a larger military pay increase (7.4 percent) than we have programmed for federal civilian employment (6.2 percent). Military retirement reform, which has been submitted, would provide career officer and enlisted personnel with new cash payments after ten years of service. The budget also includes additional funds for travel and transportation reimbursements and enlistment bonuses which, together with these other initiatives, complement non-compensation efforts to increase the supply of and reduce the demand for scarce personnel resources. Finally, we need continually to review whether military pay is competitive with wages for civilian employment alternatives, and whether the benefits are appropriate to the special circumstances of military service.

CONCLUSIONS

This, in sum, is the course we are determined to take. In line with our basic priorities and plans, we will continue to use four broad instruments of national security policy. They are:

—sustained real increases in defense spending;

—carefully planned force programs that make the best use of the added defense resources and the special national advantages we have;

—closer cooperation and coordination with allies and other friends; and

—arms control agreements that complement our defense programs.

Over the last three years, we have applied these instruments in an orderly attack on the main defense problems at hand. In our first year, we placed the full weight of our efforts behind the most pressing need: improving our early conventional combat capability in NATO. The Long-Term Defense Program (LTDP) was launched in cooperation with our NATO Allies and the first fruits of strengthened allied cooperation already are in view. With the NATO programs in train, we next turned to the problem of modernizing our strategic TRIAD. Programs to strengthen each leg — including MX, TRIDENT, and cruise missiles — are now well underway. In Asia, we have stabilized the level and begun to improve the quality of our forces in the region. Most recently, we have taken steps to modernize our theater nuclear forces in Europe.

The necessary programs — PERSHING II and GLCM — have been launched and our allies have joined us in a commitment to follow through on theater nuclear modernization.

Thus, programs in each of these areas are underway and have momentum. We can now concentrate special attention and resources on improving our capabilities to deal with threats and crises around the world and, in particular, on improving our ability to get men and equipment to potential areas of conflict as quickly as necessary.

The Administration has taken great care to develop the current program so that it is calibrated to the problems ahead of us. Carrying out this program fully and completely — not just this year, but in the years to come — is a matter of fundamental importance to the security of the nation: the most elemental and important of all our responsibilities. Therefore, should our assumptions as to future inflation, on which the program is based, later prove to have been too low, the Administration will take appropriate action to preserve the integrity of the program. Indeed, it is because of a re-estimate of inflation rates for FY 1980 and FY 1981 that the FY 1981 budget figure contained in this report is higher than the one I gave in the preview presented to the Congress in December, 1979. We will also consider submitting supplemental requests as necessary to assure a program of equivalent capability after Congressional authorization and appropriation actions have taken place. We mean to see that this program is carried out.

Critical turning points in the histories of nations are difficult to recognize at the time. Usually, they become clear only in restrospect. Nonetheless, the United States may well be at such a turning point today. We face a decision that we have been deferring for too long; we can defer it no longer. We must decide now whether we intend to remain the strongest nation in the world. The alternative is to let ourselves slip into inferiority, into a position of weakness in a harsh world where principles unsupported by power are victimized, and to become a nation with more of a past than a future. I reject that alternative, and I know that the Congress does as well.

Our new defense program is testimony enough of where this Administration believes we should be headed. This nation must remain the strongest in the world. That, I believe, is the consensus of the country, and of the Congress. In keeping with the times and this spirit, we have submitted a program that the President and I believe to be right and necessary for the security of our country.

International Politics and Defense

We are inclined to compare international politics unfavorably with domestic politics on the ground that the former is accompanied by so much more violence. As recent events in Iran have demonstrated, violence is not entirely unknown to the resolution of domestic issues, and we ourselves have not by any means been immune to it in our own history — even our recent history. It is the case, nonetheless, that force and the threat of force are more ubiquitous on the international stage. Under present conditions, lethal force is also likely to have more devastating effects when used among nation-states, although the force used within them during civil wars has inflicted deep wounds on its victims as well.

Recognition of the propensity for violence in world politics has led to recurrent efforts to devise international institutions for the peaceful settlement of disputes among states, and the United States has twice led the movement to establish and make effective worldwide political and legal bodies dedicated to these ends. We continue to support the United Nations and the World Court, and through such proceedings as the Law of the Sea Conference, we seek to modernize and give new life to traditional international law. It would be unrealistic, however, to pretend that these institutions and rules are more than partial substitutes for continuing efforts by the United States and its allies and other friends to deal separately with the many issues that confront the system of nation-states.

Some of those issues are territorial, left from the collapse of old empires, as is the case in much of Africa. Others result from differences about the proper world distribution of income and natural resources. Despite the disappearance of most imperial systems, and the existence now of 162 independent nations, demands for national self-determination continue to be heard. Even with the new military technologies that permit powerful, long-distance strikes, perceived security needs create pressures for buffer states, clients, and spheres of influence. Most explosive of all, ideological causes continue to motivate groups and states to challenge the *status quo* by violence. Terrorists and saboteurs create periodic crises. Producer nations form cartels to exploit their possession of scarce natural resources. Buyers and sellers alike look to trade barriers as a means of protecting their interests, even at the risk of beggaring their neighbors. Nations with grievances or ambitions produce or try to purchase modern conventional arms. Some actively but clandestinely seek to acquire nuclear weapons and the means to deliver them. Periodically, violence flares. But none of these dangers compare with the potential for disruption and destruction represented by the leadership and the resources of the Soviet Union.

THE SOVIET UNION

Exactly what grievances and ambitions, what fears and nightmares, are harbored by the Soviets we do not know. Indeed, one reason why they arouse so much suspicion about their motives is the closed and authoritarian nature of their system and the secrecy with which they surround most of their decisions and activities. It is easy in the circumstances to equate them with the more demonical dictatorships of the past and, because of their ideological pretensions, to attribute the most soaring ambitions to them. But despite our efforts to understand what makes this system tick, the Soviet Union remains, in Churchill's words, "a riddle wrapped in a mystery inside an enigma."

Problems

This is not to say that we remain totally ignorant of what goes on in the Soviet Union. We know a great deal, and much of our knowledge underlines the many domestic problems facing the Soviets now, and likely to confront them even more in the decade ahead. Although President Brezhnev has shown remarkable durability, no one doubts that major changes in the aging Soviet leadership are in the offing. Whether, in a political system that lacks any clear-cut procedures for political succession, the changes will be accompanied by struggles, upheavals, and a reorientation of Soviet policies remains uncertain. This much is certain, however: Mr. Brezhnev's successors will be confronted with a number of difficulties and hard choices.

During the 1950s the Soviet economy grew at a rate of six percent a year in real terms. By the 1960s the rate had fallen to five percent, and only five years ago it had fallen again to 3.5 percent. The Intelligence Community expects that during the 1980s the rate of growth will slow still further to 2.5 percent a year or less. Related to this decline in economic growth is the slowdown in the growth of Soviet energy production, particularly of oil, and emerging demographic problems. During the present five-year plan, the Soviets have increased the price of the oil and natural gas they supply to Eastern Europe, but they have maintained supplies at 1.6 million barrels a day and recently signed contracts to increase supplies by about 10 percent. Under the agreements, prices are about two-thirds those charged by OPEC, but any oil provided above the contract levels is sold at higher prices or for convertible currency. We expect the Soviets to go from a net export outside their Bloc of 800,000 barrels a day (in 1978) to a net import of a million barrels a day within the next three years.

One of the most severe and continuing of the Soviet economic problems is the fluctuation in the domestic production of grain.... Much of the corn being imported is meant to sustain the nation's livestock and poultry production, and supposedly to help raise the living standards as pledged for 1980. However, widespread shortages of meat, butter, milk and eggs are still in evidence, and the general food situation appears to be deteriorating rather than improving. At the same time, the Soviets have been trying to avert a famine in Vietnam by shipping in about $500 million in flour and rice. Most of these supplies have had to be purchased with hard currency on the world market.

Both the general economy and the agricultural sector have already suffered from shortages of labor in this labor-intensive society, and the problem is expected to grow. For the first five years of the 1970s, the working-age population increased by slightly more than two percent a year. For the last four years of the decade, the annual increase was 1.5 percent. It is now expected that through the 1980s, the working-age population will grow at no more than half a percent a year.

As Soviet population growth slows, we expect its ethnic composition to change, with as yet uncertain effects on the economy and perhaps the political system. We believe that presently a little more than half the total Soviet population is Russian. However, during the next five years, the Russian component is likely to decline by about two million, while the population of the eight Moslem republics and autonomous regions in the southern USSR will probably rise by nine million.

Posture

These developments face the Soviet leadership with severe problems in the allocation of national resources. For at least the past 20 years, they have consistently favored guns over butter. . . .

Whether the two defense efforts are measured in the U.S. or the Soviet economy, the general direction of the Soviet programs in real terms is the same — upward. The real annual rate of growth in dollar terms continues to be three percent; in rubles it is between four and five percent. As far as we can tell, the effort accounts for 11 to 14 percent of the Soviet GNP, although some experts put it at 15 percent or higher. Relative to the United States, the Soviet defense effort now appears to be about 50 percent higher measured in dollars, and around 30 percent more measured in rubles. . . .

Even more impressive than the growth in the overall Soviet defense budget is the expansion in the investment that has gone into research, development, test, and evaluation (RDT&E), procurement and military construction. . . . We estimate that measured in the U.S. economy, Soviet investments, including RDT&E, procurement and military construction, exceed those of the United States by about 85 percent. Our estimates for Soviet military R&D expenditures are less reliable than for other sectors of Soviet defense spending. Nonetheless, as far as we can tell, Soviet resources devoted to RDT&E alone have almost doubled in the last 10 years.

[Purposes]

The purposes of this large Soviet military buildup remain ambiguous (although the invasion of Afghanistan by the Soviets underlines their willingness to use force when it suits their purposes and its risk is calculated as acceptable). Clearly the buildup is something they do relatively well, but that is hardly a sufficient explanation for so substantial an investment of resources. We had hoped that well-balanced, secure, second-strike strategic nuclear forces would satisfy the security needs of the Soviet leaders in that area. They have gone well beyond such a capability, however, in the design and deployment of strategic offensive systems and active and passive defenses. They appear, indeed, to be aiming toward some sort of war-winning capability with these forces, however futile that attempt may be.

We had also hoped that as their central nuclear forces achieved second-strike sufficiency, conservatively defined, the Soviets would reduce their deployment of medium-range regional capabilities, on the ground that they would no longer need (if they ever did) either to hold the allies of the United States hostage to our good behavior or to deter attack on the Soviet Union from Western Europe. Unfortunately, no such reduction has taken place. Instead, the Soviets are modernizing both their medium-range and the tactical nuclear capabilities. And the modernization is taking place in the East as well as the West.

Apparently not content with this display of power, the Soviets continue to deploy ground and tactical air forces in Eastern Europe which seem excessively large and much too offensively oriented to serve primarily as a counterweight to NATO capabilities, let alone as occupation troops. And President Brezhnev's proposal of October 6, 1979, to withdraw 20,000 men and 1,000 tanks from Eastern Europe (allegedly to the USSR) does not — even if fully carried out, and however welcome — materially change that conclusion. Similarly, Soviet forces in the Far East, however defensive their purpose may be, are geographically positioned, exercised, and apparently designed for offensive operations. In contrast to the situation in Eastern Europe, however, most of the divisions on the Chinese border are less than fully combat-ready.

The Soviet naval buildup raises similar problems of interpretation. Some components of this increasingly modern force are clearly intended for the defense of the Soviet homeland and interdiction of the sea lanes we would use to reinforce our allies. The Soviets also have programs to increase the size and improve the quality of their anti-submarine warfare forces, and these may eventually threaten U.S. and allied ballistic missile submarines. Still other parts can only be intended for the long-range projection of Soviet military power.

One conclusion about these programs, namely that the Soviets are interested in more than the defense of their periphery, is fortified by other developments. They have gradually expanded their long-range sealift and airlift. There is recent evidence, as in Afghanistan, that they intend to use their seven airborne divisions (an eighth is a training unit) as a major instrument for possible military operations beyond their borders. And it is no secret that they consistently seek support arrangements overseas for air and naval staging, refueling and maintenance.

Policies

Soviet foreign policy serves mixed purposes, as does the Soviet military buildup. The signature of SALT II suggests that the Kremlin continues to put the control of nuclear arms high on its list of national goals. As President Carter has pointed out, speaking of the two superpowers, "Our fundamental philosophies conflict, and quite often our national interests conflict as well. But ... we do have common interests and share an overwhelming mutual concern in preventing a nuclear war."

Beyond that, some Soviet activities around the periphery of the USSR can be seen as essentially defensive in purpose. Others can be so described only on the assumption that the Soviets think they need, at least in political terms, though even then expressed through military capabilities, to dominate overwhelmingly any areas near their own frontiers. This is clearly a matter of the greatest concern to us.

In these circumstances, we and our allies must deal simultaneously with both the cooperative and the competitive aspects of Soviet policy. On the one hand, we must be prepared to negotiate our differences with the Soviet Union and, where possible, reach equitable and verifiable agreements that restrain the military competition and lessen the risk of war. On the other hand, we need to make it equally clear that we will continue to maintain (and where necessary expand) the military power required to constrain those Soviet ambitions that infringe on longstanding U.S. and allied interests, or Soviet behavior that violates international comity. We acknowledge the Soviet need for security and we welcome a constructive Soviet role in world affairs. We reject and will respond as necessary and appropriate to any Soviet insistence on the satisfaction of its claims at the expense of the rights and interests of others.

COOPERATION WITH THE SOVIET UNION

Although the Soviets have not shown much restraint in their unilateral defense decisions, they have been willing to engage in negotiations to control the military competition. Where mutual restraint is feasible, and can be made equitable and verifiable, it will no doubt remain in our national interest to negotiate formal and detailed arms control agreements that will enhance our security through limits on the Soviet threat.

SALT II is such an agreement. It provides effective restraints on strategic arms and will measurably enhance our national security, particularly when the Soviets are behaving aggressively. But the timing of ratification of SALT must be deferred until Soviet actions in Afghanistan have been adequately countered. We should recognize, meanwhile, that SALT II remains in our interest for a number of reasons. . . .

The Nuclear Capabilities

It is now well understood, I believe, that the development of nuclear weapons and intercontinental delivery vehicles has transformed once and for all the security situation of the United States and its friends. From the day when these new technologies made their appearance on the world stage — with the possibility they offered of swift knockout blows against an enemy's military forces and war production base — our safety has come to depend heavily on the deterrent power and credibility of our strategic nuclear forces.

U.S. STRATEGIC POLICIES

The most fundamental objective of our strategic policy is nuclear deterrence. Despite some initial illusions, most of us have recognized for many years that strategic nuclear capabilities alone could credibly deter only a narrow range of contingencies. While strategic nuclear weapons are not an all-purpose deterrent, they still provide the foundation on which our security is based. Only a strategic nuclear attack could threaten the extinction of the United States. For that reason, our strategic forces must be fully adequate at all times to deter — and deter persuasively — any such attack. But our nuclear forces must be able to deter nuclear attacks not only on our own country, but also on our forces overseas, as well as on our friends and allies. Nuclear forces also contribute to some degree, through justifiable concern about escalation, to deterrence of non-nuclear attacks.

Deterrence: The Countervailing Strategy

For deterrence to operate successfully, our potential adversaries must be convinced that we possess sufficient military force so that if they were to start a course of action which could lead to war, they would be frustrated in their effort to achieve their objective or suffer so much damage that they would gain nothing by their action. Put differently, we must have forces and plans for the use of our strategic nuclear forces such that in considering aggression against our interests, our adversary would recognize that no plausible outcome would represent a success — on any rational definition of success. The prospect of such a failure would then deter an adversary's attack on the United States or our vital interests. The preparation of forces and plans to create such a prospect has come to be referred to as a "countervailing strategy."

To achieve this objective we need, first of all, a survivable and enduring retaliatory capability to devastate the industry and cities of the Soviet Union. We must have such a capability even if the Soviets were to attack first, without warning, in a manner optimized to reduce that capability as much as possible. What has come to be known as assured destruction is the bedrock of nuclear deterrence, and we will retain such a capacity in the future. It is not, however, sufficient in itself as a strategic doctrine. Under many circumstances large-scale countervalue attacks may not be appropriate — nor will their prospect always be sufficiently credible — to deter the full range of actions we seek to prevent.

Recognizing this limitation on assured destruction as an all-purpose standard for deterrence, for many years the Defense Department has assessed the range of nuclear attacks an enemy might launch against the United States and its allies. We have examined the types of targets we should cover in retaliation, and shaped our strategic posture to maintain high confidence in our deterrent against the spectrum of possible attacks. We have recently completed a basic re-examination of our strategic policy. It reaffirms our basic principles, but also points out new ways to implement them.

We have concluded that if deterrence is to be fully effective, the United States must be able to respond at a level appropriate to the type and scale of a Soviet attack. Our goal is to make a Soviet victory as improbable (seen through Soviet eyes) as we can make it, over the broadest plausible range of scenarios. We must therefore have plans for attacks which pose a more credible threat than an all-out attack on Soviet industry and cities. These plans should include options to attack the targets that comprise the Soviet military force structure and political power structure, and to hold back a significant reserve. In other words, we must be able to deter Soviet attacks of less than all-out scale by making it clear to the Kremlin that, after such an attack, we would not be forced to the stark choice of either making no effective military response or totally destroying the Soviet Union. We could instead attack, in a selective and measured way, a range of military, industrial, and political control targets, while retaining an assured destruction capacity in reserve.

Such a capability, and this degree of flexibility, we have believed for some years, would enable us to:

—prevent an enemy from achieving any meaningful advantage;

—inflict higher costs on him than the value he might expect to gain from partial or full-scale attacks on the United States and its allies; and

—leave open the possibility of ending an exchange before the worst escalation and damage had occurred, even if avoiding escalation to mutual destruction is not likely.

This is what I referred to last year as a countervailing strategy. In certain respects, the name is newer than the strategy. The need for flexibility and calibrating U.S. retaliation to the provocation is not, of course, a new discovery, whatever interpretation may have been placed on general statements of prior doctrines. It has never been U.S. policy to limit ourselves to massive counter-city options in retaliation, nor have our plans been so circumscribed. For nearly 20 years, we have explicitly included a range of employment options — against military as well as non-military targets — in our strategic nuclear employment planning. Indeed, U.S nuclear forces have always been designed against military targets as well as those comprising war supporting industry and recovery resources. In particular, we have always considered it important, in the event of war, to be able to attack the forces that could do damage to the United States and its allies.

[No Contradiction]

There is no contradiction between this attention to the militarily effective targeting of the large and flexible forces we increasingly possess — to how we could fight a war, if need be — and our primary and overriding policy of deterrence. Deterrence, by definition, depends on shaping an adversary's prediction of the likely outcome of a war. Our surest deterrent is our capability to deny gain from aggression (by any measure of gain), and we will improve it. That ability is manifest in our forces and expressed in our statements. It must be recognized by any potential adversary who exhibits a self-interested regard for measuring the certain consequences of his actions before acting.

In adopting and implementing this policy we have no more illusions than our predecessors that a nuclear war could be closely and surgically controlled. There are, of course, great uncertainties about what would happen if nuclear weapons were ever again used. These uncertainties, combined with the catastrophic results sure to follow from a maximum escalation of the exchange, are an essential element of deterrence.

My own view remains that a full-scale thermonuclear exchange would constitute an unprecedented disaster for the Soviet Union and for the United States. And I am not at all persuaded that what started as a demonstration, or even a tightly controlled use of the strategic forces for larger purposes, could be kept from escalating to a full-scale thermonuclear exchange. But all of us have to recognize, equally, that there are large uncertainties on this score, and that it should be in everyone's interest to minimize the probability of the most destructive escalation and halt the exchange before it reached catastrophic proportions. Furthermore, we cannot count on others seeing the prospects of a nuclear exchange in the same light we do.

Therefore, U.S. nuclear forces, in a state of rough quantitative parity with the Soviet Union must, just as before parity, do more than dramatize the risk of uncontrolled escalation. Our forces must be in a position to deny any meaningful objective to the Soviets and impose awesome costs in the process.

As I pointed out ... [in 1979], no potential enemy should labor under the illusion that he could expect to disable portions of our nuclear forces without in turn losing assets essential to his own military and political security, even if the exchange were to stop short of an all-out destruction of cities and industry. In our planning, we take full account of the fact that the things highly valued by the Soviet leadership appear to include not only the lives and prosperity of the peoples of the Soviet Union, but the military, industrial and political sources

145

of power of the regime itself. Nor should any possible foe believe that our hands would be tied in the event that he threatened or attacked our allies with nuclear weapons. He too would place critical targets at risk, both in his own homeland and in the territory of his allies — targets, I might add, the destruction of which would undermine his political and military ability to gain control over such vital regions as Western Europe and Japan. The notion that, somehow, our only available response to enemy attacks on allied targets would be to strike at enemy cities is incorrect. We have had, and will continue to improve, the options necessary to protect our interests and, when challenged, to deny an enemy any plausible goal, no matter how he might attempt to reach it. That is the essence of our countervailing strategy to assure deterrence.

OTHER OBJECTIVES

Important as deterrence is, it is only one of our strategic objectives. We must also strive to maintain stability in the nuclear balance, both over the long term and in crisis situations. Because nuclear weapons also have political significance, we must maintain actual and perceived essential equivalence with Soviet strategic nuclear forces. We also want the structure of our nuclear forces to be such as to facilitate the negotiation of equitable and verifiable arms control agreements. Finally in the event deterrence fails, our forces must be capable (as described at length above) of preventing Soviet victory and securing the most favorable possible outcome for U.S. interests.

Essential Equivalence

In addition to their purely military capabilities, strategic nuclear forces, like other military forces, have a broader role in the world.

On the U.S. side at least, it has been recognized for more than 20 years by close students of the situation that our alleged nuclear superiority could not be converted into a war-winning strategy at an acceptable cost or at an acceptable level of confidence, given feasible Soviet actions. In other words, while we must respond to the perceived differences that follow from a world of strategic parity — and must certainly avoid parity turning into inferiority — it is simply a myth that from the standpoint of responsible policymakers, the United States has suffered a major loss of leverage because of the Soviet nuclear buildup. It is equally untrue that the supposed loss of U.S. nuclear superiority makes us any less willing to act than in those days when the Soviets threatened our allies in Europe over Suez, made life exceedingly difficult over Berlin, or deployed missiles to Cuba. If a golden age of American nuclear superiority ever existed, sober decision-makers starting with President Eisenhower never thought so at the time.

That said, it is conceivable, nonetheless, that some parts of the Soviet leadership see these matters in quite a different light. Certainly without SALT, and to some degree with it, there will be dynamism in the Soviet strategic programs. The Soviets are expanding the hard-target kill capability of their ICBM force; they are MIRVing their SLBM force and increasing its range; they are continuing to upgrade their air defenses and pushing ABM research and development; their civil defense program continues to grow.

In any event, many countries make comparative judgments about our strength and that of the Soviets. The behavior of all those nations will be influenced by their judgments about the state of the nuclear balance. It is in this regard that essential equivalence is particularly relevant.

The need for essential equivalence reflects the fact that nuclear forces have a political impact influenced by static measures (such as numbers of warheads, throw-weight, equivalent megatonnage) as well as by dynamic evaluations of relative military capability. It requires that our overall forces be at least on a par with those of the Soviet Union, and also that they be recognized to be essentially equivalent. We need forces of such a size and character that every nation perceives that the United States cannot be coerced or intimidated by Soviet forces. Otherwise the Soviets could gain in the world, and we lose, not from war, but from changes in perceptions about the balance of nuclear power. In particular we must insure that Soviet leads or advantages in particular areas are offset by U.S. leads or advantages in others. And although the United States need not match Soviet capabilities in all respects, we must also insure that the Soviet Union does not have a monopoly of any major military capability.

As long as our relationship with the Soviet Union is more competitive than cooperative — and this is clearly the case for the relevant future — maintaining essential equivalence of strategic nuclear forces is necessary to prevent the Soviets from gaining political advantage from a real or perceived strategic imbalance.

Stability

Long-term stability in the strategic balance — another objective of U.S. strategic policy — is maintained by ensuring that the balance is not capable of being overturned by a sudden Soviet technological breakthrough, either by innovation or by the clandestine development of a "breakout" potential. To accomplish this goal we must continue a vigorous program of military research and development, as well as a number of hedge programs. We must also maintain an intelligence effort which will enable us to detect Soviet technological breakthroughs or preparations for a breakout. These efforts insure that the United States is not placed at a disadvantage should the Soviets ever attempt to upset the balance.

Crisis stability means insuring that even in a prolonged and intense confrontation the Soviet Union would have no incentive to initiate an exchange, and also that we would feel ourselves under no pressure to do so. We achieve crisis stability by minimizing vulnerabilities in our own forces, by improving our ability to detect a Soviet attack (or preparations for an attack), and by enhancing our ability to respond appropriately to such a situation.

Arms Control

The United States also seeks to secure its strategic objectives through equitable and verifiable arms control agreements whenever such accords are possible. Accordingly, we will pursue negotiation and be willing to reduce or limit U.S. capabilities where Soviet programs are appropriately limited. In addition, in order to enhance the possibility of concluding meaningful limits in the future, we will maintain a capability to meet our strategic objectives in the event of failure to reach agreement. In designing our posture, we will continue to avoid giving it characteristics that might be interpreted as an intention to seek a full first-strike disarming capability.

The TRIAD

Just as we have long had targeting options, so we have insisted for many years on maintaining a TRIAD of strategic retaliatory forces, as have the Soviets, although they differ sharply from us on the strengths they give to the legs. The U.S. TRIAD has several purposes. Perhaps the most important one is to give us high confidence that a sufficient portion of our countervailing force could ride out an enemy attack and retaliate with deliberation and control against the designated portions of the target system. Our assumption, well supported in the face of impending developments, has been that while an enemy might be able to develop the capability to knock out or otherwise neutralize one leg of the TRIAD at any given time, he would find the task of simultaneously neutralizing all three legs well beyond his ingenuity and means. We, for our part, would have the time — without a renewed fear of bomber or missile gaps — to redress any shortcomings in the exposed leg. That assumption, and maintenance of the TRIAD, are still valid today.

SUMMARY

These goals set a high standard, though I believe it is one we already meet and will continue to meet. But as with other aspects of our military forces, we face critical challenges in this area. As Soviet forces have become more powerful, options appear that could seem to them to offer some hope of advantage unless we respond adequately in our forces and our plans — and are seen to do so. Moreover, the task of providing enhanced flexibility and effectiveness in response is no simple one, even from a straightforward technical point of view. And, special problems arise as we seek to ensure that we could if necessary sustain not only a brief, intense war but also a relatively prolonged exchange. All these tasks will engage our increased attention in the coming years. . . .

[Soviet Defense]

The Soviets continue to engage in an active and costly ABM research and development effort, as both sides are permitted to do under the ABM Treaty of 1972. Their main concentration appears to be on improving the performance of their large phased-array detection and tracking radars, and on developing a rapidly deployable ABM system which includes a new interceptor. Although the Soviets may be investigating the application of high-energy lasers and even charged particle beams to ABM defenses, severe technical obstacles remain in the way of converting this technology into a weapon system that would have any practical capability against ballistic missiles. We still have no evidence, moreover, that the Soviets have devised a way, even conceptually, to eliminate these obstacles.

The SA-X-10 surface-to-air missile (SAM) is expected to be deployed soon and will be able to engage aircraft-sized targets at any altitude. It will almost certainly have some capability against a cruise missile within a small engagement envelope. At the same time, a new Soviet AWACS is under development.

The Soviets have not yet managed a solution to the problem of intercepting bombers and cruise missiles penetrating their defenses. However, a number of systems near initial operating capability (IOC), if deployed, will improve their capability. A modified FOXBAT is under development with a look-down capability.

The Soviets continue their efforts to develop an anti-submarine warfare capability both against alliance SSBNs and in protection of their own SSBNs. However, the performance of their ASW forces is improving only gradually, and remains substantially below that of comparable U.S. forces. The VICTOR-class nuclear-powered attack submarine (SSN) remains the most capable Soviet ASW platform. At present, neither it nor other currently deployed Soviet ASW platforms constitute a significant threat to our SSBNs.

SOVIET DOCTRINE

I have already outlined the objectives of U.S. strategic nuclear forces — deterrence, stability, and essential equivalence — and in particular the countervailing strategy which guides our efforts to maintain deterrence.

Articulation of the principles of our countervailing strategy focuses us on an obvious but too often ignored point: to deter effectively we must affect the perceptions of Soviet leaders whose values, objectives, and incentives differ sharply from our own. Our understanding of Soviet concepts of the role and possible results of nuclear war is uncertain. This is partly because our evidence is ambiguous and our analysis clouded by that ambiguity, and partly no doubt because even in the totalitarian Soviet state different leaders address these inherently uncertain issues from different perspectives.

Soviet leaders acknowledge that nuclear war would be destructive beyond even the Russian historical experience of the horrors of war. But at the same time some things Soviet spokesmen say — and, of even more concern to us, some things they do in their military preparation — suggest they take more seriously than we have done, at least in our public discourse, the possibility that a nuclear war might actually be fought. In their discussion of that prospect, there are suggestions also that if a nuclear war occurred, the time-honored military objectives of national survival and dominant military position at the end of the fighting would govern and so must shape military preparations beforehand.

Beyond the murky teachings of these doctrinal presentations, the Soviet leaders make evident through their programs their concerns about the failure of deterrence as well as its maintenance, and their rejection of such concepts as minimum deterrence and assured destruction as all-purpose strategic theories. Those concerns are understandable; some of us share them ourselves. What must trouble us, however, is the heavy emphasis in Soviet military doctrine on the acquisition of war-winning capabilities, and the coincidence (in one sense or another of that word) between their programs and what have been alleged as the requirements of a deliberate war-winning strategy.

[SOVIET NUCLEAR CHALLENGE]

I recognize that the current generation of Soviet political leaders has been cautious about actions which could lead to nuclear war, and that published Soviet military doctrine may not fully reflect its views. Nevertheless, these leaders should know by now, as we learned some years ago, that a war-winning strategy — even with high levels of expenditures — has no serious prospect of success either in limiting damage in an all-out nuclear exchange or in providing meaningful military superiority. The enduring validity of this conclusion depends, of course, on our taking the necessary countermeasures ourselves. If Soviet efforts persist, and we do not counter them, the Soviets may succumb to the illusion that a nuclear war could actually be won at acceptable, if large, cost. Accordingly, it is essential to continue to adapt and update our countervailing capabilities so that the Soviets will clearly understand that we will never allow them to use their nuclear forces to achieve any aggressive aim at an acceptable cost. This is a feasible

U.S. goal, whatever one's view of the doctrinal issues; however, it does require that we carry out the force improvement measures I am presenting here.

To recognize that strong war-winning views are held in some Soviet circles — and that Soviet advocates of such concepts as minimum deterrence or assured destruction are rare or absent — is not necessarily to cast any accusation of special malevolence, for these are traditional military perspectives by no means unreflected even in current Western discussion of these matters. Still less is it to say that the Soviets are not subject to deterrence. The task, to paraphrase a thinker familiar to the Soviet leadership, is not to debate deterrence with the Soviets, but to maintain it in our competition with them. There is, to be sure, little evidence of any Soviet view corresponding to that sometimes expressed in the West that assured destruction as a strategy would be a positive good, making further military analysis unnecessary or even wrong. But there is at the same time every reason to believe that the Soviet leadership has in fact been deterred and can continue to be, not by theory, but by recognition of the certain costs of aggression to things most valued by the leadership. . . .

[U.S. Strategic Capabilities]

It is, of course, the Soviet nuclear force (not that of our British and French allies, or of China) that must be of primary concern to us. What, in particular, is the military impact of recent Soviet strategic nuclear developments, and what do these developments signify for the design of our nuclear strategy and force structure?

At present, there are excellent grounds for confidence in the U.S. strategic deterrent. Our alert bombers, SLBMs on patrol, and a number of our ICBMs could be expected to survive even a well-executed Soviet surprise attack. Several thousands of warheads could be launched in a comprehensive retaliation, and most of the bombers and missiles should be able to penetrate to their targets. If the U.S. force were generated to a high alert before being attacked, even more warheads could be launched. We would also have the option to withhold a number of these warheads and use a part of the force with deliberation and control against subsets of targets. However, we would not have high confidence, on a second strike, of destroying the majority of the Soviet ICBM silos and other very hard targets with our quick-reacting missile forces, although our bomber weapons (bombs now and ALCMs later) would have a good albeit delayed capability against hard targets.

The Soviets, at the present time, would have a somewhat comparable capability. Even supposing a U.S. first strike, they too would have a substantial number of surviving weapons. However, they could not cover as many targets, since their inventory of surviving alert warheads would be smaller. As with the United States, if the Soviets generated their offense prior to being attacked, the number of their surviving weapons would increase.

Because of this Soviet capability, which matches ours for all practical purposes, we have a situation of essential equivalence. It can also be said with some confidence that a state of mutual strategic deterrence is currently in effect. It follows that nuclear stability would probably prevail in a crisis as well.

Longer-term stability is not equally assured. The most immediate source of future instability is the growing Soviet threat to our fixed, hard ICBMs. Although the Soviets have only just begun to deploy a version of the SS-18 ICBM with 10 MIRVs, within a year or two we can expect them to obtain the necessary combination of ICBM numbers, reliability, accuracy, and warhead yield to put most of our MINUTEMAN and TITAN silos at risk from an attack with a relatively small proportion of their ICBM force. For planning purposes, therefore, we must assume that the ICBM leg of our TRIAD could be destroyed within a very short time as one result of a surprise Soviet attack.

To say this is not to imply that the probability of a Soviet surprise attack will increase as this hypothetical vulnerability grows greater. Prudent Soviet leaders would not be certain of obtaining the necessary performance from or coordination in their forces to make such an attack effective. Nor could they be sure that we would not launch our ICBMs on warning or under attack (as we would by no means wish to rely on having to do). However, less prudent or more desperate Soviet leaders might not be constrained by these considerations.

Still, even if the Soviets were able, in a surprise attack in the 1980s, to eliminate most of our ICBMs, all our non-alert bombers, and all our ballistic missile submarines in port, we would still be able to launch several thousand warheads at targets in the Soviet Union in retaliation. And we would still have the option of withholding a number of these warheads while directing still others to a variety of non-urban targets, including military targets of great value to the Soviet leadership.

. . . [T]he hypothetical ability of the Soviets to destroy over 90 percent of our ICBM force cannot be equated with any of the following: a disarming first strike; a Soviet advantage that could be made meaningful in an all-out nuclear exchange; a significant contribution to a damage-limiting objective; or an increased probability of a Soviet surprise attack. It would amount to none of these. What it would amount to is that the United States, in these hypothetical circumstances, could lose an important leg of the TRIAD and a significant but not crippling number of valuable warheads. We would suffer a loss in our ability to attack time-urgent hard targets and a reduction in the flexibility with which we could manage our surviving forces. However . . . despite growing MINUTEMAN vulnerability, the total number of surviving U.S. warheads would actually increase after 1981, because of TRIDENT and ALCM deployments, followed by MX.

In the decade ahead, we will have strategic retaliatory forces sufficient to deter Soviet attack, not only by the risk of escalation to massive destruction of cities and industry, but also by the certainty of our ability to destroy, on a more selective basis, a range of military and industrial targets and the seats of political control. That should surely deny the Soviet Union any advantage from embarking on a course of action that could lead to nuclear exchanges.

I must add this important caveat, however: my assessment is based on the assumption that Soviet forces remain within the limits set by SALT II. Should the treaty fail of ratification, and should Soviet force levels then increase (as I believe and, in any event, must assume they would), we would have to make a larger commitment of resources to the strategic nuclear element of our defense — a commitment which, though then necessary, would not improve our security beyond that available — at far lower cost — given ratification of SALT II. . . .

Theater Nuclear Capabilities

The reasons for being concerned about the European theater nuclear balance lie in the history of our efforts to keep Western Europe independent and secure despite the long shadow cast by the close proximity of Soviet military power. The contingency that has dominated U.S. defense planning for 35 years has been much less a surprise attack with strategic weapons on the United States than a massive Soviet invasion of Western Europe. Because of that concern, during most of those years, a strategic nuclear exchange has been envisaged, not as a separate and independent phenomenon, but as a part (and an increasingly decisive part) of a much larger and more traditional campaign of the kind we had experienced in World War II. It was quite natural, therefore, that nuclear weapons and delivery systems should have been adapted for use against tactical targets of all sorts, and deployed directly to key theaters.

Theater nuclear forces represent a critical part of the Alliance tripod* of conventional, theater nuclear, and strategic forces that supports our strategy of flexible response. The theater nuclear forces, and a wide range of targeting options, greatly strengthen deterrence. They enhance our capability for forward defense and they create the risk of escalation to higher levels of conflict.

I should stress that our objective and plans for the theater nuclear defense apply equally to our allies in Europe and Asia. Our capabilities are worldwide. However, because the Warsaw Pact has concentrated such extensive capabilities in Central Europe, the development of theater nuclear requirements has tended to focus on Europe. And it is known

---

*I use the word tripod to distinguish it from the U.S. strategic TRIAD; the word triad is often used for both.

that we have deployed for some time about 7,000 nuclear weapons to the European theater in support of NATO — the majority of the weapons being associated with relatively short-range capabilities.

Owing to the way NATO and Warsaw Pact forces have evolved, we now believe that three main conditions must be present in order for our theater deterrent to be fully effective. Not only must we be able to cover a wide range of targets — including troops on the battlefield, echeloned reinforcements, lines of communications, and (where possible) relevant enemy nuclear delivery systems. Our capabilities must be highly survivable in the aggregate, at least against conventional and limited nuclear attack. And we must have powerful non-nuclear as well as strategic nuclear forces that will provide an unbroken continuum of military options.

In the past, in order to avoid a duplication of effort, we assigned most targets in the Soviet Union to the U.S. strategic forces and the more tactical targets to the theater-based forces. The distinction, however, was dictated as much by planning convenience and the range limitations of the existing theater-based forces as by anything else, and it may cause Soviet misperceptions. We would not want the Soviets to make the mistaken judgment, based on their understanding of our targeting practices, that they would be spared retaliatory attacks on their territory as long as they did not employ strategic weapons or attack U.S. territory. Because in an era of nuclear equivalence, the Soviets might make that mistake, we are developing longer range theater nuclear delivery systems.

CURRENT U.S. CAPABILITIES

The PERSHING IA missile is the only U.S. delivery system currently dedicated solely to the tactical delivery of nuclear weapons, and its range is limited. For the rest, we rely on dual-purpose artillery, missiles such as LANCE, fighter-attack aircraft, surface ships, and SAMs to deliver our theater-designated weapons.

In addition to the 7,000 nuclear weapons in the European theater, many thousands more are allocated to tactical use worldwide. We have also committed POSEIDON strategic warheads to SACEUR, and they can reach targets in the Soviet Union.

SOVIET CAPABILITIES

The Soviets, by now, have deployed large numbers of theater-oriented nuclear delivery systems, and we believe they have stockpiled sufficient warheads to supply these systems.

The Soviets, like us, have relied on dual-capable systems for much of their shorter-range theater nuclear delivery capability. Some of their 203 mm and 240 mm artillery pieces, now deployed only in the USSR, have been adapted to fire nuclear projectiles. Their more modern fighter aircraft — the SU-17 (FITTER C/D), SU-24 (FENCER), and some versions of the FLOGGER (MIG-23 and 27) — appear to be dual-capable as well. Their nuclear-chemical-conventional launchers consist of the FROG series, the SCUD B, the SS-12 SCALEBOARD, and three follow-on missiles — the SS-21 for the FROG launchers, the SS-X-23 for the SCUD launchers, and the SS-22 for the SCALEBOARD launchers. The other members of the Warsaw Pact also have some nuclear-capable aircraft.

All members of the Warsaw Pact continue to equip and train their forces to operate in chemical and nuclear environments. They also continue to improve their capabilities for the actual use of chemical weapons.

Of even greater political significance, the Soviets maintain large nuclear-capable peripheral attack forces based in the Soviet Union.... They include more than 450 intermediate-range bombers of the BADGER and BLINDER type, and around 60 BACKFIREs, over 400 older MRBMs and IRBMs, and more than 100 SS-20 mobile IRBM launchers (with an estimated reload capability), and with each missile carrying three MIRVs. In addition, the Soviets have older submarines in the Baltic and North Sea fleets armed with ballistic missiles.

Soviet planning for war in Europe has not undergone any notable change in the past year. Its authors continue to emphasize the likelihood that any major clash in Europe would escalate to nuclear warfare. However, as I pointed out last year, some recent writings have ventured the opinion that a war in Europe might continue for some time below the nuclear threshold, and Soviet military authorities appear to have begun acknowledging such a possibility in their plans, training, and exercises. Even so, however, they stress the need to be able to destroy the tactical nuclear forces of NATO at an early stage in a European conflict.

ALLIED RESPONSES

It has always been difficult to see how either the Warsaw Pact or NATO could possibly benefit from the wholesale use of nuclear weapons in a theater such as Europe. But to provide a continuum of deterrence, we must be prepared for such an undesirable eventuality. Deterrence and escalation control are also served by forces that can survive conventional attrition or limited nuclear attack. Our surviving nuclear forces in the theater must also be able to deliver various strikes — using several tens to several hundreds of weapons — ranging from direct battlefield employment against engaged enemy forces to destruction of military targets well inside the Soviet Union. We do not plan our theater nuclear forces to defeat, by themselves, a determined Soviet attack in Europe, and we rely mainly on conventional forces to deter conventional attack.

It remains essential, nonetheless, for NATO to maintain, or as necessary acquire, the flexibility to leave the Soviets under no illusion that some way exists, by nuclear means, to gain military or political leverage on the Alliance. U.S. central systems, of course, remain the ultimate deterrent, and are inextricably linked to the defense of Europe. Augmentation of NATO's long-range theater nuclear forces based in Europe, however, would complete the Alliance's continuum of deterrence and defense, and strengthen the linkage of U.S. strategic forces to the defense of Europe. Indeed, increased NATO options for restrained and controlled nuclear responses reduce the risk that the Soviets might perceive — however incorrectly — that because NATO lacked credible theater military responses, they could use or threaten to use their own long-range theater nuclear forces to advantage.

We have already developed the flexibility with our theater nuclear forces to execute:

—limited nuclear options that permit the selective destruction of particular sets of fixed enemy military or industrial targets;

—regional nuclear options that, as one example, could aim at destroying the leading elements of an attacking enemy force; and

—theaterwide nuclear options that take under attack aircraft and missile bases, lines of communication, and troop concentrations in the follow-on echelons of an enemy attack.

We must also be able to counter the SS-20s and BACKFIREs from the theater, and place at risk Pact forces and assets deep in Eastern Europe and the western military districts of the USSR. As one example, we cannot permit a situation in which the SS-20 and BACKFIRE have the ability to disrupt and destroy the formation and movement of our operational reserves, while we cannot threaten comparable Soviet forces.

We do not plan to match the Soviet program system-by-system or warhead-by-warhead in an attempt to create a separate European nuclear balance. We do seek to preserve the continuum of capability from conventional to intercontinental forces. In parallel, NATO has given special consideration to the role arms control can play in contributing to a more stable military relationship between East and West. Modernization of the long-range theater nuclear forces will provide a firm foundation for the pursuit of serious arms control negotiations with the Soviet Union, which the United States will be prepared to undertake within the framework of SALT III.

Against this background, we are taking five steps to deal with the theater nuclear problem. First, we are continuing to modernize, protect, and improve the command and control, safety and security of, those parts of our tactical nuclear capabilities that are designed principally for battlefield use and shallow interdiction targets. Second, we are proceeding with the development of two longer range, more mobile missiles: the more accurate PERSHING II and the Ground-Launched Cruise Missile (GLCM). Third, we have agreed with our allies on a program for the deployment of these missiles in Great Britain and on the European continent. Fourth, we and our NATO allies have agreed on the outlines of an arms control approach to the Soviets on long-range theater nuclear forces in the context of SALT III. It is our hope that arms control could reduce Soviet long-range theater nuclear forces. However, it is unrealistic to think that arms control could obviate the need for any new long-range systems in NATO's inventory. Fifth, over the course of 1980, we will withdraw 1,000 nuclear warheads from Europe. These reductions can be made as part of an overall modernization program without reducing the effectiveness of our theater nuclear forces.

Since the new theater nuclear systems will be deployed with U.S. units in Europe, we will necessarily assume most of their costs. The Alliance has agreed that funding for their basing will be shared through the NATO Infrastructure Program. However, because the proposed deployment plan was only recently approved by NATO, and because we need to begin modernizing our theater nuclear forces as soon as possible, I am asking for $19 million to prefinance facilities construction, which will be paid back by the Infrastructure Program in accordance with the Alliance-agreed deployment plan.

Procurement of the GLCM will begin in FY 1981, and the missile will reach an initial operational capability in December, 1983. We will deploy 160 in Europe by the end of FY 1985, and 464 in hard shelters in Europe by the end of FY 1988. All the existing U.S. PERSHING IAs will be replaced by PERSHING IIs by the end of FY 1985. These deployments will release more of our tactical aircraft for non-nuclear missions and will increase the survivability and flexibility of our nuclear forces.

I should stress, in designing this response, that one of its purposes is to lay to rest any questions about the credibility of the U.S. commitment to the defense of Europe. In the event of nuclear threats to Europe, these forces will add to our options. We would not, in any event, be faced with a cruel choice between doing nothing and attacking Soviet cities, thereby virtually assuring the destruction of the United States. Our strategic, theater nuclear, and conventional forces are and will remain capable of thwarting the purposes of any attacks on Europe and inflicting heavy costs on the attacker. That is the essence of the flexible response embodied in NATO's military guidance (MC-14/3) and of our countervailing strategy, and it is at the heart of credible deterrence.

Accordingly, I have no hesitation in saying to all who will look at the facts, including those in Europe and in this country who should know better but still continue to question our determination to defend our allies come what may: The United States is committed to the integrity and security of Western Europe because it is in the vital interest of the United States to defend Europe. We followed that course in 1917 and again in 1941. Let no one think otherwise; we are prepared to follow it again.

PRESIDENT'S ECONOMIC REPORT, ECONOMIC ADVISERS' REPORT
January 30, 1980

In his annual economic report to Congress Jan. 30, President Carter presented a pessimistic view of the economy and predicted that the nation would undergo a mild recession early in 1980. It was the first time in the 30 years that the report had been issued that a president and his economic advisers had predicted a recession.

But if the president's message and the accompanying report of the Council of Economic Advisers were bleak, there was little evidence that would have supported a more optimistic analysis. In 1979 the Consumer Price Index had climbed 13.3 percent, the highest one-year rate since 1946. Moreover, real per capita income, adjusted for inflation, had declined 0.7 percent in the fourth quarter of 1979 compared with the same quarter in 1978, and the savings rate was at its lowest point since the 1940s.

To fill out the grim picture, the price of gasoline had risen an average 35.7 cents a gallon in 1979, home-financing costs had jumped 34.7 percent and, as the year ended, major banks had raised their prime lending rate to 15-1/4 percent. Finally, despite the forceful efforts of the Federal Reserve Board to curb the excessive creation of money, the nation's basic money supply, known as M-1, had jumped in the last reporting week of 1979 by $1 billion.

Observers said the president had been persuaded that the public perceived a recession as less of a threat than inflation. The hope was that a recession, though mild, would be severe enough to dampen the inflationary surge.

Energy 'Spillover'

Carter and his economic advisers made it clear that one of their major worries was that large increases in the price of energy, housing and food would spread or "spill over" into "wages and then into industrial goods prices generally."

The Council of Economic Advisers concluded that the "underlying" rate of inflation, excluding those volatile sectors, was 8 or 9 percent in 1979. "Sharply rising food and energy prices would not affect inflation for more than a limited period," the report said, "if they did not become built into longer term trend rates of increase in wages and other costs."

But "[i]f temporary bursts in energy prices become a relatively permanent feature of the underlying cost structure," the economists continued, "the outlook for inflation during the years immediately ahead would worsen. . . ."

The economic advisers indicated that they would consider anti-inflation policy in 1980 successful if it merely stabilized the underlying rate, preventing a spillover of the high inflation rate paced by oil. To achieve that goal, the economists said, wages and prices should remain under tight restraint.

Productivity Problem

As in its 1979 annual report, the Council of Economic Advisers said that lagging productivity was helping to fuel inflation. (Historic Documents of 1979, p. 81)

"Last year's productivity performance was particularly disappointing," the advisers wrote, adding that while productivity had increased at a rate of 1.1 percent during 1978 it had declined in 1979 by about 2 percent. The council pointed out that although the rate of productivity growth had declined in recent years in all the major industrial countries, in the United States the decline "started earlier and has lasted longer."

Indicating that much was still to be learned about the reasons for the productivity slowdown, the economists did say that increased investment in "human and physical capital" as well as in research and development was "almost surely a necessary condition" for better productivity performance.

Stronger Dollar

One of the few bright trends surveyed by the president's economists was the relative stability of the dollar on foreign exchange markets in 1979.

The dollar's generally strong performance in relation to other major currencies was in marked contrast to its weakness in the previous two years. As a crucial element in the dollar's recovery, the advisers pointed to the "strong coordinated actions" taken by the United States and other major countries in November 1978. (Historic Documents of 1978, p. 683)

Forecasts

The Council of Economic Advisers predicted that the Consumer Price Index would drop to an average of 10.4 percent during 1980. Unemployment, it predicted, would rise from 5.9 percent in the fourth quarter of 1979 to 7.5 percent in the fourth quarter of 1980. It also forecast that during 1980 the gross national product (GNP) would decline by 1 percent and that productivity would continue its fall, slipping by another 0.5 percent.

In other forecasts, the council said:
- *Rising oil prices and inflation-caused increases in tax rates would continue to dampen consumer purchasing power, but the personal savings rate probably would rise from its very low level at the end of 1979.*
- *Business would react to the slowdown in consumer spending, cutting back their capital investment plans.*
- *Housing starts, which turned sharply down in late 1979, might decline even further in response to tight mortgage credit and high interest rates.*
- *Inventory accumulation should also decline further with slackening sales.*

> *Following are excerpts from the Economic Report of the President and the Annual Report of the Council of Economic Advisers issued Jan. 30, 1980.* (Boldface headings in brackets have been added by Congressional Quarterly to highlight the organization of the texts.):

ECONOMIC REPORT OF THE PRESIDENT

To the Congress of the United States:

Last year world oil prices more than doubled. This increase will add some $200 billion to the bill for imported oil paid by consuming nations. Higher oil prices were the major reason for the worldwide speedup in inflation during 1979 and the dimming of growth prospects for 1980.

The United States was severely affected, as were other oil-importing countries. Our share of the additional oil bill will come to almost $45 billion this year. Partly, but not solely, because of higher oil prices, inflation accelerated sharply. The consumer price index rose by over 13 percent. The Nation's output of goods and services, which had been predicted in last year's *Economic Report* to grow by 2-1/4 percent over the 4 quarters of 1979, rose by less than 1 percent.

Although growth slowed, our economy offered strong resistance to the forces of recession. Despite virtually universal forecasts of imminent recession, output continued to rise throughout the second half of last year. Housing sales and construction held up better than expected until late in the year. By reducing their savings, consumers maintained spending in the face of the multibillion dollar drain of purchasing power from higher oil prices. Because business inventories have been kept remarkably lean, declines in sales did not lead to major inventory corrections. More generally, the economic recovery of recent years has been free of the distortions which, in the past, made the economy sensitive to recessionary forces.

Employment growth held up even better than output, and unemployment remained under 6 percent all year. Unfortunately, the strength of employment gains reflected a sharp decline in productivity — 2 percent over the year. This fall in productivity added to costs, and thus bore a share of the responsibility for higher inflation.

While inflation worsened in 1979, a large part of the acceleration was concentrated in a few areas — energy; homeownership and finance; and, early in the year, farm and food products. Elsewhere consumer price inflation was more moderate, as prices rose by 7.5 percent over the year. Wage gains were no higher than in 1978, despite the speedup of inflation. The government's voluntary wage and price standards were widely observed and limited sharply the extent to which inflation spread from oil and a few other troubled sectors to the rest of the economy. . . .

It is my strong conviction that inflation remains the Nation's number one economic problem. Energy and housing prices are still moving up rapidly, adding directly to inflation and continuing to threaten a new price-wage spiral in the rest of the economy. Even apart from these special problem sectors, inflation is now running at an 8 to 9 percent rate, compared to 6 or 6-1/2 percent several years ago, in part because of a disappointing productivity performance.

Our immediate objective for 1980 must be to prevent the spread of double-digit price increases from oil and other problem sectors to the rest of the economy. My budget and economic policies have that as their primary goal. We share that same urgent goal with virtually every other oil-importing country. Halting the spread of inflation is not enough, however. We must take steps to reduce it.

Each new round of inflation since the 1960s has left our country with a higher underlying inflation rate. Without long-term policies to pull down the current 8 to 9 percent rate, our Nation will remain vulnerable to still further increases. Another sharp rise in oil prices or a worldwide crop shortage could provide the next turn of the ratchet. Failure to lower inflation after the latest episode would strengthen long-run inflationary expectations and erode resistance to even larger wage and price increases. Over the longer term, we will either bring inflation down or it will assuredly get worse.

[Inflation]

To fight inflation I propose that we act along four lines. The *first* and most immediate of these is fiscal and monetary restraint:

• Under the economic conditions that now confront us we must concentrate on reducing the budget deficit by holding down Federal spending and forgoing tax reductions. We cannot afford a permissive economic environment in which the oil-led inflation of 1979 gives rise to a widespread acceleration of wage and price increases in 1980 and 1981.

• To reduce inflation in subsequent years, the budget will have to stay tight. That does not mean that it should fail to respond to changing economic circumstances or that taxes can never be reduced. But compared to an earlier less inflationary era the room for budgetary maneuver has appreciably narrowed.

• Monetary policy will have to continue firmly in support of the same anti-inflationary goals.

The *second* line of action is restraint by the private sector in its wage and price decisions. Aided by the deliberations of the Pay and Price Advisory Committees appointed last year, we have been updating and improving the voluntary wage and price standards.

As a *third* line of action we must pursue measures to encourage productivity growth, adapt our economy rapidly to the fact of scarcer oil supplies, and improve our competitive standing in the world economy. By dealing with these fundamental aspects of economic performance, we seek to ensure that the long-term monetary and fiscal restraints needed to curb inflation go hand-in-hand with a healthy growth in output, employment and living standards. These measures will also help us reduce inflationary pressures from the cost side.

Recent history has driven home the lesson that events outside our country — such as worldwide crop shortages or sudden increases in OPEC oil prices — can have major inflationary effects on the domestic economy. The *fourth* line of action, therefore, must be the use of measures relating to energy and food that reduce our vulnerability to outside inflationary shocks.

[Short-Term Outlook]

We face a difficult economic transition in the next year or two. According to my economic advisers, our economy is likely to undergo a mild recession early this year. Most private forecasters share this view. Consumer purchasing power is being drained away by rising energy prices; moreover, construction of new homes may decline somewhat further because of limited supplies of mortgage credit and high mortgage interest rates.

Since economic growth in recent years has been well balanced, there are no serious distortions in our economy to intensify the forces of recession. An economic downturn, if it occurs, should therefore be brief and mild. By year-end our economy should be growing again, and the pace of expansion is likely to increase in 1981.

Unemployment will probably rise moderately this year. Next year a stronger pace of economic expansion will create more new jobs, and unemployment will begin to come down again.

Inflation has been building in our country for a decade and a half, and it will take many years of persistent effort to bring it back down. This year energy prices will still go up faster than other prices, but less so than in 1979. Some of the other special factors that contributed to inflation last year should do so to a smaller degree, or not at all, in 1980. Enactment of the budget that I have recommended, and continued exercise of reasonable restraint by business and labor in their wage and price decisions should make it possible to lower the rate of inflation from 13 percent in 1979 to close to 10 percent in 1980, and to a range of 8 to 9 percent in 1981. But that accomplishment will still leave inflation running at an entirely unacceptable pace. We cannot, and will not, rest until reasonable price stability has been achieved.

Budget Policies

My budget proposals will reduce the Federal deficit by more than half to $16 billion in fiscal 1981. Accomplishing this reduction, despite the effect of slower economic growth on Federal tax revenues, has required severe restraint on Federal spending. Outlays will increase from $564 billion this year to $616 billion in fiscal 1981. Although real defense spending will rise, total Federal outlays, adjusted for inflation, will remain virtually constant. I propose to reduce inflation-adjusted spending outside of defense.

My 1981 budget is based squarely on the premise that bringing an end to inflation must remain the top priority of economic policy. Not only are budget expenditures held to the minimum level consistent with urgent national needs, but tax reductions are forgone. This austere budget policy, accompanied by supportive policies of monetary restraint, is a necessary condition for controlling inflation.

Citizens all across our country are facing rising tax burdens because of increased social security taxes and because inflation pushes individuals into higher income tax brackets. They want, and deserve, tax reductions when cuts can be granted within the framework of a prudent budgetary policy. Businesses need greater incentives to invest in the new and modern plant and equipment that is essential to growth in our productive capacity and to long-run improvement in economic efficiency. If we continue to keep the growth of Federal expenditures under tight rein, tax reductions will be forthcoming. But I could not and did not recommend tax relief this year.

I am aware that a mild recession is widely forecast. Indeed the estimates of revenues and expenditures in my budget assume its occurrence. But forecasts are necessarily uncertain. Our economy has shown remarkable resilience to date, and there is no evidence that a recession has begun. Under those circumstances, to have recommended a tax reduction and a much larger budget deficit would have been a signal that we were not serious in our fight against inflation. It would have increased inflationary expectations, weakened the value of the dollar in exchange markets, and risked the translation of last year's oil-led inflation into a new and higher wage-price spiral in 1980. In recognition of these realities, my budget proposals concentrate on reducing the deficit.

In this uncertain period, of course, economic policy cannot be fixed in place and then forgotten. If economic conditions and prospects should significantly worsen, I will be prepared to recommend to the Congress additional fiscal measures to support output and employment in ways and under circumstances that are consistent with a continued fight against inflation.

[Proposed Increases]

Restraint in the 1981 budget has been accomplished while still moving forward with Federal programs and expenditures that address our Nation's critical needs.

• Outlays for defense will increase by over 3 percent in real terms. Both strategic and conventional forces will be strengthened. Our commitment to our NATO allies will be met, and our ability to deploy forces rapidly anywhere in the world will be improved. Recent events in Southwest Asia have underlined the necessity for these actions.

• Expenditures will be raised to expand domestic energy supplies, increase energy conservation, and provide assistance to low-income families least able to pay higher energy prices.

• Support for basic research, enlarged in the past three fiscal years, will be further expanded to a total of $5.1 billion in 1981. Sustained commitment to basic research will assure continued American scientific and technical preeminence.

• A major new initiative, for which $1.2 billion in new budget authority is requested, addresses the serious problem of unemployment among disadvantaged youth.

These programs were made possible within the framework of a tight budget by pruning less essential programs, increasing administrative efficiencies, and reducing fraud and abuse. Legislative proposals to reduce Federal spending will save $5-1/2 billion in fiscal 1981 and even more in subsequent years.

Pay and Price Standards

A little more than a year ago, I asked business and labor to join with me in the fight against inflation by complying with voluntary standards for pay and prices. Cooperation with my request was extensive. Last year's acceleration of inflation did not represent a breakdown of the pay and price standards. Skyrocketing energy prices, and rising costs of home purchase and finance lay behind the substantial worsening of inflation. Declining productivity also added to business costs and prices.

The pay and price standards, in fact, have served the Nation well. Although the price standards had only limited applicability to food, energy, and housing prices, in the remaining sectors of the economy, for which the standards were designed, prices accelerated little during the first year of the program. Wage increases were no larger than in 1978, even though the cost of living rose faster. Increases in energy prices did *not* spill over into wages and the broad range of industrial and service prices.

On September 28, 1979, my Administration and leaders of the labor movement reached a National Accord. We agreed that our anti-inflation policies must be both effective and equitable, and that in fighting inflation we will not abandon our effort to pursue the goals of full employment and balanced growth.

As an outgrowth of that Accord, I appointed a Pay Advisory Committee to work together with my Administration to review and make recommendations on the pay standards and how they are being carried out. A Price Advisory Committee was established to make recommendations with respect to the price standards.

The most immediate problem in 1980 is to ensure that last year's sharp increase in energy prices does not result in a new spiral of price and wage increases that would worsen the underlying inflation rate for many years to come. Understandably, workers, business managers, and other groups want to make up for last year's loss of real income, and they may seek to do so by asking for larger increases in wage rates, salaries and other forms of income. Such efforts would not restore real incomes that have been reduced by rising world oil prices and declining productivity, but they would intensify inflation. Improvements in our living standards can only be achieved by making our economy more efficient and less dependent on imported oil.

Voluntary standards for wages and prices, together with disciplined fiscal and monetary policies, are the key ingredients in a strategy for reducing inflation. During the years immediately ahead, monetary and fiscal policies will seek a gradual but steady lowering of inflation. By itself, restraint on borrowing and spending would mean relatively slow economic growth and somewhat higher unemployment and idle capacity. Effective standards for moderating wage and price increases will lead to greater progress in lowering inflation and thereby reduce the burden on monetary and fiscal policies and provide scope for faster economic growth and increased jobs.

[Long-Term Goals]

Just before my Administration took office the overall unemployment rate was still close to 8 percent. For blacks and other minorities, the rate was over 13 percent and had shown little improvement since the recovery began in early 1975.

Since then increases in employment have been extraordinarily large, averaging nearly 3-1/2 percent per year. The gains for women were twice as large as for men. For blacks and other minority groups the percentage rise in employment was half again as large as for whites. Aided by a strongly expanded Federal jobs program for youth, employment among black and other minority teenagers grew by over 15 percent. Employment among Hispanic Americans rose by over 20 percent.

Unemployment rates have come down substantially for most demographic groups. Unemployment among black teenagers, however, has not fallen significantly and remains distressingly high.

To address the very serious problem of unemployment among disadvantaged youth, my Administration has substantially expanded funds for youth employment and training programs over the past 3 years. My 1981 budget includes an important new initiative to increase the skills, earning power, and employability of disadvantaged young people.

In 1978 the Humphrey-Hawkins Full Employment and Balanced Growth Act was passed with the active support of my Administration. The general objectives of the act — and those of my Administration — are to achieve full employment and reasonable price stability.

When I signed that act a little over a year ago, it was my hope that we could achieve by 1983 the interim goals it set forth: to reduce the overall unemployment rate to 4 percent and to achieve a 3 percent inflation rate.

Since the end of 1978, however, huge OPEC oil price increases have made the outlook for economic growth much worse, and at the same time have sharply increased inflation. The economic policies I have recommended for the next 2 years will help the economy adjust to the impact of higher OPEC oil prices. But no policies can change the realities which those higher prices impose.

I have therefore been forced to conclude that reaching the goals of a 4 percent unemployment rate and 3 percent inflation by 1983 is no longer practicable. Reduction of the unemployment rate to 4 percent by 1983, starting from the level now expected in 1981, would require an extraordinarily high economic growth rate. Efforts to stimulate the economy to achieve so high a growth rate would be counterproductive. The immediate result would be extremely strong upward pressure on wage rates, costs, and prices. This would undercut the basis for sustained economic expansion and postpone still further the date at which we could reasonably expect a return to a 4 percent unemployment rate.

Reducing inflation from the 10 percent expected in 1980 to 3 percent by 1983 would be an equally unrealistic expectation. Recent experience indicates that the momentum of inflation built up over the past 15 years is extremely strong. A practical goal for reducing inflation must take this fact into account.

Because of these economic realities, I have used the authority provided to me in the Humphrey-Hawkins Act to extend the timetable for achieving a 4 percent unemployment rate and 3 percent inflation. The target year for achieving 4 percent unemployment is now 1985, a 2-year deferment. The target year for lowering inflation to 3 percent has been postponed until 3 years after that.

[Economic Performance]

Achieving satisfactory economic growth, reducing unemployment, and at the same time making steady progress in curbing inflation constitutes an enormous challenge to economic policy.

To lower inflation, we will have to persist in the painful steps needed to restrain demand. But demand restraint alone is not enough. We must work to improve the supply side of our economy — speed its adjustment to an era of scarcer energy, increase its efficiency, improve the workings of its labor markets, and expand its capital stock. We must take measures to reduce our vulnerability to inflationary events that occur outside our own economy. Only an approach that deals with both demand and supply can enable the Nation to combine healthy economic growth with price stability. . . .

Over the past 3 years I have devoted a large part of my own efforts and those of my Administration toward putting in place a long-term energy policy for this Nation. With the cooperation of the Congress much has already been accomplished or stands on the threshold of final enactment.

The phased decontrol of natural gas and domestic crude oil prices will provide strong, unambiguous signals encouraging energy conservation and stimulating the development of domestic energy supplies. But decontrol of oil, in the face of very high OPEC prices, inevitably generates substantial windfall profits. The windfall profits tax I have proposed will capture a significant portion of these windfalls for public use.

The increased Federal revenues from this tax will make it possible to cushion the poor from the effects of higher oil prices, to increase our investment in mass transit, and to support programs of accelerated replacement of oil-fired electricity generation facilities and increased residential and commercial energy conservation. I have also proposed incentives for the development of energy from solar and biomass sources, and have asked the Congress for authority to create an Energy Security Corporation to provide incentives and assistance on a business-like basis for the accelerated development of synthetic fuels. Other legislation that I have proposed, which is also now before a Conference Committee of the Congress, would create an Energy Mobilization Board to cut the red tape and speed the development of essential energy projects. I urge the Congress to take the final steps to enact the enabling legislation for my energy initiatives.

These policies will sharply increase the efficiency with which our Nation uses energy and widen the range of economically feasible energy sources. In so doing, they will help make our economy less inflation-prone. They will also drastically cut our reliance on imported oil, and by making our Nation less vulnerable to sudden increases in world oil prices, reduce the probability of sudden inflationary surges. . . .

The persistence of high unemployment among some groups of workers while jobs go begging and unemployment is low elsewhere is not only a major social problem but a waste of national resources. The lack of skills, the imperfections of the labor market, and in some cases, the discrimination that gives rise to this situation, reduce national productivity and contribute to inflation.

Although our labor market currently works quite well for most people, it does not work well for disadvantaged and minority youth. . . .

[Regulation]

Regulation has joined taxation, defense, and the provision of social services as one of the principal activities of the government. Unneeded regulations, or necessary regulations that impose undue burdens, lower efficiency and raise costs.

For the past 3 years I have vigorously promoted a basic approach to regulatory reform: unnecessary regulation, however rooted in tradition, should be dismantled and the role of competition expanded; necessary regulation should promote its social objectives at minimum cost.

Working with the Congress we have deregulated the airline industry. We are now cooperating with congressional committees to complete work on fair and effective legislation that eliminates costly elements of regulation in the trucking, railroad, communications, and financial industries.

Within the executive branch, we are improving the quality and lowering the cost of regulations. The Regulatory Council, which I established a year ago, is helping us comprehend the full scope of Federal regulatory activities and how these activities, taken together, affect individual industries and sectors. A number of regulatory agencies are experimenting with new regulatory techniques that promise to achieve regulatory goals at substantially lower costs.

[Investment and Research]

We do not know all of the causes of the slowdown in productivity growth that has characterized our economy in recent years. But we do know that investment and research and development will have to play an important role in reversing the trend.

To meet the Nation's sharply increased requirement for investment in energy production and conservation, to fulfill its commitment to cleaner air and water and improved health and safety in the workplace, and at the same time to provide more and better tools for a growing American work force, our Nation in the coming decade will have to increase the share of its resources devoted to capital investment.

We took one step in this direction in the Revenue Act of 1978, which provided a larger than normal share of tax reduction for investment incentives. Passage of my pending energy legislation will make available major new incentives and financial assistance for investment in the production and conservation of energy. When economic conditions become appropriate for further tax reduction, I believe we must direct an important part of any tax cut to the provision of further incentives for capital investment generally.

One of the most important factors in assuring strong productivity growth is a continuing flow of new ideas from industry. This flow depends in the first instance on a strong base of scientific knowledge. The most important source of such knowledge is basic research, the bulk of which is federally funded.

Between 1968 and 1975 Federal spending for basic research, measured in constant dollars, actually fell. But since that latter year, and especially during the years of my Administration, Federal support for basic research has increased sharply. In spite of the generally tight economic situation, the 1981 budget I am submitting to the Congress calls for yet another substantial increase in real Federal support for basic research. Even during a period of economic difficulties, we cannot afford to cut back on the basis for our future prosperity. . . .

The International Economy

Other countries besides our own suffered important setbacks in 1979 from the dramatic increase in oil prices. Growth prospects worsened, inflation increased, and balance of payments deficits rose. In such difficult times economic cooperation between nations is especially important. Joint action among oil-consuming countries is needed to reduce the pressure of demand on supply and to restore order in world petroleum markets. Cooperation is necessary to protect international financial markets against potential disruptions arising from the need to finance massively increased payments for oil. And cooperation is also necessary to prevent a destructive round of protectionism.

Because the dollar is the major international store of value and medium of exchange, the stability of international financial markets is closely linked to the dollar's strength. The actions taken in November 1978 by the United States and our allies to strengthen and stabilize the dollar worked well during the past year. That the dollar did well despite accelerating domestic inflation is due in part to a significant improvement in our current account balance during 1979. U.S. exports grew rapidly and thus helped to offset rising payments for oil. During the autumn of 1979, however, the dollar came under downward pressure. The October actions of the Federal Reserve Board to change the techniques of monetary policy helped moderate inflationary expectations which had been partly responsible for the pressure on the dollar. As a Nation we must recognize the importance of a stable dollar, not just to the United States but to the world economy as a whole, and accept our responsibility to pursue policies that contribute to this stability.

The Multilateral Trade Negotiations of the Tokyo Round were successfully completed and became law in the United States during 1979. These trade agreements are a major achievement for the international economy. By lowering tariff barriers both in the United States and abroad, they will help increase our exports and provide Americans with access to foreign goods at lower prices. Perhaps more important, these agreements will limit restrictive and unfair trade practices and provide clearer remedies where there is abuse.

The 1970s were a decade of economic turmoil. World oil prices rose more than tenfold, helping to set off two major bouts of inflation and the worst recession in 40 years. The international monetary system had to make a difficult transition from fixed to floating exchange rates. In agriculture a chronic situation of oversupply changed to one which alternates between periods of short and ample supplies.

It was an inflationary decade. It brought increased uncertainty into business and consumer plans for the future.

We are now making the adjustment to the realities of the economic world that the 1970s brought into being. It is in many ways a more difficult world than the one that preceded it.

There are no economic miracles waiting to be performed. But with patience and self-discipline, combined with some ingenuity and care, we can deal successfully with the new world. The 1980s can be a decade of lessened inflation and healthy growth.

JIMMY CARTER

January 30, 1980

THE ANNUAL REPORT OF THE
COUNCIL OF ECONOMIC ADVISERS

Chapter I

The Economy in 1979

The economy of the United States was dealt a heavy blow by rising OPEC oil prices in 1979. Inflation increased sharply; real earnings of American workers declined and economic growth slowed. Employment continued to rise, however, while productivity fell, and the unemployment rate remained relatively stable at between 5.7 and 5.9 percent. Most major demographic groups shared in the rise in employment; the gains for blacks and adult women were particularly notable.

The economy's resilience in the face of the dramatic increase in oil prices and the attendant worsening of inflation was one of the more surprising features of economic developments in 1979. Forecasts of impending recession were becoming frequent by late 1978, long before the magnitude of the 1979 increase in oil prices by the Organization of Petroleum Exporting Countries (OPEC) was perceived. By the middle of 1979 such predictions were common. Growth did slow markedly, but the characteristics of cumulating recession were still not in evidence at the close of the year.

Developments on the inflation front were the most significant disappointment in the 1979 economic performance. At the beginning of the year it was widely expected that inflation would moderate. Those hopes were destroyed, however, by skyrocketing energy prices.

The inflation and energy problems plaguing our economy seriously threaten our ability to achieve the economic goals to which the Carter Administration is firmly committed: maintaining healthy economic growth, providing job opportunities for an expanding labor force, and reducing the unacceptably high unemployment among minorities. It is urgent that we increase our energy independence and reduce the rate of inflation as soon as possible. These are the central objectives of the Carter Administration's economic policies for the period immediately ahead.

AN OVERVIEW OF THE YEAR

It was evident at the beginning of 1979 that economic growth would slow from the 5 percent average annual rate of the preceding 3 years. Most of the resources idled by the deep recession of 1974-75 had been brought back into productive use, and monetary and fiscal policies had been shifted toward restraint in an effort to slow inflation.

The 0.8 percent growth of real gross national product (GNP) actually recorded over the 4 quarters of last year was well below the 2.2 percent forecast by the Administration at the beginning of 1979. The impact of huge energy price increases on consumers' real incomes was largely responsible.

Personal consumption expenditures for goods declined slightly in real terms, but higher outlays for services kept total personal consumption rising. Residential construction also fell last year, but about in line with expectations at the beginning of the year. The expansion of business fixed investment slowed substantially, to less than 2 percent, in 1979. Businesses continued to pursue cautious inventory policies, as they had earlier in the recovery, and the rate of inventory accumulation in the fourth quarter was well below its level a year earlier.

Net exports of goods and services increased substantially in real terms last year, and by the fourth quarter they reached the highest level since 1975. The volume of exports rose, while the volume of imports leveled off. The slowing of U.S. economic expansion, increased growth abroad, and the decline of the dollar during 1978 all contributed to these developments.

The pace of economic expansion in the United States was uneven during 1979. Real GNP declined in the second quarter, when personal consumption expenditures fell sharply in response to long gas lines, but it rebounded in the summer with the resumption of normal shopping patterns. Growth in the fourth quarter was at a more moderate rate; the rise in final sales slowed and inventory accumulation declined. Output in the industrial sector did not closely follow the quarterly pattern of GNP growth, but over the 4 quarters of 1979 industrial production rose 0.9 percent, about the same as the increase in real GNP.

Both total employment and the civilian labor force grew by about 2 million in 1979. Adult women accounted for about 70 percent of the total increase in employment. The proportion of the working-age population employed rose to 59.3 percent, a slight gain.

Very large advances in energy prices and in the costs of home purchase and finance were dominant factors in the 13 percent rise in the consumer price index (CPI) during 1979. Wholesale prices of finished goods sold by producers rose by 12.5 percent over the 4 quarters of 1979, compared with 8.7 percent in the previous year. Energy prices were primarily responsible for the larger increase last year.

Sharp movements in prices for food, energy, and houses and in mortgage interest costs can have a large influence on the overall rate of inflation recorded in a given year. It is therefore useful to trace the movements of other prices as one means of ascertaining longer-term trends in prices — that is, the underlying inflation rate.

Consumer prices excluding energy, home purchase and finance, and the farm value of food rose by 8.1 percent last year, less than 1 percentage point above the 1978 pace. . . . The rate of increase in producers' prices for finished goods excluding food and energy rose somewhat more, from 7.9 percent in 1978 to 9.0 percent in 1979. By these measures the underlying inflation rate has moved up by about 2 to 3 percentage points since 1976. . . .

Another measure of the underlying inflation rate is found in the rise of unit labor costs adjusted for cyclical variations in productivity growth. Businesses tend to calculate costs on the basis of longer-term trends in productivity and to set their prices accordingly. When nominal wage increases exceed estimated long-term productivity gains, businesses will pass the resulting cost increases through to higher prices if market conditions permit.

The rate of increase in compensation per hour for all employees in the private nonfarm business sector declined in 1977, then rose again. The 1979 increase of 8.8 percent was only slightly more than the 8.5

percent recorded in 1976. Increases in actual productivity have slackened considerably, from 2.2 percent in 1976 to minus 2.2 percent in 1979, but this is partly attributable to cyclical developments. In 1976 the economy was emerging from a deep recession and was growing strongly. In 1979 the recovery was in its fifth year and economic growth slowed.

It is not clear what rate of productivity growth is now being incorporated in business estimates of longer-term trends in costs. Studies by the Council of Economic Advisers suggest that the current trend rate of increase in productivity is only about 1 to 1-1/2 percent; productivity growth in 1979, even allowing for a cyclical slowdown, was much less than this. With compensation per hour in the private nonfarm business sector rising at about 9 percent, the long-term rate of increase in unit labor costs — and thus in this measure of the underlying rate of inflation — appears to be around 7-1/2 to 8 percent, compared to about 6 percent in 1976. If heavier weight is given to the especially poor productivity experience of 1979, the underlying rate may now be in the 8 to 9 percent range.

Wage restraint played an important role in limiting the increase in the underlying rate of inflation during 1979. Aggregate measures of wage peformance indicate that growth in nominal wages did not increase last year.

Real disposable income rose temporarily in the first quarter, when the personal income tax cut provided by the Revenue Act of 1978 took effect, but it fell in the spring. Over the final 3 quarters of 1979 real disposable income remained at about the level reached in the fourth quarter of 1978. Higher oil prices were the main cause of this stagnation in real income. Inflation, by moving individuals into higher tax brackets, added further to the drag on disposable incomes, as did overwithholding of personal income taxes. Despite the leveling off of real income, personal consumption expenditure rose by about 1-1/2 percent over the 4 quarters of 1979, as the personal saving rate fell. . . .

Why the Economy Was So Resilient

The fact that the economy did not tip into recession in 1979 has received widespread comment and attention. Periods of economic expansion since World War II have typically come to an end when inflation accelerated and monetary and fiscal policies shifted toward restraint. In 1979, despite rising inflation, restraint on aggregate demand from monetary and fiscal policies, and a huge "oil tax" levied by OPEC, the economy continued to move forward.

Fiscal policy began to shift toward restraint in 1978, but the degree of restraint was lessened somewhat in early 1979 by the tax cut provided in the Revenue Act of 1978. Thereafter the Federal budget became moderately more restrictive. The high-employment budget (discussed later in the chapter) shifted from a $7 billion deficit in the second half of 1978 to a $13 billion surplus in the second half of 1979.

Added to the restraint from the budget was the enormous drain on consumer purchasing power resulting from the 1979 rise in oil prices. The oil drag at year's end was reducing consumer spending power by almost $55 billion at an annual rate, or about 3 percent of personal after-tax income. Fiscal and oil price restraint together were thus draining large amounts from consumer incomes by the fourth quarter of last year. The magnitude of this restraint has no parallel in any postwar year — including 1974, when the first big OPEC price increase rocked the economy.

Monetary policy also moved toward restraint over the course of last year. Growth of the major monetary aggregates slowed slightly. Growth of M-1 moderated to 5.5 percent in 1979 from 7.2 percent in 1978; however, shifts to ATS and New York NOW accounts .. are estimated to have reduced M-1 growth by 1-1/2 percentage points in 1979. The rise in M-2 dropped back to 8.3 percent from 8.7 percent in the preceding year. Interest rates shot upward in the second half. Short-term market interest rates at year-end were approximately 3 percentage points higher than a year earlier, while long-term rates were up about 1-1/2 percentage points.

The reasons why the economy was able to absorb these shocks without going into a steep decline may not be fully understood for some time. Three factors, however, clearly played a role. First, individuals as consumers and home buyers appear to be more strongly affected by inflationary expectations now than in the past. Surveys of consumers' attitudes indicate that until fairly recently most people expected that an increase in inflation would be temporary. When actual inflation rates were rising, expected rates of inflation lagged well behind. After two episodes of double-digit inflation, a different response is now elicited. When inflation increases, expected inflation rates move up at the same time. As a result, consumers are now more likely to accelerate purchases when inflation increases. When inflation accelerated markedly in 1973, for example, the personal saving rate rose sharply, even after allowance is made for a large increase in the share of total income accruing to farm proprietors. In 1979, however, consumers responded to the squeeze on real incomes resulting from inflation by continuing to borrow heavily and by reducing their saving as a fraction of disposable income. . . .

Expected price increases probably exert more influence on decisions to buy houses than on purchases of other durable goods. Prices of new and existing homes have risen considerably faster than prices of other consumer goods and services over the past decade, and that fact has not been lost on most individuals. With demographic factors also supporting demand, sales of new and existing homes remained very strong until late last year, despite a rise of mortgage interest rates to unprecedented heights.

Second, monetary restraint no longer produces the abrupt changes in availability of credit that used to be instrumental in bringing an end to economic expansion. Changes in financial markets over the past

20 years have removed or reduced constraints which used to limit the availability of credit to certain borrowers during periods of monetary tightness. For example, the legal and constitutional barriers that once prevented States and their political subdivisions from paying market rates of interest have been raised or eliminated. Usury ceilings have also been liberalized. Commercial banks and thrift institutions have been given more freedom to bid for funds and are hence better able to provide credit to borrowers willing to pay going rates of interest for loans. In particular, the 6-month money market certificates (MMCs) issued by banks and thrift institutions, on which rates are tied to market yields on Treasury bills, have been a major factor sustaining mortgage credit flows since mid-1978.

Changes such as these have altered the way in which restrictive monetary policies influence aggregate demand. Monetary restraint now works more through changes in interest rates that influence a borrower's willingness to incur debt, and less through changes in a borrower's ability to obtain credit. For this reason, monetary restraint now tends to affect aggregate demand less abruptly and with a less uneven impact across major economic sectors. . . .

Third, the resilience of the economy last year reflects the relative absence of cyclical imbalances characteristic of earlier periods of economic expansion. Most notable in this regard is the comparatively balanced relationship of inventories to sales after nearly 5 years of economic expansion. Better inventory controls and very cautious inventory policies prevented a buildup of inventories relative to sales during the expansion. In fact the aggregate ratio of real nonfarm inventories to sales was lower in late 1978 and early 1979 than it was throughout most of the preceding 10 years. . . .

When consumer spending weakened in the second quarter of last year, therefore, businesses did not find themselves seriously overstocked. To be sure, auto inventories, particularly for large cars, increased substantially, and major auto producers are still trying to redress the balance between stocks and sales. In other industries, however, production cutbacks to reduce excess stocks have been modest.

As Chapter 2 indicates, the economy may head into a recession in early 1980. The factors that sustained growth in 1979 should help to make the recession moderate in depth and duration. But it is unlikely that they will cushion the economy's response to shocks to the same extent that they did in 1979. This fact increases the uncertainty surrounding forecasts of economic performance this year. . . .

Chapter 2

The Economic Outlook

Economic forecasts last year tended to underestimate the strength of private spending and, consequently, the economy's ability to withstand the effects of energy price shocks, fiscal restraint, and rising interest rates.

As indicated in Chapter 1, the resilience of the economy last year reflected forces that may continue to sustain economic activity in 1980. Nevertheless there are a number of reasons for expecting a mild recession in the first half of this year. Rising oil prices, coupled with increases in effective tax rates caused by inflation, will continue to dampen consumers' purchasing power in 1980, and the personal saving rate is likely to rise from its exceptionally low level at the end of last year. Consequently the growth in consumer spending will slow. Businesses are likely to react to the slowdown in consumer buying by trimming their capital investment plans. Housing starts turned down sharply late last year and may decline further in response to reduced availability of mortgage credit and extraordinarily high mortgage interest rates. And inventory accumulation is also likely to decline further as final sales weaken.

In most past periods of economic recession both fiscal and monetary policy have been eased significantly. At the present time, however, recession is still only a forecast; it has not yet appeared in overall measures of economic performance. Moreover the economy has recently withstood recessionary pressures far better than most analysts expected. These facts, together with the seriousness of our inflation problem, argue against an easing of policy at this time. Such a move would heighten expectations of inflation and reduce our prospects of making progress toward price stability. An easing of monetary and fiscal policy, in advance of any actual economic deterioration, would also put strong downward pressures on the dollar in foreign exchange markets. Creating an environment conducive to reduced pressures on prices and costs requires restraint in fiscal and monetary policies and great caution in making changes.

Fiscal policies cannot, of course, be set to run an unswerving course regardless of how actual economic events unfold. The Administration will monitor economic developments closely in 1980 and is prepared to recommend additional policy measures if worsening economic conditions warrant such action.

THE ECONOMY IN 1980 AND 1981

The expected recession is likely to be mild and brief. Declines in real gross national product (GNP) should not extend much past midyear, and economic growth will resume later this year, albeit slowly at first. Over the 4 quarters of 1980 real GNP is forecast to decline by 1 percent.

Employment should remain almost unchanged despite the fall in real GNP, as productivity declines and the average length of the workweek is reduced. However, because job opportunities will not grow as fast as the labor force, the unemployment rate is likely to rise from 5.9

percent in the fourth quarter of 1979 to 7-1/2 percent in the fourth quarter of this year.

In 1980 a major task of economic policy is to prevent the large energy shocks of 1979 from spilling over into wages and industrial prices. Greater slack in the economy will help to hold down inflation by discouraging large wage increases and creating resistance to price increases. The rate of increase in home financing costs should slow this year. Energy prices will continue to rise substantially, although most probably at a slower pace than in 1979. Over the 12 months of this year consumer prices are forecast to increase 10.4 percent, compared with 13.3 percent in the year just ended. Late in 1980 the annual rate of inflation should be between 9 and 9-1/2 percent.

While several factors will be working to reduce inflation, dramatic progress cannot be expected because the momentum of past inflation is substantial and expectations of inflation are deeply entrenched. . . .

[Economic Forecast]

At this time the economy appears likely to head into a mild recession. Housing starts began to turn down in the fourth quarter of last year. New car sales also fell, and auto companies have curtailed their production schedules for the first quarter of this year to reduce abnormally large inventories, especially of large models.

The downward pressure on consumers' real incomes, resulting from rising oil prices and increasing fiscal restraint, is continuing. In the 2 years beginning with the final quarter of 1978, the high-employment budget will swing to surplus by $34 billion. Increases in crude oil prices, and in domestic oil refiners' and distributors' gross margins, in excess of the general rate of inflation will increase the revenues of domestic and foreign producers by $100 billion during these years. Some of these receipts will be respent within this time, but a large part will be retained. Allowing for such respending, and adjusting for double-counting, the combination of oil and fiscal restraint is estimated to rise by almost $80 billion over the 2 years ending in the fourth quarter of 1980, about 3 percent of GNP. . . .

[Uncertainties in Outlook]

As in 1979, a major threat to the outlook is that OPEC decisions about prices and production may lead to increases in world oil prices that go well beyond those announced recently. Such a development would, in the short run, add to the restraint on the economy exerted by oil prices, exacerbate inflation, and lead to lower economic growth and higher unemployment. . . .

The new orientation of monetary policy poses additional uncertainties. If inflation does not decelerate as expected, interest rates may be under more upward pressure than is now foreseen. On the other hand, if the Federal Reserve's monetary targets are attained easily because money demand weakens more than expected, the Federal Reserve's strategy will permit market forces to lower interest rates considerably. The central bank's scope for maneuver will be determined in part by developments in monetary policy abroad and by a variety of forces influencing the value of the dollar in exchange markets.

The potential behavior of the personal saving rate further complicates the assessment of the course of the economy. The saving rate is forecast to rise moderately from its exceptionally low level at the end of 1979. Should it increase further, economic growth would be weaker than expected. . . .

Perhaps the most serious risk for the longer-term performance of the economy is the possibility of a large spillover of energy price increases into wages and then into industrial goods prices generally. If temporary bursts in energy prices became a relatively permanent feature of the underlying cost structure, the outlook for inflation during the years immediately ahead would worsen; and, as Chapter 3 points out, the costs of bringing inflation back down again would be increased. Maintenance of effective pay and price standards is essential to minimize this spillover.

CONTROLLING INFLATION

Even during the very sharp 1975 recession the underlying rate of inflation never fell below the neighborhood of 6 percent. In 1976 and 1977 inflation remained at about this level. But early in 1978 inflation began to accelerate, initially on account of a dramatic increase in food prices that resulted from limited supplies of meat and the effects of cold weather on fruit and vegetable production. In 1978 and 1979 adverse productivity developments acted to push up unit labor costs. And around the close of 1978, as the economy was operating near the limit of its capacity, excess demand added briefly to upward pressure on prices. But a dominant factor in the most recent worsening of inflation was the explosion of energy prices in 1979. In the consumer price index (CPI) energy prices in 1978 had risen by 8 percent, somewhat less than the overall rise for other consumer goods and services. During the 12 months of 1979, however, energy prices to consumers increased by 37.4 percent, directly adding about 2-1/4 percentage points to overall inflation.

Temporary excess demand or sharply rising food and energy prices would not affect inflation for more than a limited period if they did not become built into longer-term trend rates of increase in wages and other costs. However, as outside shocks drive up materials prices, businesses may seek to maintain profit margins by raising prices. The higher prices of finished goods may induce workers to try to protect their real incomes by demanding larger nominal wages. Moreover businesses are less resistant to increases in the cost of materials and labor when demand is relatively strong and these increases can be readily passed through to prices of finished products. Temporary shocks that aggravate inflation can thus become embedded in underlying inflation. . . .

Periods of economic recession over these two decades produced little permanent progress in unwinding inflation. In the very mild recession of 1970, prices of goods and services other than food and energy rose nearly as fast as they had in 1969 when the economy was overheated. Moreover in 1970, when the unemployment rate averaged almost 5 percent, the rise of hourly wages and fringe benefits was almost as large as the rise in 1969, when the unemployment rate was 3-1/2 percent. In 1975 the rate of increase of prices (excluding food and energy) declined significantly, as did the rise of compensation per hour worked. That moderation of inflation, however, came about largely because of the termination of the special factors pushing up prices and wages in 1974. During the latter half of 1975 the rates of increase in compensation per hour and in prices, excluding food and energy, were still higher than they had been in 1973.

The trend of inflation created by these developments is disturbing. Shocks from excess demand and from higher prices of food and energy have at least partly fed back into wages, costs, and prices for goods other than food and energy. Since the early 1960s the start of each period of economic expansion has been marked by higher inflation than the start of the previous upswing, and inflation has been higher at the end of each expansion than at the beginning.

Developments in productivity have been another important source of the upward trend of cost and price increases. In the early 1960s increments to productivity averaged about 3 percent per year. . . . Rates of advance have dwindled, however, since the middle years of the 1960s. Adjusted for cyclical developments, productivity growth in the 2 years ending with the fourth quarter of 1978 was only one-half of 1 percent. During 1979 cyclically adjusted productivity declined sharply. The longer-term reduction in productivity growth would not have influenced the trend of inflation if wage increases had been correspondingly scaled down. . . .

As noted earlier, rising inflation over a long period has influenced the way prices and wages are set, and these and other structural changes may have reduced the response of wages and prices to a moderate degree of slack in the economy. Formal escalator clauses in labor contracts have become more common. In 1970 only one-fourth of the workers covered by major collective bargaining contracts had such clauses; in 1979 the contracts of nearly 60 percent of such workers had these clauses. Nonunion wages have also become more sensitive to price increases, perhaps because informal agreements to provide cost-of-living protection for workers have become more common. Econometric studies of the determinants of wage changes indicate a larger response to price inflation in more recent periods, and some studies suggest a smaller response to labor market slack. The incomes of other groups have been adjusted for inflation as well. Since 1975 social security benefits have been indexed to increases in the consumer price index.

Widespread belief that inflation will continue, if not worsen, leads businesses to accede to cost increases in the expectation of being able to pass the added costs forward into higher prices. These higher prices then become the basis for additional rounds of wage increases. Expectations of inflation can also lead individuals and businesses to accelerate their spending and thus add to the pressure of aggregate demand on available supplies of goods and services.

Repeated shocks to prices from the energy and food sectors aggravate the problem. As shocks become more frequent, the probability grows that a given shock will have a greater effect on expectations of inflation. . . .

[Price and Pay Standards]

The price and pay standards announced in October 1978 recognized that our current inflation problem cannot be solved through aggregate demand policy alone. The costs in forgone output and employment would be unacceptably high. Used in conjunction with prudent monetary and fiscal policies, voluntary standards for prices and wages can help limit increases in prices that widen profit margins, lessen the need for catchup wage increases, and minimize the transmission of temporary price pressures into wages and other costs. . . .

Many firms faced with uncontrollable cost increases applied to switch from the price-deceleration standard to the profit-margin limitation. While this limitation restricted both the profit margin and the rise in dollar profits that could be secured through higher prices, firms that qualified for the exception were still able to pass through large uncontrollable cost increases to prices of final products. Moreover the constraint on the growth of dollar profits had an upward bias. Firms with low base-year profits were able to increase prices and raise their profit margins to the average of the best 2 out of 3 prior fiscal years, while those with high base-period profits were not compelled to make a comparable downward adjustment. . . .

[Outlook for Inflation]

Restraint on aggregate demand in combination with the pay and price standards can make an important contribution to the control of inflation in 1980 and help lay the foundation for later reductions in inflation. Price developments in specific sectors such as food, energy, and housing will continue to have a significant impact on inflation.

Over the 4 quarters of 1980 food prices should rise approximately in line with general inflation. Prices are expected to climb most rapidly during the fall. Both the farm value of food prices and marketers' margins are expected to move up at about the same rate.

Inflation will continue to raise food marketing costs, which account for about two-thirds of consumer food costs. Price increases in food marketing operations, including labor, packaging materials, fuels, and transport supplies, are quickly translated into higher retail food prices.

The pattern of price increases for food during the year will also depend on the general level of economic activity and the relative availability of food products, primarily meats. Beef supplies for the year will be about the same as in 1979, making 1980 the first year since 1976 that supplies have not declined substantially. However, seasonally lower cattle marketings could put upward pressure on beef prices during the spring, and a reduction in the supplies of other meats is likely to boost meat prices in the fall. While pork and poultry production will continue to increase through the first half of the year, it might slow later because farm prices for these commodities may not cover production costs during the first half of 1980. Pork and poultry prices are consequently expected to remain fairly stable through midyear but then to increase, particularly in the fourth quarter.

A major uncertainty in the outlook for food prices is consumer demand. While food prices tend to be most heavily influenced by the availability of food products and marketing costs, the slower growth of consumer incomes expected in the first half of this year will help to moderate food price increases. Prices for highly perishable products like meat, fruit, and vegetables are likely to be most affected.

Energy prices to consumers are likely to increase less in 1980 than in 1979, when they rose 37.4 percent. The outlook for prices of petroleum products is very uncertain, however, since it is not clear how much further world oil prices will rise this year. The forecast assumes no further increase in real world oil prices in 1980, after the most recent round of OPEC price increases. As decontrol of domestic oil prices proceeds, the ratio of domestic to world oil prices will rise from about two-thirds at the beginning of 1980 to slightly over four-fifths at year's end. Domestic oil prices will rise substantially over the 4 quarters of 1980.

The extent to which crude oil price increases are passed on to consumers depends heavily upon the balance of supply and demand in the oil market. In 1979 the market was tight enough not only to allow full pass-through of higher crude oil prices, but also to permit a widening of refiners' and distributors' gross margins. Barring another severe disruption in world oil supplies, the outlook for the balance of supply and demand in the world oil market, at least in the first half of 1980, is not likely to permit a further widening of inflation-adjusted margins.

The rate of increase in prices of houses may moderate somewhat early in 1980 as a consequence of reduced demand attributable to developments in mortgage credit markets late in 1979. The rise in home financing costs should also be moderated later in 1980 by declining mortgage interest rates.

Available evidence noted in Chapter 1 suggests that the pay standard reduced wage inflation by about 1 percentage point in 1979. The voluntary pay standard will continue this year, although its impact on increases in wage costs during 1980 may be somewhat less than in 1979, both because the standard has had to be made more liberal and because of pressures to restore real wage losses suffered in 1979. Increased slack in the labor market, however, will also help to hold down the rise of wage rates this year. The increase in average hourly earnings is expected to range between 8-1/2 and 9 percent in 1980.

Because of the projected cyclical decline in real GNP, the output per hour of all employees in the private business sector will probably decline in 1980, but by less than in 1979. As a consequence the increase in unit labor costs will be above 10 percent for the second year in a row. Not all of these cost increases will be passed through to consumers, however, because weak aggregate demand will limit price increases and cut into profit margins in 1980.

Taking all these factors into account, consumer prices are expected to rise about 10.4 percent over the 12 months of this year, considerably less than in 1979. Smaller increases in energy prices and in the costs of purchasing and financing homes are principally responsible for the moderation. Most of the expected slowing of inflation this year will occur during the second half, when the direct effects that OPEC's recent price increases exert on the prices of petroleum products will be largely exhausted. Some further winding down of inflation is expected in 1981, when the increase in the consumer price index is expected to be about 8-1/2 percent.

The trend rate of productivity growth in the United States, as in other major industrial countries, has been declining in recent years. In the United States, however, this decline started earlier and has lasted longer than in other industrial economies. Table 15 ... makes it evident that declines have occurred in all countries.

Table 15.—*Annual Growth in GNP per employed worker in major industrial countries, 1963-79*

(Percent change per year)

Country	1963 to 1973	1973 to 1979[1]
United States	1.9	0.1
Japan	8.7	3.4
Germany	4.6	3.2
France	4.6	2.7
United Kingdom	3.0	.3
Italy	5.4	1.6
Canada	2.4	.4

[1] Estimate.

Source: Organization for Economic Cooperation and Development

Table 16 shows growth in output per hour in the United States since the end of World War II. During the first 20 years after the war, output per hour for all employees in the private nonfarm business sector rose at an average annual rate of just under 2-1/2 percent. From 1965 to 1973 the increase was 1-1/2 percent. Since 1973 the annual growth of productivity has been less than 1 percent. In the most recent period, years of sharply declining productivity, such as 1974 and 1979, have been interspersed with years of fairly good gains, such as 1976.

Table 16.—*Labor productivity growth, 1948-79*

(Percent change per year)

Sector	1948 to 1955	1955 to 1965	1965 to 1973	1973 to 1978	1978 IV to 1979 IV[1]
Private business sector	2.5	2.4	1.6	0.8	−2.0
Nonfarm	2.4	2.5	1.6	.9	−2.2
Manufacturing	3.2	2.8	2.4	1.5	[2]
Nonmanufacturing	2.1	2.2	1.2	.5	[2]

[1] Preliminary.
[2] Not available.
Note — Data relate to output per hour for all employees.
Source: Department of Labor, Bureau of Labor Statistics.

Last year's productivity performance was particularly disappointing. While productivity increased at a rate of 1.1 percent during 1978, in line with the recent trend, it declined over the 4 quarters of 1979 by about 2 percent. Productivity growth is cyclically sensitive because businesses are generally slow to adjust their work force to changes in production. This tendency causes sharp increases in productivity when output increases vigorously in the early stages of recovery; later, near cyclical peaks, very weak growth in productivity or even declines may occur as growth in real output slows. Still, cyclical considerations cannot account for all of the decline in productivity last year.

...The productivity pattern of the last decade has not been marked by consistently lower growth, but by periods of relatively satisfactory productivity gains interrupted by several intervals of very poor performance. One of the disturbing factors about the productivity decline of 1979 was that it did not interrupt a period of high growth but followed 2 years in which productivity gains had already been quite low.

Last year's *Report* evaluated the various explanations for the slower growth of productivity in recent years. The Council has continued to examine the productivity problem and to monitor closely other analyses of this topic.

The magnitude of the slowdown and numerical estimates of the various forces behind it differ according to the period and measure of productivity examined. Most analysts have, however, identified breaks in productivity growth in the mid-1960s and again in 1973, though other sharp reductions in cyclically adjusted productivity appear to have occurred as well. A comparison of estimated productivity growth in the nonfarm economy from 1973 to 1978 with the estimated growth from 1948 to 1973 indicates a slowdown of about 1-1/4 percentage points. Statistical analyses have been able to identify factors responsible for some of the decline, but a significant part remains unexplained.

The slowdown in the growth of the capital-labor ratio may have contributed about one-fourth of a percentage point to the decline, although some estimates put the figure higher. In earlier years the entry into the labor force of many young workers had a measurable impact on the decline, but this factor has not been so important since 1973. Offsetting some of the loss, however, have been the improved training and health of the labor force.

The diversion of resources to comply with government regulation may have accounted for as much as three-tenths of a percentage point of the decline, although the impact has not been so large in recent years. Many of these regulations have of course improved the quality of our environment and the health and safety of workers and consumers, benefits that are not measured in business output and productivity statistics. But regulation has not always proceeded in the most effective and efficient manner, and there is ample room for improvement. Administration initiatives to modernize the regulatory structure in some industries have improved productivity....

The relevance of research and development spending in explaining the decline of productivity is controversial. The real volume of resources devoted to research and development fell by 7 percent between 1968 and 1975, but since the latter date it has increased steadily. However, as a percentage of GNP, total research and development spending has declined since the mid-1960s, from 3.0 percent in 1964 to 2.2 percent in 1979. In private industry, where the links between productivity and research and development are more firmly established, real expenditures have increased steadily over the last two decades and have remained relatively stable as a share of GNP. More industrial research and development, however, has been aimed at compliance with regulatory requirements, and this may affect its contribution to measured output, especially in the short term. Moreover, with the recent slowing of growth of the private capital stock, fewer technological advances may have been embodied in equipment used in production. Federal support for research and development rose steadily during the early and middle years of the 1960s, but in real terms declined by about one-fourth from fiscal 1967 to fiscal 1975. Government research and development support is concentrated in basic research and in military research, however, which affect business output and productivity only after very long lags. Thus this slowdown in Federal funding may have had little effect on measured productivity so far. And Federal obligations for research and development have increased by over 14 percent in real terms since 1975.

Finally, some events, such as sudden changes in energy prices or the impact of inflation on decisions by business and individuals, may affect productivity in ways not yet understood. For example, rapid increases in energy prices, if sustained, would make the operation of older energy-intensive equipment less profitable and may make some of our present knowledge less relevant. To the extent that energy and capital are complements in production, rising energy prices may slow the rate of growth of the capital-labor ratio, and labor productivity may fall. While this phenomenon probably played a role, the available evidence does not suggest that it represents a major source of the decline in productivity since 1973.

Since it is difficult to identify a single cause for a slowdown in productivity growth, the immediate prospects for a dramatic improvement in productivity are not good. Most recommendations for policies to improve productivity have been directed at incentives to increase investment in human and physical capital as well as in research and development. Since the slower growth of physical capital is responsible for only a part of the decline in productivity growth, efforts to stimulate business fixed investment will not solve all our productivity problem. Still, improved investment performance is almost surely a necessary condition for higher productivity growth.

February

STATE DEPARTMENT REPORT ON HUMAN RIGHTS

February 4, 1980

Surveying 154 nations of the world, the U.S. State Department's annual report on the observance of human rights concluded that "[t]here now exists an international consensus that recognizes basic human rights and obligations owed by all governments to their citizens." The report was released on Feb. 4.

Pointing to the December 1979 invasion of Afghanistan by the Soviet Union, the report blamed Moscow for the "massive violation of Afghanistan's sovereignty . . . denying the . . . fiercely independent Afghan people their right to self-determination." The study said that the Soviet Union was responsible for creating in Afghanistan a situation of total "disregard for human rights."

The document did stress that the nations of the world had made "impressive strides . . . in the building of regional and international institutions for the protection of basic rights." (Historic Documents of 1979, p. 965)

Expanded Survey

The State Department survey included for the first time reports on communist-bloc nations. In previous years it had been confined to countries receiving U.S. aid. A change by Congress required human rights reports on all countries that were members of the United Nations. Much of the criticism in the report was reserved for communist nations and for nations with which the United States had strong political differences.

Afghanistan

In Afghanistan, the human rights report said, "torture, arbitrary arrest, extended and unexplained imprisonment" had been prevalent in the Soviet-dominated regimes led by Nur Mohammad Taraki and then by his successor Hafizullah Amin. Both Afghan leaders were executed in subsequent power shifts but, the report said, "Indications are that these policies will continue under the new regime of Babrak Karmal," the Afghan leader who came to power with the Soviet invasion of Afghanistan in December 1979 and January 1980.

The document also stated that fighting continued between rebel Afghan forces and the Soviet assisted government troops and that the Afghan government forces backed by Soviet men and equipment might be using "lethal chemical agents as well as incendiary devices in their efforts to suppress the Afghan resistance."

Iran

The State Department survey said that the overthrow of the shah of Iran in January 1979 had ended a repressive regime under which "many thousands of Iranians were imprisoned for political reasons and a significant number tortured." The new regime of the Ayatollah Ruholla Khomeini, the report noted, had executed more than 700 prisoners and imprisoned up to 15,000 in summary trials without due process. (Historic Documents of 1979, p. 867; 1980, pp. 351, 999)

Asia

"Nowhere in the world are human rights more beleaguered than in Kampuchea [Cambodia]," the report said. The "fundamental human right of survival was threatened . . . following four years of brutality at the hands of the Pol Pot regime [and] . . . the Khmer people . . . were further victimized by famine, armed conflict and epidemic disease — the consequences of a massive Vietnamese invasion and occupation of their country." Population in Kampuchea had declined, the study observed, from about seven million in 1975 to about 5.5 million in 1979.

The Peoples Republic of China was reported to be "a less oppressive place in which to live than it was three years ago." Yet the improvement in the condition of human rights in China, the report continued, had "not yet broken entrenched patterns of harassment, arbitrary arrests and harsh punishment without free trial for political dissent."

The regimes in North Korea and Vietnam were cited in the report as particularly repressive and characterized by a disregard for human rights. In South Korea, the assassination of President Park Chung Hee *had made the political climate more free, but repression and censorship still persisted, the report said.*

Latin America

Regional human rights organizations had been established in the Americas and had made progress toward protecting human rights, the report declared. The American Convention on Human Rights entered into force as a treaty setting forth basic human rights standards for members of the Organization of American States (OAS), the report noted. Moreover, the Inter-American Human Rights Commission was established an Inter-American Court of Human Rights at a permanent headquarters in San Jose, Costa Rica.

Fewer human rights violations reports than in previous years emanated from Cuba and Chile, the survey stated. And in Nicaragua, where rebel Sandinista forces had overthrown the regime of Anastasio Somoza, there had been an expansion of certain freedoms, though summary executions took place when the junta assumed power.

The report also said that in Argentina there was "extensive evidence . . . that torture had been routinely used by the security forces."

Europe and the Soviet Union

Western European governments generally held human rights in high regard, the human rights survey reported. However, terrorist activities had led some governments to adopt controversial security measures. The Soviet-bloc nations of communist Eastern Europe, the report said, practiced repressive policies like those in the Soviet Union.

The State Department report estimated that there were about 10,000 political prisoners in the Soviet Union, some held in mental hospitals. According to the report prisoners were mistreated and subjected to long periods of isolation and psychological pressure.

The document also stated, perhaps noting the Soviet government's arrest and exile Jan. 22 of noted Russian human rights activist Andrei D. Sakharov, that the number of open dissenters and human rights activists in the Soviet Union remained relatively small, but the increasing level of dissent within the country had led Soviet authorities to "behave as though they believe these activities represent a serious threat to the regime." (Exile of Andrei D. Sakharov, p. 103)

> *Following are excerpts from the State Department reports on human rights violations in Afghanistan, Argentina, Cambodia, China, Iran, Nicaragua, North Korea, South Korea and the Soviet Union, released Feb. 4, 1980, by the House Committee on Foreign Affairs and the Senate Committee*

on Foreign Relations. (Boldface headings in brackets have been added by Congressional Quarterly to highlight the organization of the text.):

THE 1979 HUMAN RIGHTS REPORT

This 1979 report on human rights conditions in 154 countries is submitted to the Congress by the Department of State in compliance with Sections 116(d)(1) and 502B(b) of the Foreign Assistance Act of 1961 as amended.

This year's report includes 39 countries that were not covered in previous reports. The expanded coverage is the result of a 1979 amendment to the Foreign Assistance Act which directs that the reports include, in addition to recipients of U.S. economic or security assistance, all foreign countries which are United Nations members. . . .

The report draws on information furnished by United States Missions abroad, congressional studies, nongovernment organizations, and human rights bodies of international organizations. For most countries reported on, conditions are described up to the end of 1979. In the case of a few countries, significant developments occurring during the first month of 1980 are also included.

There now exists an international consensus that recognizes basic human rights and obligations owed by all governments to their citizens. This consensus is reflected in a growing body of international law: the Universal Declaration of Human Rights; the International Covenant on Civil and Political Rights; the International Covenant on Economic, Social and Cultural Rights; and other international and regional human rights agreements. There is no doubt that these rights are often violated; but virtually all governments acknowledge their validity.

These internationally-recognized rights can be grouped into three broad categories:

— First, the right to be free from governmental violations of the integrity of the person — violations such as torture, cruel, inhuman or degrading treatment or punishment; arbitrary arrest or imprisonment; denial of fair public trial; and invasion of the home.

— Second, the right to the fulfillment of vital needs such as food, shelter, health care and education.

— Third, the right to enjoy civil and political liberties, including freedom of speech and press, of assembly, and of religion; the right to participate in government; the right to travel freely within and outside one's own country; the right to be free from discrimination based on race or sex. . . .

[Institutions for Protecting Human Rights]

The year 1979 saw impressive strides, taken in the building of regional and international institutions for the protection of basic human rights. The creation of new bodies and the strengthening of existing ones reflect the growing recognition that human rights abuses are a legitimate subject of international concern. Over the long-run such institutions can make a vital contribution to the advancement of human freedoms.

African nations called this year for the establishment of a permanent Pan-African body for the protection of human rights. The 16th annual conference of the Organization of African Unity in Liberia in July, adopted a resolution calling for an African charter of human rights and directing the Secretary-General of the OAU to

"organize as soon as possible in an African capital a restricted meeting of highly qualified experts to prepare a preliminary draft of an African Charter of human rights, providing *inter alia* for the establishment of bodies to provide and protect human and people's rights."

In September, representatives from 29 African countries attended a second meeting in Liberia, held under U.N. auspices, to discuss creation of a human rights commission for the continent.

Various attempts have also been made to explore possibilities for setting up similar institutions in other regions. For example, the Union of Arab Jurists held a symposium on human rights which recommended adoption by Arab states of a regional human rights treaty.

In the Americas, there has entered into force a treaty, the American Convention on Human Rights, which sets forth basic human rights standards for members of the Organization of American States (OAS). And perhaps the most dramatic change has been the development of institutional and enforcement mechanisms for seeking compliance with human rights standards. The Inter-American Human Rights Commission has conducted on-site investigations and issued reports on human rights conditions in a number of countries. The year 1979 also saw establishment of an Inter-American Court of Human Rights. The Court has begun to meet at its permanent site in San Jose, Costa Rica and is developing regulations and procedures and determining its work program. Finally, a new Institute for Human Rights affiliated with the Court is being established as a research and educational center in inter-American human rights law.

In Western Europe, the Council of Europe's Commission of Human Rights and Court of Human Rights continued to hear and decide cases arising under that region's human rights treaty, the European Convention on Human Rights. The European Parliament of the European Communities, directly elected by the citizens of the nine member countries for the first time in 1979, has indicated a strong interest in human rights questions, both within the European Communities and beyond.

The thirty-three nations of Europe, the United States and Canada continued preparation for the second follow-up meeting to the Conference on Security and Cooperation in Europe (CSCE), which will take place in Madrid in November, 1980. This meeting will be concerned with the implementation of the Helsinki Final Act, including its provisions on respect for human rights and fundamental freedoms and humanitarian cooperation.

[U.N. Human Rights Commission]

There has also been further development of the international human rights standards and machinery of the United Nations. In 1976, the International Covenants on Civil and Political Rights and on Economic, Social, and Cultural Rights both entered into force. Each Covenant provides for an oversight body to monitor implementation. In addition, the U.N. Human Rights Commission considering [sic] complaints from individuals and private groups under special confidential procedures. Finally, U.N. specialized agencies may also investigate alleged human rights violations.

There remains, of course, much to be accomplished before the machinery for the international protection of human rights operates fully and effectively. But it is clear that major steps have been taken in 1979 toward the goal of an international system of legal standards and enforcement mechanisms.

United States Human Rights Policy

Mindful of both the progress achieved and the challenges that remain, this administration is continuing to implement the Congressional directive of Section 502B of the Foreign Assistance Act, that "a principal goal of the foreign policy of the United States is to promote the increased observance of internationally recognized human rights. . . ."

The foreign assistance provided by the United States is adjusted to recognize human rights conditions. The transfer of police and military equipment is carefully reviewed in order to avoid identifying the United States with repressive practices. In addition, the human rights policy employs a varied mix of diplomatic tools: frank discussions with foreign officials; meetings with victims of human rights abuses; and, where private diplomacy is unavailing or unavailable, public statements of concern.

These instruments are applied in a manner that takes into account a country's history, culture, and current political environment and recognizes that human rights concerns must be balanced with other fundamental interests. Whatever the precise measure chosen in a particular situation, human rights issues are brought to the center stage of international relations where they must be addressed. In his 1980 State of the Union address, President Carter re-affirmed both America's commitment to the human rights policy and the contribution of this policy to world peace,

"We will continue to support the growth of democracy and human rights. When peoples and governments can approach their problems together — through open and democratic methods — the basis for stability and peace is far more solid and enduring. "That is why our support for human rights in other countries is in our national interest as well as part of our national character."

Afghanistan

... Victims, as well as other eyewitnesses, have reliably reported that torture is widely employed by the authorities. Use of electrical devices to extract information or simply to punish is reportedly one of the regime's most commonly employed torture practices. More traditional personal violence, such as beatings, incarceration under extremely crowded conditions, and deprival of proper food and sanitary facilities, is also widespread.

Numerous instances of cruel, inhuman or degrading treatment or punishment have occurred, especially with regard to those who have been suspected of participating in or plotting "counter-revolutionary" activity. Executions of political prisoners, both "prisoners of conscience" — those whom the regime suspects could represent a political threat to the revolution — and those who have taken more active steps against what they perceive as a despotic government, continue and have been estimated by some to total over 5,000. The new regime headed by Babrak Karmal has claimed that "tens of thousands" of Afghans were executed under former President Amin. Most occurred at Pul-I-Charki prison, just outside Kabul, where as many as 15,000 people may be incarcerated without trial. According to reliable reports, summary executions, which for many months have been between twenty and fifty persons per night, continue at Pul-I-Charki.... For their part, the insurgents too have engaged in acts of brutality, including summary executions of captured military officers, looting of villages, maiming and disfigurement of prisoners, and disregard for the safety of innocent bystanders during attacks on government personnel and installations....

Argentina

. ... Since late 1978, the incidence of disappearances has declined significantly. They numbered many thousands in both 1976 and 1977, and over 500 in 1978; since then such occurrences have been sharply reduced. In 1979 there were 44 known disappearances, most of which occurred in the first half of the year. There are indications that the Government has committed itself to end this practice.

The number of prisoners held without charge under the Executive's "state of siege" has been reduced substantially; about 1,300 remained in late 1979. . . .

Political party activity continues to be prohibited and labor unions remain narrowly circumscribed; Government guidelines limit freedom of expression. The Government has promulgated new trade union legislation which sets forth guidelines for future labor union activity and lays a basis for lifting the present restrictions. The law has been criticized by Argentine and international labor organizations as a Government attempt to curtail organized labor's political and economic power. . . .

There is extensive evidence, primarily the statements of former detainees, that torture has been routinely used by the security forces. . . .

Democratic People's Republic of Korea

. . . [T]he North Korean people are subjected to rigid control measures similar to those in effect during the Stalin era in the USSR. Persons who fail to cooperate with the regime face imprisonment, confiscation of property, or enforced removal to remote villages. Observation by informers is so prevalent that the average citizen is distrustful of even his closest associates. Any movement from one area to another requires documentary permission. Punishment for "political crimes," a recognized category of offenses, is severe. . . .

. . . Although some internationally respected human rights are acknowledged . . . individual rights are subordinated in practice to the overriding aim of imposing a social revolution and marshalling a show of unanimous popular support for the country's governing system and its leaders. . . .

Iran

. . . There were reports of harsh treatment (i.e., beatings) and psychological abuse by revolutionary committees in Tehran and the provinces.

More than 700 executions by firing squads took the lives of political and military figures identified with the previous Government who were accused of killings or torture; counter-revolutionaries accused of plotting to overthrow the new Government; and persons accused of violating Islamic ethical norms (alleged prostitutes, homosexuals, drug dealers). Their convictions followed summary trials conducted with virtually no regard for due process.

The number of executions of persons from the previous regime declined substantially following a partial amnesty declared on July 11 by Ayatollah Khomeini. The amnesty applied to all political offenses except those directly involved with murder or orders to kill. The number of persons executed because of anti-Islamic or counter-revolutionary crimes continued at a high level into the fall months. . . .

Kampuchea [Cambodia]

Nowhere in the world are human rights more beleagured than in Kampuchea. For the individual Khmer in 1979, the fundamental human right of survival was threatened.

Following four years of brutality at the hands of the Pol Pot regime ... the Khmer people in 1979 were further victimized by famine, armed conflict and epidemic disease — the consequences of a massive Vietnamese invasion and occupation of their country....

... The Khmer also continued to suffer at the hands of Pol Pot forces which sought savage revenge on those Khmer believed to have cooperated with the Vietnamese invaders. Even villages where Vietnamese forces had merely passed through suffered brutal retribution once the Vietnamese had left the area....

Nicaragua

... Torture of political prisoners was widespread under Somoza. Some of the present government's leaders were its victims. Some cases of torture have also occurred since Somoza's fall. A senior official of the new Government acknowledged in a press conference on Nov. 14, 1979 that there were incidents of torture of imprisoned members of the Somoza National Guard....

A number of summary executions have occurred since the Sandinista takeover. Estimates of 400 executions may be supported by evidence. It appears that armed groups outside the Managua area which participated in the revolution and now consider themselves part of the revolutionary process are responsible for most of these assassinations. It is possible, however, that some security officials were responsible for a small number of deaths....

The Government has acknowledged holding approximately 7,200 prisoners as of Dec. 31....

People's Republic of China

... There has been movement in the direction of greater freedoms in the past three years since the death of Mao Zedong and the purge of the so-called "Gang of Four" and their followers. The Chinese government appears to be making a serious effort to improve the rights of citizens by instituting a working legal system, expanding access to information, allowing some political dissent, adopting a more tolerant approach to national minorities and religious groups, liberalizing emigration policies and involving a larger number of citizens in local elections. Thousands of scholars, officials, and religious figures purged during the numerous political campaigns of the past two decades have been rehabilitated. Many have been restored to positions of authority. China is a less oppressive place in which to live than it was three years ago. . . .

The reforms have not yet broken entrenched patterns of harassment, arbitrary arrests and harsh punishment without free trial for political dissent. The Chinese government still maintains, particularly in remote areas of China, a large prison system and numerous labor camps. An extensive police system continues to monitor the political activities of China's citizens. . . .

Despite signs of improvement, the Chinese media and officials still condemn "human rights" as a "bourgeois slogan" without any relevance for China today. . . .

. . . Cases of cruel punishment continue to be documented. Wall posters, court notices and refugee interviews indicate that lengthy or open-ended prison sentences for political and economic crimes often involve years of solitary confinement with little or no communication with family allowed. Executions for serious political crimes appear to have ended. . . .

The Republic of Korea

. . . On several occasions during the year, there were reports of police brutality to prison inmates. These reports followed in the wake of demonstrations or disorders in prisons in Seoul and elsewhere in the country. Korean authorities stated that prison officials used only force sufficient to restore order in the prisons and that prisoners were punished in accordance with existing law. However, in the aftermath of an incident at Seoul's Sodaemun (West Gate) Prison, two officials were demoted. . . .

Union of Soviet Socialist Republics

. . . The number of open dissenters and human rights activists remains relatively small, and they are subject to constant harassment and imprisonment. They are denied any role in the political process. The Soviet authorities, often behave as though they believe these activists represent a serious threat to the regime. . . .

. . . [R]eports from a variety of sources indicate that mistreatment of prisoners during interrogation continues to occur. Prisoners awaiting trial are often held in isolation and may be subjected to long periods of interrogation and to psychological pressure, such as threats against their families. In some cases, beatings or other forms of physical abuse reportedly are employed against prisoners during their pre-trial investigation. Agents of the Government are responsible for any such actions. Some political prisoners are confined in psychiatric hospitals, where they have been subjected to mistreatment. In places of confinement, prisoners suffer cold and hunger under penal regulations which provide for different norms of nutrition for different categories of prisoners. . . .

▼▼▼

COURT ON EMPLOYEES' RIGHTS IN DANGEROUS WORKPLACES
February 26, 1980

In a unanimous ruling Feb. 26, the Supreme Court upheld a Department of Labor regulation giving workers the right to refuse dangerous work assignments.

The decision upheld a regulation issued by Secretary of Labor F. Ray Marshall under provisions of the Occupational Safety and Health Act of 1970. The law prohibited employers from discriminating against workers who asserted any of the rights the act guaranteed.

Associate Justice Potter Stewart delivered the opinion of the court in the case, Whirlpool Corp. v. Marshall.

Background

In June 1974 a maintenance worker at a plant of the Whirlpool Corp. in Marion, Ohio, fell to his death through a screen on which he was working. The screen had been erected to protect workers from objects that might fall from overhead conveyor belts.

The company, a manufacturer of household appliances, took a number of steps to remedy the situation that had led to the fatal accident. However, two plant maintenance men, Virgil Deemer and Thomas Cornwell, expressed to plant officials and to a regional representative of the Occupational Safety and Health Administration (OSHA) their continuing concern about their safety.

Deemer and Cornwell on July 10, 1974, refused to perform their regular duties cleaning the screen. They were sent home, not paid for their shift and officially reprimanded.

The Occupational Safety and Health Act itself did not guarantee a right to refuse to work in unsafe conditions. But Secretary Marshall's regulation did grant workers such a right when there was no available alternative way of dealing with hazardous conditions.

When Marshall sued the Whirlpool Corp. for discriminating against Deemer and Cornwell, the company challenged his regulation as inconsistent with the 1970 law. The justices, however, were not persuaded by Whirlpool's argument that Congress, in approving the act, had rejected the right of workers to refuse a task because of a reasonable belief that injury or death might result.

Unanimous Ruling

Just six weeks after hearing arguments in the case, the Supreme Court unanimously held that a limited "right to refuse to work" clearly was in line with the objective of the 1970 law — to prevent death or serious injuries in the workplace.

Writing for the court, Justice Stewart said Marshall was "obviously correct" when he acknowledged in his regulation that "as a general matter, there is no right afforded by the Act which would entitle employees to walk off the job because of potential unsafe conditions at the workplace."

But, Stewart continued, "The Act does not wait for an employee to die or become injured. It authorizes the promulgation of health and safety standards and the issuance of citations in the hope that these will act to prevent deaths or injuries from ever occurring. It would seem anomalous to construe an Act so directed and constructed as prohibiting an employee, with no other reasonable alternative, the freedom to withdraw from a workplace environment that he reasonably believes is highly dangerous. . . . [T]he Secretary's regulation can be viewed as an appropriate aid to the full effectuation of the Act's 'general duty' clause."

The court ruled that the law did not entitle workers to receive pay for work they refused to do. But the placement of written reprimands in the Whirlpool workers' files did constitute the discrimination outlawed in the 1970 Act, Stewart said.

Following are excerpts from Associate Justice Potter Stewart's opinion for a unanimous court delivered Feb. 26, 1980, ruling that workers had a limited right to refuse to perform tasks because of potentially unsafe workplace conditions:

No. 78-1870

Whirlpool Corporation, Petitioner,	On Writ of Certiorari to the
v.	United States Court of Appeals
Ray Marshall, Secretary of Labor.	for the Sixth Circuit.

[February 26, 1980]

MR. JUSTICE STEWART delivered the opinion of the Court.

The Occupational Safety and Health Act of 1970 (Act) prohibits an employer from discharging or discriminating against any employee who exercises "any right afforded by" the Act. The Secretary of Labor (Secretary) has promulgated a regulation providing that, among the rights that the Act so protects, is the right of an employee to choose not to perform his assigned task because of a reasonable apprehension of death or serious injury coupled with a reasonable belief that no less drastic alternative is available. The question presented in the case before us is whether this regulation is consistent with the Act.

I

The petitioner company maintains a manufacturing plant in Marion, Ohio, for the production of household appliances. Overhead conveyors transport appliance components throughout the plant. To protect employees from objects that occasionally fall from these conveyors, the petitioner has installed a horizontal wire mesh guard screen approximately 20 feet above the plant floor. This mesh screen is welded to angle-iron frames suspended from the building's structural steel skeleton.

Maintenance employees of the petitioner spend several hours each week removing objects from the screen, replacing paper spread on the screen to catch grease drippings from the material on the conveyors, and performing occasional maintenance work on the conveyors themselves. To perform these duties, maintenance employees usually are able to stand on the iron frames, but sometimes find it necessary to step onto the steel mesh screen itself.

In 1973 the company began to install heavier wire in the screen because its safety had been drawn into question. Several employees had fallen partly through the old screen, and on one occasion an employee had fallen completely through to the plant floor below but had survived. A number of maintenance employees had reacted to these incidents by bringing the unsafe screen conditions to the attention of their foremen. The petitioner company's contemporaneous safety instructions admonished employees to step only on the angle-iron frames.

On June 28, 1974, a maintenance employee fell to his death through the guard screen in an area where the newer, stronger mesh had not yet been installed. Following this incident, the petitioner effectuated some repairs and issued an order strictly forbidding maintenance employees from stepping on either the screens or the angle-iron supporting structure. An alternative but somewhat more cumbersome and less satisfactory method was developed for removing objects from the screen. This procedure required employees to stand on power-raised mobile platforms and use hooks to recover the material.

On July 7, 1974, two of the petitioner's maintenance employees, Virgil Deemer and Thomas Cornwell, met with the plant maintenance superintendent to voice their concern about the safety of the screen. The superintendent disagreed with their view, but permitted the two men to inspect the screen with their foreman and to point out dangerous areas needing repair. Unsatisfied with the petitioner's response to the results of this inspection, Deemer and Cornwell met on July 9 with the plant safety director. At that meeting, they requested the name, address, and telephone number of a representative of the local office of the Occupational Safety and Health Administration (OSHA). Although the safety director told the men that they "had better stop and think about what [they] were doing," he furnished the men with the information they requested. Later that same day. Deemer contacted an official of the regional OSHA office and discussed the guard screen.

The next day, Deemer and Cornwell reported for the night shift at 10:45 p.m. Their foreman, after himself walking on some of the angle-iron frames, directed the two men to perform their usual maintenance duties on a section of the old screen. Claiming that the screen was unsafe, they refused to carry out this directive. The foreman then sent them to the personnel office, where they were ordered to punch out without working or being paid for the remaining six hours of the shift. The two men subsequently received written reprimands, which were placed in their employment files.

A little over a month later, the Secretary filed suit in the United States District Court for the Northern District of Ohio, alleging that the petitioner's actions against Deemer and Cornwell constituted discrimination in violation of ... [Occupational Safety and Health] Act. As relief, the complaint prayed, *inter alia,* that the petitioner be ordered to expunge from its personnel files all references to the reprimands issued to the two employees, and for a permanent injunction requiring the petitioner to compensate the two employees for the six hours of pay they had lost by reason of their disciplinary suspensions.

Following a bench trial, the District Court found that the regulation in question justified Deemer's and Cornwell's refusals to obey their foreman's order on July 10, 1974. The court found that the two employees had "refused to perform the cleaning operation because of a genuine fear of death or serious bodily harm," that the danger presented had been "real and not something which [had] existed only in the minds of the employees," that the employees had acted in good faith, and that no reasonable alternative had realistically been open to them other than to refuse to work. The District Court nevertheless denied relief, holding that the Secretary's regulation was inconsistent with the Act and therefore invalid. ...

The Court of Appeals for the Sixth Circuit reversed the District Court's judgment.... Finding ample support in the record for the District Court's factual determination that the actions of Deemer and Cornwell had been justified under the Secretary's regulation ... the appellate court disagreed with the District Court's conclusion that the regulation is invalid.... It accordingly remanded the case to the District Court for further proceedings.... We granted certiorari ... because the decision of the Court of Appeals in this case conflicts with those of two other Courts of Appeals on the important question in issue.... That question, as stated at the outset of this opinion, is whether the Secretary's regulation authorizing employee "self-help" in some circumstances ... is permissible under the Act.

II

The Act itself creates an express mechanism for protecting workers from employment conditions believed to pose an emergent threat of death or serious injury. Upon receipt of an employee inspection request stating reasonable grounds to believe that an imminent danger is present in a workplace, OSHA must conduct an inspection.... In the event this inspection reveals workplace conditions or practices that "could reasonably be expected to cause death or serious physical harm immediately or before the imminence of such danger can be eliminated through the enforcement procedures otherwise provided by" the Act ... the OSHA inspector must inform the affected employees and the employer of the danger and notify them that he is recommending to the Secretary that injunctive relief be sought.... At this juncture, the Secretary can petition a federal court to restrain the conditions or practices giving rise to the imminent danger. By means of a temporary restraining order or preliminary injunction, the court may then require the employer to avoid, correct, or remove the danger or to prohibit employees from working in the area....

To ensure that this process functions effectively, the Act expressly accords to every employee several rights, the exercise of which may not subject him to discharge or discrimination. An employee is given the right to inform OSHA of an imminently dangerous workplace condition or practice and request that OSHA inspect that condition or practice.... He is given a limited right to assist the OSHA inspector in inspecting the workplace ... and the right to aid a court in determining whether or not a risk of imminent danger in fact exists.... Finally, an affected employee is given the right to bring an action to compel the Secretary to seek injunctive relief if he believes the Secretary has wrongfully declined to do so....

In the light of this detailed statutory scheme, the Secretary is obviously correct when he acknowledges in his regulation that, "as a general matter, there is no right afforded by the Act which would entitle employees to walk off the job because of potential unsafe conditions at the workplace." By providing for prompt notice to the employer of an inspector's intention to seek an injunction against an imminently dangerous condition, the legislation obviously contemplates that the employer will normally respond by voluntarily and speedily eliminating the danger. And in the few instances where this does not occur, the legislative provisions authorizing prompt judicial action are designed to give employees full protection in most situations from the risk of injury or death resulting from an imminently dangerous condition at the worksite.

As this case illustrates, however, circumstances may sometimes exist in which the employee justifiably believes that the express statutory arrangement does not sufficiently protect him from death or serious injury. Such circumstances will probably not often occur, but such a situation may arise when (1) the employee is ordered by his employer to work under conditions that the employee reasonably believes pose an imminent risk of death or serious bodily injury, and (2) the employee has reason to believe that there is not sufficient time or opportunity either to seek effective redress from his employer or to apprise OSHA of the danger.

Nothing in the Act suggests that those few employees who have to face this dilemma must rely exclusively on the remedies expressly set forth in the Act at the risk of their own safety. But nothing in the Act explicitly provides otherwise. Against this background of legislative silence, the Secretary has exercised his rulemaking power ... and has determined that, when an employee in good faith finds himself in such a predicament, he may refuse to expose himself to the dangerous condition, without being subjected to "subsequent discrimination" by the employer.

The question before us is whether this interpretative regulation constitutes a permissible gloss on the Act by the Secretary, in light of the Act's language, structure, and legislative history. Our inquiry is informed by an awareness that the regulation is entitled to deference unless it can be said not to be a reasoned and supportable interpretation of the Act. *Skidmore* v. *Swift & Co.* [1944].

A

The regulation clearly conforms to the fundamental objective of the Act — to prevent occupational deaths and serious injuries. The Act, in its preamble, declares that its purpose and policy is "to assure so far as possible every working man and woman in the Nation safe and healthful working conditions and to *preserve* our human resources. . . ."

To accomplish this basic purpose, the legislation's remedial orientation is prophylactic in nature. See *Atlas Roofing Co.* v. *Occupational Safety Comm'n* [1977]. The Act does not wait for an employee to die or become injured. It authorizes the promulgation of health and safety standards and the issuance of citations in the hope that these will act to prevent deaths or injuries from ever occurring. It would seem anomalous to construe an Act so directed and constructed as prohibiting an employee, with no other reasonable alternative, the freedom to withdraw from a workplace environment that he reasonably believes is highly dangerous.

Moreover, the Secretary's regulation can be viewed as an appropriate aid to the full effectuation of the Act's "general duty" clause. That clause provides that "[e]ach employer . . . shall furnish to each of his employees employment and a place of employment which are free from recognized hazards that are causing or are likely to cause death or serious physical harm to his employees." . . . As the legislative history of this provision reflects, it was intended itself to deter the occurrence of occupational deaths and serious injuries by placing on employers a mandatory obligation independent of the specific health and safety standards to be promulgated by the Secretary. Since OSHA inspectors cannot be present around the clock in every workplace, the Secretary's regulation ensures that employees will in all circumstances enjoy the rights afforded them by the "general duty" clause.

The regulation thus on its face appears to further the overriding purpose of the Act, and rationally to complement its remedial scheme. In the absence of some contrary indication in the legislative history, the Secretary's regulation must, therefore, be upheld, particularly when it is remembered that safety legislation is to be liberally construed to effectuate the congressional purpose. *United States* v. *Bacto-Unidisk* [1969]; *Lilly* v. *Grand Trunk R. Co.* [1943].

B

In urging reversal of the judgment before us, the petitioner relies primarily on two aspects of the Act's legislative history.

1

. . . The petitioner reads into this legislative history a congressional intent incompatible with an administrative interpretation of the Act such as is embodied in the regulation at issue in this case. The petitioner argues that Congress' overriding concern in rejecting the "strike with pay" provision was to avoid giving employees a unilateral authority to walk off the job which they might abuse in order to intimidate or harass their employer. Congress deliberately chose instead, the petitioner maintains, to grant employees the power to request immediate administrative inspections of the workplace which could in appropriate cases lead to coercive judicial remedies. As the petitioner views the regulation, therefore, it gives to workers precisely what Congress determined to withhold from them.

We read the legislative history differently. Congress rejected a provision that did not concern itself at all with conditions posing real and immediate threats of death or severe injury. The remedy which the rejected provision furnished employees could have been invoked only after 60 days had passed following HEW's inspection and notification that improperly high levels of toxic substances were present in the workplace. Had that inspection revealed employment conditions posing a threat of imminent and grave harm, the Secretary of Labor would presumably have requested, long before expiration of the 60-day period, a court injunction pursuant to other provisions of the Daniels bill. Consequently, in rejecting the Daniels bill's "strike with pay" provision, Congress was not rejecting a legislative provision dealing with the highly perilous and fast-moving situations covered by the regulation now before us.

It is also important to emphasize that what primarily troubled Congress about the Daniels bill's "strike with pay" provision was its requirement that employees be paid their regular salary after having properly invoked their right to refuse to work under the section. It is instructive that virtually every time the issue of an employee's right to absent himself from hazardous work was discussed in the legislative debates, it was in the context of the employee's right to continue to receive his usual compensation.

When it rejected the "strike with pay" concept, therefore, Congress very clearly meant to reject a law unconditionally imposing upon employers an obligation to continue to pay their employees their regular pay checks when they absented themselves from work for reasons of safety. But the regulation at issue here does not require employers to pay workers who refuse to perform their assigned tasks in the face of imminent danger. It simply provides that in such cases the employer may not "discriminate" against the employees involved. An employer "discriminates" against an employee only when he treats that employee less favorably than he treats other similarly situated.

2

The second aspect of the Act's legislative history upon which the petitioner relies is the rejection by Congress of provisions contained in both the Daniels and the Williams bills that would have given Labor Department officials, in imminent danger situations, the power temporarily to shut down all or part of an employer's plant. These provisions aroused considerable opposition in both Houses of Congress. The hostility engendered in the House of Representatives led Representative Daniels to delete his version of the provision in proposing amendments to his original bill. The Steiger bill that ultimately passed the House gave the Labor Department no such authority. The Williams bill, as approved by the Senate, did contain an administrative shutdown provision, but the conference committee rejected this aspect of the Senate bill.

The petitioner infers from these events a congressional will hostile to the regulation in question here. The regulation, the petitioner argues, provides employees with the very authority to shut down an employer's plant that was expressly denied a more expert and objective United States Department of Labor.

As we read the pertinent legislative history, however, the petitioner misconceives the thrust of Congress' concern. Those in Congress who prevented passage of the administrative shutdown provisions in the Daniels and Williams bills were opposed to the unilateral authority those provisions gave to federal officials, without any judicial safeguards, drastically to impair the operation of an employer's business. Congressional opponents also feared that the provisions might jeopardize the Government's otherwise neutral role in labor-management relations.

Neither of these congressional concerns is implicated by the regulation before us. The regulation accords no authority to government officials. It simply permits private employees of a private employer to avoid workplace conditions that they believe pose grave dangers to their own safety. The employees have no power under the regulation to order their employer to correct the hazardous condition or to clear the dangerous workplace of others. Moreover, any employee who acts in reliance on the regulation runs the risk of discharge or reprimand in the event a court subsequently finds that he acted unreasonably or in bad faith. The regulation, therefore, does not remotely resemble the legislation that Congress rejected.

C

For these reasons we conclude that . . . [the regulation] was promulgated by the Secretary in the valid exercise of his authority under the Act. Accordingly, the judgment of the Court of Appeals is affirmed.

It is so ordered.

JOINT ECONOMIC REPORT

February 28, 1980

The Joint Economic Committee of Congress Feb. 28 issued its 1980 annual report, proclaiming a "new era" of economic thinking and recommending policies to enhance the so-called supply side of the U.S. economy.

For only the second time in 20 years, the committee unanimously endorsed the annual report. Sen. Lloyd Bentsen, D-Texas, committee chairman, said majority and minority members issued the unified report "because we believe that our Committee has developed an innovative and effective strategy to help reverse our country's declining economic fortunes and raise the standard of living for all Americans during the 1980's and beyond."

The committee claimed that by implementing supply-side policies (which it defined as policies aimed at expanding the nation's productive potential) the Consumer Price Index (CPI) could be reduced an average of 0.4 percentage points a year without increasing unemployment. Thus, inflation gradually would be brought under control. Traditional government intervention in the economy, termed by the committee "demand management policies," would be less successful, the report predicted.

Tax Cut

The centerpiece of the committee's proposals was a recommendation that consideration be given a "modest tax cut on the order of $25 billion" to take effect no later than the summer of 1981. The Carter *administration, the report noted, was concerned that a tax cut would contribute to inflation. But a properly designed reduction, the report claimed, could be targeted so that it would not add to inflation and indeed, over the long term, slow it down. One-half of the cut, the report said, should be directed toward providing greater incentives for capital investment.*

The government's "conscious adoption of policies designed to throw the economy into recession or the failure to offset the drift of the economy into recession caused by external forces such as OPEC price increases is not a responsible way to conduct policy," the committee asserted.

Eckstein Model

To buttress its supply-side arguments, some made earlier in its 1979 report, the committee commissioned Otto Eckstein, Harvard University economist and president of Data Resources Inc., to carry out a supply-side econometric study. (1979 Joint Economic Report, Historic Documents of 1979, p. 215)

The Eckstein study, the report said, was "the first step in the direction of a supply-side model of the U.S. economy. The econometric tests performed by Dr. Eckstein indicate that further developments focusing on the supply side will ultimately yield us a huge payoff in terms of new policy approaches...." Moreover, the committee said that Eckstein's study showed that demand management policies would prove to be "unacceptable."

Forecasts

The committee noted that the annual report of the White House Council of Economic Advisers had forecast a month earlier that the economy in 1980 would "experience a mild recession." (Economic Report, p. 159) *And private economic forecasters, the committee said, were largely in agreement with the president's advisers.*

The economic forecast, which the committee called "reasonable," proved correct. The nation's economy, according to the Commerce Department's Bureau of Economic Analysis, officially slid into a recession during the first quarter of 1980.

But committee analysts had refused to predict a recession in their report, saying only that in 1980, "There will be slower growth, higher inflation, and enlarged balance-of-payments deficits for the non-OPEC nations of the world."

Other Recommendations

Other recommendations of the Joint Economic Committee included:

● *Gradual reduction in the growth of the money supply and gradual reduction of the ratio of federal spending to the gross national product (GNP).*

● *A targeted program emphasizing productive private sector on-the-job training to increase the skills of the unemployed.*

● *Enactment of a regulatory budget that would encourage government agencies to reduce the costs of regulation and improve the efficiency of regulatory programs.*

● *Energy initiatives to accelerate the use of enhanced oil recovery; development of an energy security index and emergency standby programs; an energy productivity index to measure progress toward improved national energy utilization; a comprehensive energy plan to stimulate conservation; a program to encourage oil exploration in developing countries outside OPEC; a major alcohol fuels program; and a program to increase the economic security of the Western Hemisphere by strengthening long-term trade relationships, including energy trade with Mexico and Canada.*

● *Promotion of the interests of U.S. business in foreign trade.*

Background

The Joint Economic Committee was established by the Employment Act of 1946, which also required the president to submit an economic report annually. The function of the joint committee was to assess the Annual Report of the three-member Council of Economic Advisers, which the 1946 law also created.

> *Following are excerpts from Chapter I, "Introduction," Chapter II, "Review and Outlook" and Chapter III, "The Design of Macroeconomic Policy for 1980 and Beyond," of the annual report of the Joint Economic Committee, released Feb. 28, 1980:*

THE OUTLOOK FOR 1980

To be blunt, we do not know for sure, nor does anyone else, whether the economy will enter a recession in 1980. We do not know whether inflationary pressures will abate significantly or whether the unemployment rate will rise significantly. If the OPEC producers escalate their oil prices once again or curtail their shipments of oil to the United States, there could result a serious recession and a sharply increased rate of inflation. There are a number of reasons why the now widely expected recession forecast may not materialize. For example, a steep rise in military outlays coupled with continued strong consumer spending could provide a short-run stimulus. Barring a wartime mobilization effort and assuming, optimistically, that OPEC petroleum production remains at or above 30 mbd [million barrels per day], and that spot prices decline converging toward an assumed average contract price of $30 per barrel, it is possible to formulate a less uncertain outlook for 1980. For the most part, these are the conditions assumed by most model forecasters in their "baseline" predictions for 1980. The present uncertainties add to the reasons that policymakers should focus on the long term.

[CEA Forecast]

The Council of Economic Advisers has forecast that in 1980, the economy will experience a mild recession. They have predicted that real GNP [Gross National Product] will decline 1 percent during 1980 then grow at a 2.8 percent annual rate during 1981. At the same time, they foresee inflation slowing moderately. Looking at changes in the CPI [Consumer Price Index] from December to December, the Council sees the rate of inflation declining from 13.2 percent in 1979 to 10.4 percent in 1980 and 8.6 percent in 1981. The decline in real GNP is expected to be accompanied by an increase in the unemployment rate to about 7-1/2 percent in late 1980. With the resumption of economic growth, the unemployment rate is expected to fall slightly to 7-1/4 percent by the end of 1981. In the Council's view, the recession is likely to be brief, mild, and largely over by midyear.

Private forecasters are largely in agreement with the Council. They are almost unanimous in telling us that we should expect economic contraction to occur in the first half of 1980 and a resumption of moderate growth in the latter part of the year. Although there are differences in the exact quarterly pattern, the depth of the decline, and the length of the recession, there is widespread agreement that the economy will experience at least a mild recession in 1980 and move into 1981 on a positive growth track.

The forecast of a mild recession seems reasonable, but it is not certain. When we examine the potential sources of economic growth, the consumer sector is one area where caution needs to be exercised. Although it is widely anticipated that consumers will retrench and try to bring spending patterns more closely in line with disposable income, it is possible they will continue to borrow or to dip further into their savings. The unused lines of credit available to consumers remain substantial, and it is clear that people's attitudes toward the use of debt have changed dramatically in recent times. If consumers continue to behave as they did in 1979 and other parts of the economy do not deteriorate, a recession could be avoided. Although we do not consider this the most likely prospect for 1980, there is a strong possibility that it might occur.

Caution also needs to be exercised in terms of the outlook for Federal Government outlays. Defense and cold war factors could cause sharp increases in defense outlays, a factor that will contribute to growth directly, in addition to the private sector spending increases occasioned by increased contracts and military purchases. How large the military buildup will be and how rapidly it will be translated into military contracts and payments is unknown at present.

Looking at other potential sources of growth, we believe that there are likely to be some shifts between the government sector and the foreign trade sector. The embargo on grain sales to the Soviet Union means that our exports will be reduced and government purchases will be increased. Since these changes are largely offsetting, they will have little impact on next year's economic growth. However, a general slowdown in the world economy, in the wake of 1979 OPEC price increases, would mean that the growth contributed by the foreign trade sector in 1979 would not be repeated in 1980.

There is good reason to expect the business sector to be virtually flat in 1980 as it was in 1979. The slowdown in inventory accumulation observed in the last half of 1979 indicates that inventory levels will probably be kept tight next year. Surveys of investment plans also show a flat year for 1980. And finally, investment has traditionally lagged behind other sectors of the economy in turning up after a slowdown.

[Consumer Cutbacks]

This brings us back to the consumer. While it is possible for consumers to maintain their spending levels by increasing their debt burden, it seems more likely that they will cut back. The weakness in housing and automobiles that showed up in the latter part of 1979 is likely to spread to other parts of the economy, and another year of stagnant or falling real disposable income will create mounting pressure on consumers' budgets.

In view of these considerations, we think the rate of real GNP growth for 1980 could lie in the range of from +0.5 to -1.5 percent measured fourth quarter to fourth quarter. The range is a narrow one encompassing the possibility of continued sluggish growth with no recession, and a mild recession. The consensus forecast estimates growth at from -0.5 percent to -2.0 percent, and some forecasters have suggested that the situation could be much worse. However, the following factors could contribute to a more optimistic outcome: (1) The behavior of businessmen in maintaining lean inventories makes the probability of a classic inventory cycle much less likely. (2) Much of the employment growth of the past few years has been in the service industries. This part of our economy is less sensitive to cyclical fluctuations, and therefore the prospect of large layoffs during a slowdown are somewhat reduced. More stable employment patterns will be translated into more stable consumer income. (3) Just as the new financial instruments provided more credit to the housing market than had been available in past periods of high interest rates, thereby delaying the slowdown in housing starts, those same sources of funds can be expected to cushion the fall in 1980.

[Prices]

On the price front, we see little prospect for relief from inflation in 1980. The recent petroleum price increases mean that even with moderate wage increases and no unfortunate surprises in other areas, we are virtually locked into a rate of inflation of 10 percent or more. The only way our Nation can absorb external price shocks is through productivity growth. Unfortunately, policies have not been put in place to strengthen productivity and therefore the prospects are dim for a much improved productivity performance during 1980.

Of course, if consumers cut back on their expenditures by more than we now anticipate, and if investment does not increase to pick up the slack, and if net exports deteriorate by more than we now foresee, the economic outlook could be worse.

The caution we express with respect to our net export position in 1980 is well grounded. As a result of the 1979 rise in world oil prices, OPEC revenues are estimated to jump to around $280 billion in 1980 compared to $138 billion in 1977, $130 billion in 1978, and an estimated $196 billion in 1979. Even assuming no dramatic changes in OPEC policies in 1980, the magnitude of this increase in revenues virtually guarantees that the OPEC nations will run a current account surplus of $100 billion or more in 1980.

[OPEC Impact]

The consequences of the 1979 OPEC price increases for the world economy in 1980 seem clear. There will be slower growth, higher inflation, and enlarged balance-of-payments deficits for the non-OPEC nations of the world. And it is likely that the nonoil developing nations will be hit the hardest, all the more so because it is almost certain that the OPEC surpluses will not be recycled as quickly or as easily as they were following the 1973-74 OPEC price hikes. Depending on the outcomes that result from OPEC's 1979 price increases, the net export position of the United States could deteriorate dramatically.

In our estimation, it is not now possible to judge which of the many prospective outcomes is most likely for 1980. We do expect 1980 to be a year characterized by sluggish growth, at least. But even this prospect is not unconditional.

In view of this uncertainty, we do not feel that it is appropriate to rush forward with new macroeconomic policy initiatives designed explicitly on the basis of current economic forecasts. . . .

Recommendation No. 1

Because the outlook for 1980 is so uncertain, and because actual economic developments may not unfold in the manner predicted by many forecasters, we urge Congress and the Administration not to rush forward with new program initiatives specifically aimed at countering prospective short-run developments implied in those forecasts.

LONG-TERM FOCUS

In formulating our recommendations for this report, we have given careful consideration to the short-term forecasts provided by the Council of Economic Advisers and numerous private economists. However, we continue to find that looking at both the past and the future from a longer term perspective yields insights which are more valuable for policymaking.

As we turn to the longer term outlook for the U.S. economy, we cannot be unmindful of current developments. The history of the 1973-75 recession demonstrates that the economy can deteriorate more rapidly than was believed reasonable, and certainly if this situation were to recur, short-term countercyclical measures would be necessary. Contingency plans to deal with such unanticipated situations must be a permanent part of our policy formulating process. Nevertheless, it would be inappropriate to implement such countercyclical measures as long as we feel that the economy will recover from any temporary setbacks within a reasonably short period of time.

The fundamental elements which underlie the economy's long-term growth were discussed at length in the report we published ... [in 1979]. To briefly review the outlook for these fundamentals, consider estimates for the growth of potential GNP. The easiest way to arrive at such an estimate is to sum the growth rates of (a) the labor force, (b) productivity, and (c) hours worked.

Since the population supplying new workers to the labor force during the next five to ten years is largely fixed, the major factors which influence the number who actually enter the work force are changes in female and teenage participation rates. This, in turn, is influenced by such factors as the need for additional family members to enter the work force in order to maintain a certain level of real earnings in the face of rising prices, the desire of women to participate in the work force, the number of women who are occupied by childbearing and childrearing, the average length of time people remain in school, etc. Immigration also has an impact on both the population and the labor force. After reviewing all of these factors, we conclude that the labor force is likely to grow 2 to 2.3 percent per year over the next five years.

The second major factor determining longer term economic growth is, of course, productivity. We discuss this at length elsewhere, but briefly, we believe that the U.S. productivity performance must and will improve significantly during the next few years. An older, more experienced work force will be a positive factor. If combined with policies which encourage the growth of capital relative to labor, 1.5 to 2 percent average annual growth is quite reasonable. Negative factors which could reduce productivity growth such as an erratic growth pattern which would reduce capital formation or dramatic changes in the relative price of energy must be carefully managed.

Combining the projections for productivity and labor force growth with an average decline in hours worked of about 0.5 percent per year yields an estimate of 3 to 3.5 percent per year for the growth of potential GNP. Many economists will call this estimate optimistic, and we have already stated that policies designed to increase the capital to labor ratio will be necessary to achieve it. Nevertheless, if the economy is moving forward in the range of its potential growth rate by 1981, as many forecasters now expect, we believe that by implementing now the policies which are laid out in the remainder of this report, Congress can lay the foundation for economic growth and prosperity for the remainder of the decade.

[Macroeconomic Policy for 1980 and Beyond]

The failure of the economy to register as sharp a slowdown in 1979 as many forecasters earlier predicted has had one very unfortunate side effect. It has all but stalled efforts to design new fiscal and monetary policy initiatives to deal with both our current and prospective growth and inflation problems. Many policymakers are unwilling to commit themselves to any kind of tax cut proposal until presented with incontrovertible evidence that the economy is in the midst of a serious recession and that there will be no adverse inflationary effect from the tax cut. The Administration, for example, has made it clear in its fiscal 1981 budget message that it will stand firm against tax reductions until events deteriorate more than is now anticipated.

[CONSISTENT LONG-TERM ECONOMIC POLICIES]

In our estimation, there is need for a shift in the focus of monetary and fiscal policies away from short-run crisis containment toward steady long-term economic growth. In the past two decades, there has been too much emphasis placed on "fine tuning" the economy. In the future, monetary and fiscal policy should be conducted in a stable manner. Long-term policies should have a two-fold aim. First, they should promote growth at rates that are in line with the economy's actual potential for noninflationary real growth. Second, they should be structured to encourage an increase in these potential growth rates for the future.

We can use as our guide to the establishment of our steady growth target the growth rate of our Nation's productive potential, technically, the growth rate of potential real GNP. Given current and expected rates of productivity and labor force growth, this guide implies, at present, a long-term growth potential of approximately 3 percent annually. If this is correct, monetary and fiscal policies should be designed now to accommodate 3 percent average real growth per year; as well, consideration needs to be given to the structure of these policies in ways conducive to an increase in our growth potential over the long term.

From the perspective of long-term economic growth, monetary and fiscal policy should be adjusted only in accordance with changes in the long-run growth potential of the U.S. economy. Since the growth of potential real GNP only changes very gradually over time, no abrupt long-term policy changes would be anticipated.

From a short-run point of view, we do not feel that it is appropriate to try to "fine tune" the economy by attempting to adjust policy in response to all, or even most, cyclical departures from our targeted long-run growth path. However, we do feel that it is appropriate — indeed, mandatory — to adjust our macroeconomic policies if actual real growth registers a sustained departure from our long-run targeted growth path and if a change in policy is judged necessary in order to put us back on target toward the realization of our long-term growth goal. This does not mean, of course, that real economic growth must proceed at the same rate year in and year out, or that macroeconomic policies should be adjusted in ways to attempt to bring such a precise result about. It does mean that macroeconomic policies should be adjusted when, in the absence of policy changes, a realistic long-run average rate of growth would be otherwise unattainable.

And finally, since any realistic program must have a beginning and an end against which our actual performance can be assessed, we need to avoid attaching undue significance to the promised performance at the terminal date the closer we get to it. It would be wrongheaded policy, for example, to rush forward with programs to either dramatically pump up or slow down the economy in the interests of attaining a goal as though that were a desirable end in itself. Too many unexpected events can take place to render the goal unreachable, not the least of which is the fact that as we move forward in time we may witness changes in the growth of our real GNP potential as a result of both unanticipated developments and policy actions initiated in the interim. In short, there is no specific terminal goal other than that of attaining the highest possible long-run rate of real economic growth consistent with the satisfaction of our myriad other goals.

Recommendation No. 2

U.S. monetary and fiscal policies need to be designed for the purpose of achieving an average annual real growth rate equal to that of our long-run potential real GNP; we need to hold those policies steady over the long term; and we need to avoid adjusting those policies cyclically except in those instances when actual real output growth registers a sustained departure, up or down, making the attainment of our long-term growth target unattainable in the absence of policy changes.

The policy implications of this recommendation are profound. It implies the setting of monetary and fiscal policies and sticking with them, changing them only under the most extraordinary circumstances. It implies abandonment of the "fine tuning" approach to policy, an approach that is impractical because, among other reasons, the state of the art of economic forecasting is much too imprecise to permit us to make the required policy adjustments when they are needed. It implies the very close coordination of monetary and fiscal policies. And finally, it implies that conventional macroeconomic policies can no longer be used as the primary means to reduce unemployment below the 5.5 to 6.0 percent range, because the labor markets for skilled workers are tight in that range.

The latter point requires explanation. We are not abandoning the 4 percent unemployment target mandated by the Humphrey-Hawkins Full Employment and Balanced Growth Act of 1978. However, we have learned from past experience that it is inappropriate to attempt to reach that 4 percent target solely through demand stimulation. Conventional macroeconomic policies are constrained by the fact that, once the overall unemployment rate reaches the 5.5 to 6.0 range, further increases in demand add significantly to inflationary pressures. The reason for this is now clear: Although shortages of low-skilled workers are rare when the overall unemployment rate is in the neighborhood of 5.5 to 6.0 percent, at that overall rate, shortages begin to appear in many high-skilled labor markets. Demand expansion to further reduce the overall unemployment rate causes little wage inflation among low-skilled workers but highly inflationary wage increases among high-skilled workers. In order to avoid exacerbating labor shortages in high-skilled markets while attempting to reduce unemployment among low-skilled workers, it is necessary to adopt targeted structural microeconomic policies tailored to meet the specific needs of the low skilled. We also need targeted structural policies to fight inflation by generating investment in modern plant and equipment and to shift the composition of our output toward industries with high potential for productivity growth. . . .

We view the adoption of this recommendation, in conjunction with the other recommendations in this report, as essential to the ultimate attainment of the inflation and unemployment goals mandated by the Humphrey-Hawkins Act. In our estimation, an environment characterized by the application of steady, consistently applied policies is itself conducive to the establishment of an economy characterized by steady, rapid growth.

We have had enough of policy-induced economic fits and starts, enough of roller coaster policies that have left us at the end of each recovery and downturn with more inflation, higher unemployment, and a smaller growth potential than the one earlier. Steady real growth is essential to the encouragement of major new investments in factories and skills, to expand the supply side of our economy, and to enhance productivity growth and reduce inflation. The uncertainties created in the wake of economic fits and starts serve to diminish such investment incentives, the consequence of which is a slower rate of growth of potential real GNP. In other words, steady real growth, by encouraging a higher rate of capital formation than otherwise, is itself conducive to a higher rate of growth of our Nation's productive potential. According to one study by Data Resources, Inc., steady growth could add 0.2 percent to the growth of our Nation's potential real GNP each year. Additionally, appropriately structured monetary and fiscal policies aimed at enhancing productivity and capital growth could result in an even faster rate of growth of our real potential output.

In order to achieve these goals, however, it is mandatory, as noted before, that monetary and fiscal policies be closely coordinated. They must not be permitted to work at cross purposes in terms of our national goals. And the Federal Reserve Board needs to send Congress more than broadbrush assurances that their monetary growth targets are "reasonably consistent" with the economic goals of the President, as was done last year in the Board's first report to Congress under the Humphrey-Hawkins Act. We are convinced that there exists an effective anti-inflationary pro-growth mix of monetary and fiscal policies. And we know that they can be carefully coordinated with the cooperation of the Federal Reserve, the President, and Congress.

[Fiscal Policy for 1980 and Beyond]

What is required in order to maintain fiscal policy on a steady course is reasonably straightforward. Once Congress and the Administration reach agreement on the levels of government spending, they must set tax policies in such a way as to accommodate a rate of growth of real private spending consistent with the targeted long-run average rate of growth for the economy, and consistent with the monetary policy then in place. However, because both real and nominal income increases are taxed at progressively higher rates, real tax receipts will rise more than in proportion to the increase in real income. This extra rise, if not offset, will lower the future growth of real private spending, making the long-run average real growth target for the economy unattainable. Insofar as private sector incentives are reduced, the real growth potential of the economy is reduced as well. In order for fiscal policy to continue to have a steady, not contractionary, influence on the economy, it would be necessary either to periodically increase real Federal Government spending or to lower tax rates, or both, to offset the real growth and inflation-induced increases in tax receipts. Which method of offset should be used — whether it should take the form of an increase in real Federal Government spending or a reduction in taxes — depends upon the goal we set for the share of Federal Government outlays in the gross national product.

The question that now arises is: what course should fiscal policy follow in 1980 and 1981? The answer given by the Administration is that there should be no bold new fiscal policy initiatives at this time. The policy initiatives that have been proposed relate mainly to defense and energy. Proposals have not been put forward to deal with the economic slowdown.

[Taxes]

As far as taxes are concerned, the Administration remains adamantly opposed to a tax cut at this point. The economic outlook is highly uncertain. The recession failed to materialize in 1979, and there is no guarantee that it will emerge in 1980. According to the Administration, there is no need for a tax cut because such fiscal stimulus could worsen an already disturbing rate of inflation.

We fail to see why the question of a tax cut should be so intimately tied to whether or not a recession actually materializes. That there will be continued sluggish growth and that the United States will fall farther below its real GNP potential in 1980 are not in dispute. The Administration is concerned that a tax cut will contribute to inflation. A properly designed tax cut can be targeted so that it will not add to inflation and, over the long term, help slow it down. The conscious adoption of policies designed to throw the economy into recession or the failure to offset the drift of the economy into recession caused by external forces such as OPEC price increases, is not a responsible way to conduct policy. The costs of such a policy option in terms of lengthened unemployment lines, idled productive capacity, and reduced real output are both obvious and huge, serving neither the short-term nor the long-term interests of the American people. The anti-inflation gains from pursuing a sluggish growth strategy are disappointingly small.

A severe economic slowdown will result in a sharp and immediate reduction of investment spending. This is something our economy can ill afford. Not only would such a reduction of capital spending severely limit our future growth potential and our long-term rate of productivity growth, it would virtually guarantee yet another sharp increase in prices once the restrictive policy spigots are reversed. One of the first requirements for a healthy rate of capital formation is a healthy high employment economy, an outcome that we have a greater chance of fostering through the use of consistent and steady monetary and fiscal policies.

[Contractionary Fiscal Policy]

It is not the worsened outlook itself that forms the basis for our consideration of a tax cut, but the fact that fiscal policy, far from remaining steady, has become contractionary in the course of the past year, a factor that has contributed to the worsened economic outlook.

Last March, in our annual report to Congress, we endorsed the Administration's policy of overall demand restraint. We knew then that such a policy would result in a slower rate of growth for the economy in both 1979 and 1980. In the Committee's view, such an outcome was deemed appropriate in order to prevent demand (which at the end of 1978 was pressing up against our productive potential) from contributing to the then accelerating rate of inflation. Importantly, when making our recommendations we did not call for a policy of severe demand restriction. We recommended only a policy of moderate restriction aimed at slowing the rate of growth of aggregate demand to bring it into closer alignment with the growth of potential real GNP. We believe that the policy recommendations we made last March with respect to fiscal policy were correct, and on the basis of the evidence we have at our disposal concerning the current state of the economy and the long-term growth of our productive potential, we feel that fiscal policy design should continue to be guided by these same principles. However, the additional fiscal drag exerted by a higher than expected inflation rate means we are not pursuing the same fiscal policy we recommended last March. Fiscal policy has tightened considerably since then and will continue to tighten further throughout 1980 in the absence of tax or expenditure changes. Therefore, it is necessary to put fiscal policy back on its earlier recommended steady course.

The move toward fiscal restraint is most clearly evidenced in the sharp decline of the high employment budget deficit between 1978 and 1979 and its expected further decline during 1980. Between the fourth quarter of 1978 and the fourth quarter of 1979, the high employment budget shifted from an annualized deficit of $6.6 billion to a surplus of $13.8 billion, a swing of over $20 billion in the direction of fiscal restraint. This additional margin of fiscal restraint was largely the result of legislated increases in social security taxes and the effects of inflation on Federal Government tax receipts. Moreover, given a near double digit rate of inflation projected for 1980, fiscal policy will automatically tighten further this year causing yet another $10 billion increase in the high employment surplus. In order to maintain a steady fiscal policy, this additional fiscal restraint, occurring as it does in automatic response to real income increases and inflation, should be offset if it can be accomplished without worsening inflation.

[Tax Cut]

We are convinced that we need to consider a modest tax cut on the order of $25 billion to take effect no later than the summer of 1981, even though there is considerable uncertainty surrounding the economic outlook.

The tax cut we propose here is not the conventional kind which mostly benefits consumers. On the contrary, at least half of the tax reduction should be targeted to enhance productivity through savings and investment with the remainder going to help relieve taxpayers of the pressure of increased taxes and higher energy costs.

It is important to recognize why a conventional tax cut is not in order. We do not need another boom in consumer spending. Savings and investment must command a larger percentage of our GNP or we will fail to reverse our dismal productivity performance with the result that we will make little headway in our efforts to slow inflation and raise real incomes. Moreover, it is important that whatever tax relief is given to the business community it be given on the basis of its performance in expanding plant and equipment expenditures. We leave it to the tax-writing committees to work out the precise details of the tax cut proposed here.

If there is a downturn in the economy over the next 18 months and a sharp increase in the unemployment rate, Congress is likely to enact a tax cut. If there is no downturn and the unemployment rate remains in the neighborhood of 6 percent, according to the Administration, substantial budget surpluses will begin to accrue in fiscal year 1981 and Congress is also likely to enact a tax cut. In either case, Congress must make sure that the tax cut does not result in exacerbating the rate of inflation.

Recommendation No. 3

Should either of these events occur, the Joint Economic Committee recommends a targeted tax cut of approximately $25 billion to take effect no later than the summer of 1981, designed to improve productivity and partially offset the tax increase on individuals caused by inflation. At least half of the tax cut should be directed toward enhancing savings and investment.

There are a variety of approaches and methods to achieve an enhancement of savings and investment. For example, adjustments to depreciation schedules could increase business savings and investment. It would also be appropriate to consider a rollback in social security taxes and other forms of personal and corporate tax reductions.

A caveat is in order here: If in response to heightened world tensions Congress and the Administration deem it appropriate to step up sharply the rate of Federal Government outlays for defense purposes, the tax cut will need to be pared or deferred accordingly, or some other spending restrained in order to keep fiscal policy on a steady course.

The President's fiscal 1981 budget implies some increase in the Federal Government share of GNP over the course of the next year. Projected future increases in government spending imply a somewhat reduced Federal Government share of GNP in future years, an outcome that meets with our approval because, with the improved economic outlook for future years, our social program objectives need not be encumbered.

More rapid growth in the private economy is the appropriate means for achieving a reduced Federal share.

The Employment Act, as amended, requires that the President's Economic Report include interim numerical goals for reducing the share of the Nation's gross national product accounted for by Federal outlays to 21 percent or less by 1981 and to 20 percent or less by 1983, or the lowest level consistent with national needs and priorities. It was the intent of Congress when this requirement was enacted that the President's report discuss the goal of reducing Federal outlays as a share of GNP and demonstrate how policies and programs can be designed to achieve this goal without impeding the achievement of the goal of reducing unemployment. The President's Economic Report does not contain the interim numerical goals or the policy discussion called for, with respect to the share of GNP accounted for by Federal outlays. This lapse is unfortunate and we are hopeful it will be corrected in next year's report.

Recommendation No. 4

> The Committee supports the basic trend of Federal Government spending proposed by the President, for fiscal year 1981 and projected into future years, toward a gradually reduced share of Federal outlays in the gross national product.

It should be recognized that the Government's command over national resources is not accurately measured by the share of Federal outlays in GNP alone. Government regulatory activity also represents command over resources as it often requires State, local and private spending. It is conceivable that the Federal share of GNP measured by Federal spending could increase while at the same time total federally mandated spending is reduced because of a reduction in regulatory burdens.

[Monetary Policy for 1980 and Beyond]

In the overall design of macroeconomic policy, it is equally, or perhaps more, important that the monetary authorities pursue a steady course. Unfortunately, the gyrating rates of change of money growth over the past several years provide convincing evidence that the Federal Reserve's charted course has been anything but steady.

It is not difficult to discover why past Federal Reserve efforts to control the money supply proved largely unsuccessful. It was mainly a by-product of the methods used by the Federal Reserve to control money growth, methods which in practice caused short-run movements in the money supply, and perhaps long-run movements as well, to be determined largely by changes in the demand for money. The problem of monetary control arose because the Federal Reserve believed that by controlling movements of short-term interest rates — in particular, the Federal funds rate, the interest rate at which commercial banks lend to each other — it could effectively control movements in the demand for money. Using the policy instruments at its disposal to bring about changes in the Federal funds rate, the Federal Reserve believed that it could bring money demand growth into alignment with its targeted rate of money expansion.

As long as the demand for money is a stable function of the interest rate, and as long as the Federal funds rate targeted by the Board is consistent with the Board's targeted rate of money growth, such a policy approach should work. Unfortunately, neither condition was met.

The demand for money was not effectively controlled by controlling interest rates. When the demand for money rose for reasons other than movements in interest rates, the Federal funds rate would rise above its target, causing the Federal Reserve to inject new reserves into the banking system raising the supply of money. When the demand for money declined, the reverse sequence of events would occur and the money supply would fall. The absence of a stable and predictable relationship between the demand for money and the Federal funds rate meant that volatile movements in the demand for money would be mirrored in corresponding volatile movements in the money supply.

[Federal Reserve]

Additionally, if the Federal Reserve set its interest rate target "too low" or "too high," even assuming that there existed a stable relationship between the demand for money and interest rates, there would result a rate of money growth above or below the Federal Reserve's money growth targets. A targeted Federal funds rate that was too low would cause too rapid an injection of reserves, and conversely.

In an earlier era there may well have existed a more stable and predictable relationship between interest rates and the demand for money. For a variety of reasons, including recent financial reforms and rapid inflation, that relationship today is much less stable and predictable. Moreover, in a period of inflation, and particularly accelerating inflation, it is extremely difficult to interpret the significance of any given level of interest rates, in particular, what a given level of interest rates implies about the actual rate of money growth.

It is possible that the Federal Reserve's past monetary growth problems were compounded by its practice of making only small and relatively predictable policy and interest rate adjustments. This can prove particularly troublesome in a period of accelerating inflation because it means only marginal upwards adjustments in the targeted Federal funds rate when, in retrospect, much more dramatic increases would have been called for. The consequence, in the minds of many monetary experts, was a Federal funds rate that was consistently too low; too low in the sense of being inconsistent with the Federal Reserve's own targeted rate of money growth. The result was an inordinately rapid increase in the secular growth of money.

In a dramatic departure from its previous operational practices, the Federal Reserve announced on October 6, 1979, new operating procedures designed to enable it to gain more effective control over the supply of money. Instead of tying its policies to movements in the Federal funds rates, the Federal Reserve will henceforth peg its operations largely to bank reserves. That is, the Federal Reserve will supply reserves to banks at rates it believes are consistent with its money growth targets.

We applaud the Federal Reserve for having the courage to change its operating methods as it did on October 6 [1979]. By exercising firm control over the growth of reserves, the Federal Reserve should now be able to gain much more effective control over the money supply growth process than was true in the past, a laudatory goal for which there is near universal agreement. The control might not be as precise as some would like, but it should be effective enough to ensure money growth at rates that fall within the ranges of the prescribed growth targets.

We come now to the really thorny issue. Just how fast should the money supply be permitted to grow in the months and years ahead? Unfortunately, there are no clear-cut answers to this question. It depends on one's definition of money and the relationship between it and the rate of nominal spending.

[Definition of Money]

Settling on an appropriate definition of money is not as easy as one might imagine. Some argue that money should be defined narrowly as checking account (or checking account type) balances plus currency and coin only, since these constitute the only universally acceptable "means of payment" for virtually all economic transactions. True, but the relationship between this narrowly defined aggregate and the rate of nominal spending is not particularly close or reliable.

The reason why this is so is clear. The dollar amount of spending that can be financed depends not only on the stock of the "means of payment" but also on its velocity of circulation — the rate at which it changes hands and is used to make purchases. If the velocity of circulation increases, the dollar amount of purchase that can be financed rises even if the stock of the "means of payment" does not, and conversely.

The difficulty with focusing on the "means of payment" is that its velocity of circulation fluctuates sharply over time. These fluctuations are the result of the decisions people make with respect to their holdings of the "means of payment." If a large enough number of people decide to economize on their "means of payment" by temporarily putting those funds into interest bearing assets until needed for their purchases, they will thereby have put them into the hands of those who will use them to make purchases in the interim, the result of which will be a noticeable increase in the velocity of circulation. But the fact that different people behave differently at times in response to all sorts of developments, including changing laws and regulations, financial innovations and the rate of inflation, among other reasons, it is not surprising that we should discover volatile movements in the velocity of circulation of the "means of payment."

Because the velocity of circulation of the "means of payment" is so volatile and unpredictable, the Federal Reserve was not able to accomplish its objective of controlling movements in nominal spending by controlling movements in the "means of payment." This fact caused the Federal Reserve years ago to search out some more broadly defined aggregate to be used along with the "means of payment," one that included one or more financial assets that was more or less readily substitutable for the "means of payment," an aggregate that was more reliably and predictably related to nominal spending. The results of that search process led ultimately to the development of not one, but several, alternative monetary aggregate measures, no single one of which was unambiguously better than any other in all circumstances. Thus, the Federal Reserve attempted to subject to its control the growth of all of these many monetary aggregates.

As a result of continued changes in the financial and regulatory environment and changes in the behavioral responses of individuals and businesses to interest rates and inflation, even these monetary aggregates proved to be inadequate, a matter that we discussed in detail in our annual report last year. The problem, in short, is that none of them behaved as reliably and as predictably in terms of nominal spending as they once did; the velocity of circulation associated with each had increased in volatility over time. The Federal Reserve has recently introduced new aggregate measures which it hopes will prove more meaningful.

Under the circumstances, it is difficult to recommend a precise growth target for the new aggregates because their relationships to the ultimate targets of monetary control at present are unknown and ill defined. We are forced, therefore, to discuss the issue of monetary control in terms of the general principles that should govern the conduct of monetary policy now and in the future. . . .

The central question is, how can we attain "noninflationary growth in money and credit"? Should it be accomplished rapidly or only gradually over a period of several years? In our view, the rate of money and credit expansion should be slowed gradually. To do otherwise, risks pushing the economy into a prolonged and deep recession. Since wage and price inflation show considerable momentum, at least on the downside, the burden of any very abrupt slowing in the growth of money and credit would fall on production and employment, virtually guaranteeing a deep and protracted recession. As we said earlier in our discussion of fiscal policy, attempts to wring inflation out of the economy by adopting the recession route makes no sense. The emphasis should be on the attainment of a gradual reduction in money and credit growth in order to permit the economy to make the production, investment, and other real adjustments that can and do occur only gradually.

Recommendation No. 5

The Committee strongly recommends that the Federal Reserve accomplish a gradual reduction in the rate of money and credit expansion (relative to the very high rates posted in years past) over a period of years toward money and credit growth rates that are consistent with the noninflationary real growth rate of the economy.

We believe that this recommendation, coupled with our other recommendations concerning productivity, energy, savings and investment, is essential to solving inflation while maintaining real economic growth and full employment.

[Money Expansion]

Turning briefly to the rates of money expansion experienced since October 6 [1979], there exists a possibility that the Federal Reserve has moved too abruptly, that it is aiming for a rate of reduction of money growth that is too rapid from the point of view of the short-term and long-term interests of the economy. If this is so, it should ease up somewhat over the next few months in order to accomplish its ultimate long-run objectives in a more gradual and more certain manner. We say "more certain" because if the economy is thrown into a serious recession, made all the more serious by an overly restrictive monetary policy, the Federal Reserve may feel compelled to reverse itself sharply bringing us back to yet another era of monetary instability.

More explicitly, if the Federal Reserve were to maintain a rate of money expansion that was too low *for a period of several years,* there is little doubt that our inflation rate would be reduced. But unless there has been an unusual increase in the velocity of circulation, the economy would be forced to suffer through a moderate to severe recession. We find it hard to believe that the Federal Reserve would be willing to maintain such a policy in the face of such heavy costs.

But if the Federal Reserve, in the face of such an eventuality, did reverse itself sharply, we would have to ask ourselves what it was that we accomplished by such a tight money policy. Will the deflationary effect of slower money growth and higher interest rates do much to slow inflation this year and next? Probably not. The burden of the deflationary adjustment will fall almost exclusively on employment and output in the short run. And if the deflationary effects of the policy will not make a significant dent in inflation in the short run, a quick policy reversal will return us to current or higher rates of inflation, thus incurring the costs of the recession without any permanent gains against inflation.

In fairness to the Federal Reserve, there is a possibility that the relationship between the aggregates and GNP may be somewhat more flexible than in the past. If velocity, for one reason or another, has increased significantly, then any given reduction in the growth of the supply of dollars may have less of a restraining influence on GNP than formerly. This is not entirely inconceivable since high inflation, rapid financial innovation, ever-changing laws and regulations and changing behavioral responses on the part of individuals and businesses to interest rates could change the relationship between the aggregates and GNP dramatically.

[Interest Rates]

We do not know, for example, how much significance to attach to the sharp rise in interest rates since high levels of interest rates are, in part, a by-product of the inflationary process. Thus, although nominal interest rates are high, real interest rates are much lower; and real interest rates after taxes are lower still.

Interest earned is taxable. Interest paid is tax deductible. For savers and borrowers in the 50 percent bracket, a 2 percent real interest rate at zero inflation implies a real after-tax reward to savers and a real after-tax cost to borrowers of 1 percent. At a 12 percent interest rate and 10 percent inflation, the after-tax rate for both lenders and borrowers will be 6 percent in nominal terms, but a *negative* 4 percent in real terms, even if the real pretax interest rate remains at 2 percent. The reduction in real after-tax interest rates induces borrowers to demand larger quantities of money and credit, an outcome that could account for the continued strong demand for credit at record nominal interest rates and help to explain the problems the Federal Reserve had in controlling the monetary aggregates in earlier months.

Our final assessment on the matter of the appropriate rate of money expansion will have to await the announcement by the Federal Reserve of its new money growth targets and the meaning of those targets in the context of the relationship between the old and the new monetary aggregates and between the aggregates and GNP.

[Inflation]

Conventional macroeconomic policies are incapable of working a quick fix on our inflation problem. We can lick the inflation problem only gradually — through the use of *steady* policies and through a very gradual reduction in the growth of the money supply from the high rates registered in years past. Monetary policy, in general, should be neither overly expansionary nor overly contractionary, nor should it be erratic. In the past, we pursued policies that were too expansionary at first; when accelerating inflation reared its ugly head, we slammed on the brakes hard; inflation didn't decline much but output and employment did, so we pumped up the economy again for yet another repeat performance. As noted before, this roller coaster approach has caused a secular upward ratcheting of our rate of inflation. It is time we learned from our past mistakes.

One final problem area concerns the conduct of monetary policy in the face of downward pressures on the foreign exchange value of the dollar.

We should not sacrifice our long-term economic objectives for the purpose of attempting to maintain the value of the dollar in the short run. Indeed, it was precisely to avoid the need to sacrifice domestic economic objectives that made the abandonment of fixed rates of exchange an attractive option years ago.

Recommendation No. 6

The Committee sees no need to divert monetary policy from domestic goals to secure international objectives other than in truly exceptional circumstances. We are firmly convinced that the Committee's recommendations for monetary and fiscal policy will work to raise productivity and lower inflation in the United States, outcomes that will ultimately result in greater stability for the dollar internationally.

We fully recognize that the key currency role of the dollar imposes on the United States an obligation to ensure its stability. But that obligation is not ours alone; it is an obligation that must be shared by all the major industrialized countries. The key requirement that needs to be met to bring about a more stable dollar is the effective synchronization of macroeconomic policies and performances. Absent the required degree of coordination, there can be little hope of greater long-run exchange rate stability.

['Floating']

We are often told that it is unrealistic to expect the major industrialized countries to coordinate their economic policies in the manner required to ensure exchange rate stability, that to insist upon highly coordinated economic policies would necessitate that they each sacrifice the realization of their domestic goals, an outcome they would all find unacceptable. The alternative these critics suggest is a return to some more stable system of exchange rates, one that is more heavily managed than the current system. We disagree. In our estimation floating is required precisely because the industrialized economies have failed to achieve the necessary degree of coordination. Indeed, in the absence of synchronized macroeconomic policies and performances, a fixed or near-fixed exchange rate system would foster the development of growing payments imbalances, the correction of which would necessitate the use of trade and capital restrictions or the use of restrictive macroeconomic policies, or both.

We do *not* view floating as a panacea for the world's economic problems. But floating is important because it can facilitate the process of balance-of-payments adjustment by providing time for governments to correct domestic imbalances without resort to trade and capital restrictions or inappropriate macroeconomic policies.

Recommendation No. 7

The system of floating exchange rates, with periodic intervention to counter disorderly markets, should be retained. Under present world conditions, floating appears to be the only viable approach. In order to achieve greater exchange stability, we urge the Administration to continue to press for greater international coordination of macroeconomic policies.

Macroeconomic Policy Objectives: An Overview

The American people have every right to be thoroughly dissatisfied with the performance of our economy — both past and prospective. We have not been successful in our efforts to contain inflation. On the contrary, our inflation problem has worsened. We have not solved our unemployment problem. Indeed, for huge segments of the American population — most notably blacks, Hispanics, and teenagers generally — the American dream of steady, meaningful employment at high wages is nothing more than a hopeless myth. To be sure, the employment gains registered in the past several years have been truly impressive. But these employment increases have not been matched by a rising standard of living for the average American worker. The reason is the fall-off in the growth of labor productivity.

In our view, the American people are not unreasonable in demanding a reduction in the unemployment rate to 4 percent or less, a decline in the rate of inflation to something on the order of 3 percent annually and an increase in their living standards.

It would be irresponsible in the extreme to seek solutions to our problems by forcing the American people to suffer through yet another period of vicious "stagflation" characterized by continued rapid inflation, lengthened unemployment lines, and reduced levels of real production. Macroeconomic policy must be directed more toward the supply side of the economy, toward an expansion of our Nation's productive potential in a manner that raises dramatically the growth of American labor productivity. To accomplish this we need to step up sharply our Nation's rate of capital formation. Specific policies targeted at enhancing investment constitute only part of the answer, and not necessarily the most important part. Steady real growth and a lower rate of inflation are essential components of this process.

The emphasis that we accord to the supply side of the economy is important for yet another reason. The capacity of our economic system to absorb the huge costs imposed on us by the OPEC oil producers

is severely limited when our capacity for growth is limited. It is undoubtedly easier to absorb the required adjustment costs when real
production — and real production per worker — is advancing at a
rapid rate. Under those circumstances, the economy could adjust without
the need to suffer actual declines in consumable output. In the absence
of rapid real growth, purchasing power must decline for some or all
citizens. The strain this puts on our economic, social and political
fabric is all too clear. The need for a growth buffer is apparent.

Finally, as a further means of bolstering the supply side of the economy,
we need to go beyond the macroeconomic policy recommendations set
forth above, so as to deal with the real structural maladies that plague
our economy. We need better programs that address specifically the
problems of the structurally unemployed, programs forged on the basis
of a close partnership between the public and private sectors. We need
to develop an effective long-term energy strategy aimed at reducing
our vulnerability to the price and production policies of OPEC. We
must do more to enhance the development and construction of high
productivity technologies in America's businesses. We need to develop
more efficient methods for achieving the reallocation of our Nation's
resources away from declining low-productivity industries to those high
technology consumer and capital goods industries at the leading edge
of the product cycle. We need to provide more adequate transportation
networks and public utilities in order to make our industrial centers
more efficient locations for industry. And we need to shift out of, not
protect, those industries that cannot successfully compete with foreign
firms. One alternative to protectionism is to invite foreign companies
to open their high-productivity plants here. . . .

March

U.S. VOTE AT UNITED NATIONS ON ISRAELI SETTLEMENTS

March 1-3, 1980

The United States joined the 14 other members of the United Nations Security Council March 1 in adopting a resolution calling on Israel to dismantle its settlements on the West Bank and the Gaza Strip — areas occupied by Israel since the 1967 war in the Middle East. Observers saw the U.S. vote as a major stiffening of policy toward Israel.

Then, in an extraordinary and diplomatically embarrassing turnabout, President Carter March 3 issued a statement repudiating the U.S. vote in the Security Council. The president said U.N. Ambassador Donald McHenry had cast the vote as a result of a failure in communication between officials in Washington, D.C., and the U.S. delegation at the United Nations in New York.

Carter said that "the vote . . . does not represent a change in our position regarding the Israeli settlements in the occupied areas nor regarding the status of Jerusalem."

Explanation for Vote

The Department of State March 4 issued a brief statement declaring that Secretary of State Cyrus R. Vance accepted "responsibility for the failure in communications" that led to U.S. approval of the Security Council resolution.

Many diplomats at the United Nations and other observers, however, questioned the Carter administration version of what went wrong. In the days and weeks immediately after the unusual reversal, newspaper articles on the matter generally pointed to a misunderstanding between Carter, who was spending the March 1-2 weekend at Camp David in the Maryland mountains, and Vance, who was in Washington.

But the facts behind the vote and the embarrassing reversal two days later remained in considerable doubt. The March 1 vote represented the first time the United States had voted against Israel in the Security Council on the settlements issue. Previously, the United States had abstained from voting on the issue, expressing its opposition to new settlements directly to the Israeli government.

Diplomatic Gaffe

The president's repudiation of the vote caused consternation and dismay in foreign capitals and created a domestic political furor at home.

Already under pressure to act in the Iranian hostage crisis and to deal decisively with the Soviet invasion of Afghanistan, the Carter Administration, in the U.N. vote, gave the impression of ineptness and indecision. (Iran, Historic Documents of 1979, p. 867; Afghanistan, Historic Documents of 1979, p. 965)

U.S. Jewish leaders sharply criticized Carter for permitting the vote in the first place, and spokesmen in the Arab world expressed their distrust of the Carter administration after the reversal. In the words of Ambassador McHenry, the United States had gained "the worst of all possible worlds."

Members of the U.S. Senate called for hearings. Finally, the incident jarred delicate peace negotiations involving the West Bank and the Gaza Strip among Israel, Egypt and the United States.

Security Council Resolution

The U.N. Security Council resolution, which the United States initially approved, deplored Israel's decision "to officially support Israeli settlement in the Palestinian and other Arab territories occupied since 1967." The resolution said that Israeli measures taken "to change the physical character, demographic composition, institutional structure or status of the Palestinian or other Arab territories ... including Jerusalem ... have no legal validity. ..."

The resolution also urged Security Council members not to give Israel any assistance in connection with the settlements in the occupied Arab territory and ordered a three-member fact-finding commission to continue its investigation of the settlements problem and report back to the council before Sept. 1.

The resolution called on Israel to abide by the previously passed resolutions concerning Jerusalem and particularly to "respect and guarantee religious freedoms and practices [in Jerusalem] and other holy places as well as the integrity of places of worship."

After McHenry had cast the U.S. vote, he said in a formal statement, "We regard settlements in the occupied territories as illegal under international law, and we consider them to be an obstacle to the successful outcome to the current negotiations [between Egypt and Israel] which are aimed at a comprehensive, just and lasting peace in the Middle East."

McHenry Role

Before the Security Council vote March 1, Ambassador McHenry had successfully worked to delete from the resolution a paragraph that the United States found particularly objectionable. The paragraph implied criticism of Israel's administration of the holy places in Jerusalem.

McHenry also was under instructions to try to rid the resolution of language calling for Israel to dismantle its settlements. He informed Vance Feb. 29 that he had been successful with regard to the paragraph on the holy places in Jerusalem and that he proposed to deal with the settlements issue by means of a statement of reservation after the vote.

According to newspaper reports, Vance concluded that the final draft of the resolution was in accord with U.S. policy and in a telephone call to Carter told the president that it was. Carter, without reading the final version of the resolution, then authorized the vote.

The situation was further obscured by the belief of many observers that President Carter and other U.S. officials had been looking for a way to send Israel a clear signal of U.S. disapproval of Israeli settlement policy.

Arab Anger

When President Carter returned to the White House from Camp David March 3, Vice President Walter F. Mondale and other officials told him that the vote had created an uproar. After a drafting session Monday afternoon, the White House issued Carter's statement repudiating the vote.

Spokesmen in the Arab world reacted with incredulity and anger. For example, in Kuwait, the U.S. ambassador, Francois M. Dickman, was summoned to the foreign ministry to hear that country's "condemnation" of the Carter administration's change of mind. Members *of delegations at the United Nations were reported as reacting with scorn and dismay.*

The Israeli Cabinet March 4 denounced what it termed the "repugnant resolution" approved by the Security Council.

Domestic Reaction

Leaders of Jewish organizations in the United States responded skeptically to the president's disavowal of the U.S. vote. Carter assured the leaders at later meetings that U.S. policy toward Israel had not changed. Still, Howard Squadron, president of the American Jewish Congress, said, "We are not satisfied with the administration's confession of error."

Sen. Edward M. Kennedy, D-Mass., opposing Carter in Democratic primary elections, said in a campaign speech March 4 that the administration's handling of the vote "must put into serious question the decision-making process of the Administration and our commitment to Israel." Political observers attributed the margin of Kennedy's victory over the president in the New York Democratic primary March 25 as reflecting Carter's loss of support among Jewish voters.

> *Following are the texts of the U.N. Security Council resolution adopted March 1, 1980, deploring Israeli settlements in the occupied Arab territories; Carter's statement March 3, 1980, repudiating the U.S. affirmative vote in the Security Council; and excerpts from President Carter's news conference March 14, 1980, explaining the policy-making process leading to the U.N. vote and its subsequent repudiation. (Boldface headings in brackets have been added by Congressional Quarterly to highlight the organization of the text.):*

U.N. RESOLUTION

THE SECURITY COUNCIL,

TAKING NOTE of the reports of the Commission of the Security Council established under Resolution 446 (1979) to examine the situation relating to settlements in the Arab territories occupied since 1967, including Jerusalem, contained in documents S/13450 and Corr. 1 and S/13679,

TAKING NOTE also of letters from the Permanent Representative of Jordan (S/13801) and the Permanent Representative of Morocco, Chairman of the Islamic Group (S/13802),

STRONGLY DEPLORING the refusal by Israel to cooperate with the Commission and regretting its formal rejection of Resolutions 446 (1979) and 452 (1979),

AFFIRMING ONCE MORE that the Fourth Geneva Convention relative to the Protection of Civilian Persons in Time of War of 12 August 1949 is applicable to the Arab territories occupied by Israel since 1967, including Jerusalem,

DEPLORING the decision of the Government of Israel to officially support Israeli settlement in the Palestinian and other Arab territories occupied since 1967,

DEEPLY CONCERNED over the practices of the Israeli authorities in implementing that settlement policy in the occupied Arab territories, including Jerusalem, and its consequences for the local Arab and Palestinian population,

TAKING INTO ACCOUNT the need to consider measures for the impartial protection of private and public land and property, and water resources,

BEARING IN MIND the specific status of Jerusalem and, in particular, the need for protection and preservation of the unique spiritual and religious dimension of the holy places in the city,

DRAWING ATTENTION to the grave consequences which the settlement policy is bound to have on any attempt to reach a comprehensive, just and lasting peace in the Middle East,

RECALLING pertinent Security Council resolutions, specifically Resolutions 237 (1967) of 14 June 1967, 252 (1968) of 21 May 1968, 267 (1969) of 3 July 1969, 271 (1969) of 15 September 1969 and 298 (1971) of 25 September 1971, as well as the consensus statement made by the President of the Security Council on 11 November 1976,

HAVING INVITED Mr. Fahad Kawasmeh, Mayor of Al Khalil (Hebron), in the occupied territory, to supply it with information pursuant to rule 39 of the provisional rules of procedure,

1. COMMENDS the work done by the Commission in preparing the report contained in document S/13679;

2. ACCEPTS the conclusions and recommendations contained in the above-mentioned report of the Commission;

3. CALLS UPON all parties, particularly the Government of Israel, to cooperate with the Commission;

4. STRONGLY DEPLORES the decision of Israel to prohibit the free travel of Mayor Fahad Kawasmeh in order to appear before the Security Council, and requests Israel to permit his free travel to the United Nations Headquarters for that purpose;

5. DETERMINES that all measures taken by Israel to change the physical character, demographic composition, institutional structure or status of the Palestinian and other Arab territories occupied since 1967, including Jerusalem, or any part thereof, have no legal validity and that Israel's policy and practices of settling parts of its population and new immigrants in those territories constitute a flagrant violation

of the Fourth Geneva Convention relative to the Protection of Civilian Persons in Time of War and also constitute a serious obstruction to achieving a comprehensive, just and lasting peace in the Middle East;

6. STRONGLY DEPLORES the continuation and persistence of Israel in pursuing those policies and practices and calls upon the Government and people of Israel to rescind those measures, to dismantle the existing settlements and in particular to cease, on an urgent basis, the establishment, construction and planning of settlements in the Arab territories occupied since 1967, including Jerusalem;

CALLS UPON *Israel to abide by the pertinent Security Council resolutions concerning Jerusalem, in particular Resolution 252 (1968) and to respect and guarantee religious freedoms and practices in Jerusalem and other holy places in the occupied Arab territories as well as the integrity of places of religious worship;*

7. CALLS UPON all States not to provide Israel with any assistance to be used specifically in connection with settlements in the occupied territories;

8. REQUESTS the Commission to continue to examine the situation relating to settlements in the Arab territories occupied since 1967, including Jerusalem, to investigate the reported serious depletion of natural resources, particularly the water resources, with a view to insuring the protection of those important natural resources of the territories under occupation, and to keep under close scrutiny the implementation of the present resolution;

9. REQUESTS the Commission to report to the Security Council before 1 September 1980, and decides to convene at the earliest possible date thereafter in order to consider the report and the full implementation of the present resolution.

CARTER'S MARCH 3 STATEMENT

I want to make it clear that the vote of the United States in the Security Council of the United Nations does not represent a change in our position regarding the Israeli settlements in the occupied areas nor regarding the status of Jerusalem.

While our opposition to the establishment of the Israeli settlements is longstanding and well-known, we made strenuous efforts to eliminate the language with reference to the dismantling of settlements in the resolution. This call for dismantling was neither proper nor practical. We believe that the future disposition of existing settlements must be determined during the current Autonomy Negotiations.

As to Jerusalem, we strongly believe that Jerusalem should be undivided, with free access to the holy places for all faiths, and that its status should be determined in the negotiations for a comprehensive peace settlement.

The United States vote in the United Nations was approved with the understanding that all references to Jerusalem would be deleted. The failure to communicate this clearly resulted in a vote in favor of the resolution rather than abstention.

I want to reiterate in the most unequivocal of terms that in the Autonomy Negotiations and in other fora, the United States will neither support nor accept any position that might jeopardize Israel's vital security interests. Our commitment to Israel's security and well-being remains unqualified and unshakable.

MARCH 14 NEWS CONFERENCE

Q. Mr. President, is Israel keeping faith with the Camp David accords and the autonomy talks, when by government policy it continues to confiscate the land of Palestinians?

The President. There is nothing specifically in the Camp David accords concerning the settlements themselves. There is an agreement in the treaty between Israel and Egypt about settlements that have been established in the Sinai region, which is Egyptian territory. I might say concerning that, that our policy is set by me, as President. There has been no change in our policy. That policy is guided by U.N. Resolution 242 and 338, the basis of all our negotiations; by every word in the Camp David accords, signed by me on behalf of our Nation; and by Begin and Sadat on behalf of Israel and Egypt. We intend to carry out that agreement.

[Autonomy]

Right now we are indulged in some very difficult but very important discussions and negotiations to establish full autonomy on the West Bank, Gaza area. I believe that these discussions can be successful. It's crucial to our own Nation's security that they be successful, that we have peace in the Middle East; and, it's, I think, crucial to the whole region that these discussions be successful.

I might add one other point. It's not easy. We've had tedious negotiations at Camp David. We had tedious negotiations almost exactly a year ago, when we finally concluded and signed the Mideast peace treaty. Our principles are well known by Prime Minister Begin and by President Sadat, and I stay constantly in touch with them and our negotiators to make sure that we are successful.

I believe that we will have peace in the Middle East, with a secure Israel behind recognized borders, with the Palestinian question being resolved in all its aspects, and with peace between Israel and her neighbors.

Q. You say the policy is set by you.

The President. Yes.

[U.N. Vote]

Q. And this is a question about the recent mix-up on the U.N. resolution. My question really goes to process. The resolution was not the resolution that you wanted. Are you the only one who can determine that it's not the resolution you want? Does your staff not know when it's not a resolution that you want, or is it possible that some of your foreign policy advisers are trying to make policy for you?

The President. I don't think anybody in my administration doubts that I'm the one that sets the policy. The U.N. resolution, as it was passed, was not in accordance with the policy that I have established. It was not in accordance with the agreements that I had made with Prime Minister Begin, well understood by President Sadat.

We had agreed among us that we did not approve, as an American Government, of the settlements on the West Bank and Gaza area — that they were an obstacle to peace. But we also had agreed that during the time of the negotiations, we would not call for the dismantling of existing settlements. That was to be resolved as an issue in the ongoing negotiations.

Also, President Sadat, Prime Minister Begin, and I agreed on a paragraph in the Camp David accords concerning Jerusalem. It called for, and we still believe, that there should be an undivided Jerusalem, but that those who look upon those places in Jerusalem as holy places, should have unimpeded access to them for worship.

This resolution in the U.N. violated those two very important and basic principles. Those issues have not yet been resolved. There is nothing in this resolution at the U.N. that established the permanent status of the West Bank and Gaza area. That will be established after a 5-year interval period, during which full autonomy is enjoyed by the residents of the area. So, the resolution was in violation of my policy.

[Secretary Vance]

I might say that I have absolute confidence in Secretary Vance. I have seen him days and days and weeks negotiating to achieve the security of Israel and the peace of Israel. It was an honest breakdown in communications between me and the United Nations. I'm responsible for anything that goes wrong in this Government, and I'm also responsible, on occasion, for things that go right. Secretary Vance is responsible for the State Department. But to say exactly how the communications broke down is very difficult to do.

But I made it known as quickly as I discovered it, that this resolution did violate the policy and disavowed our vote for it. . . .

CARTER ANTI-INFLATION PACKAGE
March 14, 1980

By mid-February it was clear that inflation, rather than abating, was increasing in the United States at a dangerous rate and that a predicted recession with the potential to cool the surge in prices had failed to materialize. Concern that inflation might indeed be almost out of control deepened with the release of figures showing that the Consumer Price Index jumped 1.4 percent in January, for an annual rate of about 18 percent.

For three weeks beginning Feb. 24 President Carter conducted an extraordinary review at the White House to help him decide on actions to check the rapidly rising prices. On March 14, in a televised speech in the East Room before Cabinet officials, members of Congress and business leaders, and later the same day at a news conference, the president announced his new plan for fighting inflation.

The most significant elements of the president's package were a balanced budget in fiscal 1981, sharp curbs on credit and a fee on imported oil designed to raise gasoline prices 10 cents a gallon. Although economists and financial and business leaders differed widely in their assessment of the plan, most believed that it would bring about a mild recession. And a recession, it was hoped, would dampen the inflationary surge.

Background

Inflation had been singled out as the country's most serious economic problem in the annual report of the president's Council of Economic Advisers. The report, released Jan. 30, said, "The control and reduction

243

of inflation is the nation's highest economic priority, requiring fiscal and monetary policies that restrain demand not only in the immediate future but over an extended period." (Economic report, p. 159)

President Carter's economists had prepared the report before the sharp rise in prices in the early weeks of 1980. Prices that had soared in January remained at the same high level through February.

Only a few months earlier, in October 1979, the Federal Reserve Board had responded dramatically to inflation and a dollar crisis abroad by taking strong steps to slow down the creation of money. The pledge of the Federal Reserve Board chairman, Paul A. Volcker, to focus on the money supply was especially pleasing to monetarist economists who had been urging such a policy for years. But the Fed's actions, while contributing to the strength of the dollar overseas, had yet to leave their mark on the inflationary trend. (1979 Fed action, Historic Documents of 1979, p. 771)

Generally, observers said, President Carter's March 14 economic package was aimed at altering a growing expectation that inflation was not only deeply entrenched but also, perhaps, endless. A number of observers also believed that, specifically, it was designed to steady the long-term bond market where prices had been dropping sharply.

Balanced Budget

The president recommended a reduction of about $13 billion in the fiscal 1981 budget, bringing it into balance by striking out some new proposals and cutting back others. He also proposed a reduction of $2 billion in the current fiscal 1980 budget.

The reductions would come, Carter said, in almost every area of the fiscal 1981 budget "not vital to national security." He also said that he would use authority under the Budget Reform Act of 1974 to rescind or defer fiscal 1980 spending. While the Defense Department would be immune from cuts, the president said he would require the Pentagon to "offset a large part of the cost increases the department now faces."

The actual impact of the budget cuts, in view of the magnitude of the fiscal 1981 budget ($611-$613 billion), was seen as uncertain. Since he postponed specifying most of the budget cuts, Carter left himself open to the charge that he preferred not to disclose them until after the New York state Democratic primary on March 25. (Fiscal 1981 budget, p. 109)

Restraints on Credit

The part of Carter's anti-inflation package with the most bite, at least in the near term, involved the placing by the president and Federal

Reserve Board of restraints on the growth of business and consumer credit. To impose the controls, the president invoked the Credit Control Act of 1969, which had lain unused since its enactment.

Briefly, the Federal Reserve Board was to require a special set-aside of 15 percent for lenders on credit cards, check credit overdraft plans and unsecured personal loans. The Fed also was to hold down the expansion of money market funds — which in the previous five years, had become a $60 billion investment phenomenon. That was to be achieved through a special deposit requirement of 15 percent on increases in the funds' total assets above the level on March 14.

Finally, authority was granted to restrain credit extension by commercial banks that were not members of the Federal Reserve System through a special deposit requirement of 10 percent on increases in their managed liabilities, that is, large certificates of deposit. The president also pledged to cut federal loans and loan guarantees by $4 billion in fiscal 1981.

Oil Import Fee

As a measure to cut inflation over the longer term, the president said he would impose a $4.62-a-barrel oil import "conservation" fee, equal to about 10 cents a gallon, "to cut down on the use of gasoline." In his March 14 news conference, Carter pointed out that "the price of imported oil has more than doubled in the last 12 months. Last year's increase ... alone was greater than all other increases ... since oil was first discovered many years ago."

President Carter said his action would reduce oil imports by 100,000 barrels a day by the end of 1980 "and later, by as much as 250,000 barrels a day." He said he intended, with the approval of Congress, to replace the oil import fee with a new 10 cent tax on gasoline. But Congress rejected a similar proposal in 1977.

Reaction

Much of the negative reaction to Carter's program came from the nation's financial community, and it was directed particularly at the imposition of credit restraints. In an editorial titled "Credit Cop Capers," The Wall Street Journal *said, "No one at the Fed or anywhere else is wise enough to decide who should, or should not, get credit. . . ."*

In a similar vein, Walter B. Wriston, chairman and chief executive officer of Citibank in New York, interviewed on the CBS-TV program, "Face the Nation," termed the Credit Control Act of 1969 invoked by Carter "a political document and a very dangerous one" because it permitted credit "allocation."

On the other hand, Otto Eckstein, professor of economics at Harvard University and president of an economic forecasting firm, said that in the existing "miasma of doubt, we may fail to see that a historical turning point is really possibly at hand."

Eckstein said that while no one would assert the Carter program was the whole answer, the president had "after many false starts, reversed the thrust of budget policy and . . . encouraged the Federal Reserve to bring credit growth under control. The recession will buy time and provide the opportunity to get the development process going again."

Following are the text of President Carter's address on economic policy and excerpts from his news conference, March 14, 1980. (Boldface headings in brackets have been added by Congressional Quarterly to highlight the organization of the texts.):

CARTER ANTI-INFLATION ADDRESS

This afternoon I have a very serious message to deliver to our country. Present high inflation threatens the economic security of our Nation. Since my economic and budget reports were made to the Congress and to the people in January, rapid changes in world events and economic prospects have made it necessary to intensify our anti-inflation fight.

In the last 8 weeks inflation rates and interest rates have surged to unprecedented heights. This is a worldwide problem. During the last 2 reporting months, for instance, the increases in the wholesale price index in Italy, Great Britain, and Japan have all increased more than 25 percent. And even in Germany, West Germany, where the prime consideration, equal to national defense, is inflation, the wholesale price index has increased more than 13 percent.

The inflation that we face today is deep-rooted. Its many causes have been built up over more than a decade. The most important of these causes are the soaring prices for energy throughout the world, declining productivity growth in our Nation, and our failure in government and as individuals, as an entire American society, to live within our means.

Inflation is a symptom of economic distress. The truth is that we have inflation because our economy is not productive enough to do all the things that we demand of it. We want it to give us higher incomes, bigger profits, and bigger government programs in the areas where we have a special interest. The Federal Government must stop spending money we do not have and borrowing to make up the difference.

Our whole society, the entire American family, must try harder than ever to live within its means. As individuals and as a nation, we must begin to spend money according to what we can afford in the long run and not according to what we can borrow in the short run.

There are no quick answers to inflation, and, above all, there certainly are not any painless answers. If there were any such solutions, any quick or painless solutions, they would have been implemented long ago. We cannot abolish inflation overnight by just passing a law against it. Only a long-term effort, with a partnership of business and labor and individual citizens and government at all levels, can succeed in bringing this serious problem under control.

This dangerous situation calls for urgent measures. We must act firmly and decisively, and we must act now. We must remove any doubt about our Nation's will to take the painful steps that will be required to control inflation. We cannot accept high rates of inflation as a permanent fact of American life.

[Five Components]

The intensive anti-inflation program that I'm announcing today involves five major components: first, discipline by reductions in the Federal Government; second, discipline by restraints on credit; third, discipline in wage and price actions; fourth, discipline by greater conservation of energy; and fifth, structural changes over a long period of time to encourage productivity, savings, and research and development.

Let me discuss these one by one. First, the budget. I will soon set forth a revised budget for fiscal year 1981, beginning next October 1. It will be a balanced budget. And the Congress and I are determined to keep this budget in balance.

Since the last balanced budget 12 years ago — and there has been only one balanced budget since 1961 — we have added almost one-half trillion dollars to our Nation's debt. In 1981 we will thus achieve an objective that has escaped us, eluded our country in good times and in bad times, and that is a balanced budget.

By the end of this month, I will send to Congress a major revision in both my 1980 and 1981 budgets. It will propose significant reductions of budget authority from the current proposals in order to cut spending this fiscal year and next fiscal year.

I will cut spending in the 1981 budget by more than $13 billion. To reach that goal, I will defer or reduce or cancel most of the new or the expanded programs which were originally proposed in the 1981 budget. I will cut expenditures for personnel, operating, and maintenance throughout the Government. I will freeze Federal civilian employment immediately and maintain rigid ceilings, so that by the end of October of this year, we will have 20,000 fewer Federal employees on the payroll. I will reduce ongoing spending programs throughout the Federal Government.

I urgently request from the Congress the savings and the revenue measures in the budget that I proposed back in January. I want to stress in particular the legislation needed to hold down hospital costs, to reform Federal pay, and to speed up collections in revenue. When budget cuts demand sacrifices from many Americans, it's intolerable for some to evade prompt payment of the taxes which they owe. I will send to the Congress legislation to make sure that taxes that are owed on interests and on dividends are actually paid and paid in a timely manner.

[Defense Spending]

I will maintain my commitment, through all of this procedure, to a strong defense and to the level of real growth in defense spending which I committed on the honor of our Nation to our NATO Allies. But the Defense Department will not be immune from budget austerity. In particular, I will require that Department to make savings that do not affect adversely our military preparedness. I consider the proposed defense budget adequate to meet our Nation's needs. We must maintain budget restraint and fiscal responsibility in every single agency of the Federal Government.

Based on our estimates of economic and budgetary developments, the action that I have just described will produce a balanced budget in 1981. Of course, in our system the Congress controls the power of the purse. The recent intense efforts, one of the most inspiring demonstrations of congressional leadership that I have ever seen, and my close cooperation and consultation with these congressional leaders, have all convinced me that the Congress will indeed enact and maintain a balanced budget that I have just described to you. But to ensure that outcome I will use every power at my command, as President, as I did last week on a popular bill.

I will veto any legislation that exceeds the spending limits which I consider to be inconsistent [sic] with a balanced budget. I will use my full powers under the 1974 Budget Reform Act to hold down Federal spending, including some expenditures which have already been authorized by the Congress and for which money has been appropriated.

If, during the course of the year, I judge these actions and powers which I've just described as being insufficient, I will ask the Congress for a temporary grant of extraordinary powers to ensure that spending by the Federal Government of our country is contained.

Cutting back Federal spending to match revenue is not a cure-all, but it is an essential first step. The sources of inflation are far too complex to be treated by a single remedy. But nothing will work in an overall anti-inflation program until the Federal Government has demonstrated to the American people that it can discipline its own spending and its own borrowing — not just as a 1-year exercise but as a long-term policy. Together, we will do just that. We will dispel the notions that Federal budget deficits must always be with us.

I want to be absolutely honest about these budget cuts. We have been cutting out waste and fraud and trimming the bureaucratic fat.

But this time, there will also have to be cuts in good and worthwhile programs — programs which I support very strongly. In this critical situation we must all look beyond some of our most worthwhile immediate aims to the overriding permanent needs of our Nation.

[Restraints on Credit]

Our second area of action is restraining the growth of credit. Just as our governments have been borrowing to make ends meet, so have individual Americans been borrowing to make ends meet. When we try to beat inflation with borrowed money, we just make the problem worse.

Inflation is fed by credit-financed spending. Consumers have gone in debt too heavily. The savings rate in our Nation is now much lower than it has been for more than 25 years. Less than 3 percent of the earnings of Americans now go into savings. As inflationary expectations have been worsened, business and other borrowers are also tempted to use credit to finance speculative ventures as well as productive activities.

The traditional tools used by the Federal Reserve to control money and credit expansion are a basic part of the fight against inflation. But in present circumstances, these tools need to be reinforced so that effective constraint can be achieved in ways that spread the burden reasonably and fairly.

I'm therefore using my power under the Credit Control Act of 1969 to authorize the Federal Reserve to impose new restraints on the growth of credit on a limited and on a carefully targeted basis. Under this authority the Federal Reserve will first establish controls for credit cards and other unsecured loans but not for secured loans on homes, automobiles, and other durable goods, and second, to restrain credit extensions by commercial banks that are not members of the Federal Reserve System and also by certain other money market lenders.

The Chairman of the Federal Reserve will announce a voluntary program effective immediately to restrain excessive growth in loans by larger banks and by other lenders. At the same time, the program will encourage the flow of available credit supplies for investment and for other productive uses. Special attention will be given to the particular needs of small businesses, farmers, and homeowners, and I support these initiatives by the Federal Reserve.

These carefully targeted actions will not damage the productive capacity of our Nation. To help curtail the excessive uses of credit and by dampening inflation they should, along with the budget measures that I have described, speed prospects for reducing the strains which presently exist in our financial markets.

In addition, I'm taking steps to reduce the extension of credit by the Federal Government. Federal loans and loan guarantees will be cut by nearly $4 billion in fiscal year 1981. As a longer run measure, I urge Congress to institute the credit budget which I proposed in January. It will help us control more effectively the loans and the loan guarantees provided by the Federal Government.

[Wage and Price Standards]

Our third area of action is the voluntary wage and price standards. I do not have authority to impose mandatory controls. I will oppose such authority being approved at all by the Congress. We will not impose mandatory wage and price controls. Government wage and price controls have never worked in peacetime. They create unfair economic distortions, and they hurt productivity. These results always force price controls first to be eased and then to be dismantled while inflation roars ahead.

Controls create inequities, and the greatest inequity is their effect on the average American family. As even the most ardent advocates of mandatory wage and price controls will admit, the cost of vital necessities such as food and fuel would be passed on to those who are living on frozen wages and on fixed incomes.

We simply cannot outlaw inflation with a massive Federal bureaucracy or wish it away with a magic formula. On the other hand, voluntary wage and price restraints offer the flexibility we need to deal with our complex economy.

The Council on Wage and Price Stability has just issued revised pay standards and confirmed an extension of the price standards. The new pay standards were developed from the recommendation of a tripartite advisory committee, with members from business, labor, and the public. The committee unanimously recommended standards for pay increases in the rnage of 7-1/2 to 9-1/2 percent and stated that under normal circumstances increases should average 8-1/2 percent. I'm determined to meet this goal.

In the face of last year's 13-percent increase in the Consumer Price Index, and the even higher rate of recent months, this unanimous recommendation of the Pay Advisory Committee, designed to produce an average wage and salary increase of 8-1/2 percent, reflects a commendable spirit of restraint and cooperation. With business, labor, and public support, we can meet this goal of restraint.

I'm sharply expanding the price and wage monitoring activities of the Council on Wage and Price Stability. Its current staff of 80 people will be more than tripled. The Council will then establish teams of experts to track wage and price developments in each major industry. The Council will meet with leaders from specific industries to secure their cooperation in this fight against inflation. Where necessary, we will ask large firms for prenotification of significant price increases. We will investigate wage and price increases that seem out of line with the standards. I mean to apply these standards with vigor and toughness to both business and labor.

[Energy Program]

Our fourth area of action is energy. The plain truth is that we will never be completely strong at home or secure abroad until we've at last solved our Nation's excessive dependence on imported oil.

This year, we expect to spend $90 billion of America's hard-earned income [in] foreign countries to buy their oil. The price of imported oil has more than doubled — more than doubled in the last 12 months. Last year's increase alone in 1979 was greater than all other increases combined since the oil embargo of 1973. In fact, last year alone the price of oil increased more than it has since oil was first discovered.

We must forge ahead toward the goal that I set last July — cutting in half the amount of oil that we will import in 1990. To do this, we will require increased conservation and increased production of domestic oil, natural gas, and coal, and the rapid development of alternative energy supplies. For 3 years, as every Member of the Congress well knows, I have fought for a national energy policy to achieve each of these goals, and we have worked closely together. Today, at long last, we are close to enacting such a policy into law, and we must not falter now.

I'm asking the Congress to finish without delay the three essential elements of the energy policy. First, the windfall profits tax; second, the energy security corporation; and third, the energy mobilization board. These bills are the cornerstone for energy security, for our national security, and for our fight against inflation.

I have recently submitted to the Congress a proposal to conserve energy in electric powerplants and to convert them from oil to coal. This legislation, also, must be passed promptly.

[Gasoline Tax]

But we can never solve our energy dependence unless we meet the problem of America's extravagant gasoline use. Gasoline is the most important and the most wasted petroleum product in the United States. It accounts for some 40 percent of all the petroleum we use in our country. In almost every other industrial country, the average amount of gasoline used by each citizen is much less and the price for gasoline is much higher — more than twice as high in most other industrialized countries than it is today in the United States. Americans have done well in the past year in gasoline conservation. But if we're going to reduce further our dependence on foreign oil we must do more.

Therefore, I am exercising my Presidential authority to impose a gasoline conservation fee on imported oil. This will amount to about 10 cents a gallon and will be imposed only on gasoline. The fee will not add to the cost of any other petroleum product, and it will not add at all to the profit of the oil companies. It should reduce imports by 100,000 barrels per day in 1 year, and within about 3 years, it will reduce the imports of oil from foreign countries by more than 250,000 barrels every day. I will submit to Congress a request for a specific gasoline tax, in the same amount exactly, which will replace the conservation fee.

The funds from this gasoline conservation charge will be held in reserve or used to reduce the national debt. I do not intend to use these revenues to balance the budget or as a substitute for necessary spending cuts. That would not contribute substantially to the control of inflation. But these revenues, which will begin occurring immediately, will give the budget, which will be balanced, a margin of safety, ensuring that it will remain in balance if conditions or estimates change in a way that we do not anticipate.

We can now set new State targets for gasoline consumption which will, within a year, reduce consumption by 400,000 barrels per day. This action also underscores a commitment to greater conservation that our friends abroad, both the producing countries and the consuming countries, can both join and support.

Finally, the Secretary of Energy is pursuing an intensified national energy conservation plan. Our aim is to involve every level of government, business and labor — in fact, every single citizen in our country — in conserving American energy.

[Structural Changes]

Our fifth area of action involves long-term structural changes to encourage productivity, savings, and research and development. We must face the fact that over the last 10 years the pace of productivity growth in the United States has slowed sharply. Last year productivity actually declined. This trend is an important long-term factor in inflation. It must be reversed.

I'm asking my Presidential commission on an agenda for the 1980's as part of their work to develop specific recommendations for revitalizing our Nation's economy. Our priority now is to balance the budget, but once these spending limitations have actually been achieved, we can then provide tax relief to encourage investment. Through fiscal discipline today, we can free up resources tomorrow, through tax deductions, for the productivity increase which our Nation needs.

This discipline which I've described to you will not be easy. Our new budgets will be very tight. There are some things we cannot afford, at least not right now. But the most important thing we cannot afford is the national delusion which we have been harboring about inflation. We cannot afford the fairytale that inflation can somehow be passed along to the next person or somehow be passed along to the next generation.

The actions I've outlined involve costs. They involve pain. But the cost of acting is far less than the cost of not acting. The temporary pain of inconvenience and discipline is far less for all of us together that the still worst [sic] permanent pain of constantly rising inflation. For all of us, but especially for the most disadvantaged among us, inflation is indeed the most cruel tax of all.

[No Quick Victory]

When we take these necessary steps against inflation, it will not result in a quick victory. Don't look for massive changes next week. Over the next several months inflation is likely to continue at a high level. We must be patient and we must be persistent. But I'm confident that the steps that I've outlined today will make the inflation rate be declining later on this year. As that happens, we can look forward to calmer financial markets and to lower interest rates.

By taking control of this problem — which involves taking control of ourselves — we can put an end to the fear about the future that afflicts so many of our own people and so many of our institutions. In the fight against inflation, what is at stake is more than material wealth or material comfort. What is at stake is whether or not Americans — as a nation and as a people — will retain control of our own destiny.

In crises abroad, we've always shown our ability to respond with steadfastness and with courage. We must now show the same determination, the same national unity, the same national commitment, the same partnership, in meeting the challenge of inflation.

With inflation, as with defense and with energy, our responsibility is clear: to face the world as it is, not to mislead ourselves, to be honest about the hard decisions that are necessary, to make these decisions and with courage carry them out, and to build together a strong and secure and a hopeful future for every American. With proper discipline we will prevail in our fight against inflation.

Thank you very much.

NEWS CONFERENCE

The President. Last night at this time I was participating in a remarkable event, truly historic in the development of our Nation. I was in the Cabinet Room, next to the Oval Office, along with the leadership of the Democrats in the House and the Senate, discussing the features of and the implementation of a comprehensive, anti-inflation program for our Nation. We mutually pledged to assure that this program would be successful, and the Democrats, the leadership, after 10 days of intense discussions and negotiations with my administration, themselves offered adequate cuts in the existing budget to ensure a balanced budget for 1981.

I'm very grateful for this cooperation. And during the same afternoon the Republicans, the leadership there, pledged that if the Democrats would take the leadership they would also cooperate, which I think will ensure that the Congress will guarantee that with our cooperative effort this will be successful.

Just a few hours ago I described the basic elements of this program, to intensify America's battle against inflation. These actions will be painful. They will not work overnight. But they are necessary to preserve the power of the greatest economic nation on Earth.

Inflation is bad in our country, but it's not as bad as that in some of our major allies, Great Britain, Japan, Italy. We have many reasons for this high inflation rate — the unprecedented increase in the price of oil, the fact that we as individuals and a society have tried to beat inflation by borrowing. It's as though we have come to believe that a penny borrowed is a penny earned. Our whole society, beginning with the Federal Government, must live within its means. We must exert discipline on ourselves. We must act decisively, and we must act now. And I will set forth a revised budget for 1981 that will be a balanced budget.

[Budget Cuts]

To achieve this goal I will defer or reduce or cancel many new programs which have been proposed recently to the Congress. I will cut expenditures throughout the Government. I will freeze Federal employment immediately, to cut down the total number of employees on the Federal payroll by at least 20,000 between now and the 1st of October. These budget cuts will be difficult politically and also because there will be inconveniences and disappointments among many people. But some sacrifice now will be much less onerous and burdensome, particularly to the needy among us, than the serious suffering that will occur if we don't arrest the inflationary spirals.

We will have a balanced budget beginning in October. To ensure this goal I will veto any legislation that exceeds our spending limit. I will use my powers under the budget acts to hold down budget-busting appropriations, and, if necessary, I will ask the Congress for additional powers to make sure that these goals are realized.

A balanced budget is not a cure-all, but it's a necessary part of an overall commitment. Without a balanced budget commitment there would be no way to put together a credible anti-inflation program.

The Federal Government simply must accept discipline on itself as an example for others to follow.

Secondly, our governments have been borrowing, but so have people and institutions in our Nation been borrowing too much. So, credit controls will be implemented, as authorized by me and as administered by the Federal Reserve System of our country, to moderate the expansion of credit, with special emphasis provided, however, to meet the needs of small businesses, farmers, and those who would buy homes.

Third, we'll have improved compliance with our voluntary wage and price constraints. Mandatory wage and price controls will not be used. They have never worked in peacetime. Prices have always continued to rise even under an enormous Federal bureaucracy, and the greatest harm has come to the average American family living on a fixed income with frozen wages while the cost of vital necessities like food and fuel continue to go higher and higher.

And fourth, as I said earlier, the price of imported oil has more than doubled in the last 12 months. Last year's increase in prices of oil alone was greater than all other increases in the price of oil since oil was first discovered many years ago. We simply must cut these imports. We are now approaching the final stages of implementing through law a comprehensive and an adequate energy policy for our Nation. But we cannot meet the goal of reducing imports adequately unless we control the unwarranted and extravagant consumption of gasoline.

Therefore, to make reductions in oil imports, I will impose an oil import conservation fee, equal to about 10 cents a gallon, to cut down on the use of gasoline. The first year this will result in savings of 100,000 barrels a day of imported oil; after 3 years, about 250,000 barrels per day will be reduced because of this charge. And we will be able, this year, to cut our gasoline consumption, and therefore oil imports, 400,000 barrels of oil per day.

[It'll] take long-term efforts to improve the vitality of our economy and to increase productivity through tax reductions. But these tax reductions can only come after we have been sure that we can exercise and maintain the discipline of a balanced budget.

[No Quick Answers]

There are no quick answers to inflation. There are no easy answers. There are no painless answers to inflation. If so, they would have been carried out long ago. The American people are not going to be deceived on this issue. The projects that I've outlined will involve costs; they involve pain. But the cost is far less in taking action than it will be if we take no action.

I must tell you very frankly that the results will not be immediate. We can expect several more months of very high inflation. But toward the end of this year the inflation rate will begin to drop, I think drop substantially.

The hard truth is that there is no easy way. Americans must do this together.

The final point I'd like to make before I take your [questions] is that our Nation is strong and vital. We are similar to a superb athlete who has simply gotten out of shape. The American economy has an underlying strength and resiliency. With discipline and restraint and with a willingness to accept, perhaps, some aching muscles at first, our economy can perform again like a champion. In the fight against inflation what is at stake is more than material wealth, it's more than material comfort; what is at stake is whether we as Americans, as a nation, as a people, will control our own destiny. In order to do so we must control inflation. And the Congress and I and, I believe, our entire Nation is determined to make this effort successful.

Thank you very much.

Mr. Cormier [Frank Cormier, Associated Press].

Questions

Q. Mr. President, do you look forward to more than one balanced budget in a row — because if you look for more, we haven't had two in a row since Eisenhower, three in a row since Truman, and four in a row since Herbert Hoover. I just wondered how you look forward to that.

The President. My hope is that once we establish a precedent of a balanced budget under the present very difficult circumstances, that we will be able to maintain that financial discipline and that budget discipline that we have achieved. . . .

Q. Mr. President, the other three times that you proposed a new anti-inflation program, you pledged each time that they would help restrain the rate of inflation, and yet we've seen it climb from 5 percent, when you took office, to more than 18 percent now on an annual basis. What assurance can you offer the American people that the plan you announced today will bring down the rate of inflation?

The President. I have absolutely no doubt that the plan that I outlined today, when implemented, will indeed bring down the high rate of inflation which exists today. There are some elements that cause the present high inflation rate — which is a worldwide problem — over which I have no control.

One is the price of foreign oil, when we are importing so much of it. As I said earlier, it has more than doubled in price in the last 12 months. In fact, just 1 month ago, the price of energy in our own Nation increased 7-1/2 percent in 1 month, which is an annual rate of 90 percent. But I can control how much oil is imported at that high price, and we can shift to more plentiful supplies of energy in our own Nation.

We have not had a balanced budget in 12 years. We've only had one balanced budget since 1961. But I can guarantee you that we will have a balanced budget in 1981, fiscal year beginning October 1.

The Nation is aroused now, as it has never been before — at least in my lifetime — about the horrors of existing inflation and the threat of future inflation. Never in the history of our Nation has there been so much of a common commitment and a common discussion and a common negotiation between any President and his administration and the leaders of the Congress. This is a mutual commitment. It's not just something that I'm proposing to Congress with little expectation of success.

So, there are several elements, including those I've just described to you, that make it certain, in my mind, that we will have a substantial reduction in the inflation rate during this year — the latter part of this year. And I believe that we'll be under double-digit inflation next year. . . .

COURT ON POLITICAL FIRINGS
FROM PUBLIC JOBS
March 31, 1980

The Supreme Court, by a vote of 6-3, ruled March 31 that the First Amendment protected public employees from being dismissed because of their political beliefs.

The case — Branti v. Finkel — dealt with New York state employees, but because the decision was based on constitutional grounds, the court's decision also applied to federal workers.

Justice John Paul Stevens wrote the majority opinion, joined by Chief Justice Warren E. Burger and Associate Justices William J. Brennan Jr., Byron R. White, Thurgood Marshall and Harry A. Blackmun.

Associate Justice Lewis F. Powell Jr. wrote a dissenting opinion in which Justices Potter Stewart and William H. Rehnquist joined.

Background

The Supreme Court in 1976 declared it unconstitutional for a new sheriff of Cook County, Ill., to fire all non-civil-service employees of his office who did not belong to his political party.

In that case, Elrod v. Burns, Justice Brennan wrote that "political belief and association constitute the core of those activities protected by the First Amendment." But a majority of the court could not agree on the reach of the Elrod ruling. Justices Brennan, White and Marshall held unconstitutional political patronage firing of non-policy-making officials. But Justices Stewart and Blackmun further qualified their votes with the majority, stating that they found unconstitutional such firings of non-policy-making employees not in a confidential relationship with their employers.

The dissenters in the 1976 case were Chief Justice Burger and Justices Powell and Rehnquist. Justice Stevens did not take part in the ruling.

The Case

Peter Branti, a Democrat newly elected as the public defender for Rockland County, N.Y., decided to fire two of his "inherited" assistants, Aaron Finkel and Alan Tabakman, because they were Republicans.

Relying on Elrod, *Finkel and Tabakman won a court order forbidding their dismissal. Branti went to the Supreme Court, asking it to overturn the order of the lower court.*

Branti argued that Elrod v. Burns *did not apply to the situation in his office, and that, in any event, party loyalty was an acceptable requirement for the job of assistant public defender.*

Majority Opinion

The court rejected Branti's arguments. In earlier decisions it had held that a public employee was protected by the First Amendment from being fired because of what he said. In accord with that line of reasoning, wrote Stevens, the amendment "must also protect him from discharge based on what he believes."

Unless there is a vitally important governmental interest requiring that an employee's private beliefs conform to that of his employer, those beliefs cannot be the sole reason for firing him, Stevens said.

Stevens' opinion did suggest a limitation. Party loyalty might still be a permissible requirement for certain government jobs, the opinion said. "[I]f an employee's private political beliefs would interfere with the discharge of his public duties, his First Amendment rights may be required to yield to the state's vital interest in maintaining governmental effectiveness and efficiency," wrote Stevens for the court.

But the court clearly placed the burden of proof on the government employer to prove that party affiliation was an appropriate requirement for a particular job.

Party Membership

Acknowledging the difficulty of deciding whether certain jobs were those in which political loyalty was an appropriate factor for consideration, Stevens concluded that "the ultimate inquiry is not whether the label 'policy maker' or 'confidential' fits a particular position; rather the question is whether the hiring authority can demonstrate that party affiliation is an appropriate requirement for the effective performance of the public office involved."

In this case membership in the Democratic Party clearly was not an appropriate requirement for the post as assistant public defender, the majority held. In a footnote, Stevens responded to the dissenting justices by stating that the holding did not reach the question of whether a prosecutor could dismiss his deputy on grounds of party loyalty.

Dissenting Opinion

Justice Powell, in a dissenting opinion joined by Justices Stewart and Rehnquist, said the majority had engaged in "judicial lawmaking." Powell wrote that the majority ignored the "substantial governmental interests served by patronage" throughout the nation's history and was imposing a single constitutional standard upon the hiring practices of government at all levels.

The three dissenters criticized as too vague and uncertain the majority's new standard for determining which jobs might be filled on the basis of political loyalty. "Federal judges will now be the final arbiter as to who federal, state, and local governments may employ.... [T]he court is not justified in removing decisions so essential to responsible and efficient governance from the discretion of legislative and executive officials."

Powell and Rehnquist also disagreed with the court's conclusion that the First Amendment prohibited the firing of public employees on the basis of their party membership. Use of party loyalty as a criterion for public employment was not unconstitutional, they argued, if patronage worked to serve sufficiently important governmental interests.

Writing separately, Justice Stewart explained that he viewed Finkel and Tabakman as confidential employees, with whom Branti was "not constitutionally compelled to enter . . . a close professional and necessarily confidential relationship . . . if he did not with to do so."

Following are excerpts from the Supreme Court's opinion, delivered March 31, 1980, limiting the dismissal of public employees because of their political party affiliation:

No. 78-1654

Peter Branti, as Public Defender of Rockland County, Petitioner, *v.* Aaron Finkel and Alan Tabakman.	On Writ of Certiorari to the United States Court of Appeals for the Second Circuit.

[March 31, 1980]

MR. JUSTICE STEVENS delivered the opinion of the Court.

The question presented is whether the First and Fourteenth Amendments to the Constitution protect an assistant public defender who is satisfactorily performing his job from discharge solely because of his political beliefs.

Respondents, Aaron Finkel and Alan Tabakman, commenced this action in the United States District Court for the Southern District of New York in order to preserve their positions as assistant public defenders in Rockland County, New York. On January 4, 1978, on the basis of a showing that the petitioner public defender was about to discharge them solely because they were Republicans, the District Court entered a temporary restraining order preserving the status quo. After hearing evidence for eight days, the District Court entered detailed findings of fact and permanently enjoined petitioner from terminating or attempting to terminate respondents' employment "upon the sole grounds of their political beliefs.". . . The Court of Appeals affirmed in an unpublished memorandum opinion. . . .

The critical facts can be summarized briefly. The Rockland County Public Defender is appointed by the County Legislature for a term of six years. He in turn appoints nine assistants who serve at his pleasure. The two respondents have served as assistants since their respective appointments in March 1971 and September 1975; they are both Republicans.

Petitioner Branti's predecessor, a Republican, was appointed in 1972 by a Republican-dominated County Legislature. By 1977, control of the legislature had shifted to the Democrats and petitioner, also a Democrat, was appointed to replace the incumbent when his term expired. As soon as petitioner was formally appointed on January 3, 1978, he began executing termination notices for six of the nine assistants then in office. Respondents were among those who were to be terminated. With one possible exception, the nine who were to be appointed or retained were all Democrats and were all selected by Democratic legislators or Democratic town chairmen on a basis that had been determined by the Democratic caucus.

The District Court found that Finkel and Tabakman had been selected for termination solely because they were Republicans and thus did not have the necessary Democratic sponsors. . . . The court rejected petitioner's belated attempt to justify the dismissals on nonpolitical grounds. Noting that both Branti and his predecessor had described respondents as "competent attorneys," the District Court expressly found that both had "been satisfactorily performing their jobs as Assistant Public Defenders.". . .

Having concluded that respondents had been discharged solely because of their political beliefs, the District Court held that those discharges would be permissible under this Court's decision in *Elrod* v. *Burns* [1976] only if assistant public defenders are the type of policymaking, confidential employees who may be discharged solely on the basis of their political affiliations. He concluded that respondents clearly did not fall within that category. Although recognizing that they had broad responsibilities with respect to particular cases that were assigned to them, the court found that respondents had "very limited, if any, responsibility" with respect to the overall operation of the public defender's office. They did not "act as advisors or formulate plans for the implementation of the broad goals of the office" and, although they make decisions in the context of specific cases, "they do not make decisions about the orientation and operation of the office in which they work.". . .

The District Court also rejected the argument that the confidential character of respondents' work justified conditioning their employment on political grounds. He found that they did not occupy any confidential relationship to the policymaking process, and did not have access to confidential documents that influenced policymaking deliberations. Rather, the only confidential information to which they had access was the product of their attorney-client relationship with the office's clients; to the extent that such information was shared with the public defender, it did not relate to the formulation of office policy.

In light of these factual findings, the District Court concluded that petitioner could not terminate respondents' employment as assistant public defenders consistent with the First and Fourteenth Amendments. On appeal, a panel of the Second Circuit affirmed, specifically holding that the District Court's findings of fact were adequately supported by the record. That Court also expressed "no doubt" that the District Court "was correct in concluding that an assistant public defender was neither a policymaker nor a confidential employee." We granted certiorari . . . and now affirm.

Petitioner advances two principal arguments for reversal: first, that the holding in *Elrod* v. *Burns* is limited to situations in which government employees are coerced into pledging allegiance to a political party that they would not voluntarily support and does not apply to a simple requirement that an employee be sponsored by the party in power; and, second, that, even if party sponsorship is an unconstitutional condition of continued public employment for clerks, deputies, and janitors, it is an acceptable requirement for an assistant public defender.

I

In *Elrod* v. *Burns* the Court held that the newly elected Democratic sheriff of Cook County, Ill., had violated the constitutional rights of certain non-civil service employees by discharging them "because they did not support and were not members of the Democratic Party and had failed to obtain the sponsorship of one of its leaders.". . . That holding was supported by two separate opinions.

Writing for the plurality, MR. JUSTICE BRENNAN identified two separate but interrelated reasons supporting the conclusion that the discharges were prohibited by the First and Fourteenth Amendments.

First, he analyzed the impact of a political patronage system on freedom of belief and association. Noting that in order to retain their jobs, the sheriff's employees were required to pledge their allegiance to the Democratic party, work for or contribute to the party's candidates, or obtain a Democratic sponsor, he concluded that the inevitable tendency of such a system was to coerce employees into compromising their true beliefs. That conclusion, in his opinion, brought the practice within the rule of cases like *Board of Education* v. *Barnette* [1943], condemning the use of governmental power to prescribe what the citizenry must accept as orthodox opinion.

Second, apart from the potential impact of patronage dismissals on the formation and expression of opinion, MR. JUSTICE BRENNAN also stated that the practice had the effect of imposing an unconstitutional condition on the receipt of a public benefit and therefore came within the rule of cases like *Perry* v. *Sindermann* [1972]. . . .

If the First Amendment protects a public employee from discharge based on what he has said, it must also protect him from discharge based on what he believes. Under this line of analysis, unless the Government can demonstrate "an overriding interest," [*Elrod* v. *Burns*] "of vital importance," . . . requiring that a person's private beliefs conform to those of the hiring authority, his beliefs cannot be the sole basis for depriving him of continued public employment.

MR. JUSTICE STEWART's concurring opinion avoided comment on the first branch of MR. JUSTICE BRENNAN'S analysis, but expressly relied on . . . *Perry* v. *Sindermann*. . . .

Petitioner argues that *Elrod* v. *Burns* should be read to prohibit only dismissals resulting from an employee's failure to capitulate to political coercion. Thus, he argues that, so long as an employee is not asked to change his political affiliation or to contribute to or work for the party's candidates, he may be dismissed with impunity — even though he would not have been dismissed if he had had the proper political sponsorship and even though the sole reason for dismissing him was to replace him with a person who did have such sponsorship. Such an interpretation would surely emasculate the principles set forth in *Elrod*. While it would perhaps eliminate the more blatant forms of coercion described in *Elrod,* it would not eliminate the coercion of belief that necessarily flows from the knowledge that one must have a sponsor in the dominant party in order to retain one's job. More importantly, petitioner's interpretation would require the Court to repudiate entirely the conclusion of both MR. JUSTICE BRENNAN and MR. JUSTICE STEWART that the First Amendment prohibits the dismissal of a public employee solely because of his private political beliefs.

In sum, there is no requirement that dismissed employees prove that they, or other employees, have been coerced into changing, either actually or ostensibly, their political allegiance. To prevail in this type of an action, it was sufficient, as *Elrod* holds, for respondents to prove that they were discharged "solely for the reason that they were not affiliated with or sponsored by the Democratic Party."...

II

Both opinions in *Elrod* recognize that party affiliation may be an acceptable requirement for some types of government employment. Thus, if an employee's private political beliefs would interfere with the discharge of his public duties, his First Amendment rights may be required to yield to the State's vital interest in maintaining governmental effectiveness and efficiency.... In *Elrod,* it was clear that the duties of the employees — the chief deputy of the process division of the sheriff's office, a process server and another employee in that office, and a bailiff and security guard at the Juvenile Court of Cook County — were not of that character, for they were, as MR. JUSTICE STEWART stated, "nonpolicymaking, nonconfidential" employees....

As MR. JUSTICE BRENNAN noted in *Elrod,* it is not always easy to determine whether a position is one in which political affiliation is a legitimate factor to be considered.... Under some circumstances, a position may be appropriately considered political even though it is neither confidential nor policymaking in character. As one obvious example, if a State's election laws require that precincts be supervised by two election judges of different parties, a Republican judge could be legitimately discharged solely for changing his party registration. That conclusion would not depend on any finding that the job involved participation in policy decisions or access to confidential information. Rather, it would simply rest on the fact that party membership was essential to the discharge of the employee's governmental responsibilities.

It is equally clear that party affiliation is not necessarily relevant to every policymaking or confidential position. The coach of a state university's football team formulates policy, but no one could seriously claim that Republicans make better coaches than Democrats, or vice versa, no matter which party is in control of the state government. On the other hand, it is equally clear that the governor of a state may appropriately believe that the official duties of various assistants who help him write speeches, explain his views to the press, or communicate with the legislature cannot be performed effectively unless those persons share his political beliefs and party commitments. In sum, the ultimate inquiry is not whether the label "policymaker" or "confidential" fits a particular position; rather, the question is whether the hiring authority can demonstrate that party affiliation is an appropriate requirement for the effective performance of the public office involved.

Having thus framed the issue, it is manifest that the continued employment of an assistant public defender cannot properly be conditioned upon his allegiance to the political party in control of the county government. The primary, if not the only, responsibility of an assistant public defender is to represent individual citizens in controversy with the State. . . .

Thus, whatever policymaking occurs in the public defender's office must relate to the needs of individual clients and not to any partisan political interests. Similarly, although an assistant is bound to obtain access to confidential information arising out of various attorney-client relationships, that information has no bearing whatsoever on partisan political concerns. Under these circumstances, it would undermine, rather than promote, the effective performance of an assistant public defender's office to make his tenure dependent on his allegiance to the dominant political party.

Accordingly, the entry of an injunction against termination of respondents' employment on purely political grounds was appropriate and the judgment of the Court of Appeals is

Affirmed.

MR. JUSTICE STEWART, dissenting.

I joined the judgment of the Court in *Elrod* v. *Burns* because it is my view that, under the First and Fourteenth Amendments, "a nonpolicymaking, nonconfidential government employee can[not] be discharged . . . from a job that he is satisfactorily performing upon the sole ground of his political beliefs.". . . That judgment in my opinion does not control the present case for the simple reason that the respondents here clearly are not "nonconfidential" employees.

The employees in the *Elrod* case were three process servers and a juvenile court bailiff and security guard. The respondents in the present case are lawyers, and the employment positions involved are those of assistants in the office of the Rockland County Public Defender. The analogy to a firm of lawyers in the private sector is a close one, and I can think of few occupational relationships more instinct with the necessity of mutual confidence and trust than that kind of professional association.

I believe that the petitioner, upon his appointment as Public Defender, was not constitutionally compelled to enter such a close professional and necessarily confidential association with the respondents if he did not wish to do so.

MR. JUSTICE POWELL, with whom MR. JUSTICE REHNQUIST joins, and with whom MR. JUSTICE STEWART joins as to Part I, dissenting.

The Court today continues the evisceration of patronage practices begun in *Elrod* v. *Burns* (1976). With scarcely a glance at almost 200 years of American political tradition, the Court further limits the relevance of political affiliation to the selection and retention of public employees. Many public positions previously filled on the basis of membership in national political parties now must be staffed in accordance with a constitutionalized civil service standard that will affect the employment practices of federal, state, and local governments. Governmental hiring practices long thought to be a matter of legislative and executive discretion now will be subjected to judicial oversight. Today's decision is an exercise of judicial lawmaking that, as THE CHIEF JUSTICE wrote in his *Elrod* dissent, "represents a significant intrusion into the area of legislative and policy concerns.". . . I dissent.

I

The Court contends that its holding is compelled by the First Amendment. In reaching this conclusion, the Court largely ignores the substantial governmental interests served by patronage. Patronage is a long-accepted practice that never has been eliminated totally by civil service laws and regulations. The flaw in the Court's opinion lies not only in its application of First Amendment principles . . . but also in its promulgation of a new, and substantially expanded, standard for determining which governmental employees may be retained or dismissed on the basis of political affiliation.

In *Elrod* v. *Burns*, three Members of the Court joined a plurality opinion concluding that nonpolicymaking employees could not be dismissed on the basis of political affiliation. . . . Two Members of the Court joined a concurring opinion stating that nonpolicymaking, nonconfidential employees could not be so dismissed. . . . Notwithstanding its purported reliance upon the holding of *Elrod*, . . . the Court today ignores the limitations inherent in both views. The Court rejects the limited role for patronage recognized in the plurality opinion by holding that not all policymakers may be dismissed because of political affiliation. . . . And the Court refuses to allow confidential employees to be dismissed for partisan reasons. . . . The Court gives three examples to illustrate the standard. Election judges and certain executive assistants may be chosen on the basis of political affiliation; college football coaches may not. . . . And the Court decides in this case that party affiliation is not an appropriate requirement for selection of the attorneys in a public defender's office because "whatever policymaking occurs in the public defender's office must relate to the needs of individual clients and not to any partisan political interests.". . .

The standard articulated by the Court is framed in vague and sweeping language certain to create vast uncertainty. Elected and appointed officials at all levels who now receive guidance from civil service laws, no longer will know when political affiliation is an appropriate consideration in filling a position. Legislative bodies will not be certain whether they have the final authority to make the delicate line-drawing decisions embodied in the civil service laws. Prudent individuals requested to accept a public appointment must consider whether their predecessors will threaten to oust them through legal action.

One example at the national level illustrates the nature and magnitude of the problem created by today's holding. The President customarily has considered political affiliation in removing and appointing United States Attorneys. Given the critical role that these key law enforcement officials play in the administration of the Department of Justice, both Democratic and Republican Attorneys General have concluded, not surprisingly, that they must have the confidence and support of the United States Attorneys. And political affiliation has been used as one indicator of loyalty.

Yet, it would be difficult to say, under the Court's standard, that "partisan" concerns properly are relevant to the performance of the duties of a United States Attorney.... Nevertheless, I believe that the President must have the right to consider political affiliation when he selects top ranking Department of Justice officials. The President and his Attorney General, not this Court, are charged with the responsibility for enforcing the laws and administering the Department of Justice. The Court's vague, overbroad decision may cast serious doubt on the propriety of dismissing United States Attorneys, as well as thousands of other policymaking employees at all levels of government, because of their membership in a national political party.

A constitutional standard that is both uncertain in its application and impervious to legislative change will now control selection and removal of key governmental personnel. Federal judges will now be the final arbiters as to who federal, state, and local governments may employ. In my view, the Court is not justified in removing decisions so essential to responsible and efficient governance from the discretion of legislative and executive officials.

II

The Court errs not only in its selection of a standard, but more fundamentally in its conclusion that the First Amendment prohibits the use of membership in a national political party as a criterion for the dismissal of public employees. In reaching this conclusion, the Court makes new law from inapplicable precedents. The Court suggests that its decision is mandated by the principle that governmental action may not "prescribe what shall be orthodox in politics, nationalism, religion, or other matters of opinion...." *Board of Education* v. *Barnette* (1943). The Court also relies upon the decisions in *Perry* v. *Sindermann* (1972), and *Keyishian* v. *Board of Regents* (1967).... But the propriety of patronage was neither questioned nor addressed in those cases.

Both *Keyishian* and *Perry* involved faculty members who were dismissed from state educational institutions because of their political views. In *Keyishian*, the Court reviewed a state statute that permitted dismissals of faculty members from state institutions for "treasonable or seditious" utterances or acts. The Court noted that academic freedom is "a special concern of the First Amendment, which does not tolerate laws that cast a pall of orthodoxy over the classroom.".... Because of the ambiguity in the statutory language, the Court held that the law was unconstitutionally vague. The Court also held that membership in the Communist Party could not automatically disqualify a person from holding a faculty position in a state university.... In *Perry,* the Court held that the Board of Regents of a state university system could not discharge a professor in retaliation for his exercise of free speech.... In neither case did the State suggest that the governmental positions traditionally had been regarded as patronage positions. Thus, the Court correctly held that no substantial state interest justified the infringement of free speech. This case presents a question quite different from that in *Keyishian* and *Perry.*

The constitutionality of appointing or dismissing public employees on the basis of political affiliation depends upon the governmental interests served by patronage. No constitutional violation exists if patronage practices further sufficiently important interests to justify tangential burdening of First Amendment rights.... This inquiry cannot be resolved by reference to First Amendment cases in which patronage was neither involved nor discussed. Nor can the question in this case be answered in a principled manner without identifying and weighing the governmental interest served by patronage.

III

Patronage appointments help build stable political parties by offering rewards to persons who assume the tasks necessary to the continued functioning of political organizations.... The benefits of patronage to a political organization do not derive merely from filling policymaking positions on the basis of political affiliation. Many, if not most, of the jobs filled by patronage at the local level may not involve policymaking functions. The use of patronage to fill such positions builds party loyalty and avoids "splintered parties and unrestrained factionalism [that might] do significant damage to the fabric of government." *Storer* v. *Brown* (1974)....

In sum, the effect of the Court's decision will be to decrease the accountability and denigrate the role of our national political parties. This decision comes at a time when an increasing number of observers question whether our national political parties can continue to operate effectively. Broad-based political parties supply an essential coherence and flexibility to the American political scene. They serve as coalitions of different interests that combine to seek national goals. The decline of party strength inevitably will enhance the influence of special interest groups whose only concern all too often is how a political candidate votes on a single issue. The quality of political debate, and indeed the capacity of government to function in the national interest, suffers when candidates and officeholders are forced to be more responsive to the narrow concerns of unrepresentative special interest groups than to overarching issues of domestic and foreign policy. The Court ignores the substantial governmental interests served by reasonable patronage. In my view, its decision will seriously hamper the functioning of stable political parties.

IV

The facts of this case also demonstrate that the Court's decision well may impair the right of local voters to structure their government. Consideration of the form of local government in Rockland County, New York, demonstrates the antidemocratic effect of the Court's decision.

The voters of the County elect a legislative body. Among the responsibilities that the voters give to the legislature is the selection of a County Public Defender. In 1972, when the county voters elected a Republican majority in the legislature, a Republican was selected as Public Defender. The Public Defender retained one respondent and appointed the other as assistant public defenders. Not surprisingly, both respondents are Republicans. In 1976, the voters elected a majority of Democrats to the legislature. The Democratic majority, in turn, selected a Democratic Public Defender who replaced both respondents with assistant public defenders approved by the Democratic legislators. . . .

The voters of Rockland County are free to elect their Public Defender and assistant public defenders instead of delegating their selection to elected and appointed officials. Certainly the Court's holding today would not preclude the voters, the ultimate "hiring authority," from choosing both Public Defenders and their assistants by party membership. The voters' choice of public officials on the basis of political affiliation is not yet viewed as an inhibition of speech; it is democracy. Nor may any incumbent contend seriously that the voters' decision not to re-elect him because of his political views is an impermissible infringement upon his right of free speech or affiliation. In other words, the operation of democratic government depends upon the selection of elected officials on precisely the basis rejected by the Court today.

Although the voters of Rockland County could have elected both the Public Defender and his assistants, they have given their legislators a representative proxy to appoint the Public Defender. And they have delegated to the Public Defender the power to choose his assistants. Presumably the voters have adopted this course in order to facilitate more effective representative government. Of course, the voters could have instituted a civil service system that would preclude the selection of either the Public Defender or his assistants on the basis of political affiliation. But the continuation of the present system reflects the electorate's decision to select certain public employees on the basis of political affiliation.

The Court's decision today thus limits the ability of the voters of a county to structure their democratic government in the way that they please. Now those voters must elect both the Public Defender and his assistants if they are to fill governmental positions on a partisan basis. Because voters certainly may elect governmental officials on the basis of party ties, it is difficult to perceive a constitutional reason for prohibiting them from delegating that same authority to legislators and appointed officials.

V

The benefits of political patronage and the freedom of voters to structure their representative government are substantial governmental interests that justify the selection of the assistant public defenders of Rockland County on the basis of political affiliation. The decision to place certain governmental positions within a civil service system is a sensitive political judgment that should be left to the voters and to elected representatives of the people. But the Court's constitutional holding today displaces political responsibility with judicial fiat. In my view, the First Amendment does not incorporate a national civil service system. I would reverse the judgment of the Court of Appeals.

APRIL

COUP IN LIBERIA
April 12, 1980

William R. Tolbert Jr., the president of Liberia, and 27 others were killed April 12 in a coup d'etat staged by noncommissioned army officers and enlisted men.

A new regime, led by Master Sgt. Samuel K. Doe, had toppled a government controlled by the wealthy and privileged, many of whom were the lineal descendants of freed American slaves who founded Liberia before the American Civil War.

Doe, leader of a 17-member junta called the People's Redemptive Council, said in a radio broadcast that Tolbert had been overthrown because "rampant corruption and continuous failure . . . to effectively handle the affairs of the Liberian people left the enlisted men no alternative."

The junta April 25 suspended a 133-year old constitution and assumed complete executive and legislative governing powers. Some rioting and looting followed the coup, but business in the capital city of Monrovia continued without interruption. Spokesmen for the new regime said Liberia would continue to encourage foreign investment and to respect private property.

Executions

In an act of vengeance which shocked the international community, the junta announced April 18 that 91 members of the Tolbert government

275

would be tried on charges of treason, corruption and violation of human rights.

Four days later, the ruling council sanctioned the execution of 13 high-ranking members of Tolbert's cabinet and other officials of the ruling True Whig Party. All 13 had been sentenced by a five-member military court. The condemned men had spoken on their own behalf but had not been permitted defense lawyers.

The junta rejected pleas from the United Nations, the United States and European and African nations to spare the men's lives. But on April 29 it halted further mass public executions.

Those executed by a firing squad in view of members of the international press corps and thousands of spectators included Frank Tolbert, Senate president and brother of the murdered president.

Background

More than 15,000 American blacks, many of them freed slaves, settled on Cape Mesurado in West Africa between 1822 and the American Civil War. The colony, Liberia, became independent in 1847, and a constitution was adopted modeled on the U.S. Constitution. Under the Liberian constitution, however, the initial term of the president was eight years, and he was eligible for other four-year terms.

Conditions in Liberia generally improved during the long administration of President William V. S. Tubman (1944-71). Tolbert became president on the death of Tubman in 1971.

However, discontent had become widespread in recent years. Although Tolbert had promised wide ranging reforms when he became president, the old divisions and inequalities remained. The Liberian elite represented only 5 percent of the population of 1.7 million but controlled the nation's political and economic life.

Tolbert responded to widespread rioting in 1979 over food prices by permitting an opposition party. When the Progressive People's Party, headed by Gabriel Baccus Matthews, called for Tolbert's resignation, the president jailed Matthews and ordered the arrest of several other members of the party.

In one of his first official acts after taking power, Doe ordered Matthews and other leaders released from custody. The ruling council April 13 appointed Matthews foreign minister.

U.S. Reaction

The coup came as a surprise to most outside observers. But the Carter administration said it expected no change in U.S. relations with

Liberia. Forty-three U.S. companies — including Firestone, B.F. Goodrich and several banks — continued to have offices and commercial holdings in the country.

U.S. officials and representatives of U.S. banks said that the bloody coup and continued reports of corruption, instability and inefficiency had demolished confidence with respect to granting loans to the Doe regime. About $10 million in U.S. aid to Liberia, however, was not interrupted by the events.

African Reaction

Other West African nations with strong ties to the Tolbert government refused to recognize the new military regime. Guinea, Sierra Leone and the Ivory Coast all withheld recognition of the Doe government. Liberian Foreign Minister Matthews was refused permission to attend an Organization of African Unity meeting at Lagos, Nigeria, in April. And in May the 16-member economic community of West Africa excluded Doe from its meeting.

Efforts of the Liberian regime to obtain international legitimacy received another setback April 14 when Liberian troops raided the French embassy in Monrovia to arrest Tolbert's eldest son, Adolphus Tolbert, who had been granted asylum. The French government denounced the raid on its embassy, calling it a "flagrant and unacceptable violation of the status of diplomatic missions."

> *Following is the text as provided by the Republic of Liberia of a speech by Master Sgt. Samuel K. Doe, the head of a 17-man junta, delivered in Monrovia April 14, 1980, explaining why enlisted men in the Liberian army overthrew the Tolbert government. (Boldface headings in brackets have been added by Congressional Quarterly to highlight the organization of the text.):*

Our Liberia People,
Friends of Liberia,
Members, People's Redemption Council:
On the morning of April 12, 1980, the enlisted men and women of the Armed Forces of Liberia removed from our midst Mr. William R. Tolbert, Jr., and those officials, his collaborators, who worked with him in running the Government of Liberia.

We know that what we have done has never happened before in the history of Liberia, but it was most necessary because of the following reasons.

    (1) There has been uncontrolled corruption that we can see all around us in the form of conflict of interest, the selling of influence, the use of official positions for private gain, and other forms

of corruption which take from the Liberian people those things that are rightfully theirs.

Too often do we see members of the Legislature representing big companies when they should be speaking for the people. Too often have we found public officials dismissed for corrupt practices only to be reemployed to higher positions of public trust.

(2) The Tolbert Government failed to respond, in a meaningful way, to the problems of the Liberian people, especially the poor people, the masses.

We know that it is not possible for everybody at all times, but our people have a right to expect the government to always do its best in trying to meet the needs of the people.

In our country, the unemployment situation is so bad that there are more people looking for work than those who are employed.

Those who are fortunate in finding jobs, soon learn that their wages and salaries are so very low that they cannot afford to buy basic goods and services.

In other words, some people are employed and yet they are hardly surviving. Rent is rising far beyond the people's ability to pay. Houses built for poor people are being used by rich people and their friends, and very often their girlfriends. The cost of food is too high, and most of our people cannot afford $25.00 for a bag of rice.

The health situation in the country is so terrible that nearly one out of every five newly born babies dies before reaching the age of one year. Conditions in the interior are so unbearable that our people are being pushed to live in Monrovia only to face the sub-human standards of unemployment and high cost of living.

The Tolbert Government had to be removed because, as we all know, it disregarded the civil, human and constitutional rights of the Liberian people. Those who make laws must also live by the laws that they make, or they must answer to the people.

Judges were appointed who contributed to the abuse of the rights of the Liberian people. There was illegal detention, illegal search and seizure, even conviction without trial.

[People's Redemption Council]

For these and similar reasons, the People's Redemption Council was organized not only to overthrow the Government but, more importantly, to overhaul it. The members of the Council are:

MSG. Samuel K. Doe, Chairman and Head of State
SGT. Thomas Weh Syen, Co-Chairman
CPL. Mathan Poldiear, Speaker of the Council
SSG. Henry S. Zuo, Jr., Member
SSG. Thomas Quainwongba, Member
SGT. David Karmai, Member
SGT. Swen N. Dixon, Member

SGT. Jerry Gban, Member
CPL. Jacob Swen, Member
CPL. Fallah Voine, Member
CPL. Jerry C. Friday, Member
CPL. Harris S. Johnson, Member
CPL. Larry W. Bather, Member
CPL. Roberts B. Norwanu, Member
CPL. Harrison Penue, Member
PFC. Robert Zuo, Member
PFC. William S. Peters, Member

We are beginning this new Government with much knowledge and experience. We are entering this new part of Liberian history with a strong sense of those acts of previous Governments which have held our people down for too long. It is because of the fact that we have actually felt the injustices and suffering of our people that we have become committed to building a new society. As we now face our people throughout our nation, we seek to build a new society in which there is justice, human dignity, equal opportunities, and fair treatment for all before the law; as we stand here dedicated to real change, our Government will actively encourage the wide participation of the people from all parts of the country in the making of decisions that affect them.

To our friends from abroad, we say clearly that while we will depend mainly on the use of our own resources in building our country, we seek to maintain and develop friendship with foreign investors that will help us solve our burning problems, especially the problems of meeting the basic needs of our people.

We will do our best to maintain and develop friendly relations with all peace-loving countries. We support fully the aims and objectives of the United Nations and the Organization of African Unity.

We will uphold principles and goals of the non-aligned countries movement. Our Government will not rest until every inch of African soil is totally liberated. In this respect, our Government will support, with its full power, the just and glorious struggle for the liberation of all African countries from colonial rule.

Our dear Liberian people, let us assure you that this new Government is in the interest of all of the people without discrimination. This Government shall undertake to bring about equal economic and social opportunities for all.

The rights to private property and the fruits of honest labor will be respected. There will be justice for all without regards for social status or place or origin.

[No Witch-Hunting]

There is no need to fear. We are prepared to let the past go quickly into history. There will be no witch-hunting. It is our responsibility to build a new society for the benefit of all of our people. We call on all of our foreign friends to assist us in this effort.

Finally, our dear people of Liberia, we want you to know, from the very bottom of our hearts, that we have not taken over this Government only to bring back the same kind of Government that we removed. Our Government must and will do something about the high cost of living. Already, we have directed that all enlisted men and women of the Armed Forces of Liberia and law enforcement agencies be paid at least $250 a month. All other Government employees are to be paid at least $200 a month.

Within a short period of time, we will set up a broad-based committee to find out ways to reduce the over-all cost of living, especially in the areas of food, health care, education, transportation, and housing.

In our Government's efforts at reducing the cost of living and working towards bringing real progress to our people, we call upon workers, farmers, students, teachers, market people, the unemployed, the churches and civil servants, the police and soldiers to do their part by telling their Government what to do because our Government is the Government of the people.

It is upon the people of this country that this Government depends. Without the people, our Government can do nothing. But with the people, our Government can seek the interest and welfare of all.

This is time for hard work. Let us get hold of ourselves and work very hard to build up our country. Hard and honest work will bring us progress. Gone forever are the days of "Who you know?" and "Do you know who I am?" We now enter into the time of "What can you do?" ... Long live the people of Liberia! Long live African unity and freedom! In the cause of the people, the struggle continues.

SUPREME COURT ON ARRESTS IN SUSPECTS' HOMES

April 15, 1980

In a landmark decision reinforcing the constitutional protection against being seized unreasonably, the Supreme Court ruled April 15 that police must have an arrest warrant or the occupant's consent to enter a home and make an arrest.

The constitutional protection for personal privacy was given new vigor by the court's decision in the cases of Payton v. New York *and* Riddick v. New York. *The vote was 6-3.*

After hearing the two cases argued twice — in March 1979 and again in October 1979 — the court struck down as unconstitutional a New York state law that authorized police to enter a residence without a warrant and by force, if necessary, to make a routine arrest of a person charged with a felony.

Such a law — similar to those in 23 other states — violated the Fourth Amendment's guarantee of security against unreasonable searches, the court said in an opinion written by Justice John Paul Stevens.

Warrant Requirement

The warrant requirement was based on the guarantee in the Fourth Amendment to the Constitution, of "the right of the people to be secure in their persons, houses, papers and effects against unreasonable searches and seizures. . . ."

The Fourth Amendment guarantee had been the subject of many Supreme Court decisions. But most of them had concerned the search

281

and seizure of tangible evidence rather than arrests, that is, the "seizure" of the person.

The court in 1976 spoke on the issue of the Fourth Amendment and arrest warrants. In the case of United States v. Watson, *it held that police need not obtain a warrant before arresting a person in a public place, so long as they had probable cause to make the arrest.*

Justice Byron R. White, writing for the six-man majority in Watson, *made it clear that the court had not then answered the question "whether and under what circumstances an officer may enter a suspect's home to make a warrantless arrest."*

It was that question which the court resolved with its April 15 decision. In the 1980 cases, White was in the minority.

The Cases

The two cases arose after police entered the defendants' dwellings to arrest them. Entrance was made without the defendants' consent and without arrest warrants. In both cases, evidence was also seized. Payton and Riddick, one charged with murder and the other with narcotics offenses, challenged the use of that evidence.

The New York courts, citing the state law authorizing warrantless entry by police, upheld the seizure and the use of the evidence.

Majority Opinion

"The Fourth Amendment protects the individual's privacy in a variety of settings," wrote Stevens. "In none is the zone of privacy more clearly defined than when bounded by the unambiguous physical dimensions of an individual's home.... In terms that apply equally to seizures of property and to seizures of persons, the Fourth Amendment has drawn a fine line at the entrance to the house. Absent exigent circumstances, that threshold may not reasonably be crossed without a warrant."

Exigent circumstances to which Stevens referred were emergency or dangerous situations in which police must act immediately to arrest a person or make a search.

The warrant would protect an individual's privacy, Stevens explained. "If there is sufficient evidence of a citizen's participation in a felony to persuade a judicial officer that his arrest is justified, it is constitutionally reasonable to require him to open his doors to the officers of the law."

Quoting a 1972 opinion by the court, Stevens wrote, " '[P]hysical entry of the home is the chief evil against which the wording of the

Fourth Amendment is directed.' " He continued, "It is a 'basic principle of Fourth Amendment law' that searches and seizures inside a home without a warrant are presumptively unreasonable. . . ."

Stevens pointed out that the warrant requirement would not be applied to seizures in public places, where a person's privacy was less involved. That point distinguished Watson *from the New York cases.*

Stevens acknowledged that to require arrest warrants in such cases could hamper effective law enforcement but stated that "such arguments of policy must give way to a constitutional command that we consider to be unequivocal."

Dissenting Opinion

The court was imposing too rigid a warrant requirement on police, argued Chief Justice Warren E. Burger, Associate Justice White and Associate Justice William H. Rehnquist in a dissenting opinion written by White. Such a rule was unsupported by common law or the text or history of the Fourth Amendment, White wrote,

White stated that the court had exaggerated the invasion of privacy in such arrests and had underestimated the burden the warrant rule would place on effective law enforcement.

Furthermore, wrote White, the majority had ignored "the carefully crafted restrictions" which generally controlled the power of police to enter homes for the purpose of arrests without warrants or consent. Allowing such arrests only in the daytime and only for felonies, requiring police to knock and announce themselves and to have probable cause to believe that the suspect was in the dwelling minimized the invasion of privacy that occurred, argued White.

Following are excerpts from the Supreme Court's opinion, delivered April 15, 1980, ruling that police must have arrest warrants to make routine arrests in private homes; and Justice White's dissenting opinion:

Nos. 78-5420 and 78-5421

Theodore Payton, Applicant, 78-5420   On Appeals from the Court of Appeals of New York.
v.
New York
Obie Riddick, Applicant, 78-5421
v.
New York.

[April 15, 1980]

MR. JUSTICE STEVENS delivered the opinion of the Court.

These appeals challenge the constitutionality of New York statutes that authorize police officers to enter a private residence without a warrant and with force, if necessary, to make a routine felony arrest.

The important constitutional question presented by this challenge has been expressly left open in a number of our prior opinions. In *United States* v. *Watson* [1976], we upheld a warrantless "midday public arrest," expressly noting that the case did not pose "the still unsettled question ... whether and under what circumstances an officer may enter a suspect's home to make a warrantless arrest." ... The question has been answered in different ways by other appellate courts. The Supreme Court of Florida rejected the constitutional attack, as did the New York Court of Appeals in this case. The courts of last resort in 10 other States, however, have held that unless special circumstances are present, warrantless arrests in the home are unconstitutional. Of the seven United States Courts of Appeals that have considered the question, five have expressed the opinion that such arrests are unconstitutional.

Last Term we noted probable jurisdiction of these appeals in order to address that question. ... We now reverse the New York Court of Appeals and hold that the Fourth Amendment to the United States Constitution, made applicable to the States by the Fourteenth Amendment, *Mapp* v. *Ohio* [1961]; *Wolf* v. *Colorado* [1949], prohibits the police from making a warrantless and nonconsensual entry into a suspect's home in order to make a routine felony arrest.

We first state the facts of both cases in some detail and put to one side certain related questions that are not presented by these records. We then explain why the New York statutes are not consistent with the Fourth Amendment and why the reasons for upholding warrantless arrests in a public place do not apply to warrantless invasions of the privacy of the home.

I

On January 14, 1970, after two days of intensive investigation, New York detectives had assembled evidence sufficient to establish probable cause to believe that Theodore Payton had murdered the manager of a gas station two days earlier. At about 7:30 a.m. on January 15, six officers went to Payton's apartment in the Bronx, intending to arrest him. They had not obtained a warrant. Although light and music emanated from the apartment, there was no response to their knock on the metal door. They summoned emergency assistance and, about 30 minutes later, used crowbars to break open the door and enter the apartment. No one was there. In plain view, however, was a 30-caliber shell casing that was seized and later admitted into evidence at Payton's murder trial.

In due course Payton surrendered to the police, was indicted for murder, and moved to suppress the evidence taken from his apartment.

The trial judge held that the warrantless and forcible entry was authorized by the New York Code of Criminal Procedure, and that the evidence in plain view was properly seized. He found that exigent circumstances justified the officers' failure to announce their purpose before entering the apartment as required by the statute. He had no occasion, however, to decide whether those circumstances also would have justified the failure to obtain a warrant, because he concluded that the warrantless entry was adequately supported by the statute without regard to the circumstances. The Appellate Division, First Department, summarily affirmed.

On March 14, 1974, Obie Riddick was arrested for the commission of two armed robberies that had occurred in 1971. He had been identified by the victims in June of 1973 and in January 1974 the police had learned his address. They did not obtain a warrant for his arrest. At about noon on March 14, a detective, accompanied by three other officers, knocked on the door of the Queens house where Riddick was living. When his young son opened the door, they could see Riddick sitting in bed covered by a sheet. They entered the house and placed him under arrest. Before permitting him to dress, they opened a chest of drawers two feet from the bed in search of weapons and found narcotics and related paraphernalia. Riddick was subsequently indicted on narcotics charges. At a suppression hearing, the trial judge held that the warrantless entry into his home was authorized by the revised New York statute, and that the search of the immediate area was reasonable under *Chimel* v. *California* [1969]. The Appellate Division, Second Department, affirmed the denial of the suppression motion.

The New York Court of Appeals, in a single opinion, affirmed the convictions of both Payton and Riddick. The court recognized that the question whether and under what circumstances an officer may enter a suspect's home to make a warrantless arrest had not been settled either by that court or by this Court. . . . The majority supported its holding by noting the "apparent historical acceptance" of warrantless entries to make felony arrests, both in the English common law and in the practice of many American States.

Three members of the New York Court of Appeals dissented on this issue because they believed that the Constitution requires the police to obtain a "warrant to enter a home to arrest or seize a person, unless there are exigent circumstances." Starting from the premise that, except in carefully circumscribed instances, "the Fourth Amendment forbids police entry into a private home to search for and seize an object without a warrant," the dissenters reasoned that an arrest of the person involves an even greater invasion of privacy and should therefore be attended with at least as great a measure of constitutional protection. The dissenters noted "the existence of statutes and the American Law Institute imprimatur codifying the common-law rule authorizing warrantless arrests in private homes" and acknowledged that "the statutory authority of a police officer to make a warrantless arrest in this

State has been in effect for almost 100 years," but concluded that "neither antiquity nor legislative unanimity can be determinative of the grave constitutional question presented" and "can never be a substitute for reasoned analysis."

Before addressing the narrow question presented by these appeals, we put to one side related problems that are *not* presented today. Although it is arguable that the warrantless entry to effect Payton's arrest might have been justified by exigent circumstances, none of the New York courts relied on any such justification. The Court of Appeals majority treated both Payton's and Riddick's cases as involving routine arrests in which there was ample time to obtain a warrant, and we will do the same. Accordingly, we have no occasion to consider the sort of emergency or dangerous situation, described in our cases as "exigent circumstances," that would justify a warrantless entry into a home for the purpose of either arrest or search.

Nor do these cases raise any question concerning the authority of the police, without either a search or arrest warrant, to enter a third party's home to arrest a suspect. The police broke into Payton's apartment intending to arrest Payton and they arrested Riddick in his own dwelling. We also note that in neither case is it argued that the police lacked probable cause to believe that the suspect was at home when they entered. Finally, in both cases we are dealing with entries into homes made without the consent of any occupant. In *Payton,* the police used crowbars to break down the door and in *Riddick,* although his three-year-old son answered the door, the police entered before Riddick had an opportunity either to object or to consent.

II

It is familiar history that indiscriminate searches and seizures conducted under the authority of "general warrants" were the immediate evils that motivated the framing and adoption of the Fourth Amendment. Indeed, as originally proposed in the House of Representatives, the draft contained only one clause, which directly imposed limitations on the issuance of warrants, but imposed no express restrictions on warrantless searches or seizures. As it was ultimately adopted, however, the Amendment contained two separate clauses, the first protecting the basic right to be free from unreasonable searches and seizures and the second requiring that warrants be particular and supported by probable cause. . . .

It is thus perfectly clear that the evil the Amendment was designed to prevent was broader than the abuse of a general warrant. Unreasonable searches or seizures conducted without any warrant at all are condemned by the plain language of the first clause of the Amendment. Almost a century ago the Court stated in resounding terms that the principles reflected in the Amendment "reached farther than the concrete form" of the specific cases that gave it birth, and "apply to all invasions on the part of the Government and its employes of the sanctity of a man's home and the privacies of life." *Boyd* v. *United States* [1886]. Without pausing to consider whether that broad language may require some qualification, it is sufficient to note that the warrantless arrest of a person is a species of seizure required by the Amendment to be reasonable. *Beck* v. *Ohio* [1964], *Delaware* v. *Prouse* [1979]. Indeed, as MR. JUSTICE POWELL noted in his concurrence in *United States* v. *Watson* [1976] the arrest of a person is "quintessentially a seizure." . . .

The simple language of the Amendment applies equally to seizures of persons and to seizures of property. Our analysis in this case may therefore properly commence with rules that have been well established in Fourth Amendment litigation involving tangible items. As the Court unanimously reiterated just a few years ago, the "physical entry of the home is the chief evil against which the wording of the Fourth Amendment is directed." *United States* v. *United States District Court* [1972]. And we have long adhered to the view that the warrant procedure minimizes the danger of needless intrusions of that sort.

It is a "basic principle of Fourth Amendment law" that searches and seizures inside a home without a warrant are presumptively unreasonable. Yet it is also well-settled that objects such as weapons or contraband found in a public place may be seized by the police without a warrant. The seizure of property in plain view involves no invasion of privacy and is presumptively reasonable, assuming that there is probable cause to associate the property with criminal activity. The distinction between a warrantless seizure in an open area and such a seizure on private premises was plainly stated in *G. M. Leasing Corp.* v. *United States* [1977]:

> "It is one thing to seize without a warrant property resting in an open area or seizable by levy without an intrusion into privacy, and it is quite another thing to effect a warrantless seizure of property, even that owned by a corporation, situated on private premises to which access is not otherwise available for the seizing officer." . . .

The majority of the New York Court of Appeals, however, suggested that there is a substantial difference in the relative intrusiveness of an entry to search for property and an entry to search for a person. . . . It is true that the area that may legally be searched is broader when executing a search warrant than when executing an arrest warrant in the home. . . . *Chimel* v. *California.* . . . This difference may be more theoretical than real, however, because the police may need to check the entire premises for safety reasons, and sometimes they ignore the restrictions on searches incident to arrest.

But the critical point is that any differences in the intrusiveness of entries to search and entries to arrest are merely ones of degree rather than kind. The two intrusions share this fundamental characteristic: the breach of the entrance to an individual's home. The Fourth Amendment protects the individual's privacy in a variety of settings. In none is the zone of privacy more clearly defined than when bounded by the unambiguous physical dimensions of an individual's home — a zone that finds its roots in clear and specific constitutional terms: "The right of the people to be secure in their ... houses ... shall not be violated." That language unequivocally establishes the proposition that "[a]t the very core [of the Fourth Amendment] stands the right of a man to retreat into his own home and there be free from unreasonable Government intrusion." *Silverman* v. *United States* [1961]. In terms that apply equally to seizures of property and to seizures of persons, the Fourth Amendment has drawn a firm line at the entrance to the house. Absent exigent circumstances, that threshold may not reasonably be crossed without a warrant.

III

Without contending that *United States* v. *Watson* ... decided the question presented by these appeals, New York argues that the reasons that support the *Watson* holding require a similar result here. In *Watson* the Court relied on (a) the well-settled common-law rule that a warrantless arrest in a public place is valid if the arresting officer had probable cause to believe the suspect is a felon; (b) the clear consensus among the States adhering to that well settled common-law rule; and (c) the expression of the judgment of Congress that such an arrest is "reasonable." We consider each of these reasons as it applies to a warrantless entry into a home for the purpose of making a routine felony arrest.

A

An examination of the common-law understanding of an officer's authority to arrest sheds light on the obviously relevant, if not entirely dispositive, consideration of what the Framers of the Amendment might have thought to be reasonable. Initially, it should be noted that the common-law rules of arrest developed in legal contexts that substantially differ from the cases now before us. In these cases, which involve application of the exclusionary rule, the issue is whether certain evidence is admissible at trial. ... *Weeks* v. *United States* [1914]. At common law, the question whether an arrest was authorized typically arose in civil damage actions for trespass or false arrest, in which a constable's authority to make the arrest was a defense.... Additionally, if an officer was killed while attempting to effect an arrest, the question whether the person resisting the arrest was guilty of murder or manslaughter turned on whether the officer was acting within the bounds of his authority....

A study of the common law on the question whether a constable had the authority to make warrantless arrests in the home on mere suspicion of a felony — as distinguished from an officer's right to arrest for a crime committed in his presence — reveals a surprising lack of judicial decisions and a deep divergence among scholars. . . .

Thus, our study of the relevant common law does not provide the same guidance that was present in *Watson*. Whereas the rule concerning the validity of an arrest in a public place was supported by cases directly in point and by the unanimous views of the commentators, we have found no direct authority supporting forcible entries into a home to make a routine arrest and the weight of the scholarly opinion is somewhat to the contrary. Indeed, the absence of any Seventeenth or Eighteenth Century English cases directly in point, together with the unequivocal endorsement of the tenet that "a man's house is his castle," strongly suggest that the prevailing practice was not to make such arrests except in hot pursuit or when authorized by a warrant. . . . *Agnello* v. *United States* [1925]. In all events, the issue is not one that can be said to have been definitively settled by the common law at the time the Fourth Amendment was adopted.

B

A majority of the States that have taken a position on the question permit warrantless entry into the home to arrest even in the absence of exigent circumstances. At this time, 24 States permit such warrantless entries; 15 States clearly prohibit them, though three States do so on federal constitutional grounds alone; and 11 States have apparently taken no position on the question.

But these current figures reflect a significant decline during the last decade in the number of States permitting warrantless entries for arrest. Recent dicta in this Court raising questions about the practice, . . . and Federal Courts of Appeals' decisions on point, . . . have led state courts to focus on the issue. Virtually all of the state courts that have had to confront the constitutional issue directly have held warrantless entries into the home to arrest to be invalid in the absence of exigent circumstances. . . . Three state courts have relied on Fourth Amendment grounds alone, while seven have squarely placed their decisions on both federal and state constitutional grounds. A number of other state courts, though not having had to confront the issue directly, have recognized the serious nature of the constitutional question. Apparently, only the Supreme Court of Florida and the New York Court of Appeals in this case have expressly upheld warrantless entries to arrest in the face of a constitutional challenge.

A longstanding, widespread practice is not immune from constitutional scrutiny. But neither is it to be lightly brushed aside. This is particularly so when the constitutional standard is as amorphous as the word "reasonable," and when custom and contemporary norms necessarily play such a large role in the constitutional analysis. In this case, although the weight of state-law authority is clear, there is by no means the kind of virtual unanimity on this question that was present in *United*

States v. *Watson* ... with regard to warrantless arrests in public places. ... Only 24 of the 50 States currently sanction warrantless entries into the home to arrest, ... and there is an obvious declining trend. Further, the strength of the trend is greater than the numbers alone indicate. Seven state courts have recently held that warrantless home arrests violate their respective *state* constitutions. ... That is significant because by invoking a state constitutional provision, a state court immunizes its decision from review by this Court. This heightened degree of immutability underscores the depth of the principle underlying the result.

C

No congressional determination that warrantless entries into the home are "reasonable" has been called to our attention. None of the federal statutes cited in the *Watson* opinion reflects any such legislative judgment. Thus, that support for the *Watson* holding finds no counterpart in this case.

... In this case, however, neither history nor this Nation's experience requires us to disregard the overriding respect for the sanctity of the home that has been embedded in our traditions since the origins of the Republic.

IV

The parties have argued at some length about the practical consequences of a warrant requirement as a precondition to a felony arrest in the home. In the absence of any evidence that effective law enforcement has suffered in those States that already have such a requirement, ... we are inclined to view such arguments with skepticism. More fundamentally, however, such arguments of policy must give way to a constitutional command that we consider to be unequivocal.

Finally, we note the State's suggestion that only a search warrant based on probable cause to believe the suspect is at home at a given time can adequately protect the privacy interests at stake, and since such a warrant requirement is manifestly impractical, there need be no warrant of any kind. We find this ingenious argument unpersuasive. It is true that an arrest warrant requirement may afford less protection than a search warrant requirement, but it will suffice to interpose the magistrate's determination of probable cause between the zealous officer and the citizen. If there is sufficient evidence of a citizen's participation in a felony to persuade a judicial officer that his arrest is justified, it is constitutionally reasonable to require him to open his doors to the officers of the law. Thus, for Fourth Amendment purposes, an arrest warrant founded on probable cause implicitly carries with it the limited authority to enter a dwelling in which the suspect lives when there is reason to believe the suspect is within.

Because no arrest warrant was obtained in either of these cases, the judgments must be reversed and the cases remanded to the New York Court of Appeals for further proceedings not inconsistent with this opinion.

It is so ordered.

MR. JUSTICE BLACKMUN, concurring.

I joined the Court's opinion in *United States* v. *Watson* (1976), upholding, on probable cause, the warrantless arrest in a public place. I, of course, am still of the view that the decision in *Watson* is correct. The Court's balancing of the competing governmental and individual interests properly occasioned that result. Where, however, the warrantless arrest is in the suspect's home, that same balancing requires that, absent exigent circumstances, the result be the other way. The suspect's interest in the sanctity of his home then outweighs the governmental interests.

I therefore join the Court's opinion, firm in the conviction that the result in *Watson* and the result here, although opposite, are fully justified by history and by the Fourth Amendment.

MR. JUSTICE WHITE, with whom THE CHIEF JUSTICE and MR. JUSTICE REHNQUIST join, dissenting.

The Court today holds that absent exigent circumstances officers may never enter a home during the daytime to arrest for a dangerous felony unless they have first obtained a warrant. This hard-and-fast-rule, founded on erroneous assumptions concerning the intrusiveness of home arrest entries, finds little or no support in the common law or in the text and history of the Fourth Amendment. I respectfully dissent.

I

As the Court notes, ... the common law of searches and seizures, as evolved in England, as transported to the Colonies, and as developed among the States, is highly relevant to the present scope of the Fourth Amendment. *United States* v. *Watson* (1976); ... *Gerstein* v. *Pugh* (1975); *Carroll* v. *United States* (1925); *Bad Elk* v. *United States* (1900); *Boyd* v. *United States* (1886); *Kurtz* v. *Moffitt* (1885). Today's decision virtually ignores these centuries of common-law development, and distorts the historical meaning of the Fourth Amendment, by proclaiming for the first time a rigid warrant requirement for all nonexigent home arrest entries.

A

...[I]t bears noting that the doctrine against home entries on bare suspicion developed in a period in which the validity of *any* arrest on bare suspicion — even one occurring outside the home — was open

to question. Not until Lord Mansfield's decision in *Samuel* v. *Payne*
. . . (K[ing's] B[ench] 1780), was it definitively established that the
constable could arrest on suspicion even if it turned out that no felony
had been committed. To the extent that the commentators relied on
by the Court reasoned from any general rule against warrantless arrests
based on bare suspicion, the rationale for their position did not survive
Samuel v. *Payne.*

<h2 style="text-align:center">B</h2>

The history of the Fourth Amendment does not support the rule
announced today. At the time that Amendment was adopted the constable
possessed broad inherent powers to arrest. The limitations on those
powers derived, not from a warrant "requirement," but from the generally
ministerial nature of the constable's office at common law. Far from
restricting the constable's arrest power, the institution of the warrant
was used to expand that authority by giving the constable delegated
powers of a superior officer such as a justice of the peace. Hence
at the time of the Bill of Rights, the warrant functioned as a powerful
tool of law enforcement rather than as a protection for the rights of
criminal suspects. . . .

In sum, the background, text, and legislative history of the Fourth
Amendment demonstrate that the purpose was to restrict the abuses
that had developed with respect to warrants; the Amendment preserved
common-law rules of arrest. Because it was not considered generally
unreasonable at common law for officers to break doors to effect a
warrantless felony arrest, I do not believe that the Fourth Amendment
was intended to outlaw the types of police conduct at issue in the
present case.

<h2 style="text-align:center">C</h2>

Probably because warrantless arrest entries were so firmly accepted
at common law, there is apparently no recorded constitutional challenge
to such entries in the 19th-century cases. Common-law authorities on
both sides of the Atlantic, however, continued to endorse the validity
of such arrests. . . . Like their predecessors, these authorities conflicted
as to whether the officer would be liable in damages if it were shown
that the person arrested was not guilty of a felony. But all agreed
that warrantless home entries would be permissible in at least some
circumstances. None endorsed the rule of today's decision that a warrant
is always required, absent exigent circumstances, to effect a home arrest.

Apparently the first official pronouncement on the validity of
warrantless home arrests came with the adoption of state codes of
criminal procedure in the latter 19th and early 20th centuries. The
great majority of these codes accepted and endorsed the inherent authority
of peace officers to enter dwellings in order to arrest felons. By 1931,

24 of 29 state codes authorized such warrantless arrest entries. By 1975, 31 of 37 state codes authorized warrantless home felony arrests. The American Law Institute included such authority in its model legislation in 1931 and again in 1975. . . .

This Court apparently first questioned the reasonableness of warrantless nonexigent entries to arrest in *Jones* v. *United States* (1958), noting in dictum that such entries would pose a "grave constitutional question" if carried out at night. In *Coolidge* v. *New Hampshire* (1971), the Court stated, again in dictum, that:

> "[I]f [it] is correct that it has generally been assumed that the Fourth Amendment is not violated by the warrantless entry of a man's house for purposes of arrest, it might be wise to re-examine the assumption. Such a re-examination 'would confront us with a grave constitutional question, namely, whether the forcible night-time entry into a dwelling to arrest a person reasonably believed within, upon probable cause that he had committed a felony, under circumstances where no reason appears why an arrest warrant could not have been sought, is consistent with the Fourth Amendment.' *Jones* v. *United States* [1958]. . . ."

Although *Coolidge* and *Jones* both referred to the special problem of warrantless entries during the nighttime, it is not surprising that state and federal courts have tended to read those dicta as suggesting a broader infirmity applying to daytime entries also, and that the majority of recent decisions have been against the constitutionality of all types of warrantless, nonexigent home arrest entries. As the Court concedes, however, even despite *Coolidge* and *Jones* it remains the case that

> "A majority of the States that have taken a position on the question permit warrantless entry into the home to arrest even in the absence of exigent circumstances. At this time, 24 States permit such warrantless entries; 15 States clearly prohibit them, though three States do so on federal constitutional grounds alone; and 11 States have apparently taken no position on the question." . . .

This consensus in the face of seemingly contrary dicta from this Court, is entitled to more deference than the Court today provides. . . .

D

In the present case, as in *Watson*, the applicable federal statutes are relevant to the reasonableness of the type of arrest in question. Under 18 U.S.C. § 3052, 64 Stat. 1239, specified federal agents may "make arrests without warrants for any offense against the United States committed in their presence, or for any felony cognizable under the laws of the United States, if they have reasonable grounds to believe that the person to be arrested has committed or is committing such felony." On its face this provision authorizes federal agents to make warrantless arrests anywhere, including the home. Particularly in light of the accepted rule at common law and among the States permitting warrantless home arrests, the absence of any explicit exception for the home from § 3052 is persuasive evidence that Congress intended to authorize warrantless arrests there as well as elsewhere.

Further, Congress has not been unaware of the special problems involved in police entries into the home. In 18 U.S.C. § 3109, 62 Stat. 820, it provided that

> "The officer may break open any outer or inner door or window of a house, or any part of a house, or anything therein, to execute a search warrant, if, after notice of his authority and purpose, he is refused admittance. . . .". . .

In explicitly providing authority to enter when executing a search warrant, Congress surely did not intend to derogate from the officers' power to effect an arrest entry either with or without a warrant. Rather, Congress apparently assumed that this power was so firmly established either at common law or by statute that no explicit grant of arrest authority was required in § 3109. In short, although the Court purports to find no guidance in the relevant federal statutes, I believe that fairly read they authorize the type of police conduct at issue in these cases.

II

A

Today's decision rests, in large measure, on the premise that warrantless arrest entries constitute a particularly severe invasion of personal privacy. I do not dispute that the home is generally a very private area or that the common law displayed a special "reverence . . . for the individual's right of privacy in his house." *Miller* v. *United States* . . . [1958]. However, the Fourth Amendment is concerned with protecting people, not places, and no talismanic significance is given to the fact that an arrest occurs in the home rather than elsewhere. . . . It is necessary in each case to assess realistically the actual extent of invasion of constitutionally protected privacy. Further, as MR. JUSTICE POWELL observed in *United States* v. *Watson* . . . all arrests involve serious intrusions onto an individual's privacy and dignity. Yet we settled in *Watson* that the intrusiveness of a public arrest is not enough to mandate the obtaining of a warrant. The inquiry in the present case, therefore, is whether the incremental intrusiveness that results from an arrest's being made *in the dwelling* is enough to support an inflexible constitutional rule requiring warrants for such arrests whenever exigent circumstances are not present.

Today's decision ignores the carefully crafted restrictions on the common-law power of arrest entry and thereby overestimates the dangers inherent in that practice. At common law, absent exigent circumstances, entries to arrest could be made only for felony. Even in cases of felony, the officers were required to announce their presence, demand admission, and be refused entry before they were entitled to break doors. Further, it seems generally accepted that entries could be made only during daylight hours. And, in my view, the officer entering to arrest must have reasonable grounds to believe, not only that the arrestee has committed a crime, but also that the person suspected is present in the house at the time of the entry.

These four restrictions on home arrests — felony, knock and announce, daytime, and stringent probable cause — constitute powerful and complementary protections for the privacy interests associated with the home. The felony requirement guards against abusive or arbitrary enforcement and ensures that invasions of the home occur only in case of the most serious crimes. The knock and announce and daytime requirement protect individuals against the fear, humiliation and embarrassment of being roused from the beds in states of partial or complete undress. And these requirements allow the arrestee to surrender at his front door, thereby maintaining his dignity and preventing the officers from entering other rooms of the dwelling. The stringent probable cause requirement would help ensure against the possibility that the police would enter when the suspect was not home, and, in searching for him, frighten members of the family or ransack parts of the house, seizing items in plain view. In short, these requirements, taken together, permit an individual suspected of a serious crime to surrender at the front door of his dwelling and thereby avoid most of the humiliation and indignity that the Court seems to believe necessarily accompany a house arrest entry. Such a front door arrest, in my view, is no more intrusive on personal privacy than the public warrantless arrests which we found to pass constitutional muster in *Watson*.

All of these limitations on warrantless arrest entries are satisfied on the facts of the present cases. The arrests here were for serious felonies — murder and armed robbery — and both occurred during daylight hours. The authorizing statutes required that the police announce their business and demand entry; neither Payton nor Riddick makes any contention that these statutory requirements were not fulfilled. And it is not argued that the police had no probable cause to believe that both Payton and Riddick were in their dwellings at the time of the entries. Today's decision, therefore, sweeps away any possibility that warrantless home entries might be permitted in some limited situations other than those in which exigent circumstances are present. The Court substitutes, in one sweeping decision, a rigid constitutional rule in place of the common-law approach, evolved over hundreds of years, which achieved a flexible accommodation between the demands of personal privacy and the legitimate needs of law enforcement.

A rule permitting warrantless arrest entries would not pose a danger that officers would use their entry power as a pretext to justify an otherwise invalid warrantless search. A search pursuant to a warrantless arrest entry will rarely, if ever, be as complete as one under authority of a search warrant. If the suspect surrenders at the door, the officers may not enter other rooms. Of course, the suspect may flee or hide, or may not be at home, but the officers cannot anticipate the first two of these possibilities and the last is unlikely given the requirement of probable cause to believe that the suspect is at home. Even when officers are justified in searching other rooms, they may seize only items within the arrestee's possession or immediate control or items in plain view discovered during the course of a search reasonably directed at discovering a hiding suspect. Hence a warrantless home entry is likely to uncover far less evidence than a search conducted under authority of a search warrant. Furthermore, an arrest entry will inevitably tip off the suspects and likely result in destruction or removal of evidence not uncovered during the arrest. I therefore cannot believe that the police would take the risk of losing valuable evidence through a pretextual arrest entry rather than applying to a magistrate for a search warrant.

B

While exaggerating the invasion of personal privacy involved in home arrests, the Court fails to account for the danger that its rule will "severely hamper effective law enforcement." ... The policeman on his beat must now make subtle discriminations that perplex even judges in their chambers. As MR. JUSTICE POWELL noted, concurring in *United States* v. *Watson* ... police will sometimes delay making an arrest, even after probable cause is established, in order to be sure that they have enough evidence to convict. Then, if they suddenly have to arrest, they run the risk that the subsequent exigency will not excuse their prior failure to obtain a warrant. This problem cannot effectively be cured by obtaining a warrant as soon as probable cause is established because of the chance that the warrant will go stale before the arrest is made.

Further, police officers will often face the difficult task of deciding whether the circumstances are sufficiently exigent to justify their entry to arrest without a warrant. This is a decision that must be made quickly in the most trying of circumstances. If the officers mistakenly decide that the circumstances are exigent, the arrest will be invalid and any evidence seized incident to the arrest or in plain view will be excluded at trial. On the other hand, if the officers mistakenly determine that exigent circumstances are lacking, they may refrain from making the arrest, thus creating the possibility that a dangerous criminal will escape into the community. The police could reduce the likelihood of escape by staking out all possible exits until the circumstances become clearly exigent or a warrant is obtained. But the costs of such a stakeout seem excessive in an era of rising crime and scarce police resources.

The uncertainty inherent in the exigent circumstances determination burdens the judicial system as well. In the case of searches, exigent circumstances are sufficiently unusual that this Court has determined that the benefits of a warrant outweigh the burdens imposed, including the burdens on the judicial system. In contrast, arrests recurringly involve exigent circumstances, and this Court has heretofore held that a warrant can be dispensed with without undue sacrifice in Fourth Amendment values. The situation should be no different with respect to arrests in the home. Under today's decision, whenever the police have made a warrantless home arrest there will be the possibility of "endless litigation with respect to the existence of exigent circumstances, whether it was practicable to get a warrant, whether the suspect was about to flee, and the like." *United States* v. *Watson. . . .*

Our cases establish that the ultimate test under the Fourth Amendment is one of "reasonableness." *Marshall* v. *Barlow's, Inc.* (1978); *Camera* v. *Municipal Court* (1967). I cannot join the Court in declaring unreasonable a practice which has been thought entirely reasonable by so many for so long. It would be far preferable to adopt a clear and simple rule: after knocking and announcing their presence, police may enter the home to make a daytime arrest without a warrant when there is probable cause to believe that the person to be arrested committed a felony and is present in the house. This rule would best comport with the common-law background, with the traditional practice in the States, and with the history and policies of the Fourth Amendment. Accordingly, I respectfully dissent.

MR. JUSTICE REHNQUIST, dissenting.

The Court today refers to both *Payton* and *Riddick* as "routine felony arrests." I have no reason to dispute the Court's characterization of these arrests, but cannot refrain from commenting on the social implications of the result reached by the Court. Payton was arrested for the murder of the manager of a gas station; Riddick was arrested for two armed robberies. If these are indeed "routine felony arrests," which culminated in convictions after trial upheld by the state courts on appeal, surely something is amiss in the process of the administration of criminal justice whereby these convictions are now set aside by this Court under the exclusionary rule which we have imposed upon the States under the Fourth and Fourteenth Amendments to the United States Constitution.

I fully concur and join the dissenting opinion of MR. JUSTICE WHITE. There is significant historical evidence that we have over the years misread the history of the Fourth Amendment in connection with searches, elevating the warrant requirement over the necessity for probable cause in a way which the Framers of that Amendment did not intend. . . . But one may accept all of that as *stare decisis,* and still feel deeply troubled by the transposition of these same errors into the area of actual arrests of felons within their houses with respect to whom there is probable cause to suspect guilt of the offense in question.

COURT ON IMMUNITY
OF MUNICIPALITIES
April 16, 1980

The Supreme Court April 16 ruled that municipalities were not immune to federal damage suits brought by persons who felt their rights were violated by the action of city officials.

The case, Owen v. *City of Independence, Mo., was decided by a 5-4 vote. The majority rejected any qualified immunity to such suits for municipalities which might argue that their challenged actions were taken in good faith. The decision completed the removal of the absolute protection which cities had earlier enjoyed against such suits for damages.*

Justice William J. Brennan Jr. wrote the court's majority opinion. Chief Justice Warren E. Burger and Justices Potter Stewart and William H. Rehnquist joined in Justice Lewis F. Powell's dissent in the case.

The Case

Owen, the former police chief of Independence, sued the city after he was dismissed from his job. He argued that he had been denied his constitutional right to due process because he had not been notified of the reasons for his dismissal nor given an opportunity for a hearing before he was fired. Lower courts had held that the city government was immune from such a suit, but the Supreme Court reversed.

Background

In 1871 Congress approved language that provided that, "Every person who, under color of any statute, ordinance, regulation, custom, or usage,

299

of any state or territory, subjects or causes to be subjected, any citizen of the United States or other person within the jurisdiction thereof to deprivation of any rights, privileges, or immunities secured by the Constitution and laws, shall be liable to the party injured. . . ."

The court held in 1961 (Monroe v. Pate) *that cities were not "persons" within the meaning of this provision. City governments, therefore, were immune from such damage suits, although city officials as individuals did not enjoy such broad immunity.*

Seventeen years later, in 1978, the court decided that its 1961 decision had been in error. In the case of Monell v. *New York City Department of Social Services, the court held that cities might be the target of damage suits brought under the 1871 law.*

Opinion

Writing for the Owen *majority, Justice Brennan explained that "there is no tradition of immunity for municipal corporations, and neither history nor policy support a construction of [the 1871 law] that would justify the qualified immunity [sought by the city in this case]."*

Without clear evidence that Congress intended city governments to enjoy that sort of immunity, the court was "unwilling to suppose that injury occasioned by a municipality's unconstitutional conduct were not also meant to be fully redressable" through suits for damages brought under the 1871 law.

"The knowledge that a municipality will be liable for all of its injurious conduct, whether committed in good faith or not, should create an incentive for officials who may harbor doubts about the lawfulness of their intended actions to err on the side of protecting citizens' constitutional rights," Brennan wrote.

Dissent

Justice Powell, in the dissenting opinion, argued Owen had suffered no constitutional injury. He was fired two months before the Supreme Court ruled that due process required a hearing in such cases, Powell noted.

In addition, the dissenters argued that the majority's ruling "unreasonably subjects local governments to damages [sic] judgments for actions that were reasonable when performed."

> *Following are excerpts from the Supreme Court's decision April 16, 1980, ruling that cities were not immune to federal damage suits brought by persons who felt their rights were violated by the action of city officials; and excerpts from Justice Powell's dissenting opinion:*

No. 78-1779

George D. Owen, Petitioner,
v.
City of Independence,
Missouri, et al.

On Writ of Certiorari to the
United States Court of Appeals
for the Eighth Circuit.

[April 16, 1980]

MR. JUSTICE BRENNAN delivered the opinion of the Court.

Monell v. *New York City Dept. of Social Services* (1978), overruled *Monroe* v. *Pape* (1961), insofar as *Monroe* held that local governments were not among the "persons" to whom 42 U.S.C. § 1983 applies and were therefore wholly immune from suit under the statute. *Monell* reserved decision, however, on the question whether local governments, although not entitled to an absolute immunity, should be afforded some form of official immunity in § 1983 suits. . . . In this action brought by petitioner in the District Court for the Western District of Missouri, the Court of Appeals for the Eighth Circuit held that respondent city of Independence, Mo., "is entitled to qualified immunity from liability" based on the good faith of its officials: "We extend the limited immunity the district court applied to the individual defendants to cover the City as well, because its officials acted in good faith and without malice." . . . We granted certiorari. . . . We reverse.

I

The events giving rise to this suit are detailed in the District Court's findings of fact. . . . On February 20, 1967, Robert L. Broucek, then City Manager of respondent city of Independence, Mo., appointed petitioner George D. Owen to an indefinite term as Chief of Police. In 1972, Owen and a new City Manager, Lyle W. Alberg, engaged in a dispute over petitioner's administration of the police department's property room. In March of that year, a handgun, which the records of the Department's property room stated had been destroyed, turned up in Kansas City in the possession of a felon. This discovery prompted Alberg to initiate an investigation of the management of the property room. Although the probe was initially directed by petitioner, Alberg soon transferred responsibility for the investigation to the City's Department of Law, instructing the City Counselor to supervise its conduct and to inform him directly of its findings.

Sometime in early April 1972, Alberg received a written report on the investigation's progress, along with copies of confidential witness statements. Although the City Auditor found that the police department's records were insufficient to permit an adequate accounting of the goods contained in the property room, the City Counselor concluded that there was no evidence of any criminal acts or of any violation of state

301

or municipal law in the administration of the property room. Alberg discussed the results of the investigation at an informal meeting with several City Council members and advised them that he would take action at an appropriate time to correct any problems in the administration of the police department.

On April 10, Alberg asked petitioner to resign as Chief of Police and to accept another position within the department, citing dissatisfaction with the manner in which petitioner had managed the department, particularly his inadequate supervision of the property room. Alberg warned that if petitioner refused to take another position in the department his employment would be terminated, to which petitioner responded that he did not intend to resign.

On April 13, Alberg issued a public statement addressed to the Mayor and the City Council concerning the results of the investigation. After referring to "discrepancies" found in the administration, handling, and security of public property, the release concluded that "[t]here appears to be no evidence to substantiate any allegations of a criminal nature" and offered assurances that "[s]teps have been initiated on an administrative level to correct these discrepancies." . . . Although Alberg apparently had decided by this time to replace petitioner as Police Chief, he took no formal action to that end and left for a brief vacation without informing the City Council of his decision.

While Alberg was away on the weekend of April 15 and 16, two developments occurred. Petitioner, having consulted with counsel, sent Alberg a letter demanding written notice of the charges against him and a public hearing with a reasonable opportunity to respond to those charges. At approximately the same time, City Councilman Paul L. Roberts asked for a copy of the investigative report on the police department property room. Although petitioner's appeal received no immediate response, the Acting City Manager complied with Roberts' request and supplied him with the audit report and witness statements.

On the evening of April 17, 1972, the City Council held its regularly scheduled meeting. After completion of the planned agenda, Councilman Roberts read a statement he had prepared on the investigation. Among other allegations, Roberts charged that petitioner had misappropriated police department property for his own use, that narcotics and money had "mysteriously disappeared" from his office, that traffic tickets had been manipulated, that high ranking police officials had made "inappropriate" requests affecting the police court, and that "things have occurred causing the unusual release of felons." At the close of his statement, Roberts moved that the investigative reports be released to the news media and turned over to the prosecutor for presentation to the grand jury, and that the City Manager "take all direct and appropriate action" against those persons "involved in illegal, wrongful, or gross inefficient activities brought out in the investigative reports." After some discussion, the City Council passed Roberts' motion with no dissents and one abstention.

City Manager Alberg discharged petitioner the very next day. Petitioner was not given any reason for his dismissal; he received only a written notice stating that his employment as Chief of Police was "terminated under the provisions of Section 3.3 (1) of the City Charter." Petitioner's earlier demand for a specification of charges and a public hearing was ignored, and a subsequent request by his attorney for an appeal of the discharge decision was denied by the city on the grounds that "there is no appellate procedure or forum provided by the Charter or ordinances of the City of Independence, Missouri, relating to the dismissal of Mr. Owen." . . .

The local press gave prominent coverage both to the City Council's action and petitioner's dismissal, linking the discharge to the investigation. As instructed by the City Council, Alberg referred the investigative reports and witness statements to the Prosecuting Attorney of Jackson County, Mo., for consideration by a grand jury. The results of the audit and investigation were never released to the public, however. The grand jury subsequently returned a "no true bill," and no further action was taken by either the City Council or City Manager Alberg.

II

Petitioner named the city of Independence, City Manager Alberg, and the present members of the City Council in their official capacities as defendants in this suit. Alleging that he was discharged without notice of reasons and without a hearing in violation of his constitutional rights to procedural and substantive due process, petitioner sought declaratory and injunctive relief, including a hearing on his discharge, backpay from the date of discharge, and attorney's fees. The District Court, after a bench trial, entered judgment for respondents. . . .

The Court of Appeals initially reversed the District Court. . . . Although it agreed with the District Court that under Missouri law petitioner possessed no property interest in continued employment as police chief, the Court of Appeals concluded that the city's allegedly false public accusations had blackened petitioner's name and reputation, thus depriving him of liberty without due process of law. That the stigmatizing charges did not come from the City Manager and were not included in the official discharge notice was, in the court's view, immaterial. What was important, the court explained, was that "the official actions of the city council released charges against [petitioner] contemporaneous and, in the eyes of the public, connected with that discharge." . . .

Respondents petitioned for review of the Court of Appeals' decision. Certiorari was granted, and the case was remanded for further consideration in light of our supervening decision in *Monell* v. *New York City Dept. of Social Services* (1978). The Court of Appeals on the remand reaffirmed its original determination that the city had violated petitioner's rights under the Fourteenth Amendment, but held that all respondents, including the city, were entitled to qualified immunity from liability. . . .

Monell held that "a local government may not be sued under § 1983 for an injury inflicted solely by its employees or agents. Instead, it is when execution of a government's policy or custom, whether made by its lawmakers or by those whose edicts or acts may fairly be said to represent official policy, inflicts the injury that the government as an entity is responsible under § 1983." . . . The Court of Appeals held in the instant case that the municipality's official policy was responsible for the deprivation of petitioner's constitutional rights: "[T]he stigma attached to [petitioner] in connection with his discharge was caused by the official conduct of the City's lawmakers, or by those whose acts may fairly be said to represent official policy. Such conduct amounted to official policy causing the infringement of [petitioner's] constitutional rights, in violation of section 1983." . . .

Nevertheless, the Court of Appeals affirmed the judgment of the District Court denying petitioner any relief against the respondent city. . . .

III

Because the question of the scope of a municipality's immunity from liability under § 1983 is essentially one of statutory construction, see *Wood* v. *Strickland* (1975); *Tenney* v. *Brandhove* (1951), the starting point in our analysis must be the language of the statute itself. . . . By its terms, § 1983 "creates a species of tort liability that on its face admits of no immunities." *Imbler* v. *Pachtman* (1976). Its language is absolute and unqualified; no mention is made of any privileges, immunities, or defenses that may be asserted. Rather, the act imposes liability upon *"every person"* who, under color of state law or custom, "subjects, or causes to be subjected, any citizen of the United States . . . to the deprivation of any rights, privileges, or immunities secured by the Constitution and laws." And *Monell* held that these words were intended to encompass municipal corporations as well as natural "persons."

Moreover, the congressional debates surrounding the passage of § 1 of the Civil Rights Act of 1871, 17 Stat. 13 — the forerunner of § 1983 — confirm the expansive sweep of the statutory language. . . . Similar views of the act's broad remedy for violations of federally protected rights were voiced by its supporters in both Houses of Congress. . . .

However, notwithstanding § 1983's expansive language and the absence of any express incorporation of common-law immunities, we have, on several occasions, found that a tradition of immunity was so firmly rooted in the common law and was supported by such strong policy reasons that "Congress would have specifically so provided had it wished to abolish the doctrine." *Pierson* v. *Ray* (1967). Thus in *Tenney* v. *Brandhove* (1951), after tracing the development of an absolute legislative privilege from its source in 16th-century England to its inclusion in the Federal and State Constitutions, we concluded that Congress "would [not] impinge on a tradition so well grounded in history and reason by covert inclusion in the general language" of § 1983. . . .

Subsequent cases have required that we consider the personal liability of various other types of government officials. Noting that "[f]ew doctrines were more solidly established at common law than the immunity of judges from liability for damages for acts committed within their judicial jurisdiction." *Pierson* v. *Ray* . . . held that the absolute immunity traditionally accorded judges was preserved under § 1983. In that same case, local police officers were held to enjoy a "good faith and probable cause" defense to § 1983 suits similar to that which existed in false arrest actions at common law. . . . Several more recent decisions have found immunities of varying scope appropriate for different state and local officials sued under § 1983. . . . *Procunier* v. *Navarette* (1978) (qualified immunity for prison officials and officers); *Imbler* v. *Pachtman* (1976) (absolute immunity for prosecutors in initiating and presenting the State's case); *O'Connor* v. *Donaldson* (1975) (qualified immunity for superintendent of state hospital); *Wood* v. *Strickland* (1975) (qualified immunity for local school board members); *Scheuer* v. *Rhodes* (1974) (qualified "good-faith" immunity for state Governor and other executive officers for discretionary acts performed in the course of official conduct).

In each of these cases, our finding of § 1983 immunity "was predicated upon a considered inquiry into the immunity historically accorded the relevant official at common law and the interests behind it." *Imbler* v. *Pachtman*. . . . Where the immunity claimed by the defendant was well-established at common law at the time § 1983 was enacted, and where its rationale was compatible with the purposes of the Civil Rights Act, we have construed the statute to incorporate that immunity. But there is no tradition of immunity for municipal corporations, and neither history nor policy support a construction of § 1983 that would justify the qualified immunity accorded the city of Independence by the Court of Appeals. We hold, therefore, that the municipality may not assert the good faith of its officers or agents as a defense to liability under § 1983.

[Section A Omitted]

B

Our rejection of a construction of § 1983 that would accord municipalities a qualified immunity for their good-faith constitutional violations is compelled both by the legislative purpose in enacting the statute and by considerations of public policy. The central aim of the Civil Rights Act was to provide protection to those persons wronged by the " '[m]isuse of power, possessed by virtue of state law and made possible

only because the wrongdoer is clothed with the authority of state law.' "
Monroe v. *Pape* (1961) (quoting *United States* v. *Classic* (1941)). By
creating an express federal remedy, Congress sought to "enforce provisions
of the Fourteenth Amendment against those who carry a badge of authority
of a State and represent it in some capacity, whether they act in
accordance with their authority or misuse it." *Monroe* v. *Pape.* . . .

How "uniquely amiss" it would be, therefore, if the government itself
— "the social organ to which all in our society look for the promotion
of liberty, justice, fair and equal treatment, and the setting of worthy
norms and goals for social conduct" — were permitted to disavow liability
for the injury it has begotten. . . . *Adickes* v. *Kress & Co.* (1970) (opinion
of BRENNAN, J.). A damages remedy against the offending party is
a vital component of any scheme for vindicating cherished constitutional
guarantees, and the importance of assuring its efficacy is only accentuated
when the wrongdoer is the institution that has been established to
protect the very rights it has transgressed. Yet owing to the qualified
immunity enjoyed by most government officials . . . *Scheuer* v. *Rhodes*
(1974), many victims of municipal malfeasance would be left remediless
if the city were also allowed to assert a good-faith defense. Unless
countervailing considerations counsel otherwise, the injustice of such
a result should not be tolerated.

Moreover, § 1983 was intended not only to provide compensation to
the victims of past abuses, but to serve as a deterrent against future
constitutional deprivations, as well. . . . *Robertson* v. *Wegmann* (1978);
Carey v. *Piphus* (1978). The knowledge that a municipality will be
liable for all of its injurious conduct, whether committed in good faith
or not, should create an incentive for officials who may harbor doubts
about the lawfulness of their intended actions to err on the side of
protecting citizens' constitutional rights. Furthermore, the threat that
damages might be levied against the city may encourage those in a
policymaking position to institute internal rules and programs designed
to minimize the likelihood of unintentional infringements on constitutional
rights. Such procedures are particularly beneficial in preventing those
"systemic" injuries that result not so much from the conduct of any
single individual, but from the interactive behavior of several government
officials, each of whom may be acting in good faith. . . .

Our previous decisions conferring qualified immunities on various government officials . . . are not to be read as derogating the significance
of the societal interest in compensating the innocent victims of governmental misconduct. Rather, in each case we concluded that overriding
considerations of public policy nonetheless demanded that the official
be given a measure of protection from personal liability. The concerns
that justified those decisions, however, are less compelling, if not wholly
inapplicable, when the liability of the municipal entity is at issue.

In *Scheuer* v. *Rhodes* [1974], THE CHIEF JUSTICE identified the
two "mutually dependent rationales" on which the doctrine of official
immunity rested:

"(1) the injustice, particularly in the absence of bad faith, of subjecting to liability an officer who is required, by the legal obligations
of his position, to exercise discretion; (2) the danger that the threat
of such liability would deter his willingness to execute his office
with the decisiveness and the judgment required by the public
good."

The first consideration is simply not implicated when the damage
award comes not from the official's pocket, but from the public treasury.
It hardly seems unjust to require a municipal defendant which has
violated a citizen's constitutional rights to compensate him for the injury
suffered thereby. Indeed, Congress enacted § 1983 precisely to provide
a remedy for such abuses of official power. . . . *Monroe* v. *Pape*. . . .
Elemental notions of fairness dictate that one who causes a loss should
bear the loss.

It has been argued, however, that revenue raised by taxation for
public use should not be diverted to the benefit of a single or discrete
group of taxpayers, particularly where the municipality has at all times
acted in good faith. On the contrary, the accepted view is that stated
in *Thayer* v. *Boston* . . . "that the city, in its corporate capacity, should
be liable to make good the damages sustained by an [unlucky] individual,
in consequence of the acts thus done." . . . After all, it is the public
at large which enjoys the benefits of the government's activities, and
it is the public at large which is ultimately responsible for its administration. Thus, even where some constitutional development could
not have been foreseen by municipal officials, it is fairer to allocate
any resulting financial loss to the inevitable costs of government borne
by all the taxpayers, than to allow its impact to be felt solely by
those whose rights, albeit newly recognized, have been violated. . . .

The second rationale mentioned in *Scheuer* also loses its force when
it is the municipality, in contrast to the official, whose liability is
at issue. At the heart of this justification for a qualified immunity
for the individual official is the concern that the threat of *personal*
monetary liability will introduce an unwarranted and unconscionable
consideration into the decisionmaking process, thus paralyzing the governing official's decisiveness and distorting his judgment on matters
of public policy. The inhibiting effect is significantly reduced, if not
eliminated, however, when the threat of personal liability is removed.
First, as an empirical matter, it is questionable whether the hazard
of municipal loss will deter a public officer from the conscientious
exercise of his duties; city officials routinely make decisions that either
require a large expenditure of municipal funds or involve a substantial
risk of depleting the public fisc. . . . More important, though, is the
realization that consideration of the *municipality's* liability for constitutional violations is quite properly the concern of its elected or
appointed officials. Indeed, a decisionmaker would be derelict in his
duties if, at some point, he did not consider whether his decision comports
with constitutional mandates and did not weigh the risk that a violation

might result in an award of damages from the public treasury. As one commentator aptly put it, "Whatever other concerns should shape a particular official's actions, certainly one of them should be the constitutional rights of individuals who will be affected by his actions. To criticize section 1983 liability because it leads decisionmakers to avoid the infringement of constitutional rights is to criticize one of the statute's *raisons d'être*."

IV

In sum, our decision holding that municipalities have no immunity from damages liability flowing from their constitutional violations harmonizes well with developments in the common law and our own pronouncements on official immunities under § 1983. Doctrines of tort law have changed significantly over the past century, and our notions of governmental responsibility should properly reflect that evolution. No longer is individual "blameworthiness" the acid test of liability; the principle of equitable loss-spreading has joined fault as a factor in distributing the costs of official misconduct.

We believe that today's decision, together with prior precedents in this area, properly allocates these costs among the three principals in the scenario of the § 1983 cause of action: the victim of the constitutional deprivation; the officer whose conduct caused the injury; and the public, as represented by the municipal entity. The innocent individual who is harmed by an abuse of governmental authority is assured that he will be compensated for his injury. The offending official, so long as he conducts himself in good faith, may go about his business secure in the knowledge that a qualified immunity will protect him from personal liability for damages that are more appropriately chargeable to the populace as a whole. And the public will be forced to bear only the costs of injury inflicted by the "execution of a government's policy or custom, whether made by its lawmakers or by those whose edicts or acts may fairly be said to represent official policy." *Monell* v. *New York City Dept. of Social Services*. . . .

Reversed.

MR. JUSTICE POWELL, with whom THE CHIEF JUSTICE, MR. JUSTICE STEWART, and MR. JUSTICE REHNQUIST join, dissenting.

The Court today holds that the city of Independence may be liable in damages for violating a constitutional right that was unknown when the events in this case occurred. It finds a denial of due process in the city's failure to grant petitioner a hearing to clear his name after he was discharged. But his dismissal involved only the proper exercise of discretionary powers according to prevailing constitutional doctrine. The city imposed no stigma on petitioner that would require a "name clearing" hearing under the Due Process Clause.

On the basis of this alleged deprivation of rights, the Court interprets 42 U.S.C. § 1983 to impose strict liability on municipalities for constitutional violations. This strict liability approach inexplicably departs from this Court's prior decisions under § 1983 and runs counter to the concerns of the 42d Congress when it enacted the statute. The Court's ruling also ignores the vast weight of common-law precedent as well as the current state law of municipal immunity. For these reasons, and because this decision will hamper local governments unnecessarily, I dissent.

I

The Court does not question the District Court's statement of the facts surrounding Owen's dismissal. . . . It nevertheless rejects the District Court's conclusion that no due process hearing was necessary because "the circumstances of [Owen's] discharge did not impose a stigma of illegal or immoral conduct on his professional reputation." . . . Careful analysis of the record supports the District Court's view that Owen suffered no constitutional deprivation.

A

From 1967 to 1972, petitioner Owen served as Chief of the Independence Police Department at the pleasure of the City Manager. Friction between Owen and City Manager Alberg flared openly in early 1972, when charges surfaced that the Police Department's property room was mismanaged. The City Manager initiated a full internal investigation.

In early April, the City Auditor reported that the records in the property room were so sparse that he could not conduct an audit. The City Counselor reported that "there was no evidence of any criminal acts, or violation of any state law or municipal ordinances, in the administration of the property room." . . . In a telephone call on April 10, the City Manager asked Owen to resign and offered him another position in the Department. The two met on the following day. Alberg expressed his unhappiness over the property room situation and again requested that Owen step down. When Owen refused, the City Manager responded that he would be fired. . . .

On April 13, the City Manager asked Lieutenant Cook of the Police Department if he would be willing to take over as Chief. Alberg also released the following statement to the public:

"At my direction, the City Counselor's office, [i]n conjunction with the City Auditor ha[s] completed a routine audit of the police property room.

"Discrepancies were found in the administration, handling and security of recovered property. There appears to be no evidence to substantiate any allegations of a criminal nature. . . ."

The District Court found that the City Manager decided on Saturday, April 15, to replace Owen with Lieutenant Cook as Chief of Police. . . . Before the decision was announced, however, City Council Member Paul Roberts obtained the internal reports on the property room. At the April 17 Council meeting, Roberts read a prepared statement that accused police officials of "gross inefficiencies" and various "inappropriate" actions. . . . He then moved that the Council release the reports to the public, refer them to the Prosecuting Attorney of Jackson County for presentation to a grand jury, and recommend to the City Manager that he "take all direct and appropriate action permitted under the Charter. . . ." . . . The Council unanimously approved the resolution.

On April 18, Alberg "implemented his prior decision to discharge [Owen] as Chief of Police." . . . The notice of termination stated simply that Owen's employment was "[t]erminated under the provisions of Section 3.3 (1) of the City Charter." . . . That charter provision grants the City Manager complete authority to remove "directors" of administrative departments "when deemed necessary for the good of the service." Owen's lawyer requested a hearing on his client's termination. The Assistant City Counselor responded that "there is no appellate procedure or forum provided by the Charter or ordinances of the City of Independence, Missouri, relating to the dismissal of Mr. Owen." . . .

The City Manager referred to the Prosecuting Attorney all reports on the property room. The grand jury returned a "no true bill," and there has been no further official action on the matter. Owen filed a state lawsuit against Councilman Roberts and City Manager Alberg, asking for damages for libel, slander, and malicious prosecution. Alberg won a dismissal of the state law claims against him, and Councilman Roberts reached a settlement with Owen.

This federal action was filed in 1976. Owen alleged that he was denied his liberty interest in his professional reputation when he was dismissed without formal charges or a hearing. . . .

B

Due process requires a hearing on the discharge of a government employee "if the employer creates and disseminates a false and defamatory impression about the employee in connection with his termination. . . ." *Codd* v. *Velger* (1977) (*per curiam*). This principle was first announced in *Board of Regents* v. *Roth* (1972), which was decided in June of 1972, 10 weeks *after* Owen was discharged. The pivotal question after *Roth* is whether the circumstances of the discharge so blackened the employee's name as to impair his liberty interest in his professional reputation. . . .

The events surrounding Owen's dismissal "were prominently reported in local newspapers." . . . Doubtless, the public received a negative impression of Owen's abilities and performance. But a "name clearing" hearing is not necessary unless the employer makes a public statement that "might seriously damage [the employee's] standing and associations in his community." *Board of Regents* v. *Roth*. . . . No hearing is required after the "discharge of a public employee whose position is terminable at the will of the employer when there is no public disclosure of the reasons for the discharge." *Bishop* v. *Wood* (1976).

The City Manager gave no specific reason for dismissing Owen. Instead, he relied on his discretionary authority to discharge top administrators "for the good of the service." Alberg did not suggest that Owen "had been guilty of dishonesty, or immorality." *Board of Regents* v. *Roth*. . . . Indeed, in his "property room" statement of April 13, Alberg said that there was "no evidence to substantiate any allegations of a criminal nature." This exoneration was reinforced by the grand jury's refusal to initiate a prosecution in the matter. Thus, nothing in the actual firing cast such a stigma on Owen's professional reputation that his liberty was infringed.

The Court does not address directly the question whether any stigma was imposed by the discharge. Rather, it relies on the Court of Appeals' finding that stigma derived from events "connected with" the firing. . . . That court attached great significance to the resolution adopted by the City Council at its April 17 meeting. But the resolution merely recommended that Alberg take "appropriate action," and the District Court found no "causal connection" between events in the City Council and the firing of Owen. . . . Two days before the Council met, Alberg already had decided to dismiss Owen. Indeed, Councilman Roberts stated at the meeting that the City Manager had asked for Owen's resignation. . . .

Even if the Council resolution is viewed as part of the discharge process, Owen has demonstrated no denial of his liberty. Neither the City Manager nor the Council cast any aspersions on Owen's character. Alberg absolved all connected with the property room of any illegal activity, while the Council resolution alleged no wrongdoing. That events focused public attention upon Owen's dismissal is undeniable; such attention is a condition of employment — and of discharge — for high government officials. Nevertheless, nothing in the actions of the City Manager or the City Council triggered a constitutional right to a name-clearing hearing.

The statements by Councilman Roberts were neither measured nor benign, but they provide no basis for this action against the city of Independence. Under *Monell* v. *New York City Dept. of Social Services* (1978), the city cannot be held liable for Roberts' statements on a theory of *respondeat superior*. That case held that § 1983 makes municipalities liable for constitutional deprivations only if the challenged action was taken "pursuant to official municipal policy of some nature. . . ." . . . The statements of a single councilman scarcely rise to the level of municipal policy.

As the District Court concluded, "[a]t most, the circumstances . . . suggested that, as Chief of Police, [Owen] had been an inefficient administrator." ... This Court now finds unconstitutional stigma in the interaction of unobjectionable official acts with the unauthorized statements of a lone councilman who had no direct role in the discharge process. The notoriety that attended Owen's firing resulted not from any city policy, but solely from public misapprehension of the reasons for a purely discretionary dismissal. There was no constitutional injury; there should be no liability.

II

Having constructed a constitutional deprivation from the valid exercise of governmental authority, the Court holds that municipalities are strictly liable for their constitutional torts. Until two years ago, municipal corporations enjoyed absolute immunity from § 1983 claims. *Monroe* v. *Pape* (1961). But *Monell* v. *New York City Dept. of Social Services* ... held that local governments are "persons" within the meaning of the statute, and thus are liable in damages for constitutional violations inflicted by municipal policies. ... *Monell* did not address the question whether municipalities might enjoy a qualified immunity or good-faith defense against § 1983 actions. ...

After today's decision, municipalities will have gone in two short years from absolute immunity under § 1983 to strict liability. As a policy matter, I believe that strict municipal liability unreasonably subjects local governments to damages judgments for actions that were reasonable when performed. It converts municipal governance into a hazardous slalom through constitutional obstacles that often are unknown and unknowable.

The Court's decision also impinges seriously on the prerogatives of municipal entities created and regulated primarily by the States. At the very least, this Court should not initiate a federal intrusion of this magnitude in the absence of explicit congressional action. Yet today's decision is supported by nothing in the text of § 1983. Indeed, it conflicts with the apparent intent of the drafters of the statute, with the common law of municipal tort liability, and with the current state law of municipal immunities.

A

1

Section 1983 provides a private right of action against "any person" acting under color of state law who imposes or causes to be imposed a deprivation of constitutional rights. ...

The Court today abandons any attempt to harmonize § 1983 with traditional tort law. It points out that municipal immunity may be abrogated by legislation. Thus, according to the Court, Congress "abolished" municipal immunity when it includes municipalities "within the class of 'persons' subject to liability under § 1983." ...

This reasoning flies in the face of our prior decisions under this statute. We have held repeatedly that "immunities 'well grounded in history and reason' [were not] abrogated 'by covert inclusion in the general language' of § 1983." ... The peculiar nature of the Court's position emerges when the status of executive officers under § 1983 is compared with that of local governments. State and local executives are personally liable for bad-faith or unreasonable constitutional torts. Although Congress had the power to make those individuals liable for all such torts, this Court has refused to find an abrogation of traditional immunity in a statute that does not mention immunities. Yet the Court now views the enactment of § 1983 as a direct abolition of traditional municipal immunities. Unless the Court is overruling its previous immunity decisions, the silence in § 1983 must mean that the 42d Congress mutely accepted the immunity of executive officers, but silently rejected common-law municipal immunity. I find this interpretation of the statute singularly implausible.

2

Important public policies support the extension of qualified immunity to local governments. First, as recognized by the doctrine of separation of powers, some governmental decisions should be at least presumptively insulated from judicial review. ... The allocation of public resources and the operational policies of the government itself are activities that lie peculiarly within the competence of executive and legislative bodies. When charting those policies, a local official should not have to gauge his employer's possible liability under § 1983 if he incorrectly — though reasonably and in good faith — forecasts the course of constitutional law. Excessive judicial intrusion into such decisions can only distort municipal decisionmaking and discredit the courts. Qualified immunity would provide presumptive protection for discretionary acts, while still leaving the municipality liable for bad faith or unreasonable constitutional deprivations.

Because today's decision will inject constant consideration of § 1983 liability into local decisionmaking, it may restrict the independence of local governments and their ability to respond to the needs of their communities. Only this Term, we noted that the "point" of immunity under § 1983 "is to forestall an atmosphere of intimidation that would conflict with [officials'] resolve to perform their designated functions in a principled fashion." *Ferri* v. *Ackerman* (1980). ...

The Court now argues that local officials might modify their actions unduly if they face personal liability under § 1983, but that they are unlikely to do so when the locality itself will be held liable. ... This contention denigrates the sense of responsibility of municipal officers, and misunderstands the political process. Responsible local officials will be concerned about potential judgments against their municipalities for alleged constitutional torts. Moreover, they will be accountable within the political system for subjecting the municipality to adverse judgments. If officials must look over their shoulders at strict municipal liability for unknowable constitutional deprivations, the resulting degree of government paralysis will be little different from that caused by fear of personal liability. . . .

In addition, basic fairness requires a qualified immunity for municipalities. The good-faith defense recognized under § 1983 authorizes liability only when officials acted with malicious intent or when they "knew or should have known that their conduct violated the constitutional norm." *Procunier* v. *Navarette* [1978]. The standard incorporates the idea that liability should not attach unless there was notice that a constitutional right was at risk. This idea applies to governmental entities and individual officials alike. Constitutional law is what the courts say it is, and — as demonstrated by today's decision and its precursor, *Monell* — even the most prescient lawyer would hesitate to give a firm opinion on matters not plainly settled. Municipalities, often acting in the utmost good faith, may not know or anticipate when their action or inaction will be deemed a constitutional violation.

The Court nevertheless suggests that, as a matter of social justice, municipal corporations should be strictly liable even if they could not have known that a particular action would violate the Constitution. After all, the Court urges, local governments can "spread" the costs of any judgment across the local population. . . . The Court neglects, however, the fact that many local governments lack the resources to withstand substantial unanticipated liability under § 1983. Even enthusiastic proponents of municipal liability have conceded that ruinous judgments under the statute could imperil local governments. . . . By simplistically applying the theorems of welfare economics and ignoring the reality of municipal finance, the Court imposes strict liability on the level of government least able to bear it. For some municipalities, the result could be a severe limitation on their ability to serve the public.

B

The Court searches at length — and in vain — for legal authority to buttress its policy judgment. Despite its general statements to the contrary, the Court can find no support for its position in the debates on the civil rights legislation that included § 1983. Indeed, the legislative record suggests that the Members of the 42d Congress would have been dismayed by this ruling. Nor, despite its frequent citation of authorities that are only marginally relevant, can the Court rely on the traditional or current law of municipal tort liability. Both in the 19th century and now, courts and legislatures have recognized the importance of limiting the liability of local governments for official torts. Each of these conventional sources of law points to the need for qualified immunity for local governments.

[Sections 1 & 2 Omitted]

3

Today's decision also conflicts with the current law in 44 States and the District of Columbia. All of those jurisdictions provide municipal immunity at least analogous to a "good faith" defense against liability for constitutional torts. Thus, for municipalities in almost 90% of our jurisdictions, the Court creates broader liability for constitutional deprivations than for state-law torts.

Twelve States have laws creating municipal tort liability but barring damages for injuries caused by discretionary decisions or by the good-faith execution of a validly enacted, though unconstitutional, regulation. Municipalities in those States have precisely the form of qualified immunity that this Court has granted to executive officials under § 1983. Another 11 States provide even broader immunity for local governments. Five of those have retained the governmental/proprietary distinction, while Arkansas and South Dakota grant even broader protection for municipal corporations. Statutes in four more States protect local governments from tort liability except for particular injuries not relevant to this case, such as those due to motor vehicle accidents or negligent maintenance of public facilities. In Iowa, local governments are not liable for injuries caused by the execution with due care of any "officially enacted" statute or regulation.

Sixteen States and the District of Columbia follow the traditional rule against recovery for damages imposed by discretionary decisions that are confided to particular officers or organs of government. Indeed, the leading commentators on governmental tort liability have noted both the appropriateness and general acceptance of municipal immunity for discretionary acts. . . . In four states, local governments enjoy complete immunity from tort actions unless they have taken out liability insurance. Only five States impose the kind of blanket liability constructed by the Court today.

C

The Court turns a blind eye to this overwhelming evidence the municipalities have enjoyed a qualified immunity and to the policy considerations that for the life of this Republic have justified its retention. This disregard of precedent and policy is especially unfortunate because suits under § 1983 typically implicate evolving constitutional standards. A good-faith defense is much more important for those actions than in those involving ordinary tort liability. The duty not to run over a pedestrian with a municipal bus is far less likely to change than is the rule as to what process, if any, is due the bus driver if he claims the right to a hearing after discharge.

The right of a discharged government employee to a "name clearing" hearing was not recognized until our decision in *Board of Regents* v. *Roth.* . . . That ruling was handed down 10 weeks after Owen was discharged and eight weeks after the city denied his request for a hearing. By stripping the city of any immunity, the Court punishes it for failing to predict our decision in *Roth.* As a result, local governments and their officials will face the unnerving prospect of crushing damage judgments whenever a policy valid under current law is later found to be unconstitutional. I can see no justice or wisdom in that outcome.

ZIMBABWE INDEPENDENCE
April 17, 1980

The independent African nation of Zimbabwe was born at midnight on April 17 as the Union Jack was lowered over Salisbury, capital of the former British colony, Rhodesia. Britain's Prince Charles, representing Queen Elizabeth II, presented the charter of independence to President-elect Canaan Banana.

It was the swearing-in as prime minister of Robert Mugabe that particularly marked for the world the transition of power from white minority to black majority rule. Mugabe (along with Joshua Nkomo) had been a popular leader of the black nationalist guerrilla movement — the Patriotic Front — which bore the brunt of fighting against troops of the white minority Rhodesian government headed by former prime minister Ian D. Smith. (Historic Documents of 1977, p. 583; Historic Documents of 1979, p. 939)

In a conciliatory speech which echoed his remarks when he was elected, Mugabe said that "the wrongs of the past must now stand forgiven and forgotten. If yesterday I fought you as an enemy, today you have become a friend and ally, with the same national interest, loyalty, rights and duties as myself."

Mugabe Election

Mugabe won a landslide victory in parliamentary elections held Feb. 27-29. The elections were supervised by the British governor general, Lord Soames, under terms of a December 1979 agreement which tem-

porarily returned Zimbabwe Rhodesia to British colonial status until a new government was established.

The election was probably more carefully scrutinized than any other ever conducted on the African continent. More than 600 reporters from two dozen countries reported on the election campaign, and more than 150 election observers were sent into Rhodesia by governments and private groups. Moreover, a 30-member team including representatives of 11 member nations of the British Commonwealth certified the election's fairness.

The results marked a stunning defeat for supporters of Bishop Abel D. Muzorewa who, in April-May 1979, had been elected head of a biracial government in accordance with an "internal agreement" fashioned by white minority leader Ian D. Smith. Supporters of Mugabe and Nkomo boycotted Muzorewa's election, and the outcome had failed to gain international acceptance.

Independence Ceremony

Representatives of more than 100 nations, including the United Nations, attended the independence ceremony, held in a soccer stadium. Among the leaders were Prime Minister Indira Gandhi of India and Prime Minister Malcolm Fraser of Australia. U.N. Secretary-General Kurt Waldheim also attended, together with the presidents of Pakistan, Nigeria and Zambia. The U.S. delegation was headed by Averell Harriman, wartime ambassador to the Soviet Union, and it included Andrew Young, former U.S. ambassador to the United Nations.

New Budget

The new government's 21 cabinet ministers took office April 19 as independence celebrations continued throughout the country. The following day, Finance Minister Enos Nkala issued Zimbabwe's first budget. The document stressed an easing of economic burdens on Zimbabwe's poor. Sales taxes on many items were reduced to 10 percent from 15 percent, and taxes on staple food items were eliminated.

To make up for revenue losses brought about by sales tax reductions, the government imposed stiff taxes on luxuries — especially liquor, beer and tobacco.

Pledges of Aid

The United States April 14 offered $15 million in aid to help rebuild the country's rural areas shattered by years of war. Hours after independence, Robert Keeley, U.S. ambassador to Zimbabwe, pledged $2 million to rebuild rural health clinics.

The United States had been the first country to open an embassy in Zimbabwe, and it signed the new nation's first foreign aid pact. Great Britain also announced an aid package, amounting to $165 million in the next four years. Part of the funds would be used to train black civil servants and the Zimbabwean army.

South Africa

Zimbabwe on June 27 severed diplomatic ties with its neighbor, South Africa. At a meeting of the Organization of African Unity on July 4, Mugabe said that South Africa had used its diplomatic mission in Salisbury to recruit 5,000 whites in Zimbabwe to "destabilize" black governments in the region.

The South African government denied that it had engaged in subversive activities, but it did admit that the Salisbury mission office had accepted applications from former Rhodesian soldiers who wanted to join the South African armed forces.

Following are the texts of Robert Mugabe's broadcast address to the nation March 4, 1980, following his election victory; a transcript of an interview with Mugabe March 24, 1980, shown over American television on the MacNeil/Lehrer Report; Prime Minister Mugabe's independence broadcast message April 17, 1980; remarks of Prince Charles, President Banana and British Foreign Secretary Lord Carrington at the independence ceremonies April 17, 1980; and Mugabe's response. (Boldface headings in brackets have been added by Congressional Quarterly to highlight the organization of the texts.):

MUGABE'S MARCH 4 ADDRESS

Greetings in the name of freedom.

May I thank you most heartily for your votes and support.

I feel overwhelmed as at the same time I feel humbled.

I wish to address you tonight on the significance of the election victory you awarded my Party, ZANU [Zimbabwe African National Union] (PF) [Patriotic Front]. In doing so, I would like to thank all those who, either by their direct vote as our supporters or by their efficient campaigning as our organisers, have contributed to this favourable result. In addition, may I also thank all officials who participated in the mechanical exercise of handling the elections, without whose organisational and administrative efforts the whole election process would have been a failure.

Soon, a new government will come into being and lead our country to independence. In constituting this government my main concern, and that of my party, is to create an instrument capable of achieving peace and stability as it strives to bring about progress.

Peace and stability can only be achieved if all of us, first as individuals and secondly as part of the whole Zimbabwean national community, feel a definite sense of individual security on the one hand and have an assurance of national peace and security on the other.

It must be realised, however, that a state of peace and security can only be achieved by our determination, all of us, to be bound by the explicit requirements of peace contained in the Lancaster House Agreement, which express the general desire of the people of Zimbabwe.

In this regard, I wish to assure you that there can never be any return to the state of armed conflict which existed before our commitment to peace and the democratic process of election under the Lancaster House Agreement.

Surely this is now time to beat our swords into ploughshares so we can attend to the problems of developing our economy and our society.

[Coalition Government]

My party recognizes the fundamental principle that in constituting a government it is necessary to be guided by the national interest rather than by strictly party considerations. Accordingly, I am holding consultations with the leader of ZAPU (PF), Comrade Joshua Nkomo, so we can enter into a coalition. What I envisage, however, is a coalition which, in the interests of reconciliation, can include, by co-option, members of other communities whom the Constitution has denied the right of featuring as our candidates by virtue of their being given parliamentary representation. We should certainly work to achieve a national front.

Whatever government I succeed in creating will certainly adhere to the letter and spirit of our Constitution, since that government will itself have been the product of such Constitution.

Only a government that subjects itself to the rule of law has any moral right to demand of its citizens obedience to the rule of law.

Our Constitution equally circumscribes the powers of the government by declaring certain civil rights and freedoms as fundamental. We intend to uphold these fundamental rights and freedoms to the full.

Similarly, it is not our intention to interfere with pension rights and other accrued benefits of the civil servants. I may mention here that I have now held discussions with chiefs of Joint Operations Command, as well as with heads of Ministries, and all of them have given me their assurance of their preparedness to work under my government. I, in turn, have assured them of our concern about their position and the position of the civil servants.

We have assured them that it is not the intention of our government, when it comes into being, to deprive the civil servants of their pension rights and accrued benefits; nor do we want to drive anybody out of this country; nor do we intend to interfere unconstitutionally with the property rights of individuals.

[A Single Loyalty]

I urge you, whether you are black or white, to join me in a new pledge to forget our grim past, forgive others and forget, join hands in a new amity, and together, as Zimbabweans, trample upon racialism, tribalism and regionalism, and work hard to reconstruct and rehabilitate our society as we reinvigorate our economic machinery.

The need for peace demands that our forces be integrated as soon as possible so we can emerge with a single national army. Accordingly, I shall authorise General Walls, working in conjunction with the ZANLA and ZPRA commanders, to preside over the integration process. We shall also happily continue to enjoy the assistance of the British military instructors.

Finally, I wish to assure all the people that my government will strive to bring about meaningful change to their lives. But everyone should exercise patience, for change cannot occur overnight. For now, let us be united in our endeavour to lead the country to independence. Let us constitute a oneness derived from our common objectives and total commitment to build a great Zimbabwe that will be the pride of all Africa.

Let us deepen our sense of belonging and engender a common interest that knows no race, colour or creed. Let us truly become Zimbabweans with a single loyalty.

Long live our freedom!

MUGABE'S MARCH 24 U.S.-TV INTERVIEW

Robert MacNeil. Salisbury, Rhodesia, capital of the last European colony in Africa, soon to be capital of the new state of Zimbabwe. Tonight, from his private house in Salisbury, we talk to Marxist guerrilla leader Robert Mugabe, Zimbabwe's prime minister designate. The government of Zimbabwe, Rhodesia, today ended general mobilization and released thousands of men from active military service. It was a further step towards normalization in the African nation where 20,000 people were killed in the seven year war to end white rule. Now that there has been a ceasefire and national elections, the government said there was no longer need for a large standing army. The man who led much of the guerrilla struggle, Robert Mugabe, is now the prime minister designate, having won a landslide victory in parliamentary elections.

The active question is how he will use that power to rule his nation of 6 million blacks and 200,000 whites when the British formally hand over their last African colony on April 18th. Robert Mugabe is a teacher, who spent 10 years in prison for political activities. He holds five degrees, three earned by correspondence while in jail. He is a Catholic and a Marxist. In his first major American television interview since the election, Mr. Mugabe talked with Jim Lehrer and me earlier today from Salisbury.

Mr. Lehrer. Mr. Prime Minister, welcome. Your government is to take control on April 18th. Are preparations for this on schedule, sir?

Mr. Mugabe. Yes, they are. We are very busy just now preparing for independence.

Mr. Lehrer. You asked the British governor for a one month delay until the 18th. Why was that?

Mr. Mugabe. It was necessary for us to have him here. But at first we wanted him to continue because it would give us more time to prepare ourselves for the actual takeover. And then there was the question of giving the necessary reassurance to all sections of the community, especially to our white community here. I think his presence has done quite a lot of good, and it has helped us to create some degree of confidence, which we need at this stage.

[Civil Service]

Mr. Lehrer. I see. There have been reports that you've had some difficulty in finding qualified people to man the civil service. Has that problem been resolved?

Mr. Mugabe. No, we haven't looked into the question of making any adjustments or alterations. I don't think we'd run short of men, as such. But the issue is that really we would like to familiarize ourselves first with the actual work involved in every one of the departments, study the structure, study what has gone on, see how we can apply our own policies through the departments.

Mr. Lehrer. I see. What about these strikes in the last several days of industrial workers? What is behind that? Have you been able to determine that?

Mr. Mugabe. Well, I think it's our own people, supporters actually, who think the fact that we have won the elections means that we are already in a position to deliver the goods. I think it's just a misunderstanding. They think they are entitled immediately to raises in their salary scale and to the improvement that they have awaited in their conditions of service.

Mr. Lehrer. Have you been able to assure them that "just be patient a little while longer" — Is that —

Mr. Mugabe. That's what we're trying to do, to give them the necessary assurance. We cannot, at this stage, actually look into their problems.

We are not yet in control. The governor still is. And we'll have to start the process after independence.

Mr. Lehrer. Do you anticipate eventually disarming the basic civilian population of Zimbabwe?

Mr. Mugabe. The civilian population has arms for purposes of self-defense. It is not yet really an important issue to look into the question whether the civilian population should be armed, or not armed. I don't think it's really relevant. Those who need arms always apply for them, and the law provides that, where they can show the necessity for having these arms, they should be provided with arms. We don't see the necessity of disarming anybody at this stage.

[Nkomo, Muzorewa]

Mr. Lehrer. Yeah. You had of course two major rivals in the popular election. Mr. Nkomo and Bishop Muzorewa. Are you confident now of their support? Are you — Do you feel that the three of you are together now?

Mr. Mugabe. The two of us are together, Mr. Nkomo and myself. That means of course, Zanu [Zimbabwe African National Union] and Zapu [Zimbabwe African Peoples Union] are together in a coalition, but we've broadened our coalition to include two members of the white community as well, one of whom comes directly from the Rhodesia front. And I think this is the kind of broad support we envisaged earlier on. I think we've got it. And on this basis, the government is going to move on to other matters requiring attention.

Mr. Lehrer. I see. Ian Smith, as you know, the former prime minister, has said he would be willing to serve in your government. Do you see a role for him in your new government?

Mr. Mugabe. No, really. It's not a question of whether a particular individual should serve in our government or not. True, Mr. Smith might have wanted to be included, but the way we looked at it was much broader than a view that concentrates on individuals. What we tried to do was to link the two African parties which had emerged as the major parties, as a result of the elections, and also draw from the white community certain personalities, respected amongst them, whom we feel would add to the national concept that we have in mind, and to broad unity that we'd like to achieve.

Mr. Lehrer. As you know, of all the candidates going into the election, you were the one that was reportedly the most feared by the white population of Zimbabwe. Do you think that fear was justified?

Mr. Mugabe. No it wasn't. I don't see any reason why anybody should have entertained any fear about me in particular or about my party. We have never been racialistic in outlook. We have never hated individuals. We have always been opposed to the system, and those naturally who were in favor of a system which is oppressive might have misinterpreted our attitude. It was not directed at them personally, but at the system of which they were superintendents.

Mr. Lehrer. I see. Robin?

[Marxist Principles]

Mr. MacNeil. Prime Minister, one reason why you were perhaps feared politically was your reputation as a Marxist and there's been a lot of speculation before and since your election about how you intended to implement your form of Marxism in Zimbabwe. Can you enlighten us on that? How are you going to apply Marxist principles to Zimbabwe?

Mr. Mugabe. Yes, we have never denied that we have derived certain principles in our political thinking from Marxism and Leninism. We have never denied that. And we shall never deny it. We are proud we have derived certain fundamental principles which we believe are humanitarian in character. But we have never said that they are the only principles which matter. We've always added that such principles as we derive from any philosophy must be adapted to our own situation, and they're not the only principles. We have also derived definitely Christian principles and principles from our own tradition. A blend of the three makes our own socialist outlook and socialist philosophy. This is how we have approached our problem here, and this is how we are adapting ourselves. We don't have any bluebook from anybody, nor blueprint at all, except that which we conceive to be based on the realities of our own country.

Mr. MacNeil. I see. Is one of the principles multi-party, democratic government?

Mr. Mugabe. It is at the present moment, because that is what we have accepted under the Lancaster House agreement. The constitution requires that we be a multi-party democracy. And we have pledged ourselves in honoring every clause of that constitution.

Mr. MacNeil. You said "at the moment."

Mr. Mugabe. Yes, at the moment. I don't know what happens tomorrow. In any case, should we ever conceive the idea of a one-party state, it has to come from the people. We believe that it must be democracy the whole way through. Whatever you do must have the consent of your people. They must give you the final imprint to your decisions.

Mr. MacNeil. So, you don't exclude the possibility of moving towards a one-party state at some time in the future?

Mr. Mugabe. That's not relevant just now. But what happens tomorrow, of course, I cannot tell you.

[Land Reform]

Mr. MacNeil. I see. On implementing other principles, others of your principles, you and your supporters have spoken of land reform, have spoken of sharing Zimbabwe wealth more equally among the wider population. How are you going to move to do that?

Mr. Mugabe. The land reform is a simple matter, because under the constitution the government is authorized or has power to acquire land, provided it pays the necessary compensation. And there is of course a lot of unused land in the country, land which is unoccupied. Some is under absentee ownership. This is the land we are going to get for purposes of land resettlement before we can consider the necessity of acquiring any other forms of land. And hence we are going to proceed to examine what land is available, and what funds are available, before we can start the resettlement program. In terms of the sharing of wealth, well, this is one aspect, this [is] one way in which we would want to do it, insure that there is now equitable distribution of land, but we do not intend to seize any land that is being properly used. In other words, private farmers can continue, whether they be black or white. Then, of course we come to industry, to industry and commerce. Well, we would want to insure that the conditions of work are comparable, that at least there is a basic wage which enables a person with a family to make a living, and to have at least the ability to look after his family.

Mr. MacNeil. Do you intend to nationalize the basic means of production in Rhodesia, to have them owned by the public?

Mr. Mugabe. No, really. We don't intend to do that. I've already stated that we have no intention of nationalizing private property. Some nationalization has already taken place in respect of quite a number of services. Education and health are principally state, although private enterprise is allowed to play its part. There are some private schools and some private hospitals and clinics. We won't interfere with that kind of private work. It's only supplementary, really, to what the state is trying to do for the people.

Mr. MacNeil. If you are going to leave so much in the private sector, land that is privately owned and worked, industry which is privately owned, which Marxist principles are going to apply to the economy?

[Resettlement]

Mr. Mugabe. The socialist principles we'd like to apply in respect of land, I think, will find application as we start our land resettlement. What we intend to do is not to compel people to come together and constitute collective units in agriculture. We persuade them, we educate them into doing that, and we believe it's the only really most economic way of getting the peasants to cultivate their land and do so economically. But otherwise, there is no intention on our part to compel anybody. This is the area where we believe we can make a start with some of our socialist principles.

Mr. MacNeil. You mentioned, talking to Jim Lehrer a moment ago, that some of the people now on strike were your supporters who thought since the revolution was victorious they should immediately see the spoils of that. The blacks in Rhodesia outnumber the whites, who still own much of the property and wealth, 30-to-1. How are you going to be able to share that pie so that the expectations of your supporters are met?

Mr. Mugabe. All the wages have got to be fair. There's got to be participation, as much as possible, in all activities of the state by the people generally. And we would want to insure that in the public service there is no racial distinction, that there is some advancement for the African people, the African workers there, and generally that in industry and in the mining sector and agriculture, where private enterprise is concerned, the workers have fair wages and better conditions of service. I think that kind of participation will insure that a trend at least has come into existence towards equitable distribution of the wealth.

Mr. MacNeil. Do you see what's been called the "crisis of expectations" in the wake of your revolution as being a problem for your government?

Mr. Mugabe. I don't think it is a problem just now. Immediately we start moving, people will see that really we have policies which bring them better benefits than they have enjoyed so far. We are going to make education free. We are going to make health, medical service free. We are also going to insure that there is more land distributed amongst them. If we work on wage policy and insure that there is at least fair pay — a person gets what he deserves. Well, I think these will be indications to the people that we are bringing new changes, and that tomorrow will see better improvements, still.

[South Africa]

Mr. Lehrer. Mr. Prime Minister, what sort of relations do you want to have with South Africa?

Mr. Mugabe. In respect of international relations, our policy is that of non-alignment. And in respect of our immediate neighbors, we would like to pursue a policy of coexistence, and hence in respect of South Africa, we would pursue a policy of non-interference in each other's affairs. As long as South Africa is prepared to refrain from interfering with our internal affairs, we shall accordingly reciprocate and not interfere in their internal affairs. I think this is the type of policy we believe works and can make for the necessary harmonious relations between us and South Africa. In respect of our trade links, I think we could — our view is that we shall continue to use South African routes and whatever trade has been established between us and South Africa will continue.

Mr. Lehrer. I see. There were some South Africa troops in Zimbabwe. Are they still there?

Mr. Mugabe. I'm under the impression just now that most have moved out. If any are still there, you can rest assured that they are on their way out.

Mr. Lehrer. I see. When you say you want to have a peaceful coexistence with South Africa, is that possible. I mean, do you feel that you can deal with a country that endorses apartheid?

Mr. Mugabe. If we say we shall pursue a policy of coexistence with South Africa, we are not necessarily accepting the philosophy of apartheid. We know that apartheid is abominable. It is repugnant to the whole international community. It is repugnant to the generality of the people of Zimbabwe, and we cannot therefore actually espouse it. Nor can we condone it. But we accept that South Africa is a geographical reality, and as such we must have some minimum relationship with it. And we believe that we cannot ignore that reality, and we cannot ignore the historical ties that have existed between them and ourselves, and we cannot ignore the economic reality that our country has been linked with South Africa over years, you see, in trade and commerce.

Mr. Lehrer. Mr. Prime Minister. Have you considered what you might do if the members of the black majority in South Africa came to you and said, "Please, Mr. Mugabe, help us do in our country what you accomplished in Rhodesia."

Mr. Mugabe. That would be a legitimate appeal, if they came to us and said we should help them do what we have done here. I would regard it as a legitimate appeal. But it's not one which I can provide a response to. It's the whole of Africa which should be summoned to deal with the problem in South Africa. Through the OAU we shall pledge ourselves to do all we can to assist the liberation struggle in South Africa. But as a single country, we cannot be seen to be taking up arms against South Africa, which is not our responsibility. It is the responsibility of the South Africans themselves and through the OAU, through the non-aligned movement at the United Nations, we should do our best to give them the necessary assistance.

Mr. Lehrer. Have you any communications, direct or indirect, from the South African government, saying to you what you have just said about them? In other words, expressing a desire for a peaceful coexistence?

Mr. Mugabe. No direct response. We are not in touch with them. But from some of the statements they have made, I think they have accepted the policy of coexistence.

[U.S. Role in Africa]

Mr. Lehrer. You have said that you can coexist with South Africa. As you know, many western countries, particularly the United States, have been criticized in the past, even by blacks here in the United States, for continuing to trade and have normal relations with South Africa. Do you feel that the United States and other western countries should continue on the same basis that you are planning to continue?

Mr. Mugabe. Whether the United States should continue to carry on trade with South Africa is not a matter the Zimbabweans should decide. It's entirely a matter for the United States. But, obviously, where there is a decision, or an agreement, by the international community, say by the United Nations, to impose definite sanctions on South Africa, well, that's a different matter. The United States is duty bound to comply with the requirements of the agreement, and if that were to happen, we would have ourselves to examine our position and, where we can assist we will certainly do so. But, of course, it must be realized that our position is different from that of the United States. South Africa is our neighbor here. Our rail lines go to two South African ports, and our trade has been linked with South Africa for quite a long time, which is a different matter with the United States. South Africa is not their geographical neighbor, and they don't have the difficulty, therefore, of being unable to isolate South Africa geographically. In our case, we have to accept that the phenomenon of oneness, this phenomenon of being contiguous to South Africa, which is not quite the case with the United States.

[Apartheid]

Mr. MacNeil. If you had to make a prediction, Prime Minister, how long would you say apartheid would last in South Africa?

Mr. Mugabe. I cannot say, but, given the fact that the struggle here is won, that the effect of our victory here might be to bring about some transformation, there's only — on the part of the majority of people of South Africa, but also of the majority of the Afrikaaner population in South Africa. Given that phenomenon, then, one would like to believe that change will come to South Africa sooner than other people think.

Mr. MacNeil. You mean voluntary and peaceful change?

Mr. Mugabe. Well, whatever change comes will amount to change easily, as long as it transforms the prison system. Whether it will be peaceful, I think, depends entirely on what those in government decide to do.

Mr. MacNeil. Your policy of non-alignment, Prime Minister, does that mean non-alignment which would permit you to seek aid or assistance equally from the eastern bloc or the west?

[Non-Alignment]

Mr. Mugabe. I think the policy of non-alignment implies that the country which is pursuing such a policy has the right to determine the size of aid from any member of either bloc. One doesn't have to go in equal share. If we get [aid] of $1 billion from the United States, then we must get an equal amount from the Soviet Union. I don't think these go by that kind of balance. What we have in mind is really we'll get whatever aid we can from either bloc, from the two sides regardless of the balances you have in mind. However, we will get this aid on the condition that it has no strings attached to it. Because we cannot have aid with the effect of which is to force us to follow the policies of a member of either bloc.

Mr. MacNeil. How does the United States stand now in black African eyes as you see it. The Carter administration has maintained, along with the British, fairly consistently, the belief that the Rhodesian, Zimbabwe situation could only be solved with the inclusion of you and Mr. Nkomo. That having now been achieved, the solution having been reached, how does the United States look to you in its African diplomacy?

[Carter Administration]

Mr. Mugabe. Our view is that the United States has played an honorable role. Since the anglo-American proposals we have not — we have had no cause to quarrel with the United States. I think their position, or their stance, has been very correct. We have welcomed their involvement behind scenes, in the whole exercise at Lancaster House. We welcome their participation in the election exercise behind scenes. We know certain pressures were brought to bear on the British government to make them reasonable in their approach. And perhaps this is one source of pressure which, added onto the other sources of pressure which made the British steer an objective course. I believe that the role which the United States has played has in fact made us regard the United States as an ally rather than as an opponent. Regardless of the past, the fact that there's been trade with the legal, that the United States has flouted the opinion of the United Nations, we believe that the Carter administration has made amends, and we are poised ourselves for better relations with the United States. I think the position is the same on their part.

Mr. MacNeil. Well, thank you.

Mr. Mugabe. We welcome the fact that they are going to give us some aid towards our land and agricultural resettlement program.

Mr. MacNeil. Well, Prime Minister, thank you. That's the end of our time. Thank you very much for joining us this evening. Good night, Jim.

Mr. Lehrer. Good night, Robin.

Mr. MacNeil. That's all for tonight. We will be back tomorrow night. I'm Robin MacNeil. Good Night.

APRIL 17 MESSAGE BY MUGABE

Long live our Freedom.

The final countdown before the launching of the new state of Zimbabwe has now begun. Only a few hours from now, Zimbabwe will have become a free, independent and sovereign state, free to choose its own flight path and chart its own course to its chosen destiny.

Its people have made a democratic choice of those who as their legitimate government, they wish to govern them and take policy decisions as to their future. This, indeed, is the meaning of the mandate my Party secured through a free and fair election, conducted in the full glare of the world's spotlight.

Whilst my Government welcomes the mandate it has been freely given and is determined to honour it to the letter, it also accepts that the fulfilment of the tasks imposed by that mandate are only possible with the confidence, goodwill and cooperation of all of you, reinforced by the forthcoming support and encouragement of all our friends, allies and well-wishers in the international community.

The march to our national independence has been a long, arduous and hazardous one. On this march, countless lives have been lost and many sacrifices made. Death and suffering have been the prize [sic] we have been called upon to pay for the final priceless reward of freedom and national independence. May I thank all of you who have had to suffer and sacrifice for the reward we are now getting.

[A New History]

Tomorrow we shall be celebrating the historic national event which our people have striven for nearly a century to achieve. Our people, young and old, men and women, black and white, living and dead, are, on this occasion, being brought together in a new form of national unity that makes them all Zimbabweans. Independence will bestow on us a new personality, a new sovereignty, a new future and perspective, and, indeed, a new history and a new past.

Tomorrow we are being born again; born again not as individuals but collectively as a people, nay, as a viable nation of Zimbabweans. Tomorrow is thus our birthday, the birthday of great Zimbabwe, and the birthday of its nation. Tomorrow, we shall cease to be men and women of the past and become men and women of the future. It's tomorrow then, not yesterday which bears our destiny.

[New Vision]

As we become a new people we are called to be constructive, progressive and for ever forward-looking, for we cannot afford to be men of yesterday, backward-looking, retrogressive and destructive. Our new nation requires of everyone of us to be a new man, with a new mind, a new heart and a new spirit. Our new mind must have a new vision and our new hearts a new love that spurns hate, and a new spirit that must unite and not divide. This to me is the human essence that must form the core of our political change and national independence.

Henceforth, you and I must strive to adapt ourselves, intellectually and spiritually to the reality of our political change and relate to each other as brothers bound one to another by a bond of national comradeship. If yesterday I fought you as an enemy, today you have become a friend and ally with the same national interest, loyalty, rights and duties as myself. If yesterday you hated me, today you cannot avoid the love that binds you to me and me to you. Is it not folly, therefore, that in these circumstances anybody should seek to revive the wounds and grievances of the past? The wrongs of the past must now stand forgiven and forgotten.

If ever we look to the past, let us do so for the lesson the past has taught us, namely that oppression and racism are iniquities that must never again find scope in our political and social system. It could never be a correct justification that because the whites oppressed us yesterday when they had power, the blacks must oppress them today because they have power. An evil remains an evil whether practiced by white against black or by black against white. Our majority rule could easily turn into inhuman rule if we oppressed, persecuted or harassed those who do not look or think like the majority of us.

[No Mob Rule]

Democracy is never mob-rule. It is and should remain disciplined rule requiring compliance with the law and social rules. Our Independence must thus not be construed as an instrument vesting individuals or groups of individuals with the right to harass and intimidate others into acting against their will. It is not the right to negate the freedom of others to think and act as they desire. I, therefore, wish to appeal to all of you to respect each other and act in promotion of national unity rather than in negation of that unity.

On Independence Day, our integrated security forces will, in spite of their having only recently fought each other, be marching in step together to herald the new era of national unity and togetherness. Let this be an example for us all to follow. Indeed, let this enjoin the whole of our nation to march in perfect unison from year to year and decade to decade towards its own destiny.

We have abundant mineral, agricultural, and human resources, to exploit and develop for which we need perfect peace. Given such peace, our endeavours to transform our society and raise our standard of living are bound to succeed. The mineral resources lying beneath the surface of our country have hardly been scratched, nor have our agricultural and industrial resources yet been fully harnessed. Now that we have peace, we must go fully out to exploit them. We already have a sophisticated infrastructure. Our expertise is bound to increase as more and more educational and technical institutions are established to transform our unskilled manpower.

The whole world is looking on us this day. Indeed many countries in the international community are amazed at how we have so quickly and unexpectedly moved from war to peace. We have certainly won the goodwill of many countries and can confidently expect to benefit from the economic and technical aid they are able and willing to provide for us.

[Urges Patience]

May I assure you that my Government is determined to bring about meaningful change to the lives of the majority of the people in the country. But I must ask you to be patient and allow my Government time to organise the programmes that will effectively yield that change. There are people without land who need land, people without jobs who need jobs, children without schools who need schools and patients without hospitals who need them.

We are also fully aware of the need for increased wages in all sectors of employment. My Government will certainly do its best to meet the existing needs in these areas. But you have to assist us by being patient and peaceful.

I now finally wish to appeal to you, wherever you are, to participate fully, tomorrow and Saturday, in the Independence celebrations that have been organised throughout the country. There are, of course, those of you who have the duty to maintain essential services. These services must indeed be maintained so that the celebrations are facilitated. Maintaining such essential services during the celebrations is a significant contribution to their success.

[Prince Charles, Lord Soames]

I wish to thank Her Majesty the Queen for having sent us His Royal Highness, Prince Charles, the Prince of Wales, to represent her and officiate at our Independence ceremony, where he will perform the symbolic act of severing our colonial ties with Britain. As you are aware, this historic ceremony will be witnessed by Heads of State or Government and representatives of nearly 100 countries plus representatives of several international, political and voluntary organizations. The ceremony will also be reported and relayed to millions of people in the world by the mass media.

May I enjoin you all to regard this solemn occasion with honour and dignity, and participate in the celebrations that follow it with jubiliation. Let us rejoice over our Independence and recognise in it the need to dedicate ourselves to national unity, peace and progress.

I now wish to pay tribute to Lord Soames, our governor for the most important role he has played in successfully guiding this country to elections and independence. His was from the very onset a difficult and most unenviable task. And yet he performed it with remarkable ability and overwhelming dignity.

I must admit that I was one of those who originally never trusted him, and yet I have now ended up not only implicitly trusting but fondly loving him as well. He is indeed a great man through whom it has been possible, within a short period I have been Prime Minister, to organise substantial financial and technical aid from Britain and other countries. I am also personally indebted to him for the advice he has constantly given me on the art of managing the affairs of government. I shall certainly be missing a good friend and counsellor, and so will our independent Zimbabwe and all its people.

[Bond of Solidarity]

I also wish to thank all our distinguished guests for the honour they have given us by coming to attend our Independence celebrations on behalf of their countries or organisations. Their presence in our country signifies a bond of solidarity and friendship between their countries or organisations and our country. Without the support they have given us towards our liberation, this national day would never have come about. Thanks, therefore, for all the material, political, diplomatic and moral support they have given us.

Sons and daughters of Zimbabwe, I urge you to participate fully and jubilantly in our Independence celebrations and to ensure that all our visitors are well entertained and treated with utmost hospitality.

I shall be one in spirit and love, in loyalty and commitment with you all.

Forward with the Year of the People's Power!

Long live our Freedom!

Long live our Sovereignty!

Long live our Independence!

Good night!

PRINCE CHARLES' SPEECH

We have all come here together today at a moment of immense historic significance. A moment when the past and all that was negative about it can really be allowed to become the past, and we can go forward to one of those rare occasions in the lives of nations where a new and greater beginning is possible, which we must not allow to fail. The meaning and importance of what is happening in this country of yours is demonstrated by the presence of the leaders of so many other countries whose people have followed with a new upsurge of hope the processes leading to a peaceful settlement here. I am delighted and honoured as the representative of Her Majesty the Queen to join with you in celebrating on this day the independence of Zimbabwe.

Zimbabwe has reached this independence, or (?Kusitonga) [cheers], in the face of many grave and urgent difficulties which much of the world at times thought insoluble. But to have brought Zimbabwe to peace and independence is an outstanding achievement and a tribute to all those who continued to believe so bravely in peace and who worked so hard to bring it about. I know how greatly you have all suffered and the extremes of sorrow you have had to endure. But I am uplifted, as I am certain you all must be, by the spirit of reconciliation in which you have joined together in recent weeks and have united to face the future in a manner that must be an inspiration to others. To heal what has been hurt and wounded, to reunite what has been divided, and to reconcile where there has been enmity is the finest foundation on which to rebuild and improve the quality of life in your unique country and so overcome the great challenges which confront you and us all in the future.

I should like, Mr. President, to thank you and all the people of Zimbabwe for the welcome and the warm hospitality you have so generously given me. I shall remember with great pleasure my brief stay here. I shall hope to return at some time in the future, and meanwhile I shall follow with close interest the fortunes of Zimbabwe.

Her Majesty the Queen has entrusted to me a message for you all, which reads: It is with great pleasure that I send you my warmest congratulations on the occasion of the independence of Zimbabwe, and as Head of the Commonwealth welcome you as the 43rd member of our unique international fellowship. I well remember my own visit to your beautiful land with my parents in 1947 and I am all the more delighted that my son, the Prince of Wales, should be with you on this day. It is a moment for people of all races and all political persuasions to forget the bitterness of the past and to work together to build a better future for their country and all its citizens. With the great natural wealth of your land and the exceptional resources of your society you are well-equipped to achieve this. I and all my people wish you every good fortune in your endeavours. Today also marks the beginning of a new and happier relationship between my country and your own, I am confident that as you set out to create peace and prosperity you will have the full support of Britain, of your Commonwealth partners and of the international community. I wish you all happiness and success. May God bless you all [applause].

PRESIDENT BANANA'S REMARKS

Your Royal Highness, Your Excellencies, ladies and gentlemen. The citizens of this country are deeply conscious of the great honour you have accorded us by your personal presence as the representative of Her Majesty the Queen on this historic and momentous day for Zimbabwe. We are greatly heartened by the message of support you have transmitted from Her Majesty, and we look forward with great determination to building on the goodwill that has already been created during the recent months of negotiations and mutual co-operation between our two nations.

As we enter a new era of international acceptability following our long and hard-fought struggle for freedom and independence, I would like, Sir, on behalf of all the people of Zimbabwe, to thank you for your personal message of (?best wishes) and reassurance, which will fortify us as we face the challenges ahead.

Finally, Sir, I would ask you to convey to Her Majesty the Queen the good wishes of our citizens and thank her for her warm message of congratulation on the achievement of our independence. In bidding you farewell, Sir, we would ask you not to delay the fulfilment of your hopes to return once again to Zimbabwe [applause].

LORD CARRINGTON'S ADDRESS

Your Royal Highness, Mr. President. This is a great occasion. The last few months have seen a remarkable transformation in this country. The war has ended, elections have been held and the people of Zimbabwe have chosen the Government to lead them into independence. And without the courage and adaptability of the people of this country, and above all the determination of all its citizens to overcome their problems and live together in peace, these achievements would have been impossible. I wish you most sincerely a prosperous and successful future; and I would like to read to you a message that the Prime Minister, Mrs. Thatcher, has asked me to convey to you:

> I send you my warm congratulations and good wishes on the occasion of Zimbabwe's independence. The goal to which many inside and outside your country have dedicated exceptional efforts has now been achieved. We share your pleasure on this memorable day. The natural interests of our two countries lie in close co-operation and friendship. We shall do all we can to develop these and shall work closely with you on the task of reconstruction and development. I send you my best wishes on behalf of the Government of the United Kingdom for your future peace and prosperity.

MUGABE'S RESPONSE

Your Royal Highness, Your Excellencies, my lords, fellow comrades, ladies and gentlemen [cheers]. I am deeply grateful that my colleague, Mrs. Thatcher, has sent a personal message of congratulations on the occasion of Zimbabwe's independence. It is universally acknowledged that the initiative which led to the achievement of our final goal was made possible largely through her determined efforts. I welcome also, on behalf of my Government, Mrs. Thatcher's invitation for closer co-operation and friendship in the future. We for our part will strive for the closest possible ties in this regard. The task of reconstruction and development which lie ahead are formidable and we value greatly, therefore, Her Majesty's Government's pledge to assist us in achieving rapid results in our rebuilding programme. Please convey to Mrs. Thatcher my Government's good wishes and deep gratitude for their endeavours in helping to restore peace and future prosperity in Zimbabwe [applause].

CUBAN BOATLIFT
April 21—September 26, 1980

A massive flotilla of fishing boats and small pleasure craft sailing from Florida ports between April 21 and Sept. 26 brought about 126,000 Cuban refugees to the United States. Each day during that period thousands of Cubans arrived in Key West, Fla., many of them aboard boats whose profiteering owners charged exorbitant amounts for the short voyage.

At first welcoming the refugees with "open arms," President Carter later shifted U.S. policy in response to mounting concern over the number of refugees and their safety. Carter on May 14 announced a policy which called for an end to the boatlift and for an airlift of qualified refugees.

The president's plan was contingent on the cooperation of the Cuban government. But Fidel Castro's government rejected the offer. The influx of refugees continued as boat owners defied Carter's order to stop it. The owners risked stiff fines, confiscation of vessels and prison sentences.

The exodus from Cuba abated in mid-June after thousands of refugees had been taken to special processing centers set up in the United States. Castro abruptly halted the boatlift on Sept. 26 by closing the exodus port of Mariel. In November he permitted 600 refugees "stranded" at Mariel to be flown to the United States.

Role of Castro

The exodus of Cubans to Florida was precipitated April 1 when six Cubans crashed a bus through the gates of the Peruvian Embassy in Havana, Cuba, to achieve political asylum. When Peru granted the six asylum and refused the request of the Castro government to give them up, Castro withdrew Cuban guards from the embassy. That action permitted an additional 10,000 Cubans seeking asylum to jam into the embassy compound.

Premier Castro's action in withdrawing the guards provoked resolutions of condemnation from the Andean group of nations. But Castro recovered politically, it was believed, when he permitted disaffected citizens to leave Cuba by way of the private boatlift to the United States. Finally, Castro's defiance of President Carter's proposal for an orderly refugee transfer shifted attention from Cuba's economic problems and internal dissension to the groping efforts of U.S. officials to establish a refugee policy.

In moves that were seen in Washington as small gestures of conciliation, the Castro government returned to the United States two hijackers of a plane that landed in Cuba Sept. 30 and on Oct. 13 announced the pardon of 33 Americans serving sentences in Cuban jails.

Refugee Riots

The Carter administration set up refugee processing centers at Eglin Air Force Base near Pensacola, Fla., Ft. Chaffee, Ark., Ft. Indiantown Gap, Pa. and Ft. McCoy, Wis.

Two hundred refugees at Fort Chaffee, impatient with a long delay between arrival at the centers and clearance for resettlement, rioted on June 1. Bursting through the front gate of the compound, they were met by police and soldiers using tear gas. The Cubans then set fire to barracks and piles of debris in the streets. Forty Cubans were injured in the riot, and 85 were arrested.

President Carter June 7 directed the Justice Department to move to expel any Cuban refugees who had committed a serious crime in Cuba and to prosecute or expel those responsible for the rioting.

Haitian Refugees

The Carter administration came under criticism for its policy toward the Cuban refugees in relation to an earlier influx of about 26,000 Haitian refugees.

A number of civil rights groups, labor unions, mayors of large cities and black leaders in the United States told Carter that the Haitians should have been dealt with in as welcoming a manner as the Cubans. The Haitians had been classified as illegal aliens.

Rep. Shirley Chisholm, D-N.Y., told reporters she deplored the classification of white Cubans by the U.S. State Department as political refugees and of black Haitians as economic refugees.

Following are the texts of statements by Vice President Walter F. Mondale April 27, 1980, announcing that U.S. Navy and Coast Guard units would render assistance to refugees at sea; the announcement May 2, 1980, of U.S. actions in response to the emergency; an excerpt from President Carter's remarks at a news conference May 5, 1980, affirming an "open arms" policy; a White House statement and President Carter's remarks to reporters May 14, 1980, stating administration policy toward the boatlift; a statement June 5, 1980, by President Carter reiterating that illegal boat traffic in refugees was unacceptable; White House Press Secretary Jody Powell's announcement June 7, 1980, that Cuban refugees with non-political criminal violations in Cuba would not be admitted to the United States; and an announcement by the White House June 20, 1980, that Haitian and Cuban refugees alike would be granted a six-month waiting period pending clarification of their status by Congress:

MONDALE'S APRIL 27 STATEMENT

At the President's request, I chaired a meeting Saturday with the Attorney General, the Secretary of Health, Education, and Welfare, the Deputy Secretary of State, and heads of other U.S. departments concerned with the very serious humanitarian problem we are confronting with the plight of growing numbers of Cuban refugees. There is no better proof of the failure of Castro's revolution than the dramatic exodus which is currently taking place.

At the same time, we are witnessing a callous, cynical effort by Castro to play on the emotions of the Cuban American community in the United States, to lure members of this community into extraordinarily dangerous and unlawful boat trips, with the very real threat of loss of life at sea. Castro has evaded his responsibility to his citizens and has broken the commitment he made earlier to help with an orderly, prompt, and humane evacuation of refugees.

The President has directed U.S. Navy and Coast Guard units in the region to render all possible assistance to those at sea. We call upon the Cuban American community, which has contributed so much to our country, to respect the law and to avoid these dangerous and illegal boat passages. The world will hold Castro responsible for the safety of these Cubans.

Cuba must agree to a policy that permits the orderly, safe, and humane evacuation of refugees. We have stated before, and I repeat again, that the United States will contribute to this international effort. I would point out that if Castro wants to expel his people, let him begin by releasing the *plantados* — those brave Cubans in Boniato prison. These people have suffered for their freedom. The moment they are released, we will have aircraft standing ready to bring them to freedom.

The Deputy Secretary of State and other administration officials also met Saturday with leaders of the Cuban American community to continue our consultations. We will continue to give the highest priority to this humanitarian problem.

MAY 2 WHITE HOUSE ANNOUNCEMENT

The White House announced today that the Federal Government is taking additional actions to respond to the current emergency precipitated by the Cuban Government. More than 5,000 Cubans have already arrived in Florida in more than 170 small boats, and the Coast Guard estimates that as many as 2,000 additional boats are either loading passengers in Cuba or are en route to the Florida coast.

The President has directed Jack Watson, his Assistant for Intergovernmental Affairs and Secretary to the Cabinet, to work with Ambassador Victor Palmieri, U.S. Coordinator for Refugee Affairs, in managing the Federal Government's overall response to the emergency. Watson outlined the following actions:

—A processing and screening center will be established at Eglin Air Force Base in Fort Walton Beach, Fla., to supplement the receiving and processing facilities already located in Key West and Miami. The Eglin facility will accommodate approximately 1,000 persons within 24 hours and will be expanded to accommodate between 5,000 and 10,000 within 10 days. Additional facilities will be added as needed.

—Reception facilities at Key West are being expanded to accommodate daily flows of between 2,500 and 3,000, and other Federal services are being made available there, including those of a Public Health Service medical assistance team.

—Several hundred Federal personnel have been directed to the Miami/Key West area, so that more than 1,000 personnel from eight Federal agencies are now actively engaged with volunteer organizations and State and local governments in receiving, processing, and assisting the arriving Cubans. Tom Casey, Deputy Associate Director of the Federal Emergency Management Agency, has been assigned responsibility for on-site coordination of all Federal Government activities.

—The Coast Guard has expanded its capability to provide rescue and assistance missions between the Florida and Cuban coasts and, within the last few days, has performed approximately 300 rescue missions in the area. As announced earlier this week by the Department of Defense, U.S. naval vessels which had been intended for Operation

Solid Shield are now being made available to assist the Coast Guard in rescue operations.

—Because the Cuban Government is including individuals with criminal records in the boatloads of departing Cubans, careful screening of all arrivals is being conducted by appropriate Federal officials. Under U.S. immigration laws, individuals with records of criminal activity who represent a threat to the country or whose presence would not be in the best interests of the United States are subject to arrest, detention, and deportation to their countries of origin. The United States will enforce these laws.

—State Department officials will be working with national voluntary organizations to provide additional reception and resettlement assistance to Cuban, Haitian, and other groups seeking political asylum, which are so heavily affecting the Miami area.

The President appreciates the extraordinarily effective efforts of the State and local governments in Florida in dealing with this extremely difficult situation. . . .

MAY 5 REMARKS

Q. In light of thousands of illegal and legal immigrants arriving daily, a problem which is reaching critical proportions, what does your administration intend to do about enforcing current immigration laws and providing funds and programs for dealing with these newcomers, who are presently a great burden on local communities?

The President. The entire subject or issue or problem of the Cuban refugees has been greatly aggravated by the inhumane approach by Fidel Castro. We, as a nation, have always had our arms open to receiving refugees in accordance with American law. We now have more than 800,000 Cuban refugees in our country, who are making outstanding new American citizens, as you know.

I have a responsibility to administer the law, because I've taken an oath to do so, and to administer it in a fair and equitable way. It's important for me, for instance, to treat the Cuban refugees with the same degree of compassion and understanding and with the same commitment to the law as we do the refugees from Haiti and from other countries. We are the most generous nation on Earth in receiving refugees, and I feel very deeply that this commitment should be maintained.

Ours is a country of refugees. Many of those in this room have either parents or grandparents who were refugees who came here looking for a new life of freedom, a chance to worship as they pleased, or a chance to combine their own talents to build a growing and dynamic country. Those of us who have been here for a generation or six or eight generations ought to have just as open a heart to receive the new refugees as our ancestors were received in the past.

I have organized within the White House, under a senior assistant, Jack Watson, a combined group of departments who are working on this special inflow of Cuban refugees. In the last few days we have received more than 10,000 from Cuba. We've now opened up a staging area at Eglin Air Force Base in the northwestern part of Florida, and we're receiving these refugees now, primarily into the Key West area.

As you know, there are almost 400 of those who have been issued visas by our country who are hiding from mob violence instigated by Castro himself, and we're trying to get those freed by Castro to come on into our country. These are primarily former political prisoners. So, those 400 plus literally tens of thousands of others will be received in our country with understanding, as expeditiously as we can, as safely as possible on their journey across the 90 miles of ocean, and processed in accordance with the law.

So, I don't know how else to answer your question except to say we're doing the best we can. I think the local and State officials in Florida have been extraordinarily forthcoming. We do have a need to go back to the Congress for additional funds to care for this unexpected influx of refugees. You can help here; the League can help. But we'll continue to provide an open heart and open arms to refugees seeking freedom from Communist domination and from economic deprivation, brought about primarily by Fidel Castro and his government.

CARTER'S MAY 14 STATEMENT

The President. I'd like to make a statement to you and to the Nation about the extremely critical problem with the Cuban citizens who are escaping from their country and coming to our shores in a very haphazard and dangerous way.

Tens of thousands of Cubans are fleeing the repression of the Castro regime under chaotic and perilous conditions. Castro himself has refused to permit them a safe and orderly passage to the United States and to other countries who are also willing to receive them. Repeated international efforts to resolve this crisis have been rejected or ignored by the Cuban Government. At least seven people have died on the high seas. The responsibility for those deaths and the threat of further loss of life rests on the shoulders of Fidel Castro, who has so far refused to cooperate with us, with those escaping his regime, or with other countries in establishing a legal and orderly procedure for dealing with this Cuban problem.

In keeping with the laws and traditions of our own country, the United States has provided a safe haven for many of these people who have arrived on our shores. Since the beginning of this crisis we have been operating under three basic principles: first, to treat the escaping Cubans with decency, fairness, and humanity; second, to observe and to enforce the existing United States law; and third, to work with other countries and with international organizations to develop an orderly and legal solution to this very painful human dilemma. That is still our fundamental approach.

But now we must take additional steps to end Cuba's inhumane actions and to bring safety and order to a process that continues to threaten lives. Therefore we will implement a five-point program to permit safe and orderly passage from Cuba for those people who sought freedom in the U.S. Interest Section in Havana, first of all; for political prisoners who have been held by Castro for many years; for those who sought a haven of freedom in the Peruvian Embassy, some of whom are still being held there; and for close family members of Cuban Americans who live in this country and who have permanent resident status. Those four categories will be given priority in their authorization to come to our country.

First, we are ready to start an airlift and a sealift for these screened and qualified people to come to our country, and for no other escapees from Cuba. We will provide this airlift and sealift to our country and to other countries as well, just as soon as the Cubans accept this offer. The U.S. Government will have aircraft ready and will immediately charter ships — one of which will be standing by in Key West — to bring the first group of Cubans, after they are screened, to our country. These ships and the Key West planes will be ready to go to Cuba to receive properly screened Cubans for entry to the United States and to other countries, to help in their resettlement.

To ensure legality and order, all people will have to be screened before departure from Cuba. We will work with the Congress, the Cuban American community, interested nations, and the Cuban Government to determine the total number of people that we will receive, both on a monthly basis and during the next 12 months.

Second, tomorrow we will open a family registration center in Miami, and later perhaps in other communities, to begin receiving the names of people who are eligible for immigration to our Nation because they are close members of Cuban American families who have permanent residence here.

Third, the Coast Guard is now communicating with all boats who are en route to Cuba and those in Mariel Harbor in Cuba, to urge them to return to the United States without accepting additional passengers. No new trips to Cuba by these unauthorized boats should be started. Those who comply with this request or command will have nothing to fear from the law, but we will ensure that the law is obeyed. Persons who violate this requirement and who violate U.S. immigration custom laws by traveling to Cuba to pick up additional passengers will be subject to civil fines and to criminal prosecution. Furthermore, boats used to bring people unlawfully to this country will be seized. I have directed the various law enforcement agencies to take additional steps as necessary to assure that this policy and the law are obeyed.

Fourth, in an unprecedented and irresponsible act, Castro has taken hardened criminals out of prison and forced some of the boatowners who have gone to Cuba from our country to bring these criminals back to the United States. Thus far over 400 such persons have been detained. I have instructed the Attorney General to commence exclusion proceedings immediately for these criminals and others who represent any danger to our country. We will ask also appropriate international agencies to negotiate their return to Cuba.

These steps are fully consistent with the consensus which was reached by 22 nations and 7 international organizations in the San José Conference on May 8 this last week. In addition, the Secretary of State will continue consultation with other nations to determine additional steps that the international community can take to resolve this problem. We will seek the help of the United Nations, the Organization of American States, and other international organizations as well.

The Cuban American community has, of course, contributed much to Miami, to Florida, and to our own country. I respect the deep desire to reunite divided families. In the interest of that great and valiant ethnic community and in the interest of our country, we will continue to work closely with the Cuban American community to bring about a safe and orderly resolution of this crisis.

I continue to be greatly concerned about the treatment of Haitians who have also come to this country recently on small boats. I've instructed all appropriate Federal agencies to treat the Haitians now here in the same, exact, humane manner as we treat Cubans and others who seek asylum in this country. Our laws never contemplated and do not adequately provide for people coming to our shores directly for asylum the way the Cubans and the Haitians have done recently. I will work closely with the Congress to formulate a long-term solution to this problem and to determine the legal status of the boat people once this current emergency is under control.

Now the Attorney General and Stu Eizenstat, Jack Watson and others will be available to answer your specific questions about this new policy, an approach which I think will be successful in resolving this dilemma.

Reporter. Sir, will you take a question? Do you think ——

The President. Sarah [Sarah McClendon, McClendon News Service]. I'll take one question.

Q. — this will be a damaging issue in the campaign?

The President. I don't know about how it will affect the campaign. We've had this as a very serious problem now for several weeks. We've tried to deal with it in accordance with our laws, with custom, with traditions, and of course in a humane fashion, and also have tried to work, both with Castro, unsuccessfully, and with other nations and international organizations. We've done the best we could.

This is a much firmer and more consistent approach, and in my judgment, after advising with all of my Cabinet advisers involved and with the international organizations as well and with the Congress,

I believe this will resolve this problem in a legal, orderly, safe, humane, and proper fashion.

Q. Do you think that Castro will go along with it?
The President. I don't have that assurance.

Q. But if he doesn't go along with it, it's stopped, period?
The President. We'll carry out our part of the policy as I described it.

MAY 14 WHITE HOUSE STATEMENT

After consultations with senior advisers and with Congress, and in the spirit of the San José Conference, the President has decided to take the following steps to welcome the Cuban refugees in a legal and orderly process:

1. We are prepared to start an airlift or a sealift immediately as soon as President Castro accepts this offer. Our Government is chartering two large, seaworthy ships, which will go to Key West to stand by, ready to go to Cuba. To ensure a legal and orderly process, all people will have to be screened before departure from Cuba. Priority will be given to political prisoners, to close relatives of U.S. permanent residents, and to persons who sought freedom in the Peruvian Embassy and in our Interest Section last month. In the course of our discussions with the Congress and with the Cuban American community, the international community, and the Cuban Government, we will determine the number of people to be taken over the next 12 months. We will fulfill our humanitarian responsibilities, and we hope other governments will adjust their previous pledges to resettle Cuban refugees to take into account the larger problem that has developed. This will provide a safe and orderly way to accommodate Cubans wishing to enter the United States.

2. Tomorrow, we will open a Family Registration Office in Miami to receive the names of close Cuban relatives of U.S. permanent residents who will be eligible for immigration.

3. The Coast Guard is now communicating with these vessels illegally enroute to or from Cuba and those already in Mariel Harbor to tell them to return to the United States without taking Cubans on board. If they follow this directive, they have nothing to fear from the law. We will do everything possible to stop these illegal trips to Cuba. We will take the following steps to ensure that the law is obeyed:

(a) The Immigration and Naturalization Service (INS) will continue to issue notices of intent to fine those unlawfully bringing Cubans to this country. As fines become due, they will be collected.

(b) All vessels currently and unlawfully carrying Cubans to this country will henceforth be seized by the Customs Service.

(c) Anyone who tampers with or seeks to move a ship to Cuba which has been seized will be subject to separate criminal prosecution.

(d) The Coast Guard will continue to review each vessel that returns to the United States for violations of boat safety law. Those found to be in gross violation of the law will be subject to criminal prosecution and additional fines. Furthermore, boats which are found to be safety hazards will be detained.

(e) Any individual who has been notified by INS for unlawfully bringing Cubans into the country and who makes another trip will be subject to criminal prosecution, and the boat used for such a repeat trip will be seized for forfeiture proceedings.

(f) Law enforcement agencies will take additional steps, as necessary, to implement this policy and to discourage the unlawful boat traffic to Cuba.

4. Castro has taken hardened criminals out of prison and mental patients out of hospitals and has forced boatowners to take them to the United States. Thus far, over 400 such prisoners have been detained. We will not permit our country to be used as a dumping ground for criminals who represent a danger to our society, and we will begin exclusion proceedings against these people at once.

5. These steps will make clear to the Government of Cuba our determination to negotiate an orderly process. This is the mission of the three-government delegation established by the San José Conference last week. Our actions are intended to promote an international solution to this problem. We intend to continue our consultations with the participants of the San José Conference and consider additional steps the international community should take to resolve this problem.

In summary, the United States will welcome Cubans, seeking freedom, in accordance with our laws, and we will pursue every avenue to establish an orderly and regular flow.

The President continues to be greatly concerned about the Haitians who have been coming to this country on small boats. He has instructed appropriate Federal agencies to receive the Haitians in the same manner as others seeking asylum. However, our laws never contemplated and do not provide adequately for people coming to our shores in the manner the Cubans and Haitians have. We will work closely with the Congress to formulate a long-term solution to this problem and to determine the legal status of these "boat people" after the current emergency situation is controlled.

The Cuban American community has contributed much to Miami, the State of Florida, and to our country. The President understands the deep desire to reunite families which has led to this situation. He calls upon the Cuban American community to end the boat flotilla and help bring about a safe and orderly resolution to this crisis.

CARTER'S JUNE 5 STATEMENT

On Tuesday, June 3, a freighter of recent Panamanian registry landed at Key West, Florida, with 731 Cuban refugees on board. This boat was chartered by Cuban Americans apparently in direct violation of my order that the private boat flotilla from Cuba cease.

Any person who attempts to circumvent this order will be prosecuted to the full extent of the law.

Any shipowner, captain, or crewmember agreeing to travel from U.S. or foreign ports to Cuba to take refugees to the United States in violation of American immigration law will face the most severe penalties under the law. Ships engaged in such efforts will be seized regardless of the nation of registry. Ship captains will face criminal prosecutions and maximum civil fines. Those who charter boats for these purposes will also face criminal prosecution.

The penalties for aiding and abetting a conspiracy to smuggle aliens into the United States include prison sentences of up to 5 years and fines up to $2,000 per alien brought to the United States.

The captain of the freighter, the *Red Diamond,* and those responsible for chartering her services have been charged under these statutes. I have instructed the Justice Department to prosecute these cases vigorously.

There should be no misunderstanding of my intention. Illegal boat traffic in refugees is unacceptable to the United States. It will be stopped. Those who attempt to evade this order will pay very severe penalties under our laws.

PRESIDENT'S JUNE 7 ANNOUNCEMENT

Among the tens of thousands of people fleeing oppression in Cuba and seeking to reunite with their families and to seek freedom in the United States, Fidel Castro has very cynically thrown in several hundred hardened criminals from Cuban jails. These criminals will not be resettled or relocated in American communities under any circumstances. The administration will take the legal and necessary steps to make sure that this will not happen.

There is evidence that the Cuban Government exported these undesirable elements to the United States in a calculated effort to disguise the fact that the vast majority of those Cubans who have come to this country were and are law-abiding citizens whose only purpose was to seek freedom and to seek reunification with their families.

This action by the Cuban Government, in addition to its cynical and inhumane characteristics, is a direct and serious violation of international law. It would be an equally serious violation if the Government of Cuba should refuse to perform its obligations under international law to accept the return of these criminals. The President has directed the Secretary of State to press this issue urgently through diplomatic channels and in the appropriate international forum.

Unfortunately, a few of those who came to the United States seeking the right to live here in this country, to join a democratic and law-abiding society, have created disturbances and have violated the laws of the country in which they seek to live. These individuals will be dealt with in strict accordance with those laws.

The President has directed the Attorney General to take the following actions:

First, Cubans identified as having committed serious crimes in Cuba are to be securely confined. Exclusion proceedings will be expedited to the maximum extent consistent with constitutional requirements for due process of law.

Second, exclusion proceedings will also be started against those who have violated American law while waiting to be reprocessed or relocated. The Justice Department will investigate all serious violations of the law, and the Justice Department will bring prosecutions where justified. Those responsible for the disturbances at Fort Chaffee are confined and will be confined until fair decisions can be made on criminal prosecution or exclusion from this country or both. Similar measures will be taken in the event of any future disturbances.

JUNE 20 REFUGEE POLICY STATEMENT

After exhaustive review of the Refugee Act of 1980, the Immigration and Naturalization Act and other authorities and after extensive consultations with members of Congress, affected state and local officials and interested groups in the communities, the President has determined to pursue the following course of action to resettle the recent Cuban-Haitian entrants and to assist state and local governments, as well as private voluntary organizations:

Cubans who have arrived in the United States during the period April 21-June 19, 1980, and who are in I.N.S. [Immigration and Naturalization Service] proceedings as of June 19, 1980, and all Haitians who are in I.N.S. proceedings as of June 19, 1980, will have their parole into the country renewed for a six-month period as "Cuban/Haitian Entrants (status pending)."

Under this six-month parole, these Cubans and Haitians will be eligible, if they otherwise qualify, for S.S.I. [Social Security Insurance], Medicaid, A.F.D.C. [Aid to Families with Dependent Children] and emergency assistance under the rules of the states in which they are residing and with normal Federal/state matching. In order to qualify, Cuban-Haitian entrants must first report to the I.N.S. for their new parole documents. Procedures for applying for these benefits will be announced by I.N.S. and H.H.S. [Health and Human Services] next Friday, June 27.

[Resettlement Grants]

Per capita grants will be provided to private resettlement agencies for all persons leaving processing centers after June 19, 1980, and for

Cuban-Haitian entrants being relocated out of the south Florida area after that date. In addition, funds will be provided to the resettlement agencies to provide employment counseling and referral services to all Cuban-Haitian entrants already released from camps or resettled directly into the Miami area.

The President has already sought funding totaling $385 million to finance reception, processing, care and maintenance, transportation, initial relocation, health services and educational costs as part of the fiscal year 1980 supplemental appropriation. The Administration will seek necessary funding for the continuation of this program in fiscal year 1981.

[Special Legislation]

Special legislation will be submitted to the Congress as soon as possible to:

Establish a "Cuban-Haitian Entrant" status for recently arrived Cubans and Haitians.

Define services and benefits for these arrivals for one year after release from processing centers.

Provide S.S.I., Medicaid, A.F.D.C. and emergency assistance under the rules of the states in which they are residing and with normal Federal-state matching of funds and authorize retroactive reimbursement to states and localities for 75 percent of the total cost of other general assistance, medical assistance, special educational programs and social services for one year.

Provide for conversion to permanent resident alien status after two years.

Improve future asylum processing, both to expedite case-by-case review, including exclusion and deportation, and to reduce the likelihood of future problems of this nature.

Provide minor children without close relatives in this country English-language training, health services, counseling, individualized planning for permanent placement. States will be reimbursed for 100 percent of the costs of maintenance and services provided to such unaccompanied minors until they reach the age of majority.

Seek a method to identify and extend "Cuban-Haitian Entrant Status" to those other Haitian "boat people" who have arrived in Florida prior to June 19, 1980, but who are not in I.N.S. proceedings.

[Criminals]

Criminals continue to be subject to detention and exclusion or deportation from the United States.

Processing of applications for asylum will continue. Those who are granted asylum status will be eligible to adjust to permanent resident alien status after one year.

United States Government enforcement agencies will continue to interdict boats bringing undocumented aliens into the United States. Enforcement will be maintained to prevent future illegal arrivals, and violators will be subject to civil or criminal prosecution in accordance with the President's declaration of May 14, 1980. Persons who arrive illegally after June 19, 1980, will not be eligible for the program and will be subject to exclusion or deportation in accordance with United States immigration laws.

IRAN RESCUE ATTEMPT
April 25 and August 23, 1980

On April 25, 1980, President Carter made an early morning television announcement that the U.S. had made a military attempt to rescue the 52 American hostages in Iran but the mission had failed. Carter said it was a "humanitarian mission," and vowed to continue to seek release of the hostages. "We will not give up in our efforts. Throughout this extraordinarily difficult period, we have pursued and will continue to pursue every possible avenue to secure the release of the hostages," he said.

The attempted rescue on April 24 of the American hostages in Iran had a good chance to succeed, but some aspects of the operation were flawed, according to a high-level report on the operation. The report, drafted for the Joint Chiefs of Staff by a panel of six senior active and retired military officers, concluded that the planners of the mission had erred by putting an unnecessarily strong emphasis on maintaining secrecy. After some sections were removed for security reasons, the report was released to the public Aug. 23.

The report stated that the mission would have been more likely to succeed had the planners been more willing to sacrifice a margin of secrecy and had they utilized an existing joint task force, rather than assembling a special unit for the rescue.

'Professional Critique'

The writers of the Pentagon report took pains to stress that theirs was a "professional critique" of a military mission and not an "indictment

*of the able and brave men who planned and executed this operation."
They added, "We encountered not a shred of evidence of culpable
neglect or incompetence."*

*Planning to rescue the Americans in Tehran was begun shortly after
they were seized by Iranian student dissidents Nov. 4, 1979* (Historic
Documents of 1979, p. 867). *The rescue attempt began April 4 when
eight helicopters took off from the aircraft carrier* Nimitz *to rendezvous
at a desert landing site in Iran with six C-130 transport planes that
had been stationed in Egypt. The transport planes were carrying 90
commandos. According to the plan, the commandos were to board the
helicopters in the desert and fly to a hidden staging area outside Tehran.
The following evening, the troops were to rescue the hostages at the
American Embassy.*

Helicopter Failures

*The mission was called off, however, after one helicopter was ditched
before it reached the landing site due to a rotor blade malfunction,
another turned back after some instruments broke during a severe dust
storm and a third suffered a hydraulic failure that could not be repaired
at the landing site. The plan required at least six helicopters in good
condition. With three helicopters out of commission, the commander
of the task force contacted his superiors in Washington and President
Carter canceled the rest of the operation.*

*As it was being refueled for the flight out of Iran, a helicopter smashed
into one of the transport planes and, in the ensuing explosion and
fire, eight American servicemen were killed and five were injured. The
helicopter crews then abandoned their aircraft and boarded the remaining
C-130s.*

Security Issue

*The report criticized the decision to use only eight helicopters; three
more helicopters, it said, would have boosted the likelihood of success
without compromising secrecy. The desire to maintain secrecy, the report
said, also hampered training exercises among the members of the rescue
team and skewed lines of communication and command. Security considerations determined that no one with experience in special operations
reviewed the plan before it was put into effect. And mission planners
were not allowed to discuss intelligence data with the Pentagon's intelligence analysts for fear of a security leak.*

*The report also said that the lack of devices to destroy the abandoned
helicopters — some contained sensitive materials — was a serious omission. And it added that the planners should have been more mindful*

of weather conditions in the flight path over the Iranian desert; the report suggested that a weather reconnaissance aircraft could have contributed greatly to a successful mission.

Broad Recommendations

The report included two broad recommendations. First, it urged the Joint Chiefs of Staff to create a permanent "Counterterrorist Joint Task Force" staffed by members from all the branches of the armed services. And, second, the report recommended the establishment of an independent military panel to review and offer advice on plans for special operations.

Following are the text of President Carter's statement April 25, 1980, explaining the failed recue mission in Iran; and excerpts from the report, drafted for the Joint Chiefs of Staff, on the unsuccessful attempt April 25, 1980, to rescue American hostages in Iran. The document, "Rescue Mission Report," was released Aug. 23, 1980. (Boldface headings in brackets have been added by Congressional Quarterly to highlight the organization of the text.):

CARTER STATEMENT

Late yesterday, I cancelled a carefully planned operation which was underway in Iran to position our rescue team for later withdrawal of American hostages, who have been held captive there since November 4. Equipment failure in the rescue helicopters made it necessary to end the mission.

As our team was withdrawing, after my order to do so, two of our American aircraft collided on the ground following a refueling operation in a remote desert location in Iran. Other information about this rescue mission will be made available to the American people when it is appropriate to do so.

There was no fighting; there was no combat. But to my deep regret, eight of the crewmen of the two aircraft which collided were killed, and several other Americans were hurt in the accident. Our people were immediately airlifted from Iran. Those who were injured have gotten medical treatment, and all of them are expected to recover.

No knowledge of this operation by any Iranian officials or authorities was evident to us until several hours after all Americans were withdrawn from Iran.

Our rescue team knew and I knew that the operation was certain to be difficult and it was certain to be dangerous. We were all convinced that if and when the rescue operation had been commenced that it had an excellent chance of success. They were all volunteers; they were all highly trained. I met with their leaders before they went on this operation. They knew then what hopes of mine and of all Americans they carried with them.

To the families of those who died and who were wounded, I want to express the admiration I feel for the courage of their loved ones and the sorrow that I feel personally for their sacrifice.

The mission on which they were embarked was a humanitarian mission. It was not directed against Iran; it was not directed against the people of Iran. It was not undertaken with any feeling of hostility toward Iran or its people. It has caused no Iranian casualties.

Planning for this rescue effort began shortly after our embassy was seized, but, for a number of reasons, I waited until now to put those rescue plans into effect. To be feasible, this complex operation had to be the product of intensive planning and intensive training and repeated rehearsal. However, a resolution of this crisis through negotiations and with voluntary action on the part of the Iranian officials was obviously then, has been, and will be preferable.

This rescue attempt had to await my judgment that the Iranian authorities could not or would not resolve this crisis on their own initiative. With the steady unraveling of authority in Iran and the mounting dangers that were posed to the safety of the hostages themselves and the growing realization that their early release was highly unlikely, I made a decision to commence the rescue operations plans.

This attempt became a necessity and a duty. The readiness of our team to undertake the rescue made it completely practicable. Accordingly, I made the decision to set our long-developed plans into operation. I ordered this rescue mission prepared in order to safeguard American lives, to protect America's national interests, and to reduce the tensions in the world that have been caused among many nations as this crisis has continued.

It was my decision to attempt the rescue operation. It was my decision to cancel it when problems developed in the placement of our rescue team for a future rescue operation. The responsibility is fully my own.

In the aftermath of the attempt, we continue to hold the Government of Iran responsible for the safety and for the early release of the American hostages, who have been held so long. The United States remains determined to bring about their safe release at the earliest date possible.

As President, I know that our entire Nation feels the deep gratitude I feel for the brave men who were prepared to rescue their fellow Americans from captivity. And as President, I also know that the Nation shares not only my disappointment that the rescue effort could not be mounted, because of mechanical difficulties, but also my determination to persevere and to bring all of our hostages home to freedom.

We have been disappointed before. We will not give up in our efforts. Throughout this extraordinarily difficult period, we have pursued and will continue to pursue every possible avenue to secure the release of the hostages. In these efforts, the support of the American people and of our friends throughout the world has been a most crucial element. That support of other nations is even more important now.

We will seek to continue, along with other nations and with the officials of Iran, a prompt resolution of the crisis without any loss of life and through peaceful and diplomatic means.

Thank you very much.

IRAN RESCUE MISSION

Forwarding Statement

It is essential that the purpose of this report be clearly understood: it is a professional critique of the Iranian hostage rescue operation addressed to the Joint Chiefs of Staff. It is not, and should not be read as, an after-action summary, or as a white paper examining the Iranian hostage crisis at the national level. It is much too narrow and technical a report for this latter application. Except for some discussions, the review was confined to activities and persons within the Department of Defense. There was no attempt in this report to assess the events leading up to the seizure of the Embassy, the concurrent international political environment, or the ongoing efforts to secure the release of the hostages by negotiations or diplomatic means.

By its nature, therefore, this report will appear to be highly critical, more so probably than a wider review from a national perspective would deserve. But to be useful, a critique such as this must not allow any potential area of possible future improvement to go unquestioned. For this reason, a number of the issues analyzed which were evaluated as having no bearing on the success or failure of the actual mission are included in this report. The reason is that they might very well have an application for some future special operation conducted under different circumstances.

Further, it must be realized that much of the critical character of the discussions contained in the analysis is the product of hindsight. For example, the statistical evidence available to the planners of the operation may have been persuasive that eight helicopters were the best compromise between operations security and equipment redundancy, but an after-the-fact investigation is virtually obligated to assemble fresh data which will revel why eight was too low a number.

The members of the review group are unanimous in the view that the issues treated in the analysis were valid concerns, and we believe that a full discussion of these issues was necessary to provide the rationale for our conclusions and support for the recommendations.

We are, nevertheless, apprehensive that the critical tone of our discussion could be misinterpreted as an indictment of the able and brave men who planned and executed this operation. We encountered not a shred of evidence of culpable neglect or incompetence.

The facts are that, in the conduct of this review, we have seen infinitely more to be proud of than to complain about. The American servicemen who participated in this misssion — planner, crewman, or trooper — deserved to have a successful outcome. It was the ability, dedication, and enthusiasm of these people who made what everyone thought was an impossibility into what should have been a success.

Finally, we were often reminded that only the United States military, alone in the world, had the ability to accomplish what the United States planned to do. It was risky and we knew it, but it had a good chance of success and America had the courage to try.

Executive Summary

Purpose. The purpose of this review is to improve US counterterrorist (CT) capability through an independent appraisal of the hostage rescue mission, including a broad examination of its planning, organization, coordination, direction, and control. The scope of the study addresses the broader aspects of conceptual validity and operational feasibility; the planning environment, including operations security (OPSEC), policy guidance, and options available, adequacy of planning, resources, preparation, and support; and overall conduct of the executed portion of the mission.

Mission. Rescue mission planning was an ongoing process from 4 November 1979 through 23 April 1980. The planners were faced with a continually changing set of circumstances influenced mainly by the uncertain intentions of the hostages' captors and the vacillating positions of the evolving Iranian leadership. The remoteness of Tehran from the available bases and the hostile nature of the country further complicated the development of a feasible operational concept and resulted in a relatively slow generation of force readiness.

Analysis. In analyzing the planning, training, and execution of the hostage rescue mission, the review group identified 23 discrete issues that were investigated in depth. Eleven were considered to be major issues, ones that had an identifiable influence on the outcome of the hostage rescue effort or that should receive the most careful consideration at all levels in planning for any future special operation.

Issues. The major issues, which underlie the subsequent conclusions, are listed below:

OPSEC.

Independent review of plans.

Organization, command and control.

Comprehensive readiness evaluation.

Size of the helicopter force.

Overall coordination of joint training.

Command and control at Desert One.

Centralized and integrated intelligence support external to the Joint Task Force (JTF).

Alternatives to the Desert One Site.

Handling the dust phenomenon.

C-130 pathfinders.

Specific Conclusions. The major issues provide the basis for the following specific conclusions:

The concept of a small clandestine operation was valid and consistent with national policy objectives. It offered the best chance of getting the hostages out alive and the least danger of starting a war with Iran.

The operation was feasible. It probably represented the plan with the best chance of success under the circumstances, and the decision to execute was justified.

The rescue mission was a high-risk operation. People and equipment were called on to perform at the upper limits of human capacity and equipment capability.

The first realistic capability to successfully accomplish the rescue of the hostages was reached at the end of March.

OPSEC was an overriding requirement for a successful operation. Success was totally dependent upon maintaining secrecy.

Command and control was excellent at the upper echelons, but became more tenuous and fragile at intermediate levels. Command relationships below the Commander, JTF, were not clearly emphasized in some cases and were susceptible to misunderstandings under pressure.

External resources adequately supported the JTF and were not a limiting factor.

Planning was adequate except to the number of backup helicopters and provisions for weather contingencies. A larger helicopter force and better provisions for weather penetration would have increased the probability of mission success.

Preparation for the mission was adequate except for the lack of a comprehensive, full-scale training exercise. Operational readiness of the force would have benefited from a full-dress rehearsal, and command and control weaknesses probably would have surfaced and been ironed out.

Two factors combined to directly cause the mission abort: Unexpected helicopter failure rate and low-visibility flight conditions en route to Desert One.

The siting of Desert One near a road probably represented a higher risk than indicated by the JTF assessment.

General Conclusions. Although the specific conclusions cover a broad range of issues relating to the Terms of Reference, two fundamental concerns emerge in the review group's consensus which are related to most of the major issues:

The ad hoc nature of the organization and planning. By not utilizing an existing JTF organization, the Joint Chiefs of Staff [JCS] had to

start, literally, from the beginning to establish a JTF, create an organization, provide a staff, develop a plan, select the units, and train
the force before the first mission capability could be attained. An existing
JTF organization, even with a small staff and cadre units, would have
provided an organization framework of professional expertise around
which a larger tailored force organization could quickly coalesce.

OPSEC. Many things that, in the opinion of the review group, could
have been done to enhance mission success were not done because
of OPSEC considerations. The review group considers that most of
these alternatives could have been incorporated without an adverse
OPSEC impact had there been a more precise OPSEC plan selectively
exercised and more closely integrated with an existing JTF organization.

Recommendations. These conclusions lead the group to recommend
that:

*A Counterterrorist Joint Task Force (CTJTF) be established as a
field agency of the Joint Chiefs of Staff with permanently assigned
staff personnel and certain assigned forces.*

*The Joint Chiefs of Staff give careful consideration to the establishment
of a Special Operations Advisory Panel, comprised of a group of carefully
selected high-ranking officers (active and/or retired) who have career
backgrounds in special operations or who have served at the CINC
[Commander in Chief] or JCS levels and who have maintained a current
interest in special operations or defense policy matters. . . .*

Chronology

BACKGROUND

By 29 November, force commanders began to gain confidence in their
developing operational capability. CJCS [Chairman, Joint Chiefs of Staff]
approved a move of the helicopters to a US western desert training
site, so that training could be conducted in a more realistic environment.
OPSEC was observed, and the move was completed on 30 November
without apparent detection.

On 30 November, the COMJTF [Commander, Joint Task Force] training estimate was as follows: helicopter aircrew capability was judged
to be fair, with considerable work remaining; C-130 aircrew status was
judged to be mission capable, but with more training required in blacked-
out landings; the ground rescue forces had rehearsed for two weeks
and had procured and modified additional equipment; communications
planning/developments were proceeding; no logistic restraints had surfaced
from any units; weather and intelligence capabilities were improving.

By the end of November, the COMJTF overall assessment was that
a force capability was beginning to emerge, but that major deficiencies
in planning, intelligence, communications, and training were evident.

[INITIAL TRAINING]

On 1 December, the training missions were flown using the replacement helicopters. (NOTE: Those helicopters used for training in the earlier phase had been returned to owning units.)

During the period 9 December through 21 December, 153 hours were flown. Navigation and formation flying were stressed along with night landings under total blackout conditions.

On 18-19 December, the first integrated training was conducted. The exercises went poorly, with problems in night navigation encountered by the helicopters. At this time, COMJTF and planning staff recognized that pilots with increased experience in the type of mission profiles to be flown would be required. A major change in personnel took place; nine pilots were replaced.

The Palletized Inertial Navigation System (PINS) was provided to improve helicopter navigation capability, and pilots began training with this item.

By 27 December, refueling of helicopters from C-130s on the ground was surfaced as an alternative to air dropping fuel blivits; tentatively, an airfield in the objective area had been selected as a possible ground refueling site.

The ground rescue forces continued training at a secure training camp but did participate in the desert joint training effort.

By 18 December, communications arrangements and procedures to support the concept had been developed except for those of airborne elements and the ground rescue forces. . . .

By mid-December, plans were set for another joint training period using representative forces.

During this training exercise, radio equipment was tested. Except for the helicopter detachment, all units redeployed back to their home stations.

On 22 December, two additional RH-53Ds were airlifted and embarked aboard NIMITZ for transit to the Indian Ocean. During this period, OMEGA navigation systems had been acquired, and preparations were made to install them on the eight mission RH-53Ds. One OMEGA system was installed in a training aircraft at the western US training site for crew training. . . .

[CONTINUED TRAINING]

. . . On 5 January, the helicopter detachment resumed flying at the western US site to refine navigation procedures and techniques using the 10 helicopters available and using OMEGA and PINS navigation systems. (It had already been established that prior to takeoff, a forecast for visual meteorological conditions (VMC) on the mission track was required in order to execute the mission.). . .

After several more planning conferences, mission requirements had grown to include additional personnel and equipment factors which drove up the size of the force. On 12 January, the fourth C-130 arrived to provide sufficient air-refuelable, forward-looking infrared (FLIR) equipped aircraft.

In mid-January, the required number of helicopters to arrive at the hideout was confirmed to be five, six at the refueling site, and seven for launch, for a total of eight aboard the carrier. (Note: As mentioned earlier, two additonal RH-53Ds were to be put aboard NIMITZ.). . .

The JTF conducted another joint training exercise in mid-January in a new area, with long-range navigation flights similar to those planned for the mission. This event was productive, but it also identified many problems that required additional planning and training.

Problems were highlighted in the areas of OPSEC, weather, helicopter reliability, communications, refueling procedures, airfield security and control, and intelligence.

By this time, the JTF J-2 [Joint-Intelligence], searching for an alternative to the airfield site, had found only one in-country area that was sufficiently isolated for the C-130s and the helicopters to rendezvous for refueling and loading of the ground rescue forces. Such a site, named Desert One, was considered to be a possible new solution to the helicopter refueling portion of the mission. . . .

[FOURTH JOINT TRAINING EXERCISE]

During the first week in February, a joint training exercise plan was conducted to evaluate progress made during the last two weeks in January. In spite of bad weather, task force elements in general showed improvement, but more work was also indicated in the areas of helicopter navigation and combat control. Needed now was more intelligence, additional training, and a plan to refuel the helicopters at Desert One.

By 8 February, following the postexercise conference, the commanders and planners for the first time had confidence that a capability existed for the rescue.

[DESERT ONE PLAN]

On 26-27 February, another JTF exercise was conducted for the purpose of sustaining mission capabilities, incorporating Combat Control Team expertise, and refining JTF communications. JTF confidence was further increased.

At this time, increased attention by the planners was being placed on two uncontrollable and pressing environmental factors that could cause major revision of the rescue plan: available hours of darkness and ambient temperatures. By 1 May, the number of hours between evening and morning nautical twilight would drop to nine hours and 16 minutes. Eight hours were required for the helicopter mission, with a one-hour contingency factor. By 10 May, prevailing temperatures of 30° C would increase density altitude and limit helicopter performance. With these conditions, additional helicopters and C-130s would be required. COMJTF also definitely concluded that not less than six mission-capable helicopters had to reach Desert One to insure mission continuation.

On 25-27 March, the last major JTF training exercise was conducted and was considered a success, with a recognized increase in confidence.

By 28 March, the hostage rescue mission had been brought to a seven-day response status. Additional deployment was stopped until 16 April, when additional loads commenced movement. . . .

By 7 April, COMJTF concluded that Desert One was suitable for the helicopter refueling operation. . . .

[COUNTDOWN]

On 12 April, CJCS instructed COMJTF to finalize planning for deployment of the force. COMJTF recommended Thursday, 24 April, based on many considerations, a primary one being moon illumination. . . .

On 15-16 April, COMJTF conducted a two-day meeting in the Pentagon to review the plan with commanders, affirm command and control matters, evaluate force readiness, review contingencies, and make an overall assessment of mission success should it be executed on 24 April.

On 16 April, the Joint Chiefs of Staff approved the plan. That evening, the President approved the plan after he was briefed by COMJTF, Deputy COMJTF, and the commander of the ground rescue force. . . .

[EXECUTION AND ABORT]

On the evening of 24 April, after 5-1/2 months of planning and training under very tight OPSEC, eight RH-53 helicopters took off from the aircraft carrier NIMITZ and began a journey of nearly 600 nautical miles at night and low altitude to a preselected refueling site, Desert One, in the desert. The C-130 element with the ground rescue forces was also in the execution phase on a different track and time schedule to Desert One. Approximately two hours after takeoff, the crew of Helicopter #6 received cockpit indications of an impending rotor blade failure; landed; verified the malfunction (an automatic abort situation); and abandoned their aircraft. The crew was picked up by another helicopter, which then continued the mission individually.

Approximately one hour thereafter, the helicopter formation unexpectedly encountered a dust cloud of unknown size and density.

The helicopters broke out of the first area of suspended dust but, within an hour, entered a second, larger and denser area. While attempting to navigate through this second area with severely degraded visibility, a second helicopter (#5) experienced a failure of several critical navigation and flight instruments. Due to progressively deteriorating flight conditions that made safe flight extremely questionable, the helicopter pilot determined that it would be unwise to continue. He aborted the mission, reversed course, and recovered on NIMITZ. Eventually six of the original eight helicopters arrived at the refueling site in intervals between approximately 50 minutes and 85 minutes later than planned.

While en route, a third helicopter (#2) experienced a partial hydraulic failure, but the crew elected to continue to the refueling site believing repairs could be accomplished there. Upon landing, however, the crew and the helicopter unit commander determined that the helicopter could not be repaired. . . .

Earlier, it had been determined that a minimum of six operational helicopters would be required at the refueling site to continue the mission. Since at this point there were only five operational, the on-scene commander advised COMJTF by radio of the situation, and he in turn communicated to Washington the status of the force and his intention to abort the operation and return to launch base. The President concurred in the decision that the mission could not continue, and preparations began for withdrawal of the five operational helicopters, the C-130s, and the rescue force.

While repositioning one helicopter to permit another to top off his fuel tanks for the return flight, the first helicopter collided with one of the refueling C-130s. Both aircraft were immediately engulfed in flames in which eight crew members died and five other members of the team were injured. Since the C-130 was loaded with members of the rescue force awaiting extraction, even greater injury and loss of life were avoided only by swift and disciplined evacuation of the burning aircraft. Shortly afterwards, ammunition aboard both aircraft began to explode. Several helicopters were struck by shrapnel from the explosion and/or the burning ammunition, and at least one and possibly more were rendered unflyable. At this point, with time and fuel running out for the C-130s, the decision was made to transfer all helicopter crews to the remaining C-130s and to depart the area.

Analysis of Issues

. . . While the review group has attempted to maintain a constructive outlook, it has been critical where and when its collective judgment dictated. While the group believes these criticisms valid and necessary to the conclusions reached and recommendations made, no judgment of the able men who planned this mission or the brave professionals who executed it is intended nor should it be inferred.

The men charged with planning the rescue operation in November 1979 faced certain basic factors in the overall situation that must be appreciated in order that the analyses which follow are kept in proper perspective:

A forcible rescue was very much a contingency plan, only to be implemented if all other alternatives failed.

On the other hand, a sense or urgency was impressed on COMJTF and his staff at the very outset: that an immediate operation could be required.

All planning and preparation required maximum OPSEC because the *sine qua non* of the concept was to place the ground rescue force at their final assault position with total surprise. . . .

One final note of caution is appropriate. The Special Operations Review Group unanimously concluded that no one action or lack of action caused the operation to fail and that no one alternative or all the alternatives could have guaranteed its success. It was by its nature a high-risk mission that involved the possibility of failure. The object of the following issue analysis was, with the benefit of hindsight, to identify areas in which risk might have been better managed.

ISSUE 1: OPSEC

Event. Critical concern for OPSEC at all levels tended to dominate every aspect of mission planning, training, and execution. From the outset, task force members were imbued with the absolute need for total secrecy. . . .

JTF Rationale. The underlying reasons for such heavy emphasis on OPSEC were well understood throughout the JTF. Surprise was the *sine qua non* for mission success, and complete security was essential to attain surprise.

Alternative. This was, perhaps, the group's most difficult judgment: Did a seemingly nondiscriminating overemphasis on OPSEC exclude certain activities and provisions that could have materially enhanced the probability of mission success? On balance and in retrospect, the group concluded that slightly greater selectivity and flexibility in the OPSEC arena, particularly *within* the JTF, could have been beneficial in operational terms without necessarily sacrificing security. . . .

Implications. Basically, the group's alternative would have slightly reduced OPSEC restrictions in selected areas, implying incrementally improved force posture and enhanced potential effectiveness at the cost of some increased probability of operational compromise. Admittedly, it cannot be predicted at what point in easing security restrictions secrecy could have been breached, which in turn might have resulted in canceling the mission. What is known and therefore should be underscored is the fact that the level of security practiced by the JTF did preserve secrecy.

Evaluation. The question of too much or too little OPSEC was easily the most controversial issue, and the group's differences with actual JTF OPSEC practices epitomize the advantage of hindsight.

[ISSUE 2: ORGANIZATION, COMMAND AND CONTROL]

Event. When the hostage seizure incident occurred in Iran on 4 November 1979, a small planning cell, working in the Organization of the Joint Chiefs of Staff (OJCS) area, and augmented by two officers from the ground rescue force, began to formulate concepts for military options as directed by the CJCS. The planning group received intelligence support within a week, although the full array of intelligence capabilities were not integrated for over a month. . . .

JTF Rationale. OPSEC was the overriding consideration in every aspect of mission planning, training, deployment, and execution because of the absolute requirement to reach the Embassy compound undetected. OPSEC, coupled with the dynamic planning process and development of special mission capabilities, drove COMJTF to the techniques adopted for this organization, planning, and preparation by the JTF.

Alternative. The requirements for stringent OPSEC are clearly recognized. Nevertheless, it is considered essential that there be a balance between rigid compartmentalization, to include secrecy through informal or *ad hoc* arrangements, on the one hand and sound organization, planning, and preparation efforts on the other. . . .

Prolonged *ad hoc* arrangements often result in tasking from different sources and can cause confusion at the operating level. These situational arrangements may hinder preparation and can impact adversely on overall cohesion of effort. The review group's alternative would strive for a better balance between more appropriate disclosure policy, particularly at the Service Chief/CINC level, to enhance the organizing, equipping, and training of forces. . . .

Implications. On the positive side, the group's alternative would have led to a "quicker start" in the preparation phase. Additionally, task organization and force planning would have been enhanced and command relationships clarified. These in turn would have led to more effective command and control at all levels. On the negative side, the group alternative would have increased the number of people involved and, therefore, increased the OPSEC risk. . . .

[ISSUE 3: INTELLIGENCE SUPPORT]

Event. COMJTF, his staff, and subordinate commanders were fully aware that successful mission accomplishment would critically depend on precise and timely intelligence and, moreover, that intelligence would tend to drive the operation from conception to execution. The JTF fortunately had a professionally capable intelligence officer to assume the role of J-2 from the beginning. In addition, each of the Service force components — with the exception of the helicopter contingent — already had staff intelligence officers heading up small intelligence staff sections. The helicopter contingent was provided intelligence support from the JTF J-2 section. In the JTF headquarters itself, the intelligence section remained small throughout the period, beginning with one officer on 4 November and increasing to four in the course of planning.

Nonetheless, for an operation of the scope and complexity of the Iranian mission, a significant augmentation of existing intelligence capabilities was mandatory. This augmentation tended to evolve over time and in somewhat piecemeal fashion as planning got under way and as intelligence needs grew. . . . In some ways, however, certain elements of the Intelligence Community seemed slow in harnessing themselves initially for the tasks at hand. . . .

. . . By the time the operation was launched, intelligence support was adequate.

Alternative. The group believes that Intelligence Community assets and resources could have been pulled together more quickly and effectively than was actually the case. A preferred approach would have been to task the Director, DIA [Defense Intelligence Agency], to establish a small and highly select interagency Intelligence Task Force (ITF) in direct support of the JTF from the moment of operational conception. COMJTF would have retained his small intelligence section as an internal element of the JTF; the ITF would have been located externally and would have worked closely and continuously with the JTF J-2. The latter would be COMJTF's close-in intelligence staff officer; the ITF chairman would be his external senior intelligence advisor. ITF members would have been cleared and security briefed at the outset regarding the details of the contemplated operation.

Implications. The proposed arrangement would have the advantage of harnessing selected elements of the US Intelligence Community and bringing them together as an integrated intelligence supporting mechanism on extremely short notice. Fragmentation of responsibility for intelligence support would be avoided, as the Director, DIA, in his role as J-2 to the Joint Chiefs of Staff, would be clearly charged with overall supervision and given the necessary authority. Coordination of intelligence activities would be simplified by the designation of a single focal point for intelligence matters — the chairman of ITF. This individual and/or the DIA Director exercising his direct access to the CJCS would be in a position to relieve COMJTF of intelligence management concerns, freeing him to concentrate his attention in other areas.

Evaluation. Initial dificulties in the intelligence support arena had been largely overcome by the time the operation was launched. Implementation of the alternative approach to intelligence support for operations of this nature in the future could greatly facilitate achievement of acceptable readiness and forward deployment of forces in situations where time is a critical factor. . . .

ISSUE 4: INDEPENDENT REVIEW OF PLANS

Event. Early in the process of planning for the hostage rescue mission, consideration was given to establishing a small group of individuals with credible experience in special operations to act as consultants and review the plan as it developed. Overriding OPSEC concerns and the perceived need to limit as sharply as possible the number of personnel privy to the contemplated operation led to a conscious decision not to form such an element. As a consequence, planners — in effect — reviewed and critiqued their own product for feasibility and soundness as they went along. . . .

Alternative. The Special Operations Review Group, on the other hand, inclines to the view that the inclusion of several additional individuals, properly qualified to handle the plans review function on a continuing basis, would have facilitated the planning process without necessarily degrading security. . . . This small subordinate cell would have been closeted separately from the JTF planners and used as required by the Joint Chiefs of Staff to subject components of the plan to critical review, to include periodic "worst-case" analyses.

Implications. The implications of the group's alternative in the planning area can be simply stated: On the positive side, it would probably have contributed to a more thoroughly tested and carefully evaluated final plan — indeed, some of the issues now being addressed by the review group might have arisen in sharper focus during the actual planning phase. . . .

On the negative side of the group's alternative, exposure of additional individuals to the plan might have increased the risk of security leaks, inadvertent or otherwise.

Evaluation. Finally, is the issue of existence or nonexistence of a plans review element vital? Could such a unit have contributed materially to the success of the mission? In the review group's judgment, there is little doubt regarding its potential value: a comprehensive and continuing review capability impacts directly on almost all other issues. . . .

[ISSUE 5: COMPREHENSIVE READINESS]

Event. Training was planned and conducted on a highly decentralized basis within an informal component command structure that does not appear to have been clearly established. Individual and unit training was conducted and evaluated throughout the period at widely separated locations, throughout the United States. Combined training of JTF elements was conducted at various desert sites that simulated conditions expected in Iran. Thoroughly integrated training exercises of the entire JTF for the final plan were not conducted, although joint training of all plan segments was conducted by portions of the component forces in conjunction with their respective roles and tasks. Readiness evaluation was based upon observation of the training and exercises and overall assessment of the situation. COMJTF decentralized command supervision of training and evaluation, in part through the use of various advisors individually observing segments of the continuously evolving concept and plans.

JTF Rationale. Several considerations militated against thorough, integrated rehearsals and a more direct command role for COMJTF. The dynamic situation required some mission capability from mid-December 1979 to 24 April 1980. The overall situation, including intelligence and JTF assessment of various unit readiness progress, continuously changed, demanding modifications of concept and subsequent plans, including the roles played by various components. Finally, the primacy of OPSEC considerations led COMJTF to decide that regular integration of training and readiness evaluations was undesirable.

Alternative. The review group would have integrated air, ground, and naval elements throughout the preparation phase to conduct combined training as early and as often as possible. Moreover, integrated training and readiness evaluation for the entire JTF would include specialists and supporting forces, where practical. Individuals, task-oriented groups, and the force itself would drill until every aspect of the raid became an automatic process.

Implications. Thorough, integrated rehearsals would have developed precision and speed in execution, increased interunit coordination, suggested necessary changes, and resolved problem areas.... The negative implications of the alternative are implicit in the JTF rationale — that such an integrative effort would have endangered OPSEC. Moreover, the dynamic situation and compressed timeframes made such a system extremely difficult to establish. However, the difficulty of integrating training while preserving OPSEC must be measured against the contribution of that effort to mission success.

Evaluation. The criticality of this issue was difficult to assess as only a portion of the plan was executed prior to abort. Nevertheless, the review group concluded that integrated training and rehearsals reduce risk and enhance the probability of success in this or any other special operation.

[ISSUE 6: COORDINATION OF TRAINING]

Event. The overall joint training supervision function was retained at JTF level in the Pentagon. At the western US site, coordination and supervision were performed in part by two officers who were advisers to COMJTF yet retained responsibilities related to their primary office of assignment outside the JTF. Neither was responsible for the overall management of joint training activities. Tasking for joint training was accomplished by messages issued by the JTF J-3 [Joint-Operations] from the JTF headquarters in the Pentagon. Principals from the JTF staff proceeded to the western US training site to observe and supervise the directed events. Onsite support was handled individually by force elements in many instances or arranged by the JTF staff. It was related by force participants that C-130 and helicopter crews did not brief or critique jointly prior to and after every joint training exercise.... COMJTF conducted post-exercise conferences for the commander and staff a few days following training exercises. These proved very beneficial in determining procedural and equipment problems and areas needing training emphasis.

JTF Rationale. The dynamic nature of the mission concept resulting from new intelligence inputs, availability of support bases for the actual mission, testing of various helicopter refuel procedures, and JTF assessment of unit readiness militated against shifting joint training responsibility to the field. Training exercises were observed personally by COMJTF or his representative. Creating an additional staff element was not considered necessary.

Alternative. Recognizing that COMJTF had the overall responsibility for training, the myriad other important activities related to concept development, planning, and extensive coordination would indicate the need for assignment of an officer and small staff to be in charge of the very important function of joint training at the western US training site. The group would have designated the Deputy Commander of the JTF and made him responsible for coordinating joint training activities, including but not limited to training schedules, operational and administrative support, and outside support. . . . Coordination of training site support would have assured equitable allocation of available assets and contributed positively to morale and overall training progress. . . . The review group recognizes that joint doctrine assigns the Service component commanders unit training and support responsibilities; however, for this mission, forces were so interdependent that complete force integration was essential.

Implications. The group would have relieved COMJTF of the burden of day-to-day supervision of training. It would have provided a central point of contact at the training site for each element of the force, as well as for COMJTF and members of the JTF staff. . . . Additional personnel would have been required, but perhaps not more than three or four.

Evaluation. . . . [C]entralization of overall joint training responsibility and coordination would have enhanced force readiness and is recommended for future JTF operations involving joint training at a site geographically separated from the JTF headquarters. . . .

[ISSUE 7: CHANGES IN JOINT TASK FORCE]

Event. From interviews with key JTF personnel and from detailed review of after-action reports and documents, it has become clear that significant planning and training problems were created by the continuing changes in the overall political situation surrounding the plight of the hostages. The immediate objective in November was to field a capability quickly for an emergency rescue attempt. Shortly after the first of the year, as a credible rescue capability began to emerge, the emphasis shifted to contemplation of a more deliberate operation at a time and under conditions more conducive to the exercise of US initiative.

In November, as the US Embassy in Tehran was being seized, the question of how to insert and subsequently recover the ground rescue force from a hostile environment arose immediately and became the most vexing difficulty COMJTF would face.

The initial airlift requirement for the ground rescue force was approximately 80 personnel, and early training involved the number of aircraft needed to meet that requirement. Over time, however, the size of the force gradually increased, contributing to a corresponding increase in the number of helicopters from four to six, to seven, and ultimately to eight, including spares. Positioning the helicopters forward on NIMITZ well in advance of the actual operation was a delicate and time-consuming move, and the failure to fix the size and composition of the assault force at an early point, or at a minimum establish a troop lift ceiling, led to late juggling in the number of helicopters. This appeared to have exacerbated a problem that, even in early planning stages, was considered the most critical link in the entire operation.

JTF Rationale. The obvious JTF rationale for such incremental changes in force structure was to provide as finely tailored a capability as possible at the point of attack. Minor corrections and additions as planning progressed and further experience was gained from training and rehearsals were considered necessary improvements and appropriate responses to the dynamics of the situation. Further, to a large extent, intelligence drove the operation from the outset, and intelligence developments caused modifications in the operational concept.

Alternative. Nonetheless, as can be inferred from the discussion above, it would have been desirable to fix the airlift requirement at a certain ceiling well in advance of launch date and hold to that ceiling for planning purposes unless a compelling case could have been made that a given increase was indeed vital to insure mission accomplishment. For example, the ground rescue force could have been given a troop lift ceiling in early January. . . .

Implications. Adoption of the group's course of action would have facilitated greater precision in rehearsals, a more finely tuned final plan with fewer last-minute changes, and a clearer and more carefully computed airlift requirement further in advance of launch date than was the case in the actual operation.

In this particular case, it was virtually impossible for COMJTF to fix a firm date because the rescue effort was essentially a response, not an initiative. Fixing a date and force structure may have been highly desirable; it may not have been possible to adhere to such planning, especially when the terminal situation is dictated by the enemy.

Further, too rigid planning could have had the effect of reducing the JTF's flexibility to respond to last-minute changes in the situation, be they diplomatic, operational, or enemy initiated.

Evaluation. A commander is always tempted to make any adjustments possible to improve his posture up to the point when the battle is joined. The review group would simply counsel that, particularly in future undertakings of a special operations nature, such late changes be made with some trepidation and extraordinary care.

[ISSUE 8: HOSTILE SIGNAL INTERCEPTION]

Event. Analysis of operational communications planning, training, and execution, coupled with detailed interviews with key personnel, underscored JTF understanding of the need for COMSEC [communications security], particularly transmission security. The principles of signals security (SIGSEC) were vital, well understood by the JTF, and provided for in the instructions utilized by the force. However, it was clear that threat understanding and resultant radio procedures varied among units and probably resulted from a combination of knowledge, training, experience, and mind-set.

The helicopter unit commander and his plane commanders maintained strict radio silence during extreme operational difficulties in maintaining integrity and control. Additionally, the commander of #5 was not told — nor did he ask — about the weather at Desert One. The receipt of this information by the commander of Helicopter #5 could have caused him to proceed on the mission.

JTF Rationale. The JTF rationale concerning SIGSEC/COMSEC policy was driven by the requirement for total OPSEC — from initiation of planning to final assault positions — and by the assessment of the SIGSEC situation.

Alternative. The group's alternative would insure a comprehensive assessment and detailed understanding of threat capabilities by every member of the force, to include impacts and consequences.

Implications. The group's alternative would have insured, insofar as possible, that all personnel thoroughly understood the COMSEC requirements and consequences. Further, it appeared that command and control through selected use of radio communications could well have resulted in a more favorable execution of the movement to Desert One. On the other hand, total radio silence or the strictest of procedures always enhances OPSEC.

Evaluation. It is difficult to determine if the overall posture at Desert One at abort decision point would have been enhanced by additional command and control communications at critical points. . . . Nevertheless, the group would urge comprehensive analysis, assessment, and training in matters of SIGSEC operations and planning.

[ISSUE 9: ABORT CRITERIA]

Event. During the approximately 600-nm [nautical miles] flight from the carrier to Desert One, the helicopter force unexpectedly encountered visibility conditions that precluded VMC flight. The condition was caused by two separate areas of suspended dust of unknown magnitude. This condition occurred approximately three hours after takeoff. Flight integrity was lost. The helicopters broke out of the first area but soon entered the second area, which was of even greater density. The helicopter flight flew in instrument meteorological conditions (IMC) for approximately two hours. The restricted visibility ended at a point approximately 50 nm from destination. The minimum visibility conditions for the operational requirements of the mission were not defined or tested.

Two helicopters, including the leading helicopter, turned to exit the first area of dust and landed. The leader, using a special radio that afforded minimum chance of intercept, called COMJTF and told him what the flight had encountered. The radio call could not be heard by other members of the flight. In response to query by COMJTF, the leader indicated he thought that it was possible to continue the mission despite the dust. He was directed to continue. One aircraft, Helicopter #5, at the time not in visual contact with other aircraft, aborted short of destination and returned to NIMITZ a few minutes before he would have exited the dust condition. He based his abort decision on instrument malfunctions exacerbated by the visibility conditions. The crew commander indicated later that he would have continued had he known that restricted visibility conditions did not prevail at destination. His failure to arrive at Desert One proved critical in that one additional mission-capable aircraft would have permitted the entire mission to continue. The flight leader was not informed of #5's decision to abort. Strict radio silence inhibited exchange of essential information within the helicopter flight when unexpected contingencies arose.

The visibility conditions caused the helicopters to be as much as 85 minutes late at Desert One. This in itself could have been a cause for mission abort based on total hours of darkness remaining for the next phase.

JTF Rationale. There was a tendency to feel that an abort decision could best be made by the element leader based on his experience and professional knowledge. Moreover, the helicopter flight leader believed that no more precise abort criteria were necessary for his individual flight members. The absence of positive communications procedures reflected the primacy of OPSEC in all mission planning. The helicopter crews demonstrated a strong dedication toward mission accomplishment by their reluctance to abort under unusually difficult conditions.

Alternative. In the absence of comprehensive weather penetration procedures, the group would have established firm weather criteria for mission abort. The helicopter flight leader could have retained control by use of visual signals to the extent possible and by use of radio when necessary, OPSEC notwithstanding. He would have made abort decisions based on established criteria and circumstances and would have aborted the entire flight if helicopter assets fell below minimum requirements to proceed to next phase of the mission. In addition to the weather criteria, others based on an acceptable degree of punctuality were necessary to assure timely arrival of a minimum number of helicopters at Desert One. An absolute minimum of six were required for the next phase, and prudence would dictate arrival of at least seven.

Directly related to sound abort criteria is a procedure to assure that communications equipment is functional. In strict radio silence, an aircrew could be completely unaware that a radio had ceased functioning. A procedure for periodic blind radio transmissions would have served as an equipment check for all net members.

Implications. The negative implications of the group's alternative include the possibility that severely restrictive abort criteria could have limited individual initiative and the success orientation necessary to mission success. On the positive side, the review group's method would have provided positive management of mission assets.

Evaluation. ... [I]t cannot be stated categorically that adoption of the group's alternative would have assured success beyond Desert One. Even though six helicopters and seven crews arrived at the intended destination under the difficult conditions that prevailed, they proved insufficient to proceed further. If all six helicopters had been mission capable, the delayed takeoff for the next phase could well have jeopardized success and resulted in a more serious situation. The national significance of this operation demanded adoption of, and adherence to, extraordinary procedures designed to deal with relatively remote contingencies.

ISSUE 10: THE USE OF OTHER HELICOPTERS

Event. Initial study of the Iranian situation and forces available quickly led to the belief that a rescue attempt would require heavy-lift, long-range helicopters. On 19 November 1979, the CJCS approved development of a plan using helicopters. The RH-53D was selected after an in-depth review of available helicopter resources and their inherent capabilities.

JTF Rationale. Primary criteria for selection included range, payload, and ability to be positioned rapidly; i.e., airliftable. Other major considerations were suitability of candidate helicopters to carrier operations and OPSEC....

Alternative. Selection of the RH-53D for all the reasons was correct. However, it has been contended that specially configured HH-53 helicopters should have been favorably considered as primary replacements. On the other hand, these specially equipped helicopters were just coming off the production line, only a handful of pilots were proficient in flying them and operating their sophisticated systems, and they carry less payload than the RH-53D. In addition, reliability and maintainability of such a sophisticated system was doubtful at this early stage of its introduction.

Implications. On the positive side, specially equipped helicopters would have markedly improved ability. Considering that at the time there was no practical alternatives to launching the helicopter force from a carrier, the negative implications of the group's alternative are the deciding factor. An HH-53 helicopter will not fit into a carrier elevator or below decks without removal of its rotor blades — a procedure not recommended for daily operations. The option of leaving helicopters on deck is virtually infeasible because of the corrosive atmosphere; difficulty of maintenance; impact on carrier operations; and, above all, OPSEC. Logistic support of a relatively new and exotic weapon system would be further complicated by the additional delays in shipboard resupply.

Evaluation. During the planning process, the RH-53D emerged as the only helicopter with the full combination of operational capability upon which a feasible rescue plan could be structured.

ISSUE 11: HELICOPTER FORCE SIZE

Event. Approximately two weeks after US Embassy personnel in Iran were taken hostage, six RH-53D SEA STALLION helicopters were delivered to the carrier KITTY HAWK, and eventually transferred to the carrier NIMITZ when she arrived on station. These six, augmented by two more brought in on NIMITZ, launched on 24 April in support of the rescue operation. . . .

JTF Rationale. As planning for the rescue progressed, the number of helicopters perceived necessary to execute the mission grew from four, to six, to seven, and eventually to eight. These incremental increases were the result of unforeseen growth in the force believed necessary to achieve an acceptable probability of success in assaulting the Embassy and freeing the hostages. In addition, more helicopters were required to compensate for the lift capability lost because of seasonal temperature increases in the objective areas. . . .

Alternative. The review group concluded that additional helicopters and crews would have reduced the risk of abort due to mechanical failure, were operationally feasible, and could have been made available until quite late in the planning evolution. An unconstrained planner would more than likely have initially required at least 10 helicopters under JTF combat rules, 11 under the most likely case, and up to 12 using peacetime historical data. NIMITZ was capable of onloading a few more helicopters with little or no impact on other missions. Aircrew availability did not limit the force. By reducing the contingency margin, fuel available at Desert One was sufficient to accommodate at least 10 helicopters. In sum, aside from OPSEC, no operational or logistic factor prohibited launching 11 from NIMITZ and continuing beyond the halfway point to Desert One with 10 helicopters.

Implications. The negative implications of this alternative includes abandoning more helicopters in Iran, an increased threat to OPSEC generated by additional aircraft, and a reduction in contingency fuel at Desert One. On the positive side, the group's alternative would have decreased the probability that the number of mission-capable helicopters would fall below the required minimum.

Evaluation. The number of mission-capable helicopters available at Desert One was critical to allowing the mission to proceed. It is too simplistic to suggest that adding more helicopters would have reduced the likelihood of the mission aborting due to mechanical failure. The problematic advantages of an increased helicopter force must be balanced against the increased threat posed to OPSEC throughout the continuum of training, deployment, and execution and the reduced contingency fuel reserve at Desert One. In retrospect, it appears that on balance an increase in the helicopter force was warranted; however, such an increase would not itself guarantee success.

ISSUE 12: ALTERNATE HELICOPTER PILOTS

Event. At the outset, with the fate of the hostages unknown and unpredictable, an immediate capability to mount a possible rescue attempt was mandatory. Although a residue of similar capability from the Vietnam conflict existed, it was not intact; therefore, it was expedient to select an integral unit proficient in the RH-53D and carrier operations. To bolster the unit's night assault capability, Navy pilots were paired with Marine Corps pilots versed in assault missions. In this crew configuration, training progress was viewed as unsatisfactory by COMJTF. As a result, pilots progressing slowly were released in late December 1979, and USN/USMC pilots known to have demonstrated capabilities more akin to the mission were recruited. Training in preparation for the rescue progressed more rapidly with the revised crews, and no further wholesale aircrew changes were made or contemplated.

JTF Rationale. The need to be ready at any moment precluded a smooth program designed to achieve a specific capability by 24 April 1980. The requirement to be ready when windows of opportunity opened resulted not in one five-month training program, but several discrete two- or three-week programs — shingled, one overlapping the other.

Alternative. During this period, USAF pilot resources included 114 qualified H-53 pilots, instructors, and flight examiners. Of these, 96 were current in long-range flight and aerial refueling. In addition, there were another 86 former H-53 qualified pilots identified, most of whom had fairly recent Special Operations Forces (SOF) or rescue experience. These USAF pilots, more experienced in the mission profiles envisioned for the rescue operation, would have probably progressed more rapidly than pilots proficient in the basic weapons systems but trained in a markedly different role. USAF pilots, as well as those from other Services, with training and operational experience closely related to the rescue mission profile could have been identified and made available. The real question to be addressed is: is transition to a new and highly complex mission in the same aircraft more or less difficult for an experienced pilot to master than transition to an aircraft variant in the same mission? Mastering a new, difficult, and complex mission requires a pilot to acquire and hone new skills and, more importantly, a new mind-set. Transitioning from an HH- or CH-53 to an RH-53 requires only learning a few new flight parameters and slightly altering already established procedures, something every experienced pilot has done several times. This point is not new. Experience gained in Project "Jungle Jim" (circa 1961) illustrated that learning new and vastly different complex mission skills is far more difficult than transitioning to an aircraft of similar design and performance characteristics.

Implications. Teaming carefully selected pilots of all Services, with a heavy weight on USAF SOF/rescue and USMC assault experience, would most likely have produced the most competent crews at an earlier date. However, introduction of large numbers of USAF pilots would have complicated the OPSEC problem in training and aboard the carrier.

Evaluation. Should a rescue mission have been attempted in the early days after the Embassy seizure, it is probable that a complement of selected pilots with extensive or current assault and rescue experience would have been more effective. However, there is nothing to suggest that any other combination of aircrews could or would have performed the mission better than those who flew it on 24 April 1980. . . .

ISSUE 13: ESTABLISHED HELICOPTER UNIT

Event. Selection of the RH-53D helicopter for the rescue mission naturally led to selection of an RH-53D squadron as the unit to perform the mission.

JTF Rationale. The JTF selected a minesweeping helicopter squadron as the most expedient solution when it became evident the RH-53D was the helicopter to use.

Alternative. The group would marry up the appropriate helicopters and their maintenance capability with an operational unit compatible with mission requirements. When it was clear the RH-53D helicopters were required, selection of a USMC assault squadron would have facilitated training and in constructing a credible OPSEC cover story. . . . The main point is that the squadron's institutional structure would be preserved; e.g., training, tactics, and standardization. Personnel performing and experienced in these functions would greatly enhance the unit's ability to smoothly transition into its new role. . . .

Evaluation. It is believed the preservation of an established squadron's inherent unit cohesion could have facilitated training, enhanced information flow, and increased aircrew knowledge, all of which could lead to a more integrated unit operation. . . .

ISSUE 14: HANDLING THE DUST PHENOMENON

Event. There was serious and justifiable concern with the ability to accurately forecast weather along planned low-level routes to Desert One. Therefore, the JTF had to develop a catalog of weather phenomena that could likely occur in Iran and the ability to accurately and reliably forecast their occurrence. . . . Among these was the phenomenon of suspended dust actually encountered along a 200-nm stretch of the helicopter route. Information extracted from the National Intelligence Survey (NIS 33, 34 - Iran and Afghanistan) July 1970 was available to the JTF in December 1979 and was eventually included in the OPLAN [Operations Plan] weather annex. A table in this annex indicated, by location and month, the frequency of suspended-dust occurences. Helicopter pilots, however, were surprised when they encountered the dust, were unprepared to accurately assess its impact on their flight, and stated that they were not advised of the phenomenon. C-130 pilots were also unaware of the possibility of encountering suspended dust.

JTF Rationale. The AWS [Air Weather Service] team was assigned to the JTF J-2 section and did not have direct contact with the helicopter and C-130 aircrews. Weather information was passed through an intelligence officer to the pilots on regular visits to the training sites. However, pilots with extensive C-130 and H-53 experience on the JTF J-5 [Joint-Plans and Policies] section had direct access to AWS personnel. Information flow to the mission pilots was filtered as a result of organizational structure. The traditional relationship between pilots and weather forecasters was severed. This was done to enhance OPSEC.

Alternative. The question to be addressed is not where the fault lay for the lack of aircrew knowledge but, more importantly, what should be done in future situations where there exists a paucity of weather information and the price of failure is high. . . . If they were fully aware of the high degree of uncertainty associated with limited data and the attendant risk, mission planners should have more aggressively pursued options that reduced this uncertainty to a manageable and acceptable degree. One cannot build a data base overnight; it takes years of observations to accurately and reliably predict weather patterns. Therefore, active measures could have been pursued. Of equal importance, the interplay of meteorologist and operator is the process that most often surfaces the questions that need to be answered — the uncertainties that size risk. . . . The group would have required direct interface between mission pilots and their supporting weather team.

Implications. The negative aspects of the review group's alternative impact on OPSEC and administrative procedures. The AWS officer would have had to make frequent trips to the training sites for direct interface, or a second weather officer could have been temporarily assigned to the western United States training site with the aircrews. It is unlikely that either of these alternatives would have compromised OPSEC. On the other hand, there is no assurance that face-to-face interaction would have surfaced the dust phenomenon or made pilots more aware. However, the group believes that direct interface between mission pilots and air weather officers would have increased the likelihood of foreknowledge of the suspended dust phenomenon, that informed planners would have more aggressively pursued alternative approaches to reduce and manage this uncertainty, and that pilots encountering the suspended dust would have been better prepared.

Evaluation. ... While it is unlikely that direct interface between AWS personnel and mission pilots could have altered the outcome on the night of 24 April, it is possible that helicopter pilots would have gained insight into the dust phenomenon and might well have made a better informed decision when they encountered it. ...

ISSUE 15: WEATHER RECONNAISSANCE

Event. There was serious and justifiable concern about the ability to accurately forecast weather along planned routes to Desert One and the extraction site and less concern about forecast accuracy for Tehran because of the availability of weather predictions for major international airports. Forecasting difficulty was compounded by the need to predict acceptable weather for a two-day period. Accordingly, an AWS team was formed to gather data on Iran. ... Satellite imagery was extremely useful but incapable of revealing the presence of low-level clouds or other restrictions to visibility hidden beneath an overcast and was of limited value at night. Nevertheless, there was evidently sufficient confidence in the forecaster's ability to predict VMC and the frequency of VMC so that alternative means to VFR [Visual Flight Rules] flight procedures were not pursued. The weather forecast for the night of 24 April did not predict reduced visibility over extended distances of the helicopter route. Uninformed and unprepared to cope with the extremely low visibilities encountered, the leader paused, the flight became separated, Helicopter #5 aborted, and all helicopters reaching Desert One were appreciably late.

JTF Rationale. The JTF believed that the probability of VMC for the helicopter ingress was reasonably high, and that the AWS team could accurately forecast the en route weather. Therefore, the helicopter ingress would be accomplished by visual navigation using night vision goggles. If the helicopters encountered weather that could not safely be penetrated using visual navigation with night vision goggles, the flight — and mission — would be aborted. The use of a weather reconnaissance aircraft had the disadvantage of being one more sortie over the helicopter route that could arouse attention. ...

Alternative. COMJTF and his air component staff had the means to obtain more timely and accurate weather data. Weather reconnaissance is a proven and often used means of accurately determining weather along flight routes with a paucity of weather reporting stations and high risk of incomplete knowledge. In hindsight, a weather reconnaissance C-130 would have encountered the dust phenomenon in advance of the helicopters and assessed its magnitude and impact before the helicopters would have to penetrate the area of reduced visibility. ...

Implications. On the negative side, the C-130 would have been one more sortie overflying the helicopter route and could have alerted ground watchers so that the helicopter flight would have been visually detected. On the positive side, weather reconnaissance could have provided COMJTF with more accurate and timely information on which to base a decision on whether or not to abort that night and try again within the available window.

Evaluation. Weather reconnaissance along the exact helicopter route would have provided COMJTF with precise information on the prevailing weather, and influenced a decision to continue at that juncture or to wait for more favorable conditions. The group considered that provisions for handling weather contingencies could and should have been enhanced. The weather reconnaissance was one option that cost nothing in additional aircraft, fuel, or crew requirements, although there were OPSEC considerations.

ISSUE 16: C-130 PATHFINDERS

Event. During flight from respective launch points to Desert One, the C-130s made landfall in the same general vicinity and at approximately the same time as the helicopters. The helicopter force was much more austerely prepared for long-range, low-level night navigation. Their crews did not include navigators, and the aircraft were not equipped with TFR [Terrain-Following Radar] or FLIR. They were equipped with the PINS and OMEGA systems. The crews had received only limited training and expressed low confidence in the equipment and their ability to employ it. The primary method of navigation for the helicopters was dead reckoning using NVGs to terrain follow. . . .

JTF Rationale. With limitations of the navigation equipment available in the RH-53D, the JTF gained confidence in the ability of helicopter crews to navigate over long distance at night under VMC using NVGs [Night Vision Goggles] during the training phase in the western United States. . . . Use of a C-130 pathfinder for the helicopters was not considered because of the confidence in the high probability of VMC weather and because of the feeling that the use of a C-130 pathfinder would be therefore unnecessarily complicating, especially with the wide difference in operating airspeeds.

Alternative. The alternative plan would provide for a C-130/helicopter rendezvous at or just after landfall.

C-130 aircraft are capable of flying at speeds compatible with RH-53D helicopters and acting as pathfinders for them.

Implications. Using C-130s as pathfinders from the point of entry into Iran to Desert One would have increased their fuel consumption. Increased C-130 fuel consumption would be somewhat compensated for by a greater assurance that the helicopters would arrive and arrive on time, thus requiring shorter ground times for C-130s and helicopters.

Evaluation. C-130 pathfinders for the RH-53Ds would have increased the probability of all flyable helicopters arriving at Desert One regardless of unforeseen weather along the route short of a major storm. . . .

ISSUE 17: HELICOPTER ABORTS

Event. Eight mission-capable RH-53D helicopters departed NIMITZ on the evening of 24 April 1980. Of these eight, only five arrived at Desert One capable of proceeding. One helicopter aborted in the Iranian desert short of Desert One, another turned back for loss of instruments due to electrical failure, and a third RH-53D aborted at Desert One as the result of a hydraulic leak that in turn failed a primary hydraulic pump. Because only five helicopters were available to proceed against a firm minimum requirement of six, the rescue mission was aborted....

JTF Rationale. Helicopter #6, the first abort, experienced a BIM [Blade Inspection Method] indication approximately two hours into the flight. RH-53 rotor blade spars are pressurized with nitrogen, and the spar's ability to retain the nitrogen under pressure is an indication of spar integrity. A BIM warning indicates possible loss of nitrogen pressure in the blade but does not necessarily indicate that the pressure loss is the result of a crack in the spar. Nitrogen pressure loss can result from a leaky filler valve, a defective seal on the spar extrusion, or a crack in the spar that can ultimately result in rotor blade failure. The crew of #6 made a precautionary landing in the desert to investigate, verified the cockpit indication with the BIM indicator on the rotor blade, and based on normal operating procedures elected to abandon the helicopter....

Helicopter #5 aborted four hours into the mission and returned to NIMITZ because of failures to essential flight instruments that the pilots believed were critical to safely continuing the flight....

The lead C-130 crew possessed essential information on Desert One weather and the dust cloud that was not passed to Helicopter #5. Based on the helicopter pilot's testimony, these data, had they been passed, could have altered his abort decision. Once at Desert One, Helicopter #5 could have continued in the VMC conditions existing and, moreover, would have had the opportunity to exchange equipment with the non-mission-capable helicopter.

Helicopter #2 aborted at Desert One because of a hydraulic pump failure resulting from fluid depletion through a cracked "B" nut. Failures of this type usually result in metal contamination throughout the hydraulic system. Correcting the malfunction required replacing pump filters and thorough flushing of the system. The extensive maintenance required to repair a hydraulic pump malfunction justified the decision to not take a spare hydraulic pump along.

Alternative. In light of the circumstances surrounding helicopter aborts that led ultimately to the overall mission abort, it is apparent that the pilot of helicopter #5 lacked certain knowledge vital to reaching an informed decision to proceed or abort. Uncertainty regarding Iranian radar coverage and the dust phenomenon (see Issues 14 and 18) played important roles in Helicopter #5's decision to return to the carrier. However, the major factor in his abort decision was lack of readily available information on weather conditions further en route and at Desert One. Information on the number of mission-capable helicopters at Desert One or still en route also could have influenced his decision and should have been made known. Failure to pass this vital information back to the carrier and support bases and rebroadcast it via secure HF [High Frequency] was the result of a very restrictive communications doctrine related to the overriding concern for OPSEC. However, there were ways to pass the information to C-130s and helicopters en route that would have small likelihood of compromising the mission.

A BIM indication was a likely occurrence on the mission and had been experienced in training. BIM indications and other likely malfunctions should have been identified and researched in detail and information provided aircrews as part of their mission preparation.

Implications. The negative aspects of the proposed alternative are relatively insignificant. It is somewhat doubtful that secure retransmissions would have compromised OPSEC. In the positive vein, the proposed alternative would have provided for a covered and secure flow of vital information to the rescue force while en route to Desert One.

Evaluation. . . . [T]he group concludes that restricted communications flow within the task force denied information essential to reach informed decisions. The additional information might have prompted Helicopter #5 to continue on to Desert One. One more flyable helicopter would have enabled the mission to proceed.

ISSUE 18: THE ENEMY RADAR THREAT

Event. This issue, while stated in generalized fashion, derives from a single, highly explicit event in which unevaluated data has passed directly to helicopter aircrews. This data and its implications contradicted the final conclusions of intelligence analysts.

Implications. There exists the possibility that some helicopter pilot judgments regarding altitude selection were affected by the informal report.

Evaluation. It would be inappropriate to fault COMJTF and his staff in this instance, as he learned of the informal report after the mission had been concluded, obviously much too late to take corrective action. Furthermore, six helicopters did arrive at Desert One, and the abort at that point cannot be related to any alleged enemy capability along the penetration route. What is illustrated by this event deserves reemphasis, however. All concerned should refer raw information reports to the appropriate intelligence staff representative for confirmation, denial, or other qualification before accepting the report as factual.

ISSUE 19: HELICOPTER COMMUNICATONS

Event. The helicopter force planned and trained to operate in complete radio silence. Intraflight communication, where possible, was to be done with light signals. The absence of radio communication indicated to the helicopter pilots that all was well and to continue the mission. Subsequently, when helicopter flight became separated in the dust cloud, each separate element lacked vital information. The lead helicopter did not know that #8 had successfully recovered the crew from #6 and continued nor that #6 had been abandoned in the desert. More importantly, after he reversed course in the dust and landed, the lead could not logically deduce either that the other helicopter had continued or that they had turned back to return to the carrier. He did not know when the flight had disintegrated. He could have assumed that they had become separated before he reversed course and unknowingly proceeded. Alternatively, they could have lost sight of him after turning and, mistaking his intentions, continued back to the carrier. Lastly, #5 might have elected to continue had he known that his arrival at Desert One would have allowed the mission to continue and that VMC existed at the rendezvous.

JTF Rationale. In concert with the view that OPSEC was critical to achieving surprise, every effort was made to keep radio transmissions to the absolute minimum.

Alternative. Capabilities existed to pass to the helicopter crews vital information that would have enabled them to make more informed judgments. On the night of 24 April, all information deemed vital to the helicopters could have been transmitted by NIMITZ.

Implications. Negative implications of the proposed alternative are relatively minor. Secure communications would not likely have compromised OPSEC....

Evaluation. A system providing secure intelligence to the helicopter crews would have significantly enhanced the probability of the mission proceeding beyond Desert One....

ISSUE 20: ALTERNATIVES TO THE DESERT ONE SITE

Event. Early in the hostage rescue planning, it became clear that a desert rendezvous in Iran to refuel helicopters and onload the assault force had many advantages.... The site had to be located within a prescribed distance of Tehran; to have the necessary dimensions to land, park, and launch C-130s and RH-53Ds; and to satisfy a geological estimate of satisfactory bearing surface.

JTF Rationale. To succeed, the plan called for sufficient hours of nautical darkness with some moonlight, and temperatures that would enable the helicopters to lift the fuel, equipment, and assault force believed necessary to successfully execute the plan. The window where all these environmental factors overlapped closed in late spring. On the basis of the site assessment, the JTF anticipated that the force at Desert One would be observed by passing vehicles. They had a workable plan to handle personnel from these vehicles during the short period that secrecy had to be maintained, until the rescue force reached the hostages.

Alternative. The Desert One plan was feasible, but the risks of compromise along the road were high. The vehicles and helicopter abandoned along the road would more than likely draw attention to the scene and ultimately to the C-130 wheel ruts. . . . Clearly, another site away from roads would have markedly reduced compromising the rescue mission in its early phases.

Implications. The group's alternative depended on the identification of other suitable site(s) clear of roads and inhabited areas. Intelligence planners for the JTF had concluded none existed, and the group has no basis for believing that the search for alternative sites was anything less than thorough. . . .

Evaluation. . . . A refueling site in the desert was an integral part of the only feasible rescue plan, and Desert One apparently had no suitable alternative in a remote location. Therefore, the JTF's solution appears to be the only reasonable one, but the group concludes that it probably carried more risk than the JTF had assessed.

ISSUE 21: COMMAND AND CONTROL AT DESERT ONE

Event. The first aircraft to arrive at Desert One, carrying the on-scene commander, Combat Control Team, and Road Watch Team, executed a missed approach to avoid a vehicle traveling along the highway adjacent to the desert strip. As the aircraft landed on its third approach, the Road Watch Team disembarked to take up blocking positions on the roadway approaches to Desert One. They each encountered traffic, one a bus with a driver and 43 passengers, the other a small fuel truck followed closely by a pickup truck. All three vehicles showed no signs of stopping when signaled. Shots were fired, which resulted in the bus stopping and the fuel truck set on fire. The fuel truck driver jumped out, raced back to the pickup, and escaped — 44 Iranians on the bus were detained. This had all taken place rather rapidly — the operation was becoming more complex, but these contingencies had been foreseen and planned for. As the site filled up with C-130s, more than had been exercised at a western United States training area, it took on new and larger dimensions than had been experienced but was unfolding as planned. Then it became apparent the helicopters were late, but for reasons unknown at Desert One. As the helicopters started arriving in separate elements, concern increased that there would not be enough helicopters, fuel or time remaining to continue beyond Desert One. The setting in which all this took place was, at best, a difficult, but manageable one. The noise generated by 16 C-130 and 12 RH-53D engines made voice or radio communications difficult. Personnel moving about Desert One were shadowy, somewhat fuzzy figures, barely recognizable. Then came the unfortunate accident, when Helicopter

#4 crashed into a C-130 while repositioning to allow another helicopter to take on more fuel for the return flight to NIMITZ.

As complex and difficult as the Desert One scenario was, it had not been fully rehearsed. A training exercise at the western training area conducted on 13-14 April with two C-130s and four H-53s was used to validate the Desert One concept. Perhaps because the scope and complexity of Desert One was not replicated in a full-dress rehearsal, the plan for this desert rendezvous was soft. There was no identifiable command post for the on-scene commander; a staff and runners were not anticipated; backup rescue radios were not available until the third C-130 arrived; and, lastly, key personnel and those with critical functions were not identified for ease of recognition. . . .

JTF Rationale. The overriding concern for OPSEC played heavily in the JTF's decision not to fully rehearse the Desert One scenario. Moreover, the JTF apparently believed that desert operations had been practiced sufficiently and that, although there were technical differences in the refueling, a full rehearsal was not justified. With regard to identification, members of the JTF, by their own testimony, were confident that personal recognition between the key players was adequate to facilitate command and control at Desert One.

Alternative. The review group concluded that the uncertainties of conducting a clandestine operation in a hostile environment argued for the strictest adherence to doctrinal command and control procedures. The on-scene and functional commanders, their alternates and personnel of every key function should have been designated with readily identifiable markings visible in artificial or natural light. . . .

The on-scene commander's principal location should have been fixed and easily recognized. An alternate or second in command and runners to carry orders should have been available and identifiable. . . . In addition, backup communications should have been carried on both the first and second C-130s to insure reliable and secure communications from Desert One as soon as possible. Lastly, although not central to the command and control issue, a full-dress training exercise at a comparable desert training site could well have surfaced some of these problems. . . .

Implications. The review group's alternative would have reduced confusion and accelerated information flow at Desert One. Equally important, it would have virtually eliminated the disconnects that surfaced when principals such as the helicopter flight commander arrived last and the Deputy Commander for Helicopter Forces aborted.

Evaluation. Although the proposed alternative would have smoothed Desert One operations, it would not have influenced the outcome. . . .

ISSUE 22: CLASSIFIED MATERIAL SAFEGUARD

Event. In the event of mission abort at Desert One, JTF guidance called for pilots, crews, and radio operators to return their helicopter and material to NIMITZ, taking appropriate action to protect classified *[sic]*. The plan proved infeasible when one helicopter crashed into a C-130 resulting in fire, casualties, and an overall hazardous situation. The on-scene commander decided to withdraw the entire force by the remaining C-130 aircraft as soon as possible, leaving the five undamaged helicopters at Desert One. Two of the helicopters located in the southern refuel zone were properly sanitized of classified material by the individuals responsible. The other three helicopters were located in the northern refuel zone in close proximity (within 100-150 feet) to the crash and fire. Personnel responsible for the classified material in those helicopters attempted to return to them but were told to immediately board the C-130s to expedite withdrawal. Failure to sanitize the helicopters resulted in loss of classified material. There is no evidence or indication that the on-scene commander was aware that classified material was being left behind.

JTF Rationale. JTF guidance, coupled with military SOP [Standard Operating Procedure] and training, appeared sufficient to provide for adequate protection of classified material. The decision by the Desert One on-scene commander to expedite withdrawal of personnel by the remaining C-130 aircraft was made in the interest of troop safety, to protect remaining assets, and to minimize risk of detection.

Alternative. The review group's alternative would have been to refine command and control procedures at Desert One to assure adherence to provisions of the JTF plan for handling of classified material (see Issue 21).

Implications. An attempt to return to the helicopters and to sanitize them could have cost additional lives, increased the risk of discovery and of damage to the escape aircraft, and delayed departure. However, the helicopters were not destroyed, there remained a requirement to protect classified material, and a period in excess of 20 minutes was available to sanitize the helicopters.

Evaluation. The loss of classified material had no direct impact on the success of this mission. However, such loss reflects unfavorably on the performance of the personnel involved. Their actions resulted in possible enemy exploitation of sensitive material, including its use for propaganda ends.

[ISSUE 23: DESTRUCT DEVICES]

Event: Helicopter #6 developed mechanical problems en route to Desert One and landed in the desert short of destination. Ground personnel tasked with responsibility for helicopter destruction were not available. An unforseen accident and ensuing conflagration at Desert One prevented the on-scene commander from implementing the helicopter destruction plan because he perceived it to be too risky. As a result, five RH-53Ds were abandoned intact.

JTF Rationale. As planning proceeded, an option to destroy the helicopters in Iran, should a contingency situation warrant, was considered. This contingency called for individuals to place thermite grenades in the helicopters if their destruction was called for and then to detonate them. This option was never implemented at Desert One because of the perceived danger of exploding helicopters and ammunition to personnel and aircraft evacuating the site and to Iranians aboard a nearby bus.

Alternative. The review group believes it prudent to have detailed plans for contingency destruction of equipment in missions similar to the Iranian rescue. Providing the option for contingency destruction is most important when the equipment is to be abandoned in hostile country. There is good reason to believe explosives, when properly installed, are no more dangerous to crew and passengers than the onboard fuel supply. . . .

Equipping rescue mission helicopters with easily removable, separated, and disconnected explosive devices and initiators should not have jeopardized safety and would have enhanced the ability to destroy helicopters at any point in the mission.

Implications. Negative implications of the group's proposal are nil. Aircrews would have had to have been trained to connect and operate the destruct devices planned for use in their helicopters. . . . On the positive side, the proposed alternative could have eliminated the requirement to have individuals present to handle the explosives, reduced response time, and provided the option to destroy helicopters at any point in the mission. . . .

Evaluation. Equipping helicopters with destruct devices would not have altered the circumstances that ultimately led to aborting the rescue mission. However, the lack of destruct capability severely limited the Desert One on-scene commander's ability to execute destruction when an unforeseen contingency developed.

QUEEN BEATRIX CORONATION
April 30, 1980

Amid pomp and pageantry reminiscent of a medieval coronation, Queen Beatrix on April 30 became the Netherlands' sixth sovereign under its 1848 constitution. Juliana — Beatrix's 71-year-old mother and queen of the Dutch people since 1948 — abdicated in favor of her daughter at a private ceremony at the royal palace in Amsterdam earlier the same day.

But the investiture celebration did not eclipse the sounds of rock-throwing rioters who skirmished with police only blocks away from the royal ceremony. Rioters used the occasion to protest the chronic housing shortage in Amsterdam and in other Dutch cities. Shouting, "No housing, no coronation," youthful rioters smashed shop windows and burned cars. Riot police, using tear gas and water cannons, quelled the disturbances by late evening.

Beatrix made only two brief public appearances during the ceremonies — a balcony appearance with her mother, Juliana, after the signing of the Act of Abdication and, in the afternoon, a short walk of about 100 yards from the palace to the 500-year-old Nieuwe Kerk where she took the oath of obedience to the constitution and where members of the Parliament pledged allegiance.

In one of her first official acts as queen, Beatrix visited a nearby hospital to see some of those injured in the rioting.

Queen's Speech

Beatrix told Parliament and assembled dignitaries attending the coronation that she had "no idea where the road will lead us." However, she appealed to her people to build stronger ties with developing countries because "we can no longer disassociate our domestic polity from the distress of the world."

Most Netherlanders welcomed the continuation of the constitutional monarchy under the House of Orange. And Dutch political observers expected no interruption in the political and economic stability of the country or in the nation's participation in the North Atlantic Treaty Organization (NATO) and the Common Market.

Juliana's Abdication

In remarks at the abdication ceremony, Juliana, citing age as the reason for stepping aside, said that it was "better that my place should be taken by someone new and vigorous. I am well pleased in my successor; she will do her job well...."

On Jan. 31, Beatrix's 42nd birthday, Juliana had announced her intention to abdicate on her own 71st birthday. That announcement caught the nation by surprise. They had expected the popular and grandmotherly queen to continue on the throne for several more years.

Investiture Ceremony

Beatrix took office by reciting an oath of medieval origin swearing to "defend and preserve the territory of the state" and to "protect the general and specific freedoms and rights of all my subjects."

No crown was placed on the head of the new queen. But a copy of the Dutch constitution lay on a crimson cushion at the center of the dais called the Credence Table, symbolizing the supremacy of the elected government. Around it were displayed the crown, orb and scepter.

One by one, 225 members of Parliament rose to swear fealty to the new monarch. The "king of arms" then proclaimed, "The queen is invested." As trumpets sounded a fanfare, hundreds in the church and thousands outside shouted three times, "Long live the queen."

Housing Riots

Several thousand young people focused on the royal palace — empty except for ceremonial occasions — as the emblem of social injustice.

Many of them "squatters," they lived in empty buildings in a city where the waiting list for housing contained over 50,000 names. The rioters demanded more government action to ease the housing shortage. Attempts in the past by police to oust the squatters had proved unsuccessful.

Divided Nation

Although pictured on tourist posters as the land of wooden shoes and windmills, Holland was a nation deeply divided on religious and political issues.

The nation's postwar economy rode a wave of prosperity built on the sale of natural gas and on trade. But many Netherlanders questioned whether material prosperity had been purchased at too high a price — a weakening of the national spirit and a loss of direction among young people.

Moreover, the new queen had not shared in her mother's popularity. The Dutch people regarded Beatrix as strong willed and perhaps arrogant. In a country that suffered severely at German hands in World War II, the Dutch were slow to look favorably on Beatrix's marriage in 1966 to a German diplomat, Claus von Amsberg. Dutch conservatives were somewhat critical when Beatrix and her husband expressed interest in Third World problems, traveled to the Soviet Union and China and counted as friends artists and left-wing intellectuals.

With 13 political parties represented, the Dutch Parliament reflected a delicate balance of groups and interests, and the nation was ruled by coalition governments. The queen's chief political duty — often a difficult one — was to select a prime minister to form a government after national elections.

The House of Orange

Fiercely independent and determinedly informal, the Dutch accepted their royal house because it tempered its style to suit Dutch tastes. The monarchy has kept to modest proportions.

The royal house had its origins in 1658 when Prince William of Orange led a cluster of provinces in a successful revolt against King Phillip II of Spain. The Netherlands, or Holland, established the House of Orange as the royal line of succession.

In recent times the royal family overcame crises triggered when, in the 1950s, it was disclosed that Queen Juliana had consulted a faith healer and, two decades later, when Prince Bernhard, Juliana's husband, was shown to have been involved in a Lockheed bribery scandal.

Following are the texts of Queen Juliana's address at an abdication ceremony, April 30, 1980; the Act of Abdication; Juliana's speech from the balcony of the royal palace; Beatrix's address to the people from the palace balcony; and Queen Beatrix's speech at the investiture ceremony. (Boldface headings in brackets have been added by Congressional Quarterly to highlight the organization of the texts.):

QUEEN JULIANA'S ADDRESS

I should like to welcome you all — honoured guests, beloved family and especially our daughter Beatrix. As I step down, she steps up to take over her duties as Queen — duties which I can only describe as precious but onerous. She is willing to take on the task and it is one for which she is extremely well-prepared. For the sake of the Kingdom of the Netherlands, for the sake of all of us who are Dutch, it is better that my place should be taken by someone new and vigorous. I am well pleased in my successor; she will do her job well, of that I have no doubt. I am deeply grateful to her for the inner conviction with which she has accepted her new role.

Queen Beatrix will develop her own style, within the scope of her constitutional powers. But she will have to summon up much strength to meet the demands of the office which falls to her, and of this too I know she is capable.

She starts her reign at an extremely difficult time. It needs courage and imagination on the part of those who are called to high office to face both the distant and the not so distant future, particularly as there are limits to what we can achieve in the international community. The problems are great and so are the cares. The years ahead will be crucial for the future of mankind.

May God bless our daughter in her journey through life.

My husband and I, her parents, deliberately gave her a name with a very special meaning: she who brings happiness. May the meaning contained in her name come true in every possible way so that she too will experience happiness in her new function.

It only remains for me to wish her every success, both personally and in her duties as Queen and to say to her: It is time to start.

I should now like to call upon the Director of the Secretariat to read the act of abdication.

ACT OF ABDICATION

TODAY, THE THIRTIETH OF APRIL 1980, AT TEN O'CLOCK ANTE MERIDIEM, AT THE ROYAL PALACE IN AMSTERDAM, I JULIANA, Queen of The Netherlands, Princess of Orange-Nassau

... in the presence of my spouse and my eldest daughter and her spouse, called together: the Chairmen of both Chambers of the States-General, the Ministers of The Kingdom, the Vice President of the Council of State, the Members of the Delegation from the Netherlands Antilles, the Commissioner of the Queen in the Province of North-Holland, the Burgomaster of Amsterdam, and the Director of the Cabinet of the Queen, to carry out, in their presence, in a solemn declaration my determination announced to all compatriots on the Thirty-first of January last to end my reign and to abdicate from the Crown so that this passes to my eldest daughter.

I declare that, after mature consideration, from this moment forth completely of my own free will, I do abdicate from my royal authority and dignities in The Kingdom and from all rights thereunto connected, so that these pass to my eldest daughter and heiress to the throne BEATRIX, Princess of Lippe-Biesterfeld, to be occupied by her and her legal issue, in accordance with the Charter and the Constitution of the Kingdom of The Netherlands.

This, my declaration, confirmed by my signature, and fixed with the Great Seal of the Kingdom, after being signed by my spouse, and my eldest daughter and her spouse, as well as by all authorities now assembled with me, shall be preserved in the Cabinet of the Queen. Authentic copies shall be sent to both Chambers of the States-General, to the Council of State, to the Supreme Court of The Netherlands, and to the States of the Netherlands Antilles.

The Chairman of
both Chambers
of the States General

The Vice President of
the Council of State

Juliana

Beatrix

The Members of the
Delegation from the
Netherlands Antilles

Claus Bernhard

The Ministers of
The Kingdom

The Commissioner of the
Queen in the province
of North-Holland

The Burgomaster of
Amsterdam

The Director of the
Cabinet of the Queen

JULIANA'S SPEECH TO THE PEOPLE

A few moments ago I abdicated from the throne. I present to you Beatrix, your new Queen.

I rejoice that I can relinquish my task to her, since it will be in good hands.

She has not asked for this heavy responsibility, any more than I did in my time. But however much she may have looked upon her future task with apprehension, she accepts it now with complete inner dedication.

So give her your support, all of you.

We are fortunate in that she is young and strong enough to have the courage to embark on new duties in the extremely difficult times we are going through.

Together we shall all move towards the future — with all its difficulties and all its opportunities — together with Queen Beatrix.

BEATRIX'S ADDRESS TO THE PEOPLE

I am sure you will understand if I first address myself to my mother. My dear Mother,

In the almost 32 years that you have been our Queen, you have devoted yourself to the service of your fellow men. In doing so, you have won the love of us all. I am deeply grateful for what in all these years, with my father at your side, you have done for this our country.

I can only cherish the hope that I may be given the strength to perform the duties of sovereign in a manner that accords with your wisdom and your humanity, in a manner worthy of you.

You are not only my mother, you are an example to me in every way. Here, where you first appeared in public as Queen Juliana, I say to you these heartfelt words:

I wish you many, many years of happiness and contentment as Princess Juliana!

As your new Queen, I shall confine myself to a few words at this moment. I have made earnest endeavours to prepare myself for this heavy responsibility and I realize that much will be asked of me. Yet I am resolved to accept it as a great and splendid task. With the support of my husband I shall do my utmost to prove myself worthy of the trust that so many have put in me today.

May unity be the source of inspiration which will enable our richly varied nation to flourish even in the difficult times that may lie ahead. The strength that is given me I shall use to promote that unity.

I have no other ambition than to dedicate myself to you and to all our people, and to serve this country.

Long live the Netherlands!

SPEECH BY QUEEN BEATRIX

Members of the States-General,

Under our system of government, everything that the people feel is right, just and in keeping with the nation's character must stand the test of your appraisal and your trust. Indeed, the confidence of the people and parliament is the foundation of constitutional monarchy. Not power, personal will or a claim to hereditary authority but only the desire to serve the community can make present-day sovereignty meaningful.

It is in that spirit that we are gathered together to take an oath and make a promise to each other in phrases of ancient usage. I shall give my oath to the people of the Netherlands that I shall always observe and uphold the constitution;

You, the representatives of the people, now receive me as your Sovereign.

This ceremonious meeting derives its significance also from what the Statute for the Kingdom lays down. My oath will therefore, in accordance with the spirit of the Statute, also embrace the people of the Netherlands Antilles. I am glad that representatives from that part of the Kingdom are here to witness this.

[Reciprocal Promises]

But there is more to our reciprocal promises; they cover everything that a good sovereign and a good and faithful States-General are in duty bound to carry out.

I stand before you, prepared and open, firmly resolved to construe the word "everything" literally.

Mine is not an acquired function. It is an office no one would ask for. What certainly is visible is the outward splendour, but what is seldom seen is the burden and perpetual self-denial.

Nevertheless, here I stand, well prepared, but with no knowledge of where the road will lead us. I solicit your support and, through you I solicit the confidence of the people of the Netherlands.

I promise to spare no effort to discharge the duties incumbent upon me, and stake my all on meeting the exacting demands of the office.

I know my mandate: to act with complete impartiality and stand above party and group interests. I am resolved to fulfill that mandate conscientiously in the firm conviction that God directs my life.

My dear Mother —

If there is anything at all in your address on the occasion of your inauguration as Queen Juliana that has gone straight to my heart, it is the sentence in which you assert that for a Queen her role as a mother is just as important as it is for any other Dutch woman.

393

[Mother to the Dutch]

You have been a Mother, not only to me, to us your daughters, but also to the entire Dutch people. Wisdom, love of peace and faith in God were the principles underlying your 32 years of service to our country.

I have had the privilege of seeing at first hand how you looked upon your task as Queen — intense devotion to duty and profoundly human interest. Your unshakable faith was a strong support, also when adversity inevitably came your way. You were always patient, charitable, acquiescent, and much was kept in your great heart. You contrived to give substance to your office in all modesty and with complete self-effacement.

I know I am speaking today for all Dutch people within and outside the Kingdom who wish to thank you for the exceptional dedication with which you have ministered to the common weal for so many years. I make special mention of the denizens of the Netherlands Antilles, whose country acquired a new status within the Kingdom during your reign. You have also known their warm affection — and have reciprocated it.

Dear Mother, today is your birthday. In deep, deep gratitude for everything we have received from you this date will continue — also in the future — to be associated with your wisdom, your compassion and your motherly love, for it will remain The Queen's Day!

Father and Mother, as parents and in harmony you showed us, your children, the way along life's road. Although Father was away for long periods during the war, what we shall ultimately remember with profound gratitude (alongside our family ties) are his magnificent efforts for the Kingdom, both then and afterwards.

The office, dear Mother, which you have handed over to me today has been described as a lonely one; how lonely only you can know. But I am no more alone than you are. I realize how fortunate I am to have my husband beside me to support, supplement and correct me. He will continue to devote his talents to his multifarious work in and for the Netherlands.

My new task will undoubtedly make greater demands on both of us together and on our children but we are prepared to make such sacrifices in the private sphere, commensurate, of course, with our capacities and limitations. Happily, we can also reckon on the assistance of my sister Margriet and her husband.

[Shining Examples]

We have shining examples before us:
— my Grandmother, who strove in her own forceful manner to belong to and serve her people, and

— my Mother, with her very human approach to the office of sovereignty.

These examples inspire me. But I shall not be able to emulate them. What I certainly am eager to attempt is to find the link with the past in the new era with all its own demands and needs.

Members of the States-General —

If anything at all is certain today, it is a feeling of uncertainty — a foreboding that the future does not hold simply the development and growth of what already exists. The wheels of change have always whirled, but the rapidity with which yesterday's values seem to become outdated or superfluous affects our balance. It is as if there is no time to settle down.

Then there is the menace that makes our continued existence uncertain. Even one who has deliberately isolated himself and made a retreat for himself cannot feel quite secure. After all, nobody is safe; we all know that for the first time in history the human race is capable of destroying itself.

Fear of such an eventuality can paralyze our thinking and depress us. But we must not resign ourselves to despair. Every effort must be made to ensure that man can control what he himself has thought out and created. We must fight for peace. For surely it is peace that gives a future to everything that lives or will live.

He who builds needs a plan, he who sails a good compass.

Change must be progress (or so we think), progress towards equal opportunities, well-being and happiness. This calls for much experimenting (using all the imagination we possess); it calls for much inventiveness and testing (taking risks, if need be) by collective thinking and collective acting.

[Remain a Community]

No one has the answer to something so complex, but what is basic to our search for solutions is that we remain a community and prove it by exerting ourselves in unity and practising self-control in freedom. For strength and achievement need the human dimension of compassion.

The country's history proves that we have been a great nation. Not in population or area but because of essentially national characteristics such as energy, inventiveness and toleration. We have granted each other the liberty to think and speak in accordance with our individual views and convictions. Intensive communication and mobility in a small, densely populated area have made it essential to establish and confirm toleration again and again. That involved and still involves being prepared to listen, being accommodating and possessing the community spirit. That is how cooperation is born of the people and makes the present-day Dutchman no longer only governed but also a governor of those who govern him.

[Free, Pluriform Society]

The freedom of the individual to develop postulates admission of each other's right to an opportunity for development and giving each other that opportunity. Only by being discreet and respecting limitations can we create opportunities for the exercise of freedom by every individual.

In a free and pluriform society like ours there are bound to be conflicts of interests and opinions. In endeavouring to resolve such conflicts it is essential not to regard the other party as an enemy but rather as one who holds different views.

As the scales may not tip between people, so should a free society (in which the strong take care of themselves) maintain its balance by caring for the weaker ones, minorities, those who are forgotten and alone.

The partnership goes further still. We owe much of what the nation possesses — material possessions but spiritual values in particular — to our parents and forefathers; we must preserve them for the sake of our children and our children's children.

The realization that people need each other is native to us. Down the centuries the persecuted have found refuge in our country. The Dutch have from time immemorial concerned themselves actively with the world at large. This concern for other people has broadened and intensified in the last few years because of our solicitude for the people in developing countries. As we cooperate with these countries we realize even more fully that we must help to bring about fundamental changes.

[Courage to Change]

It requires courage to embark on such changes. It requires courage to face up to the fact (and take the consequences of so doing), that we can no longer dissociate our polity from the distress of the world. But willingness to take a broad view of justice and peaceful coexistence always finds its origins and roots in the home country.

Members of the States-General —

Austerity, simplicity and devotion to duty have characterized my Mother's reign.

In gratitude and respect for that example I shall endeavour to fulfil my mandate in the new era. The fulfilment [sic] of this mandate is my prime aim and object in life. I shall commit myself to this so as to be worthy of your trust in me.

When presently I take the oath before the people of the Netherlands that I will observe the constitution, I shall not be taking up the duties assigned to me with strength of my own. My faith will be the source of my strength.

Indeed, my deepest roots lie in our national anthem: "My shield and trust art Thou O Lord, my God!"

OATH OF OFFICE

I solemnly swear to the people of the Netherlands that I shall constantly preserve and uphold the Constitution. I solemnly swear that I shall defend and preserve the territory of the State to the best of My ability; that I shall protect the general and specific freedoms and rights of all My subjects, and shall employ all means placed at My disposal by the law to support and promote the general and specific welfare, as is encumbent upon a good King. So help me God!

MAY

QUEBEC SEPARATIST VOTE
May 2 - September 8, 1980

The Canadian province of Quebec May 20 voted to reject a referendum proposal that would have allowed Quebec Premier René Lévesque to negotiate the province's independence from Canada. Provincial voters defeated his "sovereignty/association" proposition by 58.2 percent to 41.8 percent.

Lévesque, head of the Parti Quebecois representing French-speaking Quebecers, had advocated sovereignty status for Quebec while maintaining a loose association with the rest of Canada. The provincial premier said the referendum results were "the last gasp of old Quebec" but he urged his supporters to hope for a "next time."

Trudeau's Response

Canadian Prime Minister Pierre Elliott Trudeau issued a low-keyed response to the election results. "We have all lost a bit as a result of this referendum," he said in Ottawa, Canada's capital. The result, Trudeau continued, "signals the end of a long period of uncertainty, of doubt, of strained relations between Quebec and other provinces and French and English-speaking Canadians." He added, "We must not delay in rebuilding our house and responding to the new needs of the family of Canadians."

The prime minister and his Liberal Party had campaigned in Quebec supporting continuation of the Canadian federation. Trudeau himself was a Quebecer, of French-Scottish ancestry.

Referendum

Political observers in Canada had expected the opponents of Lévesque's referendum to win a close contest. They were surprised by the healthy margin against the proposal. An estimated 54 percent of French-speaking Quebecers joined 80 percent of the English Canadians and other ethnic groups to defeat it.

The Quebec National Assembly, after three weeks of emotional debate March 4-20, passed the proposition by a vote of 68-37. The third paragraph was a source of controversy during the election. It read: "No change in political status resulting from these negotiations will be effected without approval by the people through another referendum."

During the intense assembly debate and in the campaign preceding the May 20 vote, Liberals argued that the referendum question was misleading. They said Lévesque's Parti Quebecois should have acknowledged openly that its goal was complete independence from the rest of Canada.

Sovereignty Issue

The Quebec-Ottawa dispute over sovereignty was the most visible of the federal-provincial quarrels. Differences of language, culture and economic status had divided the French-speaking Quebecers from English-speaking inhabitants since the British conquest of Canada in 1763.

More recently, oil- and mineral-rich western provinces such as Alberta and Saskatchewan had feuded with Ottawa over control of resource prices. And the poorer provinces — Newfoundland and Nova Scotia — had demanded a greater share of federal benefits and job-creation programs.

Constitutional Revision

Trudeau May 21 announced a new round of talks during the summer with provincial and territorial leaders on revising the constitution. He demanded in the House of Commons May 29, however, that the central government remain strong — in the face of insistent demands from Quebec and the western provinces for more autonomy. At the same time the prime minister spoke repeatedly of an urgent need to satisfy provincial aspirations. The 10 provincial premiers agreed to hold talks during July-August, 1980, culminating Sept. 8-12 in a federal-provincial summit.

The summit was called the most important constitutional conference since Canada's founding fathers first met in 1864. Its purpose was to reach a consensus on how to change Canada's constitution, the British North American Act of 1867. The document resided Britain's Parliament in London and because it was British law could be amended only by Parliament. The British appeared more than willing to let the Canadians "repatriate" or bring home their constitution. But the Canadian provinces, in 113 years of federation, had been unable to agree on the amending process. So any Canadian constitutional conference had the double duty of deciding not only what to amend, but how to go about it. Canadian history was strewn with attempts and failures to revise the constitution.

In a televised speech from the Canadian House of Commons, Trudeau set three conditions on a new constitution: 1) a federal parliament with real national powers, 2) provincial parliaments with equally valid territorial powers and 3) a charter of rights and freedoms, including the preservation of linguistic rights for French-speaking Canadians. The effort by the federal and 10 provincial governments to reach accord on constitutional change collapsed in acrimonious failure. The prime minister and the premiers had been unable to unanimously agree on a single point of Trudeau's agenda.

Trudeau, ignoring the rule of unanimity as a requirement for action, decided to move on his own. He introduced a resolution in Parliament in October, asking Britain to transfer the British North American Act of 1867 to Canada along with the power to change it. This simple act of patriation would have aroused little opposition except that Trudeau also was asking Britain to make a few amendments, among them a bill of rights including minority language rights and a formula for amending the constitution. In December, when a Gallup Poll asked 1,046 Canadians what they thought of the federal government's acting on its own without provincial consent, 58 percent disapproved. At the end of the year, the resolution still was being debated in a special committee of the Canadian Parliament.

> Following are excerpts from Prime Minister Pierre Elliot Trudeau's speech May 2, 1980, to the Montreal Chamber of Commerce, outlining the problems with the Quebec referendum; the Quebec referendum submitted to voters May 20, 1980; and excerpts from René Lévesque's opening statement to the Federal Provincial Conference of First Ministers on the Constitution, explaining the changes the Quebecers wanted after the referendum failed. (Boldface headings in brackets have been added by Congressional Quarterly to highlight the organization of the texts.):

TRUDEAU'S MAY 2 SPEECH

...The issue confronting Canada today is fundamental. That is: to remain within Canada. Every province, every group of citizens must answer this question: Do we remain in Canada? Or do we pull out?...

Well ... there are those who wish to remain Canadians and I do not know of any one among them who does not wish to take advantage of the present ferment to renew the constitution.

Mr. Ryan [Claude Ryan, leader of Quebec's Liberal Party] has submitted his proposal, in the form of his paper, The Beige Paper. The governments of other provinces, from Ontario to British Columbia, have contributed their own proposals. Our government, following the appointment of the Pepin-Robarts Commission, proposed a new theme, A Time for Action, and introduced a bill, Bill C-60, that, incidentally, included a number of proposals for a fundamental renewal.

There are those, then, who wish to remain Canadians but are prepared for a change and willing to improve federalism. And there are those, on the other hand, who want out. . . .

[Sovereignty-Association]

... [T]hese people, speaking in the name of the pride and the clearest right of Quebec Canadians, of French Canadians, to choose their destiny, ask us to vote for a proposition that would in fact place this destiny in the hands of others because, really, what are we talking about?

To say sovereignty-association is to say that one shall not happen without the other.

This is what we are told, we Quebecers: vote for sovereignty, for independence, and it can be said that this is up to you, but this independence is not to be achieved unless, at the same time, we conclude an agreement of association. This, however, is to be determined by others.

Is this not placing one's destiny in the hands of others?

Can you conceive, for instance, of Ireland in the twenties, fighting for its freedom, the country ablaze, sending this message to Great Britain: "We shall make Ireland independent, provided you join us in a monetary union."

Can you imagine Algeria, in the fifties. In the middle of its fight for independence — and the developments in that struggle were followed with passionate interest by a whole generation of Quebecers — can you imagine, then, Algeria telling France, "We shall fight to the death to make Algeria independent, provided you accept us as members of the French union.". . .

You see, what I blame the Parti Quebecois for is that, having brought Quebec to a truly historic turning point, having told the citizens of this province, and of the rest of this country, that they were going to hold a plebiscite, a referendum, to give the people a chance to choose, having said that, what are they asking?

In a conditional, ambiguous way, they are asking that the PQ government be given what belongs to the people of Quebec: access to sovereignty and independence.

This is done in a conditional way, and then they ask for a mandate to negotiate an association, down to specific details, including a monetary union; but this, essentially, depends upon the response others will provide.

[A Wrong Turn]

And this is where a wrong turn was taken. This is the outcome, after years of debate for the people of my generation, of the generation before that, of the generation that follows us. For years we discussed this issue among us, Quebecers: Was it best to remain in or to leave Canada? This took the best of our energies, intelligence and activities instead of devoting them to cultural achievements, economic development, or to deal with a question that can not be implemented by ourselves and is stated in such a way and with such guarantees that if the other party simply said: "No; we do not wish to enter into an association with you Quebecers," Quebecers would then be prevented from carrying out what they claim they want to do by themselves.

Is it not true that the premiers of the provinces, that the government of Canada, that the people of Canada outside of Quebec — if we are to rely on Mr. Gallup — is it not true that they all said, that we all said, that we would not join in arriving at sovereignty-association?

I said it before the House of Commons, about two weeks ago, on behalf of the Canadian government, and I shall come back to this in a moment. . . .

And what, then, does the PQ say to avoid the impasse.

Their answer is: "The others will agree to negotiate sovereignty-association with us." You shall see.

The prime minister of Canada said: "No." The provincial premiers said: "No."

The polls indicate that the population said: "No." Even the most carefully prepared surveys say "We do not know."

Nevertheless, I, Premier of Quebec, I assure you that they will give us our independence.

And what is the irrefutable argument?

We are told that these people respect fair play and respect the democratic process.

And, following a proud and clear yes, meaning: yes, we want sovereignty-association, who, on the other side, would be so undemocratic as to say: "Well, we reject the Quebecers' expressed wish.". . .

[BOOBY-TRAP]

This approach deserves our attention because there is great sophisry [sic] there, not to say booby-trap, and because, and I repeat it, a democratically expressed wish of the people of Quebec may possibly bind, morally or legally, those who asked the question.

But, is it binding for others?

Let us take a fairly straightforward example. Let us say that Cuba or Haiti wish to enter into an association with Canada, to create a common market with us, that they like Canadian prosperity, Canadian landscapes, Canadian girls, Canadian economic standing, and so on. Overwhelmingly, the Cuban or Haitian voter would say: "Yes, we want to join with Canada in this project."

Should we, in the name of democracy, be bound to accept this union?

Should we, in the name of fair play, be bound to say: "Of course yes, the vote was unanimous, there is nothing we can say."

Let me tell you that, whatever the measures of esteem in which you may hold the leadership of Cuba or Haiti, let me tell you that these people would not have subjected their people to the humiliation of receiving no for an answer without first trying to find out, in advance, if the answer might be yes.

In other words, Mr. Castro or Mr. Duvalier would, as minimum measures, send us few trial baloons [sic], conduct preliminary negotiations, evaluate the trends in Canadian public opinion before declaring: "We want to enter into an association with Canada," and they would do to avoid the risk of a "go and fly a kite" answer from Canada, a rather humiliating response.

And yet, this is exactly the position in which approach chosen by the PQ places the Quebec people. . . .

[A DEAD-END]

This is why we of the government of Canada, MPs and ministers elected by the people of Quebec and of the rest of the country, were under a strict obligation to tell Quebecers, in advance, that, should their answer to the referendum question be yes, then we would have reached a dead-end. And this not only because the rest of Canada does not want this association, and has said so because it is not in its best interests, but also for tactical reasons, since a rejection of association by the rest of Canada would prevent Quebec from achieving independence and breaking the country apart — the very promises of the independentists who have joined the two issues together.

And we, the Canadian government, received a clear mandate on February 18 to legislate for Quebec and we are not prepared to say that this mandate could be withdrawn in the event that Mr. Lévesque would receive an ambiguous mandate to achieve independence subject to a condition which would not be met.

The Pequistes reply to the impasse argument is to state: "Oh, well, of course elections were held on February 18, but a referendum takes precedence over a general election; that is why we are holding a referendum."

Perhaps, provided there is no ambiguity and provided those asking the question are in a position to implement the results. But not so, obviously, in this instance and it is our strict duty as the government of Canada, to state rather curtly that the tearing apart of a country cannot be based upon an ambiguity.

[AN AMBIGUOUS MANDATE]

One does not destroy a country like Canada — a country so much advanced along the paths of liberty, material prosperity, tolerance, fraternity, dialogue and exchange of cultures. One does not tear apart a country that for one hundred years placed itself among the world leaders in the practice of freedom and the achievement of prosperity. One cannot use an ambiguous mandate to tear this country apart.

And should Quebec, unfortunately, reply yes to the referendum question, our answer is already known: "You better hold your second referendum right away; we shall talk again when you can come to us with a serious proposal, show the courage of your convictions and have the willingness to face the people openly, stating as clearly as possible that your objective is independence. Then we shall talk.". . .

For our part, we have clearly indicated the steps we would take, should the answer be yes, or should it be no.

But does anyone know Mr. Lévesque's intentions should the no win? After all, it could happen; there is a choice, yes or no. . . .

If the Quebec people say no — and we are all equals in this province; one Quebecer, one vote — if they say no, will Mr. Lévesque and his party say: "Well, we lost our bet, sovereignty-association shall not be. We shall again be the effective government we claimed to be in nineteen hundred and seventy-six, before the elections.

"And, as such, we shall sit down with other more or less effective governments from the rest of the country and try to improve federalism since the Quebec people said no even to sovereignty-association."

Did Mr. Lévesque give you this commitment? . . .

Would Mr. Lévesque renounce any aim of making Quebec an independent state? Would he sit down and negotiate a renewed form of federalism? Or would he say: Heads I win, tails you lose, and in my game, if you vote "yes," it means yes, but if you vote "no," it means you will have another referendum? . . .

I would like to see every Quebecer request an answer from the supporters of the yes vote — and I wish they too would seek an answer — I wish that every one of us would ask the leader of the government of Quebec, Mr. Lévesque, this question: "What will you do if Quebec votes no? We are entitled to know, we want to know; and if you do not dare reply, we shall then know that your referendum is a trap and that you do not have the heart to tell us your true intentions."

Thank you.

REFERENDUM QUESTION

The Government of Quebec has made public its proposal to negotiate a new agreement with the rest of Canada, based on the equality of nations;

This agreement would enable Quebec to acquire the exclusive power to make its laws, levy its taxes and establish relations abroad — in other words, sovereignty — and, at the same time, to maintain with Canada an economic association, including a common currency;

No change in political status resulting from these negotiations will be effected without approval by the people through another referendum;

On these terms, do you give the Government of Quebec the mandate to negotiate the proposed agreement between Quebec and the rest of Canada?

LEVESQUE's SEPT. 8 SPEECH

Mr. Chairman, our meetings this week, like all the feverish work that has gone on this summer since the meeting of June 9 when you urged us so strongly to revive what has been referred to as the constitutional road show, stem directly, as you have pointed out, from the Quebec referendum and its results. . . .

Now in this referendum, how were a majority of the voters convinced — in the words of a slogan — that a No would be the vote of a Quebecer (que leur non serait québécois)?

Naturally, it was by making commitments, the most spectacular of which — if not the most precise — were those of the federal Prime Minister himself. Less than a week before the referendum, Mr. Trudeau had this to say at the Paul Sauvé Centre in Montreal:

> (TRANS) I say solemnly to Canadians in the other provinces, we in Quebec are sticking our necks out when we tell Quebecers to vote No. We are saying to you that we are not prepared to have you interpret a No as an indication that everything is as it should be and that everything can stay as it was before.
>
> We want changes.

In these vague, but very touching, words, the federal Prime Minister, speaking to the rest of Canada, let it be understood that the interests and the aspirations of the people of Quebec would have an important place in constitutional renewal. A Quebecer with a good head on his shoulders, listening in good faith to this statement, must have understood this. . . .

All things considered, then, what could we take from this in Quebec? What could we, and what can we still, justifiably expect as a result of the majority No vote in May?

[Constitutional Changes]

I believe that the best answer is to be found in two lines of this sentence which my colleagues from all the other provinces, unanimously agreed in fairness, in simple fairness, to include in our joint statement during the Winnipeg conference. The Winnipeg statement said that (TRANS) "there is agreement on the need to fulfil [sic] the promises that have been made to the people of Quebec that there would be constitutional changes which would meet their aspirations." This seems to me to be quite clear as far as it goes, but what are these aspirations that Quebecers have? They are those which are shared not only by a majority of those who voted No, but also, as an essential minimum, all those who voted Yes. . . .

. . . [W]hat is essential — the key, for us — is the sharing of powers. For at least the last thirty or forty years, as our society has been modernizing and has felt the need to equip itself with new or more complete tools, every government of Quebec, without exception, has constantly been calling for these tools. I am talking, for example, about what my immediate predecessor, Mr. Robert Bourassa, called cultural sovereignty, which includes communications. In 1867 communications meant telegraph, which did not have a tremendous importance for people's identity, but now we have the telecommunications galazy [sic], which for better or worse is the daily extension of academic education; that means that all our lives, individually and collectively, are affected. This is the heart of what is called popular education, which is important for the identity of a distinct society.

I am also talking, when I speak of the need for changes in powers, of instruments and means of economic development, which for reasons we know well is now at the centre of the concerns of all our fellow citizens everywhere.

Quebec needs these tools and means of economic development not only because its government, like all the provincial governments, is closer to both the problems and the opportunities for development, but also because it represents a society that, while it is just as North American as the others, is also completely different, and is therefore less mobile. . . .

In point of fact, it's a matter of obtaining a much broader range of action in the area of social policy. That stands to reason. When a society is different, necessarily its approaches and priorities may be different as well. A political administration that failed to take this into account would soon lapse into absurdity. Thus any renewal — since that is what we are coming to talk about here — any renewal of the system, to be valid, I would even say to be viable for Quebec, would have to be achieved via such a practical acknowledgment, a concrete acknowledgment of its national identity and of the requirements it entails for the future. And, needless to say — at least there should be no need to say it although it is probably better to point it out since there are some who might forget it — needless to say the people of Quebec, like any other people of the world, would not consider for a moment giving up the right it has and will always have to continue to decide its destiny freely. . . .

[Change of Direction]

In closing, I should like to say a word about good faith and credibility. After our referendum in Quebec, we in the Government of Quebec had to change direction. This change of direction was painful — I will not try to conceal that from you — but we made the change, three months ago, without hiding anything from anyone, in plain sight, with even a parliamentary commission to report on it. We have worked honestly and diligently at this new attempt at renewal, but — I have to say what I am thinking, and I am not the only one around the table — we are obliged to ask ourselves whether our federal counterparts have also made a change of direction of any kind. After weeks of discussion on these twelve topics, after we have been shown some scenarios that seem terribly prefabricated, after yet another huge advertising campaign paid for out of public funds, after the shocking intentions and the temptations to act unilaterally described in the last few days by the federal Prime Minister — could all these long weeks of intense discussion be simply a smokescreen to disguise aims that are as centralistic as ever and the old desire to provide, not a very necessary increase but a reduction, to their simplest terms, of the powers and freedom of action of the provinces?

I hope not. We all hope not, but it must be admitted that the question is still there. . . .

POPE'S ORDER ON DRINAN
May 5, 1980

Bowing to a directive of Pope John Paul II that priests should not hold public office, Democratic Rep. Robert F. Drinan of Massachusetts, a Jesuit priest, announced May 5 at a press conference in Boston that he would not seek a sixth term in Congress.

Drinan, one of the most liberal members of the House of Representatives, said he would comply with the papal decision "with great regret and pain." There was no indication that Drinan had considered running in defiance of the church's order. Father Drinan earlier had received standing approval from his order to run for office and thus had made no special request for the 1980 elections.

Priest's Role

The Rev. Edward O'Flaherty, New England Jesuit provincial, appeared with Drinan at the press conference. He said he had been told by his superiors in Rome that the principal reason for the order was Pope John Paul II's conviction that the priest's proper role lay outside politics. O'Flaherty said there was no intention of singling out Drinan for criticism.

But Richard P. McBride, writing in The New Republic, *observed that it was "difficult to avoid the conclusion that the papal order was directed explicitly at Drinan, and that the reason was not the broader theoretical question of priests in politics but the specific question of abortion." Drinan had supported federal abortion aid legislation.*

411

Jesuit Superior General Father Pedro Arrupe said in a May 5 statement in Rome that he had ordered Drinan not to seek re-election at the "express wish" of the pope.

Latin America

Vatican sources said the pope acted out of his conviction that priests should tend to the spiritual needs of their parishes and not be political activists. The pope's order stemmed from his concern over political activity in South America and in developing countries throughout the world. The directive affected all priestly orders — not just the Jesuits — but the pope had singled out the Society of Jesus for specific criticism in the matter in December 1979.

In Latin America, El Salvador's priests had long advocated social change and had been targets for right-wing assassins. In March 1980 Archbishop Oscar A. Romero, an advocate for peaceful but profound social changes in that country, was shot to death by right wing terrorists while saying mass in the cathedral.

Clerics in Nicaragua had helped to overthrow the dictatorship of Anastasio Somoza DeBayle. And Nicaragua's foreign minister, Miguel D'Escoto, was a Maryknoll priest. Other clerics worked in the ministeries of several countries.

1971 Synod

Vatican policy restricting the role of priests in politics derived from canon law. A bishop's synod in 1971 advised priests to avoid "leadership or active militancy on behalf of any political party" unless "this is truly required for the good of the community."

Pope Paul VI, who occupied the papal throne when Drinan began his political career, apparently did not think he should invoke the synod's decision. Drinan ran successfully for re-election in every House election from 1970 to 1978. Although Paul VI did not like the idea of priests in politics, he reportedly felt less strongly about it than Pope John Paul II.

Papal Warnings

The pope for the first time warned priests against direct involvement in political parties and ideological movements when he attended the Conference of Latin American Bishops (CELAM) in Puebla, Mexico, Jan. 27-28, 1979. The pontiff added, however, that members of the clergy should continue to press for the rights of the poor and oppressed. (At its second meeting in Medellin, Colombia, in 1968, CELAM had adopted a "theology of liberation" which encouraged some priests to engage in leftist-oriented political action. Rightist governments and conservative clergy opposed the principles adopted at Medellin. As the dispute widened, Latin American Catholics looked to the pope for guidance.) (Puebla speech, Historic Documents of 1979, p. 730)

The pope repeated his warnings several times after his Puebla address. Observers believed that the assassination of Archbishop Romero had deepened the pontiff's convictions.

Pope John Paul II reiterated his view during a 1980 African trip. He told Zairean priests in Kinshasa May 4 to "leave political responsibilities to those who are charged with them: You have another part. . . ." And in an impromptu press conference May 12 on his plane returning to Rome, the pontiff said that "politics is the responsibility of laymen."

Drinan's Career

A longtime dean of Boston College Law School, Drinan was the first Catholic priest elected to Congress. He upset longtime Democratic Rep. Phil Philbin in 1970 in an affluent Boston suburban district on a platform opposing the participation of the United States in the Vietnam War.

During his congressional service, the 59-year-old Democrat had been a conspicuous member of the House Judiciary Committee, especially in the impeachment proceedings against former President Nixon. In 1979 he became chairman of the committee's Criminal Justice Subcommittee, working ardently on rewriting the criminal code.

Drinan built a solid liberal voting record supporting federal abortion aid, women's rights issues, school desegregation and numerous social aid programs.

Nuns in Politics

Father Drinan's decision prompted former Rep. Robert J. Cornell, a Catholic priest, to halt his political comeback bid in Wisconsin. Cornell, a Democrat, had served two terms before he was defeated in 1978.

But the order did not seem to affect nuns who held political office. Sister Carolyn Farrell, mayor of Dubuque, Iowa, said her superiors had not asked her to step down. She argued that because nuns were not defined as clergy by the church, she was exempt.

Following are the texts of Drinan's statement to the press May 5, 1980, explaining his decision to obey the papal order; the Rev. Edward O'Flaherty's remarks made at Drinan's Boston press conference; and Society of Jesus Su-

perior General Father Pedro Arrupe's statement made in Rome. (Boldface headings in brackets have been added by Congressional Quarterly to highlight the organization of the text.):

DRINAN'S STATEMENT

It is with regret and pain that I accept the decision of the Holy See.

I went to Congress, chosen by a citizens' caucus, to work for justice in America and for peace throughout the world. These are clearly objectives ardently recommended by the Second Vatican Council and by all modern popes.

I have spent 10 of the 27 years of my priesthood as a member of Congress. I am certain that I was more influential as a priest in those 10 years than in my previous 14 years as dean of Boston College law school.

For a decade I have had a voice and a vote in the resolution of the most difficult problems confronting this country and this world. I worked for the termination of the war in Vietnam. I helped to eliminate the military draft. I was a leader in the abolition of mandatory retirement based on age.

As an attorney I was intimately involved in developing substantial improvements in the law relating to copyright, bankruptcy, civil liberties, crime, privacy and other areas.

I had a central role in the impeachment proceedings in 1974.

As a member of Congress, I have participated in important human rights missions to Argentina, Central America, the Soviet Union and elsewhere. I was one of the first to see the tragedies of the "boat people" in Indochina.

This Sunday I will fly to Amsterdam to participate in a two-day international conference to liberate Anatoly Shcharansky, the Russian human rights activist sentenced to 13 years in prison for allegedly spying.

I am grateful to have had these opportunities to be a moral architect. I can think of no other activities more worthy of the involvement of a priest and a Jesuit.

I am proud and honored to be a priest and a Jesuit. As a person of faith I must believe that there is work for me to do which somehow will be more important than the work I am required to leave.

I undertake this new pilgrimage with pain and with prayers.

Global hunger and the arms race have been the two interwoven agonies of mankind which have disturbed me more profoundly than any other problems confronting the human race. I hope that in God's providence I may be given an opportunity to work to alleviate the world hunger and to stop the arms race.

STATEMENT OF FATHER EDWARD O'FLAHERTY

Rep. Robert F. Drinan, S.J., announced today that he will not be a candidate for re-election to the U.S. House of Representatives this fall. Rep. Drinan, who is a Jesuit priest, is withdrawing from the race in deference to an order from his Roman superiors.

As provincial of the Society of Jesus in New England, I am Father Drinan's religious superior. At this time I would like to share with you the sequence of events leading to today's announcement as well as what I take to be the reasons for the superior's order.

On Sunday, April 27, 1980, I received a telephone call from the Rome headquarters of the Jesuit order communicating this order. I informed Father Drinan immediately.

Over the course of the next few days I pursued several avenues of appeal, stressing with the Roman authorities the fact that such an order would almost certainly seem in the eyes of many people to be an improper intrusion by the church into American political affairs. I also pointed out the serious inconvenience to the election process itself since the filing deadline for candidates is May 6.

On Saturday, May 3, I was told that these concerns expressed had been personally conveyed to the Vatican authorities, but that after a discussion it became clear that the decision would be final.

This information was communicated on the same day, I believe, to the Vatican's representative in Washington, Archbishop Jean Jadot.

Father Drinan and I met in Boston on Saturday afternoon. At that meeting, convinced that the decision was final, Father Drinan agreed to announce his withdrawal from the race.

It has been stressed to me that Vatican and Jesuit authorities in Rome wish to underline the point that the principal reason for the order was the pope's convictions about the proper role of the priest. Indeed, one highly placed Vatican official privately expressed the hope that it might be possible to persuade people that the pope was acting exclusively out of principle. There was no intention of singling out Father Drinan for criticism.

In Rome, the Jesuit superior general, Father Pedro Arrupe, yesterday issued a statement expressing his recognition of Rep. Drinan's achievements in the field of human rights and justice issues. I would like to add to that by thanking Father Drinan in the name of the Jesuits of Central America, where his critical interventions have recently been enormously helpful to the persecuted church. I am quite sure that such actions on Father Drinan's part were among the many things Father Arrupe was referring to.

It will be recalled that in 1970 an exception was made by local church authorities to the long-standing church law forbidding clerics to hold or seek elective office, thus permitting Father Drinan's candidacy. I had renewed that permission, as had two previous provincials before me. Nevertheless, it is obvious that in the pope's view the reasons that commended the idea of Father Drinan's candidacy up to now no longer apply.

That Pope John Paul [II] was moving toward such a view of things has been signaled more than once since his election to the papacy in October of 1978. In January of 1979, for instance, speaking in Mexico City to an immense international gathering of religious-order priests he said: "You are priests and members of religious orders. You are not social directors, political leaders or functionaries of temporal power." He asked them to remember that temporal leadership can easily become a source of division while a priest should be a sign and factor of unity of brotherhood. Finally, he said, these secular functions are the proper field of action of the laity, who ought to perfect temporal matters with a Christian spirit.

In his Holy Thursday letter to priests in April of that same year, John Paul II made a number of similar points.

I wish to associate myself completely with Father Arrupe's expression of personal admiration for Father Drinan and with his "respect for his ready, loyal compliance with the superior's directive."

STATEMENT OF FATHER PEDRO ARRUPE

Father Robert Drinan, an American Jesuit priest and also an elected member of the House of Representatives of the U.S. Congress, announced today that he will not be a candidate for re-election to the U.S. Congress this fall. He made this announcement in obedience to an order from me, his religious superior general.

I am grateful to Father Drinan for his ready and loyal compliance with my directive, a directive that reflects the express wish of his holiness, Pope John Paul II.

Father Drinan is a man of principle, and he acts firmly in keeping with his principles. This is especially true in his work in some areas involving human rights and justice. It is also true in his commitment as a Jesuit priest. As his superior general, I offer him my own deep respect and my personal support in this, his difficult hour.

REPORT ON COAL RESOURCES
May 12, 1980

The World Coal Study, an exhaustive analysis of the world's coal resources which was released May 12, concluded that coal could and must provide up to two-thirds of the new energy needed in two decades up to the year 2000.

Directed by Carroll L. Wilson, a professor at the Massachusetts Institute of Technology, the report was the product of 18 months of intensive study by experts and researchers from the 16 countries that produced and consumed the greater part of the world's coal.

The report opened with the surprising words, "This is an optimistic message about energy." Titled, "Coal — Bridge to the Future," the report said that with massive investments in coal mining technology and the transportation systems required to transport it, coal-producing nations could provide an energy bridge to ease the transition from dependence on foreign oil to the renewable energy sources of the future.

"The world needs an incremental energy source as nearly like oil as possible, but with the vital difference that it will be obtainable in increasing amounts until well into the next century," the report declared. "Only coal comes close to meeting those specifications," it said.

Cheaper Fuel

The study concluded that the pricing and production policy of the Organization of Petroleum Exporting Countries (OPEC) made it all *but inevitable that energy-consuming countries would have to do with less oil — at higher prices — for the next 20 years. Renewable energy sources, wind, water and solar power, the report said, would not develop rapidly enough to meet rising energy demands. And nuclear energy, beset by a series of delays and setbacks, might prove a politically unpalatable solution, the report added.*

Production Goals

The transition to coal would take a massive international effort. Current world raw coal production was about 3.5 billion metric tons. Output would have to double or perhaps triple over the next 20 years, the report said. World trade in coal capable of firing boilers for electricity generation (called steam coal) would have to grow more than tenfold.

The shift from oil to coal would require a huge infusion of capital and technology — most of it from the largest producers and exporters of coal, the United States, Australia, South Africa and Canada.

'Greenhouse Effect'

Coal-burning might create some serious environmental problems, the energy study warned. A buildup of carbon dioxide in the environment as the result of burning coal could threaten an environmental "greenhouse effect": a worldwide warming cycle that could destroy agricultural production and perhaps even melt the polar ice cap.

But the report noted that the direst predictions of environmental disaster caused by burning fossil fuels were based on a projected energy use growth rate of 4.2 percent. Because of conservation, energy use would grow only half that much for the rest of the century, the study estimated.

Reaction

Officials of the National Coal Association, representing coal producers in the United States, cast doubt on any possibility of the report's production goals being met. The association said there was a chance for only a 62 percent increase in U.S. mine production by 1990, reaching 1.25 billion tons of coal a year.

> *Following are excerpts from the World Coal Study ("Coal — Bridge to the Future"), released May 12, 1980, concluding that coal was the energy source the world must exploit up until the year 2000. (Boldface headings in brackets have been added by Congressional Quarterly to highlight the organization of the text.):*

Foreword

The World Coal Study (WOCOL) has been an international project involving over 80 people from 16 major coal-using and coal-producing countries. This is our Final Report: the product of 18 months of intensive work.

WOCOL came into being as a result of my belief that there was an urgent need to examine the role that coal might play in meeting world energy needs during the next 20 years. Such a choice is being forced upon us. Oil from OPEC countries can no longer be relied upon to provide expanding supplies of energy, even with rapidly rising prices. Neither can nuclear energy be planned on for rapid expansion worldwide until present uncertainties about it are resolved. Yet the world's energy needs will continue to grow, even with vigorous energy conservation programs and with optimistic rates of expansion in the use of solar energy.

Coal already supplies 25 percent of the world's energy, its reserves are vast, and it is relatively inexpensive. But no major attempt has previously been made to examine the needs for coal on a global scale, to match requirements of users with potential capacities of producers, to look at the markets coal might fill, or to examine the obstacles to a rapid expansion in coal use and how they might be overcome.

This experiment in international collaboration in WOCOL follows directly from the Workshop on Alternative Energy Strategies (WAES), which I directed. In WAES we concluded, in our report published in early 1977, that the world might find its oil supplies being constrained by limitations on exports from OPEC countries at some time during the 1980s. This report was generally regarded at the time as being too pessimistic. In fact, it proved to be optimistic — it is now clear that we are already in that position in 1980.

WAES assembled a group of people who could engage in free-ranging discussion and who worked hard together and reached agreement on a plausible range of global energy futures. These people came from key positions in governments and private and public organizations in the world's major energy-using countries, as well as from some of the largest OPEC countries. They came however as individuals, each free to represent his own views rather than those of the organization with which he was affiliated.

We learned a great deal in WAES, not just about energy, but about how to work together as an international group. These lessons have been applied in WOCOL. I was responsible for the selection of the individuals taking part. I sought a mix of nationalities, a balance of public and private sector viewpoints, a common concern with energy policy, a knowledge of the coal or energy industry, and the ability to work effectively in a group effort. The total was no greater than the number of people who could, in dialogue around a table, function as a working group. The language of the Study was English.

Members of WOCOL came from 16 countries that use 75 percent of the world's energy. They produce and use about 60 percent of the world's coal. Although not able to take a full part in the Study, observers from the People's Republic of China attended WOCOL meetings and furnished a report for their country.

The senior members of WOCOL, called Participants, gave policy direction to the Study and reviewed its work as it proceeded. It is their consensus on the Study conclusions that represents the principal summary of WOCOL. Moreover, Participants chose Associates from within their organization who devoted much of their time to WOCOL under the direction of the Participant and collaborated with other Associates both in their own country and elsewhere. Each Participant arranged for the financing of all work done at a national level and for the time, travel, and other expenses of himself and his Associate.

Formal liaison was established with the U.S. Department of Energy and with the Electric Power Research Institute (EPRI), which both provided Study members who served in the role of Associates without Participants. Costs of the headquarters, located at the Massachusetts Institute of Technology, Cambridge, Massachusetts, were sponsored by foundations, companies, and the U.S. Department of Energy. A small, capable, and extremely dedicated staff at M.I.T. coordinated this global project within some very tight deadlines.

WOCOL Participants developed together an agreed purpose, plan, and schedule for the Study. Cases were developed to project a range of future coal production, use, and trade. Like WAES these projections build on detailed country studies by WOCOL teams as well as on special studies for regions not represented in the Study. Unlike WAES the projections were based on existing national energy studies rather than on a specific global macroeconomic framework developed for the Study.

Our analysis goes to the year 2000. Over the next 5 years the use of different fuels is heavily constrained by decisions made in the past and by the fact that new energy facilities being planned now cannot be brought to completion in less than 5 to 10 years. The substantial shift to coal will therefore begin in the mid to late 1980s based on decisions being made in the early 1980s. Major effects of this expansion will be felt in the 1985-2000 period. The twenty years from now to the turn of the century are thus critical. The full effects of the switch to coal will, however, not be seen until the early decades of the next century. At that time the need for coal will still be great although renewable energy systems should be coming into use on a significant scale. . . .

Conclusions

It is now widely agreed that the availability of oil in international trade is likely to diminish over the next two decades. Vigorous conservation, the development and rapid implementation of programs for nuclear power, natural gas, unconventional sources of oil and gas, solar energy, other renewable sources, and new technologies will not be sufficient to meet the growing energy needs of the world. A massive effort to expand facilities for the production, transport, and use of coal is urgently required to provide for even moderate economic growth in the world between now and the year 2000. Without such increases in coal the outlook is bleak.

Our major conclusions after eighteen months of study are as follows.

1. Coal is capable of supplying a high proportion of future energy needs. It now supplies more than 25% of the world's energy. Economically recoverable reserves are very large — many times those of oil and gas — and capable of meeting increasing demands well into the future.

2. Coal will have to supply between one-half and two-thirds of the additional energy needed by the world during the next 20 years, even under the moderate energy growth assumptions of this Study. To achieve this goal, world coal production will have to increase 2.5 to 3 times, and the world trade in steam coal will have to grow 10 to 15 times above 1979 levels.

3. Many individual decisions must be made along the chain from coal producer to consumer to ensure that the required amounts are available when needed. Delays at any point affect the entire chain. This emphasizes the need for prompt and related actions by consumers, producers, governments, and other public authorities.

4. Coal can be mined, moved, and used in most areas in ways that conform to high standards of health, safety, and environmental protection by the application of available technology and without unacceptable increases in cost. The present knowledge of possible carbon dioxide effects on climate does not justify delaying the expansion of coal use.

5. Coal is already competitive in many locations for the generation of electricity and in many industrial and other uses. It will extend further into these and other markets as oil prices rise.

6. The technology for mining, moving, and using coal is well established and steadily improving. Technological advances in combustion, gasification, and liquefaction will greatly widen the scope for the environmentally acceptable use of coal in the 1990s and beyond.

7. The amount of capital required to expand the production, transport, and user facilities to triple the use of coal is within the capacity of domestic and international capital markets, though difficulties in financing large coal projects in some developing countries may require special solutions.

The final conclusions of this Study are cautiously optimistic. Coal can provide the principal part of the additional energy needs of the next two decades. In filling this role it will act both as a bridge to the energy systems of the future and as a foundation for the continued part that coal will play in the next century. But the public and private enterprises concerned must act cooperatively and promptly, if this is to be achieved. Governments can help in particular, by providing the confidence and stability required for investment decisions, by eliminating delays in licensing and planning permissions, by establishing clear and stable environmental standards, and by facilitating the growth of free and competitive international trade. A recognition of the urgent need for coal and determined actions to make it available in time will ensure that the world will continue to obtain the energy it requires for its economic growth and development.

The Need For Coal

The world has reached the end of an era in its energy history. Increased supplies of oil, which have been the basis for economic growth in the past few decades, are not expected to be available in the future. The development of a new energy basis for continued economic growth has therefore become an urgent necessity. Building a bridge to the energy sources and supply systems of the next century — whatever they turn out to be — is of crucial importance. We believe that coal can be such a bridge and that it will also continue to serve a vital role into the longer-term future.

A tripling of coal use and a 10-15 fold increase in world steam coal trade would allow the energy problems of the next two decades to be faced with confidence. With such increases in coal use, coupled with a mobilization of other energy sources and vigorously promoted conservation, it becomes possible to see how to meet the energy requirements of moderate economic growth throughout the world. But without such a coal expansion the outlook is bleak. This is the central message of our report.

In the industrialized countries coal can become the principal fuel for economic growth and the major replacement for oil in many uses. Coal may also provide the only way for many of the less developed countries to obtain the fuel needed for electric power and industrial development, and to reduce their dependence upon oil imports.

Increased use of coal will require large investments, but no greater than those required for other fuels such as oil, gas, and nuclear energy. Countries now heavily dependent upon oil must build coal-using facilities on a large scale before they can use the coal they will need. Power stations, coal ports, railways, and handling facilities take a long time to plan and build. So do mines and export terminals. Unless decisions to build them are made soon, these facilities will not be ready by the time when this study indicates that they will be acutely needed. It is necessary for governments and industry to act cooperatively so that the required investment decisions are made promptly.

Unlike oil, the reserve base for coal is sufficiently great to support large increases in production for a long time into the future. Moreover, the technology for its safe and environmentally acceptable production, transport, and use is proved and already widely applied in most areas.

We have examined environmental questions with great care and considered the measures that would have to be taken within each WOCOL country to comply with present and anticipated environmental regulations. The technology exists by which exacting standards of environmental protection can be met, and much work is being done to improve it and lower its costs. We are convinced that coal can be mined, moved, and used at most locations in ways that meet high standards of environmental protection at costs that still leave coal competitive with oil at mid-1979 prices.

The present knowledge of the effects on climate of carbon dioxide (CO_2) from fossil fuel combustion does not warrant a global reduction in fossil fuel use or a delay in the expansion of coal. However, support for research on the possible effects of increased atmospheric CO_2, including that of global warming, is essential so that future policies may reflect an improved understanding of such matters.

Coal is not in competition with conservation, nuclear or solar energy, or other sources as the sole solution to the world's energy problems. All these will be required if the energy needed is to be supplied. The world, however, needs an incremental energy source as nearly like oil as possible, but with the vital difference that it will be obtainable in increasing amounts until well into the next century. Ideally, and if it is to fill the role played by oil over the past decades, it should be versatile in application, easily transported and stored, and reasonably priced. The technology for using it should be mature and generally available so that it can be brought into use rapidly, widely, and safely. It should be capable of satisfying strict environmental standards with presently available technology and at a cost competitive with other fuels. It should be obtainable in large quantities and for long enough to justify the investments required to bring it into widespread use. Only coal comes close to meeting these specifications. . . .

WORLD ENERGY PROSPECTS

During the past two decades world oil consumption has grown twice as fast as that of all other sources combined. Two-thirds of the growth in energy consumption in the member countries of the Organization for Economic Cooperation and Development (OECD) came from oil during this time. In Western Europe and Japan, in fact, oil has provided over 80 percent of this increase in energy use. In all but a few of the developing countries oil has also supplied virtually all of the increase in energy consumption. It is a matter of considerable concern therefore that there now appears to be no realistic prospect of oil meeting any substantial part of future increases in the world's energy needs.

The present international oil trade amounts to about 35 million barrels a day (mbd), which is about 55 percent of the world's total oil consumption. Of that amount about 80 percent is exported by the OPEC countries, and more than 20 mbd flows through the Straits of Hormuz on the Persian Gulf. It is this concentrated and vulnerable flow of oil from the OPEC countries that has provided virtually all the flexibility within the world's energy system since 1960.

There are no secure grounds for assuming that OPEC production of oil will increase in the future, and there are good reasons to fear it may be less. As the Iranian revolution has shown, political change can be rapid and unexpected; and there are many other tensions, particularly in the Middle East, that are unlikely to be resolved soon.

Moreover, key producers, such as Saudi Arabia and Kuwait, have adopted policies that will conserve oil in the ground as a better security for their future than income they cannot spend or usefully invest. It is now the declared policy of OPEC member countries to limit oil production to amounts that will total not more than the present level of about 30 mbd. This policy is directed toward optimizing rather than maximizing revenues. The goal is to generate only as much revenue as their economies can handle without causing too rapid social change and high inflation. Increasing prices while holding production stable, or even reducing it, meets this financial objective and at the same time conserves oil reserves.

There is nothing unexpected or mysterious about this. The signs have been visible for some time. . . .

Prospects for increased oil supplies from non-OPEC areas are not sufficiently encouraging to change this picture. Production from fields in the North Sea and Alaska's Prudhoe Bay are projected to peak and level off in the next few years. It appears that Mexico and Norway will continue to limit exports to meet revenue needs. Increases in oil production in the People's Republic of China and the developing countries will be largely used to meet growing domestic demand. Furthermore some experts have suggested that production in the Soviet Union, which now exports 1 mbd to countries outside Eastern Europe, is leveling off, and that the Soviet Union/Eastern Europe area is therefore unlikely to remain self-sufficient in oil.

For all these reasons, we believe that oil will provide, at most, a small fraction of any future increase in world energy needs. Indeed, the availability of oil for import by the OECD nations is likely to be less in the year 2000 than today.

The specific amount of oil available to OECD member countries will depend on a number of factors . . . production and domestic consumption of oil by OPEC member countries, oil exports from other countries, and oil import requirements of other regions including the developing countries and the centrally planned economy countries. These assumptions lead to a projected range of net oil imports available to the OECD. . . . The most likely projection within that range is for a gradual decline in imports from 26 mbd in 1978 to about 22 mbd by the year 2000. The world must find ways other than oil to provide the additional energy required for its future economic growth. . . .

PROSPECTS FOR COAL

The dwindling prospects for any substantial increase in the supply of oil at acceptable prices constitutes the main reason for the increased importance of coal. Even with the most optimistic forecasts for the expansion of nuclear power and the aggressive development of all other energy sources, as well as vigorous conservation, it is clear that coal has a vitally important part to play in the world's energy future. World coal production in 1977 was about 3400 million metric tons of raw coal. This was a contribution of about 2500 million metric tons of coal equivalent (mtce) or 33 mbdoe [million barrels per day oil equivalent], already greater than any energy source except oil. . . .

COAL RESOURCES, RESERVES, AND PRODUCTION

There are vast resources of coal in the world, far in excess of those of any other fossil fuel. This resource base is sufficient to support greatly expanded worldwide use of coal well into the future.

Coal resources vary substantially in quality, reflecting the complex chemical structure of coal. The energy content or calorific value of the coal and the sulfur, ash, and moisture content are some of the key elements of quality. Systems of coal resources classification have been developed to deal with these complexities; however, the use of these systems varies from country to country.

The most commonly used classification standards are those established by the World Energy Conference (WEC), which has defined *geological resources* of coal as a measure of the amount of coal in place, and *technically and economically recoverable reserves* as a measure of the quantities that can be economically mined with current mining technology and at current energy prices. The WEC also subdivided coal into two major calorific categories: *hard coal,* defined as any coal with a heating value above 5,700 kilocalories per kilogram (equivalent to 10,250 Btu per pound) on a moisture and ash-free basis; and *brown coal,* any coal with a lower heating value. Bituminous and anthracite coal fall into the category of hard coal, whereas lignite and subbituminous coal are considered by the WEC as brown coals. However, some countries, for example the United States and Canada, use the term "brown coal" generally to refer only to low-calorific lignite and not to the extensive resources of subbituminous coal that they possess. . . .

Coal resources and reserves are geographically widely distributed with more than 80 countries reporting coal deposits. However, 10 countries account for about 98 percent of the currently estimated world resources and 90 percent of the reserves. Moreover, 4 countries, the Soviet Union, the United States, the People's Republic of China, and Australia, possess

almost 90 percent of the total world coal resources and 60 percent
of the reserves.

The magnitude of the world's coal resources and reserves is difficult
to comprehend. Technically and economically recoverable coal reserves
currently amount to about 660 billion tce [tons (metric) coal equivalent]
or approximately 250 times the 1977 world production. Moreover, estimates of reserves increase as exploration reveals further quantities
of extractable coal and as economics and technology change. As a result
of increased exploration, stimulated by the oil price increase since 1973,
estimates of the world's technically and economically recoverable reserves
have increased by about 185 billion tce. This increase is equivalent
to about 70 years production at the 1977 rate of production.

WORLD COAL PRODUCTION

World coal production in 1977 was about 2,500 mtce — equivalent
on an energy basis to 33 mbdoe or more than the total OPEC oil
production. . . .

Three countries — the United States, the Soviet Union, and the
People's Republic of China — were responsible for nearly 60 percent
of the total coal produced in the world in 1977. The next six largest
producers, Poland, the Federal Republic of Germany, the United Kingdom, Australia, the Republic of South Africa, and India, accounted
for a further 25 percent. In 1977 the United States accounted for 50
percent of the total production outside the centrally planned economy
countries. Production in the developing countries is similarly concentrated,
with India being by far the largest coal producer and consumer.

Even with the significant expansion in world coal production projected
by WOCOL, the cumulative production during 1977-2000 would use
up just 16 percent of the world's present technically and economically
recoverable coal reserves. . . .

WORLD ENERGY CONSUMPTION

Total world energy consumption in 1978 amounted to about 125 mbdoe
[million barrels per day oil equivalent], about 63 mbd [million barrels
per day], or one-half, of which was supplied by oil. Supplies other
than oil provided the other half — roughly divided into coal, 26 percent;
natural gas, 17 percent; hydroelectric, 4.8 percent; and nuclear energy
2.4 percent. . . .

There is a need for substantial increases in world energy supplies
over the next two decades even if the most ambitious efforts to improve
the efficiency of energy use are successful. A 50 percent increase in
world energy needs would be required by the year 2000 even if primary
energy use grows only as fast as world population. Somewhat higher
levels of world energy demand were projected for the year 2000 in
the WAES (1977) and WEC (1978) studies. . . .

COAL

Coal now provides more than 2,500 mtce, or 33 mbdoe, of energy worldwide, more than any energy source except oil. Use is distributed 40 percent in the OECD region, 55 percent in centrally planned economy countries, and 5 percent in developing countries.

Coal will be required in the future to meet a major part of world energy needs, even after allowance has been made for a vigorous conservation program, development of solar and other renewable sources, continued nuclear growth, and the expected availability of oil and gas. . . .

Environment, Health, and Safety

The large expansion of world coal production and use projected by the World Coal Study to the year 2000 means that each country will need to consider the resulting environmental, health, and safety issues. There is extensive experience with the mining, transportation, and use of coal and the application of environmental controls in the countries represented in this Study. The major problems and issues to be considered in establishing environmental policies, standards, and laws have been identified. Research conducted over the last decade has improved the state of knowledge about both the issues and the control strategies and technologies available. By 1979 many countries had adopted detailed legislative and regulatory systems, or other less formal systems, for controlling the environmental, health, and safety effects accompanying increased coal production and use.

REASONS FOR ENVIRONMENTAL CONCERN

Uncertainties remain about some issues. For example, the magnitude of long-term health effects of some of the emissions from coal combustion; the effects of fossil fuel combustion on global climate; and the environmental, health, and safety hazards posed by synthetic fuel plants have not yet been determined. There are tradeoffs that must be made in each country among the degree of control, the resource and financial costs associated with that degree of control, and the benefits from using coal. Comparisons must also be made between coal and other energy alternatives that have environmental, health, and safety effects of their own. Although uncertainties make it difficult at this time to make universally accepted statements on environmental issues, four general observations can be made.

1. Most of the environmental risks from coal use are amenable to technological control. Emission release, noise, and other effects can be reduced to whatever level is required by applying currently available technology. Each increment of reduction increases the cost, and as one approaches total control, such costs become very large. Within what

can be expected as standards we believe that coal can be produced, transported, and used cleanly at costs that leave coal competitive with other fuels. It is likely that environmental concerns or control costs will preclude the development of certain sites or certain coal resources. However, there are so many possible sites and resources remaining world-wide that such exclusions will not be a limiting factor to the expansion of coal use.

2. National perceptions of values differ on such things as exposure of the general public to health risks or visibility reduction in the at-mosphere. For example, controversy continues on the extent of health effects from various emissions from coal combustion. Moreover, envi-ronmental impacts differ because of regional characteristics such as meteorology, topography, population density, and resource distribution. For such reasons, nations and regions take different positions on the kind and extent of environmental control measures they will require as coal use increases. Even though views differ widely, the countries in the World Coal Study plan large expansions of coal use and expect to apply measures that will ensure compliance with their national en-vironmental standards.

3. There are some issues on which joint action among nations may be needed. Adequate mechanisms may not now exist for implementing international cooperation, although there are some precedents in the use of ocean resources and in the programs of OECD nations on en-vironmental matters. Agreement on the application of existing control technology for the interest of other nations in excess of what one nation might do solely on its own interest may be difficult but necessary. For example, the long-range transport of emissions and deposition of acid rain in several countries is receiving increased attention and may require early action. Similarly, improved understanding of the effects of pollutants requires continuing international cooperation. The need to integrate and coordinate some environmental actions at global, regional, national, and local levels is becoming more important.

4. Finally, there is concern about climate effects from the build-up of carbon dioxide (CO_2) in the atmosphere from combustion of all carbon fuels including oil, gas, coal, and wood. Currently there is uncertainty about CO_2 inputs from various sources, the absorption of CO_2 by various sinks, and the consequences of the effects of rising CO_2 content in the atmosphere. If the effects prove as serious as some researchers predict, the resulting situation would call for extraordinary kinds of international cooperation to control world fuel combustion or, alternatively, the amount of deforestation. Even though some people believe that immediate action is necessary, most expect that there are at least several decades to evaluate the CO_2 climate modification issue. We urge strong support of research to improve our understanding of the effects of CO_2 on climate and to expand studies of the impacts of climate change. . . .

CO₂ AND CLIMATE CHANGE

Because technical solutions for controlling CO_2 emissions are prohibitively expensive, and because large increases in the amount of atmospheric CO_2 may alter global climate, CO_2 emission poses one of the most perplexing problems resulting from the increased use of fossil fuels including coal. CO_2 is a trace gas in the atmosphere. In spite of its relatively small concentration (330 ppm [parts per million]) it has an influence on atmospheric temperature. It is largely transparent to sunlight, but it absorbs the infrared radiation emitted from the earth's surface and reradiates part of it, thereby reducing the rate of surface cooling. Consequently, it is thought that an increase in atmospheric CO_2 will contribute to a rise in the earth's temperature that has become commonly known as the greenhouse effect. Such an increase in the earth's average temperature would probably modify climate patterns, benefiting some regions but possibly bringing disaster to others.

For many reasons the issue of climate modification caused by increasing CO_2 in the atmosphere is more complex than the other environmental problems caused by fossil fuel combustion. There is a disagreement among scientists about the magnitude and urgency of the problem and about the detailed interactions involved.

CO_2 is absorbed, stored, and exchanged by the world's oceans, forests, soils, and sedimentary rocks in complex ways. . . . Major sources of CO_2 are respiration from animals and decay of vegetation as well as evaporation from the oceans. Absorption of CO_2 by photosynthesis of plants and dissolving in the ocean are the sources of removal of CO_2 from the atmosphere. The input from fossil fuel combustion is small compared with the other fluxes, whose magnitude is not well established. In addition, the global atmosphere has been cooling since 1940 after an 80-year warming cycle. One of the difficult problems is to distinguish fossil fuel combustion effects from massive natural cycles of climate change.

People have been adding CO_2 to the atmosphere at an increasing rate since earliest times by destruction of the natural vegetative cover, changes in land use, and since the industrial revolution by the burning of fossil fuels. CO_2 in the atmosphere has increased by about 15 percent during the last century and is now increasing at about 0.4 percent per year. The effects of this are not yet predictable; natural feedback mechanisms such as increased cloudiness may act to moderate the greenhouse effect but such cloud cover, despite its high reflectivity to solar radiation, may reduce surface cooling even more.

On an energy content basis, coal combustion releases 25 percent more CO_2 than oil and 75 percent more CO_2 than natural gas. Large increases in coal combustion will have an effect on the level of atmospheric CO_2, but whether this will be significant in comparison with other mechanisms at work in the earth's carbon cycle is uncertain. Moreover, even if scientists agreed about the exact effects of CO_2 on climate, we do not now have international political systems capable of acting to prevent any further increases by restricting global fossil fuel combustion or by reducing the rate of deforestation.

The issue of CO_2 climate modification requires sustained and expanded research efforts on both a national and an international scale. Progress in atmospheric theory is being made possible by improved models of global circulation supplied with much more extensive data. It may happen that some effects of CO_2 will become detectable on a regional and global scale before the end of the century, and will require a reassessment of world fossil fuel use at that time. . . .

THE NEED FOR RESEARCH

A number of improved technologies to reduce environmental effects from coal mining, transport and use are currently under development. For example, improvements in underground mining to reduce the occupational hazards of miners, and better methods to remove sulfur oxide from flue gas, are well along in development. Such research is important to reduce the cost of environmental control and to improve the ability to remove contaminants from the environment. This includes the improvement in the workplace to reduce worker exposure to accident or health risks.

Recently, concern has been expressed as to the effect of small (submicron) particles on human health. Research is needed to determine whether the risks from such emissions are sufficiently high that further control is needed.

Also, a great deal of research has been under way in the last two decades to evaluate the effects of environmental contaminants. The research has involved primarily human health effects but also effects on ecosystems. It is this work that has made society more aware of the environmental risks it is taking, and has led to the environmental control strategies taken by various nations. It is important to continue such research so that additional controls can be aimed at those areas of greatest environmental risk, and so that control can be relaxed in areas found to be less necessary. . . .

COURT ON 'INTERROGATION' IN CRIMINAL CASES

May 12, 1980

In a ruling announced May 12, the Supreme Court reaffirmed its controversial decision in the case of Miranda v. Arizona *made 14 years earlier.*

Chief Justice Warren E. Burger, earlier one of the most vocal critics of the ruling that required police to tell a suspect he had a right to remain silent and to have an attorney present during questioning, wrote that he "would neither overrule Miranda, *disparage it, nor extend it at this late date."*

But even as the court in 1980 endorsed Miranda *as a precedent, it applied it in a conservative manner in the case of* Rhode Island v. Innis.

Murder Conviction

Thomas Innis challenged his conviction for murder, arguing that police had obtained crucial evidence against him — the murder weapon — in violation of Miranda. *By a vote of 6-3, the Supreme Court rejected his challenge and upheld his conviction.*

Justice Potter Stewart delivered the opinion of the court in which Justices Byron R. White, Harry A. Blackmun, Lewis F. Powell Jr. and William H. Rehnquist joined. Chief Justice Burger wrote a concurring opinion.

Justices Thurgood Marshall, William J. Brennan Jr. and John Paul Stevens dissented.

Background

In Miranda, *the court set out a rule intended to safeguard the rights of a suspect to remain silent and to have the aid of an attorney. The* Miranda *rule, adopted by a 5-4 vote, required police to warn a suspect in custody of these rights before they began to interrogate him.*

If the suspect indicated that he wished to remain silent or to have his lawyer present, all questioning had to cease until he indicated his willingness to talk or until his attorney arrived, the court ruled.

'Interrogation'

The case of Rhode Island *v.* Innis *required the court to determine what was "interrogation" within the scope of the* Miranda *rule.*

Innis *was arrested on suspicion that he had robbed two taxi drivers and killed one of them. He was warned of his rights, and he asked to see an attorney. On the way to the police station, officers accompanying* Innis *discussed the possible danger of a child from a nearby school finding the murder weapon. The suspect then offered to show the officers where he had hidden the weapon, a sawed-off shotgun.*

Innis *argued later that the gun and his statements concerning it should be excluded from use as evidence. He described the conversation between the officers in the car as tantamount to interrogation within the meaning of* Miranda.

Innis *convinced the state Supreme Court, which set aside his conviction. The state court held that the conversation was indeed "subtle coercion," equivalent to interrogation.*

Decision

The U.S. Supreme Court overturned this finding of the state court. First, the justices defined "interrogation." Clearly, "interrogation" under Miranda *applied to more than direct express questioning of a suspect, wrote Justice Stewart for the majority.*

But, Stewart continued, "[t]his is not to say ... that all statements obtained by the police after a person has been taken into custody are to be considered the product of interrogation.... 'Interrogation,' as conceptualized in the Miranda *opinion, must reflect a measure of compulsion above and beyond that inherent in custody itself."*

Intent also was a crucial element in the court's definition of "interrogation." Interrogation was indeed more than direct questioning, Stewart wrote, "[b]ut, since the police surely cannot be held accountable for the unforeseeable results of their words or actions, the definition of interrogation can extend only to words or actions on the part of police officers that they should have known *were reasonably likely to elicit an incriminating response."*

Applying its definition to the case at hand, the court held that the conversation that indirectly persuaded Innis to locate the murder weapon was not "interrogation" within the scope of the Miranda *rule.*

Dissenting Views

Justices Marshall and Brennan agreed with the court's definition of interrogation, but disagreed with its application in this case.

They found the conversation in Innis' presence an example of "a classic interrogation technique," as "appeal to a suspect to confess for the sake of others."

The policemen knew Innis "would hear and attend to their conversation, and they are chargeable with knowledge of and responsibility for the pressures to speak which they created," the dissenters argued.

Justice Stevens also found the conversation between the officers the equivalent of interrogation. And he took issue as well with the majority's insistence upon intent as an element of its definition of interrogation. That insistence was "a plain departure" from Miranda, *Stevens said.*

Following are excerpts from the Supreme Court's ruling May 12, 1980, defining "interrogation" in criminal cases and upholding the Miranda *precedent; and from the dissenting opinions of Justices Marshall and Stevens:*

No. 78-1076

State of Rhode Island, Petitioner,   On Writ of Certiorari to the Su-
v.   preme Court of Rhode Island.
Thomas J. Innis.

[May 12, 1980]

MR. JUSTICE STEWART delivered the opinion of the Court.

In *Miranda* v. *Arizona* [1966], the Court held that, once a defendant in custody asks to speak with a lawyer, all interrogation must cease until a lawyer is present. The issue in this case is whether the respondent was "interrogated" in violation of the standards promulgated in the *Miranda* opinion.

I

On the night of January 12, 1975, John Mulvaney, a Providence, R. I., taxicab driver, disappeared after being dispatched to pick up a customer. His body was discovered four days later buried in a shallow grave in Coventry, R. I. He had died from a shotgun blast aimed at the back of his head.

On January 17, 1975, shortly after midnight, the Providence police received a telephone call from Gerald Aubin, also a taxicab driver, who reported that he had just been robbed by a man wielding a sawed-off shotgun. Aubin further reported that he had dropped off his assailant near Rhode Island College in a section of Providence known as Mount Pleasant. While at the Providence police station waiting to give a state-ment, Aubin noticed a picture of his assailant on a bulletin board. Aubin so informed one of the police officers present. The officer prepared a photo array, and again Aubin identified a picture of the same person. That person was the respondent. Shortly thereafter, the Providence police began a search of the Mount Pleasant area.

At approximately 4:30 a.m. on the same date, Patrolman Lovell, while cruising the streets of Mount Pleasant in a patrol car, spotted the respondent standing in the street facing him. When Patrolman Lovell stopped his car, the respondent walked towards it. Patrolman Lovell then arrested the respondent, who was unarmed, and advised him of his so-called *Miranda* rights. While the two men waited in the patrol car for other police officers to arrive, Patrolman Lovell did not converse with the respondent other than to respond to the latter's request for a cigarette.

Within minutes, Sergeant Sears arrived at the scene of the arrest, and he also gave the respondent the *Miranda* warnings. Immediately thereafter, Captain Leyden and other police officers arrived. Captain Leyden advised the respondent of his *Miranda* rights. The respondent stated that he understood those rights and wanted to speak with a lawyer. Captain Leyden then directed that the respondent be placed in a "caged wagon," a four-door police car with a wire screen mesh between the front and rear seats, and be driven to the central police station. Three officers, Patrolmen Gleckman, Williams, and McKenna, were assigned to accompany the respondent to the central station. They placed the respondent in the vehicle and shut the doors. Captain Leyden then instructed the officers not to question the respondent or intimidate or coerce him in any way. The three officers then entered the vehicle, and it departed.

While enroute to the central station, Patrolman Gleckman initiated a conversation with Patrolman McKenna concerning the missing shotgun. As Patrolman Gleckman later testified:

> "A. At this point, I was talking back and forth with Patrolman McKenna stating that I frequent this area while on patrol and

[that because a school for handicapped children is located nearby,] there's a lot of handicapped children running around in this area, and God forbid one of them might find a weapon with shells and they might hurt themselves." . . .

Patrolman McKenna apparently shared his fellow officer's concern:

"A. I more or less concurred with him [Gleckman] that it was a safety factor and that we should, you know, continue to search for the weapon and try to find it." . . .

While Patrolman Williams said nothing, he overheard the conversation between the two officers:

"A. He [Gleckman] said it would be too bad if the little — I believe he said girl — would pick up the gun, maybe kill herself." . . .

The respondent then interrupted the conversation, stating that the officers should turn the car around so he could show them where the gun was located. At this point, Patrolman McKenna radioed back to Captain Leyden that they were returning to the scene of the arrest, and that the respondent would inform them of the location of the gun. At the time the respondent indicated that the officers should turn back, they had traveled no more than a mile, a trip encompassing only a few minutes.

The police vehicle then returned to the scene of the arrest where a search for the shotgun was in progress. There, Captain Leyden again advised the respondent of his *Miranda* rights. The respondent replied that he understood those rights but that he "wanted to get the gun out of the way because of the kids in the area in the school." The respondent then led the police to a nearby field, where he pointed out the shotgun under some rocks by the side of the road.

On March 20, 1975, a grand jury returned an indictment charging the respondent with the kidnaping, robbery, and murder of John Mulvaney. Before trial, the respondent moved to suppress the shotgun and the statements he had made to the police regarding it. After an evidentiary hearing at which the respondent elected not to testify, the trial judge found that the respondent had been "repeatedly and completely advised of his *Miranda* rights." He further found that it was "entirely understandable that [the officers in the police vehicle] would voice their concern [for the safety of the handicapped children] to each other." The judge then concluded that the respondent's decision to inform the police of the location of the shotgun was "a waiver, clearly, and on the basis of the evidence that I have heard, and [*sic*] intelligent waiver, of his [*Miranda*] right to remain silent." Thus, without passing on whether the police officers had in fact "interrogated" the respondent, the trial court sustained the admissibility of the shotgun and testimony related to its discovery. That evidence was later introduced at the respondent's trial, and the jury returned a verdict of guilty on all counts.

On appeal, the Rhode Island Supreme Court, in a 5-2 decision, set aside the respondent's conviction. . . . Relying at least in part on this Court's decision in *Brewer* v. *Williams* [1972], the court concluded that the respondent had invoked his *Miranda* right to counsel and that, contrary to *Miranda's* mandate that, in the absence of counsel, all custodial interrogation then cease, the police officers in the vehicle had "interrogated" the respondent without a valid waiver of his right to counsel. It was the view of the state appellate court that, even though the police officers may have been genuinely concerned about the public safety and even though the respondent had not been addressed personally by the police officers, the respondent nonetheless had been subjected to "subtle coercion" that was the equivalent of "interrogation" within the meaning of the *Miranda* opinion. Moreover, contrary to the holding of the trial court, the appellate court concluded that the evidence was insufficient to support a finding of waiver. Having concluded that both the shotgun and testimony relating to its discovery were obtained in violation of the *Miranda* standards and therefore should not have been admitted into evidence, the Rhode Island Supreme Court held that the respondent was entitled to a new trial.

We granted certiorari to address for the first time the meaning of "interrogation" under *Miranda* v. *Arizona*. . . .

II

In its *Miranda* opinion, the Court concluded that in the context of "custodial interrogation" certain procedural safeguards are necessary to protect a defendant's Fifth and Fourteenth Amendment privilege against compulsory self-incrimination. More specifically, the Court held that "the prosecution may not use statements, whether exculpatory or inculpatory, stemming from custodial interrogation of the defendant unless it demonstrates the use of procedural safeguards effective to secure the privilege against self-incrimination." . . . Those safeguards included the now familiar *Miranda* warnings — namely, that the defendant be informed "that he has the right to remain silent, that anything he says can be used against him in a court of law, that he has the right to the presence of an attorney, and that if he cannot afford an attorney one will be appointed for him prior to any questioning if he so desires," — or their equivalent. . . .

The Court in the *Miranda* opinion also outlined in some detail the consequences that would result if a defendant sought to invoke those procedural safeguards. With regard to the right to the presence of counsel, the Court noted:

> "Once warnings have been given, the subsequent procedure is clear. . . . If the individual states that he wants an attorney, the interrogation must cease until an attorney is present. At that time, the individual must have an opportunity to confer with the attorney

and to have him present during any subsequent questioning. If the individual cannot obtain an attorney and he indicates that he wants one before speaking to police, they must respect his decision to remain silent.".. .

In the present case, the parties are in agreement that the respondent was fully informed of his *Miranda* rights and that he invoked his *Miranda* right to counsel when he told Captain Leyden that he wished to consult with a lawyer. It is also uncontested that the respondent was "in custody" while being transported to the police station.

The issue, therefore, is whether the respondent was "interrogated" by the police officers in violation of the respondent's undisputed right under *Miranda* to remain silent until he had consulted with a lawyer. In resolving this issue, we first define the term "interrogation" under *Miranda* before turning to a consideration of the facts of this case.

A

The starting point for defining "interrogation" in this context is, of course, the Court's *Miranda* opinion. There the Court observed that "[b]y custodial interrogation, we mean *questioning* initiated by law enforcement officers after a person has been taken into custody or otherwise deprived of his freedom of action in any significant way.".. . This passage and other references throughout the opinion to "questioning" might suggest that the *Miranda* rules were to apply only to those police interrogation practices that involve express questioning of a defendant while in custody.

We do not, however, construe the *Miranda* opinion so narrowly. The concern of the Court in *Miranda* was that the "interrogation environment" created by the interplay of interrogation and custody would "subjugate the individual to the will of his examiner" and thereby undermine the privilege against compulsory self-incrimination.... The police practices that evoked this concern included several that did not involve express questioning. For example, one of the practices discussed in *Miranda* was the use of lineups in which a coached witness would pick the defendant as the perpetrator. This was designed to establish that the defendant was in fact guilty as a predicate for further interrogation.... A variation on this theme discussed in *Miranda* was the so-called "reverse line-up" in which a defendant would be identified by coached witnesses as the perpetrator of a fictitious crime, with the object of inducing him to confess to the actual crime of which he was suspected in order to escape the false prosecution.... The Court in *Miranda* also included in its survey of interrogation practices the use of psychological ploys, such as to "posit[]" "the guilt of the subject," to "minimize the moral seriousness of the offense," and "to cast blame on the victim or on society."... It is clear that these techniques of persuasion, no less than express questioning, were thought, in a custodial setting, to amount to interrogation.

This is not to say, however, that all statements obtained by the police after a person has been taken into custody are to be considered the product of interrogation. As the court in *Miranda* noted:

> "Confessions remain a proper element in law enforcement. Any statement given freely and voluntarily without any compelling influences is, of course, admissible in evidence. *The fundamental import of the privilege while an individual is in custody is not whether he is allowed to talk with the police without the benefit of warnings and counsel, but whether he can be interrogated....* Volunteered statements of any kind are not barred by the Fifth Amendment and their admissibility is not affected by our holding today (emphasis added)." ...

It is clear therefore that the special procedural safeguards outlined in *Miranda* are required not where a suspect is simply taken into custody, but rather where a suspect in custody is subjected to interrogation. "Interrogation," as conceptualized in the *Miranda* opinion, must reflect a measure of compulsion above and beyond that inherent in custody itself.

We conclude that the *Miranda* safeguards come into play whenever a person in custody is subjected to either express questioning or its functional equivalent. That is to say, the term "interrogation" under *Miranda* refers not only to express questioning, but also to any words or actions on the part of the police (other than those normally attendant to arrest and custody) that the police should know are reasonably likely to elicit an incriminating response from the suspect. The latter portion of this definition focuses primarily upon the perceptions of the suspect, rather than the intent of the police. This focus reflects the fact that the *Miranda* safeguards were designed to vest a suspect in custody with an added measure of protection against coercive police practices, without regard to objective proof of the underlying intent of the police. A practice that the police should know is reasonably likely to evoke an incriminating response from a suspect thus amounts to interrogation. But, since the police surely cannot be held accountable for the unforeseeable results of their words or actions, the definition of interrogation can extend only to words or actions on the part of police officers that they *should have known* were reasonably likely to elicit an incriminating response.

B

Turning to the facts of the present case, we conclude that the respondent was not "interrogated" within the meaning of *Miranda*. It is undisputed that the first prong of the definition of "interrogation" was not satisfied, for the conversation between Patrolmen Gleckman and McKenna included no express questioning of the respondent. Rather, that conversation was, at least in form, nothing more than a dialogue between the two officers to which no response from the respondent was invited.

Moreover, it cannot be fairly concluded that the respondent was subjected to the "functional equivalent" of questioning. It cannot be said, in short, that Patrolmen Gleckman and McKenna should have known that their conversation was reasonably likely to elicit an incriminating response from the respondent. There is nothing in the record to suggest that the officers were aware that the respondent was peculiarly susceptible to an appeal to his conscience concerning the safety of handicapped children. Nor is there anything in the record to suggest that the police knew that the respondent was unusually disoriented or upset at the time of his arrest.

The case thus boils down to whether, in the context of a brief conversation, the officers should have known that the respondent would suddenly be moved to make a self-incriminating response. Given the fact that the entire conversation appears to have consisted of no more than a few off-hand remarks, we cannot say that the officers should have known that it was reasonably likely that Innis would so respond. This is not a case where the police carried on a lengthy harangue in the presence of the suspect. Nor does the record support the respondent's contention that, under the circumstances, the officers' comments were particularly "evocative." It is our view, therefore, that the respondent was not subjected by the police to words or actions that the police should have known were reasonably likely to elicit an incriminating response from him.

The Rhode Island Supreme Court erred, in short, in equating "subtle compulsion" with interrogation. That the officers' comments struck a responsive chord is readily apparent. Thus, it may be said, as the Rhode Island Supreme Court did say, that the respondent was subjected to "subtle compulsion." But that is not the end of the inquiry. It must also be established that a suspect's incriminating response was the product of words or actions on the part of the police that they should have known were reasonably likely to elicit an incriminating response. This was not established in the present case.

For the reasons stated, the judgment of the Supreme Court of Rhode Island is vacated, and the case is remanded to that court for further proceedings not inconsistent with this opinion. . . .

It is so ordered.

MR. JUSTICE MARSHALL, with whom MR. JUSTICE BRENNAN joins, dissenting.

I am substantially in agreement with the Court's definition of "interrogation" within the meaning of *Miranda* v. *Arizona* (1966). In my view, the *Miranda* safeguards apply whenever police conduct is intended or likely to produce a response from a suspect in custody. As I read the Court's opinion, its definition of "interrogation" for *Miranda* purposes is equivalent, for practical purposes, to my formulation, since it contemplates that "where a police practice is designed to elicit an incriminating response from the accused, it is unlikely that the practice will not also be one which the police should have known was reasonably likely to have that effect.". . . Thus, the Court requires an objective inquiry into the likely effect of police conduct on a typical individual, taking into account any special susceptibility of the suspect to certain kinds of pressure of which the police know or have reason to know.

I am utterly at a loss, however, to understand how this objective standard as applied to the facts before us can rationally lead to the conclusion that there was no interrogation. Innis was arrested at 4:30 a.m., handcuffed, searched, advised of his rights, and placed in the back seat of a patrol car. Within a short time he had been twice more advised of his rights and driven away in a four door sedan with three police officers. Two officers sat in the front seat and one sat beside Innis in the back seat. Since the car traveled no more than a mile before Innis agreed to point out the location of the murder weapon, Officer Gleckman must have begun almost immediately to talk about the search for the shotgun.

The Court attempts to characterize Gleckman's statements as "no more than a few off-hand remarks" which could not reasonably have been expected to elicit a response. . . . If the statements had been addressed to petitioner, it would be impossible to draw such a conclusion. The simple message of the "talking back and forth" between Gleckman and McKenna was that they had to find the shotgun to avert a child's death.

One can scarcely imagine a stronger appeal to the conscience of a suspect — *any* suspect — than the assertion that if the weapon is not found an innocent person will be hurt or killed. And not just any innocent person, but an innocent child — a little girl — a helpless, handicapped little girl on her way to school. The notion that such an appeal could not be expected to have any effect unless the suspect were known to have some special interest in handicapped children verges on the ludicrous. As a matter of fact, the appeal to a suspect to confess for the sake of others, to "display some evidence of decency and honor," is a classic interrogation technique. . . .

Gleckman's remarks would obviously have constituted interrogation if they had been explicitly directed to petitioner, and the result should not be different because they were nominally addressed to McKenna. This is not a case where police officers speaking among themselves are accidentally overheard by a suspect. These officers were "talking back and forth" in close quarters with the handcuffed suspect, traveling past the very place where they believed the weapon was located. They knew petitioner would hear and attend to their conversation, and they are chargeable with knowledge of and responsibility for the pressures to speak which they created.

I firmly believe that this case is simply an aberration, and that in future cases the Court will apply the standard adopted today in accordance with its plain meaning.

MR. JUSTICE STEVENS, dissenting.

An original definition of an old term coupled with an original finding of fact on a cold record makes it possible for this Court to reverse the judgment of the Supreme Court of Rhode Island. That court, on the basis of the facts in the record before it, concluded that members of the Providence, R. I. police force had interrogated respondent, who was clearly in custody at the time, in the absence of counsel after he had requested counsel. In my opinion the state court's conclusion that there was interrogation rests on a proper interpretation of both the facts and the law; thus, its determination that the products of the interrogation were inadmissible at trial should be affirmed....

I

As the Court recognizes, *Miranda* v. *Arizona* makes it clear that, once respondent requested an attorney, he had an absolute right to have any type of interrogation cease until an attorney was present. As it also recognizes, *Miranda* requires that the term "interrogation" be broadly construed to include "either express questioning or its functional equivalent."... In my view any statement that would normally be understood by the average listener as calling for a response is the functional equivalent of a direct question, whether or not it is punctuated by a question mark. The Court, however, takes a much narrower view. It holds that police conduct is not the "functional equivalent" of direct questioning unless the police should have known that what they were saying or doing was likely to elicit an incriminating response from the suspect. This holding represents a plain departure from the principles set forth in *Miranda*.

In *Miranda* the Court required the now-familiar warnings to be given to suspects prior to custodial interrogation in order to dispel the atmosphere of coercion that necessarily accompanies such interrogations. In order to perform that function effectively, the warnings must be viewed by both the police and the suspect as a correct and binding statement of their respective rights. Thus, if, after being told that he has a right to have an attorney present during interrogation, a suspect chooses to cut off questioning until counsel can be obtained, his choice must be "scrupulously honored" by the police. ... *Michigan* v. *Mosley* [1975] (WHITE, J., concurring). At the least this must mean that the police are prohibited from making deliberate attempts to elicit statements from the suspect. Yet the Court is unwilling to characterize all such attempts as "interrogation," noting only that "where a police practice is designed to elicit an incriminating response from the accused, it is unlikely that the practice will not also be one which the police should have known was reasonably likely to have that effect." . . .

From the suspect's point of view, the effectiveness of the warnings depends on whether it appears that the police are scrupulously honoring his rights. Apparent attempts to elicit information from a suspect after he has invoked his right to cut off questioning necessarily demean that right and tend to reinstate the imbalance between police and suspect that the *Miranda* warnings are designed to correct. Thus, if the rationale for requiring those warnings in the first place is to be respected, any police conduct or statements that would appear to a reasonable person in the suspect's position to call for a response must be considered "interrogation."

In short, in order to give full protection to a suspect's right to be free from any interrogation at all, the definition of "interrogation" must include any police statement or conduct that has the same purpose or effect as a direct question. Statements that appear to call for a response from the suspect, as well as those that are designed to do so, should be considered interrogation. By prohibiting only those relatively few statements or actions that a police officer should know are likely to elicit an incriminating response, the Court today accords a suspect considerably less protection. Indeed, since I suppose most suspects are unlikely to incriminate themselves even when questioned directly, this new definition will almost certainly exclude every statement that is not punctuated with a question mark from the concept of "interrogation."

The difference between the approach required by a faithful adherence to *Miranda* and the stinted test applied by the Court today can be illustrated by comparing three different ways in which Officer Gleckman could have communicated his fears about the possible dangers posed by the shotgun to handicapped children. He could have:

(1) directly asked Innis:
Will you please tell me where the shotgun is so we can protect handicapped schoolchildren from danger?
(2) announced to the other officers in the wagon:
If the man sitting in the back seat with me should decide to tell us where the gun is, we can protect handicapped children from danger.
or (3) stated to the other officers:
It would be too bad if a little handicapped girl would pick up the gun that this man left in the area and maybe kill herself.

In my opinion, all three of these statements should be considered interrogation because all three appear to be designed to elicit a response from anyone who in fact knew where the gun was located. Under the Court's test, on the other hand, the form of the statements would be critical. Statement #3 would not be interrogation because in the Court's view there was no reason for Officer Gleckman to believe that Innis was susceptible to this type of an implied appeal . . . therefore, the statement would not be reasonably likely to elicit an incriminating response. Assuming that this is true ... then it seems to me that the first two statements, which would be just as unlikely to elicit such a response, should also not be considered interrogation. But, because the first statement is clearly an express question, it *would* be considered interrogation under the Court's test. The second statement, although just as clearly a deliberate appeal to Innis to reveal the location of the gun, would presumably not be interrogation because (a) it was not in form a direct question and (b) it does not fit within the "reasonably likely to elicit an incriminating response" category that applies to indirect interrogation.

As this example illustrates, the Court's test creates an incentive for police to ignore a suspect's invocation of his rights in order to make continued attempts to extract information from him. If a suspect does not appear to be susceptible to a particular type of psychological pressure, the police are apparently free to exert that pressure on him despite his request for counsel, so long as they are careful not to punctuate their statements with question marks. And if, contrary to all reasonable expectations, the suspect makes an incriminating statement, that statement can be used against him at trial. The Court thus turns *Miranda's* unequivocal rule against any interrogation at all into a trap in which unwary suspects may be caught by police deception.

II

Even if the Court's new definition of the term "interrogation" provided a proper standard for deciding this case, I find it remarkable that the Court should undertake the initial task of applying its new standard to the facts of the present case. As noted above, the trial judge did not decide whether Officer Gleckman had interrogated respondent. Assuming *arguendo* that he had, the judge concluded that respondent had waived his request for counsel by offering to help find the gun. The Rhode Island Supreme Court disagreed on the waiver questions, and expressly concluded that interrogation had occurred. Even if the Rhode Island court might have reached a different conclusion under the Court's new definition, I do not believe we should exclude it from participating in a review of the actions taken by the Providence police. Indeed, given the creation of a new standard of decision at this stage of the litigation, the proper procedure would be to remand to the trial court for findings on the basis of evidence directed at the new standard.

In any event, I think the Court is clearly wrong in holding, as a matter of law, that Officer Gleckman should not have realized that his statement was likely to elicit an incriminating response. The Court implicitly assumes that, at least in the absence of a lengthy harangue, a criminal suspect will not be likely to respond to indirect appeals to his humanitarian impulses. It then goes on to state that the officers in this case had no reason to believe that respondent would be unusually susceptible to such appeals.... Finally, although the significance of the officer's intentions is not clear under its objective test, the Court states in a footnote that the record "in no way suggests" that Officer Gleckman's remarks were designed to elicit a response....

The Court's assumption that criminal suspects are not susceptible to appeals to conscience is directly contrary to the teachings of police interrogation manuals, which recommend appealing to a suspect's sense of morality as a standard and often successful interrogation technique. Surely the practical experience embodied in such manuals should not be ignored in a case such as this in which the record is devoid of any evidence — one way or the other — as to the susceptibility of suspects in general or of Innis in particular.

Moreover, there is evidence in the record to support the view that Officer Gleckman's statement was intended to elicit a response from Innis. Officer Gleckman, who was not regularly assigned to the caged wagon, was directed by a police captain to ride with respondent to the police station. Although there is a dispute in the testimony, it appears that Gleckman may well have been riding in the back seat with Innis. The record does not explain why, notwithstanding the fact that respondent was handcuffed, unarmed, and had offered no resistance when arrested by an officer acting alone, the captain ordered Officer Gleckman to ride with respondent. It is not inconceivable that two professionally trained police officers concluded that a few well-chosen remarks might induce respondent to disclose the whereabouts of the shotgun. This conclusion becomes even more plausible in light of the emotionally charged words chosen by Officer Gleckman ("God forbid" that a "little girl" should find the gun and hurt herself).

III

Under my view of the correct standard, the judgment of the Rhode Island Supreme Court should be affirmed because the statements made within Innis' hearing were as likely to elicit a response as a direct question. However, even if I were to agree with the Court's much narrower standard, I would disagree with its disposition of this particular case because the Rhode Island courts should be given an opportunity to apply the new standard to the facts of this case.

CHROMOSOME REPORT
ON LOVE CANAL RESIDENTS
May 14, 1980

A biomedical study suggesting that residents of a neighborhood in Niagara Falls, N.Y., had suffered chromosome damage from chemical wastes created a furor and led to deepening concern over numerous other chemical dumps across the nation.

The study report, dated May 14, had been undertaken for two federal agencies, the Department of Justice and the Environmental Protection Agency (EPA). When accounts of the study appeared in newspapers, 710 families were evacuated from the vicinity of an old, unfinished canal, the Love Canal, at the expense of the federal government.

Emotional Issue

The plight of the Love Canal residents who had purchased houses near a long-forgotten repository of chemical wastes became an unusually emotional public health and environmental issue in 1980. Moreover, a $124.5 million lawsuit was begun by the Justice Department against the Hooker Chemical Corp., accused of having dumped 21,000 tons of hazardous chemicals in the canal area 30 years earlier.

The controversy also focused attention on other chemical waste sites — estimated as high as 30,000 — throughout the country. According to Sen. Edward M. Kennedy, D-Mass., chairman of the Labor and Human Resources Subcommittee on Health and Scientific Research, "millions of Americans" might be taking "involuntary health risks every day, simply because of where they live."

Background

The Love Canal episode had its roots in the period 1947-52, when the Hooker company took over an abandoned site along the canal to dump wastes. After the company sold the filled-in site to the Niagara Falls School Board for $1, schools and private houses were built nearby.

The 1970s brought heavy rains to the area, causing chemicals to seep into basements of houses. Residents began to clamor for relocation assistance after tests in 1978 showed unusually high incidences of cancer and other medical disorders.

Cytogenetic Study

The relatively small study that broke political deadlocks in May 1980 had been commissioned by the federal government to buttress its lawsuit against the Hooker company.

Carried out by the Biogenics Corp. of Houston, Texas, as a pilot project, the study showed that 11 of 36 Love Canal residents studied had chromosome aberrations and eight of the 11 had "supernumerary acentric fragments." That appeared to mean that the eight had more chromosomal material than they were born with.

The EPA made it clear that the pilot study could not "be regarded as a complete and definitive scientific study." But chromosome damages as described in the report were suspected of being related to birth defects and, possibly, the future appearance of cancer.

Other Chemical Dumps

Writing in The New York Times June 8, Anthony J. Parisi said, "Just about everyone, including the chemical industry, agrees that deterioration at the nation's dump sites and storage facilities must be halted and the bad habits that caused the problems corrected.... But who will put up the millions — or perhaps billions — of dollars needed to clean up the lethal litter that modern man has already left in his trail?"

> Following are excerpts from Feb. 26, 1980, and May 5, 1980, statements on hazardous waste management regulations by Douglas M. Costle, administrator of the Environmental Protection Agency, and from the pilot cytogenetic study of residents of Love Canal, Niagara Falls, N.Y., prepared by the Biogenics Corp. of Houston, Texas, and dated May 14, 1980. (Boldface headings in brackets have been added by Congressional Quarterly to highlight the organization of the texts.):

FEB. 26 STATEMENT

The safe disposal of toxic chemical waste by industry is currently one of this country's most critical environmental problems.

Ever since the tragedy of Love Canal, the nation has been shocked by continuing discoveries of hazardous waste incidents which threaten public health and the environment.

We have seen the Valley of the Drums in Kentucky where barrels of chemicals hang from trees like Christmas ornaments.

We have seen miles of North Carolina roadside deadened by ditch dumping of PCB's.

We have seen entire mine shafts filled with chemical soup.

We have launched a major enforcement effort to identify these kinds of sites and to take legal action whenever the responsible party can be found.

But the eventual solution to the hazardous waste problem will require a transformation in the way that American industry handles its waste. And the size of the problem is staggering. Over 750,000 generators presently produce some 57 million tons of waste annually, of which 90 percent is disposed of by environmentally unsound methods.

As a nation, we paid too little attention to the byproducts of our chemical age. For decades, we dumped out the back door and into any vacant lot or inadequate landfill assuming that the wastes could be forgotten. Unfortunately, these wastes did not just go away. They have turned up, sometimes decades later, in people's drinking water supplies, in the nation's waterways, underneath housing developments and from there into people's homes. The toxic effects from these wastes cannot be underestimated.

Some of these wastes, byproducts from the production of pesticides, paints, industrial cleaners, solvents and other industrial chemicals, contain extremely dangerous substances.

What happened two years ago at Love Canal where hundreds of residents were displaced from their homes, some never to return, and where abnormal rates of miscarriages, birth defects and cancers have occurred, must never happen again.

We may continue to find abandoned waste sites from past decades of neglect. But the system I am announcing today is designed to prevent the creation of future Love Canals.

Today we are issuing three regulations which will give us a national roadmap of where waste is and where it is going. These regulations will:

—Create an inventory of all businesses in the nation which produce, transport, or dispose of hazardous waste.

—Establish a manifest system so that we will know at all times who is responsible for hazardous waste, where it is going, and whether it gets there safely.

The Manifest System

The manifest system is a central element in an emerging management system which will provide cradle-to-grave control over toxic chemical wastes. The manifest system is directed specifically at the midnight dumper who surreptitiously dumps wastes in sewers, in fields, or in the woods. It's designed to put the midnight dumper out of business.

Chris Beck, Assistant Administrator for Water and Hazardous Materials, will use the charts behind me to illustrate how the manifest system works.

—The generator of waste — here a chemical plant — must determine if his wastes are hazardous.

—If hazardous wastes are to be shipped, the generator must do several things:

• He must package and label the wastes in accordance with Department of Transportation shipping regulations.

• He must designate on the manifest the facility to which the wastes are to go. That facility must be permitted to handle his type of waste.

• He must prepare the manifest, which must contain
   —the name of the generator,
   —the name of all transporters,
   —the name and address of the designated facility, and
   —the description and quantity of the waste.

• Finally, he must give copies of that manifest to the transporter.

The transporter also has specified responsibilities:

• He must sign a copy of the manifest, acknowledging acceptance of the waste, and give it to the generator.

• He must deliver the waste to the designated facility, and receive from that facility a signed copy of the manifest.

• He must, in the case of a spill, take action to clean up that spill and contact the National Response Center and DOT.

—The facility, whether it be an incinerator, a treatment facility, or a disposal site, must sign a copy of the manifest and return it to the generator, thus closing the loop.

—The generator, when he receives the signed manifest, knows that his waste arrived safely. But if he does not receive a signed copy, he must

• Within 35 days, contact the transporter and the designated facility to find out the status of the waste.

• Within 45 days, submit a report to EPA.

Manifest systems are presently in operation in Europe and in several States. The system prevents illicit disposal and midnight dumping because responsibility is fixed, and evasion requires extensive collusion.

EPA and the Department of Transportation have worked closely together in developing the manifest regulations, and DOT will be revising its regulations to incorporate controls over shipments of hazardous waste.

The Schedule for Implemenation

These three regulations — standards for generators and transporters, and requirements for notification — are key elements of the management system for hazardous wastes under the Resource Conservation and Recovery Act.

In April, EPA will define what wastes are hazardous and set forth operating standards for treatment, storage, and disposal facilities. We will also issue procedural regulations for permitting and state authorization.

By July, all businesses which handle hazardous waste must notify EPA, giving us for the first time a national inventory.

By October, all firms that store, treat, or dispose must apply for a permit. Those who notify and apply for a permit can obtain interim status to continue their operations.

Also in October, the program takes effect and goes into operation. The manifest system must be used for all waste shipments, and all sites with interim status must be in compliance with the interim operating standards.

Conclusion

We are the most highly industrialized society the world has ever known. Yet until now, no system has been institutionalized for properly disposing of our toxic wastes.

These regulations, and those that will be published in April, will create a new framework which will fundamentally change the ways in which industry manages its wastes.

We do not view these regulations as the final solution. No single stroke of a pen can quickly change old habits of waste mismanagement that industry has become accustomed to. But the new regulations are an essential first step towards preventing the creation of new Love Canals.

MAY 5 ANNOUNCEMENT

Two weeks ago, on the 10th anniversary of Earth Day, the site where we intended to hold this news conference — the Chemical Control dumpsite in Elizabeth, N.J., — was transformed into a chemical inferno. It was a grim reminder on Earth Day that much remains to be done in protecting human health and the environment.

The regulations we are announcing today are designed to prevent the future creation of chemical dumps like the one in New Jersey. They establish a hazardous waste management system that provides cradle-to-grave control.

Two months ago EPA issued the first three regulations in this program. Those three regulations will give us a national roadmap of where waste is and where it is going. They will create an inventory of all businesses in the nation which produce, transport, or dispose of hazardous waste. They will establish a manifest system so that we will know at all times who is responsible for hazardous waste, where it is going, and whether it gets there safely.

Today, we are announcing the next installment of regulations to effectuate the hazardous waste program.

—These regulations identify and list the hazardous wastes which will be subject to control. They list 85 waste streams which are promulgated now, and an additional 25 waste streams which will be promulgated by May 30. They list 416 commercial products and chemicals which, if discarded, must be managed as hazardous waste. They also contain simple tests to be applied by generators to identify additional waste streams which may be ignitable, corrosive, reactive, or toxic.

—These regulations also set operating and technical standards for facilities which store, treat, or dispose of hazardous waste. In November, existing facilities will have to comply with these requirements. They will have to undertake regular inspections and provide security at their sites. They will have to train their employees properly and develop contingency plans to respond to accidents. They will have to begin to install groundwater monitoring systems. They will have to keep careful records of their operations and make regular reports. They will have to participate in the manifest system. And they will have to meet a series of technical standards regarding the storage, treatment, incineration or disposal of waste.

[Shocking Discoveries]

Let me predict now that the process we are starting will turn up information and situations which will shock our nation. We will find waste sites which are now unknown. We will document leaching of chemicals into aquifers which we have assumed were safe. We will gather hard data on a problem whose dimensions we now can only guess. But we will have begun the difficult transition from a time when wastes, once out-of-sight, were out-of-mind.

However, these regulations provide only one leg of a three-legged stool. It now is the law of the land that wastes must be managed properly. That is a critical first step. But two other conditions are necessary.

[New Commitments]

First, we must have a commitment of capital and expertise from firms willing to provide waste management. There is no reason why American technological genius, which produced these wastes, cannot provide the technological "know how" for disposing of it properly. We have tried to create a regulatory and financial climate in which responsible and capable companies step forward and take on this job.

Second, we must have sites at which good management can take place. Our citizens want the benefits to society that created those wastes. They must come to understand that all of us, in every state and locality, share responsibility for locating safe waste management sites.

Finally, let me turn to what is always the first question after EPA unveils new regulations — what will this program cost? We have studied 22 industrial sectors representing 29,000 generators responsible for gross sales of $350 billion. We estimate the cost of compliance to be $510 million — less than two-tenths of one percent of sales for these generators.

[Significant Costs]

These costs are significant. But they are also a bargain. For if we have learned nothing else since Love Canal, we have learned that an ounce of prevention in hazardous waste management is worth a pound of cure. At Love Canal, proper management of Hooker's wastes would have cost $3 million. Instead, the State of New York has already spent $36 million, EPA has filed four suits totaling $124 million, and over $14 billion in compensatory and punitive lawsuits are pending.

At another Hooker site near Muskegon, Michigan, chemical leachate has caused irreparable damage to local groundwater supplies. Total clean-up could cost $30 million.

In Dover Township, New Jersey, improper disposal of 6,000 drums of chemical wastes has cost over $400,000 to clean up. Fourteen million dollars in lawsuits have been filed.

Velsicol Chemical Corporation's improper disposal of about 300,000 55-gallon drums of pesticide wastes near Toone, Tennessee, has contaminated local drinking water supplies. Estimates of remedial costs run from $6 million to $165 million. A class action suit for $2.5 billion has been filed against Velsicol.

Clearly, we could save ourselves broke by not dealing with these problems.

Today's regulations will not clean up past disasters such as those I just described. And there are others — Coventry, Rhode Island, Lowell, Massachusetts, Valley of the Drums, Kentucky. Each with stacks and stacks of deteriorating drums, many with unknown substances — a potential risk to health and environment, and limited funds, if any, to pay for cleanup.

[Superfund Legislation]

"Superfund" legislation, proposed by President Carter 10 months ago, would provide funds to clean up these sites immediately. We are pleased that the House Transportation and Commerce Subcommittee, chaired by Rep. James Florio (D-NJ), reported a bill out last Wednesday, and that the House Public Works Committee will be marking up an oil and hazardous substances spill bill this week. We remain confident Superfund will be passed by Congress this session and signed into law.

EPA Hazardous Waste Task Force is working to clean up many of these sites through litigation when a responsible party can be identified. To date, we have filed 19 Federal hazardous waste site cases, and we anticipate the filing of 50 additional cases by the end of 1980.

However, when the public health is at stake, this kind of litigation can take too long. Superfund, if passed, would have permitted clean-up of the Chemical Control site a year ago, before time-consuming litigation and before the hazardous explosion which finally occurred.

Our regulations will prevent new unsafe sites from being created. Thus begins a new era in hazardous waste management.

Thank you.

PILOT CYTOGENETIC STUDY

Methods

Peripheral blood samples were obtained from the 36 individuals over a two day period. Samples from 19 individuals were obtained on day one, and samples from 17 individuals were obtained on day two. Five ml [milliliters] of blood was obtained via venipuncture from each individual. Blood was collected into a ten ml sterile, plastic syringe equipped with a sterile 21 gauge needle. The syringe had been pretreated with 500 units of preservative-free heparin (1000 units per ml). Samples were coded and immediately transferred to the tissue culture laboratory at the University of Buffalo and cultured according to the modification ... of the Moorhead technique. ...

Results

... 200 cells per individual were scored for the presence of chromatid breaks (deletions), chromatid intrachanges, chromatid interchanges, chromosome breaks (deletions), dicentric chromosomes, ring chromosomes, translocations, inversions, supernumerary acentric fragments, severely damaged cells, and total abnormal cells. Some of the slides from three individuals, B-29, B-31 and B-45, were broken while being transported, resulting in the reduction of the number of cells analyzed. Thus only 187 cells were analyzed for B-29, 131 for B-31, and 184 for B-45. The lower number of cells analyzed for these individuals can result only in an underestimate of the total number of aberrations present per individual.

Since a contemporary comparison group (control group) was not available for study, no unequivocal statement can be made concerning the cytogenetic results from the Love Canal residents. In the absence of a contemporary control group, we have compared our results with controls from a previous study ... historical controls. As seen ... 7102 cells were analyzed from 36 residents of Love Canal. There were 0.83% cells with chromatid breaks, 0.55% cells with chromosome breaks, 0.10% cells with marker chromosomes, 0.20% cells with supernumerary acentric chromosomes, 0 severely damaged cells and 1.10% abnormal cells. In a previous study ... on 44 non-exposed individuals, a total of 8,800 cells were examined. There were 1.1% cells with chromatid breaks, 0.35% cells with chromosome breaks, 0.06% cells with marker chromosomes, and 1.4% abnormal cells. Other types of aberrations were not reported. While there appears to be no difference in the percentage of chromatid breaks and total abnormal cells, there may be an increase in the percentage of cells with chromosome breaks (0.55% versus 0.35%) and in the percentage of cells with marker chromosomes (0.10% versus 0.06%) in the Love Canal residents.

Examination of the results of the Love Canal study on an individual basis rather than on a cellular basis ... [shows] ... the distribution of individuals with chromatid breaks, chromosome breaks, supernumerary acentric fragments and abnormal cells. ... In the previously reported study ... only the distribution of individuals related to chromosome breaks was presented. Comparison of these results with those from the Love Canal residents suggests an increase in the distribution of Love Canal residents with chromosome breaks, 17/36 (47.2%) versus 18/44 (40.9%). In addition, there appears to be a large increase in the distribution of Love Canal residents with supernumerary acentric fragments, 8/36 (22.2%). Since the distribution of individuals with supernumerary acentric fragments was not presented in the previously reported study..., we have estimated the distribution of individuals with supernumerary acentric fragments in the normal population to be approximately 1/100 (1.0%). We base this estimate upon our experience with the examination of over 6,000 individuals.

Examination of the distribution of individuals related to chromatid breaks and abnormal cells was unrevealing. ...

Recommendations

We strongly recommend the genetic toxicological examination of as many of the Love Canal residents as possible. Specifically, three genetic toxicological tests can be performed directly in these residents: cytogenetics, body fluid analysis and fluorescent study of sperm. Such mutagenic studies have the following advantages: studies are performed in intact systems, results from studies need not be extrapolated as in animal investigations, and in general, one directly observes the mutational event. . . .

COURT ON DEATH PENALTY
May 19, 1980

The U.S. Supreme Court May 19 held that Georgia — whose original death penalty law it held unconstitutional in 1972 and whose new law it upheld in 1976 — had misused its new statute in the case of Godfrey v. Georgia.

Robert Franklin Godfrey had been sentenced to die for the shotgun murders of his wife and her mother.

The vote to overturn Godfrey's death sentence was 6-3. Justice Potter Stewart announced the judgment of the court in which Justices Harry A. Blackmun, Lewis F. Powell Jr., and John Paul Stevens joined. Justices Thurgood Marshall and William J. Brennan Jr. concurred in the judgment.

Chief Justice Warren E. Burger and Justices Byron R. White and William H. Rehnquist dissented.

Four justices found Godfrey's crime insufficiently horrible — when compared with other murders — to justify the sentence of death. Marshall and Brennan voted to overturn the sentence because they believed that the death penalty is always cruel, unusual and unconstitutional punishment.

Burger, White and Rehnquist voted to uphold the sentence of death.

Background

In 1972, the court held in the case of Furman v. Georgia *that existing death penalty laws were unconstitutional because they gave judges and*

455

juries too little guidance in deciding when to impose a sentence of death.

As Justice Potter Stewart wrote, under the then-existing laws, a sentence of death was imposed in such a random way that it was "cruel and unusual in the same way that being struck by lightning is cruel and unusual." (Historic Documents of 1972, p. 499)

In 1976, the court again addressed the issue. In a series of cases involving newly enacted death penalty laws, the court refused to hold that death was always so cruel and unusual a punishment that it violated the Constitution.

But the court held that the problems pointed out in Furman *were not satisfactorily remedied by laws making death the mandatory penalty for all persons convicted of first-degree murder.*

In the case of Gregg v. Georgia, *however, the court upheld the type of capital punishment law adopted by Georgia and many other states. (Historic Documents of 1976, p. 489)*

Under Georgia's new law, a person charged with murder was first tried to determine his innocence or guilt. If convicted, a sentencing hearing followed at which evidence was presented concerning any aggravating or mitigating circumstances with regard to the crime or the defendant.

Majority Opinion

In Gregg v. Georgia, *the court upheld the provision of Georgia law that allowed imposition of the death penalty in murder cases only if the crime were found beyond reasonable doubt to be "outrageously or wantonly vile, horrible or inhuman in that it involved torture, depravity of mind, or an aggravated battery to the victim."*

Godfrey was sentenced to death after a jury found that the murders of his estranged wife and his mother-in-law were of such a horrible nature. There was no torture of the victims; Godfrey shot his wife through a window and then entered the dwelling and shot his mother-in-law. Both died within minutes.

Four justices voted in Godfrey v. Georgia *to overturn this sentence because they found that Georgia courts gave such a broad reading to the words of the law that there was "no principled way to distinguish this case, in which the death penalty was imposed, from the many cases in which it was not."*

The four found that the law had been applied in this case in such a fashion that the result was unconstitutional and must be nullified.

"A person of ordinary sensibility could fairly characterize almost every murder as 'outrageously or wantonly vile, horrible and inhuman,'" wrote

Stewart for himself, Blackmun, Powell and Stevens. But when a state's courts adopt that view in interpreting a death penalty statute, they give a jury no standards to follow in deciding whether or not to impose a death penalty, Stewart said.

Godfrey's crimes, concluded Stewart, "cannot be said to have reflected a consciousness materially more 'depraved' than that of any person guilty of murder."

Justices Brennan and Marshall also voted to overturn Godfrey's death sentence. Marshall went on to point out that in his view the Godfrey *case made clear that "[t]he task of eliminating arbitrariness in the infliction of capital punishment is proving to be one which our criminal justice system — and perhaps any criminal justice system — is unable to perform."*

In Dissent

Chief Justice Burger voted to uphold Godfrey's sentence. He criticized the court for taking on "the task of determining on a case-by-case basis whether a defendant's conduct is egregious enough to warrant a death sentence." The court should not second-guess such jury decisions, Burger wrote.

In vivid detail, Justices White and Rehnquist explained why they considered Godfrey's crimes indeed "vile," "inhuman" and "horrible." They criticized the majority's arguments as "shredded by its own illogic."

Following are excerpts from the Supreme Court's opinion announced May 19, 1980, overturning the death sentence of Robert Franklin Godfrey on grounds that the State of Georgia had misused the law in sentencing Godfrey:

No. 78-6899

Robert Franklin Godfrey, Petitioner, *v.* State of Georgia.	On Writ of Certiorari to the Supreme Court of Georgia.

[May 19, 1980]

MR. JUSTICE STEWART delivered the opinion of the Court.

Under Georgia law, a person convicted of murder may be sentenced to death if it is found beyond a reasonable doubt that the offense "was outrageously or wantonly vile, horrible or inhuman in that it involved torture, depravity of mind, or an aggravated battery to the victim." ... In *Gregg* v. *Georgia* [1976] the Court held that this statutory aggravating circumstance (§ (b)(7)) is not unconstitutional on its face. Responding to the argument that the language of the provision is "so broad that capital punishment could be imposed in any murder case," the prevailing opinion said:

> "It is, of course, arguable that any murder involves depravity of mind or an aggravated battery. But this language need not be construed in this way, and there is no reason to assume that the Supreme Court of Georgia will adopt such an open-ended construction." . . . (opinion of STEWART, POWELL and STEVENS, JJ.).

Nearly four years have passed since the *Gregg* decision, and during that time many death sentences based in whole or in part on § (b)(7) have been affirmed by the Supreme Court of Georgia. The issue now before us is whether, in affirming the imposition of the sentences of death in the present case, the Georgia Supreme Court has adopted such a broad and vague construction of the § (b)(7) aggravating circumstance as to violate the Eighth and Fourteenth Amendments to the United States Constitution.

I

On a day in early September in 1977, the petitioner and his wife of 28 years had a heated argument in their home. During the course of this altercation, the petitioner, who had consumed several cans of beer, threatened his wife with a knife and damaged some of her clothing. At this point, the petitioner's wife declared that she was going to leave him, and departed to stay with relatives. That afternoon she went to a Justice of the Peace and secured a warrant charging the petitioner with aggravated assault. A few days later, while still living away from home, she filed suit for divorce. Summons was served on the petitioner, and a court hearing was set on a date some two weeks later. Before the date of the hearing, the petitioner on several occasions asked his wife to return to their home. Each time his efforts were rebuffed. At some point during this period, his wife moved in with her mother. The petitioner believed that his mother-in-law was actively instigating his wife's determination not to consider a possible reconciliation.

In the early evening of September 20, according to the petitioner, his wife telephoned him at home. Once again they argued. She asserted that reconciliation was impossible and allegedly demanded all the proceeds from the planned sale of their house. The conversation was terminated after she said that she would call back later. This she did in an hour or so. The ensuing conversation was, according to the petitioner's account, even more heated than the first. His wife reiterated her stand that reconciliation was out of the question, said that she still wanted all the proceeds from the sale of their house, and mentioned that her mother was supporting her position. Stating that she saw no further use in talking or arguing, she hung up.

At this juncture, the petitioner got out his shotgun and walked with it down the hill from his home to the trailer where his mother-in-law lived. Peering through a window, he observed his wife, his mother-in-law, and his 11-year-old daughter playing a card game. He pointed the shotgun at his wife through the window and pulled the trigger. The charge from the gun struck his wife in the forehead and killed her instantly. He proceeded into the trailer, striking and injuring his fleeing daughter with the barrel of the gun. He then fired the gun at his mother-in-law, striking her in the head and killing her instantly.

The petitioner then called the local sheriff's office, identified himself, said where he was, explained that he had just killed his wife and mother-in-law, and asked that the sheriff come and pick him up. Upon arriving at the trailer, the law enforcement officers found the petitioner seated on a chair in open view near the driveway. He told one of the officers that "they're dead, I killed them" and directed the officer to the place where he had put the murder weapon. Later the petitioner told a police officer, "I've done a hideous crime . . . but I have been thinking about it for eight years . . . I'd do it again."

The petitioner was subsequently indicted on two counts of murder and one count of aggravated assault. He pleaded not guilty and relied primarily on a defense of temporary insanity at his trial. The jury returned verdicts of guilty on all three counts.

The sentencing phase of the trial was held before the same jury. No further evidence was tendered, but counsel for each side made arguments to the jury. Three times during the course of his argument, the prosecutor stated that the case involved no allegation of "torture" or of an "aggravated battery." When counsel had completed their statements, the trial judge instructed the jury orally and in writing in the standards that must guide them in imposing sentence. Both orally and in writing, the judge quoted to the jury the statutory language of the § (b)(7) aggravating circumstance in its entirety.

The jury imposed sentences of death on both of the murder convictions. As to each, the jury specified that the aggravating circumstance they had found beyond a reasonable doubt was "that the offense of murder was outrageously or wantonly vile, horrible and inhuman."

In accord with Georgia law in capital cases, the trial judge prepared a report in the form of answers to a questionnaire for use on appellate review. One question on the form asked whether or not the victim had been "physically harmed or tortured." The trial judge's response was "No, as to both victims, excluding the actual murdering of the two victims."

The Georgia Supreme Court affirmed the judgments of the trial court in all respects. . . . With regard to the imposition of the death sentence for each of the two murder convictions, the court rejected the petitioner's contention that § (b)(7) is unconstitutionally vague. The court noted that Georgia's death penalty legislation had been upheld in *Gregg* v. *Georgia* . . . and cited its prior decisions upholding § (b)(7) in the face of similar vagueness challenges. . . . As to the petitioner's argument that the jury's phraseology was, as a matter of law, an inadequate statement of § (b)(7), the court responded by simply observing that the language "was not objectionable.". . . The court found no evidence that the sentence had been "imposed under the influence of passion, prejudice, or any other arbitrary factor," held that the sentence was neither excessive nor disproportionate to the penalty imposed in similar cases, and stated that the evidence supported the jury's finding of the § (b)(7) statutory aggravating circumstances. . . . Two justices dissented.

II

In *Furman* v. *Georgia* [1972] the Court held that the penalty of death may not be imposed under sentencing procedures that create a substantial risk that the punishment will be inflicted in an arbitrary and capricious manner. *Gregg* v. *Georgia* . . . reaffirmed this holding. . . . A capital sentencing scheme must, in short, provide a "meaningful basis for distinguishing the few cases in which [the penalty] is imposed from the many cases in which it is not.". . .

This means that if a State wishes to authorize capital punishment it has a constitutional responsibility to tailor and apply its law in a manner that avoids the arbitrary and capricious infliction of the death penalty. Part of a State's responsibility in this regard is to define the crimes for which death may be the sentence in a way that obviates "standardless [sentencing] discretion." *Gregg* v. *Georgia.* . . . *Proffitt* v. *Florida* [1976], *Jurek* v. *Texas* [1976]. It must channel the sentencer's discretion by "clear and objective standards" that provide "specific and detailed guidance," and that "make rationally reviewable the process for imposing a sentence of death." As was made clear in *Gregg,* a death penalty "system could have standards so vague that they would fail adequately to channel the sentencing decision patterns of juries with the result that a pattern of arbitrary and capricious sentencing like that found unconstitutional in *Furman* could occur."

In the case before us, the Georgia Supreme Court has affirmed a sentence of death based upon no more than a finding that the offense was "outrageously or wantonly vile, horrible and inhuman." There is nothing in these few words, standing alone, that implies any inherent restraint on the arbitrary and capricious infliction of the death sentence. A person of ordinary sensibility could fairly characterize almost every murder as "outrageously or wantonly vile, horrible and inhuman." Such a view may, in fact, have been one to which the members of the jury in this case subscribed. If so, their preconceptions were not dispelled by the trial judge's sentencing instructions. These gave the jury no guidance concerning the meaning of any of § (b)(7)'s terms. In fact, the jury's interpretation of § (b)(7) can only be the subject of sheer speculation.

The standardless and unchanneled imposition of death sentences in the uncontrolled discretion of a basically uninstructed jury in this case was in no way cured by the affirmance of those sentences by the Georgia Supreme Court. Under state law that court may not affirm a judgment of death until it has independently assessed the evidence of record and determined that such evidence supports the trial judge's or jury's finding of an aggravating circumstance. . . .

In past cases the State Supreme Court has apparently understood this obligation as carrying with it the responsibility to keep § (b)(7) within constitutional bounds. Recognizing that "there is a possibility of abuse of [the § (b)(7)] statutory aggravating circumstance," the court has emphasized that it will not permit the language of that subsection simply to become a "catch all" for cases which do not fit within any other statutory aggravating circumstance. . . . Thus, in exercising its function of death sentence review, the court has said that it will restrict its "approval of the death penalty under this statutory aggravating circumstance to those cases that lie at the core." . . .

When *Gregg* was decided by this Court in 1976, the Georgia Supreme Court had affirmed two death sentences based wholly on § (b)(7). . . .

The . . . opinions suggest that the Georgia Supreme Court had by 1977 reached three separate but consistent conclusions respecting the § (b)(7) aggravating circumstance. The first was that the evidence that the offense was "outrageously or wantonly vile, horrible or inhuman" had to demonstrate "torture, depravity of mind, or an aggravated battery to the victim." The second was that the phrase, "depravity of mind," comprehended only the kind of mental state that led the murderer to torture or to commit an aggravated battery before killing his victim. The third . . . was that the word, "torture," must be construed *in pari materia* with "aggravated battery" so as to require evidence of serious physical abuse of the victim before death. Indeed, the circumstances proved in a number of the § (b)(7) death sentence cases affirmed by the Georgia Supreme Court have met all three of these criteria.

The Georgia courts did not, however, so limit § (b)(7) in the present case. No claim was made, and nothing in the record before us suggests, that the petitioner committed an aggravated battery upon his wife or mother-in-law or, in fact, caused either of them to suffer any physical injury preceding their deaths. Moreover, in the trial court, the prosecutor repeatedly told the jury — and the trial judge wrote in his sentencing report — that the murders did not involve "torture." Nothing said on appeal by the Georgia Supreme Court indicates that it took a different view of the evidence. The circumstances of this case, therefore, do not satisfy the criteria laid out by the Georgia Supreme Court itself. . . . In holding that the evidence supported the jury's § (b)(7) finding, the State Supreme Court simply asserted that the verdict was "factually substantiated."

Thus, the validity of the petitioner's death sentences turns on whether, in light of the facts and circumstances of the murders that Godfrey was convicted of committing, the Georgia Supreme Court can be said to have applied a constitutional construction of the phrase "outrageously or wantonly vile, horrible or inhuman in that [they] involved . . . depravity of mind. . . ." We conclude that the answer must be no. The petitioner's crimes cannot be said to have reflected a consciousness materially more "depraved" than that of any person guilty of murder. His victims were killed instantaneously. They were members of his family who were causing him extreme emotional trauma. Shortly after the killings, he acknowledged his responsibility and the heinous nature of his crimes. These factors certainly did not remove the criminality from the petitioner's acts. But, as was said in *Gardner* v. *Florida* [1978] it "is of vital importance to the defendant and to the community that any decision to impose the death sentence be, and appear to be, based on reason rather than caprice or emotion."

That cannot be said here. There is no principled way to distinguish this case, in which the death penalty was imposed, from the many cases in which it was not. Accordingly, the judgment of the Georgia Supreme Court insofar as it leaves standing the petitioner's death sentences is reversed, and the case is remanded to that court for further proceedings.

It is so ordered.

MR. JUSTICE MARSHALL, with whom MR. JUSTICE BRENNAN joins, concurring in the judgment.

I continue to believe that the death penalty is in all circumstances cruel and unusual punishment forbidden by the Eighth and Fourteenth Amendments. In addition, I agree with the plurality that the Georgia Supreme Court's construction of the provision at issue in this case is unconstitutionally vague under *Gregg* v. *Georgia* (1976). I write separately, first, to examine the Georgia Supreme Court's application of this provision, and second, to suggest why the enterprise on which the Court embarked in *Gregg* v. *Georgia* . . . increasingly appears to be doomed to failure.

I

Under Georgia law, the death penalty may be imposed only when the jury both finds at least one statutory aggravating circumstance and recommends that the sentence of death should be imposed. . . . Under [the Georgia] Code . . . § (b)(7), it is a statutory aggravating circumstance to commit a murder that "was outrageously or wantonly vile, horrible or inhuman in that it involved torture, depravity of mind, or an aggravated battery to the victim." In *Gregg* v. *Georgia* . . . the Court rejected a facial challenge to the constitutionality of this aggravating circumstance. The prevailing opinion conceded that it is "arguable that any murder involves depravity of mind or an aggravated battery.". . . Nonetheless, the plurality refused to invalidate the provision on its face, reasoning that the statutory "language need not be construed in this way, and there is no reason to assume that the Supreme Court of Georgia will adopt such an open-ended construction.".... In my view, life and death should not be determined by such niceties of language.

The Court's conclusion in *Gregg* was not unconditional; it was expressly based on the assumption that the Georgia Supreme Court would adopt a narrowing construction that would give some discernible content to § (b)(7). In the present case, no such narrowing construction was read to the jury or applied by the Georgia Supreme Court on appeal. As it has so many times in the past, that court upheld the jury's finding with a simple notation that it was supported by the evidence. The premise on which *Gregg* relied has thus proved demonstrably false.

For this reason, I readily agree with the plurality that, as applied in this case, § (b)(7) is unconstitutionally vague. The record unequivocally establishes that the trial judge, the prosecutor, and the jury did not believe that the evidence showed that either victim was tortured. Nor was there aggravated battery to the victims. I also agree that since the victims died instantaneously and within a few moments of each other, the fact that the murder weapon was one which caused extensive damage to the victim's body is constitutionally irrelevant....

I am unwilling, however, to accept the plurality's characterization of the decision below as an aberrational lapse on the part of the Georgia Supreme Court from an ordinarily narrow construction of § (b)(7). Reasoning from two decisions rendered shortly after our decision in *Gregg* ... the plurality suggests that from 1977 onward it has been the law of Georgia that a statutory aggravating circumstance can be found under § (b)(7) only if the offense involved torture and aggravated battery, manifested by "evidence of serious physical abuse of the victim before death.".... But we cannot stop reading the Georgia Reports after those two cases. In *Ruffin* v. *State* (1979) the court upheld a jury finding of a § (b)(7) aggravating circumstance stated in the words, "we the jurors conclude that this act was both horrible and inhuman." The case involved a shotgun murder of a child: no torture or aggravated battery was present.... The Georgia court's cursory treatment of § (b)(7) in *Ruffin* ... and the present case indicates either that it has abandoned its intention of reaching only "core" cases under § (b)(7) or that its understanding of the "core" has become remarkably inclusive.

In addition, I think it necessary to emphasize that even under the prevailing view that the death penalty may, in some circumstances, constitutionally be imposed, it is not enough for a reviewing court to apply a narrowing construction to otherwise ambiguous statutory language. The jury must be instructed on the proper, narrow construction of the statute. The Court's cases make clear that it is the *sentencer's* discretion that must be channeled and guided by clear, objective, and specific standards.... To give the jury an instruction in the form of the bare words of the statute — words that are hopelessly ambiguous and could be understood to apply to any murver ... would effectively grant it unbridled discretion to impose the death penalty. Such a defect could not be cured by the *post hoc* narrowing construction of an appellate court. The reviewing court can determine only whether a rational jury might have imposed the death penalty if it had been properly instructed; it is impossible for it to say whether a particular jury would have so exercised its discretion if it had known the law.

For this reason, I believe that the vices of vagueness and intolerably broad discretion are present in any case in which an adequate narrowing construction of § (b)(7) was not read to the jury, and the Court's decision today cannot properly be restricted to cases in which the particular facts appear to be insufficiently heinous to fall within a construction of § (b)(7) that would be consistent with *Gregg*.

II

The preceding discussion leads me to what I regard as a more fundamental defect in the Court's approach to death penalty cases. In *Gregg*, the Court rejected the position, expressed by my Brother BRENNAN and myself, that the death penalty is in all circumstances cruel and unusual punishment forbidden by the Eighth and Fourteenth Amendments. Instead the Court concluded that in "a matter so grave as the determination of whether a human life should be taken or spared," it would be both necessary and sufficient to insist on sentencing procedures that would minimize or eliminate the "risk that [the death penalty] would be inflicted in an arbitrary and capricious manner.". . . Contrary to the statutes at issue in *Furman* v. *Georgia* (1972), under which the death penalty was "infrequently imposed" upon "a capriciously selected random handful," . . . and "the threat of execution [was] too attenuated to be of substantial service to criminal justice," . . . the Court anticipated that the Georgia scheme would produce an even-handed, objective procedure rationally " 'distinguishing the few cases in which [the death penalty] is imposed from the many cases in which it is not.' ". . .

For reasons I expressed in *Furman* v. *Georgia* . . . and *Gregg* v. *Georgia* . . . I believe that the death penalty may not constitutionally be imposed even if it were possible to do so in an even-handed manner. But events since *Gregg* make that possibility seem increasingly remote. Nearly every week of the year, this Court is presented with at least one petition for certiorari raising troubling issues of noncompliance with the strictures of *Gregg* and its progeny. On numerous occasions since *Gregg*, the Court has reversed decisions of state supreme courts upholding the imposition of capital punishment, frequently on the ground that the sentencing proceeding allowed undue discretion, causing dangers of arbitrariness in violation of *Gregg* and its companion cases. These developments, coupled with other persuasive evidence, strongly suggest that appellate courts are incapable of guaranteeing the kind of objectivity and evenhandedness that the Court contemplated and hoped for in

Gregg. The disgraceful distorting effects of racial discrimination and poverty continue to be painfully visible in the imposition of death sentences. And while hundreds have been placed on death row in the years since *Gregg,* only three persons have been executed. Two of them made no effort to challenge their sentence and were thus permitted to commit what I have elsewhere described as "state-administered suicide." *Lenhard* v. *Wolff* (1979) (dissenting opinion). . . . *Gilmore* v. *Utah* (1976). The task of eliminating arbitrariness in the infliction of capital punishment is proving to be one which our criminal justice system — and perhaps any criminal justice system — is unable to perform. In short, it is now apparent that the defects that led my Brothers DOUGLAS, STEWART, and WHITE to concur in the judgment in *Furman* are present as well in the statutory schemes under which defendants are currently sentenced to death.

The issue presented in this case usefully illustrates the point. The Georgia Supreme Court has given no real content to § (b)(7) in by far the majority of the cases in which it has had an opportunity to do so. In the four years since *Gregg,* the Georgia court has *never* reversed a jury's finding of a § (b)(7) aggravating circumstance. With considerable frequency the Georgia court has, as here, upheld the imposition of the death penalty on the basis of a simple conclusory statement that the evidence supported the jury's finding under § (b)(7). Instances of a narrowing construction are difficult to find, and those narrowing constructions that can be found have not been adhered to with any regularity. In no case has the Georgia court required a narrowing construction to be given to the jury — an indispensable method for avoiding the "standardless and unchanneled imposition of death sentences.". . . Genuinely independent review has been exceedingly rare. In sum, I agree with the analysis of a recent commentator who, after a careful examination of the Georgia cases, concluded that the Georgia court has made no substantial effort to limit the scope of § (b)(7), but has instead defined the provision so broadly that practically every murder can fit within its reach. . . .

The Georgia court's inability to administer its capital punishment statute in an evenhanded fashion is not necessarily attributable to any bad faith on its part; it is, I believe, symptomatic of a deeper problem that is proving to be genuinely intractable. Just five years before *Gregg,* Mr. Justice Harlan stated for the Court that the task of identifying "before the fact those characteristics of criminal homicides and their perpetrators which call for the death penalty, and [of] express[ing] these characteristics in language which can be fairly understood and applied by the sentencing authority, appear to be . . . beyond present human ability." *McGautha* v. *California* (1971). From this premise, the Court in *McGautha* drew the conclusion that the effort to eliminate arbitrariness in the imposition of the death penalty need not be attempted at all. In *Furman,* the Court concluded that the arbitrary infliction of the death penalty was constitutionally intolerable. And in *Gregg,* the Court rejected the premise of *McGautha* and approved a statutory scheme under which, as the Court then perceived it, the death penalty would be imposed in an evenhanded manner.

There can be no doubt that the conclusion drawn in *McGautha* was properly repudiated in *Furman,* where the Court made clear that the arbitrary imposition of the death penalty is forbidden by the Eighth and Fourteenth Amendments. But I believe that the Court in *McGautha* was substantially correct in concluding that the task of selecting in some objective way those persons who should be condemned to die is one that remains beyond the capacities of the criminal justice system. For this reason, I remain hopeful that even if the Court is unwilling to accept the view that the death penalty is so barbaric that it is in all circumstances cruel and unusual punishment forbidden by the Eighth and Fourteenth Amendments, it may eventually conclude that the effort to eliminate arbitrariness in the infliction of that ultimate sanction is so plainly doomed to failure that it — and the death penalty — must be abandoned altogether.

MR. CHIEF JUSTICE BURGER, dissenting.

After murdering his wife and mother-in-law, petitioner informed the police that he had committed a "hideous" crime. The dictionary defines hideous as "morally offensive," "shocking," or "horrible." Thus, the very curious feature of this case is that petitioner himself characterized his crime in terms equivalent to those employed in the Georgia statute. For my part, I prefer petitioner's characterization of his conduct to the plurality's effort to excuse and rationalize that conduct as just another killing.... The jurors in this case, who heard all relevant mitigating evidence, see *Lockett* v. *Ohio* (1978), obviously shared that preference; they concluded that his "hideous" crime was "outrageously or wantonly, vile, horrible and inhuman" within the meaning of § (b)(7).

More troubling than the plurality's characterization of petitioner's crime is the new responsibility that it assumes with today's decision — the task of determining on a case-by-case basis whether a defendant's conduct is egregious enough to warrant a death sentence. In this new role, the plurality appears to require "evidence of serious physical abuse" before a death sentence can be imposed under § (b)(7).... For me, this new requirement is arbitrary and unfounded and trivializes the Constitution. Consider, for example, the Georgia case of *Harris* v. *State* (1976), where the defendant killed a young woman for the thrill of it. As he later confessed, he "didn't want nothing [she] got except [her] life."... Does the plurality opinion mean to suggest that anything in the Constitution precludes a state from imposing a death sentence on such a merciless, gratuitous killer? The plurality's novel physical torture requirement may provide an "objective" criterion, but it hardly separates those for whom a state may prescribe the death sentence from those for whom it may not.

In short, I am convinced that the course the plurality embarks on today is sadly mistaken — indeed confused. It is this Court's function to insure that the rights of a defendant are scrupulously respected; and in capital cases we must see to it that the jury has rendered its decision with meticulous care. But it is emphatically not our province to second guess a jury's judgment or to tell the States which of their "hideous," intentional murderers may be given the ultimate penalty. Because the plurality does both, I dissent.

MR. JUSTICE WHITE, with whom MR. JUSTICE REHNQUIST joins, dissenting.

The sole question presented by this petition is whether, in affirming petitioner's death sentence, the Georgia Supreme Court adopted such a broad construction of [Georgia] Code ... § (b)(7) as to violate the Eighth and Fourteenth Amendments to the United States Constitution.

I

In early September of 1977, Mrs. Godfrey, petitioner's wife, left him, moved in with her mother, and refused his entreaty to move back home. She also filed for divorce and charged petitioner with aggravated assault based on an incident in which he had cut some clothes off her body with a knife. On September 20, 1977, Mrs. Godfrey refused petitioner's request to halt divorce proceedings so that they could attempt a reconciliation. That same day petitioner carried his single-action shotgun to his mother-in-law's trailer home, where his wife, her mother, and the couple's 11-year-old daughter were playing a game around a table. Firing through a window, petitioner killed his wife with a shotgun blast to the head. As his daughter, running for help, attempted to rush past him, he struck her on the head with the barrel of the gun; she nonetheless was able to run on for help. Petitioner then reloaded his shotgun and, after entering the home, fired a fatal blast at his mother-in-law's head. After calling the police himself, petitioner was arrested, advised of his rights, and taken to the police station, where he told an officer that he had committed a "hideous crime" about which he had thought for eight years and that he would do it again.

Petitioner, over his defense of insanity, was convicted of the murders of his wife and his mother-in-law and of the aggravated assault of his daughter. He was sentenced to death for each of the murders and to 10 years' imprisonment for the aggravated assault. Under the Georgia death penalty scheme, a person can be sentenced to death only if "the jury verdict includes a finding of at least one statutory aggravating circumstance and a recommendation that such sentence be imposed."... The statutory aggravating circumstance upon which petitioner's sentence was premised reads: "The offense of murder ... was outrageously or wantonly vile, horrible, or inhuman in that it involved torture, depravity of mind, or aggravated assault to the victim."... In petitioner's case, however, the jury, upon returning its recommendation of death, described the aggravating circumstances as follows: "That the offense of murder was outrageously or wantonly vile, horrible, and inhuman." This attenuated statement of § (b)(7) in part forms the basis of petitioner's challenge to the Georgia Supreme Court's decision, for that court held that "[t]he evidence supports the jury's finding of statutory aggravating circumstances, and the jury's phraseology was not objectionable.". . .

II

In *Gregg* v. *Georgia* (1976), we upheld the constitutionality of the capital-sentencing procedures in accordance with which the State of Georgia has sentenced petitioner to death. Two aspects of that scheme impressed us in particular as curing the constitutional defects in the system that was invalidated several years earlier in *Furman* v. *Georgia* (1972). First, the sentencing system specifies statutory aggravating circumstances, one of which has to be found by the jury to exist beyond a reasonable doubt before a death sentence can ever be imposed. . . . Second, the scheme provides for automatic appeal of all death sentences to the Georgia Supreme Court, which is required by statute to undertake a specific inquiry with respect to the soundness of the decision to impose the death penalty. . . . "In short, Georgia's new sentencing procedures require as a prerequisite to the imposition of the death penalty, specific jury findings as to the circumstances of the crime or the character of the defendant. Moreover, . . . the Supreme Court of Georgia compares each death sentence with the sentences imposed on similarly situated defendants to ensure that the sentence of death in a particular case is not disproportionate.". . . *[Gregg* v. *Georgia]*. Petitioner maintains that, at least in his case, the Georgia Supreme Court has failed in its review function because, by construing § (b)(7) to authorize the imposition of the death penalty on him, the court has interpreted that provision in an unconstitutionally broad fashion.

The opinion announcing the judgment of the Court in *Gregg* recognized that § (b)(7), which would authorize imposition of the death penalty here if either of the murders was "outrageously or wantonly vile, horrible, or inhuman in that it involved torture, depravity of mind, or an aggravated battery to the victim," presented some potential interpretative difficulty because "arguabl[y] . . . any murder involves depravity of mind or an aggravated battery.". . . "But," the opinion continued, "this language need not be construed in this way, and there is no reason to assume that the Supreme Court of Georgia will adopt such an open-ended construction.". . . By concluding that the Supreme Court of Georgia has adopted "such an open-ended construction" in the present case, the Court has now turned a blind eye to the facts surrounding the murders of Mrs. Godfrey and her mother and to the constancy of the state supreme court in performance of its statutory review function.

III

This case presents a preliminary difficulty because the sentencing jury found merely that "the offense of murder was outrageously or wantonly vile, horrible, and inhuman," and did not repeat in its finding the entire incantation of § (b)(7). The Georgia Supreme Court found the jury's phraseology unobjectionable; and because this judgment was rendered in the same sentence in which the court expressed its determination that sufficient evidence supported the jury's finding of § (b)(7), the court presumably believed that the jury's finding met all necessary terms of the provision notwithstanding the jury's abbreviated statement.

Petitioner argues, however, that the Georgia Supreme Court, by not deeming the jury's abbreviated statement as reversible error, has endorsed a view of § (b)(7) that allows for the provision's application upon a finding that a murder was "outrageously or wantonly vile, horrible, or inhuman," even though the murder involved no "torture, depravity of mind, or ... aggravated battery to the victim." Such a finding, petitioner contends, would be incomplete and indicative of an unconstitutionally broad construction of the provision, for the language "outrageously or wantonly vile, horrible, or inhuman" cannot "objectively guide and channel jury discretion in the imposition of a death sentence in compliance with the command of the 8th and 14th Amendments...."
...The plurality opinion seems to agree....

I find petitioner's argument unpersuasive, for it is apparent that both the jury and the Georgia Supreme Court understood and applied § (b)(7) in its entirety. The trial court instructed the jurors that they were authorized to fix petitioner's punishment for murder as death or imprisonment for life and that they could consider any evidence in mitigation.... They were also specifically instructed to determine whether there was a statutory aggravating circumstance present beyond a reasonable doubt and that the aggravating circumstance that they could consider was "that the offense of murder was outrageously or wantonly vile, horrible or inhuman in that it involved torture, depravity of mind, or an aggravated battery to the victim."... That the jury's ultimate recitation of the aggravating circumstance was abbreviated reveals, in my view, no gap of constitutional magnitude in its understanding of its duty. It is perfectly evident, moreover, that, in exercising its review function, the Georgia Supreme Court understood that the provision applied in its entirety, just as in the past it has insisted that the provision be read as a whole and not be applied disjunctively.... The court, after quoting the language of the jury's finding, cited § (b)(7) and, more tellingly, referred to the discrepancy between the two versions as a mere problem of "phraseology." As such, the jury's version, in the court's view, "was not objectionable."...

Thus, while both sides to this litigation felt constrained to engage in elaborate structural arguments regarding § (b)(7) — focusing on grammar and syntax, nuance and implication — I ascribe no constitutional significance at all to the jury's attenuated statement of the provision, and thus regard the question whether certain language in the section is severable from the rest as immaterial to the decision of this case.

IV

The question remains whether the facts of this case bear sufficient relation to § (b)(7) to conclude that the Georgia Supreme Court responsibly and constitutionally discharged its review function. I believe that they do.

As described earlier, petitioner, in a cold-blooded executioner's style, murdered his wife and his mother-in-law and, in passing, struck his young daughter on the head with the barrel of his gun. The weapon, a shotgun, is hardly known for the surgical precision with which it perforates its target. The murder scene, in consequence, can only be described in the most unpleasant terms. Petitioner's wife lay prone on the floor. Mrs. Godfrey's head had a hole described as "[a]pproximately the size of a silver dollar" on the side where the shot entered, and much less decipherable and more extensive damage on the side where the shot exited.... Pellets that had passed through Mrs. Godfrey's head were found embedded in the kitchen cabinet.

It will be remembered that after petitioner inflicted this much damage, he took out time not only to strike his daughter on the head, but also to reload his single-shot shotgun and to enter the house. Only then did he get around to shooting his mother-in-law, Mrs. Wilkerson, whose last several moments as a sentient being must have been as terrifying as the human mind can imagine. The police eventually found her face down on the floor with a substantial portion of her head missing and her brain, no longer cabined by her skull, protruding for some distance onto the floor. Blood not only covered the floor and table, but dripped from the ceiling as well.

The Georgia Supreme Court held that these facts supported the jury's finding of the existence of statutory aggravating circumstances § (b)(7). A majority of this Court disagrees. But this disagreement, founded as it is on the notion that the lower court's construction of the provision was overly broad, in fact reveals a conception of this Court's role in backstopping the Georgia Supreme Court that is itself overly broad. Our role is to correct genuine errors of constitutional significance resulting from the application of Georgia's capital sentencing procedures; our role is not to peer majestically over the lower court's shoulder so that we might second-guess its interpretations of facts that quite reasonably — perhaps even quite plainly — fit within the statutory language.

Who is to say that the murders of Mrs. Godfrey and Mrs. Wilkerson were not "vile," or "inhuman," or "horrible"? In performing his murderous chore, petitioner employed a weapon known for its disfiguring effects on targets, human or other, and he succeeded in creating a scene so macabre and revolting that, if anything, "vile," "horrible," and "inhuman" are descriptively inadequate.

And who among us can honestly say that Mrs. Wilkerson did not feel "torture" in her last sentient moments. Her daughter, an instant ago a living being sitting across the table from Mrs. Wilkerson, lay prone on the floor, a bloodied and mutilated corpse. The seconds ticked by; enough time for her son-in-law to reload his gun, to enter the home, and to take a gratuitous swipe at his daughter. What terror must have run through her veins as she first witnessed her daughter's hideous demise and then came to terms with the imminence of her own. Was this not torture? And if this was not torture, can it honestly be said that petitioner did not exhibit a "depravity of mind" in carrying out this cruel drama to its mischievous and murderous conclusion? I should have thought, moreover, that the Georgia Court could reasonably have deemed the scene awaiting the investigating policemen as involving "an aggravated battery to the victim[s]."...

The point is not that, in my view, petitioner's crimes were definitively vile, horrible, or inhuman, or that, as I assay the evidence, they beyond *any* doubt involved torture, depravity of mind, or an aggravated battery to the victims. Rather, the lesson is a much more elementary one, an instruction that, I should have thought, this Court would have taken to heart long ago. Our mandate does not extend to interfering with factfinders in state criminal proceedings or with state courts that are responsibly and consistently interpreting state law, unless that interference is predicated on a violation of the Constitution. No convincing showing of such a violation is made here, for, as MR. JUSTICE STEWART has written in another place, the issue here is not what *our* verdict would have been, but whether "any rational factfinder" could have found the existence of aggravating circumstances § (b)(7). *Jackson* v. *Virginia* (1979). Faithful adherence to this standard of review compels our affirmance of the judgment below.

V

Under the present statutory regime, adopted in response to *Furman,* the Georgia Supreme Court has responsibly and consistently performed its review function pursuant to the Georgia capital-sentencing procedures. The State reports that, at the time its brief was written, the Georgia Supreme Court had reviewed some 99 cases in which the death penalty has been imposed. Of these, 66 had been affirmed; 5 had been reversed for errors in the guilt phase; and 22 had been reversed for errors in the sentencing phase.... This reversal rate of over 27% is not substantially lower than the historic reversal rate of state supreme courts....

The Georgia Supreme Court has also been responsible and consistent in its construction of § (b)(7). The provision has been the exclusive or nonexclusive basis for imposition of the death penalty in over 30 cases....

The majority's attempt to drive a wedge between this case and others in which § (b)(7) has been applied is thus unconvincing, as is any suggestion that the Georgia Supreme Court has somehow failed overall in performance of its review function.

VI

In the circumstances of this case, the majority today endorses the argument that I thought we had rejected in *Gregg*: namely, "that no matter how effective the death penalty may be as a punishment, government, created and run as it must be by humans, is inevitably incompetent to administer it.". . . The Georgia Supreme Court, faced with a seemingly endless train of macabre scenes, has endeavored in a responsible, rational, and consistent fashion to effectuate its statutory mandate as illuminated by our judgment in *Gregg*. Today, a majority of this Court, its arguments shredded by its own illogic, informs the Georgia Supreme Court that, to some extent, its efforts have been outside the Constitution. I reject this as an unwarranted invasion into the realm of state law, for, as in *Gregg,* "I decline to interfere with the manner in which Georgia has chosen to enforce [its] laws" until a genuine error of constitutional magnitude surfaces. . . .

I would affirm the judgment of the Supreme Court of Georgia.

▼▼▼

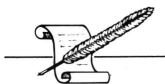 **HISTORIC DOCUMENTS OF 1980**

June

VANCE SPEECH AT HARVARD
June 5, 1980

Protesting the attempt to rescue 53 American hostages in Iran, Cyrus R. Vance resigned as secretary of state on April 28. In doing so, he became the first secretary of state to resign on a matter of principle in 60 years. Vance submitted his resignation to President Carter April 21, three days before the April 24 hostage rescue mission was launched, but acceded to Carter's request that he not make the resignation public until after the mission had been carried out.

Vance did not clearly state his specific objections to Carter's decision on the raid, but newspaper reports said he believed that the rescue mission — even if successful — was likely to antagonize American allies, destroy U.S. credibility in the Middle East and eliminate any possibility of eventual reconciliation with Iran. Carter also refused to enumerate Vance's objections but did say, at a press conference on April 29, that Vance had "preferred that we not take any kind of action inside Iran that might have had any connotation of a military nature." (Rescue mission, p. 351)

Impact of Resignation

The immediate effect of Vance's resignation was substantial. Vance had been known as a man of moderate views unwilling to air in public his differences, if any, with his superiors.

By profession a corporation lawyer, Vance also had a career in government marked by solid achievement. He served during the 1960s as secretary of the army and as deputy secretary of defense. In 1968-69 he was U.S. negotiator at the Paris Peace Conference on Vietnam.

In his letter of resignation, he told Carter that while his support remained strong "on other issues," he could not support the decision on the attempted rescue mission.

Vance waited until June 5 before making a public appearance. Then, as the principal speaker at Harvard University commencement exercises, he covered an array of international and domestic issues but avoided direct criticism of the president.

Muskie Nomination

Vance's resignation had threatened to unravel the shaky congressional and public support for Carter's policy toward Iran. But the surprise nomination of Sen. Edmund S. Muskie, D-Maine, on April 29 to succeed Vance quelled congressional opposition. Taking the spotlight away from Carter's troubles, the appointment showed that the president could still attract influential leaders to his administration. Muskie, 66, a senator since 1959, was a former Democratic vice presidential nominee and an unsuccessful presidential contender in 1972. He had been chairman of the Senate Budget Committee since its creation in 1975. Before that, he had served on the Foreign Relations Committee, heading a subcommittee on arms control. A supporter of the Strategic Arms Limitation Treaty (SALT) with the Soviet Union, Muskie resumed a seat on the Foreign Relations Committee in 1979.

The appointment was expected to please America's major allies, concerned about perceived vacillating in Carter's foreign policy and distressed by Vance's resignation. Muskie had a reputation as a moderate with views on East-West issues closer to the cooperative approach of Vance than to the more hard-line views of Zbigniew K. Brzezinski, Carter's national security adviser.

Harvard Speech

Vance's speech at Harvard was called "a summing up of a long career" by James Reston, a New York Times columnist. The former secretary of state listed the preservation of the global military balance, strong alliances among free nations, support for the independence and economic growth of poorer nations and a strong U.S. economy in a strong international economy as challenges facing the United States in the 1980s.

He specifically urged ratification of the U.S.-Soviet SALT II treaty limiting nuclear arms. Calling the treaty "the very heart of a sensible and far-seeing American foreign policy," he said it should be approved despite the December 1979 Soviet invasion of Afghanistan. (Afghanistan invasion, Historic Documents of 1979, p. 965)

If the SALT treaty were not ratified, Vance said, non-nuclear nations would have more reason to develop their own nuclear capabilities, both superpowers would have more nuclear weapons in the future and "there is bound to be less emphasis placed in both of our societies on conciliation of differences without conflict."

Vance said the United States should continue its "firm and sustained response" to the invasion of Afghanistan, but that neither Soviet aggression nor election year "considerations of the moment" should prevent Senate approval of the treaty. The former secretary of state added, "It is far too easy, in an election year, to let what may seem smart politics produce bad policies."

Following are excerpts from former Secretary of State Cyrus R. Vance's June 5, 1980, speech at Harvard University, calling for Senate approval of the SALT II treaty. (Boldface headings in brackets have been added by Congressional Quarterly to highlight the organization of the text.):

Yours is the first Harvard class to graduate in the decade of the 1980's. The decisions our nation makes now will shape the future of that decade.

We can either work to shape, in a wise and effective manner, the changes that now engulf our world or, by acting unwisely, become shackled by them.

It is a time to set and stick to basic goals. Neither we nor the world can afford an American foreign policy which is hostage to the emotions of the moment.

We must have in our minds a conception of the world we want a decade hence. The 1990 we seek must shape our actions in 1980, or the decisions of 1980 could give us a 1990 we will regret.

[Foreign Policy Goals]

Supporting the efforts of third world nations to preserve their independence and to improve the quality of life for their people, particularly those hovering at the edge of survival; strengthening the health and well-being of our economic system within a strong international economy.

These are the decisions, along with preserving the military balance while effectively managing our competition with the Soviet Union and fostering strong alliances of free nations — these are the decisions we should make now.

These goals are ambitious. It would be naive to think otherwise. But unless our reach is bold, our grasp will fall far short. . . .

There is a disturbing fear in the land that we are no longer capable of shaping our future. Some believe that we have lost our military muscle; others worry that our political will has been sapped.

I do not accept this gloom. It discards the abiding pragmatic philosophy that has characterized America ever since its founding.

I consider mistaken the view that we and we alone are responsible for all the confusing changes that we see around us. This is a serious misreading of our condition, a perverted hubris that overestimates our power and our responsibility for ill and underestimates our capacity for good.

The international diffusion of power and intellect is a fact. It will not change. It requires fresh and vital forms of action, not regret and pining for supposed "good old days."

What is to be regretted is a reluctance to relate our basic purposes to these new conditions. Yesterday's answers will not provide tomorrow's solutions.

[Illusions Exploded]

It seems to me that much of the current dissatisfaction with the world and our role in it rests on certain fallacies. These illusions must be exploded before our nation can chart a coherent and determined course in foreign policy.

The first fallacy is that a single strategy — a master plan — will yield the answers to each and every foreign-policy decision we face. Whatever value that approach may have had in a bipolar world, it now serves us badly. The world has become pluralistic, exposing the inadequacy of the single strategy, the grand design, where facts are forced to fit theory. Given the complexity of the world to which we have fallen heir, the effect of a single strategy is to blur this complexity and to divide nations everywhere into friends and enemies.

[Fear of Negotiation]

A second widely accepted fallacy is the fear of negotiation, the worry that somehow we will always come out second best in any bargain. This fallacy assumes we have a realistic alternative of going it alone, of not bothering to recognize the legitimate interests and desires of other peoples. Without the fair bargain, achieved through negotiation and diplomacy, there is only a misguided, failed effort to impose one will upon another.

Denying others a fair bargain and its benefits will not alter their behavior or reduce their power; it will simply have the effect of denying ourselves the same advantages. If America fears to negotiate with our adversaries, or to bargain fairly with third world nations, we will not have a diplomacy. And we, no less than others, will be the loser.

A third myth that needs to be exploded is that there is an incompatibility between the pursuit of America's values in our foreign policy, such as human rights, and the pursuit of our interests.

Certainly the pursuit of human rights must be managed in a practical way. We must constantly weigh how best to encourage progress while maintaining an ability to conduct business with governments — even unpopular ones — in countries where we have important security interests. . . .

Further is the dangerous fallacy of the military solution to nonmilitary problems. It arises in particularly acute form at times of frustration, when the processes of negotiation are seen as slow-moving and tedious.

American military power is essential to maintaining the global military balance. Our defense forces must be modernized — and they will be. But increased military power is a basis, not a substitute, for diplomacy.

I have heard it argued that our response to a changing world must be a new emphasis on American military power and the will to use it. This is reflected in proposed new budget priorities in the Congress, in which unnecessary defense spending squeezes out domestic programs and foreign assistance. There is near-consensus on the need for defense increases. But it is illusion to believe that they are a substitute for the diplomacy and resources needed to address such problems as internal change and basic need in other nations or a battered international economy.

[Shaping the Future]

The use of military force is not, and should not be, a desirable American policy response to the internal politics of other nations. We believe we have the right to shape our future; we must respect that right in others. We must clearly understand the distinction between our readiness to act forcefully when the vital interests of our nation, our allies and our friends are threatened, and our recognition that our military force cannot provide a satisfactory answer to the purely internal problems of other nations.

Finally there is a pervasive fallacy that America could have the power to order the world just the way we want it to be. It assumes, for example, that we could dominate the Soviet Union — that we could prevent it from being a superpower — if we chose to do so. This obsolete idea has more to do with nostalgia than with present-day reality.

Spread over the widest territory of any nation on earth, the Soviet Union has its own strategic interests and goals. From a state of underdevelopment and the ravages of war, it has built formidable military and industrial resources. We should not underestimate these resources any more than we should exaggerate them. We must preserve and manage a position of essential equivalence with the Soviet Union. It is naive to believe that the Russians will play by our rules any more than we will accept theirs. It is naive to believe that they — any more than we — would willingly accept a position of second best in military strength.

[A 'New Nostalgia']

A dangerous new nostalgia underlies all these fallacies — a longing for earlier days when the world seemed, at least in retrospect, to have been a more orderly place in which American power could, alone, preserve that order. That nostalgia continually erodes confidence in our national leadership for it encourages expectations that bear no relationship to reality. And it makes change in the world's condition seem all threat and no opportunity. It makes an unruly world seem more hostile than it is. The fact is that we are a people who not only have adapted well to change but have thrived on it.

The new nostalgia leads us to simplistic solutions and go-it-alone illusions, diverting our energies from the struggle to shape change in constructive directions. It is self-indulgent nonsense, bound to lead us into error, if not disaster.

What course is open to us now?

Our real problems are long term in nature. It will not do to reach for the dramatic act, to seek to cut through stubborn dilemmas with a single stroke. Against the real problems now facing us this approach will not only fall short but also create new problems.

Obviously, immediate crises have to be dealt with as they occur. And we should learn from these events. But they should never be allowed to distort our foreign-policy goals.

As a global power the United States has an extraordinary range of interests. That is why we must make sure that our pursuit of the desirable does not interfere with our achievement of the essential.

If, by 1990, we have not made progress in the four basic areas I listed earlier, the world will indeed be the inhospitable place many now fear it is. In each area we can make progress — if. If we listen to our hopes no less than our fears. If we are prepared to sacrifice now for our future good. And, most important, if we work with other nations to resolve problems none can solve alone.

[Global Military Balance]

First, we must preserve the global military balance and achieve, as well, balance in our political relations with the Soviet Union.

Our military strength is important to our own safety, to a strong foreign policy free from coercion, to the confidence of allies and friends, and to the future of the reciprocal arms control and other negotiations. Our strength also buttresses regional balances that could be upset by the direct or indirect use of Soviet power.

Maintaining the military balance will be expensive. To limit the costs, and to increase our safety, we must have an effective arms-control policy as an integral part of our security policy.

Yet when the historian of 1990 looks back upon the year 1980, I believe a profound mistake may well be identified: a failure to ratify the SALT II treaty. As a symbol of our hopes for a more peaceful world, as a commitment to work toward better security through arms control and as a process of trying to work out differences with an adversary, this treaty stands at the very heart of a sensible and far-seeing American foreign policy.

Without this treaty our efforts to prevent the spread of nuclear weapons will be in jeopardy. If the United States and the Soviet Union fail to make real headway toward controlling nuclear weapons and eliminating nuclear testing, non-nuclear nations will have less reason for their own restraint.

Without this treaty both sides will have more nuclear weapons than with it. In particular, the Soviet Union will have thousands of additional nuclear warheads.

Without this treaty it will be much more difficult for us to undertake reliable planning for our military forces since we will not be in as good a position to know what is going on within the Soviet Union. The treaty bans practices that would prevent each side from being able to verify compliance with its terms.

[SALT II]

Without this treaty there is bound to be less emphasis placed in both of our societies on conciliation of differences without conflict. Political elements who wish to emphasize conflict over cooperation will be strengthened.

Without this treaty the process of arms control might be dealt a blow from which it could not recover. Can anyone doubt that this will make the coming decade more dangerous?

It is not too late, but it may soon be. I believe that the Senate must ratify the SALT II treaty before the end of this year. Certainly we must continue our firm and sustained response to Soviet aggression against Afghanistan. But neither that aggression nor the fact that this is a political year are sufficient grounds for a failure to act in our own national interests. I am aware of the political difficulties in acting at this time. But if we fail to act we will someday ask ourselves why we were blinded by considerations of the moment and lost a vital long-term opportunity. It is far too easy, in an election year, to let what may seem smart politics produce bad policies.

Both the United States and the Soviet Union will have to work even harder in the years ahead to avoid extremely serious confrontations. How we conduct our relations with the Soviet Union will perhaps be the most significant test of our maturity of judgment, our clearsighted recognition of real interests and our capacity for leadership.

[Incentives for Peace]

It is foolish and dangerous to believe that we can manage this relationship by deterrence alone. We also will need to provide positive incentives.

We must use both our strength and the prospects of mutually beneficial agremeents to help shape competition with the Soviet Union. We must work for implicit if not explicit agreements to bound our competition by restraints, by a kind of common law of competition.

The means to implement this goal will rest on patience, steadiness, clarity and consistency. In our approach toward Moscow we cannot afford wild swings from being too trusting to being hysterical. And even as we maintain a steady course we must recognize that it will require constant effort to mold that common law of competition. That effort must include both deterrence and the possibility of cooperation where our interests coincide.

We must also think anew about how to manage our affairs with the People's Republic of China in relation to those with the Soviet Union. Even as we act to develop non-military ties with China we should strive to restore a more balanced approach to both countries.

[Strong Alliances]

A second and paramount goal for our nation should be to nurture strong alliances among free nations.

But there is no gainsaying that relations among the industrial democracies are uneasy. We must address the causes for this; they may well be more fundamental in origin than we care to admit.

We must find better ways to coordinate our policies in areas beyond our territories, for it is there that we increasingly face new problems. While our immediate interests may sometimes diverge in such areas, our basic interests run in parallel and, accordingly, should provide grounds for common action.

Our allies must recognize that while the American nuclear shield is unshakeable and our commitment to the common defense is firm, they cannot expect America to bear a disproportionate share of the burdens of deterrence. . . .

[Cockpit of Crises]

Partly because of the strength of our alliances, it is the third world — more than our alliance areas — that is likely to be the cockpit of crises in the coming decade.

We must first be clear on the nature of our challenge there.

Certainly, as we have seen in Afghanistan and elsewhere in the third world, Soviet actions pose threats we must meet.

But we will meet them ineffectually if we react only by imitating Soviet tactics — emphasizing the military at the expense of the political and disregarding the indigenous yearning of third world nations for true independence and economic justice. . . .

If we are prepared to accept the implications of a world of diffuse power, and work with others where we cannot succeed alone, there need be no insurmountable barriers to our progress.

There should be no mystery about how to manage East-West relations with realism and prudence, creating more cooperative alliances, addressing the problems of third world nations and acting now to strengthen our economy for later.

The mystery will be for the historian of 1990, if — blinded by the new nostalgia — we fail now to shape our future. The puzzle will be why we reacted against change in the world and did not seek to shape it. The historian will then conclude that ours was a failure not of opportunity but of seeing opportunity; a failure not of resources but of the wisdom to use them; a failure not of intellect but of understanding and of will.

It need not be so. For now, as always before, our destiny is in our hands.

CENSURE OF REP. WILSON

May 8; June 10, 1980

The U.S. House of Representatives censured Rep. Charles H. Wilson, D-Calif., June 10 after the House Committee on Standards of Official Conduct found that Wilson had improperly converted almost $25,000 in campaign funds to his personal use and accepted $10,500 worth of personal gifts from an individual who had a direct interest in legislation pending in Congress. The Standards Committee submitted its report May 8.

The House action came just one week after Wilson was defeated in his primary bid for re-election. As a result of the censure, he was stripped of his chairmanship of the House Post Office Subcommittee on Postal Operations for the remainder of the 96th Congress. Immediately following the vote, Wilson was summoned to the front of the chamber and the Speaker of the House of Representatives, Thomas P. O'Neill Jr., D-Mass., read the censure resolution to him. Wilson then walked out of the chamber.

Earlier Reprimand

This was not the first time the California Democrat had been chastised by his colleagues. In October 1978 Wilson was reprimanded by the House when he admitted — after first denying — that he had received wedding presents, including $600 in cash, from Tongsun Park, the South Korean businessman and lobbyist (Historic Documents of 1978, p. 845). Wilson was the third member of the House to be censured in the 20th century. His contemporary, Rep. Charles C. Diggs Jr., D-Mich., was censured July 31, 1979, for misuse of office funds (Historic Documents of 1979, p. 623). And

Rep. Thomas L. Blanton, D-Texas, was censured in 1921 after he had objectionable language published in the Congressional Record.

In cases of alleged official misconduct, the House is empowered to reprimand, censure, fine or expel a member. One member, Michael J. "Ozzie" Myers, D-Pa., was expelled in 1980 after being convicted in connection with the Abscam scandal. (See p. 899)

Originally scheduled for May 21, the vote on the resolution to censure Wilson was postponed twice, first to May 29 to allow Wilson's attorneys time to prepare their defense, and then to June 10 to permit time to study additional evidence disclosed May 29. The new evidence consisted of two statements filed by Wilson with the California secretary of state attesting that he had borrowed no money during his 1970 congressional campaign. During hearings before the Standards Committee, Wilson's lawyers had claimed that their client had used campaign funds to repay campaign loans. The Standards Committee staff maintained that the loans paid off with campaign money were of a personal nature.

Wilson Statement

During the House debate on the censure resolution, Wilson took the floor to proclaim his innocence. Referring to his defeat in the primary election, Wilson said, "I suppose I could have walked away from this whole thing. But I cannot because this resolution brands me as something I am not." He added, "I realize I am not a popular member of this House. But I don't think that your vote on this matter should be based on whether I am a popular member or not. It should be based on right and wrong."

> *Following are excerpts from the House Standards of Official Conduct Committee's May 8, 1980, report (H Rept 96-930) on Rep. Charles H. Wilson, D-Calif., and the text of the resolution (H Res 660) censuring Wilson, approved on a voice vote by the House June 10, 1980:*

WILSON CENSURE REPORT

Introduction and Background

During the course of the Korean Influence Investigation conducted pursuant to H. Res. 252, 95th Congress, the Special Staff conducting the inquiry (under the direction of Leon Jaworski, Esq.) became aware of possible violations of House Rules by Representative Charles H. Wilson of California.

Since the possible violations were not directly related to the scope of the Korean Influence Investigation, the matters were pursued only as far as necessary for the purposes of that particular investigation.

The Korean Influence Investigation terminated with the close of the 95th Congress and the matters were left unresolved.

On February 7, 1979, at the organizational meeting of the Committee on Standards of Official Conduct for the 96th Congress, Chairman Charles E. Bennettt appointed a two-member subcommittee, of Representative John M. Slack and Representative F. James Sensenbrenner, Jr. to conduct a study of possible violations of House Rules by Representative Wilson.

On November 28, 1979, after a brief summary of the evidence, the Committee adopted a Motion to Conduct an Inquiry. . . .

Prior to adopting the Motion to Conduct an Inquiry, the Committee requested that Representative Wilson appear in executive session to testify about the various possible violations. Representative Wilson, through counsel, declined to comply with the Committee's request.

On December 12, 1979, the Committee, in executive session, heard an unsworn statement from Representative Wilson and argument from his counsel respecting the Motion to Conduct an Inquiry. At the conclusion of the meeting the Committee agreed to a Statement of Alleged Violations against Representative Wilson by a vote of 7 to 2.

Mr. Wilson thereupon asked for full discovery of the Committee's evidence and Committee counsel was instructed to make available for inspection by Representative Wilson all documentary evidence in the possession of the Committee.

Comprised of 15 counts, the Statement of Alleged Violations alleged generally that Representative Wilson received gifts of substantial value from a person with a direct interest in legislation (a violation of House Rule XLIII, clause 4), under circumstances which might be construed by a reasonable person as influencing the performance of his governmental duties (a violation of the Code of Ethics for Government Service, clause 5), and, in so doing, reflected discredit upon the House of Representatives (a violation of House Rule XLIII, clause 1). In addition, the Statement alleged that Representative Wilson caused to be hired on his clerk-hire payroll a person whose salary was not commensurate with duties performed (a violation of House Rule XLIII, clause 8), and that Representative Wilson commingled campaign funds with personal funds and converted campaign funds to personal use in excess of allowed reimbursable amounts (violations of House rule XLIII, clause 6).

The Statement of Alleged Violations also charged that Representative Wilson gave an earlier false statement under oath to the Committee concerning the conversion of campaign funds to personal use. . . .

Representative Wilson submitted an Answer to the Statement of Alleged Violations on February 13, 1980, denying each of the counts and alleged various unspecified violations of House Rules by the Committee.

On February 26, 1980, the Committee adopted a Scope and Purpose for a Disciplinary Hearing pursuant to Committee Rule of Procedure 16(c), and scheduled the disciplinary hearing for March 25, 1980.

The date of the disciplinary hearing was subsequently rescheduled for March 31, 1980, due to the death of Representative John M. Slack. . . .

The disciplinary hearing In The Matter of Representative Charles H. Wilson commenced at 10:30 a.m. on Monday, March 31, 1980. . . .

At the disciplinary hearing Representative Wilson was afforded the opportunity, through counsel, to cross-examine witnesses called by the Committee counsel and call witnesses and offer evidence in his own behalf.

At the conclusion of the presentation of testimony and evidence by the Committee counsel and counsel for Representative Wilson, on April 1, 1980, the Committee recessed subject to a call of the chair, in order to afford the Members time to study the transcript of the hearing.

On April 16, 1980, the Committee reconvened the disciplinary hearing with the presentation of closing arguments by the Committee counsel and counsel for Representative Wilson.

At the conclusion of the arguments on April 16, 1980, the Committee immediately began deliberations in executive session and later in the day released its findings and votes thereon.

Findings

. . . In substance the Committee found in counts one through three that Representative Wilson received over a period of time a total of $10,500 from a person with a direct interest in legislation before the Congress, in violation of House Rule XLIII, clause 4, and, in so doing, reflected discredit upon the House of Representatives, in violation of House Rule XLIII, clause 1.

The payments in counts 1 and 2, contrary to the assertions of Mr. Rogers, and despite the fact that the checks were marked "loan", were found not to be true loans. In making this determination the Committee placed particular emphasis on the accepted connotation of the term "loan" as implying a temporary obligation.

The Committee determined that the permanent nature of these transactions, along with the absence of any of the normal indicia of a loan, such as a written loan agreement or note, interest, maturity date, demand or offer of repayment, proved clearly and convincingly that these payments were in fact not loans, but improper gifts.

In reaching this conclusion, the Committee also noted that Representative Wilson had an affirmative duty to report all personal liabilities which exceeded $2,500 as of the close of calendar year 1977 on the Financial Disclosure Statement filed with the Clerk of the House on April 24, 1978, pursuant to House Rule XLIV. . . .

This document disclosed that Representative Wilson had not reported any obligations or liabilities owed to Mr. Lee Rogers as would have been required had the payments in fact been loans.

The Committee additionally found that the evidence proved clearly and convincingly not only that Mr. Rogers, the donor, had a direct interest in legislation before the Congress, but also that Representative Wilson was aware of this interest when he accepted these gifts. . . .

The Committee further found that, in accepting these gifts of substantial value from a person having a direct interest in legislation before the Congress, Representative Wilson also reflected discredit upon the House of Representatives in violation of House Rule XLIII, clause 1.

The findings in counts one, two, and three (1, 2, 3) are considered of a most serious nature by the Committee, as they establish the special interest of the donor in matters over which the donee had influence by virtue of his position in the U.S. Congress. . . .

As to other counts, the Committee found that the evidence introduced at the hearing in support of counts seven, eight, and nine (7, 8, 9), proved clearly and convincingly that Representative Wilson had caused funds raised and accounted for as campaign funds to be transferred from his campaign account into his office account, upon which checks were drawn on the same day to repay personal (Rep. Wilson's) bank loans in the following respective amounts: $10,283.35, $5,129.85, and $3,047.91.

The Committee concluded in count ten (10) that Representative Wilson had caused $3,500 to be transferred from his campaign account into his office account, upon which a check was drawn on the same day, in a like amount, and deposited into Rep. Wilson's personal account at the Sergeant at Arms to cover outstanding personal obligations against that account. At the time, the balance in Rep. Wilson's personal account was insufficient to cover the checks outstanding in that account.

Finally, the Committee determined in count eleven (11) that the evidence proved clearly and convincingly that Rep. Wilson had caused $3,000 in campaign funds to be transferred into his personal account at the Sergeant at Arms to cover outstanding personal obligations against that account. At the time, the balance in Rep. Wilson's personal account was insufficient to cover the checks outstanding in that account.

House Rule XLIII, clause 6, read at all times pertinent to counts 7, 8, 9, 10, and 11, as follows:

> 6. A Member of the House of Representatives shall keep his campaign funds separate from his personal funds. He shall convert no campaign funds to personal use in excess of reimbursement for legitimate and verifiable prior campaign expenditures. He shall expend no funds from his campaign account not attributable to bona fide campaign purposes.

In order to sustain a charge alleging a conversion in violation of clause 6 it must be proved that the expenditures were not for reimbursement for legitimate prior campaign expenditures, and that the funds were in fact applied to personal use.

On the basis of the evidence introduced at the disciplinary hearing, the Committee concluded that it had been proved by at least a clear and convincing standard that the transfers from Representative Wilson's campaign account were neither intended as, nor did they represent valid reimbursements for campaign expenditures, which are proper under House Rule XLIII, clause 6.

The Committee further concluded that these transfers were made to repay personal loans of Representative Wilson and to cover outstanding obligations against his personal checking account at the Sergeant of Arms. . . .

Recommendation

. . . In determining the sanctions to recommend, the Committee carefully considered not only the nature and severity of each individual count proved, but also the offense represented by the total of these counts. The full range of sanctions available to the House was considered by the Committee.

The severity of the improper conduct was carefully weighed against past actions of the House in sanctioning Members for improper conduct and the guidelines for the recommendation of sanctions which are contained in Rule 17 of the Committee Rules of Procedure. The applicable text of the Rule reads as follows:

(b) (1) With respect to any violation with which a Member of the House was charged in a count which the Committee has voted as proved, the Committee may include in its recommendation to the House one or more of the following sanctions:

(A) Expulsion from the House.

(B) Censure.

(C) Reprimand.

(D) Fine.

(E) Denial or limitation of any right, power, privilege, or immunity of the Member if under the Constitution the House may impose such denial or limitation.

(F) Any other sanction determined by the Committee to be appropriate.

(c) (1) The purpose of this clause is to inform the Members of the House of Representatives as to the general guidelines the Committee considers appropriate for determining which, if any, sanctions to recommend to the House respecting violations proved in a disciplinary hearing. This clause does not limit the authority of the Committee to make or not to make recommendations for such sanctions.

(2) For technical violations, the Committee may direct that the violation be reported to the House without a recommendation for a sanction.

(3) With respect to the sanctions which the Committee may determine to include in a recommendation to the House respecting a violation, reprimand is appropriate for serious violations, censure is appropriate for more serious violations, and expulsion of a Member or dismissal of an officer or employee is appropriate for the most serious violations. A recommendation of a fine is appropriate in a case in which it is likely that the violation was committed to secure a financial benefit; and a recommendation of a denial or limitation

of a right, power, privilege, or immunity of a Member is appropriate when the violation bears upon the exercise or holding of such right, power, privilege, or immunity.

A majority of the Committee then determined that, in light of the nature and severity of Representative Wilson's improper conduct, the appropriate sanction would be censure and a denial of the chair on any Committee or Subcommittee for the remainder of the 96th Congress.

In recommending that Representative Wilson be denied the chair on any Committee or Subcommittee of the House for the remainder of the 96th Congress, it is the intention of the Committee that Representative Wilson be immediately removed from the chairmanship of any Committee or Subcommittee of the House, that he be ineligible to hold any such position for the remainder of the 96th Congress, and, in the absence of the chairman of any Committee or Subcommittee, that Representative Wilson not be allowed to assume the duties of the chair.

Accordingly, on a motion by Representative F. James Sensenbrenner, Jr., the Committee, by a vote of 10 ayes and 2 nays, agreed to recommend that the House adopt the following Resolution.

HOUSE RESOLUTION 660

Resolved:

(1) That Representative Charles H. Wilson be censured;

(2) That Representative Charles H. Wilson be denied the chair on any Committee or Subcommittee of the House of Representatives for the remainder of the 96th Congress;

(3) That upon adoption of this Resolution, Representative Charles H. Wilson forthwith present himself in the well of the House of Representative for the public reading of this Resolution by the Speaker; and

(4) That the House of Representatives adopt the Report of the Committee on Standards of Official Conduct dated May 8, 1980, In The Matter of Representative Charles H. Wilson.

COURT ON PATENTING OF LIVING ORGANISMS

June 16, 1980

The Supreme Court held June 16 that living organisms were patentable under existing U.S. law. The decision was expected to spur the development of a small but growing genetic engineering industry.

The immediate result of the 5-4 decision in the case, Diamond v. Chakrabarty, *was to permit a microbiologist working for the General Electric Co. to obtain a patent on a bacterium he had produced that could break down crude oil. The product was seen as useful in cleaning up oil spills.*

Writing for the slim majority, Chief Justice Warren E. Burger argued that the scientist's bacterium was a "manufacture, or composition of matter" and so could be patented. The bacterium, the chief justice explained, had markedly different characteristics from anything found in nature.

Majority Opinion

Arguing that living things were not patentable, the U.S. government relied on laws enacted in 1930 and 1970. While specifically authorizing the patenting of artificially bred plants, those laws excluded bacteria from their reach. Burger argued, however, that the patent laws distinguished between products of nature and products of human invention, not between living and inanimate things. The majority in the case included, besides Chief Justice Burger, Justices Potter Stewart, Harry A. Blackmun, William H. Rehnquist and John Paul Stevens.

Dissenting Views

Dissenting were Justices William J. Brennan Jr., Byron R. White, Thurgood Marshall and Lewis F. Powell Jr. Writing for the dissenters, Brennan said that the 1970 patent law indicated that Congress had included bacteria "within the focus of its legislative concern, but not within the scope of patent protection. . . . It is the role of Congress, not this Court, to broaden or narrow the reach of patent laws. . . ."

> *Following are excerpts from the Supreme Court's decision in* Diamond v. Chakrabarty, *June 16, 1980, holding that living micro-organisms, man-made, constituted a "manufacture" or "composition of matter" under existing U.S. patent law; and Justice Brennan's dissenting opinion:*

No. 79-136

————

Sidney A. Diamond, Commissioner
of Patents and Trademarks,
Petitioner,
v.
Ananda M. Chakrabarty et al.

On Writ of Certiorari to the
United States Court of Customs
and Patent Appeals.

[June 16, 1980]

MR. CHIEF JUSTICE BURGER delivered the opinion of the Court.

We granted certiorari to determine whether a live, human-made micro-organism is patentable subject matter under 35 U.S.C. § 101.

I

In 1972, respondent Chakrabarty, a microbiologist, filed a patent application, assigned to the General Electric Company. The application asserted 36 claims related to Chakrabarty's invention of "a bacterium from the genus *Pseudomonas* containing therein at least two stable energy-generating plasmids, each of said plasmids providing a separate hydrocarbon degradative pathway."[1] This human-made, genetically engineered bacterium is capable of breaking down multiple components of crude oil. Because of this property, which is possessed by no naturally occurring bacteria, Chakrabarty's invention is believed to have significant value for the treatment of oil spills.[2]

————

[1] Plasmids are hereditary units physically separate from the chromosomes of the cell. In prior research, Chakrabarty and an associate discovered that

Chakrabarty's patent claims were of three types: first, process claims for the method of producing the bacteria; second, claims for an inoculum comprised of a carrier material floating on water, such as straw, and the new bacteria; and third, claims to the bacteria themselves. The patent examiner allowed the claims falling into the first two categories, but rejected claims for the bacteria. His decision rested on two grounds: (1) that micro-organisms are "products of nature," and (2) that as living things they are not patentable subject matter under 35 U.S.C. § 101. . . .

II

The Constitution grants Congress broad power to legislate to "promote the Progress of Science and the useful Arts, by securing for limited times to authors and inventors the exclusive right to their respective writings and discoveries." Art. I, § 8. The patent laws promote this progress by offering inventors exclusive rights for a limited period as an incentive for their inventiveness and research efforts. *Kewanee Oil Co.* v. *Bicron Corp.* (1974); *Universal Oil Co.* v. *Globe Co.* (1944). . . .

The question before us in this case is a narrow one of statutory interpretation requiring us to construe 35 U.S.C. § 101, which provides:

"Whoever invents or discovers any new and useful process, machine, manufacture, or composition of matter, or any new and useful improvement thereof, may obtain a patent therefor, subject to the conditions and requirements of this title."

Specifically, we must determine whether respondent's micro-organism constitutes a "manufacture" or "composition of matter" within the meaning of the statute.

III

In cases of statutory construction we begin, of course, with the language of the statute. *Southeastern Community College* v. *Davis* (1979). And

---

plasmids control the oil degradation abilities of certain bacteria. In particular, the two researchers discovered plasmids capable of degrading camphor and octane, two components of crude oil. In the work represented by the patent application at issue here, Chakrabarty discovered a process by which four different plasmids, capable of degrading four different oil components, could be transferred to and maintained stably in a single *Pseudomonas* bacteria, which itself has no capacity for degrading oil.

[2] At present, biological control of oil spills requires the use of a mixture of naturally occurring bacteria, each capable of degrading one component of the oil complex. In this way, oil is decomposed into simpler substances which can serve as food for aquatic life. However, for various reasons, only a portion of any such mixed culture survives to attack the oil spill. By breaking down multiple components of oil, Chakrabarty's micro-organism promises more efficient and rapid oil-spill control.

"unless otherwise defined, words will be interpreted as taking their ordinary, contemporary, common meaning." *Perrin* v. *United States* (1979). We have also cautioned that courts "should not read into the patent laws limitations and conditions which the legislature has not expressed." *United States* v. *Dubilier Condenser Corp.* (1933).

Guided by these canons of construction, this Court has read the term "manufacture" in § 101 in accordance with its dictionary definition to mean "the production of articles for use from raw materials prepared by giving to these materials new forms, qualities, properties, or combinations whether by hand labor or by machinery." *American Fruit Growers, Inc.* v. *Brogdex Co.* (1931). Similarly, "composition of matter" has been construed consistent with its common usage to include "all compositions of two or more substances and ... all composite articles, whether they be the results of chemical union, or of mechanical mixture, or whether they be gases, fluids, powders, or solids." *Shell Dev. Co.* v. *Watson* (DC 1957).... In choosing such expansive terms as "manufacture" and "composition of matter," modified by the comprehensive "any," Congress plainly contemplated that the patent laws would be given wide scope....

This is not to suggest that § 101 has no limits or that it embraces every discovery. The laws of nature, physical phenomena, and abstract ideas have been held not patentable. See *Parker* v. *Flook* (1978); *Gottschalk* v. *Benson* (1973); *Funk Seed Co.* v. *Kalo Co.* (1948); *O'Reilly* v. *Morse* (1853); *Le Roy* v. *Tatham* (1852). Thus, a new mineral discovered in the earth or a new plant found in the wild is not patentable subject matter. Likewise, Einstein could not patent his celebrated law that $E = mc^2$; nor could Newton have patented the law of gravity. Such discoveries are "manifestations of ... nature, free to all men and reserved exclusively to none." *Funk.* ...

Judged in this light, respondent's micro-organism plainly qualifies as patentable subject matter. His claim is not to a hitherto unknown natural phenomenon, but to a nonnaturally occurring manufacture or composition of matter — a product of human ingenuity "having a distinctive name, character [and] use." *Hartranft* v. *Wiegmann* (1887). The point is underscored dramatically by comparison of the invention here with that in *Funk*. There, the patentee had discovered that there existed in nature certain species of root-nodule bacteria which did not exert a mutually inhibitive effect on each other. He used that discovery to produce a mixed culture capable of inoculating the seeds of leguminous plants. Concluding that the patentee had discovered "only some of the handiwork of nature," the Court ruled the product nonpatentable. ... Here, by contrast, the patentee has produced a new bacterium with markedly different characteristics from any found in nature and one having the potential for significant utility. His discovery is not nature's handiwork, but his own; accordingly it is patentable subject matter under § 101.

IV

Two contrary arguments are advanced, neither of which we find persuasive.

(A)

The Government's first argument rests on the enactment of the 1930 Plant Patent Act, which afforded patent protection to certain asexually reproduced plants, and the 1970 Plant Variety Protection Act, which authorized patents for certain sexually reproduced plants but excluded bacteria from its protection. In the Government's view, the passage of these Acts evidences congressional understanding that the terms "manufacture" or "composition of matter" do not include living things; if they did, the Government argues, neither Act would have been necessary.

We reject this argument. Prior to 1930, two factors were thought to remove plants from patent protection. The first was the belief that plants, even those artificially bred, were products of nature for purposes of the patent law. This position appears to have derived from the decision of the Patent Office in *Ex parte Latimer,* 1889, in which a patent claim for fiber found in the needle of the *Pinus australis* was rejected. The Commissioner reasoned that a contrary result would permit "patents [to] be obtained upon the trees of the forests and the plants of the earth, which of course would be unreasonable and impossible.". . . The *Latimer* case, it seems, came to "set[] forth the general stand taken in these matters" that plants were natural products not subject to patent protection. H. Thorne, Relation of Patent Law to Natural Products (1923). The second obstacle to patent protection for plants was the fact that plants were thought not amenable to the "written description" requirement of the patent law. . . . Because new plants may differ from old only in color or perfume, differentiation by written description was often impossible. . . .

In enacting the Plant Patent Act, Congress addressed both of these concerns. It explained at length its belief that the work of the plant breeder "in aid of nature" was patentable invention. . . . And it relaxed the written description requirement in favor of "a description . . . as complete as is reasonably possible.". . . No Committee or Member of Congress, however, expressed the broader view, now urged by the Government, that the terms "manufacture" or "composition of matter" exclude living things. The sole support for that position in the legislative history of the 1930 Act is found in the conclusory statement of Secretary of Agriculture Hyde, in a letter to the Chairmen of the House and Senate committees considering the 1930 Act, that "the patent laws . . . at the present time are understood to cover only inventions or discoveries in the field of inanimate nature.". . . Secretary Hyde's opinion, however, is not entitled to controlling weight. His views were solicited on the administration of the new law and not on the scope of patentable subject matter — an area beyond his competence. Moreover, there is language in the House and Senate Committee reports suggesting that to the extent Congress considered the matter it found the Secretary's dichotomy unpersuasive.... Congress thus recognized that the relevant distinction was not between living and inanimate things, but between products of nature, whether living or not, and human-made inventions. Here, respondent's micro-organism is the result of human ingenuity and research. Hence, the passage of the Plant Patent Act affords the Government no support.

Nor does the passage of the 1970 Plant Variety Protection Act support the Government's position. As the Government acknowledges, sexually reproduced plants were not included under the 1930 Act because new varieties could not be reproduced true-to-type through seedlings.... By 1970, however, it was generally recognized that true-to-type reproduction was possible and that plant patent protection was therefore appropriate. The 1970 Act extended that protection. There is nothing in its language or history to suggest that it was enacted because § 101 did not include living things.

In particular, we find nothing in the exclusion of bacteria from plant variety protection to support the Government's position.... The legislative history gives no reason for this exclusion. As the Court of Customs and Patent Appeals suggested, it may simply reflect congressional agreement with the result reached by that court in deciding *In re Arzberger* (1940), which held that bacteria were not plants for the purposes of the 1930 Act. Or it may reflect the fact that prior to 1970 the Patent Office had issued patents for bacteria under § 101. In any event, absent some clear indication that Congress "focused on [the] issues ... directly related to the one presently before the Court," *SEC* v. *Sloan* (1978), there is no basis for reading into its actions an intent to modify the plain meaning of the words found in § 101. *See TVA* v. *Hill* (1978); *United States* v. *Price* (1960).

(B)

The Government's second argument is that micro-organisms cannot qualify as patentable subject matter until Congress expressly authorizes such protection. Its position rests on the fact that genetic technology was unforeseen when Congress enacted § 101. From this it is argued that resolution of the patentability of inventions such as respondent's should be left to Congress. The legislative process, the Government argues, is best equipped to weigh the competing economic, social, and scientific considerations involved, and to determine whether living organisms produced by genetic engineering should receive patent protection. In support of this position, the Government relies on our recent holding in *Parker* v. *Flook* (1978), and the statement that the judiciary "must proceed cautiously when ... asked to extend patent rights into areas wholly unforeseen by Congress.". . .

It is, of course, correct that Congress, not the courts, must define the limits of patentability; but it is equally true that once Congress has spoken it is "the province and duty of the judicial department to say what the law is." *Marbury* v. *Madison* (1803). Congress has performed its constitutional role in defining patentable subject matter in § 101; we perform ours in construing the language Congress has employed. In so doing, our obligation is to take statutes as we find them, guided, if ambiguity appears, by the legislative history and statutory purpose. Here, we perceive no ambiguity. The subject matter provisions of the patent law have been cast in broad terms to fulfill the constitutional and statutory goal of promoting "the Progress of Science and the useful Arts" with all that means for the social and economic benefits envisioned by [Thomas] Jefferson. Broad general language is not necessarily ambiguous when congressional objectives require broad terms.

Nothing in *Flook* is to the contrary. That case applied our prior precedents to determine that a "claim for an improved method of calculation, even when tied to a specific end use, is unpatentable subject matter under § 101.". . . The Court carefully scrutinized the claim at issue to determine whether it was precluded from patent protection under "the principles underlying the prohibition against patents for 'ideas' or phenomena of nature.". . . We have done that here. *Flook* did not announce a new principle that inventions in areas not contemplated by Congress where the patent laws were enacted are unpatentable *per se*.

To read that concept into *Flook* would frustrate the purposes of the patent law. This Court frequently has observed that a statute is not to be confined to the "particular application[s] . . . contemplated by the legislators." *Barr* v. *United States* (1945). Accord, *Browder* v. *United States* (1941); *Puerto Rico* v. *Shell Co.* (1937). This is especially true in the field of patent law. A rule that unanticipated inventions are without protection would conflict with the core concept of the patent law that anticipation undermines patentability. . . . *Graham* v. *John Deere Co.* . . . [1966]. Mr. Justice Douglas reminded that the inventions most benefiting mankind are those that "push back the frontiers of chemistry, physics, and the like." *A. & P. Tea Co.* v. *Supermarket Corp.* (1950). . . . Congress employed broad general language in drafting § 101 precisely because such inventions are often unforeseeable.

To buttress its argument, the Government, with the support of *amicus*, points to grave risks that may be generated by research endeavors such as respondent's. The briefs present a gruesome parade of horribles. Scientists, among them Nobel laureates, are quoted suggesting that genetic research may pose a serious threat to the human race, or, at the very least, that the dangers are far too substantial to permit such research to proceed apace at this time. We are told that genetic research and related technological developments may spread pollution and disease, that it may result in a loss of genetic diversity, and that its practice may tend to depreciate the value of human life. These arguments are forcefully, even passionately presented; they remind us that, at times, human ingenuity seems unable to control fully the forces it creates — that, with Hamlet, it is sometimes better "to bear those ills we have than fly to others that we know not of."

It is argued that this Court should weigh these potential hazards in considering whether respondent's invention is patentable subject matter under § 101. We disagree. The grant or denial of patents on micro-organisms is not likely to put an end to genetic research or to its attendant risks. The large amount of research that has already occurred when no researcher had sure knowledge that patent protection would be available suggests that legislative or judicial fiat as to patentability will not deter the scientific mind from probing into the unknown any more than Canute could command the tides. Whether respondent's claims are patentable may determine whether research efforts are accelerated by the hope of reward or slowed by want of incentives, but that is all.

What is more important is that we are without competence to entertain these arguments — either to brush them aside as fantasies generated by fear of the unknown, or to act on them. The choice we are urged to make is a matter of high policy for resolution within the legislative process after the kind of investigation, examination, and study that legislative bodies can provide and courts cannot. That process involves the balancing of competing values and interests, which in our democratic system is the business of elected representatives. Whatever their validity, the contentions now pressed on us should be addressed to the political branches of the government, the Congress and the Executive, and not to the courts.

We have emphasized in the recent past that "[o]ur individual appraisal of the wisdom or unwisdom of a particular [legislative] course ... is to be put aside in the process of interpreting a statute." *TVA* v. *Hill* (1978). Our task, rather, is the narrow one of determining what Congress meant by the words it used in the statute; once that is done our powers are exhausted. Congress is free to amend § 101 so as to exclude from patent protection organisms produced by genetic engineering. Compare 42 U.S.C. § 2181, exempting from patent protection inventions "useful solely in the utilization of special nuclear material or atomic energy in an atomic weapon." Or it may choose to craft a statute specifically designed for such living things. But, until Congress takes such action, this Court must construe the language of § 101 as it is. The language of that section fairly embraces respondent's invention.

Accordingly, the judgment of the Court of Customs and Patent Appeals is affirmed.

Affirmed.

MR. JUSTICE BRENNAN, with whom MR. JUSTICE WHITE, MR. JUSTICE MARSHALL, and MR. JUSTICE POWELL join, dissenting.

I agree with the Court that the question before us is a narrow one. Neither the future of scientific research, nor even the ability of respondent Chakrabarty to reap some monopoly profits from his pioneering work, is at stake. Patents on the processes by which he has produced and employed the new living organism are not contested. The only question we need decide is whether Congress, exercising its authority under Art. I, § 8, of the Constitution, intended that he be able to secure a monopoly on the living organism itself, no matter how produced or how used. Because I believe the Court has misread the applicable legislation, I dissent.

The patent laws attempt to reconcile this Nation's deepseated antipathy to monopolies with the need to encourage progress. *Deepsouth Packing Co.* v. *Laitram Corp.* (1972); *Graham* v. *John Deere Co.* (1966). Given the complexity and legislative nature of this delicate task, we must be careful to extend patent protection no further than Congress has provided. In particular, were there an absence of legislative direction, the courts should leave to Congress the decisions whether and how far to extend the patent privilege into areas where the common understanding has been that patents are not available. . . .

In this case, however, we do not confront a complete legislative vacuum. The sweeping language of the Patent Act of 1793, as re-enacted in 1952, is not the last pronouncement Congress has made in this area. In 1930 Congress enacted the Plant Patent Act affording patent protection to developers of certain asexually reproduced plants. In 1970 Congress enacted the Plant Variety Protection Act to extend protection to certain new plant varieties capable of sexual reproduction. Thus, we are not dealing — as the Court would have it — with the routine problem of "unanticipated inventions.". . . In these two Acts Congress has addressed the general problem of patenting animate inventions and has chosen carefully limited language granting protection to some kinds of discoveries, but specifically exluding others. These Acts strongly evidence a congressional limitation that excludes bacteria from patentability.

First, the Acts evidence Congress' understanding, at least since 1930, that § 101 does not include living organisms. If newly developed living organisms not naturally occurring had been patentable under § 101, the plants included in the scope of the 1930 and 1970 Acts could have been patented without new legislation. Those plants, like the bacteria involved in this case, were new varieties not naturally occurring. Although the Court . . . rejects this line of argument, it does not explain why the Acts were necessary unless to correct a pre-existing situation. I cannot share the Court's implicit assumption that Congress was engaged in either idle exercises or mere correction of the public record when it enacted the 1930 and 1970 Acts. And Congress certainly thought it was doing something significant. The committee reports contain expansive prose about the previously unavailable benefits to be derived from extending patent protection to plants. . . . Because Congress thought it had to legislate in order to make agricultural "human-made inventions" patentable and because the legislation Congress enacted is limited, it follows that Congress never meant to make patentable items outside the scope of the legislation.

Second, the 1970 Act clearly indicates that Congress has included bacteria within the focus of its legislative concern, but not within the scope of patent protection. Congress specifically excluded bacteria from the coverage of the 1970 Act. . . . The Court's attempts to supply explanations for this explicit exclusion ring hollow. It is true that there is no mention in the legislative history of the exclusion, but that does not give us license to invent reasons. The fact is that Congress, assuming that animate objects as to which it had not specifically legislated could not be patented, excluded bacteria from the set of patentable organisms.

The Court protests that its holding today is dictated by the broad language of § 101, which "cannot be confined to the 'particular application[s] . . . contemplated by the legislators.' " . . . *Barr* v. *United States* (1945). But as I have shown, the Court's decision does not follow the unavoidable implications of the statute. Rather, it extends the patent system to cover living material even though Congress plainly has legislated in the belief that § 101 does not encompass living organisms. It is the role of Congress, not this Court, to broaden or narrow the reach of the patent laws. This is especially true where, as here, the composition sought to be patented uniquely implicates matters of public concern.

▼▼▼

VENICE ECONOMIC SUMMIT
June 22-23, 1980

International affairs and political issues overshadowed financial topics at the sixth economic summit meeting of the leaders and heads of state of the seven largest non-communist nations, held June 22-23 in Venice, Italy. Although they issued a communiqué pledging that their governments would develop alternative energy sources — coal, synthetic fuels and nuclear power — to reduce oil consumption, the world leaders were more concerned with the Soviet occupation of Afghanistan, the Americans held hostage in Iran and the stalled Middle East peace negotiations.

Going into the meeting, which was held in a Benedictine monastery on the island of San Giorgio Maggiore, President Carter and the other allied leaders were at odds over several issues. The summit was to be the centerpiece of Carter's eight-day European tour, the main theme of which was his repeated condemnation of the Soviet invasion of Afghanistan.

Afghanistan Occupation

Carter failed at the summit, however, to generate widespread allied support for his call for strong sanctions against Moscow. Differences over approaches to the Soviet Union centered on Washington's belief that Soviet actions demanded tough responses; the allies preferred to maintain commercial and diplomatic links to ease East-West tensions. President Carter reportedly was concerned that French President Valéry Giscard d'Estaing's May meeting with the Soviet leader, Leonid I. Brezh-

nev, signaled French acquiescence to the Afghanistan intervention, and he warned West German Chancellor Helmut Schmidt to avoid concessions during his parley with Brezhnev scheduled for late June.

Middle East Issues

Washington and the allies differed on other issues as well. The Carter administration characterized as lukewarm allied sanctions imposed on Iran after the U.S. hostages were taken; the allies, for their part, were uneasy in the wake of the failed U.S. mission to rescue the Americans held in Tehran. (Iran, p. 351)

Moreover, the leaders of the European Economic Community (EEC) had issued a declaration at a meeting held June 12-13 stating that the Palestine Liberation Organization (PLO) should be "associated with" the Middle East peace talks between Egypt and Israel, a position the Carter administration steadfastly had refused to consider.

The ambiguous atmosphere prevailing at the Venice summit was heightened by political considerations. Carter's approval rating in polls of American voters was hovering near 30 percent, and he and German Chancellor Schmidt both faced tough re-election campaigns. Giscard d'Estaing was up for re-election the following spring. The government of the host country, headed by Prime Minister Francesco Cossiga, was traditionally precarious, and Britain's Margaret Thatcher was battling runaway inflation. Masayoshi Ohira, the Japanese prime minister, had died June 12; his government was represented at the summit by Cabinet ministers. Only Canada's Pierre Trudeau, who had been politically resurrected after the downfall of the goernment led by Joe Clark, appeared to be in a secure position at home.

As the meeting opened June 22, Moscow announced that it was withdrawing "some" of its 85,000 troops in Afghanistan. In response, the seven leaders issued a statement calling for the "complete withdrawal of the Soviet troops" and the re-establishment of Afghanistan's "sovereignty, territorial integrity, political independence and nonaligned character."

Summit Declaration

In the final declaration of the summit meeting, the world leaders vowed to "break the existing link between economic growth and consumption of oil" by 1990 by doubling coal production and developing atomic power and synthetic fuels. They asserted that their countries could tap energy sources equal to 15 million to 20 million barrels of oil a day without endangering economic growth. The communiqué, the terms of which had been worked out during five months of consultation

*among experts from the seven nations, also called for new international
initiatives to help developing nations increase energy and food production.*

*Following are the texts of statements issued at the Venice
economic summit June 22, 1980, on the Soviet military
occupation of Afghanistan and on the taking of diplomatic
hostages, and the text of the joint declaration issued June
23, 1980, at the conclusion of the meeting:*

STATEMENT ON AFGHANISTAN

In seeking here in Venice to define a global economic strategy and
to show our united determination to make it a reality, we are consciously
accepting the responsibility that falls to the three great industrialized
areas of the world — North America, Western Europe and Japan —
to help create the conditions for harmonious and sustained economic
growth. But we cannot do this alone; others too have a part to play.

However, present circumstances oblige us to emphasize that our efforts
will only bear fruit if we can at the same time preserve a world in
which the rule of law is universally obeyed, national independence is
respected and world peace is kept. We call on all countries to join
us in working for such a world and we welcome the readiness of non-
aligned countries and regional groups to accept the responsibilities which
this involves.

We therefore reaffirm hereby that the Soviet military occupation of
Afghanistan is unacceptable now and that we are determined not to
accept it in the future. It is incompatible with the will of the Afghan
people for national independence, as demonstrated by their courageous
resistance, and with the security of the states of the region. It is also
incompatible with the principles of the United Nations Charter and
with efforts to maintain genuine détente. It undermines the very foundations of peace, both in the region and in the world at large.

We fully endorse in this respect the views already expressed by the
overwhelming majority of the international community, as set out by
the United Nations General Assembly in Resolution No. ES-6/2 of 14th
January 1980 and by the Islamic Conference at both its recent sessions.

Afghanistan should be enabled to regain the sovereignty, territorial
integrity, political independence and non-aligned character it once enjoyed. We therefore call for the complete withdrawal of Soviet troops
and for the Afghan people to be left free again to determine their
own future.

We have taken note of today's announcement of the withdrawal of
some Soviet troops from Afghanistan. In order to make a useful contribution to the solution of the Afghan crisis, this withdrawal, if confirmed,
will have to be permanent and continue until the complete withdrawal
of the Soviet troops. Only thus will it be possible to reestablish a

situation compatible with peace and the rule of law and thereby with the interests of all nations.

We are resolved to do everything in our power to achieve this objective. We are also ready to support any initiative to this end, such as that of the Islamic Conference. And we shall support every effort designed to contribute to the political independence and to the security of the states of the region.

Those Governments represented at this meeting which have taken a position against attendance at the Olympic Games vigorously reaffirm their positions.

DIPLOMATIC HOSTAGES

Gravely concerned by recent incidents of terrorism involving the taking of hostages and attacks on diplomatic and consular premises and personnel, the Heads of State and Government reaffirm their determination to deter and combat such acts. They note the completion of work on the International Convention Against the Taking of Hostages and call on all States to consider becoming parties to it as well as to the Convention on the Prevention and Punishment of Crimes Against Internationally Protected Persons of 1973.

The Heads of State and Government vigorously condemn the taking of hostages and the seizure of diplomatic and consular premises and personnel in contravention of the basic norms of international law and practice. The Heads of State and Government consider necessary that all Governments should adopt policies which will contribute to the attainment of this goal and to take appropriate measures to deny terrorists any benefits from such criminal acts. They also resolve to provide to one another's diplomatic and consular missions support and assistance in situations involving the seizure of diplomatic and consular establishments or personnel.

The Heads of State and Government recall that every State has the duty under international law to refrain from organizing, instigating, assisting or participating in terrorist acts in another State or acquiescing in organised activities within its territory directed towards the commission of such acts, and deplore in the strongest terms any breach of this duty.

SUMMIT JOINT DECLARATION

Introduction

1. In this, our first meeting of the 1980's, the economic issues that have dominated our thoughts are the price and supply of energy and the implications for inflation and the level of economic activity in our own countries and for the world as a whole. Unless we can deal with the problems of energy, we cannot cope with other problems.

2. Successive large increases in the price of oil, bearing no relation to market conditions and culminating in the recent decisions by some members of the Organization of Petroleum Exporting Countries (OPEC) at Algiers, have produced the reality of even higher inflation and the imminent threat of severe recession and unemployment in the industrialised countries. At the same time they have undermined and in some cases virtually destroyed the prospects for growth in the developing countries. We believe that these consequences are increasingly coming to be appreciated by some of the oil exporting countries. The fact is that the industrialised countries of the free world, the oil producing countries and the nonoil developing countries depend upon each other for the realisation of their potential for economic development and prosperity. Each can overcome the obstacles to that development, but only if all work together, and with the interests of all in mind.

3. In this spirit we have discussed the main problems that confront us in the coming decade. We are confident in the ability of our democratic societies, based on individual freedom and social solidarity, to meet these challenges. There are no quick or easy solutions; sustained efforts are needed to achieve a better future.

Inflation

4. The reduction of inflation is our immediate top priority and will benefit all nations. Inflation retards growth and harms all sectors of our societies. Determined fiscal and monetary restraint is required to break inflationary expectations. Continuing dialogue among the social partners is also needed for this purpose. We must retain effective international coordination to carry out this policy of restraint, and also to guard against the threat of growing unemployment and worldwide recession.

5. We are also committed to encouraging investment and innovation, so as to increase productivity, to fostering the movement of resources from declining into expanding sectors so as to provide new job opportunities, and to promoting the most effective use of resources within and among countries. This will require shifting resources from government spending to the private sector and from consumption to investment, and avoiding or carefully limiting actions that shelter particular industries or sectors from the rigors of adjustment. Measures of this kind may be economically and politically difficult in the short term, but they are essential to sustained non-inflationary growth and to increasing employment, which is our major goal.

6. In shaping economic policy, we need a better understanding of the long-term effects of global population growth, industrial expansion and economic development generally. A study of trends in these areas is in hand, and our representatives will keep these matters under review.

Energy

7. We must break the existing link between economic growth and consumption of oil, and we mean to do so in this decade. This strategy requires conserving oil and substantially increasing production and use of alternative energy sources. To this end, maximum reliance should be placed on the price mechanism, and domestic prices for oil should take into account representative world prices. Market forces should be supplemented, where appropriate, by effective fiscal incentives and administrative measures. Energy investment will contribute substantially to economic growth and employment.

8. We welcome the recent decisions of the European Community (EC), the International Energy Agency (IEA) and the Organization for Economic Cooperation and Development (OECD) regarding the need for long-term structural changes to reduce oil consumption, continuing procedures to monitor progress, the possible use of oil ceilings to deal with tight market conditions, and coordination of stock policies to mitigate the effect of market disruption. We note that the member countries of the IEA have agreed that their energy policies should result in their collective 1985 net oil imports being substantially less than their existing 1985 group objective, and that they will quantify the reduction as part of their continuing monitoring efforts. The potential for reduction has been estimated by the IEA Secretariat, given existing uncertainties, at around 4 million barrels a day (MBD).

9. To conserve oil in our countries:

— We are agreed that no new baseload, oil-fired generating capacity should be constructed, save in exceptional circumstances, and that the conversion of oil-fired capacity to other fuels should be accelerated.

— We will increase efforts, including fiscal incentives where necessary, to accelerate the substitution of oil in industry.

— We will encourage oil saving investments in residential and commercial buildings, where necessary by financial incentives and by establishing insulation standards. We look to the public sector to set an example.

— In transportation, our objective is the introduction of increasingly fuel-efficient vehicles. The demand of consumers and competition among manufacturers are already leading in this direction. We will accelerate this progress, where appropriate, by arrangements or standards for improved automobile fuel efficiency, by gasoline pricing and taxation decisions, by research and development, and by making public transport more attractive.

10. We must rely on fuels other than oil to meet the energy needs of future economic growth. This will require early, resolute, and wide-ranging actions. Our potential to increase the supply and use of energy sources other than oil over the next ten years is estimated at the equivalent of 15-20 MBD of oil. We intend to make a coordinated

and vigorous effort to realize this potential. To this end, we will seek a large increase in the use of coal and enhanced use of nuclear power in the medium-term, and a substantial increase in production of synthetic fuels, in solar energy and other sources of renewable energy over the longer term.

11. We shall encourage the exploration and development of our indigenous hydrocarbon resources in order to secure maximum production on a long term basis.

12. Together we intend to double coal production and use by early 1990. We will encourage long term commitments by coal producers and consumers. It will be necessary to improve infrastructures in both exporting and importing countries, as far as is economically justified, to ensure the required supply and use of coal. We look forward to the recommendations of the International Coal Industry Advisory Board. They will be considered promptly. We are conscious of the environmental risks associated with increased coal production and combustion. We will do everything in our power to ensure that increased use of fossil fuels, especially coal, does not damage the environment.

13. We underline the vital contribution of nuclear power to a more secure energy supply. The role of nuclear energy has to be increased if world energy needs are to be met. We shall therefore have to expand our nuclear generating capacity. We will continue to give the highest priority to ensuring the health and safety of the public and to perfecting methods of dealing with spent fuels and disposal of nuclear waste. We reaffirm the importance of ensuring the reliable supply of nuclear fuel and minimizing the risk of nuclear proliferation.

14. The studies made by the International Nuclear Fuel Cycle Evaluation Group, launched at the London Summit in 1977, are a significant contribution to the use of nuclear energy. We welcome their findings with respect to: increasing predictable supplies; the most effective utilization of uranium sources, including the development of advanced technologies; and the minimization of proliferation risks, including support of International Atomic Energy Agency (IAEA) safeguards. We urge all countries to take these findings into account when developing policies and programmes for the peaceful use of nuclear energy.

15. We will actively support the recommendations of the International Energy Technology Group, proposed at the Tokyo Summit last year, for bringing new energy technologies into commercial use at the earliest feasible time. As far as national programmes are concerned, we will by mid-1981 adopt a two-phased approach; first, listing the numbers and types of commercial scale plants to be constructed in each of our countries by the mid-1980s, and, second, indicating quantitative projections for expanding production by 1990, 1995 and 2000, as a basis for future actions. As far as international programmes are concerned, we will join others in creating an international team to promote collaboration among interested nations on specific projects.

16. A high level group of representatives of our countries and of the EEC Commission will review periodically the results achieved in these fields.

17. Our comprehensive energy strategy is designed to meet the requirements of the coming decade. We are convinced that it can reduce the demand for energy, particularly oil, without hampering economic growth. By carrying out this strategy we expect that, over the coming decade, the ratio between increases in collective energy consumption and economic growth of our countries will be reduced to about 0.6, that the share of oil in our total energy demand will be reduced from 53 percent now to about 40 percent by 1990, and that our collective consumption of oil in 1990 will be significantly below present levels so as to permit a balance between supply and demand at tolerable prices.

18. We continue to believe that international cooperation in energy is essential. All countries have a vital interest in a stable equilibrium between energy supply and demand. We would welcome a constructive dialogue on energy and related issues between energy producers and consumers in order to improve the coherence of their policies.

Relations With Developing Countries

19. We are deeply concerned about the impact of the oil price increases on the developing countries that have to import oil. The increase in oil prices in the last two years has more than doubled the oil bill of these countries, which now amounts to over $50 billion. This will drive them into ever increasing indebtedness, and put at risk the whole basis of their economic growth and social progress, unless something can be done to help them.

20. We approach in a positive spirit the prospect of global negotiations in the framework of the United Nations and the formulation of a new International Development Strategy. In particular, our object is to cooperate with the developing countries in energy conservation and development, expansion of exports, enhancement of human skills, and the tackling of underlying food and population problems.

21. A major international effort to help these countries increase their energy production is required. We believe that this view is gaining ground among oil-exporting countries. We ask the World Bank to examine the adequacy of the resources and the mechanisms now in place for the exploration, development and production of conventional and renewable energy sources in oil importing developing countries, to consider means, including the possibility of establishing a new affiliate or facility by which it might improve and increase its lending programmes for energy assistance, and to explore its findings with both oil-exporting and industrial countries.

22. We are deeply conscious that extreme poverty and chronic malnutrition afflict hundreds of millions of people of developing countries.

The first requirement in these countries is to improve their ability to feed themselves and reduce their dependence on food imports. We are ready to join with them and the International Agencies concerned in their comprehensive long term strategies to increase food production, and to help improve national as well as international research services. We will support and, where appropriate, supplement initiatives of the World Bank and of the Food and Agricultural Organization (FAO) and to improve grain storage and food handling facilities. We underline the importance of wider membership of the new Food Aid Convention so as to secure at least 10 million tons of food annually and of an equitable replenishment of the International Fund for Agricultural Development.

23. High priority should be given to efforts to cope with population growth and to existing United Nations and other programmes for supporting these efforts.

24. We strongly support the general capital increase of the World Bank, increases in the funding of the regional development banks, and the sixth replenishment of the International Development Association. We would welcome an increase in the rate of lending of these institutions, within the limits of their present replenishments, as needed to fulfill the programmes described above. It is essential that all members, especially the major donors, provide their full contributions on the agreed schedule.

25. We welcome the report of the Brandt Commission. We shall carefully consider its recommendations.

26. The democratic industrialised countries cannot alone carry the responsibility of aid and other different contributions to developing countries: it must be equitably shared by the oil exporting countries and the industrialised Communist countries. The Personal Representatives are instructed to review aid policies and procedures and other contributions to developing countries and to report back their conclusions to the next Summit.

Monetary Problems

27. The situation created by large oil-generated payments imbalances, in particular those of oil-importing developing countries, requires a combination of determined actions by all countries to promote external adjustment and effective mechanisms for balance of payments financing. We look to the international capital market to continue to play the primary role in rechanneling the substantial oil surplus funds on the basis of sound lending standards. We support the work in progress by our monetary authorities and the Bank for International Settlements designed to improve the supervision and security of the international banking system. The private banks could usefully supplement these efforts.

28. Private lending will need to be supplemented by an expanded role for international institutions, especially the International Monetary Fund (IMF). We are committed to implementing the agreed increase in the IMF quotas, and to supporting appropriate borrowing by the Fund, if needed to meet financing requirements of its members. We encourage the IMF to seek ways in which it could, within its guidelines on conditionality, make it more attractive for countries with financing problems to use its resources. In particular, we support the IMF's examination of possible ways to reduce charges on credits to low-income developing countries. The IMF and the World Bank should work closely together in responding to these problems. We welcome the Bank's innovative lending scheme for structural adjustment. We urge oil-exporting countries to increase their direct lending to countries with financial problems thus reducing the strain on other recycling mechanisms.

29. We reaffirm our commitment to stability in the foreign exchange markets. We note that the European Monetary System (EMS) has contributed to this end. We will continue close cooperation in exchange market policies so as to avoid disorderly exchange rate fluctuations. We will also cooperate with the IMF to achieve more effective surveillance. We support continuing examination by the IMF of arrangements to provide for a more balanced evolution of the world reserve system.

Trade

30. We are resolved further to strengthen the open world trading system. We will resist pressures for protectionist actions, which can only be self-defeating and aggravate inflation.

31. We endorse the positive conclusion of the multilateral trade negotiations, and commit ourselves to early and effective implementation. We welcome the participation of some of our developing partners in the new non-tariff codes and call upon others to participate. We also call for the full participation of as many countries as possible in strengthening the system of the General Agreement on Tariffs and Trade. We urge the more advanced of our developing partners gradually to open their markets over the coming decade.

32. We reaffirm our determination to avoid a harmful export credit race. To this end we shall work with the other participants to strengthen the International Arrangement on Export Credits, with a view to reaching a mutually acceptable solution covering all aspects of the arrangement by 1 December 1980. In particular, we shall seek to bring its terms closer to current market conditions and reduce distortions in export competition, recognizing the differentiated treatment of developing countries in the Arrangement.

33. As a further step in strengthening the international trading system, we commit our governments to work in the United Nations toward an agreement to prohibit illicit payments to foreign government officials in international business transactions. If that effort falters, we will seek

to conclude an agreement among our countries, but open to all, with the same objective.

Conclusions

34. The economic message from this Venice Summit is clear. The key to success in resolving the major economic challenges which the world faces is to achieve and maintain a balance between energy supply and demand at reasonable levels and at tolerable prices. The stability of the world economy, on which the prosperity of every individual country relies, depends upon all of the countries concerned, recognising their mutual needs and accepting their mutual responsibilities. Those among us whose countries are members of the European Community intend to make their efforts within this framework. We, who represent seven large industrialised countries of the free world, are ready to tackle our own problems with determination and to work with others to meet the challenges of the coming decade, to our own advantage and to the benefit of the whole world.

COURT ON PUBLIC FUNDING
OF ABORTIONS

June 30, 1980

In one of its most controversial decisions in 1980, the Supreme Court June 30 held that poor women did not have a constitutional right to publicly funded abortions. The court, in Harris v. McRae, *voted 5-4 to uphold a six-year-old congressional prohibition, known as the Hyde amendment, that barred federal funding of most abortions.*

The court found that Congress did not violate the Constitution when it refused to pay for abortions but continued to provide funding for childbirth services in an effort to encourage women to carry their pregnancies to term.

The ruling was the most important statement by the high court on the abortion controversy since 1973. In that year the court, in Roe v. Wade *struck down, 7-2, state laws making all abortions criminal except those necessary to save the mother's life. Such laws, it said, impermissibly impinged on a woman's right to privacy in deciding whether or not to have a child.*

Justice Potter Stewart spoke for the court's majority in Harris v. McRae. *He was joined by Chief Justice Warren E. Burger and Justices Byron R. White, Lewis F. Powell Jr. and William H. Rehnquist. Justice White also filed a separate concurring opinion.*

Dissenting were Justices William J. Brennan Jr., Thurgood Marshall, Harry A. Blackmun and John Paul Stevens. Each wrote a separate dissenting opinion, though Marshall and Blackmun also joined Brennan in his views.

Hyde Amendment

At issue in Harris v. McRae *was the Hyde amendment, which had been approved by Congress in some form every year since 1976. The provision was named for one of its original sponsors, Rep. Henry J. Hyde, R-Ill.*

The Hyde amendment prohibited spending of federal Medicaid funds for abortions except where the life of the mother would be endangered if the fetus were carried to term or in cases of rape or incest. Nearly a third of the one million legal abortions performed each year since 1973 in the United States had been for women on welfare. Under the court's ruling in Harris v. McRae, *states could stop paying for abortions if they chose, or they could continue to pay with state funds.*

Majority Opinion

The court held that the Hyde amendment violated neither the due process clause of the Fifth Amendment nor the establishment of religion clause of the First Amendment. Since Congress chose to withdraw federal funding for that particular service, the court held, "a state is not obligated . . . to continue to fund those medically necessary abortions for which federal reimbursement is unavailable under the Hyde Amendment." The court also ruled that the amendment restrictions did not impermissibly impinge on the due process clause.

"[A]lthough government may not place obstacles in the path of a woman's exercise of her freedom of choice, it need not remove those not of its own creation. Indigency falls in the latter category," the court held.

Dissenting Views

In his dissent, in which he was joined by Justices Marshall and Blackmun, Brennan bitterly attacked the Hyde amendment as "injecting coercive financial incentives favoring childbirth into a decision that is constitutionally guaranteed to be free from governmental intrusion. . . ." He wrote, "By funding all of the expenses associated with childbirth and none of the expenses incurred in terminating pregnancy, the government literally makes an offer that the indigent woman cannot afford to refuse."

Following are excerpts from the Supreme Court's decision June 30, 1980, ruling that women did not have a right to federally funded abortions and that states could halt payments for abortions; and excerpts from the dissenting opinions of Justices Brennan and Marshall:

No. 79-1268

Patricia R. Harris, Secretary of Health and Human Services, Appellant, *v.* Cora McRae et al.	On Appeal from the United States District Court for the Eastern District of New York.

[June 30, 1980]

MR. JUSTICE STEWART delivered the opinion of the Court.

This case presents statutory and constitutional questions concerning the public funding of abortions under Title XIX of the Social Security Act, commonly known as the "Medicaid" Act, and recent annual appropriations acts containing the so-called "Hyde Amendment." The statutory question is whether Title XIX requires a State that participates in the Medicaid program to fund the cost of medically necessary abortions for which federal reimbursement is unavailable under the Hyde Amendment. The constitutional question, which arises only if Title XIX imposes no such requirement, is whether the Hyde Amendment, by denying public funding for certain medically necessary abortions, contravenes the liberty or equal protection guarantees of the Due Process Clause of the Fifth Amendment, or either of the Religion Clauses of the First Amendment.

[Sections I and II Omitted]

III

Having determined that Title XIX does not obligate a participating State to pay for those medically necessary abortions for which Congress has withheld federal funding, we must consider the constitutional validity of the Hyde Amendment. The appellees assert that the funding restrictions of the Hyde Amendment violate several rights secured by the Constitution — (1) the right of a woman, implicit in the Due Process Clause of the Fifth Amendment, to decide whether to terminate a pregnancy, (2) the prohibition under the Establishment Clause of the First Amendment against any "law respecting an establishment of religion," and (3) the right to freedom of religion protected by the Free Exercise Clause of the First Amendment. The appellees also contend that, quite apart from substantive constitutional rights, the Hyde Amendment violates the equal protection component of the Fifth Amendment.

It is well settled that, quite apart from the guarantee of equal protection, if a law "impinges upon a fundamental right explicitly or implicitly secured by the Constitution [it] is presumptively unconstitutional." *Mobile* v. *Bolden* [1980] (plurality opinion). Accordingly, before

517

turning to the equal protection issue in this case, we examine whether the Hyde Amendment violates any substantive rights secured by the Constitution.

A

We address first the appellees' argument that the Hyde Amendment, by restricting the availability of certain medically necessary abortions under Medicaid, impinges on the "liberty" protected by the Due Process Clause as recognized in *Roe* v. *Wade* [1973] and its progeny.

In the *Wade* case, this Court held unconstitutional a Texas statute making it a crime to procure or attempt an abortion except on medical advice for the purpose of saving the mother's life. The constitutional underpinning of *Wade* was a recognition that the "liberty" protected by the Due Process Clause of the Fourteenth Amendment includes not only the freedoms explicitly mentioned in the Bill of Rights, but also a freedom of personal choice in certain matters of marriage and family life. This implicit constitutional liberty, the Court in *Wade* held, includes the freedom of a woman to decide whether to terminate a pregnancy.

But the Court in *Wade* also recognized that a State has legitimate interests during a pregnancy in both ensuring the health of the mother and protecting potential human life. These state interests, which were found to be "separate and distinct" and to "grow[] in substantiality as the woman approaches term," . . . pose a conflict with a woman's untrammeled freedom of choice. In resolving this conflict, the Court held that before the end of the first trimester of pregnancy, neither state interest is sufficiently substantial to justify any intrusion on the woman's freedom of choice. In the second trimester, the state interest in maternal health was found to be sufficiently substantial to justify regulation reasonably related to that concern. And, at viability, usually in the third trimester, the state interest in protecting the potential life of the fetus was found to justify a criminal prohibition against abortions, except where necessary for the preservation of the life or health of the mother. Thus, inasmuch as the Texas criminal statute allowed abortions only where necessary to save the life of the mother and without regard to the stage of the pregnancy, the Court held in *Wade* that the statute violated the Due Process Clause of the Fourteenth Amendment.

In *Maher* v. *Roe* [1977] the Court was presented with the question whether the scope of personal constitutional freedom recognized in *Roe* v. *Wade* included an entitlement to Medicaid payments for abortions that are not medically necessary. At issue in *Maher* was a Connecticut welfare regulation under which medicaid recipients received payments for medical services incident to childbirth, but not for medical services incident to nontherapeutic abortions. The District Court held that the regulation violated the Equal Protection Clause of the Fourteenth Amendment because the unequal subsidization of childbirth and abortion impinged on the "fundamental right to abortion" recognized in *Wade* and its progeny.

It was the view of this Court that "the District Court misconceived the nature and scope of the fundamental right recognized in *Roe*." ... The doctrine of *Roe* v. *Wade*, the Court held in *Maher*, "protects the woman from unduly burdensome interference with her freedom to decide whether to terminate her pregnancy," ... such as the severe criminal sanctions at issue in *Roe* v. *Wade*, ... or the absolute requirement of spousal consent for an abortion challenged in *Planned Parenthood of Central Missouri* v. *Danforth* [1976].

But the constitutional freedom recognized in *Wade* and its progeny, the *Maher* Court explained, did not prevent Connecticut from making "a value judgment favoring childbirth over abortion, and ... implement[ing] that judgment by the allocation of public funds.". . .

The Court in *Maher* noted that its description of the doctrine recognized in *Wade* and its progeny signaled "no retreat" from those decisions. In explaining why the constitutional principle recognized in *Wade* and later cases — protecting a woman's freedom of choice — did not translate into a constitutional obligation of Connecticut to subsidize abortions, the Court cited the "basic difference between direct state interference with a protected activity and state encouragement of an alternative activity consonant with legislative policy. Constitutional concerns are greatest when the State attempts to impose its will by force of law; the State's power to encourage actions deemed to be in the public interest is necessarily far broader." . . . Thus, even though the Connecticut regulation favored childbirth over abortion by means of subsidization of one and not the other, the Court in *Maher* concluded that the regulation did not impinge on the constitutional freedom recognized in *Wade* because it imposed no governmental restriction on access to abortions.

The Hyde Amendment, like the Connecticut welfare regulation at issue in *Maher*, places no governmental obstacle in the path of a woman who chooses to terminate her pregnancy, but rather, by means of unequal subsidization of abortion and other medical services, encourages alternative activity deemed in the public interest. The present case does differ factually from *Maher* insofar as that case involved a failure to fund nontherapeutic abortions, whereas the Hyde Amendment withholds funding of certain medically necessary abortions. Accordingly, the appellees argue that because the Hyde Amendment affects a significant interest not present or asserted in *Maher* — the interest of a woman in protecting her health during pregnancy — and because that interest lies at the core of the personal constitutional freedom recognized in *Wade*, the present case is constitutionally different from *Maher*. It is the appellees' view that to the extent that the Hyde Amendment withholds funding for certain medically necessary abortions, it clearly impinges on the constitutional principle recognized in *Wade*.

It is evident that a woman's interest in protecting her health was an important theme in *Wade*. In concluding that the freedom of a woman to decide whether to terminate her pregnancy falls within the personal liberty protected by the Due Process Clause, the Court in *Wade* emphasized the fact that the woman's decision carries with it significant personal health implications — both physical and psychological. . . . In fact, although the Court in *Wade* recognized that the state interest in protecting potential life becomes sufficiently compelling in the period after fetal viability to justify an absolute criminal prohibition of nontherapeutic abortions, the Court held that even after fetal viability a State may not prohibit abortions "necessary to preserve the life or health of the mother." . . . Because even the compelling interest of the State in protecting potential life after fetal viability was held to be insufficient to outweigh a woman's decision to protect her life or health, it could be argued that the freedom of a woman to decide whether to terminate her pregnancy for health reasons does in fact lie at the core of the constitutional liberty identified in *Wade*.

But, regardless of whether the freedom of a woman to choose to terminate her pregnancy for health reasons lies at the core or the periphery of the due process liberty recognized in *Wade*, it simply does not follow that a woman's freedom of choice carries with it a constitutional entitlement to the financial resources to avail herself of the full range of protected choices. The reason why was explained in *Maher*: although government may not place obstacles in the path of a woman's exercise of her freedom of choice, it need not remove those not of its own creation. Indigency falls in the latter category. The financial constraints that restrict an indigent woman's ability to enjoy the full range of constitutionally protected freedom of choice are the product not of governmental restrictions on access to abortions, but rather of her indigency. Although Congress has opted to subsidize medically necessary services generally, but not certain medically necessary abortions, the fact remains that the Hyde Amendment leaves an indigent woman with at least the same range of choice in deciding whether to obtain a medically necessary abortion as she would have had if Congress had chosen to subsidize no health care costs at all. We are thus not persuaded that the Hyde Amendment impinges on the constitutionally protected freedom of choice recognized in *Wade*.

Although the liberty protected by the Due Process Clause affords protection against unwarranted government interference with freedom of choice in the context of certain personal decisions, it does not confer an entitlement to such funds as may be necessary to realize all the advantages of that freedom. To hold otherwise would mark a drastic change in our understanding of the Constitution. It cannot be that because government may not prohibit the use of contraceptives, *Griswold* v. *Connecticut* [1965] or prevent parents from sending their child to a private school, *Pierce* v. *Society of Sisters* [1925] government, therefore, has an affirmative constitutional obligation to ensure that all persons have the financial resources to obtain contraceptives or send their children to private schools. To translate the limitation on governmental power implicit in the Due Process Clause into an affirmative funding obligation would require Congress to subsidize the medically necessary abortion of an indigent woman even if Congress had not enacted a Medicaid program to subsidize other medically necessary services. Nothing in the Due Process Clause supports such an extraordinary result. Whether freedom of choice that is constitutionally protected warrants federal subsidization is a question for Congress to answer, not a matter of constitutional entitlement. Accordingly, we conclude that the Hyde Amendment does not impinge on the due process liberty recognized in *Wade*.

B

The appellees also argue that the Hyde Amendment contravenes rights secured by the Religion Clauses of the First Amendment. It is the appellees' view that the Hyde Amendment violates the Establishment Clause because it incorporates into law the doctrines of the Roman Catholic Church concerning the sinfulness of abortion and the time at which life commences. Moreover, insofar as a woman's decision to seek a medically necessary abortion may be a product of her religious beliefs under certain Protestant and Jewish tenets, the appellees assert that the funding limitations of the Hyde Amendment impinge on the freedom of religion guaranteed by the Free Exercise Clause.

1

It is well settled that "a legislative enactment does not contravene the Establishment Clause if it has a secular legislative purpose, if its principal or primary effect neither advances nor inhibits religion, and if it does not foster an excessive governmental entanglement with religion." *Committee for Pub. Ed. & Rel. Lib.* v. *Regan* [1980]. Applying this standard, the District Court properly concluded that the Hyde Amendment does not run afoul of the Establishment Clause. Although neither a State nor the Federal Government can constitutionally "pass laws which aid one religion, aid all religions, or prefer one religion over another," *Everson* v. *Board of Education* [1947], it does not follow that a statute violates the Establishment Clause because it "happens to coincide or harmonize with the tenets of some or all religions." *McGowan* v. *Maryland* [1961]. That the Judaeo-Christian religions oppose stealing does not mean that a State or the Federal Government may not, consistent with the Establishment Clause, enact laws prohibiting larceny. . . . The Hyde Amendment, as the District Court noted, is as much a reflection of "traditionalist" values towards abortion, as it is an embodiment of the views of any particular religion. See also *Roe*

v. *Wade* [1973]. In sum, we are convinced that the fact that the funding restrictions in the Hyde Amendment may coincide with the religious tenets of the Roman Catholic Church does not, without more, contravene the Establishment Clause.

2

We need not address the merits of the appellees' arguments concerning the Free Exercise Clause, because the appellees lack standing to raise a free exercise challenge to the Hyde Amendment. The named appellees fall into three categories: (1) the indigent pregnant women who sued on behalf of other women similarly situated, (2) the two officers of the Women's Division of the Board of Global Ministries of the United Methodist Church (Women's Division), and (3) the Women's Division itself. The named appellees in the first category lack standing to challenge the Hyde Amendment on free exercise grounds because none alleged, much less proved, that she sought an abortion under compulsion of religious belief. See *McGowan* v. *Maryland*.... Although the named appellees in the second category did provide a detailed description of their religious beliefs, they failed to allege either that they are or expect to be pregnant or that they are eligible to receive Medicaid. These named appellees, therefore, lack the personal stake in the controversy needed to confer standing to raise such a challenge to the Hyde Amendment.... *Warth* v. *Seldin* [1975].

Finally, although the Women's Division alleged that its membership includes "pregnant Medicaid eligible women who, as a matter of religious practice and in accordance with their conscientious beliefs, would choose but are precluded or discouraged from obtaining abortions reimbursed by Medicaid because of the Hyde Amendment," the Women's Division does not satisfy the standing requirements for an organization to assert the rights of its membership. One of those requirements is that "neither the claim asserted nor the relief requested requires the participation of individual members in the lawsuit." *Hunt* v. *Washington Apple Advertising Comm'n* [1977]. Since "it is necessary in a free exercise case for one to show the coercive effect of the enactment as it operates against him in the practice of his religion," *Abington School Dist.* v. *Schempp* [1963], the claim asserted here is one that ordinarily requires individual participation. In the present case, the Women's Division concedes that "the permissibility, advisability and/or necessity of abortion according to circumstance is a matter about which there is diversity of view within ... our membership, and is a determination which must be ultimately and absolutely entrusted to the conscience of the individual before God." It is thus clear that the participation of individual members of the Women's Division is essential to a proper understanding and resolution of their free exercise claims. Accordingly, we conclude that the Women's Division, along with the other named appellees, lack standing to challenge the Hyde Amendment under the free Exercise Clause.

C

It remains to be determined whether the Hyde Amendment violates the equal protection component of the Fifth Amendment. This challenge is premised on the fact that, although federal reimbursement is available under Medicaid for medically necessary services generally, the Hyde Amendment does not permit federal reimbursement of all medically necessary abortions. The District Court held, and the appellees argue here, that this selective subsidization violates the constitutional guarantee of equal protection.

The guarantee of equal protection under the Fifth Amendment is not a source of substantive rights or liberties, but rather a right to be free from invidious discrimination in statutory classifications and other governmental activity. It is well-settled that where a statutory classification does not itself impinge on a right or liberty protected by the Constitution, the validity of classification must be sustained unless "the classification rests on grounds wholly irrelevant to the achievement of [any legitimate governmental] objective." *McGown* v. *Maryland* [1961]. This presumption of constitutional validity, however, disappears if a statutory classification is predicated on criteria that are, in a constitutional sense, "suspect," the principal example of which is a classification based on race, *e.g., Brown* v. *Board of Education* [1954].

1

For the reasons stated above, we have already concluded that the Hyde Amendment violates no constitutionally protected substantive rights. We now conclude as well that it is not predicated on a constitutionally suspect classification. In reaching this conclusion, we again draw guidance from the Court's decision in *Maher* v. *Roe....* Thus the Court in *Maher* found no basis for concluding that the Connecticut regulation was predicated on a suspect classification.

It is our view that the present case is indistinguishable from *Maher* in this repect. Here, as in *Maher,* the principal impact of the Hyde Amendment falls on the indigent. But that fact does not itself render the funding restriction constitutionally invalid, for this Court has held repeatedly that poverty, standing alone, is not a suspect classification. ...*James* v. *Valtierra* [1971]. That *Maher* involved the refusal to fund nontherapeutic abortions, whereas the present case involves the refusal to fund medically necessary abortions, has no bearing on the factors that render a classification "suspect" within the meaning of the constitutional guarantee of equal protection.

2

The remaining question then is whether the Hyde Amendment is rationally related to a legitimate governmental objective. It is the Government's position that the Hyde Amendment bears a rational relationship to its legitimate interest in protecting the potential life of the fetus. We agree.

In *Wade,* the Court recognized that the State has "an important and legitimate interest in protecting the potentiality of human life." ... That interest was found to exist throughout a pregnancy, "grow[ing] in substantiality as the woman approaches term." ... *Beal* v. *Doe* [1977]. Moreover, in *Maher,* the Court held that Connecticut's decision to fund the costs associated with childbirth but not those associated with nontherapeutic abortions was a rational means of advancing the legitimate state interest in protecting potential life by encouraging childbirth. ... *Poelker* v. *Doe* [1977].

It follows that the Hyde Amendment, by encouraging childbirth except in the most urgent circumstances, is rationally related to the legitimate governmental objective of protecting potential life. By subsidizing the medical expenses of indigent women who carry their pregnancies to term while not subsidizing the comparable expenses of women who undergo abortions (except those whose lives are threatened), Congress has established incentives that make childbirth a more attractive alternative than abortion for persons eligible for Medicaid. These incentives bear a direct relationship to the legitimate congressional interest in protecting potential life. Nor is it irrational that Congress has authorized federal reimbursement for medically necessary services generally, but not for certain medically necessary abortions. Abortion is inherently different from other medical procedures, because no other procedure involves the purposeful termination of a potential life.

After conducting an extensive evidentiary hearing into issues surrounding the public funding of abortions, the District Court concluded that "[t]he interests of ... the federal government ... in the fetus and in preserving it are not sufficient, weighed in the balance with the woman's threatened health, to justify withdrawing medical assistance unless the woman consents ... to carry the fetus to term." In making an independent appraisal of the competing interests involved here, the District Court went beyond the judicial function. Such decisions are entrusted under the Constitution to Congress, not the courts. It is the role of the courts only to ensure that congressional decisions comport with the Constitution.

Where, as here, the Congress has neither invaded a substantive constitutional right or freedom, nor enacted legislation that purposefully operates to the detriment of a suspect class, the only requirement of equal protection is that congressional action be rationally related to a legitimate governmental interest. The Hyde Amendment satisfies that standard. It is not the mission of this Court or any other to decide whether the balance of competing interests reflected in the Hyde Amendment is wise social policy. If that were our mission, not every Justice who has subscribed to the judgment of the Court today could have done so. But we cannot, in the name of the Constitution, overturn duly enacted statutes simply "because they may be unwise, improvident, or out of harmony with a particular school of thought." *Williamson* v. *Lee Optical Co.* [1955], quoted in *Dandridge* v. *Williams* [1970]. Rather, "when an issue involves policy choices as sensitive as those implicated [here]..., the appropriate forum for their resolution in a democracy is the legislature." *Maher* v. *Roe* [1977].

IV

For the reasons stated in this opinion, we hold that a State that participates in the Medicaid program is not obligated under Title XIX to continue to fund those medically necessary abortions for which federal reimbursement is unavailable under the Hyde Amendment. We further hold that the funding restrictions of the Hyde Amendment violate neither the Fifth Amendment nor the Establishment Clause of the First Amendment. It is also our view that the appellees lack standing to raise a challenge to the Hyde Amendment under the Free Exercise Clause of the First Amendment. Accordingly, the judgment of the District Court is reversed, and the case is remanded to that court for further proceedings consistent with this opinion.

It is so ordered.

MR. JUSTICE BRENNAN, with whom MR. JUSTICE MARSHALL and MR. JUSTICE BLACKMUN join, dissenting.

I agree entirely with my Brother STEVENS that the State's interest in protecting the potential life of the fetus cannot justify the exclusion of financially and medically needy women from the benefits to which they would otherwise be entitled solely because the treatment that a doctor has concluded is medically necessary involves an abortion. ... I write separately to express my continuing disagreement with the Court's mischaracterization of the nature of the fundamental right recognized in *Roe* v. *Wade* (1973), and its misconception of the manner in which that right is infringed by federal and state legislation withdrawing all funding for medically necessary abortions.

Roe v. *Wade* held that the constitutional right to personal privacy encompasses a woman's decision whether or not to terminate her pregnancy. *Roe* and its progeny established that the pregnant woman has a right to be free from state interference with her choice to have an abortion — a right which, at least prior to the end of the first trimester, absolutely prohibits any governmental regulation of that highly personal decision. The proposition for which these cases stand thus is not that the State is under an affirmative obligation to ensure access to abortions for all who may desire them; it is that the State must refrain from wielding its enormous power and influence in a manner that might burden the pregnant woman's freedom to choose whether to have an abortion. The Hyde Amendment's denial of public funds for medically necessary abortions plainly intrudes upon this constitutionally protected decision, for both by design and in effect it serves to coerce indigent pregnant women to bear children that they would otherwise elect not to have.

When viewed in the context of the Medicaid program to which it is appended, it is obvious that the Hyde Amendment is nothing less than an attempt by Congress to circumvent the dictates of the Constitution and achieve indirectly what *Roe* v. *Wade* said it could not do directly. Under Title XIX of the Social Security Act, the Federal Government reimburses participating States for virtually all medically necessary services it provides to the categorically needy. The sole limitation of any significance is the Hyde Amendment's prohibition against the use of any federal funds to pay for the costs of abortions (except where the life of the mother would be endangered if the fetus were carried to term). As my Brother STEVENS persuasively demonstrates, exclusion of medically necessary abortions from Medicaid coverage cannot be justified as a cost-saving device. Rather, the Hyde Amendment is a transparent attempt by the Legislative Branch to impose the political majority's judgment of the morally acceptable and socially desirable preference on a sensitive and intimate decision that the Constitution entrusts to the individual. Worse yet, the Hyde Amendment does not foist that majoritarian viewpoint with equal measure upon everyone in our Nation, rich and poor alike; rather, it imposes that viewpoint only upon that segment of our society which, because of its position of political powerlessness, is least able to defend its privacy rights from the encroachments of state-mandated morality. The instant legislation thus calls for more exacting judicial review than in most other cases. "When elected leaders cower before public pressure, this Court, more than ever, must not shirk its duty to enforce the Constitution for the benefit of the poor and powerless." *Beal* v. *Doe* (1977) (MARSHALL, J., dissenting). Though it may not be this Court's mission "to decide whether the balance of competing interests reflected in the Hyde Amendment is wise social policy," ... it most assuredly is our responsibility to vindicate the pregnant woman's constitutional right to decide whether to bear children free from governmental intrusion.

Moreover, it is clear that the Hyde Amendment not only was designed to inhibit, but does in fact inhibit the woman's freedom to choose abortion over childbirth. "Pregnancy is unquestionably a condition requiring medical services.... Treatment for the condition may involve medical procedures for its termination, or medical procedures to bring the pregnancy to term, resulting in a live birth. '[A]bortion and childbirth, when stripped of the sensitive moral arguments surrounding the abortion controversy, are simply two alternative medical methods of dealing with pregnancy....' " *Beal* v. *Doe* (BRENNAN, J., dissenting) (quoting *Roe* v. *Norton* (Conn. 1975)). In every pregnancy, one of these two courses of treatment is medically necessary, and the poverty-stricken woman depends on the Medicaid Act to pay for the expenses associated with that procedure. But under the Hyde Amendment, the Government will fund only those procedures incidental to childbirth. By thus injecting coercive financial incentives favoring childbirth into a decision that is constitutionally guaranteed to be free from governmental intrusion, the Hyde Amendment deprives the indigent woman of her freedom to choose abortion over maternity, thereby impinging on the due process liberty right recognized in *Roe* v. *Wade*.

The Court's contrary conclusion is premised on its belief that "[t]he financial constraints that restrict an indigent woman's ability to enjoy the full range of constitutionally protected freedom of choice are the product not of governmental restrictions on access to abortions, but rather of her indigency." . . . Accurate as this statement may be, it reveals only half the picture. For what the Court fails to appreciate is that it is not simply the woman's indigency that interferes with her freedom of choice, but the combination of her own poverty and the government's unequal subsidization of abortion and childbirth.

A poor woman in the early stages of pregnancy confronts two alternatives: she may elect either to carry the fetus to term or to have an abortion. In the abstract, of course, this choice is hers alone, and the Court rightly observes that the Hyde Amendment "places no governmental obstacle in the path of a woman who chooses to terminate her pregnancy." . . . But the reality of the situation is that the Hyde Amendment has effectively removed this choice from the indigent woman's hands. By funding all of the expenses associated with childbirth and none of the expenses incurred in terminating pregnancy, the government literally makes an offer that the indigent woman cannot afford to refuse. It matters not that in this instance the government has used the carrot rather than the stick. What is critical is the realization that as a practical matter, many poverty-stricken women will choose to carry their pregnancy to term simply because the government provides funds for the associated medical services, even though these same women would have chosen to have an abortion if the government had also paid for that option, or indeed if the government had stayed out of the picture altogether and had defrayed the costs of neither procedure.

The fundamental flaw in the Court's due process analysis, then, is its failure to acknowledge that the discriminatory distribution of the benefits of governmental largesse can discourage the exercise of fundamental liberties just as effectively as can an outright denial of those rights through criminal and regulatory sanctions. Implicit in the Court's reasoning is the notion that as long as the government is not obligated to provide its citizens with certain benefits or privileges, it may condition the grant of such benefits on the recipient's relinquishment of his constitutional rights.

It would belabor the obvious to expound at any great length on the illegitimacy of a state policy that interferes with the exercise of fundamental rights through the selective bestowal of governmental favors. It suffices to note that we have heretofore never hesitated to invalidate any scheme of granting or withholding financial benefits that incidentally or intentionally burdens one manner of exercising a constitutionally protected choice. . . . *Sherbert* v. *Verner* (1963). . . .

The Medicaid program cannot be distinguished from these other statutory schemes that unconstitutionally burdened fundamental rights. Here, as in *Sherbert*, the government withholds financial benefits in a manner that discourages the exercise of a due process liberty: The indigent woman who chooses to assert her constitutional right to have an abortion can do so only on pain of sacrificing health care benefits to which she would otherwise be entitled. . . .

I respectfully dissent.

MR. JUSTICE MARSHALL, dissenting.

Three years ago, in *Maher* v. *Roe* (1977), the Court upheld a state program that excluded nontherapeutic abortions from a welfare program that generally subsidized the medical expenses incidental to pregnancy and childbirth. At that time, I expressed my fear "that the Court's decisions will be an invitation to public officials, already under extraordinary pressure from well-financed and carefully orchestrated lobbying campaigns, to approve more such restrictions" on governmental funding for abortion. . . . (dissenting opinion in *Beal* v. *Doe* (1977), *Maher* v. *Roe, Poelker* v. *Doe* (1977)).

That fear has proved justified. Under the Hyde Amendment, federal funding is denied for abortions that are medically necessary and that are necessary to avert severe and permanent damage to the health of the mother. The Court's opinion studiously avoids recognizing the undeniable fact that for women eligible for Medicaid — poor women — denial of a Medicaid-funded abortion is equivalent to denial of legal abortion altogether. By definition, these women do not have the money to pay for an abortion themselves. If abortion is medically necessary and a funded abortion is unavailable, they must resort to back-alley butchers, attempt to induce an abortion themselves by crude and dangerous methods, or suffer the serious medical consequences of attempting to carry the fetus to term. Because legal abortion is not a realistic option for such women, the predictable result of the Hyde Amendment will be a significant increase in the number of poor women who will die or suffer significant health damage because of an inability to procure necessary medical services.

The legislation before us is the product of an effort to deny to the poor the constitutional right recognized in *Roe* v. *Wade* (1973), even though the cost may be serious and long-lasting health damage. As my Brother STEVENS has demonstrated, see *post* (dissenting opinion), the premise underlying the Hyde Amendment was repudiated in *Roe* v. *Wade*, where the Court made clear that the state interest in protecting fetal life cannot justify jeopardizing the life or health of the mother. The denial of Medicaid benefits to individuals who meet all the statutory criteria for eligibility, solely because the treatment that is medically necessary involves the exercise of the fundamental right to choose abortion, is a form of discrimination repugnant to the equal protection of the laws guaranteed by the Constitution. The Court's decision today marks a retreat from *Roe* v. *Wade* and represents a cruel blow to the most powerless members of our society. I dissent.

I

In its present form, the Hyde Amendment restricts federal funding for abortion to cases in which "the life of the mother would be endangered if the fetus were carried to term" and "for such medical procedures necessary for the victims of rape or incest when such rape or incest has been reported promptly to a law enforcement agency or public health service." ... Federal funding is thus unavailable even when severe and long-lasting health damage to the mother is a virtual certainty. Nor are federal funds available when severe health damage, or even death, will result to the fetus if it is carried to term. ...

The impact of the Hyde Amendment in indigent women falls into four major categories. First, the Hyde Amendment prohibits federal funding for abortions that are necessary in order to protect the health and sometimes the life of the mother. Numerous conditions — such as cancer, rheumatic fever, diabetes, malnutrition, phlebitis, sickle cell anemia, and heart disease — substantially increase the risks associated with pregnancy or are themselves aggravated by pregnancy. Such conditions may make an abortion medically necessary in the judgment of a physician, but cannot be funded under the Hyde Amendment. Further, the health risks of undergoing an abortion increase dramatically as pregnancy becomes more advanced. By the time a pregnancy has progressed to the point where a physician is able to certify that it endangers the life of the mother, it is in many cases too late to prevent her death because abortion is no longer safe. There are also instances in which a woman's life will not be immediately threatened by carrying the pregnancy to term, but aggravation of another medical condition will significantly shorten her life expectancy. These cases as well are not fundable under the Hyde Amendment.

Second, federal funding is denied in cases in which severe mental disturbances will be created by unwanted pregnancies. The result of such psychological distubances may be suicide, attempts at self-abortion, or child abuse. The Hyde Amendment makes no provision for funding in such cases.

Third, the Hyde Amendment denies funding for the majority of women whose pregnancies have been caused by rape or incest. The prerequisite of a report within 60 days serves to exclude those who are afraid of recounting what has happened or are in fear of unsympathetic treatment by the authorities. Such a requirement is, of course, especially burdensome for the indigent, who may be least likely to be aware that a rapid report to the authorities is indispensable in order for them to be able to obtain an abortion.

Finally, federal funding is unavailable in cases in which it is known that the fetus itself will be unable to survive. In a number of situations it is possible to determine in advance that the fetus will suffer an early death if carried to term. The Hyde Amendment, purportedly designed to safeguard "the legitimate governmental interest of protecting potential life," . . . excludes federal funding in such cases.

An optimistic estimate indicates that as many as 100 excess deaths may occur each year as a result of the Hyde Amendment. The record contains no estimate of the health damage that may occur to poor women, but it shows that it will be considerable.

II

The Court resolves the equal protection issue in this case through a relentlessly formalistic catechism. Adhering to its "two-tiered" approach to equal protection, the Court first decides that so-called strict scrutiny is not required because the Hyde Amendment does not violate the Due Process Clause and is not predicated on a constitutionally suspect classification. Therefore, "the validity of classification must be sustained unless 'the classification rests on grounds wholly irrelevant to the achievement of [any legitimate governmental] objective.'" . . . [Q]uoting *McGowan* v. *Maryland* (1961). Observing that previous cases have recognized "the legitimate governmental objective of protecting life," . . . the Court concludes that the Hyde Amendment "establishe[s] incentives that make childbirth a more attractive alternative than abortion for persons eligible for Medicaid," *ibid.*, and is therefore rationally related to that governmental interest.

I continue to believe that the rigid "two-tiered" approach is inappropriate and that the Constitution requires a more exacting standard of review than mere rationality in cases such as this one. Further, in my judgment the Hyde Amendment cannot pass constitutional muster even under the rational-basis standard of review.

A

This case is perhaps the most dramatic illustration to date of the deficiencies in the Court's obsolete "two-tiered" approach to the Equal Protection Clause. . . . With all deference, I am unable to understand how the Court can afford the same level of scrutiny to the legislation involved here — whose cruel impact falls exclusively on indigent pregnant women — that it has given to legislation distinguishing opticians from opthalmologists, or to other legislation that makes distinctions between economic interests more than able to protect themselves in the political process. . . . *Williamson* v. *Lee Optical* (1955). Heightened scrutiny of legislative classifications has always been designed to protect groups "saddled with such disabilities or subjected to such a history of purposeful unequal treatment, or relegated to such a position of political powerlessness as to command extraordinary protection from the majoritarian political process." *San Antonio School District* v. *Rodriguez* (1973). And while it is now clear that traditional "strict scrutiny" is unavailable to protect the poor against classifications that disfavor them, *Dandridge* v. *Williams* (1970), I do not believe that legislation that imposes a crushing burden on indigent women can be treated with the same deference given to legislation distinguishing among business interests.

B

The Hyde Amendment, of course, distinguishes between medically necessary abortions and other medically necessary expenses. As I explained in *Maher* v. *Roe* ... such classifications must be assessed by weighing " 'the importance of the governmental benefits denied, the character of the class, and the asserted state interests,' " ... *Massachusetts Bd. of Retirement* v. *Murgia* [1976]. Under that approach, the Hyde Amendment is clearly invalid.

... An indigent woman denied governmental funding for a medically necessary abortion is confronted with two grotesque choices. First, she may seek to obtain "an illegal abortion that poses a serious threat to her health and even her life." ... Alternatively, she may attempt to bear the child, a course that may both significantly threaten her health and eliminate any chance she might have had "to control the direction of her own life.". . .

The class burdened by the Hyde Amendment consists of indigent women, a substantial proportion of whom are members of minority races. As I observed in *Maher,* nonwhite women obtain abortions at nearly double the rate of whites. ... In my view, the fact that the burden of the Hyde Amendment falls exclusively on financially destitute women suggests "a special condition, which tends seriously to curtail the operation of those political processes ordinarily to be relied upon to protect minorities, and which may call for a correspondingly more searching judicial inquiry." *United States* v. *Carolene Products* (1938). For this reason, I continue to believe that "a showing that state action has a devastating impact on the lives of minority racial groups must be relevant" for purposes of equal protection analysis. *Jefferson* v. *Hackney* (1972) (MARSHALL, J., dissenting).

As I explained in *Maher,* the asserted state interest in protecting potential life is insufficient to "outweigh the deprivation or serious discouragement of a vital constitutional right of especial importance to poor and minority women." In *Maher,* the Court found a permissible state interest in encouraging normal childbirth. ... The governmental interest in the present case is substantially weaker than in *Maher,* for under the Hyde Amendment funding is refused even in cases in which normal childbirth will not result: one can scarcely speak of "normal childbirth" in cases where the fetus will die shortly after birth, or in which the mother's life will be shortened or her health otherwise gravely impaired by the birth. Nevertheless, the Hyde Amendment denies funding even in such cases. In these circumstances, I am unable to see how even a minimally rational legislature could conclude that the interest in fetal life outweighs the brutal effect of the Hyde Amendment on indigent women. Moreover, both the legislation in *Maher* and the Hyde Amendment were designed to deprive poor and minority women of the constitutional right to choose abortion. That purpose is not constitutionally permitted under *Roe* v. *Wade*.

C

... The Court treats this case as though it were controlled by *Maher*. To the contrary, this case is the mirror image of *Maher*. The result in *Maher* turned on the fact that the legislation there under consideration discouraged only nontherapeutic, or medically unnecessary, abortions. In the Court's view, denial of Medicaid funding for nontherapeutic abortions was not a denial of equal protection because Medicaid funds were available only for medically necessary procedures. Thus the plaintiffs were seeking benefits which were not available to other similarly situated. I continue to believe that *Maher* was wrongly decided. But it is apparent that while the plaintiffs in *Maher* were seeking a benefit not available to others similarly situated, respondents are protesting their exclusion from a benefit that is available to all others similarly situated. This, it need hardly be said, is a crucial difference for equal protection purposes.

Under Title XIX and the Hyde Amendment, funding is available for essentially all necessary medical treatment for the poor. Respondents have met the statutory requirements for eligibility, but they are excluded because the treatment that is medically necessary involves the exercise of a fundamental right, the right to choose an abortion. In short, respondents have been deprived of a governmental benefit for which they are otherwise eligible, solely because they have attempted to exercise a constitutional right. The interest asserted by the government, the protection of fetal life, has been declared constitutionally subordinate to respondents' interest in preserving their lives and health by obtaining medically necessary treatment. *Roe* v. *Wade*. ... And finally, the purpose of the legislation was to discourage the exercise of the fundamental right. In such circumstances the Hyde Amendment must be invalidated because it does not meet even the rational-basis standard of review.

III

The consequences of today's opinion — consequences to which the Court seems oblivious — are not difficult to predict. Pregnant women denied the funding necessary to procure abortions will be restricted to two alternatives. First, they can carry the fetus to term — even though that route may result in severe injury or death to the mother, the fetus, or both. If that course appears intolerable, they can resort to self-induced abortions or attempt to obtain illegal abortions — not because bearing a child would be inconvenient, but because it is necessary in order to protect their health. The result will not be to protect what the Court describes as "the legitimate governmental objective of protecting potential life," ... but to ensure the destruction of both fetal and maternal life. "There is another world 'out there,' the existence of which the Court ... either chooses to ignore or fears to recognize." *Beal* v. *Doe* ... [1977] (BLACKMUN, J., dissenting). In my view, it is only by blinding itself to that other world that the Court can reach the result it announces today.

Ultimately, the result reached today may be traced to the Court's unwillingness to apply the constraints of the Constitution to decisions involving the expenditure of governmental funds. In today's decision, as in *Maher* v. *Roe*, the Court suggests that a withholding of funding imposes no real obstacle to a woman deciding whether to exercise her constitutionally protected procreative choice, even though the government is prepared to fund all other medically necessary expenses, including the expenses of childbirth. The Court perceives this result as simply a distinction between a "limitation on governmental power" and "an affirmative funding obligation." ... For a poor person attempting to exercise her "right" to freedom of choice, the difference is imperceptible. As my Brother BRENNAN has shown ... the differential distribution of incentives — which the Court concedes is present here ... — can have precisely the same effect as an outright prohibition. It is no more sufficient an answer here than it was in *Roe* v. *Wade* to say that " 'the appropriate forum' " for the resolution of sensitive policy choices is the legislature. . . .

More than 35 years ago, Mr. Justice Jackson observed that the "task of translating the majestic generalities of the Bill of Rights ... into concrete restraints on official dealing with the problems of the twentieth century, is one to disturb self-confidence." *West Virginia State Bd. of Educ.* v. *Barnette*, (1943). These constitutional principles, he observed for the Court, "grew in soil which also produced a philosophy that the individual['s] ... liberty was attainable through mere absence of government restraints." ... Those principles must be "transplant[ed] ... to a soil in which the *laissez-faire* concept or principle of non-interference has withered at least as to economic affairs, and social advancements are increasingly sought through closer integration of society and through expanded and strengthened governmental controls.". . .

In this case, the Federal Government has taken upon itself the burden of financing practically all medically necessary expenditures. One category of medically necessary expenditure has been singled out for exclusion, and the sole basis for the exclusion is a premise repudiated for purposes of constitutional law in *Roe* v. *Wade*. The consequence is a devastating impact on the lives and health of poor women. I do not believe that a Constitution committed to the equal protection of the laws can tolerate this result. I dissent.

MR. JUSTICE STEVENS, dissenting.

... If a woman has a constitutional right to place a higher value on avoiding either serious harm to her own health or perhaps an abnormal childbirth than on protecting potential life, the exercise of that right cannot provide the basis for the denial of a benefit to which she would otherwise be entitled. The Court's sterile equal protection analysis evades this critical though simple point. The Court focuses exclusively on the "legitimate interest in protecting the potential life of the fetus." ... It concludes that since the Hyde amendments further that interest, the exclusion they create is rational and therefore constitutional. But it is misleading to speak of the Government's legitimate interest in the fetus without reference to the context in which that interest was held to be legitimate. For *Roe* v. *Wade* squarely held that the States may not protect that interest when a conflict with the interest in a pregnant woman's health exists. It is thus perfectly clear that neither the Federal Government nor the States may exclude a woman from medical benefits to which she would otherwise be entitled solely to further an interest in potential life when a physician, "in appropriate medical judgment," certifies that an abortion is necessary "for the preservation of the life or health of the mother." *Roe* v. *Wade*.... The Court totally fails to explain why this reasoning is not dispositive here.

It cannot be denied that the harm inflicted upon women in the excluded class is grievous. As the Court's comparison of the differing forms of the Hyde Amendment that have been enacted since 1976 demonstrates, the Court expressly approves the exclusion of benefits in "instances where severe and long lasting physical health damage to the mother" is the predictable consequence of carrying the pregnancy to term. Indeed, as the Solicitor General acknowledged with commendable candor, the logic of the Court's position would justify a holding that it would be constitutional to deny funding to a medically and financially needy person even if abortion were the only lifesaving medical procedure available. Because a denial of benefits for medically necessary abortions inevitably causes serious harm to the excluded women, it is tantamount to severe punishment. In my judgment, that denial cannot be justified unless Government may, in effect, punish women who want abortions. But as the Court unequivocally held in *Roe* v. *Wade*, this the Government may not do.

Nor can it be argued that the exclusion of this type of medically necessary treatment of the indigent can be justified on fiscal grounds. There are some especially costly forms of treatment that may reasonably be excluded from the program in order to preserve the assets in the pool and extend its benefits to the maximum number of needy persons. Fiscal considerations may compel certain difficult choices in order to improve the protection afforded to the entire benefited class. But, ironically, the exclusion of medically necessary abortions harms the entire class as well as its specific victims. For the records in both *McRae* and *Zbaraz* [*Williams* v. *Zbaraz* (1980)] demonstrate that the cost of an abortion is only a small fraction of the costs associated with childbirth. Thus, the decision to tolerate harm to indigent persons who need an abortion in order to avoid "serious and long lasting health damage" is one that is financed by draining money out of the pool that is used to fund all other necessary medical procedures. Unlike most invidious classifications, this discrimination harms not only its direct victims but also the remainder of the class of needy persons that the pool was designed to benefit. . . .

Having decided to alleviate some of the hardships of poverty by providing necessary medical care, the Government must use neutral criteria in distributing benefits. It may not deny benefits to a financially and medically needy person simply because he is a Republican, a Catholic, or an Oriental — or because he has spoken against a program the Government has a legitimate interest in furthering. In sum, it may not create exceptions for the sole purpose of furthering a governmental interest that is constitutionally subordinate to the individual interest that the entire program was designed to protect. The Hyde amendments not only exclude financially and medically needy persons from the pool of benefits for a constitutionally insufficient reason; they also require the expenditure of millions and millions of dollars in order to thwart the exercise of a constitutional right, thereby effectively inflicting serious and long lasting harm on impoverished women who want and need abortions for valid medical reasons. In my judgment, these amendments constitute an unjustifiable, and indeed blatant, violation of the sovereign's duty to govern impartially.

I respectfully dissent.

July

COURT ON MINORITY SET ASIDES IN FEDERAL CONTRACTS

July 2, 1980

In a 6-3 decision July 2, the Supreme Court concluded that Congress did not violate the constitutional guarantee of equal protection when it set aside 10 percent of federal funds for local public works projects to be awarded, if possible, to minority businesses. The court had deliberated on the challenge to the set-aside provision for most of its 1979-80 term.

The court majority in Fullilove v. Klutznick *did not join in a single opinion. Chief Justice Warren E. Burger wrote an opinion expressing the court's judgment that the set-aside provision of the 1977 Public Works Employment Act was constitutional. Joining in that opinion were Justices Byron R. White and Lewis F. Powell Jr. Filing separate concurring opinions were Justices Powell and Thurgood Marshall. Justices William J. Brennan Jr. and Harry A. Blackmun joined in the opinion written by Justice Marshall.*

Dissenting from the court's ruling were Justices Potter Stewart, William H. Rehnquist and John Paul Stevens.

Majority Opinion

After a review of the legislative and administrative history of the minority set-aside provision, Chief Justice Burger explained that the majority found constitutionally permissible both the objectives of the legislation and the means, the use of racial and ethnic classification. The challenged portion of the 1977 law defined minority businesses as those owned by citizens who were Negroes, Spanish-speaking, Orientals, Indians, Eskimos and Aleuts.

The objective of the set aside — to ensure that companies receiving funds under the law would not use procurement practices that might perpetuate the effects of prior discrimination — was well within the power of Congress under several powers specifically delegated to the legislature by the Constitution, wrote Burger.

Congress made no specific "findings" in enacting the set aside. But Burger said that the court majority was satisfied, nevertheless, that Congress had an "abundant historical basis" upon which to conclude that continuing use of traditional procurement practices could operate to perpetuate the effect of past discrimination.

The use of racial and ethnic criteria to remedy past discrimination was permissible, Burger continued, rejecting the dissenters' argument that "Congress must act in a wholly 'color-blind' fashion." Although some white-owned firms might lose business as a result of the set-aside provision, Burger wrote, the majority found such a limited effect acceptable as a "sharing of the burden."

Concurring Opinions

In a separate concurring opinion, Justice Powell said that the minority set-aside provision met the test he had set out in his opinion in the 1978 Bakke case for the use of racial "quotas." (Historic Documents of 1978, p. 467) He wrote that the set-aside provision was "a reasonably necessary means of furthering the compelling governmental interest" in redressing discrimination.

Similarly, Justice Marshall, joined by Justices Brennan and Blackmun, wrote that the minority set aside met the test they had formulated in their Bakke opinion.

Dissenting Views

Justices Stewart and Rehnquist disagreed, quoting Justice John Marshall Harlan's famous dissenting words in Plessy v. Ferguson, the 1896 case in which the majority upheld state laws requiring segregation of the races: " 'Our Constitution is colorblind, and neither knows nor tolerates classes among citizens. . . .' " Stewart wrote, "Today's decision is wrong, for the same reason that Plessy v. Ferguson was wrong. . . ."

Writing separately, Justice Stevens said that "When Congress creates a special preference, or a special disability, for a class of persons, it should identify the characteristic that justifies the special treatment." He said that with respect to the set aside, Congress had failed to do so and thus failed to discharge its constitutional duty to govern impartially.

Following are excerpts from the Supreme Court's ruling July 2, 1980, upholding a provision of the 1977 Public Works Employment Act setting aside for minority businesses 10 percent of federal funds for local public works projects; excerpts from the concurring opinions of Justices Powell and Marshall; and excerpts from the dissenting opinions of Justices Stewart and Stevens:

No. 78-1007

H. Earl Fullilove et al., Petitioners, *v.* Philip M. Klutznick, Secretary of Commerce of the United States, et al.	On Writ of Certiorari to the United States Court of Appeals for the Second Circuit.

[July 2, 1980]

MR. CHIEF JUSTICE BURGER announced the judgment of the Court and delivered an opinion in which MR. JUSTICE WHITE and MR. JUSTICE POWELL joined.

We granted certiorari to consider a facial constitutional challenge to a requirement in a congressional spending program that, absent an administrative waiver, 10% of the federal funds for local public works projects must be used by the state or local grantee to procure services or supplies from businesses owned and controlled by members of statutorily identified minority groups. . . .

I

In May 1977, Congress enacted the Public Works Employment Act of 1977 . . . which amended the Local Public Works Capital Development and Investment Act of 1976. . . . The 1977 amendments authorized an additional $4 billion appropriation for federal grants to be made by the Secretary of Commerce, acting through the Economic Development Administration (EDA), to state and local governmental entities for use in local public works projects. Among the changes made was the addition of the provision that has become the focus of this litigation. Section 103 (f)(2) of the 1977 Act, referred to as the "minority business enterprise" or "MBE" provision, requires that:

"Except to the extent that the Secretary determines otherwise, no grant shall be made under this Act for any local public works project unless the applicant gives satisfactory assurance to the Secretary that at least 10 per centum of the amount of each grant shall be expended for minority business enterprises. For purposes of this paragraph, the term "minority business enterprise" means a business at least 50 per centum of which is owned by minority group members or, in case of a publicly owned business, at least 51 per centum of the stock of which is owned by minority group members. For the purposes of the preceding sentence, minority group members are citizens of the United States who are Negroes, Spanish-speaking, Orientals, Indians, Eskimos, and Aleuts."

In late May 1977, the Secretary promulgated regulations governing administration of the grant program which were amended two months later. In August 1977, the EDA issued guidelines supplementing the statute and regulations with respect to minority business participation in local public works grants, and in October 1977, the EDA issued a technical bulletin promulgating detailed instructions and information to assist grantees and their contractors in meeting the 10% MBE requirement.

On November 30, 1977, petitioners filed a complaint in the United States District Court for the Southern District of New York seeking declaratory and injunctive relief to enjoin enforcement of the MBE provision. Named as defendants were the Secretary of Commerce, as the program administrator, and the State and City of New York, as actual and potential project grantees. Petitioners are several associations of construction contractors and subcontractors, and a firm engaged in heating, ventilation and air conditioning work. Their complaint alleged that they had sustained economic injury due to enforcement of the 10% MBE requirement and that the MBE provision on its face violated the Equal Protection Clause of the Fourteenth Amendment, the equal protection component of the Due Process Clause of the Fifth Amendment, and various statutory antidiscrimination provisions.

After a hearing held the day the complaint was filed, the District Court denied a requested temporary restraining order and scheduled the matter for an expedited hearing on the merits. On December 19, 1977, the District Court issued a memorandum opinion upholding the validity of the MBE program and denying the injunctive relief sought. *Fullilove* v. *Kreps* (SDNY 1977).

The United States Court of Appeals for the Second Circuit affirmed, ... holding that "even under the most exacting standard of review the MBE provision passes constitutional muster." ... Considered in the context of many years of governmental efforts to remedy past racial and ethnic discrimination, the court found it "difficult to imagine" any purpose for the program other than to remedy such discrimination. ... In its view, a number of factors contributed to the legitimacy of the MBE provision, most significant of which was the narrowed focus and limited extent of the statutory and administrative program, in size, impact and duration...; the court looked also to the holdings of other courts of appeals and district courts that the MBE program was constitutional.... It expressly rejected petitioners' contention that the 10% MBE requirement violated the equal protection guarantees of the Constitution....

II

A

The MBE provision was enacted as part of the Public Works Employment Act of 1977, which made various amendments to Title I of the Local Public Works Capital Development and Investment Act of 1976. The 1976 Act was intended as a short-term measure to alleviate the problem of national unemployment and to stimulate the national economy by assisting state and local governments to build needed public facilities. To accomplish these objectives, the Congress authorized the Secretary of Commerce, acting through the Economic Development Administration, to make grants to state and local governments for construction, renovation, repair or other improvement of local public works projects. The 1976 Act placed a number of restrictions on project eligibility designed to assure that federal monies were targeted to accomplish the legislative purposes. It established criteria to determine grant priorities and to apportion federal funds among political jurisdictions. Those criteria directed grant funds toward areas of high unemployment. The statute authorized the appropriation of up to $2 billion for a period ending in September 1977; this appropriation was soon consumed by grants made under the program.

Early in 1977, Congress began consideration of expanded appropriations and amendments to the grant program. Under administration of the 1976 appropriation, referred to as "Round I" of the local public works program, applicants seeking some $25 billion in grants had competed for the $2 billion in available funds; of nearly 25,000 applications, only some 2,000 were granted. The results provoked widespread concern for the fairness of the allocation process. Because the 1977 Act would authorize the appropriation of an additional $4 billion to fund "Round II" of the grant program, the congressional hearings and debates concerning the amendments focused primarily on the politically sensitive problems of priority and geographic distribution of grants under the supplemental appropriation. The result of this attention was inclusion in the 1977 Act of provisions revising the allocation criteria of the 1976 legislation. Those provisions, however, retained the underlying objective to direct funds into areas of high unemployment. The 1977 Act also added new restrictions on applicants seeking to qualify for federal grants; among these was the MBE provision....

The amendment was put forward not as a new concept, but rather one building upon prior administrative practice....

Although the proposed MBE provision on its face appeared mandatory, requiring compliance with the 10% minority participation requirement "[n]otwithstanding any other provision of law," its sponsor gave assurances that existing administrative practice would ensure flexibility in administration if, with respect to a particular project, compliance with the 10% requirement proved infeasible. . . .

The device of a 10% MBE participation requirement, subject to administrative waiver, was thought to be required to assure minority business participation; otherwise it was thought that repetition of the prior experience could be expected, with participation by minority business accounting for an inordinately small percentage of government contracting. The causes of this disparity were perceived as involving the longstanding existence and maintenance of barriers impairing access by minority enterprises to public contracting opportunities, or sometimes as involving more direct discrimination, but not as relating to lack — as Senator Brooke put it — "of capable and qualified minority enterprises who are ready and willing to work." In the words of its sponsor, the MBE provision was "designed to begin to redress this grievance that has been extant for so long."

B

The legislative objectives of the MBE provision must be considered against the background of ongoing efforts directed toward deliverance of the century-old promise of equality of economic opportunity. The sponsors of the MBE provision in the House and the Senate expressly linked the provision to the existing administrative programs promoting minority opportunity in government procurement, particularly those related to § 8(a) of the Small Business Act of 1958. . . .

Against this backdrop of legislative and administrative programs, it is inconceivable that Members of both Houses were not fully aware of the objectives of the MBE provision and of the reasons prompting its enactment.

C

Although the statutory MBE provision itself outlines only the bare bones of the federal program, it makes a number of critical determinations: the decision to initiate a limited racial and ethnic preference; the specification of a minimum level for minority business participation; the identification of the minority groups that are to be encompassed by the program; and the provision for an administrative waiver where application of the program is not feasible. Congress relied on the administrative agency to flesh out this skeleton, pursuant to delegated rulemaking authority, and to develop an administrative operation consistent with legislative intentions and objectives.

As required by the Public Works Employment Act of 1977, the Secretary of Commerce promulgated regulations to set into motion "Round II" of the federal grant program. The regulations require that construction projects funded under the legislation must be performed under contracts awarded by competitive bidding, unless the federal administrator has made a determination that in the circumstances relating to a particular project some other method is in the public interest. Where competitive bidding is employed, the regulations echo the statute's requirement that contracts are to be awarded on the basis of the "lowest responsive bid submitted by a bidder meeting established criteria of responsibility," and they also restate the MBE requirement.

EDA also has published guidelines devoted entirely to the administration of the MBE provision. The guidelines outline the obligations of the grantee to seek out all available, qualified, bona fide MBE's, to provide technical assistance as needed, to lower or waive bonding requirements where feasible, to solicit the aid of the Office of Minority Business Enterprise, the Small Business Administration or other sources for assisting MBE's in obtaining required working capital, and to give guidance through the intricacies of the bidding process.

EDA regulations contemplate that, as anticipated by Congress, most local public works projects will entail the award of a predominant prime contract, with the prime contractor assuming the above grantee obligations for fulfilling the 10% MBE requirement. The EDA guidelines specify that when prime contractors are selected through competitive bidding, bids for the prime contract "shall be considered by the Grantee to be responsive only if at least 10 percent of the contract funds are to be expended for MBE's." The administrative program envisions that competitive incentive will motivate aspirant prime contractors to perform their obligations under the MBE provision so as to qualify as "responsive" bidders. And, since the contract is to be awarded to the lowest responsive bidder, the same incentive is expected to motivate prime contractors to seek out the most competitive of the available, qualified, bona fide minority firms. This too is consistent with the legislative intention. . . .

. . . It will be recalled that in the report of the House Subcommittee on SBA Oversight and Minority Enterprise the subcommittee took special care to note that when using the term "minority" it intended to include "only such minority individuals as are considered to be economically or socially disadvantaged." The subcommittee also was cognizant of existing administrative regulations designed to ensure that firms maintained on the lists of bona fide minority business enterprises be those whose competitive position is impaired by the effects of disadvantage and discrimination. In its report, the subcommittee expressed its intention that these criteria continue to govern administration of the SBA's § 8(a) program. . . .

III

When we are required to pass on the constitutionality of an Act of Congress, we assume "the gravest and most delicate duty that this Court is called on to perform." *Blodgett* v. *Holden* (1927) (opinion of Holmes, J.). A program that employs racial or ethnic criteria, even in a remedial context, calls for close examination; yet we are bound to approach our task with appropriate deference to the Congress, a co-equal branch charged by the Constitution with the power to "provide for the ... general Welfare of the United States" and "to enforce by appropriate legislation" the equal protection guarantees of the Fourteenth Amendment. . . .

Here we pass, not on a choice made by a single judge or a school board but on a considered decision of the Congress and the President. However, in no sense does that render it immune from judicial scrutiny and it "is not to say we 'defer' to the judgment of the Congress ... on a constitutional question," or that we would hesitate to invoke the Constitution should we determine that Congress has overstepped the bounds of its constitutional power. . . .

The clear objective of the MBE provision is disclosed by our necessarily extended review of its legislative and administrative background. The program was designed to ensure that, to the extent federal funds were granted under the Public Works Employment Act of 1977, grantees who elect to participate would not employ procurement practices that Congress had decided might result in perpetuation of the effects of prior discrimination which had impaired or foreclosed access by minority businesses to public contracting opportunities. The MBE program does not mandate the allocation of federal funds according to inflexible percentage solely based on race or ethnicity.

Our analysis proceeds in two steps. At the outset, we must inquire whether the *objectives* of this legislation are within the power of Congress. If so, we must go on to decide whether the limited use of racial and ethnic criteria, in the context presented, is a constitutionally permissible *means* for achieving the congressional objectives and does not violate the equal protection component of the Due Process Clause of the Fifth Amendment.

A

(1)

In enacting the MBE provision, it is clear that Congress employed an amalgam of its specifically delegated powers. The Public Works Employment Act of 1977, by its very nature, is primarily an exercise of the Spending Power. U.S. Const., Art. I, § 8, cl. 1. This Court has recognized that the power to "provide for the ... general Welfare" is an independent grant of legislative authority, distinct from other broad congressional powers. *Buckley* v. *Valeo* (1976); *United States* v. *Butler* (1936). Congress has frequently employed the Spending Power to further broad policy objectives by conditioning receipt of federal monies upon compliance by the recipient with federal statutory and administrative directives. This Court has repeatedly upheld against constitutional challenge the use of this technique to induce governments and private parties to cooperate voluntarily with federal policy. . . .

The MBE program is structured within this familiar legislative pattern. The program conditions receipt of public works grants upon agreement by the state or local governmental grantee that at least 10% of the federal funds will be devoted to contracts with minority businesses, to the extent this can be accomplished by overcoming barriers to access and by awarding contracts to bona fide MBE's. It is further conditioned to require that MBE bids on these contracts are competitively priced, or might have been competitively priced but for the present effects of prior discrimination. Admittedly, the problems of administering this program with respect to these conditions may be formidable. Although the primary responsibility for ensuring minority participation falls upon the grantee, when the procurement practices of the grantee involve the award of a prime contract to a general or prime contractor, the obligations to assure minority participation devolve upon the private contracting party; this is a contractual condition of eligibility for award of the prime contract.

Here we need not explore the outermost limitations on the objectives attainable through such an application of the Spending Power. The reach of the Spending Power, within its sphere, is at least as broad as the regulatory powers of Congress. If, pursuant to its regulatory powers, Congress could have achieved the objectives of the MBE program, then it may do so under the Spending Power. And we have no difficulty perceiving a basis for accomplishing the objectives of the MBE program through the Commerce Power insofar as the program objectives pertain to the action of private contracting parties, and through the power to enforce the equal protection guarantees of the Fourteenth Amendment insofar as the program objectives pertain to the action of state and local grantees.

(2)

We turn first to the Commerce Power.... Had Congress chosen to do so, it could have drawn on the Commerce Clause to regulate the practices of prime contractors on federally funded public works projects. *Katzenbach* v. *McClung* (1964); *Heart of Atlanta Motel, Inc.* v. *United States* (1964). The legislative history of the MBE provision shows that there was a rational basis for Congress to conclude that the subcontracting practices of prime contractors could perpetuate the prevailing impaired access by minority businesses to public contracting opportunities, and that this inequity has an effect on interstate commerce. Thus Congress could take necessary and proper action to remedy the situation. ...

(3)

In certain contexts, there are limitations on the reach of the Commerce Power to regulate the actions of state and local governments. *National*

League of Cities v. *Usery* (1976). To avoid such complications, we look to § 5 of the Fourteenth Amendment for the power to regulate the procurement practices of state and local grantees of federal funds. *Fitzpatrick* v. *Bitzer* (1976). A review of our cases persuades us that the objectives of the MBE program are within the power of Congress under § 5 "to enforce by appropriate legislation" the equal protection guarantees of the Fourteenth Amendment. . . .

Although the Act recites no preambulary "findings" on the subject, we are satisfied that Congress had abundant historical basis from which it could conclude that traditional procurement practices, when applied to minority businesses, could perpetuate the effects of prior discrimination. Accordingly, Congress reasonably determined that the prospective elimination of these barriers to minority firm access to public contracting opportunities generated by the 1977 Act was appropriate to ensure that those businesses were not denied equal opportunity to participate in federal grants to state and local governments, which is one aspect of the equal protection of the laws. Insofar as the MBE program pertains to the actions of state and local grantees, Congress could have achieved its objectives by use of its power under § 5 of the Fourteenth Amendment. We conclude that in this respect the objectives of the MBE provision are within the scope of the Spending Power.

(4)

There are relevant similarities between the MBE program and the federal spending program reviewed in *Lau* v. *Nichols* (1974). In *Lau,* a language barrier "effectively foreclosed" non-English-speaking Chinese pupils from access to the educational opportunities offered by the San Francisco public school system. . . . It had not been shown that this had resulted from any discrimination, purposeful or otherwise, or from other unlawful acts. Nevertheless, we upheld the constitutionality of a federal regulation applicable to public school systems receiving federal funds that prohibited the utilization of "criteria or methods of administration *which have the effect* . . . of defeating or substantially impairing accomplishment of the objectives of the [educational] program as respect individuals of a particular race, color, or national origin.". . . Moreover, we upheld application to the San Francisco school system, as a recipient of federal funds, of a requirement that "[w]here inability to speak and understand the English language excludes national origin-minority group children from effective participation in the educational program offered by a school district, the district must take affirmative steps to rectify the language deficiency in order to open its instructional program to these students.". . .

B

We now turn to the question whether, as a *means* to accomplish these plainly constitutional objectives, Congress may use racial and ethnic criteria, in this limited way, as a condition attached to a federal grant. We are mindful that "[i]n no matter should we pay more deference to the opinion of Congress than in its choice of instrumentalities to perform a function that is within its power." *National Mutual Insurance Co.* v. *Tidewater Transfer Co.* (1949) (opinion of Jackson, J.). However, Congress may employ racial or ethnic classifications in exercising its Spending or other legislative Powers only if those classifications do not violate the equal protection component of the Due Process Clause of the Fifth Amendment. We recognize the need for careful judicial evaluation to assure that any congressional program that employs racial or ethnic criteria to accomplish the objective of remedying the present effects of past discrimination is narrowly tailored to the achievement of that goal.

Again, we stress the limited scope of our inquiry. Here we are not dealing with a remedial decree of a court but with the legislative authority of Congress. Furthermore, petitioners have challenged the constitutionality of the MBE provision on its face; they have not sought damages or other specific relief for injury allegedly flowing from specific applications of the program; nor have they attempted to show that as applied in identified situations the MBE provision violated the constitutional or statutory rights of any party to this case. In these circumstances, given a reasonable construction and in light of its projected administration, if we find the MBE program on its face to be free of constitutional defects, it must be upheld as within congressional power. . . .

Our review of the regulations and guidelines governing administration of the MBE provision reveals that Congress enacted the program as a strictly remedial measure; moreover, it is a remedy that functions prospectively, in the manner of an injunctive decree. Pursuant to the administrative program, grantees and their prime contractors are required to seek out all available, qualified, bona fide MBE's; they are required to provide technical assistance as needed, to lower or waive bonding requirements where feasible, to solicit the aid of the Office of Minority Business Enterprise, the Small Business Administration or other sources for assisting MBE's to obtain required working capital, and to give guidance through the intricacies of the bidding process. . . . The program assumes that grantees who undertake these efforts in good faith will obtain at least 10% participation by minority business enterprises. It is recognized that, to achieve this target, contracts will be awarded to available, qualified, bona fide MBE's even though they are not the lowest competitive bidders, so long as their higher bids, when challenged, are found to reflect merely attempts to cover costs inflated by the present effects of prior disadvantage and discrimination. . . .

(1)

As a threshold matter, we reject the contention that in the remedial context the Congress must act in a wholly "color-blind" fashion. In

Swann v. *Charlotte-Mecklenberg Board of Education* (1971), we rejected this argument in considering a court-formulated school desegregation remedy on the basis that examination of the racial composition of student bodies was an unavoidable starting point and that racially based attendance assignments were permissible so long as no absolute racial balance of each school was required. In *McDaniel* v. *Barresi* (1971), citing *Swann,* we observed that "[i]n this remedial process, steps will almost invariably require that students be assigned 'differently because of their race.' . . . Any other approach would freeze the status quo that is the very target of all desegregation processes." . . . And in *North Carolina Board of Education* v. *Swann* (1971), we invalidàted a state law that absolutely forbade assignment of any student on account of race because it foreclosed implementation of desegregation plans that were designed to remedy constitutional violations. We held that "[j]ust as the race of students must be considered in determining whether a constitutional violation has occurred, so also must race be considered in formulating a remedy." . . .

(2)

A more specific challenge to the MBE program is the charge that it impermissibly deprives nonminority businesses of access to at least some portion of the government contracting opportunities generated by the Act. It must be conceded that by its objective of remedying the historical impairment of access, the MBE provision can have the effect of awarding some contracts to MBE's which otherwise might be awarded to other businesses, who may themselves be innocent of any prior discriminatory actions. Failure of nonminority firms to receive certain contracts is, of course, an incidental consequence of the program, not part of its objective; similarly, past impairment of minority-firm access to public contracting opportunities may have been an incidental consequence of "business-as-usual" by public contracting agencies and among prime contractors.

It is not a constitutional defect in this program that it may disappoint the expectations of nonminority firms. . . .

(3)

Another challenge to the validity of the MBE program is the assertion that it is underinclusive — that it limits its benefit to specified minority groups rather that extending its remedial objectives to all businesses whose access to government contracting is impaired by the effects of disadvantage or discrimination. Such an extension would, of course, be appropriate for Congress to provide; it is not a function for the courts.

Even in this context, the well-established concept that a legislature may take one step at a time to remedy only part of a broader problem is not without relevance. . . . *Dandridge* v. *Williams* (1970); *Williamson* v. *Lee Optical Co.* (1955). . . .

The Congress has not sought to give select minority groups a preferred standing in the construction industry, but has embarked on a remedial program to place them on a more equitable footing with respect to public contracting opportunities. . . .

(4)

It is also contended that the MBE program is overinclusive — that it bestows a benefit on business identified by racial or ethnic criteria which cannot be justified on the basis of competitive criteria or as a remedy for the present effects of identified prior discrimination. It is conceivable that a particular application of the program may have this effect; however, the peculiarities of specific applications are not before us in this case. We are not presented here with a challenge involving a specific award of a construction contract or the denial of a waiver request; such questions of specific application must await future cases.

This does not mean that the claim of overinclusiveness is entitled to no consideration in the present case. The history of governmental tolerance of practices using racial or ethnic criteria for the purpose or with the effect of imposing an invidious discrimination must alert us to the deleterious effects of even benign racial or ethnic classifications when they stray from narrow remedial justifications. Even in the context of a facial challenge such as is presented in this case, the MBE provision cannot pass muster unless, with due account for its administrative program, it provides a reasonable assurance that application of racial or ethnic criteria will be limited to accomplishing the remedial objectives of Congress and that misapplications of the program will be promptly and adequately remedied administratively.

It is significant that the administrative scheme provides for waiver and exemption. Two fundamental congressional assumptions underlie the MBE program: (1) that the present effects of past discrimination have impaired the competitive position of businesses owned and controlled by members of minority groups; and (2) that affirmative efforts to eliminate barriers to minority-firm access, and to evaluate bids with adjustment for the present effects of past discrimination, would assure that at least 10% of the federal funds granted under the Public Works Employment Act of 1977 would be accounted for by contracts with available, qualified, bona fide minority business enterprises. Each of these assumptions may be rebutted in the administrative process. . . .

IV

Congress, after due consideration, perceived a pressing need to move forward with new approaches in the continuing effort to achieve the goal of equality of economic opportunity. In this effort, Congress has necessary latitude to try new techniques such as the limited use of racial and ethnic criteria to accomplish remedial objectives; this especially so in programs where voluntary cooperation with remedial measures is induced by placing conditions on federal expenditures. That the program may press the outer limits of congressional authority affords no basis for striking it down.

Petitioners have mounted a facial challenge to a program developed by the politically responsive branches of Government. For its part, the Congress must proceed only with programs narrowly tailored to achieve its objectives, subject to continuing evaluation and reassessment; administration of the programs must be vigilant and flexible; and, when such a program comes under judicial review, courts must be satisfied that the legislative objectives and projected administration give reasonable assurance that the program will function within constitutional limitations. . . .

Any preference based on racial or ethnic criteria must necessarily receive a most searching examination to make sure that it does not conflict with constitutional guarantees. This case is one which requires, and which has received, that kind of examination. This opinion does not adopt, either expressly or implicitly, the formulas of analysis articulated in such cases as *University of California Regents* v. *Bakke* (1978). However, our analysis demonstrates that the MBE provision would survive judicial review under either "test" articulated in the several *Bakke* opinions. The MBE provision of the Public Works Employment Act of 1977 does not violate the Constitution.

Affirmed.

MR. JUSTICE POWELL, concurring.

Although I would place greater emphasis than THE CHIEF JUSTICE on the need to articulate judicial standards of review in conventional terms, I view his opinion announcing the judgment as substantially in accord with my own views. Accordingly, I join that opinion and write separately to apply the analysis set forth by my opinion in *University of California* v. *Bakke* (1978) (hereinafter *Bakke*). . . .

The Equal Protection Clause, and the equal protection component of the Due Process Clause of the Fifth Amendment, demand that any governmental distinction among groups must be justifiable. Different standards of review applied to different sorts of classifications simply illustrate the principle that some classifications are less likely to be legitimate than others. Racial classifications must be assessed under the most stringent level of review because immutable characteristics, which bear no relation to individual merit or need, are irrelevant to almost every governmental decision. . . . In this case, however, I believe that § 103 (f)(2) is justified as a remedy that serves the compelling governmental interest in eradicating the continuing effects of past discrimination identified by Congress.

I

Racial preference never can constitute a compelling state interest. " 'Distinctions between citizens solely because of their ancestry' [are] 'odious to a free people whose institutions are founded upon the doctrine of equality.' " *Loving* v. *Virginia,* quoting *Hirabayashi* v. *United States* (1943). . . .

The Government does have a legitimate interest in ameliorating the disabling effects of identified discrimination. . . . But this Court has never approved race-conscious remedies absent judicial, administrative, or legislative findings of constitutional or statutory violations. . . .

Our past cases also establish that even if the government proffers a compelling interest to support reliance upon a suspect classification, the means selected must be narrowly drawn to fulfill the governmental purpose. . . . In *Bakke,* for example, the state university did have a compelling interest in the attainment of a diverse student body. But the method selected to achieve that end, the use of a fixed admissions quota, was not appropriate. The Regent's quota system eliminated some nonminority applicants from all consideration for a specified number of seats in the entering class, although it allowed minority applicants to compete for all available seats. . . . In contrast, an admissions program that recognizes race as a factor, but not the sole factor, in assessing an applicant's qualifications serves the University's interest in diversity while ensuring that each applicant receives fair and competitive consideration. . . .

In reviewing the constitutionality of § 103 (f)(2), we must decide: (i) whether Congress is competent to make findings of unlawful discriminations; (ii) if so, whether sufficient findings have been made to establish that unlawful discrimination has affected adversely minority business enterprises, and (iii) whether the 10% set-aside is a permissible means for redressing identifiable past discrimination. None of these questions may be answered without explicit recognition that we are reviewing an Act of Congress.

II

The history of this Court's review of congressional action demonstrates beyond question that the National Legislature is competent to find constitutional and statutory violations. Unlike the Regents of the University of California, Congress properly may — and indeed must — address directly the problems of discrimination in our society. . . .

In addition, Congress has been given the unique constitutional power of legislating to enforce the provisions of the Thirteenth, Fourteenth, and Fifteenth Amendments. At an early date, the Court stated that "[i]t is the power of Congress which has been enlarged" by the enforcement provisions of the post-Civil War Amendments. *Ex parte Virginia* (1879). In *Jones* v. *Alfred H. Mayer & Co.* (1968), the Court recognized Congress' competence to determine that private action inhibiting the right to acquire and convey real property was racial discrimination forbidden by the Thirteenth Amendment....

Congress' authority to find and provide for the redress of constitutional violations also has been confirmed in cases construing the enforcement clause of the Fifteenth Amendment....

It is beyond question, therefore, that Congress has the authority to identify unlawful discriminatory practices, to prohibit those practices, and to prescribe remedies to eradicate their continuing effects. The next inquiry is whether Congress has made findings adequate to support its determination that minority contractors have suffered extensive discrimination.

III

A

The petitioners contend that the legislative history of § 103 (f)(2) reflects no congressional finding of statutory or constitutional violations. Crucial to that contention is the assertion that a reviewing court may not look beyond the legislative history of the PWEA itself for evidence that Congress believed it was combatting invidious discrimination. But petitioners' theory would erect an artificial barrier to full understanding of the legislative process.

Congress is not an adjudicatory body called upon to resolve specific disputes between competing adversaries. Its constitutional role is to be representative rather than impartial, to make policy rather than to apply settled principles of law....

Acceptance of petitioners' argument would force Congress to make specific factual findings with respect to each legislative action. Such a requirement would mark an unprecedented imposition of adjudicatory procedures upon a coordinate branch of Government. Neither the Constitution nor our democratic tradition warrants such a constraint on the legislative process....

B

In my view, the legislative history of § 103 (f)(2) demonstrates that Congress reasonably concluded that private and government discrimination had contributed to the negligible percentage of public contracts awarded minority contractors.... The opinion of THE CHIEF JUSTICE provides a careful overview of the relevant legislative history ... to which only a few words need be added....

In light of these legislative materials and the discussion of legislative history contained in THE CHIEF JUSTICE's opinion, I believe that a court must accept as established the conclusion that purposeful discrimination contributed significantly to the small percentage of federal contracting funds that minority business enterprises have received. Refusals to subcontract work to minority contractors may, depending upon the identity of the discriminating party, violate Title VI of the Civil Rights Act of 1964 . . . or 42 U.S.C. § 1981, or the Fourteenth Amendment. Although the discriminatory activities were not identified with the exactitude expected in judicial or administrative adjudication, it must be remembered that "Congress may paint with a much broader brush than may this Court. . . ." *Oregon* v. *Mitchell* (1970) (STEWART, J., concurring in part and dissenting in part).

IV

Under this Court's established doctrine, a racial classification is suspect and subject to strict judicial scrutiny. As noted in Part I, the Government may employ such a classification only when necessary to accomplish a compelling governmental purpose. . . . The conclusion that Congress found a compelling governmental interest in redressing identified discrimination against minority contractors therefore leads to the inquiry whether use of a 10% set-aside is a constitutionally appropriate means of serving that interest. In the past, this "means" test has been virtually impossible to satisfy. Only two of this Court's modern cases have held the use of racial classifications to be constitutional. See *Korematsu* v. *United States* (1944); *Hirabayshi* v. *United States* (1943). Indeed, the failure of legislative action to survive strict scrutiny has led some to wonder whether our review of racial classifications has been strict in theory, but fatal in fact. . . .

A

Application of the "means" test necessarily demands an understanding of the type of congressional action at issue. This is not a case in which Congress has employed a racial classification solely as a means to confer a racial preference. Such a purpose plainly would be unconstitutional. . . . Nor has Congress sought to employ a racially conscious means to further a nonracial goal. In such instances, a nonracial means should be available to further the legitimate governmental purpose. . . .

Enactment of the set-aside is designed to serve the compelling governmental interest in redressing racial discrimination. As this Court has recognized, the implementation of any affirmative remedy for redress of racial discrimination is likely to affect persons differently depending upon their race. . . . We have recognized that the choice of remedies to redress racial discrimination is "a balancing process left, within appropriate constitutional or statutory limits, to the sound discretion of the trial court." . . .

I believe that the enforcement clauses of the Thirteenth and Fourteenth Amendments give Congress a similar measure of discretion to choose a suitable remedy for the redress of racial discrimination. . . .

Although the Framers of the Fourteenth Amendment may have contemplated that Congress, rather than the federal courts, would be the prime force behind enforcement of the Fourteenth Amendment, ... they did not believe that congressional action would be unreviewable by this Court. Several Members of Congress emphasized that a primary purpose of the Fourteenth Amendment was to place the provisions of the Civil Rights of 1866 "in the eternal firmament of the Constitution.". . .

I conclude, therefore, that the enforcement clauses of the Thirteenth and Fourteenth Amendments confer upon Congress the authority to select reasonable remedies to advance the compelling state interest in repairing the effects of discrimination. But that authority must be exercised in a manner that does not erode the guarantees of these Amendments. The Judicial Branch has the special responsibility to make a searching inquiry into the justification for employing a race-conscious remedy. Courts must be sensitive to the possibility that less intrusive means might serve the compelling state interest equally as well. I believe that Congress' choice of a remedy should be upheld, however, if the means selected are equitable and reasonably necessary to the redress of identified discrimination. Such a test allows the Congress to exercise necessary discretion but preserves the essential safeguard of judicial review of racial classifications.

B

When reviewing the selection by Congress of a race-conscious remedy, it is instructive to note the factors upon which the Courts of Appeals have relied in a closely analogous area. . . .

By the time Congress enacted § 103 (f)(2) in 1977, it knew that other remedies had failed to ameliorate the effects of racial discrimination in the construction industry. Although the problem had been addressed by antidiscrimination legislation, executive action to remedy employment discrimination in the construction industry, and federal aid to minority businesses, the fact remained that minority contractors were receiving less than 1% of federal contracts. . . . Congress also knew that economic recession threatened the construction industry as a whole. . . . Since the emergency public construction funds were to be distributed quickly, any remedial provision designed to prevent those funds from perpetuating past discrimination also had to be effective promptly. Moreover, Congress understood that any effective remedial program had to provide miniority contractors the experience necessary for continued success without federal assistance. And Congress knew that the ability of minority group members to gain experience had been frustrated by the difficulty of entering the construction trades. The set-aside program adopted as part of this emergency legislation serves each of these concerns because it takes effect as soon as funds are expended under PWEA and because it provides minority contractors with experience that could enable them to compete without governmental assistance.

The § 103 (f)(2) set-aside is not a permanent part of federal contracting requirements. As soon as the PWEA program concludes, this set-aside program ends. The temporary nature of this remedy ensures that a race-conscious program will not last longer than the discriminatory effects it is designed to eliminate. It will be necessary for Congress to re-examine the need for a race-conscious remedy before it extends or re-enacts § 103 (f)(2).

The percentage chosen for the set-aside is within the scope of congressional discretion. . . .

C

A race-conscious remedy should not be approved without consideration of an additional crucial factor — the effect of the set-aside upon innocent third parties. . . . In this case, the petitioners contend with some force that they have been asked to bear the burden of the set-aside even though they are innocent of wrongdoing. I do not believe, however, that their burden is so great that the set-aside must be disapproved. . . .

Consideration of these factors persuades me that the set-aside is a reasonably necessary means of furthering the compelling governmental interest in redressing the discrimination that affects minority contractors. Any marginal unfairness to innocent nonminority contractors is not sufficiently significant — or sufficiently identifiable — to outweigh the governmental interest served by § 103 (f)(2). When Congress acts to remedy identified discrimination, it may exercise discretion in choosing a remedy that is reasonably necessary to accomplish its purpose. Whatever the exact breadth of that discretion, I believe that it encompasses the selection of the set-aside in this case.

V

In the history of this Court and this country, few questions have been more divisive than those arising from governmental action taken on the basis of race. Indeed, our own decisions played no small part in the tragic legacy of government-sanctioned discrimination. See *Plessy* v. *Ferguson* (1896); *Dred Scott* v. *Sanford* (60 U.S.) (1857). At least since the decision in *Brown* v. *Board of Education* (1954), the Court has been resolute in its dedication to the principle that the Constitution envisions a Nation where race is irrelevant. The time cannot come too soon when no governmental decision will be based upon immutable characteristics of pigmentation or origin. But in our quest to achieve a society free from racial classification, we cannot ignore the claims of those who still suffer from the effects of identifiable discrimination.

Distinguishing the rights of all citizens to be free from racial classifications from the rights of some citizens to be made whole is a perplexing, but necessary, judicial task. When we first confronted such an issue in *Bakke,* I concluded that the Regents of the University of California were not competent to make, and had not made, findings sufficient to uphold the use of the race-conscious remedy they adopted. As my opinion made clear, I believe that the use of racial classifications, which are fundamentally at odds with the ideals of a democratic society implicit in the Due Process and Equal Protection Clauses, cannot be imposed simply to serve transient social or political goals, however worthy they may be. But the issue here turns on the scope of congressional power, and Congress has been given a unique constitutional role in the enforcement of the post-Civil War Amendments. In this case, where Congress determined that minority contractors were victims of purposeful discrimination and where Congress chose a reasonably necessary means to effectuate its purpose, I find no constitutional reason to invalidate § 103 (f)(2).

MR. JUSTICE MARSHALL, with whom MR. JUSTICE BRENNAN and MR. JUSTICE BLACKMUN join, concurring in the judgment.

My resolution of the constitutional issue in this case is governed by the separate opinion I coauthored in *University of California Regents v. Bakke* (1978). In my view, the 10% minority set-aside provision of the Public Works Employment Act of 1977 passes constitutional muster under the standard announced in that opinion.

I

In *Bakke,* I joined my Brothers BRENNAN, WHITE, and BLACKMUN in articulating the view that "racial classifications are not *per se* invalid under [the Equal Protection Clause of] the Fourteenth Amendment." ... We acknowledged that "a government practice or statute which ... contains 'suspect classifications' is to be subjected to 'strict scrutiny' and can be justified only if it furthers a compelling government purpose and, even then, only if no less restrictive alternative is available." ... Thus, we reiterated the traditional view that racial classifications are prohibited if they are irrelevant. ... In addition, we firmly adhered to "the cardinal principle that racial classifications that stigmatize — because they are drawn on the presumption that one race is inferior to another or because they put the weight of government behind racial hatred and separatism — are invalid without more.". ...

We recognized, however, that these principles outlawing the irrelevant or pernicious use of race were inapposite to racial classifications that provide benefits to minorities for the purpose of remedying the present effects of past racial discrimination. Such classifications may disadvantage some whites, but whites as a class lack the " 'traditional indicia of suspectness: the class is not saddled with such disabilities, or subjected to such a history of purposeful unequal treatment, or relegated to such a position of political powerlessness as to command extraordinary protection from the majoritarian political process.' " ... Because the consideration of race is relevant to remedying the continuing effects of past racial discrimination, and because governmental programs employing racial classifications for remedial purposes can be crafted to avoid stigmatization, we concluded that such programs should not be subjected to conventional "strict scrutiny" — scrutiny that is strict in theory, but fatal in fact. . . .

Nor did we determine that such programs should be analyzed under the minimally rigorous rational-basis standard of review. . . . We recognized that race has often been used to stigmatize politically powerless segments of society, and that efforts to ameliorate the effects of past discrimination could be based on paternalistic stereotyping, not on a careful consideration of modern social conditions. In addition, we acknowledged that governmental classification on the immutable characteristics of race runs counter to the deep national belief that state-sanctioned benefits and burdens should bear some relationship to individual merit and responsibility. . . .

We concluded, therefore, that because a racial classification ostensibly designed for remedial purposes is susceptible to misuse, it may be justified only by showing "an important and articulated purpose for its use." . . . "In addition, any statute must be stricken that stigmatizes any group or that singles out those least well represented in the political process to bear the brunt of a benign program." . . . In our view, then, the proper inquiry is whether racial classifications designed to further remedial purposes serve important governmental objectives and are substantially related to achievement of those objectives. . . .

II

Judged under this standard, the 10% minority set-aside provision at issue in this case is plainly constitutional. Indeed, the question is not even a close one. . . .

Because the means chosen by Congress to implement the set-aside provision are substantially related to the achievement of its remedial purpose, the provision also meets the second prong of our *Bakke* test. Congress reasonably determined that race-conscious means were necessary to break down the barriers confronting participation by minority enterprises in federally funded public works projects. That the set-aside creates a quota in favor of qualified and available minority business enterprises does not necessarily indicate that it stigmatizes. As our opinion stated in *Bakke*, "[f]or purposes of constitutional adjudication, there is no difference between" setting aside "a predetermined number of places for qualified minority applicants rather than using minority status as a positive factor to be considered in evaluating the applications of disadvantaged minority applicants." . . . The set-aside, as enacted by Congress and implemented by the Secretary of Commerce, is carefully tailored to remedy racial discrimination while at the same time avoiding stigmatization and penalizing those least able to protect themselves in the political process. . . . Since under the set-aside provision a contract may be awarded to a minority enterprise only if it is qualified to do the work, the provision stigmatizes as inferior neither a minority firm that benefits from it nor a nonminority firm that is burdened by it. Nor does the set-aside "establish a quota in the invidious sense of a ceiling," ... on the number of minority firms that can be awarded public works contracts. In addition, the set-aside affects only a minuscule amount of the funds annually expended in the United States for construction work....

In sum, it is clear to me that the racial classifications employed in the set-aside provision are substantially related to the achievement of the important and congressionally articulated goal of remedying the present effects of past racial discrimination. The provision, therefore, passes muster under the equal protection standard I adopted in *Bakke.*

III

In my separate opinion in *Bakke,* I recounted the "ingenious and pervasive forms of discrimination against the Negro" long condoned under the Constitution and concluded that "[t]he position of the Negro today in America is the tragic but inevitable consequence of centuries of unequal treatment."...

Congress recognized these realities when it enacted the minority set-aside provision at issue in this case. Today, by upholding this race-conscious remedy, the Court accords Congress the authority necessary to undertake the task of moving our society toward a state of meaningful equality of opportunity, not an abstract version of equality in which the effects of past discrimination would be forever frozen into our social fabric. I applaud this result. Accordingly, I concur in the judgment of the Court.

MR. JUSTICE STEWART, with whom MR. JUSTICE REHNQUIST joins, dissenting.

"Our Constitution is color-blind, and neither knows or tolerates classes among citizens.... The law regards man as man, and takes no account of his surroundings or of his color...." Those words were written by a Member of this Court 84 years ago. *Plessy* v. *Ferguson* (Harlan, J., dissenting). His colleagues disagreed with him, and held that a statute that required the separation of people on the basis of their race was constitutionally valid because it was a "reasonable" exercise of legislative power and had been "enacted in good faith for the promotion [of] the public good...." ... Today, the Court upholds a statute that accords a preference to citizens who are "Negroes, Spanish-speaking, Orientals, Indians, Eskimos, and Aleuts," for much the same reasons. I think today's decision is wrong for the same reason that *Plessy* v. *Ferguson* was wrong, and I respectfully dissent.

A

The equal protection standard of the Constitution has one clear and central meaning — it absolutely prohibits invidious discrimination by government. That standard must be met by every State under the Equal Protection Clause of the Fourteenth Amendment. . . .

The hostility of the Constitution to racial classifications by government has been manifested in many cases decided by this Court. . . . And our cases have made clear that the Constitution is wholly neutral in forbidding such racial discrimination, whatever the race may be of those who are its victims. In *Anderson* v. *Martin* [1964], for instance, the Court dealt with a state law that required that the race of each candidate for election to public office be designated on the nomination papers and ballots. Although the law applied equally to candidates of whatever race, the Court held that it nonetheless violated the constitutional standard of equal protection. "We see *no relevance*," the Court said, "in the State's pointing up the race of the candidate as bearing upon his qualifications for office.". . .

This history contains one clear lesson. Under our Constitution, the government may never act to the detriment of a person solely because of that person's race. The color of a person's skin and the country of his origin are immutable facts that bear no relation to ability, disadvantage, moral culpability, or any other characteristics of constitutionally permissible interest to the government. "Distinctions between citizens solely because of their ancestry are by their very nature odious to a free people whose institutions are founded upon the doctrine of equality." *Hirabayashi* v. *United States*. . . . In short, racial discrimination is by definition invidious discrimination.

The rule cannot be any different when the persons injured by a racially biased law are not members of a racial minority. The guarantee of equal protection is "universal in [its] application, to all persons . . . without regard to any differences of race, of color, or of nationality." . . . The command of the equal protection guarantee is simple but unequivocal: In the words of the Fourteenth Amendment, "No State shall . . . deny to *any* person . . . the equal protection of the laws." Nothing in this language singles out some "persons" for more "equal" treatment than others. Rather, as the Court made clear in *Shelley* v. *Kraemer* [1948], the benefits afforded by the Equal Protection Clause "are, by its terms, guaranteed to the individual. [They] are personal rights." From the perspective of a person detrimentally affected by a racially discriminatory law, the arbitrariness and unfairness is entirely the same, whatever his skin color and whatever the law's purpose, be it purportedly "for the promotion of the public good" or otherwise.

No one disputes the self-evident proposition that Congress has broad discretion under its Spending Power to disburse the revenues of the United States as it deems best and to set conditions on the receipt of the funds disbursed. No one disputes that Congress has the authority under the Commerce Clause to regulate contracting practices on federally funded public works projects, or that it enjoys broad powers under § 5 of the Fourteenth Amendment "to enforce by appropriate legislation" the provisions of that Amendment. But these self-evident truisms do not begin to answer the question before us in this case. For in the exercise of its powers, Congress must obey the Constitution just as the legislatures of all the States must obey the Constitution in the exercise of their powers. If a law is unconstitutional, it is no less unconstitutional just because it is a product of the Congress of the United States.

B

On its face, the minority business enterprise (MBE) provision at issue in this case denies the equal protection of the law. The Public Works Employment Act of 1977 directs that all project construction shall be performed by those private contractors who submit the lowest competitive bids and who meet established criteria of responsibility. . . . One class of contracting firms — defined solely according to the racial and ethnic attributes of their owners — is, however, excepted from the full rigor of these requirements with respect to a percentage of each federal grant. The statute, on its face and in effect, thus bars a class to which the petitioners belong from having the opportunity to receive a government benefit, and bars the members of that class solely on the basis of their race or ethnic background. This is precisely the kind of law that the guarantee of equal protection forbids.

The Court's attempt to characterize the law as a proper remedial measure to counteract the effects of past or present racial discrimination is remarkably unconvincing. The Legislative Branch of government is not a court of equity. It has neither the dispassionate objectivity nor the flexibility that are needed to mold a race-conscious remedy around the single objective of eliminating the effects of past or present discrimination.

But even assuming that Congress has the power, under § 5 of the Fourteenth Amendment or some other constitutional provision, to remedy previous illegal racial discrimination, there is no evidence that Congress has in the past engaged in racial discrimination in its disbursement of federal contracting funds. The MBE provision thus pushes the limits of any such justification far beyond the equal protection standard of the Constitution. Certainly, nothing in the Constitution gives Congress any greater authority to impose detriments on the basis of race than is afforded the Judicial Branch. And a judicial decree that imposes burdens on the basis of race can be upheld only where its sole purpose is to eradicate the actual effects of illegal race discrimination. . . .

The provision at issue here does not satisfy this condition. Its legislative history suggests that it had at least two other objectives in addition to that of counteracting the effects of past or present racial discrimination in the public works construction industry. One such purpose appears to have been to assure to minority contractors a certain percentage of federally funded public works contracts. But, since the guarantee of equal protection immunizes from capricious governmental treatment "persons" — not "races," it can never countenance laws that seek racial balance as a goal in and of itself. "Preferring members of any one group for no reason other than race or ethnic origin is discrimination for its own sake. This the Constitution forbids." *Regents of the University of California* v. *Bakke* (opinion of POWELL, J.). Second, there are indications that the MBE provision may have been enacted to compensate for the effects of social, educational, and economic "disadvantage." No race, however, has a monopoly on social, educational, or economic disadvantage, and any law that indulges in such a presumption clearly violates the constitutional guarantee of equal protection. Since the MBE provision was in whole or in part designed to effectuate objectives other than the elimination of the effects of racial discrimination, it cannot stand as a remedy that comports with the strictures of equal protection, even if it otherwise could.

C

The Fourteenth Amendment was adopted to ensure that every person must be treated equally by each State regardless of the color of his skin. The Amendment promised to carry to its necessary conclusion a fundamental principle upon which this Nation had been founded — that the law would honor no preference based on lineage. Tragically, the promise of 1868 was not immediately fulfilled, and decades passed before the States and the Federal Government were finally directed to eliminate detrimental classifications based on race. Today, the Court derails this achievement and places its imprimatur on the creation once again by government of privileges based on birth.

The Court, moreover, takes this drastic step without, in my opinion, seriously considering the ramifications of its decision. Laws that operate on the basis of race require definitions of race. Because of the Court's decision today, our statute books will once again have to contain laws that reflect the odious practice of delineating the qualities that make one person a Negro and make another white. Moreover, racial discrimination, even "good faith" racial discrimination, is inevitably a two-edged sword. "[P]referential programs may only reinforce common stereotypes holding that certain groups are unable to achieve success without special protection based on a factor having no relationship to individual worth." *University of California Regents* v. *Bakke* ... (opinion of POWELL, J.). Most importantly, by making race a relevant criterion once again in its own affairs, the Government implicitly teaches the public that the apportionment of rewards and penalties can legitimately be made according to race — rather than according to merit or ability — and that people can, and perhaps should, view themselves and others in terms of their racial characteristics. Notions of "racial entitlement" will be fostered, and private discrimination will necessarily be encouraged. . . .

There are those who think that we need a new Constitution, and their views may someday prevail. But under the Constitution we have, one practice in which government may never engage is the practice of racism — not even "temporarily" and not even as an "experiment."

For these reasons, I would reverse the judgment of the Court of Appeals.

MR. JUSTICE STEVENS, dissenting.

The 10% set-aside contained in the Public Works Employment Act of 1977 . . . creates monopoly privileges in a $400,000,000 market for a class of investors defined solely by racial characteristics. The direct beneficiaries of these monopoly privileges are the relatively small number of persons within the racial classification who represent the entrepreneurial subclass — those who have, or can borrow, working capital.

History teaches us that the costs associated with a sovereign's grant of exclusive privileges often encompass more than the high prices and shoddy workmanship that are familiar hand maidens of monopoly; they engender animosity and discontent as well. The economic consequences of using noble birth as a basis for classification in 18th century France, though disastrous, were nothing as compared with the terror that was engendered in the name of "egalité" and "fraternité." Grants of privilege on the basis of characteristics acquired at birth are far from an unmixed blessing.

Our historic aversion to titles of nobility is only one aspect of our commitment to the proposition that the sovereign has a fundamental duty to govern impartially. When government accords different treatment to different persons, there must be a reason for the difference. Because racial characteristics so seldom provide a relevant basis for disparate treatment, and because classifications based on race are potentially so harmful to the entire body politic, it is especially important that the reasons for any such classification be clearly identified and un-questionably legitimate.

The statutory definition of the preferred class includes "citizens of the United States who are Negroes, Spanish-speaking, Orientals, Indians, Eskimos, and Aleuts." All aliens and all nonmembers of the racial class are exluded. No economic, social, geographical or historical criteria are relevant for exclusion or inclusion. There is not one word in the remainder of the Act or in the legislative history that explains why any Congressman or Senator favored this particular definition over any other or that identifies the common characteristics that every member of the preferred class was believed to share. Nor does the Act or its history explain why 10% of the total appropriation was the proper amount to set aside for investors in each of the six racial subclasses.

Four different, though somewhat interrelated, justifications for the racial classification in this Act have been advanced: first, that the 10% set aside is a form of reparation for past injuries to the entire membership of the class; second, that it is an appropriate remedy for past discrimination against minority business enterprises that have been denied access to public contracts; third, that the members of the favored class have a special entitlement to "a piece of the action" when government is distributing benefits; and, fourth, that the program is an appropriate method of fostering greater minority participation in a competitive economy. Each of these asserted justifications merits separate scrutiny.

I

Racial characteristics may serve to define a group of persons who have suffered a special wrong and who, therefore, are entitled to special reparations. Congress has recognized, for example, that the United States has treated some Indian tribes unjustly and has created procedures for allowing members of the injured classes to obtain classwide relief. . . . But as I have formerly suggested, if Congress is to authorize a recovery for a class of similarly situated victims of a past wrong, it has an obligation to distribute that recovery among the members of the injured class in an evenhanded way. . . . Moreover, in such a case the amount of the award should bear some rational relationship to the extent of the harm it is intended to cure.

In his eloquent separate opinion in *University of California Regents v. Bakke,* MR. JUSTICE MARSHALL recounted the tragic class-based discrimination against Negroes that is an indelible part of America's history. I assume that the wrong committed against the Negro class is both so serious and so pervasive that it would constitutionally justify an appropriate classwide recovery measured by a sum certain for every member of the injured class. Whether our resources are adequate to support a fair remedy of that character is a policy question I have neither the authority nor the wisdom to address. But that serious classwide wrong cannot in itself justify the particular classification Congress has made in this Act. Racial classifications are simply too pernicious to permit any but the most exact connection between justification and classification. Quite obviously, the history of discrimination against black citizens in America cannot justify a grant of privileges to Eskimos or Indians.

Even if we assume that each of the six racial subclasses has suffered its own special injury at some time in our history, surely it does not necessarily follow that each of those subclasses suffered harm of identical magnitude. . . .

At best, the statutory preference is a somewhat perverse form of reparation for the members of the injured classes. For those who are the most disadvantaged within each class are the least likely to receive any benefit from the special privilege even though they are the persons most likely still to be suffering the consequences of the past wrong. A random distribution to a favored few is a poor form of compensation for an injury shared by many. . . .

When Congress creates a special preference, or a special disability, for a class of persons, it should identify the characteristic that justifies the special treatment. When the classification is defined in racial terms, I believe that such particular identification is imperative.

In this case, only two conceivable bases for differentiating the preferred classes from society as a whole have occurred to me: (1) that they were the victims of unfair treatment in the past and (2) that they are less able to compete in the future. Although the first of these factors would justify an appropriate remedy for past wrongs, for reasons that I have already stated, this statute is not such a remedial measure. The second factor is simply not true. Nothing in the record of this case, the legitimate history of the Act, or experience that we may notice judicially provides any support for such a proposition. It is up to Congress to demonstrate that its unique statutory preference is justified by a relevant characteristic that is shared by the members of the preferred class. In my opinion, because it has failed to make that demonstration, it has also failed to discharge its duty to govern impartially embodied in the Fifth Amendment to the United States Constitution.

I respectfully dissent.

▼▼▼

REPUBLICAN PARTY PLATFORM
July 15, 1980

The 1980 Republican platform, adopted in Detroit by the party's convention delegates July 15, called for tax cuts, federal spending restraints and less government regulation of business. Harshly critical of the Carter administration, the document consisted of policy statements designed to appeal to a broad cross-section of Republicans. The party's moderate and conservative wings agreed in writing the platform to blur their differences in order to appear united and smooth the way to the White House for their nominee, former California Gov. Ronald Reagan.

The principal theme of the document was what it called Carter's "incompetence to lead" the nation. "America is adrift," the platform's preamble stated. "Our country moves agonizingly, aimlessly, almost helplessly into one of the most dangerous and disorderly periods in history." The Carter administration, according to the platform, neglected an ailing economy and spiraling inflation, over-regulated American business, permitted U.S. foreign relations and national defenses to deteriorate and intruded excessively into Americans' lives.

Central Goal

The Republicans' central goal, as expressed in the platform, was to reform national economic policy, attain full employment, reverse the recession and end inflation. A broad program of tax relief was the cornerstone of the economic plank. Championed by Rep. Jack F. Kemp of New York and Sen. William V. Roth Jr. of Delaware, the

Kemp-Roth plan would reduce individuals' taxes by 10 percent a year for three consecutive years and limit government spending to a fixed percentage of the gross national product.

The platform proposed a tight money policy to control inflation. To pursue this policy, the Federal Reserve System must be protected from interference by Congress and the executive branch, the platform stated.

The platform also called for decentralization of the federal government and increased reliance on block grants and revenue-sharing payments to state and local governments. To return the regulation of management decisions to "the marketplace rather than the bureaucrats," the document supported the deregulation of the energy, transportation and communications industries.

Equal Rights Amendment

Gone from the Republican Party's platform for the first time since 1940 was a statement supporting ratification of a constitutional amendment guaranteeing equal rights under the law for women. Ronald Reagan opposed ratification by the states, and platform writers, who agreed that the document should be consistent with Reagan's positions, decided the platform should not take a position on the issue.

Party moderates such as Sens. Charles H. Percy of Illinois, Charles McC. Mathias Jr. of Maryland and Jacob K. Javits of New York made little secret of their unhappiness with this plank. And former Republican National Committee co-chairman Mary Dent Crisp, who resigned under pressure July 9, 1980, said the party was "about to bury the rights of over 100 million American women under a heap of platitudes."

Minorities

In an attempt to pick up votes from organized labor, blacks and the poor, the platform made new overtures to traditionally non-Republican groups. It pledged to support statehood for Puerto Rico, strengthen enforcement of civil rights laws, revitalize older cities and aid workers put out of work by competition from foreign imports. The platform supported a proposal that would create "enterprise zones" in blighted urban neighborhoods to provide local businesses and residents with incentives for economic and social renewal.

Espousing traditionally conservative views, the document supported repeal of statutory restrictions on guns, the death penalty as an effective deterrent to crime and efforts to permit non-denominational voluntary prayer in public schools.

Hard-line Positions

In two areas, however, the platform took particularly hard-line positions. Calling on a Republican administration to appoint federal judges who respect "the sanctity of innocent human life," the platform supported a constitutional amendment that would "restore protection of the right to life for unborn children." The platform also supported congressional efforts to restrict use of federal funds for abortions.

Large increases in defense spending were also pledged. The platform specifically endorsed the MX missile, the strategic cruise missile, a new manned strategic bomber such as the B-1 and an anti-ballistic missile system. Rejecting the "fundamentally flawed SALT II treaty," the plank was unrelenting in its criticism of both the Carter administration and the Soviet Union. The Carter administration, the platform said, is "mired in incompetence" and "bereft of strategic vision and purpose."

Following is the text of the platform adopted at the 1980 Republican National Convention July 15, 1980. (Boldface headings in brackets have been added by Congressional Quarterly to highlight the organization of the text.):

A Preamble

The Republican Party convenes, presents this platform, and selects its nominees at a time of crisis. America is adrift. Our country moves agonizingly, aimlessly, almost helplessly into one of the most dangerous and disorderly periods in history.

At home, our economy careens, whiplashed from one extreme to another. Earlier this year, inflation skyrocketed to its highest levels in more than a century; weeks later, the economy plummeted, suffering its steepest slide on record. Prices escalate at more than 10 percent a year. More than eight million people seek employment. Manufacturing plants lie idle across the country. The hopes and aspirations of our people are being smothered.

Overseas, conditions already perilous, deteriorate. The Soviet Union for the first time is acquiring the means to obliterate or cripple our land-based missile system and blackmail us into submission. Marxist tyrannies spread more rapidly through the Third World and Latin America. Our alliances are frayed in Europe and elsewhere. Our energy supplies become even more dependent on uncertain foreign suppliers. In the ultimate humiliation, militant terrorists in Iran continue to toy with the lives of Americans.

These events are not isolated, or unrelated. They are signposts. They mark a continuing downward spiral in economic vitality and international influence. Should the trend continue, the 1980s promise to be our most dangerous years since World War II. History could record, if we let the drift go on, that the American experiment, so marvelously successful for 200 years, came strangely, needlessly, tragically to a dismal end early in our third century.

By far the most galling aspect of it all is that the chief architects of our decline — Democratic politicians — are without program or ideas to reverse it. Divided, leaderless, unseeing, uncomprehending, they plod on with listless offerings of pale imitations of the same policies they have pursued so long, knowing full well their futility. The Carter Administration is the unhappy and inevitable consequence of decades of increasingly outmoded Democratic domination of our national life. Over the past four years it has repeatedly demonstrated that it has no basic goals other than the perpetuation of its own rule and no guiding principle other than the fleeting insights provided by the latest opinion poll. Policies announced one day are disavowed or ignored the next, sowing confusion among Americans at home and havoc among our friends abroad.

Republicans, Democrats, and Independents have been watching and reading these signs. They have been watching incredulously as disaster after disaster unfolds. They now have had enough. They are rising up in 1980 to say that this confusion must end; this drift must end; we must pull ourselves together as a people before we slide irretrievably into the abyss.

It doesn't have to be this way; it doesn't have to stay this way. We, the Republican Party, hold ourselves forth as the Party best able to arrest and reverse the decline. We offer new ideas and candidates, from the top of our ticket to the bottom, who can bring to local and national leadership firm, steady hands and confidence and eagerness. We have unparalleled unity within our own ranks, especially between our Presidential nominee and our Congressional membership. Most important, we go forth to the people with ideas and programs for the future that are as powerful and compelling as they are fresh. Together, we offer a new beginning for America.

[FOREMOST GOAL]

Our foremost goal here at home is simple: economic growth and full employment without inflation. Sweeping change in economic policy in America is needed so that Mr. Carter's promise of hard times and austerity — his one promise well kept — can be replaced with Republican policies that promise economic growth and job creation. It is our belief that the stagflation of recent years not only has consigned millions of citizens to hardship but also has bottled up the enormous ingenuity and creative powers of our people. Those energies will not be released by the sterile policies of the past: we specifically reject the Carter doctrine that inflation can be reduced only by throwing people out of work. Prosperity will not be regained simply by government fiat.

Rather, we must offer broad new incentives to labor and capital to stimulate a great outpouring of private goods and services and to create an abundance of jobs. From America's grassroots to the White House we will stand united as a party behind a bold program of tax rate reductions, spending restraints, and regulatory reforms that will inject new life into the economic bloodstream of this country.

Overseas, our goal is equally simple and direct: to preserve a world at peace by keeping America strong. This philosophy once occupied a hallowed place in American diplomacy, but it was casually, even cavalierly dismissed at the outset by the Carter Administration — and the results have been shattering. Never before in modern history has the United States endured as many humiliations, insults, and defeats as it has during the past four years: our ambassadors murdered, our embassies burned, our warnings ignored, our diplomacy scorned, our diplomats kidnapped. The Carter Administration has shown that it neither understands totalitarianism nor appreciates the way tyrants take advantage of weakness. The brutal invasion of Afghanistan promises to be only the forerunner of much more serious threats to the West — and to world peace — should the Carter Administration somehow cling to power.

Republicans are united in a belief that America's international humiliation and decline can be reversed only by strong Presidential leadership and a consistent, far-sighted foreign policy, supported by a major upgrading of our military forces, a strengthening of our commitments to our allies, and a resolve that our national interests be vigorously protected. Ultimately, those who practice strength and firmness truly guard the peace.

This platform addresses many concerns of our Party. We seek to restore the family, the neighborhood, the community, and the workplace as vital alternatives in our national life to ever-expanding federal power.

We affirm our deep commitment to the fulfillment of the hopes and aspirations of all Americans — blacks and whites, women and men, the young and old, rural and urban.

[CASE FOR THE INDIVIDUAL]

For too many years, the political debate in America has been conducted in terms set by the Democrats. They believe that every time new problems arise beyond the power of men and women as individuals to solve, it becomes the duty of government to solve them, as if there were never any alternative. Republicans disagree and have always taken the side of the individual, whose freedoms are threatened by the big government that Democratic idea has spawned. Our case for the individual is stronger than ever. A defense of the individual against government was never more needed. And we will continue to mount it.

But we will redefine and broaden the debate by transcending the narrow terms of government and the individual; those are not the only two realities in America. Our society consists of more than that; so should the political debate. We will reemphasize those vital communities like the family, the neighborhood, the workplace, and others which are found at the center of society, between government and the individual. We will restore and strengthen their ability to solve problems in the places where people spend their daily lives and can turn to each other for support and help.

We seek energy independence through economic policies that free up our energy production and encourage conservation. We seek improvements in health care, education, housing, and opportunities for youth. We seek new avenues for the needy to break out of the tragic cycle of dependency. All of these goals — and many others — we confidently expect to achieve through a rebirth of liberty and resurgence of private initiatives, for we believe that at the root of most of our troubles today is the misguided and discredited philosophy of an all-powerful government, ceaselessly striving to subsidize, manipulate, and control individuals. But it is the individual, not the government, who reigns at the center of our Republican philosophy.

To those Democrats who say Americans must be content to passively accept the gradual but inexorable decline of America, we answer: The American people have hardly begun to marshal their talents and resources or realize the accomplishments and dreams that only freedom can inspire.

To those Democrats who say we face an "age of limits," we ask: Who knows the limit to what Americans can do when their capacity for work, creativity, optimism, and faith is enhanced and supported by strong and responsive political leadership and ideals.

To those who, with Mr. Carter, say the American people suffer from a national "malaise," we respond: The only malaise in this country is found in the leadership of the Democratic Party, in the White House and in Congress. Its symptoms are an incompetence to lead, a refusal to change, and a reluctance to act. This malaise has become epidemic in Washington. Its cure is government led by Republicans who share the values of the majority of Americans.

Republicans pledge a restoration of balance in American society. But society cannot be balanced by the actions of government or of individuals alone. Balance is found at society's vital center, where we find the family and the neighborhood and the workplace.

America will not, however, achieve any of these goals on its present course nor under its present leadership. The uncharted course of Mr. Carter will lead surely to catastrophe. By reversing our economic decline, by reversing our international decline, we can and will resurrect our dreams.

And so, in this 1980 Republican Platform, we call out to the American people: With God's help, let us now, together, make America great again; let us now, together, make a new beginning.

Free Individuals in a Free Society

It has long been a fundamental conviction of the Republican Party that government should foster in our society a climate of maximum individual liberty and freedom of choice. Properly informed, our people as individuals or acting through instruments of popular consultation can make the right decisions affecting personal or general welfare, free of pervasive and heavy-handed intrusion by the central government into the decisionmaking process. This tenet is the genius of representative democracy.

Republicans also treasure the ethnic, cultural, and regional diversity of our people. This diversity fosters a dynamism in American society that is the envy of the world.

TAXES

Elsewhere in this platform we discuss the benefits, for society as a whole, of reduced taxation, particularly in terms of economic growth. But we believe it is essential to cut personal tax rates out of fairness to the individual.

Presently, the aggregate burden of taxation is so great that the average American spends a substantial part of every year, in effect, working for government.

Substantial tax rate reductions are needed to offset the massive tax increases facing the working men and women of this country. Over the next four years, federal taxes are projected to increase by over $500 billion due to the Carter Administration's policies. American families are already paying taxes at higher rates than ever in our history; as a result of these Carter policies, the rates will go even higher. The direct and indirect burden of federal taxes alone, imposed on the average family earning $20,000, has risen to $5,451 — over 27 percent of the family's gross income. During the Carter term, the federal tax alone on this family will have risen $2,000.

The Republican Party believes balancing the budget is essential but opposes the Democrats' attempt to do so through higher taxes. We believe that an essential aspect of balancing the budget is spending restraint by the federal government and higher economic growth, not higher tax burdens on working men and women.

Policies of the Democratic Party are taxing work, savings, investment, productivity, and the rewards for human ingenuity. These same tax policies subsidize debt, unemployment, and consumption. The present structure of the personal income tax system is designed to broaden the gap between effort and reward.

Therefore, the Republican Party supports across-the-board reductions in personal income tax rates, phased in over three years, which will reduce tax rates from the range of 14 to 70 percent to a range from 10 to 50 percent.

For most Americans, these reduced tax rates will slow the rate at which taxes rise. This will assure workers and savers greater rewards for greater effort by lowering the rate at which added earnings would be taxed.

These reductions have been before the Congress for three years in the Roth-Kemp legislation. The proposal will not only provide relief for all American taxpayers, but also promote non-inflationary economic growth by restoring the incentive to save, invest, and produce. These restored incentives will in turn increase investment and help reinvigorate American business and industry, leading to the creation of more jobs. In fact, Governor Reagan and Congressional Republicans have already taken the first step. Working together, they have boldly offered the American people a 10 percent tax rate cut for 1981, which will stimulate growth in our economy, and a simplification and liberalization of depreciation schedules to create more jobs.

Once tax rates are reduced, Republicans will move to end tax bracket creep caused by inflation. We support tax indexing to protect taxpayers from the automatic tax increases caused when cost-of-living wage increases move them into higher tax brackets.

Tax rate reductions will generate increases in economic growth, output, and income which will ultimately generate increased revenues. The greater justification for these cuts, however, lies in the right of individuals to keep and use the money they earn.

IMPROVING THE WELFARE SYSTEM

The measure of a country's compassion is how it treats the least fortunate. In every society there will be some who cannot work, often through no fault of their own.

Yet current federal government efforts to help them have become counterproductive, perpetuating and aggravating the very conditions of dependence they seek to relieve. The Democratic Congress has produced a jumble of degrading, dehumanizing, wasteful, overlapping, and inefficient programs that invite waste and fraud but inadequately assist the needy poor.

Proverty is defined not by income statistics alone, but by an individual's true situation and prospects. For two generations, especially since the mid-1960s, the Democrats have deliberately perpetuated a status of federally subsidized poverty and manipulated dependency for millions of Americans. This is especially so for blacks and Hispanics, many of whom remain pawns of the bureaucracy, trapped outside the social and economic mainstream of American life.

For those on welfare, our nation's tax policies provide a penalty for getting a job. This is especially so for those whose new income from a job is either equal to, or marginally greater than, the amount received on welfare. In these cases, due to taxes, the individual's earned income is actually less than welfare benefits. This is the "poverty trap" which will continue to hold millions of Americans as long as they continue to be punished for working.

The Carter Administration and the Democratic Party continue to foster that dependency. Our nation's welfare problems will not be solved merely by providing increased benefits. Public service jobs are not a substitute for employable skills, nor can increases in the food stamp program by themselves provide for individual dignity. By fostering dependency and discouraging self-reliance, the Democratic Party has created a welfare constituency dependent on its continual subsidies.

The Carter Administration has proposed, and its allies in the House of Representatives actually voted for, legislation to nationalize welfare, which would have cost additional billions and made millions more dependent upon public assistance. The Democrats have presided over — and must take the blame for — the most monstrous expansion and abuse of the food stamp program to date. They have been either unable or unwilling to attack the welfare fraud that diverts resources away from the truly poor. They have sacrificed the needy to the greedy, and sent the welfare bills to the taxpayers.

We categorically reject the notion of a guaranteed annual income, no matter how it may be disguised, which would destroy the fiber of our economy and doom the poor to perpetual dependence.

As a party we commit ourselves to a welfare policy that is truly reflective of our people's true sense of compassion and charity as well as an appreciation of every individual's need for dignity and self-respect. We pledge a system that will:

Provide adequate living standards for the truly needy;

End welfare fraud by removing ineligibles from the welfare rolls, tightening food stamp eligibility requirements, and ending aid to illegal aliens and the voluntarily unemployed;

Strengthen work incentives, particularly directed at the productive involvement of able-bodied persons in useful community work projects;

Provide educational and vocational incentives to allow recipients to become self-supporting; and

Better coordinate federal efforts with local and state social welfare agencies and strengthen local and state administrative functions.

We oppose federalizing the welfare system; local levels of government are most aware of the needs in their communities. We support a block grant program that will help return control of welfare programs to the states. Decisions about who gets welfare, and how much, can be better made on the local level.

Those features of the present law, particularly the food stamp program, that draw into assistance programs people who are capable of paying for their own needs should be corrected. The humanitarian purpose of such programs must not be corrupted by eligibility loopholes. Food stamp program reforms proposed by Republicans in Congress would accomplish the twin goals of directing resources to those most in need and streamlining administration.

Through long association with government programs, the word "welfare" has come to be perceived almost exclusively as tax-supported aid to the needy. But in its most inclusive sense — and as Americans understood it from the beginning of the Republic — such aid also encompasses those charitable works performed by private citizens, families, and social, ethnic, and religious organizations. Policies of the federal government leading to high taxes, rising inflation, and bureaucratic empire-building have made it difficult and often impossible for such individuals and groups to exercise their charitable instincts. We believe that government policies that fight inflation, reduce tax rates, and end bureaucratic excesses can help make private effort by the American people once again a major force in those works of charity which are the true signs of a progressive and humane society.

VETERANS

Republicans recognize the very special sacrifice of those who have served in our nation's armed forces. Individual rights and societal values are only as strong as a nation's commitment to defend them. Because of this our country must never forget its appreciation of and obligation to our veterans.

Today the veteran population numbers 30 million. This is the largest veteran population in our nation's history. We recognize the major sacrifices they have made for their fellow Americans.

We will maintain the integrity of the Veterans Administration. We will seek to keep it separate and distinct from other federal agencies as the single agency for the administration of all veterans' programs. In particular we feel it is of vital importance to continue and expand the health programs provided to veterans through the Veterans Administration hospitals. Here we see the need for increased access to care, especially for older veterans.

We further advocate continued and expanded health care for our Vietnam veterans and consider it vital for the Veterans Administration to continue its programs for the rehabilitation of the disabled as well as its job training efforts.

We are committed to providing timely and adequate adjustments in compensation for service-disabled veterans and the survivors of those who died as a result of their service. We are also committed to maintaining the pension program for those who have served during a period of war, for those who were disabled and impoverished, and for their widows and orphans.

We will support measures to provide for every veteran at death a final resting place for his remains in a national cemetery, and for costs of transportation thereto.

Veterans preference in federal employment in all departments and agencies will be continued and strictly enforced.

Retired military benefits deserve more than the cursory attention given them by a Department of Defense otherwise interested in on-going programs. We believe that such benefits should be administered by the Veterans Administration.

PRIVATE PROPERTY

The widespread distribution of private property ownership is the cornerstone of American liberty. Without it neither our free enterprise system nor our republican form of government could long endure.

Under Democratic rule, the federal government has become an aggressive enemy of the human right to private property ownership. It has dissipated savings through depreciation of the dollar, enforced price controls on private exchange of goods, attempted to enforce severe land use controls, and mistreated hundreds of thousands of national park and forest inholders.

The next Republican Administration will reverse this baneful trend. It will not only protect the cherished human right of property ownership, but will also work to help millions of Americans — particularly those from disadvantaged groups — to share in the ownership of the wealth of their nation.

TRANSPORTATION — PERSONAL MOBILITY

Americans enjoy greater personal mobility than any other people on earth, largely as a result of the availability of automobiles and our modern highway system. Republicans reject the elitist notion that Americans must be forced out of their cars. Instead, we vigorously support the right of personal mobility and freedom as exemplified by the automobile and our modern highway system. While recognizing the importance of fuel efficiency and alternate modes of transportation, we quickly acknowledge that for millions of Americans there is no substitute on the horizon for the automobile. We reaffirm our support for a healthy domestic automobile industry, complete with continued support for the highway trust fund, which is the fairest method yet devised for financing America's highway system.

Republicans recognize the need for further improvement in highway safety. Projections indicate that highway fatalities may exceed 60,000 per year in the coming decades. Republicans support accelerated cost-effective efforts to improve highway, automobile, and individual driver safety.

PRIVACY

The essence of freedom is the right of law-abiding individuals to life, liberty, and the pursuit of happiness without undue governmental intervention. Yet government in recent years, particularly at the federal level, has overwhelmed citizens with demands for personal information and has accumulated vast amounts of such data through the IRS, Social Security Administration, the Bureau of the Census, and other agencies. Under certain limited circumstances, such information can serve legitimate societal interests, but there must be protection against abuse.

Republicans share the concerns of our citizens as to the nature, use, and final disposition of the volume of personal information being collected. We are alarmed by Washington's growing collection and dissemination of such data. There must be protection against its misuse or disclosure.

The Republican Party commits itself to guaranteeing an individual's right of privacy. We support efforts of state governments to ensure individual privacy.

BLACK AMERICANS

For millions of black Americans, the past four years have been a long trail of broken promises and broken dreams. The Carter Administration entered office with a pledge to all minorities of a brighter economic future. Today there are more black Americans unemployed than on the day Mr. Carter became President. The unemployment rate of black teenagers is once again rising sharply. And the median income of black families has declined to less than 60 percent of white family income.

Republicans will not make idle promises to blacks and other minorities; we are beyond the day when any American can live off rhetoric or political platitudes.

Our Party specifically rejects the philosophy of the Carter Administration that unemployment is the answer to inflation. We abhor the notion that our cities should become battlegrounds in the fight against inflation and that the jobs of black Americans should be sacrificed in an attempt to counterbalance the inflationary excesses of government. Nor are we prepared to accept the practice of turning the poor into permanent wards of the state, trading their political support for continued financial assistance.

Our fundamental answer to the economic problems of black Americans is the same answer we make to all Americans — full employment without inflation through economic growth. First and foremost, we are committed to a policy of economic expansion through tax-rate reductions, spending restraint, regulatory reform and other incentives.

As the Party of Lincoln, we remain equally and steadfastly committed to the equality of rights for all citizens, regardless of race. Although this nation has not yet eliminated all vestiges of racism over the years, we are heartened by the progress that has been made, we are proud of the role that our party has played, and we are dedicated to standing shoulder to shoulder with black Americans in that cause.

Elsewhere in this platform, we set forth a number of specific proposals that will also serve to improve the quality of life for blacks. During the next four years we are committed to policies that will:

Encourage local governments to designate specific enterprise zones within depressed areas that will promote new jobs, new and expanded businesses and new economic vitality;

Open new opportunities for black men and women to begin small businesses of their own by, among other steps, removing excessive regulations, disincentives for venture capital and other barriers erected by the government;

Bring strong, effective enforcement of federal civil rights statutes, especially those dealing with threats to physical safety and security which have recently been increasing; and

Ensure that the federal government follows a non-discriminatory system of appointments up and down the line, with a careful eye for qualified minority aspirants.

HISPANIC AMERICANS

Hispanics are rapidly becoming the largest minority in the country and are one of the major pillars in our cultural, social, and economic life. Diverse in character, proud in heritage, they are greatly enriching the American melting pot.

Hispanics seek only the full rights of citizenship — in education, in law enforcement, in housing — and an equal opportunity to achieve economic security. Unfortunately, those desires have not always been fulfilled; as in so many other areas, the Carter Administration has been long on rhetoric and short on action in its approach to the Hispanic community.

We pledge to pursue policies that will help to make the opportunities of American life a reality for Hispanics. The economic policies enunciated in this platform will, we believe, create new jobs for Hispanic teenagers and adults and will also open up new business opportunities for them. We also believe there should be local educational programs which enable those who grew up learning another language such as Spanish to become proficient in English while also maintaining their own language and cultural heritage. Neither Hispanics nor any other American citizen should be barred from education or employment opportunities because English is not their first language.

THE HANDICAPPED

The Republican Party strongly believes that handicapped persons must be admitted into the mainstream of American society. It endorses efforts to enable our handicapped population to enjoy a useful and productive life.

Too often in the past, barriers have been raised to their education, employment, transportation, health care, housing, recreation, and insurance. We support a concerted national effort to eliminate discrimination in all these areas. Specifically we support tax incentives for the removal of architectural and transportation barriers. We pledge continued efforts to improve communications for the handicapped and to promote a healthy, constructive attitude toward them in our society.

WOMEN'S RIGHTS

We acknowledge the legitimate efforts of those who support or oppose ratification of the Equal Rights Amendment.

We reaffirm our Party's historic commitment to equal rights and equality for women.

We support equal rights and equal opportunities for women, without taking away traditional rights of women such as exemption from the military draft. We support the enforcement of all equal opportunity laws and urge the elimination of discrimination against women. We oppose any move which would give the federal government more power over families.

Ratification of the Equal Rights Amendment is now in the hands of state legislatures, and the issues of the time extension and rescission are in the courts. The states have a constitutional right to accept or reject a constitutional amendment without federal interference or pressure. At the direction of the White House, federal departments launched pressure against states which refused to ratify ERA. Regardless of one's position on ERA, we demand that this practice cease.

At this time, women of America comprise 53 percent of the population and over 42 percent of the work force. By 1990, we anticipate that 51 percent of the population will be women, and there will be approximately 57 million in the work force. Therefore, the following urgent problems must be resolved:

Total integration of the work force (not separate but equal) is necessary to bring women equality in pay;

Girls and young women must be given improved early career counseling and job training to widen the opportunities for them in the world of work;

Women's worth in the society and in the jobs they hold, at home or in the workplace, must be reevaluated to improve the conditions of women workers concentrated in low-status, low-paying jobs;

Equal opportunity for credit and other assistance must be assured to women in small businesses; . . .

[CHILD CARE]

One of the most critical problems in our nation today is that of inadequate child care for the working mother. As champions of the free enterprise system, of the individual, and of the idea that the best solutions to most problems rest at the community level, Republicans must find ways to meet this, the working woman's need. The scope of this problem is fully realized only when it is understood that many female heads of households are at the poverty level and that they have a very large percentage of the nation's children.

The important secret about old age in America today is that it is primarily a woman's issue, and those over 65 are the fastest growing segment of the population. With current population trends, by the year 2020, 15.5 percent of our population will be over 65; by 2035, women in this age group will outnumber men by 13 million.

In 1980, 42 percent of women between 55 and 64 are in the work force. Half of the six million elderly women who live alone have incomes of $3,700 or less, and black women in that category have a median income of $2,600. How do they survive with the present rate of inflation? The lower salaries they earned as working women are now reflected in lower retirement benefits, if they have any at all. The Social Security system is still biased against women, and non-existent pension plans combine with that to produce a bereft elderly woman. The Republican Party must not and will not let this continue.

We reaffirm our belief in the traditional role and values of the family in our society. The damage being done today to the family takes its greatest toll on the woman. Whether it be through divorce, widowhood, economic problems, or the suffering of children, the impact is greatest on women. The importance of support for the mother and homemaker in maintaining the values of this country cannot be over-emphasized.

In other sections of this platform, we call for greater equity in the tax treatment of working spouses. We deplore this marriage tax which penalizes married two-worker families. We call for a reduction in the estate tax burden, which creates hardships for widows and minor children. We also pledge to address any remaining inequities in the treatment of women under the Social Security system.

Women know better than anyone the decline in the quality of life that is occurring in America today. The peril to the United States and especially to women must be stressed. Women understand domestic, consumer, and economic issues more deeply because they usually manage the households and have the responsibility for them. With this responsibility must also come greater opportunity for achievement and total equality toward solution of problems.

EQUAL RIGHTS

The truths we hold and the values we share affirm that no individual should be victimized by unfair discrimination because of race, sex, advanced age, physical handicap, difference of national origin or religion, or economic circumstance. However, equal opportunity should not be jeopardized by bureaucratic regulations and decisions which rely on quotas, ratios, and numerical requirements to exclude some individuals in favor of others, thereby rendering such regulations and decisions inherently discriminatory.

We pledge vigorous enforcement of laws to assure equal treatment in job recruitment, hiring, promotion, pay, credit, mortgage access and housing.

Millions of Americans who trace their heritage to the nations of Eastern, Central, and Southern Europe have for too long seen their values neglected. The time has come to go beyond the ritual election year praise given to Ethnic Americans. We must make them an integral part of government. We must make recognition of their values an integral part of government policy. The Republican Party will take positive steps to see to it that these Americans, along with others too long neglected, have the opportunity to share the power, as well as the burdens of our society. The same holds true of our Asian-American citizens from the cultures of the Orient.

As a party we also recognize our commitment to Native Americans. We pledge to continue to honor our trusted relationship with them and we reaffirm our federal policy of self-determination. We support the assumption by Indians, Aleuts, and Eskimos themselves of the decisions and planning which will affect their lives and the end of undue federal influence on those plans and decisions.

Puerto Rico has been a territory of the United States since 1898. The Republican Party vigorously supports the right of the United States citizens of Puerto Rico to be admitted into the Union as a fully sovereign state after they freely so determine. We believe that the statehood alternative is the only logical solution to the problem of inequality of the United States citizens of Puerto Rico within the framework of the federal constitution, with full recognition within the concept of a multicultural society of the citizens' right to retain their Spanish language and traditions. Therefore we pledge to support the enactment of the necessary legislation to allow the people of Puerto Rico to exercise their right to apply for admission into the Union at the earliest possible date after the presidential election of 1980.

We also pledge that such decision of the people of Puerto Rico will be implemented through the approval of an admission bill. This bill will provide for the Island's smooth transition from its territorial fiscal system to that of a member of the Union. This enactment will enable the new state of Puerto Rico to stand economically on an equal footing with the rest of the states and to assume gradually its fiscal responsibilities as a state.

We continue to favor whatever action may be necessary to permit American citizens resident in the United States territories of the Virgin Islands and Guam to vote for President and Vice President in national elections.

ABORTION

There can be no doubt that the question of abortion, despite the complex nature of its various issues, is ultimately concerned with equality of rights under the law. While we recognize differing views on this question among Americans in general — and in our own Party — we affirm our support of a constitutional amendment to restore protection of the right to life for unborn children. We also support the Congressional efforts to restrict the use of taxpayers' dollars for abortion.

We protest the Supreme Court's intrusion into the family structure through its denial of the parent's obligation and right to guide their minor children.

Strong Families

The family is the foundation of our social order. It is the school of democracy. Its daily lessons — cooperation, tolerance, mutual concern, responsibility, industry — are fundamental to the order and progress of our Republic. But the Democrats have shunted the family aside. They have given its power to the bureaucracy, its jurisdiction to the courts, and its resources to government grantors. For the first time in our history, there is real concern that the family may not survive.

Government may be strong enough to destroy families, but it can never replace them.

Unlike the Democrats, we do not advocate new federal bureaucracies with ominous power to shape a national family order. Rather, we insist that all domestic policies, from child care and schooling to Social Security and the tax code, must be formulated with the family in mind.

EDUCATION

Next to religious training and the home, education is the most important means by which families hand down to each new generation their ideals and beliefs. It is a pillar of a free society. But today, parents are losing control of their children's schooling. The Democratic Congress and its counterparts in many states have launched one fad after another, building huge new bureaucracies to misspend our taxes. The result has been a shocking drop in student performance, lack of basics in the classroom, forced busing, teacher strikes, manipulative and sometimes amoral indoctrination.

The Republican Party is determined to restore common sense and quality to education for the sake of all students, especially those for whom learning is the highway to equal opportunity. Because federal assistance should help local school districts, not tie them up in red tape, we will strive to replace the crazyquilt of wasteful programs with a system of block grants that will restore decisionmaking to local officials responsible to voters and parents. We recognize the need to preserve within the structure of block grants, special educational opportunities for the handicapped, the disadvantaged, and other needy students attending public and private non-profit elementary and secondary schools.

[Teachers]

We hail the teachers of America. Their dedication to our children is often taken for granted, and they are frequently underpaid for long hours and selfless service, especially in comparison with other public employees.

We understand and sympathize with the plight of America's public school teachers, who so frequently find their time and attention diverted from their teaching responsibilities to the task of complying with federal reporting requirements. America has a great stake in maintaining standards of high quality in public education. The Republican Party recognizes that the achievement of those standards is possible only to the extent that teachers are allowed the time and freedom to teach. To that end, the Republican Party supports deregulation by the federal government of public education, and encourages the elimination of the federal Department of Education.

We further sympathize with the right of qualified teachers to be employed by any school district wishing to hire them, without the necessity of their becoming enrolled with any bargaining agency or group. We oppose any federal action, including any action on the part of the Department of Education to establish "agency shops" in public schools.

We support Republican initiatives in the Congress to restore the right of individuals to participate in voluntary, non-denominational prayer in schools and other public facilities. We applaud the action of the Senate in passing such legislation.

Our goal is quality education for all of America's children, with a special commitment to those who must overcome handicap, deprivation, or discrimination. That is why we condemn the forced busing of school children to achieve arbitrary racial quotas. Busing has been a prescription for disaster, blighting whole communities across the land with its divisive impact. It has failed to improve the quality of education, while diverting funds from programs that could make the difference between success and failure for the poor, the disabled, and minority children.

We must halt forced busing and get on with the education of all our children, focusing on the real causes of their problems, especially lack of economic opportunity.

[Tax Credits]

Federal education policy must be based on the primacy of parental rights and responsibility. Toward that end, we reaffirm our support for a system of educational assistance based on tax credits that will in part compensate parents for their financial sacrifices in paying tuition at the elementary, secondary, and post-secondary level. This is a matter of fairness, especially for low-income families, most of whom would be free for the first time to choose for their children those schools which best correspond to their own cultural and moral values. In this way, the schools will be strengthened by the families' involvement, and the families' strengths will be reinforced by supportive cultural institutions.

We are dismayed that the Carter Administration cruelly reneged on promises made during the 1976 campaign. Wielding the threat of his veto, Mr. Carter led the fight against Republican attempts to make tuition tax credits a reality.

Next year, a Republican White House will assist, not sabotage, congressional efforts to enact tuition tax relief into law.

We will halt the unconstitutional regulatory vendetta launched by Mr. Carter's IRS Commissioner against independent schools.

We will hold the federal bureaucracy accountable for its harassment of colleges and universities and will clear away the tangle of regulation that has unconscionably driven up their expenses and tuitions. We will respect the rights of state and local authorities in the management of their school systems.

The commitment of the American people to provide educational opportunities for all has resulted in a tremendous expansion of schools at all levels. And the more we reduce the federal proportion of taxation, the more resources will be left to sustain and develop state and local institutions.

HEALTH

Our country's unequalled system of medical care, bringing greater benefits to more people than anywhere else on earth, is a splendid example of how Americans have taken care of their own needs with private institutions.

Significant as these achievements are, we must not be complacent. Health care costs continue to rise, farther and faster than they should, and threaten to spiral beyond the reach of many families. The causes are the Democratic Congress' inflationary spending and excessive and expensive regulations.

Republicans unequivocally oppose socialized medicine, in whatever guise it is presented by the Democratic Party. We reject the creation of a national health service and all proposals for compulsory national health insurance.

Our country has made spectacular gains in health care in recent decades. Most families are now covered by private insurance, Medicare, or in the case of the poor, the entirely free services under Medicaid.

Republicans recognize that many health care problems can be solved if government will work closely with the private sector to find remedies that will enhance our current system of excellent care. We applaud, as an example, the voluntary effort which has been undertaken by our nation's hospitals to control costs. The results have been encouraging. More remains to be done.

What ails American medicine is government meddling and the strait-jacket of federal programs. The prescription for good health care is deregulation and an emphasis upon consumer rights and patient choice.

As consumers of health care, individual Americans and their families should be able to make their own choices about health care protection. We propose to assist them in so doing through tax and financial incentives. These could enable them to choose their own health coverage, including protection from the catastrophic costs of major long-term illness, without compulsory regimentation.

Americans should be protected against financial disaster brought on by medical expense. We recognize both the need to provide assistance in many cases and the responsibility of citizens to provide for their own needs. By using tax incentives and reforming federal medical as-sistance programs, government and the private sector can jointly develop compassionate and innovative means to provide financial relief when it is most needed.

We endorse alternatives to institutional care. Not only is it costly but it also separates individuals from the supportive environment of family and friends. This is especially important for the elderly and those requiring long-term care. We advocate the reform of Medicare to encourage home-based care whenever feasible. In addition, we encourage the development of innovative alternate health care delivery systems and other out-patient services at the local level.

We must maintain our commitment to the aged and to the poor by providing quality care through Medicare and Medicaid. These programs need the careful, detailed reevaluation they have never received from the Democrats, who have characteristically neglected their financial sta-bility. We believe that the needs of those who depend upon their programs, particularly the elderly, can be better served, especially when a Republican Administration cracks down on fraud and abuse so that program monies can be directed toward those truly in need. In the case of Medicaid, we will aid the states in restoring its financial integrity and its local direction.

We welcome the long-overdue emphasis on preventive health care and physical fitness that is making Americans more aware than ever of their personal responsibility for good health. Today's enthusiasm and emphasis on staying well holds the promise of dramatically improved health and well-being in the decades ahead. Additionally, health pro-fessionals, as well as individuals have long recognized that preventing illness or injury is much less expensive than treating it. Therefore, preventive medicine combined with good personal health habits and health education, can make a major impact on the cost of health care. Employers and employees, unions and business associations, families, schools, and neighborhood groups all have important parts in what is becoming a national crusade for better living.

YOUTH

The Republican Party recognizes that young people want the opportunity to exercise the rights and responsibilities of adults.

The Republican agenda for making educational and employment opportunities available to our youth has been addressed in detail in other sections of this platform.

Republicans are committed to the enactment of a youth differential in the minimum wage and other vitally needed incentives for the creation of jobs for our young.

In addition, we reaffirm our commitment to broaden the involvement of young people in all phases of the political process — as voters, party workers and leaders, candidates and elected officials, and participants in government at all levels.

We pledge, as we have elsewhere in this platform, efforts to create an environment which will enable our nation's youth:

To live in a society which is safe and free;

To pursue personal, educational, and vocational goals to the utmost of their abilities;

To experience the support, encouragement, and strength that comes from maintenance of the family and its values; and

To know the stimulus of challenge, renewal through encouragement, provision of opportunities, and the growth that comes from responsible participation in numerous aspects of our society.

OLDER AMERICANS

Inflation is called "the cruelest tax." It strikes most cruelly at the elderly, especially those on fixed incomes. It strikes viciously at the sick and the infirm, and those who are alone in the world.

Inflation has robbed our elderly of dignity and security. An entire generation of responsible and productive citizens who toiled and saved a full working life to build up a retirement nest egg now finds that it cannot survive on its savings. Today's inflation rates dwarf yesterday's interest rates, and the pensions and annuities of our elderly citizens cannot keep up with the rising cost of living. Millions of once-proud and independent elderly Americans face a future of welfare dependency and despair.

We propose to assist families, and individuals of all ages, to meet the needs of the elderly, primarily through vigorous private initiative. Only a comprehensive reduction in tax rates will enable families to save for retirement income, and to protect that income from ravaging inflation. Only new tax exemptions and incentives can make it possible for many families to afford to care for their older members at home.

Present laws can create obstacles to older Americans' remaining in the family home. Federal programs for the elderly, such as Medicare and Supplemental Security Income, must address, humanely and generously, the special circumstances of those who choose to stay with their families rather than enter a nursing home or other institution.

Social Security is one of this nation's most vital commitments to our senior citizens. We commit the Republican Party to first save, and then strengthen, this fundamental contract between our government and its productive citizens.

Republicans consider older Americans a community asset, not a national problem. We are committed to using the sadly wasted talents of the aged throughout our society, which sorely needs their experience and wisdom. To that end, and as a matter of basic fairness, we proudly reaffirm our opposition to mandatory retirement and our long-standing Republican commitment to end the Democrats' earnings limitation upon Social Security benefits. In addition, the Republican Party is strongly opposed to the taxation of Social Security benefits and we pledge to oppose any attempts to tax these benefits.

Republicans have resisted Democratic electioneering schemes to spend away the Social Security trust funds for political purposes. Now the bill has come due, and the workers of America are staggering under their new tax burdens. This must stop.

Precisely because Social Security is a precious lifeline for millions of the elderly, orphaned, and disabled, we insist that its financing be sound and stable. We will preserve Social Security for its original purpose.

The problems of Social Security financing are only an aspect of the overriding problems of the economy which Democratic mismangement has produced. There is but one answer, the comprehensive tax rate reduction to which Republicans are committed. To save Social Security, we have no choice but to redirect our economy toward growth. To meet this country's commitments to Social Security recipients, present and future, we need more people at work, earning more money, thereby paying more into the trust funds. That same growth can balance the federal budget with lower taxes, over time reducing inflation, which falls so cruelly on senior citizens whose income is fixed by the size of their public or private pension.

We pledge to clean up the much-abused disability system. We will also expand eligibility for Individual Retirement Accounts to enable more persons to plan for their retirement years.

THE WELFARE SYSTEM

The Republican agenda for welfare reform has been discussed in a previous section, but we think it important to stress that central to it is the preservation of the families the system is designed to serve. The current system does not do this. Neither would guaranteed annual income schemes. By supplanting parental responsibility and by denying children parental guidance and economic support, they encourage and reward the fragmentation of families. This is unconscionable. The values and strengths of the family provide a vital element in breaking the bonds of poverty.

Ultimately, the Republican Party supports the orderly, wholesale transfer of all welfare functions to the states along with the tax sources to finance them.

THE FAMILY ECONOMY

It is increasingly common for both husbands and wives to work outside the home. Often, it occurs out of economic necessity, and it creates major difficulties for families with children, especially those of preschool age. On one hand, they are striving to improve the economic well-being of their family; on the other, they are concerned about the physical and emotional well-being of their children. This dilemma is further aggravated in instances of single parenthood due to death or divorce.

Recognizing these problems, we pledge to increase the availability of non-institutional child care. We see a special role for local, private organizations in meeting this need.

We disapprove of the bias in the federal tax system against working spouses, whose combined incomes are taxed at a proportionately higher rate than if they were single. We deplore this "marriage tax" and call for equity in the tax treatment of families.

We applaud our society's increasing awareness of the role of homemakers in the economy, not apart from the work force but as a very special part of it: the part that combines the labor of a full-time job, the skills of a profession, and the commitment of the most dedicated volunteer. Recognizing that homemaking is as important as any other profession, we endorse expanded eligibility for Individual Retirement Accounts for homemakers and will explore other ways to advance their standing and security.

FAMILY PROTECTION

In view of the continuing efforts of the present Administration to define and influence the family through such federally funded conferences as the White House Conference on Families, we express our support for legislation protecting and defending the traditional American family against the ongoing erosion of its base in our society.

HANDICAPPED PEOPLE

Republicans will seek every effective means to enable families more easily to assist their handicapped members and to provide for their education and special medical and therapeutic needs. In the case of handicapped children particularly, flexibility must be maintained in programs of public assistance so that, whenever possible, these youngsters may remain at home rather than in institutions.

Targeted tax relief can make it possible for parents to keep such a child at home without foregoing essential professional assistance. Similarly, tax incentives can assist those outside the home, in the neighborhood and the workplace, who undertake to train, hire, or house the handicapped.

Secure and Prosperous Neighborhoods

The quality of American neighborhoods is the ultimate test of the success or failure of government policies for the cities, for housing, and for law enforcement.

Obsessed with the demands of special interest groups and preoccupied with the design of expensive "comprehensive" programs, the Democrats in Congress and the Administration have lost sight of that simple but important criterion. They have proposed more social and fiscal tinkering with our cities and towns.

Republicans will address the real problems that face Americans in their neighborhoods day by day — deterioration and urban blight, dangerous streets and violent crime that makes millions of Americans, especially senior citizens, fearful in their own neighborhoods and prisoners in their own homes.

In the summer of 1980, Americans suffer a rising national unemployment rate, now at nearly eight percent, and double-digit inflation and interest rates. As Republicans meet in Detroit, the policies of the Carter Administration and the Democratic Congress have pushed the economy into recession and have resulted in unemployment approaching 20 percent in our host city.

The people of Detroit have worked long and hard to revitalize their city and the evidence of its rebirth is impressive. Their efforts have been severely set back by Carter Administration policies outside of this or any city's control. The grim evidence is manifested in jobs lost as a direct consequence of bankrupt economic policies which have fostered this recession. Republicans will address and resolve the real problems of today's economy, problems that destroy jobs and deny even the hope of homeownership to millions of American families. We are, moreover, committed to nurturing the spirit of self-help and cooperation through which so many neighborhoods have revitalized themselves and served their residents.

NEIGHBORHOOD SELF-HELP

The American ethic of neighbor helping neighbor has been an essential factor in the building of our nation. Republicans are committed to the preservation of this great tradition.

To help non-governmental community programs aid in serving the needs of poor, disabled, or other disadvantaged, we support permitting taxpayers to deduct charitable contributions from their federal income tax whether they itemize or not.

In contrast, the Democrats' assault against Meals-on-Wheels highlights their insensitivity to the neighborly spirit that motivates so many Americans. For over 25 years, voluntary Meals-on-Wheels organizations have been feeding needy homebound citizens — usually the elderly — with funding from local private charitable sources. Promising for the first time to "help" these neighborhood volunteer efforts in 1978, the Democratic Congress and administration instead used the carrot of federal funding and the stick of federal regulation to crowd out private ventures.

Government must never elbow aside private institutions — schools, churches, volunteer groups, labor and professional associations — in meeting the social needs in our neighborhoods and communities.

NEIGHBORHOOD REVITALIZATION

The city is the focus for the lives of millions of Americans. Its neighborhoods are places of familiarity, of belonging, of tradition and continuity. They are arenas for civic action and creative self-help. The human scale of the neighborhood encourages citizens to exercise leadership, to invest their talents, energies, and resources, to work together to create a better life for their families.

Republican economic programs will create conditions for rebirth of citizen activity in neighborhoods and cities across the land. In a Republican economic climate, America's cities can once again produce, build, and grow.

A Republican Administration will focus its efforts to revitalize neighborhoods in five areas. We will:

Cut taxes, increase incentives to save, restore sound money, and stimulate capital investment to create jobs;

Create and apply new tax incentives for employees and employers alike to stimulate economic growth and reduce red-tape for business ventures. Local government will be invited to designate specific depressed areas as jobs and enterprise zones;

Encourage our cities to undertake neighborhood revitalization and preservation programs in cooperation with the three essential local interests: local government, neighborhood property owners and residents, and local financial institutions;

Replace the categorical aid programs with block grant or revenue sharing programs and, where appropriate, transfer the programs, along with the tax sources to pay for them, back to the state and local governments; and

Remain fully committed to the fair enforcement of all federal civil rights statutes and continue minority business enterprise and similar programs begun by Republican Administrations but bungled by overregulation and duplication during the Carter Administration.

Republican programs will revitalize the inner cities. New jobs will be created. The federal government's role will be substantially reduced. The individual citizen will reclaim his or her independence.

The revitalization of American cities will proceed from the revitalization of the neighborhoods. Cities and neighborhoods are no more nor less than the people who inhabit them. Their strengths and weaknesses provide their character. If they are to grow, it is the people who must seize the initiative and lead.

HOUSING AND HOMEOWNERSHIP

Our citizens must have a real opportunity to live in decent, affordable housing. Due to the disastrous policies of the Carter Administration and the Democratic Congress, however, the goal of homeownership and all that aspiration entails is now in jeopardy. These irrational policies have been catastrophic to the housing industry. The highest home mortgage interest rates in the history of the United States have depressed housing starts to the lowest level since World War II. Democratic policies guarantee shortages in owner-occupied and rental housing.

As many as 1.4 million people who depend upon homebuilding for work may lose their jobs in this recession. Many already have. In addition to the toll taken on millions of American families, intolerable pressures will build on state, local, and federal budgets as tax revenues decline and expenditures increase to aid the unemployed.

We support financing and tax incentives to encourage the construction of rental housing as an essential addition to our housing inventory.

Prospective first-time home buyers simply cannot afford to buy. The affordability of housing has become a crisis. The high rates of inflation have driven mortgage payments, house prices, and down-payment requirements beyond the means of close to 80 percent of young American families. In order to assist the record number of young families who wish to become home buyers, we propose to implement a young family housing initiative, which would include several elements such as: urban homesteading, savings and tax reforms, and innovative alternate mortgage instruments to help meet monthly payment requirements without federal subsidies. To assist older homeowners, again without federal subsidy, we urge more extensive availability of the reverse annuity mortgage which allows older homeowners to withdraw the substantial equity they have built up in their homes and thus supplement their retirement income. In order to slow increases in housing costs, regulations which artificially limit housing production and raise housing costs must be eliminated.

We favor expansion of the Republican-sponsored urban homesteading program as a means of restoring abandoned housing. This innovative program is locally administered, returns property to the tax rolls, and develops new ownership and stability within our neighborhoods.

The collapse of new home production and the distress of the housing finance system are closely related. The stop and go economic policies of the past year have created extreme volatility in financial markets which have made it impossible for thrift institutions to supply housing credit at a reasonable cost.

A set of policies aimed at higher and more stable levels of housing production will simultaneously reduce housing costs and unemployment in the economy. To assure a stable and continuous flow of funds for home mortgage financing, we pledge to allow responsible use of mortgage revenue bonds. We will work to change the tax laws to encourage savings so that young families will be able to afford their dreams.

Specifically, we will support legislation to lower tax rates on savings in order to increase funds available for housing. This will help particularly to make homeownership an accessible dream for younger families, encouraging them not to despair of ever having a home of their own, but to begin working and saving for it now. We oppose any attempt to end the income tax deductability of mortgage interest and property taxes.

Republicans will also end the mismanagement and waste that has characterized the Department of Housing and Urban Development during the Carter Administration. As presently structured, HUD programs present local governments and developers with a maze of bureaucracy, complicated applications, and inflexible requirements, often unsuited to local needs. Such programs often infringe upon the right of local government to retain jurisdiction over their own zoning laws and building codes. As a result, their cost is so high that relatively few of the needy are ultimately housed or helped. Republicans will replace many of HUD's categorical programs with decentralized block grants to provide more efficient and responsive housing assistance to the elderly, the handicapped, and the poor. In remaining programs, particular emphasis should be given to rehabilitation and preservation of existing housing stock as a priority in federal housing policy.

CRIME

Safety and security are vital to the health and well-being of people in their neighborhoods and communities. Republicans are committed to ensuring that neighborhoods will be safe places in which families and individuals can live, and we support and encourage community crime fighting efforts such as neighborhood crime watch and court monitoring programs.

First, we believe that Republican economic proposals, more particularly those proposals which strengthen society and smaller communities discussed elsewhere in this document, will go a long way toward stabilizing American society.

Second, we support a vigorous and effective effort on the part of law enforcement agencies. Although we recognize the vital role of federal law enforcement agencies, we realize that the most effective weapons against crime are state and local agencies.

Just as vital to efforts to stem crime is the fair but firm and speedy application of criminal penalties. The existence and application of strong penalties are effective disincentive to criminal actions. Yet these disincentives will only be as strong as our court system's willingness to use them.

We believe that the death penalty serves as an effective deterrent to capital crime and should be applied by the federal government and by states which approve it as an appropriate penalty for certain major crimes.

We believe the right of citizens to keep and bear arms must be preserved. Accordingly, we oppose federal registration of firearms. Mandatory sentences for commission of armed felonies are the most effective means to deter abuse of this right. We therefore support Congressional initiatives to remove those provisions of the Gun Control Act of 1968 that do not significantly impact on crime but serve rather to restrain the law-abiding citizen in his legitimate use of firearms.

In recent years, a murderous epidemic of drug abuse has swept our country. Mr. Carter, through his policies and his personnel, has demonstrated little interest in stopping its ravages. Republicans consider drug abuse an intolerable threat to our society, especially to the young. We pledge a government that will take seriously its responsibility to curb illegal drug traffic. We will first and most urgently restore the ability of the FBI to act effectively in this area. Republican government will work with local law enforcement agencies to apprehend and firmly punish drug pushers and drug smugglers, with mandatory sentences where appropriate. We support efforts to crack down on the sale and advertising of drug paraphernalia. Private, nonprofit drug abuse rehabilitation agencies have taken the lead in fighting drug abuse, and they deserve greater cooperation and flexibility from federal, state, and local agencies and grant programs. We pledge the enactment of legislation to ban the utilization of federal funds by grantees of the Legal Services Corporation to render their services in cases involving the pushing or smuggling of drugs as well as in cases of repeat offenders. We commend the religious leaders, community activists, parents, and local officials who are working with fervor and dedication to protect young Americans from the drug plague.

URBAN TRANSPORTATION

The complex problems of mobility, congestion, and energy resources demand creative solutions if we are to improve the living conditions of our urban areas. Many urban centers of our nation need dependable and affordable mass transit systems. The first line of responsibility must lie with the local governments. They must be given the latitude to design and implement the transportation system best suited to their singular circumstances. Republicans believe we should encourage effective competition among diverse modes of transportation. The role of the federal government should be one of giving financial and technical support to local authorities, through surface transportation block grants. Because of the long planning and construction times inherent in bus, rail, and other mass transit systems, a consistent and dependable source of revenue should be established.

Mass transportation offers the prospect for significant energy conservation. In addition, both management and labor agree that ease of access to the workplace is an important factor in employment decisions and industrial plant locations. Lack of adequate access is a major reason why businesses have moved out of crowded urban areas, resulting in lower tax bases for cities. To encourage existing businesses to remain in urban centers and to attract new businesses to urban areas, it is vital that adequate public and private transportation facilities be provided.

RURAL TRANSPORTATION

Republicans recognize the importance of transportation in the rural areas of America.

Public transit is becoming more significant to rural areas as the costs of energy rise. While public transit will not replace the importance of private vehicles in rural America, it can serve as a vital adjunct to transportation in the neighborhoods throughout rural America.

Jobs and the Workplace

We propose to put Americans back to work again by restoring real growth without inflation to the United States economy. Republican programs and initiatives detailed in this platform will create millions of additional new jobs in the American workplace. As a result of Mr. Carter's recession, more than eight million Americans are now out of work.

Sweeping change in America's economic policy is needed. We must replace the Carter Administration's promise of hard times and austerity — one promise which has been kept — with Republican policies that restore economic growth and create more jobs.

The Democratic Congress and the Carter Administration are espousing programs that candidate Carter in 1976 said were inhumane: using recession, unemployment, high interest rates, and high taxes to fight inflation. The Democrats are now trying to stop inflation with a recession, a bankrupt policy which is throwing millions of Americans out of work. They say Americans must tighten their belts, abandon their dreams, and accept higher taxes, less take-home pay, fewer jobs, and no growth in the national economy.

We categorically reject this approach. Inflation is too much money chasing too few goods. Shutting down our nation's factories and throwing millions of people out of work leads only to shortages and higher prices.

We believe inflation can only be controlled by monetary and spending restraint, combined with sharp reductions in the tax and regulatory barriers to savings, investments, production, and jobs.

[GROWTH AND ITS IMPACT ON WORKERS]

The Republican Party believes nothing is more important to our nation's defense and social well-being than economic growth.

Since 1973, the U.S. economy has grown in real terms at a rate of only 1.9 percent a year. This is barely half of the 3.7 percent annual growth rate we experienced between 1950 and 1973 and well below the 4.6 percent growth rate we enjoyed between 1961 and 1969. If our economy continues to grow at our current rate of less than two percent a year, our Gross National Product (GNP) will barely reach $3 trillion by 1990.

But if we can regain the growth we experienced during the economic boom of the 1960s, our GNP will reach nearly $4 trillion by the end of the decade, nearly one-third higher.

With this kind of economic growth, incomes would be substantially higher and jobs would be plentiful. Federal revenues would be high enough to provide for a balanced budget, adequate funding of health, education and social spending, and unquestioned military preeminence, with enough left over to reduce payroll and income taxes on American workers and retirees. Economic growth would generate price stability as the expanding economy eliminated budget deficits and avoided pressure on the Federal Reserve to create more money. And the social gains from economic growth would be enormous. Faster growth, higher incomes, and plentiful jobs are exactly what the unemployed, the underprivileged, and minorities have been seeking for many years.

All working men and women of America have much to gain from economic growth and a healthy business environment. It enhances their bargaining position by fostering competition among potential employers to provide more attractive working conditions, better retirement and health benefits, higher wages and salaries, and generally improving job security. A stagnant economy, which Democratic policies have brought about, decreases competition among business for workers, discourages improved employee benefits, reduces income levels, and dramatically increases unemployment.

SAVINGS, PRODUCTIVITY, AND JOBS

Savings and investment are the keys to economic growth. Only that part of national income which goes into savings and which is not consumed by government deficits is available to finance real economic growth.

Americans now save less than any other people in the Western world because inflation and the high rates of taxation imposed by the Carter Administration and the Democratic Congress have destroyed their ability and incentive to save and invest. This has strangled economic growth, choked off private initiative, pushed up prices, and retarded productivity and job creation.

The sharp drop in the growth of American productivity is the main reason why Americans' average real weekly earnings are no more than they were 19 years ago. This problem has worsened to the point that workers earn eight percent less in real purchasing power as the Carter term comes to a close than they did when it began.

The 25 years of Democratic domination of the Congress have cost us a generation of lost opportunities. The Carter Administration in particular has opposed every Republican effort to restore the health of the economy through lower taxes and work efforts, savings, and the modernization of America's productive machinery.

Republicans are committed to an economic policy based on lower tax rates and a reduced rate of government spending.

Therefore, the Republican Party pledges to:

Reduce tax rates on individuals and businesses to increase incentives for all Americans and to encourage more savings, investment, output and productivity, and more jobs for Americans;

Provide special incentives for savings by lowering the tax rates on savings and investment income;

Revitalize our productive capacities by simplifying and accelerating tax depreciation schedules for facilities, structures, equipment, and vehicles;

Limit government spending to a fixed and smaller percentage of the Gross National Product; and

Balance the budget without tax increases at these lower levels of taxation and spending.

We also oppose Carter proposals to impose withholding on dividend and interest income. They would serve as a disincentive to save and invest and create needless paperwork burdens for government, business, industry, and the private citizen. They would literally rob the saver of the benefits of interest compounding and automatic dividend re-investment programs.

Unless taxes are reduced and federal spending is restrained, our nation's economy faces continued inflation, recession, and economic stagnation. Tax rate reductions and spending restraint will restore the savings and investment needed to create new jobs, increase living standards, and restore our competitive position in the world.

EMPLOYMENT SAFETY-NET

To those individuals who have lost their jobs because of the Carter recession we pledge to insure that they receive their rightfully earned unemployment compensation benefits.

The Republican Party recognizes the need to provide workers who have lost their jobs because of technological obsolescence or imports the opportunity to adjust to changing economic conditions. In particular, we will seek ways to assist workers threatened by foreign competition.

The Democratic Administration's inability to ensure fairness and equity between our nation and some of our trading partners has resulted in massive unemployment in many core industries. As we meet in Detroit, this Party takes special notice that among the hardest hit have been the automotive workers whose jobs are now targeted by aggressive foreign competition. Much of this problem is a result of the present Administration's inability to negotiate foreign trade agreements which do not jeopardize American jobs. We will take steps to ensure competitiveness of our domestic industries to protect American jobs. But for workers who have already lost their jobs, we will provide assistance, incentives for job retraining and placement, and job search and relocation allowances. Toward this end, we will pursue specific tax and regulatory changes to revitalize America's troubled basic industries. We will also seek the aid of private individuals, businesses, and non-profit organizations to formulate creative new self-supporting answers to training and placement problems as well as non-governmental sources of temporary financial support.

The Republican Party believes that protectionist tariffs and quotas are detrimental to our economic well-being. Nevertheless, we insist that our trading partners offer our nation the same level of equity, access, and fairness that we have shown them. The mutual benefits of trade require that it be conducted in the spirit of reciprocity. The Republican Party will consider appropriate measures necessary to restore equal and fair competition between ourselves and our trading partners.

The international exchange of goods and services must take place under free and unfettered conditions of market entry.

TRAINING AND SKILLS

Unemployment is a growing problem for millions of Americans, but it is an unparalleled disaster for minority Americans. As this country's economic growth has slowed over the past decade, unemployment has become more intractable. The gravity of the crisis is so severe that as we entered the present recession, unemployment was over six percent for the entire labor force but it was 33 percent for minority youth. In addition, the black unemployment rate was 10.8 percent and youth between the ages of 16 and 24 continued to account for about one-half of the total unemployed.

Despite the almost $100 billion spent on well-intended public sector employment and training programs, the structural unemployment problem continues to fester among minorities and young people. In addition to providing a growth climate for job creation, specific and targeted programs must be developed to alleviate these problems.

Since four out of every five jobs are in the private sector, the success of federal employment efforts is dependent on private sector participation.

It must be recognized as the ultimate location for unsubsidized jobs, as the provider of means to attain this end, and as an active participant in the formulation of employment and training policies on the local and national level. Throughout America, the private and independent sectors have repeatedly helped in the creation of minority business through donated counseling and consulting services. They have encouraged equal opportunity hiring practices within their own industries and have built non-profit, self-supporting training centers where the products produced during training are sold to support the programs.

A coordinated approach needs to be developed which maximizes the use of existing community resources, offers adequate incentives to the private sector, focuses on both large and small business, and minimizes red tape.

In recognizing the seriousness of the youth employment problem, Republicans also realize that a job alone will do very little to move a disadvantaged young person beyond the poverty line. Republicans support the creation of comprehensive programs for disadvantaged youth which would offer pre-employment training, educational instruction, job placement, and retention services. Second, Republicans support efforts to establish and maintain programs which seek to match the needs of the private sector and our young people as efficiently and effectively as possible. We also support expansion of proven skill training practices, such as apprenticeship, as well as private schools and trade schools. These methods can provide quality training and point toward the acquisition of specific job skills leading to specific employment goals.

We will encourage and foster the growth of new organizations operated by public-private partnerships to help forge a closer link between the schools and private employers. These institutions can afford in-school and out-of-school disadvantaged youth with the opportunity to upgrade basic skills, acquire work habits and orientation to work, and move directly from successful completion of the program to private unsubsidized jobs.

We believe that present laws create additional barriers for unemployed youth. One of the keys to resolving the youth unemployment problem is to reduce the cost to private employers for hiring young people who lack the necessary skills and experience to become immediately productive. Unfortunately, current government policy makes it too expensive for employers to hire unskilled youths. We urge a reduction of payroll tax rates, a youth differential for the minimum wage, and alleviation of other costs of employment until a young person can be a productive employee.

SMALL BUSINESS

Small business is the backbone of the American economy, with unique strengths and problems which must be recognized and addressed. For more than half of all American workers, the workplace is a small business.

Small business is family business both in the sense that many of them are owned and operated by single families, and also because most American families rely not only on the goods and services, but on the jobs produced there for their livelihood and standard of living.

Republicans have demonstrated their sensitivity to the problems of the small business community. The Carter Administration held a conference to learn what Republicans have long known. In the Congress, we have been working to pass legislation to solve small business problems and achieve the very goals later identified by that conference. A 1978 initiative by the late Representative Bill Steiger reduced the capital gains tax rates which were destroying capital formation in America. Under the leadership of Republicans in Congress, efforts to simplify and liberalize the restrictive depreciation schedule are a top priority. Another proposal long advocated by our Party is the drive to encourage the entrepreneur by reform of the regulatory laws which stifle the very life of business through fines, threats, and harassment. Republicans realize the immediate necessity of reducing the regulatory burden to give small business a fighting chance against the federal agencies. We believe that wherever feasible, small business should be exempt from regulations and, where exemption is not feasible, small business should be subject to a less onerous tier of regulation. We have offered legislation to reimburse small businessmen who successfully challenge the federal government in court. Republicans believe the number one priority for small business in America is the achievement of lower business and personal tax rates for small businessmen and women and we intend to work to secure them.

All of these initiatives will receive immediate attention from a Republican Administration and Congress. Without such changes as these, the small entrepreneur, who takes the risks which help make the economy grow and provides over 90 percent of all new jobs annually, will be an endangered species.

By fostering small business growth, we are promoting permanent private sector solutions to the unemployment problem. We will continue to provide for small business needs by enacting a substantial increase in the surtax exemption. The heavy estate tax burden imposed on the American people is threatening the life savings of millions of our families, forcing spouses and children to sell their homes, businesses, and family farms to pay the estate taxes. To encourage continuity of family ownership, we will seek to ease this tax burden on all Americans and abolish excessive inheritance taxes to allow families to retain and pass on their small businesses and family farms.

We will reform the patent laws to facilitate innovation and we will further this goal by encouraging a greater share of federal research and development be done by small business. Finally, we will reform those tax laws which make it more profitable to break up a small business or merge it into a conglomerate, than to allow it to grow and develop as an independent business.

FAIRNESS TO THE WORKER

The Republican Party is committed to full employment without inflation. We will seek to provide more jobs, increase the standard of living, and ensure equitable treatment on the job for all American workers by stimulating economic growth.

We reaffirm our commitment to the fundamental principle of fairness in labor relations, including the legal right of unions to organize workers and to represent them through collective bargaining consistent with state laws and free from unnecessary government involvement. We applaud the mutual efforts of labor and management to improve the quality of work life.

Wage demands today often represent the attempt of working men and women to catch up with government-caused inflation and high tax rates. With the blessing of the Democrats' majority in Congress, the Council on Wage and Price Stability has put a de facto ceiling of seven to eight and one-half percent on workers' wages, while the Administration devalues their paychecks at a rate of 13 to 15 percent. The government, not the worker, is the principal cause of inflation.

We recognize the need for governmental oversight of the health and safety of the workplace, without interfering in the economic well-being of employers or the job security of workers.

The Republican Party reaffirms its long-standing support for the right of states to enact "Right-to-Work" laws under section 14(b) of the Taft-Hartley Act.

The political freedom of every worker must be protected. Therefore the Republican Party strongly supports protections against the practice of using compulsory dues and fees for partisan political purposes.

FAIRNESS TO THE CONSUMER

The Republican Party shares the concerns of consumers that there be full disclosure and fairness in the marketplace. We recognize that government regulation and taxes add significantly to costs of goods and services to the consumer, reducing the standard of living for all Americans. For example, safety and environmental standards, some of which are counterproductive, increase the average price of a new car by over $700. Compliance with those regulations alone costs motorists as much as $12 billion a year.

Fairness to the consumer, like fairness to the employer and the worker, requires that government perform certain limited functions and enforce certain safeguards to ensure that equity, free competition, and safety exist in the free market economy. However, government action is not itself the solution to consumer problems; in fact, it has become in large measure a part of the problem. By consistent enforcement of law and enhancement of fair competition, government can and should help the consumer.

An informed consumer making economic choices and decisions in the marketplace is the best regulator of the free enterprise system. Consumers are also taxpayers, workers, investors, shoppers, farmers, and producers. The Republican Party recognizes the need for consumer protection but feels that such protection will not be enhanced by the creation of a new consumer protection bureaucracy. Just as there can be no single monolithic consumer viewpoint, so the Republican Party opposes the funding of special self-proclaimed advocates to represent consumer interests in federal agency proceedings.

FAIRNESS TO THE EMPLOYER

The Republican Party declares war on government overregulation. We pledge to cut down on federal paperwork, cut out excessive regulation, and cut back the bloated bureaucracy.

In addressing these problems we recognize that overregulation is particularly harmful to America's small businesses whose survival is often threatened by the excessive costs of complying with government rules and handling federal paperwork.

While we recognize the role of the federal government in establishing certain minimum standards designed to improve the quality of life in America, we reaffirm our conviction that these standards can best be attained through innovative efforts of American business without the federal government mandating the methods of attainment.

The extraordinary growth of government, particularly since the middle 1960s, has brought mounting costs to society which, in turn, have added to inflationary pressures, reduced productivity, discouraged new investment, destroyed jobs, and increased bureaucratic intrusion into everyday life.

Regulatory costs are now running in excess of $100 billion each year, or about $1,800 for every American family. Federal paperwork annually costs businesses from $25 to $32 billion. According to official figures, it takes individuals and business firms over 143 million man-hours to complete 4,400 different federal forms each year. Government regulation produces many indirect, immeasurable costs as well and has led to increased bureaucratization of industry. Regulation also restricts personal choices, tends to undermine America's democratic public institutions, and threatens to destroy the private, competitive free market economy it was originally designed to protect.

GOVERNMENT REFORM

In the face of a crisis of overregulation, the Carter Administration and the Democrats who control Congress have failed to recognize the problems facing workers, employers, and consumers and seem unable to come to grips with the underlying causes. While belatedly supporting transportation deregulation programs initiated by previous Republican

Administrations, they have embarked on ambitious new schemes to tighten Washington's hold on energy and education. They have ignored or sidetracked Republican proposals to eliminate wasteful and outmoded spending programs and regulations. They have combined to push through more legislation and create additional programs which expand the size and power of the federal bureaucracy at the expense of ordinary taxpayers, consumers and businesses. In contradiction to 1976 Carter campaign promises to cut back on regulation, the number of pages in the Federal Register devoted to new rules and regulations has increased from 57,072 in 1976 to 77,497 in 1979 and will approach 90,000 by the end of 1980.

The result of Democratic rule in both the White House and the Congress is that government power has grown unchecked. Excessive regulation remains a major component of our nation's spiraling inflation and continues to stifle private initiative, individual freedom, and state and local government autonomy.

The Republican Party pledges itself to a comprehensive program of government reform. We propose to enact a temporary moratorium on all new federal regulations that diminish the supply of goods and services and add significantly to inflation. Such a moratorium will be consistent with the goal of achieving a safe and healthy working environment. We shall work to reduce substantially the regulatory and paperwork burdens on small businesses.

We encourage management and labor to form joint safety and health committees to make the workplace a better place to produce goods and services. At the same time we believe that the arbitrary and high-handed tactics used by OSHA bureaucrats must end. OSHA should concentrate its resources on encouraging voluntary compliance by employers and monitoring situations where close federal supervision is needed and serious hazards are most likely to occur. OSHA should be required to consult with, advise, and assist businesses in coping with the regulatory burden before imposing any penalty for non-compliance. Small businesses and employers with good safety records should be exempt from safety inspections, and penalties should be increased for those with consistently poor performance.

AGRICULTURE

In no American workplace is there to be found greater productivity, cooperation, neighborly concern, creative use of applied science, information and relevant research, honesty, perseverance, hard work, and independence than on the farm and ranch.

The Republican Party takes pride in the ability of American farmers to provide abundant, high quality, and nutritious food and fiber for all our citizens including those most in need and to millions throughout the world, and at the same time to supply the largest single component in our export balance of trade.

Crisis in Agriculture

Four years of the Carter Administration and 25 consecutive years of a Congress controlled by Democrats have brought farmers and ranchers to the brink of disaster and the hardest times they have known since the Great Depression. In the last four years, more than 100,000 family farms have failed as farm income has plummeted. Even the present Administration's own figures show a decrease in real net farm income of some 40 percent in the last year alone — from $33 billion in 1979 to less than $22 billion projected for 1980.

The Democratic Party and the Carter Administration have abused their authority and failed in their responsibility to provide sound agricultural policies. Republicans pledge to make life in rural America prosperous again. We will:

Increase net farm income by supporting and refining programs to bring profitable farm prices with the goal of surpassing parity levels in a market-oriented agricultural economy;

Control inflation by adopting sound fiscal and monetary policies and by eliminating excessive and unnecessary federal regulations;

Expand markets at home by effectively utilizing the advantages of the energy potential for farm, forestry, and other biomass products. We encourage the continued innovative efforts in developing alcohol and other renewable energy sources and equipment for both on-farm and commercial use;

Aggressively expand markets abroad by effectively using the Eisenhower Food for Peace program and revolving credit incentives, working to remove foreign restraints on American products and encouraging the development of dependable new markets in developing countries;

Assure a priority allocation of fuel for U.S. agriculture, including food and fiber production, transportation, and processing; and

Combine efforts to encourage the renewable resource timber production capability of privately-owned forests and woodlands with a federal program committed to multiple-use (timber, recreation, wildlife, watershed and/or range management) where federal land has not been designated as wilderness.

Rural America

Attention to the quality of life in our rural areas is a vital necessity because rural Americans impart a special strength to the national character. It is our goal to assure that all rural citizens — whether they are farmers or not — have the same consideration in matters of economic development, in energy, credit and transportation availability, and in employment opportunities which are given to those who live in towns and cities. The opportunity for non-farm jobs enhances the ability of people to live and work in rural America in the decade ahead, and our dedication to a prosperous and energetic rural America is part and parcel of our commitment to make America great again.

Expand Export Markets

Agriculture's contribution to the U.S. trade balance makes it especially fitting that an aggressive market development program to establish dependable new markets for farm exports will be a vital part of the policies to restore profitability to American agriculture. Republicans will ensure that:

International trade is conducted on the basis of fair and effective competition and that all imported agricultural products meet the same standards of quality that are required of American producers;

The General Agreement on Tariffs and Trade becomes a meaningful vehicle for handling agricultural trade problems and grievances;

An aggressive agricultural market development program and the streamlining of the export marketing system is given top national priority;

Government-to-government sales of agricultural commodities be eliminated, except as specifically provided by law;

The future of U.S. agricultural commodities is protected from the economic evils of predatory dumping by other producing nations and that the domestic production of these commodities, so important to the survival of individuals and small rural communities is preserved; and

The important and productive potential of the commercial seafood industry is given encouragement.

Farmer-Held Reserves

We support farmer-owned grain reserves, should they become necessary, and adamantly oppose government-controlled reserves.

Grain Embargo

We believe that agricultural embargoes are only symbolic and are ineffective tools of foreign policy. We oppose singling out American farmers to bear the brunt of Carter's ill-conceived, ineffective, and improperly implemented grain embargo. The Carter grain embargo should be terminated immediately.

Excessive Regulation of Agriculture

The crushing burden of excessive federal regulation such as many of those imposed on farmers, ranchers, foresters, and commercial fishermen by OSHA, EPA, the departments of Agriculture, Labor, Justice, Interior, and other government entities are unrealistic and unnecessary.

We pledge a sensible approach to reduce excessive federal regulation that is draining the profitability from farming, ranching, and commercial fishing. Especially high on the agenda for changes in policy under Republican leadership are such regulatory issues as the Interior Department's ineffective predator control policies, EPA and FDA's excessive adherence to "zero risk" policies relative to the use of pesticides, herbicides, antibiotics, food additives, preservatives, and the like.

Soil and Water Conservation

We believe the strong soil and water conservation stewardship to which farmers, ranchers, watermen, and rural Americans are devoted is exemplary, and encourage appropriate local, state, and federal programs to give conservation practices vitality. Voluntary participation with adequate incentives is essential to the effective conservation of our soil and water resources.

Water Policy

The conservation and development of the nation's water resources are vital requisites for rebuilding America's national strength. The natural abundance of water can no longer be taken for granted. The impending crisis in water could be far more serious than our energy problems unless we act now. A dynamic water policy, which addresses our national diversity in climate, geography, and patterns of land ownership, and includes all requirements across the spectrum of water use, including Reclamation policy, will be a priority of the Republican Administration working with the advice and counsel of state and local interests. We must develop a partnership between the federal and state governments which will not destroy traditional state supremacy in water law. Further, there must be cooperation between the Executive Branch and Congress in developing and implementing that policy. Lack of such partnership has resulted in four years of bitter confrontation between the states and the obstructive policies of the Democratic Administration. The Congress has been frustrated in its efforts to conserve and develop our water resources. Working together, the states and the federal government can meet the impending water crisis through innovative and alternative approaches to such problems as cleaning our lakes and rivers, reducing toxic pollution, developing multiple-use projects, and achieving a workable balance between the many competing demands on our water resources.

Agricultural Labor

Comprehensive labor legislation, which will be fair to American workers and encourage better relations with our neighbors in Mexico and Canada with whom we wish to establish a working North American Accord, is an essential endeavor. We deplore disruptive work stoppages which interrupt the supply of food to consumers.

Taxation

Federal estate and gift taxes have a particularly pernicious effect on family farms. Young farmers who inherit farm property are often forced to sell off part of the family farm to pay taxes. Once these taxes are paid, young farmers often must begin their careers deeply in debt. Our tax laws must be reformed to encourage rather than discourage family farming and ranching.

We deplore the imposition of present excessive estate and gift taxes on family farms. We support the use of lower, productivity-based valuation when farms are transferred within the family. Further, we believe that no spouse should pay estate taxes on farm property inherited from a husband or wife. We support the Republican tax cut proposal which provides accelerated depreciation and expanded investment tax credits to farm vehicles, equipment, and structures. Finally, we support legislation which would remove tax advantages foreign investors realize on the sale of U.S. forests, farmland, and other real estate.

Rural Transportation

It is essential to the well-being and security of our nation that an adequate rural transportation system be restored as a vital link between rural areas and their markets, both domestic and export. Overall, we pledge to eliminate those rules and regulations which are restrictive to the free flow of commerce and trade of agricultural products and encourage an environment that will enhance the private development and improvement of all modes of transportation to move agricultural production swiftly, safely, and economically. Recognizing the inherent advantages of each mode of transportation, the Republican Party will work to encourage and allow those advantages to be utilized on a balanced and equitable basis.

We believe the federal 55 miles per hour speed limit is counterproductive and contributes to higher costs of goods and services to all communities, particularly in rural America. The most effective, no-cost federal assistance program available would be for each state to set its own speed limit.

A Strong USDA

We pledge an Administration dedicated to restoring profitability to agriculture. A top priority will be the selection of a qualified and effective Secretary and policy staff who will speak up for American farmers — and a President who will listen.

America's preeminence in agriculture is rooted in a system of agricultural research, extension, and teaching — unique and unequalled in the world. Land Grant Universities focus on problems of national, regional, and local concern. Cooperative extension, operating in every county of the United States and its territories, brings the results of USDA and Land Grant University research to farmers and ranchers, rural women, consumers, agribusiness, and to youth through 4-H programs.

Food Safety

The Republican Party favors a legislative effort to revise and modernize our food safety laws, providing guidelines for risk assessment, benefit assessment, peer review, and regulatory flexibility which are consistent with other government health and safety policies.

Cooperatives

We believe farmer cooperatives and rural electric and telephone cooperatives provide essential benefits to farmers and the rural Americans they serve, and we support exclusive jurisdiction of USDA in the effective administration of the Capper-Volstead Act.

We Republicans pledge ourselves to work with farmers, ranchers, and our friends and neighbors to make America great again.

The Nation

Though a relatively young nation among those of western civilization we are possessed of one of the oldest institutions of government extant. Steeped in the Judeo-Christian ethic and in Anglo-Saxon theories of law and right, our legal and political institutions have evolved over many generations to form a stable system that serves free men and women well. It governs a people of multifarious heritage dispersed across a great continent of marked geographical contrasts. It presides over a diverse economy that in its collective whole is the largest, most powerful and most resilient in the world. In the two centuries of its life, though it has from time to time been sorely tested by constitutional, economic, and social crises, it has stood and not been found wanting. Its timeless strength, coupled with and reinforced by the faith and good will, the wisdom and confidence of the people from whom it derives its powers, has preserved us as a nation of enormous vitality.

The intent of the Founders, embraced and reflected by succeeding generations of Americans, was that the central government should perform only those functions which are necessary concomitants of nationality, preserve order, and do for people only those things which they cannot do for themselves. The durability of our system lies in its flexibility and its accommodation to diversity and changing circumstance. It is notable as much for what it permits as for what it proscribes. Government must ever be the servant of the nation, not its master.

BIG GOVERNMENT

Under the guise of providing for the common good, Democratic Party domination of the body politic over the last 47 years has produced a central government of vastly expanded size, scope, and rigidity. Confidence in government, especially big government, has been the chief casualty of too many promises made and broken, too many commitments unkept. It is time for change — time to de-emphasize big bureaucracies — time to shift the focus of national politics from expanding government's power to that of restoring the strength of smaller communities such as the family, the neighborhood, and the workplace.

Government's power to take and tax, to regulate and require has already reached extravagant proportions. As government's power continues to grow, the "consent of the governed" will diminish. Republicans support an end to the growth of the federal government and pledge to return the decisionmaking process to the smaller communities of society.

The emergence of policies and programs which will revitalize the free enterprise system and reverse the trend toward regulation is essential. To sustain the implementation of such policy, it is necessary to raise the public awareness and understanding that our free enterprise system is the source of all income, government and private, and raise the individual's awareness of his or her vested interest in its growth and vitality.

The Republican Party believes that it is important to develop a growing constituency which recognizes its direct relationship to the health and success of free enterprise, and realizes the negative impact of excessive regulation. Education and involvement in the system are the best means to accomplish this. To this end, we will actively pursue new and expanding opportunities for all Americans to become more directly involved in our free enterprise system.

GOVERNMENT REORGANIZATION

The Republican Party reaffirms its belief in the decentralization of the federal government and in the traditional American principle that the best government is the one closest to the people. There, it is less costly, more accountable, and more responsive to people's needs. Against the prevailing trend toward increased centralization of government under the Democrats, Republicans succeeded in the 1970s in initiating large scale revenue sharing and block grant programs to disperse the power of the federal government and share it with the states and localities.

Our states and localities have the talent, wisdom, and determination to respond to the variety of demands made upon them. Block grants and revenue sharing provide local government with the means and the flexibility to solve their own problems in ways most appropriate for each locale. Unlike categorical grants, they do not lock states and localities into priorities and needs perceived by Washington. They are also more efficient because block grants and revenue sharing relieve both local government and the federal government from the costly and complicated process of program application, implementation, and review associated with the categorical grant system.

We pledge to continue to redouble our efforts to return power to the state and local governments. The regionalization of government encouraged by federal policies diminishes the responsiveness of state and local governments and impairs the power of the people to control their destiny.

While Republican efforts have been focused on sharing revenues and the powers that go with it, the Carter Administration has been preoccupied with the reorganization and consolidation of central authority. As a result, we have the Departments of Energy and Education, for example, but no more oil and gas, or learning, to show for it.

When we mistakenly rely on government to solve all our problems we ignore the abilities of people to solve their own problems. We pledge to renew the dispersion of power from the federal government to the states and localities. But this will not be enough. We pledge to extend the process so that power can be transferred as well to non-governmental institutions.

GOVERNMENT REFORM

We favor the establishment of a commission of distinguished citizens to recommend ways of reorganizing and reducing the size and scope of the Executive Branch. Federal departments, agencies, and bureaus should be consolidated where possible to end waste and improve the delivery of essential services. Republicans pledge to eliminate bureaucratic red tape and reduce government paperwork. Agencies should be made to justify every official form and filing requirement. Where possible, we favor deregulation, especially in the energy, transportation, and communications industries. We believe that the marketplace, rather than the bureaucrats, should regulate management decisions.

The unremitting delegation of authority to the rule-makers by successive Democratic Congresses and the abuse of that authority has led to our current crisis of overregulation. For that reason, we support use of the Congressional veto, sunset laws, and strict budgetary control of the bureaucracies as a means of eliminating unnecessary spending and regulations. Agencies should be required to review existing regulations and eliminate those that are outmoded, duplicative, or contradictory. They must conduct cost-benefit analyses of major proposed regulations to determine their impact on the economy, on public health and safety, on state and local government, and on competition. We recommend legislation which would eliminate the present presumption of validity in favor of federal regulations. We also support legislation to require the federal government to provide restitution to those who have been wrongfully injured by agency actions. We oppose the use of tax monies by any federal agency to pay the expenses of intervenors in the rule-making process.

We recognize that there are dangers inherent in the rapid growth of the federal bureaucracy, especially the arbitrary nature of its discretionary power and the abuses of procedural safeguards. Accordingly, we pledge to work for fundamental changes in the federal Administrative

Procedures Act in order to give citizens the same constitutional protections before a government agency that they have in a courtroom. Among these reforms are requirements that agencies publish in the Federal Register all rules and statements of policy before they are adopted, that a person be guaranteed written notice and the opportunity to submit facts and arguments in any adjudicatory proceeding, that an agency decision be consistent with prior decisions unless otherwise provided by law, and that a person may seek judicial review without first exhausting his or her administrative remedies. At the same time we urge the Congress to strengthen its oversight to ensure that the agencies comply with the deadlines, report filing and other requirements mandated by law.

We propose to repeal federal restrictions and rewrite federal standards which hinder minorities from finding employment, starting their own businesses, gaining valuable work experience, or enjoying the fruits of their own labors.

Because there are too many federal employees in comparison to private sector employees, there should be no further increase in the number of civilian federal employees if that would increase the ratio of federal employees to private sector employees over the present ratio.

ELECTION REFORM

The Republican Party has consistently encouraged full participation in our electoral process and is disturbed by the steady decline in voter participation in the United States in recent years. We believe that the increased voter turnout during the past year in Republican campaigns is due to dissatisfaction with Democratic officials and their failure to heed popular demands to cut taxes, restrain spending, curb inflation, and drastically reduce regulation.

Republicans support public policies that will promote electoral participation without compromising ballot-box security. We strongly oppose national postcard voter registration schemes because they are an open invitation to fraud.

Republicans support public policies that encourage political activity by individual citizens. We support the repeal of those restrictive campaign spending limitations that tend to create obstacles to local grassroots participation in federal elections. We also oppose the proposed financing of congressional campaigns with taxpayers' dollars as an effort by the Democratic Party to protect its incumbent Members of Congress with a tax subsidy. We prefer the present system of having the states and party rules determine the presidential nominating process to the concept of a uniform national primary which would only add to the already high costs of, and excessive federal intrusion into, presidential campaigns.

We support the critical roles of competitive political parties in the recruitment of candidates, the conduct of campaigns, and the development of broad-based public policy responsive to the people. We urge Congress and state legislatures to frame their regulations of campaign finance, their nominating systems, and other election laws to strengthen rather than weaken parties.

ARTS AND HUMANITIES

Recent Republican Administrations led the way in bringing together private support and governmental encouragement to effect a tremendous expansion of artistic and scholarly endeavor. The Carter Administration has crudely politicized these programs, lowering their standards of excellence and increasing federal control over them.

The Republican Party will restore the sound economy which is absolutely necessary for the arts and humanities to flourish. We will restore, as well, the integrity of federal programs in this area. Most important, to ensure the continued primacy of private funding for the arts, we reiterate our support of broader tax incentives for contributions to charitable and cultural organizations.

TRANSPORTATION

America's transportation system must be designed to meet the requirements of the people, not to dictate what those requirements should be. Essential to any industrialized country is a transportation system which provides efficient and reliable service for both the movement of people and freight, urban and rural, domestic and foreign. Our nation has one of the finest transportation systems in the world but there is a danger that it will be unable to meet the future needs of a growing America.

Present levels of public and private investment will not preserve the existing system. For example, highways are deteriorating twice as fast as they are being rebuilt and inadequate rehabilitation will soon cost users more in reduced service levels than the cost of adequate rehabilitation.

The demand for transportation will grow dramatically in the next two decades with people-miles travelled increasing by over 50 percent and freight ton-miles more than doubling.

Government overregulation is inhibiting the return on investment necessary to attract capital for future growth and jobs creation.

A maze of federal agencies, Congressional committees, and conflicting policies is driving up costs and retarding innovation.

A lackluster energy policy, impeding production of oil, coal, and other forms of energy is endangering transportation's ability to keep up with demand.

Consequently, the role of government in transportation must be redefined. The forces of the free market must be brought to bear to promote competition, reduce costs, and improve the return on investment to stimulate capital formation in the private sector. The role of government must change from one of overbearing regulation to one of providing incentives for technological and innovative developments, while assuring through anti-trust enforcement that neither predatory competitive pricing nor price gouging of captive customers will occur.

Increased emphasis must be placed on the importance of having a well-balanced national transportation system where highways, passenger vehicles, buses, trucks, rail, water, pipelines, and air transportation each provide those services which they do best, while offering the widest range of reasonable choices for both passenger and freight movement. A sound transportation system is a prerequisite for the vision of America that Republicans embrace — a prosperous, growing nation where dreams can still come true.

ENERGY

Energy is the lifeblood of our economy. Without adequate energy supplies now and in the future, the jobs of American men and women, the security of their lives, and their ability to provide for their families will be threatened and their standard of living will be lowered. Every American is painfully aware that our national energy situation has deteriorated badly over the past four years of Democratic control. Gasoline prices have more than doubled. Our oil import bill has risen 96 percent. Our energy supplies have become increasingly vulnerable because U.S. oil production outside of Alaska is now 23 percent below 1973 levels. The threat of sudden shortages, curtailments, and gas lines has become a recurring reality.

This steady deterioration has not only compounded our economic problems of inflation, recession, and dollar weakness, but even more importantly, it has infected our confidence as a nation. Energy shortages, spiralling costs, and increasing insecurity are beginning to darken our basic hopes and expectations for the future.

The National Association for the Advancement of Colored People has very accurately focused on the effects that a no-growth energy policy will have on the opportunities of America's black people and other minorities. The NAACP said that "a pessimistic attitude toward energy supplies for the future ... cannot satisfy the fundamental requirement of a society of expanding economic opportunity."

In commenting on the Carter energy proposals the Association said, "We cannot accept the notion that our people are best served by a policy based upon the inevitability of energy shortage and the need for government to allocate an ever diminishing supply among competing interests. ... (The plan) reflects the absence of a black perspective in its development."

Three and one-half years ago, President Carter declared energy the "moral equivalent of war" and sent Congress 109 recommendations for action, including the creation of a new Department of Energy. Since then, the federal budget for government's energy bureaucracy has grown to about $10 billion per year and more than 20,000 pages of new energy regulations and guidelines have been issued. But these have not fostered the production of a single extra unit of energy.

The Democratic Congress has joined in the stampede, taking action on 304 energy bills since 1977. As a result, the federal bureaucracy is busy from coast to coast allocating gasoline, setting building temperatures, printing rationing coupons, and readying standby plans to ban weekend boating, close factories, and pass out "no drive day" stickers to American motorists — all the time saying, "we must make do with less." Never before in the history of American government has so much been done at such great expense with such dismal results.

Republicans believe this disappointing cycle of shrinking energy prospects and expanding government regulation and meddling is wholly unnecessary. We believe that the proven American values of individual enterprise can solve our energy problems. This optimism stands in stark contrast to the grim predictions of the Democrats who have controlled Congress for the last 25 years.

[Alternative Strategy]

They seem to believe not only that we are a nation without resources, but also that we have lost our resourcefulness. Republicans believe in the common sense of the American people rather than a complex web of government controls and interventions that threaten America's ability to grow. We are committed to an alternative strategy of aggressively boosting the nation's energy supplies; stimulating new energy technology and more efficient energy use; restoring maximum feasible choice and freedom in the marketplace for energy consumers and producers alike; and eliminating energy shortages and disruptions as a roadblock to renewed national economic growth, rising living standards, and a reawakening of the hopes and dreams of the American people for a better and more abundant future.

We believe the United States must proceed on a steady and orderly path toward energy self-sufficiency. But in the interim, our pressing need for insurance against supply disruption should not be made hostage to the whims of foreign governments, as is presently the case under the Carter Administration. We believe it is necessary to resume rapid filling of strategic oil reserves to planned levels of 500 million barrels in the short-term and ultimately to the one-billion barrel level, and to insure that non-contiguous areas of the United States have their fair share of emergency oil reserves stored within their respective boundaries, as authorized by the Energy Policy and Conservation Act of 1975.

In order to increase domestic production of energy, Republicans advocate the decontrol of the price at the well head of oil and gas.

We believe that the so-called windfall profits tax (which is unrelated to profit) should be repealed as it applies to small volume royalty owners, new oil, stripper wells, tertiary-recovery, and heavy crude oil, and that the phase-out of the tax on old oil should be accelerated. This tax legislation should be amended to include a plowback provision. We will seek decontrol of prices on all oil products and an end to government authority to allocate petroleum supplies except in national emergency. We also believe that market restrictions on the use of natural gas should be eliminated.

[Future of Coal]

Coal, our most abundant energy resource, can bridge the gap between our other present energy sources and the renewable energy sources of the future. The coal industry has been virtually ignored by the Carter Administration and the Democratic Congress. In 1977, President Carter promised to double coal production by 1985. Instead, because of obstructionist actions of the Administration, coal production has increased by only 11 percent to date and future prospects are dim. Today, thousands of coal miners are out of work and without hope for the future.

Republicans support a comprehensive program of regulatory reform, improved incentives, and revision of cumbersome and overly stringent Clean Air Act regulations. This program will speed conversion of utility, industrial, and large commercial oil-burning boilers to coal to the greatest extent feasible, thus substantially cutting our dependence on foreign oil. This program must begin immediately on a priority basis and be completed at the earliest date possible.

To effectively utilize this vast resource, our coal transportation systems must be upgraded and the government controls on them relaxed. Government regulation regarding the mining and use of coal must be simplified. We will propose a policy which will assure that governmental restraints, other than necesssary and reasonable environmental controls, do not prevent the use of coal. We also reaffirm that mined lands must be returned to beneficial use and that states, in accordance with past Congressional mandate, have the primary responsibility to implement rules concerning the mining of coal which are adapted to the states' unique characteristics.

Coal, gas, and nuclear fission offer the best intermediate solutions to America's energy needs. We support accelerated use of nuclear energy through technologies that have been proven efficient and safe. The safe operation, as well as design, of nuclear generating plants will have our highest priority to assure the continued availability of this important energy source. The design and operation of these plants can be guaranteed in less than the 10 to 12 year lead time now required to license and build them. We believe that the licensing process can and should be streamlined through consolidation of the present process and the use of standardized reactor designs.

[Nuclear Energy Development]

The Three Mile Island incident suggests the need for certain reforms, such as in the area of operator training, but illustrates that properly designed and operated nuclear plants do not endanger public health or safety. We further encourage the research, development, and demonstration of the breeder reactor with its potential for safely contributing to our nation's future energy supplies.

Nuclear power development requires sound plans for nuclear waste disposal and storage and reprocessing of spent fuel. Technical solutions to these problems exist, and decisive federal action to choose and implement solutions is essential. The Democratic-controlled Congress and Administration have failed to address the spent fuel problem. A Republican Congress and Administration will immediately begin to implement plans for regional away-from-reactor storage of spent fuel with the goal of implementation of a program no later than 1984.

Republicans are committed to the rapid development of permanent storage facilities for nuclear wastes. Since waste disposal is a national responsibility, no state should bear an unacceptable share of this responsibility.

Republicans will also move toward reprocessing of spent fuel.

Republicans will continue to support the development of new technologies to develop liquid, gaseous, and solid hydrocarbons which can be derived from coal, oil shale, and tar sands. The decontrol of oil and gas prices will eliminate any necessity for government support for a synthetic fuel industry except possibly for limited demonstration projects. Clean air, water, waste disposal, mine reclamation, and leasing rules must be made rational and final to accelerate private investment.

Gasohol is an important, immediately available source of energy that is helping to extend our petroleum reserves. We encourage development of a domestic gasohol industry.

We also believe the government must continue supporting productive research to speed the development of renewable energy technology, including solar energy, geothermal, wind, nuclear fusion, alcohol synthesis, and biomass, to provide the next generation of energy sources.

[Incentives for Conservation]

Conservation clearly plays a vital role in the consideration and formulation of national energy policy. Republicans reject, however, the position of the Democrats which is to conserve through government fiat. Republicans understand that free markets based on the collective priorities and judgments of individual consumers will efficiently allocate the energy supplies to their most highly valued uses. We also believe that the role of government is best performed by structuring creative cost-effective incentives to achieve energy efficiency and conservation.

We reject unequivocally punitive gasoline and other energy taxes designed to artificially suppress energy consumption.

Much inefficient energy use results from government subsidization of imported oil and holding the price of natural gas substantially below its market value. When the price of energy is held artificially low, there is no incentive for conservation. This kind of energy consumption stems not from the excesses of the public, but the foolish policy distortions of government. Every BTU of genuine energy "waste" in our economy would rapidly disappear if we immediately and completely dismantle all remaining energy price controls and subsidies.

[Cost of Energy]

A Republican policy of decontrol, development of our domestic energy resources, and incentives for new supply and conservation technologies will substantially reduce our dependence on imported oil. We reject the Carter Administration's incessant excuse that the high price of imported oil and OPEC are the primary cause of inflation and recession at home and a weak dollar and declining balance of payments abroad. The fastest way to bring international oil prices under control is to stop printing so recklessly the dollar in which those prices are denominated. Fully 60 percent of the world oil price increase since 1973 represents the depreciation of our dollars rather than an increase in the real price of oil.

Virtually all major environmental legislation in the past decade reflected a bipartisan concern over the need to maintain a clean and healthful environment. While the new environmental policies have resulted in improving air quality, cleaner waters, and more careful analysis of toxic chemicals, the price paid has far exceeded the direct and necessary cost of designing and installing new control technology. In the energy area, the increased complexity of regulations, together with continual changes in the standards imposed, have brought about tremendous delays in the planning and construction of new facilities ranging from electric power plants to oil refineries, pipelines, and synthetic fuel plants.

Republicans believe that an effective balance between energy and environmental goals can be achieved. We can ensure that government requirements are firmly grounded on the best scientific evidence available, that they are enforced evenhandedly and predictably, and that the process of their development and enforcement has finality.

Republicans condemn the Democrats' withdrawal of a massive amount of the most promising federal lands from prospective energy development, including the rich potential of our Outer Continental Shelf. It has been estimated that by the end of the 1980s resources from government-controlled acreage could yield over two million barrels of oil per day and four trillion cubic feet of gas per year, the equivalent of nearly all of our imports from OPEC countries. It is clear that restrictive leasing policies have driven us further to depend on OPEC by severely impairing the exploration for, and development of, domestic oil, gas, and coal resources, thereby aggravating our balance of trade deficit and making our country less secure. Republicans will move toward making available all suitable federal lands for multiple use purposes including exploration and production of energy resources.

Republicans believe that in order to address our energy problem we must maximize our domestic energy production capability. In the short term, therefore, the nation must move forward on all fronts simultaneously, including oil and gas, coal, and nuclear. In the longer term, renewable resources must be brought significantly on line to replace conventional sources. Finally, in conjunction with this all-out production initiative, we must strive to maximize conservation and the efficient use of energy.

The return to the traditions that gave vitality and strength to this nation is urgent.

The free world — indeed western civilization — needs a strong United States. That strength requires a prospering economy. That economy will be secure with a vigorous domestic energy industry. That vigor can only be achieved in an atmosphere of freedom — one that encourages individual initiatives and personal resourcefulness.

ENVIRONMENT

The Republican Party reaffirms its long standing commitment to the conservation and wise management of America's renewable natural resources.

We believe that a healthy environment is essential to the present and future well-being of our people, and to sustainable national growth.

The nature of environmental pollution is such that a government role is necessary to insure its control and the proper protection of public health. Much progress has been made in achieving the goals of clean air, clean water, and control of toxic wastes. At the same time, we believe that it is imperative that environmental laws and regulations be reviewed, and where necessary, reformed to ensure that the benefits achieved justify the costs imposed. Too often, current regulations are so rigid and narrow that even individual innovations that improve the environment cannot be implemented. We believe, in particular, that regulatory procedures must be reformed to expedite decisionmaking. Endless delay harms both the environment and the economy.

We strongly affirm that environmental protection must not become a cover for a "no-growth" policy and a shrinking economy. Our economy can continue to grow in an acceptable environment.

We believe that agricultural policy should give emphasis to the stewardship of the nation's soil and water resources. The permanent loss of productive farm land is a growing problem and we encourage states and local communities to adopt policies that help maintain and protect productive agricultural land as a national asset.

IMMIGRATION AND REFUGEE POLICY

Residence in the United States is one of the most precious and valued of conditions. The traditional hospitality of the American people has been severely tested by recent events, but it remains the strongest in the world. Republicans are proud that our people have opened their arms and hearts to strangers from abroad and we favor an immigration and refugee policy which is consistent with this tradition. We believe that to the fullest extent possible those immigrants should be admitted who will make a positive contribution to America and who are willing to accept the fundamental American values and way of life. At the same time, United States immigration and refugee policy must reflect the interests of the nation's political and economic well-being. Immigration into this country must not be determined solely by foreign governments or even by the millions of people around the world who wish to come to America. The federal government has a duty to adopt immigration laws and follow enforcement procedures which will fairly and effectively implement the immigration policy desired by American people.

The immediate adoption of this policy is essential to an orderly approach to the great problem of oppressed people seeking entry, so that the deserving can be accepted in America without adding to their hardships.

The refugee problem is an international problem and every effort should be made to coordinate plans for absorbing refugee populations with regional bodies, such as the Organization of American States and the Association of South East Asian Nations, on a global basis.

THE JUDICIARY

Under Mr. Carter, many appointments to federal judgeships have been particularly disappointing. By his partisan nominations, he has violated his explicit campaign promise of 1976 and has blatantly disregarded the public interest. We pledge to reverse that deplorable trend, through the appointment of women and men who respect and reflect the values of the American people, and whose judicial philosophy is characterized by the highest regard for protecting the rights of law-abiding citizens, and is consistent with the belief in the decentralization of the federal government and efforts to return decisionmaking power to state and local elected officials.

We will work for the appointment of judges at all levels of the judiciary who respect traditional family values and the sanctity of innocent human life.

TAXES AND GOVERNMENT SPENDING

Elsewhere in this platform, we have pledged for the sake of individual freedom and economic growth to cut personal income tax rates for all. Republicans believe that these tax rate reductions should be complemented by firm limitations on the growth of federal spending as provided by the Roth-Kemp Bill. The Republican Party, therefore, pledges to place limits on federal spending as a percent of the Gross National Product. It is now over 21 percent. We pledge to reduce it. If federal spending is reduced as tax cuts are phased in, there will be sufficient budget surpluses to fund the tax cuts, and allow for reasonable growth in necessary program spending.

By increasing economic growth, tax rate reduction will reduce the need for government spending on unemployment, welfare, and public jobs programs. However, the Republican Party will also halt excessive government spending by eliminating waste, fraud, and duplication.

We believe that the Congressional budget process has failed to control federal spending. Indeed, because of its big spending bias, the budget process has actually contributed to higher levels of social spending, has prevented necessary growth in defense spending, and has been used to frustrate every Republican attempt to lower tax rates to promote economic growth.

The immediate burden of reducing federal spending rests on the shoulders of the President and the Congress. We believe a Republican President and a Republican Congress can balance the budget and reduce spending through legislative actions, eliminating the necessity for a Constitutional amendment to compel it. However, if necessary, the Republican Party will seek to adopt a Constitutional amendment to limit federal spending and balance the budget, except in time of national emergency as determined by a two-thirds vote of Congress.

GOVERNMENT LENDING

Not only has the Democratic Congress failed to control spending, but in the last 10 years federal credit assistance programs have soared out of control.

Many federal loan guarantees and related credit programs are off-budget. As a result, no one knows the nature and extent of our obligations or the effect such practices have on our economy. The best estimate is that outstanding federal credit is now close to $600 billion.

Runaway government lending can be just as dangerous as runaway federal spending.

The Republican Party will establish a workable federal credit policy that will bring order to the reckless lending practices of the past.

INFLATION

We consider inflation and its impact on jobs to be the greatest domestic threat facing our nation today. Mr. Carter must go! For what he has done to the dollar; for what he has done to the life savings of millions of Americans; for what he has done to retirees seeking a secure old age; for what he has done to young families aspiring to a home, an education for their children, and a rising living standard, Mr. Carter must not have another four years in office.

In his three and one-half years in office, Mr. Carter has presented and supported policies which carried inflation from 4.8 percent in 1976 to a peak of 18 percent during 1980.

He has fostered a 50 percent increase in federal spending, an increase of more than $200 billion, boosting spending in an era of scarce resources, and driving up prices.

He has through both inaction and deliberate policy permitted or forced tax increases of more than 70 percent, more than $250 billion, directly increasing the cost of living and the costs of hiring and producing. This has crippled living standards, productivity, and our ability to compete in the world. It has led to reduced output, scarcity, and higher prices.

He has imposed burdensome regulations and controls on production which have reduced the availability of domestic goods and energy resources, increased our dependence on imports, particularly in the energy area, driven down the value of the dollar, and driven up prices.

He has permitted continuing federal budget deficits and increased federal borrowing, forcing higher interest rates and inflationary money creation, increasing prices.

The inflation policies of the Carter Administration have been inconsistent, counterproductive, and tragically inept. Mr. Carter has blamed everyone from OPEC to the American people themselves for this crisis of inflation — everyone, that is, but his own Administration and its policies which have been the true cause of inflation.

Inflation is too much money chasing too few goods. Much can be done to increase the growth of real output. But ultimately price stability requires a non-inflationary rate of growth of the money supply in line with the real growth of the economy. If the supply of dollars rapidly outstrips the quantity of goods, year in, year out, inflation is inevitable.

Ultimately, inflation is a decline in the value of the dollar, the monetary standard, in terms of the goods it can buy. Until the decade of the 1970s, monetary policy was automatically linked to the overriding objective of maintaining a stable dollar value. The severing of the dollar's link with real commodities in the 1960s and 1970s, in order to pursue economic goals other than dollar stability, has unleashed hyper-inflationary forces at home and monetary disorder abroad, without bringing any of the desired economic benefits. One of the most urgent tasks in the period ahead will be the restoration of a dependable monetary standard — that is, an end to inflation.

Lower tax rates, less spending, and a balanced budget are the keys to maintaining real growth and full employment as we end inflation by putting our monetary policy back on track. Monetary and fiscal policy must each play its part if we are to achieve our joint goals of full employment and price stability.

Unfortunately, Mr. Carter and the Democratic Congress seek to derail our nation's money creation policies by taking away the independence of the Federal Reserve Board. The same people who have so massively expanded government spending should not be allowed politically to dominate our monetary policy. The independence of the Federal Reserve System must be preserved.

The Republican Party believes inflation can be controlled only by fiscal and monetary restraint, combined with sharp reductions in the tax and regulatory disincentives for savings, investments, and productivity. Therefore, the Republican Party opposes the imposition of wage and price controls and credit controls.

Controls will not stop inflation, as past experience has shown. Wage and price controls will only result in shortages, inequities, black markets, and ultimately higher prices. We reject this short-sighted and misguided approach.

Peace and Freedom

PROLOGUE

At the start of the 1980s, the United States faces the most serious challenge to its survival in the two centuries of its existence. Our ability to meet this challenge demands a foreign policy firmly rooted in principle. Our economic and social welfare in the 1980s may depend as much on our foreign and defense policy as it does on domestic policy. The Republican Party reasserts that it is the solemn purpose of our foreign policy to secure the people and free institutions of our nation against every peril; to hearten and fortify the love of freedom everywhere in the world; and to achieve a secure environment in the world in which freedom, democracy, and justice may flourish.

For three and one-half years, the Carter Administration has been without a coherent strategic concept to guide foreign policy, oblivious to the scope and magnitude of the threat posed to our security, and devoid of competence to provide leadership and direction to the free world. The Administration's conduct of foreign policy has undermined our friends abroad, and led our most dangerous adversaries to miscalculate the willingness of the American people to resist aggression. Republicans support a policy of peace through strength; weakness provokes aggression.

For three and one-half years the Carter Administration has given us a foreign policy not of constancy and credibility, but of chaos, confusion, and failure. It has produced an image of our country as a vacillating and reactive nation, unable to define its place in the world, the goals it seeks, or the means to pursue them. Despite the Administration's rhetoric, the most flagrant offenders of human rights including the Soviet Union, Vietnam, and Cuba have been the beneficiaries of Administration good will, while nations friendly to the United States have suffered the loss of U.S. commercial access and economic and military assistance.

The threat to the United States and its allies is not only a military one. We face a threat from international terrorism. Our access to energy and raw material resources is challenged by civil unrest, Soviet-sponsored subversion, and economic combinations in restraint of free trade. Our first line of defense, our network of friendly nations and alliances, has been undermined by the inept conduct of foreign affairs.

American policy since World War II has rested upon the pillars of collective security, military and technological superiority, and economic strength, and upon the perception by our adversaries that the United States possesses the will to use its power where necessary to protect its freedom. These tenets have enabled a commonwealth of free and independent nations to enjoy the benefits and confidence that come from expanding economic interchange in peace and bilateral and multilateral support in time of war. The entire structure of peace was guaranteed by American and allied military power sufficient to deter conflict, or to prevail in conflict if deterrence should fail.

The Administration's neglect of America's defense posture in the face of overwhelming evidence of a threatening military buildup is without parallel since the 1930s. The scope and magnitude of the growth of Soviet military power threatens American interest at every level, from the nuclear threat to our survival, to our ability to protect the lives and property of American citizens abroad.

[Soviet Threat]

Despite clear danger signals indicating that Soviet nuclear power would overtake that of the United States by the early 1980s, threatening the survival of the United States and making possible, for the first time in post-war history, political coercion and defeat, the Administration reduced the size and capability of our nuclear forces.

Despite clear danger signals indicating that the Soviet Union was using Cuban, East German, and now Nicaraguan, as well as its own, military forces to extend its power to Africa, Asia, and the Western Hemisphere, the Administration often undermined the very governments under attack. As a result, a clear and present danger threatens the energy and raw material lifelines of the Western world.

Despite clear danger signals indicating that the Soviet Union was augmenting its military threat to the nations of Western Europe, American defense programs such as the enhanced radiation warhead and cruise missiles, which could have offset that buildup, were cancelled or delayed — to the dismay of allies who depend upon American military power for their security.

The evidence of the Soviet threat to American security has never been more stark and unambiguous, nor has any President ever been more oblivious to this threat and its potential consequences.

The entire Western world faces complex and multi-dimensional threats to its access to energy and raw material resources. The growth of Soviet military power poses a direct threat to the petroleum resources of the Persian Gulf now that its military forces deployed in Afghanistan are less than 300 miles from the Straits of Hormuz, through which half the free world's energy supplies flow.

Soviet efforts to gain bases in areas astride the major sea lanes of the world have been successful due to their use of military power, either directly or indirectly through Cuban and other Soviet bloc forces. Since the Carter Administration took office in 1977, the Soviets or their clients have taken over Afghanistan, Cambodia, Ethiopia, and South Yemen, and have solidified their grasp on a host of other nations in the developing world. The Soviet noose is now being drawn around southern Africa, the West's most abundant single source of critical raw materials.

[American Citizens Vulnerable]

The failure of the United States to respond to direct threats to its security has left American citizens vulnerable to terrorist assaults as well. American diplomatic personnel have been subject to seizure and assault by terrorists throughout the world without drawing a meaningful Administration response.

No failure of the Administration has been so catastrophic as its failure of leadership. Mired in incompetence, bereft of strategic vision and purpose, the President's failure to shoulder the burden of leadership in the Western alliance has placed America in danger without parallel since December 7, 1941. The United States cannot abdicate that role without inducing a diplomatic and eventually a military catastrophe.

Republicans realize that if the challenges of the 1980s are not met, we will continue to lose the respect of the world, our honor, and in the end, our freedom. Republicans pledge to meet these challenges with confidence and strength. We pledge to restore to the United States and its people a government with conviction in our cause, a government that will restore to our great nation its self-respect, its self-confidence, and its national pride.

National Security

DEFENSE BUDGET TRENDS

In the late 1960s, the Republicans returned to the White House, inheriting a war in Southeast Asia. Because of this war, they also inherited a Fiscal Year (FY) 1968 defense budget which, if calculated in constant 1981 dollars to account for inflation, had risen to over $194 billion from $148 billion in FY 1961, the last Eisenhower year. By the beginning of the second Nixon Administration, U.S. forces were totally disengaged from Southeast Asia. The FY 1974 defense budget had dropped back to $139 billion, and the country had reaped its desired "peace dividend" of an over $50 billion reduction in annual defense spending. During this period, between 1969 and 1973, the Democrats who controlled Congress, led by Senators Mondale and Muskie, cut almost $45 billion from Nixon defense requests. Until 1975, Congress continued to ignore long-range defense needs, and made severe cuts in Republican defense proposals. The Ford Administration, however, succeeded in reversing this trend. From a low point of $134 billion in FY 1975, the FY 1976 defense budget rose, in response to President Ford's request, to $139 billion; and in FY 1977 it rose again to $147 billion.

Despite the growing sentiment for a stronger defense, candidate Carter ran on a promise of massive cuts in U.S. defense spending, one promise he has kept. In his first three years in the White House, Mr. Carter reduced defense spending by over $38 billion from President Ford's last Five Year Defense Plan. Now, in his last year in office, faced with the total collapse of his foreign policy, and with his policy advisers and their assumptions disgraced, he has finally proposed an increase beyond the rate of inflation in defense spending. But this growth for 1981 will be less than one percent.

We deplore Mr. Carter's personal attempts to rewrite history on defense budgets. His tough speeches before military audiences cannot hide his continuing opposition to Congressional defense increases. The four chiefs of the armed services have each characterized the Carter defense program as "inadequate" to meet the military threat posed to the United States. We associate ourselves with the characterization by Democratic Congressional leaders of the President's behavior on defense as "hypocritical." We would go further; it is disgraceful.

Mr. Carter cut back, cancelled, or delayed every strategic initiative proposed by President Ford. He cancelled production of the Minuteman missile and the B-1 bomber. He delayed all cruise missiles, the MX missile, the Trident submarine and the Trident II missile. He did this while the Soviet Union deployed the Backfire bomber and designed two additional bombers equal in capability to the B-1, and while it deployed four new large ICBMs and developed four others.

Mr. Carter postponed production and deployment of enhanced radiation (neutron) warheads while the Soviet Union deployed the SS-20 mobile missile and the Backfire bomber against Western Europe. He cut President Ford's proposed shipbuilding plan in half. He vetoed a nuclear aircraft carrier. He did this while the Soviet Union pursued an aggressive shipbuilding program capable of giving them worldwide naval supremacy in the 1980s unless current trends are reversed immediately. Mr. Carter opposed efforts to correct the terribly inadequate pay rates for our military personnel and stood by as the alarming exodus of trained and skilled personnel from the services quickened. At the same time, the Soviet Union increased its military manpower to a level of 4.8 million, more than double that of the United States.

Recovery from the Carter Administration's neglect will require effort, but Americans know that effort is the unavoidable precondition to peace and economic prosperity. The Soviet Union is now devoting over $50 billion more to defense annually than the United States, achieving military superiority as a result. We have depleted our capital and must now devote the resources essential to catching up. The Secretary of Defense has stated that even if we were to maintain a constant increase in our spending of five percent in real terms, it would require 40 years for us to catch up.

Republicans commit themselves to an immediate increase in defense spending to be applied judiciously to critically needed programs. We will build toward a sustained defense expenditure sufficient to close the gap with the Soviets, and ultimately reach the position of military superiority that the American people demand.

DEFENSE STRATEGY

More is required than reversing our military decline alone. We have seen in recent years how an Administration, possessed of dwindling but still substantial strength, has stood paralyzed in the face of an inexorable march of Soviet or Soviet-sponsored aggression. To be effective in preserving our interests, we must pursue a comprehensive military strategy which guides both the design and employment of our forces. Such a strategy must proceed from a sober analysis of the diverse threats before us.

Republicans approve and endorse a national strategy of peace through strength as set forth in House Concurrent Resolution 306. We urge speedy approval of this legislation by both the U.S. House of Representatives and the U.S. Senate as a means of making clear to the world that the United States has not forgotten that the price of peace is eternal vigilance against tyranny. Therefore we commend to all Americans the text of House Concurrent Resolution 306, which reads as follows:

The foreign policy of the United States should reflect a national strategy of peace through strength. The general principles and goals of this strategy should be:

To inspire, focus, and unite the national will and determination to achieve peace and freedom;

To achieve overall military and technological superiority over the Soviet Union;

To create a strategic and civil defense which would protect the American people against nuclear war at least as well as the Soviet population is protected;

To accept no arms control agreement which in any way jeopardizes the security of the United States or its allies, or which locks the United States into a position of military inferiority;

To reestablish effective security and intelligence capabilities;

To pursue positive non-military means to roll back the growth of communism;

To help our allies and other non-Communist countries defend themselves against Communist aggression; and

To maintain a strong economy and protect our overseas sources of energy and other vital raw materials.

Our strategy must encompass the levels of force required to deter each level of foreseeable attack and to prevail in conflict in the event deterrence fails. The detailed analysis that must form the intellectual basis for the elaboration of such a strategy will be the first priority of a Republican Administration. It must be based upon the following principles.

NUCLEAR FORCES

Nuclear weapons are the ultimate military guarantor of American security and that of our allies. Yet since 1977, the United States has moved from essential equivalence to inferiority in strategic nuclear forces with the Soviet Union. This decline has resulted from Mr. Carter's cancellation or delay of strategic initiatives like the B-1 bomber, the MX missile, and the Trident II submarine missile programs and from his decisions to close the Minuteman production line and forego production of enhanced radiation weapons.

As the disparity between American and Soviet strategic nuclear forces grows over the next three years, most U.S. land-based missiles, heavy bombers, and submarines in port will become vulnerable to a Soviet first-strike. Such a situation invites diplomatic blackmail and coercion of the United States by the Soviet Union during the coming decade.

An administration that can defend its interest only by threatening the mass extermination of civilians, as Mr. Carter implied in 1979, dooms itself to strategic, and eventually geo-political, paralysis. Such a strategy is simply not credible and, therefore is ineffectual. Yet the declining survivability of the U.S. ICBM force in the early 1980s will make this condition unavoidable unless prompt measures are taken. Our objective must be to assure the survivability of U.S. forces possessing an unquestioned, prompt, hard-target counterforce capability sufficient to disarm Soviet military targets in a second-strike. We reject the mutual-assured-destruction (MAD) strategy of the Carter Administration which limits the President during crises to a Hobson's choice between mass mutual suicide and surrender. We propose, instead, a credible strategy which will deter a Soviet attack by the clear capability of our forces to survive and ultimately to destroy Soviet military targets.

In order to counter the problem of ICBM vulnerability, we will propose a number of initiatives to provide the necessary survivability of the ICBM force in as timely and effective a manner as possible. In addition, we will proceed with:

The earliest possible deployment of the MX missile in a prudent survival configuration;

Accelerated development and deployment of a new manned strategic penetrating bomber that will exploit the $5.5 billion already invested in the B-1, while employing the most advanced technology available;

Deployment of an air defense system comprised of dedicated modern interceptor aircraft and early warning support systems;

Acceleration of development and deployment of strategic cruise missiles deployed on aircraft, on land, and on ships and submarines;

Modernization of the military command and control system to assure the responsiveness of U.S. strategic nuclear forces to presidential command in peace or war; and

Vigorous research and development of an effective anti-ballistic missile system, such as is already at hand in the Soviet Union, as well as more modern ABM technologies.

For more than 20 years, commencing in the mid-1950s, the United States has maintained tactical nuclear weapons in Europe for the purpose of assuring against deep penetrations into the West by the Soviet forces. Since 1977, however, the Administration has allowed our former superiority to erode to the point where we now face a more than three-to-one disadvantage.

A Republican Administration will strive for early modernization of our theater nuclear forces so that a seamless web of deterrence can be maintained against all levels of attack, and our credibility with our European allies is restored. In consultation with them we will proceed with deployments in Europe of medium-range cruise missiles, ballistic missiles, enhanced radiation warheads, and the modernization of nuclear artillery.

CONVENTIONAL FORCES

The greatest single result of our loss of nuclear parity has been the manifest increase in the willingness of the Soviet Union to take risks at the conventional level. Emboldened by the Carter Administration's failure to challenge their use of surrogate Cuban forces in Africa and the later Soviet presence in Angola, Ethiopia, and South Yemen, the Soviets, for the first time in post-war history, employed their own army units outside of the Soviet bloc in a brutal invasion of Afghanistan. The invasion presents chilling evidence of the mounting threat and raises fundamental questions with respect to United States strategy.

We believe it is not feasible at this time, and in the long term would be unworkable, to deploy massive U.S. ground forces to such areas as the Persian Gulf on a permanent basis as we do in Europe and elsewhere. A more effective strategy must be built on the dual pillars of maintaining a limited full-time presence in the area as a credible interdiction force, combined with the clear capability to reinforce this presence rapidly with the forces necessary to prevail in battle. In addition, the strategy must envision military action elsewhere at points of Soviet vulnerability — an expression of the classic doctrine of global maneuver.

The forces essential to the support of such a strategy must include a much-improved Navy, the force most suitable for maintaining U.S. presence in threatened areas and protecting sea lines of communication.

In addition, we will require a substantial improvement in the air and sea mobility forces and improved access to regional installations. A Republican Administration will propose their substantial improvement, to include the establishment of a permanent fleet in the Indian Ocean. We will also improve contingency planning for the use and expansion of our commercial maritime fleet, and a new rational approach to emergency use of our civil aircraft fleet.

The budget cuts imposed by Mr. Carter on the Army and his restoration of the supremacy of systems analysis in the Pentagon have resulted in slowdowns, deferrals and cost increases in nine vitally needed Army procurement programs in armor, firepower, air defense, and helicopters. These critical and long-delayed modernization programs must be restored to economical production rates and must be speeded into the field. Of equal importance is the need to bring our stocks of ammunition, spare parts and supplies — now at woefully inadequate levels — to a standard that will enable us to sustain our forces in conflict.

In addition to the strategic programs needed for our Air Force, we pledge to restore tactical aircraft development and procurement to economical levels and to speed the achievement of 26 modernized wings of aircraft able to conduct missions at night, in all weather conditions, and against the most sophisticated adversary.

We pledge to increase substantially our intra- and inter-theater airlift capability and to increase our aerial tanker fleet through procurement and speedy modernization.

Of all of the services, the Navy and Marines have suffered most from Mr. Carter's cuts. Their share of the defense budget has shrunk from 40 to 33 percent during the Carter Administration. Mr. Carter slashed President Ford's 157 ship, five-year construction program to 83. He has slowed the Trident submarine and requested only one attack submarine each year in spite of a Soviet three-to-one advantage. He vetoed the Fiscal Year 1979 Defense Authorization Bill because it included an aircraft carrier which a year later Congress forced him to accept. For the fourth straight year he has requested fewer than half the number of 325 aircraft needed annually to stay even with peacetime attrition and modernization requirements. He has requested fewer than one-third of the amphibious ships needed just to keep the current level of capability for the Marines, and he has opposed Marine tactical aircraft and helicopter modernization.

The current Chief of Naval Operations has testified that, "We are trying to meet a three ocean requirement with a one-and-a-half ocean Navy." Republicans pledge to reverse Mr. Carter's dismantling of U.S. Naval and Marine forces. We will restore our fleet to 600 ships at a rate equal to or exceeding that planned by President Ford. We will build more aircraft carriers, submarines and amphibious ships. We will restore Naval and Marine aircraft procurement to economical rates enabling rapid modernization of the current forces, and expansion to meet the requirements of additional aircraft carriers.

DEFENSE MANPOWER AND THE DRAFT

The Republican Party is not prepared to accept a peacetime draft at this time. Under Mr. Carter, the all-volunteer force has not been given a fair chance to succeed. The unconscionable mismanagement and neglect of personnel policy by the Carter Administration has made a shambles of the all-volunteer force concept.

Perhaps the most compelling vulnerability of our forces results from the dramatic exodus of the core of highly skilled men and women who form the backbone of our military strength. This loss is the direct result of neglect by the Commander-in-Chief.

The sustained malign neglect of our military manpower is nothing short of a national scandal. This Administration's active assault on military benefits and military retirement has been accompanied by an enforced pay-cap set at half the inflation rate. The average military family has lost between 14 percent and 25 percent in purchasing power over the past seven years. Officers and skilled enlisted personnel are leaving in droves, and 250,000 of our servicemen qualify for public assistance. Many of our career people earn less than the minimum wage. The services are currently short 70,000 senior enlisted personnel. This scandal is the direct result of Mr. Carter's willful downgrading of the military and inept mismanagement of personnel policy. As a top priority, the Republican Party pledges to end this national disgrace.

We pledge to restore a national attitude of pride and gratitude for the service of our men and women in the armed forces. We will act immediately to correct the great inequities in pay and benefits of career military personnel. Specifically, we support immediate action to:

Provide for an increase in military pay targeted in particular toward the career grades now experiencing the greatest attrition;

Increase enlistment and reenlistment bonuses;

Improve continuation bonuses for aviators;

Increase per diem travel allowances;

Increase the allowance for moving mobile homes;

Provide family separation allowances for junior personnel; and

Expand benefit entitlement under the CHAMPUS program.

A Republican Administration will index military pay and allowances to protect military personnel from absorbing the burden of inflation. We pledge that the profession of arms will be restored to its rightful place as a preeminent expression of patriotism in America.

In order to attract recruits of high ability, a Republican Administration will act to reintroduce G.I. Bill benefits for those completing two years active service. We will press for enactment of legislation denying federal funds to any educational institution that impedes access of military recruiters to their students. We regard as a serious loss the decision of many of our finest institutions of higher learning to discontinue their military officer training programs. The leadership of our armed forces must include the best trained minds in our nation. Republicans call upon our colleges and universities to shoulder their responsibilities in the defense of freedom. We will investigate legislative inducements toward this end. We will not consider a peacetime draft unless a well-managed, Congressionally-funded, full-scale effort to improve the all-volunteer force does [not] meet expectations.

RESERVE FORCES

The armed forces of the U.S. are today critically dependent upon our nation's Reserve components for both combat arms and combat support. The Army Reserve and National Guard provide one-third of the Army's combat divisions, 80 percent of its independent combat brigades, one-half of its artillery battalions, and one-third of its special forces groups. The Navy Reserve provides 90 percent of the Navy's ocean mine sweeping and two-thirds of its mobile construction battalions. The Air Force Reserve and Air National Guard provide all of our strategic interceptors, 60 percent of our tactical airlift, and one-third of our tactical fighters. Reserve and National Guard units may be mobilized for even the smallest of conflicts and many such units today are expected to deploy immediately with the active duty units they support.

Today, however, the reserves are ill-equipped, underpaid, and un-dermanned by several hundred thousand personnel. Proper equipment, realistic, challenging training, and greater full-time support must be made available. We must ensure that all Americans take note of the proud and vital role played by the Reserve and National Guard components of the armed forces of the United States.

READINESS AND INDUSTRIAL PREPAREDNESS

History records that readiness for war is the surest means of preventing it. Lack of preparedness is the most dangerously provocative course we can take. Yet funding requests for sufficient fuel, spare parts, ammunition, and supplies for U.S. war reserves have been cut each year for the past four years from the minimum quantities the armed services have stated they need. This has left the U.S. Armed Forces at their lowest state of preparedness since 1950, seriously compromising their ability to sustain a military conflict.

Crippling shortages of spare parts, fuel, and ammunition compromise the ability of the armed forces to sustain a major military conflict. Some critical types of ammunition could not support combat operations for more than a week although we are committed to holding a 90-day inventory of major ammunition types. In addition, critical facilities such as airfields, ammunition depots, maintenance installations, and living quarters for our troops are in serious disrepair. The backlog of deferred maintenance and the underfunded purchase of vital combat consumables is so vast that years of effort will be required to rebuild U.S. forces to the required level of readiness.

The problem of maintaining the day-to-day combat readiness of U.S. armed forces is compounded by the reduced ability of American industry to respond to wartime contingencies. Reduced acquisition of equipment for the modernization of the armed forces and the Carter Administration's failure to maintain combat readiness have eroded the incentive of American industry to maintain capacity adequate to potential defense requirements.

Republicans pledge to make the combat readiness of U.S. Armed Forces and the preparedness of the industrial base to a top priority.

RESEARCH AND DEVELOPMENT

Research and Development (R & D) provides a critical means by which our nation can cope with threats to our security. In the past, the United States' qualitative and technological superiority provided a foundation for our military superiority. Yet we are now on the verge of losing this advantage to the Soviet Union because of Mr. Carter's opposition to real increases in the R & D effort. Delays imposed on the R & D process now allow seven to 10 years or more to elapse between the time when a new weapon system is proposed and when it becomes available.

The Soviet Union now invests nearly twice as much in military research and development as does the United States. This disparity in effort threatens American technological superiority in the mid-1980s and could result in Soviet breakthroughs in advanced weapon systems.

Republicans pledge to revitalize America's military research and development efforts, from basic research through the deployment of weapons and support systems, to assure that our vital security needs will be met for the balance of the century. We will seek increased funding to guarantee American superiority in this critical area and to enable us to deal with possible breakthroughs in anti-missile defense, anti-satellite killers, high-energy directed systems, and the military and civilian exploitation of space.

America's technological advantage has always depended upon its interaction with our civilian science and technology sector. The economic policy of the Carter Administration has severely encumbered private research and development efforts, thereby depriving both our civil and military sectors of the fruits of scientific innovation.

Underfunding of beneficial government-sponsored research efforts in basic and applied scientific research has disrupted the benefits of years of effective effort. In particular, America's preeminence in the exploration of space is threatened by the failure of the Carter Administration to fund fully the Space Shuttle program (with its acknowledged benefits for both the civil and military applications) as well as advanced exploration programs. Republicans pledge to support a vigorous space research program.

MANAGEMENT AND ORGANIZATION

The Republican Party pledges to reform the defense programming and budgeting management system established by the Carter Administration. The ill-informed, capricious intrusions of the Office of Management and Budget, and the Department of Defense Office of Program Analysis and Evaluation have brought defense planning full circle to the worst faults of the McNamara years. Orderly planning by the military services has become impossible. Waste, inefficiency, and paralysis have been the hallmarks of Carter Administration defense planning and budgeting. This has resulted in huge cost overruns and in protracted delays in placing advanced systems in the field.

NATIONAL INTELLIGENCE

At a time of increasing danger, the U.S. intelligence community has lost much of its ability to supply the President, senior U.S. officials, and the Congress with accurate and timely analyses concerning fundamental threats to our nation's security. Morale and public confidence have been eroded and American citizens and friendly foreign intelligence services have become increasingly reluctant to cooperate with U.S. agencies. As a result of such problems, the U.S. intelligence community has incorrectly assessed critical foreign developments, as in Iran, and has, above all, underestimated the size and purpose of the Soviet Union's military efforts.

We believe that a strong national consensus has emerged on the need to make our intelligence community a reliable and productive instrument of national policy once again. In pursuing its objectives, the Soviet Union and its surrogates operate by a far different set of rules than does the United States. We do not favor countering their efforts by mirroring their tactics. However, the United States requires a realistic assessment of the threats it faces, and it must have the best intelligence capability in the world. Republicans pledge this for the United States.

A Republican Administration will seek to improve U.S. intelligence capabilities for technical and clandestine collection, cogent analysis, coordinated counterintelligence and covert action.

We will reestablish the President's Foreign Intelligence Advisory Board, abolished by the Carter Administration, as a permanent non-partisan body of distinguished Americans to perform a constant audit of national intelligence research and performance. We will propose methods of providing alternative intelligence estimates in order to improve the quality of the estimates by constructive competition.

Republicans will undertake an urgent effort to rebuild the intelligence agencies, and to give full support to their knowledgeable and dedicated staffs. We will propose legislation to enable intelligence officers and their agents to operate safely and efficiently abroad.

We will support legislation to invoke criminal sanctions against anyone who discloses the identities of U.S. intelligence officers abroad or who makes unauthorized disclosures of U.S. intelligence sources and methods.

We will support amendments to the Freedom of Information Act and the Privacy Act to permit meaningful background checks on individuals being considered for sensitive positions and to reduce costly and capricious requests to the intelligence agencies.

We will provide our government with the capability to help influence international events vital to our national security interests, a capability which only the United States among the major powers has denied itself.

A Republican Administration will seek adequate safeguards to ensure that past abuses will not recur, but we will seek the repeal of ill-considered restrictions sponsored by Democrats, which have debilitated U.S. intelligence capabilities while easing the intelligence collection and subversion efforts of our adversaries.

TERRORISM

In the decade of the seventies, all civilized nations were shaken by a wave of widespread, international terrorist attacks. Time and again, nations and individuals have been subjected to extortion and murder at the hands of extremists who reject the rule of law, civil order, and the sanctity of individual human rights. Terrorism has been elevated to the level of overt national policy as authorities in Iran, encouraged by the Soviet Union, have held 53 Americans captive for more than eight months. Comprehensive support of international terrorist organizations has been a central, though generally covert, element of Soviet foreign policy.

Republicans believe that this tragic history contains lessons that must serve as the basis for a determined international effort to end this era of terrorism. We believe that certain principles have emerged from incidents in which states have defeated terrorist attacks, and we believe the United States should take the lead in a multilateral drive to eliminate the terrorist threat. A first requirement is the establishment of a military capability to deal promptly and effectively with any terrorist acts. We cannot afford, as in the abortive Iranian rescue mission, to allow months to pass while we prepare responses.

The United States must provide the leadership to forge an international consensus that firmness and refusal to concede are ultimately the only effective deterrents to terrorism. The United States should take the lead in combating international terrorism. We must recognize and be prepared to deal with the reality of expanded Soviet sponsorship of international terrorist movements. Development of an effective anti-terrorist military capability and establishment of a Congressional and Executive capability to oversee our internal security efforts will no longer be neglected.

[ARMS CONTROL AND DEFENSE POLICY]

The Republican approach to arms control has been markedly different from that of the Democratic Party. It has been based on three fundamental premises:

First, before arms control negotiations may be undertaken, the security of the United States must be assured by the funding and deployment of strong military forces sufficient to deter conflict at any level or to prevail in battle should aggression occur;

Second, negotiations must be conducted on the basis of strict reciprocity of benefits — unilateral restraint by the U.S. has failed to bring reductions by the Soviet Union; and

Third, arms control negotiations, once entered, represent an important political and military undertaking that cannot be divorced from the broader political and military behavior of the parties.

A Republican Administration will pursue arms control solely on the principles outlined above.

During the past three and one-half years, the Carter Administration's policy has been diametrically opposed to these principles. First, by its willful cancellation or delay of essential strategic military programs such as the B-1, the MX missile, and the Trident submarine, it has seriously damaged the credibility and effectiveness of the U.S. deterrent force. Second, by not insisting upon corresponding concessions from the Soviet Union it has, in effect, practiced unilateral disarmament and removed any incentives for the Soviets to negotiate for what they could obviously achieve by waiting. The Republican Party rejects the fundamentally flawed SALT II treaty negotiated by the Carter Administration.

The Republican Party deplores the attempts of the Carter Administration to cover up Soviet non-compliance with arms control agreements including the now overwhelming evidence of blatant Soviet violation of the Biological Warfare Convention by secret production of biological agents at Sverdlovsk.

In our platform four years ago, we stated that, "The growth of civilian nuclear technology and the rising demand for nuclear power as an alternative to increasingly costly fossil fuel resources, combine to require our recognition of the potential dangers associated with such development." We called for the formation of new multilateral arrangements to control the export of sensitive nuclear technologies. Unfortunately, the Carter Administration has failed to provide the leadership and creative diplomacy essential to forging effective international safeguards and cooperation in this vital area. In particular we oppose and deplore the pending delivery to India of nuclear material which can be directed to the manufacture of weapons.

The Republican Party reaffirms its commitment to the early establishment of effective multilateral arrangements for the safe management and monitoring of all transfers and uses of nuclear materials in the international market.

Foreign Policy

U.S.-SOVIET RELATIONS

The premier challenge facing the United States, its allies, and the entire globe is to check the Soviet Union's global ambitions. This challenge must be met, for the present danger is greater than ever before in the 200-year history of the United States. The Soviet Union is still accelerating its drive for military superiority and is intensifying its military pressure and its ideological combat against the industrial democracies and the vulnerable developing nations of the world.

Republicans believe that the United States can only negotiate with the Soviet Union from a position of unquestioned principle and unquestioned strength. Unlike Mr. Carter we see nothing "inordinate" in our nation's historic judgment about the goals, tactics, and dangers of Soviet communism. Unlike the Carter Administration, we were not surprised by the brutal Soviet invasion of Afghanistan or by other Soviet violations of major international agreements regulating international behavior, human rights, and the use of military force. And, unlike the Carter Administration, we will not base our policies toward the Soviet Union on naive expectations, unilateral concessions, futile rhetoric, and insignificant maneuvers.

As the Soviet Union continues in its expansionist course, the potential for dangerous confrontations has increased. Republicans will strive to resolve critical issues through peaceful negotiations, but we recognize that negotiations conducted from a position of military weakness can result only in further damage to American interests.

A Republican Administration will continue to seek to negotiate arms reductions in Soviet strategic weapons, in Soviet bloc force levels in Central Europe, and in other areas that may be amenable to reductions or limitations. We will pursue hard bargaining for equitable, verifiable, and enforceable agreements. We will accept no agreement for the sake of having an agreement, and will accept no agreements that do not fundamentally enhance our national security.

[High Technology]

Republicans oppose the transfer of high technology to the Soviet Union and its Eastern European satellites, such as has been done in the past, permitting development of sophisticated military hardware which threatens the United States and our allies. The Carter Administration has encouraged the most extensive raid on American technology by the Soviet bloc since World War II. The Soviet Union has gained invaluable scientific expertise in electronics, computer sciences, manufacturing techniques, mining, transportation, aviation, agriculture, and a host of other disciplines. This has contributed to the ability of the

Soviet Union to divert investment and manpower from their civilian economy to their armed forces. The fruits of Soviet access to American technology will improve the performance of the Soviet military establishment for years to come. The matter is compounded by the practice of subsidized financing of much of the Soviet bloc's acquisition of American technology through U.S. financial institutions.

Republicans pledge to stop the flow of technology to the Soviet Union that could contribute, directly or indirectly, to the growth of their military power. This objective will be pursued by a Republican Administration with our allies and other friendly nations as well. We will ensure that the Soviet Union fully understands that it will be expected to fulfill all of the commercial and diplomatic obligations it has undertaken in its international agreements.

We oppose Mr. Carter's singling out of the American farmer to bear the brunt of his failed foreign policy by imposition of a partial and incompetently managed grain embargo. Because of his failure to obtain cooperation from other grain exporting countries, the embargo has been a travesty and a substitute for policy. We call for the immediate lifting of this embargo.

[Declaration on Human Rights]

We reaffirm our commitment to press the Soviet Union to implement the United Nations Declaration on Human Rights and the Helsinki Agreements which guarantee rights such as the free interchange of information and the right to emigrate. A Republican Administration will press the Soviet Union to end its harassment and imprisonment of those who speak in opposition to official policy, who seek to worship according to their religious beliefs, or who represent diverse ethnic minorities and nationalities.

Republicans deplore growing anti-Semitism in the Soviet Union and the mistreatment of "refuseniks" by Soviet authorities. The decline in exit visas to Soviet Jews and others seeking religious freedom and the promulgation of ever more rigorous conditions inhibiting their emigration is a fundamental affront to human rights and the U.N. Charter. Republicans will make the subject of emigration from the Soviet Union a central issue in Soviet-American relations. Human rights in the Soviet Union will not be ignored as it has been during the Carter Administration. As a party to the Helsinki Conference Final Act, a Republican Administration will insist on full Soviet compliance with the humanitarian provisions of the agreement.

Republicans pledge our continued support for the people of Cuba and the captive nations of Central and Eastern Europe in their hope to achieve self-determination. We stand firmly for the independence of Yugoslavia. We support self-determination and genuine independence for new captive nations of Africa and Latin America threatened by the growing domination of Soviet power.

A Republican Administration will end the sustained Carter policy of misleading the American people about Soviet policies and behavior. We will spare no efforts to publicize to the world the fundamental differences in the two systems and will strengthen such means as the International Communication Agency, the Voice of America, Radio Free Europe, and Radio Liberty actively to articulate U.S. values and policies, and to highlight the weaknesses of totalitarianism.

We pledge to end the Carter cover-up of Soviet violations of SALT I and II, to end the cover-up of Soviet violation of the Biological Warfare Convention, and to end the cover-up of Soviet use of gas and chemical weapons in Afghanistan and elsewhere.

NATO AND WESTERN EUROPE

Since its inception three decades ago, the North Atlantic Treaty Organization has expressed the collective will of free nations to resist totalitarian aggression. As a cornerstone of the Western Alliance, NATO has stood on the firm foundations of American strategic strength, joint Allied defense efforts, and cooperative diplomacy based on shared interest and close consultations. The Republican Party recognizes that NATO serves the vital interests of the entire Western world and over the years we have continued to give the Alliance our undiminished and bipartisan support.

Republicans deplore the current drifts toward neutralism in Western Europe. We recognize that NATO and our Western Allies today face the greatest array of threats in their history, both from within and from without. Through its inept policies, the Carter Administration has substantially contributed to the evident erosion of Alliance security and confidence in the U.S. A Republican Administration, as one of its highest priorities and in close concert with our NATO partners, will therefore ensure that the United States leads a concerted effort to rebuild a strong, confident Alliance fully prepared to meet the threats and the challenges of the 1980s.

The chief external threat to NATO is that of developing Soviet military superiority. In a period of supposed "detente," the NATO nations have too often cut back or delayed essential defense programs and too often placed excessive hopes in arms control negotiations, while the Soviet-dominated Warsaw Pact has been transformed into the world's most powerful offensive military force.

Three-and-a-half years of Carter Administration policies have resulted in an increased threat to vital Alliance security interests. Mr. Carter's unilateral cancellations, reductions, and long delays in the B-1, Trident, MX, cruise-missile, and ship-building programs have increased the vulnerability of the U.S. strategic triad and have contributed to a developing strategic imbalance which undermines the foundation of Western deterrent and defense capabilities. His fundamentally flawed SALT II treaty would have codified Western inferiority. His reversals on the development and deployment of the "enhanced radiation" or neutron weapon, his treatment of future theater nuclear force modernization negotiations, and his manner of dealing with terrorist actions directed against Americans abroad, further undermined Alliance solidarity and security.

These Carter Administration inconsistencies have caused disunity in the Alliance. We have seen confusion in the fields of trade, fiscal, and energy policies. The lack of close coordination regarding Iran, the Middle East, Afghanistan, the Olympic boycott, nuclear proliferation, East-West trade, human rights, North-South issues, and a host of other international issues affecting Alliance interests, has reinforced Allied concerns. Republicans are concerned that these Carter Administration actions have increased Allied temptation to conduct independent diplomacy and to seek accommodation in the face of pressure from the Soviet Union. In this regard, we categorically reject unilateral moratoria on the deployment by the U.S. and NATO of theater nuclear weapons. Further, Republicans will oppose arms control agreements that interfere with the transfer of military technology to our allies.

In pledging renewed United States leadership, cooperation, and consultation, Republicans assert their expectation that each of the allies will bear a fair share of the common defense effort and that they will work closely together in support of common Alliance goals. Defense budgets, weapons acquisition, force readiness, and diplomatic coordination need to be substantially increased and improved. Within Europe as well as in areas beyond Europe which affect the shared vital interests of the Alliance, we will seek to increase our cooperative efforts, including increased planning for joint actions to meet common threats.

The Republican Party recognizes the vital importance of countries defending the flanks of NATO. We will search for an early resolution of problems that currently inhibit the effective participation of all the nations of NATO's southern region and we call for the integration of Spain into the North Atlantic Alliance.

MIDDLE EAST, PERSIAN GULF

In the past three years, the nations of the Middle East and Persian Gulf have suffered an unprecedented level of political, economic, and military turmoil. The Soviet Union has been prompt in turning these sources of instability to its advantage and is now in an excellent position to exploit the chaos in Iran and to foment similar upheavals in other countries in the region. Today, the countries of the Middle East and Persian Gulf are encircled as never before by Soviet advisers and troops based in the Horn of Africa, South Yemen, and Afghanistan. Moreover, the Soviets have close political and military ties with other states in the region.

The Soviet goal is clear — to use subversion and the threat of military intervention to establish a controlling influence over the region's resource-rich states, and thereby to gain decisive political and economic leverage over Western and Third World nations vulnerable to economic coercion. The first signs of Soviet success in this undertaking are already evidenced in the recent proposal by European countries to associate the Palestinian Liberation Organization in the West Bank autonomy talks.

Republicans believe that the restoration of order and stability to the region must be premised upon an understanding of the interrelationship between Soviet and radical Palestinian goals, the fundamental requirements of stable economic development and marketing of the area's resources, and the growing ferment among Islamic radical groups. Republicans believe that a wise and credible United States policy must make clear that our foremost concern is for the long-term peaceful development of all states in the region, not purely a self-serving exploitation of its resources. Our goal is to bring a just and lasting peace to the Arab-Israeli conflict.

[Rejection of PLO]

With respect to an ultimate peace settlement, Republicans reject any call for involvement of the PLO as not in keeping with the long-term interests of either Israel or the Palestinian Arabs. The imputation of legitimacy to organizations not yet willing to acknowledge the fundamental right to existence of the State of Israel is wrong. Repeated indications, even when subsequently denied, of the Carter Administration's involvement with the PLO has done serious harm to the credibility of U.S. policy in the Middle East and has encouraged the PLO's position of intransigence. We believe the establishment of a Palestinian State on the West Bank would be destabilizing and harmful to the peace process.

Our long- and short-term policies for the area must be developed in consultation with our NATO allies, Israel, Egypt, and other friends in the area, and we will spare no effort in seeking their consultation throughout the policy process, not merely demand their acquiescence to our plans.

The sovereignty, security, and integrity of the State of Israel is a moral imperative and serves the strategic interests of the United States. Republicans reaffirm our fundamental and enduring commitment to this principle. We will continue to honor our nation's commitment through political, economic, diplomatic, and military aid. We fully recognize the strategic importance of Israel and the deterrent role of its armed forces in the Middle East and East-West military equations.

Republicans recognize that a just and durable peace for all nations of the region is the best guarantee of continued stability and is vital to deterring further Soviet inroads. Peace between Israel and its neighbors requires direct negotiations among the states involved. Accordingly, a Republican Administration will encourage the peace process now in progress between Egypt and Israel, will seek to broaden it, and will welcome those Arab nations willing to live in peace with Israel. We are encouraged by the support given to the Middle East peace process by Sudan and Oman and the progress brought about by the strong and effective leadership of their governments.

[Relationship with Egypt]

We applaud the vision and courage of Egyptian President Anwar Sadat and we pledge to build our relationship with Egypt in cultural affairs, economic development, and military cooperation.

Republicans recognize that the Carter Administration's vacillations have left friend and foe alike unsure as to United States' policies. While reemphasizing our commitment to Israel, a Republican Administration will pursue close ties and friendship with moderate Arab states. We will initiate the economic and military framework for assuring long-term stability both in the internal development of regional states and an orderly marketplace for the area's resources. We will make clear that any reimposition of an oil embargo would be viewed as a hostile act. We will oppose discriminatory practices, including boycotts, and we will discourage arms sales which contribute to regional instability.

Republicans believe that Jerusalem should remain an undivided city with continued free and unimpeded access to all holy places by people of all faiths.

THE AMERICAS

Latin America is an area of primary interest for the United States. Yet, the Carter Administration's policies have encouraged a precipitous decline in United States relations with virtually every country in the region. The nations of South and Central America have been battered by the Carter Administration's economic and diplomatic sanctions linked to its undifferentiated charges of human rights violations.

In the Caribbean and Central America, the Carter Administration stands by while Castro's totalitarian Cuba, financed, directed, and supplied by the Soviet Union, aggressively trains, arms, and supports forces of warfare and revolution throughout the Western hemisphere. Yet the Carter Administration has steadily denied these threats and in many cases has actively worked to undermine governments and parties opposed to the expansion of Soviet power. This must end.

We deplore the Marxist Sandinista takeover of Nicaragua and the Marxist attempts to destabilize El Salvador, Guatemala, and Honduras. We do not support United States assistance to any Marxist government in this hemisphere and we oppose the Carter Administration aid program for the government of Nicaragua. However, we will support the efforts of the Nicaraguan people to establish a free and independent government.

[Cuba and the Soviet Union]

Republicans deplore the dangerous and incomprehensible Carter Administration policies toward Cuba. The Administration has done nothing about the Soviet combat brigade stationed there, or about the transfer of new Soviet offensive weapons to Cuba in the form of modern MIG aircraft and submarines. It has done nothing about the Soviet pilots flying air defense missions in Cuba or about the extensive improvements to Soviet military bases, particularly the submarine facilities in Cienfuegos, and the expanded Soviet intelligence facilities near Havana.

Republicans recognize the importance of our relations within this hemisphere and pledge a strong new United States policy in the Americas. We will stand firm with countries seeking to develop their societies while combating the subversion and violence exported by Cuba and Moscow. We will return to the fundamental principle of treating a friend as a friend and self-proclaimed enemies as enemies, without apology. We will make it clear to the Soviet Union and Cuba that their subversion and their build-up of offensive military forces is unacceptable.

Republicans recognize the special importance of Puerto Rico and the United States Virgin Islands in the defense of freedom in the Caribbean. We believe that Puerto Rico's admission to the Union would demonstrate our common purpose in the face of growing Soviet and Cuban pressure in that area.

Republicans recognize the fundamental importance of Mexico and restoration of good working relations with that country will be of highest priority. A new Republican Administration will immediately begin high-level, comprehensive negotiations, seeking solutions to common problems on the basis of mutual interest and recognizing that each country has unique contributions to make in resolving practical problems.

Republicans pledge to reestablish close and cooperative relations with the nations of Central and South America and repair the diplomatic damage done by the Carter Administration. We pledge understanding and assistance in the efforts of these nations, and their neighbors, to deal seriously with serious domestic problems.

[Panama Canal]

We pledge to ensure that the Panama Canal remains open, secure, and free of hostile control.

The reservations and understandings to the Panama Canal treaties, including those assuring the United States of primary responsibility of protecting and defending the Canal, are an integral part of those treaties and we will hold Panama to strict interpretation of the language of the treaties, clearly established by the legislative history of Senate adoption of amendments, reservations, and understandings at the time of Senate approval of the treaties.

We would remind the American taxpayers that President Carter gave repeated assurances that the Panama Canal treaties would not cost the American taxpayers "one thin dime," and we emphasize the fact that implementing the Panama Canal treaties will cost them $4.2 billion.

We will work closely with Canada as our most important trading partner in the hemisphere. We will foster the deep affinity that exists between our two nations and our policies will be based on mutual understanding and complete equality.

We will seek a North American Accord designed to foster close cooperation and mutual benefit between the United States, Canada, and Mexico.

A new Republican Administration will, in close cooperation with its neighbors, seek to work together to build prosperity and to strengthen common efforts to combat externally produced revolution and violence.

ASIA AND THE PACIFIC

The United States is and must remain a Pacific power. It is in our vital interest to maintain U.S. guaranteed stability in the area. Republicans recognize the dangerous shifts in power that have accelerated under the current Democratic Administration. The balance on the Korean peninsula has shifted dangerously toward the North. Soviet naval forces in Asia and the Pacific have steadily increased and are now at least equal to U.S. Naval forces there. Unilateral cancellation by the United States of the mutual defense pact with Taiwan and the abrupt announcement of withdrawal of U.S. ground forces from Korea, have led countries throughout the region to question the value of alliance with the United States.

A new Republican Administration will restore a strong American role in Asia and the Pacific. We will make it clear that any military action which threatens the independence of America's allies and friends will bring a response sufficient to make its cost prohibitive to potential adversaries.

[Close Ties with Japan]

Japan will continue to be a pillar of American policy in Asia. Republicans recognize the mutual interests and special relationships that exist between the two countries in their commitment to democracy and in trade, defense, and cultural matters. A new Republican Administration will work closely with the Japanese government to resolve outstanding trade and energy problems on an equitable basis. We strongly support a substantially increased Japanese national defense effort and reaffirm that our long-range objectives of military security and a balancing of the expanded Soviet military presence in the region are of mutual interest.

Republicans recognize the unique danger presented to our ally, South Korea. We will encourage continued efforts to expand political participation and individual liberties within the country, but will recognize the special problems brought on by subversion and potential aggression from the North. We will maintain American ground and air forces in South Korea, and will not reduce our presence further. Our treaty commitments to South Korea will be restated in unequivocal terms and we will reestablish the process of close consultations between our governments.

We reaffirm our special and historic relationships with the Philippines, Singapore, Malaysia, Indonesia, Thailand, New Zealand, and Australia. Republicans will recognize the long friendship with these countries and will cultivate and strengthen our diplomatic and trade relationships.

We deplore the brutal acts of Communist Vietnam against the people of Cambodia and Laos. We recognize that the suffering of refugees from these ravaged countries represents a major moral challenge to the world and one of the great human tragedies of modern times. A Republican Administration will work actively to bring relief to these suffering people, especially those who have sought refuge in Thailand. We value the special contribution the people of Thailand have made to the refugees by opening their borders and saving hundred of thousands of them from death, and we pledge to provide full economic aid and military material to assist Thailand in repelling Vietnamese aggression.

We believe that no expanded relations with Communist Vietnam should be pursued while it continues its course of brutal expansionism and genocide. We pledge that a Republican Administration will press for full accounting of Americans still listed as missing in action.

[China and Taiwan]

Recognizing the growing importance of the People's Republic of China in world affairs, Republicans — who took the historic initiative in opening the lines of communication with that nation — will continue the process of building a working relation with the PRC. Growing contacts between the United States and the People's Republic of China reflect the interests of both nations, as well as some common perceptions of recent changes in the global military balance. We will not ignore the profound differences in our respective philosophies, governmental institutions, policies, and concepts of individual liberty.

We will strive for the creation of conditions that will foster the peaceful elaboration of our relationship with the People's Republic of China. We will exercise due caution and prudence with respect to our own vital interests, especially in the field of expanding trade, including the transfer of sophisticated technology with potential offensive military applications. The relationship between the two countries must be based on mutual respect and reciprocity, with due regard for the need to maintain peace and stability in Asia.

At the same time, we deplore the Carter Administration's treatment of Taiwan, our long-time ally and friend. We pledge that our concern for the safety and security of the 17 million people of Taiwan will be constant. We would regard any attempt to alter Taiwan's status by force as a threat to peace in the region. We declare that the Republican Administration, in strengthening relations with Taiwan, will create conditions leading to the expansion of trade, and will give priority consideration to Taiwan's defense requirements.

AFRICA

The Republican Party supports the principle and process of self-determination in Africa. We reaffirm our commitment to this principle and pledge our strong opposition to the effort of the Soviet Union and its militant allies to subvert this process. Soviet bases, tens of thousands of Cuban troops, and Soviet-bloc subversion are unacceptable.

We recognize that much is at stake in Africa and that the United States and the industrial West have vital interests there — economically, strategically, and politically. Working closely with our allies, a Republican Administration will seek to assist the countries of Africa with our presence, our markets, our know-how, and our investment. We will work to create a climate of economic and political development and confidence. We will encourage and assist business to play a major role in support of regional industrial development programs, mineral complexes, and agricultural self-sufficiency.

Republicans believe that African nations, if given a choice, will reject the Marxist, totalitarian model being forcibly imposed by the Soviet Union and its surrogates including Cuban and Nicaraguan troops as well as East German secret police. We believe that they know the Communist powers have relatively little to offer them and that, for the most part, the African peoples are convinced that the West is central to the world stability and economic growth on which their own fortunes ultimately depend.

A Republican Administration will adhere to policies that reflect the complex origins of African conflicts, demonstrate that we know what U.S. interests are, and back those interests in meaningful ways. We will recognize the important role of economic and military assistance programs and will devote major resources to assisting African development and stability when such aid is given on a bilateral basis and contributes directly to American interests on the continent.

In Southern Africa, American policies must be guided by commonsense and by our own humanitarian principles. Republicans believe that our history has meaning for Africa in demonstrating that a multiracial society with guarantees of individual rights is possible and can work. We must remain open and helpful to all parties, whether in the new Zimbabwe, in Namibia, or in the Republic of South Africa. A Republican Administration will not endorse situations or constitutions, in whatever society, which are racist in purpose or in effect. It will not expect miracles, but will press for genuine progress in achieving goals consistent with American ideals.

FOREIGN ASSISTANCE AND REGIONAL SECURITY

The United States has included foreign assistance and regional security as a major element of its foreign policy for four decades. Properly administered and focused, foreign assistance can be an effective means of promoting United States foreign policy objectives, and serve to enhance American security by assisting friendly nations to become stronger and more capable of defending themselves and their regions against foreign subversion and attack.

The threat posed to individual Third World nations is beyond the means of any one of them to counter alone. A Republican Administration will seek to strengthen and assist regional security arrangements among nations prepared to assume the burden of their defense.

No longer should American foreign assistance programs seek to force acceptance of American governmental forms. The principal consideration should be whether or not extending assistance to a nation or group of nations will advance America's interests and objectives. The single-minded attempt to force acceptance of U.S. values and standards of democracy has undermined several friendly nations, and has made possible the advance of Soviet interests in Asia, the Middle East, Africa, and in the Western Hemisphere in the past four years.

American foreign economic assistance is not a charitable venture; charity is most effectively carried out by private entities. Only by private economic development by the people of the nations involved has poverty ever been overcome. U.S. foreign economic assistance should have a catalytic effect on indigenous economic development, and should only be extended when it is consistent with America's foreign policy interest. America's foreign assistance programs should be a vehicle for exporting the American idea.

A Republican Administration will emphasize bilateral assistance programs whenever possible. Bilateral programs provide the best assurance that aid programs will be fully accountable to the American taxpayer, and wholly consistent with our foreign policy interests.

[Negative Effects]

The effort of the Carter Administration to diminish the role of American military assistance and foreign military sales in our foreign policy has had several negative effects:

It has resulted in the export of many thousands of American jobs as the Soviet Union, Britain, and France have taken sales prohibited to American manufacturers;

It has reduced the ability of friendly nations to defend their independence against Soviet-sponsored subversion, resulting in several cases in abject takeovers by overtly pro-Soviet regimes; and

It has weakened the fabric of the U.S. alliance structure by making the U.S. appear to be an unreliable ally, a trend which can only lead to the undesirable attempt by nations fearful of their security to seek to acquire their own nuclear weapons.

Decisions to provide military assistance should be made on the basis of U.S. foreign policy objectives. Such assistance to any nation need not imply complete approval of a regime's domestic policy. Republicans pledge to strengthen America's presence abroad by well-constructed programs of military assistance to promote national and regional security.

[Foreign Arms Sales]

The manipulation of foreign arms sales has been one of the most seriously abused policy initiatives of the Carter Administration. The establishment of arbitrary ceilings on foreign sales, and the complex procedural and policy guidelines governing such sales have impeded the support of U.S. foreign policy objectives abroad. Friendly and allied nations alike have had to turn elsewhere for arms. This has stimulated the growth of a new arms industry in developing nations. Republicans pledge to reform and rebuild U.S. military assistance and foreign arms sales policies so that they will serve American interests in promoting regional security arrangements and the individual defense needs of friendly nations.

International Economic Policy

INTERNATIONAL TRADE AND ECONOMIC POLICY

The American economy has an abundance of human and material resources, but nevertheless, it is part of a larger global economy. Our domestic prosperity and international competitiveness depend upon our participation in the international economy. Moreover, our security interests are in part determined by international economic factors. Yet the Carter Administration has largely ignored the role of international economics in relations between the United States and friendly nations throughout the world. The Administration has conducted its international economic policy at cross-purposes with other dimensions of its foreign policy, resulting in strains within the Western alliance and a general decline in the domestic prosperity. Under a Republican Administration, our international economic policy will be harmonized with our foreign and defense policies to leave no doubt as to the strategy and purpose of American policy.

The economic policy of the Carter Administration has led to the most serious decline in the value of the dollar in history. The ability of Americans to purchase goods and services or to invest abroad has been diminished by Carter Administration policies devaluing the dollar. Republicans will conduct international economic policy in a manner that will stabilize the value of the dollar at home and abroad.

[Aggresive Export Policy]

The Republican Party believes the United States must adopt an aggressive export policy. For too long, our trade policy has been geared toward helping our foreign trading partners. Now, we have to put the United States back on the world export map. We helped pull other countries out of the post-World War II economic chaos; it is time to remedy our own crisis. Trade, especially exporting, must be high on our list of national priorities. The Republicans will put it there and will promote trade to ensure the long-term health of the U.S. economy.

Exports can play a key role in strengthening the U.S. economy, creating jobs and improving our standard of living. A $15 billion increase in exports can increase employment by 1,000,000, the Gross National Product by $37 billion per year, and private investment by $4 billion per year. Nevertheless, the Carter Administration has placed exporting at the bottom of its priority list. The present Administration's trade policies lack coordination, cohesiveness, and true commitment to improving our export performance. Rather than helping to create strong exporters in the United States and thereby create more jobs for Americans, the Carter Administration's trade policies have discouraged traders. At best, the Administration has adopted a passive approach to trade, merely reacting to changing world economies rather than actively seeking to promote a global structure that best addresses America's needs. As a result, we lag seriously behind our foreign competitors in trade performance and economic strength. Export promotion will be a central objective of international economic policy in a Republican Administration.

A Republican Administration will emphasize a policy of free trade, but will expect our trading partners to do so as well. The failure of the Carter Administration energetically to pursue negotiations designed to improve the access of American exports to foreign markets has contributed, in part, to protectionist sentiment.

Domestic problems — over-burdensome government regulations, excessive taxation, inflationary monetary policy, and an unstable economy — have contributed to the protectionist sentiments as well. We realize that protectionist legislation has engendered retaliation by America's trading partners in the past resulting in "beggar thy neighbor" policies that had such disastrous consequences in the 1930s.

[American Jobs and American Workers]

Republicans are committed to protect American jobs and American workers first and foremost. The Republican Party believes in free trade, and we will insist that our trade policy be based on the principles of reciprocity and equity. We oppose subsidies, tariff and non-tariff barriers that unfairly restrict access of American products to foreign markets. We will not stand idly by as the jobs of millions of Americans in domestic industries, such as automobiles, textiles, steel, and electronics are jeopardized and lost. We pledge to strengthen trade agreements and to change the Carter economic policies that have undermined the capability of American agriculture and industry to compete abroad.

Republicans believe that this nation's international trade balance can be improved through the elimination of disincentives for exporters. Statutory and regulatory requirements that inhibit exports should be reviewed and, where practical, eliminated. We further recognize that government can play a role in promoting international trade by establishing incentives for exports, especially those for small and medium size business. We pledge also to work with our trading partners to eliminate subsidies to exports and dumping.

The ability of the United States to compete in foreign markets is hampered by the excessive taxation of Americans working abroad who contributed to our domestic well-being by promoting international trade. Increased exports to our trading partners result in jobs and a rising standard of living at home. Carter Administration policy has the effect of discouraging the presence of American businessmen abroad due to the unfairly high level of taxation levied against them. A Republican Administration will support legislation designed to eliminate this inequity so that American citizens can fully participate in international commerce without fear of discriminatory taxation.

Our nation must have a strong, competitive, and efficient merchant marine to meet the needs of our international commerce and our national security. We must arrest the significant decline of recent years in the ability of American-flag shipping to compete effectively for the carriage of world commerce. A Republican Administration will revitalize our merchant marine through a responsive and sustained policy. We will encourage the development and maintenance of an American-flag ocean transportation system, staffed with trained American personnel and capable of carrying a substantial portion of our international trade in a competitive and efficient manner. We will promote the development and support of a domestic shipbuilding and ship-repair mobilization base adequate to both the commercial and the national security requirements of the United States.

[ACCESS TO ENERGY AND RAW MATERIALS]

The security of America's foreign sources of energy and raw material supply can no longer be ignored. The United States imports 50 percent of its domestic petroleum requirements, and depends upon foreign sources for 22 of the 74 non-fuel raw materials essential to a modern industrial economy. Nine of the most critical raw materials are almost entirely (i.e., more than 90 percent) located abroad. In contrast, the Soviet Union imports only two critical minerals at a level in excess of 50 percent of domestic consumption.

Reducing reliance on uncertain foreign sources and assuring access to foreign energy and raw materials requires the harmonization of economic policy with our defense and foreign policy. Domestic economic and regulatory policy must be adjusted to remove impediments to greater development of our own energy and raw materials resources. Democratic policies for federal land management, taxation, monetary policy, and economic regulation have served to increase America's dependence on foreign sources of energy and raw materials. Republicans pledge to work to eliminate domestic disincentives to the exploitation of these resources.

Multilateral negotiations have thus far insufficiently focused attention on U.S. long-term security requirements. A pertinent example of this phenomenon is the Law of the Sea Conference, where negotiations have served to inhibit U.S. exploitation of the sea-bed for its abundant mineral resources. Too much concern has been lavished on nations unable to carry out sea-bed mining, with insufficient attention paid to gaining early American access to it. A Republican Administration will conduct multilateral negotiations in a manner that reflects America's abilities and long-term interest in access to raw material and energy resources.

Resource access will assume an important place in defense and economic planning under a Republican Administration. Since America's allies are, in most cases, more dependent than the U.S. on foreign sources of energy and raw materials, they too have a vital interest in the defense of their access to these critical resources. Republicans pledge to promote allied defense cooperation to assure protection from military threats to overseas resources.

REAGAN, BUSH
ACCEPTANCE SPEECHES
July 17, 1980

Ronald Wilson Reagan and George Herbert Walker Bush accepted the Republican Party's nominations for president and vice president July 17, the final day of the Republican National Convention held in Detroit's Joe Louis Arena. Reagan's acceptance speech capped a notably unified and calm convention. The nomination of the former governor of California had been virtually guaranteed since May 26 when Bush, Reagan's most persistent challenger in the primary campaign, withdrew from the contest. Indeed, the only excitement during the four-day GOP session was generated by speculation over Reagan's choice for vice president. After he failed to persuade former President Gerald R. Ford to accept the number-two place on the ticket, Reagan turned to Bush.

The announcement that Bush had been selected was made by Reagan himself in an unprecedented late-night appearance before the convention delegates on July 16. Throughout that evening, the convention hall was rife with rumors that Ford had agreed in principle to accept Reagan's offer. Whatever agreement there might have been fell through, however, and Reagan went to the arena and said, "Let me as simply as I can straighten out and bring this to a conclusion." Reagan told the convention that Ford and he had decided that Ford would "be of more value as the former president campaigning his heart out, as he has pledged to do, and not as a member of the ticket." Reagan then announced his selection of Bush as the running mate. Bush accepted, although he had insisted throughout the campaign that he was not interested in the vice presidential nomination.

Reagan Speech

The following night, Reagan began his acceptance speech with an attempt to assuage the feelings of moderate Republicans upset by the party's failure to include a statement of support for the proposed Equal Rights Amendment in the platform. He pledged that, if elected, he would "establish a liaison with the 50 governors to encourage them to eliminate, wherever it exists, discrimination against women." Following that, the Republican nominee attacked the alleged failures of the Carter administration, reiterated his conservative beliefs and vowed to "restore to the federal government the capacity to do the people's work without dominating their lives." (Republican platform, p. 567)

The Democrats, Reagan said, bore direct responsibility for "this unprecedented calamity which has befallen us." He termed the Carter administration's economic policies an "altogether indigestible economic stew" that had "turned the national stomach." Its ingredients, he said, were inflation, high unemployment, recession, "runaway taxes," deficit spending and an energy crisis.

The resolution of those problems, Reagan said, lay in programs to permit increased mining for coal and drilling for oil and natural gas and to reduce taxes by 10 percent a year for three years. He further pledged to put the "overgrown and overweight" federal government "on a diet," to adjust business depreciation taxes to spur investment and to cut government costs as a percentage of the gross national product.

Reagan ridiculed what he termed the "trust me" policies of President Carter. He said it was time to renew a national commitment to the social "compact" — first signed by the settlers in Plymouth, Mass., in 1620 — that placed trust not in a leader but in the people themselves.

Reagan attempted to reach out to minority voters, charging that the Democrats' record of tax increases with calls for austerity and sacrifice had its most severe effect on lower-income urban dwellers. The message his administration would send to minorities, Reagan said, would be, "we have to move ahead, but we're not going to leave anyone behind."

Turning to foreign affairs, Reagan charged that the Carter administration reacted to world developments with "weakness when we need strength; vacillation when the times demand firmness." And he asked rhetorically, "Who does not feel a growing sense of unease as our allies, facing repeated instances of an amateurish and confused administration, reluctantly conclude that America is unwilling or unable to fulfill its obligation as leader of the free world?"

Reagan closed his address with a dramatic gesture. Saying, "I have thought of something that is not part of my speech, and I'm worried over whether I should do it," he asked his audience to "begin our crusade joined together in a moment of silent prayer." After a moment, Reagan raised his head and said, "God bless America."

Bush Acceptance

George Bush's brief acceptance speech, which preceded Reagan's by a few hours, was standard vice presidential nominee fare. Bush thanked the convention for its support and warned, "Though Jimmy Carter has in the past four years been a failed president, he is a formidable campaigner who can be expected to use the power of his office to suit his own political ends. . . ." And in a move designed to placate some conservative Republicans who would have preferred Sen. Jesse Helms of North Carolina or Rep. Jack Kemp of New York as Reagan's running mate, Bush declared, "I enthusiastically support your platform." He vowed to give his "total dedication and energies" to a successful campaign.

Following are the texts of speeches at the Republican National Convention in Detroit, Mich., by George Bush and Ronald Reagan, accepting their party's nominations for vice president and president, on July 17, 1980. (Boldface headings in brackets have been added by Congressional Quarterly to highlight the organization of the texts.):

BUSH ACCEPTANCE

Thank you very much ladies and gentlemen. Mr. Chairman, my fellow Republicans and fellow Americans, let me express my heartfelt thanks for the honor you have given me; the opportunity to run on our party's national ticket with a great leader like Ronald Reagan. On behalf of Barbara and the rest of the Bush family, all I can say is that we are overwhelmed and grateful for your expression of confidence.

With a deep sense of commitment, I accept your nomination to serve as our party's candidate for Vice President on a ticket headed by the leader of our party and the next President of the United States, Ronald Reagan. I accept.

I enthusiastically support our platform. I pledge to you my total dedication and energies in a united effort to see to it that next January 20th, Ronald Reagan becomes our Nation's 40th President and that a great new era will begin for America in the decade of these '80's. We need change.

Because of Ronald Reagan's leadership, we Republicans emerge from this convention as a strong, united party rededicated to the principles that made our country great. There has been a spirit of victory in the air this past week in Detroit but if that spirit is to be translated into reality, it is up to each and every one of us to help carry Ronald

Reagan's message of a strong, free America the length and the breadth of this land.

Let there be no mistake, though, Jimmy Carter, though he may in the past four years be a failed President, he is a formidable campaigner who can be expected to use the power of his office to suit his own political ends. ... [L]et's forget the pollsters and forget the pundits and remember only that political victories are hard; dedicated things come about only by tough work and that in this crucial election year, the stakes for America and the free world are too great to allow ourselves to become complacent.

We have a great mission not unlike that great mission undertaken by our party 28 summers ago, when another great Republican leader, Dwight Eisenhower, began his campaign to restore the faith of the American people in their government. Dwight Eisenhower, a man of decency, compassion and strength, led America three decades ago into a new era of peace and prosperity. And so, Ronald Reagan, a man of decency, compassion and strength, will lead America into a new era of greatness in this decade of the 1980's. This is the mission, the great mission, all of us working together, joined by millions of disillusioned Democrats and disappointed Independents, must undertake in the campaign ahead.

My fellow Republicans, this is Ronald Reagan's night. He is the man whom you and the American people are waiting to hear. Let me then conclude these words of acceptance by paraphrasing what I told this convention last evening, just moments before you nominated our party's standard-bearer for the presidency.

I said and I repeat tonight, let us, united in spirit and purpose, go forward from this convention city to make 1980 one of victory not only for Ronald Reagan and our party, but for the United States of America and the cause of freedom throughout the world.

REAGAN ACCEPTANCE SPEECH

Mr. Chairman, Mr. Vice President to be, this convention, my fellow citizens of this great Nation:

With a deep awareness of the responsibility conferred by your trust, I accept your nomination for the Presidency of the United States. I do so with deep gratitude, and I think also I might interject, on behalf of all of us, our thanks to Detroit and the people of Michigan and to this city for the warm hospitality.

And I thank you for your wholehearted response to my recommendation in regard to George Bush as a candidate for Vice President.

I am very proud of our Party tonight. This convention has shown to all America a party united, with positive programs for solving the nation's problems; a party ready to build a new consensus with all those across the land who share a community of values embodied in these words: family, work, neighborhood, peace and freedom.

Now, I know that we have had a quarrel or two, but only as to the method of attaining a goal. There was no argument about the goal. As President, I will establish a liaison with the fifty Governors to encourage them to eliminate, wherever it exists, discrimination against women. I will monitor federal laws to ensure their implementation and to add statutes if they are needed.

More than anything else, I want my candidacy to unify our country, to renew the American spirit and sense of purpose. I want to carry our message to every American, regardless of party affiliation, who is a member of this community of shared values.

Never before in our history have Americans been called upon to face three grave threats to our very existence, any one of which could destroy us. We face a disintegrating economy, a weakened defense and an energy policy based on the sharing of scarcity.

[Unprecedented Calamity]

The major issue of this campaign is the direct political, personal and moral responsibility of Democratic Party leadership — in the White House and in the Congress — for this unprecedented calamity which has befallen us. They tell us they have done the most that humanly could be done. They say that the United States has had its day in the sun; that our nation has passed its zenith. They expect you to tell your children that the American people no longer have the will to cope with their problems; that the future will be one of sacrifice and few opportunities.

My fellow citizens, I utterly reject that view.

The American people, the most generous on earth, who created the highest standard of living, are not going to accept the notion that we can only make a better world for others by moving backwards ourselves. Those who believe we can have no business leading the nation.

I will not stand by and watch this great country destroy itself under mediocre leadership that drifts from one crisis to the next, eroding our national will and purpose. We have come together here because the American people deserve better from those to whom they entrust our nation's highest offices — we stand united in our resolve to do something about it.

[Rebirth of Leadership]

We need a rebirth of the American tradition of leadership at *every* level of government and in private life as well. The United States of America is unique in world history because it has a genius for leaders — many leaders — on many levels. But, back in 1976, Mr.

Carter said, "Trust *me*." And a lot of people did. Now, many of those people are out of work. Many have seen their savings eaten away by inflation. Many others on fixed incomes, especially the elderly, have watched helplessly as the cruel tax of inflation wasted away their purchasing power. And, today, a great many who trusted Mr. Carter wonder if we can survive the Carter policies of national defense.

"Trust me" government asks that we concentrate our hopes and dreams on one man; that we trust him to do what is best for us. Well, my view of government places trust not in one person or one party, but in those values that transcend persons and parties. The trust is where it belongs — in the people. The responsibility to live up to that trust is where *it* belongs, in their elected leaders. That kind of relationship, between the people and their elected leaders, is a special kind of compact.

Three hundred and sixty years ago, in 1620, a group of families dared to cross a mighty ocean to build a future for themselves in a new world. When they arrived at Plymouth, Massachusetts, they formed what they called a "compact," an agreement among themselves to build a community and abide by its laws.

The single act — the voluntary binding together of free people to live under the law — set the pattern for what was to come.

A century and a half later, the descendants of those people pledged their lives, their fortunes and their sacred honor to found this nation. Some forfeited their fortunes and their lives; none sacrificed honor.

Four score and seven years later, Abraham Lincoln called upon the people of all America to renew their dedication and their commitment to a government of, for and by the people.

Isn't it once again time to renew our compact of freedom; to pledge to each other all that is best in our lives; all that gives meaning to them, for the sake of this, our beloved and blessed land?

[New Beginning]

Together, let us make this a new beginning. Let us make a commitment to care for the needy; to teach our children the virtues handed down to us by our families; to have the courage to defend those values and virtues and the willingness to sacrifice for them.

Let us pledge to restore, in our time, the American spirit of voluntary service, of cooperation, of private and community initiative; a spirit that flows like a deep and mighty river through the history of our nation.

As your nominee, I pledge to you to restore to the federal government the capacity to do the people's work without dominating their lives. I pledge to you a government that will not only work well, but wisely; its ability to act tempered by prudence, and its willingness to do good balanced by the knowledge that government is never more dangerous than when our desire to have it help us blinds us to its great power to harm us.

The first Republican President once said, "While the people retain their virtue and their vigilance, no administration by any extreme of wickedness or folly can seriously injure the government in the short space of four years."

If Mr. Lincoln could see what has happened in the last three and a half years, he might hedge a little on that statement. But, with the virtues that are our legacy as a free people and with the vigilance that sustains liberty, we still have time to use our renewed compact to overcome the injuries that have been done to America these three and a half years.

First, we must overcome something the present administration has cooked up: a new and altogether indigestible economic stew, one part inflation, one part high unemployment, one part recession, one part runaway taxes, one part deficit spending, seasoned by an energy crisis. It's an economic stew that has turned the national stomach!

Ours are not problems of abstract economic theory. These are problems of flesh and blood; problems that cause pain and destroy the moral fiber of real people who should not suffer the further indignity of being told by the government that it is all somehow their fault. We do not have inflation because, as Mr. Carter says, we have lived too well.

The head of the government which has utterly refused to live within its means and which has, in the last few days, told us that this coming year's deficit will be $60 billion, dares to point the finger of blame at business and labor, both of which have been engaged in a losing struggle just trying to stay even.

High taxes, we are told, are somehow good for us, as if, when government spends our money it isn't inflationary, but when we spend it, it is.

Those who preside over the worst energy shortage in our history tell us to use less, so that we will run out of oil, gasoline and natural gas a little more slowly. Conservation is desirable, of course, for we must not waste energy. But conservation is not the sole answer to our energy needs.

America must get to work producing more energy. The Republican program for solving economic problems is based on growth and productivity.

Large amounts of oil and natural gas lay beneath our land and off our shores, untouched because the present administration seems to believe the American people would rather see more regulation, taxes and controls than more energy.

Coal offers great potential. So does nuclear energy produced under rigorous safety standards. It could supply electricity for thousands of industries and millions of jobs and homes. It must not be thwarted by a tiny minority opposed to economic growth which often finds friendly ears in regulatory agencies for its obstructionist campaigns.

Now, make no mistake. We will not permit the safety of our people or our environmental heritage to be jeopardized, but we are going to reaffirm that the economic prosperity of our people is a fundamental part of our environment.

Our problems are both acute and chronic, yet all we hear from those in positions of leadership are the same tired proposals for more government tinkering, more meddling and more control — all of which led us to this state in the first place.

[Record of Carter Administration]

Can anyone look at the record of this administration and say, "Well done?" Can anyone compare the state of our economy when the Carter administration took office with where we are today and say, "Keep up the good work?" Can anyone look at our reduced standing in the world today and say, "Let's have four more years of this?"

I believe the American people are going to answer these questions ... in the first week of this November and their answer will be: "No — we have had enough!" And, then it will be up to us beginning next January 20th to offer an administration and Congressional leadership of competence and more than a little courage.

We must have the clarity of vision to see the difference between what is essential and what is merely desirable; and then the courage to bring our government back under control.

It is essential that we maintain both the forward momentum of economic growth and the strength of the safety net beneath those in society who need help. We also believe it is essential that the integrity of all aspects of Social Security be preserved.

Beyond these essentials, I believe it is clear our federal government is overgrown and overweight. Indeed, it is time for our government to go on a diet. Therefore, my first act as Chief Executive will be to impose an immediate and thorough freeze on federal hiring.

Then, we are going to enlist the very best minds from business, labor and whatever quarter to conduct a detailed review of every department, bureau and agency that lives by federal appropriation. We are going to enlist the help and ideas of many dedicated and hardworking government employees at all levels who want a more efficient government just as much as the rest of us do. I know that many are demoralized by the confusion and waste they confront in their world as a result of failed and failing policies.

Our instructions to the groups we enlist will be simple and direct. We will remind them that government programs exist at the sufferance of the American taxpayer and are paid for with money earned by working men and women. Any programs that represent a waste of their money — a theft from their pocketbooks — must have that waste eliminated or that program must go. It must be by Executive Order where possible, by Congressional action where necessary. Everything that can be run more effectively by state and local government we shall turn over to state and local government, along with the funding sources to pay for it. We are going to put an end to the money merry-go-round where our money becomes Washington's money, to be spent by the states and cities exactly the way the federal bureaucrats tell them to.

I will not accept the excuse that the federal government has grown so big and powerful that it is beyond the control of any President, any administration or Congress. We are going to put an end to the notion that the American taxpayer exists to fund the federal government. The federal government exists to serve the American people. On January 20th, we are going to reestablish that truth.

[Work and Family]

Also on that date we are going to initiate action to get substantial relief for our taxpaying citizens and action to put people back to work. None of this will be based on any new form of monetary tinkering or fiscal sleight-of-hand. We will simply apply to government the common sense we all use in our daily lives.

Work and family are at the center of our lives, the foundation of our dignity as a free people. When we deprive people of what they have earned, or take away their jobs, we destroy their dignity and undermine their families. We can't support our families unless there are jobs; and we can't have jobs unless people have both money to invest and the faith to invest it.

These are concepts that stem from an economic system that for more than 200 years has helped us master a continent, create a previously undreamed-of prosperity for our people and has fed millions of others around the globe. That system will continue to serve us in the future if our government will stop ignoring the basic values on which it was built and stop betraying the trust and goodwill of the American workers who keep it going.

The American people are carrying the heaviest peacetime tax burden in our nation's history — and it will grow even heavier, under present law, next January. We are taxing ourselves into economic exhaustion and stagnation, crushing our ability and incentive to save, invest and produce.

This must stop! We must halt this fiscal self-destruction and restore sanity to our economic system. I have long advocated a 30 percent reduction in income tax rates over a period of three years. This phased tax reduction would begin with a 10 percent "down payment" tax cut in 1981, which the Republicans in Congress and I have already proposed. A phased reduction of tax rates would go a long way toward easing the heavy burden on the American people. But, we should not stop there.

Within the context of economic conditions and appropriate budget priorities during each fiscal year of my Presidency, I would strive to go further. This would include improvement in business depreciation taxes so we can stimulate investment in order to get plants and equipment replaced, put more Americans back to work and put our nation back on the road to being competitive in world commerce. We will also work to reduce the cost of government as a percentage of our Gross National Product.

The first task of national leadership is to set realistic and honest priorities in our policies and our budget, and I pledge that my administration will do that.

When I talk of tax cuts, I am reminded that every major tax cut in this century has strengthened the economy, generated renewed productivity and ended up yielding new revenues for the government by creating new investment, new jobs and more commerce among our people.

The present administration has been forced by us Republicans to play follow-the-leader with regard to a tax cut. But, in this election year we must take with the proverbial "grain of salt" any tax cut proposed by those who have already given us the greatest single tax increase in our nation's history.

When those in leadership give us tax increases and tell us we must also do with less, have they thought about those who have always had less — especially the minorities? This is like telling them that just as they step on that first rung of the ladder of opportunity, the ladder is being pulled up from under them. That may be the Democratic leadership's message to the minorities, but it won't be ours.

Ours will be: we have to move ahead, but we are not going to leave *anyone* behind.

Thanks to the economic policies of the Democratic Party, millions of Americans find themselves out of work. Millions more have never even had a fair chance to learn new skills, hold a decent job, or secure for themselves and their families a share in the prosperity of this nation.

It is time to put America back to work, to make our cities and towns resound with the confident voices of men and women of all races, nationalities and faiths bringing home to their families a paycheck they can cash for honest money.

For those without skills, we will find a way to help them get new skills.

For those without job opportunities, we will stimulate new opportunities, particularly in the inner cities where they live.

For those who have abandoned hope, we will restore hope and we will welcome them into a great national crusade to make America great again.

[Foreign Affairs]

When we move from domestic affairs and cast our eyes abroad, we see an equally sorry chapter on the record of the present administration.

—A Soviet combat brigade trains in Cuba, just 90 miles from our shores.

—A Soviet army of invasion occupies Afghanistan, further threatening our vital interests in the Middle East.

—America's defense strength is at its lowest ebb in a generation, while the Soviet Union is vastly outspending us in both strategic and conventional arms.

—Our European allies, looking nervously at the growing menace from the East, turn to us for leadership and fail to find it.

—And, incredibly, more than 50 . . . of our fellow Americans have been held captive for over eight months by a dictatorial foreign power that holds us up to ridicule before the world.

Adversaries large and small test our will and seek to confound our resolve, but we are given weakness when we need strength; vacillation when the times demand firmness.

The Carter administration lives in the world of make-believe. Every day it dreams up a response to that day's troubles, regardless of what happened yesterday and what will happen tomorrow. But you and I live in a real world where disasters are overtaking our nation without any real response from Washington.

I condemn this make-believe, its self-deceit and, above all, its transparent hypocrisy.

For example, Mr. Carter says he supports the volunteer army, but he lets military pay and benefits slip so low that many of our enlisted personnel are actually eligible for food stamps. Reenlistment rates drop and just recently, after he fought all week against a proposed pay increase for men and women in the military, he then helicoptered out to the carrier, the U.S.S. Nimitz, which was returning from long months of duty in the Indian Ocean, and told the crew of that ship that he advocated better pay for them and their comrades! Where does he stand now that he is back on shore?

I will tell you where *I* stand. I do not favor a peacetime draft or registration, but I do favor pay and benefit levels that will attract and keep highly motivated men and women in our volunteer forces and an active reserve trained and ready for an instant call in case of an emergency.

You know, there may be a sailor at the helm of the ship of state, but the ship has no rudder. Critical decisions are made at times almost in comic fashion, but who can laugh? Who was not embarrassed when the administration handed a major propaganda victory in the United Nations to the enemies of Israel, our staunch Middle East allies [sic] for three decades, and then claimed that the American vote was a "mistake," the result of a "failure of communication" between the President, his Secretary of State and his U.N. Ambassador?

Who does not feel a growing sense of unease as our allies, facing repeated instances of an amateurish and confused administration, reluctantly conclude that America is unwilling or unable to fulfill its obligation as leader of the free world?

Who does not feel rising alarm when the question in any discussion of foreign policy is no longer, "Should we do something?", but "Do we have the capacity to do anything?"

[Four More Years of Weakness]

The administration which has brought us to this state is seeking your endorsement for four more years of weakness, indecision, mediocrity and incompetence. No American should vote until he or she has asked, is the United States stronger and more respected now than it was three and a half years ago? Is the world today a safer place in which to live?

It is the responsibility of the President of the United States, in working for peace, to ensure that the safety of our people cannot successfully be threatened by a hostile foreign power. As President, fulfilling that responsibility will be my number one priority.

We are not a warlike people. Quite the opposite. We always seek to live in peace. We resort to force infrequently and with great reluctance — and only after we have determined that it is absolutely necessary. We are awed, and rightly so, by the forces of destruction at loose in the world in this nuclear era. But neither can we be naive or foolish. Four times in my lifetime America has gone to war, bleeding the lives of its young men into the sands of beachheads, the fields of Europe and the jungles and rice paddies of Asia. We know only too well that war comes not when the forces of freedom are strong. It is when they are weak that tyrants are tempted.

We simply cannot learn these lessons the hard way again without risking our destruction.

Of all the objectives we seek, first and foremost is the establishment of lasting world peace. We must always stand ready to negotiate in good faith, ready to pursue any reasonable avenue that holds forth the promise of lessening tensions and furthering the prospects of peace. But let our friends and those who may wish us ill take note: the United States has an obligation to its citizens and to the people of the world never to let those who would destroy freedom dictate the future course of human life on this planet. I would regard my election as proof that we have renewed our resolve to preserve world peace and freedom. This nation will once again be strong enough to do that.

This evening marks the last step, save one, of a campaign that has taken Nancy and me from one end of this great land to the other, over many months and thousands of miles. There are those who question the way we choose a President; who say that our process imposes difficult and exhausting burdens on those who seek the office. I have not found it so.

It is impossible to capture in words the splendor of this vast continent which God has granted as our portion of his creation. There are no words to express the extraordinary strength and character of this breed of people we call Americans.

Everywhere we have met thousands of Democrats, Independents and Republicans who come from all economic conditions, all walks of life, bound together in that community of shared values of family, work, neighborhood, peace and freedom. They are concerned, yes, but they are not frightened. They are disturbed, but not dismayed. They are the kind of men and women Tom Paine had in mind when he wrote — during the darkest days of the American Revolution — "We have it in our power to begin the world over again."

Nearly 150 years after Tom Paine wrote those words, an American President told the generation of the Great Depression that it had a "rendezvous with destiny." I believe this generation of Americans today has a rendezvous with destiny.

Tonight, let us dedicate ourselves to renewing the American compact. I ask you not simply to "Trust *me*," but to trust your values — our values — and to hold me responsible for living up to them. I ask you to trust that American spirit which knows no ethnic, religious, social, political, regional or economic boundaries; the spirit that burned with zeal in the hearts of millions of immigrants from every corner of the earth who came here in search of freedom.

Some say that spirit no longer exists. But I have seen it — I have felt it — all across the land; in the big cities, the small towns and in rural America. It is still there, ready to blaze into life if you and I are willing to do what has to be done. We have to do the practical things, the down-to-earth things such as creating policies that will stimulate our economy, increase productivity and put America back to work.

[The Time Is Now]

The time is *now* to limit federal spending; to insist on a stable monetary reform and to free ourselves from imported oil.

The time is *now* to resolve that the basis of a firm and principled foreign policy is one that takes the world as it is and seeks to change it by leadership and example; not by harangue, harassment or wishful thinking.

The time is *now* to say that while we shall seek new friendships and expand and improve others, we shall not do so by breaking our word or casting aside old friends and allies.

And, the time is *now* to redeem promises once made to the American people by another candidate, in another time and another place.

He said, "... For three long years I have been going up and down this country preaching that government — federal, state and local — costs too much. I shall not stop that preaching. As an immediate program of action, we must abolish useless offices. We must eliminate unnecessary functions of government. . . .

"...we must consolidate subdivisions of government and, like the private citizen, give up luxuries which we can no longer afford."

And then he said, "I propose to you, my friends, and through you that government of all kinds, big and little, be made solvent and that the example be set by the President of the United States and his Cabinet."

Those were Franklin Delano Roosevelt's words as he accepted the nomination for President in 1932.

The time is *now*, my fellow Americans, to recapture our destiny, to take it into our own hands. To do this it will take many of us working together. I ask you tonight all over this land to volunteer your help in this cause so that we can carry our message throughout the land.

Isn't it time that we, the people, carried out these unkept promises? That we pledge to each other and to all America on this July day 48 years later, we intend to do just that!

I have thought of something that is not part of my speech, and I worry over whether I should do it. Can we doubt that only a Divine Providence placed this land, this island of freedom, here as a refuge for all those people in the world who yearn to breathe free — Jews and Christians enduring persecution behind the Iron Curtain, the boat people of Southeast Asia, of Cuba and of Haiti, the victims of drought and famine in Africa, the Freedom Fighters of Afghanistan, and our own countrymen held in savage captivity.

I will confess that I have been a little afraid to suggest what I am going to suggest. I am more afraid not to.

Can we begin our crusade joined together in a moment of silent prayer.

God bless America.

THE GLOBAL 2000 REPORT

July 24, 1980

Ending a three-year study on global population, natural resources and environmental trends, the president's Council on Environmental Quality (CEQ) and the State Department issued a report July 24 that painted a grim picture of life 20 years in the future. The 766-page study, The Global 2000 Report to the President: Entering the Twenty-First Century, *concluded, "If present trends continue, the world in 2000 will be more crowded, more polluted, less stable ecologically, and more vulnerable to disruption than the world we live in now."*

The Global 2000 Report, *ordered by President Carter in his 1977 Environmental Message to Congress, was described by administration officials as the most exhaustive and well-documented study ever produced of long-term changes in the world's population, natural resources and environment and the implications of those changes for public policy. It pulled together for the first time, officials said, all the government agency projections, economic models and analyses on the subject of the study.*

Gus Speth, chairman of the Council on Environmental Quality, said that while the report presented no startling new findings it was "important and indeed, unique," because of its thoroughness.

Population and Food

In a letter transmitting the report to the president, the authors warned that they found "the potential for global problems of alarming proportions by the year 2000." They added, "Environmental, resource and population stresses are intensifying and will increasingly determine the quality of human life on our planet."

The report projected the world's population over two decades to increase by 55 percent, from 4.5 billion to more than 6 billion in 2000. Most of the added population would come in the poorer, less developed countries. While food production would increase by 90 percent from 1970 to 2000, a global per capita increase in consumption of less than 15 percent was projected over the same period. Most of the increased food production would be consumed in countries where diets already were adequate or better. Individual food consumption in South Asia, Africa and the Middle East would grow hardly at all and in some areas might decline below existing levels, the report said.

While the output of goods and services was expected to grow more rapidly in many less developed countries than in the industrialized nations, the gap between rich and poor would increase because high population growth rates were likely to keep per capita income low in the poorer countries.

Resource Shortages

World oil production was projected to reach maximum capacity in the 1990s, with prices rising as demand increased sharply. The burden of energy prices would fall most heavily on the less-developed countries.

Deforestation, proceeding rapidly, would contribute to severe regional water shortages and the deterioration of water quality by destabilizing supplies, aggravating shortages in dry seasons and intensifying flooding, soil erosion and siltation of rivers and reservoirs in rainy seasons.

Environmental Threats

The report identified as perhaps the most serious environmental problem over the next 20 years "an accelerating deterioration and loss of ... resources essential for agriculture. . . ." The use of pesticides and other chemicals, while increasing yields, presented a broad range of environmental threats to crop lands and people, the report said.

The heavy use of chemicals also would mean spreading water pollution. Despite progress in reducing air pollution, the quality of air was expected to worsen, in the developing as well as industrialized countries, as increased amounts of oil, coal and hydrocarbon fuels were burned.

Finally, the report said, the world faced "an urgent problem of loss of plant and animal genetic resources" through the accelerating extinction of species.

As projections of current trends 20 years into the future, the report's findings did not take into account either scientific discoveries, wars, political upheavals, natural disasters or changes in government policy. The authors of the study emphasized that the report was not a prediction of what the world would actually be like in 2000 but rather a warning to governments to adopt policies to avert the predicted trends.

Reaction

President Carter's first response to the report was to appoint a Presidential Task Force on Global Resources and Environment, headed by Speth. Carter also instructed the State Department to arrange an international meeting of environmental and economic experts in Washington, D.C., in 1981.

Secretary of State Edmund S. Muskie told a news conference that if the challenges the report identified were ignored, "they will overwhelm our efforts to improve the quality of life and social opportunities for the world's people, including our own."

The retiring president of the World Bank, Robert S. McNamara, said of the report, "It paints an absolutely shocking picture of the world 20 years from now — unless we act."

Following are excerpts from The Global 2000 Report to the President: Entering the Twenty-First Century, *issued July 24, 1980, warning governments to adopt policies to avert predicted world trends. (Boldface headings in brackets have been added by Congressional Quarterly to highlight the organization of the text.):*

Major Findings and Conclusions

If present trends continue, the world in 2000 will be more crowded, more polluted, less stable ecologically, and more vulnerable to disruption than the world we live in now. Serious stresses involving population, resources, and environment are clearly visible ahead. Despite greater material output, the world's people will be poorer in many ways than they are today.

For hundreds of millions of the desperately poor, the outlook for food and other necessities of life will be no better. For many it will be worse. Barring revolutionary advances in technology, life for most people on earth will be more precarious in 2000 than it is now — unless the nations of the world act decisively to alter current trends.

This, in essence, is the picture emerging from the U.S. Government's projections of probable changes in world population, resources, and environment by the end of the century, as presented in the Global 2000 Study. They do not predict what will occur. Rather, they depict conditions that are likely to develop if there are no changes in public policies, institutions, or rates of technological advance, and if there are no wars or other major disruptions. A keener awareness of the nature of the current trends, however, may induce changes that will alter these trends and the projected outcome.

PRINCIPAL FINDINGS

Rapid growth in world population will hardly have altered by 2000. The world's population will grow from 4 billion in 1975 to 6.35 billion in 2000, an increase of more than 50 percent. The rate of growth will slow only marginally, from 1.8 percent a year to 1.7 percent. In terms of sheer numbers, population will be growing faster in 2000 than it is today, with 100 million people added each year compared with 75 million in 1975. Ninety percent of this growth will occur in the poorest countries.

While the economies of the less developed countries (LDCs) are expected to grow at faster rates than those of the industrialized nations, the gross national product per capita in most LDCs remains low. The average gross national product per capita is projected to rise substantially in some LDCs (especially in Latin America), but in the great populous nations of South Asia it remains below $200 a year (in 1975 dollars). The large existing gap between the rich and poor nations widens.

[World Food Production]

World food production is projected to increase 90 percent over the 30 years from 1970 to 2000. This translates into a global per capita increase of less than 15 percent over the same period. The bulk of that increase goes to countries that already have relatively high per capita food consumption. Meanwhile per capita consumption in South Asia, the Middle East, and the LDCs of Africa will scarcely improve or will actually decline below present inadequate levels. At the same time, real prices for food are expected to double.

Arable land will increase only 4 percent by 2000, so that most of the increased output of food will have to come from higher yields. Most of the elements that now contribute to higher yields — fertilizer, pesticides, power for irrigation, and fuel for machinery — depend heavily on oil and gas.

During the 1990s world oil production will approach geological estimates of maximum production capacity, even with rapidly increasing petroleum prices. The Study projects that the richer industrialized nations will be able to command enough oil and other commercial energy supplies to meet rising demands through 1990. With the expected price increases, many less developed countries will have increasing difficulties meeting energy needs. For the one-quarter of humankind that depends primarily on wood for fuel, the outlook is bleak. Needs for fuelwood will exceed available supplies by about 25 percent before the turn of the century.

[Resource Shortages]

While the world's finite fuel resources — coal, oil, gas, oil shale, tar sands, and uranium — are theoretically sufficient for centuries, they are not evenly distributed; they pose difficult economic and environmental problems; and they vary greatly in their amenability to exploitation and use.

Nonfuel mineral resources generally appear sufficient to meet projected demands through 2000, but further discoveries and investments will be needed to maintain reserves. In addition, production costs will increase with energy prices and may make some nonfuel mineral resources uneconomic. The quarter of the world's population that inhabits industrial countries will continue to absorb three-fourths of the world's mineral production.

Regional water shortages will become more severe. In the 1970-2000 period population growth alone will cause requirements for water to double in nearly half the world. Still greater increases would be needed to improve standards of living. In many LDCs, water supplies will become increasingly erratic by 2000 as a result of extensive deforestation. Development of new water supplies will become more costly virtually everywhere.

Significant losses of world forests will continue over the next 20 years as demand for forest products and fuelwood increases. Growing stocks of commercial-size timber are projected to decline 50 percent per capita. The world's forests are now disappearing at the rate of 18-20 million hectares a year (an area half the size of California), with most of the loss occurring in the humid tropical forests of Africa, Asia, and South America. The projections indicate that by 2000 some 40 percent of the remaining forest cover in LDCs will be gone.

Serious deterioration of agricultural soils will occur worldwide, due to erosion, loss of organic matter, desertification, salinization, alkalinization, and waterlogging. Already, an area of cropland and grassland approximately the size of Maine is becoming barren wasteland each year, and the spread of desert-like conditions is likely to accelerate.

Atmospheric concentrations of carbon dioxide and ozone-depleting chemicals are expected to increase at rates that could alter the world's climate and upper atmosphere significantly by 2050. Acid rain from increased combustion of fossil fuels (especially coal) threatens damage to lakes, soils, and crops. Radioactive and other hazardous materials present health and safety problems in increasing numbers of countries.

Extinctions of plant and animal species will increase dramatically. Hundreds of thousands of species — perhaps as many as 20 percent of all species on earth — will be irretrievably lost as their habitats vanish, especially in tropical forests.

The future depicted by the U.S. Government projections, briefly outlined above, may actually understate the impending problems. The methods available for carrying out the Study led to certain gaps and inconsistencies that tend to impart an optimistic bias. For example, most of the individual projections for the various sectors studied — food, minerals, energy, and so on — assume that sufficient capital, energy, water, and land will be available in each of these sectors to meet their needs, regardless of the competing needs of the other sectors. More consistent, better-integrated projections would produce a still more emphatic picture of intensifying stresses, as the world enters the twenty-first century.

CONCLUSIONS

At present and projected growth rates, the world's population would reach 10 billion by 2030 and would approach 30 billion by the end of the twenty-first century. These levels correspond closely to estimates by the U.S. National Academy of Sciences of the maximum carrying capacity of the entire earth. Already the populations in sub-Saharan Africa and in the Himalayan hills of Asia have exceeded the carrying capacity of the immediate area, triggering an erosion of the land's capacity to support life. The resulting poverty and ill health have further complicated efforts to reduce fertility. Unless this circle of interlinked problems is broken soon, population growth in such areas will unfortunately be slowed for reasons other than declining birth rates. Hunger and disease will claim more babies and young children, and more of those surviving will be mentally and physically handicapped by childhood malnutrition.

Indeed, the problems of preserving the carrying capacity of the earth and sustaining the possibility of a decent life for the human beings that inhabit it are enormous and close upon us. Yet there is reason for hope. It must be emphasized that the Global 2000 Study's projections are based on the assumption that national policies regarding population stabilization, resource conservation, and environmental protection will remain essentially unchanged through the end of the century. But in fact, policies are beginning to change. In some areas, forests are being replanted after cutting. Some nations are taking steps to reduce soil losses and desertification. Interest in energy conservation is growing, and large sums are being invested in exploring alternatives to petroleum dependence. The need for family planning is slowly becoming better understood. Water supplies are being improved and waste treatment systems built. High-yield seeds are widely available and seed banks are being expanded. Some wildlands with their genetic resources are being protected. Natural predators and selective pesticides are being substituted for persistent and destructive pesticides.

[No Quick Fixes]

Encouraging as these developments are, they are far from adequate to meet the global challenges projected in this Study. Vigorous, determined new initiatives are needed if worsening poverty and human suffering, environmental degradation, and international tension and conflicts are to be prevented. There are no quick fixes. The only solutions to the problems of population, resources, and environment are complex and long-term. These problems are inextricably linked to some of the most perplexing and persistent problems in the world — poverty, injustice, and social conflict. New and imaginative ideas — and a willingness to act on them — are essential.

The needed changes go far beyond the capability and responsibility of this or any other single nation. An era of unprecedented cooperation and commitment is essential. Yet there are opportunities — and a strong rationale — for the United States to provide leadership among nations. A high priority for this Nation must be a thorough assessment of its foreign and domestic policies relating to population, resources, and environment. The United States, possessing the world's largest economy, can expect its policies to have a significant influence on global trends. An equally important priority for the United States is to cooperate generously and justly with other nations — particularly in the areas of trade, investment, and assistance — in seeking solutions to the many problems that extend beyond our national boundaries. There are many unfulfilled opportunities to cooperate with other nations in efforts to relieve poverty and hunger, stabilize population, and enhance economic and environmental productivity. Further cooperation among nations is also needed to strengthen international mechanisms for protecting and utilizing the "global commons" — the oceans and atmosphere.

To meet the challenges described in this Study, the United States must improve its ability to identify emerging problems and assess alternative responses. In using and evaluating the Government's present capability for long-term global analysis, the Study found serious inconsistencies in the methods and assumptions employed by the various agencies in making their projections. The Study itself made a start toward resolving these inadequacies. It represents the Government's first attempt to produce an interrelated set of population, resource, and environmental projections, and it has brought forth the most consistent set of global projections yet achieved by U.S. agencies. Nevertheless, the projections still contain serious gaps and contradictions that must be corrected if the Government's analytic capability is to be improved. It must be acknowledged that at present the Federal agencies are not always capable of providing projections of the quality needed for long-term policy decisions.

[Lack of Coordination]

While limited resources may be a contributing factor in some instances, the primary problem is lack of coordination. The U.S. Government needs a mechanism for continuous review of the assumptions and methods the Federal agencies use in their projection models and for assurance that the agencies' models are sound, consistent, and well documented. The improved analyses that could result would provide not only a clearer sense of emerging problems and opportunities, but also a better means for evaluating alternative responses, and a better basis for decisions of worldwide significance that the President, the Congress, and the Federal Government as a whole must make.

With its limitations and rough approximations, the Global 2000 Study may be seen as no more than a reconnaissance of the future; nonetheless its conclusions are reinforced by similar findings of other recent global studies that were examined in the course of the Global 2000 Study. . . . All these studies are in general agreement on the nature of the problems and on the threats they pose to the future welfare of humankind. The available evidence leaves no doubt that the world — including this Nation — faces enormous, urgent, and complex problems in the decades immediately ahead. Prompt and vigorous changes in public policy around the world are needed to avoid or minimize these problems before they become unmanageable. Long lead times are required for effective action. If decisions are delayed until the problems become worse, options for effective action will be severely reduced.

The Study in Brief

The President's directive establishing the Global 2000 Study called for a "study of the probable changes in the world's population, natural resources, and environment through the end of the century" and indicated that the Study as a whole was to "serve as the foundation of our longer-term planning." The findings of the Study identify problems to which world attention must be directed. But because all study reports eventually become dated and less useful, the Study's findings alone cannot provide the foundation called for in the directive. The necessary foundation for longer-term planning lies not in study findings *per se,* but in the Government's continuing institutional capabilities — skilled personnel, data, and analytical models — for developing studies and analyses. Therefore, to meet the objectives stated in the President's directive, the Global 2000 Study was designed not only to assess probable changes in the world's population, natural resources, and environment, but also, through the study process itself, to identify and strengthen the Government's capability for longer-term planning and analysis. . . .

[UNDERLYING ASSUMPTIONS]

The Global 2000 Study has three major underlying assumptions. First, the projections assume a general continuation around the world of present public policy relating to population stabilization, natural resource conservation, and environmental protection. The projections thus point to the expected future if policies continue without significant changes.

The second major assumption relates to the effects of technological developments and of the market mechanism. The Study assumes that rapid rates of technological development and adoption will continue, and that the rate of development will be spurred on by efforts to deal with problems identified by this Study. Participating agencies were asked to use the technological assumptions they normally use in preparing long-term global projections. In general, the agencies assume a continuation of rapid rates of technological development and no serious social resistance to the adoption of new technologies. Agricultural technology, for example, is assumed to continue increasing crop yields as rapidly as during the past few decades, including the period of the Green Revolution. . . . The projections assume no revolutionary advances — such as immediate wide-scale availability of nuclear fusion for energy production — and no disastrous setbacks — such as serious new health risks from widely used contraceptives or an outbreak of plant disease severely affecting an important strain of grain. The projections all assume that price, operating through the market mechanism, will reduce demand whenever supply constraints are encountered.

Third, the Study assumes that there will be no major disruptions of international trade as a result of war, disturbance of the international monetary system, or political disruption. The findings of the Study do, however, point to increasing potential for international conflict and increasing stress on international financial arrangements. Should wars or a significant disturbance of the international monetary system occur, the projected trends would be altered in unpredictable ways.

Because of the limitations outlined above, the Global 2000 Study is not the definitive study of future population, resource, and environment conditions. Nor is it intended to be a prediction. The Study does provide the most internally consistent and interrelated set of global projections available so far from the U.S. Government. Furthermore, its major findings are supported by a variety of nongovernmental global studies based on more highly interactive models that project similar trends through the year 2000 or beyond.

POPULATION AND INCOME

Population and income projections provided the starting point for the Study. These projections were used wherever possible in the resource projections to estimate demand.

Population

One of the most important findings of the Global 2000 Study is that enormous growth in the world's population will occur by 2000 under any of the wide range of assumptions considered in the Study. The world's population increases 55 percent from 4.1 billion people in 1975 to 6.35 billion by 2000, under the Study's medium-growth projections. While there is some uncertainty in these numbers, even the lowest-growth population projection shows a 46 percent increase — to 5.9 billion people by the end of the century.

Another important finding is that the rapid growth of the world's population will not slow appreciably. The rate of growth per year in 1975 was 1.8 percent; the projected rate for 2000 is 1.7 percent. Even under the lowest growth projected, the number of persons being added annually to the world's population will be significantly greater in 2000 than today.

[Population Growth in LDCs]

Most of the population growth (92 percent) will occur in the less developed countries rather than in the industrialized countries. Of the 6.35 billion people in the world in 2000, 5 billion will live in LDCs. The LDCs' share of the world's population increased from 66 percent in 1950 to 72 percent in 1975, and is expected to reach 79 percent by 2000. LDC population growth rates will drop slightly, from 2.2 percent a year in 1975 to 2 percent in 2000, compared with 0.7 percent and 0.5 percent in developed countries. In some LDCs, growth rates will still be more than 3 percent a year in 2000. . . .

. . .The LDC populations, predominantly young with their childbearing years ahead of them, have a built-in momentum for further growth. Because of this momentum, a world population of around 6 billion is a virtual certainty for 2000 even if fertility rates were somehow to drop quickly to replacement levels (assuming there are no disastrous wars, famine, or pestilence).

The projected fertility rates and life expectancies, together with the age structure of the world's population, are extremely significant for later years since these factors influence how soon world population could cease to grow and what the ultimate stabilized global population could be. The Study's projections assume that world fertility rates will drop more than 20 percent over the 1975-2000 period, from an average of 4.3 children per fertile woman to 3.3. In LDCs, fertility rates are projected to drop 30 percent as a result of moderate progress in social and economic development and increased availability and use of contraceptive methods. The projections also assume that life expectancies at birth for the world will increase 11 percent, to 65.5 years, as a result of improved health. The projected increases in life expectancies and decreases in fertility rates produce roughly counterbalancing demographic effects.

In addition to rapid population growth, the LDCs will experience dramatic movements of rural populations to cities and adjacent settlements. If present trends continue, many LDC cities will become almost inconceivably large and crowded. By 2000 Mexico City is projected to have more than 30 million people — roughly three times the present population of the New York metropolitan area. Calcutta will approach 20 million. Greater Bombay, Greater Cairo, Jakarta, and Seoul are all expected to be in the 15-20 million range, and 400 cities will have passed the million mark. . . .

[Rapid Urban Growth]

Rapid urban growth will put extreme pressures on sanitation, water supplies, health care, food, shelter, and jobs. LDCs will have to increase urban services approximately two-thirds by 2000 just to stay even with 1975 levels of service per capita. The majority of people in large LDC cities are likely to live in "uncontrolled settlements" — slums and shantytowns where sanitation and other public services are minimal at best. In many large cities — for example, Bombay, Calcutta, Mexico City, Rio de Janeiro, Seoul, Taipei — a quarter or more of the population already lives in uncontrolled settlements, and the trend is sharply upward. It is not certain whether the trends projected for enormous increases in LDC urban populations will in fact continue for 20 years. In the years ahead, lack of food for the urban poor, lack of jobs, and increasing illness and misery may slow the growth of LDC cities and alter the trend.

Difficult as urban conditions are, conditions in rural areas of many LDCs are generally worse. Food, water, health, and income problems are often most severe in outlying agricultural and grazing areas. In some areas rural-urban migration and rapid urban growth are being accelerated by deteriorating rural conditions.

An updated medium-series population projection would show little change from the Global 2000 study projections. World population in 2000 would be estimated at about 6.18 (as opposed to 6.35) billion, a reduction of less than 3 percent. The expectation would remain that, in absolute numbers, population will be growing more rapidly by the end of the century than today.

The slight reduction in the population estimate is due primarily to new data suggesting that fertility rates in some areas have declined a little more rapidly than earlier estimates indicated. The new data indicate that fertility declines have occurred in some places even in the absence of overall socioeconomic progress. Between 1970 and 1976, for example, in the presence of extreme poverty and malnutrition, fertility declines of 10-15 percent occurred in Indonesia and 15-20 percent in the poorest income classes in Brazil.

Income

Projected declines in fertility rates are based in part on anticipated social and economic progress, which is ultimately reflected in increased income. Income projections were not possible, and gross national product projections were used as surrogates. GNP, a rough and inadequate measure of social and economic welfare, is projected to increase worldwide by 145 percent over 25 years from 1975 to 2000. But because of population growth, per capita GNP increases much more slowly, from $1,500 in 1975 to $2,300 in 2000 — an increase of 53 percent. For both the poorer and the richer countries, rates of growth in GNP are projected to decelerate after 1985.

GNP growth is expected to be faster in LDCs (an average annual growth of 4.5 percent, or an approximate tripling over 25 years) than in developed regions (an average annual growth of 3.3 percent, or somewhat more than a doubling). However, the LDC growth in gross national product develops from a very low base, and population growth in the LDCs brings per capita increases in GNP down to very modest proportions. While parts of the LDC world, especially several countries in Latin America, are projected to improve significantly in per capita GNP by 2000, other countries will make little or no gains from their present low levels. India, Bangladesh, and Pakistan, for example, increase their per capita GNP by 31 percent, 8 percent, and 3 percent, respectively, but in all three countries GNP per capita remains below $200 (in 1975 dollars). . . .

The present income disparities between the wealthiest and poorest nations are projected to widen. Assuming that present trends continue, the group of industrialized countries will have a per capita GNP of nearly $8,500 (in 1975 dollars) in 2000, and North America, Western Europe, Australia, New Zealand, and Japan will average more than $11,000. By contrast, per capita GNP in the LDCs will average less than $600. For every $1 increase in GNP per capita in the LDCs, a $20 increase is projected for the industrialized countries. . . . The disparity between the developed countries and the less developed group is so marked that dramatically different rates of change would be needed to reduce the gap significantly by the end of the century. Disparities between the rich and poor of many LDCs are equally striking.

Updated GNP projections would indicate somewhat lower economic growth than shown in the Global 2000 projections. Projections for the member nations of the Organization for Economic Cooperation and Development (OECD) have been revised downward over the past 2-3 years because of the effects of increasing petroleum prices and because of anticipated measures to reduce inflation. In turn, depressed growth in the OECD economies is expected to lead to slowed growth in LDC economies. For example, in 1976 the World Bank projected that the industrialized nations' economies would expand at 4.9 percent annually over the 1980-85 period; by 1979 the Bank had revised these projections downward to 4.2 percent annually over the 1980-90 period. Similarly, between 1976 and 1979 Bank projections for LDC economies dropped from 6.3 percent (1980-85 period) to 5.6 percent (1980-90 period).

RESOURCES

The Global 2000 Study resource projections are based to the fullest extent possible on the population and GNP projections presented previously. The resource projections cover food, fisheries, forests, nonfuel minerals, water, and energy.

Food

The Global 2000 Study projects world food production to increase at an average annual rate of about 2.2 percent over the 1970-2000 period. This rate of increase is roughly equal to the record growth rates experienced during the 1950s, 1960s, and early 1970s, including the period of the so-called Green Revolution. Assuming no deterioration in climate or weather, food production is projected to be 90 percent higher in 2000 than in 1970.

The projections indicate that most of the increase in food production will come from more intensive use of yield-enhancing, energy-intensive inputs and technologies such as fertilizer, pesticides, herbicides, and irrigation — in many cases with diminishing returns. Land under cultivation is projected to increase only 4 percent by 2000 because most good land is already being cultivated. In the early 1970s one hectare of arable land supported an average of 2.6 persons; by 2000 one hectare will have to support 4 persons. Because of this tightening land constraint, food production is not likely to increase fast enough to meet rising demands unless world agriculture becomes significantly more dependent on petroleum and petroleum-related inputs. Increased petroleum dependence also has implications for the cost of food production. After decades of generally falling prices, the real price of food is projected to increase 95 percent over the 1970-2000 period, in significant part as a result of increased petroleum dependence. If energy prices in fact rise more rapidly than the projections anticipate, then the effect on food prices could be still more marked.

On the average, world food production is projected to increase more rapidly than world population, with average per capita consumption increasing about 15 percent between 1970 and 2000. Per capita consumption in the industrialized nations is projected to rise 21 percent from 1970 levels, with increases of from 40 to more than 50 percent in Japan, Eastern Europe, and the U.S.S.R., and 28 percent in the United States. In the LDCs, however, rising food output will barely keep ahead of population growth.

An increase of 9 percent in per capita food consumption is projected for the LDCs as a whole, but with enormous variations among regions and nations. The great populous countries of South Asia — expected to contain 1.3 billion people by 2000 — improve hardly at all, nor do large areas of low-income North Africa and the Middle East. Per

capita consumption in the sub-Saharan African LDCs will actually decline, according to the projections. The LDCs showing the greatest per
capita growth (increases of about 25 percent) are concentrated in Latin
America and East Asia. . . .

[LDC Diets]

The outlook for improved diets for the poorest people in the poorest
LDCs is sobering. In the 1970s, consumption of calories in the LDCs
averaged only 94 percent of the minimum requirements set by the
U.N. Food and Agriculture Organization (FAO). Moreover, income and
food distribution within individual LDCs is so skewed that national
average caloric consumption generally must be 10-20 percent above minimum levels before the poorest are likely to be able to afford a diet
that meets the FAO minimum standard. Latin America is the only
major LDC region where average caloric consumption is projected to
be 20 percent or more above the FAO minimum standard in the year
2000. In the other LDC regions — South, East, and Southeast Asia,
poor areas of North Africa and the Middle East, and especially Central
Africa, where a calamitous drop in food per capita is projected —
the quantity of food available to the poorest groups of people will
simply be insufficient to permit children to reach normal body weight
and intelligence and to permit normal activity and good health in adults.
Consumption in the LDCs of central Africa is projected to be more
than 20 percent below the FAO minimum standard, assuming no recurrence of severe drought. In South Asia (primarily India, Pakistan,
and Bangladesh), average caloric intake is projected to remain below
the FAO minimum standard, although increasing slightly — from 12
percent below the FAO standard in the mid-1970s to about 3 percent
below the standard in 2000. In East Asia, Southeast Asia, and affluent
areas of North Africa and the Middle East, average per capita caloric
intakes are projected to be 6-17 percent above FAO minimum requirement
levels, but because the great majority of people in these regions are
extremely poor, they will almost certainly continue to eat less than
the minimum. The World Bank has estimated that the number of
malnourished people in LDCs could rise from 400-600 million in the
mid-1970s to 1.3 billion in 2000.

The projected food situation has many implications for food assistance
and trade. In the developing world, the need for imported food is expected
to grow. The most prosperous LDCs will turn increasingly to the world
commercial markets. In the poorest countries, which lack the wherewithal
to buy food, requirements for international food assistance will expand.
LDC exporters (especially Argentina and Thailand) are projected to
enlarge food production for export because of their cost advantage over
countries dependent on energy-intensive inputs. LDC grain-exporting
countries, which accounted for only a little more than 10 percent of

the world grain market in 1975, are projected to capture more than 20 percent of the market by 2000. The United States is expected to continue its role as the world's principal food exporter. Moreover, as the year 2000 approaches and more marginal, weather-sensitive lands are brought into production around the world, the United States is likely to become even more of a residual world supplier than today; that is, U.S. producers will be responding to widening, weather-related swings in world production and foreign demand.

Revised and updated food projections would reflect reduced estimates of future yields, increased pressure on the agricultural resource base, and several changes in national food policies.

[Farmers' Costs]

Farmers' costs of raising — and even maintaining — yields have increased rapidly in recent years. The costs of energy-intensive, yield-enhancing inputs — fertilizer, pesticides, and fuels — have risen very rapidly throughout the world, and where these inputs are heavily used, increased applications are bringing diminishing returns. In the United States, the real cost of producing food increased roughly 10 percent in both 1978 and 1979. Other industrialized countries have experienced comparable production cost increases. Cost increases in the LDCs appear to be lower, but are still 2-3 times the annual increases of the 1960s and early 1970s. While there have been significant improvements recently in the yields of selected crops, the diminishing returns and rapidly rising costs of yield-enhancing inputs suggest that yields overall will increase more slowly than projected.

Since the food projections were made, there have been several important shifts in national food and agricultural policy concerns. In most in-dustrialized countries, concern with protecting agricultural resources, especially soils, has increased as the resource implications of sustained production of record quantities of food here become more apparent. Debate on the 1981 U.S. farm bill, for example, will certainly include more consideration of "exporting top soil" than was foreseeable at the time the Global 2000 Study's food projections were made. The heightened concern for protection of agricultural resources is leading to a search for policies that encourage improved resource management practices. Still further pressure on the resource base can be expected, however, due to rising industrial demand for grain, especially for fermentation into alcohol-based fuels. Accelerated erosion, loss of natural soil fertility and other deterioration of the agricultural resource base may have more effect in the coming years than is indicated in the Global 2000 food projections.

In the LDCs, many governments are attempting to accelerate in-vestment in food production capacity. This policy emphasis offers im-portant long-term benefits. Some LDC governments are intervening more frequently in domestic food markets to keep food prices low, but often at the cost of low rural incomes and slowed development of agricultural production capacity.

Worldwide, the use of yield-enhancing inputs is likely to be less, and soil deterioration greater, than expected. As a result, revised food projections would show a tighter food future — somewhat less production and somewhat higher prices — than indicated in the Global 2000 projections.

Fisheries

Fish is an important component of the world's diet and has sometimes been put forth as a possible partial solution to world food shortages. Unfortunately, the world harvest of fish is expected to rise little, if at all, by the year 2000. The world catch of naturally produced fish leveled off in the 1970s at about 70 million metric tons a year (60 million metric tons for marine fisheries, 10 million metric tons for freshwater species). Harvests of traditional fisheries are not likely to increased on a sustained basis, and indeed to maintain them will take good management and improved protection of the marine environment. Some potential for greater harvests comes from aquaculture and from nontraditional marine species, such as Antarctic krill, that are little used at present for direct human consumption.

Traditional freshwater and marine species might be augmented in some areas by means of aquaculture. The 1976 FAO World Conference on Aquaculture concluded that a five- to tenfold increase in production from aquaculture would be possible by 2000, given adequate financial and technical support. (Aquaculture contributed an estimated 6 million metric tons to the world's total catch in 1975.) However, limited investment and technical support, as well as increasing pollution of freshwater ponds and coastal water, are likely to be a serious impediment to such growth.

While fish is not a solution to the world needs for calories, fish does provide an important source of protein. The 70 million metric tons caught and raised in 1975 is roughly equivalent to 14 million tons of protein, enough to supply 27 percent of the minimum protein requirements of 4 billion people. (Actually since more than one-third of the fish harvest is used for animal feed, not food for humans, the contribution of fish to human needs for protein is lower than these figures suggest.) A harvest of about 115 million metric tons would be required to supply 27 percent of the protein needs of 6.35 billion people in 2000. Even assuming that the catch of marine and freshwater fish rises to the unlikely level of 100 million metric tons annually, and that yields from aquaculture double, rising to 12 million tons, the hypothetical total of 112 metric tons would not provide as much protein per capita as the catch of the mid-1970s. Thus, on a per capita basis, fish may well contribute less to the world's nutrition in 2000 than today.

Updated fisheries projections would show little change from the Global 2000 Study projections. FAO fisheries statistics are now available for 1978 and show a world catch of 72.4 million metric tons. (The FAO statistics for the 1970-78 period have been revised downward somewhat to reflect improved data on the catch of the People's Republic of China.) While there has been some slight recovery of the anchovy and menhaden fisheries, traditional species continue to show signs of heavy pressure. As indicated in the Global 2000 projections, the catch of nontraditional species is filling in to some extent. Perhaps the biggest change in updated fisheries projections would stem from a careful analysis of the effects of the large increase in oil prices that occurred in 1979. Scattered observations suggest that fishing fleets throughout the world are being adversely affected except where governments are keeping oil prices to fishing boats artificially low.

Forests

If present trends continue, both forest cover and growing stocks of commercial-size wood in the less developed regions (Latin America, Africa, Asia, and Oceania) will decline 40 percent by 2000. In the industrialized regions (Europe, the U.S.S.R., North America, Japan, Australia, New Zealand) forests will decline only 0.5 percent and growing stock about 5 percent. Growing stock per capita is expected to decline 47 percent worldwide and 63 percent in LDCs. . . .

Deforestation is projected to continue until about 2020, when the total world forest area will stabilize at about 1.8 billion hectares. Most of the loss will occur in the tropical forests of the developing world. About 1.45 billion hectares of forest in the industrialized nations has already stabilized and about 0.37 billion hectares of forest in the LDCs is physically or economically inaccessible. By 2020, virtually all of the physically accessible forest in the LDCs is expected to have been cut.

The real prices of wood products — fuelwood, sawn lumber, wood panels, paper, wood-based chemicals, and so on — are expected to rise considerably as GNP (and thus also demand) rises and world supplies tighten. In the industrialized nations, the effects may be disruptive, but not catastrophic. In the less developed countries, however, 90 percent of wood consumption goes for cooking and heating, and wood is a necessity of life. Loss of woodlands will force people in many LDCs to pay steeply rising prices for fuelwood and charcoal or to spend much more effort collecting wood — or else to do without.

Updated forest projections would present much the same picture as the Global 2000 Study projections. The rapid increase in the price of crude oil will probably limit the penetration of kerosene sales into areas now depending on fuelwood and dung and, as a result, demand for fuelwood may be somewhat higher than expected. Some replanting of cut tropical areas is occurring, but only at low rates similar to those assumed in the Global 2000 Study projections. Perhaps the most encouraging developments are those associated with heightened international awareness of the seriousness of current trends in world forests.

Water

The Global 2000 Study population, GNP, and resource projections all imply rapidly increasing demands for fresh water. Increases of at least 200-300 percent in world water withdrawals are expected over the 1975-2000 period. By far the largest part of the increase is for irrigation. The United Nations has estimated that water needed for irrigation, which accounted for 70 percent of human uses of water in 1967, would double by 2000. Moreover, irrigation is a highly consumptive use, that is, much of the water withdrawn for this purpose is not available for immediate reuse because it evaporates, is transpired by plants, or becomes salinated.

Regional water shortages and deterioration of water quality, already serious in many parts of the world, are likely to become worse by 2000.... [P]opulation growth alone will cause demands for water at least to double relative to 1971 in nearly half the countries of the world. Still greater increases would be needed to improve standards of living.

Much of the increased demand for water will be in the LDCs of Africa, South Asia, the Middle East, and Latin America, where in many areas fresh water for human consumption and irrigation is already in short supply. Although the data are sketchy, it is known that several nations in these areas will be approaching their maximum developable water supply by 2000, and that it will be quite expensive to develop the water remaining. Moreover, many LDCs will also suffer destabilization of water supplies following extensive loss of forests. In the industrialized countries competition among different uses of water — for increasing food production, new energy systems (such as production of synthetic fuels from coal and shale), increasing power generation, expanding food production, and increasing needs of other industry — will aggravate water shortages in many areas.

Updated water projections would present essentially the same picture. The only significant change that has occurred since the projections were developed is that the price of energy (especially oil) has increased markedly. Increased energy costs will adversely affect the economics of many water development projects, and may reduce the amount of water available for a variety of uses. Irrigation, which usually requires large amounts of energy for pumping, may be particularly affected.

Nonfuel Minerals

The trends for nonfuel minerals, like those for the other resources considered in the Global 2000 Study, show steady increases in demand

and consumption. The global demand for and consumption of most major nonfuel mineral commodities is projected to increase 3-5 percent annually, slightly more than doubling by 2000. Consumption of all major steelmaking mineral commodities is projected to increase at least 3 percent annually. Consumption of all mineral commodities for fertilizer production is projected to grow at more than 3 percent annually, with consumption of phosphate rock growing at 5.2 percent per year — the highest growth rate projected for any of the major nonfuel mineral commodities. The nonferrous metals show widely varying projected growth rates; the growth rate for aluminum, 4.3 percent per year, is the largest.

The projections suggest that the LDC's share of nonfuel mineral use will increase only modestly. Over the 1971-75 period, Latin America, Africa, and Asia used 7 percent of the world's aluminum production, 9 percent of the copper, and 12 percent of the iron ore. The three-quarters of the world's population living in these regions in 2000 are projected to use only 8 percent of aluminum production, 13 percent of copper production, and 17 percent of iron ore production. The one-quarter of the world's population that inhabits industrial countries is projected to continue absorbing more than three-fourths of the world's nonfuel minerals production. . . .

The projections point to no mineral exhaustion problems but . . . further discoveries and investments will be needed to maintain reserves and production of several mineral commodities at desirable levels. In most cases, however, the resource potential is still large . . . especially for low grade ores.

Updated nonfuel minerals projections would need to give further attention to two factors affecting investment in mining. One is the shift over the past decade in investment in extraction and processing away from the developing countries toward industrialized countries (although this trend may now be reversing). The other factor is the rapid increase in energy prices. Production of many nonfuel minerals is highly energy-intensive, and the recent and projected increases in oil prices can be expected to slow the expansion of these mineral supplies.

Energy

The Global 2000 Study's energy projections show no early relief from the world's energy problems. The projections point out that petroleum production capacity is not increasing as rapidly as demand. Furthermore, the rate at which petroleum reserves are being added per unit of exploratory effort appears to be falling. Engineering and geological considerations suggest that world petroleum production will peak before the end of the century. Political and economic decisions in the OPEC countries could cause oil production to level off even before technological constraints come into play. A world transition away from petroleum dependence must take place, but there is still much uncertainty as to how this transition will occur. In the face of this uncertainty, it was not possible at the time the Global 2000 energy projections were made — late 1977 — for the Department of Energy (DOE) to develop meaningful energy projections beyond 1990. Updated DOE analyses, discussed at the end of this section, extend the global energy projections available from the U.S. Government to 1995.

[Increases in Demand]

DOE projections prepared for the Study show large increases in demand for all commercial sources over the 1975-90 period. . . . World energy demand is projected to increase 58 percent, reaching 384 quads (quadrillion British thermal units) by 1990. Nuclear and hydro sources (primarily nuclear) increase most rapidly (226 percent by 1990), followed by oil (58 percent), natural gas (43 percent), and coal (13 percent). Oil is projected to remain the world's leading energy source, providing 46-47 percent of the world's total energy through 1990, assuming that the real price of oil on the international market increases 65 percent over the 1975-90 period. The energy projections indicate that there is considerable potential for reductions in energy consumption.

Per capita energy consumption is projected to increase everywhere. The largest increase — 72 percent over the 1975-90 period — is in industrialized countries other than the United States. The smallest increase, 12 percent, is in the centrally planned economies of Eastern Europe. The percentage increases for the United States and for the LDCs are the same — 27 percent — but actual per capita energy consumption is very different. By 2000, U.S. per capita energy consumption is projected to be about 422 million Btu (British thermal units) annually. In the LDCs, it will be only 14 million Btu, up from 11 million in 1975. . . .

[Fuelwood]

While prices for oil and other commercial energy sources are rising, fuelwood — the poor person's oil — is expected to become far less available than it is today. The FAO has estimated that the demand for fuelwood in LDCs will increase at 2.2 percent per year, leading to local fuelwood shortages in 1994 totaling 650 million cubic meters — approximately 25 percent of the projected need. Scarcities are now local but expanding. In the arid Sahel of Africa, fuelwood gathering has become a full-time job requiring in some places 360 person-days of work per household each year. When demand is concentrated in cities, surrounding areas have already become barren for considerable distances — 50 to 100 kilometers in some places. Urban families, too far from collectible wood, spend 20 to 30 percent of their income on wood in some West African cities.

The projected shortfall of fuelwood implies that fuel consumption for essential uses will be reduced, deforestation expanded, wood prices increased, and growing amounts of dung and crop residues shifted from the field to the cooking fire. No explicit projections of dung and crop residue combustion could be made for the Study, but it is known that a shift toward burning these organic materials is already well advanced in the Himalayan hills, in the treeless Ganges plain of India, in other parts of Asia, and in the Andean region of South America. The FAO reports that in 1970 India burned 68 million tons of cow dung and 39 million tons of vegetable waste, accounting for roughly a third of the nation's total noncommercial energy consumption that year. Worldwide, an estimated 150-400 million tons of dung are burned annually for fuel.

Updated energy projections have been developed by the Department of Energy based on new price scenarios that include the rapid 1979 increase in the price of crude oil. The new price scenarios are not markedly different from the earlier estimates for the 1990s. The new medium-scenario price for 1995 is $40 per barrel (in 1979 dollars), which is about 10 percent higher than the $36 price (1979 dollars) implied by the earlier scenario. However, the prices for the early 1980s are almost 100 percent higher than those in the projections made by DOE in late 1977 for the Study. The sudden large increase in oil prices of 1979 is likely to have a more disruptive effect on other sectors than would the gradual increase assumed in the Global 2000 Study projections.

DOE's new projections differ in several ways from those reported in this Study. Using the higher prices, additional data, and a modified model, DOE is now able to project supply and demand for an additional five years, to 1995. Demand is projected to be lower because of the higher prices and also because of reduced estimates of economic growth. Coal is projected to provide a somewhat larger share of the total energy supply. The nuclear projections for the OECD countries are lower, reflecting revised estimates of the speed at which new nuclear plants will be built. Updated estimates of OPEC maximum production are lower than earlier estimates, reflecting trends toward resource conservation by the OPEC nations. The higher oil prices will encourage the adoption of alternative fuels and technologies, including solar technology and conservation measures.

ENVIRONMENTAL CONSEQUENCES

The population, income, and resource projections all imply significant consequences for the quality of the world environment. Virtually every aspect of the earth's ecosystems and resource base will be affected.

Impacts on Agriculture

Perhaps the most serious environmental development will be an accelerating deterioration and loss of the resources essential for agriculture. This overall development includes soil erosion; loss of nutrients and compaction of soils; increasing salinization of both irrigated land and water used for irrigation; loss of high-quality cropland to urban development; crop damage due to increasing air and water pollution; extinction of local and wild crop strains needed by plant breeders for improving cultivated varieties; and more frequent and more severe regional water shortages — especially where energy and industrial developments compete for water supplies, or where forest losses are heavy and the earth can no longer absorb, store, and regulate the discharge of water.

Deterioration of soils is occurring rapidly in LDCs, with the spread of desert-like conditions in drier regions, and heavy erosion in more humid areas. Present global losses to desertification are estimated at around 6 million hectares a year (an area about the size of Maine), including 3.2 million hectares of rangeland, 2.5 million hectares of rainfed cropland, and 125 thousand hectares of irrigated farmland. Desertification does not necessarily mean the creation of Sahara-like sand deserts, but rather it includes a variety of ecological changes that destroy the cover of vegetation and fertile soil in the earth's drier regions, rendering the land useless for range or crops. Principal direct causes are overgrazing, destructive cropping practices, and use of woody plants for fuel.

[Acceleration of Desertification]

At presently estimated rates of desertification, the world's desert areas (now some 800 million hectares) would expand almost 20 percent by 2000. But there is reason to expect that losses to desertification will accelerate, as increasing numbers of people in the world's drier regions put more pressures on the land to meet their needs for livestock range, cropland, and fuelwood. The United Nations has identified about 2 billion hectares of lands ... where the risk of desertification is "high" or "very high." These lands at risk total about two and one-half times the area now classified as desert.

Although soil loss and deterioration are especially serious in many LDCs, they are also affecting agricultural prospects in industrialized nations. Present rates of soil loss in many industrialized nations cannot be sustained without serious implications for crop production. In the United States, for example, the Soil Conservation Service, looking at wind and water erosion of U.S. soils, has concluded that to sustain crop production indefinitely at even present levels, soil losses must be cut in half.

The outlook for making such gains in the United States and elsewhere is not good. The food and forestry projections imply increasing pressures on soils throughout the world. Losses due to improper irrigation, reduced fallow periods, cultivation of steep and marginal lands, and reduced vegetative cover can be expected to accelerate, especially in North and Central Africa, the humid and high-altitude portions of Latin America, and much of South Asia. In addition, the increased burning of dung and crop wastes for domestic fuel will deprive the soil of nutrients and degrade the soil's ability to hold moisture by reducing its organic content. For the world's poor, these organic materials are often the only source of the nutrients needed to maintain the productivity of farmlands. It is the poorest people — those least able to afford chemical fertilizers — who are being forced to burn their organic fertilizers. These nutrients will be urgently needed for food production in the years ahead, since by 2000 the world's croplands will have to feed half again as many people as in 1975. In the industrialized regions, increasing use of chemical fertilizers, high-yield plant varieties, irrigation water, and herbicides and pesticides have so far compensated for basic declines in soil conditions. However, heavy dependence on chemical fertilizers also leads to losses of soil organic matter, reducing the capacity of the soil to retain moisture.

[Irrigation Problems]

Damage and loss of irrigated lands are especially significant because these lands have yields far above average. Furthermore, as the amount of arable land per capita declines over the next two decades, irrigated lands will be counted upon increasingly to raise per capita food availability. As of 1975, 230 million hectares — 15 percent of the world's arable area — were being irrigated; an additional 50 million hectares are expected to be irrigated by 1990. Unfortunately there is great difficulty in maintaining the productivity of irrigated lands. About half of the world's irrigated land has already been damaged to some degree by salinity, alkalinity, and waterlogging, and much of the additional land expected to be irrigated by 1990 is highly vulnerable to irrigation-related damage.

Environmental problems of irrigation exist in industrialized countries (for example, in the San Joaquin Valley in California) as well as in LDCs (as in Pakistan, where three-quarters of the irrigated lands are damaged). It is possible, but slow and costly, to restore damaged lands. Prevention requires careful consideration of soils and attention to drainage, maintenance, and appropriate water-saving designs.

Loss of good cropland to urban encroachment is another problem affecting all countries. Cities and industries are often located on a nation's best agricultural land — rich, well-watered alluvial soils in gently sloping river valleys. In the industrialized countries that are members of the OECD, the amount of land devoted to urban uses has been increasing twice as fast as population. The limited data available for LDCs point to similar trends. In Egypt, for example, despite efforts to open new lands to agriculture, the total area of irrigated farmland has remained almost unchanged in the past two decades. As fast as additional acres are irrigated with water from the Aswan Dam, old producing lands on the Nile are converted to urban uses.

[Yield-Enhancing Inputs]

The rising yields assumed by the Global 2000 food projections depend on wider adoption of existing high-yield agricultural technology and on accelerating use of fertilizers, irrigation, pesticides, and herbicides. These yield-enhancing inputs, projected to more than double in use worldwide and to quadruple in LDCs, are heavily dependent on fossil fuels. Even now, a rapid escalation of fossil fuel prices or a sudden interruption of supply could severely disturb world agricultural production, raise food prices, and deprive larger numbers of people of adequate food. As agriculture becomes still more dependent on energy-intensive inputs, the potential for disruption will be even greater.

Accelerating use of pesticides is expected to raise crop yields quickly and substantially, especially in LDCs. Yet, many of these chemicals produce a wide range of serious environmental consequences, some of which adversely affect agricultural production. Destruction of pest predator populations and the increasing resistance of pests to heavily used pesticides have already proved to be significant agricultural problems. On California farms, for example, 17 of 25 major agricultural pests are now resistant to one or more types of pesticides, and the populations of pest predators have been severely reduced. Many millions of dollars in crop damage are now caused annually in California by resistant pests whose natural predators have been destroyed.

Crop yields are expected to be increased significantly by much wider use of high-yield strains of grains. Unfortunately, large monocultures of genetically identical crops pose increased risks of catastrophic loss from insect attacks or crop epidemics. The corn blight that struck the U.S. corn belt in 1970 provided a clear illustration of the vulnerability of genetically identical monocultures.

Impacts on Water Resources

The quality of the world's water resources is virtually certain to suffer from the changes taking place between now and the year 2000. Water pollution from heavy application of pesticides will cause increasing difficulties. In the industrialized countries, shifts from widespread use of long-lived chemicals such as DDT are now underway, but in the LDCs — where the largest increases in agricultural chemical use is projected — it is likely that the persistent pesticides will continue to be used. Pesticide use in LDCs is expected to at least quadruple over the 1975-2000 period (a sixfold increase is possible if recent rates of increase continue). Pollution from the persistent pesticides in irrigation canals, ponds, and rice paddies is already a worrisome problem. Farmers in some parts of Asia are reluctant to stock paddies and ponds because fish are being killed by pesticides. This means a serious loss of high-quality protein for the diets of rural families.

[Water Salinity Problems]

In addition to the potential impacts on soils discussed above, irrigation adversely affects water quality by adding salt to the water returning to streams and rivers. Downstream from extensive irrigation projects the water may become too saline for further use, unless expensive desalinization measures are undertaken. As the use of water for irrigation increases, water salinity problems are certain to increase as well.

Water pollution in LDCs is likely to worsen as the urban population soars and industry expands. Already the waters below many LDC cities are heavily polluted with sewage and wastes from pulp and paper mills, tanneries, slaughterhouses, oil refineries, and chemical plants.

River basin development that combines flood control, generation of electricity, and irrigation is likely to increase in many less developed regions, where most of the world's untapped hydropower potential lies. While providing many benefits, large-scale dams and irrigation projects can also cause highly adverse changes in both freshwater and coastal ecosystems, creating health problems (including schistosomiasis, river blindness, malaria), inundating valuable lands, and displacing populations. In addition, if erosion in the watersheds of these projects is not controlled, siltation and buildup of sediments may greatly reduce the useful life of the projects.

[Destruction of Coastal Ecosystems]

Virtually all of the Global 2000 Study's projections point to increasing destruction or pollution of coastal ecosystems, a resource on which the commercially important fisheries of the world depend heavily. It is estimated that 60-80 percent of commercially valuable marine fishery species use estuaries, salt marshes, or mangrove swamps for habitat at some point in their life cycle. Reef habitats also provide food and shelter for large numbers of fish and invertebrate species. Rapidly expanding cities and industry are likely to claim coastal wetland areas for development; and increasing coastal pollution from agriculture, industry, logging, water resources development, energy systems, and coastal communities is anticipated in many areas.

Impacts of Forest Losses

The projected rapid, widespread loss of tropical forests will have severe adverse effects on water and other resources. Deforestation — especially in South Asia, the Amazon basin, and central Africa — will destabilize water flows, leading to siltation of streams, reservoirs behind hydroelectric dams, and irrigation works, to depletion of ground water, to intensified flooding, and to aggravated water shortages during dry periods. In South and Southeast Asia approximately one billion people live in heavily farmed alluvial basins and valleys that depend on forested mountain watersheds for their water. If present trends continue, forests in these regions will be reduced by about half in 2000, and erosion, siltation, and erratic streamflows will seriously affect food production.

In many tropical forests, the soils, land forms, temperatures, patterns of rainfall, and distribution of nutrients are in precarious balance. When these forests are disturbed by extensive cutting, neither trees nor productive grasses will grow again. Even in less fragile tropical forests, the great diversity of species is lost after extensive cutting.

Impacts on the World's Atmosphere and Climate

Among the emerging environmental stresses are some that affect the chemical and physical nature of the atmosphere. Several are recognized as problems; others are more conjectural but nevertheless of concern.

Quantitative projections of urban air quality around the world are not possible with the data and models now available, but further pollution in LDCs and some industrial nations is virtually certain to occur under present policies and practices. In LDC cities, industrial growth projected for the next 20 years is likely to worsen air quality. Even now, observations in scattered LDC cities show levels of sulfur dioxide, particulates, nitrogen dioxide, and carbon monoxide far above levels considered safe by the World Health Organization. In some cities, such as Bombay and Caracas, recent rapid increases in the numbers of cars and trucks have aggravated air pollution.

Despite recent progress in reducing various types of air pollution in many industrialized countries, air quality there is likely to worsen as increased amounts of fossil fuels, especially coal, are burned. Emissions of sulfur and nitrogen oxides are particularly troubling because they combine with water vapor in the atmosphere to form acid rain or produce other acid deposition. In large areas of Norway, Sweden, southern Canada, and the eastern United States, the pH value of rainfall has dropped from 5.7 to below 4.5, well into the acidic range. Also, rainfall has almost certainly become more acid in parts of Germany, Eastern Europe, and the U.S.S.R., although available data are incomplete.

[Acid Rain Effects]

The effects of acid rain are not yet fully understood, but damage has already been observed in lakes, forests, soils, crops, nitrogen-fixing plants, and building materials. Damage to lakes has been studied most extensively. For example, of 1,500 lakes in southern Norway with a pH below 4.3, 70 percent had no fish. Similar damage has been observed in the Adirondack Mountains of New York and in parts of Canada. River fish are also severely affected. In the last 20 years, first salmon and then trout disappeared in many Norwegian rivers as acidity increased.

Another environmental problem related to the combustion of fossil fuels (and perhaps also to the global loss of forests and soil humus) is the increasing concentration of carbon dioxide in the earth's atmosphere. Rising CO_2 concentrations are of concern because of their potential for causing a warming of the earth. Scientific opinion differs on the possible consequences, but a widely held view is that highly disruptive effects on world agriculture could occur before the middle of the twenty-first century. The CO_2 content of the world's atmosphere has increased about 15 percent in the last century and by 2000 is expected to be nearly a third higher than preindustrial levels. If the projected rates of increase in fossil fuel combustion (about 2 percent per year) were to continue, a doubling of the CO_2 content of the atmosphere could be expected after the middle of the next century; and if deforestation substantially reduces tropical forests (as projected), a doubling of atmosphere CO_2 could occur sooner. The result could be significant alterations of precipitation patterns around the world, and a 2°-3°C rise in temperatures in the middle latitudes of the earth. Agriculture and other human endeavors would have great difficulty in adapting to such large, rapid changes in climate. Even a 1°C increase in average global temperatures would make the earth's climate warmer than it has been any time in the last 1,000 years.

A carbon dioxide-induced temperature rise is expected to be 3 or 4 times greater at the poles than in the middle latitudes. An increase of 5°-10°C in polar temperatures could eventually lead to the melting of the Greenland and Antarctic ice caps and a gradual rise in sea level, forcing abandonment of many coastal cities.

[Ozone Layer Threatened]

Ozone is another major concern. The stratospheric ozone layer protects the earth from damaging ultraviolet light. However, the ozone layer is being threatened by chlorofluorocarbon emissions from aerosol cans and refrigeration equipment, by nitrous oxide (N_2O) emissions from the denitrification of both organic and inorganic nitrogen fertilizers, and possibly by the effects of high-altitude aircraft flights. Only the United States and a few other countries have made serious efforts to date to control the use of aerosol cans. Refrigerants and nitrogen fertilizers present even more difficult challenges. The most widely discussed effect of ozone depletion and the resulting increase in ultraviolet light is an increased incidence of skin cancer, but damage to food crops would also be significant and might actually prove to be the most serious ozone related problem.

Impacts of Nuclear Energy

The problems presented by the projected production of increasing amounts of nuclear power are different from but no less serious than those related to fossil fuel combustion. The risk of radioactive contamination of the environment due to nuclear power reactor accidents will be increased, as will the potential for proliferation of nuclear weapons. No nation has yet conducted a demonstration program for the satisfactory disposal of radioactive wastes, and the amount of wastes is increasing rapidly. Several hundred thousand tons of highly radioactive spent nuclear fuel will be generated over the lifetimes of the nuclear plants likely to be constructed through the year 2000. In addition, nuclear power production will create millions of cubic meters of low-level radioactive wastes, and uranium mining and processing will lead to the production of hundreds of millions of tons of low-level radioactive tailings. It has not yet been demonstrated that all of these high- and low-level wastes from nuclear power production can be safely stored and disposed of without incident. Some of the by-products of reactors, it should be noted, have half-lives approximately five times as long as the period of recorded history.

Species Extinctions

Finally, the world faces an urgent problem of loss of plant and animal genetic resources. An estimate prepared for the Global 2000 Study suggests that between half a million and 2 million species — 15 to 20 percent of all species on earth — could be extinguished by 2000, mainly because of loss of wild habitat but also in part because of pollution. Extinction of species on this scale is without precedent in human history.

One-half to two-thirds of the extinctions projected to occur by 2000 will result from the clearing or degradation of tropical forests. Insect, other invertebrate, and plant species — many of them unclassified and unexamined by scientists — will account for most of the losses. The potential value of this genetic reservoir is immense. If preserved and carefully managed, tropical forest species could be a sustainable source of new foods (especially nuts and fruits), pharmaceutical chemicals, natural predators of pests, building materials, speciality woods, fuel, and so on. Even careful husbandry of the remaining biotic resources of the tropics cannot compensate for the swift, massive losses that are to be expected if present trends continue.

Current trends also threaten freshwater and marine species. Physical alterations — damming, channelization, siltation — and pollution by salts, acid rain, pesticides, and other toxic chemicals are profoundly affecting freshwater ecosystems throughout the world. At present 274 freshwater vertebrate taxa are threatened with extinction, and by the year 2000 many may have been lost.

Some of the most important genetic losses will involve the extinction not of species but of subspecies and varieties of cereal grains. Four-fifths of the world's food supplies are derived from less than two dozen plant and animal species. Wild and local domestic strains are needed for breeding resistance to pests and pathogens into the high-yield varieties now widely used. These varietal stocks are rapidly diminishing as marginal wild lands are brought into cultivation. Local domesticated varieties, often uniquely suited to local conditions, are also being lost as higher-yield varieties displace them. And the increasing practice of monoculture of a few strains — which makes crops more vulnerable to disease epidemics or plagues of pests — is occurring at the same time that the genetic resources to resist such disasters are being lost.

Entering the Twenty-First Century

The preceding sections have presented individually the many projections made by U.S. Government agencies for the Global 2000 Study. How are these projections to be interpreted collectively? What do they imply about the world's entry into the twenty-first century?

The world in 2000 will be different from the world today in important ways. There will be more people. For every two persons on the earth in 1975 there will be three in 2000. The number of poor will have increased. Four-fifths of the world's population will live in less developed countries. Furthermore, in terms of persons per year added to the world, population growth will be 40 percent *higher* in 2000 than in 1975.

The gap between the richest and the poorest will have increased. By every measure of material welfare the study provides — per capita GNP and consumption of food, energy, and minerals — the gap will widen. For example, the gap between the GNP per capita in the LDCs and the industrialized countries is projected to grow from about $4,000 in 1975 to about $7,900 in 2000. Great disparities within countries are also expected to continue.

[FEWER RESOURCES]

There will be fewer resources to go around. While on a worldwide average there was about four-tenths of a hectare of arable land per person in 1975, there will be only about one-quarter hectare per person in 2000. ... By 2000 nearly 1,000 billion barrels of the world's total original petroleum resource of approximately 2,000 billion barrels will have been consumed. Over just the 1975-2000 period, the world's remaining petroleum resources per capita can be expected to decline by at least 50 percent. Over the same period world per capita water supplies will decline by 35 percent because of greater population alone; increasing competing demands will put further pressure on available water supplies. The world's per capita growing stock of wood is projected to be 47 percent lower in 2000 than in 1978.

The environment will have lost important life-supporting capabilities. By 2000, 40 percent of the forests still remaining in the LDCs in 1978 will have been razed. The atmospheric concentration of carbon dioxide will be nearly one-third higher than preindustrial levels. Soil erosion will have removed, on the average, several inches of soil from croplands all over the world. Desertification (including salinization) may have claimed a significant fraction of the world's rangeland and cropland. Over little more than two decades, 15-20 percent of the earth's total species of plants and animals will have become extinct — a loss of at least 500,000 species.

[HIGHER PRICES]

Prices will be higher. The price of many of the most vital resources is projected to rise in real terms — that is, over and above inflation. In order to meet projected demand, a 100 percent increase in the real price of food will be required. To keep energy demand in line with anticipated supplies, the real price of energy is assumed to rise more than 150 percent over the 1975-2000 period. Supplies of water, agricultural land, forest products, and many traditional marine fish species are projected to decline relative to growing demand at current prices, which suggests that real price rises will occur in these sectors, too. Collectively, the projections suggest that resource-based inflationary pressures will continue and intensify, especially in nations that are poor in resources or are rapidly depleting their resources.

The world will be more vulnerable both to natural disaster and to disruptions from human causes. Most nations are likely to be still more dependent on foreign sources of energy in 2000 than they are today. Food production will be more vulnerable to disruptions of fossil fuel energy supplies and to weather fluctuations as cultivation expands to more marginal areas. The loss of diverse germ plasm in local strains and wild progenitors of food crops, together with the increase of monoculture, could lead to greater risks of massive crop failures. Larger numbers of people will be vulnerable to higher food prices or even famine when adverse weather occurs. The world will be more vulnerable to the disruptive effects of war. The tensions that could lead to war will have multiplied. The potential for conflict over fresh water alone is underscored by the fact that out of 200 of the world's major river basins, 148 are shared by two countries and 52 are shared by three to ten countries. Long standing conflicts over shared rivers such as the Plata (Brazil, Argentina), Euphrates (Syria, Iraq), or Ganges (Bangladesh, India) could easily intensify.

[LOST OPPORTUNITIES]

Finally, it must be emphasized that if public policy continues generally unchanged the world will be different as a result of lost opportunities. The adverse effects of many of the trends discussed in this Study will not be fully evident until 2000 or later; yet the actions that are necessary to change the trends cannot be postponed without foreclosing important options. The opportunity to stabilize the world's population below 10 billion, for example, is slipping away; Robert McNamara, President of the World Bank, has noted that for every decade of delay in reaching replacement fertility, the world's ultimately stabilized population will be about 11 percent greater. Similar losses of opportunity accompany delayed perceptions or action in other areas. If energy policies and decisions are based on yesterday's (or even today's) oil prices, the opportunity to wisely invest scarce capital resources will be lost as a consequence of undervaluing conservation and efficiency. If agricultural research continues to focus on increasing yields through practices that are highly energy-intensive, both energy resources and the time needed to develop alternative practices will be lost.

The full effects of rising concentrations of carbon dioxide, depletion of stratospheric ozone, deterioration of soils, increasing introduction of complex persistent toxic chemicals into the environment, and massive extinction of species may not occur until well after 2000. Yet once such global environmental problems are in motion they are very difficult to reverse. In fact, few if any of the problems addressed in the Global 2000 Study are amenable to quick technological or policy fixes; rather, they are inextricably mixed with the world's most perplexing social and economic problems.

Perhaps the most troubling problems are those in which population growth and poverty lead to serious long-term declines in the productivity of renewable natural resource systems. In some areas the capacity of renewable resource systems to support human populations is already being seriously damaged by efforts of present populations to meet desperate immediate needs, and the damage threatens to become worse.

Examples of serious deterioration of the earth's most basic resources can already be found today in scattered places in all nations, including the industrialized countries and the better-endowed LDCs. For instance, erosion of agricultural soil and salinization of highly productive irrigated farmland is increasingly evident in the United States, and extensive deforestation, with more or less permanent soil degradation, has occurred in Brazil, Venezuela, and Colombia. But problems related to the decline of the earth's carrying capacity are most immediate, severe, and tragic in those regions of the earth containing the poorest LDCs.

Sub-Saharan Africa faces the problem of exhaustion of its resource base in an acute form. Many causes and effects have come together there to produce excessive demands on the environment, leading to expansion of the desert. Overgrazing, fuelwood gathering, and destructive cropping practices are the principal immediate causes of a series of transitions from open woodland, to scrub, to fragile semiarid range, to worthless weeds and bare earth. Matters are made worse when people are forced by scarcity of fuelwood to burn animal dung and crop wastes. The soil, deprived of organic matter, loses fertility and the ability to hold water — and the desert expands. In Bangladesh, Pakistan, and large parts of India, efforts by growing numbers of people to meet their basic needs are damaging the very cropland, pasture, forests, and water supplies on which they must depend for a livelihood. To restore the lands and soils would require decades — if not centuries — *after* the existing pressures on the land have diminished. But the pressures are growing, not diminishing.

[NO EASY SOLUTIONS]

There are no quick or easy solutions, particularly in those regions where population pressure is already leading to a reduction of the carrying capacity of the land. In such regions a complex of social and economic factors (including very low incomes, inequitable land tenure, limited or no educational opportunities, a lack of nonagricultural jobs, and economic pressures toward higher fertility) underlies the decline in the land's carrying capacity. Furthermore, it is generally believed that social and economic conditions must improve before fertility levels will decline to replacement levels. Thus a vicious circle of causality may be at work. Environmental deterioration caused by large populations creates living conditions that make reductions in fertility difficult to achieve; all the while, continuing population growth increases further the pressures on the environment and land.

The declines in carrying capacity already being observed in scattered areas around the world point to a phenomenon that could easily be much more widespread by 2000. In fact, the best evidence now available — even allowing for the many beneficial effects of technological developments and adoptions — suggests that by 2000 the world's human population may be within only a few generations of reaching the entire planet's carrying capacity.

[NATIONAL ACADEMY OF SCIENCES' REPORT]

The Global 2000 Study does not estimate the earth's carrying capacity, but it does provide a basis for evaluating an earlier estimate published in the U.S. National Academy of Sciences' report, *Resources and Man.* In this 1969 report, the Academy concluded that a world population of 10 billion "is close to (if not above) the maximum that an *intensively managed* world might hope to support with some degree of comfort and individual choice." The Academy also concluded that even with the sacrifice of individual freedom and choice, and even with chronic near starvation for the great majority, the human population of the world is unlikely to ever exceed 30 billion.

Nothing in the Global 2000 Study counters the Academy's conclusions. If anything, data gathered over the past decade suggest the Academy may have underestimated the extent of some problems, especially deforestation and the loss and deterioration of soils.

At present and projected growth rates, the world's population would rapidly approach the Academy's figures. If the fertility and mortality rates projected for 2000 were to continue unchanged into the twenty-first century, the world's population would reach 10 billion by 2030. Thus anyone with a present life expectancy of an additional 50 years could expect to see the world population reach 10 billion. This same rate of growth would produce a population of nearly 30 billion before the end of the twenty-first century.

Here it must be emphasized that, unlike most of the Global 2000 Study projections, the population projections assume extensive policy changes and developments to reduce fertility rates. Without the assumed policy changes, the projected rate of population growth would be still more rapid.

Unfortunately population growth may be slowed for reasons other than declining birth rates. As the world's populations exceed and reduce the land's carrying capacity in widening areas, the trends of the last century or two toward improved health and longer life may come to a halt. Hunger and disease may claim more lives — especially lives of babies and young children. More of those surviving infancy may be mentally and physically handicapped by childhood malnutrition.

The time for action to prevent this outcome is running out. Unless nations collectively and individually take bold and imaginative steps toward improved social and economic conditions, reduced fertility, better management of resources, and protection of the environment, the world must expect a troubled entry into the twenty-first century.

August

)

KENNEDY CONVENTION SPEECH

August 12, 1980

After failing in his attempt to deny the Democratic Party's nomination to President Carter, Sen. Edward M. Kennedy of Massachusetts delivered a dramatic speech to the Democratic National Convention Aug. 12 in which he called upon the party "not to forsake" its traditions and urged the delegates to unite and "march toward a Democratic victory in 1980."

Kennedy's speech to the convention in Madison Square Garden in New York City was the last in a series debating economic planks in the party platform. Although his bid for the nomination dissolved Aug. 11 after the delegates agreed to back a Carter-supported rule binding them to vote on the first nominating ballot for the candidate they were elected to represent, Kennedy neglected to endorse President Carter in his address. Indeed, he stressed his differences with the president over economic policy, asking the delegates to support platform planks instructing the Democratic Party to avoid attempts to stem inflation by increasing unemployment or raising interest rates. (Democratic platform, p. 711)

'The Soul of Our Party'

"Let us pledge," Kennedy declared, "that we will never misuse unemployment, high interest rates, and human misery as false weapons against inflation. Let us pledge that employment will be the first priority of our economic policy. Let us pledge that there will be security for all who are now at work. Let us pledge that there will be jobs for

all who are out of work — and we will not compromise on the issue of jobs."

These pledges, Kennedy continued, "have been the soul of our party across the generations. It is the glory and the greatness of our tradition to speak for those who have no voice, to remember those who are forgotten, to respond to the frustrations and fulfill the aspirations of all Americans seeking a better life in a better land."

Following the Kennedy speech — and the tumultous reception it received from the convention delegates — the Carter camp dropped its objections to all of Kennedy's proposed economic platform planks, except his call for a freeze on wages and prices.

Republican Strategy Derided

Kennedy unified the delegates with a sharp attack on the policies of the Republican nominee, Ronald Reagan. Reagan and the Republican Party, Kennedy said, had devised a strategy of appealing to voters by trying to appear concerned for the common man. Kennedy ridiculed the idea, citing various Reagan quotations and declaring that Reagan "is no friend" of labor, the cities, senior citizens or the environment.

Stressing the liberal economic themes that formed the centerpiece of his unsuccessful struggle for the Democratic nomination, Kennedy told the delegates: "Programs may sometimes become obsolete, but the ideal of fairness always endures. Circumstances may change, but the work of compassion must continue. It is surely correct that we cannot solve problems by throwing money at them; but it is also correct that we dare not throw out national problems on a scrap heap of inattention and indifference. The poor may be out of political fashion, but they are not without human needs. The middle class may be angry, but they have not lost the dream that all Americans can advance together."

Referring to his race for the nomination, Kennedy thanked his supporters and added, "We had our losses; but the pain of our defeats is far, far less than the pain of the people I have met. We have learned that it is important to take issues seriously, but never to take ourselves too seriously."

Kennedy's mention of his rival for the nomination, Jimmy Carter, came at the end of his speech. He said simply: "I congratulate President Carter on his victory here."

> *Following is the text of the speech Sen. Edward M. Kennedy of Massachusetts delivered Aug. 12, 1980, at the Democratic National Convention in New York City. (Boldface headings in brackets have been added by Congressional Quarterly to highlight to organization of the text.):*

Well, things worked out a little differently from the way I had planned, but I still love New York.

My fellow Democrats and my fellow Americans: I have come here tonight not to argue for a candidacy, but to affirm a cause.

I am asking you ... I am asking you to renew the commitment of the Democratic Party to economic justice. I am asking you to renew our commitment to a fair and lasting prosperity that can put America back to work.

This is the cause that brought me into the campaign and that sustained me for nine months, across a hundred thousand miles, in 40 different states. We had our losses; but the pain of our defeats is far, far less than the pain of the people that I have met. We have learned that it is important to take issues seriously, but never to take ourselves too seriously.

The serious issue before us tonight is the cause for which the Democratic Party has stood in its finest hours — the cause that keeps our party young — and makes it, in the second century of its age, the largest political party in this Republic and the longest lasting political party on this planet.

Our cause has been, since the days of Thomas Jefferson, the cause of the common man — and the common woman. Our commitment has been, since the days of Andrew Jackson, to all those he called "the humble members of society — the farmers, mechanics, and laborers." On this foundation, we have defined our values, refined our policies, and refreshed our faith.

Now I take the unusual step of carrying the cause and the commitment of my campaign personally to our national convention. I speak out of a deep sense of urgency about the anguish and anxiety I have seen across America. I speak out of a deep belief in the ideals of the Democratic Party, and in the potential of that party and of a president to make a difference. And I speak out of a deep trust in our capacity to proceed with boldness and a common vision that will feel and heal the suffering of our time — and the division of our party.

[Economic Plank]

The economic plank of this platform on its face concerns only material things; but is also a moral issue that I raise tonight. It has taken many forms over many years. In this campaign, and in this country that we seek to lead, the challenge in 1980 is to give our voice and our vote for these fundamental Democratic principles:

Let us pledge that we will never misuse unemployment, high interest rates, and human misery as false weapons against inflation.

Let us pledge that employment will be the first priority of our economic policy.

Let us pledge that there will be security for all those who are now at work. And let us pledge that there will be jobs for all who are out of work. And we will not compromise on the issue of jobs.

These are not simplistic pledges. Simply put, they are the heart of our tradition, and they have been the soul of our party across the generations. It is the glory and the greatness of our tradition to speak for those who have no voice, to remember those who are forgotten, to respond to the frustrations and fulfill the aspirations of all Americans seeking a better life in a better land.

We dare not forsake that tradition. We cannot let the great purposes of the Democratic Party become the bygone passages of history. We must not permit the Republicans to seize and run on the slogans of prosperity.

[Reagan's Stand on Issues]

We heard the orators at their convention all trying to talk like Democrats. They proved that even Republican nominees can quote Franklin Roosevelt to their own purpose. The Grand Old Party thinks it has found a great new trick. But 40 years ago, an earlier generation of Republicans attempted the same trick. And Franklin Roosevelt himself replied "Most Republican leaders ... have bitterly fought and blocked the forward surge of average men and women in their pursuit of happiness. Let us not be deluded that overnight those leaders have suddenly become the friends of average men and women.... You know," he continued, "very few of us are that gullible."

And four years later, when the Republicans tried that trick again, Franklin Roosevelt asked: "Can the Old Guard pass itself off as the New Deal? I think not. We have all seen many marvelous stunts in the circus — but no performing elephant could turn a handspring without falling flat on its back."

The 1980 Republican convention was awash with crocodile tears for our economic distress but it is by their long record and not their recent words that you shall know them.

The same Republicans who are talking about the crisis of unemployment have nominated a man who once said — and I quote: "Unemployment insurance is a prepaid vacation plan for freeloaders." And that nominee is no friend of labor.

The same Republicans who are talking about the problems of the inner cities have nominated a man who said — and I quote: "I have included in my morning and evening prayers every day the prayer that the federal government not bail out New York." And that nominee is no friend of this city and our great urban centers across this nation.

The same Republicans who are talking about security for the elderly have nominated a man who said just four years ago that participation in Social Security "should be made voluntary." And that nominee is no friend of the senior citizens of this nation.

The same Republicans who are talking about preserving the environment have nominated a man who last year made the preposterous statement, and I quote: "Eighty percent of our air pollution comes from plants and trees." And that nominee is no friend of the environment.

And the same Republicans who are invoking Franklin Roosevelt have nominated a man who said in 1976 — and these are his exact words: "Fascism was really the basis of the New Deal." And that nominee, whose name is Ronald Reagan, has no right to quote Franklin Delano Roosevelt.

[Democratic Values]

The great adventure which our opponents offer is a voyage into the past. Progress is our heritage, not theirs. What is right for us as Democrats is also the right way for Democrats to win.

The commitment I seek is not to outworn views, but to old values that will never wear out. Programs may sometimes become obsolete, but the ideal of fairness always endures. Circumstances may change, but the work of compassion must continue. It is surely correct that we cannot solve problems by throwing money at them; but it is also correct that we dare not throw out our national problems onto a scrap heap of inattention and indifference. The poor may be out of political fashion, but they are not without human needs. The middle-class may be angry, but they have not lost the dream that all Americans can advance together.

The demand of our people in 1980 is not for smaller government or bigger government, but for better government. Some say that government is always bad, and that spending for basic social programs is the root of our economic evils. But we reply: The present inflation and recession cost our economy $200 billion a year. We reply: Inflation and unemployment are the biggest spenders of all.

The task of leadership in 1980 is not to parade scapegoats or to seek refuge in reaction but to match our power to the possibilities of progress.

While others talked of free enterprise, it was the Democratic Party that acted — and we ended excessive regulation in the airline and trucking industries. And we restored competition to the marketplace. And I take some satisfaction that this deregulation was legislation that I sponsored and passed in the Congress of the United States.

As Democrats, we recognize that each generation of Americans has a rendezvous with a different reality. The answers of one generation become the questions of the next generation. But there is a guiding star in the American firmament. It is as old as the revolutionary belief that all people are created equal — and as clear as the contemporary condition of Liberty City and the South Bronx. Again and again, Democratic leaders have followed that star — and they have given new meaning to the old values of liberty and justice for all.

[Party of New Hope]

We are the party of the New Freedom, the New Deal, and the New Frontier. We have always been the party of hope. So this year, let us offer new hope — new hope to an America uncertain about the present, but unsurpassed in its potential for the future.

To all those who are idle in the cities and industries of America, let us provide new hope for the dignity of useful work. Democrats have always believed that a basic civil right of all Americans is the right to earn their own way. The party of the people must always be the party of full employment.

To all those who doubt the future of our economy, let us provide new hope for the reindustrialization of America. And let our vision reach beyond the next election or the next year to a new generation of prosperity. If we could rebuild Germany and Japan after World War II, then surely we can reindustrialize our own nation and revive our inner cities in the 1980s.

To all those who work hard for a living wage, let us provide new hope that the price of their employment shall not be an unsafe workplace and death at an earlier age.

To all those who inhabit our land, 'from California to the New York Island, from the Redwood Forest to the Gulfstream waters,' let us provide new hope that prosperity shall not be purchased by poisoning the air, the rivers and the natural resources that are the greatest gift of this continent. We must insist that our children and grandchildren shall inherit a land which they can truly call America the beautiful.

To all those who see the worth of their work and their savings taken by inflation, let us offer new hope for a stable economy. We must meet the pressures of the present by invoking the full power of government to master increasing prices. In candor, we must say that the federal budget can be balanced only by policies that bring us to a balanced prosperity of full employment and price restraint.

[Democratic Tax Reform]

And to all those overburdened by an unfair tax structure, let us provide new hope for real tax reform. Instead of shutting down classrooms, let us shut off tax shelters.

Instead of cutting out school lunches, let us cut off tax subsidies for expensive business lunches that are nothing more than food stamps for the rich.

The tax cut of our Republican opponents takes the name of tax reform in vain. It is a wonderfully Republican idea that would redistribute income in the wrong direction. It is good news for any of you with incomes over $200,000 a year. For the few of you, it offers a pot of gold worth $14,000. But the Republican tax cut is bad news for the middle income families. For the many of you, they plan a pittance of $200 a year. And that is not what the Democratic Party means when we say tax reform.

The vast majority of Americans cannot afford this panacea from a Republican nominee who has denounced the progressive income tax as the invention of Karl Marx. I am afraid he has confused Karl Marx with Theodore Roosevelt, that obscure Republican president who sought and fought for a tax system based on ability to pay. Theodore Roosevelt was not Karl Marx — and the Republican tax scheme is not tax reform.

[National Health Insurance]

Finally, we cannot have a fair prosperity in isolation from a fair society.

So I will continue to stand for a national health insurance. We must not surrender to the relentless medical inflation that can bankrupt almost anyone — and that may soon break the budgets of government at every level.

Let us insist on real controls over what doctors and hospitals can charge. And let us resolve that the state of a family's health shall never depend on the size of a family's wealth.

The president, the vice president, and the members of Congress have a medical plan that meets their needs in full. And whenever senators and representatives catch a little cold, the Capitol physician will see them immediately, treat them promptly, and fill a prescription on the spot. We do not get a bill even if we ask for it. And when do you think was the last time a member of Congress asked for a bill from the federal government?

And I say again, as I have said before: If health insurance is good enough for the president, the vice president and the Congress of the United States, then it is good enough for all of you and for every family in America.

[Democratic-GOP Differences]

There were some who said we should be silent about our differences on issues during this convention. But the heritage of the Democratic Party has been a history of democracy. We fight hard because we care deeply about our principles and purposes. We did not flee this struggle. We welcome this contrast with the empty and expedient spectacle last month in Detroit where no nomination was contested, no question was debated and no one dared to raise any doubt or dissent.

Democrats can be proud that we chose a different course — and a different platform.

We can be proud that our party stands for investment in safe energy instead of a nuclear future that may threaten the future itself. We must not permit the neighborhoods of America to be permanently shadowed by the fear of another Three Mile Island.

We can be proud that our party stands for a fair housing law to unlock the doors of discrimination once and for all. The American house will be divided against itself so long as there is prejudice against any American buying or renting a home.

And we can be proud that our party stands plainly and publicly, and persistently for the ratification of the Equal Rights Amendment. Women hold their rightful place at our convention; and women must have their rightful place in the Constitution of the United States. On this issue, we will not yield, we will not equivocate, we will not rationalize, explain, or excuse. We will stand for E.R.A. and for the recognition at long last that our nation is made up of founding mothers as well as founding fathers.

A fair prosperity and a just society are within our vision and our grasp. And we do not have every answer. There are questions not yet asked, waiting for us in the recesses of the future.

But of this much we can be certain, because it is the lesson of all our history:

Together a president and the people can make a difference. I have found that faith still alive wherever I have traveled across the land. So let us reject the counsel of retreat and the call to reaction. Let us go forward in the knowledge that history only helps those who help themselves.

There will be setbacks and sacrifices in the years ahead. But I am convinced that we as a people are ready to give something back to our country in return for all it has given to us. Let this be our commitment: Whatever sacrifices must be made will be shared — and shared fairly. And let this be our confidence: At the end of our journey and always before us shines that ideal of liberty and justice for all.

[To Those Who 'Stayed the Course']

In closing, let me say a few words to all those I have met and all those who have supported me at this convention and across the land.

There were hard hours on our journey. And often we sailed against the wind, but always we kept our rudder true. And there were so many of you who stayed the course and shared our hope. You gave your help; but even more, you gave your hearts. And because of you, this has been a happy campaign. You welcomed Joan and me and our family into your homes and neighborhoods, your churches, your campuses, your union halls. When I think back on all the miles and all the months and all the memories, I think of you. And I recall the poet's words, and I say: "What golden friends I had."

Among you, my golden friends across this land, I have listened and learned.

I have listened to Kenny Dubois, a glass blower in Charleston, W.Va., who has 10 children to support, but has lost his job after 35 years, just three years short of qualifying for his pension.

I have listened to the Trachta family, who farm in Iowa and who wonder whether they can pass the good life and the good earth on to their children.

I have listened to a grandmother in East Oakland, who no longer has a phone to call her grandchildren, because she gave it up to pay the rent on her small apartment.

I have listened to young workers out of work, to students without the tuition for college, and to families without the chance to own a home. I have seen the closed factories and the stalled assembly lines of Anderson, Ind., and South Gate, Calif. I have seen too many — far too many — idle men and women desperate to work. I have seen too many — far too many — working families desperate to protect the value of their wages from the ravages of inflation.

Yet I have also sensed a yearning for new hope among the people in every state where I have been. And I have felt it in their handshakes; I saw it in their faces. And I shall never forget the mothers who carried children to our rallies. I shall always remember the elderly who have lived in an America of high purpose and who believe that it can all happen again.

Tonight, in their name, I have come here to speak for them. And for their sake, I ask you to stand with them. On their behalf, I ask you to restate and reaffirm the timeless truth of our party.

I congratulate President Carter on his victory here. I am confident that the Democratic Party will reunite on the basis of Democratic principles — and that together we will march toward a Democratic victory in 1980.

And someday, long after this convention, long after the signs come down, and the crowds stop cheering, and the bands stop playing, may it be said of our campaign that we kept the faith. May it be said of our party in 1980 that we found our faith again.

And may it be said of us, both in dark passages and in bright days, in the words of Tennyson that my brothers quoted and loved — and that have special meaning for me now:

I am a part of all that I have met ...
Tho much is taken, much abides ...
That which we are, we are ...
One equal temper of heroic hearts ...
strong in will
To strive, to seek, to find, and not to yield.

For me, a few hours ago, this campaign came to an end. For all those whose cares have been our concern, the work goes on, the cause endures, the hope still lives, and the dream shall never die.

DEMOCRATIC PARTY PLATFORM

August 13, 1980

*After lengthy and rancorous debate, delegates to the Democratic Na-
tional Convention in New York City adopted Aug. 13 a party platform
containing several planks the Carter administration had disavowed. And
President Carter, responding to a new party rule requiring the nominee
to state his objections to the platform, pledged to honor the party's
commitment to the document while giving it only lukewarm personal
support.*

*The 40,000-word platform was divided into five chapters — the economy,
government and human needs; government operations and reform; energy;
natural resources, environment and agriculture; and foreign policy. At
the convention, interest group members and backers of Sen. Edward
M. Kennedy, D-Mass., President Carter's unsuccessful rival for the nomination, led the fight to include economic and human needs planks
opposed by the White House. After Kennedy's address on economic
issues evoked an enthusiastic reaction from the delegates, Carter forces
dropped their opposition to most of Kennedy's economic proposals, including calls for a $12 billion jobs programs and a policy of avoiding
actions that would "significantly increase" unemployment. The president
Aug. 10 had accepted a Kennedy plank eschewing the use of high
interest rates and unemployment to fight inflation. The single Kennedy
economic position rejected by the Carter camp and the convention demanded the imposition of wage and price controls. (Kennedy speech,
p. 701)*

*Other modifications pushed through at the convention included amend-
ments denying Democratic Party funds and assistance to candidates*

opposed to ratification of the equal rights amendment and supporting use of Medicaid funds to finance abortions.

Preamble to Platform

The preamble to the platform included an admission that the nation faced grave difficulties, but it charged that those were the legacy of the Nixon and Ford administrations. "We will not run from these problems," the preamble stated, "nor will we fail. The record of the past four years is a testament to what Democrats can do working together."

The economic chapter opened with the Kennedy-endorsed position on unemployment: "The Democratic Party will take no action whose effect will be a significant increase in unemployment." It went on to support "targeted tax reductions" and to criticize the Republicans' proposed broad tax reductions which, the platform claimed, "would increase inflation." The economic section also referred to the federal budget and pledged the party's support of "the discipline of attempting to live within the limits of our anticipated revenues." It added, however, that the party continued to oppose "drastic cuts in social programs" aimed at balancing the budget.

In the government and human needs chapter, the Democrats expressed their support for programs designed to aid various segments of the population — the young, the old, the poor, the handicapped, city dwellers, the gifted. The section also strongly endorsed passage of the equal rights amendment and advocated support for the rights of various minority groups, including blacks, Hispanics, American Indians, Americans living abroad, and, for the first time, homosexuals. (A plank endorsing homosexual rights had been voted down at the 1972 national convention.)

The sections also encouraged the federal government gradually to assume state and local welfare costs, increase spending on science and the humanities, and raise outlays for housing and veterans' benefits.

Under the heading "Government Operation and Reform," the platform endorsed tax reforms to encourage saving and capital formation, abolish the marriage penalty tax and eliminate deductions for "three-martini" business lunches. It also voiced support for a revised criminal code and called for public financing of congressional campaigns.

Energy Plank

The energy chapter of the platform pledged the Democratic Party's backing of greater conservation and promised federal support to solar and other renewable energy sources surpassing federal funding for synthetic fuels. The chapter also endorsed greater reliance on coal and the development of wind and thermal energy and electric- and hydrogen-

powered vehicles. And in a controversial statement, the platform added, "Through the federal government's commitment to renewable energy sources and energy efficiency, and as alternative fuels become available in the future, we will retire nuclear power plants in an orderly manner."

In the final section, foreign policy, the platform listed five major goals of U.S. international relations: strengthened links with allies, improved relations with the Third World, peace in the Middle East, improved security of the United States and its allies, and arms control. The platform lashed out at the Soviet Union's "illegal and brutal invasion of Afghanistan" and expressed support for the American boycott of the Summer Olympic Games in Moscow and restrictions on U.S.-Soviet trade.

Carter Statement

In his statement on the platform, President Carter expressed his "enthusiastic support for the thrust and ideals" of the document, but failed to endorse specifically the minority planks adopted by the delegates. He said he would "accept and support the intent" of the $12 billion jobs program but neglected to commit himself to a dollar amount. Similarly, Carter reacted to the call to place jobs above all other priorities with the remark, "We must make it clear that to achieve full employment, we must also be successful in our fight against inflation." Carter also reiterated his personal opposition to abortion but said he would abide by "the laws passed by Congress, and the Constitution of the United States as interpreted by the federal courts. . . ."

Following are excerpts from the Democratic Party platform, adopted Aug. 13, 1980, and excerpts from President Carter's statement on the 1980 Democratic Party platform, delivered Aug. 13, 1980:

DEMOCRATIC PLATFORM

Preamble

In its third century, America faces great challenges and an uncertain future. The decade that America now enters presents us with decisions as monumental and fundamental as those we faced during the Civil War, during two World Wars, and during the Great Depression. Our current task is different from each of these historic challenges. But in many ways the challenge is the same: to marshall the talents and spirit of the American people, to harness our enormous resources, and to face the future with confidence and hope.

The task now before us is as global as the worldwide energy shortage, and as local as the plight of children in Appalachia. It reaches from the condition of older Eastern cities and the industries of the snowbelt, to the complex new demands of our sunbelt region and the special needs of our Western states. It is as basic as the entitlement of minorities and women to real equality in every aspect of the nation's life. It is as immediate as the refugee crisis in Miami and the natural disaster at Mount St. Helens. It is as futuristic as the exploration of space and the oceans. It is as idealistic as the spirit of liberty which imbues our Constitution. It requires nothing less than a continued dedication to Democratic principles by each element in our society — government, business, labor, and every citizen — to the promise and potential of our nation.

We live in a time when effective policy requires an understanding of the web of competing values and interests which exist in our country. We must combine compassion with self-discipline. We must forego simplistic answers for long-term solutions to our problems.

With the Republican leadership closing its eyes to the realities of our time and running for the Presidency on a program of the easy answer ... of the pleasant-sounding political promise, it is time to take a page from Adlai Stevenson's 1952 presidential campaign — it is time "to talk sense to the American people." It is time to talk bluntly and candidly about our problems and our proposed solutions; to face up to our problems and respond to them.

If we fail in this important task ... if we fail to lay the issues squarely before the American people, we could well allow the federal government to revert to four years of Republicanism — neglect of the poor and disadvantaged, disdain for working men and women, compassion only for the rich and the privileged, failure to meet the challenges of energy, inflation and unemployment, and a breakdown of the partnership among local, state and federal governments. We as Democrats must not let this happen.

After nearly four years in office, we Democrats have not solved all of America's problems.

Most of these problems we inherited. Eight years of Republican politics left this nation weak, rudderless, unrespected and deeply divided.

As a result of this legacy, despite our progress, inflation still erodes the standard of living of every American.

As a result of this legacy, despite our progress, too many Americans are out of work.

As a result of this legacy, despite our progress, complete equality for all citizens has yet to be achieved.

As a result of this legacy, despite our progress, we still live in a very dangerous world, where competing ideologies and age-old animosities daily threaten the peace.

As a result of this legacy, our nation is still subject to the oil pricing and production decisions of foreign countries.

We will not run from these problems, nor will we fail. The record of the past four years is a testament to what the Democrats can do working together.

Time and time again in these past four years, a Democratic Congress and a Democratic President proved that they were willing to make the tough decisions.

Today, because of that Democratic partnership, we are a stronger nation.

Today, because of that Democratic partnership, we are at peace.

Today, because of that Democratic partnership, we are a more just nation.

Today, because of that Democratic partnership, honor and truth and integrity have been restored to our government and to our political process.

And so this party looks to the future with determination and confidence.

We have been and we shall remain the party of all Americans. We seek solutions that not only meet the needs of the many, but reaffirm our commitment to improve the conditions of the least fortunate in our society.

In this platform we offer programs and solutions that represent our dedication to Democratic principles. They define a spirit as well as a program ... a set of beliefs as well as a set of ideas. Time and events may alter their priority or prospects. But nothing will alter the defining spirit and values of the Democratic Party.

The platform of the Democratic Party is a contract with the people. We believe that accountability for Democratic principles goes hand in hand with dedication to those principles. The Democratic Party is proud of its historic heritage of commitment to the people of America. Fulfilling this platform will permit us to keep faith with that tradition.

The Economy

The Democratic Party will take no action whose effect will be a significant increase in unemployment — no fiscal action, no monetary action, no budgetary action — if it is the assessment of either the Council of Economic Advisers or the Congressional Budget Office that such action will cause significantly greater unemployment.

In all of our economic programs, the one overriding principle must be fairness. All Americans must bear a fair share of our economic burdens and reap a fair share of our economic benefits. High interest rates impose an unfair burden — on farmers, small businesses, and younger families buying homes. Recession imposes an unfair burden on those least able to bear it. Democratic economic policy must continue to assure fairness for workers, the elderly, the poor, minorities and the majority who are middle income Americans. In 1980, we pledge to continue a truly Democratic economic policy to secure a prosperous economic future.

ECONOMIC STRENGTH

While the past three and a half years of Democratic leadership have been years of growth for our economy, we now find ourselves in a recession.

The Democratic Party is committed to taking the necessary steps to combat the current recession. However, we cannot abandon our fight against inflation. We must fight both of these problems at the same time; we are committed to do so. We will continue to pursue the fight against inflation in ways not designed or intended to increase unemployment.

Our current economic situation is unique. In 1977, we inherited a severe recession from the Republicans. The Democratic Administration and the Democratic Congress acted quickly to reduce the unacceptably high levels of unemployment and to stimulate the economy. And we succeeded. We recovered from that deep recession and our economy was strengthened and revitalized. As that fight was won, the enormous increases in foreign oil prices — 120% last year — and declining productivity fueled an inflationary spiral that also had to be fought. The Democrats did that, and inflation has begun to recede. In working to combat these dual problems, significant economic actions have been taken.

Two tax cuts have been enacted, in 1977 and 1978, reducing taxes on individuals and business by an amount equal, this year, to about $40 billion.

While meeting our national security and pressing domestic needs, the Democratic Partnership has restrained the increase in government spending in ways which have steadily reduced the deficit we inherited.

Airline and banking regulatory reforms have been enacted; further regulatory reforms are now under consideration.

In the effort to restrain inflation, a voluntary pay advisory committee has been established with labor, business, and public representatives pursuant to a National Accord.

The first national export policy was developed; export and trade responsibilities were reorganized and strengthened; the Multilateral Trade Negotiations were completed; and the MTN Agreement was approved by the Congress.

To ensure a greater impact for scarce federal dollars, grant and loan programs have been redirected to the areas of greatest need, and the formula programs have been redesigned to *target* the areas with the most serious problems.

As a result of these economic actions:

Employment — More than 8.5 million new jobs have been added to the workforce; about 1 million of those jobs are held by Blacks, and nearly an additional 1 million are held by Hispanics. Gains have been made by all groups — more men, more women, more minorities, and more young people are working than ever before in our history.

Despite these gains, current unemployment is too high and must be lowered.

Inflation — A strong anti-inflation program has been initiated and pursued aggressively, to deal both with the short-term inflation problem and with the long-term causes of inflation. The effects of the short-term effort are now evident: inflation is beginning to come down. Although some interest rates remain high, they are falling at record rates. This progress will continue as short-term actions continue to work and long-term initiatives begin to take hold.

Economic Growth — Despite the economic declines of the past few months, for the first three years of the Carter Administration our economy was strong. For the 1977-1979 period:

- Gross National Product increased by 11.8% in real terms.
- Real after-tax income per person increased by 10.3%.
- Industrial production increased by 14.8%.
- Dividends increased by 36%.
- Real business fixed investment increased by 22.9%.

Energy — Our dependence on foreign oil has decreased — in 1977 we imported 8.8 million barrels of oil per day, and our nation is now importing approximately 6.5 million per day, a decline of 26%.

Solving Our Economic Problems

The Democratic Party commits itself to a strong economic program — one that builds on the progress we have made to date, one that corrects the very real problems we face now, one that is responsible, one that offers realistic hope, and one that can unify our Party. Such a Democratic program would contrast dramatically with the simplistic rhetoric and the traditional economic policies of the Republican Party.

Full Employment — We specifically reaffirm our commitment to achieve all the goals of the Humphrey-Hawkins Full Employment Act within the currently prescribed dates in the Act, especially those relating to a joint reduction in unemployment and inflation. Full employment is important to the achievement of a rising standard of living, to the pursuit of sound justice, and to the strength and vitality of America.

Anti-Recession Assistance — Immediately, we must undertake a short-term anti-recession program to reverse the tide of deepening recession and rising unemployment. Each percentage point increase in the unemployment rate adds $25 billion to the federal deficit.

A Democratic anti-recession program must recognize that Blacks, Hispanics, other minorities, women, and older workers bear the brunt of recession. We pledge a $12 billion anti-recession jobs program, providing at least 800,000 additional jobs, including full funding of the counter-cyclical assistance program for the cities, a major expansion of the youth employment and training program to give young people in our inner cities new hope, expanded training programs for women and displaced homemakers to give these workers a fair chance in the workplace, and new opportunities for the elderly to contribute their talents and skills.

Coupling our need to rehabilitate our railroads with the need to create new job opportunities, we must commit ourselves to a $1 billion railroad renewal program which can employ 20,000 workers.

We must take steps to restore the housing industry, including effective implementation of the Brooke-Cranston program, and the addition of 200,000 new units a year for low and moderate income families.

National Accord — The National Accord with Labor must be strengthened and continued. This enhances the unique opportunity afforded by a Democratic Administration for government, labor and business to work together to solve our inflationary and other economic problems.

Tax Reductions — We commit ourselves to targeted tax reductions designed to stimulate production and combat recession as soon as it appears so that tax reductions will not have a disproportionately inflationary effect. We must avoid untargeted tax cuts which would increase inflation. Any tax reduction must, if it is to help solve pressing economic problems, follow certain guiding principles:

● The inflationary impact must be minimized;

● Reductions provided to individuals must be weighted to help low and middle income individuals and families, to improve consumer purchasing power, and to enhance a growing economy while maintaining and strengthening the overall progressive nature of the tax code;

● Productivity, investment, capital formation, as well as incentives, must be encouraged, particularly in distressed areas and industries;

● The effect on our economy must be one which encourages job formation and business growth.

Federal Spending — Spending restraint must be sensitive to those who look to the federal government for aid and assistance, especially to our nation's workers in times of high unemployment. At the same time, as long as inflationary pressures remain strong, fiscal prudence is essential to avoid destroying the progress made to date in reducing the inflation rate.

[Flexible Fiscal Policy]

Fiscal policy must remain a flexible economic tool. We oppose a Constitutional amendment requiring a balanced budget.

Interest Rates — The Democratic Party has historically been committed to policies that result in low interest rates in order to help our nation's workers, small businesses, farmers and homeowners. Therefore, we must continue to pursue a tough anti-inflationary policy which will lead to an across-the-board reduction in interest rates on loans.

In using monetary policy to fight inflation, the government should be sensitive to the special needs of areas of our economy most affected by high interest rates. The Federal Reserve shall use the tool of reserve requirements creatively in its effort to fight inflation. The Federal Reserve should also take particular care to make certain that it is aware of the concerns of labor, agriculture, housing, consumers and small business in its decision-making process. Finally, its Open Market Committee should continue to provide regular information to the public about its activities.

Regulatory Reform — Consistent with our basic health, safety, and environmental goals, we must continue to deregulate over-regulated industries and to remove other unnecessary regulatory burdens on state and local governments and on the private sector, particularly those which inhibit competition.

Targeting and Regional Balance — From the time of Franklin Roosevelt, the Democratic Party has dedicated itself to the principle that the federal government has a duty to ensure that all regions, states and localities share in the benefits of national economic prosperity and that none bears more than its share of economic adversity. . . .

Rebuilding American Industry. . . — The Democratic Party has a long tradition of innovation, foresight, and flexibility in creating policies to solve the nation's most urgent economic needs. We now stand at another watershed in our economic history which demands our party's full attention, creative powers, resources, and skills. To revive productivity and revitalize our economy, we need a national effort to strengthen the American economy. It must include new tax depreciation rules to stimulate selective capital investment; a simplified tax code to assist business planning; removal of governmental regulations which are unnecessary and stifle business initiative; effective incentives for saving that do not discriminate against low and middle income taxpayers; reform in patent rules and new incentives for research and development, especially by small business; cooperative efforts with labor and management to retool the steel, auto and shipbuilding industries; and strengthened worker training programs to improve job opportunities and working skills. . . .

ENSURING ECONOMIC EQUITY

Budget

The budget policy that has been put forth by the Democratic Party traditionally has been based on providing adequate federal resources to meet our nation's urgent needs. The current Democratic Partnership has continued that tradition while restraining the growth of the federal budget.

We have increased support for vital domestic programs. We have increased funding for education by 75% over the Ford budget. We have increased Head Start by 73%, basic skills programs by 233%, bilingual education by 113%, Native American education by 124%, summer jobs by 66%, Job Corps by 157%, employment and training programs by 115%, Medicare by 54%, National Health Service Corps by 179%, Child

719

Nutrition by 43%, and Women, Infants and Children (WIC) Program by 300%.

We have been able to do this, while restraining the growth in federal spending, because the country has had a growing economy; tax cuts have been moderate; waste and fraud have been reduced; and aid has been targeted to those most in need.

International events have required increased defense spending. The Soviet challenge cannot be ignored. We have had to reverse the steady decline in defense spending that occurred under the Republican Administration. A Democratic Administration and a Democratic Congress have done this; real defense spending has increased, in part through the elimination of waste and the emphasis on increased efficiency.

In the eight years preceding the first Carter budget, real federal spending had been growing at an average rate of 3% each year. By contrast, between FY 1978 and 1981, real federal spending will have declined at an average annual rate of 0.6%. . . .

Worker Protection

The Democratic Administration has worked with Congress to take actions which protect our nation's workers from declining incomes, unsafe working conditions, and threats to their basic rights. The Democratic Party will not pursue a policy of high interest rates and unemployment as the means to fight inflation. We will take no action whose effect will be a significant increase in unemployment, no fiscal action, no monetary action, no budgetary action. The Democratic Party remains committed to policies that will not produce high interest rates or high unemployment.

But much more needs to be done to protect our nation's workers. The Democratic Party has a long and proud tradition in this area and we must pledge to continue our efforts over the next four years.

Over a generation ago this nation established a labor policy whose purpose is to encourage the practice and procedure of collective bargaining and the right of workers to organize to obtain this goal. The Democratic Party is committed to extending the benefit of this policy to all workers and to removing the barriers to its administration.

In the future the Democratic Party will concentrate on the following areas.

Our labor laws should be reformed to permit better administration and enforcement, and particularly to prevent the inordinate delays and *outright defiance* by some employers of our labor laws. We can no longer tolerate the fact that certain employers are willing to bear the cost of sanctions which are in our current laws in order to violate the rights of those attempting to organize.

OSHA protections should be properly administered, with the concern of the worker being the highest priority; legislative or administrative efforts to weaken OSHA's basic worker protection responsibilities are unacceptable. OSHA has significantly reduced workplace accidents and fatalities. We will not limit its scope for any reason, including the size of business, since all workers face significant workplace dangers. The Democratic Party strongly opposes and urges all actions to defeat legislation which weakens OSHA's critical protections.

Hatch Act reforms should be enacted to give federal workers their basic First Amendment rights. We must protect federal workers from interruptions in their pay due to delays in the federal appropriations process and must seek ways to assure the comparability of pay scales between the federal and private sectors.

We support the right of public employees and agricultural workers to organize and bargain collectively. We urge the adoption of appropriate federal legislation to ensure this goal.

Legislation must be enacted to allow building trades workers the same peaceful picketing rights currently afforded industrial workers.

All fair labor standards acts, such as the minimum wage and Davis-Bacon protections, must continue to be effectively enforced against employers seeking to circumvent their worker protections.

Section 14-b of the Taft-Hartley Act should be repealed.

Special assistance should be made available for unemployed workers in a distressed industry, such as the automobile, steel, and shipbuilding industries.

We must improve and strengthen our trade adjustment assistance programs.

We support federal legislation designed to give protection and human rights to those workers affected by plant closings.

Just as we must protect workers in their workplace, so must we protect them when they are disabled by accidents or sicknesses resulting from their work. The Democratic Party supports federal legislation to assure adequate minimum benefit levels to those who are unemployed, including expansion of coverage to all wage and salary workers and extended benefits for the long-term unemployed. It must not artificially disregard those who have already been unemployed for a long time.

We will continue to oppose a sub-minimum wage for youth and other workers and to support increases in the minimum wage so as to ensure an adequate income for all workers.

Small Business

The prosperity of small business is an important national priority. Over half of the major innovations in the past twenty years have come from firms with less than 1,000 employees, and technological innovation has accounted for nearly half of America's growth. . . .

Of course, larger firms may offer other economic benefits to society, but the contribution of small business is vital and unique, and no overall program for economic recovery will succeed unless it relies heavily on small businesses. For this reason, the Democratic Party commits itself to the first comprehensive program for small business in American history. That program will include the following measures.

A prompt review and response for the recommendations of the White House Conference on Small Business.

Legislation to transfer from the SBA to the Farmers Home Administration responsibility for providing loans to farmers in financial need.

Allocation of a fair percentage of federal research funds to small business.

Protection of small and independent businesses against takeover by giant conglomerates.

Continued efforts to end federal regulations which reinforce barriers to entry by new and small firms, and which thereby entrench the dominance of market leaders.

A review of regulations and requirements which impose unnecessary burdens upon smaller firms. Results should provide relief for smaller firms which now pay $12.7 billion a year to fill 850 million pages of government paperwork. We will adopt regulatory requirements to meet the needs of smaller firms, where such action will not interfere with the objectives of the regulation.

Minority Business

A Democratic Congress and a Democratic Administration have worked together to increase opportunities for minority businesses, which have suffered from inadequate capitalization. Enormous progress has been made in the last four years. . . .

The Democratic Party pledges itself to advance minority businesses, including Black, Hispanic, Asian/Pacific Americans, Native Americans and other minorities to:

• Increase the overall level of support and the overall level of federal procurement so that minority groups will receive additional benefits and opportunities.

• Triple the 1980 level of federal procurement from minority-owned firms as we have tripled the 1977 levels in the past three years.

• Increase substantially the targeting of Small Business Administration loans to minority-owned businesses.

• Increase ownership of small businesses by minorities, especially in those areas which have traditionally been closed to minorities, such as communications and newspapers.

• Expand management, technical, and training assistance for minority firms, and strengthen minority capital development under the SBA's Minority Enterprise Small Business Investment Company (MESBIC) program.

• Establish a Minority Business Development Agency in the Department of Commerce under statutory mandate.

• Implement vigorously all set-aside provisions for minority businesses.

Women in Business

The Democrats have exercised effective leadership in the field of support to women-owned businesses. A national policy was developed to support women's business enterprises, and SBA created the first program to help women entrepreneurs. President Carter has issued an Executive Order creating a national women's business enterprise policy and prescribing arrangements for developing, coordinating, and implementing a national program for women's business enterprise.

Support of this program must be expanded through effective implementation of the Executive Order to ensure an equitable distribution of government prime and subcontracts to women business owners. . . .

As the key office within the federal government for these programs, the Office of Women's Business Enterprise in SBA must be strengthened through adequate staffing and funding, and should receive continued emphasis by key White House and Office of Management and Budget personnel.

Women and The Economy

We pledge to secure the rights of working women, homemakers, minority women and elderly women to a fair share of our economy. A sound economy in the next four years is of vital importance to women, who are often at the bottom of the economic ladder. But if our economy is to be truly fair, additional steps are required to address the inequities that women now face.

Special attention must be paid to the employment needs of women. Today, women who can find work earn, on average, only 59 cents for every dollar earned by men.

The Democratic Party, therefore, commits itself to strong steps to close the wage gap between men and women, to expand child care opportunities for families with working parents, to end the tax discrimination that penalizes married working couples, and to ensure that women can retire in dignity. . . .

Perhaps most important, the Democratic Party is committed to the principle of equal pay for work of comparable value. Through new job classification studies by the Department of Labor, job reclassification by the Office of Personnel Management and new legislation from Congress if necessary, we will ensure that women in both the public and private sectors are not only paid equally for work which is identical to that performed by men, but are also paid equally for work which is of comparable value to that performed by men. . . .

Economic Inequities Facing Minorities

We must expand jobs and job training including apprenticeship training programs for those who have special problems — groups such as the

723

young, veterans, older workers, minorities, those with limited fluency in English, and the handicapped. The Democratic Party pledges that anyone who wants to learn the skills necessary to secure a job will be able to do so.

We also must improve the quality of the programs designed to help the structurally unemployed. . . .

A major effort must be undertaken to address youth employment. Half the unemployed are under 25. Teenage inner city unemployment is at disastrous levels of 50 percent or higher. The problem is one of both employment and employability — a lack of jobs and a lack of skills. . . .

Consumer Protection

Since the first administration of Franklin Roosevelt, the Democratic Party has stood as the Party which championed consumer rights. It is our tradition to support and enact policies which guarantee that the consumer is sovereign in the market place. It is our history to institute necessary government programs to protect the health, safety and economic well-being of the American consumer. And it is our way of governing to ensure that consumers have full opportunity to participate in the decision-making processes of government.

Working together, the Democratic Administration and Congress have maintained that tradition. Prominent consumer advocates have been appointed to key government positions. A new National Consumer Co-operative Bank has been created, and a Fair Debt Collection Practices Act has been enacted. Each federal agency has been directed to establish procedures so that consumer needs and interests are adequately considered and addressed on a continual basis. The basic consumer protection authorities of the Federal Trade Commission have been preserved.

Over the next four years, we must continue to guarantee and enhance the basic consumer rights to safety, to information, to choice and to a fair hearing. . . .

Antitrust Enforcement

America must commit itself to a free, open and competitive economy. We pledge vigorous antitrust enforcement in those areas of the economy which are not regulated by government and in those which are, we pledge an agency-by-agency review to prevent regulation from frustrating competition.

To accomplish these goals, we must:

• Enact the *Illinois Brick* legislation.

• Permit consumers and other interested parties to seek enforcement of consent decrees issued in antitrust cases brought by government.

• Prevent anti-competitive pricing by firms in concentrated industries, and combat price signalling and other forms of anti-competitive conduct which do not fall into the current legal categories of either monopoly or collusion.

● Control conglomerate mergers, when such mergers undermine important economic, social and political values without offsetting economic benefits.

● Reform antitrust procedures to speed up cases and deter dilatory conduct by any party.

Government and Human Needs

The Democratic Party has properly been known as the Party of the people. We Democrats believe in making government responsive to the needs of the people ... making it *work* for the people. We do not claim that government has all the answers to our problems, but we do believe that government has a legitimate role to play in searching for those answers and in applying those answers.

The Democratic Party has a proud record of responding to the human needs of our citizens. After eight years of Republican government and systematic Republican efforts to dismantle all of the hard-won New Frontier and Great Society social programs, the Carter Administration and the Democratic Congress have resurrected, preserved and strengthened those programs which have proven effective.

[GOVERNMENT SERVICE TO PEOPLE]

In the areas of health care, housing, education, welfare and social services, civil rights, and care for the disabled, elderly and veterans, a Democratic President and a Democratic Congress have put the federal government back in the business of serving our people.

Our progress has been significant, and in many areas unprecedented....

... While we recognize the need for fiscal restraint — and have proposed specific steps toward that goal — we pledge as Democrats that for the sole and primary purpose of fiscal restraint alone, we will *not* support reductions in the funding of any programs whose purpose is to serve the basic human needs of the most needy in our society — programs such as unemployment, income maintenance, food stamps, and efforts to enhance the educational, nutritional or health needs of children.

Health

The Carter Administration and the Congress have worked closely together to improve the health care provided to all Americans. In many vital areas, there has been clear progress.

The United States spent over $200 billion for health care in 1979. Despite these high expenditures and although we possess some of the finest hospitals and health professionals in the world, millions of Americans have little or no access to health care services. Incredibly, costs are predicted to soar to $400 billion by 1984, without improvement in either access to care or coverage of costs. Health care costs already consume ten cents of every dollar spent for goods and services.

The answer to runaway medical costs is not, as Republicans propose, to pour money into a wasteful and inefficient system. The answer is not to cut back on benefits for the elderly and eligibility for the poor. The answer is to enact a comprehensive, universal national health insurance plan. . . .

Child Health Assurance Program. We must continue to emphasize preventive health care for all citizens. As part of this commitment, we call for the enactment of legislation during the 96th Congress to expand the current Medicaid program and make an additional 5 million low-income children eligible for Medicaid benefits and an additional 200,000 low-income pregnant women eligible for pre-natal and post-natal care.

Mental Health Systems Act. We must enact legislation to help the mentally ill, based on the recommendations of the President's Commission on Mental Health. The legislation should focus on de-institutionalization of the chronically mentally ill, increased program flexibility at the local level, prevention, and the development of community-based mental health services. It is imperative that there be ongoing federal funding for the community-based mental health centers established under the 1963 Mental Health Act and that sufficient federal funding be provided for adequate staffing. We also endorse increased federal funding for ongoing training of mental health personnel in public facilities.

In the 1980's we must move beyond these existing health care initiatives and tackle other problems as well.

Long Term Care. We must develop a new policy on long-term care for our elderly and disabled populations that controls the cost explosion and at the same time provides more humane care. We must establish alternatives to the present provisions for long-term care, including adequate support systems and physical and occupational therapy in the home and the community, to make it unnecessary to institutionalize people who could lead productive lives at home. . . .

Multilingual Needs. We must support the utilization of bilingual interpreters in English-Spanish and other appropriate languages at federal and state-supported health care facilities. In addition, we support broader, more comprehensive health care for migrants.

Health Care Personnel. This nation must maintain an adequate supply of health professionals and personnel. Particular emphasis should be given to programs which educate nurses and other health professionals and related personnel, especially for the traditionally underserved rural and inner city areas.

The rising cost of education in health fields bars many who wish to enter these fields from doing so. In order to expand representation in the health professions of traditionally underrepresented groups, we support programs of financial assistance such as capitation grants. These programs must increase the presence of men and minorities in nursing, and must be targeted toward women and minorities in other health professions.

Minority and Women Health Care Professionals. We recognize the need for a significant increase in the number of minority and women health care professionals. We are committed to placing greater emphasis on enrollment and retention of minorities and women in medical schools and related health education professional programs.

We are also committed to placing a greater emphasis on medical research and services to meet the needs of minorities, women and children.

Reproductive Rights. We fully recognize the religious and ethical concerns which many Americans have about abortion. We also recognize the belief of many Americans that a woman has a right to choose whether and when to have a child.

The Democratic Party supports the 1973 Supreme Court decision on abortion rights as the law of the land and opposes any constitutional amendment to restrict or overturn that decision.

Furthermore, we pledge to support the right to be free of environmental and worksite hazards to reproductive health of women and men.

We further pledge to work for programs to improve the health and safety of pregnancy and childbirth, including adequate prenatal care, family planning, counseling, and services, with special care to the needs of the poor, the isolated, the rural, and the young.

Financially Distressed Public Hospitals. Frequently, the only source of medical care for much of the inner city population is the public general hospital. The ever-increasing costs of providing high quality hospital services and the lack of insurance coverage for many of the patients served have jeopardized the financial stability of these institutions. Immediate support is required for financially distressed public hospitals that provide a major community service in urban and rural areas.

In underserved areas where public hospitals have already been closed because of financial difficulty, we must explore methods for returning the needed hospitals to active service.

We must develop financial stability for these hospitals. Our approach should stress system reforms to assure that more primary medical care is provided in free-standing community centers, while the hospital is used for referral services and hospitalization.

Medicaid Reimbursement. The Democratic Party supports programs to make the Medicaid reimbursement formula more equitable.

Unnecessary Prescriptions. We must reduce unnecessary prescribing of drugs and guarantee the quality and safety of products that reach the market through improved approval procedures.

Substance Abuse

Alcoholism and drug abuse are unique illnesses which not only impair the health of those who abuse those products, but impose costs on society as a whole — in production losses, in crimes to supply habits, and in fatalities on the highway.

The Democratic Partnership has worked to reduce the serious national problem of substance abuse, and progress has been made.

As a result, in part, of a major adolescent drug abuse prevention campaign, levels of drug abuse among adolescents have begun to decline. However, as long as abuse still exists, we consider it a major problem requiring our attention. . . .

Older Americans

In other sections of this platform (for example, health and the extensive section on Social Security), we have listed programs and commitments for improving the status of older Americans. As a Party, we are aware of the demographic and biomedical developments that call for a high priority approach to the issues of retirement, work, and income maintenance for the growing number of older citizens. . . .

All Americans, regardless of age, must be afforded an opportunity to participate in the mainstream of society, and in activities at local and national levels, as useful citizens. The 1967 Age Discrimination in Employment Act, and the milestone amendments to that Act in 1978, are concrete examples of this principle. So are programs such as senior centers, nutrition services, and home attendants, as well as those programs under ACTION, the Administration on Aging, and the Community Services Administration.

Such programs have helped to diminish the conditions of dependency, isolation, and unnecessary institutionalization. We propose to continue and expand these programs to reach underserved areas and all segments of the elderly.

The Democratic Party is proud of the passage of legislation to protect and improve private pensions through the Employees Retirement Income Security Act (ERISA), as well as current proposals to extend such protection to larger numbers of workers. No worker, after long years of employment, should lose his or her pension rights because of mobility, poor management, or economic reasons.

Other priorities include working with the private sector to assure maintenance and expansion of employer-employee pension systems and continuing support of the federal-state partnership in SSI (Supplemental Security Income) for the least fortunate.

A comprehensive program of long-term care services is a goal of the Democratic Party. The fastest growing segment of our population is the "very old" and the "frail elderly." The Democratic Party will continue to be concerned with the provision of services for these groups, increasingly composed of women without access to family care. This will include home attendant care, day centers, and quality institutional care for those elderly with functional disabilities who cannot rely on non-institutional alternatives. . . .

Social Security

No group in our society deserves the commitment and respect of the Democratic Party more than the elderly. . . .

The basic program and guarantee for older citizens is Social Security. It is the single most successful social program ever undertaken by the federal government. 95% of those reaching 65 are eligible for this program; without it, 60% of the elderly would have incomes below the poverty level.

The Democratic Party will oppose any effort to tamper with the Social Security system by cutting or taxing benefits as a violation of the contract the American government has made with its people. We hereby make a covenant with the elderly of America that as we have kept the Social Security trust fund sound and solvent in the past, we shall keep it sound and solvent in the years ahead.

In 1977, the Social Security system faced bankruptcy. The Carter Administration and the Congress enacted legislation ensuring the Social Security system's financial stability and making certain that each of the 35 million recipients received his or her monthly check without interruption. They also worked together to strengthen the benefits provided to Social Security recipients. As a result of our actions:

- Workers have been protected against inflation;
- Minimum benefit payments have been reformed to protect low-paid, long-time participants;
- A 3% increase in primary benefit amounts has been added;
- The retirement test has been liberalized.

Despite our efforts, much remains to be done if the elderly are to receive the respect and dignity they have earned. . . .

In the 1980's we must continue to work for a financially strong Social Security system. The levels and types of benefits, as well as rates and systems of financing, must be continually reviewed in light of current circumstances. Decisions affecting Social Security benefits should be measured by the standards of Social Security's goals, not by the program's impact on the federal budget.

The Democratic Party is responsible for the adjustments of Social Security benefits to keep pace with increases in the cost of living. We remain committed to ensuring that these adjustments continue. We oppose any caps on Social Security benefits. No change in the index which determines cost of living adjustments should be made for the purpose of achieving smaller adjustments than those granted under the current index.

We oppose efforts to raise the age at which Social Security benefits will be provided. Our Party seeks to protect and assist those most in need. We continue to be sensitive to the economic and physical plight of the older worker and the elderly. We therefore stand unalterably opposed to the taxation of any portion of Social Security benefits. Taxing Social Security benefits would mean real hardship for millions of retired Americans. If government needs to expand the tax base, additional taxation should be borne by those most able to pay.

While these steps are critically important, they will not, standing alone, secure adequate income for the elderly women of this nation. To reach this goal, we must also move immediately to eliminate all the gender-based classifications in the Social Security system. . . .

Pensions

Our nation's complex and uneven pension system is a continuing source of concern. To help address this important problem, President Carter created a Presidential Commission on Pension Policy, charged with developing recommendations to improve public and private, federal, state and local pension systems. We applaud this initiative. . . .

Welfare Reform

The nation's welfare system continues to be inequitable and archaic. . . .

We are at a crossroad in the delivery of welfare. Serious reform is necessary if the inequities are to be remedied and administration improved.

The various components must be reorganized and simplified, with each level of government performing those services most suited to its organizational structure, taking advantage of economies allowed by large-scale delivery where appropriate, and of customized services where they are required, always treating each person with fairness and equity.

The components of an effective human service delivery system are these.

Employment — We must require work or necessary training leading to work of every capable person, except for the elderly and those responsible for the care of small children. . . .

Income Transfer — For those persons who cannot work and who have no independent means of support, we must provide assistance in an integrated, humane, dignified, and simple manner. These problems are national in scope and require a unified, national response.

Social Services — As society becomes more complex and faster paced, people such as senior citizens, handicapped, children, families, and those who need protection are under greater pressure and find it more difficult to find the help they need. As these issues vary among communities, communities should take the lead in design and provision of these services. . . .

Food Stamps — Hunger is one of the most debilitating and urgently felt human needs. A government pledged to a fairer distribution of wealth, income, and power, and to holding as a guiding concern the needs and aspirations of all, must also be a government which seeks to alleviate the hunger that results from economic conditions or personal circumstances. Over the years, the Food Stamp Program, expanded and made more responsive by a Democratic Congress and Administration, has become the bulwark of this nation's efforts to relieve hunger among its citizens.

The only form of assistance which is available to all those in financial need — food stamps — provides an important cushion for poor people, including those whose incomes are temporarily disrupted by layoffs or regional unemployment, or whose age or physical handicap leaves them unable to work.

As state and local governments modify other benefit programs on which low-income people depend, the Food Stamp Program becomes increasingly important. . . .

Medical Care — Provision of medical care for the poor remains essential. This is a critical part of the national health debate, and should be handled as such.

These reforms may require an additional investment, but they offer the prospect of stabilization of welfare costs over the long run, and the assurance that the objective of this expenditure will be accomplished.

Toward these goals, President Carter proposed welfare reform to the Congress in the form of the Work and Training Opportunities Act and the Social Welfare Reform Amendments Act. These two Acts would lift over two million people out of poverty by providing assistance to individuals and families to enable them to meet minimum income standards and by providing employment to those able to work. We must continue to work to ensure the passage of these two very important Acts.

As a means of providing immediate federal fiscal relief to state and local governments, the federal government will assume the local government's burden of welfare costs. Further, there should be in the immediate future, a phased reduction in the states share of welfare costs The Democratic Party pledges in the immediate future to introduce legislation to accomplish these purposes in the next year. . . .

Low Income Energy Assistance

Our citizens see their family budgets stretched to the breaking point by an explosion of energy costs, while the profits of oil companies multiply to record levels. Last year's 120% increase in energy prices by OPEC led to a drastic decrease in the ability of needy families to pay for other necessities of life. The recently enacted low income energy assistance legislation is helping, but it is providing only $1 of help for every $4 in increased costs that have been imposed upon the poor. Significant expansion in this program is urgently needed, and we support such action as a major priority of our Party.

Veterans

This Administration has worked to strengthen the federal government's commitment to our nation's veterans. . . .

During the 1980's, we must commit ourselves to:

• Equal opportunity and full voluntary participation in the military regardless of sex. We oppose quotas and/or percentages, rules, policies and practices which restrict or bar women from equal access to educational training and employment benefits which accrue during and after military service.

• Continue improving education and training benefits and opportunities for veterans, especially those who are economically or educationally disadvantaged and those who are disabled.

• Initiate and complete comprehensive epidemiological studies on veterans exposed to certain defoliants used during the Vietnam War as well as on veterans or civilians exposed to above-ground nuclear explosion. We then must establish appropriate and sensitive VA health care programs for those determined to have suffered from such exposure or service.

• Complete promptly the current Cabinet-level study on Agent Orange.

• Strive to maintain and improve quality health care in an independent VA health care system.

• Continue priority care to veterans with service-connected disabilities and seek ways of improving and developing special treatment for the ever-increasing aging veterans population, including burial benefit programs sensitive to the needs of veterans and their families in rural areas.

• Provide authority for the construction of a memorial in the nation's capital to those who died in service to their country in Southeast Asia.

Education

Perhaps the single most important factor in spurring productivity in our society is a skilled workforce. We must begin to think of federal expenditures as capital investments, favoring those which are productive and which reduce future costs. . . .

Over the next four years, we pledge to continue our strong commitment to education. We will continue to support the Department of Education and assist in its all-important educational enterprise that involves three out of ten Americans.

In this regard, we endorse the language of the legislation which emphasized the intent of Congress "to protect the rights of state and local governments and public and private institutions in the areas of educational policies and administration of programs. . . ."

It is now a decade and a half since the passage — by a Democratic Congress at the behest of a Democratic Administration — of the landmark Elementary and Secondary Education Act of 1965. At the time, there were sound and compelling reasons to undergird all federal aid to education with specific purposes. The specific purposes remain compelling and the specific programs addressed to them must be maintained.

Federal aid to education plays a significant role in guaranteeing that jurisdictions of differing financial capacity can spend equal amounts on schooling. We favor a steady increase in federal support with an emphasis on reducing inter- and intra-state disparities in ability to support quality education. The federal government and the states should be encouraged to equalize or take over educational expenses, relieving the overburdened property taxpayer.

The Democratic Party renews its commitment to eliminating discrimination in education because of sex and demands full and expeditious enforcement of Title IX of the 1972 Education amendments.

The Democratic Party strongly urges that the federal government be sensitive to mandating state and local programs without adequate provision for funding. Such mandates force the state and/or local governments to increase taxes to fund such required programs.

Equal educational opportunity is at the heart of the Democratic program for education. Equality of opportunity must sometimes translate to compensatory efforts. For the disadvantaged, the handicapped, those with limited English language skills, American Indians/Alaska Natives, Native Hawaiians, and other minorities, compensatory programs require concentrated federal spending.

The Democratic Administration and Congress have supported a comprehensive program of compensatory education and have expanded it to include secondary education. We will continue to target categorical assistance to low income and low achieving students.

We reaffirm our strong support for Title I concentration grants for remedial instruction for low income students. The Democratic Party pledges to achieve full funding of concentration grants under Title I and to expand the Headstart and follow-through programs. . . .

Since entry to institutions of higher learning is dependent upon a student's score on a standardized test, we support testing legislation which will assure that students will receive sufficient information relative to their performance on the test to determine their strengths and weaknesses on the tests.

Our institutions of higher education deserve both public and private backing. The Party supports the continuation of tax deductions for charitable gifts, recognizing that such gifts represent the margin of excellence in higher education and foster scholarly independence within our institutions of higher learning. . . .

Historically Black colleges and universities have played a pivotal role in educating minority students. The Democratic Party affirms its commitment to ensuring the financial viability and independence of these worthy institutions and supports expanded funding for Black institutions. The Democratic Party pledges to work vigorously for significant increases in programs which have traditionally provided funding for historically Black colleges and universities. Particular attention should be given to substantially increasing the share of funding Black colleges receive. We will substantially increase the level of participation of Black colleges in all federal programs for which they are eligible. In addition, we urge the establishment of an office within the Office of the Secretary of Education to ensure full executive implementation of the President's Black college directive. Similarly, colleges serving Hispanic, American Indian/Alaska Native, and Asian/Pacific Islander students should receive equal consideration in federal policies affecting their survival.

Finally, educational quality should be strengthened through adequate support for libraries, federal leadership in educational research and development, and improved teacher training. . . .

Child Care

While the American family structure has changed radically in recent years, the family remains the key unit of our society. When the needs of families and children are ignored, the nation as a whole ultimately suffers. It is not only morally right, but also far less expensive, for government to assist children in growing up whole, strong and able, than to pay the bill later for children and adults with health, social and educational problems. Government cannot and should not attempt to displace the responsibilities of the family; to the contrary, the challenge is to formulate policies which will strengthen the family.

The Democratic Party shall seek vigorously to enact an adequately funded, comprehensive quality child-care program based upon a national commitment to meet the health, safety, and educational needs of *all* children. . . .

Juvenile Justice

Juvenile delinquency and other problems of young people, like truancy and running away, are often manifestations of serious problems in other areas — family, school, employment, or emotional disturbance. We are committed to maintaining and strengthening the Juvenile Justice and Delinquency Prevention Act of 1974 and the Runaway Youth Act to help deal with these problems. In particular, we reaffirm our commitment to ending unnecessary institutionalization of young people who have not committed serious crimes and strengthening preventive efforts and other services at the community level to help young people and their families in the sometimes difficult transition to adulthood. . . .

Families

The Democratic Party supports efforts to make federal programs more sensitive to the needs of the family, in all its diverse forms.

Housing

Since 1976, the Administration's efforts in the area of housing have concentrated on achieving an adequate housing supply. From 1977-1979, housing starts increased substantially over the level of the prior Republican Administration. Additionally, increased emphasis has been placed on saving our existing housing stock through rehabilitation.

But the momentum to increase the housing supply for the 1980's has been threatened by the high rate of inflation. The downturn in economic activity during the first half of 1980 has created a period of severe difficulty for the housing industry and for those Americans in need of housing. These circumstances make it imperative that the Democratic Party redouble its efforts to meet the goal of a decent home in a suitable environment for every citizen. It is essential that we expand the construction and availability of affordable housing in order to match the growing needs of Americans during the 1980's and to help stabilize housing costs.

Housing shortages and deterioration, and the need for economic development, are among the most critical problems facing local government today. . . .

Transportation

Since 1977, the Carter Administration has worked closely with the Congress to improve all the transportation modes so essential to our nation. These efforts have resulted in the elimination of unnecessary regulations, the expansion of the federal commitment to mass transit, and the savings of billions of dollars for consumers. In the 1980's we must continue our efforts in the same direction.

The Democratic Party commits itself to a balanced, competitive transportation system for the efficient movement of people and goods.

The trucking industry must be deregulated, and legislation to do that is now in place. . . .

To improve their long-term viability, we must give railroads more flexibility in setting rates, without burdening excessively shippers dependent on rail service. Congress is now progressing on comprehensive legislation in this area. We expect regulatory reform of the railroad industry to speed the elimination of wasteful regulations and improve the facilities and equipment of railroads.

Coal is a centerpiece of our nation's energy policy. We are concerned about the cost of transporting coal to its markets, particularly the cost of rail transportation. Within the context of regulatory reform, we must therefore be especially sensitive to the effects of railroad rates on coal. . . .

We must ensure, through such efforts as completion of high speed rail passenger service in the Northeast Corridor, that railroads are an efficient means for personal travel. The decline in the nation's railroad system must be reversed. . . .

The vital artery of urban America is mass transit. It saves energy by providing fuel-efficient alternatives to the automobile. For the poor, the elderly, the disabled, and many other city dwellers, there is no other transportation. If they are to travel at all, to go to work or to shop, they must rely on mass transit. Mass transit serves them, as well as the employers for whom they work and the businesses where they shop. It aids all of us, by unclogging our cities, cleansing our air, and increasing the economic health of our urban areas. . . .

The auto industry and its workers must be assisted during this difficult time. We are committed to an intensive review of the automobile industry's fundamental problems, and to prompt, effective action to help ameliorate those problems. We are also committed to a strong trade adjustment program to help currently unemployed auto workers. . . .

Urban Policy

During the campaign of 1975-1976, our nation's great cities and urban counties were mired in a depression. Unemployment was well above ten percent in many cities and counties; private sector investment and jobs were leaving the great urban centers; poverty and other serious social problems were left unattended; a severe budget squeeze was causing layoffs and cutbacks in essential city services; and the public works of our cities had been allowed to decay. The nation's mayors spent a portion of the year urging Congress to override the Republican Administration's veto of vitally important anti-recession programs. Most seriously, the leadership and citizens of our great urban centers had lost the hope that the future would be better.

Upon taking office, the Democratic Administration responded to these conditions immediately with an $11 billion anti-recession package and, one year later, with the nation's first comprehensive urban policy. The urban policy was the product of a unique effort which actively involved the elected officials of state and local government, representatives of labor, neighborhood organizations, civil rights groups and the members of Congress.

These deliberations produced a blueprint to guide federal action toward cities. The Democratic Administration, in partnership with the Democratic Congress, has moved aggressively to implement parts of the urban policy. Some of these programs have already begun to contribute to the revitalization of the nation's older cities and to assure the continued health of the nation's growing cities. For example, the urban policy has:

• Created the Urban Development Action Grant (UDAG) Program to encourage private investment and jobs to locate or remain in our nation's major cities. UDAG, which is funded at $675 million annually, has already leveraged more than $7 billion of private investment and created more than 200,000 permanent jobs;

• Targeted federal government procurement, facilities and jobs to the high unemployment central cities;

• Increased funding for the Community Development Block Grant program by more than thirty percent and proposed a formula change that provides substantial new aid to the older, more distressed cities and urban counties; and

• Proposed a massive increase in the urban development programs of the Economic Development Administration. . . .

Neighborhoods

From the beginning of the Carter Administration, the government has worked to revitalize neighborhoods and to make them a central component of urban life. As a result of these efforts, the federal government now has a strong neighborhoods policy.

During the 1980's we must continue to strengthen neighborhoods by:

• Making neighborhood organizations partners with government and private sectors in neighborhood revitalization projects;

• Continuing to make neighborhood concerns a major element of our urban policy;

• Developing urban revitalization programs that can be achieved without displacing neighborhood residents; and

• Continuing to reduce discriminatory redlining practices in the mortgage and insurance industries.

Small Community and Rural Development

This Democratic Administration instituted the nation's first comprehensive small community and rural development policy. This policy establishes specific goals, directs numerous organizational and management changes, and initiates an extensive program of action to improve the quality of life for all rural Americans including American Indians/Alaska Natives, rural Hispanics, rural Blacks, and other minorities. Its principles emphasize the need for a strong partnership between the public and private sectors and among all levels of government. Recognizing rural America's great diversity and the limits of the federal role, the Administration's policy invites the nation's governors to establish rural affairs councils to define state rural development strategies and to advance federal-state coordination in addressing priority needs.

Since assuming office in 1977, the Democratic Administration has acted to increase rural access to credit and capital, expand job opportunities, alleviate persistent rural poverty, rehabilitate substandard housing, address the shortage of health professionals in rural areas, improve the mobility of the rural transportation disadvantaged, and enhance educational and training opportunities for disadvantaged rural youth. . . .

Science and Technology

The Nixon-Ford Administration permitted serious decline in the state of science and technology in our country.

There had been a decade of erosion of federal support of research and development. The funding of basic research in particular was far below its peak level of the mid-1960's.

Science and technology advice had been seriously downgraded and removed from the White House, until pressures from the science and engineering community had it restored through an act of Congress.

The previous decline in support had affected opportunities in science and engineering. It had resulted in the inadequate replacement of facilities and instrumentation and their growing obsolescence in the face of new scientific advances and needs.

Not only the work of our academic research centers, but also our technological innovation and economic competitiveness were impaired by this erosion of federal support.

To counter these conditions and help revitalize the country's science and technology, the Carter Administration, working with Congress, has taken a number of steps. The Office of Science and Technology Policy has been strengthened and upgraded. Growth has been restored in the budgets for federal research and development activities. Basic biomedical research has been strengthened to increase our fundamental knowledge of health and disease.

These are just a few of the innovations that have been made. Our scientific and technological agenda remains unfinished. The 1980's offer great promise. During the next four years, we will work to:

• Continue to strengthen our science and technology and provide for continuity and stability of support to research and development;

• Continue to monitor the flow of talent into science and engineering and provide the appropriate training and opportunities to ensure an adequate number of well-trained scientists and engineers in the coming years, with particular emphasis on women and minorities;

• Pay continued attention to the support of research facilities to make certain they remain among the best in the world;

• Successfully launch the Space Shuttle, take advantage of the many opportunities it offers to make space activities more economic and productive, and release new resources for the future scientific exploration of space; and

• Expand our programs of cooperation in science and technology with all nations who seek development and a stable, peaceful world. . . .

The Arts and the Humanities

The arts and humanities are a precious national resource.

Federal commitment to the arts and humanities has been strengthened since 1977 by expanding government funding and services to arts institutions, individual artists, scholars, and teachers. The budgets for the National Endowment for the Arts and the National Endowment for the Humanities have increased substantially. The Federal Council on the Arts and Humanities has been reactivated. Policies of the Carter Administration have fostered high standards of creativity across our nation. The Administration has encouraged the arts and humanities through appropriate federal programs for the citizens of our smallest communities, as well as those of our largest cities. . . .

ENSURING BASIC RIGHTS AND LIBERTIES

Equal Rights Amendment

The Democratic Party recognizes that every issue of importance to this nation and its future concerns women as well as men. As workers and consumers, as parents and heads of households, women are vitally concerned with the economy, energy, foreign policy, and every other issue addressed in this platform. The concerns of women cannot be limited to a portion of the platform; they must be reflected in every section of our Party's policy.

There is, however, a particular concern of women which deserves special emphasis — their entitlement to full equality in our society.

Women are a majority of the population. Yet their equality is not recognized in the Constitution or enforced as the law of the land. The choices faced by women — such as whether to seek employment or work at home, what career or profession to enter, and how to combine employment and family responsibilities — continue to be circumscribed by stereotypes and prejudices. Minority women face the dual discrimination of racism and sexism.

In the 1980's, the Democratic Party commits itself to a Constitution, economy, and society open to women on an equal basis with men.

The primary route to that new horizon is ratification of the Equal Rights Amendment. A Democratic Congress, working with women's leaders, labor, civil and religious organizations, first enacted ERA in Congress and later extended the deadline for ratification. Now, the Democratic Party must ensure that ERA at last becomes the 27th Amendment to the Constitution. We oppose efforts to rescind ERA in states which have already ratified the amendment, and we shall insist that past rescissions are invalid.

In view of the high priority which the Democratic Party places on ratification of the ERA, the Democratic National Committee renews its commitment not to hold national or multi-state meetings, conferences, or conventions in states which have not yet ratified the ERA. The Democratic Party shall withhold financial support and technical campaign assistance from candidates who do not support the ERA. The Democratic Party further urges all national organizations to support the boycott of the unratified states by not holding national meetings, conferences, or conventions in those states. . . .

Civil Rights

The Democratic Party firmly commits itself to protect the civil rights of every citizen and to pursue justice and equal treatment under the law for all citizens.

In the 1960's, enormous progress was made in authorizing civil rights for all our citizens. In many areas, the promises of the civil rights efforts of the 1960's have been met, but much more remains to be done.

An effective affirmative action program is an essential component of our commitment to expanding civil rights protections. The federal government must be a model for private employers, making special efforts in recruitment, training, and promotion to aid minority Americans in overcoming both the historic patterns and the historic burdens of discrimination.

We call on the public and private sectors to live up to and enforce all civil rights laws and regulations, i.e., Equal Employment Opportunity Programs, Title VI and Title VII of the Civil Rights Act, the Fair Housing Laws, and affirmative action requirements.

We advocate strengthening the Office of Civil Rights in the Department of Education and in the Department of Health and Human Services.

We oppose efforts to undermine the Supreme Court's historic mandate of school desegregation, and we support affirmative action goals to overturn patterns of discrimination in education and employment.

Ethnic, racial and other minorities continue to be victims of police abuse, persistent harassment and excessive use of force. In 1979, the Community Relations Service of the Department of Justice noted that "alleged use of deadly force by police and the reaction of minorities was a major force [sic] of racial unrest in the nation in 1978." In response to this finding:

● We call for the Department of Justice's Civil Rights Division to develop uniform federal guidelines and penalties for the use of undue force by local law enforcement agencies;

● We call for the Department of Justice's Civil Rights Division to establish civil rights units at appropriate U.S. Attorneys' offices; and

● We call on the Department of Justice to move concurrently with federal prosecutors so that if a failure to obtain conviction takes place at the state or local level, federal prosecution can occur swiftly. . . .

Civil Liberties

The Democratic Party has been actively committed to protecting fundamental civil liberties. Toward that end, over the past four years, the Carter Administration and the Democratic Congress have enacted legislation to control the use of wiretaps by the government in the pursuit of foreign intelligence; developed the government's first comprehensive program to protect privacy; and worked to enact a criminal code which scrupulously protects civil liberties.

As we enter the 1980's, we must enact grand jury reform; revise the Uniform Code of Military Justice; enact charters for the FBI and the intelligence agencies which recognize vital civil liberty concerns while enabling those agencies to perform their important national security tasks; shape legislation to overturn the Supreme Court *Stanford Daily* decision; and enact a criminal code which meets the very real concerns about protecting civil liberties, and which does not interfere with existing workers' rights.

We call for passage of legislation to charter the purposes, prerogatives, and restraints on the Federal Bureau of Investigation, the Central Intelligence Agency, and other intelligence agencies of government with full protection for the civil rights and liberties of American citizens living at home or abroad. Under no circumstances should American citizens be investigated because of their beliefs.

We support the concept that no employee should be discharged without just cause.

Privacy

Social and technological changes are threatening our citizens' privacy. To meet this challenge, the Carter Administration has developed the first comprehensive privacy policy. Under this policy, administrative action has been taken to cut the number of federal files on individuals and legislation has been passed to protect the privacy of telephone conversations and bank accounts.

In the 1980's we must complete this privacy agenda. Broad legislation must be enacted to protect financial, insurance, medical, and research records. We must have these safeguards to preserve a healthy balance between efficiency and privacy.

The Democratic Party recognizes reproductive freedom as a fundamental human right. We therefore oppose government interference in the reproductive decisions of Americans, especially those government programs or legislative restrictions that deny poor Americans their right to privacy by funding or advocating one or a limited number of reproductive choices only. . . .

Appointments

One of President Carter's highest priorities has been to increase significantly the number of women, Blacks, Hispanics and other minorities in the federal government. That has been done.

More women, Blacks and Hispanics have been appointed to senior government positions than during any other Administration in history. . . .

This record must be continued. The Democratic Party is committed to continue and strengthen the policy of appointing more women and minorities to federal positions at all levels including the Supreme Court.

Handicapped

Great strides have been made toward ending discrimination against the handicapped, through increased employment and education opportunities and greater access to public facilities and services.

In the 1980's, we must continue to work towards the goals of eliminating discrimination and opening opportunities. . . .

Dr. Martin Luther King, Jr.

Dr. Martin Luther King, Jr. led this nation's effort to provide all of its citizens with civil rights and equal opportunities. His commitment to human rights, peace and non-violence stands as a monument to humanity and courage. To honor this outstanding national leader, we must enact legislation that will commemorate his birthday as a national holiday.

Domestic Violence

Each year, 3 to 6 million Americans are injured in acts of domestic violence. To combat this violence the Carter Administration has initiated a government-wide effort to assist and educate victims and rehabilitate victimizers, including:

● The formation of a new Office of Domestic Violence in the Department of Health and Human Services; and

● Amendments to the Child Abuse Prevention and Treatment Act which provides funds to state and community groups. . . .

. . .The Democratic Administration must continue to support the passage of the legislation before the Congress, HR 2977, which would provide direct, immediate assistance to victims effectively and sensitively.

Insular Areas

We must be firmly committed to self-determination for the Virgin Islands, Guam, American Samoa and the Northern Mariana Islands, and vigorously support the realization of whatever political status aspirations are democratically chosen by their peoples. . . . We are committed to pursuing initiatives we have begun to stimulate insular economic development, enhance treatment under federal programs, provide vitally needed special assistance and coordinate and rationalize policies. These measures will result in greater self-sufficiency and balanced growth.

Puerto Rico

We are committed to Puerto Rico's right to enjoy full self-determination and a relationship that can evolve in ways that will most benefit U.S. citizens in Puerto Rico. The Democratic Party respects and supports the desire of the people of Puerto Rico to associate, by their own will freely expressed in a peaceful and democratic process, in permanent union with the United States either as a commonwealth or as a state, or to become an independent nation. . . .

American Indians

The Carter Administration has upheld and defended the historic special relationship between the federal government and Indian tribes. In addition, it has strongly supported the policy of self-determination and the right to practice the ancestral religions that are important to many tribal members. More than $24 million over the next ten years has been committed to assist Indian tribes with energy resources in making decisions about the development and protection of these resources. The Administration has firmly reiterated its fundamental opposition to the policy of termination which was so detrimental to Indians and their relationship with the federal government.

These policies must continue as the federal government finds better means of dealing effectively and compassionately with Indian tribes and individuals. The federal government must honor its treaty commitments. The federal government must redouble its efforts to improve the housing, health care, education and general welfare of Indians. Finally, the federal government must work as an equal partner with tribes as they decide for themselves the best means of managing their substantial energy resources.

Ethnic America

President Carter has stated that the composition of American society is analogous to a beautiful mosaic. . . .

Ethnic Americans share the concerns of all Americans. They too are concerned about decent housing, health care, equal employment opportunities, care of the elderly, and education. In addition, ethnic Americans have some concerns of their own. . . .

President Carter established the Office of Ethnic Affairs and charged it with a broad and diverse mission. The predominant functions of the office are to link the Administration and its ethnic constituents, to foster the concept of pluralism, and to enable all Americans to partake equally in the American way of life.

Americans Living Abroad

Almost three million American citizens live overseas, both as government employees and private citizens. We know only too well the dangers and sacrifices some of these government officials face in serving their country. With the threat of terrorism and political unrest always present, we are committed to improving the security of our embassies and missions abroad. Our government must work with other governments to ensure that Americans are protected while performing their vital duties in the interest of the United States. . . .

Government Operation and Reform

MAKING GOVERNMENT EFFECTIVE AND EFFICIENT

The Democratic Party has long stood for an active, responsive, vigorous government. Democrats of our generation have a special obligation to ensure that government is also efficient and well managed.

We understand full well the importance of this obligation. We realize that even the most brilliantly conceived federal programs are doomed to failure if they are not intelligently and efficiently managed.

The kind of government we Democrats stand for is a government that *cares* and knows how to translate that caring into effective action; a government whose heart and head are working in concert.

Over the last four years the Democratic Administration and the Democratic Congress have built a dramatic government reform record. In the years ahead we must carefully implement the changes we have made, and we must pursue additional measures to provide the efficient government the people have a right to expect.

Regulatory Reform

Federal regulations are needed to protect consumers and providers in the areas of health, safety, and the environment. Four years ago, however, the overall regulatory machine desperately needed an overhaul. Some rules served only to protect favored industries against competition, at the public's expense. Others imposed conflicting or needlessly costly requirements.

For decades, the economy has been hamstrung by anticompetitive regulations. A Democratic Administration and a Democratic Congress are completing the most sweeping deregulation in history. Actions already taken and bills currently pending are revamping the rules governing airlines, banking, trucking, railroads, and telecommunications. Airline deregulation in its first year of operation alone has saved passengers over 2.5 billion dollars.

For the regulatory programs our country does need, the Administration has established a new management system. Under Executive Order 12044, agencies are reviewing and eliminating outdated rules and analyzing the full impact of new rules before they are issued. They are developing alternative regulatory approaches which can reduce compliance costs without sacrificing goals. They are increasing public participation in the regulatory process. The Regulatory Council is publishing the first government-wide list of upcoming rules, the Regulatory Calendar, and is using it to eliminate conflict and duplication.

The challenges of the Eighties will place great demands on our regulatory system. The reforms we have put in place are building machinery that can meet those challenges. However, much work lies ahead to implement the steps we have taken and go further.

We must continue to conduct an agency-by-agency review to make regulation less intrusive and more effective. . . .

Tax Reform

In 1976, this Party pledged to seek fundamental tax reform, for we believed that our tax system had lost much of its needed fairness and equity. President Carter honored that pledge by proposing to Congress the most comprehensive and far-reaching set of tax reform proposals ever made by any Administration. That proposal would have closed over $9 billion worth of tax loopholes, simplified our tax laws, and provided funds for substantial tax reduction for low and middle income taxpayers.

Once again, we call on Congress to legislate meaningful tax reform. We cannot any longer allow the special interests to preserve their particular benefits and loopholes at the expense of the average taxpayers. The fight for tax reform must go forward, and the Party pledges to be a part of that important effort. Therefore, we pledge to seek tax reforms which:

● Encourage savings by low and middle income taxpayers;

● Close tax loopholes which benefit only special interest at the expense of the average taxpayer and use the proceeds to bring relief to low and middle income Americans;

● Simplify the tax code and ease the burden on taxpayers in the preparation of their tax returns;

● Encourage capital formation, innovation and new production in the United States;

745

● Curb tax deductions, like those for three-martini lunches, conventions, first class travel, and other expense account deductions, which encourage consumption, discourage saving, and thus impede productivity;

● End tax discrimination that penalizes married working couples; and

● End abuses in the tax treatment of foreign sources, such as special tax treatment and incentives for multi-national corporations that drain jobs and capital from the American economy.

Capital formation is essential both to control inflation and to encourage growth. New tax reform efforts are needed to increase savings and investment, promote the principle of progressive taxation, close loopholes, and maintain adequate levels of federal revenue.

Management

The need to restrain federal spending means that every dollar of the budget must be spent in the most efficient way possible. To achieve this, the Democratic Partnership has been working to streamline the management of the federal government and eliminate waste and fraud from federal programs. Real progress has been made in these important areas.

While these reforms have produced substantial savings for the taxpayers, they must be sustained in the coming years to realize their full potential.

The Civil Service Reform Act can be used to encourage improved productivity of the federal government.

GOVERNMENT OPENNESS AND INTEGRITY

Under the Nixon-Ford Administration the federal government was closed to all but a privileged few and the public had lost faith in the integrity of its public servants.

The Democratic Party takes pride in its long and outstanding record of leadership in opening up the processes of government to genuine participation by the people, and in making government truly responsive to the basic needs of all the American people.

For the last four years, the Carter Administration and the Democratic Congress have devoted a great deal of time and resources to opening government processes and ensuring the integrity of government officials.

The Ethics in Government Act now requires all senior government officials to make a full financial disclosure and severely limits the "revolving door" practice that has developed among former federal employees of representing private parties before the federal agencies in which they recently held significant positions.

A statutory provision has now been made for the appointment of a special prosecutor in cases of alleged wrong-doing by senior government officials.

"Whistle-blowers" in the federal government (those who report waste and illegalities) have now been given special statutory protection to prevent possible retribution.

An Executive Order has been issued significantly reducing the amount of classified information, and increasing the amount of classified material to be released over the next decade by about 250 million pages. . . .

Law Enforcement

Numerous changes were necessary when the Democrats took office in 1976. The essential trust between police officers and the public they protect had deteriorated. Funds committed by Congress had been terribly misspent during the eight Republican years.

The Carter Administration has taken solid steps toward correcting this serious problem. It has formalized the relationship between federal and state law enforcement officials to ensure maximum cooperation between federal and state agencies. It has taken long strides toward creating and implementing uniform national guidelines for federal prisons and encouraging state penal institutions to use the same guidelines.

The Democratic Party supports the enactment of a revised federal criminal code which simplifies the currently complex federal criminal law in order to make our federal criminal justice efforts more effective, and repeals antiquated laws while fully protecting all civil liberties. As that effort proceeds, we must ensure that the rights of workers to engage in peaceful picketing during labor disputes are fully protected.

The Democratic Party affirms the right of sportsmen to possess guns for purely hunting and target-shooting purposes. However, handguns simplify and intensify violent crime. Ways must be found to curtail the availability of these weapons. The Democratic Party supports enactment of federal legislation to strengthen the presently inadequate regulations over the manufacture, assembly, distribution, and possession of handguns and to ban "Saturday night specials."

Most important, the government has used its own resources to resolve satisfactorily concerns over the use of deadly force. The Administration has made progress toward the preparation of uniform guidelines for all police departments. They have also utilized the conciliation services available through the Community Relations Service to establish closer working ties among the police and community organizations. . . .

Paperwork Reduction

Over the years the federal government has imposed more and more paperwork on the private sector. The Carter Administration has stopped that trend and worked to cut the paperwork burden. . . .

We need further legislation. We urge a continuation of the effort to reduce government documents to simple English, easily understandable by all. The Administration is working with Congress to pass a Paperwork

Reduction Act, which will close wide loopholes in the current oversight process.

Election Reform

Recent reforms in the election process have aided immeasurably in opening the process to more people and have begun to reduce the influence of special interests. The limitations on campaign contributions and the public financing of Presidential elections are two reforms which have worked very well. Business political action committees continue to spend excessively, however. Further reform in this area is essential. In the 1980's we need to enact reforms which will:

- Provide for public financing of Congressional campaigns;
- Lower contributions limits for political action committees;
- Close the loophole that allows private spending in Presidential elections contrary to the intent of the election law reforms;
- Encourage voter participation in elections through use of simplified procedures for registration in states that lack mail or election day registration procedures, and by resisting efforts to reduce access to bilingual ballots; and
- Increase opportunities for full participation in all areas of party and government affairs by the low and moderate income majority of Americans.

Postal Service

The private expression statutes guarantee the protection and security of the mail for all Americans. They are essential to the maintenance of a national postal system, which will require an adequate public service subsidy to assure the delivery of mail to all Americans.

[Energy, Environment and Agriculture]

ENERGY

For the past four years, the Democratic Party's highest legislative priority has been the development of our nation's first comprehensive energy policy. Our actions were necessitated by the Republican Administration's policy that fostered dependence on foreign oil. This Republican legacy led to America's petroleum paralysis, which weakened our security, undermined our strength abroad, threatened our environment and endangered our economic health....

The struggle to develop an energy policy was difficult and time-consuming. Tough decisions, especially in the area of oil price decontrol, were necessary to reduce our dependence of foreign oil.

Not all of our energy problems have been solved. Yet the achievements of the past four years leave little doubt that we are finally serious about the problems caused by our excessive reliance on foreign oil. As a result of our national energy policy, oil imports will be cut in half by the end of this decade, saving our nation hundreds of billion of dollars. A framework is now in place that will permit further progress in the 1980's. Our economic security demands that we drastically reduce the massive flow of dollars into the OPEC treasuries and oil company bank accounts at the expense of American consumers and business. . . .

The following specific actions must be taken.

We must make energy conservation our highest priority, not only to reduce our dependence on foreign oil, but also to guarantee that our children and grandchildren have an adequate supply of energy. If we can convince one of every four drivers exceeding the 55 mile per hour speed limit to reduce their speed, we can save 100,000 barrels a day. Conservation is the cheapest form of energy production.

We must establish a massive residential energy conservation grant program. We must provide subsidized loans, direct financial assistance, and other substantial incentives to make all residences in the United States energy efficient, through upgraded insulation, heating, cooling and waterheating. Special incentives should be afforded for the use of renewable energy resources such as passive and active solar energy systems. Our goal should be to ensure that all economically justified energy efficiency investments are made by 1990.

We should use our energy programs to aid in rebuilding the industrial heartland. Industry must be given financial incentives to improve the energy efficiency of industrial processes and to build substantial amounts of generating capacity through co-generation.

We must implement mandatory Building Energy Performance Standards (BEPS) to encourage the design and construction of energy efficient buildings. Energy efficiency standards should apply to *all* new construction. Implementation of energy efficiency standards should begin with federal government buildings. In addition, the federal government should lead the way in implementing solar and energy efficiency improvements programs through its loan and insurance agencies by requiring energy conservation standards for federally assisted properties.

In recognition of the potential for substantial energy savings if our most efficient methods of transportation are utilized, we must provide direct economic assistance where private capital is unavailable to improve those means of transport.

Major new efforts must be launched to develop synthetic and alternative renewable energy sources. In pursuing a strong program of synthetic fuel plants we must also be sensitive to environmental and water concerns. The federal government must help eliminate red-tape involved in the construction of vital energy facilities. The Energy Mobilization Board, an essential mechanism to speed the construction of vital energy facilities, should be able to override state and local substantive law only with the consent of Congress and the President.

[Future of Coal]

The Democratic Party regards coal as our nation's greatest energy resource. It must play a decisive role in America's energy future. We must increase our use of coal. To accomplish this, we must see that shippers are not overburdened with excessive rates for transportation. Severance taxes levied for depletion of natural resources should be equitable. We must make clean coal conversion a reality. To this end, we will assist utilities that are large enough to permit coal conversion while maintaining or improving air quality. We must also provide incentives for industrial boiler coal conversion. Coal conversion can and must be accomplished in a manner that protects public health, nationally, regionally and locally. It can and must increase the use of coal, reduce the demand for oil, and provide employment where jobs are needed the most. . . .

We must lead the Western World in developing a program for increased use of coal in Europe, Japan, and the developing nations.

Oil exploration on federal lands must be accelerated, consistent with environmental protections.

Offshore energy leasing and development should be conditioned on full protection of the environment and marine resources. Lease sales should proceed only after appropriate safeguards necessary to preserve and protect vital natural resources are put in place. The determination of what safeguards are needed must be based on a complete assessment of the effects of offshore activity on the marine and coastal environment, and must be made in conjunction with the Environmental Protection Agency and the National Oceanic and Atmospheric Agency, the federal agencies charged with protecting our nation's fishery and other environmental resources.

Solar energy use must be increased, and strong efforts, including continued financial support, must be undertaken to make certain that we achieve the goal of having solar energy account for 20% of our total energy by the year 2000. . . .

[Alcohol Fuels]

We must encourage research and development of hydrogen or electric powered vehicles. We must fully commit ourselves to an alcohol fuel program. The federal government should expand its use of alcohol fuels in government and military vehicles. This will help reduce surplus feed grain and help to stabilize prices. The Democratic Party pledges that production of fuel-grade alcohol will be increased until at least a target of 500 million barrels of ethanol by 1981 is achieved.

A stand-by gasoline rationing plan must be adopted for use in the event of a serious energy supply interruption. In times of supply interruption, rationing is essential for equitable and prompt distribution of gas to the public. The Strategic Petroleum Reserve should be filled as market conditions permit, consistent with the requirements of existing law.

We must impose a moratorium on the acquisition of competing coal companies and solar energy companies by major oil companies.

Legislation must be enacted to prohibit purchases by oil companies of energy or non-energy companies unless the purchase would enhance competition.

The major oil companies must be responsible and accountable in their production, importation and distribution of fossil fuels. Oil is as basic to our economy, defense, and general welfare as electric power and money. Consequently, the oil companies must be invested with public purpose. To accomplish this objective, we support strengthened leasing regulations, reporting requirements and monitoring by the Departments of Energy and Justice. . . .

ENVIRONMENT

We are charged with the stewardship of an irreplaceable environment. The Democratic Party must continue to be as environmentally progressive in the future as it has been in the past. Progress in environmental quality — a major achievement of the 1970's — must continue in the 1980's. The environmental problems we face today are, if anything, more challenging and urgent than those of ten years ago.

The great strides we have taken during the past few years are the best evidence of our commitment to resource conservation and environmental restoration. We have compiled a proud record.

During the next four years, we must carry forward vigorously with these important policies, and move to address a series of new challenges.

We must move decisively to protect our countryside and our coastline from overdevelopment and mismanagement. Major efforts are now underway to solve such problems as disappearing farmland and development on our barrier islands. These efforts should help forge a strong national consensus behind the realization that protection must be balanced with the need to properly manage and utilize our land resources during the 1980's.

We must develop new and improved working relationships among federal, state, local, tribal, and territorial governments and private interests, to manage effectively our programs for increased domestic energy production and their impact on people, water, air, and the environment in general. All of our energy development efforts should be carried out without sacrificing environmental quality.

We must continue on the path to a sustainable energy future — a future based increasingly on renewable resources and energy conservation. Our national goal of having 20% of our energy from renewable resources in the year 2000 must become a working target, not a forgotten slogan. Conservation must remain the cornerstone of our national energy supply.

New efforts at home and abroad will be required in the early 1980's to face squarely such global problems as the destruction of forests, the loss of countless irreplaceable species, growing world population, acid rain, and carbon dioxide buildup.

Passage by Congress of the hazardous waste cleanup proposal will provide the basis for a major effort beginning in 1981 to clean up the thousands of hazardous waste dump sites across the country. Toxic chemicals are a serious threat to the health of our people. We must continue our programs to improve agency performance in many areas, such as protection of groundwaters, in order to better protect the public.

[Support for Standards]

We must strive to ensure that environmental regulations cost no more than necessary and are streamlined to eliminate waste, duplication and delay. We must not lose sight of the fact that the benefits of these regulations far outweigh their costs. We must work to reform regulation without deforming it.

We support the allocation of resources to the Environmental Protection Agency and other environmental agencies sufficient to carry out their mandates.

We support strict adherence to automobile pollution standards.

We will support policies to eliminate acid rain pollution from power plant emissions.

We will commit ourselves to efficient transportation alternatives, including mass transit, car pooling, van pooling, employer based commuter plans, and hydrogen and electric commuter vehicles.

We will continue to fight noise pollution in our urban centers and job sites.

We will encourage the recycling of municipal solid waste.

We will seek a strong "super-fund" law financed by government and industry.

We must continue to pursue offshore energy leasing to stimulate our domestic oil and gas production and reduce our dependence on foreign oil consistent with environmental and marine concerns.

We will fund adequately the Land and Water Conservation Fund to protect our national park system.

We will implement vigorously the Toxic Substances Control Act.

Often, actions by one nation affect the economic growth and the quality of life in other nations. Such actions can be influenced by international agreement and incentives.

To defend against environmental risks that cross national frontiers, international cooperation must be extended to new areas, such as acid rain, deforestation and desertification, buildup of carbon dioxide in the atmosphere, thinning of the ozone shield, air and water pollution, oil spills, chemicals in the environment, and disposal of radioactive waste.

Water

Water is a necessity to all, and represents life itself to much of the American Union. We recognize especially the singular dependence of the Western states on scarce water supplies. The development of navigation, irrigation, flood control, and hydroelectric projects is vital to the economic health of the West, and correspondingly to the entire nation.

Working with Congress, the Democratic Administration will implement a national water policy which recognizes the special needs of the West. Toward this end, we support the modern standards and valid cost-benefit analysis suggested by the Federal Water Resources Council. We support a federal study, in partnership with the affected states, to explore possibilities and recommend alternatives relative to importation of water into arid and semi-arid states. We also support state, local, and tribal participation in all phases of water programs within their respective jurisdictions. . . .

AGRICULTURE

America's farmers are among the most vital economic forces of the nation. Because of their extraordinary productivity, America's farm workers provide more food and fiber per person at a lower cost than their counterparts in any other country. . . .

In 1977, the Democratic Administration inherited a farm economy marked by serious over-production and badly outdated price support programs. Farm prices and incomes were plummeting, partly in response to misguided attempts at price controls. The livestock sector was in its third straight year of loss, and a herd liquidation of unprecedented scale was underway.

Because of actions taken by the Democratic Administration and Democratic Congress, this situation was turned around in 1978 and 1979. U.S. agriculture was put back on a track of steady, sustained growth and improvement. The sharp decline of farm prices and farm incomes was reversed. . . .

Recently, however, the nation's farm economy has been hurt by reduced prices; high costs of production, including energy, inflation, equipment, and high interest rates. As a result, our nation's farmers are facing a time of hardship.

Agricultural policy in the 1980's must strengthen the forces which made American farmers the most productive in the world and American agriculture the hope of hungry people everywhere. In this way, we can ensure a decade of prosperity for farmers and of agricultural abundance for America's consumers. . . .

Forestry

America's national forests contain a national treasure that provides recreation, wilderness, fish and wildlife, and timber products.

We reaffirm the Democratic Party's traditional support for multiple-use management to ensure the survival of these precious resources for this generation and generations to come.

We call for the speedy resolution by Congress of the Roadless Area Review and Evaluation, stimulated by this Administration, to determine which areas are best suited for wilderness and which should be released for timber harvest and multiple-use management.

We support continued assistance to private, non-industrial forest owners to increase their management potential. . . .

Fisheries

Under the Democratic Administration the U.S. fishing industry has made substantial progress, as evidenced by the following:

• Commercial landings of fish in 1979 were up 45% in value and 21% in quantity compared with 1977;

• The U.S. share of the catch in our 200-mile fisheries conservation zone increased from 27% in 1978 to 33% in 1979;

• Over the same period, the foreign catch of fish in the U.S. 200-mile zone dropped 6%, and 29% from the average for the five preceding years;

• The U.S. has moved from fifth in the world in 1977 to fourth in 1978 in total commercial fish landings; and

• Exports of U.S. edible fishery products in 1979 were up 116% in value and 67% in quantity compared with 1977.

While such trends are encouraging, there remains a tremendous potential for growth. By volume, 67%, and by value, 34%, of the harvest in the fishery conservation zone is still taken by foreign vessels. The value of the catch to foreign fishermen was $470 million in 1979. . . .

Foreign Policy

Introduction

When the Democratic Party came into office almost four years ago, the most dangerous threat to America's position in the world was the profound disillusionment and mistrust which the American people felt for their own government. This had reached the point where the very term "national security" became synonymous with the abuse of power, deceit and violation of public trust. It undermined our capacity to defend our interests and to play our proper role in the world at a time when Soviet power was continuing to grow.

The hallmark of the previous eight years of Republican Administration had been to emphasize the primacy of power politics irrespective of compatibility with American values and with the increasing power of the Soviet Union. The result was disrespect abroad and discontent at home.

The Democratic Party was determined to make our values a central factor in shaping American foreign policy. The one-sided emphasis of the previous Republican Administration had led many Americans to a suspicion of power, and in some respects, even to rejection of military strength. The American people longed to see their country once again identified with widespread human aspirations. The Democratic Party understood, if the Republicans did not, that this is essential to preserve our long-term interests in the world.

The Democratic Administration sought to reconcile these two require-ments of American foreign policy — principle and strength. Both are required to maintain a constructive and secure relationship between America and the rest of the world. We have tried to make clear the continuing importance of American strength in a world of change. Without such strength, there is a genuine risk that global change will deteriorate into anarchy to be exploited by our adversaries' military power. Thus, the revival of American strength has been a central pre-occupation of the Democratic Administration.

The use of American power is necessary as a means of shaping not only a more secure, but also a more decent world. To shape a decent world, we must pursue objectives that are moral, that make clear our support for the aspirations of mankind and that are rooted in the ideals of the American people.

That is why the Democrats have stressed human rights. That is why America once again has supported the aspirations of the vast majority of the world's population for greater human justice and freedom. As we continue to strive to solve our own internal problems, we are proud of the values for which the United States has always stood. We should continue to be a beacon of liberty around the world and to effectively and positively state America's case for freedom to the world through various governmental and nongovernmental channels.

A foreign policy which seeks to blend our ideals and our strength does not easily reduce itself to simple statements.

First, we must consistently strengthen our relations with likeminded industrial democracies. In meeting the dangers of the coming decade the United States will consult closely with our Allies to advance common security and political goals. As a result of annual summit meetings, coordinated economic policies and effective programs of international energy conservation have been fashioned. With the cooperation of rich and poor nations alike, a new international trade agreement has been reached which safeguards our free enterprise system from protectionism and gives us greater economic opportunity in the world, while it gives the developing world a stake in the stability of the world's economy.

Second, we must continue to improve our relations with the Third World by being sensitive to their legitimate aspirations. The United States should be a positive force for peaceful change in responding to ferment in the Third World. Today, thanks to a number of steps that have been taken — strengthening the international aid institutions, the Panama Canal treaties, the Zimbabwe settlement, the normalization of relations with China — the United States has a healthier and more productive relationship with these countries.

Our third objective must be peace in the Middle East. The Carter Administration has pursued this objective with determination and together with the leaders of Israel and Egypt, has overcome great obstacles in the last three years. America made this commitment for two fundamental reasons — morality and national security.

Our nation feels a profound moral obligation to sustain and assure the security of Israel. That is why our relationship with Israel is, in most respects, a unique one. Israel is the single democracy, the most stable government, the most strategic asset and our closest ally in the region.

To fulfill this imperative, we must move towards peace in the Middle East. Without peace, there is a growing prospect, indeed inevitability, that this region will become radicalized, susceptible to foreign intrusion, and possibly involved in another war. Thus, peace in the Middle East also is vital for our national security interests. . . .

Defense

America's military strength is and must be unsurpassed. The Democratic Administration has moved to reverse the threatened decline in America's world position. While claiming concern for our nation's defense preparedness, the Nixon-Ford Administration presided over a steady decline of 33 percent in real U.S. military spending between 1968 and 1976.

As a result of the joint efforts of the Democratic Administration and Congress, there has been a real increase in our defense spending in every year since 1976. This increase is necessary in order to compensate for the decline in U.S. military strength over the previous eight years and to assure a high quality of military personnel, an effective nuclear deterrent capability, a capable conventional fighting force and an improved intelligence capability. We will act to further improve intelligence gathering and analysis.

We must be careful that our defense dollars are spent wisely. We must make sure that we develop and deploy practical weapons and that we have the resources to ensure that the men and women who must operate these weapons have the skill to do so.

The serious question of manpower shortages must be addressed promptly. In order to prevent the necessity of a peacetime draft, the all-volunteer force must have wage standards which will retain experienced personnel or recruit new personnel upon whom an increasingly sophisticated military heavily depends.

We will upgrade the combat readiness of our armed forces. We will give the highest priority to combat training, to an effective Reserve and Guard force, and to sufficient supplies, spare parts, fuel and ammunition. Registration of 19-year-olds is intended to enable the United States to mobilize more rapidly in the event of an emergency, which is the only time it should be used. We do not favor a peacetime draft or the exclusion of women from registration. We will seek ways to expand voluntary service in both the armed forces and non-military programs such as VISTA, the Young Adult Conservation Corps, and the Peace Corps.

We need to go forward to protect our retaliatory capabilities in the face of continuing Soviet advances in their strategic forces.

The nation has moved to modernize its strategic deterrent through the MX, Trident, and cruise missile systems. The MX missile deployment wil enhance the survivability of our land-based intercontinental ballistic missile force. Cruise missiles will modernize our strategic air deterrent, and the new Trident submarine, with a missile range of over 4,000 miles, will both improve and help guarantee the invulnerability of our nuclear deterrent.

The United States has acted to correct the dangerous military imbalance which had developed in Europe, by initiating and obtaining Allied support for a long overdue NATO long-term defense program and proceeding toward the deployment in Europe of long-range theater nuclear deterrents to counter the Soviet buildup of such weaponry in Europe. Our commitment to increase defense spending by at least three percent per year is crucial to the maintenance of Allied consensus and confidence in this regard. We need to modernize our conventional military capabilities so that we can better protect American lives and American interests abroad. . . .

. . . We have given particular attention to developing the facilities and capabilities to further support the policy of the United States with regard to the Persian Gulf enunciated by President Carter in the State of the Union address on January 23, 1980: "Let our position be absolutely clear: an attempt by any outside force to gain control of the Persian Gulf region will be regarded as an assault on the vital interests of the United States of America and such an assault will be repelled by any means necessary, including military force."

We are confident that the negotiation of American overseas military facilities in support of this effort as well as other areas of the world will be conducted with respect for the independence, integrity and cultural values of the host countries.

The Democratic Party recognizes the strategic value of Israel and that peace in the Middle East requires a militarily secure Israel. Because Middle East nations that have not joined the peace process have been able to purchase the latest sophisticated Soviet and other weaponry, the technological advantage which Israel holds over its adversaries has been jeopardized. The progress of the peace talks means that Israel has gained considerable security advantages from peace with Egypt. At the same time, Israel will lose some of the tactical advantages previously provided by territory occupied in 1967. Any further war Israel fights could take place close to its population centers. Therefore, we pledge a continued high level of U.S. military support for Israel.

Our military supply relationship with other nations of the Middle East is also important to our national security. It should continue to be carried out in a manner which does not jeopardize the security of Israel.

U.S.-Soviet Relations

A strong, consistent, and principled policy toward the Soviet Union is a vital element of our foreign policy everywhere. The Democratic Administration will use all its resources — including both firm diplomacy and military power — to deter adventurism and to make restraint the only acceptable course available to our adversaries. . . .

We must continue to support U.S. actions such as the Olympic boycott and trade restrictions in order to show determined opposition to Soviet aggression. We insist on immediate Soviet withdrawal from Afghanistan and the reestablishment of a non-aligned, independent government which is supported by the people of Afghanistan. The Soviet invasion of Afghanistan makes it extremely important that the United States be ready to aid those in the Third World resisting Soviet, Cuban, and East German domination.

While the invasion of Afghanistan has side-tracked our pursuit of a productive relationship with the Soviet Union, the Democratic Party supports efforts to strengthen ties to the nations of Eastern Europe. Treating each of those nations with sensitivity to its individual situation, the U.S. has steadily improved relations with the people of Hungary, Poland, and Romania. While Soviet conduct has profoundly damaged East-West relations, the U.S. should continue to draw distinctions, to the extent possible, between the sanctions it imposes on economic dealings with Moscow and similar relations with some other members of the Warsaw Pact, as long as they are not diverting that trade, in grain or items under export control, to the use of the Soviet Union and as long as they are willing to maintain a constructive dialogue on issues of concern and significance to the United States.

Through the measures now being taken, including both denial of economic benefits and the Olympic boycott, as well as our efforts to enhance the security of the region more directly affected, the objective should be to make the Soviets pay a price for their act of international aggression. We should continue to do so along with efforts to strengthen our national defense. We cannot permit this attack across an international border, with the threat it poses to the region and thus to the strategic balance, to go unanswered. Only firmness now can prevent new adventures later.

The Democratic Administration will also seek to reverse the recent sharp downturn in Soviet Jewish emigration and to obtain the release of dissidents now detained in the Soviet Union, including 41 members of the Helsinki Watch Groups who are in Soviet prisons, labor camps and banishment for their human rights activity. We will pursue our human rights concerns as a necessary part of overall progress on the range of political, military and economic issues between the United States and the Soviet Union — including the possibility of improved, mutually beneficial economic relations between our two countries.

Consideration of human rights should be a permanent feature of U.S.-Soviet relations. We salute those Soviet citizens active in the Moscow, Ukrainian, Lithuanian, Armenian, and Georgian Helsinki Monitoring Groups, assert our support of the courageous human rights advocate, Nobel Peace Prize Winner, Dr. Andrei Sakharov, and call for Dr. Sakharov's release from forced exile as well as the release of all political prisoners in the U.S.S.R.

We pledge that a Democratic Administration will raise the question of the Soviet violation of human rights at all appropriate international forums.

Arms Control

The SALT II Treaty also serves our security interests. It is a vital step in an arms control process that can begin to lift from humanity the shadow of nuclear war. That process, also, must be sustained.

Soviet aggression against Afghanistan has delayed the course of ratification of the SALT II Treaty, but we must continue to pursue both security priorities: deterrence of Soviet aggression and balanced arms control agreements. Both the response to Afghanistan and the SALT II Treaty serve this purpose.

The SALT Treaty is in the U.S. interest because it is an important way of restraining Soviet behavior.

Without SALT II, the Soviets could have hundreds more missiles and thousands more nuclear warheads than the Treaty permits. Under the Treaty, they would have to eliminate many nuclear weapons they already have.

The Treaty helps sustain a strong American position in the world. Our Allies and other nations around the world know the SALT II Treaty serves their security interests as well as ours. American support for arms control is important to our standing in the international community, the same community that has rebuked the Soviets for their attempted suppression of Afghanistan. It is also important to our efforts to organize an enduring response to the growing threat to Europe of the Soviet SS-20 nuclear missiles and to Soviet aggression in Afghanistan.

Along with support for SALT, we seek to maintain a stable conventional and theater nuclear balance in Europe. We will support modernization programs in which European countries bear their fair share of the cost and other burdens. At the same time, we will ensure that no possibility for effective limits on theater nuclear weapons is left unexplored. The Democratic Administration will join with our NATO allies in making far-reaching, equitable, and verifiable proposals for nuclear and conventional arms control in Europe.

The Democratic Party wants an arms control process to continue, just as it wants to sustain strong policies against Soviet aggression in Afghanistan. We understand that both build peace and make our nation more secure. Accordingly, we must persist in a strong policy regarding the Soviet aggression, and we must seek ratification of SALT as soon as it is feasible.

A Democratic Administration will not accept an indefinite deferral of strategic arms control. On the basis of review and planning of U.S. security requirements in the coming decade, we are determined to pursue negotiations with the Soviet Union, aimed at the achievement of strategic stability and, for the first time, of major reductions and qualitative limits on strategic systems. The American SALT proposals in March 1977 were the first effort to seek such reductions, which remain the goal and justification of arms control. A Democratic Administration will treat the Soviet government's readiness to negotiate verifiable, substantial and significant reductions and qualitative limits as a test of its seriousness about arms control and the compatibility of its approach to arms control with that of the United States. . . .

Human Rights

In the area of international affairs, the Democratic Administration has placed America's power in the service of a more decent world by once again living up to our own values and working in a formal, deliberate way to foster the principles set out in the Universal Declaration of Human Rights.

This has been accomplished through a strong commitment to human rights, which must be seen not only as a moral imperative but as the only secure and enduring basis upon which a truly stable world order can be fashioned. There have been successes in Asia, Latin America, and elsewhere in the world. We must be undaunted by the increasing repression in the Soviet Union. We support measures designed to restrict trade with the Soviet Union until such time as Soviet emigration policy is made fair and non-restrictive.

We must be vigilant about human rights violations in any country in which they occur including South Africa. We note in particular that many of the Communist-dominated countries are persistent violators of the most basic human freedoms — the right to free speech, the right to religious freedom, the right to travel and emigrate, and the right to be free from arbitrary harrassment [*sic*].

We support Senate ratification of the Genocide Convention and the International Convenants on Human Rights as soon as possible. . . .

Refugees and Migration

America's roots are found in the immigrants and refugees who have come to our shores to build new lives in a new world. The Democratic Party pledges to honor our historic commitment to this heritage.

The first comprehensive reform of this nation's refugee policies in over 25 years was completed with the signing in March 1980 of the Refugee Act of 1980, based on legislation submitted to Congress by the Carter Administration in March 1979.

This Act offers a comprehensive alternative to the chaotic movement and the inefficient and inequitable administration of past refugee programs in the United States. We favor the full use of refugee legislation now to cope with the flow of Cuban and Haitian refugees, and to help the states, local communities and voluntary agencies resettle them across our land. We urge that monies be distributed to voluntary agencies fairly so that aid is distributed to all refugees without discrimination.

The Administration also established the first refugee coordination office in the Department of State under the leadership of a special ambassador and coordinator for refugee affairs and programs.

The new legislation and the coordinator's office will bring common sense and consolidation to our nation's previously fragmented, inconsistent, and, in many ways, outdated refugee and immigration policies.

A Select Commission on Immigration and Refugee Policy is now at work to further reform the system. We pledge our support to the goals and purposes of the Commission, and we urge the Administration to move aggressively in this area once the Commission submits its report.

Once that report has been completed, we must work to resolve the issue of undocumented residents in a fair and humane way. We will oppose any legislation designed to allow workers into the country to undercut U.S. wages and working conditions, and which would re-establish the bracero program of the past.

World population projections, as well as international economic indicators — especially in the Third World — forewarn us that migration pressures will mount rapidly in many areas of the world in the decade ahead. Our own situation of undocumented workers underscores how difficult it is to deal with economic and employment forces that are beyond any nation's immediate control. Most of Europe, and many parts of Latin America and Asia, face similar dilemmas. For example, Mexico faces the pressure of migration from Central America.

We will work with other nations to develop international policies to regularize population movement and to protect the human rights of migrants even as we protect the jobs of American workers and the economic interest of the United States. In this Hemisphere, such a policy will require close cooperation with our neighbors, especially Mexico and Canada.

We must also work to resolve the difficult problems presented by the immigration from Haiti and from the more recent immigration from Cuba. In doing so, we must ensure that there is no discrimination in the treatment afforded to the Cubans or Haitians. We must also work to ensure that future Cuban immigration is handled in an orderly way, consistent with our laws. To ameliorate the impact on state and local communities and school districts of the influx of new immigrants from Cuba and Haiti, we must provide the affected areas with special fiscal assistance. . . .

The Middle East

When the Democratic Administration began in 1977, the prospects for peace in the Middle East were bleak. Despite efforts over thirty years, Israel still faced an Arab world that was totally hostile to it; it was still denied any movement towards its dream of living at peace with its neighbors, behind secure and recognized frontiers.

Almost immediately after his inauguration, President Carter undertook to move the peace process forward. Following the historic visit of President Sadat to Jerusalem, the Administration's efforts led to Camp David, where the two Presidents and Prime Minister Begin in thirteen days created the Camp David Accords — the most promising effort in three decades for creating a genuine and lasting peace in the Middle East.

Following President Carter's trip to the Middle East in March 1979, Prime Minister Begin and President Sadat signed the Israel-Egypt peace treaty at the White House. A year later, that treaty has led to the transfer of two-thirds of the Sinai to Egypt — along with the Sinai oil fields; ambassadors have been exchanged; borders have been opened; and normalization of relations is well underway. Israel has finally gained peace with its largest Arab neighbor. In sum, this Democratic Administration has done more to achieve Israel's dream of peace than any other Administration in thirty years.

Negotiations are continuing under the Camp David framework on full autonomy for the inhabitants of the West Bank and Gaza, in order to preserve fully Israel's security while permitting the Palestinians living in the territories to participate in determining their own future. The United States is a full partner in negotiations between Israel and Egypt to provide for a five-year transitional regime in the West Bank and Gaza.

It is recognized that the Democratic Administration has to proceed with special care and sensitivity resulting from its deep engagement in the delicate process of promoting a wider peace for Israel. . . .

We condemn the government of Iran for its outrageous conduct in the taking of our diplomatic personnel as hostages. We insist upon respect for the principle — as repeatedly enunciated by the UN Security Council and the International Court of Justice — of the inviolability for diplomatic personnel. We call upon all governments to abide by and uphold this basic tenet of civilized international conduct.

In the region as a whole, we must end our dangerous dependence on foreign oil. Only in this way can our foreign policy counter effectively the pressures of OPEC and of Soviet power poised above the Persian Gulf in Afghanistan. The Democratic Administration will fulfill its commitments to the Strategic Petroleum Reserve to protect America against an oil embargo. As we reduce oil consumption and dependence on OPEC, we will be able to bargain on equal terms with the OPEC states for an assurance of more certain supplies of oil at more stable prices.

Europe and Japan

America and her allies must continue the mutual confidence and commitment, the sense of common purpose, that marked our relations for decades. The problems we face are global in scope. We cannot begin to solve them if each of us goes a separate way. We must learn to work in partnership, on an increasing range of problems, in areas such as Africa and the Persian Gulf, and on worldwide economic and security issues.

The Democratic Administration will be committed to a strong NATO and a stable military balance in Europe. We will pursue both modernization of NATO conventional and nuclear forces and equitable limitations between NATO and the Warsaw Pact.

The Democratic Administration will seek collective solutions to the common economic problems of inflation, unemployment, energy, trade and monetary relations which confront us and our allies. This will require increased cooperation and coordination among all OECD countries.

The Democratic Administration will continue to support the growth and cohesion of the European community, and will increase our support for Greece, Spain and Portugal, which have rejoined the ranks of democracy.

We have been particularly concerned about the need to maintain strategic stability in the Eastern Mediterranean. To this end, we have worked with Congress toward the resolution of differences between Greece and Turkey over Cyprus and other divisive issues. We have worked toward a balanced treatment of both countries in our assistance programs.

We will give priority to the reintegration of Greece into NATO's military structure and to the strengthening of NATO's southern flank, including the economic progress of each of our allies in southern Europe. . . .

The International Economy

A vigorous American foreign policy and a sustained defense effort depend on the strength of the U.S. economy and its ability to compete in the international marketplace.

Through annual economic summits in London, Bonn, Tokyo, and Venice, we have established a sound basis for economic progress in the 1980's by improving the coordination of our economic policies. . . .

The Democratic Administration, which has wrestled with these issues over the past three and a half years, pledges a renewed effort to revitalize the world economy and to maintain our position as the leader of the free world's economic forces.

Trade

In 1976, we called for trade policies that would benefit economic growth. Trade promotes new jobs for American workers, new markets for farmers and businessmen, and lower prices for consumers. But trade can also cause dislocations within the economy, and we have sought — and will continue to seek — ways to ease the burden of adjustment to foreign competition without impeding the process of structural change so vital to our economic health. We favor a free international trading system, but that system must also be fair. We will not allow our workers and industries to be displaced by unfair import competition. We have entered orderly marketing agreements and other arrangements in areas such as color television, footwear and textiles, to help promote the competitive position of American industry. Others may be necessary.

Last year, we successfully concluded the Multilateral Trade Negotiations, an ambitious set of negotiations designed to reduce barriers to international trade. Before the Democratic Administration took office, these negotiations had proceeded at a snail's pace, and there had been a growing risk of failure which could have sparked a trade war damaging to our interests. It was the imaginative leadership of this Administration which breathed new life into an otherwise somnolent negotiation.

To strengthen the U.S. economy and improve our competitive position in the world economy, U.S. export-import policy must be based on the principle of fair trade that will enhance our exports while safeguarding domestic industry from unfair trade practices. In assuring orderly foreign trade, the U.S. must require observance of our trade laws, as well as cooperation with our trade policies if economic disruption is to be avoided. . . .

Monetary Affairs

We will continue to take whatever actions are necessary to maintain a sound and stable dollar. We will cooperate with other nations to minimize exchange rate disturbances. We fully support efforts underway to strengthen the ability of international financial institutions to adapt to changing needs and to facilitate the recycling of funds from the surplus oil-producing nations to those countries facing large, oil-induced deficits. We will urge OPEC countries to participate constructively in this process.

International Energy Cooperation

We have cooperated with other industrial countries, at summit meetings and in the International Energy Agency, in developing joint programs to conserve oil and increase production of alternative energy sources. Only through a truly global effort can the present imbalance between energy supply and demand be redressed. We will continue to support such efforts, showing our leadership by continuing the actions that have reduced oil consumption and imports by a greater proportion in the U.S. than in any other industrial country in the last year. We will work with our partners abroad to elicit increased effort by them, even as we seek increased U.S. effort at home, to the same ends.

The Developing World

Under the previous Republican Administration, the nations of the Third World viewed the United States as uninterested in or hostile to the need to treat the North-South economic issues which are of greatest importance to developing countries. Since then, the United States has adopted a range of economic policies on trade (MTN, Generalized System of Preferences expansion), commodities (Common Fund, sugar, coffee, tin), aid (International Financial Institutions replenishments) which have demonstrated that the Carter Administration is responsive to the aspirations of peoples in developing countries.

But this task is only begun. . . .

Latin America and the Caribbean

In stark contrast to the policies of previous Republican Administrations, this Democratic Administration has begun to forge a new, collaborative relationship with nations of Latin America and the Caribbean; one resting on a firm commitment to human rights, democratization, increased economic and industrial development, and non-intervention.

We must now move innovatively to strengthen our ties with our neighbors in the Western Hemisphere, first to obviate any vacuum for outside intervention and second to promote bilateral approaches for social progress and economic development including energy resources.

Through systematic and structural high level attention to the problems of the Western Hemisphere we will mobilize the resources of our government to achieve this end. One such possibility to be considered is to appoint an Under Secretary of State for the Western Hemisphere.

This would encourage both economic and political freedom throughout the Hemisphere. . . .

Asia

The establishment of normal diplomatic and economic relations with China is an historic foreign policy achievement.

Progress in U.S.-China relations was stalled in 1977, but with patience, political courage and historic vision, the deadlock was broken by this Democratic Administration.

In the fifteen months since normalization, the benefits of normalization have already become clear: trade, travel, cultural exchange, and, most important of all, the security and stability of the Pacific region is greater now than in any time in this century.

The Democratic Party commits itself to a broadening and deepening of our relationship with China in a way that will benefit both our peoples and the peace and security of the world. We will continue to seek new areas where the United States and China can cooperate in support of common interests. We have not and will not play "China cards" or other dangerous games; nor will we allow our relationship with any other country to impede our efforts to continue the process of normalization of relations with China.

In 1976, the so-called Koreagate affair had badly hurt our ties to Korea. A friendly and increasingly frank dialogue with the Korean government has been promoted. We will continue not only to fulfill our commitment to security, but equally to the promotion of a more democratic government. North and South Korea have renewed their dialogue and made a difficult but hopeful start down a long, uncertain road. In our relationships with the Philippines, Taiwan and others in the region, we will also press for political liberalization and human rights. . . .

Africa

Africa will be of central importance to American foreign policy in the 1980's. By the end of the previous Republican Administration in 1977, the United States had little credibility in Black Africa for they had made little or no attempt to see African problems from an African perspective. Our policy had no clearly defined goals. As a consequence, our attempts to bring an end to the war in Southern Africa were ineffective. We were becoming, in African eyes, irrelevant — even antagonistic — to African aspirations.

The Democratic Administration developed a long-term African policy — a policy that is viable on its own merits and does not treat Africa as an appendage to great power competition. It recognized the need for a new approach to the Continent, an approach based on mutual respect, fundamental concern for human rights and the necessity for economic justice.

Considerable success has been achieved, perhaps most notably in Southern Africa. Our diplomatic efforts there have been instrumental in helping to bring about a peaceful settlement in Rhodesia — now Zimbabwe — while lessening Soviet/Cuban influence in the area. We will continue to assist in the reconstruction and development of an independent Zimbabwe, as a means of promoting stability in the region.

Much remains to be done. . . .

The Democratic Party pledges itself to continue efforts to improve U.S. relations with all African nations, on the basis of mutual respect and a mutual commitment to enhance economic justice and human dignity everywhere, with particular emphasis on the recurrent problem of drought and starvation. U.S. aid in the form of grain and foodstuffs must be continued but, in addition, we must seek with African governments ways of removing famine permanently from the African Continent.

The Democratic Party pledges itself to the process of economic reconstruction in Zimbabwe within the context of a coherent multi-donor development plan for all the cooperating nations of the Southern African region.

The Democratic Party pledges active support for self-determination in Namibia, and for full social and economic justice for all the peoples of Southern Africa.

The Democratic Administration will press for the withdrawal of Soviet and Cuban troops.

In Southern Africa, we will exert our influence to promote progress toward majority rule and to end the racist system of apartheid. . . .

The United Nations and International Agencies

In each of the regions of the globe, international organizations and agencies will be tested in the coming decade and will play an increasingly crucial role. The United Nations remains the only forum where rich and poor, East and West, and neutral nations can come together to air their grievances, participate in respected forums of world opinion, and find mechanisms to resolve disputes without resort to force. . . .

We support the call in Section 503 of the Foreign Relations Authorization Act of 1978, for the United States to make "a major effort toward reforming and restructuring the United Nations system."

We also endorse that portion of the President's report to Congress in March, 1978 on U.N. reform and restructuring which calls for the Senate "to re-examine the Connally reservation," "the creation of a U.N. Peacekeeping Reserve composed of national contingents trained in peacekeeping functions," the establishment of "a new U.N. senior post as High Commissioner of Human Rights," and the development of autonomous sources of income for the international community. . . .

Into the 1980's

As we look to the 1980's, we have a full and challenging agenda.

With our Allies, we face the challenge of building greater unity of action while preserving the diversity of our democracies. Europe is increasingly united and is finding its own identity and voice. We must forge new links of consultation and revive the political process within the North Atlantic Alliance so that Europe remains America's partner in meeting the challenges to our common security and economic interests. We must find ways to include Japan in this process, broadening the mechanisms for cooperation which exist in current international forums, such as the Seven-Nation Summit.

With the Third World countries, we must continue to do our part in the realization of their aspirations for justice, respect, and freedom. We must continue to work for full political participation by all in South Africa, including independence and majority rule in Namibia. We must work to strengthen democracy in the Caribbean and Central America in the face of efforts by the Cubans to export their failed revolution. Throughout Latin America, we must continue to cooperate for the realization of greater human rights and the fulfillment of basic human needs. In Asia, we must continue to strengthen our relationships with our friends and Allies as they confront the twin dangers flowing from the Soviet invasion of Afghanistan and the Soviet-backed invasion of Cambodia.

We must persevere with the Middle East peace process. There is no viable alternative. We can welcome initiatives from other countries so long as they contribute to the Camp David process that is leading toward a comprehensive peace in that region. But we will oppose efforts that undermine Camp David while offering no viable alternative. Our goal is to see the achievement of a comprehensive peace for all parties.

With our defenses, we will continue to meet the requirements of the Administration's five-year defense program, including the deployment of the MX missile, cruise missiles, the Trident submarine, and long-range theater nuclear forces in Europe. At the same time, we intend to increase readiness and strengthen the All-Volunteer Force with a standby system of draft registration. We will continue with our Allies to meet the commitments of the long-term NATO defense program and, as we strengthen our military capabilities and presence in Southwest Asia and the region of the Persian Gulf, we will look to our Allies to assume more of the burden for the defense and security of Europe. Finally, we must recognize that development assistance represents a crucial part of our national security. As such, we may have to make a greater contribution of resources to these programs.

In the field of arms control, in addition to ratification of SALT II, we must proceed to more comprehensive and drastic reductions and qualitative limitations on strategic nuclear forces. SALT III must also include effective limitations and reductions in long-range theater nuclear forces based on the principle of equality. We must pursue to a conclusion a comprehensive test ban, effective curbs in the international traffic of conventional arms and a more rigorously effective international regime to prevent the spread of nuclear weapons and weapons technology. We must bring to at least an initial conclusion the negotiations for mutual and balanced force reductions in Europe. The decade of the 1980's is not to become the decade of violence. We must make renewed efforts to stabilize the arms competition and widen the scope of arms control arrangements.

As we look to the future, we hope the progress in arms control and the strength and determination we shall demonstrate in the face of Soviet aggression in Afghanistan will soon result in the fashioning of a stronger, more productive relationship with the Soviet Union. We favor a genuine detente — one with equivalent benefits to ourselves and the Soviets, one that is based on genuine restraint, one that benefits all mankind by harnessing the enormous potential of our two societies for cooperation rather than competition and confrontation. This will take patience, but we shall persevere for the prize is peace.

By reaffirming America's values as the centerpiece of our foreign policy and by pursuing realistically the requirements of military strength, the Democratic Party is forging a new and broader consensus among the American people in support of our foreign policy. We are turning the tide against the paralysis of despair that came from a tragic war in Asia and political scandal at home. We are restoring America to its rightful place, not only as the strongest nation in the world, but as the nation which is the champion of human justice and freedom.

CARTER STATEMENT

... I am pleased to present my comments on the Platform to the delegates to the 1980 Democratic National Convention.

I give you my enthusiastic support for the thrust and ideals expressed in the Platform you have adopted.

It has been my desire throughout the platform process to produce a working unity among various elements of the Party on the hundreds of issues which were initially debated. As a result of the agreements reached during the initial drafting process, agreements made thereafter on a number of Minority Reports, and through further debate on the Convention floor, this goal was substantially achieved.

[Stronger Economy/Full Employment]

... The Platform as passed by the Convention commits the Democratic Party to a full employment and balanced growth policy under the Humphrey-Hawkins Act; to strong efforts to speed recovery from the recession; to strengthen the National Accord with Labor; to carefully designed tax reductions; to responsible management of the Federal budget; to policies that result in fair and reasonable interest rates to help our Nation's workers, small businesses, farmers and homeowners; to regulatory reform; to targeted assistance for areas with high unemployment; and to increase economic productivity and competitiveness.

All of these commitments are compatible with the goals and achievements of my Administration and I support them enthusiastically....

I am in full agreement that our economic programs must be based on the principle of fairness and that we should do everything possible to avoid actions which significantly increase unemployment. However, I have concerns with Minority Report No. 2 because responsibility in these matters must ultimately rest with the President and the Congress. This responsibility should not be delegated to staff officials of either branch of government....

[Minority Report No. 9]

... With regard to Minority Report No. 9, I want to emphasize that I have no higher domestic priority than full employment. But we must make it clear that to achieve full employment we must also be successful in our fight against inflation. To be lasting, a jobs policy must not only promote economic growth and provide opportunities to the disadvantaged, but also create an environment of reasonable price stability.

[Equal Rights/Abortion]

I am proud of the ringing endorsement of the Equal Rights Amendment contained in the Platform. My family and I have spent countless hours working to obtain Congressional agreement for extending the time for ratification and to securing the necessary state approvals for ratification. I will not be satisfied until the ERA is part of our Constitution.

Since the beginning of my Administration, I have personally opposed Federal funding of abortion. I am sworn to uphold the laws passed by Congress, and the Constitution of the United States as interpreted by the federal courts, but my personal view remains unchanged....

CARTER, MONDALE ACCEPTANCE SPEECHES

August 14, 1980

President Jimmy Carter, trailing his Republican opponent Ronald Reagan in the opinion polls, warned in his speech accepting the Democratic Party's nomination Aug. 14 that the upcoming election would present the electorate with a "stark choice" between "two futures" for the United States. A future based on the policies his administration had pursued, Carter claimed, would be characterized by "security, justice and peace." But a Reagan administration, he asserted, would usher in a future of "despair," "risk" and "surrender." "It is up to all of us," Carter said, "to make sure America rejects this alarming, even perilous, destiny."

The president's speech, delivered to the delegates meeting in New York's Madison Square Garden, the same hall in which Carter accepted the Democratic nomination in 1976, capped the four-day convention. Carter used his address to introduce the "two futures" theme (which campaign officials hoped to emphasize throughout the presidential race) and to mend fences with warring factions within the Democratic Party, particularly the backers of Sen. Edward M. Kennedy's unsuccessful bid for the nomination.

Control of Convention

The Carter forces gained control of the convention at its opening session, Aug. 11, when delegates voted to accept a rule requiring them to vote on the first nominating ballot for the candidate they were

*elected to support. Kennedy subsequently withdrew from the contest,
but he received a rousing reception from the convention when he delivered
a speech on economic issues Aug. 12. The president's supporters conceded
that Carter would be hard pressed to match Kennedy's oratory. "That's
a tough act to follow," a White House official told reporters. (Kennedy
speech, p. 701)*

*Attempting to put the sometimes bitter dispute with Kennedy behind
him, Carter, early in his speech, appealed to the Massachusetts senator
for his support. Addressing Kennedy, the president said, "Ted, you're
a tough competitor and a superb campaigner, and I can attest to that. . . .
I reach out to you tonight and I reach out to all those who supported
you and your valiant and passionate campaign. Ted your party needs —
and I need — you. . . ."*

*The chief theme of the Carter speech was the contrast between his
and what he said was Reagan's approach to the problems facing the
nation. Democrats, the president said, "grapple with the real challenges
of a real world," but Republicans "talk about a world of tinsel and
make-believe." In this "fantasy America," Carter charged, social, economic and international crises are glossed over or ignored. "If we succumb
to a world of fantasy, we will wake up to a nightmare," Carter warned.*

Republican Programs

*Carter saved his harshest criticism for proposed Republican energy
and economic programs. He said that a Reagan administration would
abolish existing programs for synthetic fuels, solar power, conservation
and mass transit, scrap the windfall profits tax on petroleum, and
free the oil companies "to solve the energy problem for us." And Carter
charged that the Republicans' Kemp-Roth tax-cut proposal "offers rebates
to the rich, deprivation to the poor, and fierce inflation to the rest
of us."*

*Noticeably missing from the president's address was any mention
of the independent candidacy of Illinois Rep. John Anderson.*

Mondale Speech

*Vice President Walter F. Mondale, who addressed the convention
before the president, offered a passionate attack on Republican Party
candidates and a spirited defense of the Carter administration's accomplishments. The Republicans, Mondale claimed, have "been out
of step with America for 50 years. And their nominee is out of step
with America today."*

*Mondale asserted that most Americans — "but not Ronald Reagan"
— supported a variety of progressive programs, including the proposed*

equal rights amendment, federal education aid, the new Department of Education, government-financed medical insurance, labor law reforms, federal programs to protect workers' health and safety, energy conservation and a "judiciary free from right-wing loyalty tests" (a reference to a Republican platform plank calling for the selection of federal judges who supported a constitutional amendment banning abortions). (See p. 515)

In addition, the vice president claimed that to fulfill promises to cut taxes, increase defense expenditures and balance the federal budget, Reagan would have to repeal "Medicare and Medicaid and all our programs for schools and cities and veterans and the unemployed."

Defending the Carter administration record, Mondale said that its successes included creation of 8 million jobs, initiation of peace talks between Egypt and Israel, and increased spending for defense.

Following are the texts of President Carter's Aug. 14, 1980, speech accepting the Democratic presidential nomination and Vice President Mondale's Aug. 14 speech accepting the vice presidential nomination. (Boldface headings in brackets have been added by Congressional Quarterly to highlight the organization of the texts.):

CARTER SPEECH

Fellow Democrats, fellow citizens:

I thank you for the nomination you've offered me. And I especially thank you for choosing as my running mate the best partner any president ever had — Fritz Mondale.

With gratitude and with determination, I accept your nomination.

And I am proud to run on a progressive and sound platform that you have hammered out at this convention.

Fritz and I will mount a campaign that defines the real issues — a campaign that responds to the intelligence of the American people — a campaign that talks sense — and we're going to beat, whip the Republicans in November.

We'll win because we are the party of a great president who knew how to get re-elected — Franklin D. Roosevelt. And we're the party of a courageous fighter who knew how to "give 'em hell" — Harry Truman. And as Truman said, he just told the truth and they thought it was hell. And we're the party of a gallant man of spirit — John Fitzgerald Kennedy. And we're the party of a great leader of compassion — Lyndon Baines Johnson. And the party of a great man who should have been president and would have been one of the greatest presidents in history — Hubert Horatio Hornblower — Humphrey. I have appreciated what this convention has said about Senator Humphrey, a great man who epitomized the spirit of the Democratic Party, and I would like to say that we're also the party of Governor Jerry Brown and Senator Edward M. Kennedy.

[Salute to Senator Kennedy]

I'd like to say a personal word to Senator Kennedy. Ted, you're a tough competitor and a superb campaigner and I can attest to that. Your speech before this convention was a magnificent statement of what the Democratic Party is and what it means to the people of this country — and why a Democratic victory is so important this year. I reach out to you tonight and I reach out to all those who have supported you in your valiant and passionate campaign. Ted, your party needs — and I need — you and your idealism and dedication working for us. There is no doubt that even greater service lies ahead of you — and we are grateful to you and to have your strong partnership now in the larger cause to which your own life has been dedicated.

I thank you for your support. We'll make great partners this fall in whipping the Republicans. We're Democrats and we have had our differences, but we share a bright vision of America's future — a vision of good life for all our people — a vision of a secure nation, a just society, a peaceful world, a strong America — confident and proud and united. And we have a memory of Franklin Roosevelt forty years ago when he said that there are times in our history when concern over our personal lives are overshadowed by concern of "what will happen to the country we have known." This is such a time — and I can tell you that the choice to be made this year can transform our own personal lives and the life of our country as well.

During the last Presidential campaign, I crisscrossed this country and I listened to thousands and thousands of people — housewives and farmers, teachers and small-business leaders, workers and students, the elderly and the poor — people of every race and every background and every walk of life. It was a powerful experience — a total immersion in the human reality of America.

['No Easy Answers' in White House]

And I have now had another kind of total immersion — being president of the United States of America. Let me talk for a moment about what that job is like — and what I have learned from it.

I've learned that only the most complex and difficult tasks come before me in the Oval Office. No easy answers are found there — because no easy questions come there.

I've learned that for a President experience is the best guide to the right decisions. I'm wiser tonight than I was four years ago.

And I have learned that the Presidency is a place of compassion. My own heart is burdened for the troubled Americans. The poor and the jobless and the afflicted — they've become part of me. My thoughts and my prayers for our hostages in Iran are as though they were my own sons and daughters.

The life of every human being on Earth can depend on the experience and judgment and vigilance of the person in the Oval Office. The President's power for building and his power for destruction are awesome. And the power is greatest exactly where the stakes are highest — in matters of war and peace.

And I have learned something else — something that I have come to see with extraordinary clarity. Above all, I must look ahead — because the President of the United States is the steward of the nation's destiny.

He must protect our children — and the children they will have — and the children of generations to follow. He must speak and act for them. That is his burden — and his glory.

And that is why a President cannot yield to the short-sighted demands, no matter how rich or powerful the special interests might be that make those demands. And that is why the President cannot bend to the passions of the moment, however popular they might be. And that is why the President must sometimes ask for sacrifice when his listeners would rather hear the promise of comfort.

The President is a servant of today. But his true constituency is the future. That is why the election of 1980 is so important.

Some have said it makes no difference who wins this election. They are wrong. This election is a stark choice between two men, two parties, two sharply different pictures of what America is and what the world is. But it is more than that. It is a choice between two futures.

[Choice of Two Futures]

The year 2000 is just less than 20 years away — just four presidential elections after this one. Children born this year will come of age in the 21st century. The time to shape the world of the year 2000 is now. The decisions of the next few years will set our courses, perhaps an irreversible course — and the most important of all choices will be made by the American people at the polls less than three months from tonight.

The choice could not be more clear — nor the consequences more crucial. In one of the futures we can choose — the future that you and I have been building together — I see security and justice and peace. I see a future of economic security — security that will come from tapping our own great resources of oil and gas, coal and sunlight — and from building the tools, the technology and factories for a revitalized economy based on jobs and stable prices for everyone.

I see a future of justice — the justice of good jobs, decent health care, quality education, and the full opportunity for all people, regardless of color or language or religion; the simple human justice of equal rights for all men — and for all women, guaranteed equal rights at last — under the Constitution of the United States of America.

And I see a future of peace — a peace born of wisdom and based on the fairness toward all countries of the world — a peace guaranteed both by American military strength and by American moral strength as well. That is the future I want for all people — a future of confidence and hope and a good life. It is the future America must choose — and with your help and with your commitment, it is the future America will choose.

[Republican Future]

But there is another possible future. In that other future, I see despair — the despair of millions who would struggle for equal opportunity and a better life — and struggle alone. And I see surrender — the surrender of our energy future to the merchants of oil; the surrender of our economic future to a bizarre program of massive tax cuts for the rich, service cuts for the poor and massive inflation for everyone.

And I see risk — the risk of international confrontation; the risk of an uncontrollable, unaffordable, and unwinnable nuclear arms race.

No one, Democrat or Republican leader, consciously seeks such a future. And I do not claim that my opponent does. But I do question the disturbing commitments and policies already made by him and by those with him who have now captured control of the Republican Party. The consequences of those commitments and policies would drive us down the wrong road. It's up to all of us to make sure America rejects this alarming, and even perilous, destiny.

The only way to build a better future is to start with realities of the present. But while we Democrats grapple with the real challenges of a real world, others talk about a world of tinsel and make-believe.

Let's look for a moment at their make-believe world. In their fantasy America, inner-city people and farm workers and laborers do not exist. Women, like children, are to be seen but not heard. The problems of working women are simply ignored. The elderly do not need Medicare. The young do not need more help in getting a better education. Workers do not require the guarantee of a healthy and a safe place to work.

In their fantasy world, all the complex global changes of the world since World War II have never happened. In their fantasy America, all problems have simple solutions. Simple — and wrong.

It is a make-believe world. A world of good guys and bad guys, where some politicians shoot first and ask questions later.

No hard choices. No sacrifice. No tough decisions. It sounds too good to be true — and it is.

The path of fantasy leads to irresponsibility. The path of reality leads to hope and peace. The two paths could not be more different. Nor could the futures to which they lead. Let's take a hard look at the consequences of our choice.

[Rebuilding Military Strength]

You and I have been working toward a secure future by rebuilding our military strength — steadily, carefully and responsibly. The Republicans talk about military strength — but they were in office for eight out of the last 11 years — and in the face of a growing Soviet threat they steadily cut real defense spending by more than a third.

We've reversed the Republican decline in defense. Every year since I've been President, we've had real increases in our commitment to a stronger nation — increases which are prudent and rational. There is no doubt that the United States of America can meet any threat from the Soviet Union. Our modernized strategic forces, a revitalized NATO, the Trident submarine, the cruise missile, Rapid Deployment Force — all these guarantee that we will never be second to any nation. Deeds, not words — fact, not fiction. We must and we will continue to build our own defenses. We must and we will continue to seek balanced reductions in nuclear arms.

[Nuclear Arms Control]

The new leaders of the Republican Party, in order to close the gap between their rhetoric and their record, have now promised to launch an all-out nuclear arms race. This would negate any further effort to negotiate a strategic arms limitation agreement. There can be no winners in such an arms race — and all the people of the Earth can be the losers.

The Republican nominee advocates abandoning arms control policies which have been important and supported by every Democratic president since Harry Truman and also by every Republican president since Dwight D. Eisenhower. This radical and irresponsible course would threaten our security — and could put the whole world in peril. You and I must never let this come to pass.

It's simple to call for a new arms race. But when armed aggression threatens world peace, tough-sounding talk like that is not enough. A president must act — responsibly.

[Keeping the Peace]

When Soviet troops invaded Afghanistan, we moved quickly to take action. I suspended some grain sales to the Soviet Union. I called for draft registration.

We joined wholeheartedly with the Congress. And I joined wholeheartedly with the Congress and with the U.S. Olympics Committee and led more than 60 other nations in boycotting the big propaganda show in Russia — the Moscow Olympics.

The Republican leader opposed two of these forceful but peaceful actions and he waffled on the third. But when we asked him what he would do about aggression in Southwest Asia, he suggested blockading Cuba. Even his running mate wouldn't go along with that.

He doesn't seem to know what to do with the Russians. He's not sure if he wants to feed them or play with them or fight with them.

As I look back on my first term, I'm grateful that we've had a country with a full four years of peace. And that's what we're going to have for the next four years — peace.

It's only common sense that if America is to stay secure and at peace, we must encourage others to be peaceful as well.

As you know, we've helped in Zimbabwe-Rhodesia, where we stood firm for racial justice and democracy. And we have also helped in the Middle East. Some have criticized the Camp David accords and they've criticized some delays in the implementation of the Middle East peace treaty. Well, before I became President there was no Camp David accord and there was no Middle East peace treaty.

Before Camp David, Israel and Egypt were poised across barbed wire, confronting each other with guns and tanks and planes. But afterward, they talked face-to-face with each other across a peace table — and they also communicated through their own ambassadors in Cairo and Tel Aviv.

Now that's the kind of future we're offering — of peace to the Middle East if the Democrats are re-elected in the fall.

I am very proud that nearly half the aid that our country has ever given to Israel in the 32 years of her existence has come during my administration. Unlike our Republican predecessors, we have never stopped nor slowed that aid to Israel. And as long as I am President, we will never do so. Our commitment is clear: security and peace for Israel; peace for all the peoples of the Middle East.

[Human Rights]

But if the world is to have a future of freedom as well as peace, America must continue to defend human rights.

Now listen to this: The new Republican leaders oppose our human rights policy. They want to scrap it. They seem to think it's naive for America to stand up to freedom and — for freedom and democracy. Just what do they think we should stand up for? Ask the former political prisoners who now live in freedom if we should abandon our stand on human rights. Ask the dissidents in the Soviet Union about our commitment to human rights. Ask the Hungarian-Americans, ask the Polish-Americans. Listen to Pope John Paul II. Ask those who are suffering for the sake of justice and liberty around the world. Ask the millions who've fled tyranny if America should stop speaking out for human principles. Ask the American people. I tell you that as long as I am President, we will hold high the banner of human rights, and you can depend on it.

[Energy Future]

Here at home the choice between the two futures is equally important. In the long run, nothing is more crucial to the future of America than energy — nothing was so disastrously neglected in the past. Long after the 1973 Arab oil embargo, the Republicans in the White House had still done nothing to meet the threat to national security of our nation. Then, as now, their policy was dictated by the big oil companies.

We Democrats fought hard to rally our nation behind a comprehensive energy program and a good program — a new foundation for challenging and exciting progress. Now, after three years of struggle, we have that program. The battle to secure America's energy future has been fully and finally joined. Americans have cooperated with dramatic results.

We've reversed decades of dangerous and growing dependence on foreign oil. We are now importing 20 percent less oil. That is one and a half million barrels of oil every day less than the day I took office.

And with our new energy policy now in place, we can discover more, produce more, create more, and conserve more energy — and we will use American resources, American technology, and millions of American workers to do it with.

[Republican Energy Program]

Now what do the Republicans propose? Basically their energy program has two parts. The first part is to get rid of almost everything that we've done for the American public in the last three years. They want to reduce or abolish the synthetic fuels program. They want to slash the solar energy incentives, the conservation programs, aid to mass transit, aid to the elderly Americans to help pay their fuel bills. They want to eliminate the fifty-five mile speed limit. And while they're at it, the Republicans would like to gut the Clean Air Act. They never liked it to begin with. That's one part of the program.

The other part is worse. To replace what we have built, this is what they propose: to destroy the windfall profits tax, and to "unleash" the oil companies and let them solve the energy problem for us. That's it. That's the whole program. There is no more. Can this nation accept such an outrageous program? No! We Democrats will fight it every step of the way, and we'll begin tomorrow morning with the campaign for re-election in November.

['New Economic Age']

When I took office, I inherited a heavy load of serious economic problems besides energy — and we've met them all head-on. We've slashed government regulation and put free enterprise back into the airlines, the trucking and the financial systems of our country — and we're now doing the same thing for the railroads. This is the greatest change in the relationship between government and business since the New Deal. We've increased our exports dramatically. We've reversed the decline in the basic research and development. And we have created more than 8 million new jobs — the biggest increase in the history of our country.

But the road's bumpy, and last year's skyrocketing OPEC price increases have helped to trigger a worldwide inflation crisis.

We took forceful action, and interest rates have now fallen, the dollar is stable and, although we still have a battle on our hands, we are struggling to bring inflation under control.

We are now at a critical turning point in our economic history. Because we made the hard decisions — because we guided our economy through a rough but essential period of transition — we have laid the groundwork for a new economic age.

Our economic renewal program for the 1980s will meet our immediate need for jobs by attacking the very same long-term problems that caused unemployment and inflation in the first place. It will move America simultaneously towards our five great economic goals — lower inflation, better productivity, revitalization of American industry, energy security and jobs.

It is time to put all America back to work — not in make work, but in real work.

There is real work in modernizing American industry and creating new industries for America.

Here are just a few things we will build together:

New industries to turn our coal and shale and farm products into fuel for our cars and trucks, and to turn the light of the sun into heat and electricity for our homes;

A modern transportation system for railbeds and ports to make American coal into a powerful rival of OPEC oil;

Industries that will provide the convenience of communications and futuristic computer technology to serve millions of American homes, offices and factories;

Job training for workers displaced by economic changes;

New investment pinpointed in regions and communities where jobs are needed most;

Better mass transit in our cities and between cities;

And a whole new generation of American jobs to make homes and vehicles and buildings that will house us and move us in comfort — with a lot less energy.

This is important, too — I have no doubt that the ingenuity and dedication of the American people can make every single one of these things happen. We are talking about the United States of America — and those who count this country out as an economic superpower are going to find out just how wrong they are.

We are going to share in the exciting enterprise of making the 1980s a time of growth for America. The Republican alternative is the biggest tax giveaway in history. They call it "Reagan-Kemp-Roth." I call it a free lunch Americans cannot afford.

[Republican Tax Proposal]

The Republican tax program offers rebates to the rich, deprivation for the poor and fierce inflation for all of us.

Their party's own vice presidential nominee said that "Reagan-Kemp-Roth" would result in an inflation rate of more than 30 percent. He called it "voodoo economics." He suddenly changed his mind toward the end of the Republican convention, but he was right the first time.

Along with this gigantic tax cut, the new Republican leaders promise to protect retirement and health programs, and to have massive increases in defense spending. And they claim they can balance the budget. If they are serious about these promises — and they say they are — then a close analysis shows that the entire rest of the government would have to be abolished — everything from education to farm programs, from the G.I. Bill to the night watchman at the Lincoln Memorial. And the budget would still be in the red. The only alternative would be to build more printing presses to print cheap money. Either way the American people lose. But the American people will not stand for it.

The Democratic Party has always embodied the hope of our people for justice, opportunity and a better life. And we've worked in every way possible to strengthen the American family, to encourage self-reliance, and to follow the Old Testament admonition: "Defend the poor and fatherless: give justice to the afflicted and needy." [Psalms 82:3] We have struggled to assure that no child in America ever goes to bed hungry, that no elderly couple in America has to live in a substandard home, and that no young person in America is excluded from college because the family is poor.

What have the Republicans proposed? Just an attack on everything we have done in the achievement in social justice and decency that we've won in the last 50 years — ever since Franklin Delano Roosevelt's first term. They would make Social Security voluntary. They would reverse our progress on the minimum wage, full employment laws, safety in the work place and a healthy environment.

Lately, as you know, the Republicans have been quoting Democratic presidents, but who can blame them? Would you rather quote Herbert Hoover or Franklin Delano Roosevelt? Would you rather quote Richard Nixon or John Fitzgerald Kennedy?

The Republicans have always been the party of privilege, but this year their leaders have gone even further. In their platform, they have repudiated the best traditions of their own party. Where is the conscience of Lincoln in the party of Lincoln? What's become of that traditional Republican commitment to fiscal responsibility? What's happened to their commitment to a safe and sane arms control?

[Democratic Decisions]

Now I don't claim perfection for the Democratic Party. I don't claim that every decision that we have made has been right or popular. Certainly they've not all been easy. But I will say this: We've been tested under fire. We've neither ducked nor hidden. And we've tackled the great, central issues in our time, the historic challenges of peace and energy which had been ignored for years. We've made tough decisions and we've taken the heat for them. We've made mistakes and we've learned from them. So we have built the foundation now for a better future.

We've done something else — perhaps even more important. In good times and bad, in the valleys and on the peaks, we've told people the truth — the hard truth — the truth that sometimes hurts.

One truth that we Americans have learned is that our dream has been earned for progress and for peace. Look what our land has been through within our own memory — a great depression, a world war, the technological explosion, the civil rights revolution, the bitterness of Vietnam, the shame of Watergate, the twilight peace of nuclear terror.

Through each of these momentous experiences we've learned the hard way about the world and about ourselves. For we've matured and we've grown as a nation. And we've grown stronger.

We've learned the uses and the limitations of power. We've learned the beauty and responsibility of freedom. We've learned the value and the obligation of justice — and we have learned the necessity of peace.

Some would argue that to master these lessons is somehow to limit our potential. That is not so. A nation which knows its true strengths, which sees its true challenges, which understands legitimate constraints — that nation, our nation — is far stronger than one which takes refuge in wishful thinking or nostalgia.

The Democratic Party — the American people — have understood these fundamental truths.

All of us can sympathize with the desire for easy answers. There's often the temptation to substitute idle dreams for hard reality.

The new Republican leaders are hoping that our nation will succumb to that temptation this year. But they profoundly misunderstand and underestimate the character of the American people.

Three weeks after Pearl Harbor, Winston Churchill came to North America — and he said, "We've not journeyed all this way across the centuries, across the oceans, across the mountains, across the prairies because we are made of sugar candy." We Americans have courage.

[Hopes for Future]

Americans have always been on the cutting edge of change. We've always looked forward with anticipation and confidence. I still want the same thing that all of you want — a self-reliant neighborhood and strong families; work for the able-bodied and good medical care for the sick; opportunity for our youth and dignity for our old; equal rights and justice for all people.

I want teachers eager to explain what a civilization really is — and I want students to understand their own needs and their own aims, but also the needs and yearnings of their neighbors. I want women free to pursue without limit the full life of what they want for themselves.

I want our farmers growing crops to feed our nation and the world, secure in the knowledge that the family farm will thrive and with a fair return on the good work they do for all of us. I want workers to see meaning in the labor they perform — and work enough to guarantee a job for every worker in this country. And I want the people in business free to pursue with boldness and freedom new ideas. And I want minority citizens fully to join the mainstream of American life, and I want from the bottom of my heart to remove the blight of racial and other discrimination from the face of our nation, and I'm determined to do it.

I need for all of you to join me in fulfilling that vision. The choice — the choice between the two futures — could not be more clear. If we succumb to a dream world, then we'll wake up to a nightmare. But if we start with reality and fight to make our dreams a reality — then Americans will have a good life, a life of meaning and purpose in a nation that's strong and secure.

Above all, I want us to be what the founders of our nation meant us to become — the land of freedom, the land of peace, and the land of hope.

Thank you very much.

MONDALE SPEECH

Mr. Speaker, fellow Americans, fellow Democrats:

I am honored to accept your nomination. I am proud to be running with Jimmy Carter. And I am proud to be running on our Party's progressive platform. And we're going to win!

This has been an extraordinary week in American politics. We have just held the most representative and the most open political convention in American history.

Last month in Detroit another convention was held, isolated in a bubble of privilege from the city that hosted it.

A comfortable convention, composed of America's wealthy, told us they symbolized the nation.

A malapportioned convention, where the cities were denied their share of the delegates, told us they symbolized democracy.

A token convention, whose workers and women and minorities sat at the back of the bus, they told us they symbolized the people.

They spoke of realism and cheered the gold standard. They spoke of truth and said Franklin Roosevelt caused World War II. They spoke of modernization and vindicated Barry Goldwater. They spoke of justice with a script by Phyllis Schlafly, and they spoke of fairness with a text by Jesse Helms.

[Mirror of America]

This Democratic Convention is a mirror of all America — all of it, black and white, Asian and Hispanic, native and immigrant, male and female, young and old, urban and rural, rich and poor.

When we speak of peace, the voice is Ed Muskie's. When we speak of workers, the voices are Lane Kirkland's and Doug Fraser's. When we speak of freedom, the dream is Coretta King's. When we speak of compassion, the fire is Ted Kennedy's. And when we speak of courage, the spirit is Jimmy Carter's. When we in this hall speak for America — it is America that is speaking.

Tonight, at this Democratic Convention, let us openly declare our faith: We believe in the fundamental decency of the American people. And we believe in strong, efficient and compassionate government.

We believe that America's greatest strength is its values. Our love of freedom, our sense of fairness, our spirit of service: these beliefs have been passed in every accent that America speaks — in Polish, in Italian, in Yiddish, in Greek, at the kitchen tables in Boston, on family farms in my own Midwest.

We Democrats believe that government can serve those values. No government can guarantee a perfect life for anyone. No government can substitute for our families, our churches, our synagogues, our neighborhoods or our volunteers. But a progressive government must do two things. It must create the conditions to help all people build better lives for themselves. And it must do so efficiently, honestly and fairly.

Those are the beliefs that we share together as Democrats. But the Republican nominee for President has a different view of Government. He tells us instead — and let me use his own words — that "the best thing that Government can do is nothing."

We disagree. Let him tell the auto workers in Detroit that the right to collective bargaining is "nothing." Let him tell the senior citizen in Philadelphia that the Social Security index for inflation is "nothing." Let him tell the freshman in Chicago that student assistance is "nothing." Let him ask the family in Boulder if clean air and pure water and protected wilderness are "nothing." And let him ask the people of Selma, Ala., if the right to vote is "nothing."

These rights and these programs are the work of Democrats and were fiercely opposed by the Republicans. The Republican Party has been out of step with America for 50 years, and their nominee is out of step more than any of them.

['But Not Ronald Reagan']

Today, most Americans, indeed most Republicans, believe that the Constitution of the United States should incorporate an Equal Rights Amendment for the women of this country — but not Ronald Reagan.

Most Americans today believe that we should have strong Federal aid to education and a Department of Education to support it — but not Ronald Reagan.

Most Americans believe that no family should be impoverished in medical debts because of tragic illness — but not Ronald Reagan.

Most Americans believe in labor law reform to protect the rights won by workers in the 30's — but not Ronald Reagan.

Most Americans believe that workers' health and safety should be protected on the job by Federal law — but not Ronald Reagan.

You're getting better.

Most Americans believe that we need energy conservation to cut out dependence on foreign oil — but not Ronald Reagan.

Most Americans, including the American Bar Association, believe in a judiciary free from right-wing loyalty tests — but not Ronald Reagan.

And yet, the Republican nominee wants us to forget all that, forget 40 years of extreme positions.

All of a sudden, that party is for jobs. The party that gave us the Great Depression and four years ago the highest unemployment since then, would have us believe that they're now for working people and for leaving no one behind.

Well, I've been in politics many years, and I've noticed that the closer the Republican oratory moves toward Franklin Roosevelt, the closer their policies move to Herbert Hoover.

[Reagan-Kemp-Roth]

This year's version of "prosperity's just around the corner" is called Reagan-Kemp-Roth. It's simple and it goes like this: Cut taxes by one trillion dollars.

That's it — their entire strategy. Every one of their promises — your next pay check, your grocery bills, your home — they all hang on that slender thread.

It's a trillion-dollar tax cut based on a two-cent theory. Every leading economist rejects it; most Americans disbelieve it and for a good reason. First of all, it is obviously, murderously inflationary. Even Business Week said it "would touch off an inflationary explosion that would wreck the country."

Second, it's the most regressive tax proposal in history. It is the stalest Republican idea of all: tax cuts for the wealthy, trickle-down for the rest of Americans. If you're earning $200,000 a year, you save enough money to buy a new Mercedes. But if you're a teacher, you save enough money to buy a hubcap. And if you're unemployed or on Social Security, you don't even get your bus fare back.

Kemp-Roth is an insult to the American people. The only way to cut taxes by a trillion dollars, add billions to defense and balance the budget all at the same time — as they propose — is to destroy everything that Roosevelt, and Truman, and Kennedy, and Johnson, and Humphrey, and Carter, and every delegate in this room has worked for all of our lives.

Only if Mr. Reagan repealed Medicare and Medicaid and all of our programs for schools and cities and veterans and the unemployed — only then could he finance that tax scheme. Only if he destroyed the Social Security system and all who depend on it — only then would the job be done.

[Ronald Reagan Said . . .]

It's hard to believe, I confess, it's hard to believe that Ronald Reagan would do that. After all, what kind of a person would try to wipe out every program since Roosevelt? Well, he'd have to be a person who'd believe, and I quote, "Fascism was really the basis for the New Deal." Now who would say something like that? Ronald Reagan would.

He'd have to be a person who calls the weak and the disadvantaged, and I quote, "a faceless mass waiting for handouts." Who on earth would say something like that? Ronald Reagan did.

He'd have to be a person who would call programs that help blacks and Hispanics "demeaning" and "insulting." Who on earth would say that? Ronald Reagan did.

He'd have to be a person who believes, and I quote, get this, "The minimum wage has caused more misery and unemployment than anything since the Great Depression." Who on earth would say anything like that? Ronald Reagan.

He'd have to be a person who thinks antitrust suits should bust up trade unions in America. Who would propose anything like that? Ronald Reagan.

He'd have to be a person who would wreck the Social Security system by making it voluntary. Who would ever suggest anything like that? Ronald Reagan.

He'd have to be a person who would destroy the family farm programs because they're, quote, "subsidizing the inefficient." Who would propose anything like that? Ronald Reagan, of course.

He would have to be a person who called the Civil Rights Act of 1964 "a bad piece of legislation." Who would say anything like that? Ronald Reagan.

One of the finest student bodies I've ever lectured to in my life.

Now get this one: Who on earth would call the League of Women Voters "Rhine Maidens." Who would say anything like that? You guessed it, Ronald Reagan.

[Progressive Record of Democrats]

That negative-thinking, I must say, was not a part of that small town of rural Minnesota where I grew up. That tone of resentment was never heard in my father's church. That cynicism was not what I felt in the high schools, the farms, the factories and the homes that I visited all over this nation in the last three and a half years.

The fact of it is that the people of this country want to work together. They want to build. They are confident. And as the Republican nominee will learn in November, the American people do not and will not turn back. They want to move forward, and moving forward is what we're doing under President Carter.

This Administration has a good, solid, progressive record, and we're going to run on it and we're going to win with it.

In 1976, I will remind you, from this podium, we said we believed in jobs. And today there are over 8 million more people at work than on the day that President Carter was inaugurated. A higher percentage of working age Americans are on the job today than ever before. We have added more jobs to the workforce than any administration in American history.

That is a good — the best record of producing jobs in American history and Jimmy Carter deserves credit for that accomplishment.

But we all know there are still too many unemployed in America, and I pledge to you, I pledge to every delegate in this convention hall and to the American people that this administration and this Democratic Party will not stop until everybody who needs and wants a job in America has one.

In 1976, we promised Americans that we would support education. And after eight years of Republican vetoes and impoundment, President Carter has added more funds to education than any President in American history. President Carter goes down as the most pro-education President in the nation's history.

We said we believed in the dignity of our seniors. We rescued the Social Security system from the brink of bankruptcy where the Republicans left it, and we made sure the benefits kept on growing. We increased health care programs for the elderly by 50 percent, doubled housing aid, eliminated the cash downpayment for food stamps. We proposed and passed the nation's first program to help older Americans pay their fuel bills, and up and down this progressive agenda, this administration has delivered.

And I would point out that President Carter has appointed more women, more blacks and more minorities to the federal bench than all the previous presidents in American history combined.

We created the first farmer-held reserves and each year we built an all-time record in farm exports. We passed the biggest increase in minimum wages. We doubled legal services for the poor. We built the most effective across-the-board, pro-city policy in our history. Every mayor and county executive, practically, in America is supporting President Carter because he's done more for the cities than any president in American history. We did this within a tight budget to bring down inflation.

It is a good, solid record, my Democrats. It is a good, solid record. Let's be proud of it, let's work for it, and let's fight those who wish to destroy it. Let's stick with this good President and this political party and the platform that we've developed.

Let us not go for this quick-fix tax cut for the rich. The American people do not want to wipe out a half-century of progress in the know-nothing season of resentment. The American people do want their Government to be efficient and honest, and I am confident they also want their Government to fight for social and economic justice. And on that belief I will stake this election.

[National Strength]

We will also stake the contest on the paramount issue that the Republicans tried to raise in Detroit — the question of national strength. We gladly accept the challenge.

The President of the United States has an enormous job. He's charged with the most powerful responsibility and most sober responsibility to be found in the world — the burden of nuclear power. He is the leader of the civilized world. He must defend its freedom. He must grasp the complexities of our difficult world. He must protect our security by freeing our dependence on foreign oil.

And to do all of that we must have a strong President. Yet last month, Ronald Reagan spent two days on national television drawing up a plan to divide the Presidency and weaken its powers. Anyone who seeks the Presidency and in his first serious act convenes a Constitutional Convention in his hotel room to weaken the office he's seeking does not understand the Constitution, the Presidency, or what national security is all about.

The first responsibility of a strong President is to defend our nation.

For the eight years of Republican rule while the Soviets were building up their power, real American defense spending dropped 35 percent. That's the Republican record. We not only have increased real defense support by 10 percent, we also have invested in the most sophisticated weapons in the world. No American general or admiral would dream of exchanging our forces for any on Earth.

But Mr. Reagan scolds us for having canceled an outmoded bomber that would be obsolete and vulnerable the day it was launched. President Carter chose instead the modern cruise missile which renders the whole expensive Soviet air defense system obsolete.

Up and down the defense agenda the Republicans repeat the same mistake. They want to resurrect decommissioned ships. They want to revive the ABM system, which even Nixon junked. With obsolete missiles, mothballed ships, vulnerable bombers, and petrified ideas, they would waste billions on defense relics that would drain and weaken us.

President Carter does not want to mimic the Soviets' bulk. He has chosen to offset it with the greatest resource we have — genius of American technology. And as a result, this nation today is building security, not for yesterday, but for the rest of the century.

National strength requires more than just military might: It requires the commitment of the President to arms control.

If there is one thing that bothers me more than anything else, and I think bothers you, it is the fear that someday, somehow, for reasons that do not matter, the world will resort to the final madness of a nuclear holocaust. Reason, common sense and a decent respect for humanity demand that we stall this nuclear arms race before it bankrupts and destroys us all.

Without arms control, everything is out of control. Without the SALT treaty, we would be forced to waste billions on weapons that buy us nothing.

And even though it took seven years to negotiate this treaty, and even though our President and our Secretary of Defense and all the Joint Chiefs of Staff and every NATO ally wants this treaty ratified, Mr. Reagan for the life of him cannot understand why.

Well, let me say, Mr. Reagan: We must have arms control for the life of all of us. And we need a President Jimmy Carter who believes in controlling the madness of controlling nuclear arms.

[Human Rights]

Above all, America's strength depends on American values. Every time we have a foreign policy that reflects American beliefs, we strengthen this nation.

Last month I was in Nigeria — the world's most powerful black nation, and the second largest source of American oil. A few years ago the Secretary of State under the Republicans was told he was not welcome in Nigeria because they did not stand up for the principle of human rights and majority rule.

But when I went to Nigeria I was welcome because the United States has a President, President Carter, who in his first act in office said from here on out the United States is going to stand for human rights and majority rule all over this Earth.

And now, and now, in Rhodesia, we see the same developments, a new democracy based on democratic institutions and the Soviets suffering another reversal. Today, our human rights policy is drawing the nations of Africa and the world together like a magnet and toward us.

The Republicans say a strong nation is one that never apologizes to any one. I say it's a nation whose leaders who are not doing things for which we must apologize. That's the difference.

A foreign policy that reflects American values advances American interests.

When President Carter saw to it that we ratified the Panama Canal treaties, not only did we rid ourselves of the last vestiges of colonialism, we also strengthened our influence in Latin America. When the President normalized relations with China, he not only told one fourth of the human race that they exist, he also established a powerful counterforce to Soviet aggression. And when the President denounced the persecution of Andrei Sakharov, he not only affirmed individual liberty, he also unmasked the Kremlin to other nations.

[Four Years of Peace]

Today, my fellow Democrats, thank God, for four years, our nation is at peace. Our armed forces are engaged in combat nowhere in the world. But I want you to note this. In the years of preparing to run for the Presidency, Mr. Reagan suggested that American forces be sent — now listen to this — Mr. Reagan said that we should send American forces to Ecuador, to Angola, to Rhodesia, to Panama, to Cyprus, to Pakistan, to North Korea, to the Middle East; and I don't think the American people stand for that for a moment.

They want a President who is steady, who's sober, who's experienced, and who has demonstrated that he knows how to keep the peace. And that's why they're going to re-elect President Carter. They want a President, who like Jimmy Carter, took Egypt and Israel, that had fought four tragic wars in 30 years, brought them together, got them talking, caused a peace treaty to be signed. And tonight they are exchanging ambassadors and not bullets between Israel and Egypt because of Jimmy Carter's courage and leadership.

And let me say a special word about Israel. Israel is our friend, our conscience, our partner. Its well-being is in our moral, our political and our strategic interest. And I stand before you tonight and say that the people of the United States, the President of the United States will stand by Israel in this term, in the next term and always.

In the last three and a half years, you permitted me to serve you as your Vice President. I've been privileged to represent you to the people of every continent on this earth, and every time I've traveled abroad, the more I've loved my home.

I spent my whole life in the struggle for civil rights, but when I heard the President of Senegal invoke the words of Martin Luther King, seldom have I loved our conscience more.

My whole life, I've been proud of the refuge we've been to exiles, but when I saw the men of the USS *Midway* who had saved boat people from the sea, seldom have I prized our compassion more.

I have been my whole life an advocate of family farming in America, but when I spent a week in China answering questions about our triumphs, seldom have I respected and admired our genius more.

All my life I believed that America must be strong, but when I met the people of Norway, whose independence our strength protects, seldom have I been more thankful for our power.

Like every American, I value freedom above all else, but when the U.S. Olympic Committee and American athletes sacrificed for an Afghan nation half a world away, seldom have I loved our people more.

We are blessed to be Americans. We are an example to the world. Don't let anyone tell you that we're less than we've been. And don't let anyone make us less than we can be.

POLISH WORKERS' DEMANDS
August 31, December 3, 12, 1980

After a wave of strikes paralyzed Poland during August, the Polish Communist Party agreed to most of the workers' demands, including a key proposal allowing the strikers to establish labor unions independent of the government-controlled workers' groups. The regime's concessions raised problems for Poland's deteriorating economy — already $20 billion in debt — and evoked fears of a Soviet intervention.

The unrest was triggered July 1 when the government removed subsidies on the price of meat. As in 1970 and 1976, when increases in the prices of food and basic goods aroused the workers, reaction from the working force was explosive. Scattered strikes erupted throughout the country protesting the price hike. Workers at the Lenin shipyard in Gdansk, Poland's largest, took over the yard Aug. 14. The trouble at Gdansk quickly became the center of the controversy; the government cut telephone lines in and out of the northern city Aug. 16. The following day, strikers formed an Inter-factory Strike Committee. On Aug. 17, the leader of the committee, Lech Walesa, a 37-year-old electrician, announced the group's terms for negotiation. In addition to demands for increased wages and reduced meat prices, the committee called for the formation of independent labor unions, relaxed government censorship and the right to strike. A list of 21 demands promulgated by the Inter-factory Strike Committee was made public Aug. 28.

Half-Million Strikers

Officials of the Polish Communist Party, led by First Secretary Edward Gierek, refused to negotiate with the committee and began to make advances to individual groups of strikers. The strike committee held firm, however, and the government finally agreed Aug. 23 to open talks with the labor group. As a precondition to negotiations, the workers demanded that telephone lines to the rest of the country be restored; the government agreed Aug. 25. In the meantime, the strike began to take its toll on the Polish economy. It was estimated that by late August 500,000 workers had walked off their jobs, and the country reportedly was losing tens of millions of dollars a day. Although the strike was centered in the Baltic region around Gdansk, workers in other parts of the country, particularly in the coal- and copper-mining region of Silesia, began to take part. In the Baltic region alone, strikes affected shipyards, auto parts and truck manufacturing plants, rubber factories, textile plants and turbine works.

Settlement

A settlement between the government and the Gdansk workers was reached Aug. 30; the agreement was signed the following day by strike leader Walesa and the government's designated negotiator, First Deputy Premier Mieczyslaw Jagielski. For the first time in an eastern-bloc nation, the government agreed to permit workers to form labor unions free of government domination. The settlement also reduced government censorship, permitted churches and other groups access to the government-controlled news media and freed imprisoned dissidents who had supported the strike. In addition, the government promised to increase wages, upgrade medical services and improve supplies of basic foods.

Gierek Ouster

Gdansk strikers returned to work Sept. 1. Striking miners in Silesia also reached a settlement, and they went back on the job Sept. 3. As things appeared to return to normal, the Communist Party announced Sept. 6 that First Secretary Gierek had been replaced. Ironically, Gierek had been named first secretary in 1970 after labor unrest had led to the downfall of his predecessor, Wladyslaw Gomulka. The new Polish leader, Stanislaw Kania, formerly the head of the country's security forces, pledged to honor the strike settlement and vowed to retain Poland's close ties with the Soviet Union and the Eastern-bloc nations. It was announced in early September that Moscow had agreed to lend Warsaw $100 million and to step up deliveries of food and basic goods.

The controversy heated up again in late September when representatives of the new independent unions attempted to gain legal recognition for their charter. The court objected because, it said, the charter neglected to recognize the "leading role" of the Polish Communist Party. The *workers refused to include the language in the charter, arguing that it would subvert the unions' proclaimed independence from government control. The government, for its part, desired the pledge of subservience to the party to mollify nervous Eastern-bloc allies. Other communist regimes in Eastern Europe were fearful that if liberalization in Poland went "too far" it would spread uncontrollably. In a show of force, the strike committee orchestrated a one-hour nationwide work stoppage Oct. 3. As tensions rose, the Communist Party Oct. 6 purged eight members, most of them close associates of former First Secretary Gierek. And in a speech to the Party Central Committee, leader Kania admitted that Poland's economic problems were caused by "our own mistakes."*

Soviet Invasion Threat

The situation remained tense throughout the remainder of 1980 as Walesa's new union, which took the name Solidarity, accused the Kania government of failing to fulfill the promises made in the Aug. 31 agreement. As sporadic work stoppages continued and arrests of union members were reported, fears rose that the Soviet Union would intervene to put down the uprising with military force.

The crisis eased somewhat on Nov. 10 when Poland's highest court ruled that Solidarity's charter could stand without the disputed clause recognizing the supremacy of the Communist Party. A general strike set for Nov. 12 was called off, but the general atmosphere of unrest was unabated. The union's demand for a five-day work week, with paid Saturdays off, became one of the most volatile unresolved issues.

On Dec. 3 President Carter issued a warning to the Soviet Union that any intervention in Poland's affairs would have "most negative consequences" and that U.S.-Soviet relations would be "directly and adversely affected." He followed up by sending Secretary of State Edmund S. Muskie to Brussels to rally the North Atlantic Treaty Organization behind the U.S. position. The mission was successful. In a communiqué issued Dec. 12, the NATO ministers said that Soviet intervention in Poland "would fundamentally alter the entire international situation. The allies would be compelled to react in the manner which the gravity of this development would require."

> *Following are excerpts from the Polish Interpress Agency text of the agreement signed Aug. 31, 1980, at Gdansk, Poland, by the Polish Government Commission and the Inter-factory Strike Committee; the text of President Carter's Dec. 3, 1980, statement on the situation in Poland; and excerpts from the Dec. 12, 1980, communiqué by NATO foreign ministers. (Boldface headings in brackets have been added by Congressional Quarterly to highlight the organization of the texts.):*

AUG. 31 AGREEMENT

The Government Commission and the Inter-factory Strike Committee after considering the 21 demands of the striking worker crews of the Coast have agreed to the following:

[Union Freedom]

Concerning point one, which reads: "Acceptance of free trade unions independent of the party and employers, in accordance with convention No. 87 of the International Labour Organization concerning union freedoms, ratified by the Polish People's Republic", it has been determined that:

1. The activity of the trade unions in the PPR [Polish People's Republic] has not fulfilled the hopes and expectations of the employees.

It is deemed desirable to establish new, self-governing trade unions, which would be an authentic representative of the working class. No one's right to remain in the present union is questioned, and in the future there could be a possibility of cooperation between the unions.

2. Creating the new, independent, self-governing trade unions the Inter-factory Strike Committee states that they will adhere to the principles defined in the Constitution of the PPR. The new trade unions will defend the social and material interests of employees and do not intend to play the role of a political party. They endorse the principle of social ownership of the means of production constituting the foundation of Poland's socialist system. Recognizing the leading role of the Polish United Workers' Party in the state and without undermining the determined system of international alliances, they strive to secure for the working people appropriate means of control, of expressing their opinions and defending their interests.

The Government Commission states that the Government will guarantee and ensure full respect for the independence and self-government of the new trade unions, both concerning their organizational structure and functioning at all levels of their activity. . . .

3. The creation and activity of independent, self-governing trade unions is compatible with convention No. 87 of the International Labour Organization on union freedom and protection of union rights, and convention No. 98 on the rights of association and collective bargaining, both ratified by Poland. . . .

4. The established strike committees have the possibility of transforming themselves into works bodies of employee representation such as workers' committees, employees' commissions, workers' councils or founding committees of the new, self-governing trade unions.

The Inter-factory Strike Committee [IFSC] as the founding committee of these unions has the freedom of choosing either one union or an association encompassing the Coast. . . .

5. The new trade unions should have genuine possibilities of publicly expressing their opinions on key decisions determining the living conditions of the working people, . . . The Government pledges ensurance of conditions for the fulfilment of these functions.

6. The Inter-factory Committee establishes a centre for socio-vocational studies, which will have the task of conducting an objective analysis of the situation of employees, the living conditions of the working people and ways of representing employee interests. . . .

7. The Government will ensure observance in Poland of Article 1 Point 1 of the 1949 bill on trade unions which reads that workers and employees are guaranteed the right to voluntary association in trade unions. The newly emerging trade unions will not be part of the association represented by the Central Council of Trade Unions. It is understood that the new bill will uphold this principle. At the same time the participation will be ensured of representative of IFSC, or of the founding committees of the self-governing trade unions or other representation of employees in working out this bill.

Concerning Point 2, which reads: "guaranteeing of the right to strike and of the security of the strikers and persons supporting them", it has been decided:

The right to strike will be guaranteed in the bill on trade unions now being prepared. The bill should define the conditions of proclaiming and organizing strikes, methods of settling disputes and responsibility for violation of the law. . . .

Concerning Point 3, which reads: "to respect the freedom of speech, print and publication guaranteed in the Constitution of the PPR, and by the same token not to apply repressive measures against independent publications and to give access to the mass media to representatives of all religious denominations", it has been agreed that:

1. The Government will submit to the Sejm [parliament] within three months a draft bill on the control of press, publications and shows, based on the following principles. Censorship should protect the interests of the state. This means protection of state and industrial secrets, the scope of which will be defined by law, of matters concerning security of the state and its important international interest protection of religious feelings and of the feelings of non-believers, and prevention of the distribution of morally harmful materials. The draft bill would also include the provision for appealing against the decisions of the organs of the control of press, publications and shows to the Chief Administrative Court. . . .

2. The use of the mass media by denominational unions within the scope of their religious activity will be realized upon settling

the substantive and organizational problems between state organs and the interested denominational unions. The Government will ensure radio broadcasting of the Sunday Mass, within the framework of a detailed agreement with the Episcopate.

3. The activity of the radio and television, as well as press and publishing enterprises should serve the expression of different ideas, views and judgements. It should be subjected to public control.

4. The press, like the citizens and their organizations, should have access to public documents (acts), especially administrative ones, to socio-economic plans etc., issued by the Government and its subordinate administrative organs. Exemptions . . . will be specified in the bill in accordance with Point 1.

[Dismissals and Prisoners]

Concerning Point 4, which reads: "A. To restore former rights to people dismissed from work after the strikes of 1970 and 1976, and to students expelled from universities for their convictions, B. To release all political prisoners (including Edmund Zadrozynski, Jan Kozlowski and Marek Kozlowski), C. To eliminate repressions for convictions" it has been agreed to:

A. Immediately check the propriety of all dismissals from work after the strikes in 1970 and 1976 in all cases submitted, and in cases of inproprieties to immediately rehire those persons who will wish this, taking into account any qualifications gained in the meantime. This will correspondingly apply to the relegated students.

B. Submit the cases of persons mentioned in point B to the Minister of Justice, who within two weeks will take the appropriate action; in the cases of those among the mentioned persons who are detained — to suspend the serving of the sentences until the end of trials;

C. consideration of the propriety of the detainment and release of the persons mentioned in the Annex

D. full observance of the freedom of expressing convictions in public and vocational life.

[Publication]

Concerning Point 5, which reads: "To announce in the mass media the establishment of the Inter-factory Strike Committee and to publish its demands" it has been agreed that the implementation of this postulate will consist in publishing this protocol in the national mass media.

Concerning Point 6 which reads: "To undertake realistic actions aimed at leading the country out of the crisis by means of: a) supply the public with full information on the socio-economic situation, b) making it possible for all communities and social strata to participate in the discussion on the programme of reforms", it has been agreed that:

We deem it necessary to markedly accelerate the work on the economic reform. The authorities will define and publish in the next few months the basic provisions of the reform. Broad public discussion on the reform should be made possible. The trade unions should especially participate in the work on the bills concerning socialist economic organizations and workers' self-management. . . .

[Pay Increases]

As regards Point 7, which reads: "To pay all employees participating in the strike wages for the period of the strike the equivalent of paid holiday from the fund of the Central Trade Union Council", it has been agreed that:

The decision is to grant the workers in striking crews an advance payment amounting to 40 percent of wage for the period of strike while after resuming work the employees will receive the remaining 60 percent of the wage calculated as that received on paid holiday, on the eight-hour work day basis. The IFSC appeals to the crews associated in it to undertake actions aimed at increasing productivity, improving raw-material and energy economy and shop-floor discipline after the strike ends. . . .

As regards Point 8, which reads: "To raise basic wages of each employee by two thousand zlotys to offset the hitherto price increases", it has been agreed that:

Gradual pay increases will be introduced for all worker groups, and first of all for those in the lowest income bracket. . . .

As regards Point 9, which reads: "To guarantee pay increases parallel to price increases in inflation", it has been established that:

It had been recognized as necessary to stop price increases of basic goods through a more intensive control over the socialized and private sector, and through abolishion [sic] of the unannounced price increases in particular;

In keeping with the government decision the shaping of the costs of living will be monitored. . . . By the end of 1980, the government will have elaborated the principles of offsetting living cost increases, which will then be submitted to public discussion and following an agreement on them, implemented. . . .

[Food Supplies]

As regards Point 10, which reads: "To implement full supplies of food for the domestic market and export only and exclusively surplus goods"; 11, which reads: "To abolish commercial prices and hard-currency sales under the so-called domestic exports system"; 13, which reads: "to introduce rationing of meat and meat products (until the situation in the market is under control) — it has been agreed that:

> Meat supplies will be improved by December 31st, 1980, through, among others: increasing profitability of agricultural production, limiting meat exports to indispensable minimum and additional meat imports. . . .

As regards Point 12, which reads: "To introduce the principles of management staff selection on the basis of their qualifications and not party affiliation as well as to abolish the privileges enjoyed by the Citizens' Militia, Security Service and party apparatus through:
—raising workers' family allowances to the level the former enjoy,
—abolishing of special shops, etc." it has been established that:

> A postulate is accepted of consistent appointing of the managerial staff on the basis of qualifications and competence. . . . The programme of equalizing family allowances for all occupational groups will be presented by the Government by December 31st, 1980. . . .

[Retirement Policy]

Concerning Point 14, which reads: "To lower the age of retirement to 50 years for women, and 55 years for men or to grant retirement rights to women who have worked 30 years in the PPR and to men who have worked for 35 years", it has been determined that:

> The Government Commission regards the postulate impossible to realize in the current economic and demographic situation of the country. The issue may be submitted for discussion in the future. The IFSC postulates that this issue be examined by December 31st, 1980 and consideration be given to the possibility of lowering by five years the retirement age of employees working in arduous conditions (or 30 years of work for women and 35 years for men, including at least 15 years of exceptionally arduous work). This should take place exclusively at the request of an employee.

Concerning Point 15, which reads: "To raise the pensions from the so-called old portfolio to the level of the present pensions", it has been determined that:

> The Government Commission states that the raising of the lowest pensions will be conducted every year in accordance with the economic possibilities of the country, and with regard to the increases of the lowest wages. The Government will present a programme of implementation by December 31st, 1980. . . . The IFSC underscores the urgent nature of this matter. . . .

[Health Service]

Concerning Point 16, which reads: "to improve the working conditions of the health service, which will ensure full medical care for the working people", the following has been agreed upon:

It is considered necessary to immediately increase the capacity of enterprises involved in health service projects, to improve the supplies of pharmaceuticals by means of increased imports of raw materials, to increase the wages of all health service employees (change of the system of nurses), and to prepare as soon as possible Government and ministry programmes for the improvement of the state of health of the people. . . .

[Hours and Allowances]

As regards Point 17, which says: "To ensure an adequate number of places at creches and kindergartens for children of working mothers", it has been decided:

The commission fully agreed with this postulate. A programme will be submitted by voivodship authorities by November 30th, 1980.

As regards Point 18, which says: "To introduce a 3-year paid maternity leave for raising children", it has been decided:

A programme on improving the housing situation which would aim at shortening the waiting time for an apartment, will be submitted by voivodship authorities by December 31st, 1980. . . .

As regards Point 20, which says: "To raise travel allowances from 40 to 100 zlotys and the allowance for work away from home", it was decided:

The amount of travel allowances and allowances for work away from home will be raised as of January 1st, 1981. Proposals on this issue will be submitted by the government by October 31st, 1980.

As regards Point 21, which says: "To introduce all Saturdays free from work. To compensate lack of free Saturdays for workers in non-stop production cycles and in a 4-shift system with longer holidays or other fully paid days off", it has been decided:

The principles and ways of implementing programmes on the introduction of free paid Saturdays or another way of regulating a shortened worktime will be elaborated and submitted by December 31st, 1980. The programme will take into consideration an increased number of free paid Saturdays already in 1981. . . .

After reaching the above settlement, it has been decided as follows:
The government pledges to:

—ensure personal safety and maintain to-date working conditions for participants in the present strike, as well as to people supporting the strike,

—consider at ministries specific industry issues submitted by crews of all striking enterprises grouped in the IFSC,

—publish immediately the full text of the protocol of the agreement in Polish mass media (press, radio, TV).

The Inter-factory Strike Committee pledges to end the strike on August 31st, 1980 at 5 p.m. . . .

CARTER STATEMENT

The United States is watching with growing concern the unprecedented building of Soviet forces along the Polish border and the closing of certain frontier regions along the border. The United States has also taken note of Soviet references to alleged "anti-Socialist" forces within Poland. We know from postwar history that such allegations have sometimes preceded military intervention.

The United States continues to believe that the Polish people and authorities should be free to work out their internal difficulties without outside interference. The United States, as well as some Western governments, and also the Soviet Union, have pledged economic assistance to Poland in order to alleviate internal Polish difficulties. The United States has no interest in exploiting in any fashion the Polish difficulties for its political ends.

Foreign military intervention in Poland would have most negative consequences for East-West relations in general and U.S.-Soviet relations in particular. The Charter of the United Nations establishes the right of all states, both large and small, to exist free of foreign interference, regardless of ideology, alliances, or geographic location. I want all countries to know that the attitude and future policies of the United States toward the Soviet Union would be directly and very adversely affected by any Soviet use of force in Poland.

NATO COMMUNIQUE

The continuing military buildup of the Soviet Union, its clear willingness, as seen in Afghanistan, to use force in disregard of the principles of the United Nations Charter, the Helsinki Final Act and international law, and the Soviet menace which hangs over Poland give cause for grave concern to the members of the alliance and to the entire international community.

Genuine détente must be worldwide in scope and indivisible. It can succeed only if the Soviet Union strictly abides, in Europe and elsewhere, by the United Nations Charter and the principles of the Helsinki Final Act in their entirety.

Allied efforts to persuade the Soviet Union to change its policy from one of intervention in the affairs of other states to one of respect for their sovereignty serve the general interest of the international community. . . .

Détente has brought appreciable benefits in the field of East-West cooperation and exchange. But it has been seriously damaged by Soviet actions. It could not survive if the Soviet Union were again to violate the basic rights of any state to territorial integrity and independence. Poland should be free to decide its own future. The allies will respect the principle of nonintervention and strongly urge others to do likewise. Any intervention would fundamentally alter the entire international situation. The allies would be compelled to react in the manner which the gravity of this development would require. . . .

September

MILITARY TAKEOVER IN TURKEY

September 12, 1980

A *military junta of five generals and an admiral took over the government of Turkey Sept. 12. In a bloodless coup shortly after midnight,
infantrymen and troops in tanks and personnel carriers took up positions
throughout Istanbul, the capital. The next day the tanks and carriers
were ordered back to their bases.*

*Calling itself the National Security Council, the junta dismissed par-
liament and suspended the nation's 19-year-old constitution. Gen. Kenan
Evren, the new head of state, said at a news conference Sept. 14,
"I would like to underline the fact that this is not a coup d'etat
as described in history books." He added that the takeover was "carried
out to remove the threat to our democracy."*

Government Paralysis

*Most observers believed that the military leaders intervened because
the government had indeed become virtually paralyzed. Neither the
conservative Justice Party of Prime Minister Suleyman Demirel nor
its chief rival, the center-left Republican People's Party of Bulent Ecevit,
a former prime minister, had been able to win a parliamentary majority.
Moreover, in a five-month parliamentary impasse, the civilian politicians
had been unable to choose a new president.*

*Even more ominous, political violence had cost at least 1,800 lives
in Turkey in the first eight months of 1980, and terrorism had been
accelerating rapidly in the weeks before the coup. The government was*

*widely seen as incapable of coping either with the mounting violence
or with a rapidly deteriorating economy.*

National Security Council

*In announcing the military takeover, Gen. Evren promised a return
to democratic rule under a new constitution and electoral laws that
he said would be designed to bring about a stable government.*

*The National Security Council included, besides Chairman Evren,
Gen. Nurettin Ersin, Gen. Tahsin Sahinkaya, Gen. Sedat Ceasun, Adm.
Nejat Tumer and Gen. Haydar Saltik. The junta on Sept. 20 appointed
a retired admiral, Bulent Ulusu, as prime minister. It named a cabinet
of 27 members, only two of whom had been serving in parliament.
But it appointed Turgut Ozal, who had been an economic adviser to
Prime Minister Demirel and had put together a $6 billion program
to rescue Turkey's economy, as deputy premier for economic affairs.*

Demirel and Ecevit

*During the coup, the junta took Demirel and Ecevit, the former
prime ministers, into custody, placing them in a military resort near
Gallipoli. Almost a month later, the new leaders released the two politicians, allowing them to return to their homes. Gen. Saltik on Oct.
28 called the men "normal citizens" and said that they would be allowed
"to return to political life after the political armistice."*

Background

*Military leaders in Turkey had intervened twice before, in 1960 and
1971, in the face of what they saw as severe threats to the nation.
In the earlier takeovers, the generals ran into difficulties in the administration of the country and seemed glad to return power to elected
civilian officials. The National Security Council in 1980 was quick to
allow top civil servants to make most of the decisions in their own
departments.*

*The Turkish army generally was considered "above politics" in the
tradition of Kemal Atatürk, the country's president in 1923-38 and
a legendary figure in Turkish history. Gen. Evren himself was well
known in the United States, having fought alongside American forces
in the Korean War.*

*Following are excerpts from a press release on the military
takeover in Turkey issued Sept. 12, 1980, by the Turkish
Embassy in Washington, D.C., and the text of a Sept.
12, 1980, statement made by the U.S. Department of State:*

EMBASSY PRESS RELEASE

A military takeover has taken place in Turkey in the early hours of September 12, Turkish time.

A National Security Council under the Chairmanship of General Kenan Evren, Chief of General Staff, has been established. Members of this Council are the Chiefs of the four Services, Ground, Air, Naval and Gendarmerie. General Haydar Saltik has been appointed as the Secretary General of this Council. Martial Law has been declared throughout the country.

The following are the highlights from the Communiqués issued by this Council, as well as the statement of General Evren to the nation:

The Turkish Armed Forces, in face of the vital dangers confronting the territorial integrity and national unity of the Republic of Turkey has taken over the Government and has established complete control of the entire country. The Turkish Armed Forces has undertaken this historic task, which the overwhelming majority of the Turkish nation expected and yearned, with a great responsibility and love for the country. This historic task is entrusted to the Turkish Army by the Internal Service Law.

In carrying out this task the members of the Armed Forces have acted and will act free from all personal interests and ambitions, with a superior sense of discipline, and great determination to strive and succeed for the preservation of a free and independent Turkish Republic based on Atatürk's principles.

The Republic of Turkey, committed to all its alliances and treaties including NATO, is resolved to develop economic, social and cultural relations on the principles of equality and reciprocal respect for independence and non-interference in the internal affairs of others with all countries, in particular with her neighbors. . . .

The present Parliament and the Government have been abolished. The Turkish Armed Forces are devoted to the free democratic parliamentary system. Therefore they commit themselves to a speedy restoration of the democratic process. . . .

A new Constitution, electoral law and a law on political parties, befitting the Turkish nation, will be prepared and parallel arrangements to these will be taken so that the degeneration of the free democratic parliamentary system, as has recently been the case, be prevented. It will transfer the administration of the country to a freely elected Government. . . .

Until these preparation are completed, all political activities at all levels are suspended. Political activities will resume in sufficiently ahead of time before the elections, the time and conditions of which will be later announced. No action will be taken against the members of the Parliament unless they adopt an attitude constituting a crime against the new Administration. However, those members of the Parliament who in the past have under the laws committed crime, will be prosecuted. Leaders of the Justice Party, Republican Peoples Party, National Salvation Party, National Action Party, for their personal safety, are under protective custody. When conditions so permit they will be set free.

STATE DEPARTMENT STATEMENT

At 0400 local time in Ankara, General Kenan Evren, Chief of the Turkish General Staff, announced that Turkish military authorities were taking control of the country. The announcement stated that the civilian government and Parliament had been dissolved. Our Embassy reports that the country appears calm, that there has been no bloodshed and that American citizens and property are not in danger.

The United States must be concerned about the seizure of power from any democratically-elected government. We note that in taking power the Turkish military have stated that they do so to restore a functioning democratic government. For the last several years Turkey has been beset by increasing politically-motivated terrorism and severe economic difficulties. We have admired the Turkish people for their persistent efforts to deal with a deepening economic and political crisis through a democratic system of government. The United States, along with Turkey's other NATO allies and friends, has provided significant levels of assistance to help stabilize its economy and provide for the common defense. This assistance will continue. We look forward to the early restoration of democracy in Turkey and to the establishment of economic and political stability.

REPORT ON ECONOMIC IMPACT
OF MT. ST. HELENS ERUPTIONS
September 15, 1980

The economic effects of the repeated eruptions of Mount St. Helens in southwestern Washington during 1980 were not nearly so devastating as the spectacular eruptions themselves, according to an International Trade Commission (ITC) report released September 15. "The immediate economic effects of the recent eruptions of Mount St. Helens," the report began, "have been small in relation to the economy of the Pacific Northwest and, in relation to the U.S. economy, virtually insignificant."

"The long-term effects," the report continued, "depend primarily upon the volcano's future activity. If volcanic activity continues for a significant period, there may be a reduction in investment, and a lower rate of growth in the region. However, if Mount St. Helens returns to a dormant state the long-term impact will be minimal, with a probable growth in tourism due to the unique nature of the mountain."

Eruptions

Mount St. Helens, one of several volcanoes in the Cascade Mountain Range, began to send out small amounts of steam and ash in late March and early April. The volcano had been quiet since a series of eruptions between 1831 and 1856. With a blast equal to that of a hydrogen bomb, the volcano erupted May 18, sending a pillar of ash 60,000 feet into the atmosphere. The eruption, consisting of mountain debris and hot gases, blew 1,500 feet off the top of Mount St. Helens and formed a large crater on the mountain's northwest slope. The immediate impact in the surrounding region was threefold: First, parts of the mountain mixed with melting ice and snow to form massive mudslides that destroyed homes and bridges and clogged nearby Spirit Lake and the Toutle, Cowlitz and Columbia rivers; second, the blast decimated 120,000 acres of timberland north of the volcano; and third, the ash emitted from Mount St. Helens spread throughout the area, fouling the engines of vehicles and machinery and reducing visibility to dangerous levels. The eruption killed at least 30 people; 38 others were missing and presumed dead.

In the first few days following the initial volcanic activity, state and federal officials expressed fears that the eruption would seriously disrupt the region's economic well-being. Officials continued to voice such apprehensions as five additional, though lesser, eruptions took place. Their fears were unfounded, according to the ITC report. However, the total losses and repair and cleanup costs, the report said, amounted to $1.2 billion.

Report's Findings

The report, prepared in response to a request from the U.S. House of Representatives' Committee on Ways and Means, stated that the timber industry was hardest hit, with losses totaling an estimated $659 million. Most of the loss — $652 million — was in trees destroyed. Damaged roads and buildings accounted for the remainder. But the amount of downed timber — 3.2 billion board feet — the report stated, was less than the 4 billion to 5 billion board feet lost annually in the Pacific Northwest as a result of disease, insect damage and fire. Moreover, the report said, some of the destroyed timber might be salvaged.

Agricultural Losses

Losses in the agriculture sector would be small, according to the report, amounting to 3.5 percent of 1979 totals. In fact, "the eruption of Mount St. Helens is expected to provide some long-term benefits to agriculture in those areas receiving ash since the ash does contain some trace elements and mineral nutrients that are necessary for plant growth. In addition, the ash will help to loosen the soil which will allow better root penetration by plants and better moisture penetration which will help enhance plant growth."

The fish population in local rivers was nearly wiped out, the report noted. But it added that prospects for the restoration of fish habitats were good. Similarly, though the eruptions kept all but the most curious *tourists away from the area, the ITC report asserted that, over the long-term, an idle Mount St. Helens could develop into a very lucrative tourist attraction.*

Effects on Health

The report also claimed that the area's transportation system and its level of international trade were only slightly harmed due to the volcano. It noted, however, that the long-term effects on human health could not be easily determined. It warned that lengthy exposure to volcanic ash could lead to respiratory ailments such as industrial bronchitis and silicosis.

> *Following are excerpts from a report of the U.S. International Trade Commission, The Economic Effects of the Eruptions of Mt. St. Helens, released Sept. 15, 1980. (Boldface headings in brackets have been added by Congressional Quarterly to highlight the organization of the text.):*

Executive Summary

The immediate economic effects of the recent eruptions of Mt. St. Helens have been small in relation to the economy of the Pacific Northwest and, in relation to the U.S. economy, virtually insignificant. There has been little overall impact on the area's imports and exports, despite the fact that specific activities such as agriculture (including timber production) and shipping experienced immediate, short-term losses. The long-term effects depend primarily upon the volcano's future activity. If volcanic activity continues for a significant period, there may be a reduction in investment, and a lower rate of growth in the region. However, if Mt. St. Helens returns to a dormant state the long-term impact will be minimal, with a probable growth in tourism due to the unique nature of the mountain.

The strongest and most violent of the eruptions was the one on May 18. The three major physical effects — the mudflows, the pyroclastic blast, and the ash fallout — each has had distinct economic consequences. The blast blew down 120,000 acres of forest. The mudflows, along with knocking down bridges and roads, let loose tons of silt blocking transport along the Columbia River, killing fish, and destroying their habitat. The ash fallout caused crop losses and forced many manufacturing facilities to close for hours and some for days.

The subsequent eruptions were of a lesser magnitude and resulted largely in more ash being carried by winds to sections of the country west, south, and northeast of the volcano.

The estimated losses and repair/cleanup costs, as currently reported, are as follows:

	Value (Million dollars)
Timber and related losses	695
Agricultural losses	192
Fishery losses	95
Dredging Columbia River	44
Damage to public roads and bridges	112
Cleaning ash from roads	75
Total	1,213

The resolution of the Committee on Ways and Means of the House of Representatives requested the U.S. International Trade Commission to investigate the economic impact of the Mt. St. Helens' eruptions on the Pacific Northwest and the United States. . . .

Introduction

. . . Mt. St. Helens is located in southwestern Washington State, 45 miles north of Portland, Oreg., and approximately 100 miles south of Seattle. It is one of a chain of volcanos in the Cascade Mountain Range which extends from northern California to British Columbia. . . . Because geologists have been able to identify many previous periods of violent volcanic activity at Mt. St. Helens, it has long been considered one of the most active and potentially violent in the United States. Prior to 1980, the most recent activity was from 1831 to 1856, when several other Cascade volcanos erupted as well.

Most geologists believe that most volcanos are created where the plates of the earth's crust come together. As the plates shift, melted rock may be released through weakened spots to form new volcanos or through passages in existing volcanos. Violent eruptions occur when the passageways to the volcano's cap from the high-pressure areas below the earth's surface become clogged. If sufficient pressure mounts, an explosion occurs in which heat, ash, rock, and gases may be expelled.

The early signs that Mt. St. Helens was returning to activity in 1980 were a series of earthquakes, the first of which occurred on March 20, approximately 20 miles north of the volcano. . . .

In early April, scientists noticed a large and growing bulge caused by pressure from within on the north side of Mt. St. Helens. By May 18, when two strong earthquakes centered at Mt. St. Helens loosened the bulge, the protrusion had extended over 300 feet. As the north face of the mountain began to collapse, pressure was vented laterally from the area formerly occupied by the bulge and three, more or less simultaneous, events occurred.

First, the material from the collapsing bulge slid down the north face of the volcano, mixing with water from Spirit Lake, the Toutle River, and from melted snow and glaciers. This combination of earth and water formed massive mudflows which followed the drainage system down the Toutle and Cowlitz Rivers, and into the Columbia River. Along the Toutle and Cowlitz the mudflows and associated floods scoured the river banks leaving mud, sediment, logs, and other debris some of which eventually contributed to a shoal blocking the Columbia River.

Second, a "pyroclastic blast" or mixture of mountain debris and hot volcanic gases traveling at speeds up to 150 miles an hour, shot out from the area of the displaced bulge, and destroyed most of the forest in a fan-shaped area extending 20 miles north of the mountain.

Third, a large vertical cloud of ash was emitted 11 miles into the atmosphere and was carried east along with the prevailing winds to eastern Washington State, northern Idaho, and west and central Montana. The coarsest ash particles landed within 100 miles of the mountain while finer ash material fell as far east as Oklahoma. The finest particles are still airborne and are expected to remain so for years.

In five subsequent major eruptions of lesser magnitude, the blasts were principally directed vertically with only ashfall as their primary consequence. On May 25, the ash was carried by winds to the west, on June 12 to the south, and on July 22, August 7, and August 15 to the northeast. . . .

With regard to the future of Mt. St. Helens, scientists are unable to predict the probability, magnitude, and timing of continued volcanic activity. They have observed, however, a pattern of gas emissions and harmonic tremors which preceded by several hours five of the six eruptions. As a result, people working in the immediate vicinity of Mt. St. Helens were forewarned and removed to avoid further loss of life. There is also a growing consensus among geologists that the magnitude of future volcanic activity will tend to be closer to the five later eruptions than to the first. . . .

DAMAGE APPRAISAL

The May 18 eruption of Mt. St. Helens laid waste to perhaps as much as 120,000 acres of forest land. Most of the damage was done by the pyroclastic blast, a high velocity lateral discharge consisting of a mass of earth and rocks, accompanied by a cloud of hot ash and gases with temperatures which may have approximated 1,000 degrees centigrade. Substantial damage was also caused by the enormous mudflows (consisting of hot mixtures of earth, rocks, and water) which poured down Mt. St. Helens' drainage systems. As the mudflows moved downstream they scoured riverbanks of standing timber and ripped out bridges and roads.

Estimates of damage to the timber resources and related losses (including repair/replacement costs to access roads, buildings, and so forth) currently total about $695 million, with the bulk of the loss — some $652 million — in timber. Of the down and damaged timber, about 70 percent is privately held and the remainder divided about equally between Federal and State ownership. In terms of ownership of the forest areas damaged by the May 18 blast, privately owned timberlands constitute about 60 percent, Federal lands about 35 percent, and the remainder State lands.

Approximately 3.2 billion board feet of timber are believed to have been destroyed or blown down by the pyroclastic blast or uprooted and washed downstream by the mudflows. About half of this timber is Douglas-fir with the remainder consisting of hemlock and other white-wood species. The downed timber included stands of various age groups — overmature, mature, and plantations.

To provide a frame of reference for appraisal of the magnitude of the downed timber, the current loss of 3.2 billion board feet should be compared with the annual loss owing to disease, insects, and fire in the Pacific Northwest of about 4 to 5 billion board feet and to the 10 to 12 billion board feet which were harvested because of the 1962 Columbus Day storm that hit northern California, Oregon, Washington, and then Canada. Another frame of reference is the total annual cut of softwood timber in the United States: about 56 to 58 billion board feet cut annually with Washington, Oregon, and Idaho supplying about 12 percent, 14 percent, and 3 percent, respectively.

In regard to the salvage possibilities of the downed timber, available estimates vary from a low of about 20 percent to a high of about 80 percent of the preblast volume of the stands; however, it appears that substantially less than 50 percent may be salvaged. The force of the pyroclastic blast virtually destroyed many acres of timber and left many others with badly shattered and broken trees. Even those downed trees which appear to be essentially intact may have suffered extensive splintering, shake damage, microscopic tissue damage, or other types of structural failure. Another possible type of damage may be the extent and depth of penetration of ash particles into the wood of the downed trees. The incidence of the various types of damage is unknown at this time. As the areas of the downed timber are harvested with extensive laboratory tests being made on samples of the downed timber, a clearer picture will emerge of the extent and seriousness of the various types of damage that occurred.

[EFFECTS ON PRODUCTION]

The effect of the Mt. St. Helens' eruptions upon the output of the forest products industries of the Pacific Northwest and upon the United States has been minimal. Immediately after the May 18 blast, a few mills were shut down for a short time, one or two shifts or 1 or 2 days, principally owing to ash-related problems. One mill was closed down because all roads leading to it were cut by mudflows or ashfall.

For the long term, however, there are problems facing various forest products firms in securing their logs. Companies which had been logging in the down area now must procure their logs from other sources available to them. For instance, those firms owning timberlands have begun to cut on lands that had not been scheduled for cutting until a later date. Those firms which had been securing their logs from the blast area and now have no other timberlands available may have difficulty in purchasing logs.

The consensus, however, appears to be that the large amount of downed timber will not be harvested at a rate exceeding the normal rate for the region; i.e., as the blast timber is harvested, logging cutbacks will occur elsewhere in the region. Although the downed timber has caused fluctuations in the market prices of logs, such variations have been outweighed in large measure by the downward pressure on market prices generated by the depressed level of housing starts and of the economy in general.

There are a number of problems of a somewhat extended nature affecting the future output of forest products from the vicinity of Mt. St. Helens. Foremost, perhaps, is the need to remove the wood before it rots. All dead timber, of course, presents serious disease and insect hazards not only affecting the harvest of such timber but also the risk of spreading to nearby green timber. Depending upon species, the harvest will have to be completed within 18 months to perhaps 3 years. There is a substantial fire hazard as well because of the extensive acreage of dead trees, both standing and down, and both with and without branches and twigs intact. Such areas present a significant forest fire hazard not only to the dead trees but also to adjacent stands of green timber.

The presence of ash on the ground or on the logs or in the wood presents serious problems in harvesting of the logs and their processing into products. The ash, being gritty in nature, is quite abrasive and causes extensive wear on chain saws, chipper knives, and other wood cutting and slicing equipment, thus appreciably raising the costs of logging and of manufacture. Further, the presence of ash particles also would seriously limit the utilization of the log for processing into those products where the ash particles would adversely affect the utility or the appearance of the end product. . . .

[EFFECTS ON AGRICULTURAL PRODUCTS]

The effects of the eruptions of Mt. St. Helens on agricultural production in the Pacific Northwest have been minimal, thus far. Short-term losses are estimated at about $192 million for the region, equivalent to approximately 3.5 percent of the total value of agricultural production for the region in 1979. The heaviest losses occurred to the animal and animal products sector, to hay, and to tree fruits,. . .

Although individual farmers were adversely affected by the various eruptions of Mt. St. Helens, it is possible that the total value of agricultural production in the region may be higher in 1980 than it was in 1979 because of the large wheat and barley crops and the possibility of a near record apple crop. Also, the drought in the central United States may cause prices for nearly all farm products to increase this year. This general rise in farm price levels may also result in damage estimates from the eruptions being increased.

Animal and animal products. It is estimated that this sector incurred nearly $38 million in losses from the eruptions. Almost all of the losses were confined to the State of Washington and occurred in part because farmers were not able to deliver their products to market. For example, it has been reported that dairy farmers dumped milk during the week following the eruptions of May 18 and of May 25 because delivery trucks could not reach the farms and because air filters on the milk-holding tanks clogged. However, the bulk of the $38 million is estimated as potential losses because of livestock needing longer periods of time to obtain market weight and owing to lower milk production because of the ash-caused decreased palatability and poor quality of the pasture and the first hay crop this year. Only a small part of the total loss is attributed to livestock deaths, primarily to sheep and cattle. Most of these deaths resulted from the animals drowning during the flooding along the Toutle and Cowlitz Rivers following the May 18 eruption.

Hay. Hay is the principal crop which was adversely affected by the eruptions. At the time of the May 18 eruption, much of the first hay cutting was ready for harvest. Losses are estimated at more than $35 million with the loss being confined almost entirely to the State of Washington. It is estimated that half of the first cutting of hay in Washington was damaged or destroyed by the ash (the first cutting usually accounts for about 40 percent of the entire crop). The ash has lowered the quality and palatability of the hay, hence, livestock do not readily eat it. Therefore, many farmers have purchased hay from areas that were not affected by the eruptions to mix with the ash-contaminated hay so that the livestock will accept it. This has also caused their operating costs to increase sharply. Hence, these farmers are at a competitive disadvantage when compared with farmers that are not in the affected areas.

It has been reported that the second cutting of alfalfa hay was excellent on those fields that were disced after the eruptions. On those fields that were not disced, however, the alfalfa hay is not doing nearly as well. It is believed, however, that generally the quality of the second and subsequent cuttings will be very good.

Tree fruits. Losses to tree fruits are estimated at $25 million, primarily to apples. Cherries, prunes, and pears were also affected by the ash but only to a minor extent. The ash is believed to have been in part responsible for the larger than normal apple drop in June in parts of the Yakima Valley. However, it is believed that weather conditions were also a major factor in the larger drop. On the other hand, industry sources report that the Washington apple crop may reach a near record since the apples that remain on the trees are much larger than would be expected for this time of the season in the Yakima Valley and because of a larger than normal fruit set in the other apple-producing areas of Washington. Although about 40 percent of the cherry crop was lost due to splitting this year, the splitting resulted from excess moisture and not from the ash. Growers are somewhat concerned that the pear crop, although showing little sign of damage at present, may be affected adversely owing to ash clinging to the blossom end of the fruit at harvest time, thus causing discoloration and lowering the final grade of the fruit.

Wheat and barley. Total losses to wheat, barley, and other small grains are estimated at $19 million, and reflect potential losses owing to reduced yield more than actual losses. Most of the actual losses were to spring planted grains such as spring wheat and barley that were suffocated in the heaviest ashfall areas. Estimates (based on August 1 growing conditions) put Washington's winter wheat crop production — which was virtually unaffected by the eruptions — at 135.0 million bushels — up more than one-third from the amount of production in 1979. Winter wheat accounts for more than 90 percent of the State's wheat output.

Estimates of losses to spring wheat production from plants being suffocated are not available. However, spring wheat production in Washington is estimated at 15.6 million bushels in 1980 — down one-third from the previous crop. It should be noted, however, that this production is from 410,000 acres, or 45 percent fewer acres than the number of acres in 1979.

Washington's barley production in 1980 is estimated at 28.0 million bushels, or nearly 65 percent higher than output in 1979, although acreage planted only increased by 3.7 percent from 1979 to 1980.

Other crops. There was also some damage to other crops such as dried legumes (peas and lentils) and miscellaneous horticultural crops (i.e., vegetables, berries, and seed crops). Damage to dried legumes is estimated at about $15 million. Damage varied from field to field depending on the height of the plants at the time of the ashfall. In addition to the damage from the ashfall, producers of dried legumes face substantial losses as a result of poor weather conditions and disease problems.

Berry crops were also affected by the May 25 and June 12 eruptions. Losses are estimated at more than $8 million, primarily to strawberries. The principal effect of the ash on strawberries was reduced quality for processed berries. Although the ash can be washed off the berries at an increased expense, a very fine residue remains which precludes the processed berries from being graded "A" or "B" by the U.S. Department of Agriculture. . . .

Other losses. The extent of losses to machinery is a major unknown. At present, losses to farm machinery, primarily for repairs, and the cost of increased preventive maintenance are estimated at $30 million. Routine maintenance such as changing air and fuel filters and changing oil has been greatly accelerated to prevent damage from the ash. In the heaviest ashfall areas it is recommended that routine maintenance be performed at least twice as often as normal. The ash is very abrasive to moving machinery parts. Machinery which operates close to the ground is particularly susceptible to rapid ash-caused wear (as hay producers have discovered, to their dismay). Dried legume producers are particularly concerned, since their crops must be cut close to the ground. Producers of forage and grass seeds are also concerned since their crops not only have to be cut off close to the ground and placed in windrows to dry but they also have to use expensive combines to harvest the seed from windrows.

Long-term losses to agriculture as a result of the eruptions are not known but it is believed that such losses will be negligible. The most likely long-term losses will be increased maintenance costs and premature equipment failure because of prolonged exposure to the ash. It is believed that the ash can be incorporated into the existing soil with only minor difficulty on almost all of the affected farmland. The incorporation of the ash is not expected to significantly affect soil composition since most of the soil types in the regions are of volcanic origin and the ash is basically composed of inert material. The salinity of the ash may cause some problems in the drier areas of the Pacific Northwest. In the humid areas the salinity of the ash may result in the ground water containing slightly higher salt levels than currently found in irrigation water in the region. It is anticipated that normal rainfall will leach most of the salts from the soil quickly. Hence, increased salinity should not cause any prolonged adverse effects.

Although 25 to 30 farms along the Toutle and Cowlitz Rivers were covered by mud deposits of 1 foot to 8 feet as a result of the mudflows from the May 18 eruption, it is believed that many of the farmers will farm over the deposits. Therefore, there will be little, if any, loss of farmland.

The eruption of Mt. St. Helens is expected to provide some long-term benefits to agriculture in those areas receiving ash since the ash does contain some trace elements and mineral nutrients that are necessary for plant growth. In addition, the ash will help to loosen the soil which will allow better root penetration by plants and better moisture penetration which will help enhance plant growth. . . .

[EFFECTS ON FISHERY PRODUCTS]

The damaging effects of the May 18 eruption of Mt. St. Helens on the Columbia River fishery were substantial and resulted primarily from the mudflows and floods. . . . The eruption adversely affected the entire Mt. St. Helens' drainage system, to varying degrees; these effects are discussed in the following section of the report.

Direct fish kill. Virtually all fish in the Toutle and in the Cowlitz Rivers from its junction with the Toutle downstream to the Columbia River were killed following the May 18th eruption. Salmon was the principal fish impacted, with the major kill consisting of the young salmon that were on their way downstream at the time of the eruption.

The Washington Department of Fisheries estimates a loss of about 12 million juvenile salmon. The salmon losses include all the salmon in the affected rivers at the time — wild fish, fish released from the Cowlitz hatchery just prior to the May 18 eruption, all the fish in the flooded-out Toutle hatchery on the Green River, and about 400,000 young salmon that were lost when they were forced through the turbines of a dam on the Lewis River when the reservoir was sharply lowered to stave off possible flooding on the river. . . .

Fish in the Columbia River undoubtedly were adversely affected by turbid waters and by the raised water temperatures caused by the eruption. The count of fish passing Bonneville Dam showed a small decline after the May 18 eruption. It is not known, however, whether the decline was due to the eruption or to other factors. It is believed that sturgeon, shad, and smelt moved down the Columbia River from the turbid area below the Cowlitz to cleaner waters nearer the mouth of the Columbia following the May 18 eruption, and hence they were not harmed by the eruption. . . .

Damage to fish habitat. The May 18 eruption destroyed fish habitat in the waters north of Mt. St. Helens. Spirit Lake (a sport fishing and recreation center) was partially filled with volcanic debris, as was most of the Toutle River. In addition, mud flows in the Toutle and Cowlitz Rivers destroyed much of the fish habitat. The Washington State Game Department estimates that the eruption of May 18 heavily damaged or destroyed 26 lakes and moderately damaged 27 others and destroyed 154 miles of resident trout streams. Another 142 lakes and 1,029 miles of resident trout streams received little or no damage but currently are inaccessible due to road closures in the Gifford Pinchot National Forest. . . .

At the time of heavy sedimentation, young salmon were able to survive in the ash-laden water for only a few hours. Young trout in hatcheries as far away as Yakima apparently were weakened from the sedimentation and a few died. Although the water has cleared considerably in the Toutle and Cowlitz Rivers, there is still a danger from glasslike particles of ash cutting the gills of young fish.

Large fish are able to survive the sharp particles of ash and many negotiated the Cowlitz when it was in particularly poor condition. While the rivers have cleared considerably, they are not in a condition suitable for fish to spawn. The fish need river bottoms of pebbles or gravel in order to spawn, and many of the old river beds are believed to be covered with at least 18 inches of silt — many of the old resting pools are also filled with silt. . . .

Long-term effects. Long-term losses to the Columbia River fishery as a result of the eruptions are not known, but it is believed that such losses will be small. The major loss will be the decrease in fish habitat and thus in the size of the fish population that it can support. Fish habitat was destroyed by the mudflows down the Toutle and Cowlitz Rivers and by sedimentation in the Columbia River. In addition, the dredging of the Columbia and Cowlitz Rivers is destroying additional habitat since the silt dredged is being deposited in the marshes along the river banks. These marshes are a primary source of nutrients for fish. In addition, the construction of temporary debris-retaining structures and settling basins on the Toutle River will affect fish habitat.

It is believed, however, that much of the fish habitat that was damaged or destroyed will recover in time and that the various fish species will resume their natural migrations in and out of the region. To speed up this process, it is expected that various fish species will be transferred to help repopulate the Mt. St. Helens' area from hatcheries in areas that were not affected by the eruptions.

It is also anticipated that beneficial nutrients from the volcanic ash will enter the water system and become available to aquatic organisms. The ash is composed predominantly of silica — the basic component of the diatoms which are a major base in the food chain of young salmon and other small fish.

EFFECTS ON MANUFACTURING

Introduction

An assessment of the immediate effects of the eruptions of Mt. St. Helens on manufacturing activities suggests that the losses to income and damage to equipment of individual manufacturers were small. However, while the individual losses were not great, they were suffered in one form or another by almost all manufacturers within the paths of the ash fallouts in the affected areas of Washington and Oregon.

The principal long-term effect of the change of Mt. St. Helens to an active volcano has been the uncertainty it has created with regard to future investment in the region. One of the main selling points of the area to potential investors was its clean air, "quality of life" image. The prospect of intermittent air quality alerts resulting from ash fallout has tarnished that image, at least temporarily. Nonetheless, if the volcanic activity were to cease soon, it is quite possible that the long-run effect, like that of the short run, will be small. On the other hand, if Mt. St. Helens continues to erupt ash, investors may go elsewhere. . . .

Difficulty in predicting long-term effects. Precise estimates of the long-term effects of the eruptions of Mt. St. Helens are difficult and are likely to remain so for some time. One reason for this is the impossibility of predicting future volcanic activity. In this regard, answers to such questions as whether there will be more ash eruptions, and in what quantities and areas it will fall, are crucial to predicting future economic effects. Furthermore, even if these questions could be answered, it would also be essential to know the implications of further volcanic activity for different sectors of the economy.

The result of these combined uncertainties is to raise the level of risk associated with investments in the region. Conventional finance theory states that when such risk is increased, investment will tend to go elsewhere or at least seek a higher return, thereby lowering regional long-term economic growth prospects. The extent to which these areas in the weeks, months, and years to come will be perceived as more risky than other areas for prospective investment is difficult to estimate. Even for the present, the situation, as reflected in the prices and ratings of securities in the region, is not clear. For example, in spite of the fact that the national bond rating institutions have not downgraded the regional issues, local bond brokers estimate that municipalities and school districts close to the volcano have had to raise the yields of their recent 20-year bond issues by 0.1 to 0.5 percentage points to attract buyers. Also, the recommendations to buy the stocks of the major regional banks were downgraded by one national brokerage firm because of the Mt. St. Helens' eruptions. Nonetheless, the prices of the stock of these banks, after falling in June, have either returned to, or surpassed, their preeruption levels. . . .

Summary of the long-term effects. The long-term effects of the eruption of Mt. St. Helens are yet to be determined by Mt. St. Helens' future activity. If Mt. St. Helens soon returns to a state of dormancy, the long-term effects of the eruptions experienced so far will be small. However, should Mt. St. Helens remain active, the long-term economic effects on the region could be severe. . . .

EFFECTS ON TOURISM

According to statistics from the Washington State Department of Revenue, the tourist industry revenues, as measured by State tax receipts for hotel and motel rooms, have decreased greatly in May and June 1980 compared with the corresponding months of 1979. . . . Similarly, an accounting firm's survey of 35 hotels and motels in Portland, Oreg. shows a decrease of about 15 percent in the room occupancy level this June compared with last June. Officials contacted in the convention and visitors centers of Spokane, Yakima, and other regional tourist centers attributed these late spring and early summer problems primarily to the ash fallout and the negative publicity that ensued from the first eruptions. They also noted that other factors may have played a contributory role such as the bad weather experienced by the region in June 1980, high gasoline prices, and the national economic recession.

The same officials felt however that late July and August revenues from tourism had increased to a level closer to last year's. Although no statistics could be provided to substantiate this, the consensus was that by late summer the nationwide recession was having a more serious effect on tourism in the Pacific Northwest than Mt. St. Helens was. In fact, it is increasingly commented by area tourist officials that Mt. St. Helens is becoming an asset for tourism. For example, the U.S. Forest Service, which established observation booths 40 miles from Mt. St. Helens, reported having more than 4,000 visitors per day in August 1980. Many feel that Mt. St. Helens may soon parallel Mt. Lassen in California and Volcan Irazu in Costa Rica as an often-visited volcano attraction enhancing the Northwest's tourist appeal. . . .

DEATH SENTENCE FOR KIM
IN SOUTH KOREA
September 17, 1980

Kim Dae Jung, a prominent critic of the military-backed government in South Korea, was sentenced to death by a military court Sept. 17. Kim, 54, was arrested May 17 and charged with sedition. His 23 co-defendants received sentences ranging from three years to 23 years in prison.

Reaction to the sentence was swift. Secretary of State Edmund S. Muskie criticized the court's "extreme verdict" of death by hanging and the Japanese Prime Minister, Masayoshi Ito, hinted that Tokyo would cut off economic aid to South Korea.

Although the courts rejected Kim's appeal, South Korean President Chun Doo Hwan on Jan. 23, 1981, commuted his sentence to life imprisonment. There was speculation that Chun's unexpected act of clemency came in large part as the result of pressure on the South Korean president by both the Carter administration and incoming officials of the Reagan administration. An invitation from President Ronald Reagan for Chun to visit the White House on Feb. 2, 1981, was seen as likely having been conditioned on a reciprocal gesture by Chun.

New Strongman

President Chun emerged as the country's new strongman in the months following the assassination of Park Chung Hee, the president assassinated Oct. 26, 1979, by the head of the Korean secret service. (Historic Documents of 1979, p. 895) In early December 1979, Maj. Gen. Chun and his supporters in the armed forces took over Seoul, arrested the martial law commander and forced about 40 senior military officers to resign. Meanwhile, demonstrations occurred throughout the country in favor of measures to relax Park's authoritarian legacy. Reaction to the demonstrations reached a climax May 17. The military declared martial law, seized control of the government and arrested Kim and other opposition politicians. Kim's arrest sparked further large-scale protests that were finally put down violently by the armed forces.

Election Runner-Up

Following Park's murder, the transitional government had pledged to reinstate presidential elections. Kim was considered one of the leading candidates; in the country's most recent free elections, held in 1971, he garnered 46 percent of the vote against President Park. Most observers felt that his arrest and subsequent trial were a signal from President Chun (who named himself to the nation's highest post in September) that he intended to be the "people's choice" in any new elections. Kim's showcase trial and harsh sentence were taken to mean also that, despite hopes of liberalization following Park's death, South Korea's new ruler would brook little opposition from any quarter.

> *Following are the text of the "Conclusion" section of "Report on the Investigation of Kim Dae-jung" made available in July 1980 by the Korean Overseas Information Service; excerpts from statements to the press July 7, 1980, by U.S. State Department spokesman David Passage; and the text of a Sept. 17, 1980, statement by Secretary of State Edmund S. Muskie on the verdict against Kim:*

CONCLUSION OF REPORT

The investigation results ... show that Kim Dae-jung, as part of his attempted insurrection, established four phases in his struggle for power, and to fulfill them mounted both legitimate and illegal campaigns.

First, he succeeded in having his civil rights restored, thus preparing the way for legal political struggles. He then sought to seize control of the New Democratic Party.

However, when the New Democratic Party mainstreamers refused to yield to Kim, and when his obsessive pursuit of personal political ambition was clearly no longer to be tolerated, Kim Dae-jung relinquished his grasping for control of the party and concentrated on illegal struggles for power through his private organizations and demagoguery. He restructured an assortment of private organizations, including the People's Alliance, to facilitate their more effective use in agitating popular uprisings.

Convinced that transforming student demonstrations into violent riots to create a state of anarchy was the only way to spark a popular uprising, Kim Dae-jung set up various private organizations, chiefly among reinstated professors and students. He then infiltrated his followers onto the campuses, covertly engineered student disturbances and induced violent street demonstrations. He also tried to stir public distrust of the legitimacy of the incumbent Government and its schedule for political development with wild rumors and outrageous demagoguery.

In particular, Kim Dae-jung orchestrated student demonstrations and slogans with the phases of his struggle for power. He fabricated and spread assorted rumors in a bid to estrange the people from the military, the last bulwark of national security and political and social stability. He also ensured that student slogans were designed to achieve the same result.

The campus disturbances worsened as Kim Dae-jung schemed. Despite Martial Law, students began taking to the streets in force on May 13. On May 14 and 15, students staged extremely violent demonstrations in Seoul and other major cities, paralyzing the cities and challenging the authority of the Republic.

In the course of struggling to overthrow the Government and seize power, Kim Dae-jung went so far as to conceive the idea of an interim regime formed around his private organizations. The investigation found Kim completely prepared to seize power promptly once the incumbent Government was overthrown.

Moreover, by assigning some persons to several organizations and putting them in charge of different would-be recruits and covert action channels, Kim sought to represent his network of organizations as vast and broadly supported, while boosting his followers' sense of participation and pride by distributing many "high posts."

To sum up, despite the fact that the Government took the people's aspirations into full account and made public pledges to implement the political schedule announced immediately after the October 26 assassination of President Park, and has been doing its utmost to honor those pledges, Kim Dae-jung and a group of his followers conspired to overthrow the incumbent Government by violence and set up an interim regime headed by Kim himself. The Government was thus compelled to declare Nationwide Martial Law on May 17 and launched a thorough investigation of Kim and his followers.

To achieve stable and steady political development, there must be a political climate in which all politicians can work in concert to overcome crises by transcending partisan interests and tactics.

In spite of the results of the investigation of Kim Dae-jung and his supporters, the previously announced political timetable — with a constitutional referendum by the end of October this year and a new administration by June next year — will be implemented as originally planned.

MUSKIE STATEMENT

As is well known, we have followed the court martial trial of Kim Dae Jung with intense interest and deep concern. The Government of the Republic of Korea is fully aware of our views. We obviously have strong feelings about the extreme verdict which has been handed down. Nevertheless, since the case is subject to judicial review, we will have no additional comment on the matter at this time.

EXCERPT FROM NEWS CONFERENCE

(The spokesman was asked about reports that South Korea had decided to put opposition politician Kim Dae-jung on trial.)

A: "We have heard such reports from time to time. We have repeatedly expressed our strong concerns to Korean authorities about the handling of political prisoners, including Kim Dae-jung. We shall continue to make our views known. We believe it particularly important that those charged be given access to their families and legal counsel, and that any judicial proceedings be fair and open to international observers. We have, as I said, made these points repeatedly to Korean authorities." . . .

Q: Do you have any independent information that helps to corroborate the charges the South Korean Government is making against the people they arrested, especially Kim Dae-jung?

A: "Well, the short answer to that would be probably no. We have seen the quite sweeping charges that have been levelled against Kim Dae-jung and against some of the others. On the basis of information of which we would be aware those charges seem to be pretty far-fetched. Some of the others hardly amount to anything more than the charge that Kim Dae-jung was campaigning to be president. We're just not sure, under the circumstances, that there is any useful purpose in our attempting to analyze all of the charges that have been levelled. I think our concern remains that if there be a trial that those charged be given access to both their families and to legal counsel and that any trials that are held be fair and open to international observers."

U.S.-CHINA AGREEMENTS
September 17 and October 22, 1980

Relations between the United States and the People's Republic of China were strengthened by the signing of five agreements in September and October. The September accords, signed in Washington Sept. 17 by President Carter and Vice Premier Bo Yibo, established regular commercial airline service between China and the United States, opened all American ports to Chinese ships and all Chinese ports to the American merchant fleet, set terms for the marketing of Chinese textiles in the United States, and outlined rights and responsibilities of American consular offices in China and their Chinese counterparts in the United States. On Oct. 22 in Peking, the two nations signed a trade agreement permitting Peking to purchase up to nine million metric tons of American grain annually.

In his remarks made at the Sept. 17 signing ceremony in the White House Rose Garden, President Carter said, "With the four agreements that we are about to sign, the normalization of relations between the United States of America and the People's Republic of China is at last complete. The two countries resumed normal relations almost two years earlier (Historic Documents of 1978, p. 781). That relationship, Carter added, "is a new and vital force for peace and stability in the international scene." With the election less than two months away, the president emphasized that the agreements promised benefits for U.S. citizens and industry. The maritime pact, he said, would strengthen American shipping; the textile accord would "benefit American retailers and consumers without damaging our own textile industry"; and the consular convention would "promote trade, travel, and cultural and *educational exchange" and "ensure the protection of the rights and interests of American citizens in China." Carter also asserted that "[t]rade between the United States and China this year will be nearly four times what it was two years ago. China will buy some $3 billion worth of American goods. That means jobs for American workers and opportunities for American businesses. And it means help for China's efforts to modernize and develop her economy."*

Vice Premier's Remarks

Vice Premier Bo hailed the agreements as a "task of major significance" that moved U.S.-Sino economic relations "from ordinary exchanges to institutionalization."

The U.S.-China grain deal provided a major sales outlet for American grain producers angry with President Carter over his embargo of grain sales to the Soviet Union after Moscow's military intervention in Afghanistan. The president's critics claimed that the agreement was announced less than two weeks before Election Day in an attempt to rally support for Carter in grain-producing states. The president's opponent, Ronald Reagan, had said previously that the embargo on grain shipments to the USSR was ineffective and that he would not have ordered it. (Afghanistan invasion, Historic Documents of 1979, p. 965)

Terms of Grain Agreement

Under the terms of the pact, signed by Ambassador Leonard Woodcock and Foreign Trade Minister Li Qiang, China agreed to purchase six million to eight million metric tons of American wheat and corn each year for four years. (A metric ton equals 2,205 pounds.) Although no limit was placed on the amount of grain the Chinese could buy, it was agreed that, if the Chinese wished to purchase more than nine million metric tons in one year, they would be required to obtain permission from Washington before doing so. Moreover, the agreement stipulated that 15 to 20 percent of the Chinese purchases would be corn and that wheat would account for the remainder.

The chief effect of the trade agreement was to formalize Chinese purchases of wheat and corn and guarantee a Chinese market for American grain growers. Since 1972, when trade between the two nations was resumed after a hiatus of more than 30 years, grain sales to China had been erratic. For example, in some years the Chinese bought no grain from the United States; in others, they purchased as much as four million tons.

White House Statement

The White House said in a statement released after the agreement was signed that the pact "will promote the sale of U.S. grain to a large and growing market" and "will further the process of building a long-term structure for U.S.-China relations." The statement added that the grain deal "will help to moderate the wide swing [sic] in grain prices that are often associated with annual fluctuations in agricultural exports." The statement referred to the strengthening of ties between Washington and Peking and said that "[w]e have also begun carefully and deliberately to build a consultative relationship which will enable us to work together to identify and cooperate on issues of common interest, such as the Soviet invasion of Afghanistan."

> *Following are the texts of remarks by President Jimmy Carter of the United States and Vice Premier Bo Yibo of the People's Republic of China at a White House ceremony Sept. 17, 1980, at which four agreements were signed; excerpts from a maritime agreement; excerpts from an agreement establishing regular airline service between the two countries; excerpts from an agreement setting terms for the marketing of Chinese textiles in the United States; the text of a letter by Secretary of State Edmund S. Muskie to Chai Zemin, ambassador of the People's Republic of China, accompanying a consular convention; and the text of a White House statement Oct. 22, 1980, on a trade agreement permitting China to buy American grain. (Boldface headings in brackets have been added by Congressional Quarterly to highlight the organization of the texts.):*

REMARKS OF CARTER AND BO

The President. Vice Premier Bo, Mr. Ambassador, distinguished guests and friends:

I'm delighted to welcome you here to our country, Mr. Vice Premier, and also your delegation. You are among friends, as you know.

We are here today to share some good news with each other. With the four agreements that we are about to sign, the normalization of relations between the United States of America and the People's Republic of China is at last complete. That relationship is a new and vital force for peace and stability in the international scene. In addition it holds a promise of ever-increasing benefits in trade and other exchanges for both the United States and for the People's Republic of China.

I am personally committed, Mr. Vice Premier, to the proposition that our relationship will not be undermined, but will be strengthened.

Both the United States and China have made firm and written commitments which form the basis of this relationship. These commitments have the support of the people of my country and of your country and therefore they will be honored.

What we have accomplished together since the beginning of diplomatic relations between our countries has been extraordinary. But, as I said to Vice Premier Deng Xiaoping when he was here in January 1979, our aim is to make these exchanges not extraordinary, but ordinary. In other words, to make the benefits of this new relationship a routine part of the everyday lives of the citizens of this country and of the People's Republic of China. That is exactly what these four agreements will do.

Let me say a brief word about each one of them.

First, the civil aviation agreement. This agreement will mean regularly scheduled direct flights between the United States and China, beginning in the very near future. I have instructed the Civil Aeronautics Board to move quickly to name the first of the two United States airlines which, along with the Chinese carriers, will fly the new routes. At the airports in New York or Los Angeles or San Francisco or Honolulu a few months from today, we will hear flights announced for Shanghai and for Peking as well as to London and Paris.

Second, the maritime agreement. For the first time in more than 30 years, all United States ports will be open to Chinese merchant ships and American ships will have access to all Chinese ports of call. This will mean a stronger American maritime industry. It will mean revenue for United States shippers from the growing Chinese market for American goods, and growing trade and commerce will benefit the people of both China and the United States.

Third, the textile agreement. By permitting orderly marketing in this country of Chinese textile products, this agreement will benefit American retailers and consumers without damaging our own textile industry, which was fully represented in these negotiations.

The fourth agreement is the consular convention. It spells out the duties of consular officers in providing services to citizens of both our countries. One immediate benefit is to ensure the protection of the rights and interests of American citizens in China.

[New Consulates]

We have two consulates in China already, and now we will open three more. These offices will promote trade, travel, and cultural and educational exchange. They will serve the needs of hundreds of thousands of Americans who will be visiting China in the next few years. On this side of the Pacific Ocean, China now has two consulates in the United States, one in San Francisco and one in Houston. Soon, thanks to this agreement, there will be new Chinese consulates in New York, Chicago, and Honolulu as well.

These agreements, as you well know, are the fruit of some very hard work. A year ago when Vice President Mondale visited China, both nations pledged an effort to complete the political and legal framework of normalization by the end of 1980. We have met that goal with 3-1/2 months to spare. The negotiators on both sides deserve the thanks and the appreciation of us all.

I'm privileged to lead my great Nation in taking this step. I consider this to be one of the most important achievements of my administration, but it's an achievement with a bipartisan history. President Nixon concluded the Shanghai Communique of 1972, and President Ford accepted and supported the principles of that communique. My administration, working closely with the Congress, has taken the decisive steps which made that goal a reality.

One result has been the activity by private and public organizations on both sides to build human contacts between our peoples after 30 years of near-total, mutual isolation. Another was the establishment of the Joint Economic Committee, which is meeting here this week under the chairmanship of Vice President Bo and Secretary Miller. Our economic ties, like our cooperation in science and technology, grow broader and closer every day. Trade between the United States and China this year will be nearly four times what it was 2 years ago. China will buy some $3 billion worth of American goods. That means jobs for American workers and opportunities for American businesses. And it means help for China's efforts to modernize and to develop her economy.

[Kinship with China]

Almost 700,000 American citizens trace their roots to China. There are strong bonds of blood kinship and history between the United States and China. Yet both countries have acted not out of sentiment, but out of mutual interest.

In a few moments, normalization between our two countries will be a fact. We're building something together — a broadly-based, consultative relationship that will enable us to expand our cooperation as the years go by. Both of us will gain from this relationship. So, I firmly believe, will the peace of the world. America and China, so recently at odds, will have shown the world something about the possibilities of peace and friendship. In a world that badly needs a good deal of both, this is an achievement, Mr. Vice Premier, of which we can all be proud.

Thank you very much.

The Vice Premier. Mr. President, ladies and gentlemen:

Today, in the field of Sino-U.S. economic cooperation, President Carter and I have completed a task of major significance. Starting from today the economic relations between our two countries will have moved from ordinary exchanges to institutionalization.

Just as President Carter pointed out in his very warm message to the Chinese trade exhibition which opened in San Francisco a few days ago, the cornerstone of our relationship is the communique on the establishment of diplomatic relations between our two countries which was solemnly declared to the whole world by the heads of government of our two countries on December 15, 1978. Since that time the relations between our two countries in various fields have developed rapidly on the basis of both sides abiding by the obligations undertaken in the communique. It is our firm opinion that these friendly relations should continue to develop forward.

Here it is my pleasure to declare that with the signing of the consular convention, we'll be setting up three more general consulates in your country. This will give a further impetus to the friendly contacts and trade and economic cooperation between our two peoples. Facts have proven and will continue to prove that such relations are not only beneficial to the two peoples but also to the peace and stability of the world.

Not long ago we held the third session of the Fifth National People's Congress. Our newly elected Premier, Zhao Ziyang, explicitly pointed out that we will continue to carry out unswervingly the domestic and foreign policies which we have set forth in recent years. Through this session of the Peoples' Congress, the whole series of the effective new policies which we have been carrying out have been or will shortly be fully legalized and institutionalized. All our people are with full confidence working hard to build our country into a highly democratic and civilized modern nation. For this purpose, we need peace; we need stability; we need friendship; we need cooperation.

It is my conviction that the American people too need peace, need stability, need friendship, need cooperation. Let our two great nations and two great peoples on both sides of the Pacific advance hand in hand and make common efforts for world peace and stability and for the prosperity and strength of our two peoples.

Thank you, ladies and gentlemen.

MARITIME AGREEMENT

ARTICLE 2

a. The Parties agree that when vessels of either Party, for the purpose of transportation of passengers and cargo, enter into or depart from the ports, mooring places and waters of the other Party, the latter shall adopt all appropriate measures to provide favorable treatment to such vessels with regard to servicing of vessels, port operations, the simplification and expedition of administrative, customs and all required formalities. . . .

b. Each Party undertakes to ensure that tonnage duties upon vessels of the other Party will be as favorable as the charges imposed in like situations with respect to vessels of any other country . . . .

ARTICLE 4

a. Each Party shall recognize the nationality of the vessels which fly the national flag of the other Party and hold certificates of their nationality issued according to the laws and regulations of the other Party.

b. Each Party shall recognize the tonnage certificates and other ship's documents issued by the competent authorities of the other Party to the extent permitted by applicable laws and regulations. . . .

ARTICLE 5

Each Party shall recognize the identity documents of crew members issued by the competent authorities of the other Party. Those issued by the United States of America shall be the "U.S. Merchant Mariner's Document" while those issued by the People's Republic of China shall be the "Seaman's Book." . . .

ARTICLE 6

a. Members of the crew of vessels of either Party shall be permitted to go ashore during the stay of their vessel in the ports of the other Party, in accordance with its applicable laws and regulations.

b. Each Party may deny entry into its territory of a member of the crew of a vessel of the other Party in accordance with its applicable laws and regulations. . . .

ARTICLE 7

a. Should a vessel of either Party be involved in a maritime accident or encounter any other danger in the ports, mooring places and waters of the other Party, the latter shall give friendly treatment and all possible assistance to the passengers, crew members, cargo and vessel.

b. When a vessel of one Party is involved in a maritime accident or encounters any other danger and its cargo and other property is removed therefrom and landed in the territory of the other Party, such cargo and other property shall not be subject to any customs duties by that Party, unless it enters into its domestic consumption. Storage charges incurred shall be just, reasonable and non-discriminatory.

c. Each Party shall promptly notify the consular officials or in their absence the diplomatic representatives, of the other Party when one of its vessels is in distress, and inform them of measures taken for the rescue and protection of the crew members, passengers, vessel, cargo and stores. . . .

ARTICLE 13

This Agreement shall be in force for three years from the date of signing and shall expire on September 17, 1983. This Agreement may be extended, subject to negotiations between the Parties prior to the expiration date. The Agreement may also be terminated by either Party on 90 days written notice.

DONE at Washington, this seventeenth day of September 1980 in duplicate, each copy in the English and Chinese languages, both texts being equally authentic.

For the Government of the United States of America:

JIMMY CARTER

For the Government of the People's Republic of China:

BO YIBO

CIVIL AIR TRANSPORT AGREEMENT

ARTICLE 2

Grant of Rights

(1) Each Party grants to the other Party the rights specified in this Agreement to enable its designated airline(s) to establish and operate scheduled air services on the route(s) specified in Annex I to this Agreement. . . .

(2) Subject to the provisions of the Agreement, the designated airline(s) of each Party, while operating the agreed services on the specified route(s), shall enjoy the following rights:

(a) to make stops at points on the specified route(s) in the territory of the other Party for the purpose of taking on board and discharging international traffic in passengers, baggage, cargo and mail; and

(b) subject to the approval of the aeronautical authorities of the other Party, to make stops for non-traffic purposes at points on the specified route(s) in the territory of the other Party.

(3) Nothing in paragraph (2) (a) of this Article shall be deemed to confer on the designated airline(s) of one Party the right of taking on at one point in the territory of the other Party traffic in passengers, baggage, cargo or mail destined for another point in the territory of the other Party (stopover and cabotage traffic), except the non-revenue traffic in personnel of such airline(s), their families, baggage and household effects, articles used by the representative offices of such airline(s) and aircraft stores and spare parts of such airline(s) for use in the operation of the agreed services. . . .

(4) The operation of the agreed services by the designated airline(s) on routes over third countries shall be conducted on routes available to the airlines of both Parties, unless otherwise agreed. . . .

ARTICLE 3

Designation and Authorization

(1) Each Party shall have the right to designate in writing through diplomatic channels to the other Party two airlines to operate the agreed services on the specified route(s), and to withdraw or alter such designations. In the operation of the agreed services, the designated airlines may operate combination or all-cargo service or both.

(2) Substantial ownership and effective control of an airline designated by a Party shall be vested in such Party or its nationals.

(3) The aeronautical authorities of the other Party may require an airline designated by the first Party to satisfy them that it is qualified to fulfill the conditions prescribed under the laws and regulations normally applied to the operation of international air services by the said authorities. . . .

ARTICLE 5

Application of Laws

(1) The laws and regulations of each Party relating to the admission to, operation within and departure from its territory of aircraft engaged in the operation of international air service shall be complied with by the designated airline(s) of the other Party, while entering, within, and departing from the territory of the first Party.

(2) The laws and regulations of each Party relating to the admission to, presence within, and departure from its territory of passengers, crew, baggage, cargo and mail shall be applicable to the designated airline(s) of the other Party, and the passengers, crew, baggage, cargo and mail carried by such airline(s), while entering, within and departing from the territory of the first Party.

(3) Each Party shall promptly supply to the other Party at the latter's request the texts of the laws and regulations referred to in paragraphs (1) and (2) of this Article.

ARTICLE 6

Technical Services and Charges

(1) Each Party shall designate in its territory regular airports and alternate airports to be used by the designated airline(s) of the other Party for the operation of the agreed services, and shall provide the latter with such communications, navigational, meteorological and other auxiliary services in its territory as are required for the operation of the agreed services, as set forth in Annex III to this Agreement.

(2) The designated airline(s) of each Party shall be charged for the use of airports, equipment and technical services of the other Party at fair and reasonable rates. Neither Party shall impose on the designated airline(s) of the other Party rates higher than those imposed on any other foreign airline operating international air service. . . .

ARTICLE 7

Safety

(1) Mutually acceptable aeronautical facilities and services shall be provided by each Party for the operation of the agreed services, which facilities and services shall at least equal the minimum standards which may be established pursuant to the Convention, to the extent that such minimum standards are applicable.

(2) Each Party shall recognize as valid, for the purpose of operating the agreed services, certificates of airworthiness, certificates of competency, and licenses issued or rendered valid by the other Party and still in force, provided that the requirements for such certificates or licenses at least equal the minimum standards which may be established pursuant to the Convention. Each Party may, however, refuse to recognize as valid, for the purpose of flight above its own territory, certificates of competency and licenses granted to or rendered valid for its own nationals by the other Party. . . .

ARTICLE 8

Aviation Security

The Parties reaffirm their grave concern about acts or threats against the security of aircraft, which jeopardize the safety of persons or property, adversely affect the operation of air services and undermine public confidence in the safety of civil aviation. The Parties agree to implement appropriate aviation security measures and to provide necessary aid to each other with a view to preventing hijackings and sabotage to aircraft, airports and air navigation facilities and threats to aviation security. When incidents or threats of hijackings or sabotage against aircraft, airports or air navigation facilities occur, the Parties shall assist each other by facilitating communications intended to terminate such incidents rapidly and safely. . . .

ARTICLE 10

Personnel

(1) The crew members of the designated airline(s) of either Party on flights into and out of the territory of the other Party shall be nationals of the Party designating such airline(s). If a designated airline of either Party desires to employ crew members of any other nationality on flights into and out of the territory of the other Party, prior approval shall be obtained from that other Party.

(2) The staff of the representative offices of the designated airline(s) of each party in the territory of the other Party shall be nationals of either Party, unless otherwise agreed. The number of such staff shall be subject to the approval of the competent authorities of both Parties. . . .

ARTICLE 13

Pricing

(1) Each Party may require the filing with its aeronautical authorities of fares to be charged for transportation of passengers to and from its territory. Such filing shall be made sixty (60) days prior to the date on which the fares are proposed to go into effect. . . . If the competent authorities of a Party are dissatisfied with a fare, they shall notify the competent authorities of the other Party as soon as possible, . . . If agreement is not reached during consultations, the fare in question shall not go into effect, and the fare previously in force shall remain effective until a new fare is established.

(2) If the competent authorities do not express dissatisfaction within thirty (30) days after the date of receipt of the filing of a fare made in accordance with paragraph (1) above, it shall be considered as approved. . . .

ARTICLE 18

Entry into Force and Termination

This Agreement shall enter into force on the date of its signature and shall remain in force for three years. Thereafter, it shall continue in force but may be terminated by either Party by giving twelve months' written notice to the other Party of its intention to terminate.

DONE at Washington, this seventeenth day of September 1980 in duplicate, each copy in the English and Chinese languages, both texts being equally authentic.

For the Government of the United States of America:

JIMMY CARTER

For the Government of the People's Republic of China:

BO YIBO

ANNEX I

I. First Route

A. *For the United States of America:*

The first airline designated by the United States of America shall be entitled to operate the agreed services on the following route, in both directions:

New York, San Francisco, Los Angeles, Honolulu, Tokyo or another point in Japan, Shanghai, Beijing.

B. *For the People's Republic of China:*

The first airline designated by the People's Republic of China shall be entitled to operate the agreed services on the following route, in both directions:

Beijing, Shanghai, Tokyo or another point in Japan, Honolulu, Los Angeles, San Francisco, New York. Anchorage may be utilized as a technical stop in both directions on this route.

II. Second Route

The Parties shall consult during the first two years following the commencement of any agreed service to decide on a route for operation by the second designated airline of each Party....

III. Extra Section

In case any of the designated airline(s) of either Party desires to operate additional sections on its specified route(s), it shall submit application to the aeronautical authorities of the other Party three (3) days in advance of such operation, and the additional sections can be commenced only after approvals have been obtained therefrom....

ANNEX II

Charter Air Transportation

(1) In addition to the operation of the agreed services by the designated airlines of the two Parties, any airline(s) of one Party may request

permission to operate passenger and/or cargo (separately or in combination) charter flights between the territories of the Parties as well as between a third country and the territory of the Party to which the requests are addressed. Each Party may provide to the other Party by diplomatic note a list of airlines qualified under the laws of the first Party to provide charter air transportation.

(2) The application for charter flight(s) shall be filed with the aeronautical authorities of the other Party at least fifteen (15) days before the anticipated flight(s). The flight(s) can be operated only after permission has been obtained. Permission shall be granted without undue delay in the spirit of equality of opportunity for the airlines of both Parties to operate international charter air transportation, mutual benefit and friendly cooperation. . . .

ANNEX III

Technical Services

I. Airports for Scheduled Service

(1) In accordance with Article 6, paragraph (1) of this Agreement, airlines designated by the Government of the People's Republic of China are assigned the following regular and alternate airports in the United States:

Regular Airports

New York, New York: JFK International Airport
Los Angeles, California: Los Angeles International Airport
San Francisco, California: San Francisco International Airport
Honolulu, Hawaii: Honolulu International Airport
Anchorage, Alaska: Anchorage International Airport

Alternate Airports

Baltimore, Maryland: Baltimore-Washington International Airport
Boston, Massachusetts: Logan International Airport
Newark, New Jersey: Newark International Airport
Philadelphia, Pennsylvania: Philadelphia International Airport
Pittsburgh, Pennsylvania: Greater Pittsburgh Airport
Moses Lake, Washington: Grant County Airport
Oakland, California: Metropolitan Oakland International Airport
Ontario, California: Ontario International Airport
Stockton, California: Stockton Metropolitan Airport
Hilo, Hawaii: Hilo International/General Lyman Airport
Seattle, Washington: Sea-Tac International Airport
Kansas City, Kansas: Kansas City International Airport
Fairbanks, Alaska: Fairbanks International Airport
Washington, D.C.: Dulles International Airport

(2) In accordance with Article 6, paragraph (1) of this Agreement, airlines designated by the Government of the United States of America are assigned the following regular and alternate airports in China:

Regular Airports

Beijing: Capital Airport
Shanghai: Hongqiao Airport

Alternate Airports

Guangzhou: Baiyun Airport
Hangzhou:Jianqiao Airport
Tianjin: Zhangguizhuang Airport

II. Airports for Charter Air Transportation
Aircraft of the airline(s) of each Party engaged in the operation of charter air transportation approved by the aeronautical authorities of the other Party may utilize airports appropriately identified in the Aeronautical Information Publication of that other Party as available for international flights, and such other airports as may be approached by such aeronautical authorities.

III. Air Routes
All flight operations by aircraft of the designated airline(s) of one Party operated in the airspace of the other Party shall be over established airways/prescribed routes or as cleared by the appropriate air traffic control service. Each Party will make reasonable efforts to ensure that air routes entering and within their sovereign airspace are as direct as practicable in the interest of economy, efficiency and fuel conservation, . . .

MUSKIE LETTER

September 17, 1980

His Excellency Chai Zemin
    Ambassador of the
    People's Republic of China

Excellency:

I have the honor to confirm on behalf of the Government of the United States of America that in the course of negotiating the Consular Convention between the United States of America and the People's Republic of China, the two sides reached agreement on the following questions:

1. The two governments agree to facilitate the reunion of families and will process all applications as quickly as possible under mutually agreed arrangements and in accordance with each side's laws and regulations.

2. The two governments agree to facilitate travel between their respective countries of persons who may have a claim simultaneously to the nationality of the United States of America and the People's Republic of China, but this does not imply that the governments of the two countries recognize dual nationality. Exit formalities and documentation shall be dealt with in accordance with the laws of the country in which such person resides. Entry formalities and documentation shall be dealt with in accordance with the laws of the country of destination.

3. All nationals of the sending State entering the receiving State on the basis of travel documents of the sending State containing properly executed entry and exit visas of the receiving State will, during the period for which their status has been accorded, and in accordance with the visa's period of validity, be considered nationals of the sending State by the appropriate authorities of the receiving State for the purpose of ensuring consular access and protection by the sending State as provided for in Article 35 of the Consular Convention between the United States of America and the People's Republic of China. If judicial or administrative proceedings prevent the above-mentioned persons from leaving the country within the visa's period of validity, they shall not lose the right of consular access and protection by the sending State. Such persons shall be permitted to leave the receiving State without the necessity of obtaining documentation from the receiving State other than the exit documentation normally required of departing aliens.

4. Both governments agree that persons residing in one country who are entitled to receive financial benefits from the other country shall receive their benefits under mutually agreed arrangements and in accordance with each country's laws and regulations.

If your Excellency confirms the above by a note in reply on behalf of the Government of the People's Republic of China, this note shall constitute an integral part of the above-mentioned Consular Convention and shall come into effect simultaneously with the Consular Convention. At that time, the Annex on Practical Arrangements to the Agreement Between the Government of the United States of America and the Government of the People's Republic of China on the Mutual Establishment of Consular Relations and the Opening of Consulates-General, signed on January 31, 1979 will cease to be in effect.

Accept, Excellency, the renewed assurances of my highest consideration.

EDMUND S. MUSKIE
Secretary of State

TEXTILE AGREEMENT

The Government of the United States of America and the Government of the People's Republic of China, as a result of discussions concerning exports to the United States of America of cotton, wool, and man-made fiber textiles and textile products manufactured in the People's Republic of China, agree to enter into the following Agreement relating to trade in cotton, wool, and man-made fiber textiles and textile products between the United States of America and the People's Republic of China (hereinafter referred to as "the Agreement"):

1. The two Governments reaffirm their commitments under the Agreement on Trade Relations between the United States of America and the People's Republic of China as the basis of their trade and economic relations.

2. The term of the Agreement shall be the three-year period from January 1, 1980 through December 31, 1982. Each "Agreement Year" shall be a calendar year. . . .

10. The Government of the United States of America shall promptly supply the Government of the People's Republic of China with monthly data on imports of textiles from China, and the Government of the People's Republic of China shall promptly supply the Government of the United States of America with quarterly data on exports of China's textiles to the United States in categories for which levels have been established. Each Government agrees to supply promptly any other pertinent and readily available statistical data requested by the other Government.

11. (a) Tops, yarns, piece goods, made-up articles, garments, and other textile manufactured products (being products which derive their chief characteristics from their textile components) of cotton, wool, man-made fibers, or blends thereof, in which any or all of these fibers in combination represent either the chief value of the fibers or 50 percent or more by weight (or 17 percent or more by weight of wool) of the product, are subject to the Agreement.

(b) For purposes of the Agreement, textiles and textile products shall be classified as cotton, wool or man-made fiber textiles if wholly or in chief value of either of these fibers.

(c) Any product covered by subparagraph 11 (a) but not in chief value of cotton, wool, or man-made fiber shall be classified as: (I) cotton textiles if containing 50 percent or more by weight of cotton or if the cotton component exceeds by weight the wool and the man-made fiber components; (II) wool textiles if not cotton and the wool equals or exceeds 17 percent by weight of all component fibers; (III) man-made fiber textiles if neither of the foregoing applies. . . .

14. If the Government of the People's Republic of China considers that, as a result of a limitation specified in this Agreement, China is being placed in an inequitable position vis-a-vis a third country

or party, the Government of the People's Republic of China may request consultations with the Government of the United States of America with a view to taking appropriate remedial action such as reasonable modification of this Agreement and the Government of the United States of America shall agree to hold such consultations.

15. At the request of either Government, the two Governments will undertake a major review of the Agreement at the end of the second Agreement Year.

16. Each Government will take such measures as may be necessary to ensure that the Specific Limits established for any categories under this Agreement are not exceeded. Calculations will be based on the date of export from the People's Republic of China. Neither Government shall act to restrain the trade in textile products covered by the Agreement except in accordance with the terms of the Agreement.

17. Either Government may terminate the Agreement effective at the end of any Agreement Year by written notice to the other Government to be given at least 90 days prior to the end of such Agreement Year. Either Government may at any time propose revisions in the terms of the Agreement.

DONE at Washington, in duplicate, in the English and Chinese languages, both texts being equally authentic, this seventeenth day of September, 1980.

For the Government of the United States of America:

JIMMY CARTER

For the Government of the People's Republic of China:

BO YIBO

WHITE HOUSE STATEMENT ON GRAIN

Today, we signed in Beijing a grain agreement with the People's Republic of China which accomplishes two important things. First, it will promote the sale of U.S. grain to a large and growing market. Second, it will further the process of building a long-term structure for U.S.-China relations.

Under the terms of this agreement, China will purchase at least 6 million metric tons (MMT) of U.S. wheat and corn annually for a 4-year period beginning January 1, 1981. The Chinese may purchase up to 9 MMT without prior notice.

Since the establishment of diplomatic relations in January 1979, U.S. agricultural exports to China have expanded rapidly and will reach a record $2 billion in 1980. China is now our most important customer for cotton and one of the most important for other farm products.

The agreement grew out of a dialog dating back to Secretary Bergland's visit to the People's Republic of China in 1978. It will provide important benefits for both U.S. farmers and consumers. It will help to moderate the wide swing [sic] in grain prices that are often associated with annual fluctuations in agricultural exports. The agreement will also provide further stimulus to our dynamic agricultural export sector and contribute to our growing surplus in agricultural trade, which will reach $22 billion in 1980.

The President takes great personal pride in the fact that in his administration he was able to take the difficult but enormously successful step of establishing full diplomatic relations with China, the largest country in the world.

The establishment of diplomatic relations with China almost 2 years ago made it possible for us to move ahead to build a new relationship which truly enriches us in knowledge, trade, and culture:

—Trade more than doubled from $1.1 billion in 1978 to $2.3 billion in 1979. This year we estimated it will almost double again to $4 billion.

—About 25 cultural and sports delegations from China visit our country every 6 months, and we are reciprocating with visits by orchestras and other cultural groups as well as our Olympic athletes.

—We have 13 separate working agreements in science and technology, which not only give us current and future commercial benefits but make it possible for our scientists and technicians to share in China's research in medicine, earthquake prediction, and agriculture.

Important as they are, there is more to our relationship than trade and cultural ties. We have also begun carefully and deliberately to build a consultative relationship which will enable us to work together to identify and cooperate on issues of common interest, such as the Soviet invasion of Afghanistan.

This effort to construct a long-term strategic relationship is still new and therefore fragile. It is based on carefully written and painstakingly negotiated understandings set down in the joint communique establishing diplomatic relations between the United States and China. This administration has consistently made clear its resolve to honor those understandings.

We have come a long way since that day almost 2 years ago when the President announced that we had reached agreement with the Chinese on the establishment of diplomatic relations. Thirty years of mutual isolation and hostility have been replaced with a deepening consultative relationship which is already contributing significantly to American security and to the peace and stability in East Asia and the world beyond.

ANDERSON-REAGAN DEBATE
September 21, 1980

In the first of two major debates in the 1980 presidential campaign, Republican nominee Ronald Reagan and independent candidate John B. Anderson stressed their opposing views on domestic issues while criticizing the policies of the candidate who declined to participate — President Carter.

The Reagan-Anderson debate, sponsored by the League of Women Voters, sponsor of the 1976 presidential debates (Historic Documents of 1976, pp. 693, 733, 797), was held Sept. 21 in Baltimore, Md. The one-hour exchange, during which the candidates were questioned by six journalists, was viewed on television by an estimated 50 million Americans. The debate was broadcast by NBC, CBS and PBS; ABC chose not to carry live coverage.

Questions were posed by Carol Loomis of Fortune magazine, Daniel Greenberg, a science columnist, Charles Corddry of The Sun (Baltimore), Lee May of the Los Angeles Times, Jane Bryant Quinn of Newsweek, The Washington Post and CBS, and Soma Golden, a member of The New York Times' editorial board. Ruth J. Hinerfeld, League of Women Voters Education Fund chair, opened the forum which was moderated by Bill Moyers, host and executive editor of the PBS program "Bill Moyers' Journal."

Carter Strategy

President Carter's strategists advised him to avoid the debate, arguing that his presence would add stature to Anderson's candidacy. They *also claimed that the president would benefit more from a two-man confrontation with Reagan in which, they reasoned, Carter could exhibit his grasp of government complexities. The league laid down the ground rules for the debate, deciding that Anderson would be invited if the presidential preference polls showed him the favorite among at least 15 percent of those polled. After several more weeks of wrangling between the Carter and Reagan camps, a two-man Carter-Reagan debate was finally scheduled for Oct. 28. (p. 919)*

Reagan-Anderson Differences

Reagan and Anderson disagreed on every major point discussed during the debate except the peacetime draft, which they opposed, and higher pay for the military, which they favored. Reagan also called for the reinstitution of the so-called GI Bill to attract young people to the armed services. On other defense-related issues, Anderson expressed his disapproval of the MX mobile missile system. Reagan endorsed the MX, saying that "we are so out of balance strategically that we lack a deterrent to a possible first assault." But the GOP nominee attacked "that fantastic plan of the Administration to take thousands and thousands of square miles out in the Western states" to house the MX system.

In response to an economic question, Anderson criticized as inflationary both the Democrats' and the Republicans' proposed tax cuts. The independent candidate declared that his program of $11.3 billion in specific tax reductions would strengthen the economy. Reagan, for his part, defended his "phased-in tax cut over a three-year period" and said the federal government was the chief cause of inflation.

On energy, Reagan declared, "To say that we are limited, and at a dangerous point in this country with regard to energy, I think, is to ignore the fact. The fact is, that in today's oil wells, there is more oil still there than we have so far taken out and used." And he charged that the government, "with its own restrictions and regulations," created the energy crisis. In contrast, Anderson said that "we are going to have to create a new conservation ethic" in the United States, and he plugged his call for a 50-cents-per-gallon excise tax on gasoline to reduce consumption.

Urban Problems

The debaters differed widely on their approaches to solving the problems of the nation's cities. Anderson called for a $4 billion urban reinvestment trust fund (financed by alcohol and tobacco taxes) "to rebuild the streets, to rebuild the cities, the leaking water mains" and a $1 billion youth employment program. Reagan, on the other hand, advocated tax *incentives to attract business and industry to deteriorating urban areas. And he proposed a plan to sell abandoned government-owned houses to urban homesteaders for $1. Such a plan had been administered by the Department of Housing and Urban Development since 1974.*

A further point of contention was raised during the candidates' responses to a question concerning the influence of religion on politics and government. Anderson said that "to try to tell the parishioners of any church, of any denomination, how they should vote, or for whom they should vote, I think violates the principle of separation of church and state." Anderson restated his opposition to a constitutional amendment banning abortions. Reagan, however, contended that organized religions "have been too reluctant to speak up in behalf of what they believe is proper in government." He added, "I've noticed that everybody that is for abortion has already been born."

> *Following is the transcript of the debate between independent presidential candidate Rep. John B. Anderson, R-Ill., and Republican nominee Ronald Reagan, held Sept. 21, 1980, in Baltimore, Md. (Boldface headings in brackets have been added by Congressional Quarterly to highlight the organization of the text.):*

Hinerfeld: Good evening. I'm Ruth Hinerfeld of the League of Women Voters Education Fund. We're pleased to be in Baltimore for the first of our 1980 Presidential Debates. The League is a non-partisan organization. We're presenting these debates to provide citizens an opportunity to see and hear the candidates state their positions on important issues of concern to us all. Our moderator is Bill Moyers.

Moyers: Thank you, Mrs. Hinerfeld. My colleagues and I agreed to participate tonight, although the questioners are limited by the constraints of the format, because we thought with the League of Women Voters, that it is desirable to seek a comparison of views on a few issues in a joint appearance by the men who would be the next President of the United States.

Former Governor Ronald Reagan, a Republican Party candidate, and Congressman John Anderson, who is running as an Independent, accepted the League of Women Voters' invitation to be here. President Carter declined. Mr. Reagan and Mr. Anderson will respond with their views on certain issues posed by questions from my colleagues: Carol Loomis of Fortune Magazine; Daniel Greenberg, a syndicated columnist; Charles Corddry of the Baltimore Sun; Lee May of the Los Angeles Times; James Bryant Quinn ... Jane Bryant Quinn of Newsweek; and Soma Golden of The New York Times. None of the questions has been submitted in advance to either the League of Women Voters, or to the candidates, or to their representatives.

Gentlemen, thank you both for coming. The ground rules you agreed upon with the League are brief. Each panelist will ask a single question.

You will have two and a half minutes in which to respond. After you've stated your positions in those two and a half minutes, each of you will have one minute and 15 seconds for response. At the close of the debate, each of you will have three minutes for closing remarks.

We ask the Convention Center audience to abide by one simple ground rule: Please do not applaud or express approval or disapproval during the debate. You may do that on November 4.

Having won the toss of the coin, Mr. Anderson will respond to the first question from Carol Loomis.

[Inflation]

Loomis: Mr. Anderson, opinion polls show that the American public sees inflation as the country's number one economic problem, yet, as individuals, they oppose cures that hurt them personally. Elected officials have played along by promising to cure inflation while backing away from tough programs that might hurt one special interest group or another, and by actually adding inflationary elements to the system, such as indexing. They have gone for what is politically popular, rather than for what might work and amount to leadership.

My question, and please be specific, is what politically unpopular measures are you willing to endorse, push and stay with, that might provide real progress in reducing inflation?

Anderson: Miss Loomis, I think it's very appropriate that the first question in this first debate of Campaign '80 should relate to the economy of the country, because it seems to me that the people who are watching us tonight — 221 million Americans — are truly concerned about the poor rate of performance of the American economy over the last four years.

Governor Reagan is not responsible for what has happened over the last four years, nor am I. The man who should be here tonight to respond to those charges chose not to attend.

But I want to answer as specifically as I can the question that you have just put to me. Let me tell you that I, first of all, oppose an election year tax cut, whether it is the 10% across-the-board tax cut promised to the taxpayers by my opponent in this debate tonight, or whether it is the $27.5 billion tax cut promised on the 20th of August by President Carter.

I simply think that when we are confronting a budget deficit this year — and this fiscal year will end in about 10 days, and we are confronted with the possibility of a deficit of $60 billion, perhaps as much as $63 billion — that that simply would be irresponsible. That, once again, the printing presses will start to roll; once again we will see the monetization of that debt result in a higher rate of inflation. Even though we've seen some hopeful signs, perhaps, in the flash report on the third quarter, that perhaps the economy is coming out of the recession, we've also seen the rise in the rate of the prime; we have seen mortgage rates back up again, a sure sign of inflation in the housing industry.

What I would propose, and I proposed it way back in March when I was a candidate in my own state of Illinois, I proposed $11.3 billion, specifically, in cuts in the Federal budget. I think we've got to have fiscal restraint. And I said at that time that one of the things that we could do, that perhaps would save as much as $5 billion to $7 billion, according to one of the leading members of the House Budget Committee, was to recalculate the index that is used to determine the cost of living benefits that are paid to civil service retirees, to military retirees. That we ought to ... in addition to that, we ought to pay those retirement benefits on the basis of once a year, rather than twice a year, and save $750 billion [*sic*]. In other words. . . .

Moyers: Mr. Anderson. . . .

Anderson: . . . fiscal restraint, I think is necessary.

Moyers: . . . your time is up. Ms. Loomis?

Loomis: Governor Reagan, repeating the question, and I would ask you, again, to engage in as many specifics as you possibly can. What politically unpopular measures are you willing to endorse, push and stay with that might provide real progress in reducing inflation?

Reagan: I believe that the only unpopular measures, actually, that could be, or would be applied, would be unpopular with the government, and with those ... perhaps, some special interest groups who are tied closely to government. I believe that inflation today is caused by government simply spending more than government takes in, at the same time that government has imposed upon business and industry, from the shopkeeper on the corner to the biggest industrial plant in America, countless harassing regulations and punitive taxes that have reduced productivity at the same time they have increased the cost of production. And when you are reducing productivity at the same time that you are turning out printing-press money in excessive amounts, you're causing inflation. And it isn't really higher prices, it's just, you are reducing the value of the money. You are robbing the American people of their savings.

And so, the plan that I have proposed — and contrary to what John says, my plan is for a phased-in tax cut over a three-year period, tax increase and depreciation allowances for business and industry to give them the capital to refurbish plant and equipment, research and development, improved technology — all of which we see our foreign competitors having, and we have the greatest percentage of outmoded industrial plant and equipment of any of the industrial nations — produce more, have stable money supply, and give the people of this country a greater share of their own savings.

Now, I know that this has been called inflationary by my opponent and by the man who isn't here tonight. But I don't see where it is inflationary to have people keep more of their earnings and spend it, and it isn't inflationary for government to take that money away from them and spend it on the things it wants to spend it on. I believe we need incentive for the individual, and for business and industry, and I believe the plan that I have submitted, with detailed backing, and which has been approved by a number of our leading economists in the country, is based on projections ... conservative projections out for the next five years, that indicates that this plan would, by 1983, result in a balanced budget.

We have to remember, when we talk a tax cut, we're only talking about reducing a tax increase, because this Administration has left us with a built-in tax increase that will amount to $86 billion next year. ...

Moyers: Your time is up.

Reagan: ... and $500 billion over the next five.

Moyers: Mr. Anderson?

Anderson: Mr. Moyers, in addition to saying that this is no time for a tax cut, in view of the incipient signs of renewed inflation, in addition to calling for restraint in Federal spending, 15 months ago, I also suggested we ought to have an emergency excise tax on gasoline. I say that because I think, this year, we will send $90 billion out of this country to pay for imported oil, even though that ... those imports have been reduced. And since I first made that proposal 15 months ago, the price of gasoline, which was then $.80, has gone up to about $1.30. In other words, we've had a huge increase of about $.50 a gallon since that time, and all of that increase has gone out of this country — or much of it — into the pockets of OPEC oil producers.

Whereas I have proposed we ought to take ... put that tax on here at home, reduce our consumption of that imported oil. Recycle those proceeds, then, back into the pockets of the American workers by reducing their tax payments ... their Social Security tax payments by 50%.

That, I think, in addition, would be an anti-inflationary measure that would strengthen the economy of this country.

Moyers: Mr. Reagan.

Reagan: Well, I cannot see where a $.50 a gallon tax applied to gasoline would have changed the price of gasoline. It would still have gone up as much as it has, and the $.50 would be added on top of that. And it would be a tax paid by the consumers, and then we're asked to believe that some way, they would get this back to the consumers. But why? Why take it in the first place if you're going to give it back? Why not leave it with them?

And John spoke about 15 years ago, on the position that he ... or 15 months ago, on what he believed in. Fifteen months ago, he was a cosigner and advocating the very tax cut that I am proposing, and said that that would be a forward step in fighting inflation, and that it would be beneficial to the working people of this country.

Moyers: The next question goes to Mr. Reagan from Daniel Greenberg.

[Energy Shortages]

Greenberg: Well, gentlemen, what I'd like to say first is, I think the panel and the audience would appreciate responsiveness to the questions, rather than repetitions of your campaign addresses.

My question for the Governor is: Every serious examination of the future supply of energy and other essential resources — including air, land and water — finds that we face shortages and skyrocketing prices, and that, in many ways, we're pushing the environment to dangerous limits. I'd like to know, specifically, what changes you would encourage and require in American lifestyles in automobile use, housing, land use and general consumption, to meet problems that aren't going to respond to campaign lullabies about minor conservation efforts and more production?

Reagan: Well, I believe that conservation, of course, is worthy in and of itself. Anything that would preserve, or help us use less energy, that would be fine, and I'm for it. But I do not believe that conservation alone is the answer to the present energy problem, because all you're doing then is staving off, by a short time, the day when you would come to the end of the energy supply. To say that we are limited, and at a dangerous point in this country with regard to energy, I think, is to ignore the fact. The fact is, that in today's oil wells, there is more oil still there than we have so far taken out and used. But it would require what is known as secondary or tertiary efforts to bring it out of the ground. And this is known oil reserves, known supplies.

There are hundreds of millions of acres of land that have been taken out of circulation by the Government for whatever reason they have, that is believed by the most knowledgeable oil geologists to contain probably more oil and natural gas than we have used so far since we drilled that first well 121 years ago.

We have a coal supply that is equal to 50% of the world's coal supply, good for centuries, in this country. I grant you that prices may go up, because as you go further and have to go deeper, you are adding to the cost of production.

We have nuclear power, which, I believe, with the safest ... the most stringent of safety requirements, could meet our energy needs for the next couple of decades while we go forward exploring the areas of solar power and other forms of energy that might be renewable and that would not be exhaustible.

All of these things can be done. When you stop and think that we are only drilling on 2% ... have leased only 2% of the possible ... possibility for oil of the whole continental shelf around the United States; when you stop to think that the government has taken over 100 million acres of land out of circulation in Alaska, alone, that is believed by geologists to contain much in the line of minerals and

853

energy sources, then I think it is the Government, and the Government with its own restrictions and regulations, that is creating the energy crisis. That we are, indeed, an energy-rich nation.

Moyers: I would like to say at this point that the candidates requested the same questions to be repeated, for the sake of precision, on the part of the interrogator. So, Mr. Greenberg, you may address Mr. Anderson.

Greenberg: Mr. Anderson, I'd like to know specifically, what changes you would encourage and require in American lifestyles in automobile use, housing, land use and consumption, to meet problems that aren't going to respond to campaign lullabies about minor conservation efforts and more production?

Anderson: Well, Mr. Greenberg, I simply cannot allow to go unpassed the statements that have just been made by Mr. Reagan, who once again, has demonstrated, I think, a total misunderstanding of the energy crisis that confronts, not only this country, but the world, when he suggests that we have 27 years' supply of natural gas, 47 years' supply of oil, and all the rest, and that we really ... all we have to do is to get the Government off the back of the oil industry, and that's going to be enough.

I agree with what I think is the major premise of your question, sir, that we are going to have to create a new conservation ethic in the minds of the American people, and that's simply why I proposed, 15 months ago, the emergency excise tax on gasoline that I did. I did it as a security measure to be sure, because I would rather see us reduce the consumption of imported oil than have to send American boys to fight in the Persian Gulf.

But at the same time, I think it's going to take a dramatic measure of that kind to convince the American people that we will have to reduce the use of the private automobile. We simply cannot have people sitting one behind the wheel of a car in these long traffic jams going in and out of our great cities. We are going to have to resort to van pooling, to car pooling. We're going to have to develop better community transportation systems, so that with buses and light rail, we can replace the private automobile in those places where it clearly is not energy-efficient.

I think that, with respect to housing, when we are consuming, even though our per capita income today is about the same as that of the Federal Republic of Germany, we are consuming about, by a factor of two, the amount of energy that they consume in that country. Surely, there are things that we can do in the retrofitting, in the redesign of our homes, not only of our houses, but of our commercial structures, as well, that will make it possible for us to achieve.

According to one study that was published a short time ago — the Harvard Business School study — indicated that just in the commercial sector alone of the economy, we could save between 30% and 40% of the energy that we consume in this country today.

So I think, yes, we will have to change in a very appreciable way, some of the lifestyles that we now enjoy.

Moyers: Mr. Reagan.

Reagan: Well, as I've said, I am not an enemy of conservation. I wouldn't be called a conservative if I were. But, when my figures are challenged, as the President himself challenged them after I made them, I think it should be called to the attention of John and the others here that my figures are the figures of the Department of Energy, which has not been overly optimistic in recent years as to how much supply we have left. That is the same Government that, in 1920, told us we only had enough oil left for 13 years, and 19 years later, told us we only had enough left for another 15 years.

As for saving energy and conserving, the American people haven't been doing badly at that. Because in industry today, we're producing more, over the last several years, and at 12% less use of energy than we were back in about 1973. And motorists are using 8% less than they were back at that time of the oil embargo. So, I think we are proving that we can go forward with conservation and benefit from that. But also, I think it is safe to say that we do have sources of energy that have not yet been used or found.

Moyers: Mr. Anderson.

Anderson: Mr. Greenberg, I think my opponent in this debate tonight is overlooking one other very important fact. And that is, that we cannot look at this as simply a national problem. Even though it's true that, perhaps, between now and the end of the decade, our total consumption of oil may not increase by more than, perhaps, a million or 2 million barrels of oil a day. The rest of the Western world, we are told, may see its consumption increase from 51 million barrels to about 66 million. And that additional 15 million barrels is going to cause scarcity.

It is going to cause scarcity in world markets because there are at least five reputable studies, one even by the American Petroleum Institute itself, that, I think, clearly indicate that somewhere along around the end of the present decade, total world demand for oil is simply going to exceed total available supplies.

I think that conservation — I think that a change in lifestyles — is necessary, and we had better begin to plan for that now, rather than later.

Moyers: This question goes to you, Mr. Anderson, from Charles Corddry.

[Military Draft]

Corddry: Mr. Anderson, you and Mr. Reagan both speak for better defense . . . for stronger defense and for programs that would mean spending more money. You do not, either of you, however, come to grips with the fundamental problem of manning the forces, of who shall serve, and how the burden will be distributed. This will surely be a critical issue in the next Presidential term. You both oppose the draft.

The questions are, how would you fill the under-strength combat forces with numbers and quality, without reviving conscription? And will you commit yourself, here, tonight, should you become the Commander in Chief, to propose a draft, however unpopular, if it becomes clear that voluntary means are not working?

Anderson: Mr. Corddry, I am well aware of the present deficiencies in the Armed Forces of this country. When you have a report, as we did recently, that six out of 10 CONUS Divisions in this country — Continental United States Army Divisions — simply could not pass a readiness test; that two out of three divisions that were to be allocated to the so-called Rapid Deployment Force could not meet a readiness test. And in most cases, that failure to meet the test was because of a lack of manning requirements, an inability to fill many of the slots in those divisions.

Yes, I have seen figures that indicate that perhaps as of September, 1980 — this very month — that there is a shortage of about 104,000 in the ranks between E-4 and E-9. And there were reports ... public reports not long ago about ships that could not leave American ports because of a lack of crews. I talked to one of the leading former chiefs of Naval operations in my office a few weeks ago, who told me about 25,000 Chief Petty Officers being short.

But, I think that that is clearly related to the fact that, going back to the time when the all-volunteer Army was created in 1973 — and I worked hard for it and supported it — we simply have failed to keep pace with the cost of living. And today, on the average, the average serviceman is at least 15% — and I happen to think that's a very modest estimate — 15% below what has happened to the cost of living over that period of time. And as a result, the families of some of our young servicemen are on food stamps today. And I think that's shocking; it's shameful.

So, yes, I told the American Legion National Convention, the VFW National Convention — when I spoke to each of those bodies — I outlined a very specific program of increasing pay and allowances, re-enlistment bonuses. That only makes sense.

But I would leave you with this thought, sir, to be quite specific in my answer to your question: that, of course, to protect the vital interests of this country, if that became impossible; if I could not, despite the very best efforts that I asked the Congress to put forward, to raise those pay and incentives and allowances, of course, I would not leave this country go undefended.

Moyers: Mr. Corddry?

Corddry: Mr. Reagan, I will just repeat the two questions: How would you fill the under-strength combat forces with numbers and with quality, without reviving conscription? And will you commit yourself, here, tonight, should you become the Commander in Chief, to propose a draft, however unpopular, if it becomes clear that voluntary means are not solving our manpower problems?

Reagan: Mr. Corddry, it's a shame now that there are only two of us here debating, because the two that are here are in more agreement than disagreement on this particular issue, and the only one who would be disagreeing with us is the President, if he were present.

I, too, believe in the voluntary military. As a matter of fact, today the shortages of non-commissioned officers that John mentioned are such that if we tried to have a draft today, we wouldn't have the non-commissioned officers to train the draftees.

I believe the answer lies in just recognizing human nature and how we make everything else work in this country, when we want it to work. Recognize that we have a voluntary military. We are asking for men and women to join the military as a career, and we're asking them to deal with the most sophisticated of equipment. And a young man is out there on a $1 billion carrier in charge of the maintenance of a $20 million aircraft, working 100 hours a week at times, and he's earning less for himself and his family, while he's away from his family, than he could earn if he were in one of the most menial jobs, working 40 hours a week here at home.

As an aid to enlistment ... we had an aid — 46% of the people who enlisted in the voluntary military up until 1977 said they did so for one particular reason, the G.I. Bill of Rights — the fact that, by serving in the military, they could provide for a future college education. In 1977, we took that away from the military. That meant immediately 46% of your people that were signing up had no reason for signing up.

So I think it is a case of pay scale, of recognizing that if we're going to have young men and women responsible for our security, dealing with this sophisticated equipment, then for heaven's sakes, let's go out and have a pay scale that is commensurate with the sacrifice that we're asking of them.

Along with this, I think we need something else that has been allowed to deteriorate. We need a million-man active reserve that could be called up on an instant's notice, and that would be also trained, ready to use that type of equipment. Both of these, I think, would respond to the proper kind of incentives that we could offer these people.

The other day, I just — I'll hasten — I just saw one example. Down in Texas, I saw a high school that is military.

Moyers: Your time is up, Mr. Reagan.

Reagan: Fine.

Moyers: I'm sorry.

Reagan: I'll catch up with it later.

Moyers: You can finish it after it's over. Mr. Anderson?

Anderson: Mr. Moyers, I must say that I think I have better opportunity, however, of finding the necessary funds to pay what, admittedly, will be very, very substantial sums of money. We signed one bill, or we passed one bill, just a couple of weeks ago in the House of Representatives for $500 million — a half a billion dollars. That is just a downpayment, in my opinion.

But, unlike Governor Reagan, I do not support a boondoggle like the MX missile. I've just gotten a report from the Air Force that indicates that the 30-year lifecycle cost of that system is going to be $100 billion. The initial cost is about $54 billion, and then when you add in the additional costs — not only the construction of the system, the missiles and the personnel, and so on — when you add in the additional costs over the lifecycle of that system, over $100 billion. I would propose to save the taxpayers of this country from that kind of costly boondoggle.

Moyers: Mr. Reagan?

Reagan: Well, let me just say that, with regard to that same missile system, I happen to support and believe in the missile, itself. But that's not the $54 billion cost that John is talking about. He's talking about that fantastic plan of the Administration to take thousands and thousands of square miles out in the Western states. And first, he was going to dig a racetrack and have it going around in the racetrack so it would meet the requirements of SALT II treaty, and now he's decided it'll have a straight up and down thing, so it can be both verifiable and yet hideable from the Soviet Union.

We need the missile, I think, because we are so out of balance strategically that we lack a deterrent to a possible first assault. But I am not in favor of the plan that is so costly.

And therefore, if I only had another second left, I'd say that that high school class in a military training — 40 of its 80 graduates last year entered the United States service academies; West Point, Annapolis and the Air Force Academy, and to see those young men made me very proud to realize that there are young people in this country that are prepared to go into that kind of a career in service of their country.

Moyers: This question comes to you, Mr. Reagan, from my colleague, Lee May.

[Deteriorating Cities]

May: Mr. Reagan, the military is not the only area in crisis. American cities are physically wearing out, as housing, streets, sewers and budgets all fall apart. And all of this is piled upon the emotional strain that comes from refugees and racial confrontations.

Now, I'm wondering what specific plans do you have for Federal involvement in saving our cities from these physical and emotional crises, and how would you carry out those plans in addition to raising military pay, without going against your pledge of fiscal restraint?

Reagan: I don't think I'd have to go against that pledge. I think one of the problems today with the cities is Federal aid. The mayors that I've talked to in some of our leading cities tell me that the Federal grants that come with ... for a specific cause or a specific objective, come with such red tape, such priorities established by a bureaucracy in Washington, that the local government's hands are tied with regard to using that money as they feel it could best be used, and for what they think might be the top priority. If they had that money without those government restrictions, every one of them has told me they could make great savings and make far greater use of the money.

What I have been advocating is, why don't we start with the Federal Government turning back tax sources to states and local governments, as well as the responsibilities for those programs? Seventy-five percent of the people live in the cities. I don't know of a city in America that doesn't have the kind of problems you're talking about. But, where are we getting the money that the Federal Government is putting out to help them? New York is being taxed for money that will then go to Detroit. But Detroit is being taxed for money that, let's say, will go to Chicago, while Chicago is being taxed to help with the problems in Philadelphia. Wouldn't it make a lot more sense if the government let them keep their own money there in the first place?

But there are other things that we can do with the inner cities, and I've believed ... I have talked of having zones in those cities that are run down, where there is a high percentage of people on welfare, and offer tax incentives. The government isn't getting a tax now from businesses there because they aren't there, or from individuals who are on welfare rather than working. And why don't we offer incentives for business and industry to start up in those zones? Give them a tax moratorium for a period if they build and develop there. The individuals that would then get jobs — give them a break that encourages them to leave the social welfare programs and go to work.

We could have an urban homestead act. We've got thousands and thousands of homes owned by government boarded up, being vandalized, that have been taken in in mortgage foreclosures. What if we had a homestead act, and said to the people, for $1 we sell you this house. All you have to do is agree to refurbish it, make it habitable, and live in it — just as 100 or more years ago, we did with the open land in this country — urban ... or country homesteading.

Moyers: Mr. May?

May: Mr. Anderson, let me ask you, what specific plans do you have for Federal involvement in saving cities from the physical and emotional crises that confront them, and how would you carry out those plans, in addition to raising military pay, without going against your pledge of fiscal restraint?

Anderson: Mr. May, I recently saw a Princeton University study that indicated that the cities of America — the large cities of this country — are in worse shape today than they were in 1960. It seems to totally belie the claim that I heard President Carter make a few days ago, that he was the first President that had come forth with a real urban strategy to meet the problems of urban America. Incidentally, just this past week, the crown jewel in that program that he had devised was stolen, I guess, because a conference committee turned down the ambitious plan that he had to increase the amount of money that would be available to the Economic Development Administration for loan guarantees and direct loans and credits.

I'm happy to say that, in contrast to that, the Anderson-Lucey platform for America, program for the '80s, has devoted considerable time, and in very specific detail, we have talked about two things that ought to be done to aid urban America. We call, first of all, for the creation of a $4 billion urban reinvestment trust fund, to do exactly what you spoke about in your question — to rebuild the streets, to rebuild the cities, the leaking water mains.

I was in North Pittsburgh — I think it was a few weeks ago, on my campaign — the water mains in that city had begun to leak, and literally, there wasn't money available to fix them. And until we can begin to recreate the basic infrastructure of the great cities of America, particularly in the upper Midwest and in the Northeast, they simply are not going to provide the kind of economic climate that will enable them to retain industry, enable them to retain the kind of solid industrial base that they need, so that they can provide jobs.

We have also provided in our program for a $4 billion Community Trust Fund, and we've told you where the money is coming from. It's going to come from the dedication, by 1984, of the excise revenues that today are being collected by the Federal Government on alcohol and tobacco. That money, I think, ought to be put into rebuilding the base of our cities.

In addition to that, jobs programs to re-employ the youth in our cities would be very high on my priority list, both the Youth Opportunities Act of 1980 and a billion-dollar program that I would recommend to put youth to work in energy projects, in conservation projects, in projects that would carry out some of the great national goals of our country.

Moyers: Mr. Reagan, your response.

Reagan: Yes. Government claims ... John claims that he is making plain where the money will come from. It will come from the pockets of the people. It will come from the pockets of the people who are living in those very areas. And the problem is, with Governments — Federal, State and Local — taking $.44 out of every dollar earned, that the Federal Government has pre-empted too many of the tax sources, and that the cities ... if Pittsburgh does not have the money to fix the leaking water mains, it's because the Federal Government has pre-empted.

Now, the Federal Government is going to turn around and say, well you have this problem; we will now hand you the money to do it. But the Federal Government doesn't make money. It just takes — from the people. And in my view, this is not the answer to the problem.

Stand in the South Bronx as I did, in the spot where Jimmy Carter made his promise that he was going to, with multi-billion dollar programs, refurbish that area that looks like bombed-out London in World War II. I stood there, and I met the people. And I heard them ask just for something that would give them hope. And I believe that, while all of the promises have been broken, they've never been carried out. But I believe that my plan might offer an opportunity for that, if we would move into those areas and let, encourage — with the tax incentive — the private sector, to develop and to create the jobs for the people.

Moyers: Mr. Anderson.

Anderson: Well, of course, where has the private sector been, Governor Reagan, during the years that our cities have been deteriorating? It seems to me that to deny the responsibility of the Federal Government to do something about our crumbling cities is to deny the opportunity for one thing: To 55% of the black population of our country that is locked within the inner cities of the metropolitan areas of our country. We simply cannot ignore the fact that, in those cities today, we have 55% youth unemployment among black and Hispanic youth.

And why is that? It's because they have lost their industry. And why have they lost their industry? It's because they no longer present the kind of viable economic climate that makes it possible for industry to remain there, or to locate there. I think Government has a responsibility to find jobs for the youth of this country, and that the place to start is to assist in the very important and necessary task of helping cities rebuild.

Moyers: Jane Bryant Quinn has the next question, for you, Mr. Anderson.

[Impact of Inflation]

Quinn: Mr. Anderson, many voters are very worried that tax cuts, nice as they are, will actually add to inflation. And many eminent conservatives have testified that even business tax cuts, as you have proposed, can be inflationary as long as we have a budget deficit.

Now, Mr. Reagan has mentioned that he put out a five-year economic forecast, which indeed he did, but it contained no inflation number. You have published a detailed program, but it too does not have any hard numbers on it about how these things work with inflation. So I would like to ask you, if you will commit to publish specific forecasts within two weeks, so that the voters can absorb them and understand them and analyze them, showing exactly what all these problems you've mentioned tonight — on energy, on defense, on the cities — how these impact on inflation, and what inflation's actually going to be over five years.

Anderson: Miss Quinn, I would be very happy to accept the challenge of your question tonight, to tell the voters of this country exactly what

I think it's going to cost, because I believe that all too often in past elections, politicians have simply been promising people things that they cannot deliver. When these Presidential Debates were held just four years ago, I remember the incumbent President, who was willing to debate President Ford, telling the American people that they simply ought not to vote for somebody who promised more than they could deliver.

Well, we've seen what has happened. We haven't gotten either the economies in Government that were promised; we haven't gotten the 4% inflation that we were supposed to get at the end of Mr. Carter's first term. Instead we had, I think, in the second quarter, a Consumer Price Index registering around 12%. And nobody really knows, with the latest increase in the Wholesale Price Index — that's about 18% on an annualized basis — what it's going to be.

Let me say this. I think my programs are far less inflationary than those of Governor Reagan. His own running mate, when he was running for the Presidency, said that they would cost 30% inflation inside of two years, and he cited his leading economic advisor, a very distinguished economist, Paul Macavoy [sic], as the source of that information. He went so far as to call it "brutal economics."

I've been very careful — I have been very careful in saying that what I'm going to do is to bring Federal spending under control first. I would like to stand here and promise the American people a tax cut, as Governor Reagan has done. But, you know, it's gotten to be about $122 difference. Somebody worked it out. And they figured out that between the tax cut that Governor Reagan is promising the American people, and the tax cut that Jimmy Carter is promising in 1981, his is worth about $122 more.

So you, dear voters, are out there on the auction block, and these two candidates are bidding for your votes. And one is going to give you $122 more if you happen to be in that range of about a $20,000-a-year income. I'm going to wait until I see that that inflation rate is going down, before I even begin to phase in the business tax cuts that I've talked about. But I think, by improving productivity, they would be far less inflationary than the consumption-oriented tax cut that Governor Reagan is recommending.

Moyers: Ms. Quinn.

Quinn: Mr. Anderson, I'll call you for that forecast.

Mr. Reagan, will you publish specific forecasts within two weeks, so that the voters can have time to analyze and absorb them before the election, showing exactly what all these things you've discussed tonight — for energy, cities and defense — mean for inflation over the next five years?

Reagan: Miss Quinn, I don't have to. I've done it. We have a back-up paper to my economic speech of a couple of weeks ago in Chicago, that gives all of the figures. And we used — yes, we used — the Senate Budget Committee's projections for five years, which are based on an average inflation rate of 7.5% — which, I think, that under our plan, can be eliminated. And eliminated probably more quickly than our plan, but we wanted to be so conservative with it, that people would see how ... how well it could be done.

Now, John's been in the Congress for 20 years. And John tells us that first, we've got to reduce spending before we can reduce taxes. Well, if you've got a kid that's extravagant, you can lecture him all you want to about his extravagance. Or you can cut his allowance and achieve the same end much quicker.

But Government has never reduced ... Government does not tax to get the money it needs. Government always needs the money it gets. And when John talks about his non-inflationary plan, as far as I have been able to learn, there are 88 proposals in it that call for additional Government spending programs.

Now, I speak with some confidence of our plan, because I took over a state — California — 10% of the population of this nation — a state that, if it were a nation, would be the seventh-ranking economic power in the world. And that state ... we controlled spending. We cut the rate of increase in spending in half. But at the same time, we gave back to the people of California — in tax rebates, tax credits, tax cuts — $5.7 billion. I vetoed 993 measures without having a veto overturned. And among those vetoes, I stopped $16 billion in additional spending. And the funny thing was that California, which is normally above the national average in inflation and unemployment, for those six years for the first time, was below the national average in both inflation and unemployment.

We have considered inflation in our figures. We deliberately took figures that we, ourselves, believed were too conservative. I believe the budget can be balanced by 1982 or 1983, and it is a combination of planned reduction of the tax increase that Carter has built into the economy, and that's what he's counting on for his plan. But he's going to get a half-a-trillion dollars more over the next five years that he can use for additional programs, or hopefully, someplace down the line, balancing the budget. We believe that that's too much additional money to take out of the pockets of the people.

Moyers: Mr. Anderson.

Anderson: Mr. Moyers, I'm not here to debate Governor Reagan's record as Governor. This is 1980 and not 1966. But I do know that, despite his pledge to reduce state Government spending, that it rose from $4.6 billion when he took office in 1967, to $10.2 billion during his eight years in office. Spending, in other words, more than doubled, and it rose at a faster rate than spending was rising in the Federal Government.

But on his very optimistic figures about his tax cut producing a balanced budget by 1983, and the fact that he is using, he says, the figures of the Senate Budget Committee, that Senate Budget Committee Report does not accommodate all of the Reagan defense plans. It doesn't accommodate the expenditures that he calls for, for accelerated development and deployment of a new manned strategic bomber, for a permanent fleet in the Indian Ocean, for the restoration of the fleet to 600 ships, to the development and deployment of a dedicated modern aircraft interceptor.

In other words, I have seen his program costed out to the point where it would amount to more than $300 million a year, just for the military. And I think the figures that he has given are simply not going to stand up.

Moyers: Would . . . would you have a comment, Mr. Reagan:

Reagan: Well, some people look up figures, and some people make up figures. And John has just made up some very interesting figures. We took the Senate report, of course. But we did factor in our own ideas with regard to increases in the projected military spending that we believe would, over a period of time, do what is necessary.

Now also, with regard to the figures about California. The truth of the matter is, we did cut the increase in spending in half. It . . . at the . . . John doesn't quite realize — he's never held an executive position of that kind. And I think being Governor of California is probably the closest thing to the Presidency, if that's possible, of any executive job in America today — because it is the most populous state.

And I can only tell him that we reduced, in proportion of other states, the per capita spending, the per capita size of Government — we only increased the size of Government one-twelfth what it had increased in the preceding eight years. And one journal, the *San Francisco Chronicle,* a respected newspaper, said there was no question about the fact that Governor Reagan had prevented the State of California from going bankrupt.

Moyers: Our final question comes from Soma Golden, and it's directed to Mr. Reagan.

[Organized Religion in Politics]

Golden: I'd like to switch the focus from inflation to God. This week, Cardinal Medeiros of Boston warned Catholics that it's sinful to vote for candidates who favor abortion. This did not defeat the two men he opposed, but it did raise questions about the roles of church and state.

You, Mr. Reagan, have endorsed the participation of fundamentalist churches in your campaign. And you, Mr. Anderson, have tried three times to amend the Constitution to recognize the, quote, "law and authority," unquote, of Jesus Christ.

My question: Do you approve of the Church's actions this week in Boston? And should a President be guided by organized religion on issues like abortion, equal rights, and defense spending?

Moyers: Mr. Reagan.

Golden: Mr. Reagan.

Reagan: Oh, I'm . . . it's my question. But whether I agree or disagree with some individual, or what he may say, or how he may say it, I don't think there's any way that we can suggest that because people believe in God and go to church, that they should not want reflected in those people and those causes they support, their own belief in morality, and in the high traditions and principles which we've abandoned so much in this country.

Going around this country, I think that I have found a great hunger in America for a spiritual revival. For a belief that law must be based on a higher law. For a return to traditions and values that we once had. Our Government, in its most sacred documents — the Constitution and the Declaration of Independence and all — speak of man being created, of a Creator. That we're a nation under God.

Now, I have thought for a long time that too many of our churches have been too reluctant to speak up in behalf of what they believe is proper in Government, and they have been too . . . too lax in interfering, in recent years, with Government's invasion of the family itself, putting itself between parent and child. I vetoed a number of bills of that kind myself, when I was in California.

Now, whether it is rightful, on a single issue, for anyone to advocate that someone should not be elected or not, I won't take a position on that. But I do believe that no one in this country should be denied the right to express themselves, or to even try to persuade others to follow their leader. That's what elections are all about.

Moyers: Ms. Golden.

Golden: Okay. I would point out that churches are tax-exempt institutions, and I'll repeat my question.

Do you approve the Church's action this week in Boston, and should a President be guided by organized religion on issues like abortion, equal rights and defense spending?

Anderson: Ms. Golden, certainly the church has the right to take a position on moral issues. But to try, as occurred in the case that you mentioned — that specific case — to try to tell the parishioners of any church, of any denomination, how they should vote, or for whom they should vote, I think violates the principle of separation of church and state.

Now, Governor Reagan is running on a platform that calls for a Constitutional amendment banning abortion. I think that is a moral issue that ought to be left to the freedom of conscience of the individual. And for the state to interfere with a Constitutional amendment, and tell a woman that she must carry that pregnancy to term, regardless of her personal belief, that, I think, violates freedom of conscience as much as anything that I can think of.

And he is also running on a platform that suggests a litmus test for the selection of judges — that only judges that hold a certain, quote, "view," on the sanctity of family life, ought to be appointed

to the Federal Judiciary, one of the three great independent branches
of our Government.

No. I believe in freedom of choice. I don't believe in Constitutional
Amendments that would interfere with that. I don't believe in trying
to legislate new tests for the selection of the Federal Judiciary.

On the Amendment that you mentioned, I abandoned it 15 years
ago. And I have said freely, all over this country, that it was a mistake
for me or anyone to ever try to put the Judeo-Christian heritage of
this country, important as it is, and important as my religious faith
is to me — it's a very deeply personal matter. But for me to try,
in this very pluralistic society of ours, to try to frame any definition,
whatever, of what that belief should be, is wrong.

And so, not once, but twice — in 1971 — I voted on the floor
of the House of Representatives against a Constitutional amendment
that tried to bring prayer back into the public schools. I think mother
ought to whisper to Johnny and to Susie, as they button their coats
in the morning and leave for the classroom, "Be sure to say a prayer
before you start your day's work." But I don't think that the state,
the Board of Regents, a Board of Education, or any state official,
should try to compose that prayer for a child to recite.

Moyers: Mr. Reagan.

Reagan: The litmus test that John says is in the Republican platform,
says no more than the judges to be appointed should have a respect
for innocent life. Now, I don't think that's a bad idea. I think all
of us should have a respect for innocent life.

With regard to the freedom of the individual for choice with regard
to abortion, there's one individual who's not being considered at all.
That's the one who is being aborted. And I've noticed that everybody
that is for abortion has already been born. I . . . I think that, technically,
I know this is a difficult and an emotional problem, and many people
sincerely feel on both sides of this, but I do believe that maybe we
could find the answer through medical evidence, if we would determine
once and for all, is an unborn child a human being? I happen to
believe it is.

Moyers: Mr. Anderson.

Anderson: I also think that that unborn child has a right to be
wanted. And I also believe, sir, that the most personal, intimate decision
that any woman is ever called upon to make is the decision as to
whether or not she shall carry a pregnancy to term. And for the state
to interfere in that decision, under whatever guise, and with whatever
rationale, for the state to try to take over in that situation, and by
edict, command what the individual shall do, and substitute itself for
that individual's conscience, for her right to consult her rabbi, her
minister, her priest, her doctor — any other counselor of her choice
— I think goes beyond what we want to ever see accomplished in
this country, if we really believe in the First Amendment; if we really
believe in freedom of choice and the right of the individual.

Moyers: Mr. Reagan, you now have three minutes for closing remarks.

[Closing Remarks]

Reagan: Before beginning my closing remarks, here, I would just like to remark a concern that I have that we have criticized the failures of the Carter policy here rather considerably, both of us this evening. And there might be some feeling of unfairness about this because he was not here to respond. But I believe it would have been much more unfair to have had John Anderson denied the right to participate in this debate. And I want to express my appreciation to the League of Women Voters for adopting a course with which I believe the great majority of Americans are in agreement.

Now, as to my closing remarks: I've always believed that this land was placed here between the two great oceans by some divine plan. That it was placed here to be found by a special kind of people — people who had a special love for freedom and who had the courage to uproot themselves and leave hearth and homeland, and come to what, in the beginning, was the most undeveloped wilderness possible.

We came from 100 different corners of the earth. We spoke a multitude of tongues. We landed on this Eastern shore and then went out over the mountains and the prairies and the deserts and the far western mountains to the Pacific, building cities and towns and farms, and schools and churches. If wind, water or fire destroyed them, we built them again. And in so doing, at the same time, we built a new breed of human called an American — a proud, an independent, and a most compassionate individual, for the most part.

Two hundred years ago, Tom Paine, when the 13 tiny colonies were trying to become a nation, said, we have it in our power to begin the world over again. Today, we're confronted with the horrendous problems that we've discussed here tonight. And some people in high positions of leadership, tell us that the answer is to retreat. That the best is over. That we must cut back. That we must share in an ever-increasing scarcity. That we must, in the failure to be able to protect our national security as it is today, we must not be provocative to any possible adversary.

Well, we, the living Americans, have gone through four wars. We've gone through a Great Depression in our lifetime that literally was worldwide and almost brought us to our knees. But we came through all of those things and we achieved even new heights and new greatness.

The living Americans today have fought harder, paid a higher price for freedom, and done more to advance the dignity of man than any people who ever lived on this earth. For 200 years, we've lived in the future, believing that tomorrow would be better than today, and today would be better than yesterday.,

I still believe that. I'm not running for the Presidency because I believe that I can solve the problems we've discussed tonight. I believe the people of this country can, and together, we can begin the world over again. We can meet our destiny — and that destiny to build a land here that will be, for all mankind, a shining city on a hill. I think we ought to get at it.

Moyers: Mr. Anderson, you have the final three minutes.

Anderson: Mr. Moyers, President Carter was not right a few weeks ago when he said that the American people were confronted with only two choices, with only two men, and with only two parties.

I think you've seen tonight in this debate that Governor Reagan and I have agreed on exactly one thing — we are both against the reimposition of a peacetime draft. We have disagreed, I believe, on virtually every other issue. I respect him for showing tonight — for appearing here, and I thank the League of Women Voters for the opportunity that they have given me.

I am running for President as an Independent because I believe our country is in trouble. I believe that all of us are going to have to begin to work together to solve our problems. If you think that I am a spoiler, consider these facts: Do you really think that our economy is healthy? Do you really think that 8 million Americans being out of work and the 50% unemployment among the youth of our country are acceptable? Do you really think that our armed forces are really acceptably strong in those areas of conventional capability where they should be? Do you think that our political institutions are working the way they should when literally only half of our citizens vote?

I don't think you do think that. And therefore, I think you ought to consider doing something about it, and voting for an Independent in 1980.

You know, a generation of office seekers has tried to tell the American people that they could get something for nothing. It's been a time, therefore, of illusion and false hopes, and the longer it continues, the more dangerous it becomes. We've got to stop drifting.

What I wish tonight so desperately is that we had had more time to talk about some of the other issues that are so fundamentally important. A great historian, Henry Steele Commager, said that in their lust for victory, neither traditional party is looking beyond November. And he went on to cite three issues that their platforms totally ignore: atomic warfare, Presidential Directive 59 notwithstanding. If we don't resolve that issue, all others become irrelevant. The issue of our natural resources; the right of posterity to inherit the earth, and what kind of earth will it be? The issue of nationalism — the recognition, he says, that every major problem confronting us is global, and cannot be solved by nationalism here or elsewhere — that is chauvinistic, that is parochial, that is as anachronistic as states' rights was in the days of Jefferson Davis.

Those are some of the great issues — atomic warfare, the use of our natural resources, and the issue of nationalism — that I intend to be talking about in the remaining six weeks of this campaign, and

I dare hope that the American people will be listening and that they will see that an Independent government of John Anderson and Patrick Lucey can give us the kind of coalition government that we need in 1980 to begin to solve our problems. Thank you.

Moyers: Mr. Anderson, we, too, wish there were more time, and for all the limitations of the form — and there are other forms to try — the Chair, for one, would like to see such meetings become a regular and frequent part of every Presidential campaign.

Mr. Reagan, Mr. Anderson, we thank you for coming, and thanks to our panelists, Carol Loomis, Daniel Greenberg, Charles Corddry, Lee May, Jane Bryant Quinn and Soma Golden. And thank you in the audience at home for joining us.

This first Presidential Debate of 1980 has been brought to you as a public service by the League of Women Voters Education Fund. I'm Bill Moyers. Good night.

SYNOD OF CATHOLIC BISHOPS
September 26-October 26, 1980

The Fifth World Synod of Bishops, meeting at the Vatican in Rome for a month beginning Sept. 26, reaffirmed traditional Roman Catholic positions on birth control and divorce. A number of the delegates, however, were said to have argued in the closed sessions for an easing of the church's approach to matters involving sexuality and the family. The synod had been called to discuss problems of modern families.

The leader of the American delegation, Archbishop John R. Quinn, seemed, in an address at the synod Sept. 29, to criticize by indirection the church's stand on birth control and to ask for a study of the question. But at a later news conference Archbishop Quinn "clarified" his statements, stressing that he did not call for any change in the Catholic position.

The delegates discussed "pastoral ways" of meeting the problems of divorced Catholics who remarried. Permitted to attend mass and to go to confession, such Catholics usually were barred from communion. In connection with the issue of divorce, the bishops heard a report that church annulments of marriage had increased dramatically in the previous 10 years.

Background

Composed of all the church's bishops, the World Synod of Bishops was created in 1965 by the Second Vatican Council, which also directed it to meet every three years. With no actual policymaking power, the synod was

*able to report to the pope, who was free to reject or revise its recommenda-
tions. The 1980 synod was the first devoted to the whole range of family
issues.*

*The choice of topics appeared to reflect an awareness on the part of the
church's leaders of a disaffection among many Catholics, especially in
Western nations, over Catholic prohibitions in the area of sexuality and
family life. Perhaps central among the churchmen's concerns was promoting a better understanding of the reaffirmation by Pope Paul VI in 1968 of
the church's ban on artificial birth control, in his encyclical letter,
"Humanae Vitae" ("On Human Life"). Pope John Paul II repeated his
support for the encyclical in a meeting with U.S. bishops in Chicago Oct. 5,
1979, and in an address in the 1980 synod. (Historic Documents of 1979, p.
755)*

Archbishop Quinn

*In his address Archbishop Quinn, president of the National Conference
of Bishops of the United States, pointed to opposition to the church's
teachings on birth control "found not only outside the Catholic Church but
also within the family of the church itself."*

*The individual priest, Archbishop Quinn said, found himself on the one
hand "expected to uphold the teaching of the magisterium" and on the
other "as a pastor . . . also expected to aid people in the shaping of their
conscience." In a news conference, he referred to a study that suggested
that more than three-quarters of American Catholic women used methods
of birth control prohibited by the church.*

*Archbishop Quinn's address was attacked by conservative churchmen at
the synod. He explained at a news conference Oct. 1 that neither he "nor
the American bishops' conference reject or challenge the doctrine of the
[church] on contraception." The "intent" of his address, he said, was to
"suggest possible ways of making the church's teachings on contraception
better understood and more widely accepted."*

Annulments of Marriage

*Cardinal Pericle Felici, prefect of the Vatican Appeals Court, told the
synod that the rise in annulments of Catholic marriages in a 10-year period
had been "astronomical." Although Cardinal Felici did not name the
courts or countries where annulments had increased so dramatically, Pope
Paul VI had charged before his death that courts in North America were
granting annulments "easily and excessively." An Associated Press article
published in The New York Times said that the number of annulments in
the United States increased from 338 in 1968 to 17,190 in 1978.*

'Message to Christian Families'

As it closed, the synod released a 2,800-word "Message to Christian Families in the Modern World." The message reaffirmed the Catholic Church's opposition to divorce, contraception and abortion. It also expressed compassion for "many Christian couples who, although they sincerely want to observe the moral norms taught by the church, find themselves unequal to the task because of weakness in the face of difficulties."

> *Following are excerpts from Pope John Paul II's homily during a eucharistic celebration in the Sistine Chapel opening the 1980 International Synod of Bishops, Sept. 26; excerpts from a proposal by Ukranian-Rite Archbishop Maxim Hermaniuk of Winnipeg, Manitoba, Canada, that the synod urge the United Nations to proclaim a charter of family rights, delivered Sept. 29; excerpts from a speech to the Synod of Bishops in Rome Sept. 29 by Archbishop John R. Quinn of San Francisco; and excerpts from a Message to Christian Families, issued by the synod at closing cermonies at the Vatican Oct. 25. (Boldface headings in brackets have been added by Congressional Quarterly to highlight the organization of the text.):*

POPE'S HOMILY AT SYNOD

1. Venerable brothers in the episcopate and dearly beloved brothers and sisters participating in this session of the Synod of Bishops, which is about to begin:

It would be fitting to start our work by going straight to the heart of the priestly prayer of Christ. We know how important and how profound the moment was when he uttered the words of this prayer.

Let us listen to the deep meaning which fills these words: "Oh Father most holy, protect them with your name which you have given me, that they may be one, as we are one" (Jn. 17:11).

When the church prays for her unity, she simply goes back to these words. With these words we pray for the unity of Christians. And using the same words, we seek from the Father, in the name of Christ, that unity which we should bring about during the assembly of the Synod of Bishops, which begins today and starts after a period of long and thorough preparation for its work on the theme: "The Role of the Christian Family."

2. This theme has been chosen as a result of thorough examination of the suggestions sent to the secretary general of the Synod of Bishops by many bishops and episcopal conferences. It will form the basis for our consider-

ations during the next few weeks also because we are deeply convinced that through the Christian family the church lives and fulfills the mission given to her by Christ.

Therefore we can say in all honesty that the theme of the present session of the synod is a continuation of the preceding two sessions. Both evangelization, theme of the 1974 synod, and catechesis, theme of the 1977 synod, not only look to the family but also receive their authentic vitality from the family. The family is the fundamental object of the church's evangelization and catechesis, but it is also the necessary subject for which nothing else can be substituted: the creative subject.

3. As the subject, the family must be conscious of the mission of the church and of its participation in this mission, not only to persevere in the church and to draw from its spiritual resources, but also to constitute the church in its fundamental dimension, like a "miniature church" (domestic church).

The present synod's job is to show all the families their particular role in the mission of the church. This participation includes, at the same time, the realization of the actual ends of the Christian family, as much as possible in its full dimension.

In the work of the synodal assembly, we would like to perceive again the rich teachings of the Second Vatican Council which pertain to the truths about the family and how the families have translated these teachings into daily life. The Christian families must fully find their place in this work of great importance. Above all, the synod intends to render service to this end. . . .

Beloved brothers and sisters, we will be grateful to you if during the work of this synod in which we are involved, in our episcopal and pastoral duty, you would share with us these gifts of your condition and your vocation, at least through the testimony of your presence and your experience, rooted in the sanctity of this great sacrament. This sacrament which is proper to you: the sacrament we call matrimony.

5. When Christ the Lord, before his death, at the threshold of the paschal mystery, prays: "Oh Father most holy, protect them with your name which you have given me, that they may be one, even as we are one" (Jn. 17:11), he is seeking in a special way the unity of married couples and of families. He prays for the unity of his disciples, for the unity of the church; and the mystery of the church is compared by St. Paul with marriage (cf. Eph 5:21-33) and its duties. The church not only has special responsibilities to the family, but it also finds its reflection in the family.

Inflamed with love for Christ her spouse, who loved us till the end, the church looks toward spouses who promise love to one another through the course of their whole life, even unto death. The church considers it her particular duty to foster this love, this faithfulness, this honesty and all good things which come from the human person and society. It is actually the family which gives life to society because in the family through the work of education, the actual structure of humanity is formed, proper to every person on this world.

In today's Gospel, the Son speaks thus to the Father: "I entrusted to them the message you entrusted to me and they have received . . . and have believed it was you who sent me . . . just as all that belongs to me is yours, so all that belongs to you is mine . . ." (Jn. 17:8-10).

Doesn't the echo of this dialogue resound in the hearts of all generations? Don't these words vividly portray the history of each family and through the family, of each person?

Don't we feel, through these words, specially connected to the mission of Christ himself: of Christ the priest, the prophet, the king? Isn't the family born by reason of this mission? . . .

The word of God, announced in today's liturgy, describes the duties which it is fitting that we propose to Christian families in the church and in the modern world:

—Consciousness of one's own mission, which comes from the saving mission of Christ and is fulfilled as a special service.

—This consciousness is fed by the word of the living God and by the power of Christ's sacrifice. In this way the testimony of life is developed, capable of forming the life of others and of sanctifying others in truth.

—From this consciousness flows the good which alone "guards from the evil one." The duty of the family is altogether like the duty of he who in the Gospel said of himself: "As long as I was with them, I guarded them with your name which you gave me. . . . Not one of them was lost." (Jn. 17:12).

Yes, the duty of each Christian family is to guard and preserve the fundamental values. To do this is to guard and preserve humanity itself. . . .

CHARTER OF FAMILY RIGHTS PROPOSAL

I am speaking in the name of the assembly of the Ukrainian-Rite bishops in Canada.

In the following we wish to speak about the social function of the family. . . .

As is known, there is a close connection between the well-being of the family and the welfare of the state, because, as Vatican II teaches, the family is "the first vital cell of society from which not only the citizens are born but which is also the first school of those virtues without which human society cannot exist. . . . Wherefore, the well-being of the individual and of human and Christian society are very closely connected with the healthy condition of the community formed by marriage and the family. . . .

Hence, both societies have a complementary function. Therefore also, on one hand, the Christian family, as the first unit of society and the first school of the social virtues, ought *de facto* to be the first school of these virtues through its exemplary Christian life; while, on the other hand, the state ought to help the family with all its resources, completely respecting "its own special fundamental right" to carry out its own responsibilities.

But, unfortunately, in today's society the family is often, very often, the victim of the unjust organization of government and the economy throughout the whole world.

For there are not a few things in the organization of society, as the working document rightly notes, that violate the integrity of the human person, offend human dignity or create conditions of life that are subhuman and harmful. . . .

And thus in the so-called consumer society, favor is shown to the individual as contributing to quantitative economic progress, with the practical neglect of his marital and familial community, with its integrity, with its intimacy, with its mutual giving and sacrifice. There the purpose of all human endeavor is money, accumulation of wealth and the enjoyment of life's pleasures. In this context of things, the unity of the family and the fidelity of the spouses are often considered optional. Children are considered a burden and not a gift of God. Hence, contraception, divorce and abortion are proposed as the means of personal liberation, especially for women.

However, in nations under a political regime of dictatorship, to all the evils of the consumer world there is added a new calamity for the Christian family, namely, the deprivation of the liberty to react against abuses of the civil power in matters political and economic, reducing the family to a condition of slavery to the state.

This condition of the family, very sad in a consumer society and in a society with a dictatorship, becomes indeed tragic in the communist world, where the human person, either in marriage or in the family or in all external matters, is deprived of all liberty in religious, political, economic and social matters. There the family for all practical purposes is deprived of its primordial right to a life special to itself according to the divine law. The Christian family, moreover, is deprived under such a regime of the liberty of living and acting according to its baptismal and apostolic vocation. In such a state of affairs, the human person and the family are reduced to total slavery. Such conditions exist today, for example, in the Ukraine and in other regions of the atheistic world of communism.

These evils and difficulties which today afflict families in so many nations, even in every continent, are effects not only by accident or from natural causes, but from the unjust organization of governments and economics throughout the world. Thus the disorganized social order of our time has a certain worldwide dimension. Therefore the social responsibilities of the family, which as the first cell of society can alone with the help of God's grace restore that disorganized condition according to the divine law, have a universal significance.

But to fulfill this immense responsibility the Christian family needs the help of the whole church and of all of society.

The Christian family today begs mother church with the voice of these very evils to give it the help it needs. To this request the church, in our humble opinion, can give its help to the Christian family in the following ways:

1. Through an intense education to make the Christian family aware of its fundamental value for the very existence of society, of its power for the formation of its laws and the establishment of its institutions, and especially of its irrevocable responsibility for its transformation according to the law of Christ.

2. Through the organization for this purpose of Catholic families into national associations; and through the formation of one international association of Catholic families, made up of these national ones, with the purpose of promoting the well-being of the family in the religious, political, economic, social and cultural levels throughout the world.

3. And last, through the elaboration and proclamation by the United Nations of a certain charter of family rights with the recognition of the true value of marriage and the family, with the protection of its individual primordial rights, with the promotion of its spiritual and economic prosperity and with full liberty in political matters.

By the proclamation of such a charter of the rights of the family modern society would fulfill a great work for the well-being of the family and for itself.

ARCHBISHOP QUINN'S SPEECH

. . . From the moment the topic of the synod was announced, it was clear that some consideration of the subject of contraception would form part of the deliberations.

Yet to speak about contraception can easily create the impression that one is attacking the doctrine of the church, while not to speak about it at all would be irresponsible.

To avoid any misinterpretation of what follows, I want to affirm clearly that this paper is based on an acceptance of the teaching of the church as it has been enunciated by Pope Paul VI in the encyclical letter Humanae Vitae and by Pope John Paul II in his address to the bishops of the United States in October 1979, a teaching which he has repeated also in his visits to other countries.

But are there only three options available: silence, a mere repetition of magisterial teaching or dissent? This paper is based on the belief that there is another course.

While the encyclical Humanae Vitae was addressed to the Catholic Church, it was also addressed to "all men and women of good will." Yet a very large number of these "men and women of good will" do not accept the teaching of the encyclical on the intrinsic evil of each and every use of contraceptives.

Much of this rejection stems from misunderstandings, aggravated by the fact that the encyclical lies largely unread and its rich teaching reduced to the single principle forbidding artificial contraception.

[Opposition Within Church]

But the problem becomes even more serious when one considers that this widespread opposition is found not only outside the Catholic Church but also within the family of the church itself. The situation in the United States is not unique and is paralleled in many other countries today. Unless one is willing to dismiss the attitude of all these people as obduracy, ignorance or bad will, this widespread opposition must give rise to serious concern.

There is no doubt that the teaching of Humanae Vitae on contraception is authentic teaching of the magisterium of the church.

We cannot credibly treat the problem of contraception without clear and honest recognition of the grave demographic problem of our times. For many couples in the industrialized countries it is the demographic factor as well as their own personal circumstances which influence them in the determination of the size of their family.

It is with this that I would propose the synod begin its treatment of the issue of contraception: place it in the context of a developed teaching on responsible parenthood.

Public, repeated and widespread dissent by well-known theologians not only serves to confirm the Catholic faithful in their own disagreement with the magisterium, but, far worse, leads many to call into question the very reliability of the teaching office of the church and causes doubts about other teachings of the church as well.

[Dilemma for Priests]

As the representative of the teaching authority of the church, the priest is expected to uphold the teaching of the magisterium. As a pastor he is also expected to aid people in the shaping of their conscience. Thus, on the one side he is confronted by the fact of widespread nonobservance of the teaching on contraception, and on the other side he is confronted in the theological literature with widespread dissent from the teaching.

I would then propose the following approach to resolving the problem: that the Holy See initiate a formal dialogue with Catholic theologians. The dialogue should have two stages or phases.

The first would be a listening phase, including both theologians who support the church's teaching and those who do not.

The second phase of the dialogue should be comprised of the patient, loving efforts of those who are brothers and sisters in the church, the magisterium and the theologians, to work towards a resolution of this problematic situation in the light both of the dialogue itself and in the light of the church's experience since Humanae Vitae. This hopefully would lead to a meeting of minds which would result in a greater effectiveness for the church's mission to her own sons and daughters and to the whole world. . . .

MESSAGE TO CHRISTIAN FAMILIES

I. Introduction

1. We have come to the end of the synod. For the past month we bishops from all over the world have met here in Rome in union with the Holy Father and under his leadership. Before returning to our own countries, we wish to address these few words to you. It is not our intention to give answers to all the complex questions raised in our day about marriage and the family. We only want to share with you the love, confidence and hope which we feel. As your bishops and pastors, who are also your brothers in the faith, we have been united with you during these weeks; nor have we forgotten that we too grew up in families with all their joys and sorrows. To you and to our own families we are deeply grateful.

II. The Situation of Families Today

2. In our discussion of family life today we have found joys and consolations, sorrows and difficulties. We must look first for the good things and seek to build on them and make them perfect, confident always that God is present everywhere in his creatures and that we can discern his will in the signs of our times. We are encouraged by the many good and positive things that we see. We rejoice that so many families, even in the face of great pressure to do otherwise, gladly fulfill the God-given mission entrusted to them. Their goodness and fidelity in responding to God's grace and shaping their lives by his teaching gave us a great hope.

The number of families who consciously want to live the life of the Gospel, giving witness to the fruits of the Spirit, continues to grow in all our lands.

3. During this past month we have learned much about the many and varied cultural conditions in which Christian families live. The church must accept and foster this rich diversity, while at the same time encouraging Christian families to give effective witness to God's plan within their own cultures. But all cultural elements must be evaluated in light of the Gospel, to ensure that they are consistent with the divine plan for marriage and the family. This duty — of acceptance and evaluation — is part of the same task of discernment.

4. A more serious problem than that of culture is the condition of those families who live in need in a world of such great wealth. In many parts of the globe, as well as within individual countries, poverty is increasing as a result of social, economic and political structures which foster injustice, oppression and dependence. Conditions in many places are such as to prevent many young men and women from exercising their right to marry and lead decent lives. In the more developed countries, on the other hand, one finds another kind of deprivation: a spiritual emptiness in the midst of abundance, a misery of mind and spirit which makes it difficult for people

to understand God's will for human life and causes them to be anxious about the present and fearful of the future. . . .

5. Often certain governments and some international organizations do violence to families. The integrity of the home is violated. Family rights in regard to religious liberty, responsible parenthood and education are not respected. Families regard themselves as wards and victims rather than as human beings responsible for their own affairs. Families are compelled — and this we oppose vehemently — to use such immoral means for the solution of social, economic and demographic problems as contraception or, even worse, sterilization, abortion and euthanasia. The synod therefore strongly urges a charter of family rights to safeguard these rights everywhere.

6. Underlying many of the problems confronting families and indeed the world at large is the fact that many people seem to reject their fundamental vocation to participate in God's life and love. They are obsessed with the desire to possess, the will for power, the quest for pleasure. Instead of looking upon their fellow human beings as brothers and sisters, members of the human family, they regard them as obstacles and adversaries. Where people lose their sense of God, the heavenly Father, they also lose their sense of the human family. . . .

10. God's plan for marriage and the family can only be fully understood, accepted and lived by persons who have experienced conversion of heart, that radical turning of the self to God by which one puts off the "old" self and puts on the "new." All are called to conversion and sanctity. We must all come to the knowledge and love of the Lord and experience him in our lives, rejoicing in his love and mercy, his patience, compassion and forgiveness, and loving one another as he loves us. Husbands and wives, parents and children, are instruments and ministers of Christ's fidelity and love in their mutual relationships. It is this which makes Christian marriage and family life authentic signs of God's love for us and of Christ's love for the church. . . .

IV. The Family's Response to God's Plan

12. Just as we are doing, you also are seeking to learn what your duties are in today's world. In looking at the world, we see facing you certain important tasks of education. You have the tasks of forming free persons with a keen moral sense and a discerning conscience, together with a perception of their duty to work for the betterment of the human condition and the sanctification of the world. Another task for the family is to form persons in love and also to practice love in all its relationships, so that it does not live closed in on itself but remains open to the community, moved by a sense of justice and concern for others as well as by a consciousness of its responsibility toward the whole of society. It is your duty to form persons in the faith — that is, in knowledge and love of God and eagerness to do his will in all things. It is also your task to hand on sound human and Christian values and to form persons in such a way that they can integrate

new values into their lives. The more Christian the family becomes, the more human it becomes.

13. In fulfilling these tasks the family will be, as it were, a "domestic church," a community of faith living in hope and love, serving God and the entire human family. Shared prayer and the liturgy are sources of grace for families. In fulfilling its tasks the family must nourish itself on God's word and participate in the life of the sacraments, especially reconciliation and the eucharist. Traditional and contemporary devotions, particularly those associated with the Blessed Virgin, are rich sources of growth in piety and grace. . . .

V. The Church and the Family

16. During the synod we have grown in awareness of the church's duty to encourage and support couples and families. We have deepened our commitment in this regard.

17. Family ministry is of very special interest to the church. By this we mean efforts made by the whole people of God through local communities, especially through the help of pastors and lay people devoted to pastoral work for families. They work with individuals, couples and families to help them live out their conjugal vocation as fully as possible. This ministry includes preparation for marriage; help given to married couples at all stages of married life; catechetical and liturgical programs directed to the family; help given to childless couples, single-parent families, the widowed, the separated and divorced, and, in particular, to families and couples laboring under burdens like poverty, emotional and psychological tensions, physical and mental handicaps, alcohol and drug abuse, and the problems associated with migration and other circumstances which strain family stability.

18. The priest has a special place in family ministry. It is his duty to bring the nourishment and consolation of the word of God, the sacraments, and other spiritual aids to the family, encouraging it and in a human and patient way, strengthening it in charity so that families which are truly outstanding can be formed. . . .

19. In speaking of God's plan, the church has many things to say to men and women about the essential equality and complementarity of the sexes, as well as about the different charisms and duties of spouses within marriage. Husband and wife are certainly different, but they are also equal. The difference should be respected but never used to justify the domination of one by the other. In collaboration with society, the church must effectively affirm and defend the dignity and rights of women.

VI. Conclusion

20. As we reach the end of our message, we wish to say to you, brothers and sisters, that we are fully aware of the frailty of our common human condition. In no way do we ignore the very difficult and trying situation of

the many Christian couples who, although they sincerely want to observe the moral norms taught by the church, find themselves unequal to the task because of weakness in the face of difficulties. All of us need to grow in appreciation of the importance of Christ's teachings and his grace and to live by them. Accompanied and assisted by the whole church, those couples continue along the difficult way toward a more complete fidelity to the commands of the Lord.

"The journey of married couples, like the whole journey of human life, meets with delays and difficult and burdensome times. But it must be clearly stated that anxiety or fear should never be found in the souls of people of good will. For is not the Gospel also good news for family life? For all the demands it makes, is it not a profoundly liberating message? The awareness that one has not achieved his full interior liberty and is still at the mercy of his tendencies and finds himself unable to obey the moral law in an area so basic causes deep distress. But this is the moment in which the Christian, rather than giving way to sterile and destructive panic, humbly opens up his soul before God as a sinner before the saving love of Christ" (Pope Paul VI, "Address to the Equipes de Notre Dame," May 4, 1970).

21. Everything we have said about marriage and the family can be summed up in two words: love and life. As we come to the end of this synod, we pray that you, our brothers and sisters, may grow in the love and life of God. In turn we humbly and gratefully beg your prayers that we may do the same. We make St. Paul's words to the Colossians our final words to you: "Over all these virtues put on love, which binds the rest together and makes them perfect. Christ's peace must reign in your hearts, since as members of the one body you have been called to that peace. Dedicate yourselves to thankfulness" (Col. 3:14-15).

IMF-WORLD BANK CONFERENCE
September 30-October 3, 1980

In an atmosphere of heightened concern over the economic plight of the world's poorest countries, more than 2,000 delegates attended the 35th annual joint conference of the International Monetary Fund (IMF) and the World Bank in Washington Sept. 30-Oct. 3.

The conference was highlighted by a farewell address by Robert S. McNamara, for 13 years president of the World Bank. Under McNamara, the bank had become the single largest conveyor of loans to the Third World. But McNamara said that was not enough; in his address he called for a tripling of the bank's annual lending rate by the mid-1980s.

Larger IMF Role

For its part, the IMF was given authority by its governing body to increase sharply the amount of its loans and to ease conditions of its lending. The British periodical, The Economist, *said the action was taken in the face of "grim economic prospects and pressure from the poorer countries."*

Both the IMF and the World Bank had been launched in 1944. The mission of the bank was to make loans for economically sound development projects in the poorer countries. The purpose of the IMF, on the other hand, was to help its members, both rich and poor, cope with balance-of-payments problems.

Disruption Threats

Although threats of disruption of the meeting had been made over the issue of the Palestine Liberation Organization (PLO), they did not materialize.

Jacques de Larosiere, executive director of the IMF, had made it known before the conference opened that a quorum of member countries had voted to bar an observer sent to Washington by the PLO. The move to invite the observer had been supported by a group of Arab countries.

New Member: China

The People's Republic of China was welcomed for the first time as a member of both the IMF and the World Bank. Wang Bingquian, minister of finance and governor of the Bank of China, led a delegation of 22 Chinese. With a nod to "the positive aspects of a market economy," Wang said that "we are going to give the enterprises a greater say in running their own affairs, and we will apply the economic leverage exercised through fixing prices, setting taxes and interest rates and having recourse to banking credits under the overall guidance of state planning."

McNamara's Valedictory

McNamara, who had told the bank that he would retire when he reached 65 in June 1981, singled out the United States, Britain, Japan and the Soviet Union (not a member of the bank) for failing to meet their responsibilities in providing aid to poor countries. (Foreign development aid provided by the United States was .18 of 1 percent of gross national product in 1980, lower proportionately than the aid from other industrial countries except Italy.)

In an emotional speech that drew a thunderous ovation, McNamara pointed to a "new surge" in oil prices that in one year had more than doubled the cost of imported energy for the developing world and to the "continuous recession" in the industrialized nations as creating the "urgent needs" of the "poorest countries."

More Credit

The IMF's policy-setting interim committee granted that institution authority to increase international credit. Countries that had been able to borrow up to 125 percent of their quota in a year were now permitted to borrow up to 200 percent for three consecutive years. (Based on relative economic strength, quotas determined both the borrowing rights and the voting power of member countries.)

In his address, de Larosiere, IMF managing director, said that he saw "no course of policy that could make the economic situation truly satisfactory over the next several years." But de Larosiere added that "the tackling of inflation — provided it is coupled with effective policies on the supply side — holds out the promise of bringing substantial improvement" to the world economy by the mid-1980s.

Dollar Stability

In some previous years, the IMF-World Bank annual meeting had taken place in a near-crisis atmosphere because of weakness of the U.S. dollar and turbulence in the foreign exchange markets. (Historic Documents of 1978, p. 659; Historic Documents of 1979, p. 771)

In 1980, however, the dollar achieved relative stability. De Larosiere took note of the fact, saying that there had been, "over the last two years, a greater degree of stability in the foreign exchange markets than most people would have dared to predict."

> *Following are excerpts from addresses delivered Sept. 30, 1980, by Robert S. McNamara, president of the World Bank, and Jacques de Larosiere, president of the International Monetary Fund, at a joint annual meeting of the bank and the IMF in Washington, D.C. (Boldface headings in brackets have been added by Congressional Quarterly to highlight the organization of the texts.):*

McNAMARA ADDRESS

Introduction

This is the thirteenth, and final, address that I will have the privilege of making in this forum.

The occasion, I believe, places on me a special responsibility, and hence what I have to say this morning will be particularly frank and candid, especially as it relates to the future role of the World Bank.

During the past 18 months the external environment affecting economic growth in the oil-importing developing countries — and thus their rate of social advance — has become substantially more difficult.

The new surge in oil prices, and the downturn in trade with the developed nations, have imposed on these countries huge and potentially unsustainable current account deficits. The result is that their critical development tasks, never easy in the past, are now seriously threatened.

Meanwhile, the industrialized nations continue to grapple with problems of inflation, unemployment, and recession. Governments are searching for politically feasible ways to reduce public expenditures. And though Official Development Assistance remains a miniscule *[sic]* and insignificant fraction of gross national product — and is, in fact, wholly inadequate to the urgent needs at hand — there is little legislative initiative to increase it.

Further, the global financial system as a whole, still trying to cope with past imbalances, must now find a way to recycle to appropriate recipients over $100 billion a year of additional surpluses being earned by the capital-surplus oil-exporting countries.

The cumulative effect of all of this is a climate of apprehension in which the temptation will be strong for both the developed and developing nations to react unwisely. . . .

[Economic Prospects]

Global economic prospects have seriously deteriorated since we met last year in Belgrade. The outlook now is that the oil-importing developing countries in the years immediately ahead are going to have a very difficult time. The Bank is currently projecting, for the decade of the 1980s, lower levels of economic growth in those countries than it did twelve months ago. . . .

The most probable outcome for at least the next five years is that the annual average per capita growth of the oil-importing developing countries — which was 3.1% in the 1960s, and 2.7% in the 1970s — will drop in 1980-85 to 1.8%.

More depressing still is the outlook for the 1.1 billion people who live in the poorest countries. Their already desperately low per capita income, less than $220 per annum, is likely to grow by no more than 1% a year — an average of only two or three dollars per individual. There would even be negative growth for the 141 million people in the low-income countries of sub-Saharan Africa.

There are two principal causes. The new surge in oil prices has more than doubled the cost of imported energy for the oil-importing developing countries. And the continuing recession in the industrialized nations, which comprise their most important markets, is severely limiting demand for their exports.

In 1973 the oil-import bill of these developing countries (in current dollars) was $7 billion. In 1980 it is likely to be $67 billion. The price of oil is not going to come down — on the contrary it is likely to continue to rise in real terms by perhaps 3% a year. The projection for 1985, therefore, is $124 billion, and by 1990 — even assuming these countries more than double their own domestic energy production, and make a considerable effort at conservation — the bill is projected to be nearly $230 billion. . . .

The Drive Against Poverty

Over the past decade I have drawn attention repeatedly in this forum — sometimes at the risk of tedium — to the principal goals of development. They are: to accelerate economic growth, and to eradicate what I have termed absolute poverty.

Economic growth, of course, is obvious enough. And once one has been in contact with developing societies, so is absolute poverty: it is a condition of life so limited by malnutrition, illiteracy, disease, high infant mortality, and low life expectancy as to be beneath any rational definition of human decency.

The two goals are intrinsically related, though governments are often tempted to pursue one without adequate attention to the other. But from a development point of view that approach always fails in the end. The pursuit of growth without a reasonable concern for equity is ultimately socially destabilizing, and often violently so. And the pursuit of equity without a reasonable concern for growth merely tends to redistribute economic stagnation.

Neither pursuit, taken by itself, can lead to sustained, successful development. . . .

Let us be clear about one point. Sustaining the attack on poverty is not economic luxury — something affordable when times are easy, and superfluous when times become troublesome.

It is precisely the opposite. It is a continuing social and moral responsibility, and an economic imperative — its need now is greater than ever. It is true that sluggish economic growth in both the developing and developed nations in the early years of the 1980s may mean that the privileged and affluent in most societies will have to accept slower rates of advance or even some selective reduction in their already favored standard of living. If they have to, they can absorb such inconveniences.

But for the 800 million absolute poor such a downward adjustment is a very different matter. For them downward does not mean inconvenience, but appalling deprivation. They have little margin for austerity. They lie at the very edge of survival already. . . .

All of this illustrates the tragic waste of poverty. If millions of a country's citizens are uneducated, malnourished, and ill, how can they possibly make a reasonable contribution to their nation's economic growth and social advance? The poverty they are immersed in, through no fault of their own, simply denies them that.

As I have pointed out before, it is the poverty itself that is the liability. Not the individuals who happen to be poor. They represent immense human potential.

It used to be said that lack of capital was the chief obstacle to economic growth. But we now know that capital formation explains less than one-third of the variation in growth rates among developing countries. Human resource development explains a great deal more.

Investment in the human potential of the poor, then, is not only morally right; it is very sound economics.

Certainly what is very unsound economics is to permit a culture of poverty to so develop within a nation that it begins to infect and erode the entire social and political fabric.

No government wants to perpetuate poverty. But not all governments, at a time of depressed economic growth, are persuaded that there is much that they can really do against so vast a problem.

But there is.

A number of avenues of attack deserve attention. Today I want to emphasize two that reflect our research of the past year. Both of these are concerned with human resource development. They are: the redesign of social programs to reduce their per capita cost while expanding their coverage; and the restructuring of the total set of social sector programs to establish priorities that take advantage of the linkages and complementarities between them, thereby reducing their overall cost. Unless essential services are both redesigned and reorganized to complement each other, governments will not be able to afford them on the scale required, particularly in periods of austerity.

Our studies confirm the synergistic effects on productivity of actions designed to meet basic needs in each of the five core areas: education, health care, clean water, nutrition, and shelter. Each has linkages to the others. Advance in one contributes to advance in the others, and all contribute to higher output. . . .

Urban employment, particularly in the modern sector, is not only often dependent on the degree of education, but on health and nutrition as well. Workers who are easily fatigued and have low resistance to chronic illness are inefficient, and add substantially to the accident rate, absenteeism, and unnecessary medical expenditure. More serious still, to the extent that their mental capacity has been impaired by malnutrition in childhood, their ability to perform technical tasks is reduced. Dexterity, alertness, and initiative have been drained away.

And yet not only are essential public services often out of reach of the poor, but such facilities as are in place may be so inappropriately designed as to be virtually irrelevant to their needs: impressive four-lane highways, but too few market roads; elaborate curative-care urban hospitals, but too few preventive-care rural clinics; prestigious institutions of higher learning, but too few primary schools and village literacy programs.

Public services that are not designed modestly and at low cost per unit will almost certainly end by serving the privileged few rather than the deprived many.

To reverse this trend, governments must be prepared to make tough and politically sensitive decisions, and to reallocate scarce resources into less elaborate — but more broadly based — delivery systems that can get the services to the poor, and the poor to the services.

The developing countries do not, of course, have the financial and administrative resources at hand today to eliminate rapidly all the inadequacies in education, health, and other public services that penalize the poor. They must — out of very real necessity — be selective in determining where to concentrate their efforts. . . .

PRIMARY EDUCATION

School enrollments throughout the developing world still fall far below the objective of universal primary education for both boys and girls, and this picture is made even worse by dropout rates which are often over 50%.

Research makes it clear that economic returns on primary education for boys are high. This is not always recognized. But I want to emphasize today something much less recognized and understood. And that is the immensely beneficial impact on reducing poverty that results from educating girls.

In most developing societies women simply do not have equitable access to education. The number of illiterate females is growing faster than illiterate males. Nearly two-thirds of the world's illiterates are women, and virtually everywhere males are given preference both for general education and vocational training.

One reason for this is that the prevailing image of women distorts their full contribution to society. Women are esteemed — and are encouraged to esteem themselves — predominantly in their roles as mothers. Their economic contribution, though it is substantial in a number of developing societies, is almost always understated.

The fact is that in subsistence societies women generally do at least 50% of the work connected with agricultural production and processing, as well as take care of the children and the housekeeping.

Schooling clearly enhances a girl's prospects of finding employment outside the home. In a comparative study of 49 countries, the level of female education in each nation demonstrated a significant impact on the proportion of women earning wages or salaries.

Greater educational opportunity for women will also substantially reduce fertility. In Latin America, for example, studies indicate that in districts as diverse as Rio de Janeiro, rural Chile, and Buenos Aires, women who have completed primary school average about two children fewer than those who have not.

Of all the aspects of social development, the educational level appears most consistently associated with lower fertility. And it is significant that an increase in the education of women tends to lower fertility to a greater extent than a similar increase in the education of men. In societies in which rapid population growth is draining away resources, expenditure on education and training for boys that is not matched by comparable expenditure for girls will very likely be diminished in the end by the girls' continued high fertility.

Women represent a seriously undervalued potential in the development process. And to prolong inequitable practices that relegate them exclusively to narrow traditional roles not only denies both them and society the benefits of that potential, but very seriously compounds the problem of reducing poverty.

PRIMARY HEALTH CARE

In the health sector, as well, carefully designed and sharply focused efforts can contribute immensely to an overall antipoverty program.

In most developing countries health expenditures have been heavily concentrated on supplying a small urban elite with expensive curative-care systems — highly skilled doctors and elaborate hospitals — that fail to reach 90% of the people. What are required are less sophisticated, less costly, but more effective preventive-care delivery systems that reach the mass of the population.

Even quite poor countries can succeed in this, provided sound policies are pursued. Some 25 years ago, for example, Sri Lanka decided to improve rural health facilities. As a result of its efforts in health care, along with those in education and in nutrition, there has been over the past two decades a decline in infant mortality to 47 per 1,000, an increase in life expectancy to 69 years, and an associated decline in the crude birth rate to 26.

But many other countries — countries with a much higher per capita national income than Sri Lanka — have spent as much or more on health, and by failing to stress simple, inexpensive, but effective primary care systems, have reaped much poorer results.

Turkey, for example, had a GNP per capita of $1,200 in 1978, compared to Sri Lanka's $190, but has concentrated on urban health, with conventional facilities, and today has an infant mortality rate of 118 per 1,000, life expectancy of 61 years, and a crude birth rate of 32 — all far short of Sri Lanka's accomplishments.

As part of their preventive-care programs, governments should make a special effort to reduce sharply current infant and child mortality rates. Average rates of infant mortality — deaths per 1,000 in the first year — are well above 140 in Africa, and roughly 120 in Asia and 60 in Latin America. In the developed countries they average only about 13.

Why are they so high in the developing world? Largely because of low nutritional standards, poor hygiene, health practices and services. But infant and child mortality rates can be brought down relatively quickly with a combination of redesigned and reoriented health, education, and nutrition policies. And the return in lowered fertility, healthier children, and increased productivity is clearly worth the effort and costs.

The truth is that a basic learning package for both males and females — and particularly for females — and a carefully designed program of primary health care for both the countryside and the cities are investments that no developing country can afford to neglect. . . .

I want to turn now to the role the World Bank itself can play in the 1980s. And to establish the background against which this must be viewed, let me briefly summarize the principal points that emerged earlier in our discussion.

[World Bank Role in the 1980s]

The current account deficits of the oil-importing developing countries have risen dramatically. The increase in these deficits is the mirror image of a portion of the rise in the surpluses of the oil-exporting nations. A major objective of the world's intermediation effort to deal with these surpluses must be to assure that appropriate portions of them flow, directly or indirectly, back to these developing countries.

The assistance the developing societies will need in the 1980s — both to alleviate their burden of absolute poverty, and to facilitate the structural changes in their economies required by the changes in the external environment — is much larger than was projected before the events of the past 18 months.

The developing countries, already financing 90% of their own development efforts, will now have to mobilize substantial additional resources. But they cannot succeed in this enormous task by their own efforts alone. That is why all previously planned programs of international assistance, including that of the Bank, must be reexamined in order to determine how the most urgent needs of the developing world can be met. . . .

Finally, let me turn to the matter of China.

The change in the representation of China in the Bank has increased by nearly a billion the number of people who now have a claim on the Bank's resources. That claim is no less compelling, and their needs are no less urgent than those of the Bank's other members. It will take time to translate these needs into specific Bank projects, but when that has been done it is clear that they will amount to several billion dollars per year.

If we had to accommodate these needs within the lending program planned earlier, we would have to reduce sharply our lending to other member countries. This would seriously disrupt their development programs, and this we must not do. An addition to the lending program is clearly required.

The inescapable conclusion of all these considerations is this: the Bank Group must mobilize substantial additional resources if it is effectively to assist its developing member countries through the critical years of the 1980s. But it must do this in a manner that takes full account of the current budgetary constraints faced by the governments of the developed nations.

What we need to do now is to reach broad agreement on the following objective.

The Bank should:

• Increase its lending program in order to offset fully the higher-than-anticipated inflation levels;

• Finance structural adjustment, but not at the cost of reducing the development finance already planned for the oil-importing developing countries;

• Assist in financing an expanded energy development program, but not at the cost of cutting its assistance to other equally vital programs; and

• Respond to the development needs of China, but not at the cost of its other borrowers.

If we agree on this objective — and I believe we can — then our task is to find the means for financing the expansion in lending without imposing undue burdens on the budgets of our member governments. . . .

The question is how can this best be done, while at the same time fully safeguarding the strength and integrity of the Bank's financial structure?

There are at least three actions that should be considered.

The relationship between the Bank's loans — and hence its outstanding debt — and its equity base could be changed.

The Articles of Agreement, drafted over 35 years ago in immensely different financial circumstances, provide that the Bank's total disbursed and outstanding loans cannot exceed its total subscribed capital and reserves.

The question the Brandt Commission, investment bankers, and other financial experts have been asking us in the Bank is this: in the circumstances of today, as contrasted with those of 1944, does it still make financial sense to limit any increase whatever in the Bank's lending authority to an equal increase in its capital?

The tentative answer appears to be that the 1 to 1 ratio, established at Bretton Woods in the closing months of World War II, is no longer really relevant to the Banks' financial condition or to the economic situation of its principal shareholders, and that the result now is an unnecessary underutilization of the Bank's capital base. . . .

A second possibility would be the organization of a separately capitalized energy affiliate. . . .

A third approach would be to raise the Bank's lending and borrowing authority again, as was done in 1960, by increasing subscribed stock, but without the necessity of additional paid-in capital.

Any one of these three actions, or a combination of them, would make it possible for the Bank to be more responsive to the urgent needs of its developing member countries which were not anticipated when the General Capital Increase was put forward. The variety of means available to equip the Bank to be more responsive should encourage those who, like myself, believe that the current climate of budgetary constraint in the developed nations need not stand in the way of necessary action. . . .

Let me now summarize and conclude the central points I have made this morning.

Summary and Conclusions

Global economic conditions over the past 18 months have become substantially more difficult, and the prospects for growth in the oil-importing development countries during the decade of the 1980s now appear less promising. . . .

Due to your support, and that of the governments you represent, the World Bank over the past ten years has become by far the world's largest and most influential development institution.

That is important.

But what is far more important is what has transpired throughout the developing world in the millions of individual lives that this institution has touched.

What these countless millions of the poor need and want is what each of us needs and wants: the well-being of those they love; a better future for their children; an end to injustice; and a beginning of hope.

We do not see their faces, we do not know their names, we cannot count their number. But they are there. And their lives have been touched by us.

And ours by them.

[Personal Note]

And now — if I may — let me add a purely personal note.

These past 13 years have been the most stimulating of my life. I wouldn't have traded them for anything.

And I want to say to all of you how deeply grateful I am for the privilege of having served with you throughout these years.

This World Bank — born out of the ruins of World War II — has grown into one of the most constructive instruments of human aspiration and progress.

And yet, it has only barely begun to develop its full potential for service and assistance.

There is so much more it can do, so much more it ought to do to assist those who need its help.

Each one of us here can help make that happen.

And how can we begin?

We must begin — as the founders of this great institution began — with vision. With clear, strong, bold vision.

George Bernard Shaw put it perfectly:

"You see things and say why? But I dream things that never were, and I say why not?". . .

DE LAROSIERE STATEMENT

... Three problems dominate the state of the world economy: inflation, energy, and the plight of the non-oil developing countries.

The present level of *inflation* is intolerable, not because of some theoretical preference, but because it undermines the prospect for medium-term economic growth. In the industrial countries, the average rate of increase in consumer prices from 1979 to 1980 is estimated at 12 per cent. This is greater than the 1979 figure (9 per cent), and is close to the highest in recent history (13 per cent in 1974). The inflation record of the developing countries has been far worse — on average, consumer prices in those countries are expected to rise by 35 per cent from 1979 to 1980.

In time inflation destroys the roots of savings and productive investment. Indexing mechanisms engendered by inflation become widespread and elaborate; they accelerate the phenomenon, anesthetize the body politic and the whole society, and postpone the essential policy actions. The primary aim of economic policy must be to bring about and maintain a reduction of inflation and inflationary expectations.

It must be recognized that many countries have noticeably tightened their economic policies since we met in Belgrade last year. These countries have given top priority to the fight against inflation, and elimination of negative real interest rates in most industrial countries is a sign of this awareness. But the member countries that have taken this firm stance against inflation now face a crucial test. Activity is weakening and unemployment is rising in most of the industrial countries; there is a danger that great pressure may now be exerted on national authorities to relax demand management policies.

[Energy Problem]

I come now to the *energy* situation. If we do not address this problem, directly and comprehensively, we will be encouraging economic instability. No anti-inflation effort, no sustained policy of growth, no plan to organize the world's monetary system could succeed if the present energy situation were to persist. The problem of energy has become all-pervasive; measures to deal with it must embrace the whole process of formulating and conducting policies at both the national and international levels.

The energy problem stems primarily from one fact: the present level of oil consumption greatly exceeds rates of production that appear sustainable in the long run. The implications of this for national policies are of great importance. Most of our countries must speed up the process of adjustment to an age of high-cost energy. They must recognize that oil has become an expensive product and is bound to remain so.

This message is underscored by the impact which the steep rise in oil prices during 1979 and 1980 has had on countries' international payments. The combined current account surplus of the oil exporting countries has gone up from $5 billion in 1978 to about $110 billion in 1980; and, as we look ahead to the next few years, it seems likely that this surplus will prove to be longer lasting than in the 1974-78 period.

Unfortunately, it is certain — and I come now to the third problem — that many of the *non-oil developing countries,* in particular, will continue to be sharply affected by international economic developments. The rise in oil prices has reduced, in some cases massively, the foreign exchange available for their imports of other goods. The growth in their exports has been slowed by anti-inflation policies — albeit justified policies — in the industrial countries and by the depressive effects of higher prices of energy in those countries. We are projecting a current account deficit of $80 billion for the non-oil LDCs [less developed countries] in 1981 — higher than this year and more than twice as large as their combined deficit in 1978.

For developing countries where levels of per capita income are already close to the margin of human subsistence, these depressive forces could prove disastrous. . . .

[Assistance to Members]

. . . with flexibility and realism the Fund is endeavoring to make its assistance to members increasingly effective. I am fully aware of the claims by some critics that our policy advice has been too harsh. But this criticism, I believe, is largely misplaced. It is the condition of a country's balance of payments — sometimes in conjunction with the low level of official assistance from abroad — that is the true cause of the harsh adjustment measures that sometimes must be adopted in the attempt to restore its payments equilibrium and to open up prospects of improved future growth.

We have learned from experience how difficult it is to reconcile conflicting claims when countries are forced to cut back on their use of resources. The Fund helps with finance and thereby moderates the severity of the adjustment. But it cannot determine the manner in which the pain of adjustment is distributed within the society. For this extends to the heart of the political process, and there we are vigilant to pay due regard to the domestic social and political objectives, to the economic priorities, and to the individual circumstances of members. There is little that the Fund — or, for that matter, any external agency — can do to help with decisions in this area.

The difficulties associated with many adjustment programs could be eased, or even avoided, if members came to the Fund earlier, before the external situation had become so severe as to require drastic action. It is my hope that the various changes now being introduced into our policies on the use of the Fund's resources will induce members to come to the Fund for assistance whenever needed, and without delay.

[Areas of Stability]

We live in a system that is under strain. There are, nevertheless, important and growing areas of stability and consensus in this system, and I will begin by speaking of these. First, the surge of inflation in the 1970s provoked, or hastened, an increasing awareness of the importance of monetary discipline. By this, I do not mean a naive and mechanistic faith but a growing recognition that continuous monitoring and restraint of monetary expansion is a necessary, though not sufficient, condition for sustainable growth. Monetary targets and the monitoring of monetary aggregates are widespread in the industrial countries, and increasingly so in the developing world. Second, in close relation to this, there has been, over the last two years, a greater degree of stability in the foreign exchange market than most people would have dared to predict. This market has coped remarkably well with large shifts in deficits and surpluses and with other serious international tensions. The European Monetary System is one example of this stability; and, more generally, the principal world currencies have only in rare cases fluctuated beyond a range conducive to appropriate balance of payments adjustment. Third, despite the regrettable failure to decide on the establishment of a substitution account, the Fund's members have reaffirmed their conviction that a strong SDR [special drawing rights] should be the centerpiece of the international monetary system. The recent decision to simplify the SDR to a five-currency basket will increase its use both by the private sector and by official holders. Furthermore, the Interim Committee has just requested the Executive Board to give early attention to the question of adjusting the SDR interest rate to the full market rate and of eliminating the remaining reconstitution requirement. Also, the importance of the SDR as a stable and attractive international reserve asset will continue to be enhanced through the Fund's borrowing activities. . . .

October

MYERS' EXPULSION FROM HOUSE
October 2, 1980

When the last representative had cast his vote, Oct. 2 became a historic day in the U.S. House: For the first time, a colleague had been expelled for corruption. Only three other members of that body had ever been dismissed — all of them 119 years earlier for support of the South during the Civil War.

By its vote, the House was exercising its ultimate disciplinary authority over U.S. representatives. The power of the House and Senate to punish members had been used sparingly over the years, even in less severe forms than outright expulsion. Including the 1980 case, only seven senators, 20 representatives and one territorial delegate had been formally censured for misconduct. Expulsions numbered 15 in the Senate and four in the House.

The House member expelled in 1980 was Rep. Michael J. "Ozzie" Myers, a Pennsylvania Democrat. The charge against him, in the eyes of many colleagues, was simply selling his office for profit. The House's decision grew from an FBI undercover investigation of political corruption in which law enforcement agents, posing as businessmen or wealthy Arabs, attempted to get some members of Congress and other elected officials to use their influence — for pay — for such things as helping Arabs obtain U.S. residency, obtaining federal grants and arranging real estate deals. The probe became known as "Abscam" (for "Arab scam").

Many of the meetings between the agents and the political figures were recorded by hidden videotape cameras. Some of the tapes showed

Myers accepting large amounts of cash. Moreover, a court jury already had convicted Myers of illegality for his actions. The overwhelming evidence left the House little room for a lesser punishment.

FBI Investigation

The FBI investigation had begun in the summer of 1978 as an attempt to lure individuals involved in organized crime into selling stolen securities and art objects to undercover FBI agents. News reports about the Abscam probe began to appear in February 1980. In the weeks afterward, federal grand juries indicted six House members and one senator in connection with the case. Within a year of the original disclosures, all six of the House members had been convicted; the indicted senator was awaiting trial.

Besides Myers, those indicted were Reps. John W. Jenrette Jr., D-S.C.; Richard Kelly, R-Fla.; Raymond F. Lederer, D-Pa.; John M. Murphy, D-N.Y.; Frank Thompson Jr., D-N.J., and Sen. Harrison A. Williams Jr., D-N.J. Of the indicted House members, only Lederer won re-election. The trial of Williams, whose six-year Senate term had two years to run, was set for early 1981.

Convictions

Myers and Jenrette were convicted in separate trials during the summer and fall of 1980. Myers' conviction came Aug. 30 on charges of bribery, conspiracy and interstate travel to aid racketeering. After the trial, jurors said they had been heavily influenced by government videotapes, which offered scenes of the defendant actually taking cash from undercover FBI agents and discussing what services could be performed in return. The tapes, which the public saw on television after the trial, showed Myers accepting an envelope containing $50,000. On the stand, Myers acknowledged that he had accepted money from the undercover agents. However, he maintained he was not bribed because he had never intended to do anything in return for the money.

Jenrette was convicted Oct. 7 following a five-week trial on two counts of bribery and a single count of conspiracy. Convicted along with Jenrette was a business associate, John R. Stowe. During the trial, government prosecutors charged Jenrette and Stowe had accepted $50,000 in cash from an undercover FBI agent. Prosecutors described the payment as the first installment of a $100,000 bribe to be paid the two men in return for a promise from Jenrette to introduce a private immigration bill on behalf of the agent's supposed Arab employer.

"I've got larceny in my blood," jurors saw Jenrette say during a meeting with the agent that was secretly videotaped by the FBI. Jenrette's

attorney attempted to portray the congressman as a drunk with financial problems whom the government lured into committing a crime. Jenrette denied he had ever received any bribe money.

Thompson and Murphy were tried together and found guilty Dec. 3. Thompson was convicted of bribery, conspiracy and receiving an unlawful gratuity. Murphy was cleared of the bribery charge but convicted of conspiracy, acceptance of an outside compensation for the performance of official duties and receiving an unlawful gratuity. Both denied receiving any money.

Lederer was found guilty Jan. 9, 1981, on all four counts in his indictment: bribery, bribery conspiracy, accepting an unlawful gratuity and interstate travel to aid racketeering. Lederer argued that he had been entrapped by the government.

Kelly, the only Republican in the group, was convicted Jan. 26, 1981, of bribery, conspiracy and interstate travel to aid racketeering. Two businessman co-defendants were found guilty of similar charges. During the trial jurors saw videotapes of Kelly stuffing $25,000 into his pockets. Kelly maintained that he accepted the money as part of his own investigation of underworld characters, and that he had been entrapped.

Expulsion, Resignation

The 376-30 vote to expel Myers on Oct. 2 was well above the two-thirds required by the Constitution. The House Committee on Standards of Official Conduct had recommended Myers' expulsion Sept. 24. In its report, the committee said that by "trading a promise of votes and influence for money," Myers had placed "personal greed" above his duties as a House member. The committee said it found Myers' defense that he never intended to do anything in return for the money to be "inherently unbelievable." It added: "Even if we were to accept Mr. Myers' testimony at face value, we still would conclude that his conduct was in violation of the most fundamental standards for congressional conduct."

To head off a similar expulsion effort, Jenrette resigned from the House Dec. 10. The Standards Committee was considering a staff recommendation that Jenrette be given the same punishment as Myers. Jenrette said he was innocent but was resigning "to spare the House further embarrassment. . . ."

Thompson and Murphy, two of the most senior members implicated in the scandal, avoided disciplinary action because the House adjourned Dec. 16 without considering their cases and they were not returning for the 97th Congress. Pending their trials they had been forced by House Democratic Caucus rules to step aside from several chairmanships, including the House Administration Committee (Thompson) and the

Merchant Marine and Fisheries Committee (Murphy). Thompson had taken over the House Administration Committee in 1976 after its chairman, Wayne L. Hays, D-Ohio, resigned from the House in an earlier scandal involving his former mistress, Elizabeth Ray. (Historic Documents of 1976, p. 365)

> *Following are the text of House Resolution 794, calling for the expulsion of Rep. Michael "Ozzie" Myers, D-Pa., and excerpts from the floor debate on H Res 794 prior to its adoption by the House on Oct. 2, 1980.* (Boldface headings in brackets have been added by Congressional Quarterly to highlight the organization of the text.):

HOUSE RESOLUTION 794

Resolved, That, pursuant to article I, section 5, clause 2 of the United States Constitution, Representative Michael J. Myers be, and he hereby is, expelled from the House of Representatives.

OCT. 2 FLOOR DEBATE

[Charles E. Bennett, D-Fla., chairman of the House Committee on Standards of Official Conduct] .... I find this an extremely difficult statement to make. Indeed, calling on this body to expel one of our colleagues is one of the most unpleasant tasks I have faced in many years in Congress. Nevertheless, I submit, Mr. Speaker, based upon the evidence presented at Mr. Myers' criminal trial — at the conclusion of which a jury found him guilty of bribery, conspiracy and violation of the Travel Act — as well as the evidence presented before our committee, this House can appropriately consider no other sanction except expulsion.

The committee, as well as the Federal court jury which convicted Mr. Myers, had available to it and reviewed at length, videotapes, and audiotapes of Mr. Myers' own statements and acts with which he was charged. Moreover, Mr. Myers appeared and testified before our committee and essentially admitted his involvement in what we were forced to conclude were blatant breaches of the rules and indeed of the fundamental integrity of the House of Representatives.

As is by now all too familiar about what happened, in 1978, the FBI began an undercover operation known as Abscam in which FBI agents and an informer posed as representatives of Middle Eastern businessmen or sheiks who were interested in investing in the United States.

On July 26, 1979, Anthony Amoroso, an undercover FBI agent using the name of Tony DeVito held a meeting in Florida to talk about these sheiks with Angelo Errichetti, the mayor of Camden, N.J., and Howard Criden of Pennsylvania, lawyer, and Louis Johanson, his law partner.

Errichetti later told Criden that on a prior occasion he had been paid a substantial fee to introduce the sheiks to a Congressman and he inquired if Criden and Johanson knew any Congressman who would be willing to meet with the sheiks in exchange for a portion of a fee. . . .

[Assistance Offered]

Johanson contacted Congressman Myers, and Myers agreed to the arrangement. Errichetti then informed DeVito that Myers was prepared to "do anything" for the sheiks and a meeting with Myers was arranged.

On August 22, 1979, Myers and Errichetti met with DeVito at the TraveLodge Hotel at Kennedy Airport, N.Y. DeVito described to Myers in general terms the sheiks' desire to insure that if they fled their country, they would be able to enter and remain in the United States, and he asked how Myers could be of assistance in this.

Myers replied, "Where I could be of assistance in this type of a matter, first of all, is private bills that can be introduced." Myers explained that as soon as the sheiks had entered the United States, "I'd have to put a bill in at that point." Elaborating on the process, he indicated that once the bill had been introduced, he would be able to use the hearing process to delay any action for a year or 18 months, after which time it would be much easier to arrange for the sheiks to stay in this country. In addition to the introduction of a private bill, Myers indicated that he knew people in the State Department and volunteered to meet with them when he returned to Washington.

Myers then suggested that the sheiks invest in Myers' district. He said, "That gives me the out that I need to go full guns."

Throughout the meeting, the Congressman repeatedly promised to assist the unidentified sheiks. "I'll be in the man's corner a hundred percent," he said, "and I'll deliver a lot of other people in his corner," he assured DeVito. "Feel free to call me, and, you know, matter of fact, you can come down, we'll meet down in Washington if you want." He also commended DeVito for going about things the right way. "Money talks in this business and bull s--- walks. And it works the same way down in Washington," he explained.

[Money Accepted]

As the meeting drew to a close, Myers again gave his guarantee that he would assist the sheiks. DeVito then handed Myers an envelope containing $50,000 in cash. "Spend it well," DeVito said as Myers accepted the envelope and replied: "Pleasure."

Five months later, on January 24, 1980, two other undercover agents, Michael Wald, using the name of "Michael Cohen" and Ernest Haridopolos, using the name of "Ernie Poulos," met with Myers and Criden at the Barclay Hotel in Philadelphia. Early in the meeting, Cohen raised the subject of the sheiks' immigration problem, indicating that the situation had become worse in the sheiks' country and suggesting that, because of the sheiks' confidence in Myers, they were planning to come to the United States.

Cohen said the sheiks were considering building a $34 million hotel complex in Myers' district, but were concerned about the Mafia and about securing the necessary zoning variances and approval of the city council. Myers agreed to deal with the Mafia on behalf of the sheiks. He also promised to "use his office" to help with zoning variances and the city council, expressing confidence that he could convince the council members from his district to vote in favor of any necessary provisions. He said he would use "my influence, my office, and my personal friendship" with council members, and he assured Cohen that the city council would be no problem. "City council we can handle. Forget city council. Those that we can't handle, we can buy."

Another issue discussed at this meeting was the amount of money Myers had received in the August meeting. Myers expressed some dissatisfaction with the amount that he had received.

Representative Myers testified in his own defense at the criminal trial, and at our committee proceedings. He did not deny having received an envelope containing $50,000 — which he thought was $100,000 — for his personal use. He attempted, however, to explain the circumstances surrounding the receipt of these moneys. In essence, Mr. Myers claimed that in advance of the crucial meetings he was told he was about to engage in play-acting and he would never have to do anything affirmative in return for the money except to make promises.

['Acted Corruptly']

The Committee on Standards of Official Conduct found, as the jury did, that Mr. Myers' story is inherently unbelievable and is contradicted by events revealed in the tapes. Moreover, even if we were to accept Mr. Myers' testimony at face value, we still would conclude that his conduct was in violation of the most fundamental standards for congressional conduct. Mr. Myers has not explained why wealthy foreigners would pay substantial sums of money in return for a wholly fictitious charade if they knew it was a charade, or, if they did not know it was a charade, why Mr. Myers was entitled to take these sums upon promising to use his influence in the performance of his official duties.

The committee can only conclude — as the tapes conclusively show — that Mr. Myers was sincere in his belief that he was dealing with persons willing to pay for his influence as a Representative, that he took money in return for promising to use that influence on their behalf, and that he thereby acted corruptly, in violation of law, and in total disregard of his duties and obligations as spelled out in clauses 1 through 3 of House Rule XLIII. . . .

[Myers' Defense]

Mr. Myers of Pennsylvania . . . When I stand here today, I am going to cut my remarks down, because obviously I am not going to change anybody's mind on how they are going to vote, but I would like to start off, first of all, and say I am sorry I put the House in this position. I do not feel good about it. I told that to the committee, and certainly I owe this House an apology for my action.

But my actions that were viewed on that video tape certainly were not "Ozzie" Myers. That was play-acting from the word "go," and I was following a script which was given to me. I was led into a trap that was cleverly disguised with bait, the bait being: First, money; second, employment for my district; and third, to help a friend land a hotel casino in Atlantic City.

I was set up from the word "go." I cannot change that. I cannot change anybody's feelings, but that is what happened. . . .

. . . I am saying to you that what is on those tapes is play-acting, which I was instructed to do prior to going to those meetings. When you talk about my behavior on the second set of tapes, I was intoxicated, I was drinking FBI bourbon, if you know what that is, big glasses full of it. I could hardly talk. You saw my condition. . . .

Let me just go on now. In closing, I was sitting on the floor. I know what it feels like now to sit on death row. In a way I am awaiting execution, and you, the Members of this body, are the ones who will decide my fate.

As you go to that voting machine to put your cards in, keep in mind, use a comparison when you hit the button, when you vote to expel, that it will have the same effect as hitting the button if I were strapped in an electric chair in this well.

That is all I have to say. . . .

[Expulsion Voted]

Mr. Bennett. Mr. Speaker, every life has its tragedies. The most painful of the tragedies are those that we earn ourselves by our own defects. When the concluding remarks were prepared for me to make in the early part of this statement, there was a sentence, "There can be no other choice of sanctions for such a man." I struck through the phrase "a man" and changed it to read "There can be no other choice of sanctions for such actions."

God never made a bad man or a bad woman. We make our mistakes in life. We have to pay for those mistakes. In this instance, the integrity of the House of Representatives is at stake, an institution which is not only important for our country but for mankind.

So, as painful as it is for me to do this, I must ask the House of Representatives to expel Representative Myers.

Mr. Speaker, I move the previous question on the resolution.

The Speaker [Thomas P. O'Neill Jr., D-Mass.]. The question is on the resolution offered by the gentleman from Florida (Mr. Bennett).

The question was taken.

Mr. Charles H. Wilson of California. Mr. Speaker, at the request of the gentleman from Pennsylvania (Mr. Myers). I demand the yeas and nays.

The yeas and nays were ordered.

The vote was taken by electronic device, and there were — yeas 376, nays 30, not voting 26, as follows: . . .

So (two-thirds having voted in favor thereof) the resolution was agreed to.

The result of the vote was announced as above recorded.

A motion to reconsider was laid on the table.

The Speaker. The Clerk will notify the Governor of the Commonwealth of Pennsylvania of the action of the House.

The matter is closed.

SENATE PROBE REPORT
ON BILLY CARTER'S ACTIVITIES
October 2, 1980

The special Senate Judiciary subcommittee established to investigate the relations of the president's brother with the Libyan government and the Carter administration's handling of the matter concluded Oct. 2 that Billy Carter's conduct "was contrary to the interests of the President and the United States and merits severe criticism." And, although the subcommittee uncovered no evidence that administration officials had engaged in illegal activities, it chided the president and some of his aides for their actions.

The Senate panel, composed of five Democrats and four Republicans, was established after Billy Carter registered as a Libyan agent July 14 and acknowledged that he had received $220,000 from the Libyan government. Critics of the administration charged that the president's brother registered only after he received advance notice that the Justice Department had discovered the payments and was preparing a complaint against him. In exchange for Carter's registration, the department agreed not to pursue criminal or civil actions against him under the Foreign Agents Registration Act.

Background

Carter's dealing with the Libyans went back to September 1980 when he declared himself Libya's friend and announced he would strive to improve ties between the radical Arab state and the United States. He subsequently took two trips to Libya and was the host for a five-week visit by Libyans to the United States. When it was disclosed *that Carter had received money from Libya, he said the $220,000 was a loan; Justice Department officials said the payments amounted to compensation for his representing Libya's interests in the United States. Moreover, Carter tried to set up a deal between the Charter Oil Co. of Jacksonville, Fla., and Libya to help the company obtain more Libyan petroleum. Had the deal been successfully concluded, the financially insecure Carter would have received millions of dollars in commissions.*

The Justice Department learned through intelligence sources of the Libyan payments to Carter in late May and early June. At a June 11 meeting arranged by Billy Carter with Justice Department officials, Carter admitted receiving the money. Carter had denied at a January 1980 interview with representatives of the Justice Department receiving funds from the Libyans; it was later revealed that he had accepted $20,000 from Libya on Dec. 27, 1979.

The subcommittee report said that the Justice Department's investigation was "honestly and conscientiously conducted" without regard to the fact the subject of the investigation was the president's brother. It noted, however, that Attorney General Benjamin R. Civiletti had mentioned the Billy Carter case to the president June 17 — four weeks before the president's brother finally agreed to register as a foreign agent. In that conversation, Civiletti told the president that his brother was "foolish" not to register and advised President Carter that, should his brother register, no criminal charges would be filed. The subcommittee report said it was not improper for the attorney general to discuss Justice Department business with the president, but it added that "the Attorney General should not have made, in that conversation, what amounted to a prediction that criminal proceedings would not be instituted if Billy Carter registered, when the question of whether to bring criminal proceedings had not yet been determined by those in the Department of Justice who were familiar with the facts of the case and primarily responsible for that determination."

Criticism of President

Regarding the president's action, the report said that Carter should have "either issued a public statement or sent a private message to the Libyan government, or both, that Billy Carter did not represent the United States and that the Libyans should not expect to gain any influence in the United States by cultivating their relationship with him." The report added that the president was "ill-advised" in his decision to use his brother's contacts with Libya to set up a Nov. 27, 1979, meeting between Zbigniew Brzezinski, the national security adviser, and Ali A. El-Houderi, Libya's representative in Washington. The goal was to enlist Libya's help in resolving the hostage crisis in Iran. Billy Carter's role as a diplomatic intermediary, the report said, enhanced his stature with Tripoli and appeared to "confer a measure of presidential condonation on his relationship with the Libyans.... [who were likely to attach significance to the fact] ... that the President would involve his brother in an important matter of state."

Following are excerpts from the report of the Special Senate Judiciary Subcommittee, released Oct. 2, 1980, on Billy Carter's Libyan dealings and the Carter administration's handling of the matter:

Conclusions

It has been an objective of the Subcommittee to agree on a set of conclusions. While there will be a number of additional statements, the members of the Subcommittee agree to the following:

I

Libyan officials went to considerable trouble and expense in establishing and maintaining a relationship with Billy Carter. The initial contact was the result of persistent efforts and a devious series of personal contacts aided by the participation of an important Libyan official. The relationship was then cultivated not only through personal participation by important Libyan officials and expense-paid trips but by holding out the prospect of a highly lucrative oil commission arrangement and a large loan, as well as the actual transfers of large sums of money.

The Libyan plan to establish a relationship with Billy Carter may have received its original impetus from the Libyan program aimed at influencing U.S. policy through people-to-people contacts, which is described earlier in this report. Enlisting Billy Carter as a spokesman supportive of Libya and its policies and conduct might have been viewed as aid to Libya's public relations effort. Billy Carter's usefulness for this purpose soon ended, however, and surely did not extend beyond early 1979, when it became apparent that he would not be effective as a salesman of the Libyan cause to the American people. Other purposes must have remained, because the remarkable relationship between important Libyan officials and the brother of the President of the United States continued, and the Libyans eventually conferred substantial pecuniary benefits upon him and held out to him the possibility of even greater financial rewards.

To a large degree the other possible Libyan purposes must be left to inference. Among the diverse advantages the relationship may have provided for the Libyans were an avenue by which communications between them and the President might be facilitated should the opportunity and need arise, a means of embarrassing the United States or the President at an opportune time, and, perhaps, opportunities to obtain through friendly conversations with Billy Carter insights into the personality of the President. We can assume with some assurance that the Libyan purpose in creating and maintaining the relationship was to benefit the Libyan government and Libyan policy.

The Subcommittee believes that operation of the Foreign Agents Registration Act in this instance served the valid objective of requiring public disclosure. The Department of Justice correctly rejected the view that Billy Carter's oil commission arrangement with the Charter Crude Oil Company was an ordinary commercial arrangement. Rather, the arrangement with Charter was the basis for a benefit which the Libyan government could bestow on Billy Carter whenever Libya concluded that its needs would thereby be served. The Subcommittee also believes that the payments totaling $220,000 by Libya to Billy Carter are additional indicia of the influence or control by Libya over him. This is so whether the payments are viewed as compensation for services rendered or to be rendered by Billy Carter for Libya, or as a major financial obligation which Billy Carter must satisfy to a nation whose interests are often inimical to ours.

II

Billy Carter was repeatedly warned, by friends, officials, and his brother, that his actions could embarrass the United States. The potential for embarrassment was increased by his failure to inform the government officials whom he contacted, particularly those in the White House, that he was negotiating for oil allocations and a large loan from the Libyans and in fact received substantial sums of money from them. Billy Carter was repeatedly advised about the duty of a foreign agent to register, yet he failed to register. His conduct was contrary to the interests of the President and the United States and merits severe criticism.

III

The Subcommittee concludes that the Justice Department's investigation of Billy Carter would have proceeded with considerably more dispatch if the Foreign Agents Registration Act [FARA] had provided authority for adequate investigative tools, if the subject had been more cooperative, and if relevant intelligence information known to intelligence gathering agencies of the government had been provided to the Criminal Division's FARA unit within a reasonable time after it became available. It should be noted, however, in considering the time consumed between the opening of the file by the FARA unit in January, 1979, and the registration and the entry of the consent judgment on July 14, 1980, that some of the most important relevant events did not occur until late 1979 and 1980. Nevertheless, the case could have been brought to a conclusion substantially earlier if any or all of the obstacles described below had not been present.

The Act does not provide for administrative subpoenas or civil investigative demands. Short of the commencement of a civil action and discovery under the Federal Rules of Civil Procedure, the only way to obtain information about the activities of an uncooperative subject is to utilize a grand jury, a drastic step that ordinarily will not be taken unless some evidence of agency is available. It is also noteworthy that FARA enforcement is given a low priority by the department of Justice and the staff of the FARA unit is small in relation to the number of registrations and investigations for which it is responsible, although there is no direct evidence that these conditions were responsible for any part of the delay in the Billy Carter case.

Billy Carter was not a cooperative subject. He repeatedly ignored letters from the Department. When interviewed in January, 1980, he did not disclose important information, including his receipt of $20,000 from Libya on December 27, 1979. Neither the payments, totalling $220,000 by April, nor the oil allocation negotiations were disclosed by him until June 11, and even then they were disclosed only when the interviewers indicated they had other information inconsistent with his initial denials. Even after disclosing the payments, he asserted that the $20,000 payment, which he later testified was a loan, was partial reimbursement for advances on behalf of the Libyans. Some delay in the progress of the investigation is attributable to Phillip J. Wise, Jr., the President's Appointments Secretary, who was less cooperative than he should have been in returning calls by an FBI agent seeking to reinterview him and professed not to remember events relevant to the investigation which he could reasonably have been expected to remember.

When the Attorney General [Benjamin R. Civiletti] failed to share the classified information that came to him in April, 1980, with any trustworthy subordinate who had the necessary security clearance, he did so without attempting to learn whether the Department had available to it other information which might have permitted it to make investigative use of the April, 1980 intelligence. A call by the Attorney General for information may have elicited the fact that the FBI had information from intelligence channels as early as November and December 1979, that Billy Carter was trying both to negotiate a loan from the Libyans and to arrange for a Libyan crude oil contract on behalf of the Charter Crude Oil Company. When brought together, these several items of intelligence information might have been usable in the investigation without compromising sources and were in fact so used, together with other intelligence information, in June, 1980, when investigators confronted Billy Carter with an assertion of knowledge that he had received payments from Libya.

The Subcommittee concludes that the investigation was honestly and conscientiously conducted by the Criminal Division. Moreover, we believe the disposition of the Billy Carter case as a civil rather than a criminal proceeding was the result of an honest judgment on the merits by the officials who participated in that decision. There is no evidence that either the investigation or disposition of the case by the Criminal Division was skewed in favor of Billy Carter because he is the brother of the President.

IV

The Subcommittee has found no evidence that the decisions of the Department of Commerce and the Department of State with respect to export licenses for aircraft or motor vehicles sold to Libya were made other than on the merits of the proposed licenses. Nor has the Subcommittee found evidence that the White House attempted to alter those decisions by reason of any act of Billy Carter. Although concern may have existed in some quarters that a decision to grant an export license might erroneously be attributed to Billy Carter's influence, it has not been established that any decision was affected by such a concern.

V

In April, 1979, the President had made one of several attempts to dissuade Billy Carter from making a return trip to Libya by stating in a letter to him that such a trip "would create severe problems for us because of their threats against Sadat and because they are fighting in Uganda for Idi Amin." Billy Carter nevertheless announced in July, 1979, that he intended to return to Libya. There was some sentiment among White House staff personnel favoring advising the President to try to dissuade Billy Carter from making the trip, but the President does not recall receiving advice from any staff member concerning Billy Carter's planned trip to Libya. The President did not make a further effort to dissuade Billy Carter from making the trip. Neither did the President make a public announcement disassociating himself and the administration from Billy Carter's visit to Libya, an omission that was exacerbated by Billy Carter's attendance at the celebration of the tenth anniversary of the Libyan Revolution, which was also attended by terrorist leaders and a number of representatives of radical governments. Nor did the President send an appropriate similar private message to the Libyan government. The Department of State was instructed, however, that the trip should be treated as a private one.

The Subcommittee recognizes the difficulty of dissuading Billy Carter. However, the Subcommittee concludes that having failed to dissuade him from returning to Libya, the President should have either issued a public statement or sent a private message to the Libyan government, or both, that Billy Carter did not represent the United States and that the Libyans should not expect to gain any influence in the United States by cultivating their relationship with him.

VI

The decision to involve Billy Carter in the hostage crisis was made and carried out in haste. The decision was made despite the known facts that diplomatic initiatives already underway to persuade Libya to take a position on the seizure of the hostages had borne some fruit and that relations between the Iranians and Libyan leaders were strained because of the Iranian belief that the Libyan government was responsible for the murder of a Shiite religious leader. The reasons for the decision are stated by the President and Dr. Brzezinski [the president's national security adviser] in the August 4 Report and in the testimony of Dr. Brzezinski before the Subcommittee. There is no evidence that in making the decision consideration was given to a number of negative factors which the Subcommittee believes should have been given careful consideration. They include the following:

(a) A predictable effect of using Billy Carter would be to confer a measure of presidential condonation on his relationship with the Libyans.

(b) Another predictable effect would be to enhance Billy Carter's stature and prestige with the Libyans. It was likely that they would attach significance to the fact that the relationship between the brothers was such that the President would involve his brother in an important matter of state.

(c) Serious questions concerning Billy Carter's judgment, his lack of concern for whether his conduct would embarrass the President or the country, and his primary concern for his own self-interest had been raised by his previous conduct in establishing his relationship with the Libyans and maintaining it in the face of admonitions from the President.

(d) The enhancement of Billy Carter's importance in the eyes of the Libyans might be exploited by him for his own economic advantage. This possibility was made more serious by the financial difficulties that, as the President knew, Billy Carter was experiencing.

The Subcommittee believes that full and careful reflection leads to the conclusion that the decision to use Billy Carter in the hostage crisis was ill-advised in light of those risks and the available means of communication between our government and that of Libya.

VII

As events showed, Billy Carter's telephonic communications concerning proposed transactions involving Libya from which he would receive economic benefits increased dramatically immediately after the November 27, 1979, meeting and continued at a relatively high level. On December 27, 1979, the Libyan government paid him $20,000. On April 7, 1980, he received another $200,000. The Libyan government appears to have held out the promise of an increased oil allotment well beyond that date.

Whether there was in fact a relationship between these events and Billy Carter's involvement in the hostage situation is a question that perhaps only the Libyan officials could answer. The appearance of a relationship that arises from the circumstances is, however, unfortunate.

VIII

When Admiral Turner [the CIA director] decided to furnish the intelligence report received by him in March, 1980, only to Dr. Brzezinski with the request that it be shown to the President, he denied another intelligence element [the] missing portions of the information, which were unknown to it and which it had requested. He thus decided that the information had no utility for intelligence purposes. In so doing he did not consult with the other intelligence element, which had called for the missing portions but had not received them; he thus preempted the professional judgment of the other element that the information combined with the missing portions might have an intelligence use and indeed may have been referred to the FBI.

Admiral Turner also decided not to refer the information to the Attorney General based on his view that the information was not useful for law enforcement purposes. Admiral Turner made these decisions without calling for other information that might have been available within the intelligence community, and in fact was available. That information might well have had a material bearing on both decisions.

IX

Dr. Brzezinski testified that after receiving the intelligence information from Admiral Turner on March 31, 1980, he spoke to Billy Carter by telephone and then reported both the information and the telephone conversation to the President. The President's recollection is also that Dr. Brzezinski told him in a single conversation of both the information and the telephone conversation. If these recollections are accurate, then Dr. Brzezinski (a) took it upon himself, without consulting the President or appropriate intelligence officials, such as the Director of the FBI [William H. Webster], to do an act outside his normal functions as National Security Adviser that should have been done, if at all, only with their authority, and (b) kept to himself significant information about the President's brother for nearly two days, during which time he had met alone with the President at least once on an occasion when Dr. Brzezinski's handwritten note shows he intended to discuss it.

The Subcommittee concludes that communicating a portion of the intelligence information to Billy Carter, the subject of the information, carried with it the significant risk that sources could have been compromised. It was Dr. Brzezinski's belief that he was not compromising the sources. It will be recalled that Attorney General Civiletti determined that the same intelligence information, and another item of intelligence information as well, were so sensitive that he should not communicate any portion of the information to his most trusted subordinates, who had the requisite clearance for receiving classified information. Communicating the information to Billy Carter also involved the risk that he would take measures to make his activities more difficult for FARA investigators to discover and, in the event of a civil or criminal action, more difficult for the government to prove.

It is to be noted that within two weeks after receiving Dr. Brzezinski's admonition, Billy Carter accepted $200,000 from the Libyan government.

The Subcommittee reaches no conclusion as to whether, once having communicated the information to Billy Carter and admonished him to desist, and he having rejected the admonition, the President or Dr. Brzezinski should have made further efforts to dissuade Billy from the oil enterprise.

X

The Subcommittee questions the judgment of the Attorney General in withholding the substance of the intelligence information contained in the two items received by him in April, 1980, from a subordinate with knowledge of the case and the requisite security clearances and trustworthiness. The Subcommittee believes it likely that at least some of the information could have been used in some manner and in some degree by law enforcement personnel without compromising the sources. The Attorney General did not have knowledge of the facts which had been developed in the investigation and should have consulted with someone who did before making his decision. A judgment as to the usefulness of the intelligence information, and whether it could have been used without jeopardizing sources and methods, could have been best made by or in consultation with a person who knew the facts thus far developed in the investigation, and with the assistance of an intelligence expert.

The Subcommittee believes that the Billy Carter case would have come to an earlier conclusion if the Attorney General had shared the information with a subordinate having knowledge of the case.

The Subcommittee finds persuasive the evidence that the Attorney General did direct his subordinates on June 11, 1980, to take no action for ten days, by which he meant that no step should be taken toward disposition, such as presentation to a grand jury, but not that investigative activities should be halted. The Subcommittee makes no determination as to the reason for that direction. It is to be noted that within the ten-day period he held the conversation with the President described in the next Conclusion. The Subcommittee concludes that the direction to the Justice Department attorneys did not affect the manner in which the Criminal Division completed the investigation.

XI

The Attorney General talked with the President about the Billy Carter case on June 17, 1980. The Subcommittee concludes that it would not have been improper for the Attorney General to advise the President of significant information received by the Department of Justice about Billy Carter's activities promptly upon the receipt and analysis of that information. As pointed out in Conclusion XII below, the President should receive significant information relevant to the exercise of his constitutional responsibilities with respect to both foreign relations and law enforcement, even if that information pertains to a member of his family.

The Subcommittee also concludes, however, that the Attorney General should not have made, in that conversation, what amounted to a prediction that criminal proceedings would not be instituted if Billy Carter registered, when the question of whether to bring criminal proceedings had not yet been determined by those in the Department of Justice who were familiar with the facts of the case and primarily responsible for that determination. It should also be noted that, although the alternative of criminal prosecution seems to have been carefully weighed in the Billy Carter case, the history of the Department's enforcement of FARA since the amendment of the Act in 1966 to provide for a civil remedy has been that, when a subject has registered, a criminal prosecution has not been brought.

XII

Prior conclusions have treated the officers of the Executive Branch separately. Their actions have some similarities. One is that the Attorney General, Admiral Turner, and Dr. Brzezinski all made decisions about the use of intelligence information without calling for the facts available to the organizations they head, or to the government generally, which may have enabled them to make more fully informed judgments. This unwillingness of key officials to draw on the talents and knowledge of the organizations they head is a matter of significant concern to the Subcommittee. In saying this we recognize that from time to time circumstances may arise in which top officials with intelligence re-sponsibilities, including the Attorney General, could reasonably conclude that the responsible treatment of intelligence information, including the protection of vital sources and methods, require that they take direct and individual action with the information they receive. While we have in the Conclusions above stated our views as to this case, we do not wish to prejudge the informed discretion of intelligence officers in cases which may arise in the future.

916

A second similarity is that while the Attorney General and Dr. Brzezinski handled, in quite different manners, the information they received, their treatment of the information had one important element in common. The President has the constitutional responsibility to conduct the foreign policy of the United States, as well as the responsibility to take care that the laws are faithfully executed. The Assistant to the President for National Security Affairs advises with respect to the President's foreign policy responsibilities, and the Attorney General is the President's principal legal adviser. By himself neither possesses the range of responsibilities which the President has and which were implicated in this matter. Yet, neither saw it to be his responsibility to present to the President for decision the issues arising from the intelligence information each had received. Both Dr. Brzezinski, by not consulting with the President before calling Billy Carter, and the Attorney General, by not informing the President of the intelligence information brought to him in April, acted to protect the President from taking personal responsibility for the proper course of conduct in a situation which involved both foreign policy and law enforcement aspects.

XIII

The Subcommittee has not undertaken a thorough study of the several legislative problems identified during the course of the investigation. These problems are as follows:

(a) The inadequacy of the civil investigative procedures available under FARA prior to the filing of suit, and the need for provisions for civil investigative demands or administrative subpoenas, which, as a matter relating to implementation, is an appropriate subject for consideration by the Committee on the Judiciary.

(b) A possible need for improved procedures for coordination and centralized availability in the intelligence community of information gathered for either intelligence purposes or national-security-related law enforcement and usable for the other purpose, which is an appropriate subject for consideration by the Select Committee on Intelligence.

(c) A possible need for improved coordination and clearer allocation of responsibility between the National Security Council and the State Department, a subject that has received and will no doubt continue to receive the attention of the Committee on Foreign Relations.

CARTER-REAGAN DEBATE

October 28, 1980

After months of wrangling between their campaign advisers, the Democratic and Republican presidential candidates, President Jimmy Carter and Ronald Reagan, met in a nationally televised debate held in Cleveland, Ohio, Oct. 28. Held just one week before the election, the debate had been believed critically important for both men. Most national polls reported the candidates neck and neck, and Carter and Reagan each hoped that a successful debate would provide a last-minute boost to his candidacy.

The Cleveland debate was the second of the campaign. Reagan met independent candidate John Anderson Sept. 21 in Baltimore in a debate sponsored by the League of Women Voters. In the Cleveland exchange, also sponsored by the League, Anderson was excluded because his standing in the polls had dropped and because Carter had steadfastly refused to participate in a debate with the Illinois representative. (Anderson-Reagan debate, p. 847)

In the aftermath of Reagan's landslide victory in the Nov. 4 election, polls showed that the debate had been a major factor in a massive shift of votes away from Carter in the final days of the campaign.

120 Million Viewers

Unlike the Baltimore debate, the Cleveland session allowed journalists on the panel to ask follow-up questions and permitted exchanges and rebuttals between the candidates. Ninety minutes long, the debate was

*broadcast to an audience estimated as large as 120 million viewers.
The journalists on the panel were Marvin Stone, editor of U.S. News
& World Report, Harry Ellis of the Christian Science Monitor, William
Hilliard, assistant managing editor of the Portland Oregonian, and Bar-
bara Walters of ABC News. The moderator was Howard K. Smith,
also of ABC News.*

*In the only face-to-face confrontation between the major candidates,
President Carter tried to keep his opponent on guard by directing the
discussion toward Reagan's alleged readiness to rely on U.S. military
power to resolve international crises while deflecting attention away
from his administration's attempts to revive the faltering economy. Yet
the president's strategy apparently failed. Many observers said they
thought Reagan gained an edge by appearing friendly, reasonable and
even-tempered while responding to Carter's attacks.*

National Security Issues

*During the course of the debate, neither candidate missed an op-
portunity to criticize his opponent or point out differences in their
positions. Responding to a question about national security, Reagan
attacked the Carter administration's record and added, "I believe with
all my heart that our first priority must be world peace, and that
use of force is always and only a last resort, when everything else has
failed. . . ."*

*In rebuttal to the president's claim that his administration had reversed
a trend in the preceding Republican administrations of reducing military
expenditures, Reagan charged that Carter blocked or delayed the production of the B-1 bomber, the Cruise missile, the Trident submarine
and the Minuteman missile. Carter, in response, brought up a point
he would stress throughout the debate; he said, "I think, habitually,
Governor Reagan has advocated the injection of military forces into
troubled areas, when I and my predecessors — both Democrats and
Republicans — have advocated resolving those troubles in those difficult
areas of the world peacefully, diplomatically, and through negotiation."*

Economic Issues

*The candidates went on to disagree on economic issues, Carter de-
scribing a large tax cut, endorsed by Reagan, favored by "supply-side"
economists and embodied in the so-called Kemp-Roth tax proposal,
as "ridiculous." Carter added that the Republican nominee's proposal
to do away with the minimum wage to combat inflation was "a heartless
kind of approach to the working families of our country. . . ." And when
Carter attacked Reagan's economic policies during his tenure as governor
of California, Reagan replied, "our spending in California increased*

less per capita than the spending in Georgia while Mr. Carter was governor of Georgia in the same four years. The size of government increased only one-sixth in California of what it increased in proportion to the population in Georgia."

SALT II Treaty

President Carter attacked Reagan's opposition to the strategic arms limitation treaty (SALT II) as a "very dangerous and disturbing thing." Reagan's suggestion that SALT II be renegotiated, he added, reflected an attitude that "is extremely dangerous and belligerent in its tone, although it's said with a quiet voice." Reagan replied that the president's reaction to his call for a new round of arms limitation talks reminded him of "the witch doctor that gets mad when a good doctor comes along with a cure that'll work." Carter also attacked his rival's opposition to the equal rights amendment, forcing Reagan to defend himself while Carter made an appeal to Southerners, women and members of minority groups.

In his closing statement, Carter claimed he was a mainstream Democrat who endorsed national strength, human rights and peace. Reagan posed several questions in his final declaration, asking voters," ... are you better off than you were four years ago? Is it easier for you to go and buy things in the stores than it was four years ago? Is there more or less unemployment in the country than there was four years ago? ..."

> *Following is the transcript of the debate between presidential candidates Jimmy Carter and Ronald Reagan in Cleveland, Ohio, Oct. 28, 1980. (Boldface headings in brackets have been added by Congressional Quarterly to highlight the organization of the text.):*

Hinerfeld: Good evening. I'm Ruth Hinerfeld of the League of Women Voters Education Fund. Next Tuesday is Election Day. Before going to the polls, voters want to understand the issues and know the candidates' positions. Tonight, voters will have an opportunity to see and hear the major party candidates for the Presidency state their views on issues that affect us all. The League of Women Voters is proud to present this Presidential Debate. Our moderator is Howard K. Smith.

Smith: Thank you, Mrs. Hinerfeld. The League of Women Voters is pleased to welcome to the Cleveland Ohio Convention Center Music Hall President Jimmy Carter, the Democratic Party's candidate for reelection to the Presidency, and Governor Ronald Reagan of California, the Republican Party's candidate for the Presidency. The candidates will debate questions on domestic, economic, foreign policy, and national security issues.

The questions are going to be posed by a panel of distinguished journalists who are here with me. They are: Marvin Stone, the editor of U.S. News & World Report; Harry Ellis, national correspondent of the Christian Science Monitor; William Hilliard, assistant managing editor of the Portland Oregonian; Barbara Walters, correspondent, ABC News.

The ground rules for this, as agreed by you gentlemen, are these: Each panelist down here will ask a question, the same question, to each of the two candidates. After the two candidates have answered, a panelist will ask follow-up questions to try to sharpen the answers. The candidates will then have an opportunity each to make a rebuttal. That will constitute the first half of the debate, and I will state the rules for the second half later on.

Some other rules: The candidates are not permitted to bring prepared notes to the podium, but are permitted to make notes during the debate. If the candidates exceed the allotted time agreed on, I will reluctantly but certainly interrupt. We ask the Convention Center audience here to abide by one ground rule. Please do not applaud or express approval or disapproval during the debate.

Now, based on the toss of the coin, Governor Reagan will respond to the first question from Marvin Stone.

[Use of Military Power]

Stone: Governor, as you're well aware, the question of war and peace has emerged as a central issue in this campaign in the give and take of recent weeks. President Carter has been criticized for responding late to aggressive Soviet impulses, for insufficient build-up of our armed forces, and a paralysis in dealing with Afghanistan and Iran. You have been criticized for being all too quick to advocate the use of lots of muscle — military action — to deal with foreign crises. Specifically, what are the differences between the two of you on the uses of American military power?

Reagan: I don't know what the differences might be, because I don't know what Mr. Carter's policies are. I do know what he has said about mine. And I'm only here to tell you that I believe with all my heart that our first priority must be world peace, and that use of force is always and only a last resort, when everything else has failed, and then only with regard to our national security.

Now, I believe, also, that this meeting . . . this mission, this responsibility for preserving the peace, which I believe is a responsibility peculiar to our country, and that we cannot shirk our responsibility as a leader of the Free World because we're the only ones that can do it. Therefore, the burden of maintaining the peace falls on us. And to maintain that peace requires strength. America has never gotten in a war because we were too strong. We can get into a war by letting events get out of hand, as they have in the last three and a half years under the foreign policies of this Administration of Mr. Carter's, until we're faced each time with a crisis. And good management in preserving the peace requires that we control the events and try to intercept before they become a crisis.

I have seen four wars in my lifetime. I'm a father of sons; I have a grandson. I don't ever want to see another generation of young Americans bleed their lives into sandy beachheads in the Pacific, or rice paddies and jungles in the . . . in Asia or the muddy battlefields of Europe.

Smith: Mr. Stone, do you have a follow-up question for the Governor?

Stone: Yes. Governor, we've been hearing that the defense build-up that you would associate yourself with would cost tens of billions of dollars more than is now contemplated. Assuming that the American people are ready to bear this cost, they nevertheless keep asking the following question: How do you reconcile huge increases in military outlays with your promise of substantial tax cuts and of balancing the budget, which in this fiscal year, the one that just ended, ran more than $60 billion in the red?

Reagan: Mr. Stone, I have submitted an economic plan that I have worked out in concert with a number of fine economists in this country, all of whom approve it, and believe that over a five year projection, this plan can permit the extra spending for needed refurbishing of our defensive posture, that it can provide for a balanced budget by 1983 if not earlier, and that we can afford — along with the cuts that I have proposed in Government spending — we can afford the tax cuts I have proposed and probably mainly because Mr. Carter's economic policy has built into the next five years, and on beyond that, a tax increase that will be taking $86 billion more out of the people's pockets than was taken this year. And my tax cut does not come close to eliminating that $86 billion increase. I'm only reducing the amount of the increase. In other words, what I'm talking about is not putting government back to getting less money than government's been getting, but simply cutting the increase in . . . in spending.

Smith: The same question now goes to President Carter. President Carter, would you like to have the question repeated?

Stone: Yes, President Carter, the question of war and peace, a central issue in this campaign. You've been criticized for, in the give and take, for responding late to aggressive Soviet impulses, for an insufficient build-up of our armed forces, and a paralysis in dealing with Afghanistan and Iran. Governor Reagan, on the other hand, has been criticized for being all too quick to advocate the use of lots of muscle — military action — to deal with foreign crises such as I have mentioned. Specifically, what are the differences between the two of you on the uses of American military power?

Carter: Mr. Stone, I've had to make thousands of decisions since I've been President, serving in the Oval Office. And with each one of those decisions that affect the future of my country, I have learned in the process. I think I'm a much wiser and more experienced man than I was when I debated four years ago against President Ford. I've also learned that there are no simple answers to complicated questions. H. L. Mencken said that for every problem there's a simple answer. It would be neat and plausible and wrong.

The fact is that this nation, in the eight years before I became President, had its own military strength decreased. Seven out of eight years, the budget commitments for defense went down, 37% in all. Since I've been in office, we've had a steady, carefully planned, methodical but very effective increase in our commitment for defense.

But what we've done is use that enormous power and prestige and military strength of the United States to preserve the peace. We've not only kept peace for our own country, but we've been able to extend the benefits of peace to others. In the Middle East, we've worked for a peace treaty between Israel and Egypt, successfully, and have tied ourselves together with Israel and Egypt in a common defense capability. This is a very good step forward for our nation's security, and we'll continue to do as we have done in the past.

I might also add that there are decisions that are made in the Oval Office by every President which are profound in nature. There are always trouble spots in the world, and how those troubled areas are addressed by a President alone in that Oval Office affects our nation directly, the involvement of the United States and also our American interests. That is a basic decision that has to be made so frequently, by every President who serves. That is what I have tried to do successfully by keeping our country at peace.

Smith: Mr. Stone, do you have a follow-up for. . . ?

Stone: Yes. I would like to be a little more specific on the use of military power, and let's talk about one area for a moment. Under what circumstances would you use military forces to deal with, for example, a shut-off of the Persian Oil Gulf [sic], if that should occur, or to counter Russian expansion beyond Afghanistan into either Iran or Pakistan? I ask this question in view of charges that we are woefully unprepared to project sustained — and I emphasize the word sustained — power in that part of the world.

Carter: Mr. Stone, in my State of the Union address earlier this year, I pointed out that any threat to the stability or security of the Persian Gulf would be a threat to the security of our own country. In the past, we have not had an adequate military presence in that region. Now we have two major carrier task forces. We have access to facilities in five different areas of that region. And we've made it clear that working with our allies and others, that we are prepared to address any foreseeable eventuality which might interrupt commerce with that crucial area of the world.

But in doing this, we have made sure that we address this question peacefully, not injecting American military forces into combat, but letting the strength of our nation be felt in a beneficial way. This, I believe, has assured that our interests will be protected in the Persian Gulf region, as we have done in the Middle East and throughout the world.

Smith: Governor Reagan, you have a minute to comment or rebut.

Reagan: Well yes, I question the figure about the decline in defense spending under the two previous Administrations in the preceding eight years to this Administration. I would call to your attention that we were in a war that wound down during those eight years, which of course made a change in military spending because of turning from war to peace. I also would like to point out that Republican presidents in those years, faced with a Democratic majority in both houses of the Congress, found that their requests for defense budgets were very often cut.

Now, Gerald Ford left a five-year projected plan for a military build-up to restore our defenses, and President Carter's Administration reduced that by 38%, cut 60 ships out of the Navy building program that had been proposed, and stopped the ... the B-1, delayed the Cruise missile, stopped the production line for the Minuteman missile, stopped the Trident or delayed the Trident submarine, and now is planning a mobile military force that can be delivered to various spots in the world, which does make me question his assaults on whether I am the one who is quick to look for use of force.

Smith: President Carter, you have the last word on this question.

Carter: Well, there are various elements of defense. One is to control nuclear weapons, which I hope we'll get to later on because that is the most important single issue in this campaign. Another one is how to address troubled areas of the world. I think, habitually, Governor Reagan has advocated the injection of military forces into troubled areas, when I and my predecessors — both Democrats and Republicans — have advocated resolving those troubles in those difficult areas of the world peacefully, diplomatically, and through negotiation. In addition to that, the build-up of military forces is good for our country because we've got to have military strength to preserve the peace. But I'll always remember that the best weapons are the ones that are never fired in combat, and the best soldier is one who never has to lay his life down on the field of battle. Strength is imperative for peace, but the two must go hand in hand.

Smith: Thank you gentlemen. The next question is from Harry Ellis to President Carter.

[Inflation and Government Spending]

Ellis: Mr. President, when you were elected in 1976, the Consumer Price Index stood at 4.8%. It now stands at more than 12%. Perhaps more significantly, the nation's broader, underlying inflation rate has gone up from 7% to 9%. Now, a part of that was due to external factors beyond U.S. control, notably the more than doubling of oil prices by OPEC last year. Because the United States remains vulnerable to such external shocks, can inflation in fact be controlled? If so, what measures would you pursue in a second term?

Carter: Again it's important to put the situation in perspective. In 1974, we had a so-called oil shock, wherein the price of OPEC oil was raised to an extraordinary degree. We had an even worse oil shock in 1979. In 1974, we had the worst recession, the deepest and most penetrating recession since the Second World War. The recession that resulted this time was the briefest since the Second World War.

In addition, we've brought down inflation. Earlier this year, in the first quarter, we did have a very severe inflation pressure brought about by the OPEC price increase. It averaged about 18% in the first quarter of this year. In the second quarter, we had dropped it down to about 13%. The most recent figures, the last three months, on the third quarter of this year, the inflation rate is 7% — still too high, but it illustrates very vividly that in addition to providing an enormous number of jobs — nine million new jobs in the last three and a half years — that the inflationary threat is still urgent on us.

I notice that Governor Reagan recently mentioned the Reagan-Kemp-Roth proposal, which his own running mate, George Bush, described as voodoo economics, and said that it would result in a 30% inflation rate. And Business Week, which is not a Democratic publication, said that this Reagan-Kemp-Roth proposal — and I quote them, I think — was completely irresponsible and would result in inflationary pressures which would destroy this nation.

So our proposals are very sound and very carefully considered to stimulate jobs, to improve the industrial complex of this country, to create tools for American workers, and at the same time would be anti-inflationary in nature. So to add nine million new jobs, to control inflation, and to plan for the future with an energy policy now intact as a foundation is our plan for the years ahead.

Smith: Mr. Ellis, do you have a follow-up question for Mr. Carter?

Ellis: Yes. Mr. President, you have mentioned the creation of nine million new jobs. At the same time, the unemployment rate still hangs high, as does the inflation rate. Now, I wonder, can you tell us what additional policies you would pursue in a second administration in order to try to bring down that inflation rate? And would it be an act of leadership to tell the American people they are going to have to sacrifice to adopt a leaner lifestyle for some time to come?

Carter: Yes. We have demanded that the American people sacrifice, and they have done very well. As a matter of fact, we're importing today about one-third less oil from overseas than we did just a year ago. We've had a 25% reduction since the first year I was in office. At the same time, as I have said earlier, we have added about nine million net new jobs in that period of time — a record never before achieved.

Also, the new energy policy has been predicated on two factors: One is conservation, which requires sacrifice, and the other one, increase

in production of American energy, which is going along very well —
more coal this year than ever before in American history, more oil
and gas wells drilled this year than ever before in history.

The new economic revitalization program that we have in mind, which
will be implemented next year, would result in tax credits which would
let business invest in new tools and new factories to create even more
new jobs — about one million in the next two years. And we also
have planned a youth employment program which would encompass
600,000 jobs for young people. This has already passed the House,
and it has an excellent prospect to pass the Senate.

Smith: Now, the same question goes to Governor Reagan. Governor
Reagan, would you like to have the question repeated?

Ellis: Governor Reagan, during the past four years, the Consumer
Price Index has risen from 4.8% to currently over 12%. And perhaps
more significantly, the nation's broader, underlying rate of inflation
has gone up from 7% to 9%. Now, a part of that has been due to
external factors beyond U.S. control, notably the more than doubling
of OPEC oil prices last year, which leads me to ask you whether,
since the United States remains vulnerable to such external shocks,
can inflation in fact be controlled? If so, specifically what measures
would you pursue?

Reagan: Mr. Ellis, I think this idea that has been spawned here
in our country that inflation somehow came upon us like a plague
and therefore it's uncontrollable and no one can do anything about
it, is entirely spurious and it's dangerous to say this to the people.
When Mr. Carter became President, inflation was 4.8%, as you said.
It had been cut in two by President Gerald Ford. It is now running
at 12.7%.

President Carter also has spoken of the new jobs created. Well, we
always, with the normal growth in our country and increase in population,
increase the number of jobs. But that can't hide the fact that there
are 8 million men and women out of work in America today, and
2 million of those lost their jobs in just the last few months. Mr.
Carter had also promised that he would not use unemployment as
a tool to fight against inflation. And yet, his 1980 economic message
stated that we would reduce productivity and gross national product
and increase unemployment in order to get a handle on inflation, because
in January, at the beginning of the year, it was more than 18%. Since
then, he has blamed the people for inflation, OPEC, he has blamed
the Federal Reserve system, he has blamed the lack of productivity
of the American people, he has then accused the people of living too
well and that we must share in scarcity, we must sacrifice and get
used to doing with less. We don't have inflation because the people
are living too well. We have inflation because the Government is living
too well. And the last statement, just a few days ago, was a speech
to the effect that we have inflation because Government revenues have
not kept pace with Government spending.

I see my time is running out here. I'll have to get this out very fast. Yes, you can lick inflation by increasing productivity and by decreasing the cost of government to the place that we have balanced budgets, and are no longer grinding out printing press money, flooding the market with it because the Government is spending more than it takes in. And my economic plan calls for that. The President's economic plan calls for increasing the taxes to the point that we finally take so much money away from the people that we can balance the budget in that way. But we will have a very poor nation and a very unsound economy if we follow that path.

Smith: A follow-up, Mr. Ellis?

Ellis: Yes. You have centered on cutting Government spending in what you have just said about your own policies. You have also said that you would increase defense spending. Specifically, where would you cut Government spending if you were to increase defense spending and also cut taxes, so that, presumably, Federal revenues would shrink?

Reagan: Well, most people, when they think about cutting Government spending, they think in terms of eliminating necessary programs or wiping out something, some service that Government is supposed to perform. I believe that there is enough extravagance and fat in government. As a matter of fact, one of the secretaries of HEW under Mr. Carter testified that he thought there was $7 billion worth of fraud and waste in welfare and in the medical programs associated with it. We've had the General Accounting Office estimate that there is probably tens of billions of dollars that is lost in fraud alone, and they have added that waste adds even more to that.

We have a program for a gradual reduction of Government spending based on these theories, and I have a task force now that has been working on where those cuts could be made. I'm confident that it can be done and that it will reduce inflation because I did it in California. And inflation went down below the national average in California when we returned the money to the people and reduced Government spending.

Smith: President Carter.

Carter: Governor Reagan's proposal, the Reagan-Kemp-Roth proposal, is one of the most highly inflationary ideas that ever has been presented to the American public. He would actually have to cut Government spending by at least $130 billion in order to balance the budget under this ridiculous proposal. I notice that his task force that is working for his future plans had some of their ideas revealed in The Wall Street Journal this week. One of those ideas was to repeal the minimum wage, and several times this year, Governor Reagan has said that the major cause of unemployment is the minimum wage. This is a heartless kind of approach to the working families of our country, which is typical of many Republican leaders of the past, but, I think, has been accentuated under Governor Reagan.

In California — I'm surprised Governor Reagan brought this up — he had the three largest tax increases in the history of that state under his administration. He more than doubled state spending while he was Governor — 122% increase — and had between a 20% and 30% increase in the number of employees...

Smith: Sorry to interrupt, Mr. Carter.

Carter: ...in California. Thank you, sir.

Smith: Governor Reagan has the last word on this question.

Reagan: Yes. The figures that the President has just used about California is a distortion of the situation there, because while I was Governor of California, our spending in California increased less per capita than the spending in Georgia while Mr. Carter was Governor of Georgia in the same four years. The size of government increased only one-sixth in California of what it increased in proportion to the population in Georgia.

And the idea that my tax-cut proposal is inflationary: I would like to ask the President why is it inflationary to let the people keep more of their money and spend it the way that they like, and it isn't inflationary to let him take that money and spend it the way he wants?

Smith: I wish that question need not be rhetorical, but it must be because we've run out of time on that. Now, the third question to Governor Reagan from William Hilliard.

[Urban Decay]

Hilliard: Yes. Governor Reagan, the decline of our cities has been hastened by the continual rise in crime, strained race relations, the fall in the quality of public education, persistence of abnormal poverty in a rich nation, and a decline in the services to the public. The signs seem to point toward a deterioration that could lead to the establishment of a permanent underclass in the cities. What, specifically, would you do in the next four years to reverse this trend?

Reagan: I have been talking to a number of Congressmen who have much the same idea that I have, and that is that in the inner city areas, that in cooperation with the local government and the national Government, and using tax incentives and with cooperating with the private sector, that we have development zones. Let the local entity, the city, declare this particular area, based on the standards of the percentage of people on welfare, unemployed, and so forth, in that area. And then, through tax incentives, induce the creation of businesses providing jobs and so forth in those areas. The elements of government through these tax incentives.... For example, a business that would not have, for a period of time, an increase in the property tax reflecting its development of the unused property that it was making wouldn't be any loss to the city because the city isn't getting any tax from that now. And there would simply be a delay, and on the other hand, many of the people who would then be given jobs are presently wards of the Government, and it wouldn't hurt to give them a tax incentive, because they ... that wouldn't be costing Government anything either.

I think there are things to do in this regard. I stood in the South Bronx on the exact spot that President Carter stood on in 1977. You have to see it to believe it. It looks like a bombed-out city — great, gaunt skeletons of buildings, windows smashed out, painted on one of them "Unkept promises;" on another, "Despair." And this was the spot at which President Carter had promised that he was going to bring in a vast program to rebuild this department. There are whole . . . or this area . . . there are whole blocks of land that are left bare, just bulldozed down flat. And nothing has been done, and they are now charging to take tourists there to see this terrible desolation. I talked to a man just briefly there who asked me one simple question: "Do I have reason to hope that I can someday take care of my family again? Nothing has been done."

Smith: Follow-up, Mr. Hilliard?

[Racial Inequities]

Hilliard: Yes, Governor Reagan. Blacks and other non-whites are increasing in numbers in our cities. Many of them feel that they are facing a hostility from whites that prevents them from joining the economic mainstream of our society. There is racial confrontation in the schools, on jobs, and in housing, as non-whites seek to reap the benefits of a free society. What do you think is the nation's future as a multi-racial society?

Reagan: I believe in it. I am eternally optimistic, and I happen to believe that we've made great progress from the days when I was young and when this country didn't even know it had a racial problem. I know those things can grow out of despair in an inner city, when there's hopelessness at home, lack of work, and so forth. But I believe that all of us together, and I believe the Presidency is what Teddy Roosevelt said it was. It's a bully pulpit. And I think that something can be done from there, because a goal for all of us should be that one day, things will be done neither because of nor in spite of any of the differences between us — ethnic differences or racial differences, whatever they may be — that we will have total equal opportunity for all people. And I would do everything I could in my power to bring that about.

Smith: Mr. Hilliard, would you repeat your question for President Carter?

Hilliard: President Carter, the decline of our cities has been hastened by the continual rise in crime, strained race relations, the fall in the quality of public education, persistence of abnormal poverty in a rich nation, and a decline in services to the public. The signs seem to point toward a deterioration that could lead to the establishment of a permanent underclass in the cities. What, specifically, would you do in the next four years to reverse this trend?

Carter: Thank you, Mr. Hilliard. When I was campaigning in 1976, everywhere I went, the mayors and local officials were in despair about the rapidly deteriorating central cities of our nation. We initiated a very fine urban renewal program, working with the mayors, the governors, and other interested officials. This has been a very successful effort. That's one of the main reasons that we've had such an increase in the number of people employed. Of the nine million people put to work in new jobs since I've been in office, 1.3 million of those has been among black Americans, and another million among those who speak Spanish.

We now are planning to continue the revitalization program with increased commitments of rapid transit, mass transit. Under the windfall profits tax, we expect to spend about $43 billion in the next 10 years to rebuild the transportation systems of our country. We also are pursuing housing programs. We've had a 73% increase in the allotment of Federal funds for improved education. These are the kinds of efforts worked on a joint basis with community leaders, particularly in the minority areas of the central cities that have been deteriorating so rapidly in the past.

It's very important to us that this be done with the full involvement of minority citizens. I have brought into the top level, top levels of government, into the White House, into administrative offices of the Executive branch, into the judicial system, highly qualified black and Spanish citizens and women who in the past had been excluded.

I noticed that Governor Reagan said that when he was a young man that there was no knowledge of a racial problem in this country. Those who suffered from discrimination because of race or sex certainly knew we had a racial problem. We have gone a long way toward correcting these problems, but we still have a long way to go.

Smith: Follow-up question?

Hilliard: Yes. President Carter, I would like to repeat the same follow-up to you. Blacks and other non-whites are increasing in numbers in our cities. Many of them feel that they are facing a hostility from whites that prevents them from joining the economic mainstream of our society. There is racial confrontation in the schools, on jobs, and in housing, as non-whites seek to reap the benefits of a free society. What is your assessment of the nation's future as a multi-racial society?

Carter: Ours is a nation of refugees, a nation of immigrants. Almost all of our citizens came here from other lands and now have hopes, which are being realized, for a better life, preserving their ethnic commitments, their family structures, their religious beliefs, preserving their relationships with their relatives in foreign countries, but still holding themselves together in a very coherent society, which gives our nation its strength.

In the past, those minority groups have often been excluded from participation in the affairs of government. Since I've been President, I've appointed, for instance, more than twice as many black Federal judges as all previous presidents in the history of this country. I've done the same thing in the appointment of women, and also Spanish-speaking Americans. To involve them in the administration of government and the feeling that they belong to the societal structure that makes decisions in the judiciary and in the executive branch is a very important commitment which I am trying to realize and will continue to do so in the future.

Smith: Governor Reagan, you have a minute for rebuttal.

Reagan: Yes. The President talks of Government programs, and they have their place. But as governor, when I was at that end of the line and receiving some of these grants for Government programs, I saw that so many of them were dead-end. They were public employment for these people who really want to get out into the private job market where there are jobs with a future.

Now, the President spoke a moment ago about ... that I was against the minimum wage. I wish he could have been with me when I sat with a group of teenagers who were black, and who were telling me about their unemployment problems, and that it was the minimum wage that had done away with the jobs that they once could get. And indeed, every time it has increased you will find there is an increase in minority unemployment among young people. And therefore, I have been in favor of a separate minimum for them.

With regard to the great progress that has been made with this Government spending, the rate of black unemployment in Detroit, Michigan is 56%.

Smith: President Carter, you have the last word on this question.

Carter: It's obvious that we still have a long way to go in fully incorporating the minority groups into the mainstream of American life. We have made good progress, and there is no doubt in my mind that the commitment to unemployment compensation, the minimum wage, welfare, national health insurance, those kinds of commitments that have typified the Democratic party since ancient history in this country's political life are a very important element of the future. In all those elements, Governor Reagan has repeatedly spoken out against them, which, to me, shows a very great insensitivity to giving deprived families a better chance in life. This, to me, is a very important difference between him and me in this election, and I believe the American people will judge accordingly.

There is no doubt in my mind that in the downtown central cities, with the, with the new commitment on an energy policy, with a chance to revitalize homes and to make them more fuel efficient, with a chance for our synthetic fuels program, solar power, this will give us an additional opportunity for jobs which will pay rich dividends.

[Terrorism Policy]

Smith: Now, a question from Barbara Walters.

Walters: Mr. President, the eyes of the country tonight are on the hostages in Iran. I realize this is a sensitive area, but the question of how we respond to acts of terrorism goes beyond this current crisis. Other countries have policies that determine how they will respond. Israel, for example, considers hostages like soldiers and will not negotiate with terrorists. For the future, Mr. President, the country has a right to know, do you have a policy for dealing with terrorism wherever it might happen, and, what have we learned from this experience in Iran that might cause us to do things differently if this, or something similar, happens again?

Carter: Barbara, one of the blights on this world is the threat and the activities of terrorists. At one of the recent economic summit conferences between myself and the other leaders of the Western world, we committed ourselves to take strong action against terrorism. Airplane hijacking was one of the elements of that commitment. There is no doubt that we have seen in recent years — in recent months — additional acts of violence against Jews in France and, of course, against those who live in Israel, by the PLO and other terrorist organizations.

Ultimately, the most serious terrorist threat is if one of those radical nations, who believe in terrorism as a policy, should have atomic weapons. Both I and all my predecessors have had a deep commitment to controlling the proliferation of nuclear weapons. In countries like Libya or Iraq, we have even alienated some of our closest trade partners because we have insisted upon the control of the spread of nuclear weapons to those potentially terrorist countries.

When Governor Reagan has been asked about that, he makes the very disturbing comment that non-proliferation, or the control of the spread of nuclear weapons, is none of our business. And recently when he was asked specifically about Iraq, he said there is nothing we can do about it.

This ultimate terrorist threat is the most fearsome of all, and it's part of a pattern where our country must stand firm to control terrorism of all kinds.

Smith: Ms. Walters, a follow up?

Walters: While we are discussing policy, had Iran not taken American hostages, I assume that, in order to preserve our neutrality, we would have stopped the flow of spare parts and vital war materials once war broke out between Iraq and Iran. Now we're offering to lift the ban on such goods if they let our people come home. Doesn't this reward terrorism, compromise our neutrality, and possibly antagonize nations now friendly to us in the Middle East?

Carter: We will maintain our position of neutrality in the Iran and Iraq war. We have no plans to sell additional materiel or goods to Iran, that might be of a warlike nature. When I made my decision to stop all trade with Iran as a result of the taking of our hostages, I announced then, and have consistently maintained since then, that if the hostages are released safely, we would make delivery on those items which Iran owns — which they have bought and paid for — also, that the frozen Iranian assets would be released. That's been a consistent policy, one I intend to carry out.

Smith: Would you repeat the question now for Governor Reagan, please, Ms. Walters?

Walters: Yes. Governor, the eyes of the country tonight remain on the hostages in Iran, but the question of how we respond to acts of terrorism goes beyond this current crisis. There are other countries that have policies that determine how they will respond. Israel, for example, considers hostages like soldiers and will not negotiate with terrorists.

For the future, the country has the right to know, do you have a policy for dealing with terrorism wherever it might happen, and what have we learned from this experience in Iran that might cause us to do things differently if this, or something similar, should happen again?

Reagan: Barbara, you've asked that question twice. I think you ought to have at least one answer to it. I have been accused lately of having a secret plan with regard to the hostages. Now, this comes from an answer that I've made at least 50 times during this campaign to the press, when I am asked have you any ideas of what you would do if you were there? And I said, well, yes. And I think that anyone that's seeking this position, as well as other people, probably, have thought to themselves, what about this, what about that? These are just ideas of what I would think of if I were in that position and had access to the information, and which I would know all the options that were open to me.

I have never answered the question, however; second, the one that says, well, tell me, what are some of those ideas? First of all, I would be fearful that I might say something that was presently under way or in negotiations, and thus expose it and endanger the hostages, and sometimes, I think some of my ideas might require quiet diplomacy where you don't say in advance, or say to anyone, what it is you're thinking of doing.

Your question is difficult to answer, because, in the situation right now, no one wants to say anything that would inadvertently delay, in any way, the return of those hostages if there ... if there is a chance that they're coming home soon, or that might cause them harm. What I do think should be done, once they are safely here with their families, and that tragedy is over — we've endured this humiliation for just lacking one week of a year now — then, I think, it is time for us to have a complete investigation as to the diplomatic efforts that were made in the beginning, why they have been there so long, and when they come home, what did we have to do in order to bring that about — what arrangements were made? And I would suggest that Congress should hold such an investigation. In the meantime, I'm going to continue praying that they'll come home.

Smith: Follow up question.

Walters: I would like to say that neither candidate answered specifically the question of a specific policy for dealing with terrorism, but I will ask Governor Reagan a different follow-up question. You have suggested that there would be no Iranian crisis had you been President, because we would have given firmer support to the Shah. But Iran is a country of 37 million people who are resisting a government that they regarded as dictatorial.

My question is not whether the Shah's regime was preferable to the Ayatollah's, but whether the United States has the power or the right to try to determine what form of government any country will have, and do we back unpopular regimes whose major merit is that they are friendly to the United States?

Reagan: The degree of unpopularity of a regime when the choice is total authoritarianism ... totalitarianism, I should say, in the alternative government, makes one wonder whether you are being helpful to the people. And we've been guilty of that. Because someone didn't meet exactly our standards of human rights, even though they were an ally of ours, instead of trying patiently to persuade them to change their ways, we have, in a number of instances, aided a revolutionary overthrow which results in complete totalitarianism, instead, for those people. I think that this is a kind of a hypocritical policy when, at the same time, we're maintaining a detente with the one nation in the world where there are no human rights at all — the Soviet Union.

Now, there was a second phase in the Iranian affair in which we had something to do with that. And that was, we had adequate warning that there was a threat to our embassy, and we could have done what other embassies did — either strengthen our security there, or remove our personnel before the kidnap and the takeover took place.

Smith: Governor, I'm sorry, I must interrupt. President Carter, you have a minute for rebuttal.

Carter: I didn't hear any comment from Governor Reagan about what he would do to stop or reduce terrorism in the future. What the Western allies did decide to do is to stop all air flights — commercial air flights — to any nation involved in terrorism or the hijacking of airplanes, or the harboring of hijackers. Secondly, we all committed ourselves, as have all my predecessors in the Oval Office, not to permit the spread of nuclear weapons to a terrorist nation, or to any other nation that does not presently have those weapons or capabilities for explosives. Third, not to make any sales of materiel or weapons to a nation which is involved in terrorist activities. And, lastly, not to deal with the PLO until and unless the PLO recognizes Israel's right to exist and recognizes U.N. Resolution 242 as a basis for Middle East peace.

These are a few of the things to which our nation is committed, and we will continue with these commitments.

Smith: Governor Reagan, you have the last word on that question.

Reagan: Yes. I have no quarrel whatsoever with the things that have been done, because I believe it is high time that the civilized countries of the world made it plain that there is no room worldwide for terrorism; there will be no negotiation with terrorists of any kind. And while I have a last word here, I would like to correct a misstatement of fact by the President. I have never made the statement that he suggested about nuclear proliferation and nuclear proliferation, or the trying to halt it, would be a major part of a foreign policy of mine.

Smith: Thank you gentlemen. That is the first half of the debate. Now, the rules for the second half are quite simple. They're only complicated when I explain them. In the second half, the panelists with me will have no follow-up questions. Instead, after the panelists have asked a question, and the candidates have answered, each of the candidates will have two opportunities to follow up, to question, to rebut, or just to comment on his opponent's statement.

Governor Reagan will respond, in this section, to the first question from Marvin Stone.

[SALT II Treaty]

Stone: Governor Reagan — arms control: The President said it was the single most important issue. Both of you have expressed the desire to end the nuclear arms race with Russia, but by methods that are vastly different. You suggest that we scrap the Salt II treaty already negotiated, and intensify the build-up of American power to induce the Soviets to sign a new treaty — one more favorable to us. President Carter, on the other hand, says he will again try to convince a reluctant Congress to ratify the present treaty on the grounds it's the best we can hope to get.

Now both of you cannot be right. Will you tell us why you think you are?

Reagan: Yes. I think I'm right because I believe that we must have a consistent foreign policy, a strong America, and a strong economy. And then, as we build up our national security, to restore our margin of safety, we at the same time try to restrain the Soviet build-up, which has been going forward at a rapid pace, and for quite some time.

The Salt II treaty was the result of negotiations that Mr. Carter's team entered into after he had asked the Soviet Union for a discussion of actual reduction of nuclear strategic weapons. And his emissary, I think, came home in 12 hours having heard a very definite nyet. But taking that one no from the Soviet Union, we then went back into negotiations on their terms, because Mr. Carter had cancelled the B-1 bomber, delayed the MX, delayed the Trident submarine, delayed the Cruise missile, shut down the Missile Man — the three — the Minute Man missile production line, and whatever other things that might have been done. The Soviet Union sat at the table knowing that we had gone forward with unilateral concessions without any reciprocation from them whatsoever.

Now, I have not blocked the Salt II treaty, as Mr. Carter and Mr. Mondale suggest I have. It has been blocked by a Senate in which there is a Democratic majority. Indeed, the Senate Armed Services Committee voted 10 to 0, with seven abstentions, against the Salt II treaty, and declared that it was not in the national security interests of the United States. Besides which, it is illegal, because the law of the land, passed by Congress, says that we cannot accept a treaty in which we are not equal. And we are not equal in this treaty for one reason alone — our B-52 bombers are considered to be strategic weapons; their Backfire bombers are not.

Smith: Governor, I have to interrupt you at that point. The time is up for that. But the same question now to President Carter.

Stone: Yes. President Carter, both of you have expressed the desire to end the nuclear arms race with Russia, but through vastly different methods. The Governor suggests we scrap the Salt II treaty which you negotiated in Vienna ... or signed in Vienna, intensify the build-up of American power to induce the Soviets to sign a new treaty, one more favorable to us. You, on the other hand, say you will again try to convince a reluctant Congress to ratify the present treaty on the grounds it is the best we can hope to get from the Russians.

You cannot both be right. Will you tell us why you think you are?

Carter: Yes, I'd be glad to. Inflation, unemployment, the cities are all very important issues, but they pale into insignificance in the life and duties of a President when compared with the control of nuclear weapons. Every President who has served in the Oval Office since Harry Truman has been dedicated to the proposition of controlling nuclear weapons.

To negotiate with the Soviet Union a balanced, controlled, observable, and then reducing levels of atomic weaponry, there is a disturbing pattern in the attitude of Governor Reagan. He has never supported any of those arms control agreements — the limited test ban, Salt I, nor the Antiballistic Missile Treaty, nor the Vladivostok Treaty negotiated with the Soviet Union by President Ford — and now he wants to throw into the wastebasket a treaty to control nuclear weapons on a balanced and equal basis between ourselves and the Soviet Union, negotiated over a seven-year period, by myself and my two Republican predecessors.

The Senate has not voted yet on the Strategic Arms Limitation Treaty. There have been preliminary skirmishings in the committees of the Senate, but the Treaty has never come to the floor of the Senate for either a debate or a vote. It's understandable that a Senator in the preliminary debates can make an irresponsible statement, or, maybe, an ill-advised statement. You've got 99 other senators to correct that mistake, if it is a mistake. But when a man who hopes to be President says, take this treaty, discard it, do not vote, do not debate, do not explore the issues, do not finally capitalize on this long negotiation — that is a very dangerous and disturbing thing.

Smith: Governor Reagan, you have an opportunity to rebut that.

Reagan: Yes, I'd like to respond very much. First of all, the Soviet Union ... if I have been critical of some of the previous agreements, it's because we've been out-negotiated for quite a long time. And they have managed, in spite of all of our attempts at arms limitation, to go forward with the biggest military build-up in the history of man.

Now, to suggest that because two Republican presidents tried to pass the Salt treaty — that puts them on its side — I would like to say that President Ford, who was within 90% of a treaty that we could be in agreement with when he left office, is emphatically against this Salt treaty. I would like to point out also that senators like Henry Jackson and Hollings of South Carolina — they are taking the lead in the fight against this particular treaty.

I am not talking of scrapping. I am talking of taking the treaty back, and going back into negotiations. And I would say to the Soviet Union, we will sit and negotiate with you as long as it takes, to have not only legitimate arms limitation, but to have a reduction of these nuclear weapons to the point that neither one of us represents a threat to the other. That is hardly throwing away a treaty and being opposed to arms limitation.

Smith: President Carter?

Carter: Yes. Governor Reagan is making some very misleading and disturbing statements. He not only advocates the scrapping of this treaty — and I don't know that these men that he quotes are against the treaty in its final form — but he also advocates the possibility, he said it's been a missing element, of playing a trump card against the Soviet Union of a nuclear arms race, and is insisting upon nuclear superiority by our own nation, as a predication for negotiation in the future with the Soviet Union.

If President Brezhnev said, we will scrap this treaty, negotiated under three American Presidents over a seven-year period of time, we insist upon nuclear superiority as a basis for future negotiations, and we believe that the launching of a nuclear arms race is a good basis for future negotiations, it's obvious that I, as President, and all Americans, would reject such a proposition. This would mean the resumption of a very dangerous nuclear arms race. It would be very disturbing to American people. It would change the basic tone and commitment that our nation has experienced ever since the Second World War, with all Presidents, Democratic and Republican. And it would also be very disturbing to our allies, all of whom support this nuclear arms treaty. In addition to that, the adversarial relationship between ourselves and the Soviet Union would undoubtedly deteriorate very rapidly.

This attitude is extremely dangerous and belligerent in its tone, although it's said with a quiet voice.

Smith: Governor Reagan?

Reagan: I know the President's supposed to be replying to me, but sometimes, I have a hard time in connecting what he's saying, with what I have said or what my positions are. I sometimes think he's like the witch doctor that gets mad when a good doctor comes along with a cure that'll work.

My point I have made already, Mr. President, with regard to negotiating: it does not call for nuclear superiority on the part of the United States. It calls for a mutual reduction of these weapons, as I say, that neither of us can represent a threat to the other. And to suggest that the Salt II treaty that your negotiators negotiated was just a continuation, and based on all of the preceding efforts by two previous Presidents, is just not true. It was a new negotiation because, as I say, President Ford was within about 10% of having a solution that could be acceptable. And I think our allies would be very happy to go along with a fair and verifiable Salt agreement.

Smith: President Carter, you have the last word on this question.

Carter: I think, to close out this discussion, it would be better to put into perspective what we're talking about. I had a discussion with my daughter, Amy, the other day, before I came here, to ask her what the most important issue was. She said she thought nuclear weaponry — and the control of nuclear arms.

This is a formidable force. Some of these weapons have 10 megatons of explosion. If you put 50 tons of TNT in each one of railroad cars, you would have a carload of TNT — a trainload of TNT stretching across this nation. That's one major war explosion in a warhead. We have thousands, equivalent of megaton, or million tons, of TNT warheads. The control of these weapons is the single major responsibility of a President, and to cast out this commitment of all presidents, because of some slight technicalities that can be corrected, is a very dangerous approach.

Smith: We have to go to another question now, from Harry Ellis to President Carter.

[Alternative Fuels]

Ellis: Mr. President, as you have said, Americans, through conservation, are importing much less oil today than we were even a year ago. Yet U.S. dependence on Arab oil as a percentage of total imports is today much higher than it was at the time of the 1973 Arab oil embargo, and for some time to come, the loss of substantial amounts of Arab oil could plunge the U.S. into depression.

This means that a bridge must be built out of this dependence. Can the United States develop synthetic fuels and other alternative energy sources without damage to the environment, and will this process mean steadily higher fuel bills for American families?

Carter: I don't think there's any doubt that, in the future, the cost of oil is going to go up. What I've had as a basic commitment since

I've been President is to reduce our dependence on foreign oil. It can only be done in two ways: one, to conserve energy — to stop the waste of energy — and, secondly, to produce more American energy. We've been very successful in both cases. We've now reduced the importing of foreign oil in the last year alone by one-third. We imported today 2 million barrels of oil less than we did the same date just a year ago.

This commitment has been opening up a very bright vista for our nation in the future, because with the windfall profits tax as a base, we now have an opportunity to use American technology and American ability and American natural resources to expand rapidly the production of synthetic fuels, yes; to expand rapidly the production of solar energy, yes; and also to produce the traditional kinds of American energy. We will drill more oil and gas wells this year than any year in history. We'll produce more coal this year than any year in history. We are exporting more coal this year than any year in history.

And we have an opportunity now, with improved transportation systems and improved loading facilities in our ports, to see a very good opportunity on a world international market, to replace OPEC oil with American coal as a basic energy source. This exciting future will not only give us more energy security, but will also open up vast opportunities for Americans to live a better life and to have millions of new jobs associated with this new and very dynamic industry now in prospect because of the new energy policy that we've put into effect.

Smith: Would you repeat the question now for Governor Reagan?

Ellis: Governor Reagan, Americans, through conservation, are importing much less oil today than we were even a year ago. And yet, U.S. reliance on Arab oil as a percentage of total imports is much higher today than it was during the 1973 Arab oil embargo. And the substantial loss of Arab oil could plunge the United States into depression.

The question is whether the development of alternative energy sources, in order to reduce this dependence, can be done without damaging the environment, and will it mean for American families steadily higher fuel bills?

Reagan: I'm not so sure that it means steadily higher fuel costs, but I do believe that this nation has been portrayed for too long a time to the people as being energy-poor when it is energy-rich. The coal that the President mentioned — yes, we have it — and yet one-eighth of our total coal resources is not being utilized at all right now. The mines are closed down; there are 22,000 miners out of work. Most of this is due to regulations which either interfere with the mining of it or prevent the burning of it. With our modern technology, yes, we can burn our coal within the limits of the Clean Air Act. I think, as technology improves, we'll be able to do even better with that.

The other thing is that we have only leased out — begun to explore — 2% of our outer continental shelf for oil, where it is believed, by everyone familiar with that fuel and that source of energy, that there are vast supplies yet to be found. Our Government has, in the last year or so, taken out of multiple use millions of acres of public lands that once were — well, they were public lands subject to multiple use — exploration for minerals and so forth. It is believed that probably 70% of the potential oil in the United States is probably hidden in those lands, and no one is allowed to even go and explore to find out if it is there. This is particularly true of the recent efforts to shut down part of Alaska.

Nuclear power: There were 36 power plants planned in this country. And let me add the word safety; it must be done with the utmost of safety. But 32 of those have given up and cancelled their plans to build, and again, because Government regulations and permits, and so forth, take — make it take — more than twice as long to build a nuclear plant in the United States as it does to build one in Japan or in Western Europe.

We have the sources here. We are energy rich, and coal is one of the great potentials we have.

Smith: President Carter, your comment?

Carter: To repeat myself, we have this year the opportunity, which we'll realize, to produce 800 million tons of coal — an unequalled record in the history of our country. Governor Reagan says that this is not a good achievement, and he blames restraints on coal production on regulations — regulations that affect the life and the health and safety of miners, and also regulations that protect the purity of our air and the quality of our water and our land. We cannot cast aside those regulations. We have a chance in the next 15 years, insisting upon the health and safety of workers in the mines, and also preserving the same high air and water pollution standards, to triple the amount of coal we produce.

Governor Reagan's approach to our energy policy, which has already proven its effectiveness, is to repeal, or to change substantially, the windfall profits tax — to return a major portion of $227 billion back to the oil companies; to do away with the Department of Energy; to short-circuit our synthetic fuels program; to put a minimal emphasis on solar power; to emphasize strongly nuclear power plants as a major source of energy in the future. He wants to put all our eggs in one basket and give that basket to the major oil companies.

Smith: Governor Reagan.

Reagan: That is a misstatement, of course, of my position. I just happen to believe that free enterprise can do a better job of producing the things that people need than government can. The Department of Energy has a multi-billion-dollar budget in excess of $10 billion. It hasn't produced a quart of oil or a lump of coal, or anything else in the line of energy. And for Mr. Carter to suggest that I want to do away with the safety laws and with the laws that pertain to clean water and clean air, and so forth. As Governor of California, I took charge of passing the strictest air pollution laws in the United States

— the strictest air quality law that has even been adopted in the United States. And we created an OSHA — an Occupational Safety and Health Agency — for the protection of employees before the Federal Government had one in place. And to this day, not one of its decisions or rulings has ever been challenged.

So, I think some of those charges are missing the point. I am suggesting that there are literally thousands of unnecessary regulations that invade every facet of business, and indeed, very much of our personal lives, that are unnecessary; that Government can do without; that have added $130 billion to the cost of production in this country; and that are contributing their part to inflation. And I would like to see us a little more free, as we once were.

Smith: President Carter, another crack at that?

Carter: Sure. As a matter of fact, the air pollution standard laws that were passed in California were passed over the objections of Governor Reagan, and this is a very well-known fact. Also, recently, when someone suggested that the Occupational Safety and Health Act should be abolished, Governor Reagan responded, amen.

The offshore drilling rights is a question that Governor Reagan raises often. As a matter of fact, in the proposal for the Alaska lands legislation, 100% of all the offshore lands would be open for exploration, and 95% of all the Alaska lands, where it is suspected or believed that minerals might exist. We have, with our five-year plan for the leasing of offshore lands, proposed more land to be drilled than has been opened up for drilling since this program first started in 1954. So we're not putting restraints on American exploration, we're encouraging it in every way we can.

Smith: Governor Reagan, you have the last word on this question.

Reagan: Yes. If it is a well-known fact that I opposed air pollution laws in California, the only thing I can possibly think of is that the President must be suggesting the law that the Federal Government tried to impose on the State of California — not a law, but regulations — that would have made it impossible to drive an automobile within the city limits of any California city, or to have a place to put it if you did drive it against their regulations. It would have destroyed the economy of California, and, I must say, we had the support of Congress when we pointed out how ridiculous this attempt was by the Environmental Protection Agency. We still have the strictest air control, or air pollution laws in the country.

As for offshore oiling, only 2% now is so leased and is producing oil. The rest, as to whether the lands are going to be opened in the next five years or so — we're already five years behind in what we should be doing. There is more oil now, in the wells that have been drilled, than has been taken out in 121 years that they've been drilled.

Smith: Thank you Governor. Thank you, Mr. President. The next question goes to Governor Reagan from William Hilliard.

[Social Security]

Hilliard: Governor Reagan, wage earners in this country — especially the young — are supporting a Social Security system that continues to affect their income drastically. The system is fostering a struggle between the young and the old, and is drifting the country toward a polarization of these two groups. How much longer can the young wage earner expect to bear the ever-increasing burden of the Social Security system?

Reagan: The Social Security system was based on a false premise, with regard to how fast the number of workers would increase and how fast the number of retirees would increase. It is actuarially out of balance, and this first became evident about 16 years ago, and some of us were voicing warnings then. Now, it is trillions of dollars out of balance, and the only answer that has come so far is the biggest single tax increase in our nation's history — the payroll tax increase for Social Security — which will only put a bandaid on this and postpone the day of reckoning by a few years at most.

What is needed is a study that I have proposed by a task force of experts to look into this entire problem as to how it can be reformed and made actuarially sound, but with the premise that no one presently dependent on Social Security is going to have the rug pulled out from under them and not get their check. We cannot frighten, as we have with the threats and the campaign rhetoric that has gone on in this campaign, our senior citizens — leave them thinking that in some way, they're endangered and they would have no place to turn. They must continue to get those checks, and I believe that the system can be put on a sound actuarial basis. But it's going to take some study and some work, and not just passing a tax increase to let the load — or the roof — fall in on the next administration.

Smith: Would you repeat that question for President Carter?

Hilliard: Yes. President Carter, wage earners in this country, especially the young, are supporting a Social Security System that continues to affect their income drastically. The system is fostering a struggle between young and old and is drifting the country toward a polarization of these two groups. How much longer can the young wage earner expect to bear the ever-increasing burden of the Social Security System?

Carter: As long as there is a Democratic president in the White House, we will have a strong and viable Social Security System, free of the threat of bankruptcy. Although Governor Reagan has changed his position lately, on four different occasions, he has advocated making Social Security a voluntary system, which would, in effect, very quickly bankrupt it. I noticed also in The Wall Street Journal early this week, that a preliminary report of his task force advocates making Social Security more sound by reducing the adjustment in Social Security for the retired people to compensate for the impact of inflation.

These kinds of approaches are very dangerous to the security, the well being and the peace of mind of the retired people of this country and those approaching retirement age. But no matter what it takes in the future to keep Social Security sound, it must be kept that way. And although there was a serious threat to the Social Security System and its integrity during the 1976 campaign and when I became President, the action of the Democratic Congress working with me has been to put Social Security back on a sound financial basis. That is the way it will stay.

Smith: Governor Reagan?

Reagan: Well, that just isn't true. It has, as I said, delayed the actuarial imbalance falling on us for just a few years with that increase in taxes, and I don't believe we can go on increasing the tax, because the problem for the young people today is that they are paying in far more than they can ever expect to get out. Now, again this statement that somehow, I wanted to destroy it and I just changed my tune, that I am for voluntary Social Security, which would mean the ruin of it.

Mr. President, the voluntary thing that I suggested many years ago was that with a young man orphaned and raised by an aunt who died, his aunt was ineligible for Social Security insurance because she was not his mother. And I suggested that if this is an insurance program, certainly the person who is paying in should be able to name his own beneficiary. That is the closest I have every come to anything voluntary with Social Security. I, too, am pledged to a Social Security program that will reassure these senior citizens of ours that they are going to continue to get their money.

There are some changes that I would like to make. I would like to make a change in the regulation that discriminates against a wife who works and finds that she then is faced with a choice between her father's or her husband's benefits, if he dies first, or what she has paid in; but it does not recognize that she has also been paying in herself, and she is entitled to more than she presently can get. I'd like to change that.

Smith: President Carter's rebuttal now.

Carter: These constant suggestions that the basic Social Security System should be changed does call for concern and consternation among the aged of our country. It is obvious that we should have a commitment to them, that Social Security benefits should not be taxed and that there would be no peremptory change in the standards by which Social Security payments are made to retired people. We also need to continue to index Social Security payments, so that if inflation rises, the Social Security payments would rise a commensurate degree to let the buying power of a Social Security check continue intact.

In the past, the relationship between Social Security and Medicare has been very important to providing some modicum of aid for senior citizens in the retention of health benefits. Governor Reagan, as a matter of fact, began his political career campaigning around this nation against Medicare. Now, we have an opportunity to move toward national health insurance, with an emphasis on the prevention of disease, an emphasis on out-patient care, not in-patient care; an emphasis on hospital cost containment to hold down the cost of hospital care for those who are ill, an emphasis on catastrophic health insurance, so that if a family is threatened with being wiped out economically because of a very high medical bill, then the insurance would help pay for it. These are the kinds of elements of a national health insurance, important to the American people. Governor Reagan, again, typically is against such a proposal.

Smith: Governor?

Reagan: When I opposed Medicare, there was another piece of legislation meeting the same problem before the Congress. I happened to favor the other piece of legislation and thought that it would be better for the senior citizens and provide better care than the one that was finally passed. I was not opposing the principle of providing care for them. I was opposing one piece of legislation versus another.

There is something else about Social Security. Of course, it doesn't come out of the payroll tax. It comes out of a general fund, but something should be done about it. I think it is disgraceful that the Disability Insurance Fund in Social Security finds checks going every month to tens of thousands of people who are locked up in our institutions for crime or for mental illness, and they are receiving disability checks from Social Security every month while a state institution provides for all of their needs and their care.

Smith: President Carter, you have the last word on this question.

Carter: I think this debate on Social Security, Medicare, national health insurance typifies, as vividly any other subject tonight, the basic historical differences between the Democratic Party and Republican Party. The allusions to basic changes in the minimum wage is another, and the deleterious comments that Governor Reagan has made about unemployment compensation. These commitments that the Democratic Party has historically made to the working families of this nation, have been extremely important to the growth in their stature and in a better quality of life for them.

I noticed recently that Governor Reagan frequently quotes Democratic presidents in his acceptance address. I have never heard a candidate for President, who is a Republican, quote a Republican president, but when they get in office, they try to govern like Republicans. So, it is good for the American people to remember that there is a sharp basic historical difference between Governor Reagan and me on these crucial issues — also, between the two parties that we represent.

Smith: Thank you Mr. President, Governor Reagan. We now go to another question — a question to President Carter by Barbara Walters.

[Opponent's Weaknesses]

Walters: Thank you. You have addressed some of the major issues tonight, but the biggest issue in the minds of American voters is yourselves — your ability to lead this country. When many voters go into that booth just a week from today, they will be voting their gut instinct about you men. You have already given us your reasons why people should vote for you, now would you please tell us for this your final question, why they should not vote for your opponent, why his Presidency could be harmful to the nation and, having examined both your opponent's record and the man himself, tell us his greatest weakness.

Carter: Barbara, reluctant as I am to say anything critical about Governor Reagan, I will try to answer your question. First of all, there is the historical perspective that I just described. This is a contest between a Democrat in the mainstream of my party, as exemplified by the actions that I have taken in the Oval Office the last four years, as contrasted with Governor Reagan, who in most cases does typify his party, but in some cases, there is a radical departure by him from the heritage of Eisenhower and others. The most important crucial difference in this election campaign, in my judgment, is the approach to the control of nuclear weaponry and the inclination to control or not to control the spread of atomic weapons to other nations who don't presently have it, particularly terrorist nations.

The inclination that Governor Reagan has exemplified in many troubled times since he has been running for President — I think since 1968 — to inject American military forces in places like North Korea, to put a blockade around Cuba this year, or in some instances, to project American forces into a fishing dispute against the small nation of Ecuador on the west coast of South America. This is typical of his longstanding inclination, on the use of American power, not to resolve disputes diplomatically and peacefully, but to show that the exercise of military power is best proven by the actual use of it.

Obviously, no president wants war, and I certainly do not believe that Governor Reagan, if he were President, would want war, but a President in the Oval Office has to make a judgment on almost a daily basis about how to exercise the enormous power of our country for peace, through diplomacy, or in a careless way in a belligerent attitude which has exemplified his attitudes in the past.

Smith: Barbara, would you repeat the question for Governor Reagan?

Walters: Yes, thank you. Realizing that you may be equally reluctant to speak ill of your opponent, may I ask why people should not vote for your opponent, why his Presidency could be harmful to the nation, and having examined both your opponent's record and the man himself, could you tell us his greatest weakness?

Reagan: Well, Barbara, I believe that there is a fundamental difference — and I think it has been evident in most of the answers that Mr. Carter has given tonight — that he seeks the solution to anything as another opportunity for a Federal Government program. I happen to believe that the Federal Government has usurped powers of autonomy and authority that belong back at the state and local level. It has imposed on the individual freedoms of the people, and there are more of these things that could be solved by the people themselves, if they were given a chance, or by the levels of government that were closer to them.

Now, as to why I should be and he shouldn't be, when he was a candidate in 1976, President Carter invented a thing he called the misery index. He added the rate of unemployment and the rate of inflation, and it came, at that time, to 12.5% under President Ford. He said that no man with that size misery index has a right to seek reelection to the Presidency. Today, by his own decision, the misery index is in excess of 20%, and I think this must suggest something.

But, when I had quoted a Democratic President, as the President says, I was a Democrat. I said many foolish things back in those days. But the President that I quoted had made a promise, a Democrat promise, and I quoted him because it was never kept. And today, you would find that that promise is at the very heart of what Republicanism represents in this country today. That's why I believe there are going to be millions of Democrats that are going to vote with us this time around, because they too want that promise kept. It was a promise for less government and less taxes and more freedom for the people.

Smith: President Carter?

Carter: I mentioned the radical departure of Governor Reagan from the principles or ideals of historical perspective of his own party. I don't think that can be better illustrated than in the case of guaranteeing women equal rights under the Constitution of our nation. For 40 years, the Republican Party platforms called for guaranteeing women equal rights with a constitutional amendment. Six predecessors of mine who served in the Oval Office called for this guarantee of women's rights. Governor Reagan and his new Republican Party have departed from this commitment — a very severe blow to the opportunity for women to finally correct discrimination under which they have suffered.

When a man and a women do the same amount of work, a man gets paid $1.00, a women only gets paid 59 cents. And the equal rights amendment only says that equality of rights shall not be abridged for women by the Federal Government or by the state governments. That is all it says — a simple guarantee of equality of opportunity which typifies the Democratic Party, and which is a very important commitment of mine, as contrasted with Governor Reagan's radical departure from the long-standing policy of his own party.

Smith: Governor Reagan?

Reagan: Yes. Mr. President, once again, I happen to be against the amendment, because I think the amendment will take this problem out of the hands of elected legislators and put it in the hands of

947

unelected judges. I am for equal rights, and while you have been in
office for four years and not one single state — and most of them
have a majority of Democratic legislators — has added to the ratification
or voted to ratify the equal rights amendment. While I was Governor,
more than eight years ago, I found 14 separate instances where women
were discriminated against in the body of California law, and I had
passed and signed into law 14 statutes that eliminated those discriminations, including the economic ones that you have just mentioned
— equal pay and so forth.

I believe that if in all these years that we have spent trying to
get the amendment, that we had spent as much time correcting these
laws, as we did in California — and we were the first to do it. If
I were President, I would also now take a look at the hundreds of
Federal regulations which discriminate against women and which go
right on while everyone is looking for an amendment. I would have
someone ride herd on those regulations, and we would start eliminating
those discriminations in the Federal Government against women.

Smith: President Carter?

Carter: Howard, I'm a Southerner, and I share the basic beliefs
of my region about an excessive government intrusion into the private
affairs of American citizens and also into the private affairs of the
free enterprise system. One of the commitments that I made was to
deregulate the major industries of this country. We've been remarkably
successful, with the help of a Democratic Congress. We have deregulated
the air industry, the rail industry, the trucking industry, financial institutions. We're now working on the communications industry.

In addition to that, I believe that this element of discrimination
is something that the South has seen so vividly as a blight on our
region of the country which has now been corrected — not only racial
discrimination but discrimination against people that have to work for
a living — because we have been trying to pick ourselves up by our
bootstraps, since the long depression years, and lead a full and useful
life in the affairs of this country. We have made remarkable success.
It is part of my consciousness and of my commitment to continue
this progress.

So, my heritage as a Southerner, my experience in the Oval Office,
convinces me that what I have just described is a proper course for
the future.

Smith: Governor Reagan, yours is the last word.

Reagan: Well, my last word is again to say this: We were talking
about this very simple amendment and women's rights. And I make
it plain again: I am for women's rights. But I would like to call the
attention of the people to the fact that that so-called simple amendment
could be used by mischievous men to destroy discriminations that properly
belong, by law, to women respecting the physical differences between
the two sexes, labor laws that protect them against things that would
be physically harmful to them. Those would all, could all be challenged

by men. And the same would be true with regard to combat service in the military and so forth.

I thought that was the subject we were supposed to be on. But, if we're talking about how much we think about the working people and so forth, I'm the only fellow who ever ran for this job who was six times president of his own union and still has a lifetime membership in that union.

Smith: Gentlemen, each of you now has three minutes for a closing statement. President Carter, you're first.

[Closing Statements]

Carter: First of all, I'd like to thank the League of Women Voters for making this debate possible. I think it's been a very constructive debate and I hope it's helped to acquaint the American people with the sharp differences between myself and Governor Reagan. Also, I want to thank the people of Cleveland and Ohio for being such hospitable hosts during these last few hours in my life.

I've been President now for almost four years. I've had to make thousands of decisions, and each one of those decisions has been a learning process. I've seen the strength of my nation, and I've seen the crises it approached in a tentative way. And I've had to deal with those crises as best I could.

As I've studied the record between myself and Governor Reagan, I've been impressed with the stark differences that exist between us. I think the result of this debate indicates that that fact is true. I consider myself in the mainstream of my party. I consider myself in the mainstream even of the bipartisan list of Presidents who served before me. The United States must be a nation strong; the United States must be a nation secure. We must have a society that's just and fair. And we must extend the benefits of our own commitment to peace, to create a peaceful world.

I believe that since I've been in office, there have been six or eight areas of combat evolved in other parts of the world. In each case, I alone have had to determine the interests of my country and the degree of involvement of my country. I've done that with moderation, with care, with thoughtfulness; sometimes consulting experts. But, I've learned in this last three and a half years that when an issue is extremely difficult, when the call is very close, the chances are the experts will be divided almost 50-50. And the final judgment about the future of the nation — war, peace, involvement, reticence, thoughtfulness, care, consideration, concern — has to be made by the man in the Oval Office. It's a lonely job, but with the involvement of the American people in the process, with an open Government, the job is a very gratifying one.

The American people now are facing, next Tuesday, a lonely decision. Those listening to my voice will have to make a judgment about the future of this country. And I think they ought to remember that one vote can make a lot of difference. If one vote per precinct had changed in 1960, John Kennedy would never have been President of this nation. And if a few more people had gone to the polls and voted in 1968, Hubert Humphrey would have been President; Richard Nixon would not.

There is a partnership involved in our nation. To stay strong, to stay at peace, to raise high the banner of human rights, to set an example for the rest of the world, to let our deep beliefs and commitments be felt by others in other nations, is my plan for the future. I ask the American people to join me in this partnership.

Smith: Governor Reagan?

Reagan: Yes, I would like to add my words of thanks, too, to the ladies of the League of Women Voters for making these debates possible. I'm sorry that we couldn't persuade the bringing in of the third candidate, so that he could have been seen also in these debates. But still, it's good that at least once, all three of us were heard by the people of this country.

Next Tuesday is Election Day. Next Tuesday all of you will go to the polls, will stand there in the polling place and make a decision. I think when you make that decision, it might be well if you would ask yourself, are you better off than you were four years ago? Is it easier for you to go and buy things in the stores than it was four years ago? Is there more or less unemployment in the country than there was four years ago? Is America as respected throughout the world as it was? Do you feel that our security is as safe, that we're as strong as we were four years ago? And if you answer all of those questions yes, why then, I think your choice is very obvious as to whom you will vote for. If you don't agree, if you don't think that this course that we've been on for the last four years is what you would like to see us follow for the next four, then I could suggest another choice that you have.

This country doesn't have to be in the shape that it is in. We do not have to go on sharing in scarcity with the country getting worse off, with unemployment growing. We talk about the unemployment lines. If all of the unemployed today were in a single line allowing two feet for each of them, that line would reach from New York City to Los Angeles, California. All of this can be cured and all of it can be solved.

I have not had the experience the President has had in holding that office, but I think in being Governor of California, the most populous state in the Union — if it were a nation, it would be the seventh-ranking economic power in the world — I, too, had some lonely moments and decisions to make. I know that the economic program that I have proposed for this nation in the next few years can resolve many of the problems that trouble us today. I know because we did it there. We cut the cost — the increased cost of government — in half over the eight years. We returned $5.7 billion in tax rebates, credits and cuts to our people. We, as I have said earlier, fell below the national average in inflation when we did that. And I know that we did give back authority and autonomy to the people.

I would like to have a crusade today, and I would like to lead that crusade with your help. And it would be one to take Government off the backs of the great people of this country, and turn you loose again to do those things that I know you can do so well, because you did them and made this country great. Thank you.

Smith: Gentlemen, ladies and gentlemen, for 60 years the League of Women Voters has been committed to citizen education and effective participation of Americans in governmental and political affairs. The most critical element of all in that process is an informed citizen who goes to the polls and votes. On behalf of the League of Women Voters, now, I would like to thank President Carter and Governor Reagan for being with us in Cleveland tonight. And, ladies and gentlemen, thank you and good night.

November

MAO'S WIDOW ON TRIAL IN CHINA

November 2, 1980

Jiang Qing and other members of China's so-called "Gang of Four" were indicted Nov. 2 on a charge of "counter-revolutionary" crimes, including causing the death of 34,000 Chinese during the Cultural Revolution (1967-76) and conspiracy to overthrow the "proletarian dictatorship." The carefully orchestrated trial that began Nov. 20 in Beijing (Peking) was the keystone of a strategy designed by China's current leaders to steer the country toward a more moderate course and away from the radical policies endorsed by Chairman Mao Zedong.

The outcome of the trial was never in doubt; all defendants were found guilty. In January 1981, Jiang, the 67-year-old widow of Chairman Mao, received a suspended death sentence, as did another of the Gang of Four, Zhang Chunqiao. The other members of the "gang" and six other former officials — Mao's political secretary and five senior military officers implicated in an alleged plot to assassinate Mao in 1971 — received sentences ranging from 16 years in jail to life imprisonment.

A former film actress, Jiang Qing joined Mao's communist rebels in 1937. She rose to prominence in the 1960s as one of the leaders of her husband's Cultural Revolution, a country-wide campaign to enliven revolutionary fervor in China. She led attacks against government officials, including Deng Xiaoping, senior vice premier and China's current de facto leader. Jiang and her associates were arrested in October 1976, just a month after Mao's death.

Reformed Legal System

The charges leveled against the Gang of Four and the others were contained in a 20,000-word, 48-point indictment. The defendants were tried before a panel of 35 judges, many of whom had been persecuted or purged during the Cultural Revolution. Many observers believed that the trial represented an attempt by China's leaders to show off the country's reformed legal system. In the past, politicians who fell out of favor usually were dispatched to the hinterlands without legal proceedings.

All the defendants, with the exceptions of Jiang and Zhang, confessed their guilt in court. Zhang refused to address the court. In contrast, Jiang frequently castigated the judges, government prosecutors and witnesses. And she defended her actions during the Cultural Revolution, saying that she was carrying out the wishes of her husband. At one point in her testimony in late December she reportedly told the court, "I was Chairman Mao's dog. Whomever he told me to bite, I bit."

Position Toward Mao

Though anticipated, Jiang's line of defense presented a delicate problem for China's leaders. Apparently reluctant to damage Mao's image too quickly, they delayed the trial while trying to decide whether they could afford to put to death the widow of the late chairman. The government's position toward Mao was outlined in a Dec. 22 article in People's Daily, *the Communist Party newspaper. The article said that Mao was responsible for the Cultural Revolution and added that while the decade-long upheaval had led to mistakes, the chairman had committed no crimes. And the government prosecutor read a statement that blamed Mao for the excesses of the Cultural Revolution but implied that his earlier achievements outweighed his later "mistakes."*

Hua a Casualty

Another casualty of the trial appeared to be Hua Guofeng, the man Mao chose as his successor as premier and party chairman. Hua resigned as premier in August and was replaced by Zhao Ziyang, the favorite of Deng Xiaoping. In early December, Chairman Hua dropped from public view amid speculation that he was being pressured to relinquish leadership of the party. It was anticipated that he would resign as chairman before the party congress scheduled for the spring of 1981.

Following are excerpts from the indictment of the "Gang of Four" by the special procuratorate under the Supreme People's Procuratorate of the People's Republic of China broadcast Nov. 2, 1980:

...The Ministry of Public Security of the People's Republic of China, after concluding its investigation, has referred the case of the plot by the Lin Biao and Jiang Qing counter-revolutionary cliques to overthrow the political power of the dictatorship of the proletariat to the Supreme People's Procuratorate of the People's Republic of China for examination and prosecution.

Having examined the case, the Special Procuratorate under the Supreme People's Procuratorate confirms that the principal culprits of the Lin Biao and Jiang Qing counter-revolutionary cliques, namely, Lin Biao, Jiang Qing, Kang Sheng, Zhang Chunqiao, Yao Wenyuan, Wang Hongwen, Chen Boda, Xie Fuzhi, Ye Qun, Huang Yongsheng, Wu Faxian, Li Zuopeng, Qiu Huizuo, Lin Liguo, Zhou Yuchi and Jiang Tengjiao, acted in collusion during the "Great Cultural Revolution" and, taking advantage of their positions and the power at their disposal, framed and persecuted Communist Party and state leaders in a premeditated way in an attempt to usurp party leadership and state power and overthrow the political power of the dictatorship of the proletariat.

They did this by resorting to all kinds of intrigues and using every possible means, legal or illegal, overt or covert, by pen or by gun. In September 1971, after the failure of their plot to murder Chairman Mao Zedong and stage an armed counter-revolutionary coup d'etat, Lin Biao, Ye Qun, Lin Liguo, Zhou Yuchi and Jiang Tengjiao fled the country in defection, and the counter-revolutionary clique headed by Lin Biao was exposed and crushed. The counter-revolutionary gang of four of Jiang Qing, Zhang Chunqiao, Yao Wenyuan and Wang Hongwen, with Jiang Qing at the head, carried on its counter-revolutionary conspiratorial activities until it was exposed and smashed in October 1976. The Lin Biao and Jiang Qing counter-revolutionary cliques brought untold disasters to our country and nation.

The Lin Biao and Jiang Qing counter-revolutionary cliques are found guilty of the following crimes:

I. Frame-Up and Persecution of Party and State Leaders and Plotting To Overthrow the Political Power of the Dictatorship of the Proletariat

To overthrow the political power of the dictatorship of the proletariat, the Lin Biao and Jiang Qing counter-revolutionary cliques framed and persecuted party and state leaders and leading cadres in all walks of life in a premeditated way. . . .

II. The Persecution and Suppression of Large Numbers of Cadres and Masses

In order to seize party and state leadership and establish their counter-revolutionary rule, the Lin Biao and Jiang Qing counter-revolutionary cliques incited beating, smashing and looting, whipped up violence, and trumped up false charges, thus persecuting and suppressing large numbers of cadres and people. . . .

III. Plotting To Assassinate Chairman Mao Zedong and Engineer an Armed Counter-Revolutionary Coup D'Etat

After the failure of their conspiracy to usurp party and state leadership through "peaceful transition", the Lin Biao counter-revolutionary clique plotted to stage an armed counter-revolutionary coup d'etat and assassinate chairman Mao Zedong. . . .

IV. Plotting Armed Rebellion in Shanghai

Zhang Chunqiao, Yao Wenyuan and Wang Hongwen, as well as Ma Tianshui, Xu Jiangxian, Wang Xiuzhen and company, made Shanghai their base, built up their own armed force and plotted an armed rebellion in the face of their impending doom. . . .

ELECTION VICTORY AND
CONCESSION STATEMENTS
November 4, 1980

With the dimensions of his landslide victory clear, Ronald Reagan told an election night gathering of supporters in a Los Angeles hotel Nov. 4 that "there has never been a more humbling moment in my life." And Jimmy Carter, the first elected incumbent president since Herbert Hoover in 1932 to fail to win re-election, made a graceful concession speech in which he said, "I promised you four years ago that I would never lie to you. So, I can't stand here and say it doesn't hurt."

President Carter appeared before a group of campaign workers in a Washington, D.C., hotel at 9:50 p.m. with his family and close aides. "The people of the United States have made their choice, and, of course, I accept that decision but, I have to admit, not with the same enthusiasm that I accepted that decision four years ago," Carter said. He added that, one hour earlier, he had called President-elect Reagan to congratulate him on his victory. Reagan won the electoral votes of 44 states; Carter carried only six states and the District of Columbia.

Praise for Mondale

After praising Walter Mondale as the "best Vice President anybody ever had," Carter said that his administration had "achieved some very important goals for our country." He told his listeners to "come together as a united and a unified people to solve the problems that are still before us, to meet the challenges of a new decade. And I urge all of you to join with me in a sincere and fruitful effort to support my successor when he

959

undertakes this great responsibility as President of the greatest nation on Earth."

Carter ended his brief concession address by saying, "I've wanted to serve as President because I love this country and because I love the people of this Nation. Finally, let me say that I am disappointed tonight, but I have not lost either love."

Carter's early concession, made while the polls on the West Coast were still open, was criticized by some. Carter decided to concede after the television networks "called" the election for Reagan early in the evening. Some observers claimed that his concession kept potential voters away from polling places.

Victory Speech

In his speech, Reagan thanked his supporters, his family and his running mate, George Bush, for their efforts on his behalf during the presidential campaign. And Reagan claimed that he was "not frightened by what lies ahead." He added that he did not believe the American people "are frightened by what lies ahead. Together, we are going to do what has to be done. We're going to put America back to work again."

Few expected the election to be a one-sided contest. Reagan referred to his margin of victory when he said, "I would have been not only humbled by the extent of what has happened tonight — even if it had been the cliffhanger that all of us I think were expecting, it would have been the same way — but just to have had the support of the people of this country."

Midway through his speech, Reagan was interrupted by supporters who presented him with a cake baked in the shape of the United States. As the cake was displayed to the president-elect and the audience, it began to slide off the tray. Reagan quipped, "When that began to slide, I thought that maybe the world was going out just as I was getting in."

> *Following are the texts of Reagan's victory speech as it appeared in the* Washington Star *and Carter's concession remarks.* (Boldface headings in brackets have been added by Congressional Quarterly to highlight the organization of the text.):

REAGAN VICTORY SPEECH

... Let me just say first of all this has been — well, there has never been a more humbling moment in my life.

I would have been not only humbled by the extent of what has happened tonight — even if it had been the cliffhanger that all of us I think were expecting, it would have been the same way — but just to have had the support of the people of this country.

I consider the trust that you have placed in me sacred and I give you my sacred oath that I will do my utmost to justify your faith.

I spoke on the phone with President Carter. He called, John Anderson called. But the president pledged the utmost in cooperation in the transition that will take place in these coming months.

I offered him my own cooperation, he graciously said that he wanted this to be the . . .

But anyway, as I say, the president was most gracious about this.

And now all across America there are some people that I owe a great debt of thanks to. There they are, they're meeting tonight in our national headquarters in Arlington, Virginia. The national committee people, the dedicated professionals who made the campaign run.

And in every state, in the counties, in the cities and the precincts, to all of them who worked so tirelessly, literally hundreds of thousands of volunteers — and I've seen them at work throughout the country on this campaign — I just owe them an immeasurable debt of thanks.

[Partnership in White House]

To George and Barbara Bush, our running mates down in Texas, no one has worked harder than they have. We only crossed paths a few times, on this campaign, and had to go out of our way to do it because their schedule was so heavy. And I can tell you that we are going to have a true partnership and a true friendship in the White House.

And now, as I said before, my family. I'm so grateful to them, for the love, for the support and for the hard work because some of them were out on the campaign trail easily as much as Nancy and I were.

And speaking of Nancy, she's going to have a new title in a couple of months. And it isn't really new, because she's been the first lady in my life for a long time. Now we'll share that a little bit in the future.

You know Abe Lincoln, the day after his election to the presidency, gathered in his office the newsmen who had been covering his campaign. And he said to them: "Well boys, your troubles are over now, mine have just begun."

I think I know what he meant. Lincoln may have been concerned in the troubled times in which he became president, but I don't think he was afraid. He was ready to confront the problems and the troubles of a still youthful country, determined to seize the historic opportunity to change things.

And I am not frightened by what lies ahead, and I don't believe the American people are frightened by what lies ahead.

Together, we are going to do what has to be done. We're going to put America back to work again.

[Great American Spirit]

You know, I aim to try and tap that great American spirit that opened up this completely undeveloped continent from coast to coast and made it a great nation, survived several wars, survived the Great Depression, and we'll survive the problems we face right now.

When I accepted your nomination for president, I hesitatingly but I asked for your prayers at that moment. I won't ask them for this in this particular moment but I will just say that I will be very happy to have them in the days ahead.

All I can say to all of you is thank you, and thank you for more than just George Bush and myself, thank you because if the trend continues, we may very well control one house of Congress for the first time in a quarter of a century.

We have already, we have picked up some governorships and Bill Brock told me on the phone just a few minutes ago that it looks like in a number of states we have turned the state legislatures around and for the first time they are majorities for us.

You did it. I have one message that I have to give before I leave. I have been upstairs on the phone trying to get ahold of two celebrations, two parties that are going on, one in Tampico, Ill., where I was born, and one in Dickson [sic], Ill., where I grew up. I've got two home towns. And finally we managed to get the radio station in that area and they told us that they would broadcast my message into the two parties that are going on.

So to all of them, thank you too, back there in the hometowns:

Thank you all.

CARTER CONCESSION

I promised you 4 years ago that I would never lie to you. So I can't stand here and say it doesn't hurt.

The people of the United States have made their choice, and, of course, I accept that decision but, I have to admit, not with the same enthusiasm that I accepted that decision 4 years ago. I have a deep appreciation of the system, however, that lets people make a free choice about who will lead them for the next 4 years.

About an hour ago I called Governor Reagan in California, and I told him that I congratulated him for a fine victory. I look forward to working closely with him during the next few weeks. We'll have a very fine transition period. I told him I wanted the best one in history. And I then sent him this telegram, and I'll read it to you. "It's now apparent that the American people have chosen you as the next President. I congratulate you and pledge to you our fullest support and cooperation in bringing about an orderly transition of government in the weeks ahead. My best wishes are with you and your family as you undertake the responsibilities that lie before you." And I signed it Jimmy Carter.

I have been blessed as only a few people ever have, to help shape the destiny of this Nation. In that effort I've had your faithful support. In some ways I've been the most fortunate of Presidents, because I've had the daily aid of a wise man and a good man at my side, in my judgment the best Vice President anybody every had, Fritz Mondale.

I've not achieved all I set out to do; perhaps no one ever does. But we have faced the tough issues. We've stood for and we've fought for and we have achieved some very important goals for our country. These efforts will not end with this administration. The effort must go on. Nor will the progress that we have made be lost when we leave office. The great principles that have guided this Nation since its very founding will continue to guide America to the challenges of the future.

This has been a long and hard-fought campaign, as you well know. But we must come together as a united and a unified people to solve the problems that are still before us, to meet the challenges of a new decade. And I urge all of you to join in with me in a sincere and fruitful effort to support my successor when he undertakes this great responsibility as President of the greatest nation on Earth.

Ours is a special country, because our vast economic and military strength give us a special responsibility for seeking solutions to the problems that confront the world. But our influence will always be greater when we live up to those principles of freedom, of justice, of human rights, for all people.

God has been good to me and God has been good to this country, and I'm truly thankful. I'm thankful for having been able to serve you in this capacity, thankful for the successes that we have had, thankful that to the end you were with me and every good thing that I tried to do.

There's an old Yiddish proverb that I've often thought of in the days and months that I've held this office. It says simply: 'God gives burdens, also shoulders.' In all the days and months when I have served you and served this country, you've readily given me your shoulders, your faith, and your prayers. No man could ask any more of his friends.

I've wanted to serve as President because I love this country and because I love the people of this Nation. Finally, let me say that I am disappointed tonight, but I have not lost either love.

December

POPE'S ENCYCLICAL
AND TRAVELS

June 2—December 2, 1980

Pope John Paul II, the leader of the Roman Catholic Church, issued the second encyclical of his pontificate Dec. 2. Entitled, "Dives in Misericordia" (literally, "Rich in Mercy": the English version was entitled "On the Mercy of God"), the 15,000-word encyclical urged Catholics to use God's mercy as the basis for their efforts to achieve social justice.

The draft of the encyclical was written by the pope in Polish, his native tongue. His first encyclical, "Redemptor Hominis" or "Redeemer of Man," issued in March 1979, was composed in the same manner. Both encyclicals dealt essentially with the same subject.

In "Dives in Misericordia," the pope stressed the importance of God's love as the sole motivation for justice. Social activism not based on mercy, he said, could turn oppressive.

Citing the parable of the prodigal son, the pope noted that "the term 'justice' is not used even once; just as in the original text the term 'mercy' is not used either. Nevertheless, the relationship between justice and love that is manifested as mercy is inscribed with great exactness in the content of the gospel parable. . . ."

"The experience of the past and of our own time," the pope continued, "demonstrates that justice alone is not enough, that it can even lead to the negation and destruction of itself, if that deeper power, which is love, is not allowed to shape human life in its various dimensions."

Social justice was very much on the pontiff's mind during his 13-day visit to Brazil. He endorsed the campaign led by some of Brazil's bishops to temper the oppressive policies of the military regime. But he warned against using social activism for "political partisanship and subjection to this or that ideology or system."

Priests and Politics

John Paul II, the first pope of modern times to travel regularly and extensively outside Italy, had stressed some of the same themes of social reform and clerical avoidance of partisan politics during his visits to North and South America in 1979. In keeping with the pope's directives, one member of the U.S. House of Representatives, Robert F. Drinan, D-Mass., did not seek re-election in 1980. (Pope's journeys, Historic Documents of 1979, pp. 725-761; Drinan retirement, this volume, p. 411)

Besides visiting Brazil, the pope in 1980 also traveled to Africa, France and West Germany. During his African tour, May 2-12, he caused a slight stir when he suggested that certain traditional African rites be omitted from Catholic religious services. And, as he has since his election in 1978, he stressed the sanctity of the family in most of his public statements.

The pope was in France May 30-June 2 where he urged unity and peace in the church and the world. Similar themes characterized the pontiff's Nov. 15-19 trip to West Germany, the home of the Reformation. The pope also defended the right of the church to intervene in theological disputes, a reference to Hans Küng, a German theologian censured by the Vatican in December 1979 and subsequently stripped of his post as a theology teacher.

Following are excerpts from Pope John Paul II's address to the United Nations Educational, Scientific and Cultural Organization (UNESCO) in Paris, France, June 2; his address to the bishops of Brazil at Fortaleza, July 10; his address to the West German bishops at Fulda, Nov. 17; and the second encyclical of Pope John Paul II, "Dives in Misericordia," released at the Vatican Dec. 2, 1980:

ADDRESS TO UNESCO IN PARIS

... 8. All of us here meet on the basis of culture, a basic reality which unites us and is the foundation for the establishment of UNESCO and its goals. By the same token, we gather around man and, so to speak, in man. This very man, who expressed himself in culture and through culture, is unique, complete and undivided. He is at the same time the subject and the artisan of culture. Thus he cannot be considered only as the result of all the concrete conditions of his existence, nor as a result — let me give just this one example — of relations of factors which are outstanding at a given time. Would not this criterion of relations of factors, be the key to understanding the historicity of man, the understanding of his culture and different ways of developing it? This criterion certainly is key, even precious, but it is neither the fundamental key nor the constitutive one. Human cultures reflect, doubtlessly, different systems of relations of factors; however, the origin of culture is not one system or another, but man, who lives within a system, who accepts it or who tries to change it. Culture without human subjectivity is unthinkable nor can it exist without human causality; concerning cultural aspects, man is always first, man is the first and fundamental part of culture.

And such will man always remain in his entirety: in the whole of his spiritual and material subjectivity. If the distinction between spiritual and material culture only exists in relation to the character and content of the products by which culture is manifested, we must state, on the one hand, that the works of material culture bring about a spiritualizing effect of matter, a submission of material elements to the spiritualizing powers of man: i.e., his intelligence and his will; and on the other hand, the works of spiritual culture manifest in a specific way a certain "materializing element" of that which is spiritual, an incarnation of what is spiritual. Cultural works present both these characteristics, which are equally important and permanent. . . .

9. I would like to mention here something else, a vital consideration, though belonging to an entirely different order. We can mention it because the Holy See is represented at UNESCO by a permanent observer, whose presence reflects the very nature of the Apostolic See. This presence, in a wider sense, is in harmony with the nature and the mission of the Catholic Church, and indirectly, with the mission of all of Christianity. I take advantage of the occasion offered me today to express a personal and deep conviction of mine. The presence of the Holy See in your organization has — even if it is also a result of the Holy See's specific sovereignty — above all a raison-d'etre, in the organic and constitutive relation existing between religion in general, and Christianity in particular, on the one hand, and culture on the other. This relation covers numerous realities which have to be considered as concrete expressions of culture throughout the different periods of history and in all parts of the earth.

ADDRESS AT FORTALEZA

1. . . . No encounter is more important than this with you, bishops of Brazil. You form today the most numerous episcopal body in the world. With numbers there is a corresponding, intense activity. You show this in your pastorate of the young and dynamic church which is yours. For this reason and because of the promising prospects of your country, the episcopate of which you are part gains prestige, but it also receives a responsibility going well beyond the bounds of your dioceses and your country. It is a responsibility concerning the entire church. . . .

. . .Your vocation to be bishops prohibits you, with total clarity and without the least attenuation, from everything that has to do with political partisanships and subjection to this or that ideology or system. But it does not prohibit you, rather does it call you to be near and at the service of all men and women, especially the weakest and most needy. . . .

The church of Brazil does well to show itself as the church of the poor. . . . By doing so in the exercise of her mission the church also serves the good of society. She does not claim to take on political activities as part of her own function. She does not oppose authority.

On the contrary, she proclaims that authority is necessary for the good of society, for maintaining and exerting its sovereignty. But the church does claim that the practice of a social pastorate is her right and duty, not in view of a purely temporal project, but for the formation and orientation of consciences for their own specific ends, in order that society may become more just. . . .

The bold reforms that are necessary have not the sole aim of collectivizing the means of production, even less if this means concentrating all in the hands of the state, thus turned into being the sole true capitalist force. These reforms ought to have the goal of enabling all to have access to property, since this in a certain fashion constitutes the indispensable condition for man's liberty and creativity, such as will permit him to rise out of obscurity and alienation when it is a question of collaborating for the common good.

Last, the church's social action ought to be the accomplishment of all who bear significant shares of the church's mission on their shoulders, each in accordance with his specific function and responsibility. . . .

ADDRESS AT FULDA

. . . Inner renewal of religious and church life and ecumenical effort toward rapprochement and understanding among divided Christians also form the main objects of my apostolic journeys to the various local churches and continents. They are the objects of my pastoral visit to the church of your land and of our encounter today. Spiritual renewal of the church and Christian unity were the explicit tasks of the Second Vatican Council. Pope, bishops, priests and faithful are equally committed and pledged thereto. To make these tasks a matter of common responsibility is the pressing demand of the hour. They are the great challenge and duty facing our whole collegial responsibility as pastors of the church. My reflections and considerations which follow are meant to apply to and serve those ends.

Ever since the first hours of my pontificate I have understood the supreme pastoral office particularly as service to the collegiality of the bishops united with the successor of Peter. On the other hand, I understand the *collegialitas effectiva et affectiva* (effective and affective collegiality) of the bishops as a weighty help to my own service.

So I am drawn, as I visit your land, to bring out my nearness to you above all, my communion with you, and to strengthen it through my witness. . . .

3. Be lovingly careful of the unity of the presbyterium in each diocese. What is expected and demanded from priests has increased in a very burdensome way for you over recent decades. Because of their shrinking number, more tasks are falling to priests. Because of the many vocational and honorable services performed by the laity in the care of souls, priests are more often in request for their office of spiritual guidance. Ever more multifaceted spiritual intercommunication is necessary for priests in a society that is encompassed with an ever thicker net of social communications. Many priests wear themselves out with work, but become lonely and lose their sense of direction. So it is all the more important for the unity of the presbyterium to be lived and experienced. Support everything that strengthens priests to come together and help each other to live by the word and spirit of the Lord.

Three things are especially dear to my heart:

—Seminaries ought to be nurturers of true priestly interpersonal communion and friendship as well as places for making clear, enduring decisions for life.

—Theology ought to prepare for witness of faith and lead to deepening of faith, so that priests may understand men's problems, and the Gospel's and the church's answers as well.

—Priests ought to have help to fulfill the lofty demands of the celibate life and dedication to Christ and mankind and to give evidence of that through priestly simplicity, poverty and readiness. The spiritual community can do valuable service here. . . .

SECOND ENCYCLICAL OF JOHN PAUL II

I

He Who Sees Me Sees the Father
(Cf. Jn. 14:9)

1. THE REVELATION OF MERCY

. . . Following the teaching of the Second Vatican Council and paying close attention to the special needs of our times, I devoted the encyclical *Redemptor Hominis* to the truth about man, a truth that is revealed to us in its fullness and depth in Christ. A no less important need in these critical and difficult times impels me to draw attention once again in Christ to the countenance of the "Father of mercies and God of all comfort." We read in the constitution *Guadium et Spes:* "Christ the new Adam . . . fully reveals man to himself and brings to light his lofty calling," and does it "in the very revelation of the mystery of the Father and of his love." The words I have quoted are clear testimony to the fact that man cannot be manifested in the full dignity of his nature without reference — not only on the level of concepts but also in an integrally existential way — to God. Man and man's lofty calling are revealed in Christ through the revelation of the mystery of the Father and his love. . . .

Since, therefore, in the present phase of the church's history we put before ourselves as our primary task the implementation of the doctrine of the great council, we must act upon this principle with faith, with an open mind and with all our heart. In the encyclical already referred to, I have tried to show that the deepening and the many-faceted enrichment of the church's consciousness resulting from the council must open our minds and our hearts more widely to Christ. Today I wish to say that openness to Christ, who as the redeemer of the world fully "reveals man to himself," can only be achieved through an ever more mature reference to the Father and his love. . . .

The truth revealed in Christ about God the "Father of mercies," enables us to "see" him as particularly close to man, especially when man is suffering, when he is under threat at the very heart of his existence and dignity. And this is why, in the situation of the church and the world today, many individuals and groups guided by a lively sense of faith are turning, I would say almost spontaneously, to the mercy of God. They are certainly being moved to do this by Christ himself, who through his Spirit works within human hearts. For the mystery of God the "Father of mercies" revealed by Christ becomes, in the context of today's threats to man, as it were a unique appeal addressed to the church.

In the present encyclical I wish to accept this appeal; I wish to draw from the eternal and at the same time — for its simplicity and depth — incomparable language of revelation and faith, in order through this same language to express once more before God and before humanity the major anxieties of our time. . . .

III
The Old Testament

4. The concept of "mercy" in the Old Testament has a long and rich history. We have to refer back to it in order that the mercy revealed by Christ may shine forth more clearly. By revealing that mercy both through his actions and through his teaching, Christ addressed himself to people who not only knew the concept of mercy, but who also, as the people of God in the Old Covenant, had drawn from their agelong history a special experience of the mercy of God. This experience was social and communal, as well as individual and interior.

Israel was, in fact, the people of the covenant with God, a covenant that it broke many times. Whenever it became aware of its infidelity — and in the history of Israel there was no lack of prophets and others who awakened this awareness — it appealed to mercy. . . .

IV
The Parable of the Prodigal Son

5. AN ANALOGY

At the very beginning of the New Testament, two voices resound in St. Luke's Gospel in unique harmony concerning the mercy of God, a harmony which forcefully echoes the whole Old Testament tradition. They express the semantic elements linked to the differentiated terminology of the ancient books. Mary, entering the house of Zechariah, magnifies the Lord with all her soul for "his mercy," which "from generation to generation" is bestowed on those who fear him. . . .

In the teaching of Christ himself, this image inherited from the Old Testament becomes at the same time simpler and more profound. This is perhaps most evident in the parable of the Prodigal Son. Although the word "mercy" does not appear, it nevertheless expresses the essence of the divine mercy in a particularly clear way. This is due not so much to the terminology, as in the Old Testament books, as to the analogy that enables us to understand more fully the very mystery of mercy, as a profound drama played out between the father's love and the prodigality and sin of the son.

That son, who receives from the father the portion of the inheritance that is due to him and leaves home to squander it in a far country "in loose living," in a certain sense is the man of every period, beginning with the one who was the first to lose the inheritance of grace and original justice. The analogy at this point is very wide-ranging. The parable indirectly touches upon every breach of the covenant of love, every loss of grace, every sin.

In this analogy there is less emphasis than in the prophetic tradition on the unfaithfulness of the whole people of Israel, although the analogy of the prodigal son may extend to this also. "When he had spent everything," the son "began to be in need," especially as "a great famine arose in that country" to which he had gone after leaving his father's house. And in this situation "he would gladly have fed on" anything, even "the pods that the swine ate," the swine that he herded for "one of the citizens of that country." But even this was refused him.

The analogy turns clearly toward man's interior. The inheritance that the son had received from his father was a quantity of material goods, but more important than these goods was his dignity as a son in his father's house. The situation in which he found himself when he lost the material goods should have made him aware of the loss of that dignity. He had not thought about it previously, when he had asked his father to give him the part of the inheritance that was due to him, in order to go away.

He seems not to be conscious of it even now, when he says to himself: "How many of my father's hired servants have bread enough and to spare, but I perish here with hunger." He measures himself by the standard of the goods that he has lost, that he no longer "possesses," while the hired servants in his father's house "possess" them. These words express above all his attitude to material goods; nevertheless, under their surface is concealed the tragedy of lost dignity, the awareness of squandered sonship.

It is at this point that he makes the decision: "I will arise and go to my father, and I will say to him, 'Father, I have sinned against heaven and before you; I am no longer worthy to be called your son. Treat me as one of your hired servants.' "

These are words that reveal more deeply the essential problem. Through the complex material situation in which the prodigal son found himself because of his folly, because of sin, the sense of lost dignity had matured. When he decides to return to his father's house, to ask his father to be received — no longer by virtue of his right as a son, but as an employee — at first sight he seems to be acting by reason of the hunger and poverty that he had fallen into; this motive, however, is permeated by an awareness of a deeper loss: To be a hired servant in his own father's house is certainly a great humiliation and source of shame.

Nevertheless, the prodigal son is ready to undergo that humiliation and shame. He realizes that he no longer has any right except to be an employee in his father's house. His decision is taken in full consciousness of what he has deserved and of what he can still have a right to in accordance with the norms of justice. Precisely this reasoning demonstrates that at the center of the prodigal son's consciousness the sense of lost dignity is emerging, the sense of that dignity that springs from the relationship of the son with the father. And it is with this decision that he sets out.

In the parable of the prodigal son, the term "justice" is not used even once; just as in the original text the term "mercy" is not used either. Nevertheless, the relationship between justice and love that is manifested as mercy is inscribed with great exactness in the content of the gospel parable. It becomes more evident that love is transformed into mercy when it is necessary to go beyond the precise norm of justice — precise and often too narrow. . . .

Since this [the prodigal son's] conduct had in his own eyes deprived him of his dignity as a son, it could not be a matter of indifference to his father. It was bound to make him suffer. It was also bound to implicate him in some way. And yet, after all, it was his own son who was involved, and such a relationship could never be altered or destroyed by any sort of behavior. The prodigal son is aware of this and it is precisely this awareness that shows him clearly the dignity which he has lost and which makes him honestly evaluate the position that he could still expect in his father's house.

6. PARTICULAR CONCENTRATION ON HUMAN DIGNITY

This exact picture of the prodigal son's state of mind enables us to understand exactly what the mercy of God consists in. There is no doubt that in this simple but penetrating analogy the figure of the father reveals to us God as Father. The conduct of the father in the parable and his whole behavior, which manifests his internal attitude, enables us to rediscover the individual threads of the Old Testament vision of mercy in a synthesis which is totally new, full of simplicity and depth.

The father of the prodigal son is faithful to his fatherhood, faithful to the love that he had always lavished on his son. This fidelity is expressed in the parable not only by his immediate readiness to welcome him home when he returns after having squandered his inheritance; it is expressed even more fully by that joy, that merrymaking for the squanderer after his return, merrymaking which is so generous that it provokes the opposition and hatred of the elder brother, who had never gone far away from his father and had never abandoned the home. . . .

Going on, one can therefore say that the love for the son, the love that springs from the very essence of fatherhood, in a way obliges the father to be concerned about his son's dignity. This concern is the measure of his love, the love of which St. Paul was to write: "Love is patient and kind . . . love does not insist on its own way; it is not irritable or resentful . . . but rejoices in the right . . . hopes all things, endures all things" and "love never ends."

Mercy — as Christ has presented it in the parable of the prodigal son — has the interior form of the love that in the New Testament is called *agape*. This love is able to reach down to every prodigal son, to every human misery, and above all to every form of moral misery, to sin. When this happens, the person who is the object of mercy does not feel humiliated, but rather found again and "restored to value." . . .

What took place in the relationship between the father and the son in Christ's parable is not to be evaluated "from the outside." Our prejudices about mercy are mostly the result of appraising them only from the outside. At times it happens that by following this method of evaluation we see in mercy above all a relationship of inequality between the one offering it and the one receiving it. And, in consequence, we are quick to deduce that mercy belittles the receiver, that it offends the dignity of man.

The parable of the prodigal son shows that the reality is different: The relationship of mercy is based on the common experience of that good which is man, on the common experience of the dignity that is proper to him. This common experience makes the prodigal son begin to see himself and his actions in their full truth (this vision in truth is a genuine form of humility); on the other hand, for this very reason he becomes a particular good for his father: The father sees so clearly the good which has been achieved thanks to a mysterious radiation of truth and love, that he seems to forget all the evil which the son had committed.

The parable of the prodigal son expresses in a simple but profound way the reality of conversion. Conversion is the most concrete expression of the working of love and of the presence of mercy in the human world. The true and proper meaning of mercy does not consist only in looking, however penetratingly and compassionately, at moral, physical or material evil: Mercy is manifested in its true and proper aspect when it restores to value, promotes and draws good from all the forms of evil existing in the world and in man.

Understood in this way, mercy constitutes the fundamental content of the messianic message of Christ and the constitutive power of his mission. His disciples and followers understood and practiced mercy in the same way. Mercy never ceased to reveal itself, in their hearts and in their actions, as an especially creative proof of the love which does not allow itself to be "conquered by evil," but overcomes "evil with good."

The genuine face of mercy has to be ever revealed anew. In spite of many prejudices, mercy seems particularly necessary for our times. . . .

COURT ON DOUBLE JEOPARDY
December 9, 1980

The Supreme Court, in a 5-4 decision, ruled Dec. 9 that the Constitution's prohibition against double jeopardy did not prevent prosecutors from appealing sentences they considered too lenient.

The ruling cut across usual conservative-liberal lines. It was seen not only as giving prosecutors a second chance to obtain a tough sentence but also as adjusting disparities that had resulted from the broad sentencing discretion of judges.

The decision grew out of a $480,000 arson scheme and the 1970 bombing of a federal building in Rochester, N.Y. Eugene DiFrancesco was sentenced in federal district court to nine years on the bombing charges and to a 10-year concurrent term for running an arson ring. An appellate court dismissed a government appeal that the sentence was too lenient.

Majority Decision

Writing for the majority, Justice Harry A. Blackmun said that the reason for the double jeopardy clause (the Fifth Amendment guarantees that no one will be "subject for the same offense to be twice put in jeopardy of life or limb") was to save an acquitted defendant the "ordeal" of another trial. But Blackmun — joined by Chief Justice Warren E. Burger and Justices Potter Stewart, Lewis F. Powell Jr. and William H. Rehnquist — wrote that a sentence can be reopened because "a sentence does not have the qualities of constitutional finality that attend an acquittal."

Dissenting Opinions

Justices William J. Brennan Jr., Byron R. White, Thurgood Marshall and John Paul Stevens dissented. In their opinion, written by Brennan, they said the court had not demonstrated a basis for differentiating between the finality of acquittals and the finality of sentences. "[A] punishment enhanced by an appellate court is an unconstitutional multiple punishment," Brennan wrote.

In a separate dissent, Justice Stevens wrote that he agreed with Justice John Marshall Harlan's "powerful analysis" of the double jeopardy issue in North Carolina v. *Pearce (1969). As quoted by Stevens, Harlan referred to cases in which defendants had received "punishment less than the maximum." Harlan wrote that "in each case it was determined . . . that the defendant or his offense was of a certain limited degree of 'badness' or gravity only, and therefore merited only a certain limited punishment."*

> *Following are excerpts from the Supreme Court's Dec. 9, 1980, opinion that the Constitution's prohibition against double jeopardy did not prevent prosecutors from appealing sentences they considered too lenient; from the dissenting opinion of Justices William J. Brennan Jr., Byron R. White, Thurgood Marshall and John Paul Stevens; and from the separate dissenting opinion of Justice Stevens:*

No. 79-567

United States, Petitioner,	On Writ of Certiorari to the
v.	United States Court of Appeals
Eugene DiFrancesco.	for the Second Circuit.

[December 9, 1980]

MR. JUSTICE BLACKMUN delivered the opinion of the Court.

The Organized Crime Control Act of 1970, Pub. L. 91-452, 84 Stat. 922, contains, among other things, a definition of "dangerous special offender," 18 U.S.C. §§ 3575 (e) and (f); authorizes the imposition of an increased sentence upon a convicted dangerous special offender, § 3575 (b); and grants the United States the right, under specified conditions, to take that sentence to the Court of Appeals for review, § 3576. The issue presented by this case is whether § 3576, authorizing the United

States so to appeal, violates the Double Jeopardy Clause of the Fifth Amendment of the Constitution.

I

At a 1977 jury trial in the United States District Court for the Western District of New York, respondent Eugene DiFrancesco was convicted of conducting the affairs of an enterprise through a pattern of racketeering activity, and of conspiring to commit that offense, in violation of 18 U.S.C. §§ 1962 (c) and (d). At another jury trial in 1978, — before a different judge in the same district — based on an indictment returned prior to the racketeering indictment, respondent was convicted of damaging federal property, in violation of 18 U.S.C. § 1361, of unlawfully storing explosive materials, in violation of 18 U.S.C. § 842 (j), and of conspiring to commit those offenses, in violation of 18 U.S.C. § 371. . . .

Respondent was first sentenced, in March 1978, on his convictions at the later trial. He received eight years on the charge for damaging federal property and five years on the conspiracy charge, these sentences to be served concurrently, and one year on the unlawful storage charge, to be served consecutively to the other sentences. This made a total of nine years' imprisonment. In April, respondent was sentenced as a dangerous special offender under § 3575 to two 10-year terms on the racketeering counts upon which he was convicted at the earlier trial; the court specified that these sentences were to be served concurrently with each other and with the sentences imposed in March. The dangerous special offender charge and sentences thus resulted in additional punishment of only about a year.

Respondent appealed the respective judgments of conviction to the Court of Appeals for the Second Circuit, and the United States sought review, under § 3576, of the sentences imposed upon respondent as a dangerous special offender. The Court of Appeals unanimously affirmed the judgments of conviction. By a divided vote, however, that court dismissed the Government's appeal on double jeopardy grounds. . . . The two judges in the majority thus did not address the merits of the special offender issue. The third judge, while agreeing that the Government's appeal was to be dismissed, based that conclusion not on constitutional grounds, as did the majority, but on the grounds that §§ 3575 and 3576 were inapplicable to the facts of the case. . . . Because of the importance of the constitutional question, we granted the Government's petition for certiorari, which confined itself to that single issue. . . . Respondent has not filed a cross-petition.

II

At the earlier racketeering trial, the evidence showed that respondent was involved in an arson-for-hire scheme in the Rochester, N.Y., area that was responsible for at least eight fires between 1970 and 1973; that the ring collaborated with property owners to set fire to buildings in return for shares of the insurance proceeds; and that insurers were defrauded of approximately $480,000 as a result of these fires. At the second trial, the evidence showed that respondent participated in the 1970 "Columbus Day bombings," including the bombing of the federal building at Rochester.

Prior to the first trial, the Government, in accordance with § 3575 (a), filed with the trial court a notice alleging that respondent was a dangerous special offender. This notice recited the Government's intention to seek enhanced sentences on the racketeering counts in the event respondent was convicted at that trial. After respondent was found guilty, a dangerous special offender hearing, pursuant to § 3575 (b), was held. At the hearing, the Government relied upon the testimony adduced at the trial and upon public documents that attested to other convictions of respondent for the Columbus Day bombings, for loansharking, and for murder. . . . The defense offered no evidence. It conceded the validity of the public records, . . . but objected to any consideration of the murder offense because that conviction had been vacated on appeal. . . .

The District Court made findings of fact and ruled that respondent was a dangerous special offender within the meaning of the statute. The findings set forth respondent's criminal record and stated that that record revealed "virtually continuous criminal conduct over the past eight years, interrupted only by relatively brief periods of imprisonment in 1975, 1976 and 1977." . . . The court found, in addition, that respondent's "criminal history, based upon proven facts, reveals a pattern of habitual and knowing criminal conduct of the most violent and dangerous nature against the lives and property of the citizens of this community. It further shows the defendant's complete and utter disregard for the public safety. The defendant, by virtue of his own criminal record, has shown himself to be a hardened habitual criminal from whom the public must be protected for as long a period as possible. Only in that way can the public be protected from further violent and dangerous criminal conduct by the defendant." . . . The court thereupon sentenced respondent under § 3575 (b) to the concurrent 10-year terms hereinabove described. . . .

The United States then took its appeal under § 3576, claiming that the District Court abused its discretion in imposing sentences that amounted to additional imprisonment of respondent for only one year, in the face of the findings the court made after the dangerous special offender hearing. The dismissal of the Government's appeal by the Court of Appeals rested specifically upon its conclusion, which it described as "inescapable," that "to subject a defendant to the risk of substitution of a greater sentence, upon an appeal by the government, is to place him a second time 'in jeopardy of life or limb.' ". . .

III

While this Court, so far as we are able to ascertain, has never invalidated an Act of Congress on double jeopardy grounds, it has had frequent occasion recently to consider and pass upon double jeopardy claims raised in various contexts. . . .

That the Clause is important and vital in this day is demonstrated by the host of recent cases. That its application has not proved to be facile or routine is demonstrated by acknowledged changes in direction or in emphasis. . . . Nonetheless, the following general principles emerge from the Court's double jeopardy decisions and may be regarded as essentially settled:

This concept has ancient roots centering in the common law pleas of *autre fois acquit, autre fois convict,* and pardon, 4 W. Blackstone, Commentaries 329-330 (1st ed. 1769), and found expression in the legal tradition of colonial America. . . .

—The stated design, in terms of specific purpose, has been expressed in various ways. It has been said that "a" or "the" "primary purpose" of the Clause was "to preserve the finality of judgments,". . . or the "integrity of judgments,". . . But it has also been said that "central to the objective of the prohibition against successive trials" is the barrier to "affording the prosecution another opportunity to supply evidence which it failed to muster in the first proceeding." . . . Implicit in this is the thought that if the Government may reprosecute, it gains an advantage from what it learns at the first trial about the strengths of the defense case and the weaknesses of its own. . . .

Still another consideration has been noted:

—The general design of the Double Jeopardy Clause of the Fifth Amendment is that described in *Green* v. *United States:* [1957]

> "The constitutional prohibition against 'double jeopardy' was designed to protect an individual from being subjected to the hazards of trial and possible conviction more than once for an alleged offense. . . . The underlying idea, one that is deeply ingrained in at least the Anglo-American system of jurisprudence, is that the State with all its resources and power should not be allowed to make repeated attempts to convict an individual for an alleged offense, thereby subjecting him to embarrassment, expense and ordeal and compelling him to live in a continuing state of anxiety and insecurity, as well as enhancing the possibility that even though innocent he may be found guilty.". . .

"Because jeopardy attaches before the judgment becomes final, the constitutional protection also embraces the defendant's 'valued right to have his trial completed by a particular tribunal.' " *Arizona* v. *Washington* [1978] quoting from *Wade* v. *Hunter* (1949).

See *Swisher* v. *Brady* [1978]. . . .

On occasion, stress has been placed upon punishment:

"It is the punishment that would legally follow the second conviction which is the real danger guarded against by the Constitution.". . .

—The Court has summarized:

"That guarantee [against double jeopardy] has been said to consist of three separate constitutional protections. It protects against a second prosecution for the same offense after acquittal. It protects against a second prosecution for the same offense after conviction. And it protects against multiple punishments for the same offense." . . . *North Carolina* v. *Pearce* [1969]. . . .

See *Illinois* v. *Vitale* [1980].

—An acquittal is accorded special weight. "The constitutional protection against double jeopardy unequivocally prohibits a second trial following an acquittal," for the "public interest in the finality of criminal judgments is so strong that an acquitted defendant may not be retried even though 'the acquittal was based upon an egregiously erroneous foundation.' See *Fong Foo* v. *United States* [1962]. . . .

—The result is definitely otherwise in cases where the trial has not ended in an acquittal. This Court has long recognized that the Government may bring a second prosecution where a mistrial has been occasioned by "manifest necessity." *United States* v. *Perez* [1824]. See *Arizona* v. *Washington*; *Illinois* v. *Somerville*, [1973]. Furthermore, reprosecution of a defendant who has successfully moved for a mistrial is not barred, so long as the Government did not deliberately seek to provoke the mistrial request. *United States* v. *Dinitz* [1976].

Similarly, where the trial has been terminated prior to a jury verdict at the defendant's request on grounds unrelated to guilt or innocence, the Government may seek appellate review of that decision even though a second trial would be necessitated by a reversal. See *United States* v. *Scott* [1978]. *A fortiori*, the Double Jeopardy Clause does not bar a Government appeal from a ruling in favor of the defendant after a guilty verdict has been entered by the trier of fact. See *United States* v. *Wilson* [1975]; *United States* v. *Rojas* (1977); *United States* v. *DeGarces* (1975).

Finally, if the first trial has ended in a conviction, the double jeopardy guarantee "imposes no limitations whatever upon the power to *retry* a defendant who has succeeded in getting his first conviction set aside" (emphasis in original). *North Carolina* v. *Pearce*. "It would be a high price indeed for society to pay were every accused granted immunity from punishment because of any defect sufficient to constitute reversible error in the proceedings leading to conviction." *United States* v. *Tateo* [1964]. "[T]o require a criminal defendant to stand trial again after he has successfully invoked a statutory right of appeal to upset his first conviction is not an act of governmental oppression of the sort against which the Double Jeopardy Clause was intended to protect." *United States* v. *Scott*. There is, however, one exception to this rule: the Double Jeopardy Clause prohibits retrial after a conviction has been reversed because of insufficiency of the evidence. *Burks* v. *United States* [1978]; *Greene* v. *Massey* [1978].

—Where the Clause does apply, "its sweep is absolute." *Burks* v. *United States*. . . .

—The United States "has no right of appeal in a criminal case, absent explicit statutory authority." *United States* v. *Scott*. But with the enactment of the first paragraph of what is now 18 U.S.C. § 3731 by Pub. L. 91-644 in 1971, . . . permitting a Government appeal in a criminal case except "where the double jeopardy clause of the United States Constitution prohibits further prosecution," the Court necessarily concluded that "Congress intended to remove all statutory barriers to Government appeals and to allow appeals whenever the Constitution would permit." *United States* v. *Wilson*. See also *United States* v. *Scott*.

IV

From these principles, certain propositions pertinent to the present controversy emerge:

A. The Double Jeopardy Clause is *not* a complete barrier to an appeal by the prosecution in a criminal case. "[W]here a Government appeal presents no threat of successive prosecutions, the Double Jeopardy Clause is not offended.". . . From this it follows that the Government's taking a review of respondent's sentence does not in itself offend double jeopardy principles just because its success might deprive respondent of the benefit of a more lenient sentence. . . .

B. The double jeopardy focus, thus, is not on the appeal but on the relief that is requested, and our task is to determine whether a criminal sentence, once pronounced, is to be accorded constitutional finality and conclusiveness similar to that which attaches to a jury's verdict of acquittal. We conclude that neither the history of sentencing practices, nor the pertinent rulings of this Court, nor even considerations of double jeopardy policy support such an equation. . . .

Historically, the pronouncement of sentence has never carried the finality that attaches to an acquittal. The common law writs of *autre fois acquit* and *autre fois convict* were protections against retrial. . . . Although the distinction was not of great importance early in the English common law because nearly all felonies, to which double jeopardy principles originally were limited, were punishable by the critical sentences of death or deportation, . . . it gained importance when sentences of imprisonment became common. The trial court's increase of a sentence, so long as it took place during the same term of court, was permitted. This practice was not thought to violate any double jeopardy principle. . . . The common law is important in the present context, for our Double

Jeopardy Clause was drafted with the common law protections in mind. . . . This accounts for the established practice in the federal courts that the sentencing judge may recall the defendant and increase his sentence, at least (and we venture no comment as to this limitation) so long as he has not yet begun to serve that sentence. . . . Thus it may be said with certainty that history demonstrates that the common law never ascribed such finality to a sentence as would prevent a legislative body from authorizing its appeal by the prosecution. Indeed, countries that trace their legal systems to the English common law permit such appeals.

C. This Court's decisions in the sentencing area clearly establish that a sentence does not have the qualities of constitutional finality that attend an acquittal. In *Bozza* v. *United States* (1947), the defendant was convicted of a crime carrying a mandatory minimum sentence of fine and imprisonment. The trial court, however, sentenced the defendant only to imprisonment. Later on the same day, the judge recalled the defendant and imposed both fine and imprisonment. This Court held that there was no double jeopardy. . . . And in *North Carolina* v. *Pearce* the Court held that there was no absolute constitutional bar to the imposition of a more severe sentence on reconviction after the defendant's successful appeal of the original judgment of conviction. . . .

D. The double jeopardy considerations that bar reprosecution after an acquittal do not prohibit review of a sentence. We have noted above the basic design of the double jeopardy provision, that is, as a bar against repeated attempts to convict, with consequent subjection of the defendant to embarrassment, expense, anxiety, and insecurity, and the possibility that he may be found guilty even though innocent. These considerations, however, have no significant application to the prosecution's statutorily granted right to review a sentence. This limited appeal does not involve a retrial or approximate the ordeal of a trial on the basic issue of guilt or innocence. Under § 3576, the appeal is to be taken promptly and is essentially on the record of the sentencing court. The defendant, of course, is charged with knowledge of the statute and its appeal provisions, and has no expectation of finality in his sentence until the appeal is concluded or the time to appeal has expired. To be sure, the appeal may prolong the period of any anxiety that may exist, but it does so only for the finite period provided by the statute. The appeal is no more of an ordeal than any Government appeal under § 3731 from the dismissal of an indictment or information. The defendant's primary concern and anxiety obviously relate to the determination of innocence or guilt, and that already is behind him. The defendant is subject to no risk of being harassed and then convicted, although innocent. Furthermore, a sentence is characteristically determined in large part on the basis of information, such as the presentence report, developed outside the courtroom. It is purely a judicial determination, and much that goes into it is the result of inquiry that is nonadversarial in nature.

E. The Double Jeopardy Clause does not provide the defendant with the right to know at any specific moment in time what the exact limit of his punishment will turn out to be. Congress has established many types of criminal sanctions under which the defendant is unaware of the precise extent of his punishment for significant periods of time, or even for life, yet these sanctions have not been considered to be violative of the Clause. Thus, there is no double jeopardy protection against revocation of probation and the imposition of imprisonment. . . . There are other situations where probation or parole may be revoked and sentence of imprisonment imposed. . . . While these criminal sanctions do not involve the increase of a final sentence, and while the defendant is aware at the original sentencing that a term of imprisonment later may be imposed, the situation before us is different in no critical respect. Respondent was similarly aware that a dangerous special offender sentence is subject to increase on appeal. His legitimate expectations are not defeated if his sentence is increased on appeal any more than are the expectations of the defendant who is placed on parole or probation that is later revoked.

All this highlights the distinction between acquittals and sentences. . . .

V

We turn to the question whether the increase of a sentence on review under § 3576 constitutes multiple punishment in violation of the Double Jeopardy Clause. The Court of Appeals found that it did. . . . This conclusion appears to be attributable primarily to that court's extending to an appeal this Court's dictum in *United States* v. *Benz* (1931) to the effect that the federal practice of barring an increase in sentence by the trial court after service of the sentence has begun is constitutionally based. The real and only issue in *Benz,* however, was whether the trial judge had the power to *reduce* a defendant's sentence after service had begun. The Court held that the trial court had such power. It went on to say gratuitously, however, . . . and with quotations from a textbook and from *Ex parte Lange,* . . . that the trial court may not *increase* a sentence, even though the increase is effectuated during the same court session, if the defendant has begun service of his sentence. But the dictum's source, *Ex parte Lange,* states no such principle. . . .

The guarantee against multiple punishment that has evolved in the holdings of this Court plainly is not involved in this case. As *Ex parte Lange* demonstrates, a defendant may not receive a greater sentence than the legislature has authorized. No double jeopardy problem would have been presented in *Ex parte Lange* if Congress had provided that the offense there was punishable by both fine and imprisonment, even though that is multiple punishment. . . . The punishment authorized by Congress under §§ 3575 and 3576 is clear and specific and, accordingly, does not violate the guarantee against multiple punishment expounded by *Ex parte Lange.*

VI

The conclusion that § 3576 violates neither the guarantee against multiple punishment nor the guarantee against multiple trials is consistent with those opinions in which the Court has upheld the constitutionality of two-stage criminal proceedings. . . .

Swisher v. *Brady* (1978), affords particular support and, indeed, precedent for the decision we reach. . . .

We conclude that § 3576 withstands the constitutional challenge raised in the case before us. The judgment of the Court of Appeals is reversed and the case is remanded for further proceedings consistent with this opinion.

It is so ordered.

JUSTICE BRENNAN, with whom JUSTICE WHITE, JUSTICE MARSHALL, and JUSTICE STEVENS join, dissenting.

. . . Because the Court fundamentally misperceives the appropriate degree of finality to be accorded the imposition of sentence by the trial judge, it reaches the erroneous conclusion that enhancement of a sentence pursuant to § 3576 is not an unconstitutional multiple punishment. I respectfully dissent.

I

The Court acknowledges, as it must, that the Double Jeopardy Clause has two principal purposes: to "protect an individual from being subjected to the hazards of trial and possible conviction more than once for an alleged offense," *Green* v. *United States* (1957), and to prevent imposition of multiple punishments for the same offense, *North Carolina* v. *Pearce* (1969). An overriding function of the Double Jeopardy Clause's prohibition against multiple trials is to protect against multiple punishments: "It is the punishment that would legally follow the second conviction which is the real danger guarded against by the Constitution."

An unconstitutional punishment need not derive exclusively from a second prosecution, but may stem from the imposition of more than one sentence following a single prosecution. *Ex parte Lange, supra,* and *In re Bradley* (1943), provide examples of unconstitutional multiple punishments flowing from a single trial — imprisonment *and* fine for an offense punishable by either imprisonment *or* fine — but neither case purports to exhaust the reach of the Double Jeopardy Clause's prohibition against multiple punishments. Indeed, this Court has consistently assumed that an increase in the severity of a sentence subsequent to its imposition — the issue presented in this case — also constitutes multiple punishment in violation of the Double Jeopardy Clause. . . .

My Brother REHNQUIST only recently noted that "the Double Jeopardy Clause as interpreted in *Ex parte Lange* prevents a sentencing court from increasing a defendant's sentence for any particular statutory offense, even though the second sentence is within the limits set by the legislature.". . .

II

Not only has the Court repeatedly said that sentences may not be increased after imposition without violating the double jeopardy prohibition against multiple punishments, but the analytic similarity of a verdict of acquittal and the imposition of sentence requires this conclusion. A verdict of acquittal represents the factfinder's conclusion that the evidence does not warrant a finding of guilty. *United States v. Martin Linen Supply Co.* (1977). Similarly, a guilty verdict of second-degree murder where the charge to the jury permitted it to find defendant guilty of first-degree murder represents the factfinder's *implicit* finding that the facts do not warrant a first-degree murder conviction. . . .

I suggest that most defendants are more concerned with how much time they must spend in prison than with whether their record shows a conviction. This is not to say that the ordeal of trial is not important. And obviously it is the conviction itself which is the predicate for time in prison. But clearly, the defendant does not breathe a sigh of relief once he has been found guilty. Indeed, an overwhelming number of criminal defendants are willing to enter plea bargains in order to keep their time in prison as brief as possible. Surely, the Court cannot believe then that the sentencing phase is merely incidental and that defendants do not suffer acute anxiety. To the convicted defendant, the sentencing phase is certainly as critical as the guilt-innocence phase. . . .

The Court's contrary view rests on the circular notion that the defendant "has no expectation of finality in his sentence until the [government] appeal [pursuant to § 3576] is concluded or the time to appeal has expired.". . .

Finally, the Court attempts to differentiate the finality of acquittals from the finality of sentences through reliance on *North Carolina* v. *Pearce, supra,* and *Swisher* v. *Brady* (1978). Neither decision supports the Court's result. . . .

III

Because the Court has demonstrated no basis for differentiating between the finality of acquittals and the finality of sentences, I submit that a punishment enhanced by an appellate court is an unconstitutional multiple punishment. To conclude otherwise, as the Court does, is to create an exception to basic double jeopardy protection which, if carried to its logical conclusion, might not prevent Congress, on double jeopardy grounds, from authorizing the Government to appeal verdicts of acquittal.

Such a result is plainly impermissible under the Double Jeopardy Clause.
   I, therefore, dissent.

JUSTICE STEVENS, dissenting.
   While I join JUSTICE BRENNAN's dissent, I also note that neither
today nor in its opinion in *North Carolina* v. *Pearce* (1969), has the
Court adequately responded to Justice Harlan's powerful analysis of
the double jeopardy issue in that case. ... Its purported response in
Pearce — that although the rationale for allowing a more severe punishment after a retrial "has been variously verbalized, it rests ultimately
upon the premise that the original conviction has, at the defendant's
behest, been wholly nullified," — clearly has no application to the
question whether a more severe sentence may be imposed at the *prosecutor's* behest when the original conviction has *not* been nullified.
   The straightfoward analysis by Justice Harlan is worthy of emphasis:

   "Every consideration enunciated by the court in support of the
   decision in *Green* [1957] applies with equal force to the situation
   at bar. In each instance, the defendant was once subjected to the
   risk of receiving a maximum punishment, but it was determined
   by legal process that he should receive only a specified punishment
   less than the maximum. ... And the concept or fiction of an 'implicit
   acquittal' of the greater offense, *ibid.,* applies equally to the greater
   sentence: in each case it was determined at the former trial that
   the defendant or his offense was of a certain limited degree of 'badness'
   or gravity only, and therefore merited only a certain limited
   punishment.

   "If, as a matter of policy and practicality, the imposition of an
   increased sentence on retrial has the same consequences whether
   effected in the guise of an increase in the degree of offense or an
   augmentation of punishment, what other factors render one route
   forbidden and the other permissible under the Double Jeopardy Clause?
   It cannot be that the provision does not comprehend 'sentences' —
   as distinguished from "offenses' — for it has long been established
   that once a prisoner commences service of sentence, the Clause prevents
   a court from vacating the sentence and then imposing a greater
   one. See *United States* v. *Benz* (1931); *Ex parte Lange.*

   The Court's response to this analysis is nothing more than a rather
wooden extrapolation from a rationale that, however it may be "variously
verbalized," ... is wholly irrelevant to the important question presented
by this case.
   Because I agree with what JUSTICE BRENNAN has written today
as well as with what Justice Harlan wrote in 1969, I respectfully dissent.

▼▼▼

FLIGHT OF VOYAGER I
December 15, 1980

America's one-ton space explorer, Voyager I, on Nov. 12 cruised to within 77,000 miles of the cloud tops of the planet Saturn, sailing through its moons and beneath its fabled rings. Photographs and other information obtained by the spacecraft's cameras and sensors dazzled scientists and the public alike. On Dec. 15, the NASA Jet Propulsion Laboratory issued "Voyager I Saturn Science Summary," a report on the Saturn photo reconnaisance mission of Voyager I.

By the time the spacecraft had left Saturn's vicinity and begun a long sweep toward interstellar space, its instruments had told space scientists enough to alter sharply their earlier conceptions of the planet, its rings and its moons. Yet in some ways the Voyager I mission left Saturn and its concentric rings more mysterious than ever.

Discussing one Voyager discovery about the planet's rings, Bradford A. Smith, leader of the Voyager photo-interpretation team, told reporters, "It boggles the mind. . . ."

Voyage of Discovery

Launched from Cape Canaveral, Fla., in September 1977, the small spacecraft had passed Jupiter two years later and journeyed 1.3 billion miles to keep its historic appointment with Saturn. After it explored Saturn and its moons, the spacecraft sped away at 36,700 miles an hour on a nine-year journey beyond the Earth's solar system into in-

989

terstellar space. *Voyager I began to transmit information about Saturn to the Earth on Aug. 22, 1980, and continued to do so until Dec. 15.*

An earlier Saturn fly-by had been made by a less sophisticated space-craft, Pioneer II, in September 1979. A third photo reconnaissance mission was scheduled for August 1981 by Voyager II, equipped with equipment similar to that carried by its twin, Voyager I.

Rings and Moons

The planet itself is the sixth from the sun, with an orbit between those of Jupiter and Uranus. Galileo was the first to see its concentric rings, in 1610. By the middle of the 19th century, three distinct rings had been identified by astronomers, and in the 20th century three more were seen. But Voyager I revealed rings within rings whose number could reach 1,000.

Before Voyager I, scientists had thought that the rings were composed of ice particles no larger than snowballs. However, information sent back by the spacecraft disclosed that they may contain larger chunks with sufficient gravity to draw smaller particles into newly revealed patterns.

Voyager I revelations concerning Saturn's moons provided scientists with as many surprises as the discoveries about the rings. The spacecraft sailed within 2,500 miles of Titan, a moon larger than the planet Mercury and the only moon in the Earth's solar system with an atmosphere. Among its discoveries on other moons were a huge crater on Mimas and a 465-mile-long canyon on Tethys. Moreover, Voyager I identified three new moons, bringing to 15 the number of Saturn's satellites.

U.S. Space Program

The stunning success of the Voyager I photo reconnaissance mission was made somewhat bittersweet for National Aeronautics and Space Administration scientists by the knowledge that the American space program was running out of funds. The Voyager program itself was a scaled-down version of the originally planned "grand tour" of all the outer planets. In recent years, the bulk of the NASA budget had been earmarked for the reusable space plane known as the shuttle.

Following are excerpts from a report of the NASA Jet Propulsion Laboratory, Pasadena, Calif., "Voyager I Saturn Science Summary," issued December 15, 1980, on the Saturn photo reconnaissance mission of Voyager I in 1980:

Voyager 1's encounter with Saturn began Aug. 22, 1980, and ended Dec. 15, 1980. The spacecraft took more than 17,000 photographs of Saturn and its satellites.

Initial scientific results of the encounter are as follows:

Saturn

From the spacecraft, as from Earth, Saturn's atmosphere appears grossly similar to Jupiter's, with alternating dark belts and light zones, circulating storm regions and other discrete dark and light cloud markings. Unlike Jupiter, however, Saturn's markings are strongly muted by a thick haze layer above the visible cloud tops. (Jupiter has a similar haze layer, but it is not as optically thick as Saturn's.)

While the gross features of both planets are similar, Saturn and Jupiter have pronounced differences. The belt-zone structure on Saturn extends to much higher latitudes than on Jupiter, for example.

Wind speeds in the atmosphere of Saturn are substantially higher than on Jupiter, and do not appear closely tied to the belt-zone boundaries as they are on Jupiter. Highest winds (about 1,600 kilometers or 1,000 miles an hour) occur at the equator and are four to five times stronger than on Jupiter.

Voyager 1 found auroral emissions near Saturn's poles and auroral-type emissions in ultraviolet were found near the illuminated limbs of the planet. Scientists faced a difficult problem in attempts to detect lightning on the dark side of Saturn. The rings reflect so much light onto the night side — especially on the region above the illuminated face of the rings — that it washed out lightning bolts that might have appeared in Voyager photos. Lightning has not been detected in images of Saturn's dark face, but radio emissions typical of lightning discharges have been observed. Those discharges are believed to originate in the rings rather than in the atmosphere.

Radio emissions, primarily from the north polar region and near 90 degrees longitude, indicate that the body of Saturn and its magnetosphere rotate with a period of 10 hours, 39 minutes and 26 seconds. (That is a refinement of earlier Voyager results that indicated the length of a day is 10 hours, 39 minutes, 24 seconds.)

The Rings

Voyager 1 found that the classically observed A-, B- and C-rings consist of hundreds of small ringlets, a few of which are elliptical in shape. The F-ring, discovered by Pioneer 11 in 1979, is composed of three separate ringlets that are intertwined. The inner and outer limits of the F-ring appear to be controlled by two shepherd satellites, S-13 on the outside and S-14 on the inside. The intertwining or "braiding" phenomenon is, as yet, unexplained — although it may be related to electrostatic charging of the dust particles comprising the ring.

The outer edge of the A-ring is similarly shepherded by the newly discovered satellite S-15. All three of those satellites (S-13, S-14 and S-15) were discovered by Voyager 1.

Voyager 1 also photographed the D-ring, during passage through Saturn's shadow. Although the existence of a D-ring had been claimed by a few Earth-based observers and doubted by many others who had been unable to see it, preliminary analysis suggests that the ring observed by Voyager 1 is too faint to be seen from Earth. Voyager 1 also photographed the tenuous E-ring, which can be seen from Earth only when the rings are edge-on, and discovered a new ring just inside, and casting a shadow on, the satellite S-11.

Measurement show that the D-, E- and F-rings have large populations of particles smaller than 2/10,000th to 3/10,000th of an inch in diameter. Radio measurements of the C-ring indicate that it has an effective particle size of about one meter (three feet), and, at the same time, suggest a wide distribution of particle sizes.

On its inbound leg, Voyager 1 discovered a series of transient, spokelike features that radiate outward across the B-ring; they first appear as the ring emerges from darkness and seem to dissipate within a few hours. In photos taken during the inbound portion of the flight, the spoke-like features appeared darker than the surrounding ring material.

After it passed Saturn, Voyager 1 took photographs of the features that showed them to be brighter than the surrounding material. That suggests that the material in the spokes is extremely fine, and is forward-scattering sunlight.

New Satellites

In the photographs of new satellites, only S-10 and S-11 were large enough to determine their shapes. Both are irregular and have their long axes pointed toward the center of Saturn. S-10, the leading of the two co-orbital satellites, is the larger, with an average diameter of about 200 kilometers (124 miles). S-11, the trailing satellite, is about 70 kilometers (43 miles) wide. . . .

Other Satellites

Mimas, Enceladus, Tethys, Dione and Rhea are approximately spherical in shape and appear to be composed mostly of water ice. Tethys in particular seems to be almost pure ice, while Dione may range from 30 to 70 percent rock. All five represent a size of satellite not previously explored by spacecraft. Their measured diameters, accurate to about 20 kilometers (12 miles), are: Mimas, 390 kilometers (240 miles); Enceladus, 500 kilometers (310 miles); Tethys, 1,050 kilometers (650 miles); Dione, 1,120 kilometers (696 miles); and Rhea, 1,530 kilometers (950 miles).

Mimas, Tethys, Dione and Rhea are all cratered; Enceladus appears smooth in the photos taken by Voyager 1.

One very prominent crater on Mimas is so large it covers about one-fourth the diameter of the satellite.

Stretching for 750 kilometers (465 miles) across the surface of Tethys is a valley that is 60 kilometers (40 miles) wide. The valley appears to be a great fracture in the crust of the satellite.

Several sinuous valleys, some of which appear to branch, are visible on Dione's surface, as are plains, suggestive of internal processes and renewal of portions of the surface.

Both Dione and Rhea have bright, wispy streaks that stand out against an already-bright surface. The streaks are probably the results of relatively fresh ice which have evolved from the interior fairly recently (on a geologic time scale).

Enceladus shows no evidence, at 12 kilometers (7.4 miles) resolution, of any impact craters. . . .

Titan

Titan is not only far different from the satellite scientists had expected, it may turn out to be the most important and interesting body (from a terrestrial perspective) in the solar system.

For almost two decades, space scientists have searched for clues to the primeval Earth. At Titan, they found a body with an atmosphere similar to the one that would have evolved on Earth, had Earth formed at Titan's distance from the Sun.

Titan was thought from Earth-based observations to be the largest satellite in the solar system. Voyager's close approach and diametric occultation show it to have a diameter of 5,120 kilometers (3,180 miles) — smaller than Ganymede, Jupiter's largest satellite. Both are larger than the planet Mercury.

Titan's density thus appears to be about twice that of water ice, requiring Titan to be composed of nearly equal amounts of rock and ice, as is Ganymede.

Titan's surface cannot be seen in photos from Voyager because it is hidden by a dense, optically thick haze. . . .

OPEC OIL PRICE ACTIONS

June 9-10, September 15-17, December 15-16, 1980

The price of petroleum continued to rise in 1980 as militant members of the Organization of Petroleum Exporting Countries (OPEC) called for even higher charges for their crude oil. The differences among the members over production and pricing levels — and the war between Iraq and Iran, both founding members of OPEC — threatened the cartel's unity.

In the wake of the December 1979 meeting at which the OPEC ministers failed to agree on a standard price (Historic Documents of 1979, p. 251), *charges in the first half of 1980 ranged from $28 for a barrel of Saudi Arabian oil to $38 for a barrel of Algerian crude. The stated goal of the OPEC ministers at their first 1980 session, held June 9-10 in Algiers, was to re-establish a common pricing formula. The moderate Saudi Arabians pressed to keep prices low. The militant OPEC members, led by Libya, Algeria and Nigeria, argued for a higher benchmark price (the amount charged for a barrel of Saudi Arabian light crude). The militants also pressured Saudi Arabia to reduce production to maintain worldwide demand. (The Saudis had increased their production by one million barrels a day after the Iranian revolution had drastically cut Iran's production.)*

'Oil Glut'

In the end, it was announced that the cartel members had agreed on a new base price of $32 a barrel. However, Sheik Ahmed Zaki Yamani, the Saudi oil minister, told reporters, "I have agreed to nothing. I will not raise my prices." The Saudis also determined to keep their production high, apparently to create an oversupply of oil and thereby keep prices down.

In July news reports began to circulate about an "oil glut." Prices on the spot market — where merchants buy and sell excess oil at whatever prices they can command — dropped to or below official levels. Experts attributed the decline in demand to the Saudi production, conservation measures instituted in the industrialized world, a recession in the United States and the worldwide economic slowdown.

Other Meetings

As the OPEC ministers gathered in Vienna for a second meeting, held Sept. 15-17, the supply of oil was reported to be 1 million to 2.5 million barrels a day over demand. The Saudi Arabians pledged that they would not raise prices or lower production unless agreement was reached on long-term pricing and production accords. No accords were approved; nevertheless, the Saudis agreed to raise their prices $2 a barrel and the militant members accepted the $30-a-barrel rate as the new benchmark. The members agreed, moreover, to freeze prices until the end of the year.

The September meeting was marked by tension between Iran and Iraq, whose armies engaged in border skirmishes earlier in the month. After the meeting, full-scale war broke out between the two countries and soon each had damaged badly the other's oil refineries and pipelines. Saudi Arabia, Bahrain, Qatar and the United Arab Emirates agreed to increase production to offset the loss of oil from the warring nations. And OPEC announced that a November meeting of OPEC heads of state, scheduled to mark the cartel's 20th anniversary, had been canceled.

OPEC's final 1980 meeting, in Bali, Indonesia, Dec. 15-16, was held amid growing doubts about the cartel's future. Iran and Iraq remained at war and Saudi Arabia had recently broken off relations with Libya. In another move to reunify the cartel, the Saudis again announced a moderate price rise, up to $32 a barrel, retroactive to Nov. 1. The benchmark price for the other members rose to $36 a barrel; with surcharges allowed by the cartel, it was possible the top price for a barrel of high-quality crude would reach $41 in early 1981.

Following are excerpts, as published by The New York Times, *from the communiqué issued Dec. 16, 1980, at the conclusion of the OPEC ministerial meeting in Bali, Indonesia:*

The 59th meeting of the conference of the Organization of the Petroleum Exporting Countries was held in Bali, Indonesia, from December 15th to 16th, 1980. President of the Republic of Indonesia, Suharto, addressed and formally opened the conference.

The conference unanimously elected as its president Dr. Subroto, Minister of Mines and Energy of Indonesia and head of its delegation. Edouard Alexis M'Bouy-Boutzit, Minister of Mines, Energy and Hydraulic

Resources of Gabon and head of its delegation, was elected alternate president.

The conference reviewed the progress report on the creation of an institute for higher education in science and technology for the developing countries, as decided upon by its 57th meeting, and instructed the secretary general to convene a working party to deal with the matter during the first half of next year. On the basis of this working party's findings a feasibility study will be conducted under the general supervision of the secretariat and the outcome be presented for the consideration of the conference.

The conference, after having reviewed the report of the 52th [*sic*] meeting of the economic commission board, and on the basis of the oil market situation decided:

A) To fix official price of the marker crude (Arabian light 34 API Ex Ras Tanura) at a level of $32 a barrel.

B) Prices of OPEC crude may be set on the basis of an oil price ceiling for a deemed marker crude of up to $36 a barrel.

C) To set a maximum price for OPEC crudes at $41 a barrel.

The conference endorsed the sincere and honest appeal made by the president of the Republic of Indonesia in his inauguration speech to the two member countries who are presently in dispute — Iran and Iraq — to seek the best possible solution quickly to their conflict leading to a peaceful settlement of their differences.

The conference approved the budget of the organization for the year 1981.

The conference decided that the term of office of the present secretary general, René G. Ortiz, be extended until the end of June 1981.

The conference passed resolutions which will be published on January 16, 1981, after ratification by member countries.

The next ordinary meeting of the conference will be convened on May 25, 1981.

NEGOTIATIONS WITH IRAN ON RELEASE OF HOSTAGES

December 21, 1980

As 1980 came to an end, it appeared that a resolution of the "hostage crisis" — the case of the 52 Americans held in Iran — would prove beyond the grasp of the Carter administration. Negotiations concerning the fate of the hostages, captured when Iranian militants seized the U.S. Embassy in Tehran Nov. 4, 1979 (Historic Documents of 1979, p. 867), reached an impasse in late December.

Formal talks with Iranian officials, conducted through Algerian intermediaries, began in November. After months of conflicting statements, the Ayatollah Ruhollah Khomeini, leader of Iran's revolutionary government, Sept. 12 announced four conditions for the release of the American captives. The conditions — the United States must pledge to relinquish property and assets of the former Shah Mohammed Reza Pahlavi, must cancel all financial claims against Iran, must release Iran's assets frozen by President Carter Nov. 14, 1979, and must refrain from interfering in Iran's affairs — were endorsed Nov. 2 by the Majlis, Iran's parliament. Deputy Secretary of State Warren M. Christopher Nov. 10 delivered Washington's response to Iran's conditions to the Algerian intermediaries. The United States agreed to restore Iran's financial position as of Nov. 4, 1979, and to adopt a hands-off policy toward Iran's internal affairs. Iran's assets in U.S. banks and branches overseas were estimated to total between $8 billion and $14 billion.

New Iranian Demand

Hopes for a quick end to the confrontation were dashed Dec. 19 when Iran, in what it said was its "final reply" to U.S. proposals,

*demanded that Washington deposit $24 billion worth of financial guar-
antees in Algeria's central bank prior to the release of the hostages.
The money, the Iranians said, would be held until the United States
returned all of the frozen Iranian funds and the property of the shah's
family.*

*American reaction was strong. Secretary of State Edmund S. Muskie,
named to replace Cyrus R. Vance after Vance resigned April 28 in
protest of the failed mission to rescue the hostages (see p. 351), termed
Iran's conditions "unreasonable." Muskie, appearing on NBC-TV's "Meet
the Press" Dec. 21, the same day Iran's formal reply was made public,
added that the demands "would require us to go beyond the President's
legal authority." Other officials said the Iranians were demanding
"ransom."*

Release of Hostages

*Unwilling to give up in the last days of their tenure, officials of
the Carter White House made yet another proposal to Iran on Dec.
28. This proposal, presented to the Algerians on Jan. 3, 1981, led to
further negotiations and the eventual release of the hostages on Jan.
20, 1981, just minutes after the inauguration of President Ronald Reagan.*

*Fear among Iran's leaders that the Reagan administration might take
a tougher stance toward the hostage situation was seen by some observers
as having contributed to its resolution. Internal pressures also may
have convinced the Iranians to negotiate with the United States. It
appeared that, after the former shah died on July 27 in Cairo, the
hostages had become a liability for Iran's fundamentalist Islamic rulers
since they no longer could be used in an effort to force the shah
to return to Iran to stand trial. Iran's political and economic isolation,
which developed in the months following the hostage-taking, grew in
intensity in late 1980. And a war between Iran and neighboring Iraq,
which began Sept. 22 after a series of border clashes, crippled Iran's
oil-producing capacity and drained its treasury. These factors were seen
by many as leading the Iranians to back down from their Dec. 19
demands and seek an accommodation.*

> *Following are the text of the Iranian response Dec. 21,
> 1980, to the United States on conditions for release of
> the 52 American hostages, as translated by the official
> Iranian news agency Pars, and excerpts from the interview
> with Secretary of State Edmund S. Muskie on NBC-TV's
> "Meet the Press" Dec. 21, 1980. (Boldface headings in
> brackets have been added by Congressional Quarterly to
> highlight the organization of the texts.):*

IRANIAN STATEMENT

In the name of God, most gracious, most merciful.

On 2 November 1980, the Islamic Consultative Assembly announced its resolution on the conditions for the release of the 52 Americans. On 3 November 1980, this resolution, in both Persian and English texts, was delivered by the Iranian Government to the Ambassador of the Algerian Government in Washington for delivery to the U.S. Government.

On 12 November 1980, the response of the U.S. Government, dated 8 November 1980, was delivered to the Iranian Government by the representatives of the Algerian People's Democratic Republic under their memorandum dated 12 November 1980. Since in the responses of the U.S. Government, no allusion was made to the proposals contained in the resolution of the Islamic Consultative Assembly, and no clear reference was made to them, according, during a meeting in Teheran with the representatives of the Algerian People's Democratic Republic on 22 November 1980, the U.S. Government, through the Algerian representatives, was asked to declare its clear response to those points.

The Algerian representatives, in their memorandum dated 4 December 1980, delivered the complementary response of the U.S. to the Government of the Islamic Republic of Iran.

After reviewing both responses and hearing the explanations of the Algerian delegation, the following conclusions were reached:

Despite the acceptance of the principles of the resolution of the Islamic Consultative Assembly by the U.S. Government, the proposed undertakings of the U.S. Government are not adequately responsive to all the points asked by the Islamic Consultative Assembly of Iran, and in some cases amendments to the responses, and changes in the executive procedures, are necessary.

It is only after such amendments and changes that the after-mentioned undertakings can be acceptable to the Government of the Islamic Republic of Iran as the minimum requirements. The amendments, changes and executive procedures asked by the Government of the Islamic Republic of Iran, on the basis of the resolution of the Islamic Consultative Assembly, are as follows:

Amendments Relating to the American Response to Section One of the Resolution of the Islamic Consultative Assembly of Iran:

With due regard to the fact that the official recognition of the Islamic revolution and the government of the Islamic Republic is a fait accompli, and there is no request for such recognition in the resolution of the Islamic Consultative Assembly, and at the same time in the resolution of the Consultative Assembly, in the condition of noninterference, the phrase: "from now on" has been used, accordingly "recognition of the Islamic revolution and Government of the Islamic Republic of Iran" be deleted from the declaration, and the stipulation "from now on" be added to the condition on nonintervention.

With due regard to this explanation, the U.S. Declaration on non-intervention in Iran be amended as follows:

"The Government of the United States of America hereby pledges not to intervene, from now on, directly or indirectly, militarily or politically, in the internal affairs of the Islamic Republic of Iran."

In addition to the above amendment in the declaration, it is necessary that the overall response of the U.S. be amended accordingly.

Executive Procedures
of Section Two and Three
of the Resolution of the Islamic
Consultative Assembly:

With due regard to the fact that the U.S. Government has accepted the principles of sections two and three of the resolution of the Islamic Consultative Assembly, the following executive procedures are proposed:

SECTION ONE

Steps to Be Taken by the U.S. Government:

The U.S. Government, in taking all the legal and administrative steps necessary for carrying out all of the provisions of sections two and three of the resolution of the Islamic Consultative Assembly, will also take the following measures:

A

The return of $9,069,000,000 of Iranian assets plus relevant interest at the standard rates, as well as the return of the gold belonging to Iran, deposited with the Federal Reserve Bank of New York, and deliver the above to the Central Bank of Algeria before the release of the 52 Americans, hostages of the Iranian nation.

Immediately upon the release of the 52 Americans, these assets, after deduction of the amounts mentioned in subsections A and B of section two, will be placed at the disposal of the Iranian Government by the Government of Algeria.

These assets, in detail, are as follows:

1. Deposits of Bank Markazi of Iran with American banks in London: $3,518,000,000.

2. Deposits of Bank Markazi of Iran with American banks in Paris: $400 million.

3. Deposits of Bank Markazi of Iran with American banks in the United States: $167 million.

4. Deposits of other Iranian banks with American banks: $300 million.

5. Deposits of the National Iranian Oil Company: $407 million.

6. Funds relating to oil sales: $2,108,000,000.

7. Treasury notes of the Bank Markazi of Iran with the Federal Reserve Bank: $1,000,000,000.

8. Deposits of the Bank Markazi of Iran with the Federal Reserve Bank: $269 million.

9. Trust fund of the Ministry of Defense of the Islamic Republic of Iran: $800 million.

Total: $9,069,000,000.

10. Bank Markazi of Iran's gold with the Federal Reserve Bank equal to 1,632,827 ounces.

B

With regard to the other assets and funds of Iran at the disposal of, or under attachment by the American Government, American nationals or institutions inside or outside the United States, the U.S. Government, in pledging to return all such assets and funds, will deposit with the Central Bank of Algeria a guarantee equal to $4 billion in cash, or any other valid guarantee acceptable to the above bank, as a guarantee of the bona fide discharge of its obligations.

Immediately upon the release of the 52 Americans the aforementioned assets and funds will be placed at the disposal of representatives of the Government of the Islamic Republic of Iran for transfer to Iran. On the transfer of each part of the aforementioned assets and funds, an amount equal in value to such transfers will be deducted from the amount of the guarantee deposited with the Central Bank of Algeria.

C

The U.S. Government will make the necessary commitment to respond to any kind of claims for losses arising from the Islamic revolution of Iran to American nationals, American Government, organizations and institutions, but not due to decisions adopted by the Islamic Government of Iran.

Relevant explanations were delivered to the Algerian delegation on 10 December 1980 as follows: (by "related to the Islamic revolution" is meant all the claims related to any damage to and loss by U.S. persons and entities caused by the revolutionary movement of the Iranian people, and not by the decisions of the Government of the Islamic Republic of Iran, from February 11, 1979 until the present time).

D

For the purpose of comparing and checking the list of Iranian assets and funds existing within the jurisdiction of the U.S.A. or at the disposal of the American Government, nationals and institutions outside the U.S.A. and with due regard to the fact that the agents of the deposed Shah, before the downfall of the Pahlevi regime, have destroyed much of the documents relating to the Iranian assets and funds in the U.S.A.:

Therefore the U.S. Government will, within one week from the date of receipt of this memorandum, provide the Iranian Government, through the Government of Algeria, with a detailed list of all the assets and funds of the Islamic Republic of Iran and Iranian institutions.

At the same time, the U.S.A. will undertake to immediately place at the disposal of the Government of the Islamic Republic of Iran all Iranian assets and funds which may not have been stipulated in the present lists, but may come to light at a future date.

SECTION TWO

Steps to Be Taken By the Government of the Islamic Republic of Iran

Concurrent with all the aforementioned steps to be taken by the U.S. Government, the Iranian government pledges to take the following steps:

A

With due regard to the fact that all declarations of default of loan agreements, loan accelerations, and set-offs effected by American banks will be nullified and cancelled, the Government of the Islamic Republic of Iran undertakes to pay the bona fide loan instalments on loans and credits contracted in the past, and hereby authorizes the Algerian Government to keep the amount of one billion dollars from the aforementioned amounts as a guarantee for the delayed instalments on the aforementioned loans, and after reviewing each loan agreement, the agreed sums be paid to the American banks. After settlement of outstanding debts, the balance will be returned to Iran.

B

Since the Government of the Islamic Republic of Iran undertakes to settle its bona fide debts to American persons or institutions, the Iranian Government accepts that the claims of American entities and citizens against Iran, and the claims of Iranian nationals and institutions, be settled, in the first stage through agreement between the parties and, failing such agreement, through arbitration acceptable to the respective parties.

For the purpose of repaying the above debts, the Government of the Islamic Republic of Iran will deposit with the Algerian Government an initial cash guarantee equal to $1 billion, or any other guarantee acceptable to the Central Bank of Algeria. In repaying such debts, this guarantee will be adjusted in such a way that it will never drop below $500 million.

It should be noted that the above guarantee will not include claims arising from the results of the seizure of the former U.S. Embassy in Teheran, results arising from the hostage-taking by the Iranian people and the reactions of the U.S. Government, as well as claims originating from the effects of the Islamic revolution of Iran.

Executive Procedure of Section Four of the Resolution of the Islamic Consultative Assembly:

Since the properties and assets of the deposed Shah and his close relatives have been confiscated and those portions of the properties and assets that have been determined have been appropriated for the benefit of the Iranian nation, and since a large part of such properties remains outside of Iran, specially in the U.S.A., accordingly and with due regard to the fact that the Government of the Islamic Republic of Iran presently has no complete information on the amount of properties and assets plundered by the aforementioned persons, therefore, for the purpose of speeding up the execution of the resolution of the Islamic Consultative Assembly and the attachment order of the Attorney General in respect of the above properties, the U.S. Government was asked through the Algerian delegation, on 10 December 1980, to place at the disposal of the Iranian Government, as soon as possible, a complete list of the properties and assets of the deposed Shah and his close relatives (a list of the relationships was previously submitted) on the basis of information available before 4 November 1979 and as at present.

Since the U.S. Government has up till now placed no useful information in this respect at the disposal of Iran, therefore the Government of the Islamic Republic of Iran asks that the U.S. Government:

A

As in the case of collecting information on frozen Iranian assets and funds, when the U.S. Government set a time limit and asked its nationals and institutions to place all relevant information at the disposal of the U.S. Treasury and stipulated that failure to do so would entail fines and imprisonment, in this respect also the U.S. Government should take all legal and administrative measures, setting a 30-day time limit and determine fines and imprisonment, for the purpose of collecting information on the aforementioned properties and assets and issue the necessary instructions in this respect.

B

Until final results are reached, the U.S. Government will continue the attachment of all the properties and assets of the deposed Shah and his close relatives.

C

In addition to all the above measures relating to determination of the properties and assets of the deposed Shah and his close relatives at the present time in the U.S.A., the U.S. Government will also determine all the properties and assets of the deposed Shah and his close relatives in the U.S.A. as at 3 November 1979 and notify this to the Government of the Islamic Republic of Iran within the period stipulated.

D

The U.S. Government pledges to provide information on the amounts, origin and destination of the properties and assets of the deposed Shah and his close relatives transferred out of U.S. jurisdiction, probably after triumph of the Islamic revolution and until the date of acceptance of this response, as well as information on the agents involved in such transfers.

E

The U.S. Government to deposit with the Central Bank of Algeria a cash guarantee equal to $10 billion, or any other guarantee acceptable to the Algerian Government, which is a percentage of the properties of the Iranian nation plundered by the deposed Shah and his relatives, as a guarantee of the bona fide discharge of its obligations, so that:

1. In case the U.S. Government refrains from declaring a part or parts of the properties and assets of the deposed Shah and his relatives to the Iranian government, and the fact is later discovered and proven by the Iranian Government,

2. In case the U.S. Government refrains from issuing the attachment order on the properties of the deposed shah and his relatives, or later cancels such an order,

3. In case the U.S. Courts refrain from carrying out the U.S. Government's attachment order, and the order, confirmed by the Iranian courts, for the transfer of all the properties to the Government of the Islamic Republic of Iran,

Then, in such an eventuality the Algerian Government will place at the disposal of the Iranian Government an amount from the guarantee equal to the loss sustained from any one case or a number of cases of the aforementioned eventualities.

The amount of loss will be determined by arbitration acceptable to the parties.

The above guarantee is for the bona fide execution of the undertakings, and on the declaration of the Iranian Government on the nonexistence of any kind of properties and assets, as well as by issuing the executive order and execution of the verdict of Iranian courts, the guarantee will be lifted.

The maximum period for notifying the nonexistence of properties and assets and issue of the attachment order by Iranian courts is one year, and after clearing all attachment orders and transfer of all the properties to the Government of the Islamic Republic of Iran, will the above guarantee be lifted.

After all the conditions stipulated in this memorandum have been carried out and officially confirmed by the Government of the Algerian People's Democratic Republic, then the 52 Americans, hostages of the Iranian nation, will be released.

MUSKIE INTERVIEW

Q. Mr. Secretary, what is your assessment of the latest conditions from Iran for return of the 52 American hostages and the options they make available to this country?

A. In a brief word, let me say that we regard the response as unreasonable and as requiring of us actions beyond the power of the President to take.

Q. Mr. Secretary, are the difficulties now posed by Iran so severe in your judgment that the Administration would consider, in effect, suspending negotiations at this point and leaving the resolution of the matter up to the incoming Reagan administration?

A. No, indeed. We continue to work at what we think is a high-priority goal. And that is the release of the hostages.

The Iranians previously have made requests that we could not meet. Nevertheless, we continued to use the private channel through the Algerian Government in an attempt to persuade them to our position. What we've tried to do is make a good-will effort, a good-faith effort to examine what we can do to restore their frozen assets within the legal authority of the President of the United States. We'll continue to do that.

Q. Are you saying that the Administration will present a detailed response to Iran's latest terms?

A. The nature of the response is, of course, still under study. We've had this response which, as you now know from the public prints, is quite long and extensive and complicated. And which also requires an understanding of the Iranian use of concepts before we can respond.

[Take It or Leave It?]

Q. Mr. Secretary, you seem to be implying that you will respond again in some fashion, whatever the details, and that you won't simply say: "This is as far as we can go, you know what it is, take it or leave it; if you don't like it, deal with the next administration." Is that what you mean to imply?

A. What I mean to say is that a part of this frustrating and at times agonizing effort is to make clear to the Iranians, through a third party, which complicates the task, the limits beyond which the President cannot legally go.

And it's not always clear whether that message has gotten through or whether they accept it. This is not the first time that they've suggested items that would require us to go beyond the President's legal authority.

Q. How do you expect them to release the hostages if they're not given something of a nature that they can pass off politically to their own people. I mean, we're saying we want the hostages back because they were illegally taken and you can't have the money until the hostages are back.

A. Well, they have the responsibility for leadership and accountability in their own political system, just as I do in our system, and just as our President does in our system. The President cannot politically, let alone legally, exceed his own powers in dealing with their requests. And they must understand that.

And so they've got to decide, first, are they going to respond to world opinion, which has judged that they've taken an illegal act and which has had an impact upon their own country: economically, in terms of isolation from the world community, in terms of denial of access to markets that they would find useful now, in terms of impacting on an unstable political situation in their own country, in terms of threats on their own borders.

Q. Mr. Secretary, but they have for a year thumbed their noses at world opinion. We have Radio Teheran saying that if you don't accept what you've called unreasonable, the Christmas trees here will be unlit again next year, meaning the hostages will still be there. Would you give me your candid assessment as to whether you think there can be ever a negotiated settlement?

A. Well, there will have to be a negotiated settlement. Unless they take the other step, which they've given no indication at all they're willing to take, to release the hostages without condition. That is what they ought to do, given the fact that they did an illegal act over a year ago.

With respect to their public rhetoric, I have found that, like politicians everywhere, their public statements made for domestic consumption may not necessarily disclose what may be possible through appropriate negotiations.

[Military Action Not Imminent]

Q. A lot of us sitting on the outside see a situation where it appears you've done everything that you can possibly do, and you're still left with a situation where the U.S. has to accept something close to abject capitulation to kidnappers. And that we may be at the point where nothing is left but military action. Are we close to that point?

A. No, I would not say so. May I add this: We've had a previous experience in the case of North Korea, a hostage situation, involving roughly the same number of people. They were held for 11 months and were eventually released.

Q. Now you are aware that there are some mumblings out there in America that the honor of the United States is more important than the lives of 52 hostages; and that at some time this government is going to have to say the 52 don't matter that much, we're going to have to do what we have to do. Do you think that having given priority to saving the hostages all these months, that the U.S. ever can make that hard decision?

A. Well, I don't think the two are that separable. I think that to permit them, you know, to jeopardize the safety and the lives of the hostages would be counter to our national interests and our national honor.

Q. Mr. Secretary, just to clear up this one point that seems to be lingering about: Are you ruling out the use of American military force by this Administration to resolve this problem?

A. Well, we tried a form of that in the rescue effort which failed. And that effort did not succeed and, in addition, making the effort, I think, prolonged the agony of the problem.

Now, it is not easy if one looks at a map of Iran to consider military options, unless one were to consider options with consequences that need to be carefully weighed, for our other national interests, before making it.

I mean, an automatic military response is not an easy thing to devise, or an easy thing to execute, or one that one easily contemplates when one considers other national interests that might be impacted.

But the President has made it clear for a year that we will hold Iran accountable for the safety of the hostages, with whatever that implies in the circumstances that may arise. I don't think it is helpful to try to hypothesize what circumstances may arise.

I mean, at this point in our negotiations with Iran, we are within reach, if they could but see it, of a solution to the problem which would eliminate any such possibility, which would make possible the return of the hostages and would make possible the beginnings of a meaningful process of bringing Iran back into the community of nations in a dignified, responsible way.

And they've got to do that, they've got to face it at some point.

CUMULATIVE INDEX, 1976-80

CUMULATIVE INDEX, 1976-80

A

CUMULATIVE INDEX 1976-1980

ANDERSON, JOHN B., 847-869 *(1980)*
ANDRUS, CECIL D.
Alaskan Federal Lands, 732 *(1978)*
ANTIQUITIES ACT OF 1906, 734 *(1978)*
ANTITRUST ENFORCEMENT. *See*
Justice Department
AQUACULTURE
Global 2000 Report, 680 *(1980)*
ARAB STATES. *See* Middle East.
ARAFAT, YASIR. *See* Palestine Liberation
Organization (PLO).
ARGENTINA
Human Rights Report, 3, 5 *(1977)*; 195
(1980)
ARMED FORCES. *See also* Military Draft.
Congressional Budget Report, 184, 187
(1976)
Defense Posture Report, 123, 135 *(1980)*
Iran Rescue Attempt, 351-385 *(1980)*
State of the Union, 89 *(1980)*
ARMS CONTROL. *See also* Defense Policy.
Strategic Arms Limitation Talks.
Brezhnev at Party Congress, 144, 149 *(1976)*
Carter Arms Sales Policy, 105-109 *(1978)*
Carter Nuclear Policy, 271-276 *(1977)*
Carter Press Conference, 254 *(1977)*
Carter U.N. Speech, 193, 737-745 *(1977)*
Democratic Midterm Conference, 774
(1978)
Democratic Party Platform, 583 *(1976)*; 759
(1980)
Ford Nuclear Curbs Proposal, 823 *(1976)*
Giscard d'Estaing on Nuclear Exports, 332
(1976)
Mideast Warplane Sales, 125-134 *(1978)*
Republican Party Platform, 635 *(1980)*
Review of Nuclear Nonproliferation Treaty
(NPT), 275, 368 *(1977)*
State of the Union, 40 *(1978)*; 101 *(1980)*
U.S.-Soviet Nuclear Test Treaty (PNE),
369 *(1976)*
Vladivostok Agreement, 252, 257 *(1977)*
ARTS AND HUMANITIES
Court on Historic Preservation, 453-465
(1978)
Democratic Party Platform, 566 *(1976)*; 739
(1980)
Republican Party Platform, 649 *(1976)*; 612
(1980)
State of the Union, 30 *(1978)*; 54 *(1979)*; 70
(1980)
ASSAD, HAFEZ
Sadat Peace Initiative, 829 *(1977)*
ASSASSINATION PLOTS (C.I.A.)
Senate Intelligence Committee Report, 251
(1976)
ATLANTIC COMMUNITY. *See* North
Atlantic Treaty Organization.
AUSTRALIA
Carter Arms Sales Policy, 105 *(1978)*
Coal Resources Report, 418, 426 *(1980)*
Skylab's Return, 553-558 *(1979)*

B

BAKER, RUSSELL T. JR., 55 *(1978)*
BAKKE, ALLAN, 467-492 *(1978)*
BANGLADESH. *See* India-Pakistan War.
BARON, FREDERICK D., 60 *(1978)*
BEGIN, MENACHEM
Camp David Accords, 605-632 *(1978)*
Carter U.N. Speech, 738 *(1977)*
Egyptian-Israeli Peace Treaty, 223-247
(1979)
Sadat's Peace Initiative, 827-859 *(1977)*
BELGIUM
NATO Communiqué, Polish Strikes Crisis,
795, 802 *(1980)*
New European Monetary System, 741
(1978)
BELL, GRIFFIN
Carter Cabinet Reshuffle, 561 *(1979)*
Carter Warehouse Probe, 802 *(1979)*
Marston Dismissal Inquiry, 51 *(1978)*
BICENTENNIAL
Ford Message, 509 *(1976)*
Giscard d'Estaing Visit, 331 *(1976)*
Queen Elizabeth II Visit, 537 *(1976)*
BIRTH CONTROL. *See also* Abortion.
Pope John Paul II on, 725 *(1979)*; 873 *(1980)*
BLACKMUN, HARRY A. *See also* Supreme
Court.
Abortion Guidelines, 483 *(1976)*
Affirmative Action, 489-492 *(1978)*
Alimony Payments to Men, 200 *(1979)*
Campaign Finance Law, 73, 110 *(1976)*
Capital Punishment, 508 *(1978)*
Death Penalty for Murder, 400 *(1977)*
Double Jeopardy, 977 *(1980)*
Drug Advertising, 351 *(1976)*
Endangered Species, 446-452 *(1978)*
Gag Orders, 464 *(1976)*
Gilmore Execution, 923 *(1976)*
Home Arrests, 291 *(1980)*
Minimum Wage for State, Municipal
Employees, 385 *(1976)*
Minority Set Asides, 558 *(1980)*
Nixon Tapes and Papers, 487, 500 *(1977)*
Parochial School Aid, 433 *(1977)*
Pretrial Hearings Closed to Press and
Public, 525-533 *(1979)*
Public Funds for Abortions, 418 *(1977)*
Taiwan Treaty Termination, 918 *(1979)*
BLACKS, *See also* Busing. Equal
Opportunity₀ Minority Groups.
Court on Minority Set Asides, 539-566
(1980)
Court on School Attendance Zones, 413
(1976)
Court on School Desegregation, 535-552
(1979)
Court on Seniority and Employment
Discrimination, 383 *(1977)*
Republican Party Platform, 578 *(1980)*

1014

F

G

J

K

L

N

T

X, Y, Z